THE O'LEARY SERIES

INTRODUCTORY EDITION

Microsoft®
Office 2010:
A Case Approach

THE O'LEARY SERIES

INTRODUCTORY EDITION

Microsoft®
Office 2010:
A Case Approach

Timothy J. O'Leary

Professor Emeritus,
Arizona State University

Linda I. O'Leary

Mc
Graw
Hill

Connect
Learn
Succeed™

THE O'LEARY SERIES MICROSOFT® OFFICE 2010: A CASE APPROACH, INTRODUCTORY

3 4 5 6 7 8 9 0 RMN/RMN 1 0 9 8 7 6 5 4 3 2 1

ISBN   978-0-07-351930-2
MHID   0-07-351930-8

Vice president/Editor in chief: *Elizabeth Haefele*
Vice president/Director of marketing: *John E. Biernat*
Senior sponsoring editor: *Scott Davidson*
Director of development: *Sarah Wood*
Developmental editor II: *Alaina Grayson*
Editorial coordinator: *Alan Palmer*
Marketing manager: *Tiffany Wendt*
Lead digital product manager: *Damian Moshak*
Digital developmental editor: *Kevin White*
Director, Editing/Design/Production: *Jess Ann Kosic*
Project manager: *Marlena Pechan*
Senior buyer: *Michael R. McCormick*
Senior designer: *Srdjan Savanovic*
Senior photo research coordinator: *Jeremy Cheshareck*
Media project manager: *Cathy L. Tepper*
Cover design: *Evan Modesto*
Interior design: *Laurie Entringer*
Typeface: *10/12 New Aster LT STD*
Compositor: *Laserwords Private Limited*
Printer: *R. R. Donnelley*
Cover credit: © Kjpargeter/Dreamstime.com
Credits: The credits section for this book begins on page OFC.1 and is considered an extension of the copyright page.

Library of Congress Cataloging-in-Publication Data

O'Leary, Timothy J., 1947-
    Microsoft Office 2010 : a case approach / Timothy J. O'Leary, Linda I. O'Leary.— Introductory ed.
       p. cm.—(The O'Leary series)
    Includes bibliographical references and index.
    ISBN-13: 978-0-07-351930-2 (spiral bound)
    ISBN-10: 0-07-351930-8 (spiral bound)
    1. Microsoft Office. 2. Business—Computer programs. I. O'Leary, Linda I. II. Title.
HF5548.4.M525O445 2011
005.5—dc22   2010034305

LAB 3 — CREATING REPORTS AND TABLES   WD3.1

WORKING TOGETHER 1: WORD 2010 AND YOUR WEB BROWSER WDWT1.1

EXCEL

LAB 1 CREATING AND EDITING A WORKSHEET EX1.1

LAB 2 ENHANCING THE WORKSHEET WITH GRAPHICS AND CHARTS EX2.1

LAB 3 MANAGING AND ANALYZING A WORKBOOK EX3.1

WORKING TOGETHER 1: LINKING AND EMBEDDING BETWEEN WORD 2010 AND EXCEL 2010 *EXWT1.1*

ACCESS

LAB 1 CREATING A DATABASE *AC1.1*

LAB 2 — MODIFYING AND FILTERING A TABLE AND CREATING A FORM AC2.1

LAB 3 — QUERYING TABLES AND CREATING REPORTS AC3.1

WORKING TOGETHER 1: EXPORTING DATA

ACWT1.1

POWERPOINT

LAB 1   CREATING A PRESENTATION   PP1.1

LAB 2 · MODIFYING AND REFINING A PRESENTATION · *PP2.1*

WORKING TOGETHER 1: COPYING, EMBEDDING, AND LINKING BETWEEN APPLICATIONS · *PPWT1.1*

Acknowledgments

We would like to extend our thanks to the professors who took time out of their busy schedules to provide us with the feedback necessary to develop the 2010 Edition of this text. The following professors offered valuable suggestions on revising the text:

Joan Albright
Greenville Technical College

Wilma Andrews
Virginia Commonwealth University

Robert M. Benavides
Collin College

Kim Cannon
Greenville Technical College

Paulette Comet
The Community College of Baltimore County

Michael Dunklebarger
Alamance Community College

Joel English
Centura College

Deb Fells
Mesa Community College

Tatyana Feofilaktova
ASA Institute

Sue Furnas
Collin College

Debbie Grande
The Community College of Rhode Island

Rachelle Hall
Glendale Community College

Katherine Herbert
Montclair State University

Terri Holly
Indian River State College

Mark W. Huber
University of Georgia

Joyce Kessel
Western International University

Hal P. Kingsley
Trocaire College

Diane Lending
James Madison University

Dr. Mo Manouchehripour
The Art Institute of Dallas

Sue McCrory
Missouri State University

Gary McFall
Purdue University

Margaret M. Menna
The Community College of Rhode Island

Philip H. Nielson
Salt Lake Community College

Craig Piercy
University of Georgia

Mark Renslow
Globe University/Minnesota School of Business

Ann Rowlette
Liberty University

Chakra Pani Sharma
ASA Institute

Eric Weinstein
Suffolk County Community College

Sheryl Wright
College of the Mainland

Laurie Zouharis
Suffolk University

We would like to thank those who took the time to help us develop the manuscript and ensure accuracy through painstaking edits: Brenda Nielsen of Mesa Community College–Red Mountain, Stephen J. Adams of Cleveland State University, Candice Spangler of Columbus State Community College, and Kate Scalzi.

Finally, we would like to thank team members from McGraw-Hill, whose renewed commitment, direction, and support have infused the team with the excitement of a new project. Leading the team from McGraw-Hill are Tiffany Wendt, Marketing Manager; and Developmental Editor Alaina Grayson.

The production staff is headed by Marlena Pechan, Project Manager, whose planning and attention to detail have made it possible for us to successfully meet a very challenging schedule; Srdjan Savanovic, Designer; Michael McCormick, Production Supervisor; Kevin White, Digital Developmental Editor; Jeremy Cheshareck, Photo Researcher; and Betsy Blumenthal and Becky Komro, copyeditors—team members on whom we can depend to do a great job.

Word

Sarah Clifford is an independent writer, editor, and educator based in the San Francisco Bay area. She has designed and delivered academic programs for large organizations in both the private and public sectors. Additionally, Sarah has served as a faculty member of Golden Gate University. Over the past 20 years, she has co-authored several texts on information technology for McGraw-Hill, including the Advantage Series of books, resources geared towards training college students and others in using and integrating personal computer applications. For the past six years, Sarah also has served as the curriculum director for Vita Academy, a private co-educational grammar school she helped found in Oakland, California.

Excel

Kaari Busick is a freelance technical writer and editor with over 15 years of experience in technical documentation, from end-user manuals to programmer training materials. After receiving a BA from Colby College, she went on to receive a certificate in Technical Communication from the University of Washington. She has co-authored two nonfiction books with VeloPress and Prima Publishing, as well as various articles and reviews. She lives in Chicago, and her Web site is at kaaribusick.com.

Access

Paula Gregory was influenced early on by her mother, who enrolled in computer classes at the local community college, using the first home computer released by Radio Shack—a TRS-80. Paula received her associates degree with honors in 1990 at Yavapai College, majoring in computer science. In 1991, she began teaching and helping students one-on-one with computers at Yavapai College, and went on to get her teaching certification in 1998. Since then, Paula has enjoyed teaching college students all about computers and Microsoft Office and Adobe products. MCAS-certified in Microsoft Word and Access and ACA-certified in Adobe Photoshop, as well as an accomplished artist and writer, Paula enjoys combining all her skills to develop material that engages the audience and makes learning fun.

PowerPoint

Christy Parrish spent 20 years developing, designing, and delivering corporate training programs. She has contributed to several books on Microsoft Office and other productivity software packages. As a freelance author, she also has written a magazine series and numerous online articles on a wide variety of topics. Christy is also a member of her community artists group and is recognized for her unique photographic skills that are on display at various galleries. She is married and has two sons that both share her love of writing and art.

The 20th century brought us the dawn of the digital information age and unprecedented changes in information technology. There is no indication that this rapid rate of change will be slowing—it may even be increasing. As we begin the 21st century, computer literacy is undoubtedly becoming a prerequisite in whatever career you choose.

The goal of the O'Leary Series is to provide you with the necessary skills to efficiently use these applications. Equally important is the goal to provide a foundation for students to readily and easily learn to use future versions of this software. This series does this by providing detailed step-by-step instructions combined with careful selection and presentation of essential concepts.

Times are changing, technology is changing, and this text is changing too. As students of today, you are different from those of yesterday. You put much effort toward the things that interest you and the things that are relevant to you. Your efforts directed at learning application programs and exploring the Web seem, at times, limitless.

On the other hand, students often can be shortsighted, thinking that learning the skills to use the application is the only objective. The mission of the series is to build upon and extend this interest by not only teaching the specific application skills but by introducing the concepts that are common to all applications, providing students with the confidence, knowledge, and ability to easily learn the next generation of applications.

Instructor's Resource Center

The Online **Instructor's Resource Center** contains access to a computerized Test Bank, an Instructor's Manual, Solutions, and PowerPoint Presentation Slides. Features of the Instructor's Resource are described below.

- **Instructor's Manual**   The Instructor's Manual, authored by the primary contributor, contains lab objectives, concepts, outlines, lecture notes, and command summaries. Also included are answers to all end-of-chapter material, tips for covering difficult materials, additional exercises, and a schedule showing how much time is required to cover text material.

- **Computerized Test Bank**   The test bank, authored by the primary contributor, contains hundreds of multiple choice, true/false, and discussion questions. Each question will be accompanied by the correct answer, the level of learning difficulty, and corresponding page references. Our flexible EZ Test software allows you to easily generate custom exams.

- **PowerPoint Presentation Slides**   The presentation slides, authored by the primary contributor, include lab objectives, concepts, outlines, text figures, and speaker's notes. Also included are bullets to illustrate key terms and FAQs.

Online Learning Center/Web Site

Found at **www.mhhe.com/oleary**, this site provides additional learning and instructional tools to enhance the comprehension of the text. The OLC/Web site is divided into these three areas:

- **Information Center**   Contains core information about the text, supplements, and the authors.

- **Instructor Center**   Offers the aforementioned instructional materials, downloads, and other relevant links for professors.

- **Student Center**   Contains data files, chapter competencies, chapter concepts, self-quizzes, additional Web links, and more.

Simnet Assessment for Office Applications

Simnet Assessment for Office Applications provides a way for you to test students' software skills in a simulated environment. Simnet is available for Microsoft Office 2010 and provides flexibility for you in your applications course by offering:

    Pretesting options
    Post-testing options
    Course placement testing
    Diagnostic capabilities to reinforce skills
    Web delivery of tests
    Certification preparation exams
    Learning verification reports

For more information on skills assessment software, please contact your local sales representative, or visit us at **www.mhhe.com**.

O'Leary Series

The O'Leary Application Series for Microsoft Office is available separately or packaged with *Computing Essentials*. The O'Leary Application Series offers a step-by-step case-based approach to learning computer applications and is available in both introductory and complete versions.

Computing Concepts

Computing Essentials 2012 offers a unique, visual orientation that gives students a basic understanding of computing concepts. *Computing Essentials* encourages "active" learning with exercises, explorations, visual illustrations, and screen shots. While combining the "active" learning style with current topics and technology, this text provides an accurate snapshot of computing trends. When bundled with software application lab manuals, students are given a complete representation of the fundamental issues surrounding the personal computing environment.

Tim and Linda O'Leary live in the American Southwest and spend much of their time engaging instructors and students in conversation about learning. In fact, they have been talking about learning for over 25 years. Something in those early conversations convinced them to write a book, to bring their interest in the learning process to the printed page. Today, they are as concerned as ever about learning, about technology, and about the challenges of presenting material in new ways, in terms of both content and method of delivery.

A powerful and creative team, Tim combines his 30 years of classroom teaching experience with Linda's background as a consultant and corporate trainer. Tim has taught courses at Stark Technical College in Canton, Ohio, and at Rochester Institute of Technology in upstate New York, and is currently a professor emeritus at Arizona State University in Tempe, Arizona. Linda offered her expertise at ASU for several years as an academic advisor. She also presented and developed materials for major corporations such as Motorola, Intel, Honeywell, and AT&T, as well as various community colleges in the Phoenix area.

Tim and Linda have talked to and taught numerous students, all of them with a desire to learn something about computers and applications that make their lives easier, more interesting, and more productive.

Each new edition of an O'Leary text, supplement, or learning aid has benefited from these students and their instructors who daily stand in front of them (or over their shoulders). The O'Leary Series is no exception.

Dedication

We dedicate this edition to our parents, Irene Perley Coats, Jean L. O'Leary, and Charles D. O'Leary, for all their support and love. We miss you.

Objectives

After completing the Introduction to Microsoft Office 2010, you should be able to:

1 Describe the Office 2010 applications.

2 Start an Office 2010 application.

3 Use the Ribbon, dialog boxes, and task panes.

4 Use menus, context menus, and shortcut keys.

5 Use Backstage view.

6 Open, close, and save files.

7 Navigate a document.

8 Enter, edit, and format text.

9 Select, copy, and move text.

10 Undo and redo changes.

11 Specify document properties.

12 Print a document.

13 Use Office 2010 Help.

14 Exit an Office 2010 application.

What Is Microsoft Office 2010?

Microsoft's Office 2010 is a comprehensive, integrated system of programs designed to solve a wide array of business needs. Although the programs can be used individually, they are designed to work together seamlessly, making it easy to connect people and organizations to information, business processes, and each other. The applications include tools used to create, discuss, communicate, and manage projects. If you share a lot of documents with other people, these features facilitate access to common documents. If you are away on business or do not have your PC with you, you can use Office 2010 Web applications, browser versions of Word, Excel, PowerPoint, and OneNote, to edit documents and collaborate with others.

Microsoft Office 2010 is packaged in several different combinations of programs or suites. The major programs and a brief description are provided in the following table.

Program	Description
Word 2010	Word processor program used to create text-based documents
Excel 2010	Spreadsheet program used to analyze numerical data
Access 2010	Database manager used to organize, manage, and display a database
PowerPoint 2010	Graphics presentation program used to create presentation materials
Outlook 2010	Desktop information manager and messaging client
InfoPath 2010	Used to create XML forms and documents
OneNote 2010	Note-taking and information organization tools
Publisher 2010	Tools to create and distribute publications for print, Web, and e-mail
Visio 2010	Diagramming and data visualization tools
SharePoint Designer 2010	Web site development and management for SharePoint servers
Project 2010	Project management tools

The four main components of Microsoft Office 2010—Word, Excel, Access, and PowerPoint—are the applications you will learn about in this series of labs. They are described in more detail in the following sections.

Word 2010

Word 2010 is a word processing software application whose purpose is to help you create text-based documents such as letters, memos, reports, e-mail messages, or any other type of correspondence. Word processors are one of the most flexible and widely used application software programs.

WORD 2010 FEATURES

The beauty of a word processor is that you can make changes or corrections as you are typing. Want to change a report from single spacing to double spacing? Alter the width of the margins? Delete some paragraphs and add others from yet another document? A word processor allows you to do all these things with ease.

Edit Content

Word 2010 excels in its ability to change or **edit** a document. Basic document editing involves correcting spelling, grammar, and sentence-structure errors and revising or updating existing by inserting, deleting, and rearranging areas of text. For example, a document that lists prices can easily be updated to reflect new prices. A document that details procedures can be revised by deleting old procedures and inserting new ones. Many of these changes are made easily by cutting (removing) or copying (duplicating) selected text and then pasting (inserting) the cut or copied text in another location in the same or another document. Editing allows you to quickly revise a document, by changing only the parts that need to be modified.

To help you produce a perfect document, Word 2010 includes many additional editing support features. The AutoCorrect feature checks the spelling and grammar in a document as text is entered. Many common errors are corrected automatically for you. Others are identified and a correction suggested. A thesaurus can be used to display alternative words that have a meaning similar or opposite to a word you entered. The Find and Replace feature can be used to quickly locate specified text and replace it with other text throughout a document. In addition, Word 2010 includes a variety of tools that automate the process of many common tasks, such as creating tables, form letters, and columns.

Format Content

You also can easily control the appearance or **format** of the document. Perhaps the most noticeable formatting feature is the ability to apply different fonts (type styles and sizes) and text appearance changes such as bold, italics, and color to all or selected portions of the document. Additionally, you can add color shading behind individual pieces of text or entire paragraphs and pages to add emphasis. Other formatting features include changes to entire paragraphs, such as the line spacing and alignment of text between the margins. You also can format entire pages by displaying page numbers, changing margin settings, and applying backgrounds.

To make formatting even easier, Word 2010 includes Document Themes and Styles. Document Themes apply a consistent font, color, and line effect to an entire document. Styles apply the selected style design to a selection of text. Further, Word 2010 includes a variety of built-in preformatted content that helps you quickly produce modern-looking, professional documents. Among these are galleries of cover page designs, pull quotes, and header and footer designs. While selecting many of these design choices, a visual live preview is displayed, making it easy to see how the design would look in your document. In addition, you can select from a wide variety of templates to help you get started on creating many common types of documents such as flyers, calendars, faxes, newsletters, and memos.

Insert Illustrations

To further enhance your documents, you can insert many different types of graphic elements. These include drawing objects, SmartArt, charts, pictures, clip art, and screenshots. The drawing tools supplied with Word 2010 can be used to create your own drawings, or you can select from over 100 adjustable shapes and modify them to your needs. All drawings can be further enhanced with 3-D effects, shadows, colors, and textures. SmartArt graphics allow you to create a visual representation of your information. They include many different layouts such as a process or cycle that are designed to help you communicate an idea. Charts can be inserted to illustrate and compare data. Complex pictures can be inserted in documents by scanning your own, using supplied or purchased clip art, or downloading images from the World Wide Web. Additionally, you can produce fancy text effects using the WordArt tool. Finally, you can quickly capture and insert a picture, called a screenshot, from another application running on your computer into the current document.

Collaborate with Others

Group collaboration on projects is common in industry today. Word 2010 includes many features to help streamline how documents are developed and changed by group members. A discussion feature allows multiple people to insert remarks in the same document without having to route the document to each person or reconcile multiple reviewers' comments. You can easily consolidate all changes and comments from different reviewers in one simple step and accept or reject changes as needed.

Two documents you will produce in the first two Word 2010 labs, a letter and flyer, are shown here.

A letter containing a tabbed table, indented paragraphs, and text enhancements is quickly created using basic Word features

January 27, 2012

Dear Adventure Traveler:

Imagine camping under the stars in Africa, hiking and paddling your way through the rainforests of Costa Rica, or following in the footsteps of the ancient Inca as you backpack along the Inca trail to Machu Picchu. Turn these thoughts of adventure into memories you will cherish forever by joining Adventure Travel Tours on one of our four new adventure tours.

To tell you more about these exciting new adventu... area. These presentations will focus on the features and cu... of the places you will visit and activities you can participate... Plan to attend one of the following presentations:

Date	Time	Locatio...
February 5	8:00 p.m.	Renaissan...
February 19	7:30 p.m.	Airport Pla...
March 8	8:00 p.m.	Crowne Co...

In appreciation of your past patronage, we are ple... of the new tour packages. You must book the trip at least ... this letter to qualify for the discount.

Our vacation tours are professionally developed s... everything in the price of your tour while giving you the be... these features:

➤ All accommodations and meals
➤ All entrance fees, excursions, transfers and tips
➤ Professional tour manager and local guides

We hope you will join us this year on another spe... Travel Tours each day is an adventure. For reservations, pl... Travel Tours directly at 1-800-555-0004.

Be...

St...
Ad...

ADVENTURE TRAVEL TOURS

NEW ADVENTURES

Attention adventure travelers! Attend an Adventure Travel presentation to learn about some of the earth's greatest unspoiled habitats and find out how you can experience the adventure of a lifetime. This year Adventure Travel Tours is introducing four new tours that offer you a unique opportunity to combine many different outdoor activities while exploring the world.

Costa Rica Rivers and Rainforests

India Wildlife Adventure

Safari in Tanzania

Inca Trail to Machu Picchu

Presentation dates and times are January 5 at 7:00 p.m., February 3 at 7:30 p.m., and March 8 at 7:00 p.m. All presentations are held at convenient hotel locations. The hotels are located in downtown Los Angeles, in Santa Clara, and at the LAX airport.

Call Adventure Travel Tours at 1-800-555-0004 for presentation locations, a full color brochure, and itinerary information, costs, and trip dates. Student Name will gladly help with all of your questions.

A flyer incorporating many visual enhancements such as colored text, varied text styles, and graphic elements is both eye-catching and informative

Excel 2010 is an electronic spreadsheet, or **worksheet**, that is used to organize, manipulate, and graph numeric data. Once used almost exclusively by accountants, worksheets are now widely used by nearly every profession. Nearly any job that uses rows and columns of numbers can be performed using an electronic spreadsheet. Once requiring hours of labor and/or costly accountants' fees, data analysis is now available almost instantly using electronic spreadsheets and has become a routine business procedure. This powerful business tool has revolutionized the business world. Typical uses include the creation of budgets and financial planning for both business and personal situations. Marketing professionals record and evaluate sales trends. Teachers record grades and calculate final grades. Personal trainers record the progress of their clients.

EXCEL 2010 FEATURES

Excel 2010 includes many features that not only help you create a well-designed worksheet, but one that produces accurate results. The features include the ability to quickly edit and format data, perform calculations, create charts, and print the spreadsheet. Using Excel 2010, you can quickly analyze and manage data and communicate your findings to others. The program not only makes it faster to create worksheets, but it also produces professional-appearing results.

Enter and Edit Data

The Microsoft Excel 2010 spreadsheet program uses a workbook file that contains one or more worksheets. Each worksheet can be used to organize different types of related information. The worksheet consists of rows and columns that create a grid of cells. You enter numeric data or descriptive text into a cell. These entries can then be erased, moved, copied, or edited.

Format Data

Like text in a Word document, the design and appearance of entries in a worksheet can be enhanced in many ways. For instance, you can change the font style and size and add special effects such as bold, italic, borders, boxes, drop shadows, and shading to selected cells. You also can use cell styles to quickly apply predefined combinations of these formats to selections. Additionally, you can select from different document themes, predefined combinations of colors, fonts, and effects, to give your workbooks a consistent, professional appearance.

Unlike the Word application, Excel includes many formatting features that are designed specifically for numeric data. For example, numeric entries can be displayed with commas, dollar signs, or a set number of decimal places. Special formatting, such as color bars, can be applied automatically to ranges of cells to emphasize data based on a set of criteria you establish and to highlight trends.

Analyze Data

The power of a spreadsheet application is its ability to perform calculations from very simple sums to the most complex financial and mathematical formulas. Formulas can be entered that perform calculations using data contained in specified cells. The results of the calculations are displayed in the cell containing the formula. Predefined formulas, called functions, can be used to quickly perform complex calculations such as calculating loan payments or statistical analysis of data.

Analysis of data in a spreadsheet once was too expensive and time-consuming. Now, using electronic worksheets, you can use what-if or sensitivity analysis by changing the values in selected cells and immediately observing the effect on related cells in the worksheet. Other analysis tools such as Solver and Scenarios allow you to see the effects of possible alternative courses of action to help forecast future outcomes.

Chart Data

Using Excel, you also can produce a visual display of numeric data in the form of graphs or charts. As the values in the worksheet change, charts referencing those values automatically adjust to reflect the changes. You also can enhance the appearance of a chart by using different type styles and sizes, adding three-dimensional effects, and including text and objects such as lines and arrows.

Two worksheets you will produce using Excel 2010 are shown below.

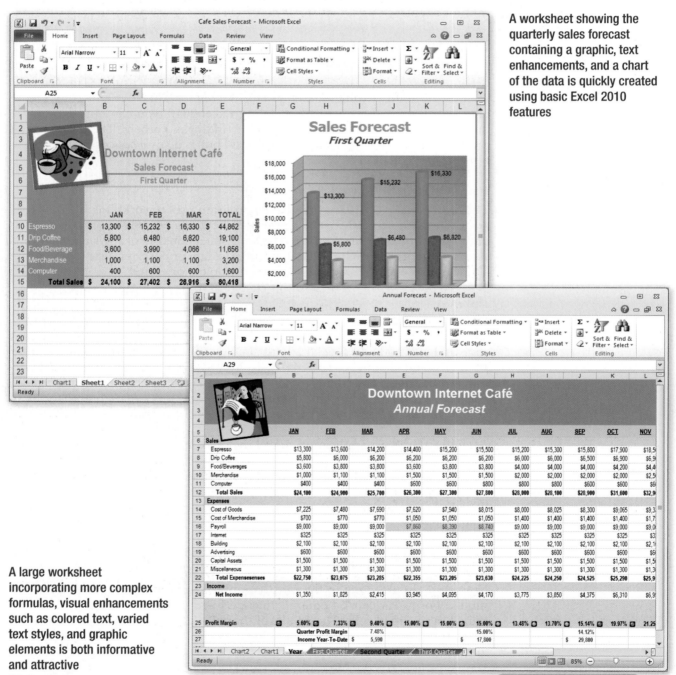

A worksheet showing the quarterly sales forecast containing a graphic, text enhancements, and a chart of the data is quickly created using basic Excel 2010 features

A large worksheet incorporating more complex formulas, visual enhancements such as colored text, varied text styles, and graphic elements is both informative and attractive

Access 2010 is a relational database management application that is used to create and analyze a database. A **database** is a collection of related data. **Tables** consist of columns (called **fields**) and rows (called **records**). Each row contains a record, which is all the information about one person, thing, or place. Each field is the smallest unit of information about a record.

In a relational database, the most widely used database structure, data is organized in linked tables. The tables are related or linked to one another by a common field. Relational databases allow you to create smaller and more manageable database tables, since you can combine and extract data between tables.

For example, a state's motor vehicle department database might have an address table. Each row (record) in the table would contain address information about one individual. Each column (field) would contain just one piece of information, for example, zip codes. The address table would be linked to other tables in the database by common fields. For example, the address table might be linked to a vehicle owner's table by name and linked to an outstanding citation table by license number (see example below).

Address Table

Name	License Number	Street Address	City	State	Zip
Aaron, Linda	FJ1987	10032 Park Lane	San Jose	CA	95127
Abar, John	D12372	1349 Oak St	Lakeville	CA	94128
Abell, Jack	LK3457	95874 State St	Stone	CA	95201

key fields linked

key fields linked

Owner's Table

Name	Plate Number
Abell, Jack	ABK241
Abrams, Sue	LMJ198
Abril, Pat	ZXA915

Outstanding Citation Table

License Number	Citation Code	Violation
T25476	00031	Speed
D98372	19001	Park
LK3457	89100	Speed

ACCESS 2010 FEATURES

Access 2010 is a powerful program with numerous easy-to-use features including the ability to quickly locate information; add, delete, modify, and sort records; analyze data; and produce professional-looking reports. Some of the basic Access 2010 features are described next.

Find Information

Once you enter data into the database table, you can quickly search the table to locate a specific record based on the data in a field. In a manual system, you can usually locate a record by knowing one key piece of information. For example, if the records are stored in a file cabinet alphabetically by last name, to quickly find a record, you must know the last name. In a computerized database, even if the records are sorted or organized by last name, you can still quickly locate a record using information in another field.

Add, Delete, and Modify Records

Using Access, it is also easy to add and delete records from the table. Once you locate a record, you can edit the contents of the fields to update the record or delete the record entirely from the table. You also can add new records to a table. When you enter a new record, it is automatically placed in the correct organizational location within the table. Creation of forms makes it easier to enter and edit data as well.

Sort and Filter Records

The capability to arrange or sort records in the table according to different fields can provide more meaningful information. You can organize records by name, department, pay, class, or any other category you need at a particular time. Sorting the records in different ways can provide information to different departments for different purposes.

Additionally, you can isolate and display a subset of records by specifying filter criteria. The criteria specify which records to display based on data in selected fields.

Analyze Data

Using Access, you can analyze the data in a table and perform calculations on different fields of data. Instead of pulling each record from a filing cabinet, recording the piece of data you want to use, and then performing the calculation on the recorded data, you can simply have the database program perform the calculation on all the values in the specified field. Additionally, you can ask questions or query the table to find only certain records that meet specific conditions to be used in the analysis. Information that was once costly and time-consuming to get is now quickly and readily available.

Generate Reports

Access includes many features that help you quickly produce reports ranging from simple listings to complex, professional-looking reports. You can create a simple report by asking for a listing of specified fields of data and restricting the listing to records meeting designated conditions. You can create a more complex professional report using the same restrictions or conditions as the simple report, but you can display the data in different layout styles, or with titles, headings, subtotals, or totals.

A database and a report that you will produce using Access 2010 are shown on the next page.

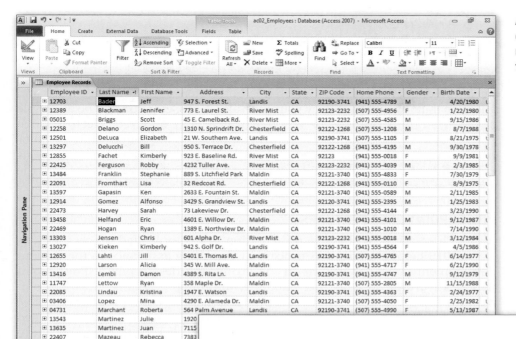

A relational database can be created and modified easily using basic Access 2010 features

Job Position Report

For **Landis**

Employee ID	First Name	Last Name	Position
11703	Jeff	Bader	Fitness Instructor
12389	Jennifer	Blackman	Sales Associate
05015	Scott	Briggs	Personal Trainer Director
12501	Elizabeth	DeLuca	Personal Trainer
12855	Kimberly	Fachet	Sales Associate
13484	Stephanie	Franklin	Food Service Server
12914	Alfonso	Gomez	Cleaning
22469	Ryan	Hogan	Personal Trainer
13303	Chris	Jensen	Greeter
13027	Kimberly	Kieken	Food Service Server
07650	Chris	Lamm	Sales Director
22085	Kristina	Lindau	Child Care Provider
13635	Juan	Martinez	Fitness Instructor
03225	Dan	Morgan	Food Service Director
99999	Student	Name	Human Resources Administrator
12420	Allison	Player	Maintenance
13005	Emily	Reilly	Assistant Manager
12297	Patricia	Rogondino	Greeter
07287	Anita	Roman	Child Care Director
12918	Carlos	Ruiz	Assistant Manager
00212	Chad	Schiff	Club Director
12585	Marie	Sullivan	Greeter
03890	Erona	Thi	Fitness Director
12380	Jessica	Thomas	Fitness Instructor

Saturday, December 01, 2012

Page 1 of 1

A professional-looking report can be quickly generated from information contained in a database

PowerPoint 2010 is a graphics presentation program designed to help you produce a high-quality presentation that is both interesting to the audience and effective in its ability to convey your message. A presentation can be as simple as overhead transparencies or as sophisticated as an on-screen electronic display. Graphics presentation programs can produce black-and-white or color overhead transparencies, 35 mm slides, onscreen electronic presentations called **slide shows**, Web pages for Web use, and support materials for both the speaker and the audience.

POWERPOINT 2010 FEATURES

Although creating an effective presentation is a complicated process, PowerPoint 2010 helps simplify this process by providing assistance in the content development phase, as well as in the layout and design phase. PowerPoint includes features such as text handling, outlining, graphing, drawing, animation, clip art, and multimedia support. In addition, the programs suggest layouts for different types of presentations and offer professionally designed templates to help you produce a presentation that is sure to keep your audience's attention. In addition, you can quickly produce the support materials to be used when making a presentation to an audience.

Develop, Enter, and Edit Content

The content development phase includes deciding on the topic of your presentation, the organization of the content, and the ultimate message you want to convey to the audience. As an aid in this phase, PowerPoint 2010 helps you organize your thoughts based on the type of presentation you are making by providing both content and design templates. Based on the type of presentation, such as selling a product or suggesting a strategy, the template provides guidance by suggesting content ideas and organizational tips. For example, if you are making a presentation on the progress of a sales campaign, the program would suggest that you enter text on the background of the sales campaign as the first page, called a **slide**; the current status of the campaign as the next slide; and accomplishments, schedule, issues and problems, and where you are heading on subsequent slides.

Design Layouts

The layout for each slide is the next important decision. Again, PowerPoint 2010 helps you by suggesting text layout features such as title placement, bullets, and columns. You also can incorporate graphs of data, tables, organizational charts, clip art, and other special text effects in the slides.

PowerPoint 2010 also includes professionally designed themes to further enhance the appearance of your slides. These themes include features that standardize the appearance of all the slides in your presentation. Professionally selected combinations of text and background colors, common typefaces and sizes, borders, and other art designs take the worry out of much of the design layout.

Deliver Presentations

After you have written and designed the slides, you can use the slides in an onscreen electronic presentation or a Web page for use on the Web. An onscreen presentation uses the computer to display the slides on an overhead projection screen. As you prepare this type of presentation, you can use the rehearsal feature that allows you to practice and time your presentation. The length of time to display each slide can be set and your entire presentation can be completed within the allotted time. A presentation also can be modified to display on a Web site and run using a Web browser. Finally, you can package the presentation to a CD for distribution.

A presentation that you will produce using PowerPoint 2010 is shown below.

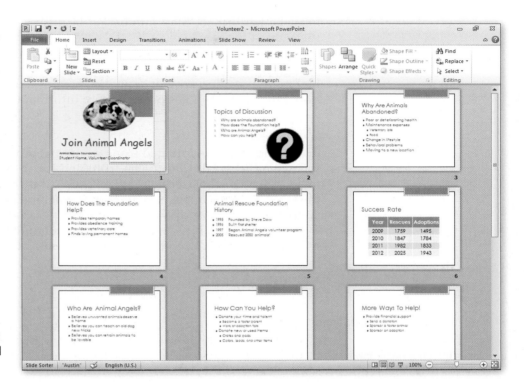

A presentation consists of a series of pages or "slides" presenting the information you want to convey in an organized and attractive manner

When running an on-screen presentation, each slide of the presentation is displayed full-screen on your computer monitor or projected onto a screen

Instructional Conventions

As you follow the directions in the following hands-on section and in the application labs, you need to know the instructional conventions that are used. Hands-on instructions you are to perform appear as a sequence of numbered steps. Within each step, a series of bullets identifies the specific actions that must be performed. Step numbering begins over within each topic heading throughout the lab.

Three types of marginal notes appear throughout the labs. Another Method notes provide alternate ways of performing the same command. Having Trouble? notes provide advice or cautions for steps that may cause problems. Additional Information notes provide more information about a topic.

COMMANDS

Commands that are initiated using a command button and the mouse appear following the word "Click." The icon (and the icon name if the icon does not include text) is displayed following "Click." If there is another way to perform the same action, it appears in an Another Method margin note when the action is first introduced as shown in Example A.

When a feature has already been covered and you are more familiar with using the application, commands will appear as shown in Example B.

Example A

1

● **Select the list of four tours.**

● **Open the Home tab.**

● **Click** **B** **Bold in the Font group.**

> **Another Method**
> The keyboard shortcut is Ctrl + B.

Example B

1

● **Select the list of four tours.**

● **Click** **B** **Bold in the Font group of the Home tab.**

OR

1

● **Bold the list of four tours.**

Sometimes, clicking on an icon opens a drop-down list or a menu of commands. Commands that are to be selected follow the word "Select" and appear in black text. You can select an item by pointing to it using the mouse or by moving to it using the directional keys. When an option is selected, it appears highlighted; however, the action is not carried out. Commands that you are to complete appear following the word "Choose." You can choose a command by clicking on it using the mouse or by pressing the [Enter] key once it is selected. Initially these commands will appear as in Example A. Choosing a command carries out the associated action. As you become more familiar with the application, commands will appear as shown in Example B.

Example A

1

● Click ▣ ▾ Font Color in the Font group of the Home tab.

● Select Green.

● Choose Dark Blue.

Example B

1

● Click ▣ ▾ Font Color and choose Dark Blue.

FILE NAMES AND INFORMATION TO TYPE

Plain blue text identifies file names you need to select or enter. Information you are asked to type appears in blue and bold. (See Example C.)

Example C

1

● **Open the document** wd01_Flyer.

● **Type** **Adventure Travel presents four new trips**

Common Office 2010 Features

Now that you know a little about each of the applications in Microsoft Office 2010, you will take a look at some of the features that are common to all Office 2010 applications. In this hands-on section you will learn to use the common interface and application features to allow you to get a feel for how Office 2010 works. Although Word 2010 will be used to demonstrate how the features work, only features that are common to all the Office applications will be addressed.

COMMON INTERFACE FEATURES

All the Office 2010 applications have a common **user interface**, a set of graphical elements that are designed to help you interact with the program and provide instructions as to the actions you want to perform. These features include the use of the Ribbon, Quick Access Toolbar, task panes, menus, dialog boxes, and the File tab.

Additional Information

The procedure to start Excel, Access, and PowerPoint is the same as starting Word, except that you must select the appropriate program name or shortcut.

Starting an Office 2010 Application

To demonstrate the common features, you will start the Word 2010 application. There are several ways to start an Office 2010 application. The two most common methods are by clicking the ● Start button to see a menu of available programs or by clicking a desktop shortcut for the program if it is available.

1

● Click ● Start to display the Start menu.

● Choose Microsoft Word 2010.

Having Trouble?

If you do not see the program name on the Start menu, select All Programs, choose Microsoft Office, and then choose Microsoft Word 2010.

OR

1

● Double-click the [icon] shortcut on the desktop.

2

● If necessary, click ▣ Maximize in the title bar to maximize the window.

Your screen should be similar to Figure 1

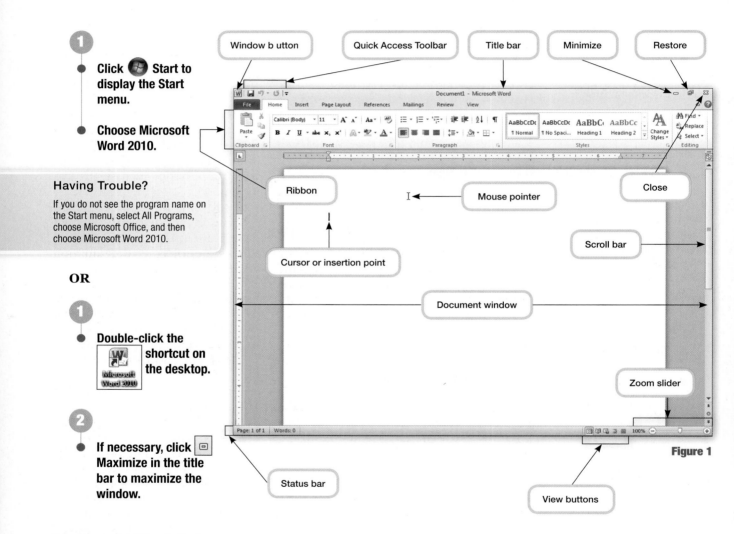

Figure 1

The Word 2010 program is started and displayed in a window on the desktop. All application windows display a title bar at the top of the window that includes the file name followed by the program name, in this case Microsoft Word. They also include the ⬜ Minimize, ⬚ Restore Down, and ⊠ Close buttons at the right end of the title bar. **Buttons** are graphical elements that perform the associated action when you click on them using the mouse. At the left end of the title bar is the W Window button. Clicking this button opens a menu of commands that allow you to size, move, and close the window just as the buttons on the right end of the title bar. To the right of the W Window button is the **Quick Access Toolbar** (QAT), which provides quick access to frequently used commands. By default, it includes the 🖫 Save, ↺ Undo, and ↻ Redo buttons, commands that Microsoft considers to be crucial. It is always available and is a customizable toolbar to which you can add your own favorite buttons.

Below the title bar is the **Ribbon**, which provides a centralized location of commands that are used to work in your document. The Ribbon has the same basic structure and is found in all Office 2010 applications. However, many of the commands found in the Ribbon vary with the specific applications. You will learn how to use the Ribbon shortly.

The large center area of the program window is the **document window** where open application files are displayed. When you first start Word 2010, a new blank Word document named Document1 (shown in the title bar) automatically opens, ready for you to start creating a new document. In Excel, a new, blank workbook named Book1 would be opened and in PowerPoint a new, blank presentation file named Presentation1 would be opened. In Access, however, a new blank database file is not opened automatically. Instead, you must create and name a new database file or open an existing database file.

The **cursor**, also called the **insertion point**, is the blinking vertical bar that marks your location in the document and indicates where text you type will appear. Across all Office applications, the mouse pointer appears as I I-beam when it is used to position the insertion point when entering text and as a ⌖ when it can be used to select items. There are many other mouse pointer shapes that are both common to and specific to the different applications.

On the right of the document window is a vertical scroll bar. A **scroll bar** is used with a mouse to bring additional information into view in a window. The vertical scroll bar is used to move up or down. A horizontal scroll bar is also displayed when needed and moves side to side in the window. The scroll bar is a common feature to all Windows and Office 2010 applications; however, it may not appear in all applications until needed.

At the bottom of the application window is another common feature called the **status bar**. It displays information about the open file and features that help you view the file. It displays different information depending upon the application you are using. For example, the Word status bar displays information about the number of pages and words in the document, whereas the Excel status bar displays the mode of operation and the count, average, and sum of values in selected cells. All Office 2010 applications include **View buttons** that are used to change how the information in the document window is displayed. The View buttons are different for each application. Finally, a **Zoom Slider**, located at the far right end of the status bar, is used to change the amount of information displayed in the document window by "zooming in" to get a close-up view or "zooming out" to see more of the document at a reduced view.

Displaying ScreenTips

You are probably wondering how you would know what action the different buttons perform. To help you identify buttons, the Office applications display ScreenTips when you point to them.

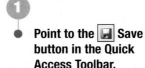

1 ● Point to the 🖫 Save button in the Quick Access Toolbar.

Your screen should be similar to Figure 2

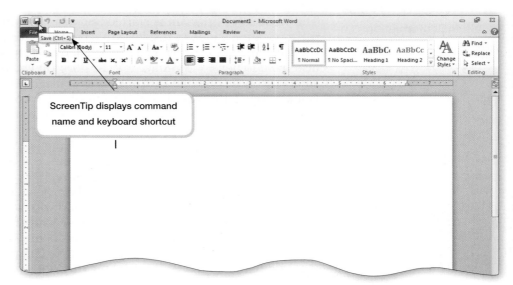

ScreenTip displays command name and keyboard shortcut

Figure 2

A **ScreenTip**, also called a **tooltip**, appears displaying the command name and the keyboard shortcut, Ctrl + S. A **keyboard shortcut** is a combination of keys that can be used to execute a command in place of clicking the button. In this case, if you hold down the Ctrl key while typing the letter S, you will access the command to save a file. ScreenTips also often include a brief description of the action a command performs.

Using Menus

Notice the small button ⏷ at the end of the Quick Access Toolbar. Clicking this button opens a menu of commands that perform tasks associated with the Quick Access Toolbar.

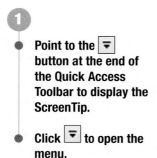

1 ● Point to the ⏷ button at the end of the Quick Access Toolbar to display the ScreenTip.

● Click ⏷ to open the menu.

Your screen should be similar to Figure 3

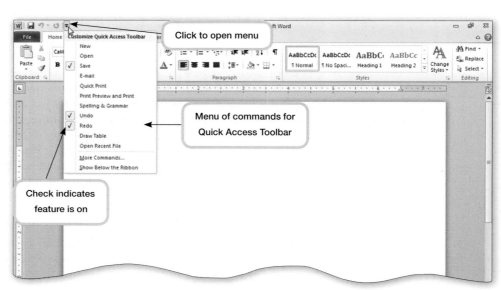

Click to open menu

Menu of commands for Quick Access Toolbar

Check indicates feature is on

Figure 3

The first 11 items in the menu allow you to quickly add a command button to or remove a command button from the Quick Access Toolbar. Those commands that are already displayed in the Quick Access Toolbar are preceded with a checkmark. The last two commands allow you to access other command features to customize the Quick Access Toolbar or change its location.

Once a menu is open, you can select a command from the menu by pointing to it. As you do the selected command appears highlighted. Like buttons, resting the mouse pointer over the menu command options will display a ScreenTip. Then to choose a selected command, you click on it. Choosing a command performs the action associated with the command or button. You will use several of these features next.

2

● Point to the commands in the Quick Access Toolbar menu to select (highlight) them and see the ScreenTips.

● Click on the Open command to choose it and add it to the Quick Access Toolbar.

Your screen should be similar to Figure 4

Figure 4

The command button to open a document has been added to the Quick Access Toolbar. Next, you will remove this button and then you will change the location of the Quick Access Toolbar. Another way to access some commands is to use a context menu. A **context menu**, also called a **shortcut menu**, is opened by right-clicking on an item on the screen. This menu is context sensitive, meaning it displays only those commands relevant to the item or screen location. For example, right-clicking on the Quick Access Toolbar will display the commands associated with using the Quick Access Toolbar and the Ribbon. You will use this method to remove the Open button and move the Quick Access Toolbar.

3

● Point to the Open button on the Quick Access Toolbar and right-click.

● Click on the Remove from Quick Access Toolbar command to choose it.

● Right-click on any button in the Quick Access Toolbar again and choose the Show Quick Access Toolbar Below the Ribbon option.

Another Method

You also can type the underlined letter of a command to choose it or press [Enter] to choose a selected command.

Your screen should be similar to Figure 5

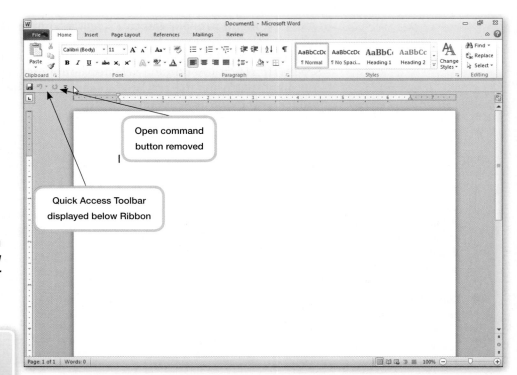

Open command button removed

Quick Access Toolbar displayed below Ribbon

Figure 5

The Quick Access Toolbar is now displayed full size below the Ribbon. This is useful if you have many buttons on the toolbar; however, it takes up document viewing space. You will return it to its compact size.

4

● Display the Quick Access Toolbar menu.

● Choose Show Above the Ribbon.

Your screen should be similar to Figure 6

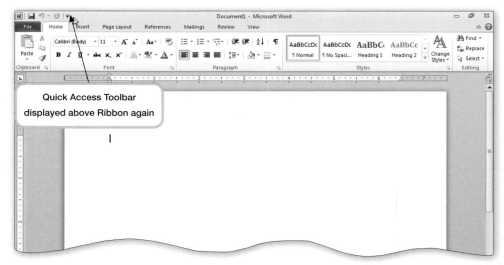

Quick Access Toolbar displayed above Ribbon again

Figure 6

The Quick Access Toolbar is displayed above the Ribbon again.

Using the Ribbon

The Ribbon has three basic parts: tabs, groups, and commands (see Figure 7). **Tabs** are used to divide the Ribbon into major activity areas. Each tab is then organized into **groups** that contain related items. The related items are **commands** that consist of command buttons, a box to enter information, or a menu. Clicking on a command button performs the associated action or displays a list of additional options.

The Ribbon tabs, commands, and features vary with the different Office applications. For example, the Word Ribbon displays tabs and commands used to create a text document, whereas the Excel Ribbon displays tabs and commands used to create an electronic worksheet. Although the Ribbon commands are application specific, many are also common to all Office 2010 applications. In all applications, the Ribbon also can be customized by changing the built-in tabs or creating your own tabs and groups to personalize your workspace and provide faster access to the commands you use most.

Opening Tabs

The Word application displays the File tab and seven Ribbon tabs. The Home tab (shown in Figure 6), consisting of five groups, appears highlighted, indicating it is the open or active tab. This tab is available in all the Office 2010 applications and because it contains commands that are most frequently used when you first start an application or open a file, it is initially the open tab. In Word, the commands in the Home tab help you perform actions related to creating the text content of your document. In the other Office 2010 applications, the Home tab contains commands related to creating the associated type of document, such as a worksheet, presentation, or database. To open another tab you click on the tab name.

1

● **Click on the Insert tab.**

Your screen should be similar to Figure 7

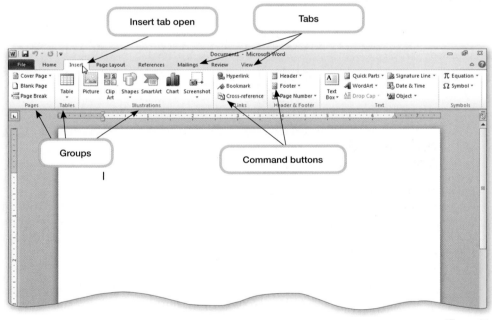

Figure 7

This Insert tab is now open and is the active tab. It contains seven groups whose commands have to do with inserting items into a document. As you use the Office applications, you will see that the Ribbon contains many of the same tabs, groups, and commands across the applications. For example, the Insert tab is available in all applications except Access. Others, such as the References tab in Word, are specific to the application. You also will see that many of the groups and commands in the common tabs, such as the Clipboard group of commands in the Home tab, contain all or many of the same commands across applications. Other groups in the common tabs contain commands that are specific to the application.

To save space, some tabs, called **contextual tabs** or **on-demand tabs**, are displayed only as needed. For example, when you are working with a picture, the Picture Tools tab appears. The contextual nature of this feature keeps the work area uncluttered when the feature is not needed and provides ready access to it when it is needed.

2

● **Click on each of the other tabs, ending with the View tab, to see their groups and commands.**

Additional Information

If you have a mouse with a scroll wheel, pointing to the tab area of the ribbon and using the scroll wheel will scroll the tabs.

Your screen should be similar to Figure 8

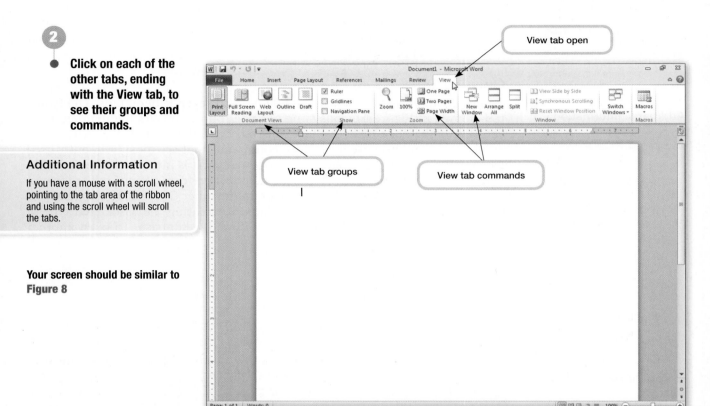

Figure 8

Each tab relates to a type of activity; for example, the View tab commands perform activities related to viewing the document. Within each tab, similar commands are grouped together to make it easy to find the commands you want to use.

Displaying Enhanced ScreenTips

Although command buttons display graphic representations of the action they perform, often the graphic is not descriptive enough. As you have learned, pointing to a button displays the name of the button and the keyboard shortcut in a ScreenTip. To further help explain what a button does, many buttons in the Ribbon display **Enhanced ScreenTips**. For example, the Paste button in the Clipboard group of the Home tab is a two-part button. Clicking on the upper part will immediately perform an action, whereas clicking on the lower part will display additional options. You will use this feature next to see the Enhanced ScreenTips.

1

- Click on the **Home** tab to open it.

- Point to the upper part of the 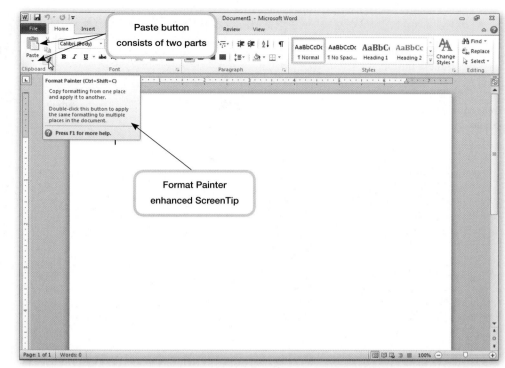 Paste button in the Clipboard group.

- Point to the lower part of the Paste button in the Clipboard group.

- Point to Format Painter in the Clipboard group.

Your screen should be similar to Figure 9

Figure 9

Because the Paste button is divided into two parts, both parts display separate Enhanced ScreenTips containing the button name; the keyboard shortcut key combination, Ctrl + V; and a brief description of what action will be performed when you click on that part of the button. Pointing to Format Painter displays an Enhanced ScreenTip that provides more detailed information about the command. Enhanced ScreenTips may even display information such as procedures or illustrations. You can find out what the feature does without having to look it up using Office Help, a built-in reference source. If a feature has a Help article, you can automatically access it by pressing F1 while the Enhanced ScreenTip is displayed.

Using Command Buttons

Clicking on most command buttons immediately performs the associated action. Many command buttons, however, include an arrow as part of the button that affects how the button works. If a button includes an arrow that is separated from the graphic with a line when you point to the button (as in Bullets), clicking the button performs the associated default action and clicking the arrow displays a menu of options. If a button displays an arrow that is not separated from the graphic with a line when you point to it (as in Line Spacing), clicking the button immediately displays a menu of options. To see an example of a drop-down menu, you will open the Bullets menu.

1

● Click ⏷ in the ▤ ▾ Bullets button.

Your screen should be similar to Figure 10

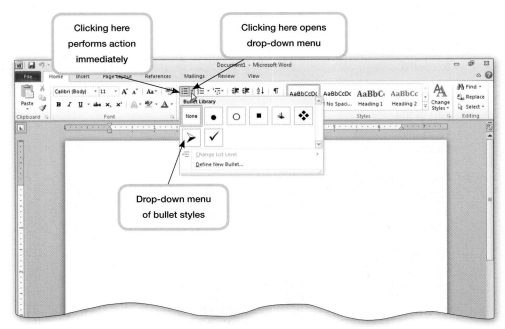

Clicking here performs action immediately

Clicking here opens drop-down menu

Drop-down menu of bullet styles

Figure 10

A drop-down menu of different bullet styles is displayed. The drop-down menu will disappear when you make a selection or click on any other area of the window.

2

● Click outside the Bullet menu to clear it.

● Click ▤ ▾ Line and Paragraph Spacing.

Your screen should be similar to Figure 11

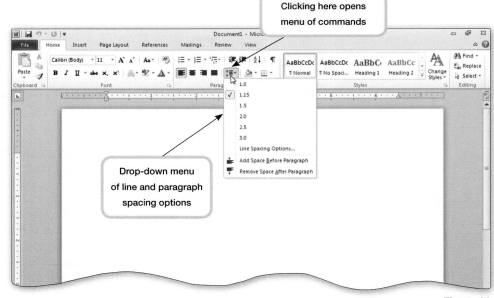

Clicking here opens menu of commands

Drop-down menu of line and paragraph spacing options

Figure 11

Another Method

You also can open tabs and choose Ribbon commands using the access key shortcuts. Press Alt or F10 to display the access key letters in KeyTips over each available feature. Then type the letter for the feature you want to use.

The menu of options opened automatically when you clicked ▤ ▾ Line and Paragraph Spacing.

Using the Dialog Box Launcher

Because there is not enough space, only the most used commands are displayed in the Ribbon. If more commands are available, a ⊡ button, called the **dialog box launcher**, is displayed in the lower-right corner of the group. Clicking ⊡ opens a dialog box or task pane of additional options.

1

● **Click outside the Line and Paragraph Spacing menu to clear it.**

● **Point to the ⊡ of the Paragraph group to see the ScreenTip.**

● **Click ⊡ of the Paragraph group.**

Your screen should be similar to Figure 12

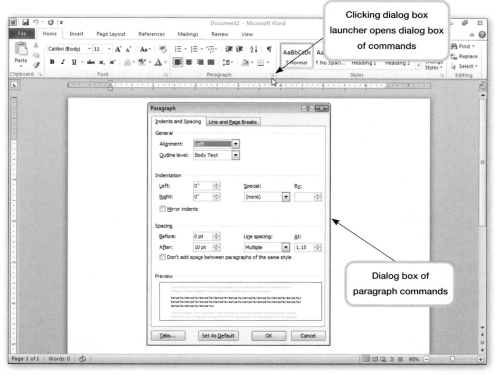

Figure 12

The Paragraph dialog box appears. It provides access to the more advanced paragraph settings options. Selecting options from the dialog box and clicking ⟦ OK ⟧ will close the dialog box and apply the options as specified. To cancel the dialog box, you can click ⟦ Cancel ⟧ or ⟦✖⟧ Close in the dialog box title bar.

2

● **Click ✖ to close the dialog box.**

● **Click ⊡ in the Clipboard group.**

Your screen should be similar to Figure 13

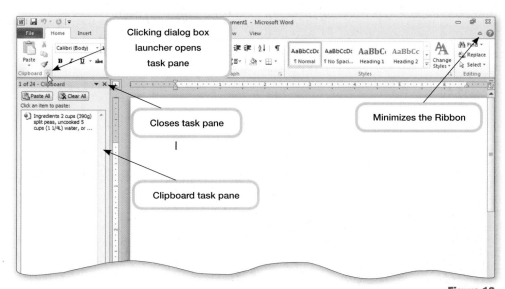

Figure 13

A task pane is open that contains features associated with the Clipboard. Unlike a dialog box, a task pane is a separate window that can be sized and moved. Generally, task panes are attached or docked to one edge of the application window. Also, task panes remain open until you close them. This allows you to make multiple selections from the task pane while continuing to work on other areas of your document.

• Click ☒ **Close in the upper-right corner of the task pane to close it.**

Minimize and Expand the Ribbon

Sometimes you may not want to see the entire Ribbon so that more space is available in the document area. You can minimize the Ribbon by double-clicking the active tab.

• **Double-click the Home tab.**

Your screen should be similar to Figure 14

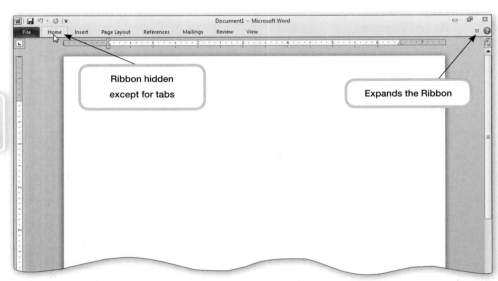

Figure 14

Now, the only part of the Ribbon that is visible is the tab area. Then, to expand the Ribbon, simply double click on the tab you want to make active. Another way to hide and redisplay the Ribbon is to click ☒ Minimize the Ribbon or ☒ Expand the Ribbon located at the far right end of the Ribbon tabs. You will unhide it using this feature.

• Click ☒ **Expand the Ribbon.**

The full Ribbon reappears and the tab that was active when you minimized the Ribbon is active again.

Using Backstage View

To the left of the Home tab in the Ribbon is the File tab. Unlike the other tabs that display a Ribbon of commands, the File tab opens Backstage view. **Backstage view** contains commands that allow you to work *with* your document, unlike the Ribbon that allows you to work *in* your document.

Backstage view contains commands that apply to the entire document. For example, you will find commands to open, save, print, and manage your files and set your program options. This tab is common to all the Office 2010 applications, although the menu options may vary slightly.

1

● **Click the File tab to open Backstage view.**

Your screen should be similar to Figure 15

Command buttons

Tabs

Command buttons

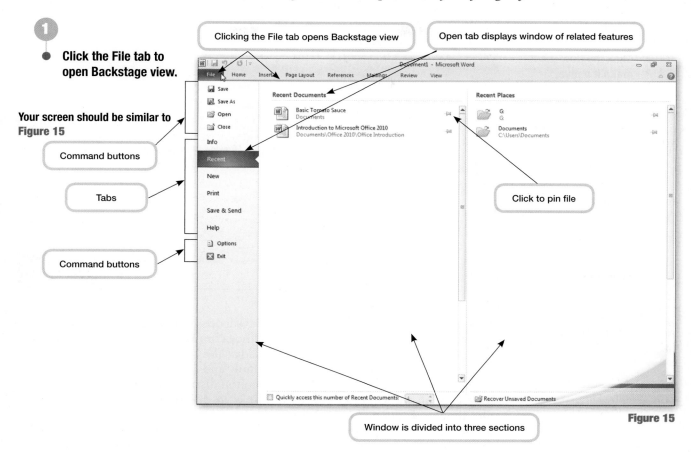

Clicking the File tab opens Backstage view

Open tab displays window of related features

Click to pin file

Window is divided into three sections

Figure 15

Another Method

You also can use the directional keys to move up, down, left, or right within Backstage view and press Enter to choose a selected command or tab.

Additional Information

A list of recent files also may appear above the Info tab if this option is selected.

Additional Information

Clicking [ ] next to a file name pins the file and permanently keeps the file name in the recently used list until it is unpinned.

The document window is hidden and the Backstage view window is open. The Backstage view window completely covers the document window and is divided into sections or panes. In all Office 2010 applications, the first (left) section always displays command buttons and tabs. You can select a tab or a button by pointing to it. As you do, the selected tab or button appears highlighted. Then to choose a selected tab or button, you click on it. Choosing a command button either opens a dialog box or immediately performs the associated action. Clicking a tab opens the tab and displays the related commands and features.

When you first open Backstage view and you have not yet opened a document or started to create a new document, the Recent tab is open. It displays a list of links to recently opened Word files in the second section, making it easy to quickly locate and resume using a file. The third section displays a list of folder locations that have been recently visited. In Excel, PowerPoint, and Access, the recently opened file list displays files for the associated application. The list of files and folders changes as you work to reflect only the most recent files and folder locations. The most recently used files and folder locations appear at the top of the list.

Next, you will try out some of these features by selecting and opening different tabs and command buttons.

2

• Point to all the tabs
and commands in
the Backstage view
menu.

• Click the New tab to
make it active.

**Your screen should be similar to
Figure 16**

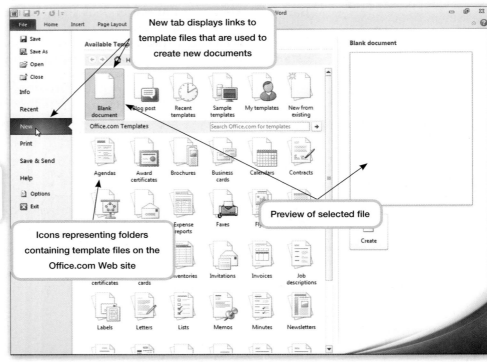

Figure 16

The second section of the New tab displays icons representing links to available
templates on your computer or on the Office.com Web site. A **template** is a professionally designed document that is used as the basis for a new document. The
Blank document icon is selected by default and is used to create a new Word
document file from scratch. The third section displays a preview of the selected
file. Icons in the Office.com area are links to different categories of template
files that are contained in folders. Clicking on a folder icon opens the folder and
displays file icons. Double-clicking on a file icon opens the file in Word. Again,
the available templates are specific to the Office application you are using.

3

• Click the Info tab.

**Your screen should be similar to
Figure 17**

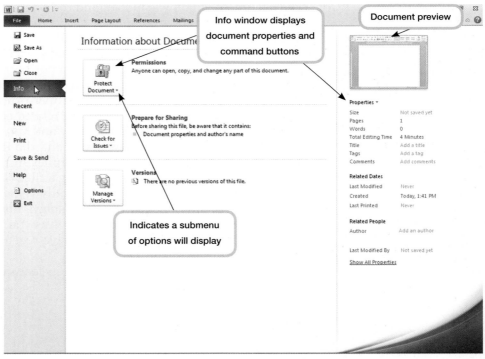

Figure 17

The Info tab displays information about your current document. The three buttons in the second section are used to define permissions, check for issues related to distribution, and manage document versions for the current document. A description of these buttons and the current document settings is shown to the right of the button. Notice that the buttons display a ▾. This indicates that a menu of commands will be displayed when you click the button. The third section displays a preview picture of the current document and a list of the settings, called **properties**, associated with the document. The current properties displayed in the Info window show the initial or **default** properties associated with a new blank document.

4

Click 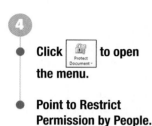 to open the menu.

Point to Restrict Permission by People.

Your screen should be similar to Figure 18

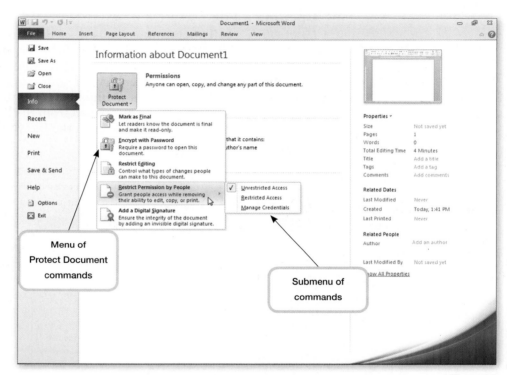

Figure 18

The Protect Document drop-down menu displays five commands. The highlighted command displays a submenu of additional commands. Next, you will clear the Protect Document menu and close Backstage view.

5

Click 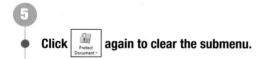 again to clear the submenu.

Click the Home tab to close Backstage view and open the Home tab again.

COMMON APPLICATION FEATURES

So far you have learned about using the Office 2010 user interface features. Next, you will learn about application features that are used to work in and modify documents and are the same or similar in all Office 2010 applications. These include how to open, close, and save files; navigate, scroll, and zoom a document; enter, select, edit, and format text; and document, preview, and print a file. To do this, you will open a Word document file and make a few changes to it. Then you will save and print the revised document. Once you have gained an understanding of the basic concepts of the common features using Word, you will be able to easily apply them in the other Office applications.

Opening a File

In all Office 2010 applications, you either need to create a new file using the blank document file or open an existing file. Opening a file retrieves a file that is stored on your computer hard drive or an external storage device and places it in RAM (random access memory) of your computer so it can be read and modified. There are two main methods that can be used to open an existing file. One is to select the file to be opened from the list of recently opened documents. If you have not recently opened the file you want to use, then you use the Open command in Backstage view.

1

- **Click the File tab to open Backstage view.**

- **Click** [Open].

Your screen should be similar to Figure 19

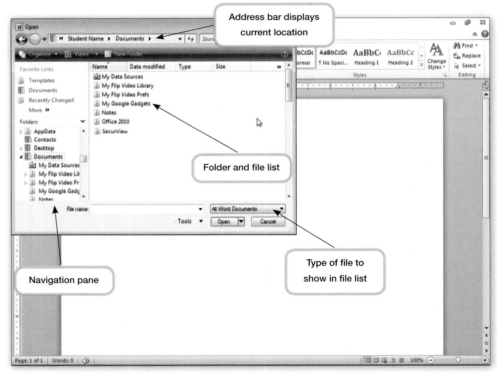

Figure 19

Additional Information

The Open dialog box is common to all programs using the Windows operating system. Your dialog box may look slightly different depending on the version of Windows on your computer.

The Open dialog box is displayed in which you specify the location where the file you want to open is stored and the file name. The location consists of identifying the hard drive of your computer or an external storage device or a remote computer followed by folders and subfolders within that location. The Address bar displays the default folder as the location to open the file. The file list displays folder names as well as the names of any Word documents in the current location. Only Word documents are listed because All Word Documents is the specified file type in the File Type list box. In Excel and PowerPoint, only files of that application's file type would be displayed.

First you need to change the location to where your data files for completing these labs are stored. The file location may be on a different drive, in an external storage device, or in a folder or subfolder. There are several methods that can be used to locate files. One is to use the Address bar to specify another location by either typing the complete folder name or path or by opening the drop-down list of previously accessed locations and clicking a new location. Another is to use the Favorite Links list in the Navigation pane, which provides shortcut links to specific folders on your computer. A third is to use the Folders list in the navigation pane to navigate through the hierarchical structure of drives and folders on your computer. Clicking a link or folder from the list displays files at that location in the file list. Then, from the file list, you can continue to select subfolders until the file you want to open is located.

2

● **Change to the location where your student data files for this lab are located.**

Your screen should be similar to Figure 20

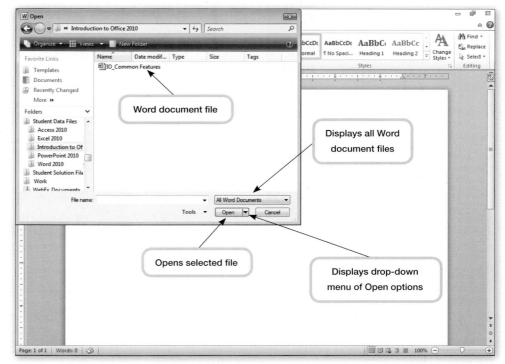

Figure 20

Now the file list displays the names of all Word files at that location. Next, you open the file by selecting it and clicking the Open button. In addition, in the Office applications you can specify how you want to open a file by choosing from the Open drop-down menu options described in the following table.

Open Options	Description
Open	Opens with all formatting and editing features enabled. This is the default setting.
Open Read-only	Opens file so it can be read or copied only, not modified in any way.
Open as Copy	Automatically creates a copy of the file and opens the copy with complete editing capabilities.
Open in Browser	Opens HTML type files in a Web browser.
Open with Transform	Opens certain types of documents and lets you change it into another type of document.
Open in Protected View	Opens files from potentially unsafe locations with editing functions disabled.
Open and Repair	Opens file and attempts to repair any damage.

You will open the file IO_Common Features. Clicking the [Open ▼] button opens the file using the default Open option so you can read and edit the file.

3

● **Select** IO_Common Features.

● **Click** [Open ▼].

Your screen should be similar to Figure 21

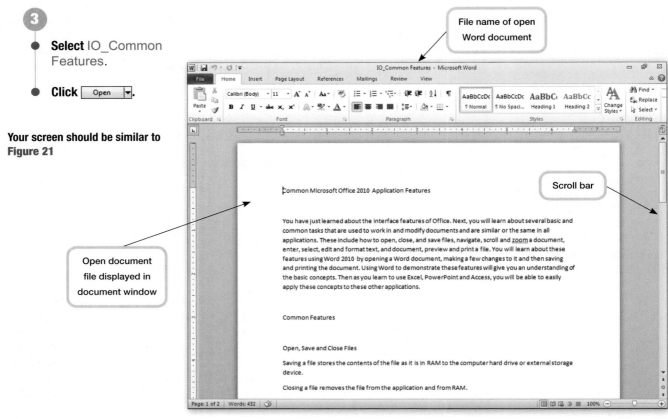

File name of open Word document

Open document file displayed in document window

Scroll bar

Figure 21

A Word document file describing the common Microsoft Office application features is displayed in the document window.

Scrolling the Document Window

As documents increase in size, they cannot be easily viewed in their entirety in the document window and much time can be spent moving to different locations in the document. All Office 2010 applications include features that make it easy to move around and view the information in a large document. The basic method is to scroll through a document using the scroll bar or keyboard. Both methods are useful, depending on what you are doing. For example, if you are entering text using the keyboard, using the keyboard method may be more efficient than using the mouse.

The table below explains the basic mouse and keyboard techniques that can be used to vertically scroll a document in the Office 2010 applications. There are many other methods for navigating through documents that are unique to an application. They will be discussed in the specific application text.

Mouse or Key Action	Effect in:			
	Word	**Excel**	**PowerPoint**	**Access**
Click ▼ Or ↓	Moves down line by line.	Moves down row by row	Moves down slide by slide	Moves down record by record
Click ▲ Or ↑	Moves up line by line.	Moves up row by row	Moves up slide by slide	Moves up record by record
Click above/below scroll box Or Page Up / Page Down	Moves up/down window by window	Moves up/down window by window	Displays previous/next slide	Moves up/down window by window
Drag ▤ Scroll Box	Moves up/down line by line	Moves up/down row by row	Moves up/down slide by slide	Moves up/down record by record
Ctrl + Home	Moves to beginning of document	Moves to first cell in worksheet or beginning of cell entry	Moves to first slide in presentation or beginning of entry in placeholder	Moves to first record in table or beginning of field entry
Ctrl + End	Moves to end of document	Moves to last-used cell in worksheet or end of cell entry	Moves to last slide in presentation or to end of placeholder entry	Moves to last record in table or end of field entry

You will use the vertical scroll bar to view the text at the bottom of the Word document. When you use the scroll bar to scroll, the actual location in the document where you can work does not change, only the area you are viewing changes. For example, in Word, the cursor does not move and in Excel the cell you can work in does not change. To move the cursor or make another cell active, you must click in a location in the window. However, when you scroll using the keyboard, the actual location as identified by the position of the cursor in the document also changes. For example, in Word the cursor attempts to maintain its position in a line as you scroll up and down through the document. In Excel the cell you can work in changes as you move through a worksheet using the keyboard.

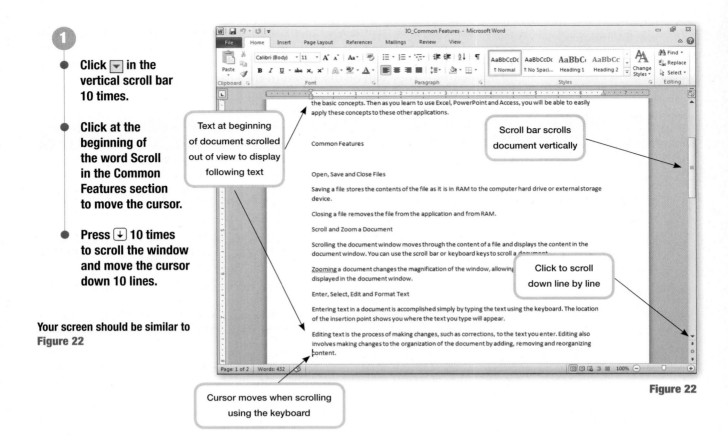

1

- Click ▾ in the vertical scroll bar 10 times.

- Click at the beginning of the word Scroll in the Common Features section to move the cursor.

- Press ↓ 10 times to scroll the window and move the cursor down 10 lines.

Your screen should be similar to Figure 22

Text at beginning of document scrolled out of view to display following text

Scroll bar scrolls document vertically

Click to scroll down line by line

Cursor moves when scrolling using the keyboard

Figure 22

Having Trouble?

If your screen scrolls differently, this is a function of the type of monitor you are using.

The text at the beginning of the document has scrolled line by line off the top of the document window, and the following text is now displayed. In a large document, scrolling line by line can take a while. You will now try out several additional mouse and keyboard scrolling features that move by larger increments through the document.

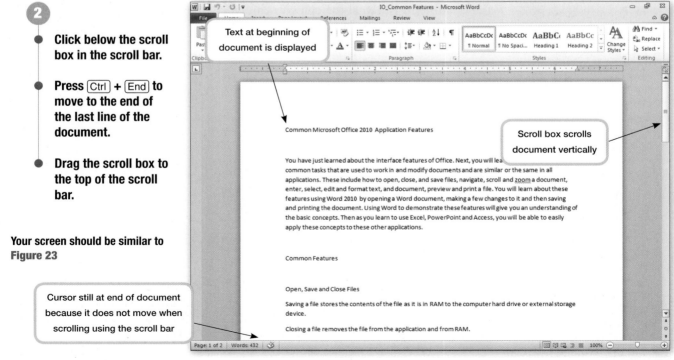

2

- Click below the scroll box in the scroll bar.

- Press Ctrl + End to move to the end of the last line of the document.

- Drag the scroll box to the top of the scroll bar.

Your screen should be similar to Figure 23

Text at beginning of document is displayed

Scroll box scrolls document vertically

Cursor still at end of document because it does not move when scrolling using the scroll bar

Figure 23

The document window displays the beginning of the document; however, the cursor is still at the end of the document. Using these features makes scrolling a large document much more efficient.

Using the Zoom Feature

Another way to see more or less of a document is to use the zoom feature. Although this feature is available in all Office 2010 applications, Excel and PowerPoint have fewer options than Word. In Access, the zoom feature is available only when specific features are used, such as viewing reports.

The Zoom Slider in the status bar is used to change the magnification. To use the Zoom Slider, click and drag the slider control. Dragging to the right zooms in on the document and increases the magnification whereas dragging to the left zooms out on the document and decreases the magnification. You also can change the zoom percentage by increments of 10 by clicking the ⊕ or ⊖ on each end of the slider control. In Word, the default display, 100 percent, shows the characters the same size they will be when printed. You can increase the onscreen character size up to five times the normal display (500 percent) or reduce the character size to 10 percent.

You will first "zoom out" on the document to get an overview of the file, and then you will "zoom in" to get a close-up look. When a document is zoomed, you can work in it as usual.

Additional Information

The degree of magnification varies with the different applications.

● Click ⊖ in the Zoom Slider five times to decrease the zoom percentage to 50%.

● Press Ctrl + Home to move the cursor to the beginning of the document.

● Drag the Zoom Slider all the way to the right to increase the zoom to 500%.

Your screen should be similar to Figure 24

Another Method

You can also hold down Ctrl while using the scroll wheel on your mouse to zoom a document.

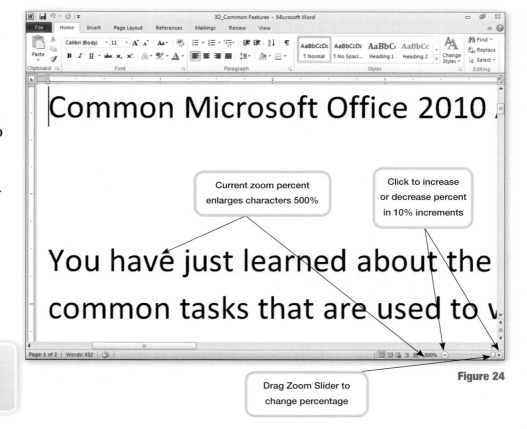

Current zoom percent enlarges characters 500%

Click to increase or decrease percent in 10% increments

Drag Zoom Slider to change percentage

Figure 24

Another Method

You can also click on the zoom percentage in the status bar to open the Zoom dialog box.

Another way to change the magnification is to use the 🔍 button in the View tab. This method opens the Zoom dialog box containing several preset zoom options, or an option that lets you set a precise percentage using the Percent scroll box. You will use this feature next to zoom the document. This method is available in Word only.

2

- Open the View tab.

- Click  in the Zoom group.

- Click Whole Page and note that the percent value in the Percent text box and the preview area reflect the new percentage setting.

- Click the ▲ up scroll button in the Percent scroll box to increase the zoom percentage to 57.

Another Method

You could also type a value in the Percent text box to specify an exact percentage.

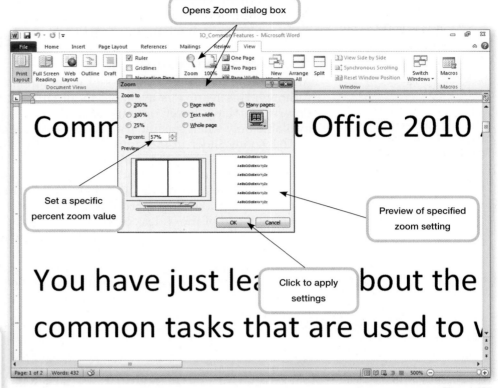

Opens Zoom dialog box

Set a specific percent zoom value

Preview of specified zoom setting

Click to apply settings

Figure 25

Your screen should be similar to Figure 25

The Zoom dialog box preview areas show how the document will appear on your screen at the specified zoom percent. Not until you complete the command by clicking [OK] will the zoom percent in the document actually change. You will complete the command to apply the 57% zoom setting. Then, you will use the 🔲 button in the Zoom group to quickly return to the default zoom setting.

3

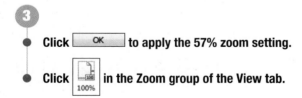

- Click [OK] to apply the 57% zoom setting.

- Click [100%] in the Zoom group of the View tab.

The document is again at 100% magnification.

Entering and Editing Text

Now that you are familiar with the entire document, you will make a few changes to it. The keyboard is used to enter information into a document. In all applications, the location of the cursor shows you where the text will appear as you type. After text is entered into a document, you need to know how to move around within the text to edit or make changes to the text. Again, the process is similar for all Office applications.

Currently, in this Word document, the cursor is positioned at the top of the document. You will type your name at this location. As you type, the cursor moves to the right and the characters will appear to the left of the cursor. Then you will press [Enter] to end the line following your name and press [Enter] again at the beginning of a line to insert a blank line.

Additional Information

The effect of pressing [Enter] varies in the different Office applications. For example, in Excel, it completes the entry and moves to another cell. You will learn about these differences in the individual application labs.

1

● Type your first and
   last name.

● Press **Enter** two
   times.

Your screen should be similar to
Figure 26

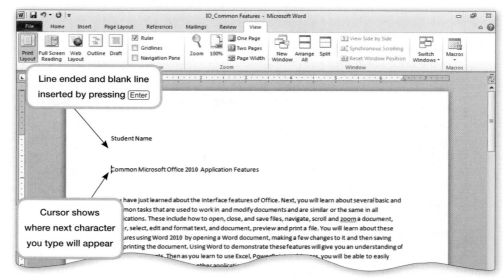

Line ended and blank line
inserted by pressing **Enter**

Student Name

Common Microsoft Office 2010 Application Features

...have just learned about the interface features of Office. Next, you will learn about several basic and
...mon tasks that are used to work in and modify documents and are similar or the same in all
...cations. These include how to open, close, and save files, navigate, scroll and zoom a document,
...r, select, edit and format text, and document, preview and print a file. You will learn about these
...res using Word 2010 by opening a Word document, making a few changes to it and then saving
...printing the document. Using Word to demonstrate these features will give you an understanding of
...s. Then as you learn to use Excel, PowerP... ...s, you will be able to easily
...other application...

Cursor shows
where next character
you type will appear

Figure 26

Additional Information

You can use the directional keys on
the numeric keypad or the dedicated
directional keypad area. If using the
numeric keypad, make sure the Num
Lock feature is off; otherwise, numbers
will be entered in the document. The
Num Lock indicator light above the
keypad is lit when on. Press **Num Lock**
to turn it off.

As you typed your name, to make space for the text on the line, the existing
text moved to the right. Then, when you pressed **Enter** the first time, all the
text following your name moved down one line. A blank line was inserted after
pressing **Enter** the second time.

Next, you want to add a word to the first line of the first paragraph. To do
this, you first need to move the cursor to the location where you want to make
the change. The keyboard or mouse can be used to move through the text in
the document window. Depending on what you are doing, one method may
be more efficient than another. For example, if your hands are already on the
keyboard as you are entering text, it may be quicker to use the keyboard rather
than take your hands off to use the mouse.

Additional Information

The mouse pointer also has other
shapes whose meaning varies with the
different applications. These specific
features will be described in the
individual application labs.

You use the mouse to move the cursor to a specific location in a document
simply by clicking on the location. When you can use the mouse to move the
cursor, the mouse pointer is shaped as an I I-beam. You use the arrow keys
located on the numeric keypad or the directional keypad to move the cursor
in a document. The keyboard directional keys are described in the following
table.

Key	Word/PowerPoint	Excel	Access
→	Right one character	Right one cell	Right one field
←	Left one character	Left one cell	Left one field
↑	Up one line	Up one cell	Up one record
↓	Down one line	Down one cell	Down one record
Ctrl + →	Right one word	Last cell in row	One word to right in a field entry
Ctrl + ←	Left one word	First cell in row	One word to left in a field entry
Home	Beginning of line	First cell in row	First field of record
End	End of line		Last field of record

Additional Information

Many of the keyboard keys and key
combinations have other effects
depending on the mode of operation at
the time they are used. You will learn
about these differences in the specific
application labs as they are used.

In the first line of the first paragraph, you want to add the word "common"
before the word "interface" and the year "2010" after the word "Office." You
will move to the correct locations using both the keyboard and the mouse and
then enter the new text.

2

- **Click at the beginning of the word You in the first paragraph.**

- **Press → four times to move to the beginning of the second word.**

- **Press Ctrl + → five times to move to the beginning of the seventh word.**

Additional Information

Holding down a directional key or key combination moves quickly in the direction indicated, saving multiple presses of the key.

- **Type basic and press Spacebar.**

Having Trouble?

Do not be concerned if you make a typing error; you will learn how to correct them next.

- **Position the I-beam between the e in Office and the period at the end of the first sentence and click.**

- **Press Spacebar and type 2010**

Your screen should be similar to Figure 27

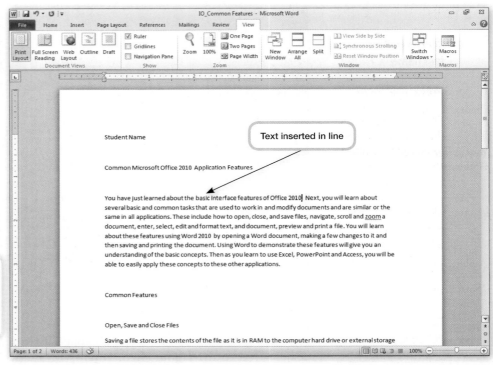

Figure 27

Next, you want to edit the text you just entered by changing the word "basic" to "common." Removing typing entries to change or correct them is one of the basic editing tasks. Corrections may be made in many ways. Two of the most basic editing keys that are common to the Office applications are the Backspace and Delete keys. The Backspace key removes a character or space to the left of the cursor. It is particularly useful when you are moving from right to left (backward) along a line of text. The Delete key removes the character or space to the right of the cursor and is most useful when moving from left to right along a line.

You will use these features as you make the correction.

● Move the cursor between the s and i in "basic" (in the first sentence).

● Press ⟨Del⟩ to remove the two characters to the right of the insertion point.

● Press ⟨Backspace⟩ three times to remove the three characters to the left of the cursor.

● Type common

● Correct any other typing errors you may have made using ⟨Backspace⟩ or ⟨Delete⟩.

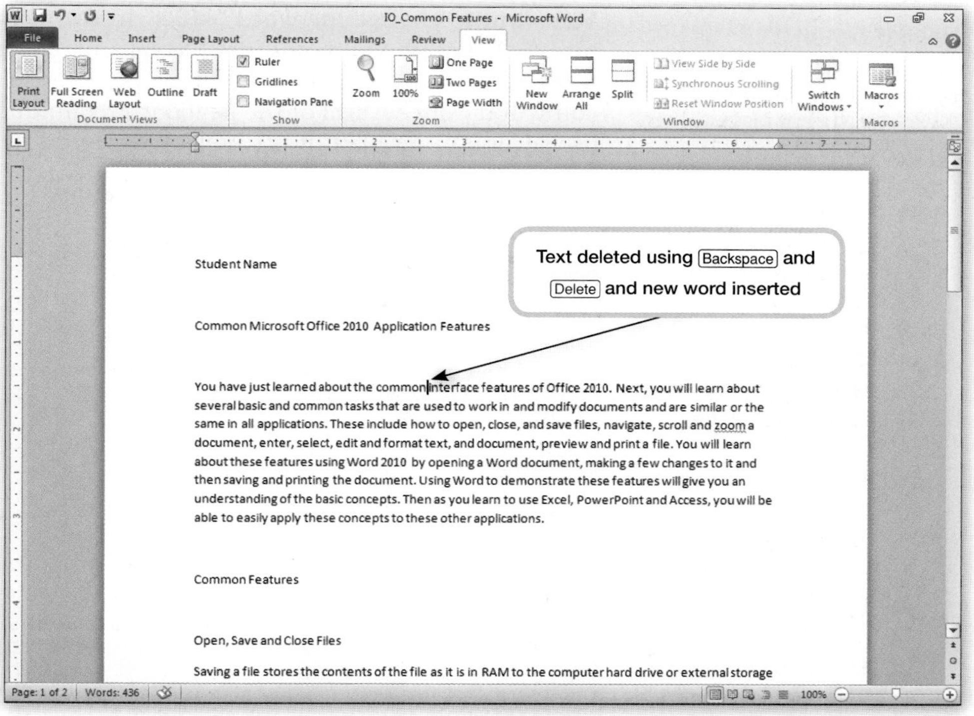

Your screen should be similar to Figure 28

Figure 28

The word "basic" was deleted from the sentence and the word "common" was entered in its place.

Selecting Text

Additional Information

The capability to select text is common to all Office 2010 applications. However, many of the features that are designed for use in Word are not available in the other applications. Some are available only when certain modes of operation are in effect or when certain features are being used.

While editing and formatting a document, you will need to select text. Selecting highlights text and identifies the text that will be affected by your next action. To select text using the mouse, first move the cursor to the beginning or end of the text to be selected, and then drag to highlight the text you want selected. You can select as little as a single letter or as much as the entire document. You also can select text using keyboard features. The following table summarizes common mouse and keyboard techniques used to select text in Word.

To Select	Mouse	Keyboard
Next/previous space or character	Drag across space or character.	⟨Shift⟩ + ⟨→⟩/⟨Shift⟩ + ⟨←⟩
Next/previous word	Double-click in the word.	⟨Ctrl⟩ + ⟨Shift⟩ + ⟨→⟩/⟨Ctrl⟩ + ⟨Shift⟩ + ⟨←⟩
Sentence	Press ⟨Ctrl⟩ and click within the sentence.	
Line	Click to the left of a line when the mouse pointer is ⟨pointer⟩.	
Multiple lines	Drag up or down to the left of a line when the mouse pointer is ⟨pointer⟩.	
Text going backward to beginning of paragraph	Drag left and up to the beginning of the paragraph when the mouse pointer is ⟨pointer⟩.	⟨Ctrl⟩ + ⟨Shift⟩ + ⟨↑⟩
Text going forward to end of paragraph	Drag right and down to the end of the paragraph when the mouse pointer is ⟨pointer⟩.	⟨Ctrl⟩ + ⟨Shift⟩ + ⟨↓⟩
Paragraph	Triple-click on the paragraph or double-click to the left of the paragraph when the mouse pointer is ⟨pointer⟩.	
Multiple paragraphs	Drag to the left of the paragraphs when the mouse pointer is ⟨pointer⟩.	
Document	Triple-click or press ⟨Ctrl⟩ and click to the left of the text when the mouse pointer is ⟨pointer⟩.	⟨Ctrl⟩ + A

Having Trouble?

If you accidentally select the incorrect text, simply click anywhere in the document or press any directional key to clear the selection and try again.

You want to change the word "tasks" in the next sentence to "application features". Although you could use Delete and Backspace to remove the unneeded text character by character, it will be faster to select and delete the word. First you will try out several of the keyboard techniques to select text. Then you will use several mouse features to select text and finally you will edit the sentence.

- **Move the cursor to the beginning of the word "basic" in the second sentence.**

- **Press Shift + → five times to select the word basic.**

- **Press Shift + Ctrl + → to extend the selection word by word until the entire line is selected.**

- **Press Shift + Ctrl + ↓ to extend the selection to the end of the paragraph.**

Your screen should be similar to Figure 29

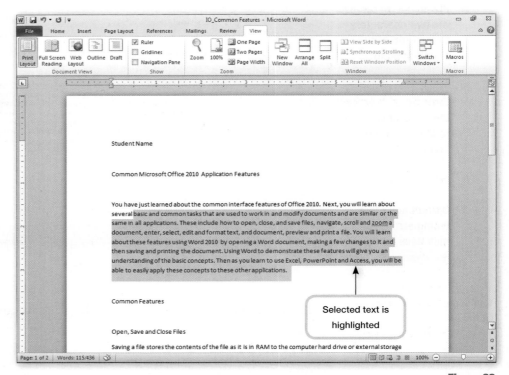

Figure 29

The text from the cursor to the end of the paragraph is selected. Next, you will clear this selection and then use the mouse to select text.

2

- Click anywhere in the paragraph to clear the selection.

- Click at the beginning of the word "basic" and drag to the right to select the text to the end of the line.

- Click in the left margin to the left of the fourth line of the paragraph when the mouse pointer is 🔏 to select the entire line.

- Double-click in the margin to the left of the paragraph when the mouse pointer is 🔏 to select the paragraph.

Your screen should be similar to Figure 30

Additional Information

When positioned in the left margin, the mouse pointer shape changes to 🔏, indicating it is ready to select text.

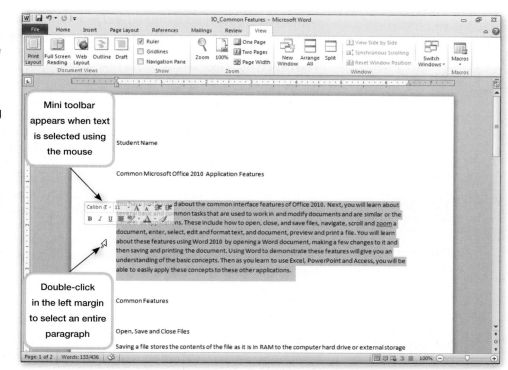

Figure 30

When you select text using the mouse, the **Mini toolbar** appears automatically in Word, Excel, and PowerPoint. You will learn about using this feature in the next section.

Text that is selected can be modified using many different features. In this case, you want to replace the word "tasks" in the second sentence with "application features".

3

- Double-click on the word "tasks" in the second sentence.

- Type **application features**

Your screen should be similar to Figure 31

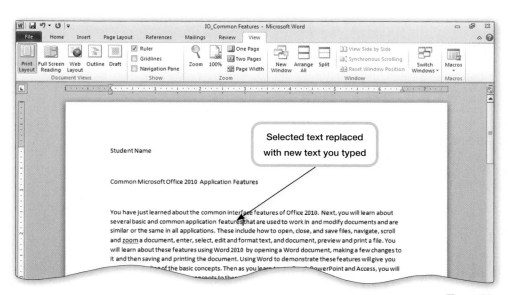

Figure 31

Common Office 2010 Features

IO.39

As soon as you began typing, the selected text was automatically deleted. The new text was inserted in the line just like any other text.

Formatting Text

An important aspect of all documents you create using Office 2010 is the appearance of the document. To improve the appearance you can apply many different formatting effects. The most common formatting features are font and character effects. A **font**, also commonly referred to as a **typeface**, is a set of characters with a specific design. The designs have names such as Times New Roman and Courier. Each font has one or more sizes. **Font size** is the height and width of the character and is commonly measured in points, abbreviated "pt." One point equals about 1/72 inch. **Character effects** are enhancements such as bold, italic, and color that are applied to selected text. Using font and character effects as design elements can add interest to your document and give readers visual cues to help them find information quickly.

First you want to change the font and increase the font size of the title of this document.

1

Click in the left margin next to the title line when the mouse pointer is  **to select it.**

Open the Home tab.

Open the Calibri (Body) ▼ **Font drop-down menu in the Font group.**

Point to the Arial Black font option in the menu.

Your screen should be similar to Figure 32

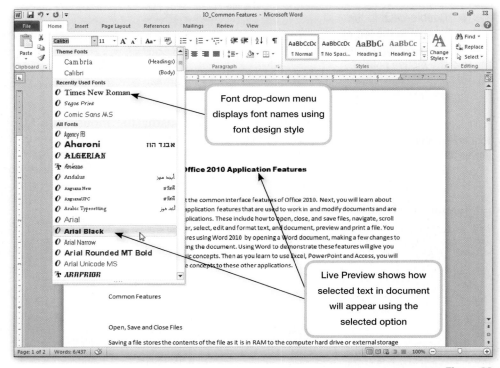

Figure 32

As you point to the font options, the **Live Preview** feature shows you how the selected text in the document will appear if this option is chosen.

2

- Point to several different fonts in the menu to see the Live Preview.

- Scroll the menu and click Segoe Print to choose it.

Additional Information

Font names are listed in alphabetical order.

Having Trouble?

If this font is not available on your computer, choose a similar font.

Your screen should be similar to Figure 33

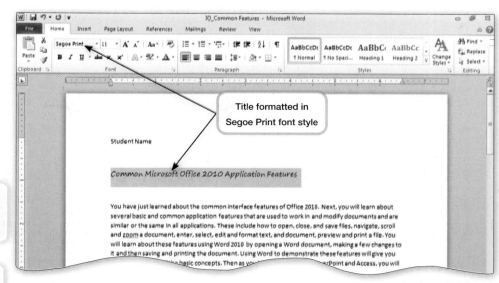

Title formatted in Segoe Print font style

Figure 33

The title appears in the selected font and the name of the font used in the selection is displayed in the [Segoe Print ▼] Font button. Next you want to increase the font size. The current (default) font size of 11 is displayed in the [11 ▼] Font Size button. You will increase the font size to 16 points.

3

- Open the [11 ▼] Font Size drop-down menu in the Font group of the Home tab.

- Point to several different font sizes to see the Live Preview.

- Click 16 to choose it.

Another Method

The keyboard shortcut is [Ctrl] + [Shift] + P.

Your screen should be similar to Figure 34

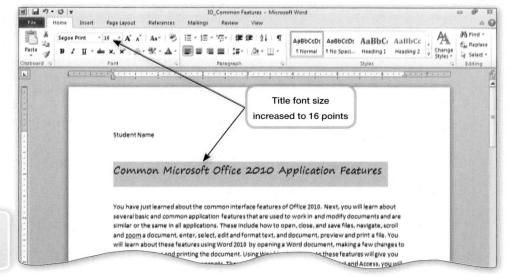

Title font size increased to 16 points

Figure 34

Now the title stands out much more from the other text in the document. Next you will use the Mini toolbar to add formatting to other areas of the document. As you saw earlier, the Mini toolbar appears automatically when you select text. Initially the Mini toolbar appears dimmed (semi-transparent) so that it does not interfere with what you are doing, but it changes to solid when you point at it. It displays command buttons for often-used commands from the Font and Paragraph groups that are used to format a document.

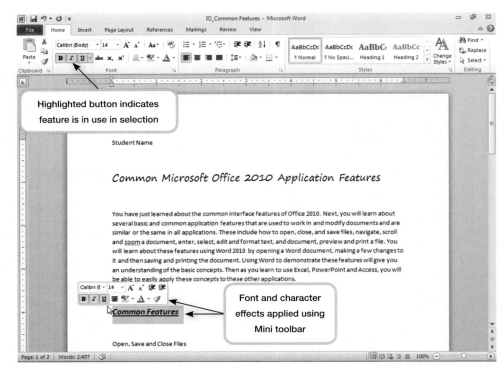

4

- Select the line "Common Features" and point to the Mini toolbar.

- Click `11` Font Size and choose 14.

- Click **B** Bold.

- Click *I* Italic.

- Click U Underline.

Your screen should be similar to Figure 35

Figure 35

The increase in font size as well as the text effects makes this topic head much more prominent. Notice the command button for each selected effect is highlighted, indicating the feature is in use in the selection.

Using the Mini toolbar is particularly useful when the Home tab is closed because you do not need to reopen the Home tab to access the commands. It remains available until you clear the selection or press [Esc]. If you do nothing with a selection for a while, the Mini toolbar will disappear. To redisplay it simply right-click on the selection again. This will also open the context menu.

You will remove the underline effect from the selection next.

5

- Right-click on the selection to redisplay the Mini toolbar.

- Click **U** Underline on the Mini toolbar.

Your screen should be similar to Figure 36

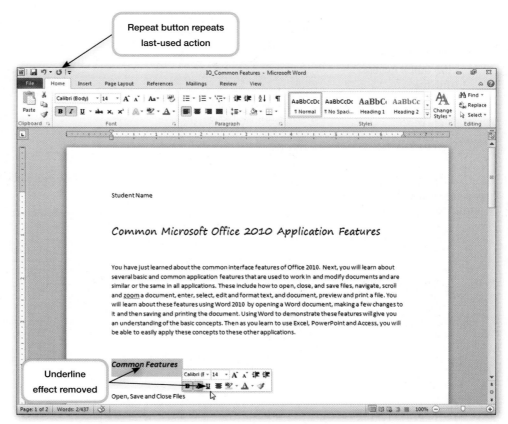

Figure 36

The context menu and Mini toolbar appeared when you right-clicked the selection. The context menu displayed a variety of commands that are quicker to access than locating the command on the Ribbon. The commands that appear on this menu change depending on what you are doing at the time. The context menu disappeared after you made a selection from the Mini toolbar. Both the Mini toolbar and context menus are designed to make it more efficient to execute commands.

Also notice that the 🔁 Redo button in the Quick Access Toolbar has changed to a 🔁 Repeat button. This feature allows you to quickly repeat the last-used command at another location in the document.

Undoing and Redoing Editing Changes

Instead of reselecting the **U** Underline command to remove the underline effect, you could have used 🔁 ▾ Undo to reverse your last action or command. You will use this feature to restore the underline (your last action).

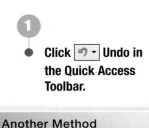

1 ● Click ↶ ▾ Undo in the Quick Access Toolbar.

Another Method
The keyboard shortcut is Ctrl + Z.

Your screen should be similar to **Figure 37**

Undo restores last-used action

Underline effect restored using Undo

Figure 37

Undo reversed the last action and the underline formatting effect was restored. Notice that the Undo button includes a drop-down menu button. Clicking this button displays a menu of the most recent actions that can be reversed, with the most-recent action at the top of the menu. When you select an action from the drop-down menu, you also undo all actions above it in the menu.

2 ● Open the ↶ ▾ Undo drop-down menu.

● Choose Bold.

Your screen should be similar to **Figure 38**

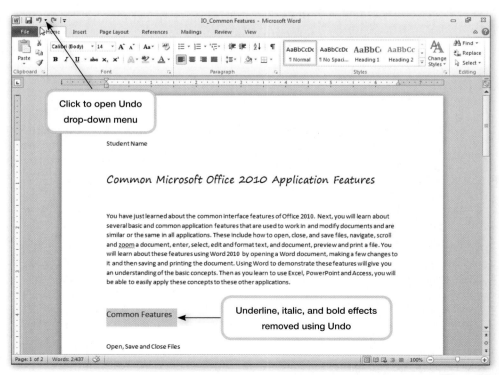

Click to open Undo drop-down menu

Underline, italic, and bold effects removed using Undo

Figure 38

The underline, italic, and bold effects were all removed. Immediately after you undo an action, the ↺ Repeat button changes to the ↻ Redo button and is available so you can restore the action you just undid. You will restore the last-removed format, bold.

● **Click ↻ Redo.**

Another Method

The keyboard shortcut is Ctrl + Y.

Copying and Moving Selections

Common to all Office applications is the capability to copy and move selections to new locations in a document or between documents, saving you time by not having to recreate the same information. A selection that is moved is cut from its original location, called the **source**, and inserted at a new location, called the **destination**. A selection that is copied leaves the original in the source and inserts a duplicate at the destination.

Additional Information

You will learn about using the Office Clipboard in the individual application texts.

When a selection is cut or copied, the selection is stored in the system **Clipboard**, a temporary Windows storage area in memory. It is also stored in the **Office Clipboard**. The system Clipboard holds only the last cut or copied item, whereas the Office Clipboard can store up to 24 items that have been cut or copied. This feature allows you to insert multiple items from various Office documents and paste all or part of the collection of items into another document.

First, you will copy the text "Office 2010" to two other locations in the first paragraph.

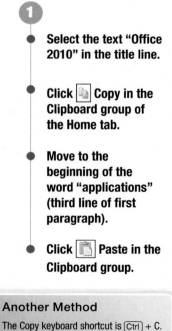

● **Select the text "Office 2010" in the title line.**

● **Click 📄 Copy in the Clipboard group of the Home tab.**

● **Move to the beginning of the word "applications" (third line of first paragraph).**

● **Click 📋 Paste in the Clipboard group.**

Another Method

The Copy keyboard shortcut is Ctrl + C.
The Paste keyboard shortcut is Ctrl + V.

Figure 39

Your screen should be similar to Figure 39

The copied selection is inserted at the location you specified with the same formatting as it has in the title. The  Paste Options button appears automatically whenever a selection is pasted. It is used to control the format of the pasted item.

2

Click the ⬚ (Ctrl) ▾ **Paste Options button.**

Your screen should be similar to Figure 40

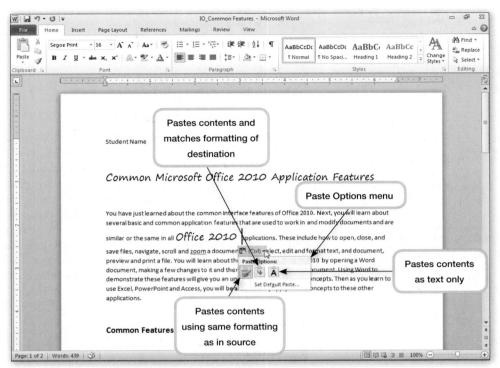

Figure 40

Additional Information

The Paste Options vary with the different applications. For example, Excel has 14 different Paste Options. The Paste Options feature is not available in Access and Paste Preview is not available in Excel.

The Paste Options are used to specify whether to insert the item with the same formatting that it had in the source, to change it to the formatting of the surrounding destination text, or to insert text only (from a selection that is a combination of text and graphics). The default as you have seen is to keep the formatting from the source. You want to change it to the formatting of the surrounding text. As you point to a Paste Options button, a **Paste Preview** will show how that option will affect the selection. Then you will copy it again to a second location.

3

- Click  Merge Formatting.

- Select "other" in the last line of the first paragraph.

- Right-click on the selection and point to each of the Paste Options in the context menu to see the Paste Preview.

- Click ⬓ Merge Formatting.

Your screen should be similar to Figure 41

Figure 41

The selected text was deleted and replaced with the contents of the system Clipboard. The system Clipboard contents remain in the Clipboard until another item is copied or cut, allowing you to paste the same item multiple times.

Now you will learn how to move a selection by rearranging several lines of text in the description of common features. You want to move the last sentence in the document, beginning with "Opening a file", to the top of the list. The Cut and Paste commands in the Clipboard group of the Home tab are used to move selections.

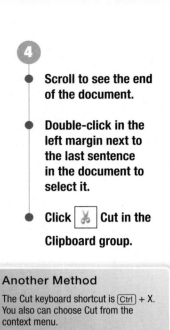

4

- Scroll to see the end of the document.

- Double-click in the left margin next to the last sentence in the document to select it.

- Click ✂ Cut in the Clipboard group.

Another Method

The Cut keyboard shortcut is Ctrl + X. You also can choose Cut from the context menu.

Your screen should be similar to Figure 42

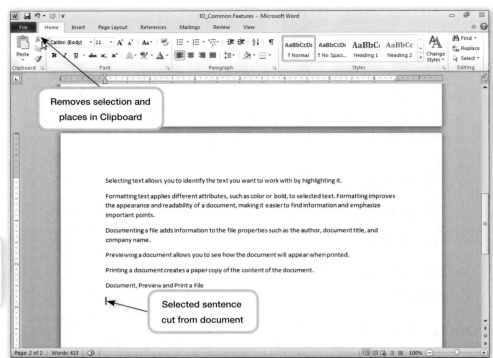

Removes selection and places in Clipboard

Selected sentence cut from document

Figure 42

The selected paragraph is removed from the source and copied to the Clipboard. Next, you need to move the cursor to the location where the text will be inserted and paste the text into the document from the Clipboard.

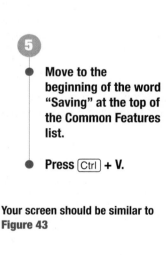

5

- Move to the beginning of the word "Saving" at the top of the Common Features list.

- Press Ctrl + V.

Your screen should be similar to Figure 43

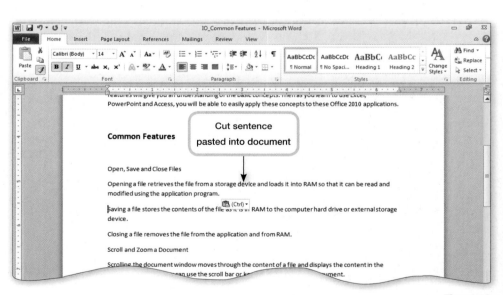

Cut sentence pasted into document

Figure 43

The cut sentence is reentered into the document at the cursor location. That was much quicker than retyping the whole sentence! Because the source has the same formatting as the text at the destination, the default setting to keep the source formatting is appropriate.

Using Drag and Drop

Another way to move or copy selections is to use the drag-and-drop editing feature. This feature is most useful for copying or moving short distances in a document. To use drag and drop to move a selection, point to the selection and drag it to the location where you want the selection inserted. The mouse pointer appears as as you drag, and a temporary insertion point shows you where the text will be placed when you release the mouse button.

1

- Select the last line of text in the document.

- Drag the selection to the beginning of the word "Documenting" (four lines up).

Your screen should be similar to Figure 44

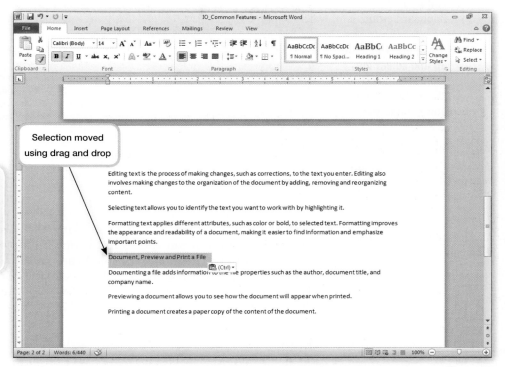

Figure 44

The selection moved to the new location. However, the selection is not copied and stored in the Clipboard and cannot be pasted to multiple locations in the document.

Copying Formats

Many times, you will find you want to copy the formats associated with a selection, but not the text. It is easy to do this using the Format Painter tool.

1

- Apply bold and italic effects and increase the font size to 14 of the currently selected text.

- Click Format Painter in the Clipboard group.

- Scroll the document up and select the topic line of text "Enter, Select, Edit and Format text".

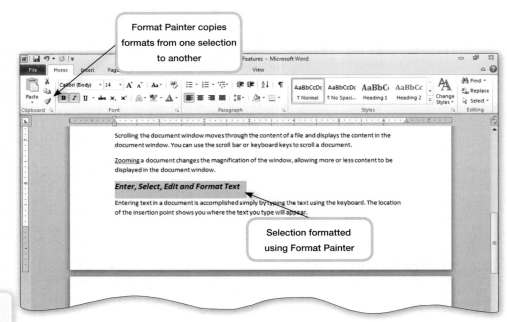

Format Painter copies formats from one selection to another

Selection formatted using Format Painter

Figure 45

Additional Information

The mouse pointer appears as when this feature is on.

Your screen should be similar to Figure 45

The text you selected is formatted using the same formats. This feature is especially helpful when you want to copy multiple formats at one time. Next, you want to format the other topic heads in the Common Features list using the same formats. To do this, you can make the Format Painter "sticky" so that it can be used to copy the format multiple times in succession.

2

- Double-click Format Painter in the Clipboard group.

- Select the remaining two topic heads in the Common Features list:

  Scroll and Zoom a Document

  Open, Save and Close Files

- Click Format Painter to turn off this feature.

- Clear the selection.

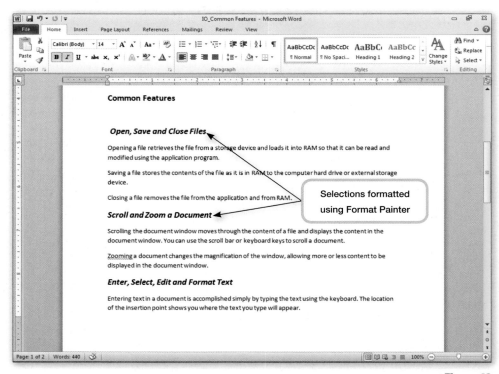

Selections formatted using Format Painter

Figure 46

Your screen should be similar to Figure 46

Specifying Document Properties

In addition to the content of the document that you create, all Office 2010 applications automatically include details about the document that describe or identify it called **metadata** or document **properties**. Document properties include details such as title, author name, subject, and keywords that identify the document's topic or contents (described below). Some of these properties are automatically generated. These include statistics such as the number of words in the file and general information such as the date the document was created and last modified. Others such as author name and tags or keywords are properties that you can specify. A **tag** or **keyword** is a descriptive word that is associated with the file and can be used to locate a file using a search.

By specifying relevant information as document properties, you can easily organize, identify, and search for your documents later.

Property	Action
Title	Enter the document title. This title can be longer and more descriptive than the file name.
Tags	Enter words that you associate with the presentation to make it easier to find using search tools.
Comments	Enter comments that you want others to see about the content of the document.
Categories	Enter the name of a higher-level category under which you can group similar types of presentations.
Author	Enter the name of the presentation's author. By default this is the name entered when the application was installed.

You will look at the document properties that are automatically included and add documentation to identify you as the author, and specify a document title and keywords to describe the document.

1

● **Open the File tab.**

● **Click the "Show all properties" link at the bottom of the Properties panel in the Info window to display all properties.**

Your screen should be similar to Figure 47

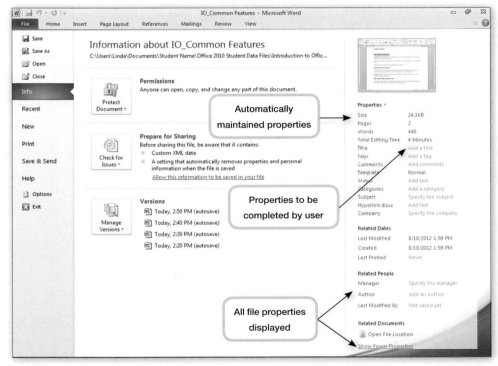

Figure 47

The Properties panel in the right section of the Info tab is divided into four groups and displays the properties associated with the document. Properties such as the document size, number of words, and number of pages are automatically maintained. Others such as the title and tag properties are blank waiting for you to specify your own information.

You will add a title, a tag, and your name as the author name.

2

- Click in the Title text box and type **Common Office Features**

- In the same manner, enter **common, features, interface** as the tags.

- Click in the Add an Author text box and enter your name.

Your screen should be similar to Figure 48

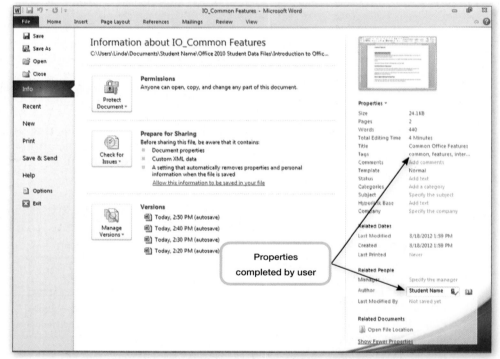

Figure 48

Once the document properties are specified, you can use them to identify and locate documents. You also can use the automatically updated properties for the same purpose. For example, you can search for all files created by a specified user or on a certain date.

Saving a File

As you enter and edit text to create a document in Word, Excel, and PowerPoint, the changes you make are immediately displayed onscreen and are stored in your computer's memory. However, they are not permanently stored until you save your work to a file on a disk. After a document has been saved as a file, it can be closed and opened again at a later time to be edited further. Unlike Word, Excel, and PowerPoint, where you start work on a new document and then save your changes, Access requires that you name the new database file first and create a table for your data. Then, it saves your changes to the data automatically as you work. This allows multiple users to have access to the most up-to-date data at all times.

As a backup against the accidental loss of work from power failure or other mishap, Word, Excel, and PowerPoint include an AutoRecover feature. When this feature is on, as you work you may see a pulsing disk icon briefly appear in the status bar. This icon indicates that the program is saving your work to a temporary recovery file. The time interval between automatic saving can be set to any period you specify; the default is every 10 minutes. After a problem has occurred, when you restart the program, the recovery file is automatically opened containing all changes you made up to the last time it was saved by AutoRecover. You then need to save the recovery file. If you do not save it, it is deleted when closed. AutoRecover is a great feature for recovering lost work but should not be used in place of regularly saving your work.

You will save the work you have done so far on the document. You use the Save or Save As commands to save files. The ⬜ Save command on the File tab or the 🖫 Save button on the Quick Access Toolbar will save the active file using the same file name by replacing the contents of the existing disk file with the document as it appears on your screen. The 🖫 Save As command on the File tab is used to save a file using a new file name, to a new location, or as a different file type. This leaves the original file unchanged. When you create a new document, you can use either of the Save commands to save your work to a file on the disk. It is especially important to save a new document very soon after you create it because the AutoRecover feature does not work until a file name has been specified.

You will save this file using a new file name to your solution file location.

Additional Information

You can specify different AutoRecover settings by choosing Options/Save in Backstage view and specifying the AutoRecover settings of your choice.

Another Method

The keyboard shortcut for the Save command is Ctrl + S.

Additional Information

Saving a file is the same in all Office 2010 applications, except Access.

1

> **Click**  **in the left section of Backstage view.**
>
> **Your screen should be similar to Figure 49**

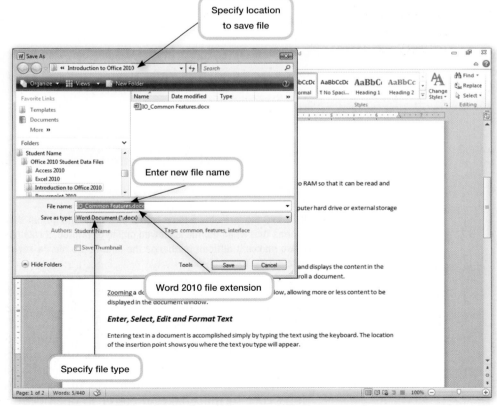

Figure 49

The Save As dialog box is used to specify the location where you will save the file and the file name. The Address bar displays the folder location from which the file was opened and the File name text box displays the name of the open file. The file name is highlighted, ready for you to enter a new file name. The Save as type box displays "Word Document.docx" as the default format in which the file will be saved. Word 2010 documents are identified by the file extension .docx. The file type you select determines the file extension that will be automatically added to the file name when the file is saved. The file types and extensions for the four Office 2010 applications are described in the following table.

Extensions	File Type
Word 2010	
.docx	Word 2007-2010 document without macros or code
.dotx	Word 2007-2010 template without macros or code
.docm	Word 2007-2010 document that could contain macros or code
.xps	Word 2007-2010 shared document (see Note)
.doc	Word 95–2003 document
Excel 2010	
.xlsx	Excel 2007-2010 default workbook without macros or code
.xlsm	Excel 2007-2010 default workbook that could contain macros
.xltx	Excel 2007-2010 template without macros
.xltm	Excel 2007-2010 template that could contain macros
.xps	Excel 2007-2010 shared workbook (see Note)
.xls	Excel 97–2003 workbook
PowerPoint	
.pptx	PowerPoint 2007-2010 default presentation format
.pptm	PowerPoint 2007-2010 presentation with macros
.potx	PowerPoint 2007-2010 template without macros
.potm	PowerPoint 2007-2010 template that may contain macros
.ppam	PowerPoint 2007-2010 add-in that contains macros
.ppsx	PowerPoint 2007-2010 slide show without macros
.ppsm	PowerPoint 2007-2010 slide show that may contain macros
.thmx	PowerPoint 2007-2010 theme
.ppt	PowerPoint 2003 or earlier presentation
Access	
.accdb	Access 2007-2010 database
.mdb	Access 2003 or earlier database

NOTE XPS file format is a fixed-layout electronic file format that preserves document formatting and ensures that when the file is viewed online or printed, it retains exactly the format that you intended. It also makes it difficult to change the data in the file. To save as an XPS file format, you must have installed the free add-in.

Office 2007 and 2010 save Word, Excel, and PowerPoint files using the XML format (Extensible Markup Language) and a four-letter file extension. This format makes your documents safer by separating files that contain macros (small programs in a document that automate tasks) to make it easier for a virus checker to identify and block unwanted code or macros that could be dangerous to your computer. It also makes file sizes smaller by compressing the content upon saving and makes files less susceptible to damage. In addition, XML format makes it easier to open documents created with an Office application using another application.

Additional Information

Depending upon your Office 2010 setup, a prompt to check for compatibility may appear automatically when you save a file.

Previous versions of Word, Excel, and PowerPoint did not use XML and had a three-letter file extension. If you plan to share a file with someone using an Office 2003 or earlier version, you can save the document using the three-letter file type; however, some features may be lost. Otherwise, if you save it as a four-letter file type, the recipient may not be able to view all features. There also may be loss of features for users of Office 2007 (even though it has an XML file type) because the older version does not support several of the new features in Office 2010. Office 2010 includes a feature that checks for compatibility with previous versions and advises you what features in the document may be lost if opened by an Office 2007 user or if the document is saved in the 2003 format.

Additional Information

Using Save As in Access creates a copy of the open database file and then opens the copy. Access automatically closes the original database.

If you have an Office Access 2007 (.accdb) database that you want to save in an earlier Access file format (.mdb), you can do so as long as your .accdb database does not contain any multivalued lookup fields, offline data, or attachments. This is because older versions of Access do not support these new features. If you try to convert an .accdb database containing any of these elements to an .mdb file format, Access displays an error message.

First you may need to change the location to the location where the file will be saved. The same procedures you used to specify a location to open a file are used to specify the location to save a file. Then, you will change the file name to Common Features using the default Word document type (.docx).

2

- If necessary, select the location where you save your solution files.

- If necessary, triple-click or drag in the File Name text box to highlight the existing file name.

- Type **Common Features**

- Click 〔 Save 〕.

Your screen should be similar to Figure 50

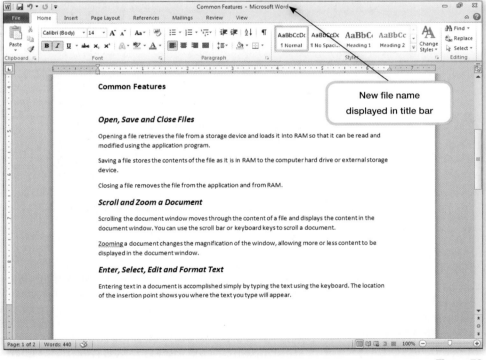

Figure 50

The document is saved as Common Features.docx at the location you selected, and the new file name is displayed in the Word application window title bar.

Additional Information

Windows files can have up to 256 characters in the file name. Names can contain letters, numbers, and spaces; however, the symbols \, /, ?, :, *, ", <, and > cannot be used. The file name can be entered in either uppercase or lowercase letters and will appear exactly as you type it.

Printing a Document

Once a document appears how you want, you may want to print a hard copy for your own reference or to give to others. All Office 2010 applications include the capability to print and have similar options. You will print this document next.

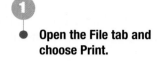

Open the File tab and choose Print.

Another Method

The keyboard shortcut for the Print command is Ctrl + P.

Your screen should be similar to Figure 51

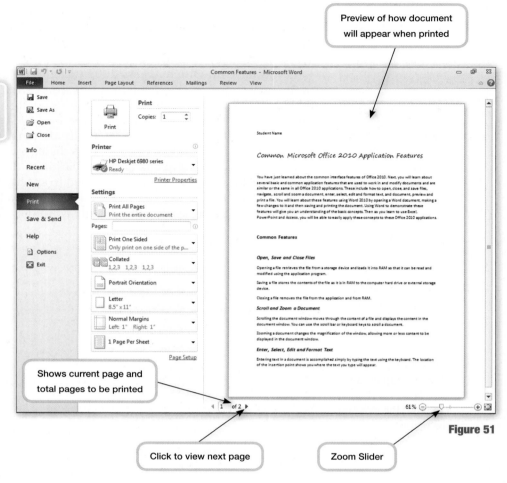

Preview of how document will appear when printed

Shows current page and total pages to be printed

Click to view next page

Zoom Slider

Figure 51

Having Trouble?

If necessary, use the Zoom Slider to change the preview zoom to 60%.

The right section of the Print window displays a preview of the current page of your document. To save time and unnecessary printing and paper waste, it is always a good idea to preview each page of your document before printing. Notice below the preview, the page scroll box shows the page number of the page you are currently viewing and the total number of pages. The scroll buttons on either side are used to scroll to the next and previous pages. Additionally, a Zoom Slider is available to adjust the size of the preview.

2

- Click ▶ to view the second page of the document.

- Increase the zoom to 70%.

Your screen should be similar to Figure 52

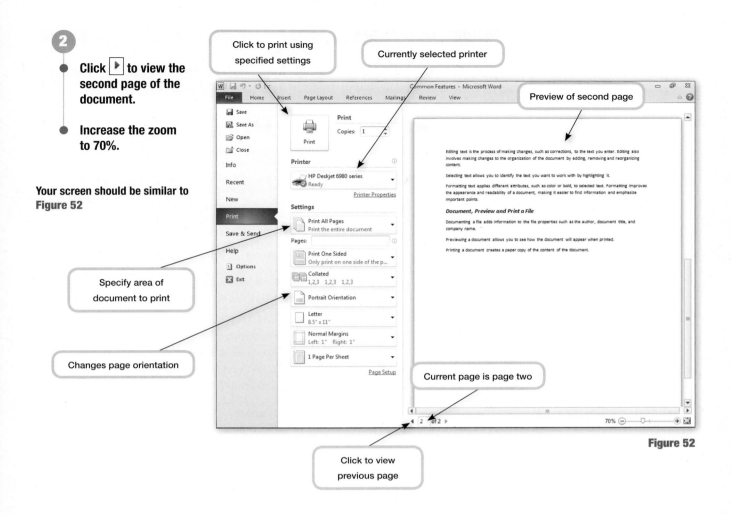

Click to print using specified settings

Currently selected printer

Preview of second page

Specify area of document to print

Changes page orientation

Current page is page two

Click to view previous page

Figure 52

If you see any changes you want to make to the document, you would need to close the File tab and make the changes. If the document looks good, you are ready to print.

The second section of the Print window is divided into three areas: Print, Printer, and Settings. In the Print section you specify the number of copies you want printed. The default is to print one copy. The Printer section is used to specify the printer you will use and the printer properties such as paper size and print quality. The name of the default printer on your computer appears in the list box. The Settings area is used to specify what part of the document you want to print, whether to print on one or both sides of the paper or to collate (sort) the printed output, the page orientation, paper size, margins, and sheet settings. The Word print setting options are explained in the following table. The Print settings will vary slightly with the different Office applications. For example, in Excel, the options to specify what to print are to print the entire worksheet, entire workbook, or a selection. The differences will be demonstrated in the individual labs.

Option	Setting	Action
Print what	All	Prints entire document (default)
	Current page	Prints selected page or page where the cursor is located.
	Pages	Prints pages you specify by typing page numbers in Pages text box
	Selection	Prints selected text only (default)
Sides	One	Prints on one side of the paper.
	Both (short)	Prints on both sides by flipping the page vertically using a duplex printer
	Both (long)	Prints on both sides by flipping the page horizontally using a duplex printer
	Manually both	Reload the paper when prompted to print on the other side
Collate	Collated	Prints all of specified document before printing second or multiple copies; for example, pages 1,2 then 1,2 again (default)
	Uncollated	Prints multiple copies of each specified page sequentially (for example, pages 1,1 then 2,2)
Orientation	Portrait	Prints across the width of the paper (default)
	Landscape	Prints across the length of the paper
Paper	Size	Select the paper size (8.5 × 11 is default)
	Envelope	Select an envelope size
Margins	Normal	One-inch margins all around (default)
	Narrow, Wide	Select alternative margin settings
Sheet	One Page Per Sheet	Prints each page of the document on a separate sheet (default)
	Multiple pages per sheet	Specify number of pages to print on a sheet

NOTE **Please consult your instructor for printing procedures that may differ from the following directions.**

You will specify several different print settings to see the effect on the preview, then you will print using the default print settings.

3

• If you need to change the selected printer to another printer, open the Printer drop-down menu and choose the appropriate printer (your instructor will tell you which printer to select).

• Click 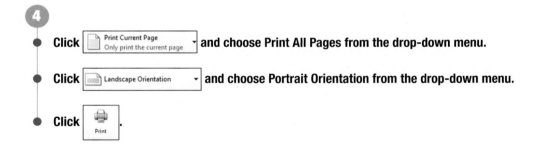 and choose Print Current Page from the drop-down menu.

• Click and choose Landscape Orientation from the drop-down menu.

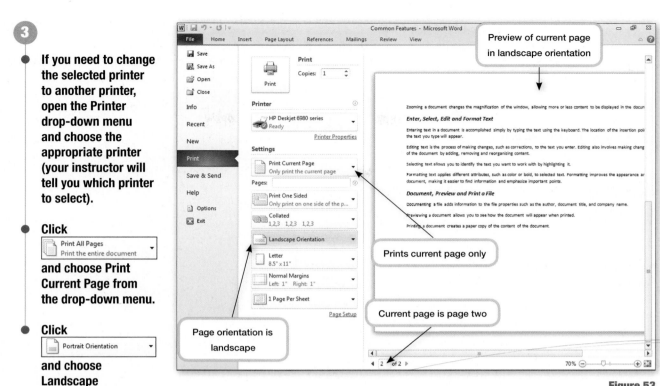

Figure 53

Your screen should be similar to Figure 53

The preview window displays the current page in landscape orientation and the page indicator shows that page two of two will print. You will return these settings to their defaults and then print the document.

4

• Click **Print Current Page** *Only print the current page* and choose Print All Pages from the drop-down menu.

• Click **Landscape Orientation** and choose Portrait Orientation from the drop-down menu.

• Click **Print**.

Your printer should be printing the document.

Closing a File

Finally, you want to close the document.

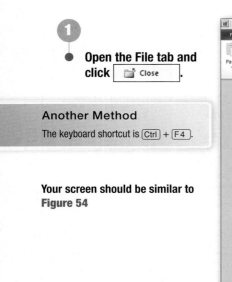

● **Open the File tab and click** ⬜ Close .

Another Method

The keyboard shortcut is Ctrl + F4.

Your screen should be similar to Figure 54

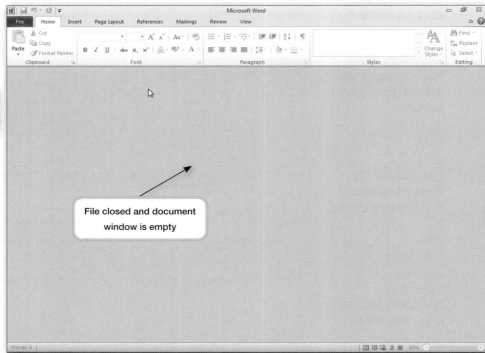

File closed and document window is empty

Figure 54

Additional Information

Do not click ⬜ Close in the window title bar as this closes the application.

Now the Word window displays an empty document window. Because you did not make any changes to the document since saving it, the document window closed immediately. If you had made additional changes, the program would ask whether you wanted to save the file before closing it. This prevents the accidental closing of a file that has not been saved first.

USING OFFICE HELP

Another Method

You also can press F1 to access Help.

Notice the 🔘 in the upper-right corner of the Ribbon. This button is used to access the Microsoft Help system. The Help button is always visible even when the Ribbon is hidden. Because you are using the Microsoft Word 2010 application, Word Help will be accessed.

1

Click Microsoft Word Help.

If a Table of Contents pane is not displayed along the left side of the Help window, click ▨ Show Table of Contents in the Help window toolbar to open it.

Your screen should be similar to **Figure 55**

Additional Information

Click ⊡ Hide Table of Contents in the Help window toolbar to hide the Table of Contents pane when it is open.

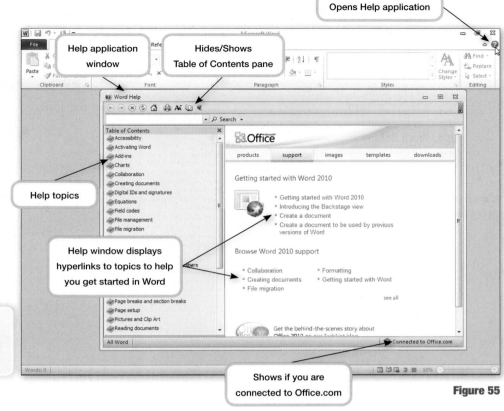

Figure 55

Additional Information

Because Help is an online feature, the information is frequently updated. Your screens may display slightly different information than those shown in the figures in this lab.

Additional Information

Depending on the size of your Help window, you may need to scroll the window to see all the Help information provided.

Having Trouble?

In addition to being connected to the Internet, the Help feature to show content from the Internet must be selected. If necessary, click 🌐 Offline at the bottom of the Help window and choose Show content from Office.com.

The Word Help feature is a separate application and is opened and displayed in a separate window. The Help window on your screen will probably be a different size and arrangement than in Figure 56. A list of help topics is displayed in the Table of Contents pane along the left side of the window and the Help window on the right side displays several topics to help you get started using Word. If you are connected to the Internet, the Microsoft Office Online Web site, Office.com, is accessed and help information from this site is displayed in the window. If you are not connected, the offline help information that is provided with the application and stored on your computer is located and displayed. Generally, the listing of topics is similar but fewer in number.

Selecting Help Topics

There are several ways you can get help. The first is to select a topic from the listing displayed in the Help window. Each topic is a **hyperlink** or connection to the information located on the Office.com Web site or in Help on your computer. When you point to a hyperlink, it appears underlined and the mouse pointer appears as 🖑. Clicking the hyperlink accesses and displays the information associated with the hyperlink.

1

● Click "Getting started
with Word 2010."

● Scroll the Help
window and click
"Basic tasks in Word
2010" in the Never
Used Word Before
area.

Your screen should be similar to
Figure 56

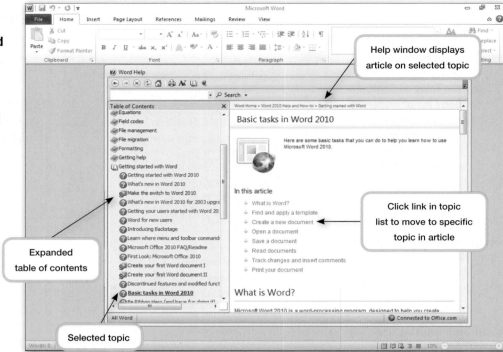

Expanded
table of contents

Help window displays
article on selected topic

Click link in topic
list to move to specific
topic in article

Selected topic

Figure 56

An article containing information about basic features of Word 2010 is displayed and the table of contents has expanded and current topic is underlined to show your location in Help. A topic list appears at the top of the article. You can either scroll the article to read it, or you can jump to a specific location in the article by clicking on a topic link.

2

● Click "Create a new
document."

Your screen should be similar to
Figure 57

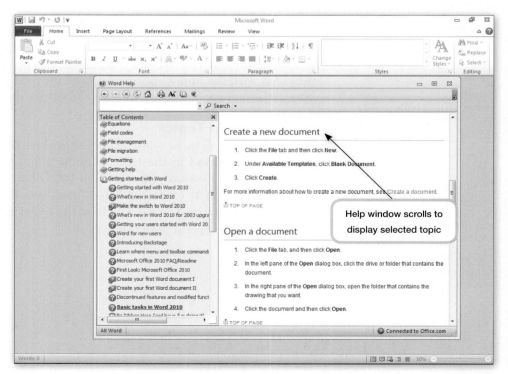

Help window scrolls to
display selected topic

Figure 57

WWW.MHHE.COM/OLEARY

The information on the selected topic is displayed in the window. Notice, as you made selections in the Help window, that the Table of Contents pane shows your current location in Help.

Using the Help Table of Contents

Choosing a topic from the Table of Contents is another method of locating Help information. Using this method allows you to browse the entire list of Help topics to locate topics of interest to you. In this case, the Getting Started with Word topic has expanded to show the subtopics and the topic you are currently viewing is underlined, indicating it is selected. Notice the 📖 Open Book and 📘 Closed Book icons in the Table of Contents. The 📖 Open Book icon identifies those chapters that are open. Clicking on an item preceded with a 📘 Closed Book icon opens a chapter, which expands to display additional chapters or topics. Clicking on an item preceded with ❓ displays the specific Help information.

- Click "Word for new users" in the Table of Contents list.

- Click "A tour of the Word user interface" in the Help window.

Your screen should be similar to Figure 58

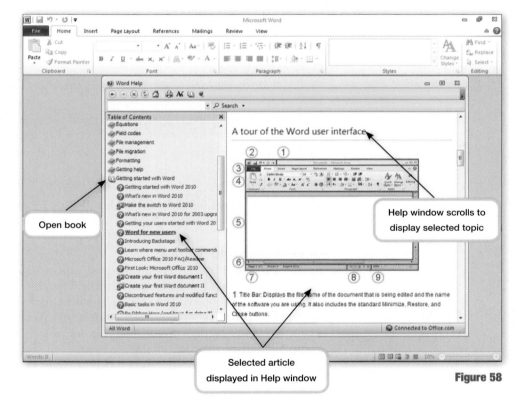

Open book

Help window scrolls to display selected topic

Selected article displayed in Help window

Figure 58

Now information about the user interface features of Word 2010 is displayed in the Help window. To move through previously viewed Help topics, you can use the ⬅ Back and ➡ Forward buttons in the Help toolbar. You can quickly redisplay the opening Help window using 🏠 Home on the Help toolbar.

- Click ⬅ Back to display the previous topic.

- Click ⌂ Home in the Help window toolbar.

- Click "Getting started with Word" in the Table of Contents pane to close this topic.

Your screen should be similar to Figure 59

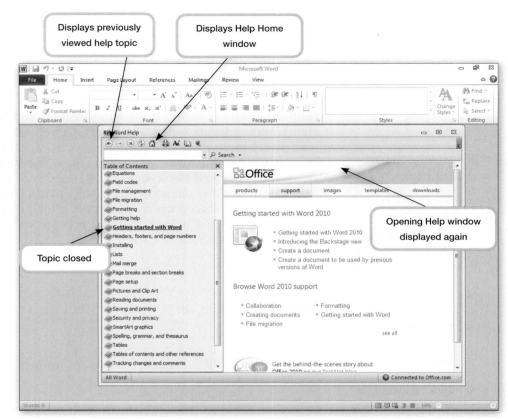

Displays previously viewed help topic

Displays Help Home window

Opening Help window displayed again

Topic closed

Figure 59

The opening Help window is displayed, the Table of Contents topic is closed, and the ➡ Forward button in the Help window toolbar is now available for use.

Searching Help Topics

Another method to find Help information is to conduct a search by entering a word or phrase you want help on in the Search text box. When searching, you can specify the scope of the search by selecting from the 🔍 Search ▾ drop-down menu. The broadest scope for a search, All Word under Content from Office .com, is preselected. You will use this feature to search for Help information about the Office user interface.

①

Click in the Search text box to display the cursor and type user interface

Click 🔍 Search ▾ **.**

Scroll the Help window to see the search results.

Your screen should be similar to Figure 60

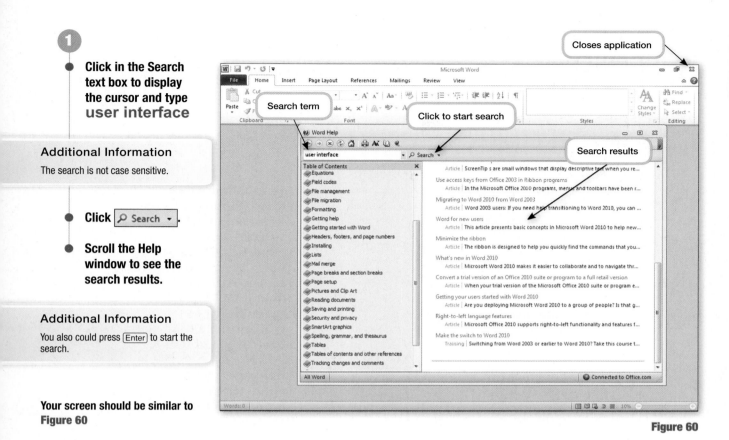

Figure 60

The Help window displays links to articles that contain both the words "user" and "interface." The results are shown in order of relevance, with the most likely matches at the top of the list.

EXITING AN OFFICE 2010 APPLICATION

Now you are ready to close the Help window and exit the Word program. The 🔲 Close button located on the right end of the window title bar can be used to exit most application windows. Alternatively, you can use the 🔲 Exit command on the File tab. If you attempt to close an application without first saving your document, a warning appears asking if you want to save your work. If you do not save your work and you exit the application, any changes you made since last saving it are lost.

①

Click 🔲 **Close in the Help window title bar to close the Help window.**

Click 🔲 **Close in the Word window title bar to exit Word.**

The program window is closed and the Windows desktop is visible again.

KEY TERMS

Backstage view IO.24	Mini toolbar IO.39
buttons IO.15	Office Clipboard IO.45
character effects IO.40	on-demand tabs IO.20
Clipboard IO.45	Paste Preview IO.46
commands IO.18	properties IO.27, 51
context menu IO.17	Quick Access Toolbar IO.15
contextual tabs IO.20	records IO.7
cursor IO.15	Ribbon IO.15
database IO.7	ScreenTip IO.16
default IO.27	scroll bar IO.15
destination IO.45	shortcut menu IO.17
dialog box launcher IO.23	slide IO.10
document window IO.15	slide shows IO.10
edit IO.3	source IO.45
Enhanced ScreenTip IO.20	status bar IO.15
fields IO.7	tables IO.7
font IO.40	tabs IO.18
font size IO.40	tag IO.51
format IO.3	task pane IO.23
groups IO.18	template IO.26
hyperlink IO.61	tooltip IO.16
insertion point IO.15	typeface IO.40
keyboard shortcut IO.16	user interface IO.14
keyword IO.51	View buttons IO.15
Live Preview IO.40	worksheet IO.5
metadata IO.51	Zoom Slider IO.15

COMMAND SUMMARY

Command/Button	Shortcut	Action
Quick Access Toolbar		
↺ ▾ Undo	Ctrl + Y	Restores last change
↻ Redo	Ctrl + Y	Restores last Undo action
↻ Repeat	Ctrl + Y	Repeats last action
⊘ Microsoft Word Help	F1	Opens Microsoft Help

COMMAND SUMMARY (CONTINUED)

Command/Button	Shortcut	Action
File tab		
🖫 Save	Ctrl + S or 🖫	Saves document using same file name
🖫 Save As	F12	Saves document using a new file name, type, and/or location
📂 Open	Ctrl + O	Opens existing file
📁 Close	Ctrl + F4 or ⊠	Closes document
Info		Displays document properties
Print/ 🖶 Print	Ctrl + P	Prints document using specified settings
⊠ Exit	Alt + F4 or ⊠	Exits Office program
View tab		
Zoom group		
🔍 Zoom		Changes magnification of document
Home tab		
Clipboard group		
📋 Paste	Ctrl + V	Inserts copy of Clipboard at location of cursor
✂ Cut	Ctrl + X	Removes selection and copies to Clipboard
📋 Copy	Ctrl + C	Copies selection to Clipboard
✒ Format Painter		Duplicates formats of selection to other locations
Font group		
Calibri (Body) ▾ Font	Ctrl + Shift + F	Changes typeface
11 ▾ Font Size	Ctrl + Shift + P	Changes font size
B Bold	Ctrl + B	Adds/removes bold effect
I Italic	Ctrl + I	Adds/removes italic effect
U Underline	Ctrl + U	Adds/removes underline effect

STEP-BY-STEP

EXPLORING EXCEL 2010

1. In this exercise you will explore the Excel 2010 application and use many of the same features you learned about while using Word 2010 in this lab.

   a. Use the Start menu or a shortcut icon on your desktop to start Office Excel 2010.

   b. What shape is the mouse pointer when positioned in the document window area? _____

   c. Excel has _____ tabs. Which tabs are not the same as in Word? _____

   d. Open the Formulas tab. How many groups are in the Formulas tab? _____

   e. Which tab contains the group to work with charts? _____

   f. From the Home tab, click the Number group dialog box launcher. What is the name of the dialog box that opens? _____ How many number categories are there? _____ Close the dialog box.

   g. Display ScreenTips for the following buttons located in the Alignment group of the Home tab and identify what action they perform.

   _____

   _____

   _____

   h. Open the Excel Help window. From the Help window choose "Getting started with Excel 2010" and then choose "Basic tasks in Excel 2010." Read this article and answer the following question: What is Excel used for? _____

   i. In the Table of Contents, open the "Worksheets" topic and then "Entering Data." Read the topic "Enter data manually in worksheet cells" and answer the following:

   • What is the definition of worksheet? Hint: Click on the grayed term "worksheet" to view a definition.

   _____

   • What four types of data can be entered in a worksheet? _____, _____,

   _____, _____

   j. Read the topic "Quick Start: Edit and enter data in a worksheet." If you have an Internet connection, click the Watch the video link and view the video. Close your browser window.

   k. Enter the term "formula" in the Search text box. Look at several articles and answer the following question: All formula entries begin with what symbol? _____

   l. Close the Help window. Exit Excel.

EXPLORING POWERPOINT 2010

2. In this exercise you will explore the PowerPoint 2010 application and use many of the same features you learned about while using Word 2010 in this lab.

   a. Use the Start menu or a shortcut icon on your desktop to start Office PowerPoint 2010.

   b. PowerPoint has _____ tabs. Which tabs are not the same as in Word?

     _____

   c. Open the Animations tab. How many groups are in this tab? _____

   d. Which tab contains the group to work with themes? _____

   e. Click on the text "Click to add title." Type your name. Select this text and change the font size to 60; add italic and bold. Cut this text. Click in the box containing "Click to add subtitle" and paste the cut selection. Use the Paste Options to keep the source formatting.

   f. Click on the text "Click to add title" and type the name of your school. Select the text and apply a font of your choice.

   g. Open the PowerPoint Help window. From the Help window, choose "Getting Started with PowerPoint 2010" and then choose "Basic tasks in PowerPoint 2010." Read the information in this article and answer the following questions:

     • In the "What is PowerPoint?" topic, what is the primary use of PowerPoint?_____.

     • In the "Save a presentation" topic, what is the default file format for a presentation?

       _____

     • What is the first tip in the "Tips for creating an effective presentation" topic?

      _____

   h. Enter the term "placeholder" in the Search text box. Look at several articles and write the definition of this term. Hint: Click on a word in an article that appears in light gray to view a definition.

    _____

   i. In the Table of Contents, open the "Delivering your presentation" topic. Choose "Create and print notes pages" and answer the following questions:

     • What are notes pages?

      _____

     • What is the Green Idea?

      _____

   j. Close the Help window. Exit PowerPoint and do not save the changes you made to the presentation.

LAB EXERCISES

EXPLORING ACCESS 2010

3. As noted in this Introduction to Microsoft Office 2010, when you start Access 2010 you need to either open an existing database file or create and name a new database. Therefore, in this exercise, you simply explore the Access 2010 Help information without opening or creating a database file.

   a. Use the Start menu or a shortcut icon on your desktop to start Office Access 2010.

   b. Open the Help tab in Backstage view and choose Microsoft Office Help.

   c. From the Help window, choose "Basic tasks in Access 2010." Read the information in this article and answer the following questions:

   - In the "What is Access?" topic, what are the two locations where you can keep your data? _____ and _____.

   - In the "Create a Database from Scratch" topic, what are the two choices? _____ or _____.

   d. In the Table of Contents pane, open the "Access basics" topic. Choose "Database basics" and answer the following questions:

   - In the "What is a database?" topic, define "database."
     _____

   - In "The parts of an Access database" topic, what are the six main parts? _____, _____, _____, _____, _____, _____.

   - In "The parts of an Access database" topic, how is data in a table stored? _____ and _____.

   - In "The parts of an Access database" topic, each row in a table is referred to as a _____.

   e. Enter the term "field" in the Search text box. Look at several articles and write the definition of this term. Hint: Click on a word in an article that appears in light gray to view a definition.
   _____

   f. Close the Help window. Exit Access.

ON YOUR OWN

EXPLORING WORD HELP

1. In addition to the Help information you used in this lab, Office 2010 Help also includes many interactive tutorials. Selecting a Help topic that starts a tutorial will open the browser program on your computer. Both audio and written instructions are provided. You will use one of these tutorials to learn more about using Word 2010.

   Start Word 2010. Open Help and choose "Getting started with Word" from the Help window. Click on the training topic "Create your first Word document I." Follow the directions in your browser to run the tutorial. When you are done, close the browser window, close Help, and exit Word 2010.

Creating and Editing a Document

Objectives

After completing this lab, you will know how to:

1. Develop a document as well as enter and edit text.

2. Insert and delete text and blank lines.

3. Use spelling and grammar checking.

4. Use AutoCorrect.

5. Cut and copy text.

6. Change fonts and type sizes.

7. Bold and color text.

8. Change alignment.

9. Insert and size pictures.

10. Print a document.

11. Use a template.

Adventure Travel Tours

As a recent college graduate, you have accepted a job as advertising coordinator for Adventure Travel Tours, a specialty travel company that organizes active adventure vacations. The company is headquartered in Los Angeles and has locations in other major cities throughout the country. You are responsible for coordination of the advertising program for all locations. This includes the creation of many kinds of promotional materials: brochures, flyers, form letters, news releases, advertisements, and a monthly newsletter. You are also responsible for creating Web pages for the company Web site.

Adventure Travel Tours is very excited about four new tours planned for the upcoming year. They want to promote them through informative presentations held throughout the country. Your first job as advertising coordinator will be to create a flyer advertising the four new tours and the presentations about them. The flyer will be modified according to the location of the presentation.

The software tool you will use to create the flyer is the word processing application Microsoft Office Word 2010. It helps you create documents such as letters, reports, and research papers. In this lab, you will learn how to enter, edit, and print a document while you create the flyer (shown right) to be distributed in a mailing to Adventure Travel Tours clients.

ADVENTURE TRAVEL TOURS

NEW ADVENTURES

Attention adventure travelers! Attend an Adventure Travel presentation to learn about some of the earth's greatest unspoiled habitats and find out how you can experience the adventure of a lifetime. This year Adventure Travel Tours is introducing four new tours that offer you a unique opportunity to combine many different outdoor activities while exploring the world.

Safari in Tanzania

India Wildlife Adventure

Costa Rica Rivers and Rainforests

Inca Trail to Machu Picchu

...5 at 7:00 p.m., February 3 at 7:30 p.m., ...ent hotel locations. ...ara, and at the LAX

...tion locations, a full ...ates. Student Name ...s.

Entering and editing text is simplified with many of Word's AutoCorrect features.

Formatting enhances the appearance of a document.

Pictures add visual interest to a document.

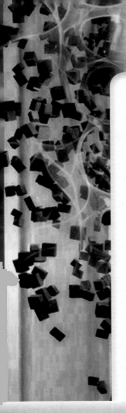

The following concepts will be introduced in this lab:

1 **Grammar Checker** The grammar checker advises you of incorrect grammar as you create and edit a document, and proposes possible corrections.

2 **Spelling Checker** The spelling checker advises you of misspelled words as you create and edit a document, and proposes possible corrections.

3 **AutoCorrect** The AutoCorrect feature makes some basic assumptions about the text you are typing and, based on these assumptions, automatically corrects the entry.

4 **Word Wrap** The word wrap feature automatically decides where to end a line and wrap text to the next line based on the margin settings.

5 **Alignment** Alignment is the positioning of text on a line between the margins or indents. There are four types of paragraph alignment: left, centered, right, and justified.

6 **Graphics** A graphic is a nontext element or object such as a drawing or picture that can be added to a document.

7 **Templates** A template is a document file that stores predefined settings and other elements such as graphics for use as a pattern when creating documents.

Creating New Documents

Adventure Travel Tours has recently upgraded their computer systems at many of their locations across the country. As part of the upgrade, they have installed the latest version of the Microsoft Office 2010 suite of applications. You are very excited to see how this new and powerful application can help you create professional letters and reports as well as eye-catching flyers and newsletters. Your first project with Adventure Travel Tours is to create a flyer about four new tours.

DEVELOPING A DOCUMENT

The development of a document follows several steps: plan, enter, edit, format, and preview and print.

Step	Description
Plan	The first step in the development of a document is to understand the purpose of the document and to plan what your document should say.
Enter	After planning the document, you enter the content of the document by typing the text using the keyboard.
Edit	While creating a document, you will need to **edit** it to correct typing, spelling, and grammar errors. You will also probably spend much time revising the document by adding and deleting information and by reorganizing it to make the meaning clearer.
Format	Enhancing the appearance of the document by **formatting** the text makes it more readable and attractive and makes it easier to find information and emphasize important points. This is usually performed when the document is near completion, after all edits and revisions have been completed. It includes many features such as boldfaced text, italics, and bulleted lists.
Preview and Print	The last step is to preview and print the document. When previewing, you check the document's overall appearance and make any final changes before printing.

You will find that you will generally follow these steps in the order listed above for your first draft of a document. However, you will probably retrace steps such as editing and formatting as the final document is developed.

During the planning phase, you spoke with your manager regarding the purpose of the flyer and the content in general. The primary purpose of the flyer is to promote Adventure Travel's new tours. A secondary purpose is to advertise the company in general.

You plan to include specific information about the new tours in the flyer as well as general information about Adventure Travel Tours. The content also needs to include information about the upcoming new tour presentations. Finally, you want to include information about the Adventure Travel Web site.

EXPLORING THE WORD 2010 WINDOW

You will use the word processing application Microsoft Office Word 2010 to create a flyer promoting the new tours and presentations.

1

● **Start Word 2010.**

● **If necessary, maximize the Word 2010 application window.**

Your screen should be similar to Figure 1.1

Having Trouble?

See "Common Interface Features," on page IO.14, for information on how to start the application and use features that are common to all Office 2010 applications.

Blank document is displayed in document window

Additional Information

The Ribbon may display additional tabs if other application add-ins associated with Office are enabled.

Additional Information

If the ruler is not displayed, click [image] View Ruler above the vertical scroll bar to turn it on. You also can temporarily display the horizontal or vertical ruler by pointing to the top or left edge of the document window.

Additional Information

The mouse pointer also may appear in other shapes, depending upon the task being performed.

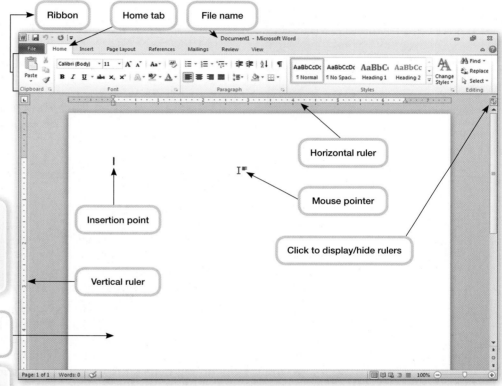

Figure 1.1

The Word 2010 Ribbon below the title bar displays command tabs that provide access to the commands and features you will use to create and modify a document.

The large area below the Ribbon is the **document window**. It currently displays a blank Word document. The **insertion point**, also called the **cursor**, is the blinking vertical bar that marks your location in the document. A vertical and horizontal **ruler** may be displayed along both edges of the document window. The horizontal ruler at the top of the document window shows the line length in inches and is used to set margins, tab stops, and indents. The vertical ruler along the left edge shows the page length in inches and shows your line location on the page.

The mouse pointer may appear as an I-beam (see Figure 1.1) or a left- or right-facing arrow, depending on its location in the window. When it appears as an I-beam, it is used to move the cursor, and when it appears as an arrow, it is used to select items.

2

- Move the mouse pointer into the left edge of the blank document to see it appear as ⬈.

- Move the mouse pointer to the Ribbon to see it appear as ▷.

Your screen should be similar to **Figure 1.2**

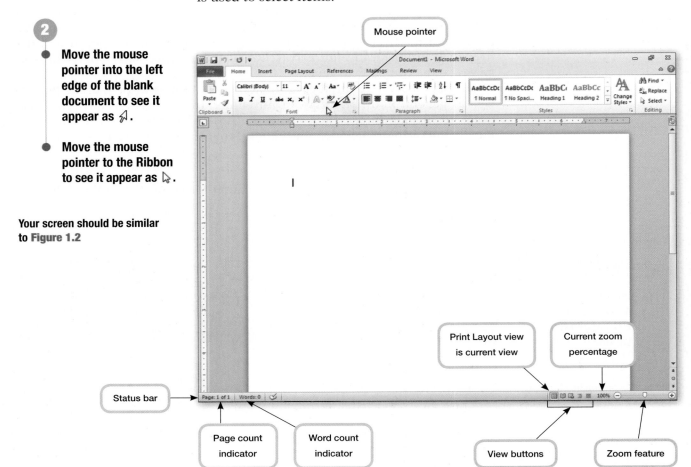

Figure 1.2

CHANGING THE DOCUMENT VIEW

Additional Information

You also can change views using commands in the Document Views group of the View tab.

The status bar at the bottom of the window displays the page and word count indicators. The page indicator identifies the page of text that is displayed onscreen of the total number of pages in the document. The word count indicator displays the number of words in a document. When you first start Word, a new blank document consisting of a single page and zero words is opened.

The right end of the status bar displays five buttons that are used to change the document view and a document zoom feature. Word includes several views that are used for different purposes. The different document views are described in the table below.

Document View	Button	Effect on Text
Print Layout		Shows how the text and objects will appear on the printed page. This is the view to use when adjusting margins, working in columns, drawing objects, and placing graphics.
Full Screen Reading		Shows the document only, without Ribbon, status bar, or any other features. Useful for viewing and reading large documents. Use to review a document and add comments and highlighting.
Web Layout		Shows the document as it will appear when viewed in a Web browser. Use this view when creating Web pages or documents that will be displayed on the screen only.
Outline		Shows the structure of the document. This is the view to use to plan and reorganize text in a document.
Draft		Shows text formatting and simple layout of the page. This is the best view to use when typing, editing, and formatting text.

Print Layout view is the view you see when first starting Word or opening a document. You can tell which view is in use by looking at the view buttons. The button for the view that is in use appears highlighted (see Figure 1.2). The zoom setting for each view is set independently and remains in effect until changed to another zoom setting. Initially the zoom percentage for Print Layout view is 100%. At this percentage, the document appears as it will when printed.

You will "zoom out" on the document to see the entire page so you can better see the default document settings.

Additional Information

Pointing to the items on the status bar displays a ScreenTip that identifies the feature.

1

● Drag the Zoom Slider to the left to reduce the zoom until the entire page is visible.

Having Trouble?

See "Using the Zoom Feature" on page I0.33 in the Introduction to Microsoft Office 2010 to review the document zoom feature.

Your screen should be similar to Figure 1.3

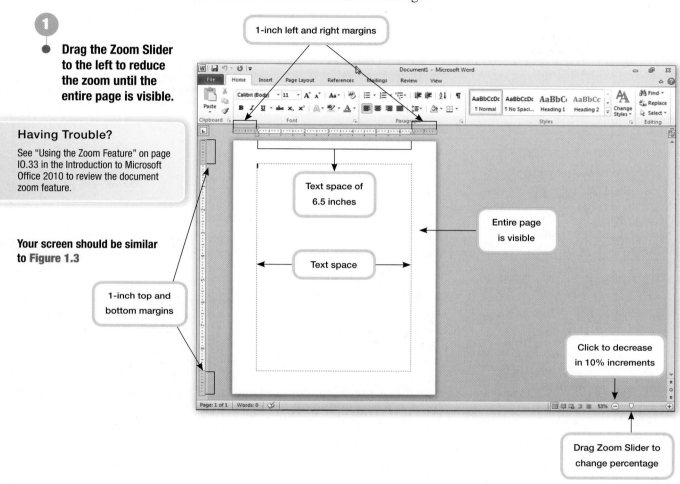

Figure 1.3

At this zoom percentage, the entire page is displayed and all four edges of the paper are visible. It is like a blank piece of paper that already has many predefined settings. These settings, called **default** settings, are generally the most commonly used settings. The default settings include a standard paper-size setting of 8.5 by 11 inches, 1-inch top and bottom margins, and 1-inch left and right margins.

You can verify many of the default document settings by looking at the information displayed in the rulers. The shaded area of the ruler identifies the margins and the white area identifies the text space. The text space occupies 6.5 inches of the page. Knowing that the default page size is 8.5 inches wide, this leaves 2 inches for margins: 1 inch for equal-sized left and right margins. The vertical ruler shows the entire page length is 11 inches with 1-inch top and bottom margins, leaving 9 inches of text space.

You will use Draft view to create the flyer about this year's new tours. You will use the View tab to change both the view and the Zoom percentage.

2

- Open the **View tab.**

- From the **Document Views group,** click [Draft].

- If necessary, choose **Ruler** in the **Show group to display the ruler.**

Having Trouble?

Click the box next to an option to select or deselect (clear the checkmark).

- From the **Zoom group,** click [Page Width].

Your screen should be similar to **Figure 1.4**

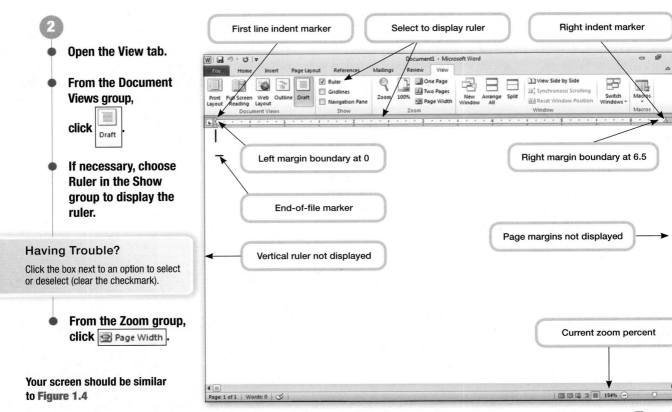

First line indent marker

Select to display ruler

Right indent marker

Left margin boundary at 0

Right margin boundary at 6.5

End-of-file marker

Page margins not displayed

Vertical ruler not displayed

Current zoom percent

Figure 1.4

Increasing the zoom to page width increases the magnification to 154% and displays the full text area in the document window. In Draft view, the margins and the edges of the page are not displayed. This allows more space on the screen to display document content. This view also displays the **end-of-file marker**, the solid horizontal line that marks the last-used line in a document.

The ruler also displays other default settings. The symbol ▽ at the zero position is the first-line indent marker and marks the location of the left paragraph indent. The ▲ symbol on the right end of the ruler line at the 6.5-inch position marks the right paragraph indent. Currently, the indent locations are the same as the left and right margin settings.

Additional Information

The vertical ruler is not displayed in Draft view.

Entering Text

Now that you understand the purpose of the flyer and have a general idea of the content, you are ready to enter the text. As you type, you will probably make simple typing errors that you want to correct. Word includes many features that make entering text and correcting errors much easier. These features include checking for spelling and grammar errors, auto correction, and word wrap. You will see how these features work while entering the title and first paragraph of the flyer.

TYPING TEXT

The first line of the flyer will contain the text "Adventure Travel Tours New Adventures." As you enter this line of text, include the intentional error identified in italic.

1

- Type **Adventure Traveel** (do not press space after typing the last letter).

Having Trouble?

To review the basics of moving the cursor and editing a document, refer to the "Entering and Editing Text" section on page IO.34 of the Introduction to Microsoft Office 2010.

Your screen should be similar to Figure 1.5

Additional Information

The status bar also can display additional information such as the horizontal position of the cursor on the line and the line number. To customize the status bar, right-click the status bar and select the features you want displayed from the status bar context menu.

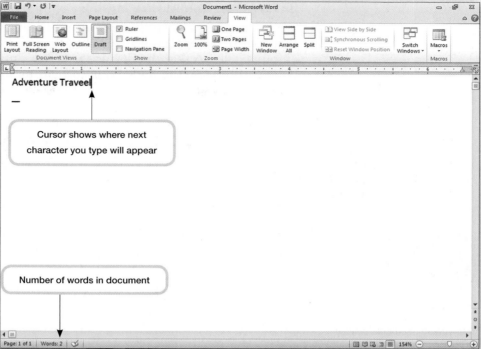

Figure 1.5

Notice that the status bar now tells you that there are two words in the document.

Next, you need to correct the typing error by deleting the extra e in the word travel. Then you will complete the first line of the flyer.

2

- Press ← or position the I-beam between the e and l and click.

- Press Backspace to remove the extra e.

- Press → or click at the end of the line.

- Press Spacebar.

- Type **Tours four new adventures** and correct any typing errors as you make them using Backspace or Delete.

- With the cursor positioned at the end of the line, press Enter 3 times.

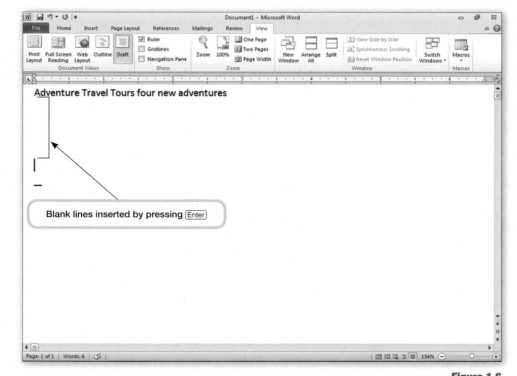

Figure 1.6

The first line of the flyer is now complete. Pressing the first Enter ended the first line of text and inserted a blank line. The next two inserted blank lines.

Your screen should be similar to Figure 1.6

REVEALING FORMATTING MARKS

While creating a document, Word automatically inserts formatting marks that control the appearance of your document. These marks are not displayed automatically so that the document is not cluttered. Sometimes, however, it is helpful to view the underlying formatting marks. Displaying these marks makes it easy to see, for example, if you have added an extra space between words or at the end of a sentence.

1

● **Open the Home tab and click ¶ Show/Hide in the Paragraph group.**

Another Method

You also can use the keyboard shortcut ⎡Ctrl⎤ + * to display formatting marks.

Your screen should be similar to Figure 1.7

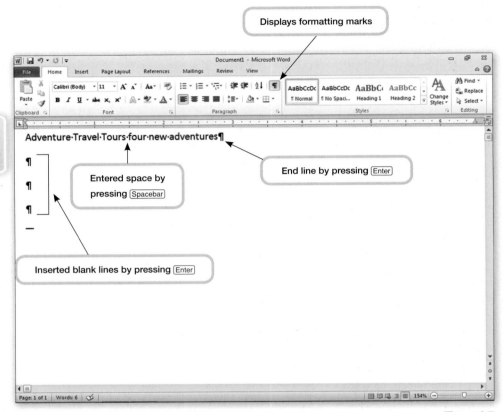

Figure 1.7

The document now displays the formatting marks. The ¶ paragraph mark character on the line above the cursor represents the pressing of ⎡Enter⎤ that created the blank line. The ¶ character at the end of the text represents the pressing of ⎡Enter⎤ that ended the line and moved the cursor to the beginning of the next line. Between each word, a dot shows where the ⎡Spacebar⎤ was pressed. Formatting marks do not appear when the document is printed. You can continue to work on the document while the formatting marks are displayed, just as you did when they were hidden.

You have decided you want the flyer heading to be on two lines, with the words "four new adventures" on the second line. To do this, you will insert a blank line after the word Tours. You will move the cursor to the location in the text where you want to insert the blank line.

2

- Click to the left of the dot after the "s" in "Tours".

- Press [Enter] 2 times.

- Press [Delete] to remove the space at the beginning of the line.

- Press [↓].

Your screen should be similar to Figure 1.8

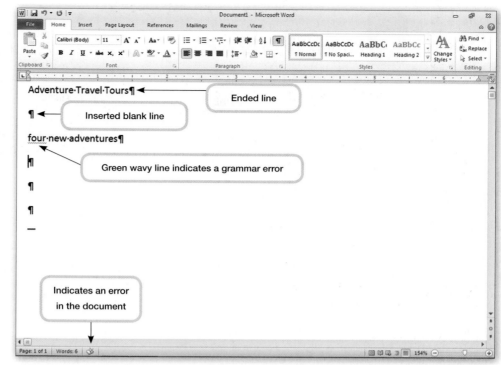

Figure 1.8

All the text to the right of the cursor when you pressed [Enter] moved down to the beginning of the next line. Then as you continued to work on the document, the formatting marks adjusted automatically.

Identifying and Correcting Errors Automatically

Having Trouble?

If the green underline is not displayed, open the File tab, click [📄 Options], Proofing, and select the "Check spelling as you type", "Mark grammar errors as you type", and "Check grammar with spelling" options.

Notice that a green wavy underline appears under the word "four." This indicates an error has been detected.

As you enter text, Word constantly checks the document for spelling and grammar errors. The Spelling and Grammar Status icon in the status bar displays an animated pencil icon [✏️] while you are typing, indicating Word is checking for errors as you type. When you stop typing, it displays either a blue checkmark [✓], indicating the program does not detect any errors, or a red X [✗], indicating the document contains an error.

In many cases, Word will automatically correct errors for you. In other cases, it identifies the error by underlining it. The different colors and designs of underlines indicate the type of error that has been identified. In addition to identifying the error, Word provides suggestions as to the possible correction needed.

CHECKING GRAMMAR

In addition to the green wavy line under "four," the Spelling and Grammar Status icon appears as [✗] in the status bar. This indicates that a spelling or grammar error has been located. The green wavy underline below the error indicates it is a grammar error.

Concept Grammar Checker

The **grammar checker** advises you of incorrect grammar as you create and edit a document, and proposes possible corrections. Grammar checking occurs after you enter punctuation or end a line. If grammatical errors in subject-verb agreements, verb forms, capitalization, or commonly confused words, to name a few, are detected, they are identified with a wavy green line. You can correct the grammatical error by editing it or you can open the context menu for the identified error and display a suggested correction. Because not all identified grammatical errors are actual errors, you need to use discretion when correcting the errors.

Right-click the word "four" to open the context menu.

Having Trouble?

Review context menus in the "Common Office 2010 Features" section on page IO.51 in the Introduction to Microsoft Office 2010. If the wrong context menu appears, you probably did not have the I-beam positioned on the error with the green wavy line. Press Esc or click outside the menu to cancel it and try again.

Your screen should be similar to Figure 1.9

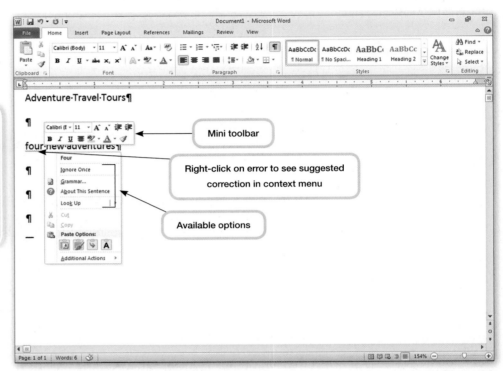

Figure 1.9

Additional Information
You will learn about using the Mini toolbar shortly.

Additional Information
A dimmed menu option means it is currently unavailable.

The Word Mini toolbar and a context menu containing commands related to the grammar error are displayed. The first item on the menu is the suggested correction, "Four." The grammar checker indicates you should capitalize the first letter of the word because it appears to be the beginning of a sentence. It also includes four available commands that are relevant to the item, described below.

Command	Effect
Ignore Once	Instructs Word to ignore the grammatical error in this sentence.
Grammar	Opens the grammar checker and displays an explanation of the error.
About This Sentence	Provides help about the grammatical error.
Look up	Looks up word in dictionary.

To make this correction, you could simply choose the correction from the menu and the correction would be inserted into the document. Although, in this case, you can readily identify the reason for the error, sometimes the reason is not so obvious. In those cases, you can open the grammar checker to find out more information.

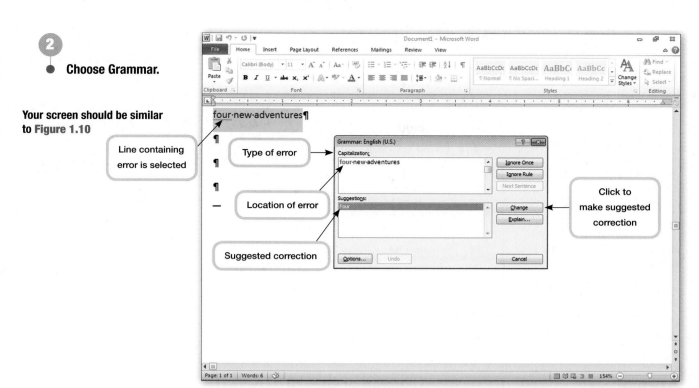

2

● Choose Grammar.

Your screen should be similar to Figure 1.10

Line containing error is selected

Type of error

Location of error

Suggested correction

Click to make suggested correction

Figure 1.10

The Grammar dialog box identifies the type and location of the grammatical error in the upper text box and the suggested correction in the Suggestions box. The line in the document containing the error is also highlighted (selected) to make it easy for you to see the location of the error. You will make the suggested change.

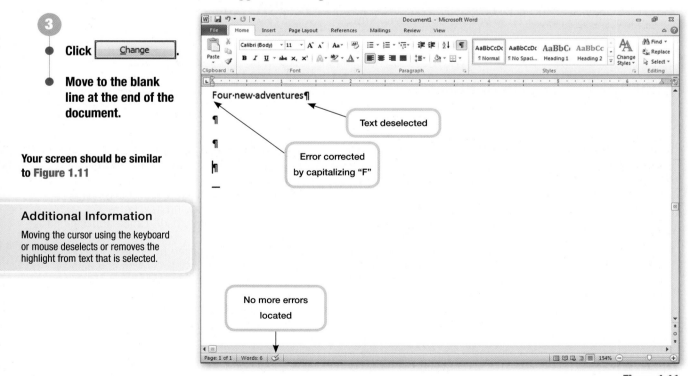

3

● Click **Change**.

● **Move to the blank line at the end of the document.**

Your screen should be similar to Figure 1.11

Additional Information

Moving the cursor using the keyboard or mouse deselects or removes the highlight from text that is selected.

Text deselected

Error corrected by capitalizing "F"

No more errors located

Figure 1.11

The error is corrected, the wavy green line is removed, and the Spelling and Grammar Status icon returns to ⬛.

Identifying and Correcting Errors Automatically   **WD1.13**

CHECKING SPELLING

Now you are ready to type the text for the first paragraph of the flyer. Enter the following text, including the intentional spelling errors.

● **Type Attention adventire travellars!**

● **Press** [Spacebar].

Your screen should be similar to Figure 1.12

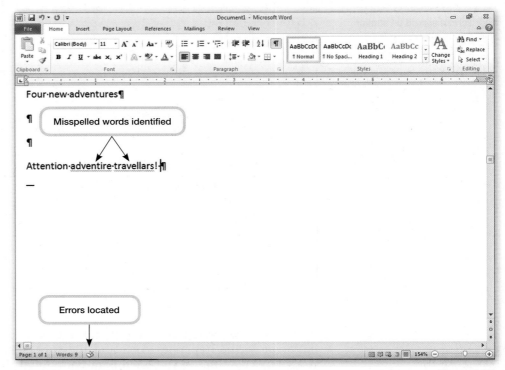

Figure 1.12

As soon as you complete a word by entering a space, the program checks the word for spelling accuracy.

Concept 2 Spelling Checker

The **spelling checker** advises you of misspelled words as you create and edit a document, and proposes possible corrections. The spelling checker compares each word you type to a **main dictionary** of words supplied with the program. The main dictionary includes most common words. If the word does not appear in the main dictionary, it then checks the custom dictionary. The **custom dictionary** consists of a list of words such as proper names, technical terms, and so on, that are not in the main dictionary and that you want the spelling checker to accept as correct. Adding words to the custom dictionary prevents the flagging as incorrect of specialized words that you commonly use. Word shares custom dictionaries with other Microsoft Office applications such as PowerPoint.

If the word does not appear in either dictionary, the program identifies it as misspelled by displaying a red wavy line below the word. You can then correct the misspelled word by editing it. Alternatively, you can display a list of suggested spelling corrections for that word and select the correct spelling from the list to replace the misspelled word in the document.

Word automatically identified the two words "adventire travellars" as misspelled by underlining them with a wavy red line. The quickest way to correct a misspelled word is to select the correct spelling from a list of suggested spelling corrections displayed on the context menu.

Right-click on "adventire" to display the context menu.

Your screen should be similar to Figure 1.13

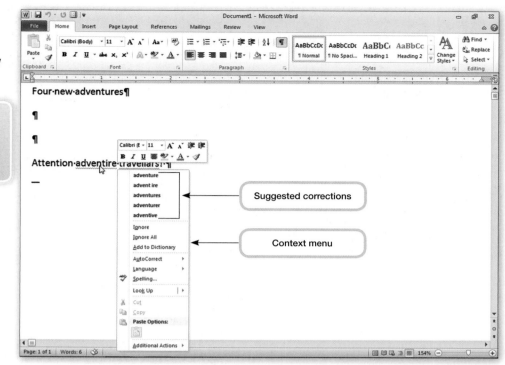

Figure 1.13

A context menu containing suggested correct spellings is displayed. The context menu also includes several related menu options, described in the following table.

Option	Effect
Ignore	Instructs Word to ignore the misspelling of this word for this occurrence only.
Ignore All	Instructs Word to ignore the misspelling of this word throughout the rest of this session.
Add to Dictionary	Adds the word to the custom dictionary list. When a word is added to the custom dictionary, Word will always accept that spelling as correct.
AutoCorrect	Adds the word to the AutoCorrect list so Word can correct misspellings of it automatically as you type.
Language	Sets the language format, such as French, English, or German, to apply to the word.
Spelling	Starts the spell-checking program to check the entire document.
Look Up	Searches reference tools to locate similar words and definitions.

Sometimes there are no suggested replacements because Word cannot locate any words in its dictionary that are similar in spelling; or the suggestions are not correct. If this occurs, you need to edit the word manually. In this case, the first suggestion is correct.

3

- Choose "adventure".

- Correct the spelling for "travellars".

Your screen should be similar to Figure 1.14

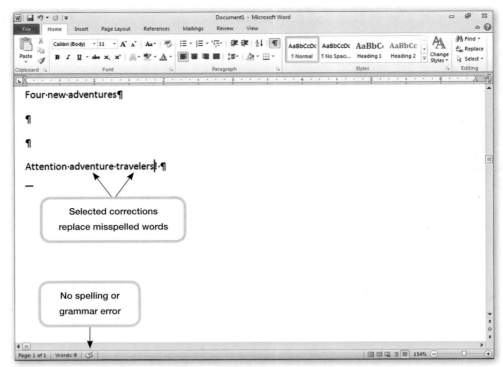

Four·new·adventures¶

¶

¶

Attention·adventure·travelers|·¶

Selected corrections replace misspelled words

No spelling or grammar error

Figure 1.14

The spelling corrections you selected replace the misspelled words in the document. The Spelling and Grammar status icon returns to [ ], indicating that, as far as Word is able to detect, the document is free from errors.

USING AUTOCORRECT

As you have seen, as soon as you complete a word by entering a space or punctuation, the program checks the word for grammar and spelling accuracy. Also, when you complete a sentence and start another, additional checks are made. Many spelling and grammar corrections are made automatically for you as you type. This is part of the AutoCorrect feature of Word.

Concept 3 AutoCorrect

The **AutoCorrect** feature makes some basic assumptions about the text you are typing and, based on these assumptions, automatically corrects the entry. The AutoCorrect feature automatically inserts proper capitalization at the beginning of sentences and in the names of days of the week. It also will change to lowercase letters any words that were incorrectly capitalized because of the accidental use of the [Shift] key. In addition, it also corrects many common typing and spelling errors automatically.

One way the program automatically makes corrections is by looking for certain types of errors. For example, if two capital letters appear at the beginning of a word, Word changes the second capital letter to a lowercase letter. If a lowercase letter appears at the beginning of a sentence, Word capitalizes the first letter of the first word. If the name of a day begins with a lowercase letter, Word capitalizes the first letter. When Spelling Checker provides a single suggested spelling correction for the word, the program will automatically replace the incorrect spelling with the suggested replacement.

Another way the program makes corrections is by checking all entries against a built-in list of AutoCorrect entries. If it finds the entry on the list, the program automatically replaces the error with the correction. For example, the typing error "withthe" is automatically changed to "with the" because the error is on the AutoCorrect list. You also can add words to the AutoCorrect list that you want to be automatically corrected.

WWW.MHHE.COM/OLEARY

Enter the following text, including the errors (identified in italics).

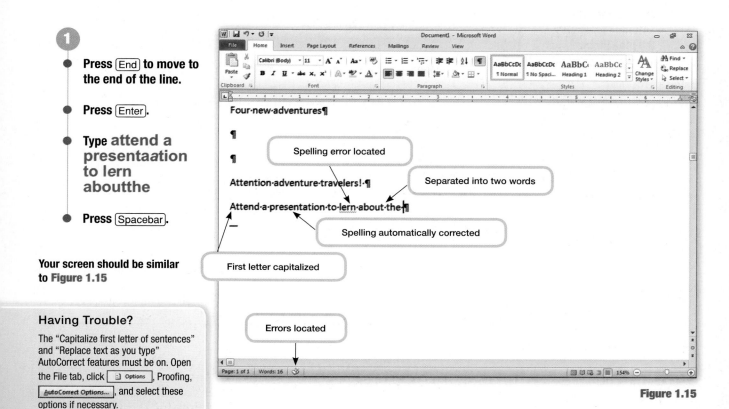

1

- Press [End] to move to the end of the line.

- Press [Enter].

- Type **attend a presentaation to lern aboutthe**

- Press [Spacebar].

Your screen should be similar to Figure 1.15

Having Trouble?

The "Capitalize first letter of sentences" and "Replace text as you type" AutoCorrect features must be on. Open the File tab, click [Options], Proofing, [AutoCorrect Options...], and select these options if necessary.

Four·new·adventures¶

¶

¶

Attention·adventure·travelers!·¶

Attend·a·presentation·to·lern·about·the·¶

Spelling error located

Separated into two words

Spelling automatically corrected

First letter capitalized

Errors located

Page: 1 of 1 | Words: 16 | 154%

Figure 1.15

The first letter of the word "attend" was automatically capitalized because, as you were typing, the program determined that it is the first word in a sentence. In a similar manner, it corrected the spelling of "presentation" and separated the words "about the" with a space. The AutoCorrect feature corrected the spelling of "presentation" because it was the only suggested correction for the word supplied by the Spelling Checker. The word "lern" was not corrected because there are several suggested spelling corrections.

When you rest the mouse pointer near text that has been corrected automatically or move the cursor onto the word, a small blue box appears under the first character of the word. The blue box changes to the AutoCorrect Options button when you point to it.

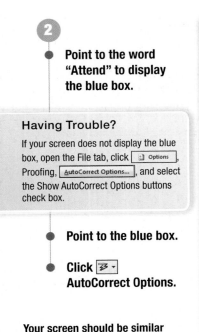

2

● Point to the word "Attend" to display the blue box.

Having Trouble?

If your screen does not display the blue box, open the File tab, click Options, Proofing, AutoCorrect Options..., and select the Show AutoCorrect Options buttons check box.

● Point to the blue box.

● Click AutoCorrect Options.

Your screen should be similar to **Figure 1.16**

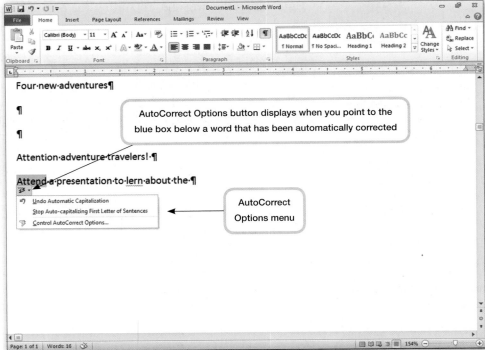

Figure 1.16

Each time Word uses the AutoCorrect feature, the AutoCorrect Options button is available. The AutoCorrect Options menu allows you to undo the AutoCorrection or to permanently disable the AutoCorrection for the remainder of your document. The Control AutoCorrect Options command is used to change the settings for this feature. In some cases, you may want to exclude a word from automatic correction. You can do this by adding the word to the exceptions list so the feature will be disabled for that word. If you use Backspace to delete an automatic correction and then type it again the way you want it to appear, the word will be automatically added to the exceptions list.

You want to keep all the AutoCorrections that were made and correct the spelling for "lern".

Another Method

You also can open the File tab, click Options, Proofing, AutoCorrect Options..., Exceptions... to add a word to the exceptions list.

3

● Click outside the menu to close it.

● Open the spelling context menu for "lern" and choose "learn".

The spelling is corrected, and the spelling indicator in the status bar indicates that the document is free of errors.

Using Word Wrap

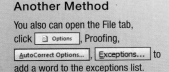

Now you will continue entering more of the paragraph. As you type, when the text gets close to the right margin, do not press Enter to move to the next line. Word will automatically wrap words to the next line as needed.

Concept ④ Word Wrap

The **word wrap** feature automatically decides where to end a line and wrap text to the next line based on the margin settings. This feature saves time when entering text because you do not need to press [Enter] at the end of a full line to begin a new line. The only time you need to press [Enter] is to end a paragraph, to insert blank lines, or to create a short line such as a salutation. In addition, if you change the margins or insert or delete text on a line, the program automatically readjusts the text on the line to fit within the new margin settings. Word wrap is common to all word processors.

Enter the following text to complete the sentence.

1

- Press [End] to move to the end of the line.

- Type **earth's greatest unspoiled habitats and find out how you can experience the adventure of a lifetime.**

- Correct any spelling or grammar errors that are identified.

Your screen should be similar to Figure 1.17

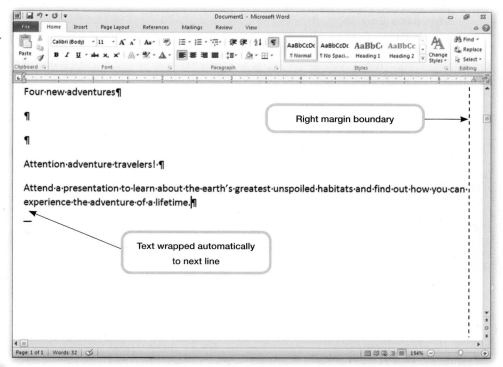

Right margin boundary

Text wrapped automatically to next line

Figure 1.17

Additional Information

Generally, when using a word processor, separate sentences with one space after a period rather than two spaces, which was common when typewriters were used.

Additional Information

You can continue typing to ignore the date suggestion.

The program has wrapped the text that would overlap the right margin to the beginning of the next line.

You have a meeting you need to attend in a few minutes and want to continue working on the document when you get back. You decide to add your name and the current date to the document. As you type the first four characters of the month, Word will recognize the entry as a month and display a ScreenTip suggesting the remainder of the month. You can insert the suggested month by pressing [Enter]. Then enter a space to continue the date and another ScreenTip will appear with the complete date. Press [Enter] again to insert it.

2

- Move to the end of the sentence and press Enter twice.

- Type **your name**

- Press Enter.

- Type the **current date** beginning with the month and when the ScreenTips appear for the month and the complete date, press Enter to insert them.

- Press Enter twice.

- Click ¶ **Show/Hide** to turn off the display of formatting marks.

Your screen should be similar to Figure 1.18

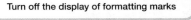

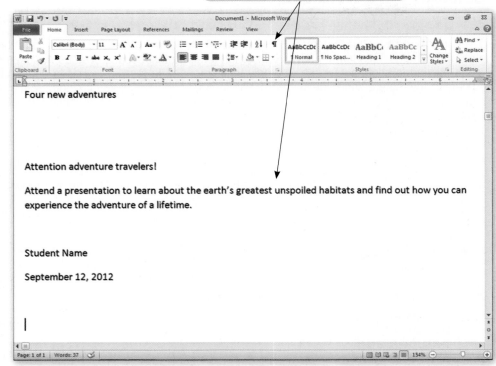

Four new adventures

Attention adventure travelers!

Attend a presentation to learn about the earth's greatest unspoiled habitats and find out how you can experience the adventure of a lifetime.

Student Name

September 12, 2012

Figure 1.18

Having Trouble?

Review saving files in the "Saving a File" section on pg. IO.52 in the Introduction to Microsoft Office 2010.

As you have seen, in many editing situations, it is helpful to display the formatting marks. However, for normal entry of text, you will probably not need the marks displayed. Now that you know how to turn this feature on and off, you can use it whenever you want when entering and editing text.

Before leaving to attend your meeting, you want to save your work to a file. You will name the file Flyer and use the default document type (.docx).

3

- Click 🖫 **Save in the Quick Access Toolbar.**

- **Select the location where you want to save your file.**

- **If necessary, drag to select the proposed file name in the File Name text box to highlight the text.**

- **Type** Flyer.

- **Click**  **to save your document as a Word document.**

Your screen should be similar to Figure 1.19

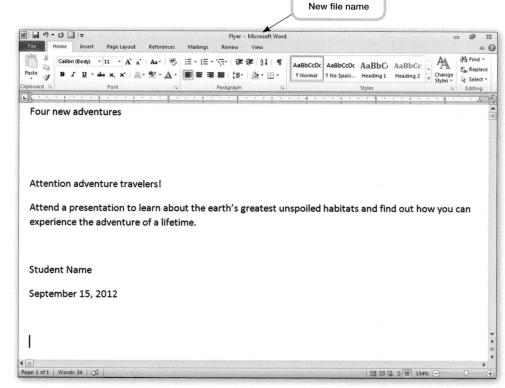

New file name

Four new adventures

Attention adventure travelers!

Attend a presentation to learn about the earth's greatest unspoiled habitats and find out how you can experience the adventure of a lifetime.

Student Name

September 15, 2012

Figure 1.19

The document is saved as Flyer.docx at the location you selected, and the new file name is displayed in the Word title bar.

Finally, you want to close the document while you attend your meeting.

4

- **Open the File tab and click** 📁 Close **.**

Now the Word window displays an empty document window.

Having Trouble?

Review closing files in the "Closing a File" section on pg. IO.60 in the Introduction to Microsoft Office 2010.

Editing Documents

You asked your assistant to enter the remaining information in the flyer for you while you attended the meeting. Upon your return, you find a note from your assistant on your desk. The note explains that he had a little trouble entering the information and tells you that he saved the revised file as Flyer1. You want to open the file and continue working on the flyer.

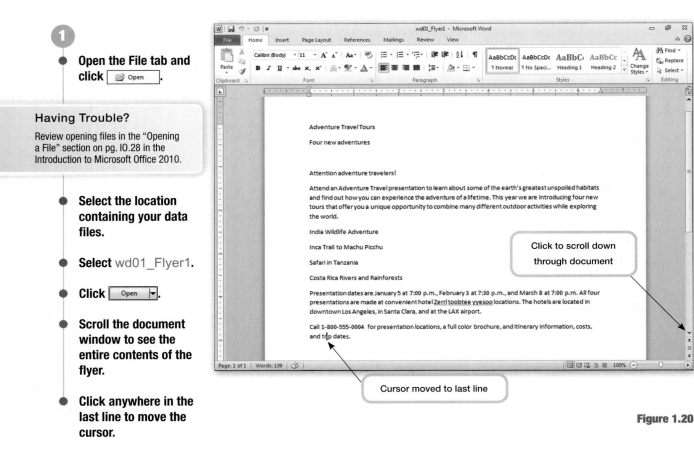

1

- Open the File tab and click [📂 Open].

Having Trouble?
Review opening files in the "Opening a File" section on pg. IO.28 in the Introduction to Microsoft Office 2010.

- Select the location containing your data files.

- Select wd01_Flyer1.

- Click [Open ▼].

- Scroll the document window to see the entire contents of the flyer.

- Click anywhere in the last line to move the cursor.

Your screen should be similar to Figure 1.20

Having Trouble?
Review how to navigate a document in the "Scrolling the Document Window" section on page IO.30 of the Introduction to Microsoft Office 2010.

Figure 1.20

The file containing the additional content you asked your assistant to add to the flyer is opened and displayed in the document window. After looking over the flyer, you have identified several errors that need to be corrected and changes you want to make to the content. The changes you want to make are shown below.

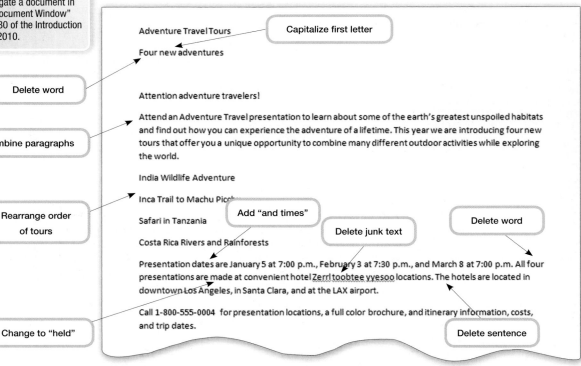

INSERTING AND REPLACING TEXT

Additional Information

You can replace existing text using Overtype mode, in which each character you type replaces an existing character. This feature is turned on by opening the File tab, then clicking 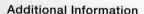 Options, Advanced, and then selecting Use overtype mode.

As you check the document, you see that the first sentence of the paragraph below the list of trips is incorrect. It should read: "Presentation dates and times are . . . " The sentence is missing the words "and times." In addition, you want to change the word "made" to "held" in the following sentence. These words can easily be entered into the sentence without retyping the entire line. This is because Word uses **Insert mode** to allow new characters to be inserted into the existing text by moving the existing text to the right to make space for the new characters. You will insert the words "and times" after the word "dates" in the first sentence.

- **Press** Ctrl + Home **to move to the top of the document.**

- **Move the cursor to the "a" in "are" in the first sentence of the paragraph below the list of tours.**

Additional Information

Throughout these labs, when instructed to move to a specific letter in the text, this means to move the cursor to the left side of the character.

- **Type** and times

- **Press** Spacebar.

Your screen should be similar to Figure 1.21

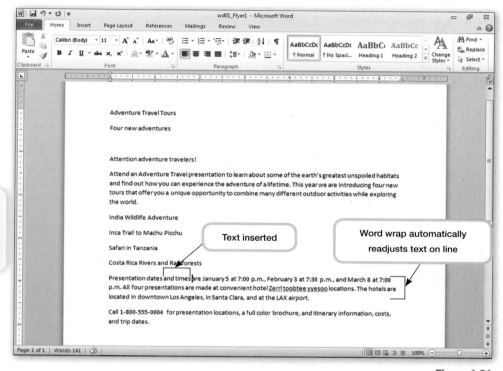

Figure 1.21

The inserted text pushes the existing text on the line to the right, and the word wrap feature automatically readjusts the text on the line to fit within the margin settings.

In the second sentence, you want to change the word "made" to "held." You could delete this word and type in the new word, or as you will do next, you can select the text and type the new text.

Additional Information

If necessary, refer to the section "Selecting Text" on page IO.37 in the Introduction to Microsoft Office 2010 to review this feature.

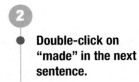

2

● Double-click on "made" in the next sentence.

Having Trouble?
If you accidentally select the wrong text, simply click anywhere in the document or press any directional key to clear the selection.

● Type **held**

Your screen should be similar to **Figure 1.22**

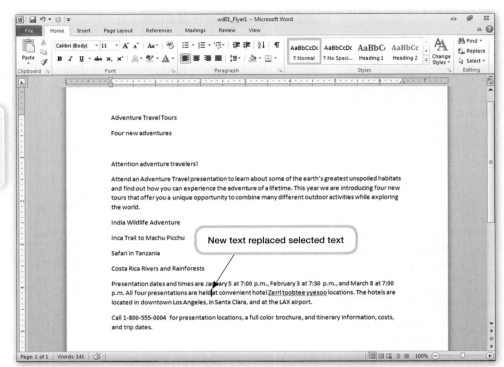

New text replaced selected text

Figure 1.22

As soon as you began typing, the selected text was automatically deleted. The new text was inserted in the line just like any other text.

DELETING TEXT

As you continue proofreading the flyer, you see several changes you would like to make. The first change is to combine the line "Attention adventure travellers!" with the text in the following paragraph. To do this, you need to delete the paragraph mark symbol ¶ after the text "travelers!".

1

● Move to the "A" of "Attend" at the beginning of the first paragraph.

● Press Backspace.

Your screen should be similar to **Figure 1.23**

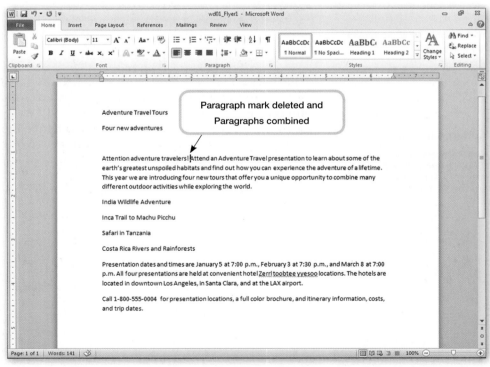

Paragraph mark deleted and Paragraphs combined

You deleted the ¶ that ended the previous line and the paragraph has now moved up to the line above.

You next want to delete the word "four" from the second sentence in the paragraph below the list of tours. The [Ctrl] + [Delete] key combination deletes text to the right of the cursor to the beginning of the next group of characters. In order to delete an entire word, you must position the cursor at the beginning of the word.

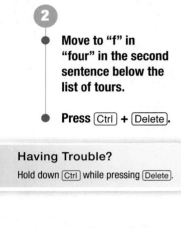

2

● **Move to "f" in "four" in the second sentence below the list of tours.**

● **Press [Ctrl] + [Delete].**

Having Trouble?

Hold down [Ctrl] while pressing [Delete].

Your screen should be similar to Figure 1.24

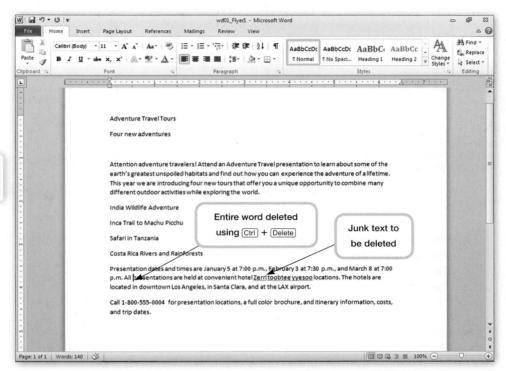

Figure 1.24

The word "four" has been deleted.

You see that the end of the same sentence contains a section of junk characters. To remove these characters, you could use [Delete] and [Backspace] to delete each character individually, or [Ctrl] + [Delete] or [Ctrl] + [Backspace] to delete each word or group of characters. This is very slow, however. Several characters, words, or lines of text can be deleted at once by first selecting the text and then pressing [Delete].

The section of characters you want to remove follows the word "hotel" in the same sentence. You also decide to delete the entire last sentence of the paragraph.

3

● **Move to "Z"**
(following the word
"hotel").

● **Drag to the right until**
all the text including
the space before the
word "locations" is
highlighted.

Having Trouble?

Hold down the left mouse button while
moving the mouse to drag.

Additional Information

When you start dragging over a word,
the entire word including the space after
it is automatically selected.

● **Press** Delete .

● **Hold down** Ctrl **and**
click anywhere in
the third sentence of
the paragraph below
the list of trips.

● **Press** Delete .

Your screen should be similar
to Figure 1.25

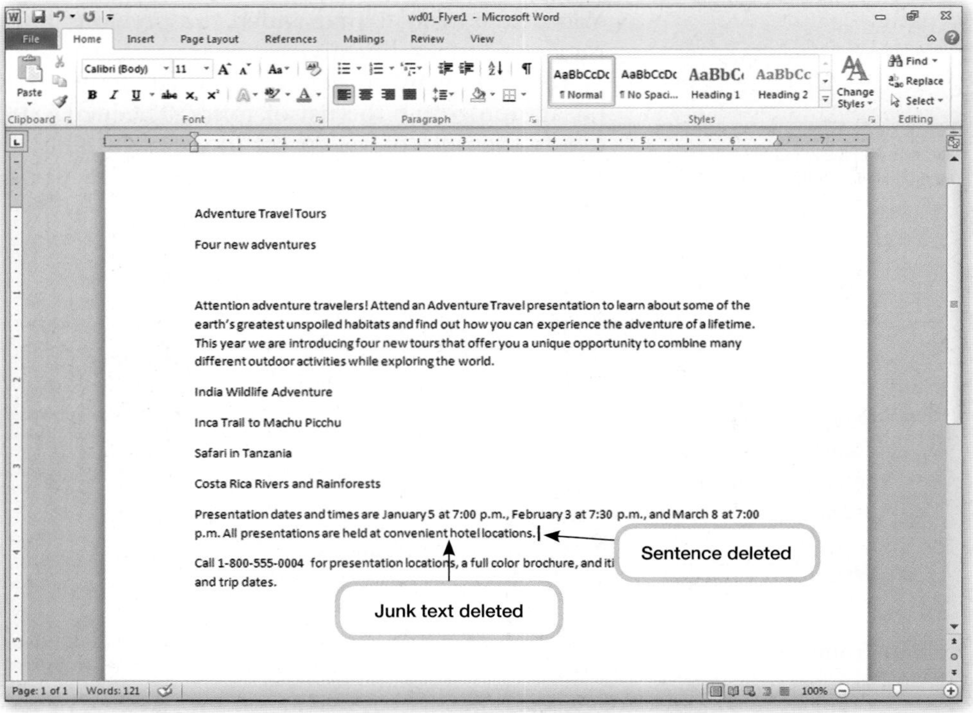

Adventure Travel Tours

Four new adventures

Attention adventure travelers! Attend an Adventure Travel presentation to learn about some of the
earth's greatest unspoiled habitats and find out how you can experience the adventure of a lifetime.
This year we are introducing four new tours that offer you a unique opportunity to combine many
different outdoor activities while exploring the world.

India Wildlife Adventure

Inca Trail to Machu Picchu

Safari in Tanzania

Costa Rica Rivers and Rainforests

Presentation dates and times are January 5 at 7:00 p.m., February 3 at 7:30 p.m., and March 8 at 7:00
p.m. All presentations are held at convenient hotel locations.
← Sentence deleted

Call 1-800-555-0004 for presentation locations, a full color brochure, and iti
and trip dates.

Junk text deleted

Figure 1.25

The selected junk text and the complete sentence were removed from the flyer.

UNDOING EDITING CHANGES

After removing the sentence, you decide it may be necessary after all. To
quickly restore this sentence, you can use [icon] Undo to reverse your last action
or command. Notice that the Undo button includes a drop-down list button. Clicking this button displays a list of the most recent actions that can be
reversed, with the most recent action at the top of the list. When you select an
action from the drop-down list, you also undo all actions above it in the list.

Additional Information

Review the Undo feature in the
"Undoing Editing Changes"section
on page IO.43 of the Introduction to
Microsoft Office 2010.

Another Method

The keyboard shortcut for the Undo
command is Ctrl + Z.

1

- Open the ↺ ▾ Undo drop-down list.

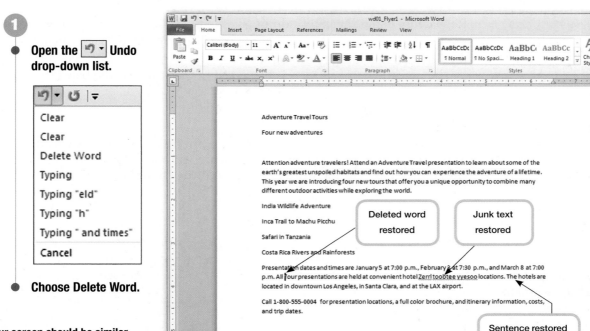

- Choose Delete Word.

Your screen should be similar to **Figure 1.26**

Figure 1.26

The deleted sentence, junk characters, and the word "four" are restored. You will restore two of your corrections and then save the changes you have made to the document to a new file.

2

- Click ↻ Redo 2 times.

Another Method
The keyboard shortcut is Ctrl + Y.

- Open the File tab and choose Save As.

- Save the document as Flyer1 to your solution file location.

Your screen should be similar to **Figure 1.27**

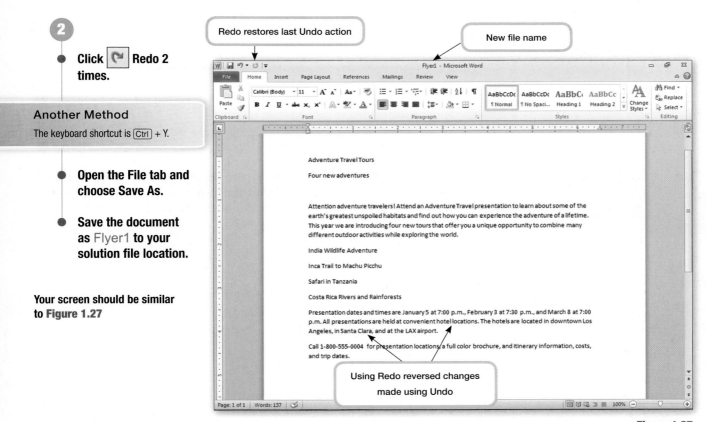

Figure 1.27

Repeatedly using the 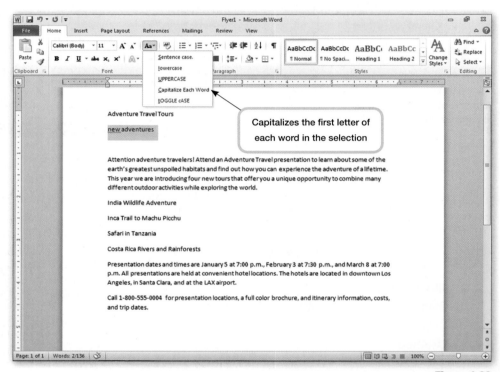 Undo or Redo buttons performs the actions in the list one by one. So that you can see what action will be performed, the button's ScreenTips identify the action.

The new file name, Flyer1, is displayed in the window title bar. The original document file, wd01_Flyer1 is unchanged.

CHANGING CASE

You also want to delete the word "Four" from the second line of the flyer title and capitalize the first letter of each word. Although you could change the case individually for the words, you can quickly change both using the Change Case command in the Font group.

1

● **Move the cursor to the beginning of the word "Four".**

● **Press** Ctrl **+** Delete **.**

● **Click in the left margin to select the entire title line.**

● **From the Font group, click** Aa▾ **Change Case.**

Your screen should be similar to Figure 1.28

Figure 1.28

Additional Information

You also can use Shift + F3 to cycle through and apply the different change case options.

The Change Case drop-down menu allows you to change the case of selected words and sentences to the desired case without having to make the change manually. You want both words in the title to be capitalized.

2

- **Choose Capitalize Each Word.**

- **Click anywhere to deselect the title line.**

Your screen should be similar to Figure 1.29

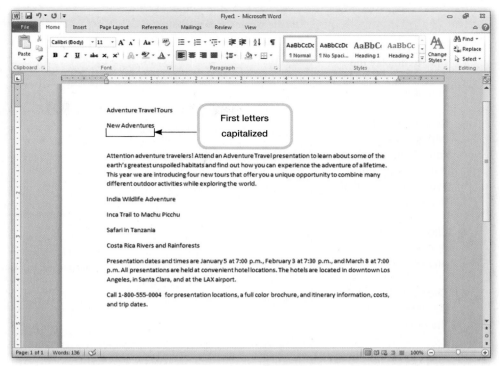

Figure 1.29

The first letter of each word in the title is now capitalized and the highlight is removed from the text.

Copying and Moving Selections

After looking over the letter, you decide to add the company name in several other locations and to change the order of the list of tours. To make these changes quickly, you can copy and move selections.

USING COPY AND PASTE

Additional Information

Review how to copy and move selections in the "Copying and Moving Selections" section on page IO.45 of the Introduction to Microsoft Office 2010.

You want to include the company name in the last paragraph of the letter. Because the name has already been entered on the first line of the document, you will copy the name instead of typing the name again. Before you copy the text, you will reveal formatting marks in your document to make sure you're copying exactly what you want.

- Click ¶ Show/Hide to display the formatting marks in your document.

- Select the text "Adventure Travel Tours" not including the ¶ paragraph symbol at the end of the line.

- Click ¶ Show/Hide to hide the formatting marks again.

- Click 🗐 Copy in the Clipboard group of the Home tab.

- Move the cursor to the left of "1" in the phone number (last paragraph).

- Click 📋 Paste in the Clipboard group.

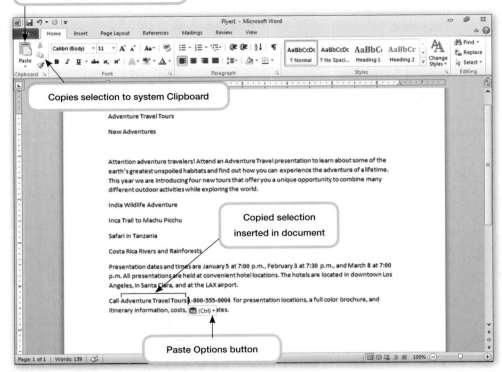

Figure 1.30

Another Method

The Copy keyboard shortcut is [Ctrl] + C. The Paste keyboard shortcut is [Ctrl] + V.

Your screen should be similar to **Figure 1.30**

The copied selection is inserted at the location you specified. The 📋 (Ctrl) ▾ Paste Options button appears automatically whenever a selection is pasted. It is used to control the format of the pasted item. By default, pasted items maintain the original formatting from the source.

2

● Click the [icon] (Ctrl) ▾
  Paste Options button.

**Your screen should be similar
to Figure 1.31**

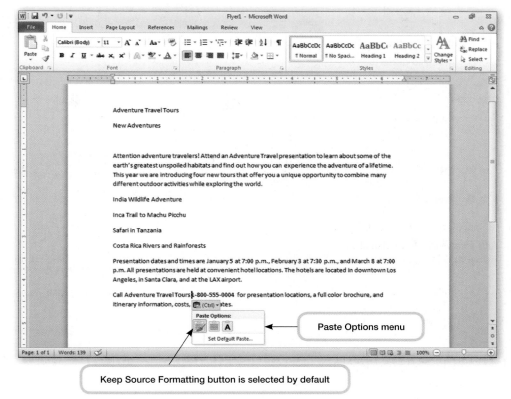

Paste Options menu

Keep Source Formatting button is selected by default

Figure 1.31

The following table describes the options on the Paste Options menu.

Paste Option	Description
Keep Source Formatting [icon]	Pastes the item with the same formatting that it had in the source.
Merge Formatting [icon]	Pastes the item, changing the formatting to match the surrounding destination text.
Keep Text Only [icon]	Pastes text only (from a selection that is a combination of text and graphics). This option also strips formatting from the pasted text.
Set Default Paste	Enables you to change the default paste formatting setting to another.

The selection was pasted using the same formatting it had in the source, which is appropriate for this sentence. You will close the Paste Options menu without changing the selection.

3
- **Click outside the menu to close it.**

Additional Information

The Paste Options button will disappear as soon as you begin to type.

- **Type at**
- **Press Spacebar.**

Your screen should be similar to Figure 1.32

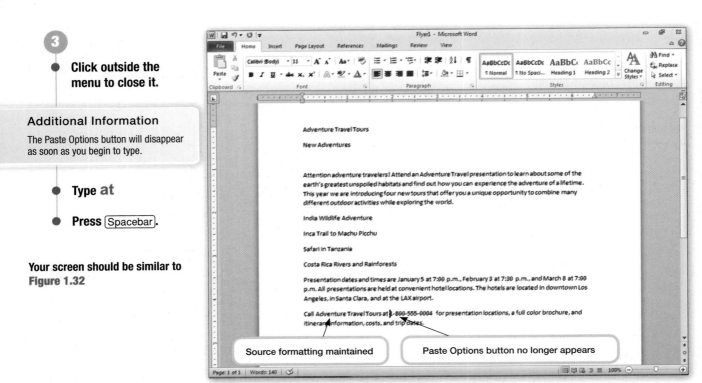

Source formatting maintained

Paste Options button no longer appears

Figure 1.32

Next, you want to insert the company name in place of the word "we" in the first paragraph and then change the word "are" to "is".

4
- **Select "we" (third sentence, first paragraph).**

- **Right-click on the selection and click Keep Source Formatting from the context menu.**

Another Method

You could simply have clicked Paste in the Clipboard group of the Home tab to insert the Clipboard contents again.

- **Change "are" in the same sentence to "is".**

Your screen should be similar to Figure 1.33

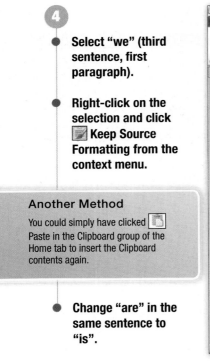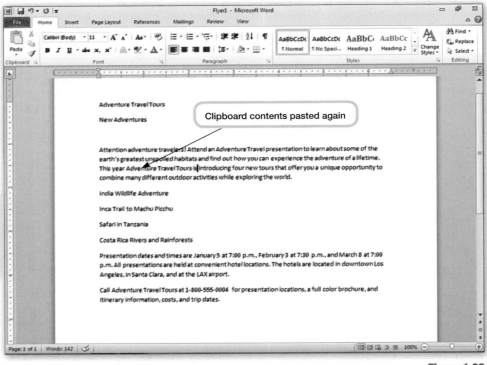

Clipboard contents pasted again

Figure 1.33

The selected text was deleted and replaced with the contents of the system Clipboard. The system Clipboard contents remain in the Clipboard until another item is copied or cut, allowing you to paste the same item multiple times.

USING CUT AND PASTE

You've decided to move the "Costa Rica Rivers and Rainforests" tour name to be second in the tour list. To do this, you will move the name from its current location to the new location. The Cut and Paste commands in the Clipboard group of the Home tab are used to move selections.

1

- Select the line of text "Costa Rica Rivers and Rainforests".

Having Trouble?
Click in the margin space to the left of the paragraph to select it.

- Click ✂ Cut in the Clipboard group.

Another Method
The Cut keyboard shortcut is Ctrl + X. You also can choose Cut from the context menu.

- Move to the "I" in the "Inca Trail to Machu Picchu" title.

- Press Ctrl + V.

Your screen should be similar to **Figure 1.34**

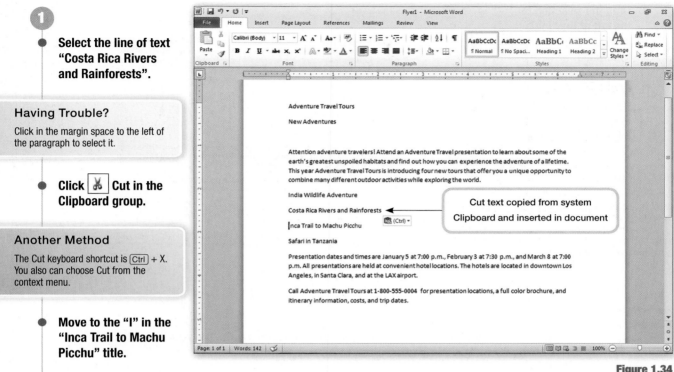

Cut text copied from system Clipboard and inserted in document

Figure 1.34

The selected text was removed from the source and copied to the Clipboard. Then it was reentered into the document at the cursor location. That was much quicker than retyping the tour name over!

USING DRAG AND DROP

Additional Information
Review the drag and drop feature in the "Using Drag and Drop" section on page I0.49 of the Introduction to Microsoft Office 2010.

Additional Information
You also can use drag and drop to copy a selection by holding down Ctrl while dragging. The mouse pointer shape is ⬚.

Finally, you also decide to move the tour name "Safari in Tanzania" to first in the list. Rather than use Cut and Paste to move this text, you will use the drag-and-drop editing feature. This feature is most useful for copying or moving short distances in a document.

- Select the entire line "Safari in Tanzania", including the space at the end of the line.

- Drag the selection to the left of the "India Wildlife Adventure" tour name.

- Click 🖫 Save in the Quick Access Toolbar to save the file using the same file name.

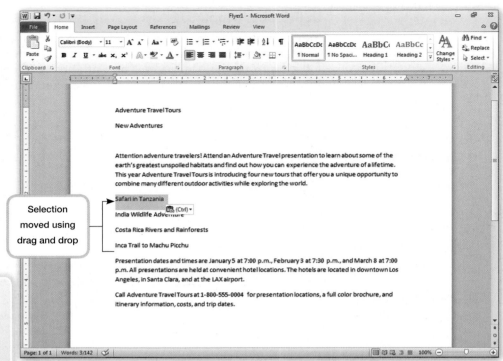

Figure 1.35

Your screen should be similar to Figure 1.35

The selection is moved to the new location. As you are working on a document, it is a good idea to save your document frequently to prevent the accidental loss of work from a power outage or other mishap. While AutoRecover is a great feature for recovering lost work, it should not be used in place of regularly saving your work.

Formatting a Document

Because this document is a flyer, you want it to be interesting to look at and easy to read. Applying different formatting to characters and paragraphs can greatly enhance the appearance of the document. **Character formatting** consists of formatting features that affect the selected characters only. This includes changing the character style and size, applying effects such as bold and italics to characters, changing the character spacing, and adding animated text effects. Paragraph formatting features affect an entire paragraph. A paragraph consists of all text up to and including the paragraph mark. **Paragraph formatting** features include how the paragraph is positioned or aligned between the margins, paragraph indentation, spacing above and below a paragraph, and line spacing within a paragraph.

CHANGING FONTS AND FONT SIZES

The first formatting change you want to make is to use different fonts and font sizes in the flyer. Using fonts as a design element can add interest to your document and give readers visual cues to help them find information quickly.

Two basic types of fonts are serif and sans serif. **Serif fonts** have a flair at the base of each letter that visually leads the reader to the next letter. Two common serif fonts are Roman and Times New Roman. **Sans serif fonts** don't have a flair at the base of each letter and are generally used for text in paragraphs. Arial and Calibri are two common sans serif fonts. Because sans serif fonts have a clean look, they are often used for headings in documents. A good practice is to use only two types of fonts in a document, one for text and one for headings. Using too many different font styles can make your document look cluttered and unprofessional.

Several common fonts in different sizes are shown in the table below.

Font Name	Font Type	Font Size
Arial	Sans serif	This is 10 pt. This is 16 pt.
Courier New	Serif	This is 10 pt. This is 16 pt.
Times New Roman	Serif	This is 10 pt. This is 16 pt.

To change the font before typing the text, use the command and then type. All text will appear in the specified setting until another font setting is selected. To change a font setting for existing text, select the text you want to change and then use the command. If you want to apply font formatting to a word, simply move the cursor to the word and the formatting is automatically applied to the entire word.

First you want to increase the font size of all the text in the flyer to make it easier to read. Currently, you can see from the Font Size button in the Font group that the font size is 11 points.

1

● **Triple-click in the left margin when the mouse pointer is ⬦ to select the entire document.**

Another Method

The keyboard shortcut is [Ctrl] + A.

● **From the Font group, open the 11 ⏷ Font Size drop-down list.**

Another Method

The keyboard shortcut is [Ctrl] + [Shift] + P.

Your screen should be similar to Figure 1.36

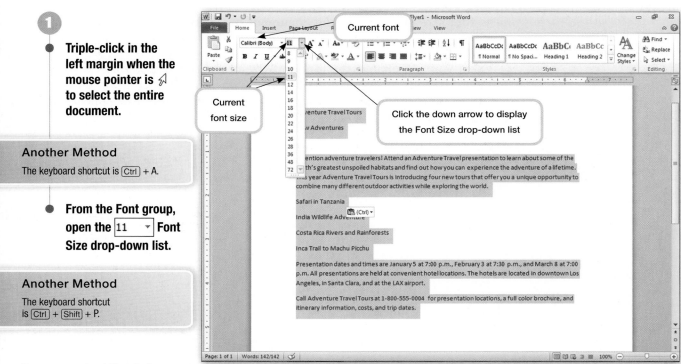

Figure 1.36

Formatting a Document   **WD1.35**

Refer to the Section

"Formatting Text" on page IO.40 in the Introduction to Microsoft Office 2010 to review the Live Preview feature.

The current (default) font size of 11 is selected. You will increase the font size to 14 points. As you point to the size options, the Live Preview feature shows how the selected text in the document will appear if chosen.

2

- **Point to several different point sizes in the list to see the Live Preview.**

- **Click 14 to choose it.**

Your screen should be similar to Figure 1.37

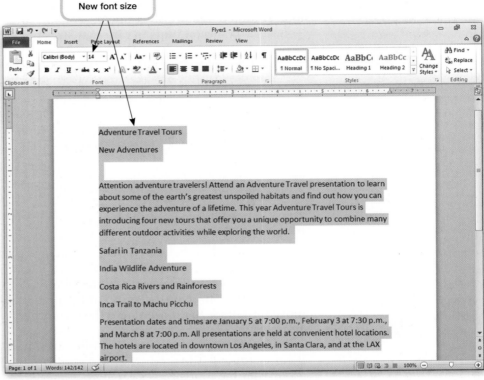

Figure 1.37

Additional Information

If a selection includes text of various sizes, the Font Size button will be blank.

The font size of all text in the document has increased to 14 points, making the text much easier to read. The Font Size button displays the new point size setting for the text at the location of the cursor.

Next you will change the font and size of the two title lines. First you will change the font to Comic Sans MS and then you will increase the font size. Many of the formatting commands are on the Mini toolbar that appears whenever you select text.

3

- Select the two title lines and point to the Mini toolbar.

- Open the Calibri (Body) Font drop-down menu in the Mini toolbar.

- Scroll the list and choose Comic Sans MS.

Additional Information

Font names are listed in alphabetical order.

Having Trouble?

If this font is not available on your computer, choose a similar font.

Your screen should be similar to **Figure 1.38**

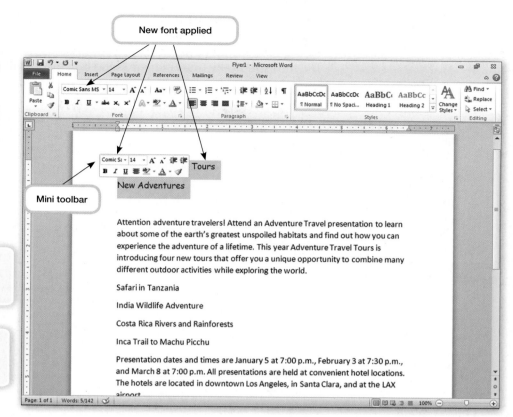

Figure 1.38

Using the Mini toolbar to apply the formats is a quick and convenient alternative to using the Ribbon. Next, you will change the font size.

4

- Open the 14 Font Size drop-down menu in the Mini toolbar.

- Choose 36.

Your screen should be similar to **Figure 1.39**

Figure 1.39

The selected font and size have been applied to the selection, making the title lines much more interesting and eye-catching. The Font and Font Size buttons reflect the settings in use in the selection. As you look at the title lines, you decide the font size of the first title line is too large. You will reduce it to 20 points.

5
- Select the first title line.

- Click `36` ▼ and choose 20 points Font Size drop-down menu.

Your screen should be similar to Figure 1.40

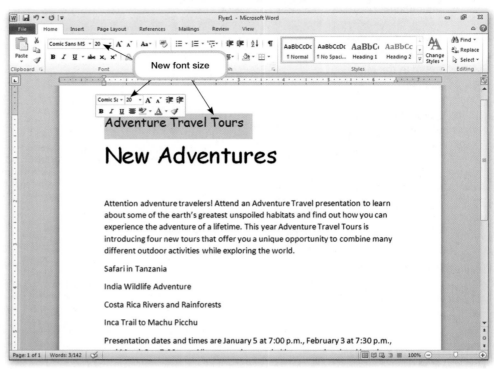

Figure 1.40

Finally, you want to change the font of the list of four tours.

6
- Select the list of four tours.

- Click `Calibri (Body)` ▼ Font in the Mini toolbar and change the font to Comic Sans MS.

Additional Information

Theme fonts and recently used fonts appear at the top of the list. You will learn about themes in Lab 3.

- Click anywhere on the highlighted text to deselect it.

- Reduce the zoom so the entire page is visible.

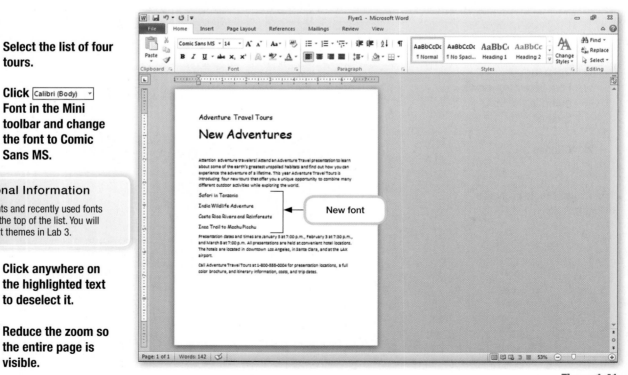

Figure 1.41

Your screen should be similar to Figure 1.41

The changes you have made to the font and font size have made the flyer somewhat more interesting. However, you want to further enhance the document.

APPLYING CHARACTER EFFECTS

Next you want to liven up the flyer by adding character effects such as color and bold to selected areas. The table below describes some of the effects and their uses.

Format	Example	Use
Bold, italic	**Bold** *Italic*	Adds emphasis.
Underline	<u>Underline</u>	Adds emphasis.
Strikethrough	~~Strikethrough~~	Indicates words to be deleted.
Double strikethrough	~~Double Strikethrough~~	Indicates words to be deleted.
Superscript	"To be or not to be."[1]	Used in footnotes and formulas.
Subscript	H_2O	Used in formulas.
Shadow	Shadow	Adds distinction to titles and headings.
Outline	Outline	Adds distinction to titles and headings.
Emboss	Emboss	Adds distinction to titles and headings.
Engrave	Engrave	Adds distinction to titles and headings.
Small caps	SMALL CAPS	Adds emphasis when case is not important.
All caps	ALL CAPS	Adds emphasis when case is not important.
Hidden		Prevents selected text from displaying or printing. Hidden text can be viewed by displaying formatting marks.
Color	Color Color **Color**	Adds interest

First you will add color and bold to the top title line. The default font color setting is Automatic. This setting automatically determines when to use black or white text. Black text is used on a light background and white text on a dark background.

- Return the zoom to 100%.

- Select the first title line and point to the Mini toolbar.

- Open the 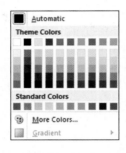 Font Color drop-down list on the Mini toolbar.

Additional Information

A ScreenTip displays the name of the color when selected.

- Choose ☐ Orange from the Standard Colors bar.

- Click **B** Bold on the Mini toolbar.

Another Method

The keyboard shortcut is Ctrl + B.

- Click on the title line to clear the selection.

Your screen should be similar to Figure 1.42

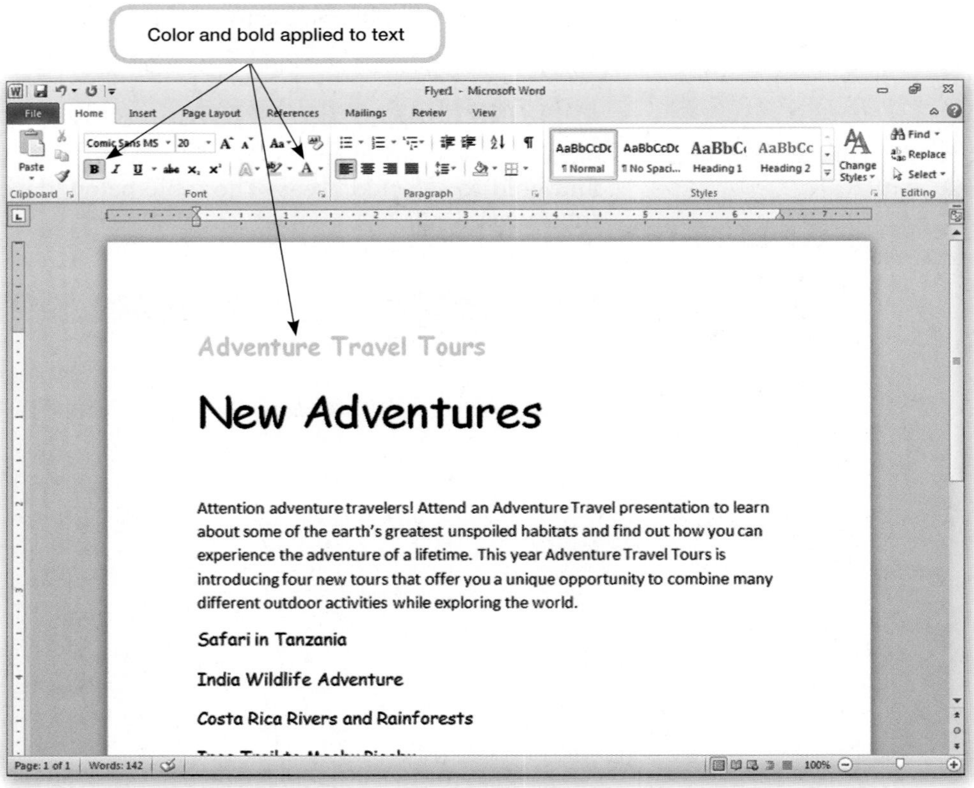

Color and bold applied to text

Figure 1.42

The buttons reflect the settings associated with the text at the insertion point. The Font Color button appears in the last selected color. This color can be quickly applied to other selections now simply by clicking the button.

Next you will add color and bold to several other areas of the flyer.

2

- Select the second title line.

- Using the Mini toolbar, change the font color to green using the Standard Colors bar.

- Add bold to the selected title.

- Select the list of four tours.

- Click 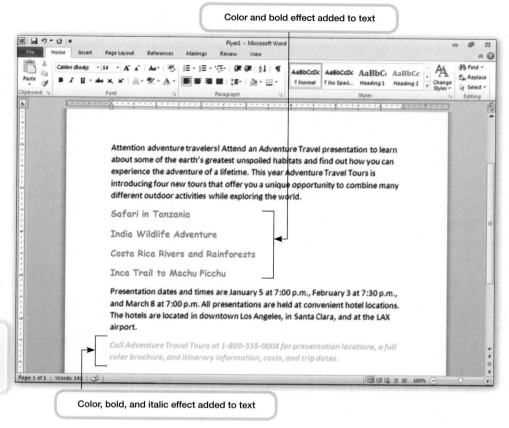 Font Color to change the color to green.

Color and bold effect added to text

Additional Information

The currently selected font color can be applied to the selection simply by clicking the button.

- Click **B** Bold, *I* Italic.

- Click *I* Italic again to remove the italic effect.

Additional Information

Many formatting commands are toggle commands. This means the feature can be turned on and off simply by clicking on the command button.

- Apply bold, italic, and orange font color to the last sentence of the flyer.

- Click in the document to deselect the text.

Your screen should be similar to Figure 1.43

Color, bold, and italic effect added to text

Figure 1.43

The character formatting effects you added to the flyer make it much more interesting.

The next formatting change you want to make is to apply the Small Caps effect to the title lines. Since the Ribbon does not display a button for this feature, you need to open the Font dialog box to access this feature.

3

- Select both title lines.

- Click ⊡ in the bottom-right corner of the Font group to open the Font dialog box.

Your screen should be similar to Figure 1.44

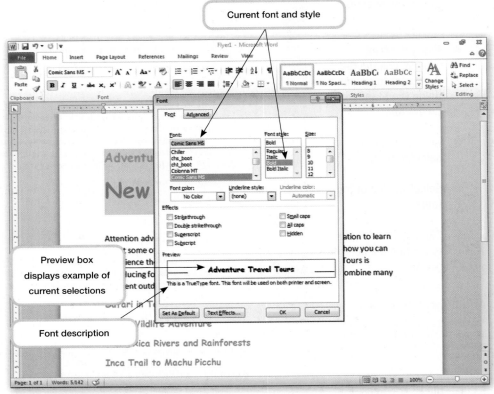

Figure 1.44

The Font dialog box contains all of the Font commands in the Font group and more. Using the Dialog Box Launcher to open a dialog box allows you to access the more-advanced or less-used features of a group. The font and font style used in the selected text are identified in the list boxes. However, because the selection includes two different font sizes and colors, these settings are not identified.

The Preview box displays an example of the currently selected font setting. Notice the description of the font below the Preview box. It states that the selected font is a TrueType font. **TrueType** fonts are fonts that are automatically installed when you install Windows. They appear onscreen exactly as they will appear when printed. Some fonts are printer fonts, which are available only on your printer and may look different onscreen than when printed. Courier is an example of a printer font.

You will add the Small caps effect to the selected lines.

4

● **Choose Small caps.**

● **Click** [OK].

Your screen should be similar to Figure 1.45

Small Caps effect applied to selection

Figure 1.45

The Small caps effect has been applied to all text in the selection and adds more emphasis to the title lines.

SETTING PARAGRAPH ALIGNMENT

The final formatting change you want to make is to change the paragraph alignment.

Concept 5 Alignment

Alignment is the positioning of text on a line between the margins or indents. There are four types of paragraph alignment: left, centered, right, and justified. The alignment settings affect entire paragraphs and are described in the table below.

Alignment	Effect on Text Alignment
Left	Aligns text against the left margin of the page, leaving the right margin ragged or uneven. This is the most commonly used paragraph alignment type, and therefore the default setting in all word processing software packages.
Center	Centers each line of text between the left and right margins. Center alignment is used mostly for headings or centering graphics on a page.
Right	Aligns text against the right margin, leaving the left margin ragged. Use right alignment when you want text to line up on the outside of a page, such as a chapter title or a header.
Justify	Aligns text against the right and left margins and evenly spaces out the words by inserting extra spaces, called **soft spaces**, that adjust automatically whenever additions or deletions are made to the text. Newspapers commonly use justified alignment so the columns of text are even.

The commands to change paragraph alignment are available in the Paragraph dialog box. However, it is much faster to use the keyboard shortcuts or command buttons in the Paragraph group shown below.

Alignment	Keyboard Shortcut	Button
Left	Ctrl + L	
Center	Ctrl + E	
Right	Ctrl + R	
Justify	Ctrl + J	

You want to change the alignment of all paragraphs in the flyer from the default of left-aligned to centered.

1

- **Triple-click in the left margin to select the entire document.**

- **Click ☰ Center in the Mini toolbar.**

Another Method

You also can use ☰ in the Paragraph group of the Home tab or choose Centered from the Alignment list box in the Paragraph dialog box.

- **Reduce the zoom so the entire page is visible.**

Your screen should be similar to Figure 1.46

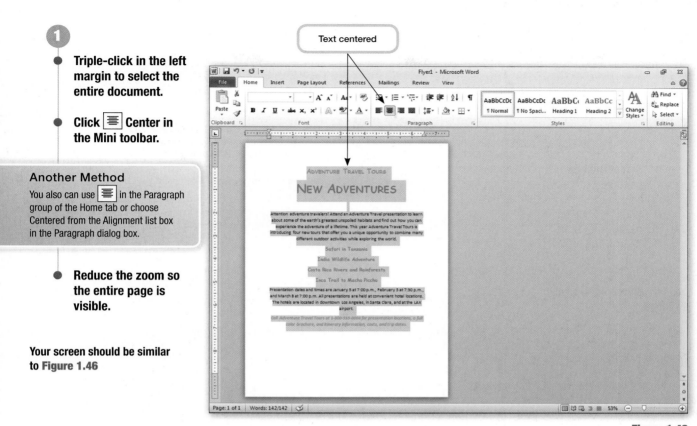

Figure 1.46

Each line of text is centered evenly between the left and right page margins.

CLEARING FORMATS

Additional Information

The alignment settings also can be specified before typing in new text. As you type, the text is aligned according to your selection until the alignment setting is changed to another setting.

As you look at the entire flyer, you decide the last line is overformatted. You think it would look better if it did not include italics and color. Since it has been a while since you applied these formats, using Undo also would remove many other changes that you want to keep. Instead, you will quickly clear all formatting from the selection and then apply only those you want.

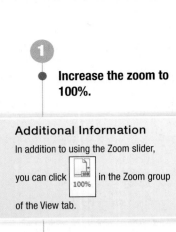

1

● **Increase the zoom to 100%.**

Additional Information

In addition to using the Zoom slider, you can click [100%] in the Zoom group of the View tab.

● **Select the last sentence.**

● **Click**  **Clear Formatting in the Font group.**

Your screen should be similar to Figure 1.47

Another Method

Instead of clearing all formats, you could simply reselect the command button to remove the formats that you did not want or select another format to replace it.

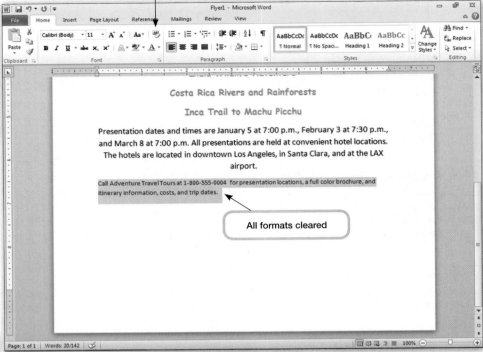

Clears all formatting from selection

Costa Rica Rivers and Rainforests

Inca Trail to Machu Picchu

Presentation dates and times are January 5 at 7:00 p.m., February 3 at 7:30 p.m., and March 8 at 7:00 p.m. All presentations are held at convenient hotel locations. The hotels are located in downtown Los Angeles, in Santa Clara, and at the LAX airport.

Call Adventure Travel Tours at 1-800-555-0004 for presentation locations, a full color brochure, and itinerary information, costs, and trip dates.

All formats cleared

Figure 1.47

All formatting associated with the selection, including text alignment and font size, has been removed and the text appears in the default document font and size.

2

● **Format the last sentence to bold, centered, and a font size of 14.**

● **Click** 🖫 **Save in the Quick Access Toolbar to save the file using the same file name.**

The formatting of the last sentence looks much better now.

Working with Graphics

Finally, you want to add a graphic to the flyer to add interest.

Concept 6 Graphics

A **graphic** is a nontext element or object such as a drawing or picture that can be added to a document. An **object** is an item that can be sized, moved, and manipulated.

A graphic can be a simple **drawing object** consisting of shapes such as lines and boxes. A drawing object is part of your Word document. A **picture** is an illustration such as a graphic illustration or a scanned photograph. Pictures are graphics that were created using another program and are inserted in your Word document as **embedded objects**. An embedded object becomes part of the Word document and can be opened and edited from within the Word document using the **source program**, the program in which it was created. Any changes made to the embedded object are not made to the original picture file because they are independent. Several examples of drawing objects and pictures are shown below.

Drawing object

Graphic illustration

Photograph

Add graphics to your documents to help the reader understand concepts, to add interest, and to make your document stand out from others.

Pictures can be obtained from a variety of sources. Many simple drawings called **clip art** are available in the Clip Organizer, a Microsoft Office tool that arranges and catalogs clip art and other media files stored on the computer's hard disk. Additionally, you can access Microsoft's Clip Art and Media Web site for even more graphics.

Digital images created using a digital camera are one of the most common types of graphic files. You also can create picture files using a scanner to convert any printed document, including photographs, to an electronic format. Most images that are scanned and inserted into documents are stored as Windows bitmap files (.bmp). All types of pictures, including clip art, photographs, and other types of images, can be found on the Internet. These files are commonly stored as .jpg or .pcx files. Keep in mind that any images you locate on the Internet may be copyrighted and should only be used with permission. You also can purchase CDs containing graphics for your use.

Additional Information

You also can scan a picture and insert it directly into a Word document without saving it as a file first.

INSERTING A PICTURE FROM FILES

You want to add a picture to the flyer below the two title lines. You will move to the location in the document where you want to insert a photograph of a lion you recently received from a client. The photograph has been saved as a picture image.

1

- Move to the blank line below the second title line.

- Open the Insert tab.

- From the Illustrations group, click 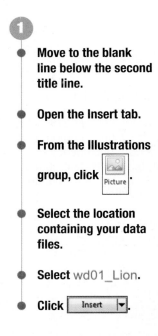.

- Select the location containing your data files.

- Select wd01_Lion.

- Click **Insert** ▾.

Your screen should be similar to Figure 1.48

Figure 1.48

The picture is inserted in the document at the location of the cursor. It is centered because the paragraph in which it was placed is centered. Notice the picture is surrounded by a **selection rectangle** and four circles and four squares, called **sizing handles**, indicating it is a selected object and can now be deleted, sized, moved, or modified. A Picture Tools tab automatically appears and can be used to modify the selected picture object.

Additional Information

You will learn more about the Picture Tools tab features in later labs.

INSERTING A PICTURE FROM CLIP ART

Although you like the picture of the lions that you might see on one of the tours, you want to check the Clip Art Gallery to see if you can locate a better animal picture.

1

- Click to the right side of the graphic to deselect it.

- Open the Insert tab.

- From the Illustrations group, click ⬚.

Your screen should be similar to Figure 1.49

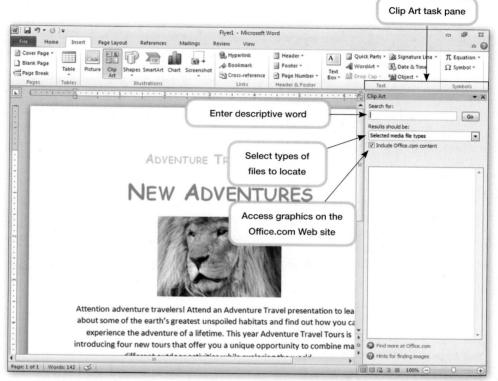

Figure 1.49

The Clip Art task pane appears in which you can enter a word or phrase that is representative of the type of picture you want to locate. You also can specify the locations to search and the type of media files, such as clip art, movies, photographs, or sound, to display in the results. You want to find clip art and photographs of animals.

2

- If necessary, select any existing text in the Search For text box.

- Type **animals**

- If necessary, select the Include Office. com content check box.

Having Trouble?

Click the box next to an option to select or deselect (clear the checkmark).

- **Open the Results Should Be drop-down list, select Illustrations and Photographs, and deselect all other options.**

- Click **Go**.

Your screen should be similar to Figure 1.50

Having Trouble?

Your Clip Art task pane may display different pictures than shown in Figure 1.50.

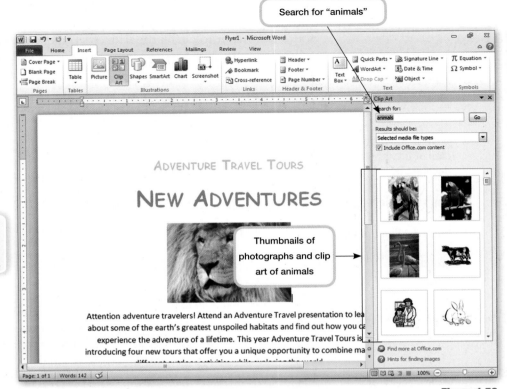

Search for "animals"

Thumbnails of photographs and clip art of animals

Figure 1.50

The program searches the Microsoft Clip Organizer on your computer and, if you have an Internet connection established, Microsoft's Office Online site for clip art and graphics that match your search term. The Results area displays **thumbnails**, miniature representations of pictures, of all located graphics. The pictures stored in the Microsoft Clip Organizer appear first in the results list, followed by the Office Online clip art.

Pointing to a thumbnail displays a ScreenTip containing the keywords associated with the picture and information about the picture properties. It also displays a drop-down list bar that accesses the item's context menu.

- Scroll the list to view additional images.

- Point to any thumbnail to see a ScreenTip.

Your screen should be similar to Figure 1.51

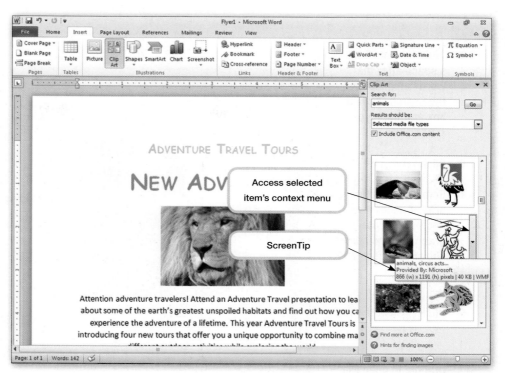

Figure 1.51

Each graphic has several keywords associated with it. All the displayed graphics include the keyword "animals." Because so many pictures were located, you decide to narrow your search to display pictures with keywords of "animals" and "parrots" only. Additionally, because it is sometimes difficult to see the graphic, you can preview it in a larger size.

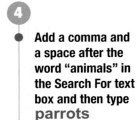

4

- Add a comma and a space after the word "animals" in the Search For text box and then type **parrots**

- Click **Go**.

- Scroll the results area, if necessary, and point to the graphic of the parrot shown in Figure 1.52.

- Click next to the graphic to open the context menu.

- Choose Preview/Properties.

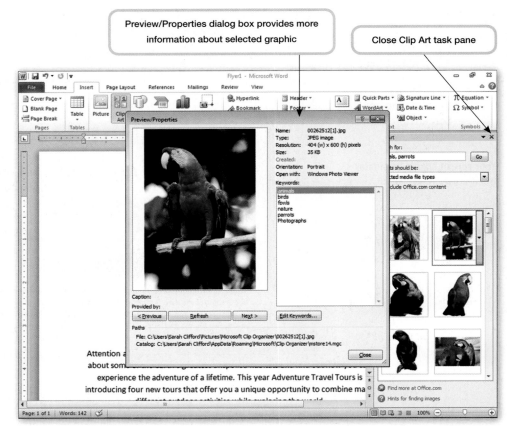

Preview/Properties dialog box provides more information about selected graphic

Close Clip Art task pane

Figure 1.52

Your screen should be similar to **Figure 1.52**

Because the search term is more specific, fewer results are displayed. The Preview/Properties dialog box displays the selected graphic larger so it is easier to see. It also displays more information about the properties associated with the graphic, including the keywords used to identify the graphic. You think this looks like a good choice and will insert it into the document.

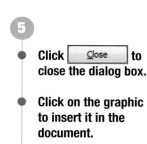

⑤

- Click [Close] to close the dialog box.

- Click on the graphic to insert it in the document.

Another Method

You also could choose Insert from the thumbnail's context menu.

- Click [×] in the Clip Art task pane title bar to close it.

- Scroll the document, if necessary, to view the pictures in their entirety.

Your screen should be similar to Figure 1.53

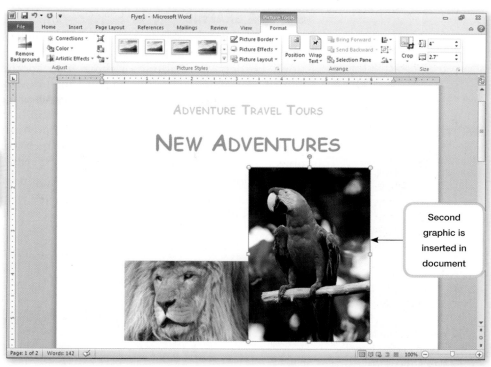

Figure 1.53

The clip art graphic is inserted next to the lion picture. You will reduce the size of the clip art graphic shortly.

DELETING A GRAPHIC

There are now two graphics in the flyer. You decide to use the parrot graphic and need to remove the picture of the lion. To do this, you select the graphic and delete it.

①

- Click on the lion graphic to select it.

- Press [Delete].

Your screen should be similar to Figure 1.54

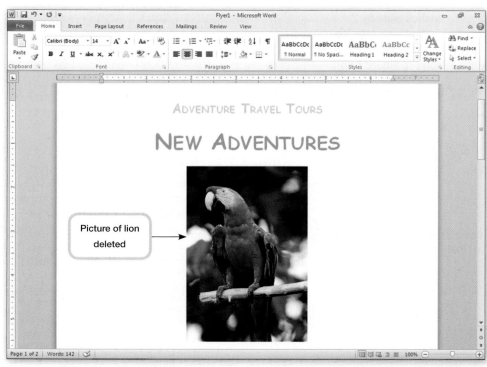

Figure 1.54

The lion graphic is removed and the parrot graphic is centered on the page.

Working with Graphics   **WD1.53**

SIZING A GRAPHIC

Usually, when a graphic is inserted, its size will need to be adjusted. A graphic object can be manipulated in many ways. You can change its size; add captions, borders, or shading; or move it to another location. A graphic object can be moved anywhere on the page, including in the margins or on top of or below other objects, including text. The only places you cannot place a graphic object are into a footnote, endnote, or caption.

In this case, you want to decrease the picture's size. To size a graphic, you select it and drag the sizing handles to increase or decrease the size of the object. The mouse pointer changes to when pointing to a handle. The direction of the arrow indicates the direction in which you can drag to size the graphic. You want to increase the image to approximately 1 inch wide by 1.5 inches high.

Additional Information

A selected graphic object can be moved by dragging it to the new location.

Another Method

You also can size a picture to an exact measurement using commands in the Size group of the Picture Tools tab.

1

- **Click on the graphic to select it.**

- **Point to the lower-right corner handle.**

Additional Information

Dragging a corner handle maintains the original proportions of the graphic.

- **With the pointer as a , drag inward to decrease the size to approximately 1.25 inches wide by 2 inches high (use the ruler as a guide and refer to Figure 1.55).**

- **Click anywhere in the document to deselect the graphic.**

- **Reduce the zoom to display the entire page.**

Your screen should be similar to Figure 1.55

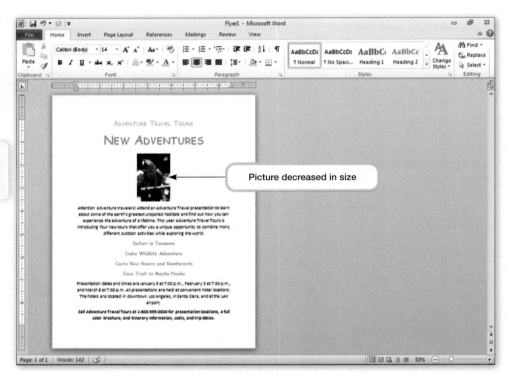

Figure 1.55

ADDING A WATERMARK

The final change you want to make to the flyer for now is to add a watermark in the page background. **Watermarks** are text or pictures that appear behind document text. They often add interest or identify the document status, such as marking a document as a Draft. You can insert a predesigned watermark from a gallery of watermark text, or you can insert a watermark with custom text. The watermark feature affects an entire page and is found in the Page Layout tab.

You have decided to add a watermark to the background of the flyer identifying the document as a draft.

1

- Open the Page Layout tab.

- Click 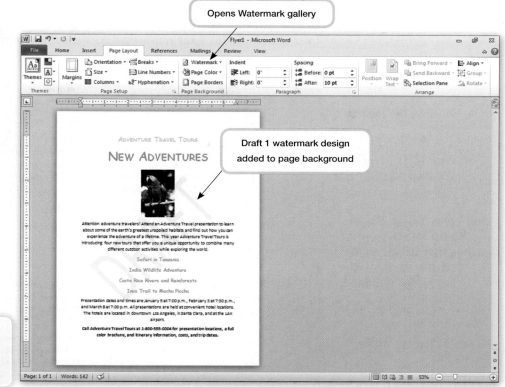 Watermark ▾ from the Page Background group.

- Scroll the Watermark gallery and choose the Draft 1 design from the Disclaimers section.

- Click 💾 Save.

Your screen should be similar to **Figure 1.56**

Opens Watermark gallery

Draft 1 watermark design added to page background

Figure 1.56

The DRAFT watermark appears diagonally across the background of the page. The entire page is displayed as it will appear when printed. The flyer looks good and does not appear to need any further modifications immediately.

MODIFYING DOCUMENT PROPERTIES

Before printing the document for your manager, you will add a sentence to the flyer that includes your name and edit the document properties.

1

● **Increase the zoom to 100%.**

● **Press** Ctrl **+** End **and then press** Spacebar**.**

● **Type Your Name will gladly help with all of your questions. as the last sentence of the flyer.**

Your screen should be similar to Figure 1.57

Having Trouble?

If your document now extends beyond a single page, reduce the size of the graphic slightly. If resizing the graphic does not work, check for and delete any extra blank lines at the end of the document.

Additional Information

Review document properties in the "Specifying Document Properties" section on page IO.51 of the Introduction to Microsoft Office 2010.

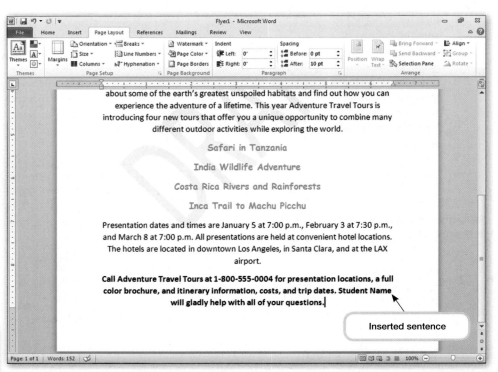

Figure 1.57

Next, you will look at the document properties that are automatically included with the Flyer1 file. You also will add documentation to identify you as the author, and specify a document title and keywords to describe the document.

2

- Open the File tab and then click the **Show All Properties** link below the list of properties.

- Enter **New Tours Flyer** in the Title text box.

- Enter **Flyer** in the Tags text box.

- Enter **First Draft** as the Status.

- Enter **Advertising** as the category.

- Enter **Four new tours** as the Subject.

- Type **your name** in the Author text box.

Your screen should be similar to Figure 1.58

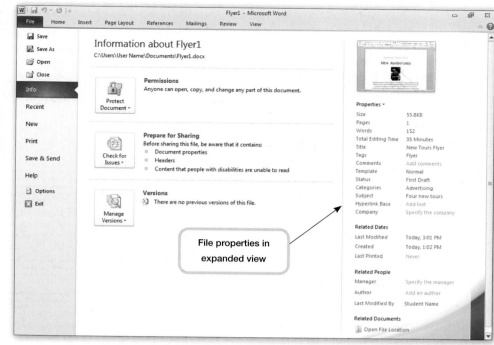

File properties in expanded view

Figure 1.58

You are now finished entering document properties.

Printing a Document

Although you still plan to make several formatting changes to the document, you want to give a copy of the flyer to your manager to get feedback regarding its content and layout.

PREVIEWING THE DOCUMENT

Additional Information

Review previewing and printing in the "Printing a Document" section on page IO.56 of the Introduction to Microsoft Office 2010.

As part of the printing process, Word automatically displays a preview image of your document, showing you exactly how the document will appear when printed.

1

● If necessary, make sure your printer is on and ready to print.

● Choose Print on the File tab.

Your screen should be similar to **Figure 1.59**

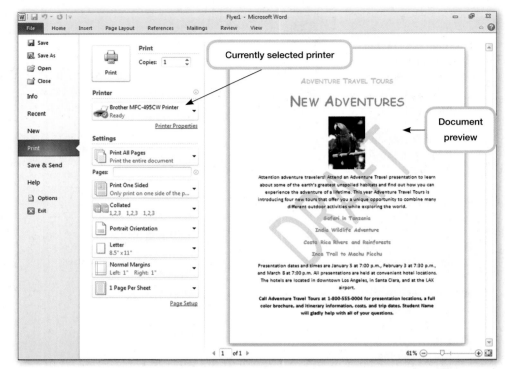

Figure 1.59

A preview image of your document displays on the right side of your screen. This image of the flyer should be similar to the document shown in the Case Study at the beginning of the lab.

NOTE **Please consult your instructor for printing procedures that may differ from the following directions.**

You will now print the document using the default print settings.

2

● If you need to change the selected printer to another printer, open the Printer drop-down list box and select the appropriate printer (your instructor will tell you which printer to select).

● Click .

Your printer should be printing the document.

You are finished working on the flyer for now and want to save the properties you entered.

3

● Click 🖫 Save.

● Open the File tab and click ☐ Close .

The flyer is saved and the document window is empty.

Working with Templates

You would like to give a copy of the completed flyer to your manager Maria Salverez for feedback along with a cover memo. You will begin by creating a memo using one of the document templates included in Word.

Concept 7 Templates

A **template** is a document file that stores predefined settings and other elements such as graphics for use as a pattern when creating documents. The **Normal document template** automatically opens whenever you start Word 2010. Settings such as a Calibri 11-point font, left-alignment, and 1-inch margin are included in the Normal template. So far, you have only used the Normal document template as a basis for your documents.

In addition to this template, Word also includes many other templates that are designed specifically to help you create professional-looking business documents such as letters, faxes, reports, brochures, press releases, manuals, newsletters, resumes, invoices, purchase orders, and Web pages. Many of the templates are already installed and are available within Word. Many more are available at the Microsoft Office Online Templates Web page. The settings included in these specialized templates are available only to documents based on that template. You also can design and save your own document templates.

All template files have a .dotx file extension and are stored in the Templates folder. The Normal document template, for example, is named Normal.dotx. When you create a new document from a template file, a copy of the file is opened and the file type changes to a Word document (.docx). This prevents accidentally overwriting the template file when the file is saved.

You will now start a new document using one of Word's memo templates. This template file is available at the Microsoft Office.com Web site. You will then change different elements in the template to give it your own personal style.

1

 Open the File tab and choose New to display the available templates.

Your screen should be similar to Figure 1.60

Having Trouble?

If you do not have access to Office Online, no templates will display in the Office.com Templates area. If this is your situation, open the file wd01_Elegant Memo from your data files location.

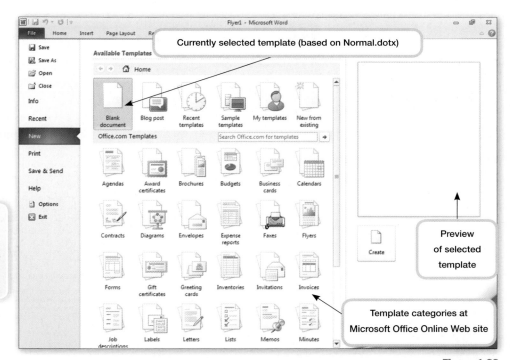

Figure 1.60

The templates are categorized by topic. You will look in the Memo category to find a template to use for your memo to the manager.

2

- **From the Office.com Templates section, choose Memos.**

- **Select the Memo (Elegant design) template.**

Your screen should be similar to Figure 1.61

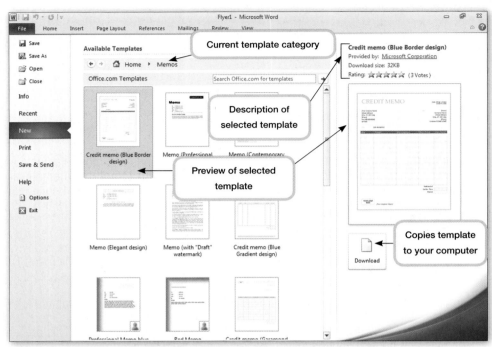

Figure 1.61

Word displays a gallery of memo templates in different designs and the Preview area displays how the selected template looks. You will use the Memo (Elegant design) template to create your memo. Because this template is stored on the Office Online Web site, you need to download it to your computer. It will then open automatically for you in Word.

3

- **Click** .

- **Change the zoom to page width.**

Your screen should be similar to Figure 1.62

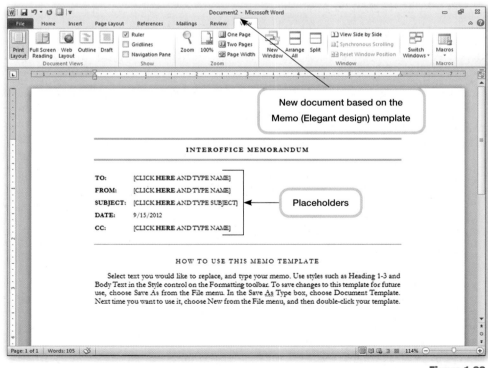

Figure 1.62

A copy of the memo template is opened as a new Word document and is displayed in Print Layout view. The file name "Document2" appears in the Title bar, indicating that the current document hasn't yet been saved. The template itself, however, is saved to your computer so that you can open and use it again without having to download it again.

REPLACING PLACEHOLDERS

Templates often include **placeholders**, which are graphic elements, commonly enclosed in brackets, that are designed to contain specific types of information. You edit placeholders to contain the information you want by clicking on the placeholder to select it and then typing the new information.

You will modify the memo header, which includes placeholders for identifying the recipient, sender, subject, date and a "CC:" (carbon or courtesy copy) recipient.

1

- **Click the To: placeholder.**

- **Type Maria Salverez**

- **Click the From: placeholder and type your name**

- **Click the Subject: placeholder and type Adventure Travel Tours Flyer**

Your screen should be similar to Figure 1.63

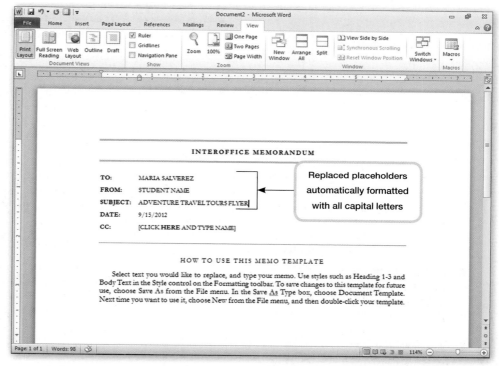

Figure 1.63

As a result of formatting selections stored in the memo template, the text you typed was automatically formatted in all capital letters. After you type text into a placeholder, the placeholder usually changes into normal text. This is true of all the placeholders in the Memo (Elegant design) template.

The computer's system date was automatically inserted in the Date: placeholder. As a result, the current date might not be displaying in the memo. You have decided not to use the CC: placeholder, so you will delete it and its identifying text.

2

- If the date displaying in the Date: placeholder isn't the current date, double-click on the placeholder and type in the correct date.

- Click the CC: placeholder and then press [Delete].

- Select the text "CC:" and then press [Delete].

Your screen should be similar to Figure 1.64

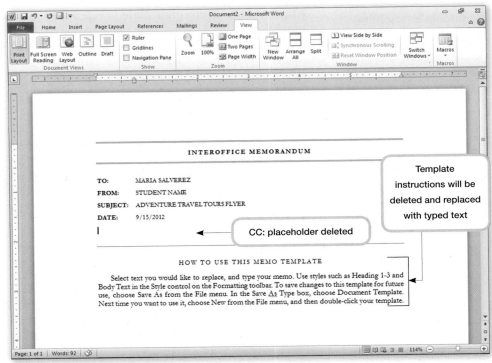

Figure 1.64

ENTERING BODY TEXT

Next you will type a few sentences into the body of the memo. The template currently includes a title and some instructions on how to use the memo template. You will select this text and replace it with your own.

1

- Select the title and following paragraph located below the last horizontal line.

- Type Maria, please review the draft of the flyer I created announcing our new travel adventures. I look forward to receiving your feedback. Thanks!

Your screen should be similar to Figure 1.65

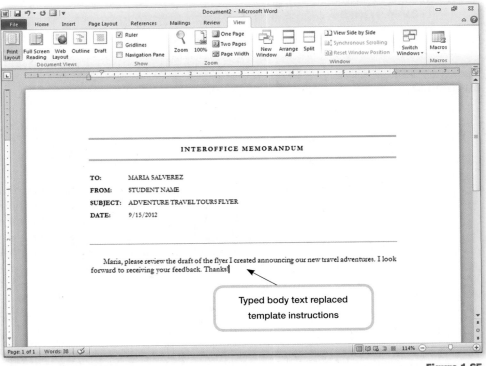

Figure 1.65

The text you typed replaced the selected text. The memo is now complete. You want to save it and exit the Word application.

Exiting Word

Additional Information

Review exiting in the "Exiting an Office 2010 application" section on page IO.65 of the Introduction to Microsoft Office 2010.

The ☒ Exit command in the File menu or the ☒ Exit button in the application window title bar are used to quit the Word program. If you attempt to exit the application without first saving your document, Word displays a warning asking if you want to save your work. If you do not save your work and you exit the application, any changes you made since last saving it are lost.

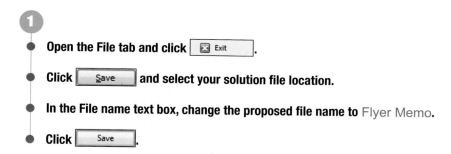

1

- Open the File tab and click ☒ Exit .

- Click Save and select your solution file location.

- In the File name text box, change the proposed file name to Flyer Memo.

- Click Save .

The memo is saved as Flyer Memo.docx to the location you selected, the document is closed and the application exited. The original template file is unchanged on your computer so you can use it again to create another memo.

OCUS ON CAREERS

EXPLORE YOUR CAREER OPTIONS

Food Service Manager

Have you noticed flyers around your campus advertising job positions? Many of these jobs are in the food service industry. Food service managers are traditionally responsible for overseeing the kitchen and dining room. However, these positions increasingly involve administrative tasks, including recruiting new employees. As a food service manager, your position would likely include creating newspaper notices and flyers to attract new staff. These flyers should be eye-catching and error-free. The typical salary range of a food service manager is $34,000 to $41,700. Demand for skilled food service managers is expected to increase through 2012.

Grammar Checker (WD1.12)

The grammar checker advises you of incorrect grammar as you create and edit a document, and proposes possible corrections.

Spelling Checker (WD1.14)

The spelling checker advises you of misspelled words as you create and edit a document, and proposes possible corrections.

AutoCorrect (WD1.16)

The AutoCorrect feature makes some basic assumptions about the text you are typing and, based on these assumptions, automatically corrects the entry.

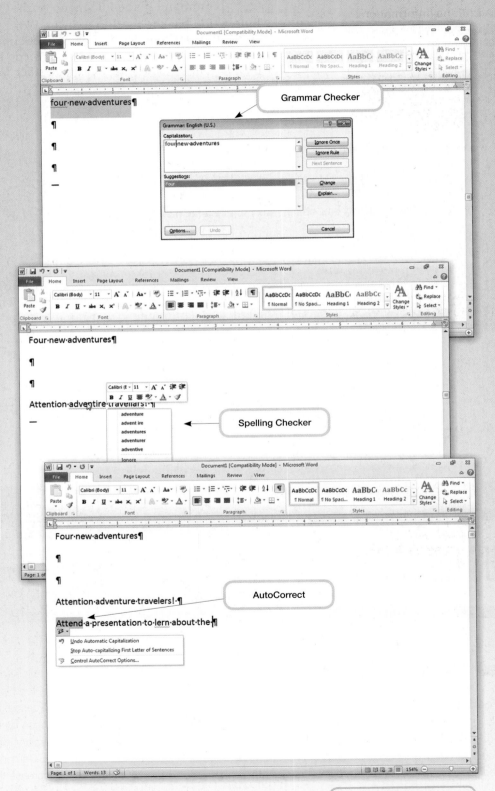

Word Wrap (WD1.19)

The word wrap feature automatically decides where to end a line and wraps text to the next line based on the margin settings.

Alignment (WD1.44)

Alignment is the positioning of text on a line between the margins or indents. There are four types of paragraph alignment: left, centered, right, and justified.

Graphics (WD1.47)

A graphic is a nontext element or object such as a drawing or picture that can be added to a document.

Templates (WD1.59)

A template is a document file that stores predefined settings and other elements such as graphics for use as a pattern when creating documents.

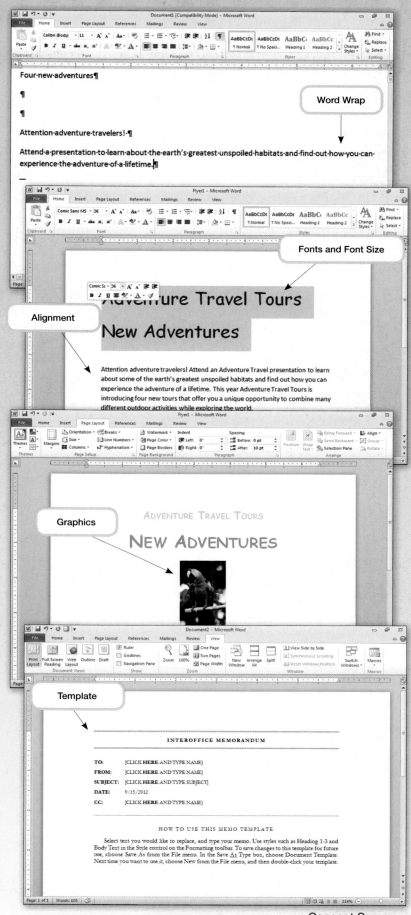

KEY TERMS

alignment WD1.44
AutoCorrect WD1.16
character formatting WD1.34
clip art WD1.47
cursor WD1.5
custom dictionary WD1.14
default WD1.7
document window WD1.5
drawing object WD1.47
edit WD1.4
embedded object WD1.47
end-of-file marker WD1.8
format WD1.4
grammar checker WD1.12
graphic WD1.47
Insert mode WD1.23
insertion point WD1.5
main dictionary WD1.14

Normal document template WD1.59
object WD1.47
paragraph formatting WD1.34
picture WD1.47
placeholder WD1.61
ruler WD1.5
sans serif font WD1.35
selection rectangle WD1.48
serif font WD1.35
sizing handles WD1.48
soft space WD1.44
source program WD1.47
spelling checker WD1.14
template WD1.59
thumbnail WD1.50
TrueType WD1.42
watermark WD1.54
word wrap WD1.19

COMMAND SUMMARY

Command	Shortcut	Action
Quick Access Toolbar		
💾 Save	Ctrl + S	Saves document using same file name
↩ Undo	Ctrl + Z	Restores last editing change
↪ Redo	Ctrl + Y	Restores last Undo or repeats last command or action
File tab		
New	Ctrl + N	Opens new blank document or specialized template
📂 Open	Ctrl + O	Opens existing document file
💾 Save	Ctrl + S	Saves document using same file name
💾 Save As	F12	Saves document using a new file name, type, and/or location
Print	Ctrl + P	Prints document
🛠 Options		Change options for working with Word
📁 Close	Ctrl + F4	Closes document
✖ Exit	Alt + F4	Exit Word application
Home tab		
Clipboard group		
📋 Copy	Ctrl + C	Copies selection to Clipboard
✂ Cut	Ctrl + X	Cuts selection to Clipboard
📋 Paste	Ctrl + V	Pastes items from Clipboard
Font group		
Calibri (Body) ▾ Font		Changes typeface
11 ▾ Font Size		Changes font size
🅰 Clear Formatting		Removes all formatting from selection
B Bold	Ctrl + B	Adds/removes bold effect
I Italic	Ctrl + I	Adds/removes italic effect

LAB REVIEW

COMMAND SUMMARY (CONTINUED)

Command	Shortcut	Action
Aa ▾ Change Case	Shift + F3	Changes case of selected text
A ▾ Font Color		Changes text to selected color
Paragraph group		
¶ Show/Hide	Ctrl + *	Displays or hides formatting marks
▤ Align Text Left	Ctrl + L	Aligns text to left margin
▤ Center	Ctrl + E	Centers text between left and right margins
▤ Align Text Right	Ctrl + R	Aligns text to right margin
▤ Justify	Ctrl + J	Aligns text equally between left and right margins
Insert Tab		
Illustrations group		
Picture		Inserts selected picture
Clip Art		Accesses Clip Organizer and inserts selected clip
Page Layout Tab		
Page Background group		
Watermark ▾		Inserts watermark behind page content
Review Tab		
Proofing group		
ABC Spelling & Grammar		Opens Spelling and Grammar dialog box
View Tab		
Document Views group		
Print Layout	▤	Shows how text and objects will appear on printed page
Full Screen Reading	📖	Displays document only, without application features

WWW.MHHE.COM/OLEARY

COMMAND SUMMARY (CONTINUED)

Command	Shortcut	Action
Web Layout		Shows document as it will appear when viewed in a Web browser
Outline		Shows structure of document
Draft		Shows text formatting and simple layout of page
Show group		
☑ Ruler		Displays/hides ruler
Zoom group		
Zoom		Opens Zoom dialog box
100%		Zooms document to 100% of normal size
One Page		Zooms document so an entire page fits in window
Page Width		Zooms document so width of page matches width of window

LAB EXERCISES

SCREEN IDENTIFICATION

1. In the following Word screen, letters identify important elements. Enter the correct term for each screen element in the space provided.

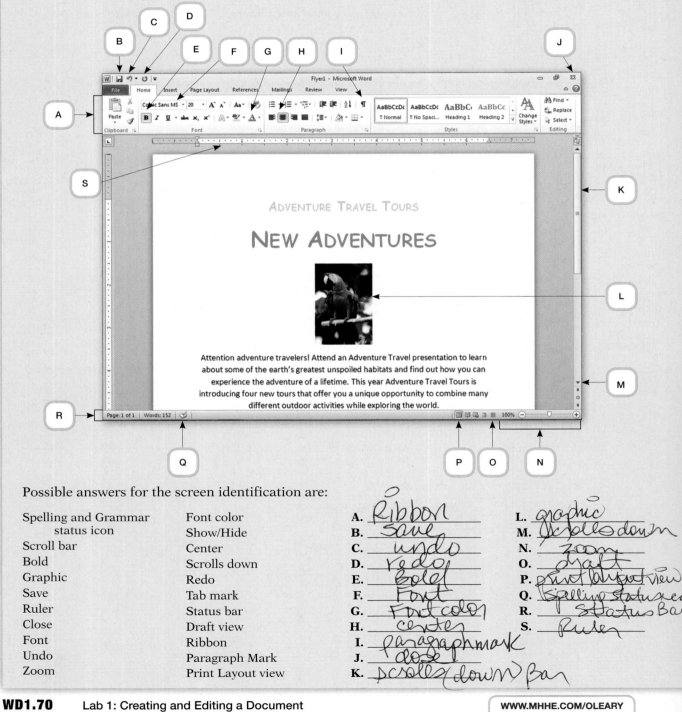

Possible answers for the screen identification are:

Spelling and Grammar
    status icon
Scroll bar
Bold
Graphic
Save
Ruler
Close
Font
Undo
Zoom

Font color
Show/Hide
Center
Scrolls down
Redo
Tab mark
Status bar
Draft view
Ribbon
Paragraph Mark
Print Layout view

A. Ribbon
B. Save
C. undo
D. redo
E. Bold
F. Font
G. Font color
H. center
I. paragraph mark
J. close
K. scrolls down bar
L. graphic
M. scrolls down
N. zoom
O. draft
P. print layout view
Q. spelling status icon
R. status Bar
S. Ruler

MATCHING

Match the item on the left with the correct description on the right.

1. word wrap   _5_   a. undoes last command
2. ▣   _10_   b. moves to the top of the document
3. 💾   _1_   c. feature that automatically begins a new line when text reaches the right margin
4. alignment   _7_   d. simplifies the creation of new documents
5. ↩ ▾   _2_   e. shows dialog box
6. sans serif   _9_   f. type style that can be applied to text
7. template   _8_   g. font size measurement
8. point   _4_   h. controls paragraph positioning between the margins
9. font   _3_   i. saves a document using the same file name
10. Ctrl + Home   _6_   j. font without a flair at the base of each letter

TRUE/FALSE

Circle the correct answer to the following questions.

1. The AutoCorrect feature automatically identifies and corrects certain types of errors.   **True**   **False**
2. The automatic word wrap feature checks for typing errors.   **True**   **False**
3. Font sizes are measured in inches.   **True**   **False**
4. A wavy red line indicates a potential spelling error.   **True**   **False**
5. The default document settings are stored in the Normal.docx file.   **True**   **False**
6. A selected picture is surrounded by a selection rectangle and eight moving handles.   **True**   **False**
7. The Delete key erases the character to the right of the cursor.   **True**   **False**
8. The Word document file name extension is .wrd.   **True**   **False**
9. Word inserts hidden marks into a document to control the display of text.   **True**   **False**
10. Hard spaces are used to justify text on a line.   **True**   **False**

LAB EXERCISES

FILL-IN

Complete the following statements by filling in the blanks with the correct terms.

1. To size a graphic evenly, click and drag the _____ in one corner of the graphic.

2. A small blue box appearing under a word or character indicates that the _____ feature was applied.

3. A _____ is a miniature representation of all located graphics in the Clip Art task pane.

4. The _____ feature displays each page of your document in a reduced size so you can see the page layout.

5. It is good practice to use only _____ types of fonts in a document.

6. The default document settings are stored in the _____ template file.

7. The _____ at the top of the window contains commands that are organized into related groups.

8. The _____ feature shows how your formatting choices will appear on selected text.

9. Use _____ when you want to keep your existing document with the original name and make a copy with a new name.

10. Word 2010 documents are identified by the _____ file extension.

MULTIPLE CHOICE

Circle the correct response to the questions below.

1. Words that are not contained in the main dictionary can be added to the _____ dictionary.
   a. custom
   b. additional
   c. supplemental
   d. user-defined

2. A(n) _____ is text or pictures that appear behind document text.
   a. graphic
   b. watermark
   c. embedded object
   d. thumbnail

3. A(n) _____ is a nontext element or object that can be added to a document.
   a. illustration
   b. picture
   c. drawing
   d. all of the above

4. Document development follows these steps.
   a. plan, edit, enter, format, preview, and print
   b. enter, edit, format, preview, and print
   c. plan, enter, edit, format, preview, and print
   d. design, enter, edit, format, preview, and print

5. This feature makes some basic assumptions about the text entered and automatically makes changes based on those assumptions.
   a. AutoChange
   b. AutoFormat
   c. AutoText
   d. AutoCorrect

6. When text is evenly aligned on both margins, it is _____.
   a. centered
   b. justified
   c. left-aligned
   d. right-aligned

7. A set of characters with a specific design is called a(n) _____.
   a. style
   b. font
   c. AutoFormat
   d. Design

8. Font sizes are measured in _____.
   a. inches
   b. points
   c. bits
   d. pieces

9. The _____ feature shows how various formatting choices would look on selected text.
   a. Actual Preview
   b. Real Preview
   c. Active Preview
   d. Live Preview

10. Words that may be spelled incorrectly in a document are indicated by a _____.
    a. green wavy line
    b. red wavy line
    c. blue wavy line
    d. purple dotted underline

LAB EXERCISES

Hands-On Exercises

STEP-BY-STEP

ASKING FOR INPUT MEMO ★

1. The Lifestyle Fitness Club is planning to perform maintenance work on its facilities in the near future. You have been asked to solicit suggestions from existing customers about what changes they would like to see made to the club. You decide to send all of the current club members a memo asking them for their input. Your completed memo will be similar to the one shown here.

   a. Open a blank Word 2010 document and create the following memo in Draft view. Press Tab after you type the colon (:) in the memo header. This will make the information following the colons line up evenly. Enter a blank line between paragraphs.

   To: Club Members
   From: Student Name
   Date: [Current date]

   The Lifestyle Fitness Club is seeking to improve some of its current facilities. Several of the improvements we will make next year fall under the category of routine maintenance. For example, the current swimming pool has begun to age requiring us to close the pool for a week to repair several areas of cracking and chipping. We will be performing maintenance work on the sauna and steam room. As we enter into this season of improvements, we'd also like your feedback on how we might serve you better. For example, one member recently asked whether it would be possible to have additional tables near the snack bar. All of your suggestions are welcome and will be considered in the upcoming months.

   Thank you in advance for your input.

   > To: Club Members
   >
   > From: Student Name
   >
   > Date: November 11, 2012
   >
   > The Lifestyle Fitness Club is seeking to improve some of its facilities. Several of the improvements we will make next year fall under the category of routine maintenance. For example, the swimming pool has begun to age requiring us to close the pool for a week to repair several areas of cracking and chipping. Simultaneously, we will be performing maintenance work on the sauna and steam room.
   >
   > As we enter into this season of improvements, we'd also like your feedback on how we might serve you better. For example, one member recently asked whether it would be possible to have additional tables and chairs near the snack bar. All of your suggestions for changes are welcome and will be considered in the upcoming months.
   >
   > Thank you in advance for your input.

   b. Correct any spelling and grammar errors that are identified.

   c. Turn on the display of formatting marks. Check the document and remove any extra blank spaces between words or at the end of lines.

   d. Save the document as Fitness Club Memo in your solution file location.

   e. Switch to Print Layout view.

   f. At the beginning of the fourth sentence of the paragraph, insert the word "Simultaneously" followed by a comma. Change the following "W" in "We" to lowercase. In the second to last sentence of the paragraph, insert the words "and chairs" after the word "tables". Delete the word "current" from the first and third sentences.

g. Start a new paragraph beginning with the fifth sentence.

h. Change the font size for the entire memo to 14 pt and the alignment of the body of the memo to justified.

i. Turn off the display of formatting marks.

j. Add an ASAP watermark.

k. Include your name in the document properties as author and the file name as the title.

l. Save the document again and print the document.

PROMOTING CELEBRATE BIKES SUNDAY ★ ★

2. You are the program coordinator for the city of Westbrook's Parks and Recreation Department. In next week's newspaper, you plan to run an article to promote bike riding in the community through the Celebrate Bikes Sunday event. Your completed article will be similar to the one shown here.

a. Enter the following information in a new Word 2010 document. Press Enter at the end of each paragraph.

Celebrate Bicycling!

May is traditionally National Bike Month, so take out your bicycle, tune it up and get a breath of fresh air! And plan to take part in Celebrate Bikes Sunday on 5/8 to learn about the benefits of bike riding.

As part of the activities on this day, the Westbrook Parks and Recreation Department is sponsoring a bike ride from the West Avenue YMCA to the Main Street Park beginning at 11 am.

Businesses and organizations participating in the event are all "related to biking in Westbrook and most of them are involved in the development of the trail system," says event director Mary Jo Miller.

At the end of the bike ride, the riders are encouraged to stay for the fun and informative activities in the park. Activities include a bike safety program, entertainment,

CELEBRATE BICYCLING!

May is National Bike Month, so take out your bicycle, tune it up and get a breath of fresh air! And plan to take part in Celebrate Bikes Sunday on *May 8* to learn about the benefits of riding and bicycle safety.

Businesses and organizations participating in the event are all "related to biking in Westbrook and most of them are involved in the development of the trail system," says event director Mary Jo Miller.

As part of the activities on this day, the Westbrook Parks and Recreation Department is sponsoring a bike ride from West Avenue YMCA to the Main Street Park. The ride begins promptly at *11 am*.

At the end of the bike ride, stay for the fun and informative activities in the park. Activities include a bike safety program, entertainment, and food booths. The Safe Route to School program will work with parents and children to find the safest route to either walk or bike to school.

Registration is free and available by calling *(603) 555-0113*, visiting the YMCA during regular business hours or beginning at 10 am on Sunday at the YMCA.

Student Name

Date

and food booths. The Safe Route to School program will work with parents and children to find the safest route to either walk or bike to school.

Registration is free and available by calling (603) 555-0113, visiting the YMCA during regular business hours or beginning at 10 am on Sunday at the YMCA.

b. Correct any spelling or grammar errors. Save the document as Bike Event.

c. Turn on the display of formatting marks. Check the document and remove any extra blank spaces between words or at the end of lines.

d. In Print Layout view, center the title. Change the title font to Castellar (or a font of your choice), 22 pt, and light blue font color. Apply bold to the title.

e. In the first paragraph, delete the word "traditionally" and change the number 5/8 to "May 8." Add the text "and bicycle safety" to the end of the second sentence in this paragraph.

f. End the sentence in paragraph 3 after the word "Park". Change the following sentence to "The ride begins promptly at 11 am."

g. Delete the phrase "the riders are encouraged to" from the first sentence of the fourth paragraph.

h. Move the paragraph beginning with "Businesses and organizations" to the second paragraph, with "As part of the activities" becoming the third paragraph.

i. Add italics, bold, and light blue font color to the date in the first paragraph, the time in the third paragraph, and the phone number in the last paragraph.

j. Justify the paragraphs.

k. Increase the font size of the paragraphs to 12 pt.

l. Insert a blank line below the title.

m. With the cursor on the blank line, insert a clip art graphic of your choice of a child riding a bike by searching on the keyword "bike" or use the graphic file wd01_Child on Bike. Center it and adjust the size of the graphic if necessary.

n. Add your name and the current date on separate lines several lines below the last line. Left-align both lines. Turn off the display of formatting marks.

o. Review the document and, if necessary, adjust the size of the graphic to fit the document on a single page.

p. Include your name in the file properties as author and the file name as the title.

q. Save the document again. Print the document.

ANNOUNCING MONTHLY MUSIC PERFORMANCES ★ ★

3. The Downtown Internet Cafe combines the relaxed atmosphere of a coffee house with the fun of using the Internet. The cafe will now be hosting monthly performances featuring local musicians. You want to create a flyer about the monthly music performances that you can give to customers and also post in the window of other local businesses. Your completed flyer will be similar to the one shown here.

You will also create the memo coversheet shown here using a Word template. You will then give the memo coversheet and flyer to Evan, the cafe owner for review.

a. Open a new Word document and enter the following text, pressing [Enter] where indicated.

Monthly music performances every fourth Sunday! [Enter]

Downtown Internet Cafe [Enter] (2 times)

Come enjoy an excellent dark Italian Roast coffee, premium loose teas, blended drinks and quality light fare of sandwiches, pitas and salads. [Enter]

Your favorite coffeehouse has recently added a superb sound system composed of quality speakers and amplifiers. Starting Sunday, January 24 at 3:00 p.m. we will be hosting performances by local musicians. Come by every fourth Sunday and be entertained! [Enter]

Cafe Hours: Sunday - Thursday 8:00 a.m. to 9:00 p.m. Friday and Saturday 8:00 a.m. to 12:00 a.m. [Enter]

2314 Telegraph Avenue [Enter]

b. Correct any spelling and grammar errors that are identified.

c. Save the document as Music Performances.

d. Turn on the display of formatting marks. Center the entire document.

e. Capitalize each word of the first line. Change the case of the text "Downtown Internet Café" to uppercase.

f. Using drag and drop, move the second paragraph, including the paragraph mark, to the left of "C" of "Come" in the previous paragraph.

Monthly Music Performances Every Fourth Sunday!

DOWNTOWN INTERNET CAFÉ

Your favorite coffeehouse has recently added a superb sound system composed of quality speakers and amplifiers. Starting Sunday, January 24 at 3 p.m. we will be hosting performances by local musicians. Come by every fourth Sunday and be entertained!

February 28, West Coast Bluegrass Experience

March 28, Vocal String Quartet

April 25, International Guitar Night

Come enjoy an excellent dark Italian Roast coffee, premium loose teas, blended drinks and quality light fare of sandwiches, pitas and salads.

2314 Telegraph Avenue

Café Hours: Sunday – Thursday 8:00 a.m. to 9:00 p.m. Friday and Saturday 8:00 a.m. to 12:00 a.m.

Student Name - Current Date

Memorandum

To:	Mike Van Noord
CC:	Raquel Van Noord
From:	Student Name
Date:	9/15/2012
Re:	Downtown Internet Café Flyer

Please review the attached flyer. I'd like to begin handing the flyer out right away, so the sooner I receive your feedback, the better. Thanks!

LAB EXERCISES

g. Using cut and paste, move the street address, including the following paragraph mark, to the "C" of "Café Hours".

h. Insert the following three lines of text between the first and second paragraphs:

February 28, West Coast Bluegrass Experience

March 28, Vocal String Quartet

April 25, International Guitar Night

i. Change the first line of the document to a font color of dark red, font type of Arial Black or a font of your choice, and size of 24 pt.

j. Change the text "Downtown Internet Café" to a font color of blue, font type of Arial Narrow or a font of your choice, and size of 28 pt.

k. Select all the remaining text in the document and increase the font size to 14 pt.

l. Change the three date lines below the first paragraph to a font color of purple and a font size of 16 pt. Change the last two lines (address and hours) to a font color of dark blue. Add bold to the selection.

m. Insert the graphic file wd01_Saxophone (from your data files) on the blank line below the title Downtown Internet Café at the top of the document. Size the graphic to be approximately 2 by 2 inches using the ruler as a guide.

n. Add your name and the current date, left-aligned, on one line, below the last line.

o. If a paragraph mark is displayed to the right of the date, delete it.

p. Turn off the display of formatting marks.

q. If necessary, reduce the size of the graphic so the entire flyer fits on one page.

r. Include your name in the file properties as author and the file name as the title. Save, print, and then close the flyer document.

s. Start a new document based on the Memo (Contemporary design) template.

t. Delete the "CC" line of the memo.

u. Edit the placeholders as follows:

To: **Evan**

From: **your name**

Re: **Downtown Internet Café Flyer**

v. Edit the date, if necessary, to reflect the current date.

w. Select the text below the horizontal border and then type **Please review the attached flyer. I'd like to begin handing the flyer out right away, so the sooner I receive your feedback, the better. Thanks!**

x. Save the completed memo as Café Memo. Print the memo.

PREPARING A LECTURE ON NOTE-TAKING SKILLS ★ ★ ★

4. You teach a college survival skills class and have recently read about the results of a survey conducted by the Pilot Pen Company of America about note-taking skills. The survey of 500 teenagers found that students typically begin taking classroom notes by sixth grade and that only half had been taught how to take classroom notes. It also found that those students trained in note-taking earned better grades. Note-taking becomes increasingly important in high school and is essential in college. Lecture notes are a key component for mastering material. In response to the survey, the pen manufacturer came up with 10 tips for better note-taking. You started a document of these tips that you plan to use to supplement your lecture on this topic. You will continue to revise and format the document. The revised document will be similar to the one shown here.

a. Open the Word document wd01_Note Taking Skills.

b. Correct any spelling and grammar errors that are identified. Save the document as Note Taking Skills.

c. Switch to Draft view. Change the font of the title line to a font of your choice, 26 pt. Center and add color of your choice to the title line.

d. Apply the small caps effect to the title line.

e. In the Be Ready tip, delete the word "lots". In the Write Legibly tip, delete the word "cursive" and add the words "an erasable" before the word "pen." Change the tip heading "Margins" to "Use Wide Margins."

f. Above the Write Legibly tip, insert the following tip:

Fill in Gaps

Check with a classmate or your teacher after class to get any missing names, dates, facts or other information you could not write down.

TIPS FOR TAKING BETTER CLASSROOM NOTES

Be Ready

Review your assigned reading and previous notes you've taken before class. Bring plenty of paper and a sharpened pencil, an erasable pen or a pen that won't skip or smudge. Write the class name, date and that day's topic at the top the page.

Write Legibly

Print if your handwriting is poor. Use a pencil or an erasable pen if you cross out material a lot so that your notes are easier to read. Take notes in one-liners rather than paragraph form. Skip a line between ideas to make it easier to find information when you're studying for a test.

Use Wide Margins

Leave a wide margin on one side of your paper so you'll have space to write your own thoughts and call attention to key material. Draw arrows or stars beside important information like dates, names and events. If you miss getting a date, name, number or other fact, make a mark in the margin so you'll remember to come back to it.

Fill in Gaps

Check with a classmate or your teacher after class to get any missing names, dates, facts or other information you could not write down.

Mark Questionable Material

Jot down a "?" in the margin beside something you disagree with or do not think you recorded correctly. When appropriate, ask your teacher, classmate, or refer to your textbook, for clarification.

Student Name

Current Date

g. Move the Fill in Gaps tip to after the Use Wide Margins tip.

h. Change the font of the tip heading lines to Broadway with a font size of 16 pt and a color of your choice.

i. Change the alignment of the paragraphs to justified. Use Undo Changes to return the alignment to left. Use Redo Changes to return the paragraphs to justified again.

LAB EXERCISES

j. Switch to Print Layout view. Insert a clip art graphic of your choice (search on "pencil") below the title, or insert the picture named wd01_Pencils from your data files location. Size it and center it by referring to the completed document.

k. Add your name and the current date, centered, on separate lines two lines below the last line. If needed, reduce the size of the graphic to fit the entire document on one page.

l. Include your name in the file properties as author and the document title as the title. Save the document. Print the document.

WRITING AN ARTICLE ON THE HISTORY OF ICE CREAM ★ ★ ★

5. Each month the town's free paper prints a fun article on the history of something people are familiar with but might not know anything about. You researched the topic online and found the information you needed about the history of ice cream from the International Dairy Foods Association's Web site at www.idfa.org/news--views/media-kits/ice-cream/the-history-of-ice-cream. You started writing the article a few days ago and just need to continue the article by adding a few more details. Then you need to edit and format the text and include a graphic to enhance the appearance of the article. Your completed article will be similar to the one shown here.

a. Open the file named wd01_History of Ice Cream.

b. Correct any spelling and grammar errors. (Hint: Click ⟲ in the status bar to move to each error.) Save the document as Ice Cream History.

c. Enter the following headings at the location shown in parentheses.

History of Ice Cream (above first paragraph)

The Evolution of Ice Cream (above second paragraph)

Ice Cream in America (above third paragraph)

d. Center the title "History of Ice Cream". Change the font to Lucida Sans with a point size of 24, and add the Small Caps effect. Add a color of your choice to the title.

e. Change the other two headings to bold with a type size of 14 pt. Use the same color as in the title for the heads.

HISTORY OF ICE CREAM

Ice cream probably began as snow and ice flavored with honey and nectar. Alexander the Great, King Solomon and Nero Claudius Caesar were known to have enjoyed this treat. Although the origin of ice cream has been traced back as far as the second century B.C., a specific date is not known and no one inventor has been indisputably credited with its discovery.

The Evolution of Ice Cream

It is thought that the recipe for ice cream evolved from a recipe that was brought back to Italy by Marco Polo when he returned from the Far East over a thousand years later. This recipe closely resembled our current day sherbet. Sometime in the 16th century, ice cream, similar to what we have today, appeared in both Italy and England. However, only royalty and wealthy enjoyed this treat until 1660 when ice cream was made available to the general public at *Café Procope*, the first café in Paris.

Ice Cream in America

It took a while before ice cream made its way to the New World. a letter written in 1744 by a guest of Maryland Governor William Bladen describes ice cream, and the first advertisement for ice cream appeared in the *New York Gazette* on May 12, 1777. President George Washington was particularly fond of ice cream and inventory records from his Mount Vernon estate included two pewter pots used to make ice cream. Both Presidents Thomas Jefferson and James Madison were also known to have served ice cream during important presidential events.

This dessert continued to be enjoyed mostly by the elite until insulated ice houses were invented in early 1800. Finally, in 1851 Jacob Fussell, a Baltimore milk dealer, began to manufacture and provide ice cream to the public. Technological innovations, such as steam power, mechanical refrigeration, the homogenizer, electric power and motors, and motorized delivery vehicles were used to manufacture ice cream soon making ice cream a major industry in America.

Student Name

Current Date

f. Move "The Evolution of Ice Cream" heading and paragraph to below the second "Ice Cream in America" paragraph.

g. Undo the move operation you performed in the last step.

h. Change the alignment of the first paragraph to justified.

i. Add a blank line below the main title of the article and insert the picture wd01_Ice Cream (from your data files) at this location.

j. Size the picture to be 1 inch wide (use the ruler as a guide). Center it below the title.

k. Add a Draft watermark.

l. Add your name and the current date below the last line of the article. View the whole page and, if necessary, reduce the size of the graphic so the entire article fits on one page.

m. Include your name in the file properties as author and the document title as the title. Save the document again. Print the document.

ON YOUR OWN

CREATING A FLYER ★

1. Adventure Travel Tours is offering a great deal on a Day of the Dead Bicycle Tour in Mexico. Research the Day of the Dead celebration using the Web as a resource. Then, using the features of Word you have learned so far, create a flyer that will advertise this tour. Be sure to use at least two colors of text, two sizes of text, and two kinds of paragraph alignment. Include a graphic from the Clip Organizer. Include your name at the bottom of the flyer. Include your name in the file properties as author and the file name as the title. Save the document as Mexico Adventure.

CREATING A FAX COVERSHEET ★ ★

2. You work at the community pool and have been asked by your boss (Anna Najarian) to fax some information over to Asher Hayes at the local high school describing the rules swimmers should follow when using the pool. Start a new document using the Fax (Equity theme) template. (If necessary, open the wd01_Equity Fax template from your data files location.) Edit the template to include the following recipient information: **Asher Hayes** (To:), **650-555-0198** (Fax:) **650-555-0197** (Phone:), **Pool Rules** (Re:). Include the following sender information: **Your Name** (From:), **1** (Pages:), **Today's Date** (Date:), and **Anna Najarian** (CC:). Select the "For Review" check box by clicking on it. (The box should appear shaded.)

Edit the Comments: placeholder to include the five most important rules to follow while swimming at the pool. Use the Web as a resource for obtaining pool safety information. Place each rule on separate lines. Insert a piece of clip art after the list of rules. Size the image if necessary so that the document remains one page in length. Include your name in the file properties as author and the file name as the title. Save the document as Pool Rules.

LAB EXERCISES

ASTRONOMY CLASS MEMO ★ ★ ★

3. The city of Gilbert, Arizona, has recently built a $100,000 observatory that includes a $20,000 tele-scope in a local park. The observatory is open evenings for small groups of five to six people to take turns looking through the 16-inch telescope's eyepiece. The use of the observatory is free.

    The city has decided to offer classes for the community to learn how to use the telescope and to teach about astronomy. As a trial run, the class will first be offered to city employees and their families. You want to notify all employees about the observatory and the class by including a memo with their paycheck. Using Step-by-Step Exercise 1 as a model, provide information about when and where the class will be held. Include information about how people sign up for the class. Include your name in the file properties as author and the file name as the title. Save the memo as Astronomy Basics.

VOLUNTEER OPPORTUNITIES ★ ★ ★

4. Many community groups, hospitals, libraries, and churches are looking for volunteers to assist in their programs. Volunteering has rewards for both the volunteer and the community. Using the Web as a resource, research volunteer opportunities in your community. Then write a one-page report that includes information about two volunteer groups for which you would like to volunteer. Include information about what the organization does for the community. Also include the skills you have to offer and the amount of time you can commit as volunteer. Include a title at the top of the document and your name and the current date below the title. Center the title lines. Use at least two colors of text, two sizes of text, and two kinds of paragraph alignment. Include a graphic from the Clip Organizer. Include your name in the file properties as author and the file name as the title. Save the document as Volunteer Opportunities.

WRITING A CAREER REPORT ★ ★ ★

5. Using the library or the Web, research information about your chosen career. Write a one-page report about your findings that includes information on three areas: Career Description; Edu-cational Requirements; Salary and Employment projections. Include a title at the top of the document and your name and the current date below the title. Center the title lines. Justify the paragraphs. Include your name in the file properties as author and the file name as the title. Save the document as Career Report.

Revising and Refining a Document Lab 2

Objectives

After completing this lab, you will know how to:

1 Use the Spelling and Grammar tool and the Thesaurus.

2 Work with multiple documents.

3 Control document paging.

4 Find and replace text.

5 Insert the current date.

6 Change indents, line spacing, and margins.

7 Create a tabbed table.

8 Add color highlighting and underlines.

9 Create numbered and bulleted lists.

10 Create and use Building Blocks.

11 Insert and modify a shape.

12 Add a page border.

13 Secure content and share documents.

14 Prepare and print envelopes.

CASE STUDY

Adventure Travel Tours

After creating the rough draft of the new tours flyer, you showed the printed copy to your manager at Adventure Travel Tours. Your manager then made several suggestions for improving the flyer's style and appearance. In addition, you created a letter to be sent to clients along with your flyer. The letter briefly describes Adventure Travel's four new tours and invites clients to attend an informational presentation. Your manager likes the idea, but also wants the letter to include information about the new Adventure Travel Tours Web site and a 10 percent discount for early booking.

In this lab, you will learn more about editing documents so you can reorganize and refine both your flyer and a rough draft of the letter to clients. You also will learn to use many more of the formatting features included in Office Word 2010 so you can add style and interest to your documents. Formatting features can greatly improve the appearance and design of any document you produce so that it communicates its message more clearly. The completed letter and revised flyer are shown here.

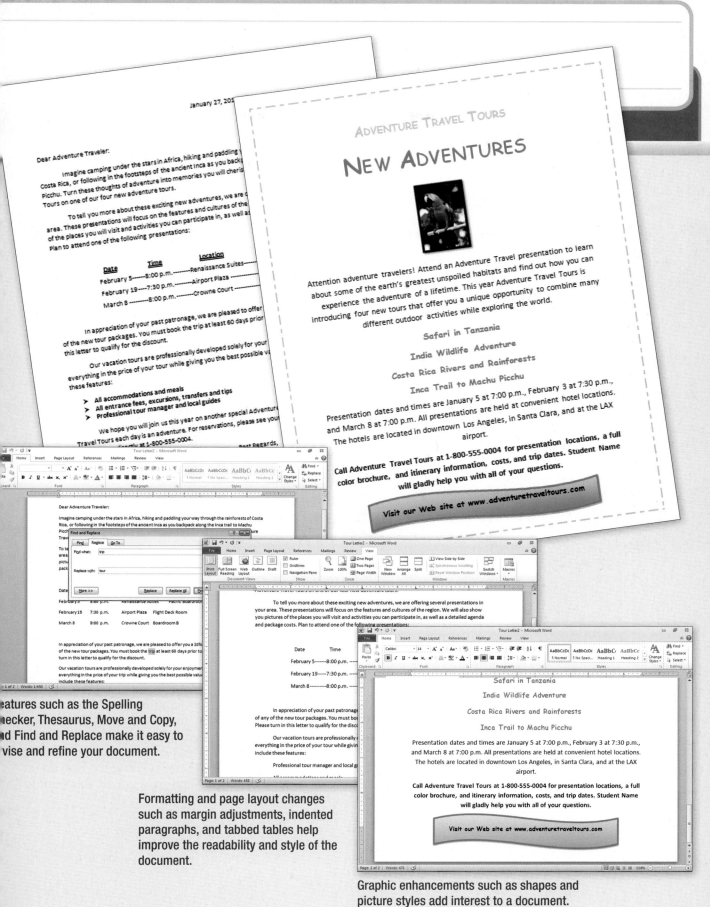

Features such as the Spelling Checker, Thesaurus, Move and Copy, and Find and Replace make it easy to revise and refine your document.

Formatting and page layout changes such as margin adjustments, indented paragraphs, and tabbed tables help improve the readability and style of the document.

Graphic enhancements such as shapes and picture styles add interest to a document.

The following concepts will be introduced in this lab:

1 Thesaurus Word's Thesaurus is a reference tool that provides synonyms, antonyms, and related words for a selected word or phrase.

2 Page Break A page break marks the point at which one page ends and another begins. Two types of page breaks can be used in a document: soft page breaks and hard page breaks.

3 Find and Replace To make editing easier, you can use the Find and Replace feature to find text in a document and replace it with other text as directed.

4 Field A field is a placeholder that instructs Word to insert information into a document.

5 Indents To help your reader find information quickly, you can indent paragraphs from the margins. Indenting paragraphs sets them off from the rest of the document.

6 Line and Paragraph Spacing Adjusting the line spacing, or the vertical space between lines of text and paragraphs, helps set off areas of text from others and when increased or decreased makes it easier to read and edit text.

7 Bulleted and Numbered Lists Whenever possible, add bullets or numbers before items in a list to organize information and make your writing clear and easy to read.

8 Sort Word can quickly arrange or sort text, numbers, or data in lists or tables in alphabetical, numeric, or date order based on the first character in each paragraph.

9 Quick Styles Applying a quick style, a predefined set of formatting options allows you to quickly apply a whole group of formats to a text selection or object in one simple step.

10 Section To format different parts of a document differently, you can divide a document into sections.

11 Page Margin The page margin is the blank space around the edge of the page. Standard single-sided documents have four margins: top, bottom, left, and right.

Revising a Document

After speaking with the manager about the letter's content, you planned the basic topics that need to be included in the letter: to advertise the new tours, invite clients to the presentations, describe the early-booking discount, and promote the new Web site. You quickly entered the text for the letter, saved it as Tour Letter, and printed out a hard copy. As you are reading the document again, you mark up the printout with the changes and corrections you want to make. The marked-up copy is shown here.

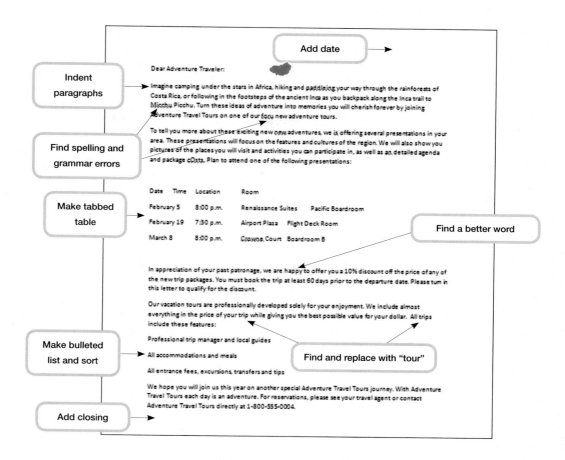

The following callouts point to the document image:

- Add date
- Indent paragraphs
- Find spelling and grammar errors
- Make tabbed table
- Find a better word
- Make bulleted list and sort
- Find and replace with "tour"
- Add closing

Document text shown:

Dear Adventure Traveler:

Imagine camping under the stars in Africa, hiking and paddleing your way through the rainforests of Costa Rica, or following in the footsteps of the ancient Inca as you backpack along the Inca trail to Micchu Picchu. Turn these ideas of adventure into memories you will cherish forever by joining Adventure Travel Tours on one of our foru new adventure tours.

To tell you more about these exciting new new adventures, we is offering several presentations in your area. These presentations will focus on the features and cultures of the region. We will also show you pictures of the places you will visit and activities you can participate in, as well as an detailed agenda and package cOsts. Plan to attend one of the following presentations:

Date	Time	Location	Room
February 5	8:00 p.m.	Renaissance Suites	Pacific Boardroom
February 19	7:30 p.m.	Airport Plaza	Flight Deck Room
March 8	8:00 p.m.	Crowne Court	Boardroom B

In appreciation of your past patronage, we are happy to offer you a 10% discount off the price of any of the new trip packages. You must book the trip at least 60 days prior to the departure date. Please turn in this letter to qualify for the discount.

Our vacation tours are professionally developed solely for your enjoyment. We include almost everything in the price of your trip while giving you the best possible value for your dollar. All trips include these features:

Professional trip manager and local guides

All accommodations and meals

All entrance fees, excursions, transfers and tips

We hope you will join us this year on another special Adventure Travel Tours journey. With Adventure Travel Tours each day is an adventure. For reservations, please see your travel agent or contact Adventure Travel Tours directly at 1-800-555-0004.

SPELL-CHECKING THE ENTIRE DOCUMENT

The first correction you want to make is to clean up the spelling and grammar errors that Word has identified.

1

- **Start Microsoft Word 2010 and open the file** wd02_Tour Letter

- **If necessary, change to Print Layout view at 100% zoom.**

Your screen should be similar to **Figure 2.1**

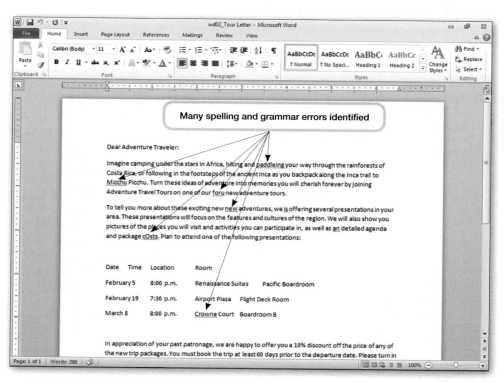

Many spelling and grammar errors identified

Figure 2.1

To correct the misspelled words and grammatical errors, you can use the context menu to correct each individual word or error, as you learned in Lab 1. However, in many cases, you may find it more efficient to wait until you are finished writing before you correct errors. Rather than continually breaking your train of thought to correct errors as you type, you can manually turn on the spelling and grammar checker to locate and correct all the errors in the document at once.

2

● **Open the Review tab.**

● **Click** [ABC Spelling & Grammar].

Another Method

The keyboard shortcut is F7.

● **If necessary, select the Check grammar option to turn on grammar checking.**

Additional Information

You also can click the Spelling and Grammar status icon 📖 to move to the next spelling or grammar error and open the spelling context menu.

Your screen should be similar to Figure 2.2

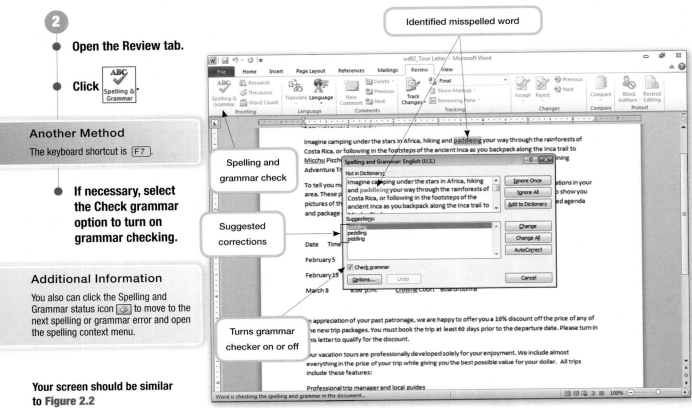

Figure 2.2

Additional Information

Because the contents of the list are determined only by spelling, any instances of terms that seem inappropriate in context are completely coincidental.

The Spelling and Grammar dialog box is displayed, and the spelling and grammar checker has immediately located the first word that may be misspelled, "paddleing." The sentence with the misspelled word in red is displayed in the Not in Dictionary text box, and the word is highlighted in the document.

The Suggestions list box displays the words the spelling checker has located in the dictionary that most closely match the misspelled word. The most likely match is highlighted. Sometimes the spelling checker does not display any suggested replacements. This occurs when it cannot locate any words in the dictionaries that are similar in spelling. If no suggestions are provided, the Not in Dictionary text box simply displays the word that is highlighted in the text.

Additional Information

The [Change All] option replaces the same word throughout the document with the word you select in the Suggestions box.

To change the spelling of the word to one of the suggested spellings, highlight the correct word in the list and then click [Change]. If there were no suggested replacements, and you did not want to use any of the option buttons, you could edit the word yourself by typing the correction in the Not in Dictionary box. In this case, the correct replacement, "paddling," is already highlighted.

3 ● Click [Change].

Having Trouble?

You may need to scroll the Not in Dictionary box to see the highlighted word.

Your screen should be similar to Figure 2.3

Additional Information

On your own computer system, you would want to add words to the custom dictionary that you use frequently and that are not included in the standard dictionary so they will be accepted when typed correctly and offered as a suggested replacement when not typed correctly.

Figure 2.3

The spelling checker replaces the misspelled word with the selected suggested replacement and moves on to locate the next error. This time the error is the name of the Inca ruins at Machu Picchu. "Micchu" is the incorrect spelling for this word; there is no correct suggestion, however, because the word is not found in the dictionary. You will correct the spelling of the word by editing it in the Not in Dictionary text box.

4
● **Edit the spelling of the word to Machu in the Not in Dictionary box.**

● Click [Change].

Your screen should be similar to Figure 2.4

Additional Information

You also can edit words directly in the document and then click [Resume] to continue using the Spelling and Grammar Checker.

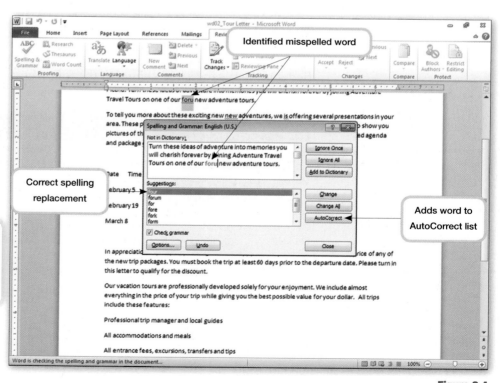

Figure 2.4

The next located error, "foru," is a typing error that you make frequently when typing the word four. The correct spelling is selected in the Suggestions list box. You want to change it to the suggested word and add it to the list of words that are automatically corrected.

5

Click AutoCorrect .

Your screen should be similar to Figure 2.5

Having Trouble?

If a dialog box appears telling you an AutoCorrect entry already exists for this word, simply click Yes to continue.

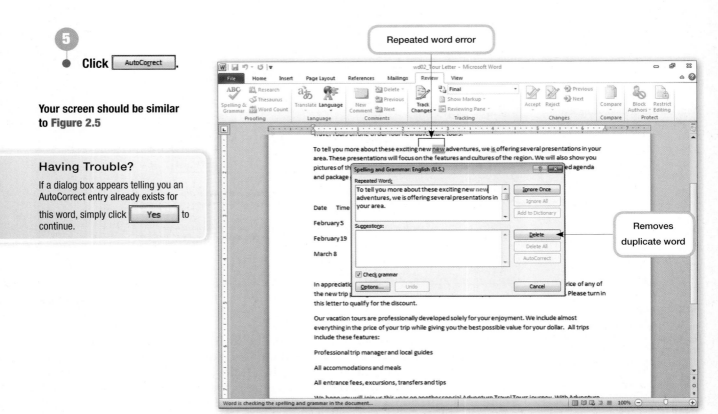

Repeated word error

Removes duplicate word

Figure 2.5

The word is corrected in the document. Because you also added it to the AutoCorrect list, in the future whenever you type this word incorrectly as "foru," it will automatically be changed to "four." The next five errors that will be identified and their causes are shown in the following table:

Identified Error	Cause	Action	Result
new	Repeated word	Delete	duplicate word "new" is deleted
we is	Subject-verb disagreement	Change	we are
cOsts	Inconsistent capitalization	Change	costs
an detailed	Grammatical error	Change	a
Crowne	Spelling error	Ignore Once	accepts the word as correct for this occurrence only

6

- Respond to the spelling and grammar checker by taking the actions in the table on the previous page for the five identified errors.

- Click [OK] in response to the message telling you that the spelling and grammar check is complete.

- Move to the top of the document.

Your screen should be similar to Figure 2.6

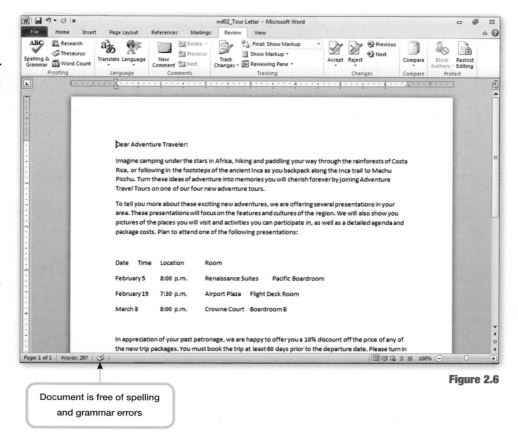

Document is free of spelling and grammar errors

Figure 2.6

USING THE THESAURUS

The next text change you want to make is to find a more descriptive word for "ideas" in the first paragraph and "happy" in the second paragraph. To help find a similar word, you will use the thesaurus tool.

Concept 1 Thesaurus

Word's **thesaurus** is a reference tool that provides synonyms, antonyms, and related words for a selected word or phrase. **Synonyms** are words with a similar meaning, such as "cheerful" and "happy." **Antonyms** are words with an opposite meaning, such as "cheerful" and "sad." Related words are words that are variations of the same word, such as "cheerful" and "cheer." The thesaurus can help to liven up your documents by adding interest and variety to your text.

First you need to identify the word you want looked up by moving the insertion point onto the word. Then you use the thesaurus to suggest alternative words. The quickest way to get synonyms is to use the context menu for the word you want to replace.

- **Right-click on the word "ideas" (first paragraph, second sentence) to display the context menu.**

- **Select Synonyms on the context menu.**

Having Trouble?

Simply point to the menu option to select it.

Additional Information

Whenever you right-click an item, both the context menu and the Mini toolbar are displayed.

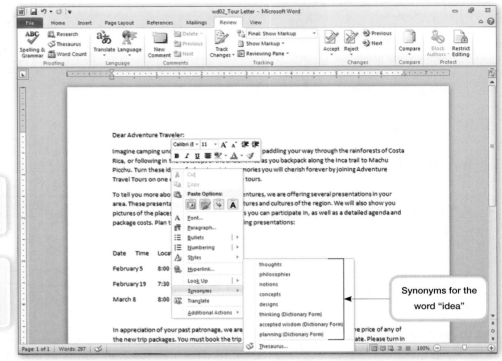

Figure 2.7

Your screen should be similar to Figure 2.7

The Synonyms submenu lists several words with similar meanings. You decide to replace "ideas" with "thoughts." Then you will look for a synonym for "happy." You will use the Research pane to locate synonyms this time.

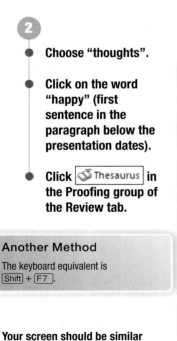

- **Choose "thoughts".**

- **Click on the word "happy" (first sentence in the paragraph below the presentation dates).**

- **Click [Thesaurus] in the Proofing group of the Review tab.**

Another Method

The keyboard equivalent is Shift + F7.

Your screen should be similar to Figure 2.8

Figure 2.8

The thesaurus opens in the Research task pane and the word the insertion point is on is displayed in the Search For text box. The list box displays words that have similar meanings for the word "happy" with a meaning of "content (adj.)." The best choice from this list is "pleased." To see whether any other words are closer in meaning, you will look up synonyms for the word "pleased."

3

● **Choose "pleased".**

Additional Information

You also can choose Look Up from the word's drop-down menu to look up synonyms for the word.

Your screen should be similar to Figure 2.9

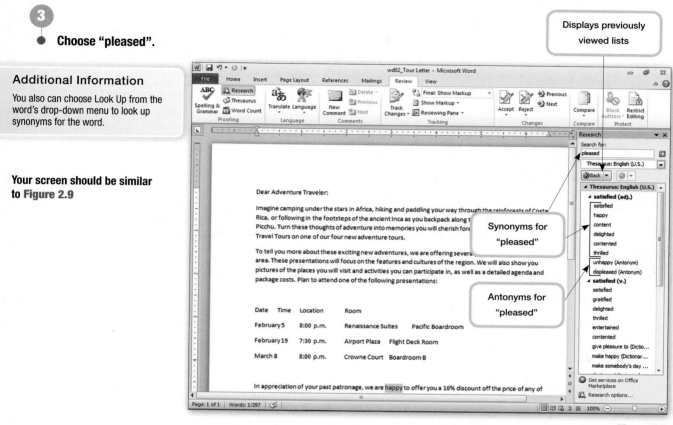

Figure 2.9

The word "pleased" is the new search term, and the list displays synonyms, as well as a few antonyms, for this word. You decide to use "pleased" and will return to the previous list and insert the word into the document.

- Click **Back** to display the list for the word "happy."

- Open the "pleased" synonym drop-down menu.

- Choose Insert.

- Close the Research task pane.

- Move to the top of the document and save the revised document as Tour Letter2 to your solution file location.

Your screen should be similar to Figure 2.10

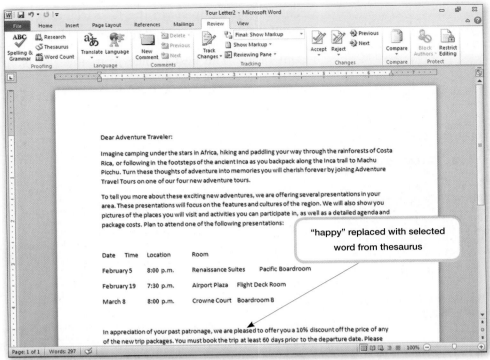

Figure 2.10

The word "happy" is replaced with the selected word from the thesaurus.

Working with Multiple Documents

You plan to include the flyer with the letter to be mailed to clients. To do this, you will open the flyer document and copy it into the letter document file. All Office 2010 applications allow you to open and use multiple files at the same time. This feature makes it easy to compare documents or to move or copy information between documents.

ARRANGING AND SCROLLING WINDOWS

First you will open the file containing the flyer document.

1

● **Open the** wd02_
Flyer2 **document.**

**Your screen should be similar
to Figure 2.11**

Document open and displayed in a
second application window

Point or click here to
see a list of open files

Figure 2.11

The flyer document is opened and displayed in a separate Word 2010 application window. You would like to see both documents in the window at the same time.

2

- Open the View tab.

- Click [☐ View Side by Side] in the Window group.

Having Trouble?

Do not be concerned if your windows are reversed.

- Reduce the Zoom to 75% using the zoom slider for the wd02_ Flyer2 window.

- Scroll to the bottom of the wd02_Flyer2 window.

- Move to the beginning of the first sentence of the last paragraph.

Your screen should be similar to **Figure 2.12**

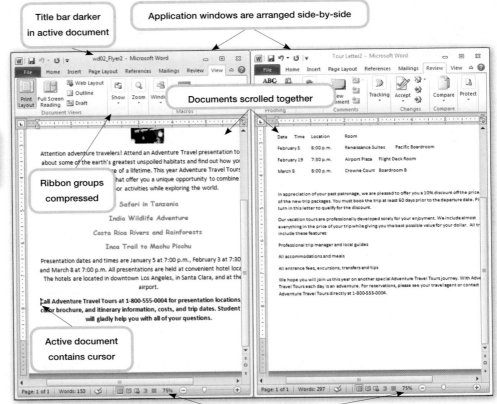

Figure 2.12

Additional Information

Using [Arrange All] arranges all open windows horizontally on the screen.

Now, the two Word application windows are arranged side by side on the screen. The flyer contains the cursor, which indicates that it is the **active window**, or the window in which you can work. Simply clicking on the other document makes it active. Because the windows are side by side and there is less horizontal space in each window, the Ribbon groups are compressed. To access commands in these groups, simply click on the group button and the group commands appear.

Did you notice when you scrolled the document that both documents scrolled together? This is because the windows are **synchronized**, meaning both windows will act the same. When synchronized, the documents in both windows will scroll together so you can compare text easily. If you are not comparing text, this feature can be turned off so that they scroll independently.

Click [Window] **to display the Window group commands.**

Click [Synchronous Scrolling] **to turn off this feature.**

Move to the top of the Wd02_Flyer2 **document.**

Your screen should be similar to Figure 2.13

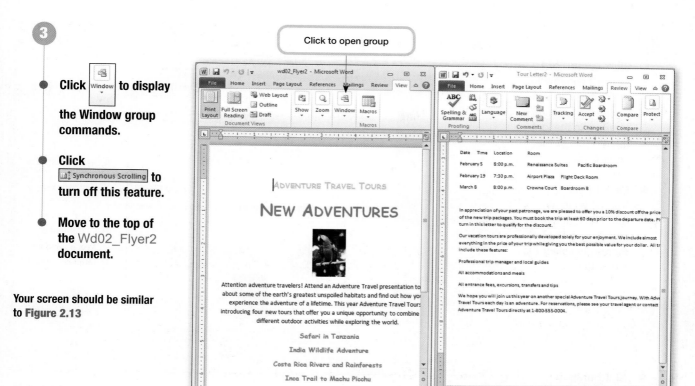

Figure 2.13

The flyer document scrolled while the letter document remained stationary.

COPYING BETWEEN DOCUMENTS

You plan to include the flyer with the letter to be mailed to clients. Since the document windows are displaying side by side, you can simply copy the entire flyer to the bottom of the letter document using drag and drop. To copy between documents using drag and drop, hold down the right mouse button while dragging. When you release the button, a context menu appears where you specify the action you want to perform. If you drag using the left mouse button, the selection is moved by default.

- **Click in the** Tour Letter2 **window to make it active and press** Ctrl + End **to move to the last (blank) line of the document.**

- **Click in the** Wd02_Flyer2 **window to make it active and drag in the left margin to select the entire flyer.**

- **Right-drag the selection to the last blank line at the end of the letter.**

- **Release the mouse button and choose Copy Here from the context menu.**

- **Click** ☐ **Maximize in the** Tour Letter2 **title bar to maximize the application window.**

- **Scroll the window to see the bottom of page one and the top of page two.**

Your screen should be similar to Figure 2.14

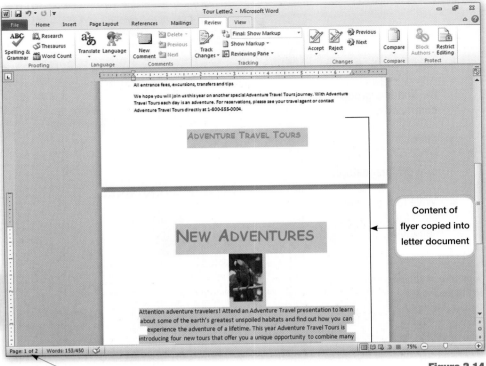

All entrance fees, excursions, transfers and tips

We hope you will join us this year on another special Adventure Travel Tours journey. With Adventure Travel Tours each day is an adventure. For reservations, please see your travel agent or contact Adventure Travel Tours directly at 1-800-555-0004.

ADVENTURE TRAVEL TOURS

Content of flyer copied into letter document

NEW ADVENTURES

Attention adventure travelers! Attend an Adventure Travel presentation to learn about some of the earth's greatest unspoiled habitats and find out how you can experience the adventure of a lifetime. This year Adventure Travel Tours is introducing four new tours that offer you a unique opportunity to combine many

Page: 1 of 2 | Words: 153/450

Document consists of 2 pages

Figure 2.14

The letter now consists of two pages. Notice the status bar shows the insertion point location is on page 1 of 2 pages.

Since you no longer need to use the Wd02_Flyer2 document, you will now close it.

2

- Click on the Windows taskbar.

- Right-click on Wd02_Flyer2 and choose Close from the shortcut menu.

Having Trouble?

If your taskbar displays separate buttons for each open document, simply right-click the Wd02_Flyer2 button and choose Close from the shortcut menu.

- If prompted to save your document, choose Don't Save .

- Scroll to the bottom of the Tour Letter2 document and replace Student Name with your name in the last sentence.

- Move the insertion point to the top of the document and then save the document.

The Tour Letter2 document is now the only open document.

CONTROLLING DOCUMENT PAGING

As text and graphics are added to a document, Word automatically starts a new page when text extends beyond the bottom margin setting. The beginning of a new page is identified by a page break.

Concept **2** Page Break

A **page break** marks the point at which one page ends and another begins. Two types of page breaks can be used in a document: soft page breaks and hard page breaks. As you fill a page with text or graphics, Word inserts a **soft page break** automatically when the bottom margin is reached and starts a new page. As you add or remove text from a page, Word automatically readjusts the placement of the soft page break.

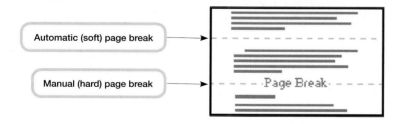

Many times, however, you may want to force a page break to occur at a specific location. To do this you can manually insert a **hard page break**. This action instructs Word to begin a new page regardless of the amount of text on the previous page. When a hard page break is used, its location is never moved regardless of the changes that are made to the amount of text on the preceding page. All soft page breaks that precede or follow a hard page break continue to adjust automatically. Sometimes you may find that you have to remove the hard page break and reenter it at another location as you edit the document.

In Print Layout view, the page break is identified by a space between pages. However you cannot tell if it is a hard or soft page break. You will switch to Draft view to see the soft page break that was entered in the document. Also notice that images are not shown in Draft view.

1

- **Click in the document to deselect the text.**

- **Switch to Draft view at 100% zoom.**

- **If necessary, scroll the document to see the soft page break line.**

Your screen should be similar to Figure 2.15

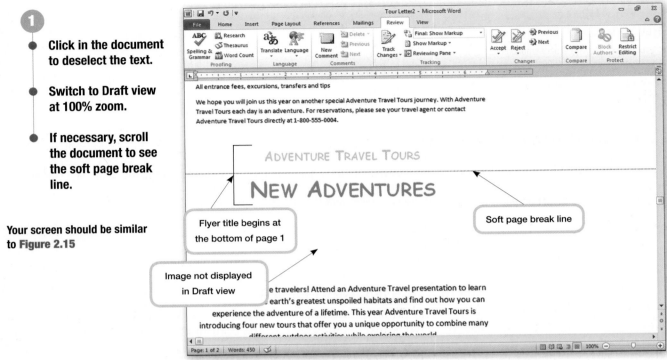

Figure 2.15

To show where one page ends and another begins, Word displays a dotted line across the page to mark the soft page break.

INSERTING A HARD PAGE BREAK

Many times, the location of the soft page break is not appropriate. In this case, the location of the soft page break displays the flyer title on the bottom of page 1 and the remaining portion of the flyer on page 2. Because you want the entire flyer to print on a page by itself, you will manually insert a hard page break above the flyer title.

1

- Move to the beginning of the first line of the flyer text, Adventure Travel Tours.

- Display formatting marks in the document.

Having Trouble?

Click ¶ in the Paragraph group of the Home tab or press Ctrl + * to display and hide formatting marks.

- Press Ctrl + Enter to insert a hard page break line.

Another Method

The Ribbon equivalent is Insert/📄 Page Break or Page Layout/📄 Breaks ▾/Page.

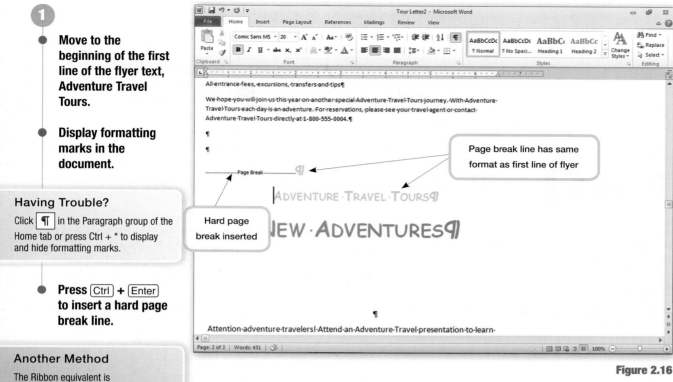

Figure 2.16

Your screen should be similar to Figure 2.16

Additional Information

To remove a hard page break, simply select the hard page break line and press Delete.

A dotted line and the words "Page Break" appear above the flyer title, indicating that a hard page break was entered at that position. Also notice the page break line has the same format as the first line in the flyer. You will clear the formats from the page break line so that it has the same format as the text on this page and does not interfere with changes you may want to make later.

2

- If necessary, open the Home tab.

- Select the page break line and click 🧹 Clear Formatting in the Font group.

- Turn off the display of formatting marks and save the document again.

Finding and Replacing Text

As you continue proofing the letter, you notice that the word "trip" is used too frequently. You think that the letter would read better if the word "tour" was used in place of "trip" in some instances. To do this, you will use the Find and Replace feature.

Concept 3 Find and Replace

To make editing easier, you can use the **Find and Replace** feature to find text in a document and replace it with other text as directed. For example, suppose you created a lengthy document describing the type of clothing and equipment needed to set up a world-class home gym, and then you decided to change "sneakers" to "athletic shoes." Instead of deleting every occurrence of "sneakers" and typing "athletic shoes," you can use the Find and Replace feature to perform the task automatically.

You also can find and replace occurrences of special formatting, such as replacing bold text with italicized text, as well as find and replace formatting marks. Additionally, special characters and symbols, such as an arrow or copyright symbol, can be easily located or replaced. This feature is fast and accurate; however, use care when replacing so that you do not replace unintended matches.

FINDING TEXT

First, you will use the Find command to locate all occurrences of the word "trip" in the document.

1

- **Switch to Print Layout view at 100% zoom.**

- **Move the insertion point to the top of the document.**

Another Method

Reminder: Use [Ctrl] + [Home] to quickly move to the top of the document.

- **Click** 🔍 Find **in the Editing group.**

Another Method

The keyboard shortcut is [Ctrl] + F.

Your screen should be similar to Figure 2.17

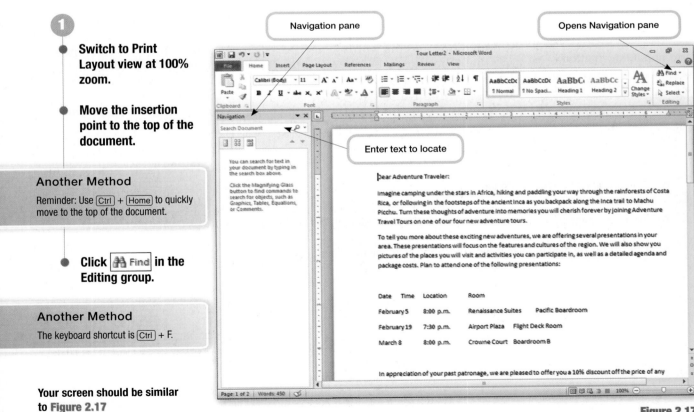

Figure 2.17

The **Navigation Pane**, located to the left of your document, provides a convenient way to quickly locate and move to specified text. The Search text box at the top of the Navigation pane is used to specify the text you want to locate. As you type each letter of your search text in the Search box, the Navigation pane displays and narrows down the matches.

2

● **Type trip in the search text box.**

Your screen should be similar to Figure 2.18

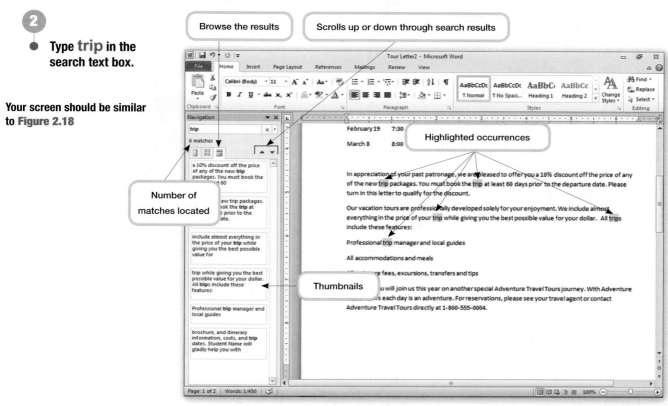

Browse the results

Scrolls up or down through search results

Number of matches located

Highlighted occurrences

Thumbnails

Figure 2.18

Additional Information

The highlight color in your document is determined by the currently selected color in [abʲ] Text Highlight.

Word searches for all occurrences of the text to find beginning at the insertion point and locates the word "trip" six times in the document. Search results display as thumbnails in the Navigation Pane. You also can see the first five search results highlighted in your document. The last use of the word trip is on the last line of the flyer. By clicking a thumbnail in the Navigation Pane, you can move to that location in your document. You can also scroll through your search results using the [▲] Previous Search Result and [▼] Next Search Result buttons located to the right of the tabs in the Navigation Pane.

Unless you specify otherwise, the [▤] Browse the results in your document tab is selected in the Navigation Pane. As a result, thumbnails show text matches next to surrounding text. Alternatively, the [▦] Browse the pages in your document tab displays thumbnails of each page containing the search text, and the [▤] Browse by headings in your document tab displays thumbnails of the headings in your document containing the search text. These latter options are especially useful when working with longer documents because they give you an overview of where search text has been found.

You will now use the Navigation Pane to browse through the search results.

3

- **Click the third thumbnail down to move the highlight to the third occurrence of the search text in your document.**

- **Click ▼ Next Search Result to move to the next occurrence of the search text.**

- **Click ⊞ Browse the pages in your document to display each page in your document that contains the search text.**

- **Click the thumbnail for page 2.**

Your screen should be similar to Figure 2.19

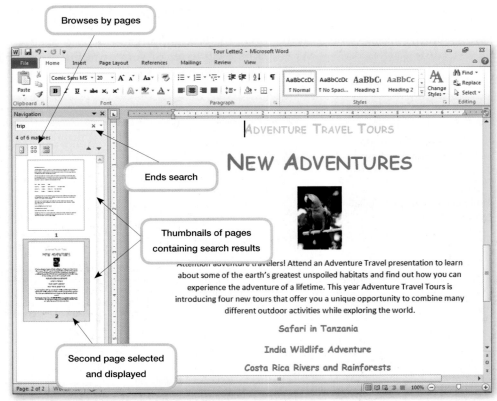

Browses by pages

Ends search

Thumbnails of pages containing search results

Second page selected and displayed

Figure 2.19

The top of the second page is displayed and the search text is highlighted at the bottom of the current page. To see the highlighted text, you would have to scroll down in your document. If you look closely, you can even see the search terms highlighted in the thumbnails.

There may be cases when you need to refine how using Find locates the search text. Clicking 🔍 Find Options at the right end of the search box opens a drop-down menu of commands that accesses options for customizing your search as well as options for searching for other types of document elements including graphics and tables.

Your screen should be similar to Figure 2.20

4

- Click ⊠ to end the current search.

- Click 🔍 Find Options in the Navigation Pane.

Additional Information

The 🔍 button only displays before you type text into the search text box.

- Choose Options.

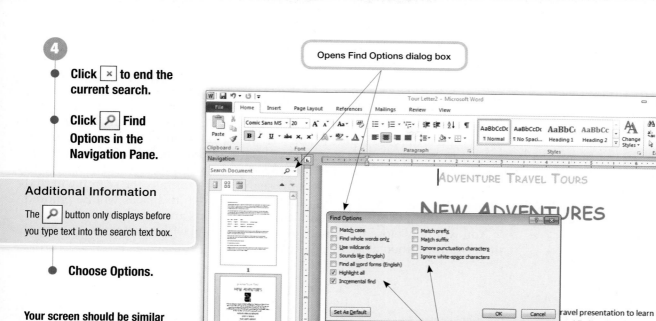

Opens Find Options dialog box

Use these options to refine your search

Figure 2.20

The Find Options dialog box displays 11 search options that can be combined in many ways to help you find and replace text in documents. They are described in the table below.

Option	Effect on Text
Match case	Finds only those words in which the capitalization matches the text you typed.
Find whole words only	Finds matches that are whole words and not part of a larger word. For example, finds "cat" only and not "catastrophe" too.
Use wildcards	Fine-tunes a search; for example, c?t finds "cat" and "cot" (one-character matches), while c*t finds "cat" and "court" (searches for one or more characters).
Sounds like (English)	Finds words that sound like the word you type; very helpful if you do not know the correct spelling of the word you want to find.
Find all word forms (English)	Finds and replaces all forms of a word; for example, "buy" will replace "purchase," and "bought" will replace "purchased."
Highlight all	Highlights all matches in your document.
Incremental find	Finds and refines your search incrementally with each letter you type in the search box.
Match prefix	Finds all words that begin with the same letters you type.
Match suffix	Finds all words that end with the same letters you type.
Ignore punctuation characters	Finds words that are similar to your search text, but that might contain punctuation, such as a hyphen (-) or apostrophe ('), in it.
Ignore white-space characters	Finds text that is similar to your search text but that may also contain spaces.

The two options that are checked are on by default. To use any of the other Find options, you would need to turn on the option by clicking on the box. Likewise, clicking on an option that is already on (checked) will turn it off.

In this case, when you entered the text to find, you can type everything lowercase because the Match Case option is not selected and the search will not be **case sensitive**. This means that lowercase letters will match both upper- and lowercase letters in the text. To further control the search, you can specify to match prefixes and suffixes. Because these options aren't currently selected, a letter or group of letters added at the beginning or end of a word to form another word will not affect the search. For example, the search will find "quick" and "quickly". Finally, punctuation and white spaces will be ignored when searching the document unless these options are selected.

You will now close the Find Options dialog box without making any selections. You will then close the Navigation Pane.

5

● Click [Cancel] in the Find Options dialog box.

● Click [X] Close in the title bar of the Navigation Pane.

REPLACING TEXT

Additional Information

The [▼] Task Pane Options button in the title bar of the Navigation Pane lets you move, size, and close the pane.

You decide to replace several occurrences of the word "trip" in the letter with "tour" where appropriate. You will use the Find and Replace feature to do this.

1

● **Move to the top of the document.**

● **Click** 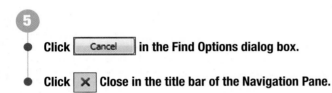 **Replace in the Editing group.**

Your screen should be similar to Figure 2.21

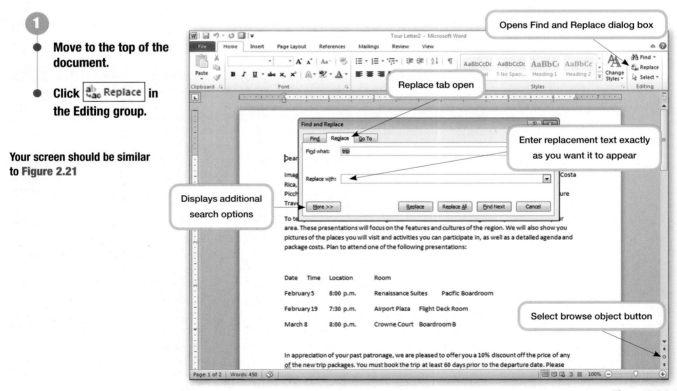

Figure 2.21

The Replace tab is open in the Find and Replace dialog box. Note that the search text "trip" that you had entered in the Search box is already displayed in the Find what text box. You want to find and replace selected occurrences of the word "trip" with "tour." Again, you can refine how the search is conducted by accessing the Find options from the Find and Replace dialog box.

2

• Open the Find tab.

• Click ⌊ More >> ⌋ to display additional search options.

Your screen should be similar to Figure 2.22

Figure 2.22

The Find tab provides another method for finding text in a document. The same Find options that you looked at in the Navigation Pane are available here. Note that the Search option is set to All. This means that by default Word will search the entire document, including headers and footers. You also can choose to search Up to the top of the document or Down to the end of the document from your current location in the document. These options search in the direction specified but exclude the headers, footers, footnotes, and comments from the area to search. Because you want to search the entire document, All is the appropriate setting.

Next, you will open the Replace tab again and enter the replacement text in the Replace with text box. This text must be entered exactly as you want it to appear in your document. It will also display the Search options that you opened in the Find tab. You will hide the search options and enter the replacement text. Then you will replace the first located match with the replacement text.

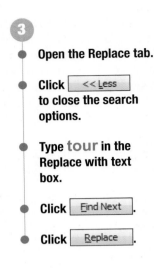

3

- Open the Replace tab.

- Click **<< Less** to close the search options.

- Type **tour** in the Replace with text box.

- Click **Find Next**.

- Click **Replace**.

Your screen should be similar to **Figure 2.23**

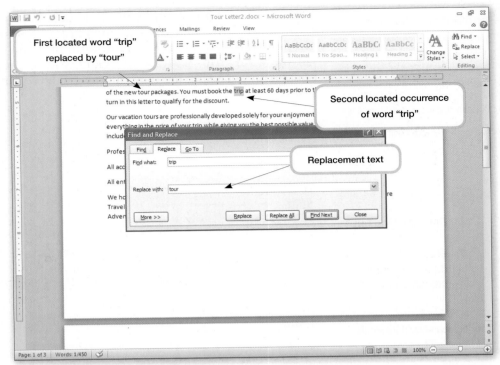

First located word "trip" replaced by "tour"

Second located occurrence of word "trip"

Replacement text

Figure 2.23

Word replaced the first located word with "tour" and has highlighted the second occurrence of the word "trip." You do not want to replace this occurrence of the word. You will continue the search without replacing the highlighted text.

4

- Click [Find Next] to skip this occurrence and locate the next occurrence.

- Replace the next located occurrence.

- Continue to review the document, replacing all other occurrences of the word "trip" with "tour," except in the final paragraph of the flyer.

- Click [Find Next].

- Click [OK] to close the information dialog box.

- Click [X] to close the Find and Replace dialog box.

- Save the document.

Your screen should be similar to Figure 2.24

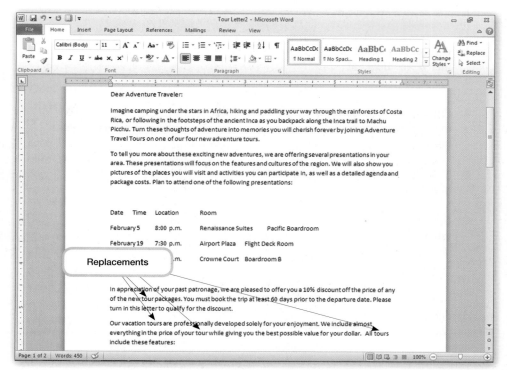

Dear Adventure Traveler:

Imagine camping under the stars in Africa, hiking and paddling your way through the rainforests of Costa Rica, or following in the footsteps of the ancient Inca as you backpack along the Inca trail to Machu Picchu. Turn these thoughts of adventure into memories you will cherish forever by joining Adventure Travel Tours on one of our four new adventure tours.

To tell you more about these exciting new adventures, we are offering several presentations in your area. These presentations will focus on the features and cultures of the region. We will also show you pictures of the places you will visit and activities you can participate in, as well as a detailed agenda and package costs. Plan to attend one of the following presentations:

Date	Time	Location	Room
February 5	8:00 p.m.	Renaissance Suites	Pacific Boardroom
February 19	7:30 p.m.	Airport Plaza	Flight Deck Room
	.m.	Crowne Court	Boardroom B

Replacements

In appreciation of your past patronage, we are pleased to offer you a 10% discount off the price of any of the new tour packages. You must book the trip at least 60 days prior to the departure date. Please turn in this letter to qualify for the discount.

Our vacation tours are professionally developed solely for your enjoyment. We include almost everything in the price of your tour while giving you the best possible value for your dollar. All tours include these features:

Page: 1 of 2   Words: 450   100%

Figure 2.24

When using the Find and Replace feature, if you wanted to change all the occurrences of the located text, it is much faster to use [Replace All]. Exercise care when using this option, however, because the search text you specify might be part of another word and you may accidentally replace text you want to keep. If this happens, you could use Undo to reverse the action.

Inserting the Current Date

The last text change you need to make is to add the date to the letter. The Date and Time command on the Insert tab inserts the current date as maintained by your computer system into your document at the location of the insertion point. You want to enter the date on the first line of the letter, five lines above the salutation.

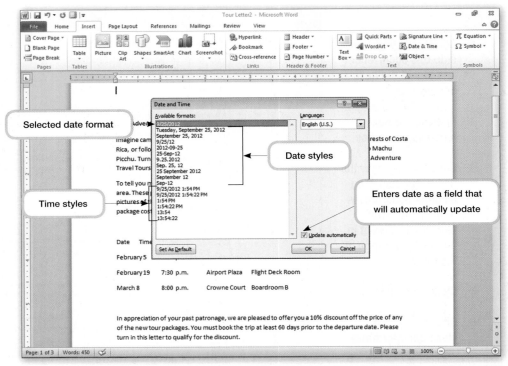

1

- If necessary, move to the "D" in "Dear" at the top of the letter.

- Press [Enter] 2 times to insert two blank lines.

- Move to the first blank line.

- Open the Insert tab and click Date & Time in the Text group.

Your screen should be similar to Figure 2.25

Figure 2.25

Additional Information

The current time also can be inserted into a document using the same procedure.

From the Date and Time dialog box, you select the style in which you want the date displayed in your document. The Available Formats list box displays the format styles for the current date and time. You want to display the date in the format Month XX, 2XXX, the third format setting in the list.

You also want the date to be updated automatically whenever the letter is opened or printed. You use the Update Automatically option to do this, which enters the date as a field.

Concept **4** Field

A **field** is a placeholder that instructs Word to insert information into a document. The **field code** contains the directions as to the type of information to insert or action to perform. Field codes appear between curly brackets {}, also called braces. The information that is displayed as a result of the field code is called the **field result**. Many field codes are automatically inserted when you use certain commands; others you can create and insert yourself. Many fields update automatically when the document changes. Using fields makes it easier and faster to perform many common or repetitive tasks.

2

- Select the third format setting.

- If necessary, select **Update Automatically** to display the checkmark.

- Click OK.

- Point to the date.

- Click on the date.

- If necessary, scroll the window up slightly to better see the field.

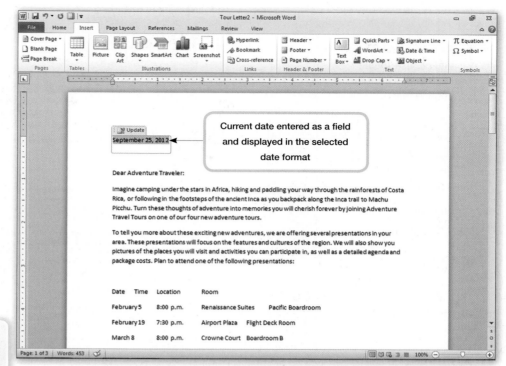

Figure 2.26

Additional Information

You can use Alt + Shift + D to insert the current date as a field in the format MM/DD/YY.

Your screen should be similar to Figure 2.26

Having Trouble?

The date on your screen will reflect the current date on your system. If your date is not shaded, this is because the setting for this feature is off in your program.

Additional Information

To show or remove field shading, open the File tab, click Options, Advanced, and then select Never, Always, or When Selected from the Field Shading drop-down list in the Show Document Content section.

The current date is entered in the document in the format you selected. When you point to a field, the entire entry is shaded to identify the entry as a field. When the insertion point is positioned in a field entry, the entire entry is highlighted, indicating it is selected and can be modified.

The date is the field result. You will display the field code to see the underlying instructions.

● **Right-click on the date and choose Toggle Field Codes from the context menu.**

Another Method

The keyboard shortcut is Shift + F9.

Your screen should be similar to Figure 2.27

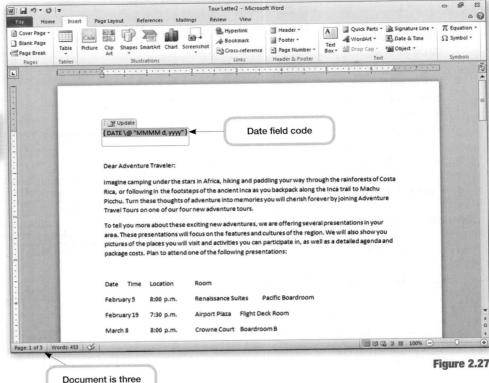

Date field code

Document is three pages long

Figure 2.27

Additional Information

You can press Alt + F9 to show or hide field codes for all fields in a document.

The field code includes the field name "DATE", followed by the field properties, which in this case direct how the date will be formatted. Whenever this document is printed, Word will print the current system date using this format.

Also notice that the page indicator in the status bar shows the document is now three pages long. When you inserted two lines at the top of the document in order to enter the date, the page break you entered earlier was pushed down onto a blank page. As a result a blank page is displaying as page 2 of your document and the flyer is displaying on page 3. You will display the date field result again and then delete the extra lines at the bottom of the letter.

● Press **Shift** + **F9** to display the field result again.

● Move to the bottom of the letter on page 1, to the right of the period in the last sentence of the letter.

● Display formatting marks in your document.

● Press **Delete** twice to delete the two paragraph marks at the bottom of page 1.

● Turn off the display of formatting marks.

● Save the document.

Your screen should be similar to Figure 2.28

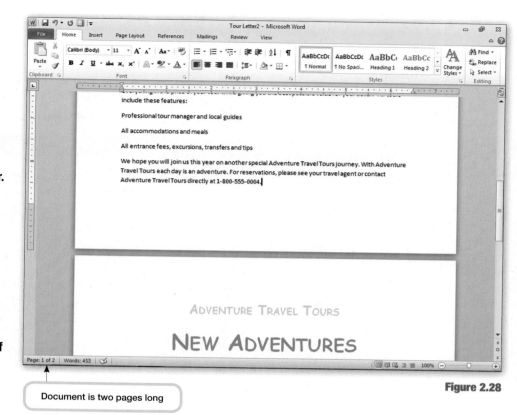

Document is two pages long

Figure 2.28

The blank lines before the page break have been deleted and the document is again two pages long.

Modifying Page Layout

Next the manager has suggested that you make several changes to improve the overall appearance of the letter and flyer. Two common page layout features are paragraph settings, such as indents and line spacing, and page margin settings. Other page layout features include page background colors, themes, and vertical alignment and orientation of text on a page.

To give the document more interest, you can indent paragraphs, use tabs to create tabular columns of data, and change the line spacing. These formatting features are all paragraph formats that affect the entire selected paragraph.

INDENTING PARAGRAPHS

Business letters typically use a block layout style or a modified block style with indented paragraphs. In a block style, all parts of the letter, including the date, inside address, all paragraphs in the body, and closing lines, are evenly aligned with the left margin. The block layout style has a very formal appearance. The modified block style, on the other hand, has a more casual appearance. In this style, certain elements such as the date, all paragraphs in the body, and the closing lines are indented from the left margin.

Concept 5 Indents

To help your reader find information quickly, you can **indent** paragraphs from the margins. Indenting paragraphs sets them off from the rest of the document. The four types of indents, and their effects are described below.

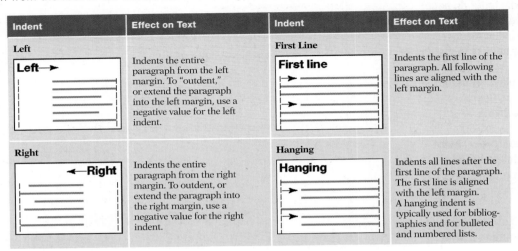

Indent	Effect on Text	Indent	Effect on Text
Left	Indents the entire paragraph from the left margin. To "outdent," or extend the paragraph into the left margin, use a negative value for the left indent.	**First Line**	Indents the first line of the paragraph. All following lines are aligned with the left margin.
Right	Indents the entire paragraph from the right margin. To outdent, or extend the paragraph into the right margin, use a negative value for the right indent.	**Hanging**	Indents all lines after the first line of the paragraph. The first line is aligned with the left margin. A hanging indent is typically used for bibliographies and for bulleted and numbered lists.

You want to change the letter style from the block paragraph style to the modified block style. You will begin by indenting the first line of the first paragraph. The quickest way to indent the first line of a paragraph is to press Tab when the insertion point is positioned at the beginning of the first line. Pressing Tab indents the first line of the paragraph to the first tab stop from the left margin. A tab stop is a marked location on the horizontal ruler that indicates how far to indent text each time the Tab key is pressed. The default tab stops are every 0.5 inch.

1

● Change the zoom to Page Width.

Another Method

Click on the Zoom percentage in the status bar to open the Zoom dialog box.

● Move to the beginning of the first paragraph on page 1.

● Press Tab.

Another Method

You can also right-click in the first paragraph, choose Paragraph, and then choose Special/First Line/By 0.5 in the Indents and Spacing tab.

Your screen should be similar to Figure 2.29

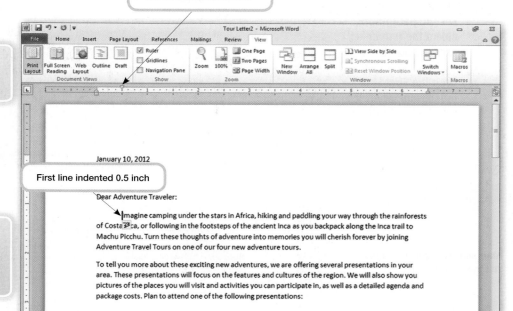

Indent marker positioned at 0.5-inch location on ruler

First line indented 0.5 inch

January 10, 2012

Dear Adventure Traveler:

Imagine camping under the stars in Africa, hiking and paddling your way through the rainforests of Costa Rica, or following in the footsteps of the ancient Inca as you backpack along the Inca trail to Machu Picchu. Turn these thoughts of adventure into memories you will cherish forever by joining Adventure Travel Tours on one of our four new adventure tours.

To tell you more about these exciting new adventures, we are offering several presentations in your area. These presentations will focus on the features and cultures of the region. We will also show you pictures of the places you will visit and activities you can participate in, as well as a detailed agenda and package costs. Plan to attend one of the following presentations:

Date	Time	Location	Room
February 5	8:00 p.m.	Renaissance Suites	Pacific Boardroom

Figure 2.29

Additional Information

To indent an entire paragraph, click in front of any line except the first line and press Tab.

The first line of the paragraph indents a half inch from the left margin. The text in the paragraph wraps as needed, and the text on the following line begins at the left margin. Notice that the First Line Indent marker on the ruler moved to the 0.5-inch position. This marker controls the location of the first line of text in the paragraph.

If the insertion point was positioned anywhere else within the line of text, pressing Tab would move the text to the right of the insertion point to the next tab stop and the indent marker would not move.

You can indent the remaining paragraphs individually, or you can select the paragraphs and indent them simultaneously by dragging the upper indent marker on the ruler.

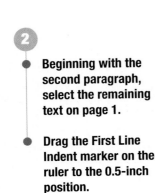

2

- Beginning with the second paragraph, select the remaining text on page 1.

- Drag the First Line Indent marker on the ruler to the 0.5-inch position.

Additional Information

A ScreenTip identifies the First Line Indent marker when you point to it.

Your screen should be similar to Figure 2.30

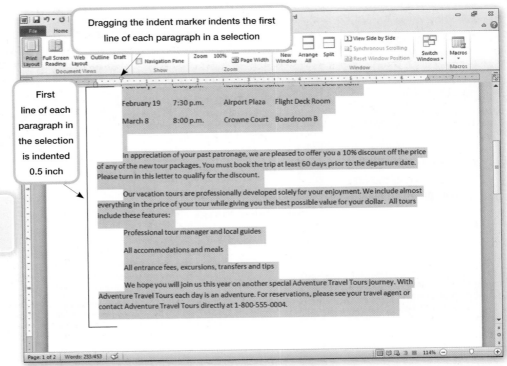

Dragging the indent marker indents the first line of each paragraph in a selection

First line of each paragraph in the selection is indented 0.5 inch

Figure 2.30

The first line of each paragraph in the selection is indented. Notice that each line of the presentation date and time information and the list of tour features also are indented. This is because Word considers each line a separate paragraph (each line ends with a paragraph mark). You decide to further indent the date and time information to the 1-inch position.

3

- Select the line of table headings and the three lines of data.

- Drag the First Line Indent marker on the ruler to the 1-inch position.

Having Trouble?

If the selection does not move to the 1-inch position, repeat dragging the First Line Indent marker to the 1-inch position.

Your screen should be similar to Figure 2.31

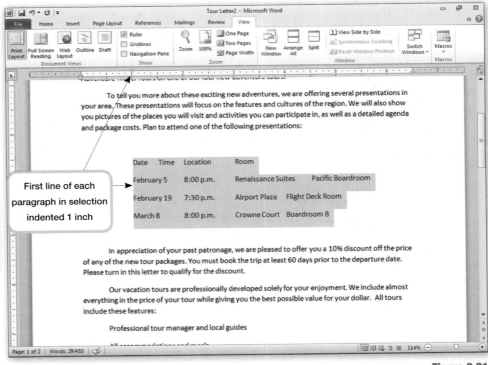

First line of each paragraph in selection indented 1 inch

Figure 2.31

SETTING TAB STOPS

Next you want to improve the appearance of the list of presentation times and dates. The date and time information was entered using the ⟨Tab⟩ key to separate the different columns of information. However, because the default tab stops are set at every 0.5 inch, the columns are not properly aligned. To improve the appearance of the information, you will set manual **tab stops** that will align the information in evenly spaced columns. You also can select from five different types of tab stops that control how characters are positioned or aligned with the tab stop. The following table explains the five tab types, the tab marks that appear in the tab selector box (on the left end of the horizontal ruler), and the effects on the text.

Tab Type	Tab Mark	Effects on Text	Example
Left	⌊L⌋	Extends text to right from tab stop	left
Center	⌊⊥⌋	Aligns text centered on tab stop	center
Right	⌊⌐⌋	Extends text to left from tab stop	right
Decimal	⌊⊥⌋	Aligns text with decimal point	35.78
Bar	⌊I⌋	Draws a vertical line through text at tab stop		

You want to reformat the list of presentation times and dates to appear as a tabbed table of information so that it is easier to read, as shown below.

Date	Time	Location	Room
February 5------	8:00 p.m.-------	Renaissance Suites -----	Pacific Boardroom
February 19 ----	7:30 p.m.-------	Airport Plaza-------------	Flight Deck Room
March 8---------	8:00 p.m.-------	Crowne Court -----------	Boardroom B

Additional Information

The default tab stops are visible on the ruler as light vertical lines below the numbers.

To align the information, you will set three left tab stops at the 2-inch, 3-inch, and 4.5-inch positions. You can quickly specify manual tab stop locations and types using the ruler. To select a type of tab stop, click the tab selector box, located directly above the vertical ruler, to cycle through the types. Then, to specify where to place the selected tab stop type, click on the location in the ruler. As you specify the new tab stop settings, the information will align to the new settings.

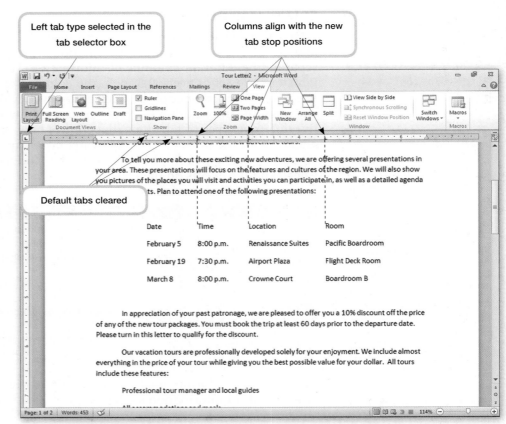

1

- If necessary, select the line of table headings and the three lines of information.

- If necessary, click the tab alignment selector box until the left tab icon ⌊L⌋ appears.

- Click on the 2-inch position on the ruler.

- Click on the 3-inch and the 4.5-inch positions on the ruler.

- Click anywhere in the table to deselect it.

Your screen should be similar to **Figure 2.32**

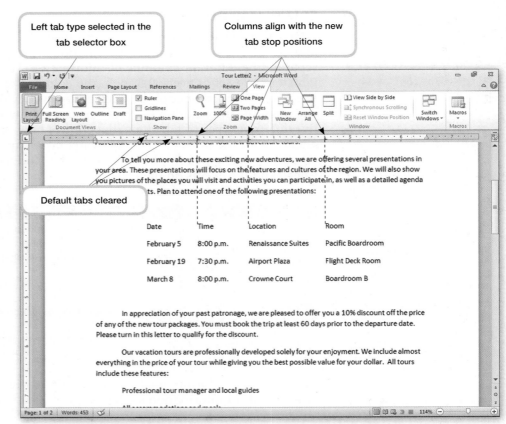

Left tab type selected in the tab selector box

Columns align with the new tab stop positions

Default tabs cleared

Date	Time	Location	Room
February 5	8:00 p.m.	Renaissance Suites	Pacific Boardroom
February 19	7:30 p.m.	Airport Plaza	Flight Deck Room
March 8	8:00 p.m.	Crowne Court	Boardroom B

Figure 2.32

Additional Information

The tab selector box also can be used to insert first line or hanging indents by selecting ♡ First Line Indent or ⊡ Hanging Indent.

The three tabbed columns appropriately align with the new tab stops. All default tabs to the left of the manual tab stops are cleared. After looking at the columns, you decide the column headings would look better centered over the columns of information. To make this change, you will remove the three left tab stops for the heading line and then add three center tab stops.

Manual tab stops can be removed by dragging the tab stop up or down off the ruler. They also can be moved by dragging them left or right along the ruler. In addition the Tabs dialog box can be used to make these same changes. You will first drag a tab stop off the ruler to remove it and then you will use the Tabs dialog box to clear the remaining tab stops.

2

● Move to anywhere in the table heading line.

● Drag the 2-inch tab stop mark down off the ruler.

● Double-click any tab stop to open the Tabs dialog box.

● Click **Clear All** to remove the remaining two tab stops.

● Click **OK**.

● Click the tab alignment selector box until the center tab icon ⊥ appears.

● Set center tab stops at the 1.25-inch, 2.25-inch, 3.5-inch, and 5-inch positions.

Your screen should be similar to Figure 2.33

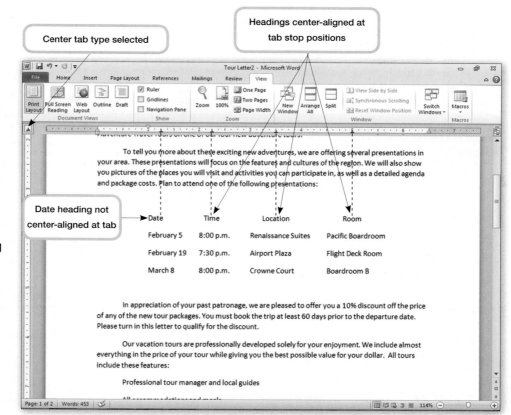

Center tab type selected

Headings center-aligned at tab stop positions

Date heading not center-aligned at tab

Date   Time   Location   Room

February 5   8:00 p.m.   Renaissance Suites   Pacific Boardroom

February 19   7:30 p.m.   Airport Plaza   Flight Deck Room

March 8   8:00 p.m.   Crowne Court   Boardroom B

Figure 2.33

The Time, Location, and Room headings are appropriately centered on the tab stops. However, the Date heading still needs to be indented to the 1.25-inch tab stop position by pressing Tab.

3

● If necessary, move to the "D" in "Date."

● Press Tab.

Your screen should be similar to Figure 2.34

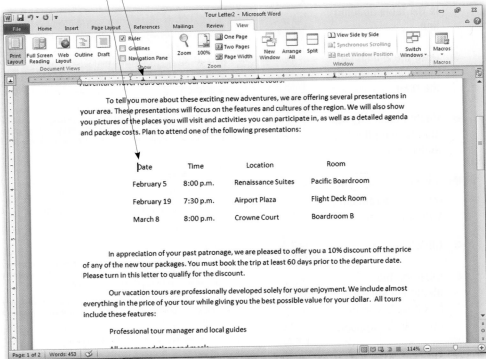

Heading center-aligned at 1.25 inch position

Figure 2.34

As you can see, setting different types of tab stops is helpful for aligning text or numeric information vertically in columns. Using tab stops ensures that the text will indent to the same set location. Setting manual tab stops instead of pressing Tab or Spacebar repeatedly is a more professional way to format a document, as well as faster and more accurate. It also makes editing easier because you can change the tab stop settings for several paragraphs at once.

ADDING LEADER CHARACTERS

To make the presentation times and location information even easier to read, you will add leader characters before each of the tab stops. **Leader characters** are solid, dotted, or dashed lines that fill the blank space between tab stops. They help the reader's eye move across the blank space between the information aligned at the tab stops. To do this, you use the Tabs dialog box.

1

Select the three lines of presentation information, excluding the heading line.

Double-click any tab stop on the ruler.

Your screen should be similar to Figure 2.35

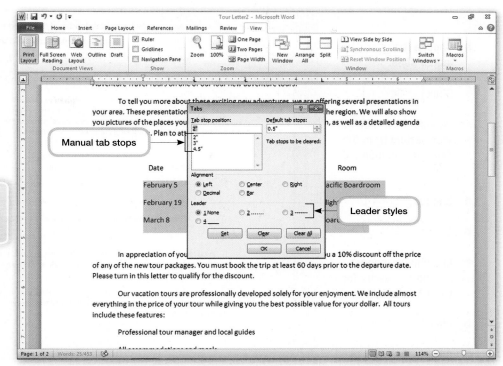

Figure 2.35

Notice that the Tabs dialog box displays the manual tabs you set on the ruler. You also can set tab stops using the Tabs dialog box by entering the tab positions in the text box and selecting the tab alignment. You also can clear an individual tab stop by selecting the tab stop position from the list and clicking Clear.

The 2-inch tab stop appears in the Tab Stop Position text box, indicating it is the tab stop that will be affected by your actions. The Leader setting is None for the 2-inch tab stop. You can select from three styles of leader characters. You will use the third leader style, a series of dashed lines. The leader characters fill the empty space to the left of the tab stop. Each tab stop must have the leader style individually set.

- **Choose the** ⚪ 3 ------- **leader style.**

- **Click** [Set] .

- **Choose the 3-inch tab stop setting from the Tab Stop Position list box.**

- **Choose** ⚪ 3 ------- .

- **Click** [Set] .

- **In a similar manner, set the tab leader for the 4.5-inch tab.**

- **Click** [OK] .

- **Click in the table to deselect the text.**

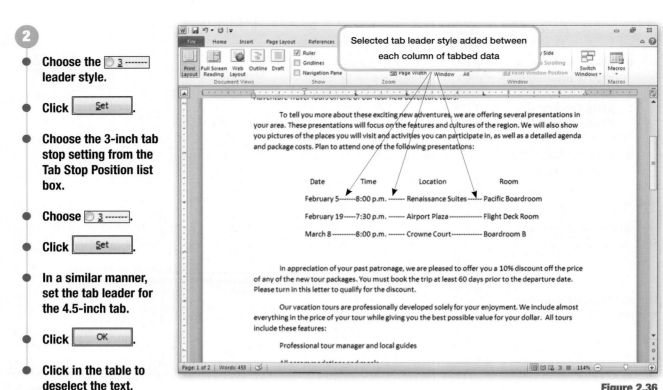

Selected tab leader style added between each column of tabbed data

Figure 2.36

Your screen should be similar to Figure 2.36

The selected leader style has been added to the blank space between each column of tabbed text.

CHANGING LINE AND PARAGRAPH SPACING

You decide you want to adjust the spacing above and below the table as well as between the lines in the table to help make the table stand out from the other text in the letter.

Concept 6 — Line and Paragraph Spacing

Adjusting the **line spacing**, or the vertical space between lines of text and paragraphs, helps set off areas of text from others and when increased makes it easier to read and edit text. If a line contains a character or object, such as a graphic, that is larger than the surrounding text, the spacing for that line is automatically adjusted. Additional line spacing settings are described in the table below.

Spacing	Effect
Single	Accommodates the largest font in that line, plus a small amount of extra space; the amount of extra space varies with the font that is used.
1.5 lines	Spacing is one and a half times that of single line spacing.
Double (2.0)	Spacing is twice that of single line spacing.
At least	Uses a value specified in points as the minimum line spacing that is needed to fit the largest font or graphic on the line.
Exactly	Uses a value specified in points as a fixed line spacing amount that is not adjusted, making all lines evenly spaced. Graphics or text that is too large will appear clipped.
Multiple	Uses a percentage value to increase or decrease the spacing from single spacing. For example, 1.3 will increase the spacing by 33 percent.

The default line spacing for a Word 2010 document is set to multiple with a 15 percent increase (1.15) over single spacing.

In addition to changing line spacing within paragraphs, you also can change the spacing before or after paragraphs. The default paragraph spacing adds a small amount of space (10 pt) after a paragraph and no extra space before a paragraph.

The Line and Paragraph Spacing command in the Paragraph group of the Home tab can be used to specify standard spacing settings, such as double and triple spacing. It also lets you turn on or off the extra spacing between paragraphs. You want to look at the line spacing settings and make the adjustments from the Paragraph dialog box.

①

- Select the table including the blank lines above and below it.

- Open the 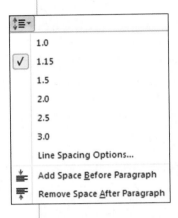 Line and Paragraph Spacing drop-down menu in the Paragraph group of the Home tab.

- Choose Line Spacing Options.

Another Method

You also could click ⬚ in the Paragraph group to open the Paragraph dialog box to access this feature.

Another Method

You also can use Ctrl + 1 or 2 to change the line spacing to single or double spaced.

Your screen should be similar to Figure 2.37

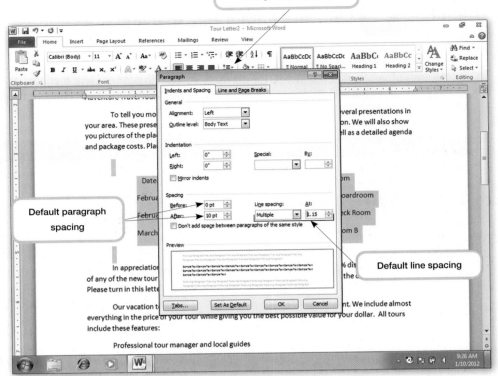

Changes line spacing

Default paragraph spacing

Default line spacing

Figure 2.37

The default document line spacing setting, multiple at 1.15; before paragraph spacing of 0 pt; and after paragraph spacing of 10 pt are displayed in the Spacing section of the dialog box.

You want to decrease the spacing between each line of the table. Because Word considers each line of the table and the blank lines above and below it as separate paragraphs, you can decrease the Spacing After paragraph setting to achieve this effect. You also will change the line spacing to single to remove the 15 percent spacing increase. As you make these changes, the Preview box will show you a sample of the effect they will have on the text.

2

- Select Single from the Line Spacing drop-down menu.

- Click the down scroll button of the After box to decrease the spacing to 6 pt.

- Click [OK].

Your screen should be similar to Figure 2.38

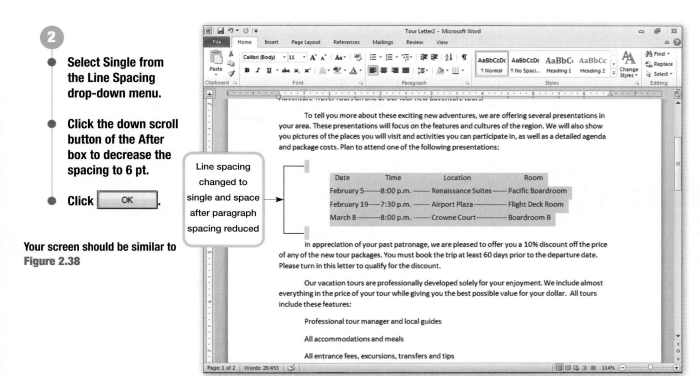

Line spacing changed to single and space after paragraph spacing reduced

Figure 2.38

Changing the line and paragraph spacing improves the appearance of the table and makes the information stand out more from the other text in the letter. You think this same change also would be effective in the list of tour features.

3

- Select the list of three tour features.

- Click [≡] Line and Paragraph Spacing and choose 1.0.

- Select the first two items in the feature list and change the space after paragraph to 6 pt.

Another Method

You can also use

[After: 10 pt] in the Paragraph group of the Page Layout tab to adjust paragraph spacing.

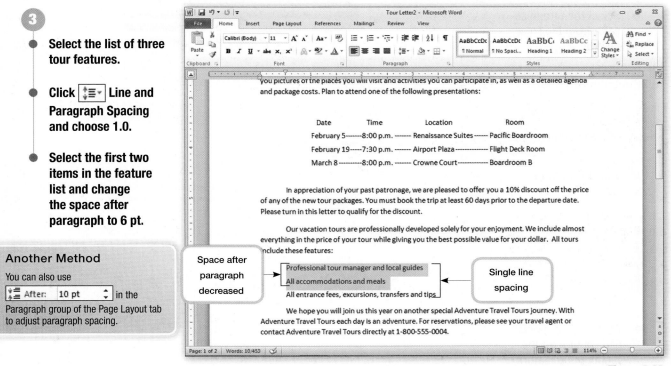

Space after paragraph decreased

Single line spacing

Your screen should be similar to Figure 2.39

Figure 2.39

As you look at the letter, you still feel that the table of presentation dates and times does not stand out enough. You can add emphasis to information in your documents by formatting specific characters or words. Applying color shading or highlighting behind text is commonly used to identify areas of text that you want to stand out. It is frequently used to mark text that you want to locate easily as you are revising a document. Italics, underlines, and bold are other character formats that add emphasis and draw the reader's attention to important items. Word applies character formatting to the entire selection or to the entire word at the insertion point. You can apply formatting to a portion of a word by selecting the area to be formatted first.

Additional Information

When you use highlights in a document you plan to print in black and white, select a light color so the text is visible.

ADDING COLOR HIGHLIGHTING

First, you want to see how a color highlight behind the tabbed table of presentation times and locations would look.

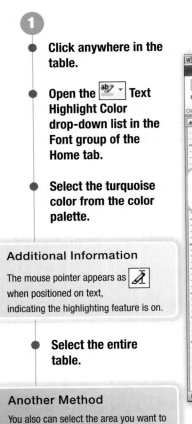

- **Click anywhere in the table.**

- **Open the [ab] ▾ Text Highlight Color drop-down list in the Font group of the Home tab.**

- **Select the turquoise color from the color palette.**

Additional Information

The mouse pointer appears as [🖉] when positioned on text, indicating the highlighting feature is on.

- **Select the entire table.**

Another Method

You also can select the area you want to highlight first and then click [ab] ▾ to select and apply a color.

- **Click [ab] ▾ or press [Esc] to turn off the highlighting feature.**

Adds selected color highlight

Color highlight added to table

you pictures of the places you will visit and activities you can participate in, as well as a detailed agenda and package costs. Plan to attend one of the following presentations:

Date	Time	Location	Room
February 5	8:00 p.m.	Renaissance Suites	Pacific Boardroom
February 19	7:30 p.m.	Airport Plaza	Flight Deck Room
March 8	8:00 p.m.	Crowne Court	Boardroom 8

In appreciation of your past patronage, we are pleased to offer you a 10% discount off the price of any of the new tour packages. You must book the trip at least 60 days prior to the departure date. Please turn in this letter to qualify for the discount.

Our vacation tours are professionally developed solely for your enjoyment. We include almost everything in the price of your tour while giving you the best possible value for your dollar. All tours include these features:

Professional tour manager and local guides

All accommodations and meals

All entrance fees, excursions, transfers and tips

We hope you will join us this year on another special Adventure Travel Tours journey. With Adventure Travel Tours each day is an adventure. For reservations, please see your travel agent or contact Adventure Travel Tours directly at 1-800-555-0004.

Figure 2.40

Although the highlight makes the table stand out, it does not look good.

Your screen should be similar to Figure 2.40

UNDERLINING TEXT

Instead, you decide to bold and underline the headings. The default underline style is a single black line. In addition, Word includes 15 other types of underlines.

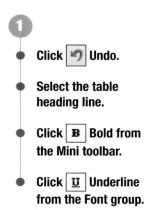

- Click ↶ Undo.

- Select the table heading line.

- Click **B** Bold from the Mini toolbar.

- Click U Underline from the Font group.

Your screen should be similar to Figure 2.41

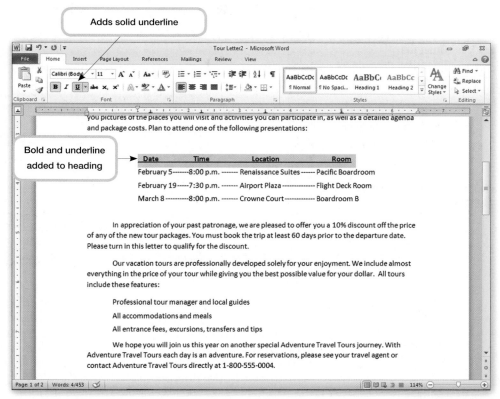

Figure 2.41

All the words are bold, and a single black underline has been added below the entire selection. You decide you want the underline to appear under each word only and to stand out more. To do this, you will select another underline style and apply the underline to the word individually. When the insertion point is positioned on a word, the selected underline style is applied to the entire word.

- Click 🔄 Undo to remove the underline.

- Click on the "Room" heading in the table.

- Open the U ▾ Underline drop-down menu.

- Point to the dotted underline style to see the Live Preview.

Your screen should be similar to Figure 2.42

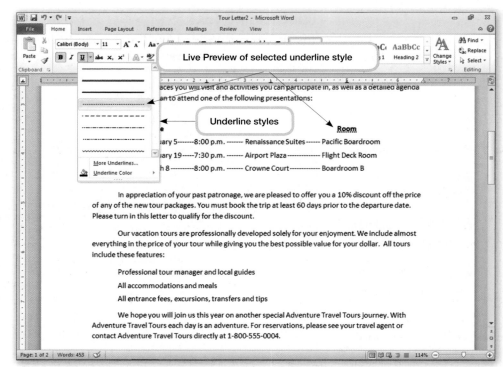

Figure 2.42

The eight most popular underline styles are listed in the menu. Using More Underlines will open the Font dialog box, where you can select other styles, clear underlining from a selection using the None option, or select the Words Only option to display a single underline below words in the selection, not under the spaces between words. Live Preview shows you how the selection will appear in the document.

3

- Select several other underline styles and see how they appear in the Live Preview.

- Click the double underline style.

Additional Information

Using the keyboard shortcut Ctrl + U adds the default single underline style.

Your screen should be similar to Figure 2.43

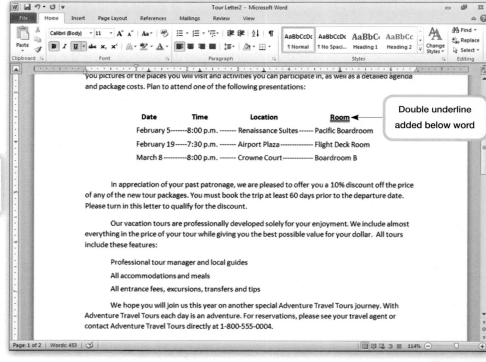

Figure 2.43

The selected word is underlined using the double underline style.

COPYING FORMATS WITH FORMAT PAINTER

You want to quickly apply the same formats to the other headings. To do this, you can use the **Format Painter**. This feature applies the formats associated with the current selection to new selections. If the selection is a paragraph (including the paragraph mark), the formatting is applied to the entire paragraph. If the selection is a character, the format is applied to a character, word, or selection you specify.

To use this feature, move the insertion point to the text whose formats you want to copy and click the 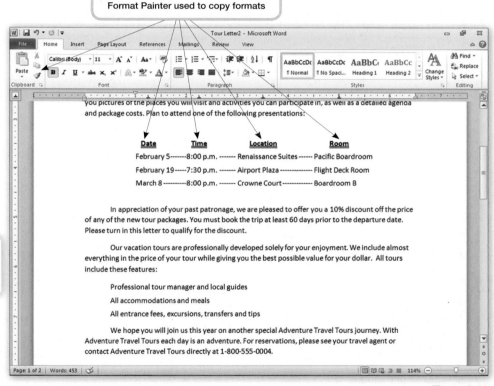 Format Painter button. Then select the text to which you want the formats applied. The format is automatically applied to an entire word simply by clicking on the word. To apply the format to more or less text, you must select the area. Whereas clicking Format Painter once lets you format one selection, clicking the button twice lets you format multiple selections until you turn off this feature by clicking Format Painter again.

Additional Information

When Format Painter is on, the mouse pointer appears as [icon].

1

- **If necessary, click on the "Room" heading.**

- **Double-click Format Painter in the Clipboard group.**

- **Click on the Date, Time, and Location headings.**

- **Click to turn off Format Painter.**

Another Method

You can press [Esc] to turn off Format Painter.

- **Save the document again.**

Your screen should be similar to Figure 2.44

Format Painter used to copy formats

Figure 2.44

Creating Lists

Additional Information

A list can be used whenever you present three or more related pieces of information.

The next change you want to make is to display the three lines of information about tour features as an itemized list so that they stand out better from the surrounding text.

Whenever possible, add bullets or numbers before items in a list to organize information and to make your writing clear and easy to read. Word includes many basic bullets, a dot or other symbol, and number formats from which you can select. Additionally, there are many picture bullets available. If none of the predesigned bullet or number formats suits your needs, you also can create your own customized designs.

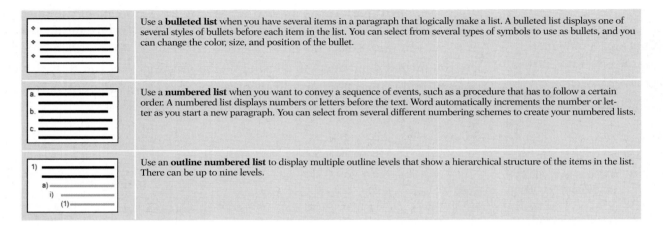

(bullet list icon)	Use a **bulleted list** when you have several items in a paragraph that logically make a list. A bulleted list displays one of several styles of bullets before each item in the list. You can select from several types of symbols to use as bullets, and you can change the color, size, and position of the bullet.
(numbered list icon)	Use a **numbered list** when you want to convey a sequence of events, such as a procedure that has to follow a certain order. A numbered list displays numbers or letters before the text. Word automatically increments the number or letter as you start a new paragraph. You can select from several different numbering schemes to create your numbered lists.
(outline list icon)	Use an **outline numbered list** to display multiple outline levels that show a hierarchical structure of the items in the list. There can be up to nine levels.

NUMBERING A LIST

Because both bullet and number formats will indent the items automatically when applied, you first need to remove the indent from the three tour features. Then you will try a numbered list format to see how it looks.

- **Select the three tour features.**

- **Drag the First Line Indent marker on the ruler back to the margin boundary.**

- **Right-click on the selection and point to Numbering in the context menu.**

Another Method

The Ribbon equivalent is 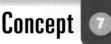 Numbering in the Paragraph group.

Your screen should be similar to Figure 2.45

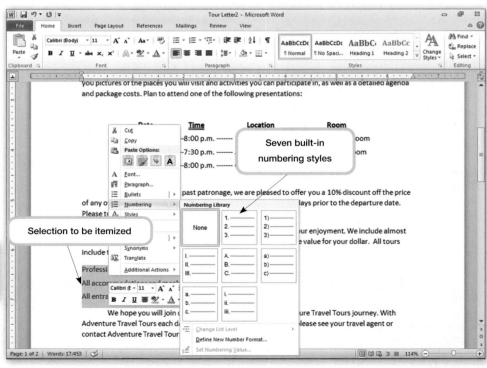

Figure 2.45

The Numbering gallery displays examples of seven built-in numbered list formats in the Numbering Library category. The None option is used to remove an existing numbering format. Numbers followed by periods is the default style that is applied when clicking ▥ Numbering in the Paragraph group. However, if another style has been used since starting Word, the last-used numbering format is inserted.

The numbering gallery also may include a Recently Used category if this feature has already been used since Word 2010 was started. If the document contains another numbered list, the gallery will display the used number style in a Document Number Formats category.

The three options at the bottom of the menu are used to change the indent level of the items, to customize the appearance of the built-in formats, and to set a start number for the list (1 is the default). For example, you could increase the indent level of the list, change the color of the numbers, and start numbering with 3 instead of 1.

You will use the second number format that has a number followed by a parenthesis.

2

● **Choose the second (parenthesis style) numbered list format option.**

Your screen should be similar to Figure 2.46

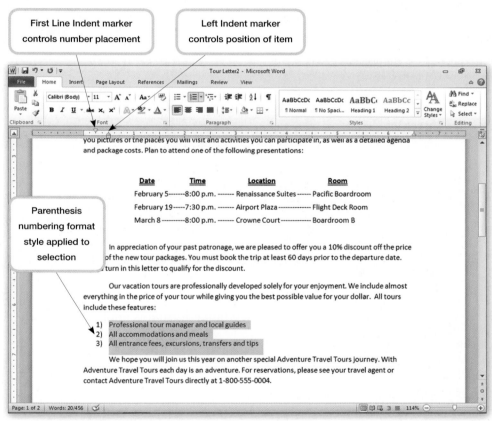

Figure 2.46

A number is inserted at the 0.25-inch position before each line, and the text following the number is indented to the 0.5-inch position. In an itemized list, the First Line Indent marker on the ruler controls the position of the number or bullet, and the Left Indent marker controls the position of the item following the number or bullet. The Left Indent marker creates a hanging indent. If the text following each bullet were longer than a line, the text on the following lines would also be indented to the 0.5-inch position. Additionally, the extra space between the lines was removed because the feature that adds space between paragraphs of the same style was automatically turned off.

BULLETING A LIST

After looking at the list, you decide it really would be more appropriate if it were a bulleted list instead of a numbered list. The solid round bullet format is the default when clicking ⊞ ▾ Bullets. However, if another style was previously used since starting Word 2010, that style is inserted. The bullet submenu is divided into the same three groups as the Numbering submenu and has similar options.

1

● If necessary, select the list of three features.

● Right-click the selection and select Bullets to display the bullet gallery.

Another Method

You also can use ⊞ ▾ Bullets in the Paragraph group of the Home tab.

● Choose the ➤ bullet format.

Your screen should be similar to Figure 2.47

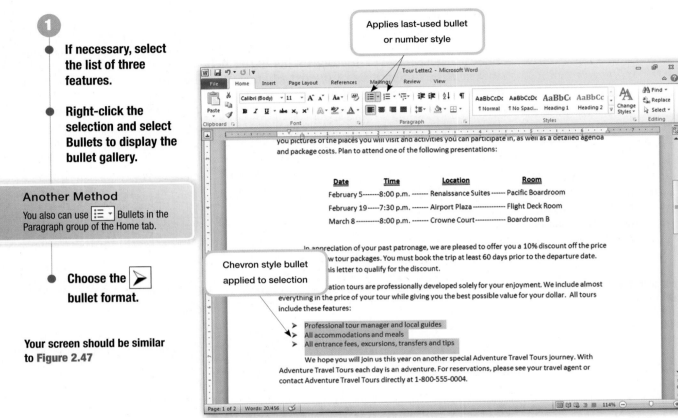

Figure 2.47

The selected bullet format is applied to the selection.

Additional Information

To remove bullets or numbers, select the text, open the ⊞ ▾ Bullets drop-down menu, and select None, or click ⊞ ▾ Bullets again.

SORTING A LIST

As you look at the bulleted list, you decide you want the three items to appear in alphabetical order. To make this change quickly, you can sort the list.

Concept 8 Sort

Word can quickly arrange or **sort** text, numbers, or data in lists or tables in alphabetical, numeric, or date order based on the first character in each paragraph. The sort order can be ascending (A to Z, 0 to 9, or earliest to latest date) or descending (Z to A, 9 to 0, or latest to earliest date). The following table describes the rules that are used when sorting.

Sort by	Rules
Text	First, items beginning with leading spaces and punctuation marks or symbols (such as !, #, $, %, or &) are sorted.
	Second, items beginning with numbers are sorted. Dates are treated as three-digit numbers.
	Third, items beginning with letters are sorted.
Numbers	All characters except numbers are ignored. The numbers can be in any location in a paragraph.
Date	Valid date separators include hyphens, forward slashes (/), commas, and periods. Colons (:) are valid time separators. If unable to recognize a date or time, Word places the item at the beginning or end of the list (depending on whether you are sorting in ascending or descending order).
Field results	If an entire field (such as a last name) is the same for two items, Word next evaluates subsequent fields (such as a first name) according to the specified sort options.

When a tie occurs, Word uses the first nonidentical character in each item to determine which item should come first.

You will use the default Sort settings that will sort by text and paragraphs in ascending order.

- If necessary, select the entire bulleted list.

- Click 🔼 Sort in the Paragraph group.

- Click [OK] to accept the default settings.

- Click on the document to clear the highlight.

- Increase the space after for the third list item to 12 pt.

- Save the file.

Your screen should be similar to Figure 2.48

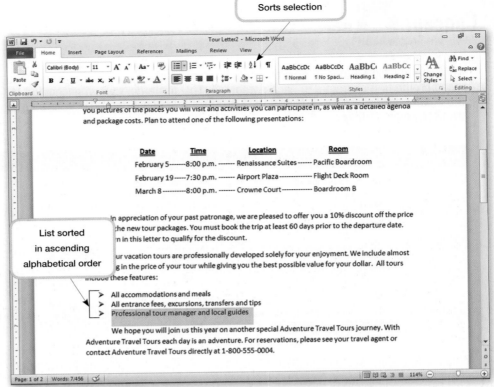

Sorts selection

List sorted in ascending alphabetical order

Figure 2.48

The three items in the list now appear in ascending sorted order.

Using Quick Parts

While looking at the letter, you realize that the closing lines have not been added to the document. You can quickly insert text and graphics that you use frequently using the Quick Parts feature. The **Quick Parts** feature includes reusable pieces of content or document parts, called **building blocks**, that give you a head start in creating content such as page numbers, cover pages, headers and footers, and sidebars. In addition to the supplied building blocks, you also can create your own custom building blocks.

USING SUPPLIED BUILDING BLOCKS

As a result of the new line spacing settings, there is now room below the letter to insert lines for the closing. You will create the closing for the letter using the Author and Company supplied building blocks that get their information from the file's document properties.

1

- Move to the end of the last line of the letter and press [Enter] to insert a blank line.

- Return the indent to the left margin.

- Type **Best Regards,**

- Press [Enter].

- Open the Insert tab and click [Quick Parts ▾] in the Text group.

- Select Document Property and choose Author from the submenu.

Your screen should be similar to **Figure 2.49**

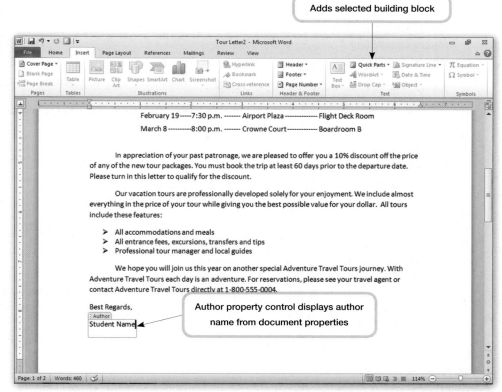

Adds selected building block

Author property control displays author name from document properties

Figure 2.49

An Author property control containing the name that is currently stored in the file's Author document property is inserted in the document. A **control** is a graphic element that is a container for information or objects. Controls, like fields, appear shaded when you point to them.

You can update or modify the information displayed in a property control by editing the entry. Any changes you make in the property control are automatically updated in the document's properties. You will change the information in the Author property to your name and then continue to create the closing.

- Select the text in the Author control and type **your name**

- Press → to deselect it.

- Type **, Advertising Coordinator** following your name.

- Press [Enter].

- Insert the Company document property control.

- Select the last two lines and remove the space after the paragraphs.

- Increase the spacing after of the Best Regards line to 18 pt. to make space for a signature.

Your screen should be similar to Figure 2.50

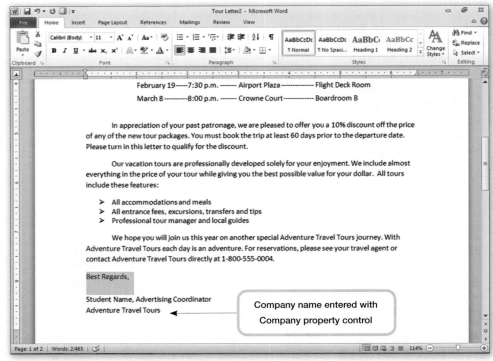

Figure 2.50

The closing is now complete and the document properties now include your name as the author. Using document property controls in a document is particularly helpful when the same controls are used multiple times, as in a contract. Then, when one control is updated or edited, all controls of the same type throughout the document are automatically updated.

CREATING A CUSTOM BUILDING BLOCK

In addition to the supplied building blocks, you can create your own. In this case, because you frequently use the same closing when creating correspondence, you will create a building block that you can use to quickly insert this information.

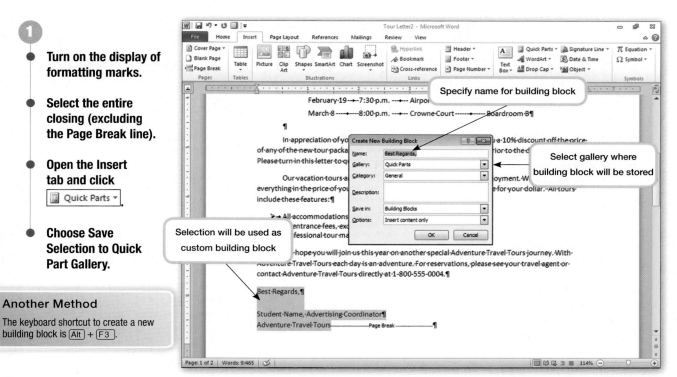

1

- Turn on the display of formatting marks.

- Select the entire closing (excluding the Page Break line).

- Open the Insert tab and click [Quick Parts ▾].

- Choose Save Selection to Quick Part Gallery.

Another Method

The keyboard shortcut to create a new building block is Alt + F3.

Your screen should be similar to Figure 2.51

Figure 2.51

In the Create New Building Block dialog box, you define the properties for the building block. This includes entering a unique name for the building block, specifying the gallery where you want the building block stored, and other information that is needed to identify and use the building block.

You will use the proposed name, Best Regards, and store it in the Quick Parts Gallery. All the other default settings for this building block are appropriate. After saving the building block, you will erase the closing you typed in the letter and then reinsert it using the stored Quick Part.

- Click [OK].

- Delete the closing in the letter.

- Click [📄 Quick Parts ▾].

- Click on the Best Regards building block.

- If necessary, scroll to see the bottom of page 1 again.

- Turn off the display of formatting marks, if necessary, and then save the document again.

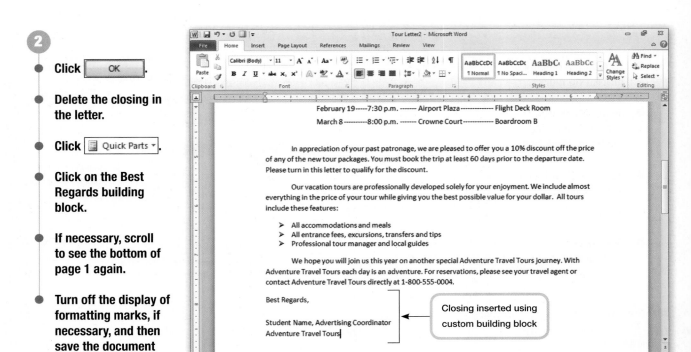

Figure 2.52

Your screen should be similar to Figure 2.52

Additional Information

You will learn more about Quick Parts and use several of the other supplied building blocks in later labs.

The custom building block you created appeared as a gallery item at the top of the Quick Parts menu, making it easy for you to access and use. The selected block was inserted into the document at the location of the insertion point. As you can see, using Quick Parts was much quicker than typing the closing.

Adding and Modifying Shapes

You also want to add a special graphic to the flyer containing information about the company Web site to catch the reader's attention. To quickly add a shape, you will use one of the ready-made shapes that are supplied with Word. These include basic shapes such as rectangles and circles, a variety of lines, block arrows, flowchart symbols, stars and banners, and callouts. Additional shapes are available in the Clip Organizer. You also can combine shapes to create more complex designs. To see and create shapes, the view needs to be Print Layout view. In Draft view, shapes are not displayed. If you are using Draft view when you begin to create a shape, the view will change automatically to Print Layout view.

INSERTING A SHAPE

You want to add a graphic of a banner to the bottom of the flyer.

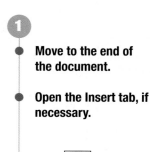

1

- Move to the end of the document.

- Open the Insert tab, if necessary.

- Click in the Illustrations group.

- From the Stars and Banners group, point to the Wave shape.

Your screen should be similar to Figure 2.53

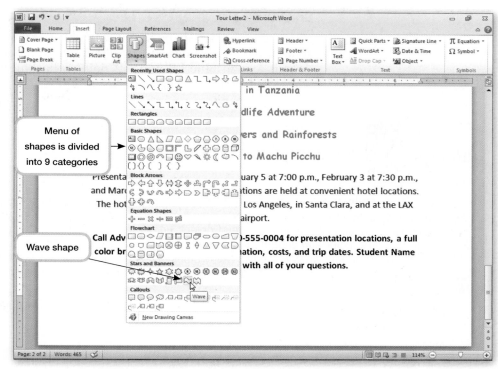

Figure 2.53

The Shapes menu displays nine categories of shapes. Pointing to a shape displays the shape name in a ScreenTip. The recently selected shapes appear at the top of the menu. You will insert the Wave shape at the end of the flyer.

2

- Click the Wave shape.

- Click below the last line of the flyer to insert the shape.

- Drag the sizing handles to obtain a shape similar to that shown in Figure 2.54.

Additional Information

To maintain the height and width proportions of a shape, hold down [Shift] while you drag.

Your screen should be similar to Figure 2.54

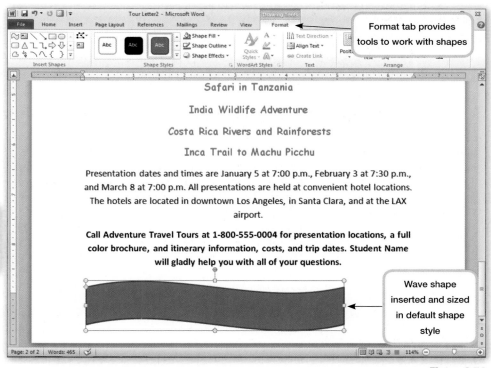

Figure 2.54

Notice the Drawing Tools Format tab is displayed and open so you can continue working with the shape.

CHANGING THE SHAPE STYLE

When you insert a shape in a document, Word automatically applies a quick style to the shape that defines all aspects of its appearance. For example, by default a solid blue fill and a 2 point solid blue border were applied to the wave shape you inserted in the last section.

Concept 9 Quick Styles

Applying a **quick style**, a named group of formatting options allows you to quickly apply a whole group of formats to a text selection or an object in one simple step. The formatting options associated with the different quick styles varies depending upon the type of object. For example, a text quick style may consist of a combination of font, font size, color and alignment options whereas a shape quick styles may consist of a combination of fill color, line color and line weight options. Many quick styles are automatically applied when certain features, such as shapes, are used. Others must be applied manually to selected text or object. You also can create your own custom styles.

Quick styles are available for text selections as well as many different types of objects. Some of the most common are described in the following table.

Type of Style	Description
Graphic	Affects all aspects of a graphic object's appearance, including fill color, outline color, and other effects.
Text	Affects selected text within a paragraph, such as the font and size of text, and bold and italic formats.
Paragraph	Controls all aspects of a paragraph's appearance, such as text alignment, tab stops, and line spacing. It also can include character formatting. The default paragraph quick style is named Normal, which includes character settings of Calibri, 11 pt, and paragraph settings of left indent at 0, 1.15 line spacing, and left alignment. In addition, many paragraph styles are designed to affect specific text elements such as headings, captions, and footnotes.
Table	Provides a consistent look to borders, shading, alignment, and fonts in tables.
List	Applies similar alignment, numbering or bullet characters, and fonts to lists.

You can easily change the default quick style of the shape using the Shape Styles group on the Format tab.

1

- Click ▾ More in the Shape Styles group to open the shape style gallery.

- Point to several of the styles to see the Live Preview.

- Click the Light 1 Outline, Colored Fill–Orange, Accent 6 style to apply it to the wave shape (third row, last column).

Your screen should be similar to **Figure 2.55**

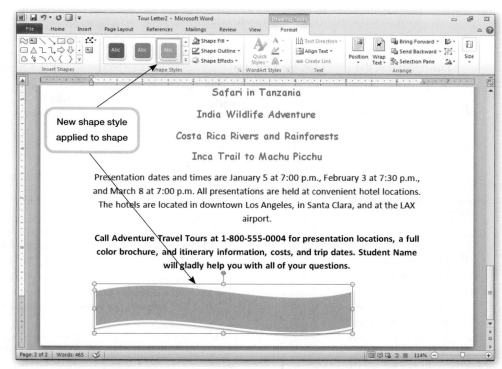

Figure 2.55

FILLING THE SHAPE WITH COLOR

You decide to change the fill color of the wave shape to match the text color used in the flyer. If there isn't a quick style that meets your needs, no need to worry. You can easily customize shapes using many of the features on the Format tab, such as adding a background fill color, gradient, and line color. A **gradient** is a gradual progression of colors and shades, usually from one color to another, or from one shade to another of the same color.

1

- Open the 🪣 drop-down menu in the Shape Styles group.

- Choose the green fill color from the standard colors bar.

- Open the 🪣 drop-down menu, select Gradient, and choose the Linear Up gradient from the Light Variations section (3rd row).

- In the same manner, open the ✏️ menu and choose green.

Your screen should be similar to **Figure 2.56**

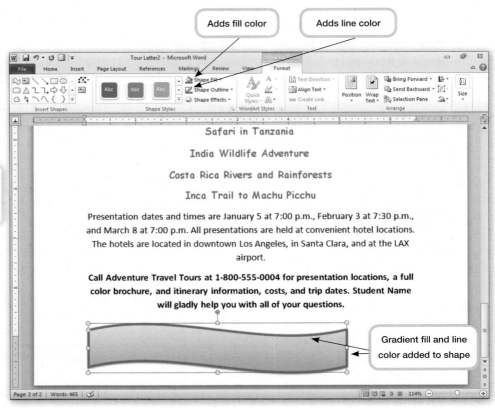

Figure 2.56

ADDING TEXT TO A SHAPE

Next you will add information about the company's Web site to the shape. It will include the Web site's address, called a **URL** (Uniform Resource Locator). Word automatically recognizes URLs you enter and creates a hyperlink of the entry. A **hyperlink** is a connection to a location in the current document, another document, or a Web site. It allows the reader to jump to the referenced location by clicking on the hyperlink text when reading the document on the screen.

1

- Right-click on the shape to open the context menu.

- Choose Add Text.

- Type **Visit our Web site at www.adventureltraveltours.com** and press `Spacebar`.

- If necessary, adjust the shape size to fully display the text.

- Click outside the shape to deselect it.

Your screen should be similar to Figure 2.57

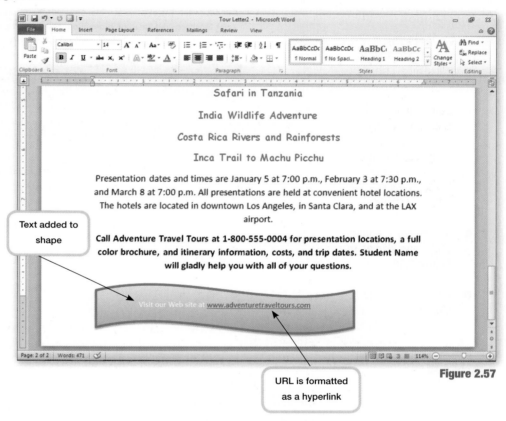

Text added to shape

URL is formatted as a hyperlink

Figure 2.57

The text appears in the default font settings. The text color is white because the default font color setting is Automatic. This setting will make the text color black if the background fill color is light and white if the fill color is dark.

The Web address is automatically formatted in blue and underlined, indicating the entry is a hyperlink. The AutoFormat feature makes certain formatting changes automatically to your document. These formats include formatting a Web address, replacing ordinals (1st) with a superscript (1st) and fractions (1/2) with fraction characters (½), and applying a bulleted list format to a list if you type an asterisk (*) followed by a space at the beginning of a paragraph. These AutoFormat features can be turned off if the corrections are not needed in your document.

Because this is a document you plan to print, you do not want the text displayed as a link. Since the hyperlink was created using the AutoFormat feature, you can undo the correction or turn it off using the AutoCorrect Options button. You also can choose Remove Hyperlink from the hyperlink's context menu.

Additional Information

You can turn off the AutoFormat feature so the hyperlinks are not created automatically. To do this, open the File tab, click `Options`, and then choose Proofing, AutoCorrect Options. Next, open the AutoFormat tab and then clear the Internet and network paths with hyperlinks option.

Right-click on the hyperlink and choose Remove Hyperlink from the context menu.

Additional Information

A ScreenTip appears when you point to a hyperlink with instructions on how to follow a link.

Another Method

You also could click ⤺ Undo immediately after entering a URL to remove the hyperlink formatting.

Select all the text in the shape and, using the Mini toolbar, change the font color to black, font to Comic Sans MS, 12 pt, and bold.

If necessary, adjust the shape size as in Figure 2.58.

Click outside the shape.

Your screen should be similar to Figure 2.58

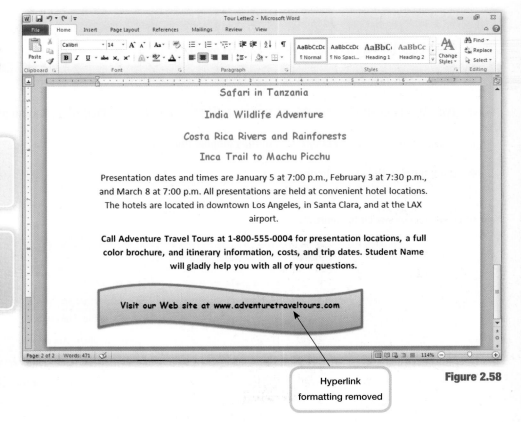

Safari in Tanzania

India Wildlife Adventure

Costa Rica Rivers and Rainforests

Inca Trail to Machu Picchu

Presentation dates and times are January 5 at 7:00 p.m., February 3 at 7:30 p.m., and March 8 at 7:00 p.m. All presentations are held at convenient hotel locations. The hotels are located in downtown Los Angeles, in Santa Clara, and at the LAX airport.

Call Adventure Travel Tours at 1-800-555-0004 for presentation locations, a full color brochure, and itinerary information, costs, and trip dates. Student Name will gladly help you with all of your questions.

Visit our Web site at www.adventuretraveltours.com

Hyperlink formatting removed

Figure 2.58

The Web address now appears as normal text and the font changes make the entire line much easier to read.

MOVING AN OBJECT

Finally, you need to center the shape at the bottom of the flyer. You will do this by dragging the object to the desired location.

Point to the shape and when the mouse pointer appears as 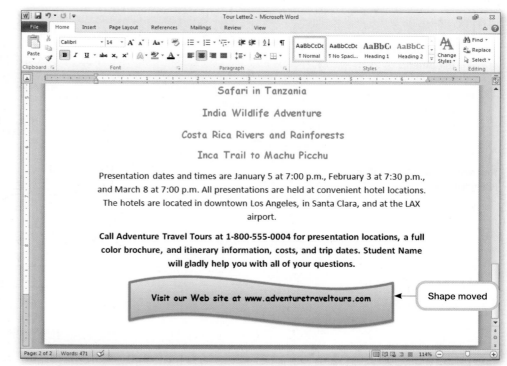 **, drag the shape to the position shown in Figure 2.59.**

Click outside the shape to deselect it.

Save the document again.

Your screen should be similar to Figure 2.59

Figure 2.59

The banner complements the colors used in the flyer and adds the needed information about the Web site.

Finalizing the Document

Next you will check out the layout of the document and make any final changes to the letter and flyer before printing it.

VIEWING THE ENTIRE DOCUMENT

First, you want to display both pages of your document at the same time in the window.

1

- **Move to the top of the document.**

- **Use the Zoom slider to reduce the zoom to 50%.**

Your screen should be similar to Figure 2.60

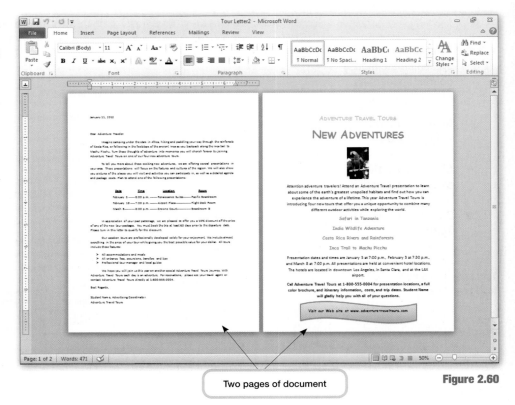

Two pages of document

Figure 2.60

Now that you can see the entire letter, you decide to indent the date and closing to the 3.5-inch tab position. You will select both these items at the same time and then change the indent. To select nonadjacent areas in a document, hold down Ctrl while selecting each additional area.

2

- **Select the date.**

- **Hold down Ctrl and select the closing.**

- **Drag the upper indent marker to the 3.5-inch position.**

Your screen should be similar to Figure 2.61

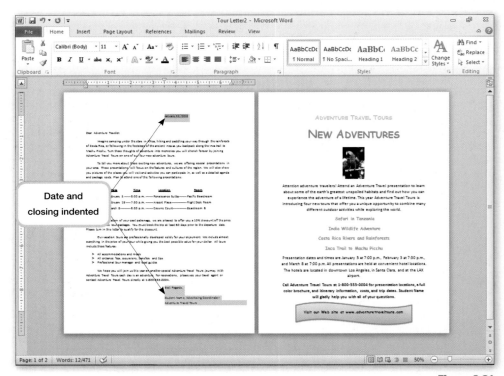

Date and closing indented

Figure 2.61

While looking at the document, you decide to emphasize the list of tour features by adding bold. You also want to decrease the space between the tour names in the flyer.

3

- Select the three bulleted items.

- Click **B** Bold on the Mini toolbar.

Having Trouble?

If the date at the top of the document moved back to the left margin, select the date and then repeat dragging the upper-indent marker to the 3.5-inch position.

- Select the list of four tours in the flyer.

- Decrease the spacing after to 6 pt.

- Click in the list to clear the selection.

Your screen should be similar to **Figure 2.62**

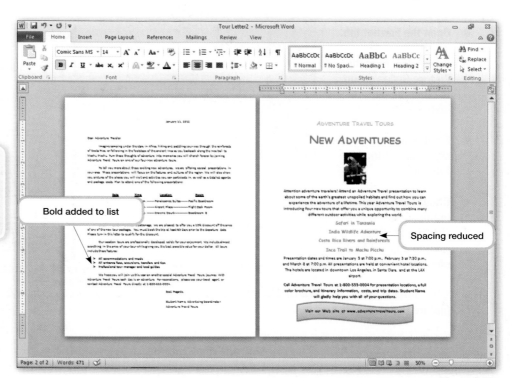

Figure 2.62

APPLYING A PICTURE STYLE

Additional Information

You can also customize many other individual aspects of a picture using the 🖌 Picture Border ▾ and 🖌 Picture Effects ▾ buttons on the Format toolbar. In addition, the Format Picture dialog box, which you can access from the picture's context menu, provides even more options for enhancing your pictures.

While looking at the document, you decide to enhance the picture in the flyer using a picture quick style. Picture quick styles let you easily change the appearance of a picture's border and apply special effects such as a shadowed or beveled edge.

- **Click on the parrot picture to select it.**

- **Open the Format tab.**

- **Click** ⬚ **More in the Picture Styles group to open the picture style gallery.**

- **Point to several of the styles to see the Live Preview.**

- **Choose the Simple Frame, Black style (fourth in the second row) to apply it to the picture.**

- **Click outside the picture to deselect it.**

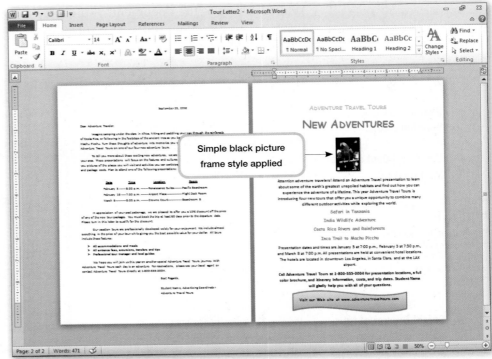

Figure 2.63

Your screen should be similar to Figure 2.63

The chosen picture style has improved the appearance of the flyer.

INSERTING A SECTION BREAK

You decide the document may look better if the margins for the letter are narrower. Many format and layout settings, including margin settings, when applied affect an entire document. To apply layout or formatting changes to a portion of a document, you need to create separate sections in the document by inserting section breaks.

Concept 10 Section

To format different parts of a document differently, you can divide a document into sections. Initially a document is one section. To separate a document into different parts, you insert section breaks. The **section break** identifies the end of a section and stores the document format settings associated with that section of the document. Once a document is divided into sections, the following formats can be changed for individual sections: margins, paper size and orientation, paper source for a printer, page borders, vertical alignment, headers and footers, columns, page numbering, line numbering, and footnotes and endnotes.

The three types of section breaks, described below, control the location where the text following a section break begins.

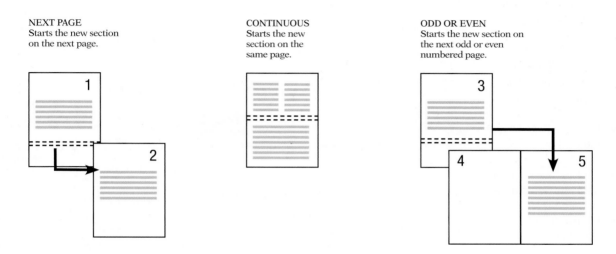

NEXT PAGE
Starts the new section
on the next page.

CONTINUOUS
Starts the new
section on the
same page.

ODD OR EVEN
Starts the new section on
the next odd or even
numbered page.

If you delete a section break, the preceding text becomes part of the following section and assumes its section formatting.

Because you do not want the new margin settings to affect the flyer portion of your document, you will divide the document into two sections. To do this, you will delete the Page Break code located at the bottom of page 1 and insert a Next Page section break at the same location.

- **Turn on the display of paragraph marks.**

- **Increase the zoom to 100% and then scroll to view the bottom of page 1 and the top of page 2.**

- **Position the insertion point to the right of the Page Break line at the bottom of page 1.**

- **Press** Backspace **to delete the Page Break.**

- **Open the Page Layout tab.**

- **Click** Breaks **from the Page Setup group.**

- **Choose Next Page from the Section Breaks category.**

- **Press** Delete **to delete the paragraph mark located at the top of page 2.**

Your screen should be similar to Figure 2.64

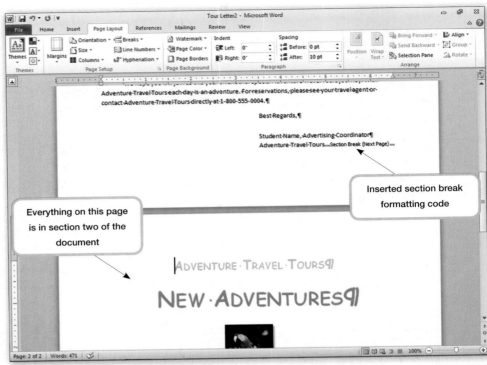

Everything on this page is in section two of the document

Inserted section break formatting code

Figure 2.64

A double dotted line and the words "Section Break (Next Page)" were inserted on the last line of the page 1, identifying the type of document break that was inserted. A section break, like a hard page break, can be deleted. The report now contains one section break that divides the letter into two sections. Each section can be formatted independently.

SETTING PAGE MARGINS

The default document setting for the left and right margins is 1 inch. You would like to see how the document would look if you decreased the size of the right and left margin widths for just the letter portion of the document (page 1). Because a section break appears at the bottom of page 1, you can format page 1 independently of page 2.

Concept 11 Page Margins

The **page margin** is the blank space around the edge of a page. Generally, the text you enter appears in the printable area inside the margins. However, some items can be positioned in the margin space. You can set different page margin widths to alter the appearance of the document.

Standard single-sided documents have four margins: top, bottom, left, and right. Double-sided documents with facing pages, such as books and magazines, also have four margins: top, bottom, inside, and outside. These documents typically use mirror margins in which the left page is a mirror image of the right page. This means that the inside margins are the same width and the outside margins are the same width. (See the illustrations below.)

You also can set a "gutter" margin that reserves space on the left side of single-sided documents, or on the inside margin of double-sided documents, to accommodate binding. There are also special margin settings for headers and footers. (You will learn about these features in Lab 3.)

Single-sided with gutter

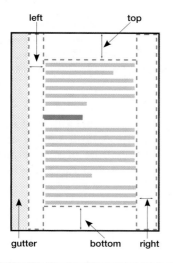

Double-sided with facing pages

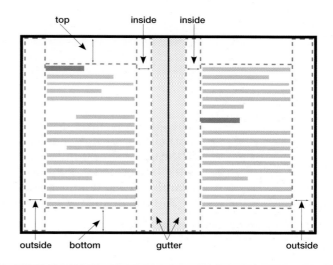

The Page Setup group is used to change settings associated with the layout of the entire page.

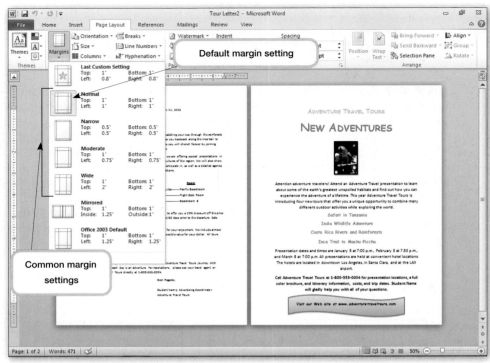

1

- Reduce the zoom to 50% and turn off the display of paragraph marks.

- Move the insertion point to anywhere on page 1.

- Open the Page Layout tab.

- Click [Margins] in the Page Setup group.

Your screen should be similar to Figure 2.65

Figure 2.65

The Margins drop-down menu displays several common margin setting options for a single-sided document, including the default setting of Normal. The Mirrored option is used for documents that will be printed double-sided with facing pages, such as a book. Additionally, if you have used a custom margin setting, it appears at the top of the menu.

You decide to try the Narrow option first.

Your screen should be similar to Figure 2.66

First page conforms to changed margin settings

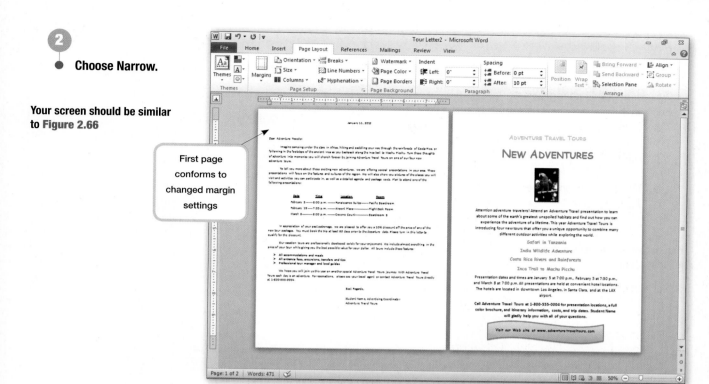

Figure 2.66

The first page of the document was reformatted to the narrow margin settings, however the second page remains unchanged. It remains unchanged because the margin setting affects only the current section, which in this case consists of page 1. If you hadn't inserted the section break in the last section, the entire document would conform to the narrow margin settings.

You do not like how this setting looks at all and will undo the change. Then you will create a custom setting to change the first page of the document to have 0.8-inch side margins. Custom margin settings are specified using the Custom Margins option on the Margins drop-down menu. You also can double-click on the margin section of the ruler to access this feature.

Additional Information

Use the Custom Margins option if you want the new margin settings to be saved for future use.

3

- Click ⟲ Undo to cancel this change.

- Double-click the margin section of the ruler.

- If necessary, open the Margins tab.

Your screen should be similar to Figure 2.67

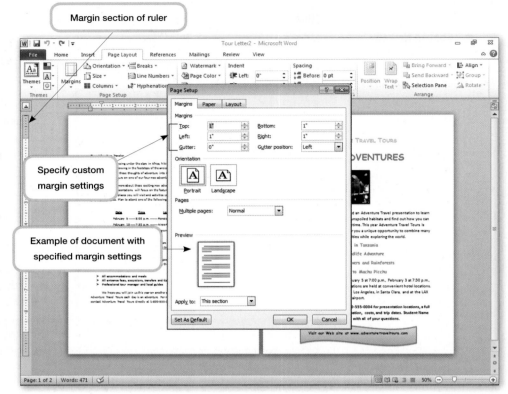

Margin section of ruler

Specify custom margin settings

Example of document with specified margin settings

Figure 2.67

The Margins tab of the Page Setup dialog box displays the default margin settings for a single-sided document. The Preview box shows how the current margin settings will appear on a page. New margin settings can be entered by typing the value in the text box, or by clicking the ▲ Up and ▼ Down scroll buttons or pressing the ↑ or ↓ key to increase or decrease the settings by tenths of an inch.

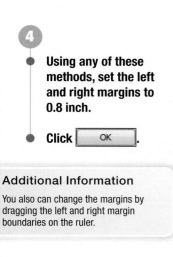

4 ● Using any of these methods, set the left and right margins to 0.8 inch.

● Click **OK**.

Additional Information

You also can change the margins by dragging the left and right margin boundaries on the ruler.

Your screen should be similar to Figure 2.68

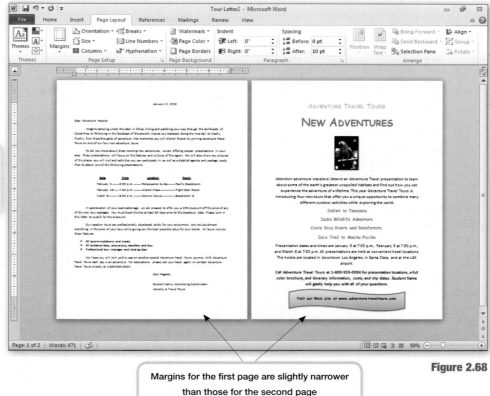

Figure 2.68

Margins for the first page are slightly narrower than those for the second page

Although the text is difficult to read, you can easily see the layout of the pages and that the margin settings for the first page have been narrowed slightly. The margins for the flyer have not changed. You are happy with the new settings.

ADDING A PAGE BORDER

Finally, you want to add a decorative border around only the flyer to enclose it and enhance its appearance.

1

- Click anywhere on the flyer.

- If necessary, open the Page Layout tab.

- Click 🔲 Page Borders in the Page Background group.

Your screen should be similar to Figure 2.69

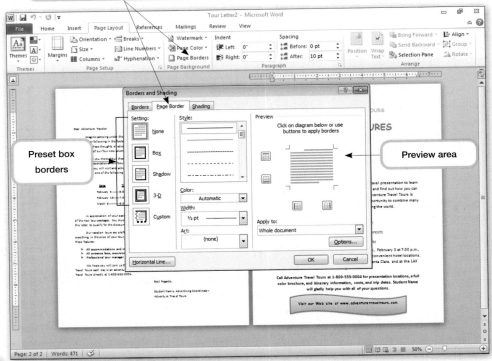

Opens Page Border tab of Borders and Shading dialog box

Preset box borders

Preview area

Figure 2.69

Additional Information

There are also a variety of graphical borders available in the Art drop-down list.

Additional Information

You will learn about creating custom borders in later labs.

From the Page Border tab of the Borders and Shading dialog box, you first select either a preset box border or a custom border. Then you specify the style, color, weight, and location of the border. A page border can be applied to all pages in a document, to all pages in the current section, to the first page of a section, or to every page except the first page of a section.

You want to create a box border around the entire page of text. As you specify the border settings, the Preview area will reflect your selections.

Choose Box in the Setting area.

Scroll the Style list box and select `─ · ─ · ─ · ─ · ─`.

Open the Color gallery and select Orange from the Standard Colors bar.

From the Width drop-down list box, choose 3 pt.

Your screen should be similar to Figure 2.70

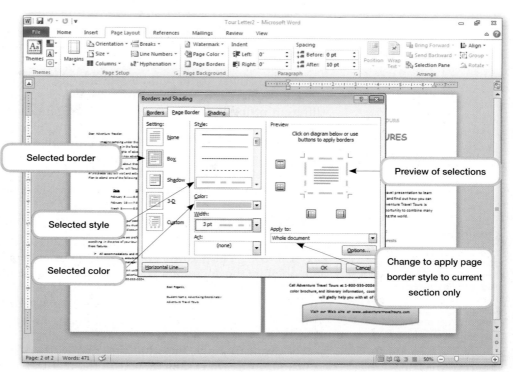

Labels in figure: Selected border · Selected style · Selected color · Preview of selections · Change to apply page border style to current section only

Figure 2.70

Having Trouble?

Use the None option to remove all border lines, or remove individual lines by selecting the border location again.

The Preview area shows how the box page border will appear in the style, color, and point size you selected. The default selection of Whole Document needs to be changed since you only want the border setting to affect page 2 of the document (the current section).

Choose "This section" from the Apply To drop-down list.

Click OK **.**

If necessary, reposition or resize the wave shape so that it is not touching the page border, and then click outside the shape to deselect it.

Save the document.

Your screen should be similar to Figure 2.71

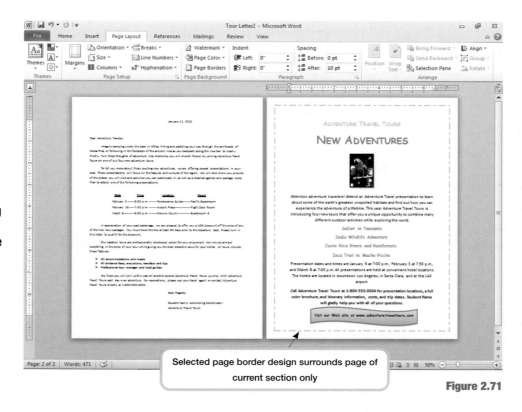

Label in figure: Selected page border design surrounds page of current section only

Figure 2.71

The selected page border appears only around the second page of the document.

Adventure Travel Tours will be offering presentations around the country in the cities where it has offices. Your Tour Letter2 document will be used by the different offices to promote upcoming presentations. A staff member in each ATT office will need to modify your document to include revised presentation dates and locations. Because this document will be distributed for use, you need to take several steps to prepare it. These steps include making sure that your file is compatible with the software versions used in the other offices, removing private information, and sending the file as an e-mail attachment.

SETTING FILE COMPATIBILITY

Although you created your file using Word 2010, some of the other ATT offices are still using Word 2007. Fortunately, your co-workers should have no problem opening the document you send them because documents in both versions of Word are saved by default to a file format defined by the ".docx" extension. However, it's possible that some of the Word 2010 features you've applied to your document won't either look the same or show up in the 2007 version of Word.

You want to make sure that those co-workers who are using previous versions of Word will be able to see all the features you've included in the document you send them. You will use the Compatibility Checker to find out. The **Compatibility Checker** lists any features that aren't compatible with the previous version of Word and the number of occurrences in the document.

Additional Information

When saving a file for the first time, Word may display a dialog box asking if you want to maintain compatibility with previous versions of Word. If you know in advance that you will be sharing your document with others who are using an earlier version of Word, you would click [Cancel] in this dialog box and then choose the Maintain compatibility check box. If you don't do this, some formatting features of your 2010 document may appear somewhat different in Word 2003 and 2007.

1

- **Change the zoom level to 100%.**

- **Open the File tab and click** **in the Info tab.**

- **Choose Check Compatibility from the drop-down list.**

Your screen should be similar to Figure 2.72

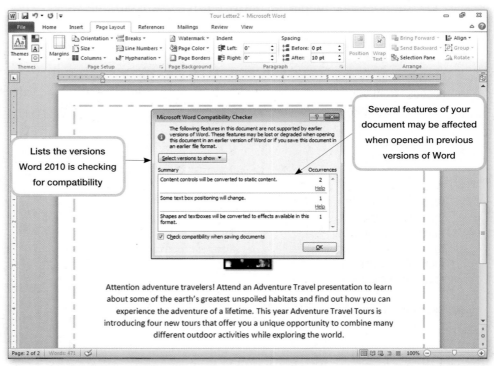

Figure 2.72

The Compatibility Checker lists several features of your document that may be affected. Before we look at these closer, let's see if these problems will affect Word 2007 users.

Click  **to open the drop-down list.**

Deselect Word 97-2003.

Your screen should be similar to Figure 2.73

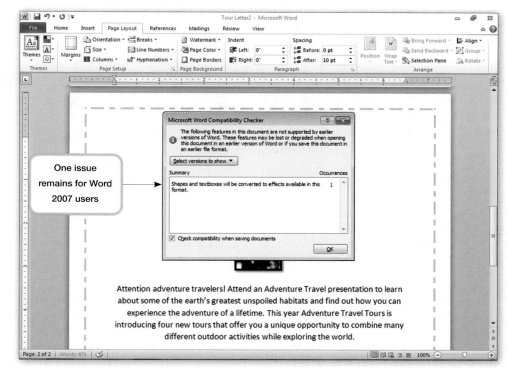

> One issue remains for Word 2007 users

Attention adventure travelers! Attend an Adventure Travel presentation to learn about some of the earth's greatest unspoiled habitats and find out how you can experience the adventure of a lifetime. This year Adventure Travel Tours is introducing four new tours that offer you a unique opportunity to combine many different outdoor activities while exploring the world.

Figure 2.73

3

Click OK **.**

The dialog box indicates that the shapes and textboxes in your Word 2010 document might not look exactly the same in Word 2007. As a result, the wave shape might appear somewhat different to your co-workers when they open your document in Word 2007.

CHECKING FOR PRIVATE INFORMATION

Before you give a file to another user, it is a good idea to check the document for hidden data or personal information that may be stored in the computer itself or in the document's properties that you may not want to share. To help locate and remove this information, you can use the Document Inspector.

Additional Information

It is a good idea to save a backup copy of a document before using Document Inspector, as it is not always possible to restore data that was removed by this feature.

1

Open the File tab and click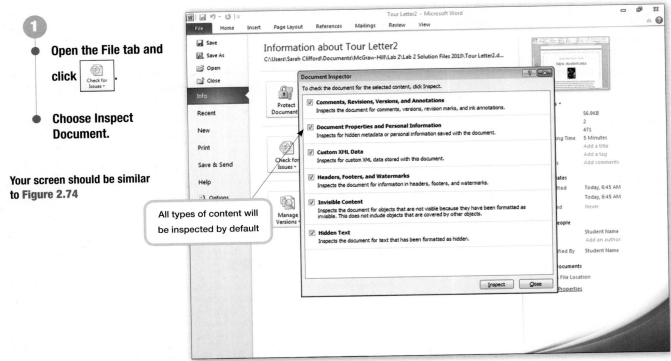

Choose Inspect Document.

Your screen should be similar to Figure 2.74

All types of content will be inspected by default

Figure 2.74

Using the Document Inspector dialog box, you can specify the type of content you want inspected by checking each of the types described in the following table.

Type	Removes
Comments, Revisions, Versions, and Annotations	Comments, tracked changes revision marks, document version information, and ink annotations
Document Properties and Personal Information	All document properties, including statistical information, e-mail headers, routing slips, send-to-review information, document server properties, content type information, user name, template name
Custom XML Data	All custom XML data that was stored within the document
Headers, Footers, and Watermarks	All information in headers and footers as well as watermarks
Invisible Content	All content that has been formatted as invisible
Hidden text	Any text that was formatted as hidden

You will inspect the Tour Letter2 document for all types of information.

2

- If necessary, select all six types of content to check.

- Click [Inspect].

Your screen should be similar to Figure 2.75

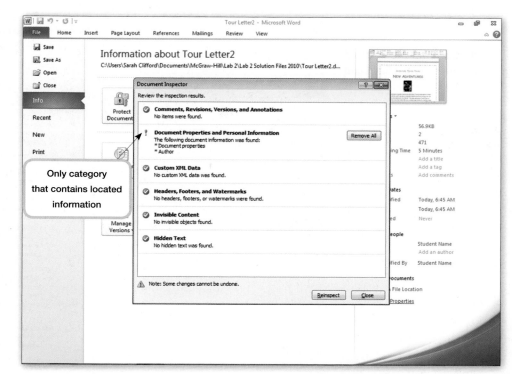

Figure 2.75

The Inspector results show that only Document Properties and Personal Information were located. For any located items, you have the option of removing the information. To remove any located information, you would click [Remove All] next to each item in the list; otherwise, the information is maintained. You want to maintain your name and the company name in the document properties and will close the Document Inspector without removing this information.

3

- Click [Close].

- Save the document.

NOTE Skip this section if you do not have an e-mail program installed on your system and an Internet connection.

SHARING A DOCUMENT

You will now send the document to your co-workers via e-mail.

1

● Open the File tab and
then choose Save and
Send.

**Your screen should be similar
to Figure 2.76**

Figure 2.76

Word provides several other options for sharing your document, as described
in the table below.

Save & Send Option	Description
Send Using E-Mail	Sends the document via your e-mail program.
Save to Web	Saves your document to a Web site so that you can access it remotely from another computer or allow others easy access to your document.
Save to SharePoint	Saves your document to a SharePoint Web site for easy collaboration with others.
Publish as Blog Post	Publishes your document to the Web as a blog post.

When using e-mail to share your document, Word provides several options. You can send the document as an **attachment**, which is a file that is sent with the e-mail message but is not part of the e-mail text. You can attach the document in a Word format using [Send as Attachment], in a PDF format using [Send as PDF], or in an XPS format using [Send as XPS]. The PDF and XPS formats allow others to view your document but not make changes to it. Alternatively, if your document is saved on a shared storage device, such as on a SharePoint server, you can include a hyperlink in your e-mail message that references your document using [Send a Link]. Finally, if you subscribe to an Internet fax service, you can choose to send your document as a fax using [Send as Internet Fax]. You will send your document as an e-mail attachment.

2

Click  .

Your screen should be similar to Figure 2.77

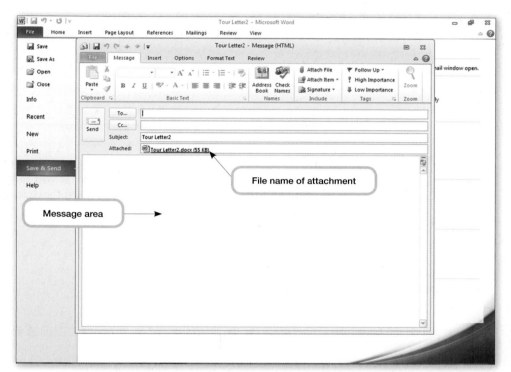

Figure 2.77

Having Trouble?

Your e-mail message window may look different than that shown in Figures 2.77 and 2.78 depending on the e-mail program on your computer.

An e-mail window is displayed in which you can address your e-mail message. Notice that the Subject and the Attached fields display the file name of the attached document. The extension indicates the application in which the file will open, which is helpful to know.

3

- In the To field, type your e-mail address.

- In the message area, type **Here is the document you can use to advertise your upcoming ATT presentations. I hope you have a good turnout!**

Your screen should be similar to Figure 2.78

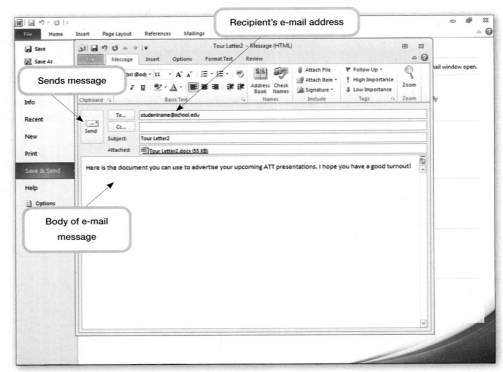

Figure 2.78

Now you are ready to send the message. If you have access to the Internet, you will send the message; otherwise, you will save it to be sent at a later time.

4

- If you have Internet access, click .

- If you do not have Internet access, save the message as Tour Letter2 E-Mail **to your solution files location.**

- Close the e-mail window.

- Close the Word document.

Having Trouble?

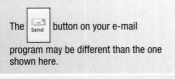

The [Send] button on your e-mail program may be different than the one shown here.

The recipient of the e-mail message will be able to open the attached file in Word 2010 or Word 2007 and view and make changes to it like any other document.

Preparing and Printing Envelopes

You plan to mail out the letter and flyer to the ATT clients in your area. Before doing this, you decide to see how Word's envelope feature works.

1

- Start a new blank document.

- Open the Mailings tab.

- Click 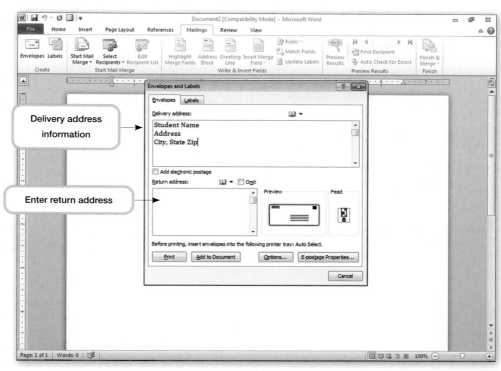 in the Create group.

- Type your name and address into the Delivery Address text box.

Your screen should be similar to Figure 2.79

Figure 2.79

Additional Information

You also can copy an address into the Delivery Address text box.

Additional Information

The Labels tab is used to create a mailing label rather than to print the address directly on the envelope. This feature is accessed by clicking Labels.

To complete the information for the envelope, you need to add the return address. Then you will check the options for printing and formatting the envelope.

2

● Type the following in the Return Address text box:

Adventure Travel Tours

1338 San Pablo Ave

Los Angeles, CA 90007

● Click [Options...].

● If necessary, open the Envelope Options tab.

Your screen should be similar to Figure 2.80

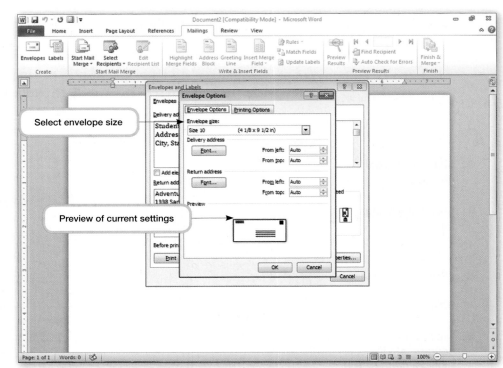

Figure 2.80

Additional Information

You can select other envelope sizes from the Envelope Size drop-down list.

Using the Envelope Options dialog box, you can change the envelope size and the font and placement of the delivery and return addresses. The Preview area shows how the envelope will appear when printed using the current settings.

The default envelope size 10 is for standard 8½-by-11-inch letter paper. This is the appropriate size for the letter. Next, you will check the print options.

3

● Open the Printing Options tab.

Your screen should be similar to Figure 2.81

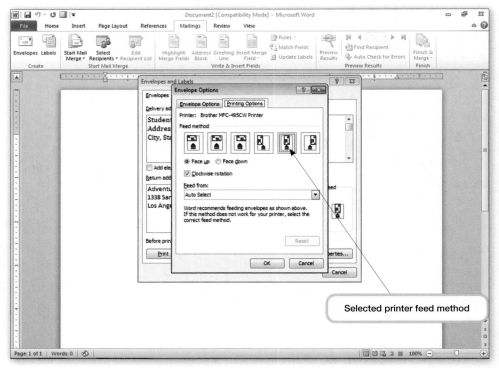

Figure 2.81

The options in this tab are used to specify how the envelope is fed into the printer. Word automatically selects the best option for the selected printer. You do not need to change any of the envelope options. If you were printing an actual envelope, you would need to insert the correct-size envelope in the printer at this time. However, you will simply print it on a sheet of paper.

● **Close the Envelope Options dialog box.**

Additional Information

Use Add to Document to add the envelope to the beginning of the active document so that you can print the envelope at the same time you print the document.

● **Click** Print **.**

● **Click** No **in response to the prompt to save the return address as the default.**

Additional Information

Responding Yes displays that address automatically whenever envelopes are printed.

● **Close the document window without saving it.**

● **Exit Word 2010.**

CUS ON CAREERS

EXPLORE YOUR CAREER OPTIONS

Assistant Broadcast Producer

Have you wondered who does the background research for a film or television broadcast? Or who is responsible for making sure a film production runs on schedule? Assistant producers are responsible for background research and the daily operations of a shooting schedule. They also may produce written materials for broadcast. These written materials are often compiled from multiple documents and sources. The typical salary range for an assistant broadcast producer is $30,000 to $40,000. Demand for those with relevant training and experience is expected to continue.

Thesaurus (WD2.9)

Word's Thesaurus is a reference tool that provides synonyms, antonyms, and related words for a selected word or phrase.

Page Break (WD2.17)

A page break marks the point at which one page ends and another begins. Two types of page breaks can be used in a document: soft page breaks and hard page breaks.

Find and Replace (WD2.20)

To make editing easier, you can use the Find and Replace feature to find text in a document and replace it with other text as directed.

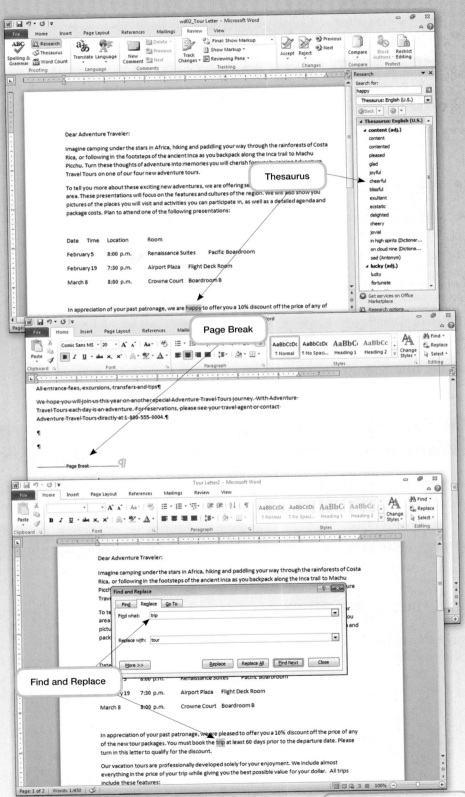

Field (WD2.28)

A field is a placeholder that instructs Word to insert information into a document.

Indents (WD2.32)

To help your reader find information quickly, you can indent paragraphs from the margins. Indenting paragraphs sets them off from the rest of the document.

Line and Paragraph Spacing (WD2.41)

Adjusting the line spacing, or the vertical space between lines of text and paragraphs, helps set off areas of text from others and, when increased, makes it easier to read and edit text.

Bulleted and Numbered Lists (WD2.48)

Whenever possible, add bullets or numbers before items in a list to organize information and make your writing clear and easy to read.

Sort (WD2.51)

Word can quickly arrange or sort text, numbers, or data in lists or tables in alphabetical, numeric, or date order based on the first character in each paragraph.

Quick Styles (WD2.58)

Applying a quick style, a predefined set of formatting options, allows you to quickly apply a whole group of formats to a text selection or an object in one simple step.

Section (WD2.67)

To format different parts of a document differently, you can divide a document into sections.

Page Margin (WD2.69)

The page margin is the blank space around the edge of the page. Standard single-sided documents have four margins: top, bottom, left, and right.

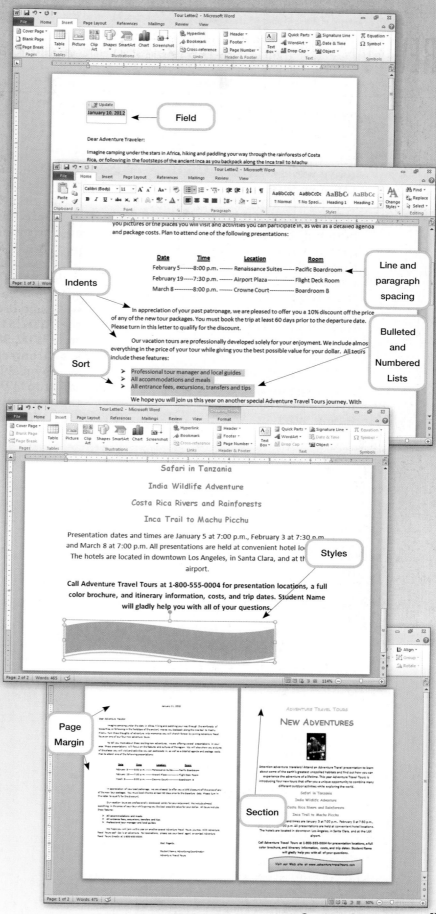

KEY TERMS

active window WD2.14
antonym WD2.9
attachment WD2.81
building blocks WD2.52
bulleted list WD2.48
case sensitive WD2.24
Compatibility Checker WD2.76
control WD2.53
field WD2.28
field code WD2.28
field result WD2.28
Find and Replace WD2.20
Format Painter WD2.47
gradient WD2.59
hard page break WD2.17
hyperlink WD2.60
indent WD2.32

leader character WD2.38
line spacing WD2.41
Navigation Pane WD2.21
numbered list WD2.48
outline numbered list WD2.48
page break WD2.17
page margin WD2.69
Quick Parts WD2.52
section break WD2.67
soft page break WD2.17
sort WD2.51
style WD2.58
synchronized WD2.14
synonym WD2.9
tab stop WD2.35
thesaurus WD2.9
URL WD2.60

COMMAND SUMMARY

Command	Shortcut	Action
File tab		
/Inspect Document		Checks your document for hidden data or personal information
/Check Compatibility		Checks your document for features that aren't compatible with previous versions
Save & Send/ Send as Attachment		Sends a document as an e-mail attachment
Home tab		
Editing group		
Find	Ctrl + F	Locates specified text
Replace	Ctrl + H	Locates and replaces specified text
Font group		
U Underline	Ctrl + U	Underlines selected text with single line
Paragraph group		
Bullets		Creates a bulleted list
Numbering		Creates a numbered list
Sort		Rearranges information in a list in alphabetical order
Increase Indent		Increases indent of paragraph to next tab stop
Decrease Indent		Decreases indent of paragraph to previous tab stop
Line Spacing	Ctrl + 1 or 2	Changes spacing between lines of text
Tabs...		Specifies types and positions of tab stops

LAB REVIEW

COMMAND SUMMARY (CONTINUED)

Command	Shortcut	Action
▣/Indents and Spacing/ Special/First Line	Tab	Indents first line of paragraph from left margin
▣/Indents and Spacing/ Line Spacing	Ctrl + 1 or 2	Changes the spacing between lines of text
Insert tab		
Pages group		
⊟ Page Break	Ctrl + Enter	Inserts hard page break
Illustrations group		
Shapes		Inserts graphic shapes
Text group		
Quick Parts ▾		Inserts Building Blocks
Date & Time		Inserts current date or time, in selected format
Page Layout tab		
Page Setup group		
Margins		Sets margin sizes
Breaks ▾		Inserts page and section breaks
Page Borders		Inserts and customizes page borders
Mailings tab		
Create group		
Envelopes		Prepares and prints an envelope
Review tab		
Proofing group		
ABC Spelling & Grammar	F7	Starts Spelling and Grammar Checker
Thesaurus	Shift + F7	Opens Thesaurus tool

COMMAND SUMMARY (CONTINUED)

Command	Shortcut	Action
View tab		
Window group		
Arrange All		Arranges all open windows horizontally on the screen
View Side by Side		Displays two document windows side by side to make it easy to compare content
Format tab		
Picture Styles group		
Picture Border ▾		Customizes a picture's border
Picture Effects ▾		Adds special effects to a picture

LAB EXERCISES

MATCHING

Match the item on the left with the correct description on the right.

1. leader character   ____ a. inserts a hard page break
2. synonyms   ____ b. placeholder that instructs Word to insert information into a document
3. [icon]   ____ c. arranges selection in sorted order
4. [Tab]   ____ d. changes line spacing
5. field   ____ e. copies formatting to another place
6. [icon]   ____ f. indents first line of paragraph
7. soft page break   ____ g. words with similar meaning
8. line spacing   ____ h. solid, dotted, or dashed lines between tab stops
9. [Ctrl] + [Enter]   ____ i. vertical space between lines of text
10. [icon]   ____ j. automatically starts a new page when a previous page is filled with text

TRUE/FALSE

Circle the correct answer to the following questions.

1. Styles are collections of formatting characteristics.   **True**   **False**
2. Indents are used to set paragraphs off from the rest of the text.   **True**   **False**
3. A sorted list conveys a sequence of events.   **True**   **False**
4. The thesaurus identifies synonyms for common words.   **True**   **False**
5. The Find and Replace feature is used to locate misspelled words in a document.   **True**   **False**
6. A hyperlink is a connection to a location in the current document, to another document, or to a Web site.   **True**   **False**
7. Draft view does not display graphics.   **True**   **False**
8. Soft page breaks are automatically inserted whenever the text reaches the bottom margin.   **True**   **False**
9. The Quick Parts feature can be used to quickly insert text and graphics.   **True**   **False**
10. By default the Find capability is case sensitive.   **True**   **False**

FILL-IN

Complete the following statements by filling in the blanks with the correct terms.

1. The _____ lets you see what features will be disabled in previous versions of Word.

2. Windows that are _____ scroll together.

3. Double-sided documents with facing pages typically use _____ margins.

4. _____ are reuseable pieces of content that can be quickly inserted in a document.

5. The _____ lets you check a document for hidden data or personal information that may be stored in your document's properties.

6. In a(n) _____ style letter, all parts are aligned with the left margin.

7. A(n) _____ is a gradual progression of colors and shades.

8. A(n) _____ code instructs Word to insert the current date in the document using the selected format whenever the document is printed.

9. As you add or remove text from a page, Word automatically _____ the placement of the soft page break.

10. Two types of page breaks that can be used in a document are _____ and _____.

LAB EXERCISES

MULTIPLE CHOICE

Circle the correct response to the questions below.

1. The information that is displayed as a result of a field is called a _____.
   a. field code
   b. field result
   c. quick part
   d. wildcard

2. Word includes preformatted content, called _____, that gives you a head start in cre-ating content such as page numbers, cover pages, headers and footers, and sidebars.
   a. drag and drop
   b. Format Painter
   c. building blocks
   d. AutoContent

3. To convey a sequence of events in a document, you should consider using a _____.
   a. bulleted list
   b. numbered list
   c. sorted list
   d. paragraph list

4. A _____ marks the point at which one page ends and another begins.
   a. leader character
   b. selection point
   c. field code
   d. page break

5. The _____ is a reference tool that provides synonyms and antonyms.
   a. find and replace feature
   b. research
   c. thesaurus
   d. clipboard

6. The blank space around the edge of the page is called the _____.
   a. gutter
   b. indent
   c. margin
   d. white space

7. _____ is a feature that applies the formats associated with a selection to another selection.
   a. Format Painter
   b. Find and Replace
   c. AutoFormat
   d. Format Designer

8. A predefined set of formatting characteristics is called a(n) _____.
   a. attachment
   b. margin
   c. style
   d. section break

9. The field _____ contains the directions that identify the type of information to insert.
   a. results
   b. code
   c. placeholder
   d. format

10. A _____ is a Web site address.
    a. URL
    b. RUL
    c. WSL
    d. ULR

LAB EXERCISE
Hands-On Exercises

STEP-BY-STEP

EXPANDING THE NOTE-TAKING SKILLS HANDOUT ★

1. You are continuing to work on the handout to supplement your lecture on note-taking skills and tips. Although the content is nearly complete, there are several more tips you need to add to the document. This handout is also going to be included in the freshman orientation information packet and needs to include formatting to make the document interesting and appealing to students. Your completed document will be similar to the one shown here.

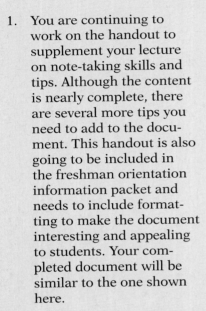

TIPS FOR TAKING BETTER CLASSROOM NOTES

Be Ready

- Review your assigned reading and previous notes you've taken before class.
- Bring plenty of paper and a sharpened pencil, an erasable pen or a pen that won't skip or smudge.
- Write the class name, date and that day's topic at the top the page.

Write Legibly

- Print if your handwriting is poor. Use a pencil or an erasable pen if you cross out material a lot so that your notes are easier to read.
- Take notes in one-liners rather than paragraph form.
- Skip a line between ideas to make it easier to find information when you're studying for a test.

Use Wide Margins

- Leave a wide margin on one side of your paper so you'll have space to write your own thoughts and call attention to key material.
- Draw arrows or stars beside important information like dates, names and events.
- If you miss getting a date, name, number or other fact, make a mark in the margin so you'll remember to come back to it.

Fill in Gaps

- Check with a classmate or your teacher after class to get any missing names, dates, facts or other information you could not write down.

Mark Questionable Material

- Jot down a "?" in the margin beside something you disagree with or do not think you recorded correctly.
- When appropriate, ask your teacher, classmate, or refer to your textbook, for clarification.

   a. Open the file wd02_Note Taking Tips. Spell-check the document.

   b. Use the thesaurus to find a better word for "gist" in the first tip.

   c. Open the document Note Taking Skills you created in Step-by-Step Exercise 4 in Lab 1. Display the document windows side by side. Copy the tips from the wd02_Note Taking Tips document to the end of the tips (before your name and date) in the Note Taking Skills document. Close the wd02_Note Taking Tips document without saving your changes.

   d. Use Format Painter to change the format of the five new headings to the same as the existing headings.

   e. Change the margins to Narrow. Change the space after paragraphs to 6 points for the entire document. Remove any blank lines between topics.

   f. Change the margins back to Moderate.

g. Break the tips under each topic heading into separate bulleted items using a variety of bullet styles of your choice. (A bulleted item may be more than one sentence if it contains an explanation or is a continuation of the same tip topic.)

h. Insert a hard page break before the Listen for Cues topic.

i. Delete your name and replace it using the Author quick part. Replace the date with a date field using a format of your choice.

j. Add the shape "7-Point Star" from the Stars and Banners category to the bottom of the document. Size the shape so that it fills much of the space at the bottom of the document.

k. Add the text Good Notes = Better Grades to the shape. Bold and size the text to 20 pt. If necessary, size the shape again to display the text on two lines.

l. Add a fill color to the shape and color to the text to complement the colors you used in the document. Center the shape at the bottom of the document.

m. Apply the shape style of your choice to the star.

n. Insert a black 3-point wide page border in a style of your choice around both pages of the document.

o. Add document properties. Save the document as Note Taking Skills2 and print it.

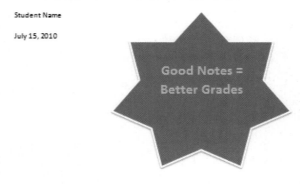

Listen for Cues

- Don't try to write everything down.
- Listen for cues from your teacher about what is important. When you hear "The reasons why…" "Here is how…" or a change in tone of voice, that indicates something noteworthy is about to be said.
- Write down dates, names, definitions, and formulas, and why they are important.
- Write down the meaning of any examples or stories your teacher gives when explaining a point or concept. These will help you remember the material.

Use Abbreviations

- Abbreviations let you write more quickly.
- To abbreviate, condense a word or phrase into initials, or use a symbol. For instance, use b/c for because; w/ for with; w/o for without; and govt for government.
- Always use the same abbreviations for the same words and phrases so you'll immediately know what they stand for.

Keep Organized

- Keep notes for the same class together, along with any handouts.

Check the Board

- ✓ When your teacher writes something on the board or projects it, that's a signal that the information is important. Copy everything down, and note that it was on the board.

Review and Highlight

- Go over your notes after class or after school while the lecture is still fresh in your mind.
- Complete any partially recorded noes and clarify any unintelligible sections as quickly as possible.
- Add information that will help you comprehend the material. Use a highlighter or a different color of ink to highlight, underline or circle important words and phrases.

Student Name

July 15, 2010

Good Notes = Better Grades

LAB EXERCISES

DOG PARK RULES ★★

2. You are a part-time city employee and have been asked to create a document that lists the rules dog owners must follow before using any of the city's 5 dog parks. You started the document a few days ago and you need to look it over and apply formatting. You also want to check the document to make sure others in your department who are using previous versions of Word will be able to open it for review. Your completed document will be similar to that shown below.

a. Open the document wd02_ Dog Park Rules. Spell- and grammar-check the document.

b. Replace all occurrences of the word "canine" with the word "dog".

c. Insert the current date on a separate line below the title using the Date and Time command. Pick the date format of your choice.

d. Select the title and date and change the spacing before and after the selection to 0 pt.

e. Center the title and date. Change the font to Arial Black with a point size of 24. Add a color of your choice to the title.

f. Select the remainder of the document and change the spacing before and after each paragraph to 6 pt.

g. Use the Format Painter to apply the same formatting from the title to the third line in the document describing the hours of operation. Change the font size to 14 pt. Increase the spacing after for this line to 24 pt.

h. Select the remainder of the document and change it to a numbered list using the numbering format of your choice.

i. Save the document using the file name Dog Park Rules.

j. Change the top and bottom margins to 1.25 inch. Change the right and left margins to 1.5 inch.

**Dog Park Rules
July 15, 2010**

Hours: Sunrise to Sunset

1) Dogs must be current on all vaccinations
2) Dogs must have a current dog license. Dogs should also wear an owner identification tag at all times.
3) Dogs must be leashed when entering and exiting the Dog Park.
4) Aggressive dogs are not permitted on the premises. Dogs must be removed at the first sign of aggression.
5) Dog owners must be in the park and within view of their dogs at all times.
6) All off-leash dogs must be under voice control of their owners. If you cannot control your dog off leash, keep your pet leashed at all times.
7) Dog owners must keep their leash in hand at all times.
8) Please do not bring dog food into the park.
9) Owner must clean up dog feces. Seal waste in the provided plastic bags before disposing in designated receptacles.
10) Fill any holes your dog digs.
11) Proof of a current rabies vaccination and license is required upon request of a police or animal control officer. Tags may serve as proof.
12) Failure to abide by the park rules may result in loss of privileges or owners may be ticketed.

**Follow the rules to help keep our dog parks safe!
Contact Student Name if you have questions.**

k. Insert the Double Wave shape at the bottom of your document. Size it to span the left to the right margin and apply the shape style of your choice.

l. Add the following text to the shape: Follow the rules to help keep our dog parks safe! Contact Student Name if you have questions. Increase the font size of the shape text to 16 pt. If necessary, change the size of the shape so that the text displays on two lines. Apply formatting, such as color and bold, of your choice to this line. Fill the shape with a gradient color.

m. Add a page border of your choice to the document.

n. Use the Document Inspector to check the document for hidden properties or personal information. Remove any items that are found.

o. Run the Compatibility Checker to see what items might be affected in previous versions of Word, and then close the dialog box.

p. Add document properties. Save, print, and then close the document.

PROMOTING NEW FITNESS CLASSES ★★

3. The Lifestyle Fitness Club has just started a new series of informal classes for the members and their families. You want to spread the word by creating a flyer for club members to pick up at the front desk. You have created a Word document with the basic information that you want to include in the flyer. Now you just need to make it look better. Your completed flyer will be similar to the one shown here.

    a. Open the file wd02_Fitness Fun.

    b. Find each occurrence of "class" and replace it with "Class" where appropriate. Be sure to use the match case and whole words only options. Find and replace all occurrences of "mins" with "minutes."

    c. Use the spelling and grammar checker to correct the identified errors.

    d. Save the document as Fitness Fun Flyer.

    e. Change the title font to Forte (or a font of your choice), 48 pt, and a color of your choice. Center the title.

    f. Center the introductory paragraph and set line spacing to 1.5.

    g. Use Format Painter to format the "Class Descriptions" heading the same as the title. Reduce the font size to 14 and left-align it. Add space before the paragraph.

Fitness Fun!

Need a break from the everyday stresses of life? Interested in exploring new and exciting activities with the whole family? Try one of Lifestyle Fitness Club's new informal classes. Come and dance with a spouse or friend. Spend some quality time with the kids. Or come alone and decompress.

Class Descriptions
Move to Movies
Soundtracks, movie clips, and scene participation make this course something special! Sing along, dance along, and act along to movie classics suitable for the whole family.

Tai Chi
An introduction to Chen style movements that are practiced slowly in a relaxed manner coordinated with deep breathing.

Families in Motion
An exercise class for the whole family, this course offers something for moms, dads, and kids.

Dads and Lads Class
This course is a father/son workout featuring batting and putting practice, plus strength training.

Water Dance
This truly unique workout is a graceful, low-impact course. Learn some of the basics of synchronized swimming under the stars.

Hip-Hop and Swing
Hip-Hop Dance instructors share the basics in this high-energy exciting class.

October Class Schedule

Day	Class	Time	Length of Class
Sunday	Tai Chi	6:30	60 minutes
Monday	Families in Motion	6:00 and 7:00	50 minutes
Tuesday	Water Dance	7:00	50 minutes
Wednesday	Dads and Lads	6:00 and 7:00	50 minutes
Thursday	Hip-Hop and Swing	7:00	50 minutes
Friday	Move to Movies	7:00	90 minutes
Saturday	Move to Movies	6:00 and 7:00	90 minutes

Student Name – September 25, 2012

Fun for the whole family!

LAB EXERCISES

h. Increase the font size of the rest of the document to 12.

i. Apply a different font to the eight class titles, plus bold and a color highlight.

j. Delete the class title and description for Beginning Ballroom Dance as well as the scheduling information (at the bottom of the document) because you do not have an instructor for this month.

k. Set the margins to Narrow.

l. Use drag and drop to move the Tai Chi class description below the Move to Movies description. Adjust the line spacing as needed between descriptions.

m. Create a tabbed table of the schedule. Add left tab marks at 1.5, 3, and 5 inches. Bold, add color, and underline the words only of the table heads: Day, Class, Time, and Length of Class. Move the tab marker from the 5-inch position to the 4.5-inch position for the entire table. Change the tab at the 3-inch position to a center tab stop at the 3.5-inch position. Add tab leaders of your choice between the columns of data. Add space after the heading line only of the tabbed table.

n. Above the table, add the heading October Class Schedule. Format it the same as the "Class Descriptions" heading. Insert a hard page break above the table heading.

o. Add the shape "Explosion 2" from the Stars and Banners section below the Line Dancing description at the bottom of page one. Add the text Fun for the whole family!. Bold and size the text to 12 pt. Add fill color and font color of your choice to the shape. Move and size the shape to fit in the bottom right of the flyer.

p. Delete the Line Dancing class title and description. Delete the hard page break.

q. Increase the left and right margins to 1-inch. Reposition and size the shape as needed.

r. Remove the color highlights from the class titles. Add a colored, 6 pt page border to the flyer.

s. Use the Document Inspector to check the document for hidden properties or personal information. Remove any items that are found.

t. Add your name using the Author quick part and the current date (as a field) on the last line on the page. Adjust the line spacing as needed to fit the document on one page.

u. Run the Compatibility Checker to see what items might be affected in previous versions of Word, and then close the dialog box.

v. Add a title to the document properties. Save and print the document.

ENERGY CONFERENCE ANNOUNCEMENT ★ ★ ★

4. The Energy Conservation Council is actively seeking volunteers to help with an upcoming conference on alternative energy sources. You are preparing the information that will appear on the Web site and the flyer that will be distributed to local businesses. Your completed document will be similar to the one shown here.

a. Open a new document and set the margins to Moderate.

b. On the first line, type the title ECC Needs Your Help!. Increase the font to 36 points and apply formats of your choice.

c. Several lines below the title, type the following paragraphs:

The Energy Conservation Council needs volunteers to help with our upcoming conference.

Registration and Hospitality

We need help at registration throughout the meeting, assembling packets several days prior to the meeting, and with answering questions and giving directions at hospitality tables.

Education: Session Moderators

We need help in preparing rooms for presentations, assisting and introducing speakers, collecting evaluation sheets, assisting with poster session.

Special

Events

We need help greeting, collecting tickets, loading buses and decorating.

If you are interested in serving in any of these areas, please contact:

[Your Name], Volunteer Coordinator at (800) 555-8023

ECC Needs Your Help!

The Energy Conservation Council needs volunteers to help with our upcoming conference.

Registration and Hospitality

We need help at registration throughout the conference, assembling packets several days prior to the conference, and with answering questions and giving directions at hospitality tables.

Education: Session Moderators

We need assistance preparing rooms for presentations, assisting and introducing speakers, collecting evaluation sheets, assisting with poster session.

Special Events

We need help greeting, collecting tickets, loading buses and decorating.

Volunteer Times Available

Day	Date	Time
Monday	May 8	10:00 AM to 1:00PM
Tuesday	May 9	7:00 PM to 9:00 PM
Saturday	May 13	10:00 AM to 7:00 PM
Sunday	May 14	9:00 AM to 4:00 PM

If you are interested in serving in any of these areas, please contact:

Student Name, Volunteer Coordinator at (800) 555-8023

Visit www.ecc.com for more information!

d. Spell-check the document. Use the thesaurus to find a better word for "help" in the Education: Session Moderators paragraph.
e. Find and replace all occurrences of "meeting" with "conference."
f. Save the document as Conference Volunteers.
g. Increase the font size of all the text in the document to 14, not including the title. Add bold and color to the three headings. Indent the paragraphs below each heading 0.5 inch.
h. Below the Special Events topic, enter the title Volunteer Times Available . Use the same formatting as the main title with a font size of 14 points, indented at 0.5 inch.
i. Below this heading, you will create a table describing when help is needed with upcoming special events. Place center tab stops at 1, 2.5, and 4.25 inches on the ruler. Enter the word Day at the first tab stop, Date at the second tab stop, and Time at the third tab stop.

LAB EXERCISES

j. Press (Enter), then clear the tab stops. Create a left tab at 0.75 and 2.25 and a right tab stop at 5. Enter the schedule information shown here into the table.

Monday	May 8	10:00 AM to 1:00 PM
Tuesday	May 9	7:00 PM to 9:00 PM
Saturday	May 13	10:00 AM to 7:00 PM
Sunday	May 14	9:00 AM to 4:00 PM

k. Apply the same color as the title to the table headings. Add an underline style of your choice to the table headings.

l. Create a shape of your choice and add the text Visit www.ecc.com for more information! using a font size of 12 points, and bold. Move and size the shape appropriately. Remove the hyperlink format from the URL. Add color to the URL. Apply a shape style of your choice to the shape.

m. Add document properties. Save and print the document.

ADVERTISING WEEKLY SPECIALS ★ ★ ★

5. In addition to monthly music concerts at the Downtown Internet Café, the owner wants to continue to bring in new and repeat customers by offering weekly specials. You want to create a flyer describing the coffee varieties and specials for the week. Your completed flyer will be similar to the one shown here.

a. Open a new document.

b. Enter the title Downtown Internet Cafe on the first line. Add four blank lines. Change the font of the title to Lucida Sans.

c. Enter Italian Market Reserve on line 4 followed by two blank lines.

d. On line 6, place a left tab stop at 0.5 and center tabs at 3.25 and 5.75 inches.

e. Enter the word Coffee at the first tab stop, Description at the second tab stop, and Cost/Pound at the third tab stop.

f. On the next line, clear all the tab stops and enter the rest of the information for the table shown below using left tabs at 0.5, 2, and 5.5.

Original	Our Signature Coffee! With Old World charm	$10.49
Decaffeinated	All the original has to offer—decaffeinated natural	$13.49
Reduced Caffeine	All the original has to offer with half of the caffeine	$13.49

g. Add tab leaders of your choice between the data in the table. Remove the space after each line in the table.

h. Right-align the first title line and change the font color to blue with a font size of 24 pt.

i. Center the text "Italian Market Reserve" and change it to blue with a font size of 20 pt.

j. Increase the font of the table headings to 14 pt. Add bold, color, and an underline style of your choice to the table headings.

k. Save the document as Weekly Specials.

l. Open the file wd02_Coffee Flyer. Display the document windows side by side. Copy the title and first two paragraphs and insert them above "Italian Market Reserve" in the Weekly Specials document.

m. Spell-check the Weekly Specials document. Use the thesaurus to find better words for "desire" and "giant" in the first paragraph.

n. Use Find and Replace to replace all occurrences of "java" with "coffee" (except the one following "high-powered").

o. Right-align the words Weekly Specials below the title. Use the same font as the title, change the font size to 24 points, and select a color of your choice.

p. Make the paragraph that begins with "Tired" bold, justified, and 14 pt, and set the line spacing to double. Add dark red color to the URL.

q. Increase the font size of the line above "Italian Market Reserve" to 16 pt. Center the text.

r. Copy the remaining paragraph from the wd02_Coffee Flyer document and insert it at the bottom of the Weekly Specials document. Include two blank lines between the table and the paragraph. Close the wd02_Coffee Flyer document.

Downtown Internet Café

Weekly Specials

Tired of brewing a wimpy cup of coffee that just doesn't have the punch you crave? Then point your Web browser to *www.somecoffee.com* for our huge sale, and have our high-powered java delivered right to your front door. You'll never buy bland supermarket coffee again.

Through January, take $2 off the regular coffee prices shown below.

Italian Market Reserve

Coffee	Description	Cost/Pound
Original	Our Signature Coffee! With Old World charm	$10.49
Decaffeinated	All the original has to offer – decaffeinated natural	$13.49
Reduced Caffeine	All the original has to offer with half of the caffeine	$13.49

You can also order online at *www.somecoffee.com* today, and get coffee delivered right to your door! But hurry, our sale won't last forever.

Student Name 7/15/2010

s. Bold and center the final paragraph. Remove the hyperlink format from the URL. Format the URL as italic and dark red.

t. Create the Explosion 1 shape from the Stars and Banners group. Enter the text Coffee Sale! and change the font size to a 22 pt. Add a fill color of your choice. Move the shape to the left of the title. Size the shape appropriately.

u. Adjust the line spacing and formatting of the document as needed to improve its appearance.

v. Add your name using the Author quick part and the current date (as a field) on a single line below the final paragraph. Left align this line.

w. Add the title "Weekly Specials Flyer" to the document properties. Save and print the document.

LAB EXERCISES

ON YOUR OWN

REQUESTING A REFERENCE ★

1. Your first year as a business major is going well and you are looking for a summer internship with a local advertising firm. You have an upcoming interview and want to come prepared with a letter of reference from your last position. Write a business letter directed to your old supervisor, Kevin Westfall, at your former position, R & A Publishing. Use the modified block letter style shown in the lab. Be sure to include the date, a salutation, two paragraphs, a closing, and your name as a signature. Spell-check the document, save the document as Reference Letter, and print it.

CELL PHONE RATES ★

2. MyRatePlan.com provides comparative pricing information for a variety of products. For example, it posts up-to-date rate information on cell phone rates and available minutes at each price break. Using your Web browser, go to myrateplan.com/wireless_plans and then type in your zip code. Scroll down to view the rates offered by different wireless carriers. Create a tabbed table of this rate plan information. Bold and underline the column heads. Add style 2 tab leaders to the table entries. Above the table, write a paragraph explaining the table contents.

Include your name and the date below the table. Save the document as Cell Phone Rates and print the document.

YARD SALE ★ ★

3. Create a flyer to advertise a yard sale you plan for Saturday morning. Include the following features on your flyer:
   - Different fonts in different sizes, colors, and styles.
   - Bulleted or numbered list.
   - Indents.
   - A shape with appropriate text.
   - A graphic.
   - A tabbed table with tab leaders.

Include your name as the contact information. Save the document as Yard Sale Flyer and print it.

WYOMING RELOCATION ★ ★

4. You work for the Department of Tourism for the State of Wyoming. You have been asked to produce a relocation packet to aid people planning to move to the state. This packet includes information on state history, the weather, geography, major cities, population statistics, and so forth. Research information on the Web about Wyoming and create a one-page fact sheet of your findings. Your completed project should include an introductory paragraph on relocation, graphics, a table with the average weather statistics, a bulleted list of attractions, and shapes. Include your name as the contact and save the file as Wyoming Facts. Print the file.

DOWNLOADING MUSIC ★ ★ ★

5. Your ethics class is studying the ethics of downloading free music from online sources. Your instructor has divided the class into groups and assigned each group a research project. Your group is to find out about court cases related to copyright infringement. Use the Web to research this topic and write a one-page report on your findings. Include a table of the data you found. Use other features demonstrated in this lab, including shapes, indents, bulleted lists, font colors, and so forth to make your report attractive and easy to read. Be sure to reference your sources on the Web for the data you located. Include your name and the current date below the report. Save the report as Ethics Report and print your report.

Creating Reports and Tables Lab 3

Objectives

After you have completed this lab, you will know how to:

1. Apply and customize quick styles.

2. Navigate by browsing headings and pages.

3. Create a cover page.

4. Apply and customize document themes.

5. Create and update a table of contents, table of figures, and an index.

6. Add citations and create a bibliography.

7. Add footnotes, captions, and cross-references.

8. Wrap text around graphics.

9. Create and format a simple table.

10. Add headers, footers, and page numbers.

Adventure Travel Tours

Adventure Travel Tours provides information on their tours in a variety of forms. Travel brochures, for instance, contain basic tour information in a promotional format and are designed to entice potential clients to sign up for a tour. More detailed regional information packets are given to people who have already signed up for a tour, so they can prepare for their vacation. These packets include facts about each region's climate, geography, and culture. Additional informational formats include pages on Adventure Travel's Web site and scheduled group presentations.

Part of your responsibility as advertising coordinator is to gather the informa-

tion that Adventure Travel will publicize about each regional tour. Specifically, you have been asked to provide background information for two of the new tours: the Tanzania Safari and the Machu Picchu trail. Because this information is used in a variety of formats, your research needs to be easily adapted. You will therefore present your facts in the form of a general report on Tanzania and Peru.

In this lab, you will learn to use many of the features of Word 2010 that make it easy to create an attractive and well-organized report. A portion of the completed report is shown here.

Adventure Travel Tours

Tanzania and Peru

La Costa

Occupying the slender area along Peru's western coastline, La Costa, p[...] between the mountains and sea. Although some of this area is fertile, m[...] and arid. This region's temperature averages approximately 68°F, and i[...] of rainfall annually. The Andes Mountains prevent greater annual precip[...] east. Some areas in the south are considered drier than the Sahara. Conv[...] areas in this region where mountain rivers meet the ocean that are green[...] the impression of being in a desert at all.

La Selva

La Selva, a region of tropical rainforest, is the easternmost region in Pe[...] eastern foot of the Andes Mountains, forms the Amazon Basin, into wh[...] The Amazon River begins at the meeting point of the two dominant rive[...] Marañón. La Selva is extremely wet, with some areas exceeding an ann[...] inches. Its wettest season occurs from November to April. The weather [...] extremely hot.

La Sierra

Inland and to the east is the mountainous region called La Sierra, encom[...] the Andes mountain range. The southe[...] some volcanoes are active today. La S[...] which is winter in that part of the worl[...] in some areas during the night. The we[...] precipitation. The former Incan capital[...] the Incas. This region also contains La[...]

Region	Annu[...] ([...]
La Costa	
La Selva	
La Sierra	

Table 1: Peru Climate

---

[2] Lake Titicaca is 12,507 feet above sea level.

Table of Contents

A cover page and table of contents listing can be created quickly using Word's built-in features.

Animal Life

Figure 2: Peruvian Flamingos

Peru is home to many exotic animals, but is particularly known for its large population of birds. More than 1,700 species can be found, including parakeets, toucans, and Amazon parrots. Many extremely rare families of birds also live here. Each geographical region of Peru boasts its own distinct habitat, and some types of birds cannot be seen anywhere else.

The popular Manu National Park spanning over 4.5 million acres of unbroken Peruvian rain forest is alive with several species of monkeys, the ocelot, alligators, boars, iguana, and the anaconda. It is also considered one of the best places in the world to spot the elusive jaguar. Both the squirrel monkey, named for its relatively small size, and the howler monkey, which is quite loud vocally, can be spotted throughout the rainforests. Piranhas populate many of the Amazon River basins and lakes. Though they are known to be vicious feeders, it is a common misconception that they are man-eaters; in fact, they will graciously share their waters with human swimmers. Also found in the remote Yarapa and Amazon Rivers is the mysterious pink dolphin, so named because of its striking pink hue.

Table of Figures

Tables, footnotes, cross-references, and headers and footers are many standard features that are quick and easy to include in a report.

Wrapping text around graphics, adding figure captions, and applying a document theme are among many features that can be used to enhance a report.

Works Cited

Camerapix, comp. Spectrum Guide to Tanzania. Edison: Hunter, 1992.

Country Studies US. Peru. 2003-2005. 16 March 2012 <http://countrystudies.us/peru/23.htm>.

Wikipedia: The Free Encyclopedia. Tanzania. 5 March 2010. 16 March 2012 <http://en.wikipedia.org/wiki/Tanzania>.

A bibliography can be quickly generated from cited sources.

The following concepts will be introduced in this lab:

1 Theme A theme is a predefined set of formatting choices that can be applied to an entire document in one simple step.

2 Table of Contents A table of contents is a listing of the topic headings that appear in a document and their associated page references.

3 Citations and Bibliography Parenthetical source references, called citations, give credit for specific information included in the document. Complete information for citations is included in a bibliography at the end of the report.

4 Footnotes and Endnotes Footnotes and endnotes are used in documented research papers to explain or comment on information in the text, or provide source references for text in the document.

5 Text Wrapping You can control the appearance of text around a graphic object by specifying the text wrapping style.

6 Captions and Cross-References A caption is a numbered label for a figure, table, picture, or graph. A cross-reference is a reference from one part of a document to related information in another part.

7 Table A table is used to organize information into an easy-to-read format of horizontal rows and vertical columns.

8 Table of Figures A table of figures is a list of the figures, tables, or equations used in a document and their associated page references.

9 Index An index appears at the end of a long document as a list of major headings, topics, and terms with their page numbers.

10 Header and Footer A header is a line or several lines of text in the top margin of each page. A footer is a line or several lines of text in the margin space at the bottom of every page.

Using Quick Styles

After several days of research, you have gathered many notes from various sources including books, magazines, and the Web. You have created a document using these notes; however, you find it difficult to read because all the text seems to run together making it difficult to identify topics.

APPLYING HEADING STYLES

You organized the report into two main topics, Tanzania and Peru, and many subtopics. You decide to use Full Screen Reading view to quickly look over the document and decide how to better differentiate the topics. This view initially displays two pages of your document on the screen side-by-side, as it would appear on the printed page.

- **Open the** wd03_ Tour Research **data file.**

- **Click** **Full Screen Reading (in the status bar).**

Another Method

Alternatively, you can switch to Full Screen Reading view by clicking Full Screen Reading on the View tab.

- **If necessary, click** **View Options** ▼ **(upper-right corner of page) and choose Show Two Pages.**

- **Click** ▶ **twice (lower-right corner of page) to move forward in the document.**

- **Click** ◀ **(lower-left corner of page) to move backward in the document.**

Another Method

In Full Screen Reading view, you can also press the Pg Up and Pg Dn keys, and the ◀ Previous Screen and ▶ Next Screen buttons in the Title bar.

- **Press** Pg Up **to view the beginning of the document again.**

Your screen should be similar to Figure 3.1

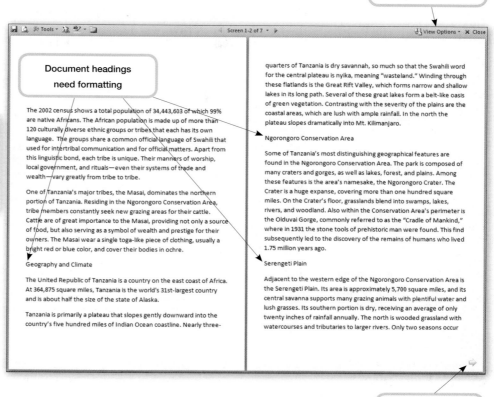

Opens View Options drop-down menu

Document headings need formatting

Moves forward through document

Figure 3.1

As you scrolled through the document, you may have noticed that the headings in the document could use some formatting to help identify where a new topic begins. Rather than apply individual sets of formats to the topic headings, you will use Word's **heading styles** to change the appearance of the different headings in your document to make them easier to locate. Heading styles are quick styles that consist of combinations of fonts, type sizes, color, bold, italics, and spacing. The heading styles that are associated with Word's default document settings and the formats associated with each are shown in the table below:

Heading Level	Appearance
Heading 1	Cambria, 14 pt, bold, left align, spacing 24 pt before, 0 pt after, blue
Heading 2	Cambria, 13 pt, bold, left align, spacing 10 pt before, 0 pt after, blue
Heading 3	Cambria, 13 pt, left align, spacing 10 pt before, 0 pt after, blue
Heading 4	Cambria, 11 pt, bold italic, left align, spacing 10 pt before, 0 pt after, blue

The Heading 1 style is the largest and most prominent and should be used for the main headings in your document. Subheadings are assigned the Heading 2 style, and so on. Headings give the reader another visual cue about how information is organized in your document. You will improve the appearance of the headings by applying quick styles.

2

- Click ☒ Close to exit Full Screen Reading view.

- If necessary, open the Home tab.

- Move to anywhere in the Tanzania main heading.

- Click ▾ More in the Styles group to open the Styles gallery.

Another Method

You also can scroll the list of styles.

Your screen should be similar to **Figure 3.2**

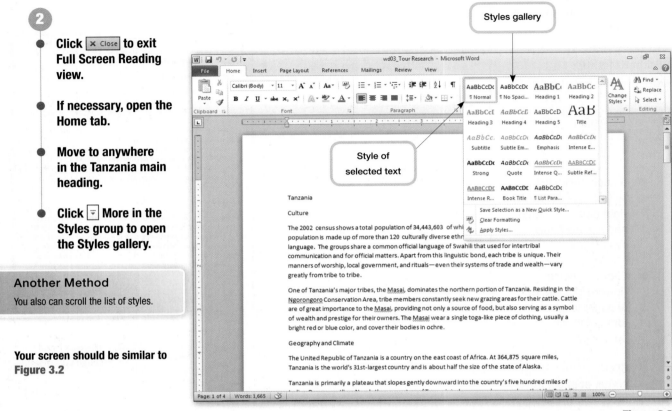

Figure 3.2

The Styles gallery appears with the current style of Normal for the selected text highlighted. Each quick style is named and displays a sample of the style above the name. The formatting of the different styles in the gallery reflects a selection of colors, fonts, and effects. When you point to a style, the document displays a Live Preview of how that style would appear if selected.

3

- **Point to several quick styles to see how they would look.**

- **Choose Heading 1.**

Your screen should be similar to Figure 3.3

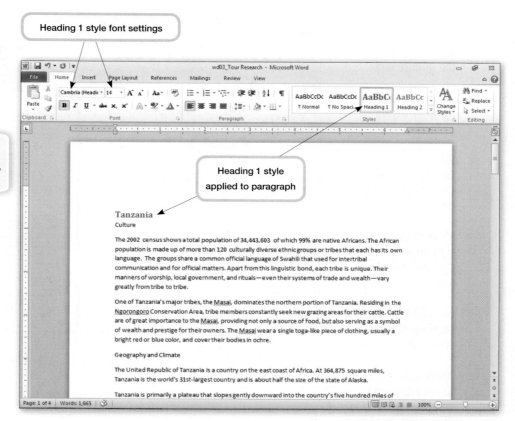

Figure 3.3

Notice that the entire title appears in the selected style. This is because the Heading 1 style is a paragraph style, affecting the entire paragraph at the insertion point. The Heading 1 style includes font settings of Cambria, 14 pt. bold in blue.

You will now apply heading styles to the remaining headings in the document. You can choose from the displayed quick styles in the Ribbon without opening the Styles gallery. You also can click ⊡ to scroll through the gallery.

4

- Move to anywhere in the Culture topic.

- Choose Heading 2 from the Styles gallery.

- Move to the Geography and Climate topic and choose Heading 2.

- Move to the Ngorongoro Conservation Area topic.

- Click ⊡ to scroll the Styles gallery and choose Heading 3.

- Apply heading styles to the remaining headings in the document, as shown below.

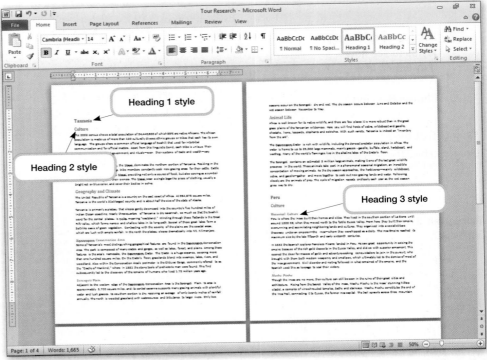

Figure 3.4

It's now much easier to identify the different topics of information in the document.

Serengeti Plain	Heading 3
Animal Life	Heading 2
Peru	Heading 1
Culture	Heading 2
Historical Culture	Heading 3
Machu Picchu	Heading 4
Current Culture	Heading 3
Geography and Climate	Heading 2
La Costa	Heading 3
La Selva	Heading 3
La Sierra	Heading 3
Animal Life	Heading 2

- Save the document as Tour Research

- Move to the top of the document and reduce the zoom level to 50%.

Your screen should be similar to Figure 3.4

UPDATING THE NORMAL STYLE

Another change you would like to make to the document to make it easier to read is to increase the font size of all the body text from 11 points to 12 points. The body text in your document is determined by the Normal style, which currently specifies an 11-point font. The easiest way to increase the point size of all the body text in the document is to first increase the point size of a paragraph of body text and then update the Normal style to match that text.

1

- **Increase the zoom level to 100%.**

- **Select the first paragraph below the Tanzania heading and increase the font size to 12 points.**

- **Right-click on the paragraph and select Styles from the context menu.**

- **Choose Update Normal to Match Selection.**

Additional Information

You also can change the style of a heading by choosing a new style from the shortcut menu.

- **Clear the selection.**

Your screen should be similar to Figure 3.5

Figure 3.5

All body text in the document that uses the Normal style has been immediately updated to the new font size of 12 points.

Navigating a Document

In a large document, locating and moving to an area of text you want to view can take a lot of time. However, after headings have been applied to different areas of a document, there are several features that can make navigation easier. As a help when scrolling by dragging the scroll box, a ScreenTip identifies the topic heading in addition to the page number that will be displayed when you stop dragging the scroll box. Even more convenient, however, is to use the Navigation Pane to jump to a selected location.

BROWSING BY HEADINGS

The Navigation Pane, which opens after you press Ctrl + F, or by clicking Find in the Editing group of the Home tab, lets you quickly view and browse document headings, expand and contract headings, change heading levels, and move topics.

1

- Press **Ctrl** + F to display the Navigation Pane.

- Click in the Navigation Pane to browse the headings in the document.

Your screen should be similar to **Figure 3.6**

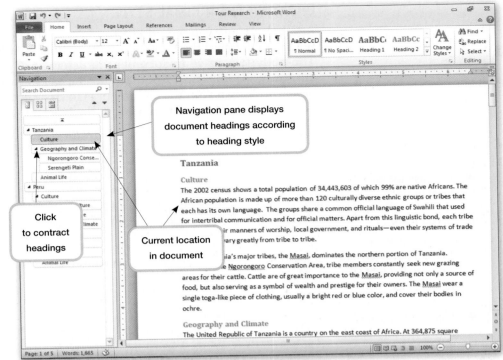

Figure 3.6

The Navigation Pane displays the topic headings you identified using heading styles. The headings are indented, as they would be in an outline, to show the different levels. The highlighted heading shows your location in the document. Clicking on a heading quickly jumps to that location in the document. Notice the ◢ symbol to the left of many of the headings; this symbol indicates that all subordinate headings are displayed. A ▷ symbol would indicate that subordinate headings are not displayed. Clicking these buttons expands or contracts the subordinate headings.

2

- Click the Peru heading in the Navigation pane.

- In the Navigation Pane, click ◢ in the Peru topic to contract the headings.

Your screen should be similar to **Figure 3.7**

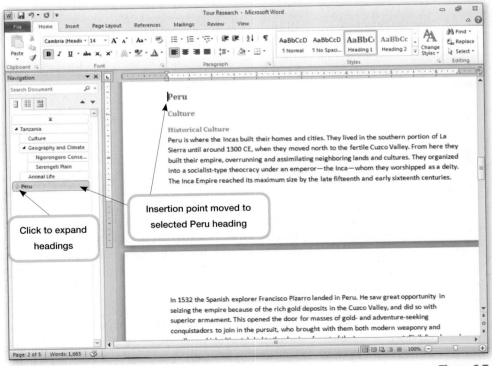

Figure 3.7

You quickly moved from one topic location in the document to another. The selected topic appears at the top of the window. Contracting the headings is particularly helpful when navigating a long document.

● Click ▷ again in the Peru topic to expand the headings.

Additional Information

You can also double-click a heading in the Navigation pane to expand and contract the headings.

● On your own, practice expanding and contracting headings.

● Expand all headings again so that your screen again looks similar to Figure 3.6.

Additional Information

There may be times that you want to change the level of a heading in your document. For example, you might want to turn a Heading 1 into a Heading 2 heading or vice-versa. To do this, right-click the heading in the Navigation Pane and then choose ⇦ Promote or ⇨ Demote.

As you look at the organization of the report, you decide to move the discussion of culture in the Tanzania section so that it follows the Geography and Climate section. Moving headings using the Navigation Pane quickly selects and moves the entire topic, including subtopics and all body text.

● Click the Culture heading in the Tanzania section and drag it down to above the Animal Life heading in the same section.

Additional Information

A solid line will display showing where the topic will be moved.

● Click the Culture heading in the Peru section and drag it down to above the Animal Life heading in the same section.

● Click the Culture heading again in the Peru section.

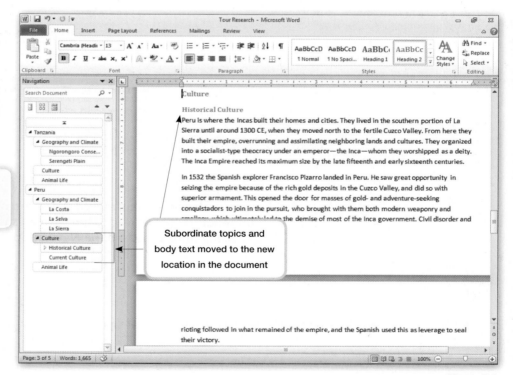

Figure 3.8

Your screen should be similar to Figure 3.8

In the Navigation pane, the subtopics appear below the heading you moved. When you move or change the level of a heading that includes subordinate headings and body text, the headings and text are also selected. Any changes you make to the heading, such as moving, copying, or deleting it, also affect the subordinate text.

BROWSING BY PAGES

The Navigation Pane also can display thumbnails of each page in your document. Clicking on a thumbnail moves directly to that page.

1

● Click 🔳 in the Navigation Pane.

● Scroll the Navigation Pane and click on page 4.

● Scroll again and click on page 2.

Your screen should be similar to Figure 3.9

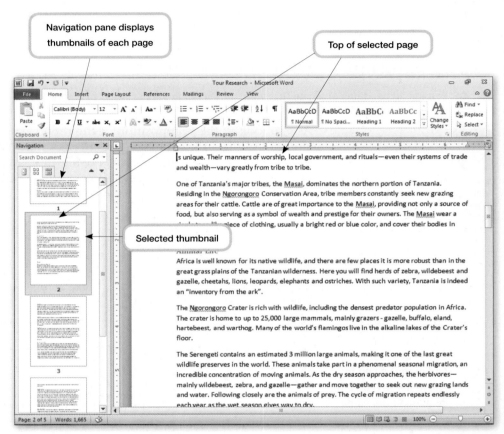

Figure 3.9

In the document, the cursor has moved to the top of the selected page and the selected thumbnail is highlighted. The Navigation Pane remains open in the view you are using until you close the Navigation Pane or close the document window.

2

● Click the thumbnail for page 1 and then close the Navigation Pane.

● Save the document.

Creating a Cover Page

Now that you have finished applying heading styles to your document, you want to add a title or cover page. Generally, this page includes information such as the report title, the name of the author, and the date.

When preparing research reports, two styles of report formatting are commonly used: MLA (Modern Language Association) and APA (American Psychological Association). Although they require the same basic information, they differ in how this information is presented. For example, MLA style does not include a separate title page, but APA style does. The report you will create in this lab will use many of the style requirements of the MLA. However, because this report is not a formal report to be presented at a conference or other academic proceeding, some liberties have been taken with the style to demonstrate Word 2010 features.

INSERTING A COVER PAGE

Word 2010 includes many preformatted building blocks that help you quickly create professional-looking documents. The preformatted content includes cover pages, pull quotes, and headers and footers. They are fully formatted and include placeholders where you enter the title, date, and other information. You will use this feature to insert a cover page. Regardless of the location of the cursor in a document, a cover page is always automatically inserted at the beginning of the document.

1

- **Open the Insert tab.**

- **Click** [Cover Page] **in the Pages group.**

- **Scroll the gallery and choose the Mod cover page design.**

- **Change the zoom to display two pages.**

Having Trouble?

Use the Zoom slider or [Two Pages] on the View tab.

Your screen should be similar to Figure 3.10

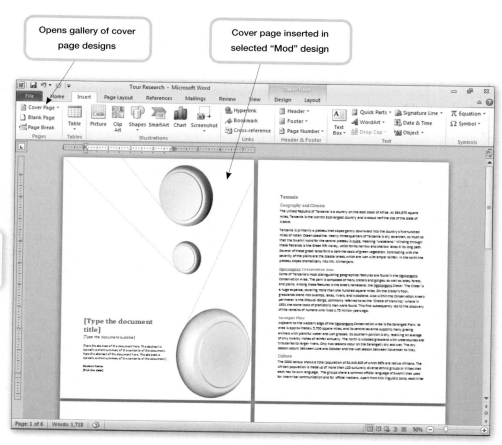

Opens gallery of cover page designs

Cover page inserted in selected "Mod" design

Figure 3.10

A new page is inserted at the beginning of the document with the selected cover page design. After looking at this design, you decide to change it to a more traditional cover page look.

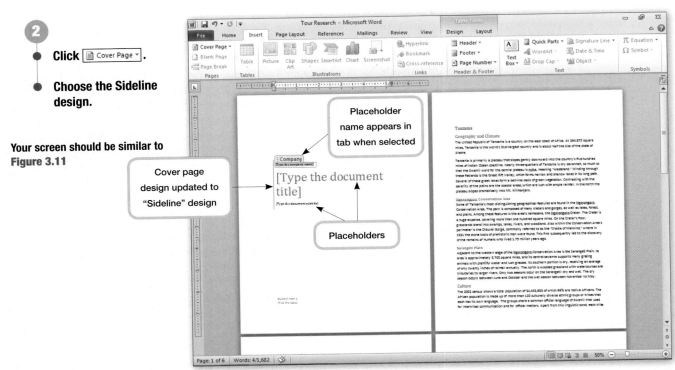

Figure 3.11

The new cover page design you selected replaces the first cover page you inserted. This design includes a blue vertical line to the left of the placeholders for the company name, document title and subtitle. The title text is a larger font size and blue. Additionally, the design includes the author and date information in blue at the bottom of the page.

MODIFYING A COVER PAGE

Next, you need to replace the placeholder text with the information you want to appear on the cover page. If the company name and document title have already been entered in the document properties, the placeholders will automatically display this information. When you click on a placeholder, the placeholder name appears in a tab and the placeholder text is selected and ready to be replaced. Currently the Company placeholder is selected. You will replace the Company and Title placeholder text.

1

- Increase the zoom to 80% and scroll the page so you can see both the report title and the author and date areas.

- Click the Company placeholder, if necessary, and type **Adventure Travel Tours**

- Click the Title placeholder and type **Tanzania and Peru**

Your screen should be similar to Figure 3.12

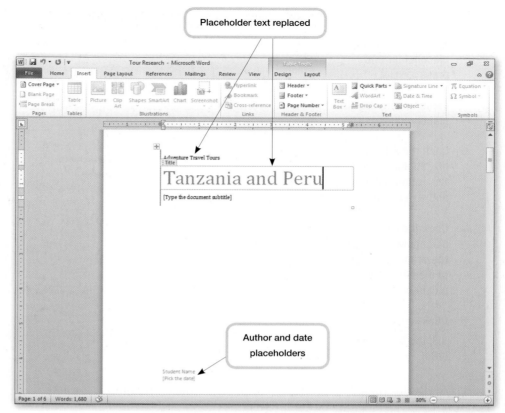

Figure 3.12

The placeholder text was replaced with the text you typed. Additionally, the company name and title information you entered have been automatically added to the document properties.

Finally, you will delete the Subtitle placeholder and add your name as author and the current date. Notice Student Name appears as the Author because this is the name that is stored in the document properties. Since the name is not placeholder text, you will need to select it before replacing it with your name. When you click on the date placeholder, you will use the date picker feature to quickly enter the current date from the pop-up calendar.

2

- Select the Subtitle placeholder and press Delete twice to delete the contents and then the placeholder.

- Click the Author placeholder, select the author name text, and enter your name.

- Click the Date placeholder and open the drop-down list to display the date-picker calendar.

- Click Today to display the current date.

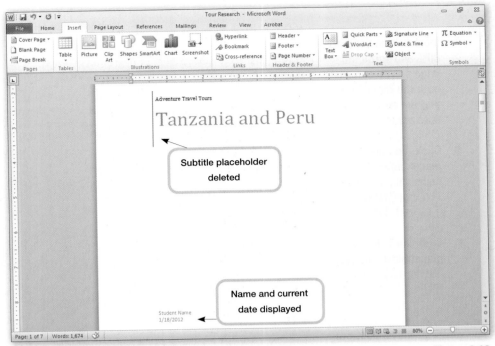

Figure 3.13

The cover page is now complete.

Additional Information

You also can click on a specific date in the calendar that you want and use the right and left arrow buttons to scroll through the months.

- Click outside the placeholder.

- Save the document.

Your screen should be similar to Figure 3.13

Using Document Themes

Because color and design are important elements of documents, Word includes a collection of built-in document themes.

Concept 1 Theme

A **theme** is a predefined set of formatting choices that can be applied to an entire document in one simple step. Heading styles and other effects available to your document are determined by the current theme. Word includes 40 named built-in document themes. Each document theme includes three subsets of themes: colors, fonts, and effects. Each color theme consists of 12 colors that are applied to specific elements in a document. Each fonts theme includes different body and heading fonts. Each effects theme includes different line and fill effects. You also can create your own custom themes by modifying an existing document theme and saving it as a custom theme.

The default document (Normal.dotm), which opens when you start a new Office document, uses the Office theme. If you change the current theme, style choices that you've previously made will be updated to match settings in the new theme. However, colors that you've selected from the standard colors gallery will remain the same.

Using themes gives your documents a professional and modern look. Because document themes are shared across 2010 Office applications, all your office documents can have the same uniform look.

APPLYING A THEME

You decide to see how the report would look using a different document theme.

1

- Change the zoom to display two pages.

- Open the Page Layout tab.

- Click ![Themes] from the Themes group.

Your screen should be similar to Figure 3.14

Figure 3.14

A gallery of 40 built-in named themes is displayed. A sample shows the color and font effects included in each theme. The Office theme is the default theme and is the theme that is used in this document. Pointing to each theme will display a Live Preview of how it will appear in the document.

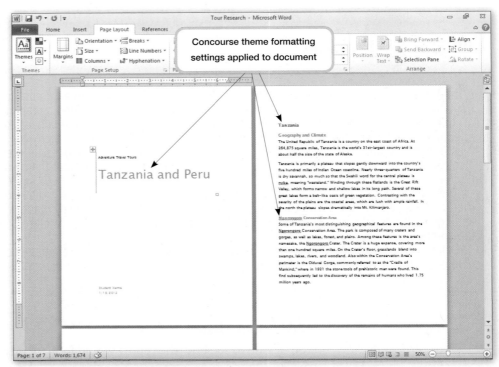

② ● Point to several themes to preview them.

● Choose the Concourse theme.

Your screen should be similar to Figure 3.15

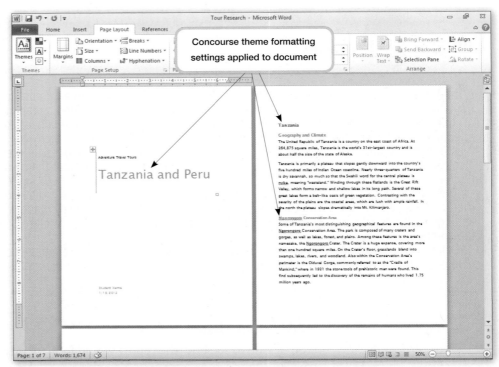
(inside figure) Concourse theme formatting settings applied to document

Adventure Travel Tours

Tanzania and Peru

Student Name
1-18-2012

Tanzania

Geography and Climate

The United Republic of Tanzania is a country on the east coast of Africa. At 364,875 square miles, Tanzania is the world's 31st-largest country and is about half the size of the state of Alaska.

Tanzania is primarily a plateau that slopes gently downward into the country's five hundred miles of Indian Ocean coastline. Nearly three-quarters of Tanzania is dry savannah, so much so that the Swahili word for the central plateau is nyika, meaning "wasteland." Winding through these flatlands is the Great Rift Valley, which forms narrow and shallow lakes in its long path. Several of these great lakes form a belt-like oasis of green vegetation. Contrasting with the severity of the plains are the coastal areas, which are lush with ample rainfall. In the north the plateau slopes dramatically into Mt. Kilimanjaro.

Ngorongoro Conservation Area

Some of Tanzania's most distinguishing geographical features are found in the Ngorongoro Conservation Area. The park is composed of many craters and gorges, as well as lakes, forest, and plains. Among these features is the area's namesake, the Ngorongoro Crater. The Crater is a huge expanse, covering more than one hundred square miles. On the Crater's floor, grasslands blend into swamps, lakes, rivers, and woodland. Also within the Conservation Area's perimeter is the Olduvai Gorge, commonly referred to as the "Cradle of Mankind," where in 1931 the stone tools of prehistoric man were found. This find subsequently led to the discovery of the remains of humans who lived 1.75 million years ago.

Figure 3.15

Additional Information

If you made manual changes to text, for example, by increasing the font size of the body text, or changing the font and font size of the title as opposed to applying a Title style, these changes are not updated to the new theme design.

The formatting settings associated with the selected theme have been applied to the entire document. The two obvious changes are the color and font changes for the titles and heading levels, and the increased line spacing. The font of all heading styles and body text has changed to Lucida Sans Unicode from the default of Calibri. The color associated with the different heading levels also has changed.

CUSTOMIZING A THEME

Sometimes, you cannot find just the right combination of features in a built-in theme. To solve this problem, you can customize a theme by changing the color scheme, fonts, and effects. Although you like much of the Concourse theme design, you decide to try customizing the theme by changing the color scheme and fonts. First you will change the color scheme. Each theme has an associated set of colors that you can change by applying the colors from another theme to the selected theme.

1

● Click 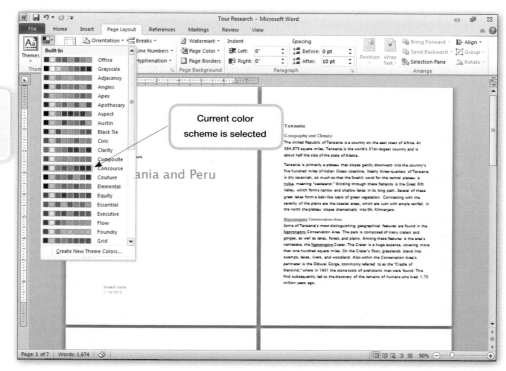 Theme Colors.

Additional Information

The colors you see in the Theme Colors button represent the current text and background colors.

Your screen should be similar to Figure 3.16

Figure 3.16

The colors used in each of the themes are displayed in the Built-In drop-down list. The set of eight colors that appears next to each theme color name represents the text, background, accent, and hyperlink colors. The Concourse color scheme is selected because it is the color scheme currently in use. You want to see how the Equity color scheme would look.

2

● **Point to several color schemes to preview them.**

● **Choose the Equity theme.**

Your screen should be similar to Figure 3.17

Figure 3.17

The new color scheme has been applied to different elements such as the headings. All other aspects of the Concourse theme are unchanged.

Next, you will change the theme fonts. Just like theme colors, you could change fonts by applying fonts from another theme to the selected theme. This time, however, you will specify your own font settings for the selected theme. Each theme contains a heading font and a body text font.

3

● Click A▾ **Theme Fonts.**

Additional Information

The name of the heading and body text fonts for each theme appears below the Theme Fonts name in the Theme Fonts gallery.

● Choose **Create New Theme Fonts.**

Your screen should be similar to Figure 3.18

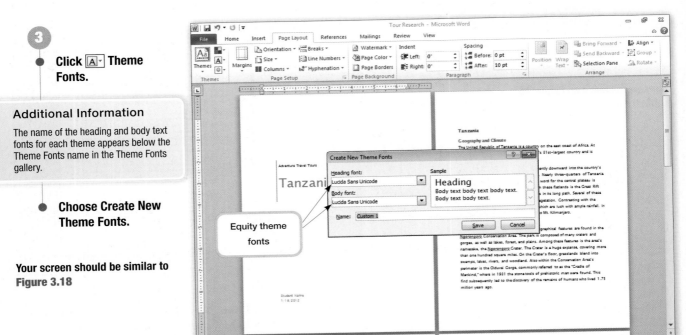

Figure 3.18

The fonts used in the current theme are displayed in the Heading and Body font text boxes. You will change the heading font to Constantia and the body font to Times New Roman.

4

- From the Heading font: drop-down list, choose Constantia.

- From the Body font: drop-down list, choose Times New Roman.

- Replace the default name with **Report Font**

- Click Save .

- Click ☐ Theme Fonts.

Your screen should be similar to Figure 3.19

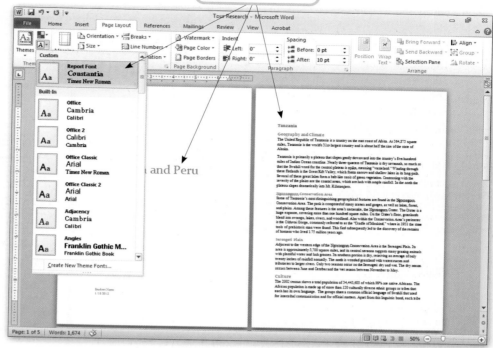

Figure 3.19

Additional Information

To remove a custom theme font, choose Delete from the custom theme font's shortcut menu.

The name of the custom theme font appears at the top of the Theme Fonts gallery list and could be applied simply by selecting it from the list. As you add other features to the document, they will be formatted using the customized Concourse theme colors and fonts.

SAVING A CUSTOM THEME

After making all these changes to the Concourse theme, you decide to save the changes as a custom theme. This will make it easy to reapply the same settings to another document in the future.

- **Click** 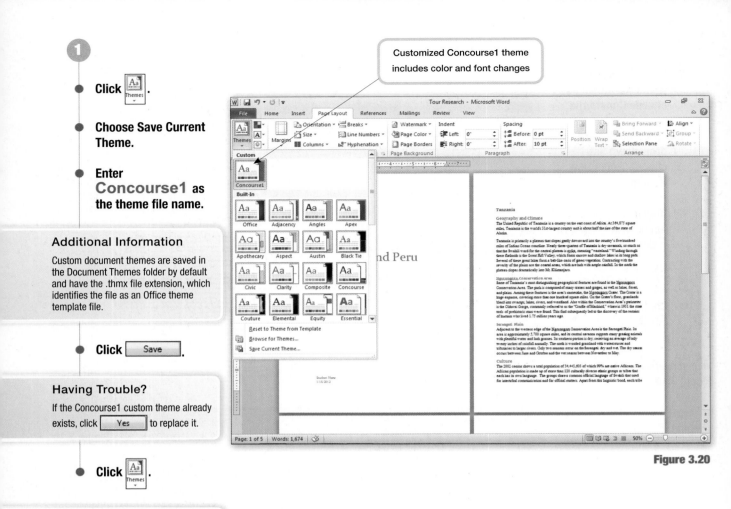.

- **Choose Save Current Theme.**

- **Enter Concourse1** as the theme file name.

Additional Information
Custom document themes are saved in the Document Themes folder by default and have the .thmx file extension, which identifies the file as an Office theme template file.

- **Click Save**.

Having Trouble?
If the Concourse1 custom theme already exists, click **Yes** to replace it.

- **Click** 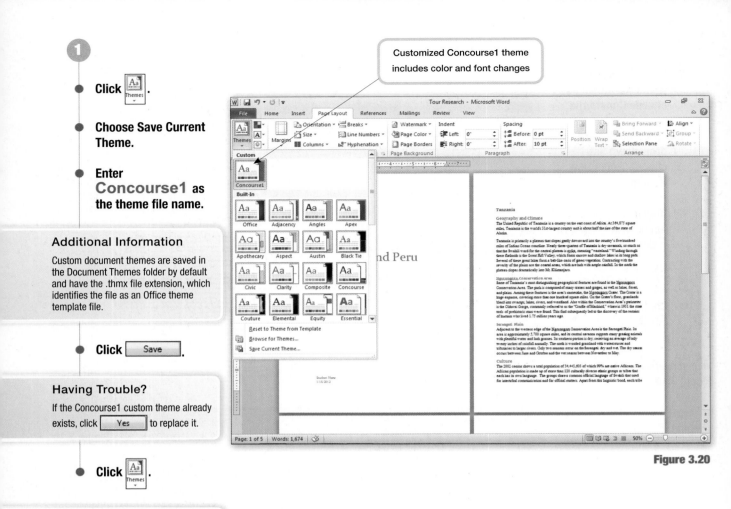.

Additional Information
To remove a custom theme, choose Delete from the theme's shortcut menu.

Your screen should be similar to Figure 3.20

Additional Information
You can quickly return a document back to the default style using Reset to Theme from Template on the 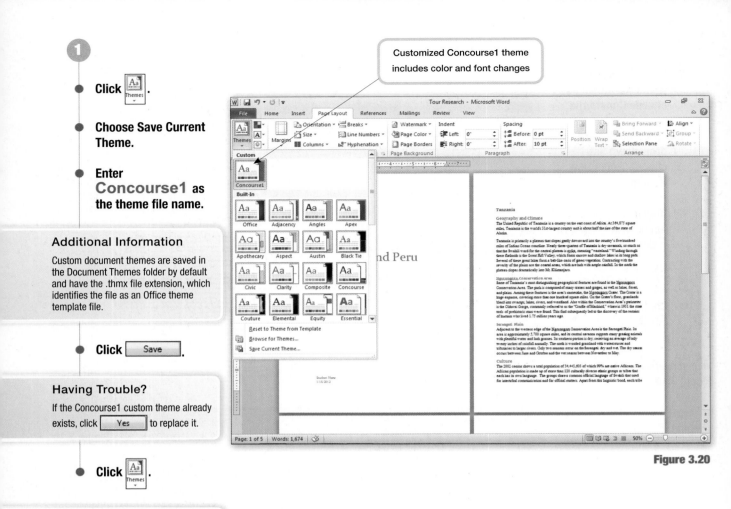 menu.

> Customized Concourse1 theme includes color and font changes

Figure 3.20

The custom theme you created appears at the top of the Themes gallery. Now you can quickly reapply this entire theme in one step to another document, just like the built-in themes.

Creating a Table of Contents

Now you are ready to create the table of contents.

Concept 2 Table of Contents

A **table of contents** is a listing of the topic headings that appear in a document and their associated page references (see the sample below). It shows the reader at a glance the topics that are included in the document and makes it easier for the reader to locate information. Word can generate a table of contents automatically after you have applied heading styles to the document headings. To do this, Word first searches the document for headings. Then it formats and inserts the heading entry text into the table of contents. The level of the heading style determines the table of contents level.

The table of contents that is generated is a field that can be easily updated to reflect changes you may make to the document after the list is generated. Additionally, each entry in the table is a hyperlink to the heading in the document.

INSERTING A BLANK PAGE

First you will create a new page to contain a table of contents. Then you will enter a title for the page and improve the appearance of the title by applying a style. You want the new page to be inserted above the Tanzania topic heading. Blank pages are inserted above the location of the cursor.

1

- **Move to the blank line above the Tanzania heading at the top of page 2.**

- **Open the Insert tab and click** ☐ Blank Page **in the Pages group.**

Another Method

You also could press Ctrl + Enter to insert a blank page.

Your screen should be similar to Figure 3.21

Inserts blank page above location of insertion point

Tanzania and Peru

Figure 3.21

Having Trouble?

If a second blank page is also inserted, change to Draft view and delete one of the hard page break lines.

A blank page has been inserted in the document at the location of the cursor, making the document six pages long.

Additional Information

MLA and APA styles do not use a table of contents.

GENERATING A TABLE OF CONTENTS

The report already includes heading styles to identify the different topics in the report. Now, all you need to do is select the style you want to use for the table of contents.

① **Move to the top of the newly inserted page (see Figure 3.22).**

● **Open the References tab.**

● **Click** in the **Table of Contents group.**

Your screen should be similar to Figure 3.22

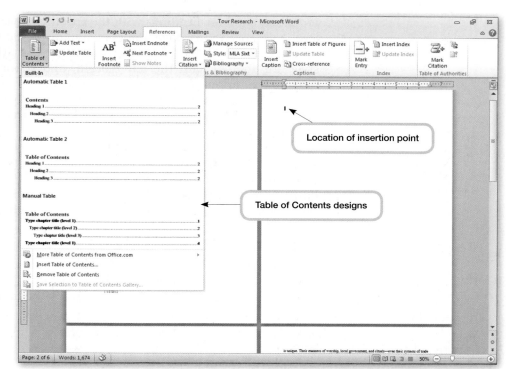

Figure 3.22

A gallery of three preformatted table of contents styles is displayed. The first two options automatically create a table of contents list using the Heading 1–3 styles in the document. The main difference between these two options is that the title used in Automatic Table 1 is Contents and in Automatic Table 2 it is Table of Contents. The third option, Manual Table, creates a table of contents that you can fill out independent of the content in the document.

② **Choose Automatic Table 2.**

● **Increase the zoom to 100% and then scroll upward to see the table of contents.**

● **Click anywhere in the table of contents to select it.**

Your screen should be similar to Figure 3.23

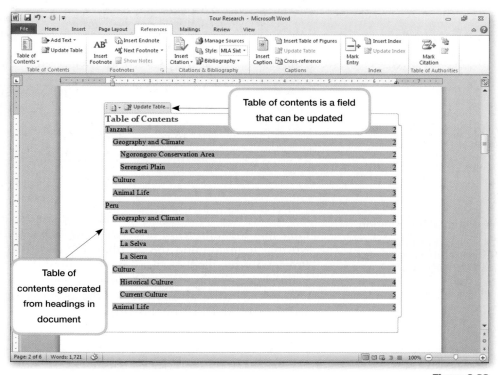

Figure 3.23

Word searched for headings with the specified styles, sorted them by heading level, referenced their page numbers, and displayed the table of contents using the selected style in the document. The headings that were assigned a Heading 1 style are aligned with the left margin, and subordinate heading levels are indented as appropriate. The table of contents displays the page numbers flush with the right margin with a dotted-line tab leader between the heading entry and the page number. It includes all entries in the document that are formatted with Headings 1, 2, and 3.

The table of contents is a field that is highlighted and enclosed in a box when selected. The field tab provides quick access to the Table of Contents menu by clicking [▤ ▾] Table of Contents and the [📄 Update Table...] command button. Because it is a field, the table of contents can be easily updated to reflect changes you may make to the document after the list is generated.

MODIFYING A TABLE OF CONTENTS

You want the table of contents to include topics formatted with the Heading 4 style also. Additionally, you want to change how the Table of Contents heading is formatted. To do this, you need to modify the table of contents settings.

1

● **Click** [Table of Contents] .

● **Choose Insert Table of Contents.**

Your screen should be similar to Figure 3.24

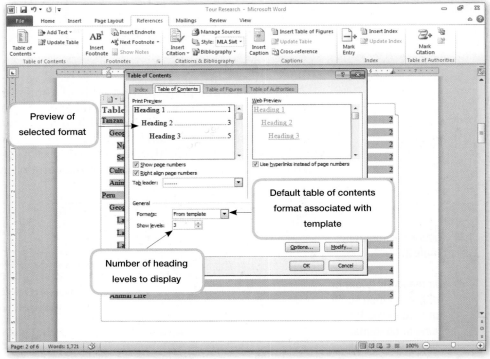

Figure 3.24

Additional Information

You also can create a new table of contents list directly from the Table of Contents dialog box.

From the Table of Contents dialog box, you select the format (style) of the table and the number of levels to show. The default style is determined by the Normal template and the number of levels to show is set to three. The two Preview boxes display an example of how the selected format will look in a printed document or in a document when viewed in a Web browser. You will change the format to another and the level to four. You also will apply the Title style to the table of contents title.

2

- Select Formal from the Formats list.

- Specify 4 in the Show levels: box.

- Click [OK].

- Click [OK] to replace the current contents list.

- Click anywhere in the title "Table of Contents" and apply the Title style.

Your screen should be similar to Figure 3.25

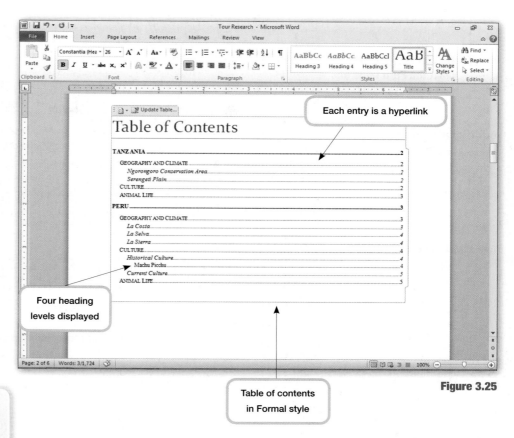

Each entry is a hyperlink

Four heading levels displayed

Table of contents in Formal style

Figure 3.25

Additional Information

To remove a table of contents, choose Remove Table of Contents from the

[Table of Contents ▾] menu or from the table of contents field's tab menu.

The table is regenerated using the new style and the one level 4 heading for Machu Picchu is now displayed in the table of contents.

USING A TABLE OF CONTENTS HYPERLINK

Additional Information

Pointing to an entry in a table of contents displays a ScreenTip with directions on how to follow the hyperlink.

Not only does the table of contents display the location of topic headings in the report, but it also can be used to quickly move to these locations. This is because each entry in the table is a hyperlink to the heading in the document. A hyperlink, as you have learned, is a connection to a location in the current document, another document, or a Web site. To use a hyperlink in Word, hold down [Ctrl] while clicking on the hyperlink.

1

● **Hold down** Ctrl **and click the Peru table of contents hyperlink.**

Your screen should be similar to Figure 3.26

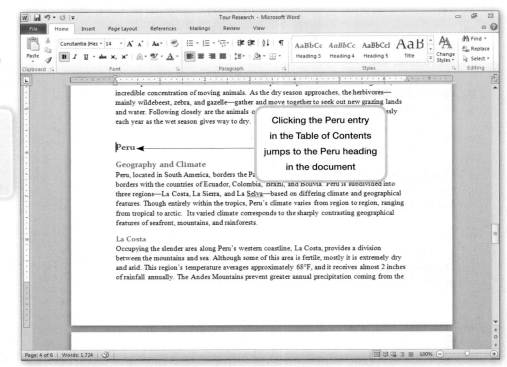

Figure 3.26

The cursor jumps to the Peru heading in the document. Now, however, the table of contents is no longer visible. If you wanted to jump to a different topic, you would need to return to the table of contents page and select another hyperlink or use the Navigation pane.

CREATING A CUSTOM QUICK STYLE

Although the Title style you applied to the table of contents title looks good, you decide instead that you want the title to be the same color as the title on the cover page. To do this, you will modify the Title style and then save the modified design as a custom quick style so you can quickly apply the style in the future.

1

- Display the Table of Contents page again.

- Right-click the Table of Contents title and select Styles.

- Choose Save Selection as a New Quick Style from the submenu.

- Click Modify... from the Create New Style from Formatting dialog box.

Your screen should be similar to Figure 3.27

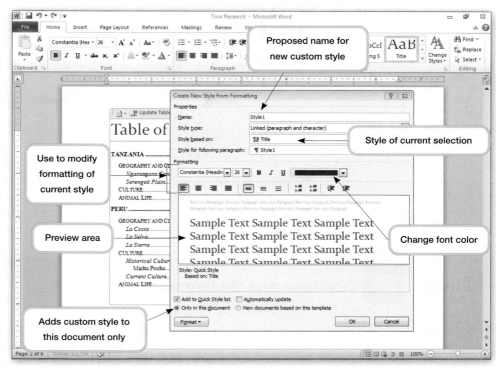

Figure 3.27

The Create New Style from Formatting dialog box displays the settings associated with the current selection. You will change the font color associated with the Title style and then give the custom style a descriptive name. The options to add the new style to the quick style list for this document only are appropriately selected. The preview area will show you how your selections will look.

2

- Open the Font Color drop-down menu and choose the Orange, Accent 1 theme color.

- In the Name text box, replace the default name with **TOC Title**

- Click OK .

- Save the document.

Your screen should be similar to Figure 3.28

Figure 3.28

Creating a Table of Contents **WD3.29**

The new TOC Title style is applied to the selection and added to the gallery of quick styles. If you ever need to change a style back to the default document style, you can easily clear the style by moving to the text whose style you want removed and choosing Clear Formatting from the Style gallery or clicking Clear Formatting in the Font group.

Including Source References

Documented research papers typically provide credit for the sources of information that were used in developing the document. These sources are cited both within the text of the document and in a bibliography.

Concept ③ Citations and Bibliography

Parenthetical source references, called **citations**, give credit for specific information included in the document. Complete source information for citations is included in a **bibliography** at the end of the report. Citations and bibliographies must be entered using the appropriate reference style, such as MLA or APA style. Word includes a feature that will automatically format citations and bibliographies according to different reference styles. This saves you the time it would take to learn the style from the documentation manuals, and of entering the citations and bibliographies using the correct format.

As you insert citations, Word asks for the bibliography information for each source. Once a source is created, it is stored in two places: a Master List and a Current List. The Master List is a database of all sources ever created. The Current List includes all of the sources that will be used in the current document. The purpose of the Master List is to save you from retyping and reentering information about sources that you commonly use. This is because you can select and copy sources in your Master List to add them to your Current List.

Word uses the information in the Current List to quickly generate a complete bibliographic list (similar to the sample shown here) of the information for each source according to the selected reference style.

Works Cited

Camerapix. Spectrum Guide to Tanzania. Edison: Hunter, 1992.

Country Studies US. Peru. 2003-2005. 16 March 2012 <http://countrystudies.us/peru/23.htm>.

Wikipedia: The Free Encyclopedia. Tanzania. 5 March 2010. 16 March 2012 <http://en.wikipedia.org/wiki/Tanzania>.

Both citations and bibliography entries are inserted as fields in the document. This means that any changes you may make to the source information is automatically updated in both the citation and the bibliography.

Additional Information

Changing reference styles allows you to repurpose documents to be submitted to a number of publications requiring different reference standards.

SELECTING A REFERENCE STYLE

You have been following the MLA reference style guidelines for this report and will specify the MLA reference style before you begin inserting citations. You can change the reference style at any point while working on your document and your citations and bibliography will be automatically updated to reflect the new style.

● **Open the References tab.**

● **Open the** Style: APA Fifth **drop-down list in the Citations and Bibliography group.**

● **Choose MLA Sixth Edition from the drop-down list.**

Having Trouble?

If the drop down list does not include MLA Sixth Edition, choose any MLA reference style listed.

Now, as you enter citations and create a bibliography, they will be formatted using the MLA style guidelines.

CREATING CITATIONS

Research papers using the MLA style require citations to include the author's last name and a page number or range within parentheses. The first citation that needs to be included in the document is to credit the source of the geography statistics about Tanzania. The source of this information was from the Wikipedia Web site.

To create a citation, you first need to move to the end of the sentence or phrase in the document that contains the information you want to cite. Then you enter the bibliography information for the source.

1

- **Open the Navigation Pane and display the document headings.**

- **Click the Tanzania Geography and Climate heading.**

- **Move to the end of the first paragraph (before the period) of the Geography and Climate section.**

- **Open the References tab, if necessary, and click** 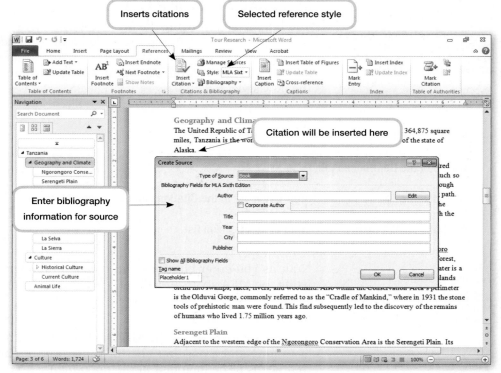 **in the Citations and Bibliography group.**

- **Choose Add New Source.**

Your screen should be similar to **Figure 3.29**

Figure 3.29

Additional Information

Word includes the capability to search an external library through the Research and Reference pane to locate data and import it with one click. The source information is automatically entered in the Create Source form for you.

In the Create Source dialog box, you first select the type of source, for example, a book, a journal article, or a Web site. Then you enter the bibliography information for the source in the appropriate text boxes for the selected source type.

2

• Choose Web site as the type of source.

• Enter the following in the appropriate locations to complete the bibliography information for this citation.

Author	**Wikipedia**
Name of Web Page	**Tanzania**
Year	**2010**
Month	**March**
Day	**5**
Year Accessed	**Enter the current year**
Month Accessed	**Enter the current month**
Day Accessed	**Enter the current day**
URL	**http://en.wikipedia.org/wiki/Tanzania**

• Click **OK**.

Your screen should be similar to Figure 3.30

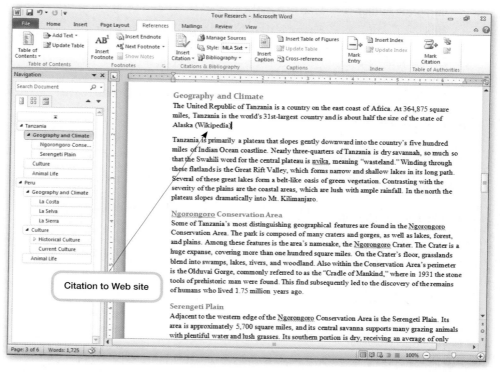

Figure 3.30

The citation is inserted at the location of the insertion point. It is a field that is linked to the source information. The source information is now stored in both the Master List and the Current List.

The next citation is also to the Wikipedia Web site. Once source information has been specified, it is easy to insert the citation again. This is because the Insert Citation drop-down menu displays a brief bibliographic entry for each source in the Current List. You will insert another citation for the same source in the report and then you will add a citation for the quote at the end of the first paragraph of the Tanzania Animal Life topic. This quote was found on page 252 of a book that was compiled by Camerapix Publishers International. Because this citation is to a quote, the page number must be included in the citation. You will enter the source information and then edit the citation to include the page.

- **Click the Tanzania Culture heading in the Navigation Pane.**

- **Move to the end of the third sentence (after the word "matters" and before the period) in the first paragraph of the Culture section.**

- **Click** 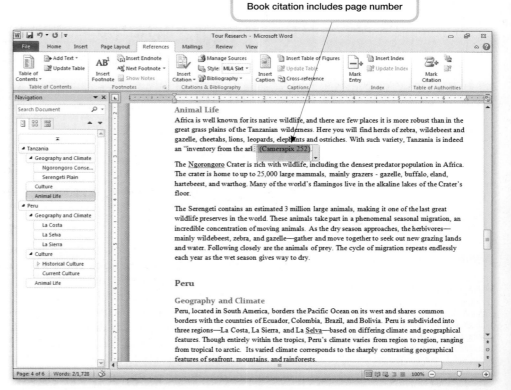 **and choose the Wikipedia entry from the Citation list.**

- **Click the Tanzania Animal Life heading in the Navigation Pane, and then move to the end of the first paragraph (before the period) of the Animal Life section.**

- **Click** and choose Add New Source.

- **Scroll to the top of the Type of Source drop-down list and choose Book.**

- **Enter the following in the appropriate locations to complete the bibliography information for this citation.**

Corporate Author	**Camerapix**
Title	**Spectrum Guide to Tanzania**
Year	**1992**
City	**Edison**
Publisher	**Camerapix Publishers International**

- **Click** OK .

- **Click on the citation and open the drop-down menu.**

- **Choose Edit Citation.**

- **Enter 252 as the page number.**

- **Click** OK .

Your screen should be similar to Figure 3.31

Book citation includes page number

Animal Life

Africa is well known for its native wildlife, and there are few places it is more robust than in the great grass plains of the Tanzanian wilderness. Here you will find herds of zebra, wildebeest and gazelle, cheetahs, lions, leopards, elephants and ostriches. With such variety, Tanzania is indeed an "inventory from the ark" (Camerapix 252).

The Ngorongoro Crater is rich with wildlife, including the densest predator population in Africa. The crater is home to up to 25,000 large mammals, mainly grazers - gazelle, buffalo, eland, hartebeest, and warthog. Many of the world's flamingos live in the alkaline lakes of the Crater's floor.

The Serengeti contains an estimated 3 million large animals, making it one of the last great wildlife preserves in the world. These animals take part in a phenomenal seasonal migration, an incredible concentration of moving animals. As the dry season approaches, the herbivores—mainly wildebeest, zebra, and gazelle—gather and move together to seek out new grazing lands and water. Following closely are the animals of prey. The cycle of migration repeats endlessly each year as the wet season gives way to dry.

Peru

Geography and Climate

Peru, located in South America, borders the Pacific Ocean on its west and shares common borders with the countries of Ecuador, Colombia, Brazil, and Bolivia. Peru is subdivided into three regions—La Costa, La Sierra, and La Selva—based on differing climate and geographical features. Though entirely within the tropics, Peru's climate varies from region to region, ranging from tropical to arctic. Its varied climate corresponds to the sharply contrasting geographical features of seafront, mountains, and rainforests.

Figure 3.31

The last citation you will complete for now is to credit the source of the geography statistics about Peru. The source of this information was from the Country Studies Web site. This Web site contains the online versions of books that were published by the Federal Research Division of the Library of Congress as part of the Country Studies/Area Handbook series.

4

- Click the **Peru Geography and Climate** heading in the Navigation Pane, and then move to the end of the second sentence (after the word "features" and before the period) in the first paragraph in the section.

- Insert a Web site citation using the following source information:

Corporate Author	**Country Studies US** (you will need to first select the Corporate Author check box)
Name of Web Page	**Peru**
Year	**2003–2005**
Year Accessed	Enter the current year
Month Accessed	Enter the current month
Day Accessed	Enter the current day
URL	**http://countrystudies.us/peru/23.htm**

- Click [OK].

Your screen should be similar to Figure 3.32

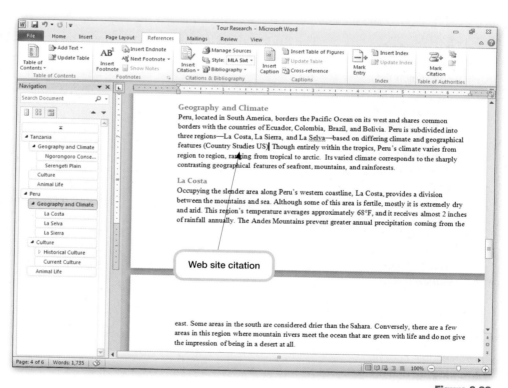

Figure 3.32

EDITING A SOURCE

As you look back at the citations you just entered, you realize the author for the Wikipedia Web site should have been entered as a corporate author, not an individual author. Additionally, the Web site name is incomplete. You will quickly return to this citation using the Go To feature and edit the source.

● Click 🔍 (at the end of the Search box) in the Navigation Pane and then choose Go To.

Another Method

You also can click on the page count indicator in the status bar to open the Go To dialog box.

● Select Field from the Go to What list.

● Click Previous three times to search backward through the document.

● Click Close when the Wikipedia citation is located.

● Choose Edit Source from the citation's drop-down list.

● Click Corporate Author to move the information in the Author text box to the Corporate Author text box.

● Type :The Free Encyclopedia following Wikipedia in the Corporate Author box.

● Click OK.

● Click Yes to update both the Master and Current Lists.

Your screen should be similar to Figure 3.33

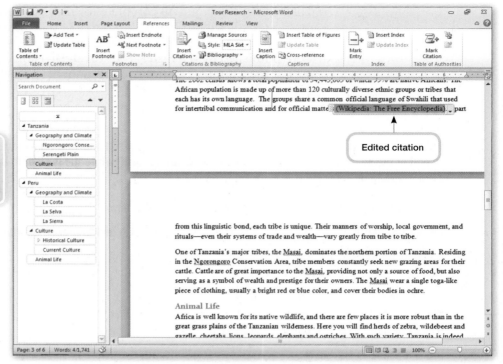

Figure 3.33

The information for the source is now correct and both citations to this source have been updated appropriately.

Including Footnotes

You still have several reference notes you want to include in the report as footnotes to help clarify some information.

Concept 4   Footnotes and Endnotes

Footnotes and endnotes are used in documented research papers to explain or comment on information in the text, or provide source references for text in the document. A **footnote** appears at the bottom of a page containing the material that is being referenced. An **endnote** appears at the end of a document. You can have both footnotes and endnotes in the same document.

Footnotes and endnotes consist of two parts, the **note reference mark** and the note text. The default note reference mark is a superscript number appearing in the document at the end of the material being referenced (for example, text ^{1}). You also can use custom marks consisting of any nonnumeric character or combination of characters, such as an asterisk. The note text for a footnote appears at the bottom of the page on which the reference mark appears. The footnote text is separated from the document text by a horizontal line called the **note separator**. Endnote text appears as a listing at the end of the document.

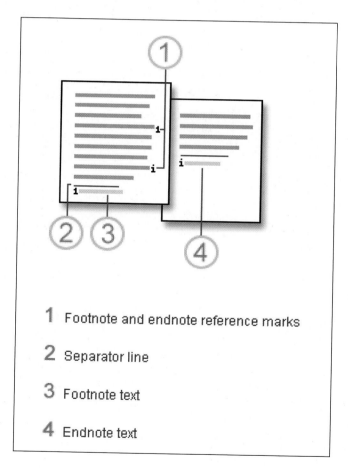

1 Footnote and endnote reference marks

2 Separator line

3 Footnote text

4 Endnote text

Note text can be of any length and formatted just as you would any other text. You also can customize the appearance of the note separators.

INSERTING FOOTNOTES IN DRAFT VIEW

The first footnote reference you want to add is the height of Mt. Kilimanjaro. This note will follow the reference to the mountain at the end of the second paragraph in the Geography and Climate section for Tanzania. To create a footnote, you first need to move to the location in the document where you want the footnote reference mark to be displayed. Then you enter the footnote text. You want to create numbered footnotes, so the default settings are acceptable.

1

- **Using the Navigation Pane, move to the Tanzania Geography and Climate heading.**

- **Switch to Draft view.**

- **Move to the end of the second paragraph.**

- **If necessary, open the References tab.**

- **Click** [Insert Footnote] **from the Footnotes group.**

Another Method

The keyboard shortcut to insert a footnote using the default settings is [Alt] + [Ctrl] + F.

Your screen should be similar to Figure 3.34

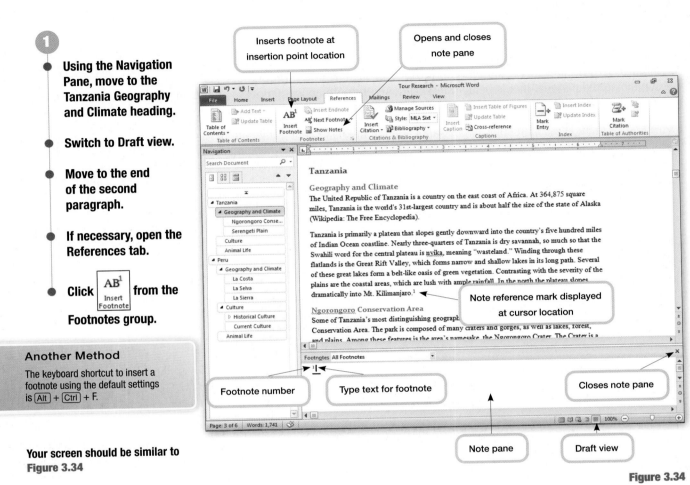

Figure 3.34

The document window is now horizontally divided into upper and lower panes. The report is displayed in the upper pane. The note reference mark, 1, appears as a superscript in the document where the cursor was positioned when the footnote was created. The note pane displays the footnote number and the insertion point. This is where you enter the text for the footnote.

When you enter the footnote text, you can insert, edit, and format it just like any other text.

2

- Type **Mt. Kilimanjaro is 19,340 feet high, making it the fourth tallest mountain in the world.**

- Click 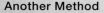 **Close** to close the note pane.

- Point to note reference mark 1 in the document.

Your screen should be similar to Figure 3.35

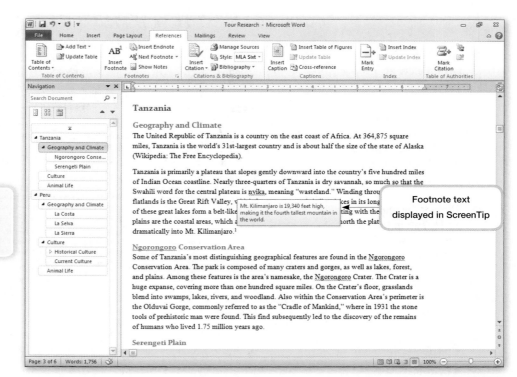

Figure 3.35

In Draft view, the only way to see the footnote text when the footnote pane is not open is in the reference mark's ScreenTip.

INSERTING FOOTNOTES IN PRINT LAYOUT VIEW

The second footnote you want to add is in the Geography and Climate section under Peru. You also can insert footnotes in Print Layout view. After using the command to insert a footnote, the footnote number appears in the footnote area at the bottom of the page, ready for you to enter the footnote text. You want to add a note about Lake Titicaca.

- **Switch to Print Layout view at 100% zoom.**

- **Using the Navigation Pane, move to the La Sierra heading in the Peru Geography and Climate section.**

- **Click at the end of the paragraph in the La Sierra section after the word "lake."**

- **Click** AB^1 **Insert Footnote**.

- **Type Lake Titicaca is 12,507 feet above sea level.**

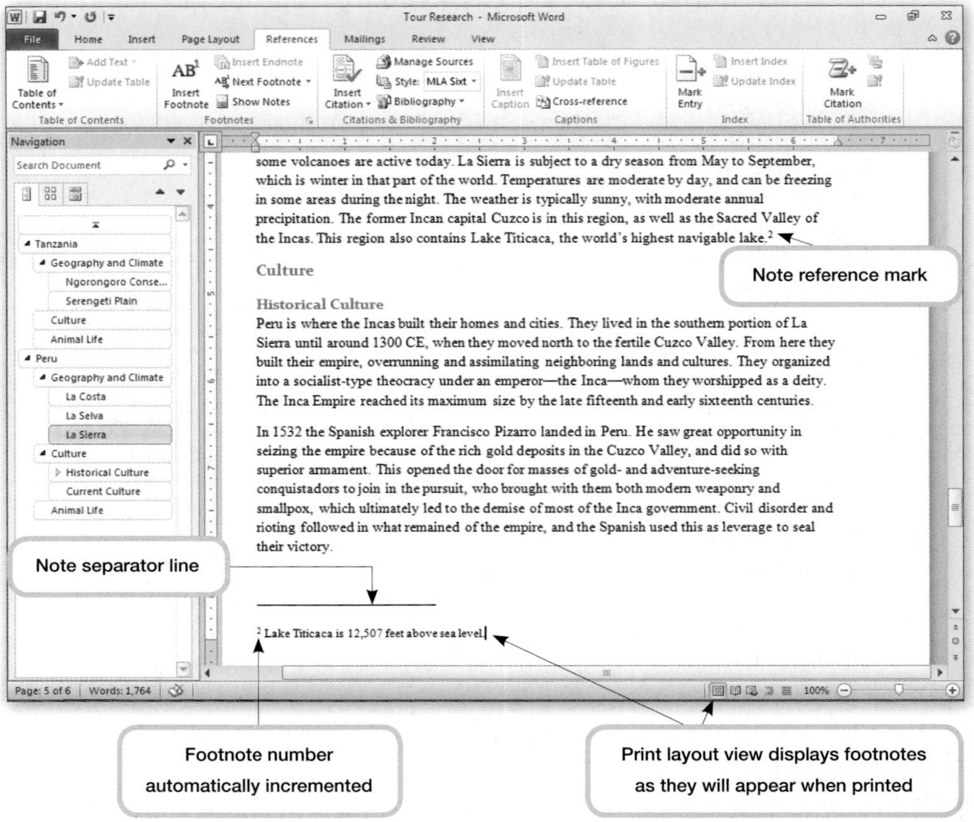

Your screen should be similar to Figure 3.36

some volcanoes are active today. La Sierra is subject to a dry season from May to September, which is winter in that part of the world. Temperatures are moderate by day, and can be freezing in some areas during the night. The weather is typically sunny, with moderate annual precipitation. The former Incan capital Cuzco is in this region, as well as the Sacred Valley of the Incas. This region also contains Lake Titicaca, the world's highest navigable lake.[2]

Culture

Historical Culture
Peru is where the Incas built their homes and cities. They lived in the southern portion of La Sierra until around 1300 CE, when they moved north to the fertile Cuzco Valley. From here they built their empire, overrunning and assimilating neighboring lands and cultures. They organized into a socialist-type theocracy under an emperor—the Inca—whom they worshipped as a deity. The Inca Empire reached its maximum size by the late fifteenth and early sixteenth centuries.

In 1532 the Spanish explorer Francisco Pizarro landed in Peru. He saw great opportunity in seizing the empire because of the rich gold deposits in the Cuzco Valley, and did so with superior armament. This opened the door for masses of gold- and adventure-seeking conquistadors to join in the pursuit, who brought with them both modern weaponry and smallpox, which ultimately led to the demise of most of the Inca government. Civil disorder and rioting followed in what remained of the empire, and the Spanish used this as leverage to seal their victory.

[2] Lake Titicaca is 12,507 feet above sea level.

Note reference mark

Note separator line

Footnote number automatically incremented

Print layout view displays footnotes as they will appear when printed

Figure 3.36

Additional Information

A footnote or endnote can be copied or moved by selecting the note reference mark and using Cut or Copy and Paste. You also can use drag and drop to copy or move a note.

Additional Information

In Print Layout view, you also can display the footnote text in a ScreenTip by pointing to the note reference mark.

The footnote number 2 was automatically entered at the location of the insertion point in the text and the footnote text is displayed immediately above the bottom margin separated from the text by the note separator line. Footnotes are always displayed at the bottom of the page containing the footnote reference mark. Print Layout view displays footnotes as they will appear when the document is printed.

Now you realize that you forgot to enter a footnote earlier in the document, on page 2.

2

- Using the Navigation Pane, move to the Ngorongoro Conservation Area heading.

- Move to after the period following the word "Area" (end of first sentence of first paragraph).

- Insert the following footnote at this location: **The Conservation Area is a national preserve spanning 3,196 square miles.**

- Save the document.

Your screen should be similar to Figure 3.37

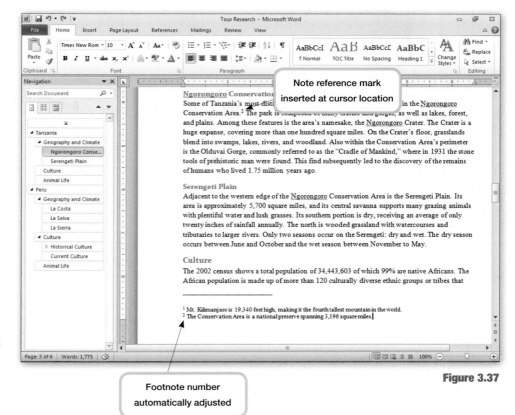

Note reference mark inserted at cursor location

Footnote number automatically adjusted

Figure 3.37

Additional Information

To delete a footnote or endnote, highlight the reference mark and press [Delete]. The reference mark and associated note text are removed, and the following footnotes are renumbered.

Notice that this footnote is now number 2 in the document. Word automatically adjusted the footnote numbers when the new footnote was inserted.

You are finished entering footnotes for now. Footnotes can quickly be converted to endnotes and vice versa by right-clicking on the note you want to convert and choosing Convert from the context menu.

Formatting Picture Layout

Next you want to add two pictures to the report and you want the text to wrap around the pictures. To do this, you change the text-wrapping layout for the picture.

Concept **5** Text Wrapping

You can control the appearance of text around a graphic object by specifying the **text wrapping style**. The text in the paragraph may wrap around the object in many different ways as shown below.

| Inline with Text | Square | Tight | Through | Top and Bottom | Behind Text | In Front of Text |

When a picture is inserted into a Word document, it is an **inline object**. This means it is positioned directly in the text at the position of the insertion point. It becomes part of the paragraph and any paragraph alignment settings that apply to the paragraph also apply to the picture.

By changing a graphic to a **floating object**, it is inserted into the **drawing layer**, a separate layer from the text that allows graphic objects to be positioned precisely on the page. You can change an inline object to a floating picture by changing the wrapping style of the object.

WRAPPING TEXT AROUND GRAPHICS

You will insert a picture of a giraffe next to the second paragraph on page 2.

1

- **Use the Navigation Pane to move to the Geography and Climate heading under Tanzania.**

- **Close the Navigation pane.**

- **Move to the beginning of the second paragraph.**

- **Insert the picture** wd03_Mt Kilimanjaro **from your data files.**

Having Trouble?

Refer to the section Working with Graphics in Lab 1 to review inserting graphic files.

- **Reduce the size of the picture to approximately 2 inches high by 3 inches wide.**

Having Trouble?

You can check the size of your photo by looking at the Size group in the Format tab.

Additional Information

Dragging the corner handle maintains the original proportions of the picture.

Your screen should be similar to Figure 3.38

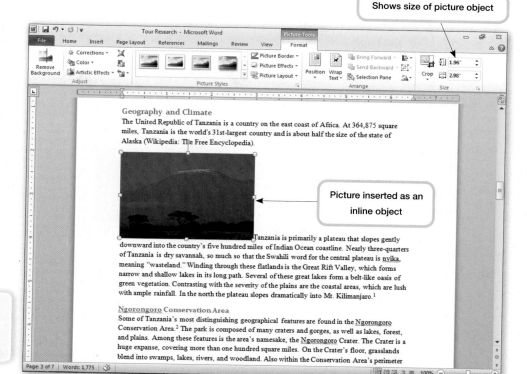

Shows size of picture object

Picture inserted as an inline object

Geography and Climate

The United Republic of Tanzania is a country on the east coast of Africa. At 364,875 square miles, Tanzania is the world's 31st-largest country and is about half the size of the state of Alaska (Wikipedia: The Free Encyclopedia).

Tanzania is primarily a plateau that slopes gently downward into the country's five hundred miles of Indian Ocean coastline. Nearly three-quarters of Tanzania is dry savannah, so much so that the Swahili word for the central plateau is nyika, meaning "wasteland." Winding through these flatlands is the Great Rift Valley, which forms narrow and shallow lakes in its long path. Several of these great lakes form a belt-like oasis of green vegetation. Contrasting with the severity of the plains are the coastal areas, which are lush with ample rainfall. In the north the plateau slopes dramatically into Mt. Kilimanjaro.[1]

Ngorongoro Conservation Area

Some of Tanzania's most distinguishing geographical features are found in the Ngorongoro Conservation Area.[2] The park is composed of many craters and gorges, as well as lakes, forest, and plains. Among these features is the area's namesake, the Ngorongoro Crater. The Crater is a huge expanse, covering more than one hundred square miles. On the Crater's floor, grasslands blend into swamps, lakes, rivers, and woodland. Also within the Conservation Area's perimeter

Figure 3.38

The picture has been inserted as an inline object and appears at the beginning of the paragraph like the first text character of the paragraph. The text continues to the right of the picture. The Picture Tools Format tab is automatically displayed and is used to modify the selected picture object.

You want to change the wrapping style so that the text wraps around the picture. To do this, you will change the wrapping style to Square.

Click  **from the Arrange group.**

Choose Square from the submenu.

If necessary, resize and position the picture until the text wraps around it as in Figure 3.39.

Your screen should be similar to **Figure 3.39**

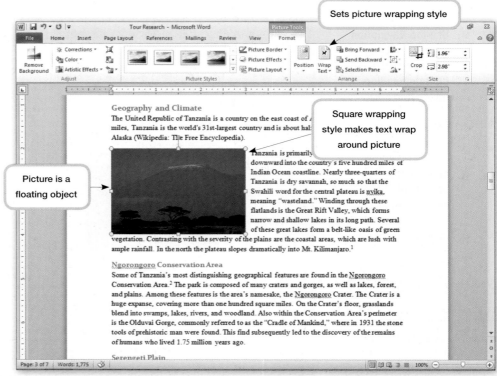

Sets picture wrapping style

Square wrapping style makes text wrap around picture

Picture is a floating object

Geography and Climate
The United Republic of Tanzania is a country on the east coast of A[...] miles, Tanzania is the world's 31st-largest country and is about hal[...] Alaska (Wikipedia: The Free Encyclopedia).

Tanzania is primarily [...] downward into the country's five hundred miles of Indian Ocean coastline. Nearly three-quarters of Tanzania is dry savannah, so much so that the Swahili word for the central plateau is nyika, meaning "wasteland." Winding through these flatlands is the Great Rift Valley, which forms narrow and shallow lakes in its long path. Several of these great lakes form a belt-like oasis of green vegetation. Contrasting with the severity of the plains are the coastal areas, which are lush with ample rainfall. In the north the plateau slopes dramatically into Mt. Kilimanjaro.[1]

Ngorongoro Conservation Area
Some of Tanzania's most distinguishing geographical features are found in the Ngorongoro Conservation Area.[2] The park is composed of many craters and gorges, as well as lakes, forest, and plains. Among these features is the area's namesake, the Ngorongoro Crater. The Crater is a huge expanse, covering more than one hundred square miles. On the Crater's floor, grasslands blend into swamps, lakes, rivers, and woodland. Also within the Conservation Area's perimeter is the Olduvai Gorge, commonly referred to as the "Cradle of Mankind," where in 1931 the stone tools of prehistoric man were found. This find subsequently led to the discovery of the remains of humans who lived 1.75 million years ago.

Serengeti Plain

Page: 3 of 7 | Words: 1,775 | 100%

Figure 3.39

Additional Information

Sometimes a floating object is hidden behind another. If this happens, you can press [Tab] to cycle forward or [Shift] + [Tab] to cycle backward through the stacked objects.

The picture is changed to a floating object that can be placed anywhere in the document, including in front of or behind other objects including the text. Because the picture is even with the left margin, the text wraps to the right side of the object. If you moved the picture, because the wrapping style is Square, the text would wrap around the object on all sides.

Move the picture to the center of the page to see how the text wraps around it.

Your screen should be similar to **Figure 3.40**

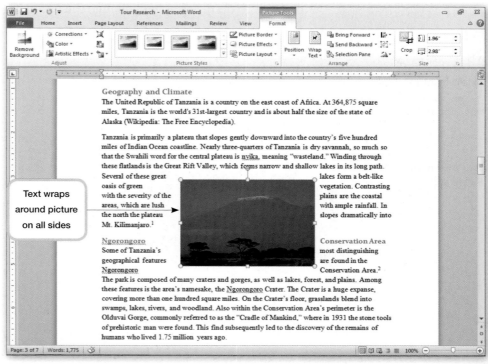

Text wraps around picture on all sides

Geography and Climate
The United Republic of Tanzania is a country on the east coast of Africa. At 364,875 square miles, Tanzania is the world's 31st-largest country and is about half the size of the state of Alaska (Wikipedia: The Free Encyclopedia).

Tanzania is primarily a plateau that slopes gently downward into the country's five hundred miles of Indian Ocean coastline. Nearly three-quarters of Tanzania is dry savannah, so much so that the Swahili word for the central plateau is nyika, meaning "wasteland." Winding through these flatlands is the Great Rift Valley, which forms narrow and shallow lakes in its long path. Several of these great oasis of green with the severity of the areas, which are lush with the north the plateau Mt. Kilimanjaro.[1]

lakes form a belt-like vegetation. Contrasting plains are the coastal with ample rainfall. In slopes dramatically into

Ngorongoro
Some of Tanzania's geographical features Ngorongoro

Conservation Area
most distinguishing are found in the Conservation Area.[2]

The park is composed of many craters and gorges, as well as lakes, forest, and plains. Among these features is the area's namesake, the Ngorongoro Crater. The Crater is a huge expanse, covering more than one hundred square miles. On the Crater's floor, grasslands blend into swamps, lakes, rivers, and woodland. Also within the Conservation Area's perimeter is the Olduvai Gorge, commonly referred to as the "Cradle of Mankind," where in 1931 the stone tools of prehistoric man were found. This find subsequently led to the discovery of the remains of humans who lived 1.75 million years ago.

Page: 3 of 7 | Words: 1,775 | 100%

Figure 3.40

The text wraps on all sides of the object, depending on its location in the text. You will align this picture with the left margin again. Then you will add a second picture in the Peru Animal Life section.

4

- **Move the picture back to the left margin and aligned with the top of the paragraph (see Figure 3.39).**

- **Move to the beginning of the first paragraph in the Peru Animal Life section.**

- **Insert the picture** wd03_Flamingos **to the left of the first paragraph.**

- **Size the picture to approximately 1.15 inches wide by 1.75 inches high.**

- **Change the wrapping style to Square and position the picture as in Figure 3.41.**

- **Save the document.**

Your screen should be similar to Figure 3.41

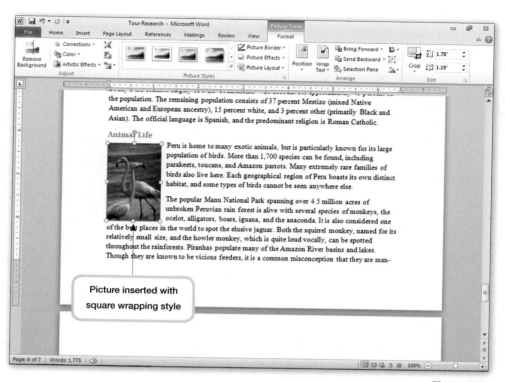

Figure 3.41

Picture inserted with square wrapping style

Referencing Figures

After figures and other illustrative items have been added to a document, it is helpful to include figure references to identify the items. Figure references include captions and cross-references. If the reader is viewing the document online, the captions and cross-references become hyperlinks to allow the reader to jump around in the document.

Concept 6 Captions and Cross-References

Using captions and cross-references in a document identifies items in a document and helps the reader locate information quickly. A **caption** is a numbered label for a figure, table, picture, or graph. Word can automatically add captions to graphic objects as they are inserted, or you can add them manually. The caption label can be changed to reflect the type of object to which it refers, such as a table, chart, or figure. In addition, Word automatically numbers graphic objects and adjusts the numbering when objects of the same type are added or deleted.

A **cross-reference** is a reference from one part of a document to related information in another part. Once you have captions, you also can include cross-references. For example, if you have a graph in one part of the document that you would like to refer to in another section, you can add a cross-reference that tells the reader what page the graph is on. A cross-reference also can be inserted as a hyperlink, allowing you to jump to another location in the same document or in another document.

ADDING A FIGURE CAPTION

Next, you want to add a caption below the picture of Mt. Kilimanjaro.

1

- Select the picture of Mt. Kilimanjaro in the Tanzania section.

- Open the References tab.

- Click [Insert Caption].

Your screen should be similar to Figure 3.42

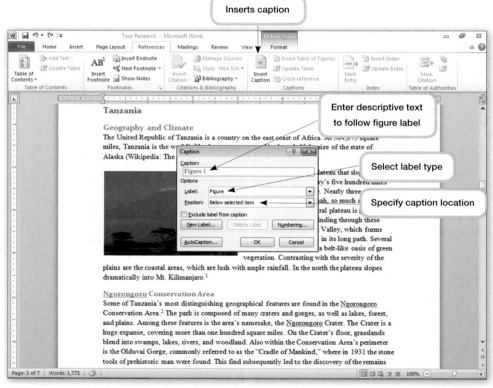

Figure 3.42

The Caption options are described in the following table.

Option	Description
Label	Select from one of three default captions: Table, Figure, or Equation.
Position	Specify the location of the caption, either above or below a selected item. When an item is selected, the Position option is available.
New Label	Create your own captions.
Numbering	Specify the numbering format and starting number for your caption.
AutoCaption	Turns on the automatic insertion of a caption (label and number only) when you insert selected items into your document.

The default caption label is Figure 1. You will use this caption and add additional descriptive text. The default setting of "Below selected item" is also correct.

2

● In the Caption text box, following "Figure 1," type : Mt. Kilimanjaro

● Click OK.

● If necessary, size and position the picture and caption as in Figure 3.43.

Your screen should be similar to Figure 3.43

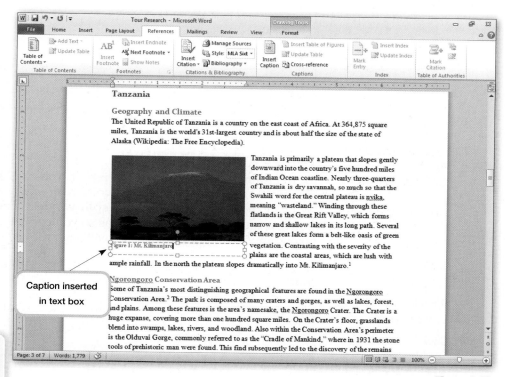

Caption inserted in text box

Figure 3.43

Additional Information

Only captions that are associated with floating graphic objects are in text boxes. Otherwise, they are text entries.

Additional Information

You will learn more about text boxes in later labs.

The caption label appears below the figure. It is formatted using the caption style associated with the selected theme. The figure number is a field that will update automatically as you add or delete captions in the document. The caption is contained in a **text box**, a container for text and other graphic objects that can be moved like any other object.

3

- In a similar manner, add a **Figure 2: Peruvian Flamingos** caption below the flamingos picture.

- **Size and position the picture and caption as in Figure 3.44.**

Your screen should be similar to Figure 3.44

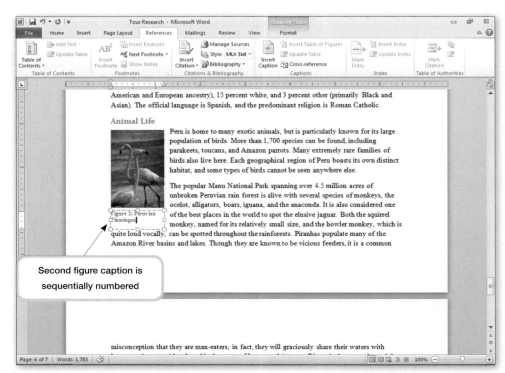

Second figure caption is sequentially numbered

Figure 3.44

ADDING A CROSS-REFERENCE

In the Animal Life section of the report, you discuss the animals found in the Serengeti. You want to include a cross-reference to the picture at this location. While doing this, you will use the **split window** feature to divide the document window into separate viewing areas so you can see the figure you will reference in one area and the text where you will enter the cross-reference in the other area.

1

- **Open the View tab.**

- Click  in the Window group.

- **Drag the split bar to the position shown in Figure 3.45.**

- **Click to position the split bar at that location.**

Another Method

You also can drag the split box , located at the top of the vertical scroll bar, or use Alt + Ctrl + S to split a window.

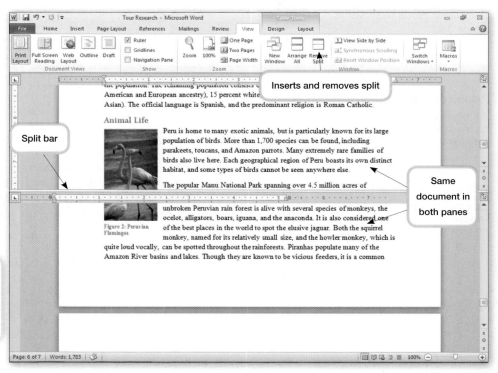

Inserts and removes split

Split bar

Same document in both panes

Your screen should be similar to Figure 3.45

Figure 3.45

WWW.MHHE.COM/OLEARY

The document area is divided into two horizontal sections. Each section is displayed in a pane that can be scrolled and manipulated independently.

Next, you will scroll the document in the panes to display the areas you want to view. While using panes, the insertion point and the ruler are displayed in the active pane or the pane in which you are currently working.

2

- **Scroll the upper pane to display the Figure 1 caption below the Mt. Kilimanjaro picture.**

- **Scroll the lower pane to display the third paragraph in the Tanzania Animal Life section (page 4).**

Your screen should be similar to Figure 3.46

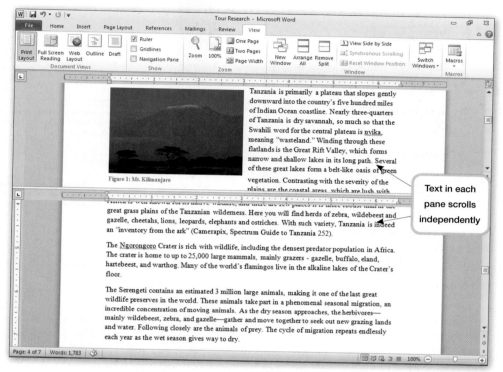

Figure 3.46

The text in each pane scrolls independently. Now you can conveniently see both areas of the document while you enter the cross-reference.

- **Move to after the word "water" (before the period) in the third paragraph in the Tanzania Animal Life section.**

- **Press** Spacebar.

- **Type** (see **and press** Spacebar.

- **Open the References tab.**

- **Click** Cross-reference **from the Captions group.**

Your screen should be similar to Figure 3.47

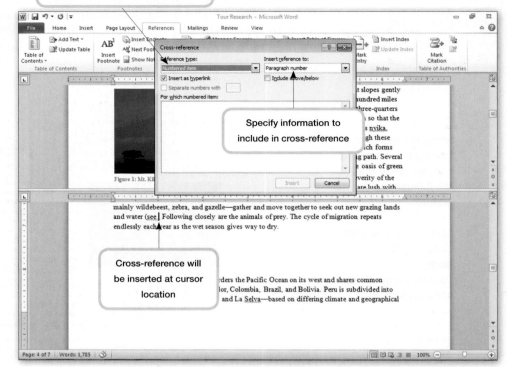

Select type of item to be referenced

Specify information to include in cross-reference

Cross-reference will be inserted at cursor location

Figure 3.47

In the Cross-reference dialog box, you specify the type of item you are referencing and how you want the reference to appear. You want to reference the Mt. Kilimanjaro picture, and you want only the label "Figure 1" entered in the document. From the For which caption list box, you select the figure you want to reference from the list of all figure captions in the document. Notice that the Insert as Hyperlink option is selected by default. This option creates a hyperlink between the cross-reference and the caption. The default setting is appropriate.

- **From the Reference type: drop-down list box, choose Figure.**

- **From the Insert reference to: drop-down list box, choose Only label and number.**

- **If necessary, from the For which caption: list box, select Figure 1: Mt. Kilimanjaro.**

- **Click** Insert **.**

- **Click** Close **.**

- **Type)**

- **Click on the Figure 1 cross-reference.**

Your screen should be similar to Figure 3.48

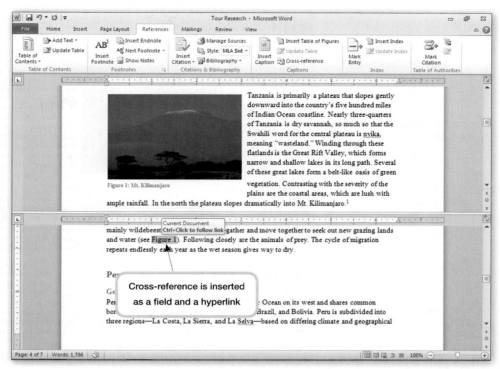

Figure 3.48

The cross-reference to Figure 1 is entered into the document as a field. Therefore, if you insert another picture or item that is cross-referenced, the captions and cross-references will renumber automatically. If you edit, delete, or move cross-referenced items, you should manually update the cross-references using Update Field. When you are working on a long document with several figures, tables, and graphs, this feature is very helpful.

USING A CROSS-REFERENCE HYPERLINK

The cross-reference field is also a hyperlink and, just like a table of contents field, can be used to jump to the source it references.

1

● Hold down Ctrl and click on the Figure 1 cross-reference.

Your screen should be similar to Figure 3.49

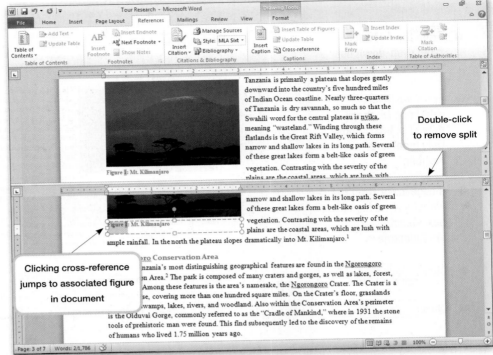

Double-click to remove split

Clicking cross-reference jumps to associated figure in document

Figure 3.49

The document in the lower pane jumped to the caption beneath the figure. You will clear the split and save the document next.

2

● Double-click on the split bar (above the ruler) to remove the split.

● Save the document.

Another Method

You also can click [Remove Split] in the Window group of the View tab, drag the split bar to the top of the document window or use Alt + Ctrl + S to remove the split.

The split is removed and the document window returns to a single pane. As you can see, splitting the document window is most useful for viewing different sections of the document at the same time and allows you to quickly switch between panes to access information in the different sections without having to repeatedly scroll to the areas.

Creating a Simple Table

Next, you want to add a table comparing the rainfall and temperature data for the three regions of Peru.

Concept (7) Table

A **table** is used to organize information into an easy-to-read format of horizontal rows and vertical columns. The insertion of a row and column creates a **cell** in which you can enter data or other information. Cells in a table are identified by a letter and number, called a **table reference**. Columns are identified from left to right beginning with the letter A, and rows are numbered from top to bottom beginning with the number 1. The table reference of the top-leftmost cell is A1 because it is in the first column (A) and first row (1) of the table. The second cell in column 2 is cell B2. The fourth cell in column 3 is C4.

A	B	C	D	E
(A1)	Jan	Feb	Mar	Total
East	7 (B2)	7	5	19
West	6	4	7	17
South	8	7 (C4)	9	24
Total	21	18	21	60

Tables are a very effective method for presenting information. The table layout organizes the information for readers and greatly reduces the number of words they have to read to interpret the data. Use tables whenever you can to make your documents easier to read.

The table you want to create will display columns for regions, rainfall, and temperature. The rows will display the data for each region. Your completed table will be similar to the one shown below.

Region	Annual Rainfall (Inches)	Average Temperature (Fahrenheit)
La Costa	2	68
La Selva	137	80
La Sierra	35	54

INSERTING A TABLE

Word includes several methods you can use to create tables. One method will quickly convert text that is arranged in tabular columns into a table. Another uses the Draw Table feature to create any type of table, but is most useful for creating complex tables that contain cells of different heights or a varying number of columns per row. Another method inserts a preformatted table containing sample data that you replace with your data.

The last method, which you will use, creates a simple table consisting of the same number of rows and columns by highlighting boxes in a grid to define the table size.

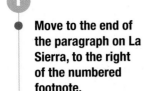

1

● Move to the end of the paragraph on La Sierra, to the right of the numbered footnote.

● Press [Enter] twice to insert two blank lines.

● Open the Insert tab.

● Click [Table].

● Point to the boxes in the grid in the drop-down menu and drag to select a 3 by 3 table.

Additional Information

The dimensions are reflected at the top of the grid and Live Preview shows you how it will look in the document.

● Click on the lower-right corner of the selection to insert it.

Your screen should be similar to Figure 3.50

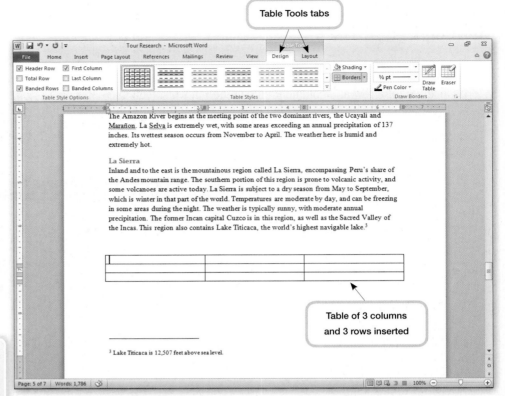

Figure 3.50

A table the full width of the page is inserted in the document. It has equal-sized columns and is surrounded by a black borderline. The Table Tools tab is automatically open and includes a Design tab and a Layout tab that are used to work with the table.

ENTERING DATA IN A TABLE

Now you are ready to enter information in the table. Each cell contains a single line space where you can enter data. You can move from one cell to another by using the arrow keys or by clicking on the cell. The insertion point appears in the cell that is selected. In addition, you can use the keys shown in the table below to move around a table.

Additional Information

Pressing [Tab] when in the last cell of a row moves to the first cell of the next row or if you are positioned in the last row of the table to the first cell of a new row.

To Move to	Press
Next cell in row	[Tab ⇥]
Previous cell in row	[⇧ Shift] + [Tab ⇥]
First cell in row	[Alt] + [Home]
Last cell in row	[Alt] + [End]
First cell in column	[Alt] + [Page Up]
Last cell in column	[Alt] + [Page Down]
Previous row	[↑]
Next row	[↓]

The mouse pointer also may appear as a solid black arrow when pointing to the table. When it is a ↓, you can click to select the entire column. When it is ↗, you can click to select a cell. You will learn more about this feature shortly.

You will begin by entering the information for La Costa in cells A1 through C1. You can type in the cell as you would anywhere in a normal document.

1

- If necessary, click cell A1 to select it.

- Type **La Costa**

- Press Tab.

- In the same manner, type **2** in cell B1 and **68** in cell C1.

- Continue entering the information shown below, using Tab to move to the next cell.

Cell	Entry
A2	La Sierra
B2	35
C2	54
A3	La Selva
B3	137
C3	80

Your screen should be similar to Figure 3.51

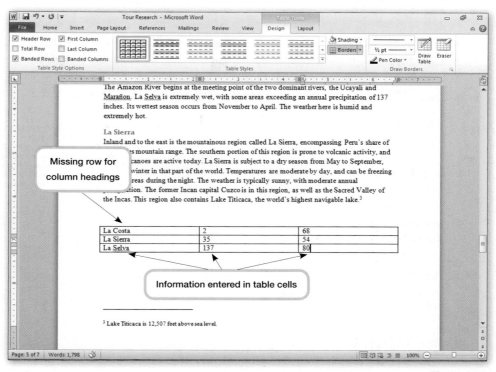

Figure 3.51

INSERTING A ROW

After looking at the table, you realize you need to include a row above the data to display the descriptive column headings. To add a row, simply click in any cell above or below the location where you want to add the row and then use the appropriate command to insert a row. Once the row is inserted, you will enter the column headings in the cells.

1

- Move to any cell in row 1.

- Open the Table Tools Layout tab.

- Click [Insert Above] from the Rows & Columns group.

- In cell A1 type **Region**

- In cell B1 type **Annual Rainfall**

- Press [Enter] to insert a second line in the cell.

- Type **(Inches)**

- In cell C1 type **Average Temperature** on the first line and **(Fahrenheit)** on the second.

Your screen should be similar to Figure 3.52

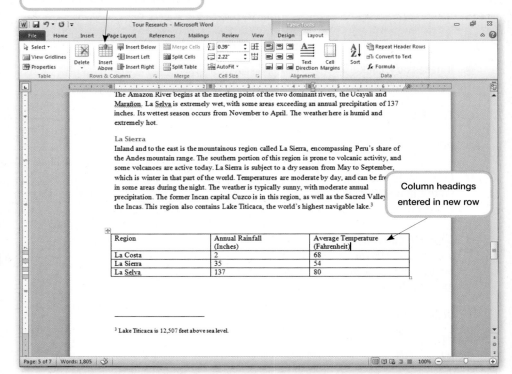

Inserts blank row above current row

Column headings entered in new row

Figure 3.52

SIZING A COLUMN

You decide to change the width of the columns to better fit the data. To change the width of a column you simply point to the vertical divider until the mouse pointer looks like ◄╫►. Then drag the divider to the left or right, depending on whether you want to narrow or widen a column.

1

● Point to the vertical divider between the first and second columns until the mouse pointer looks like ⊹.

● Using the ruler as your guide, narrow the column by dragging the column divider to position 1.5 inches.

● Drag the divider between the second and third columns to position 3.5 inches.

● Drag the right edge of the table to position 6 inches.

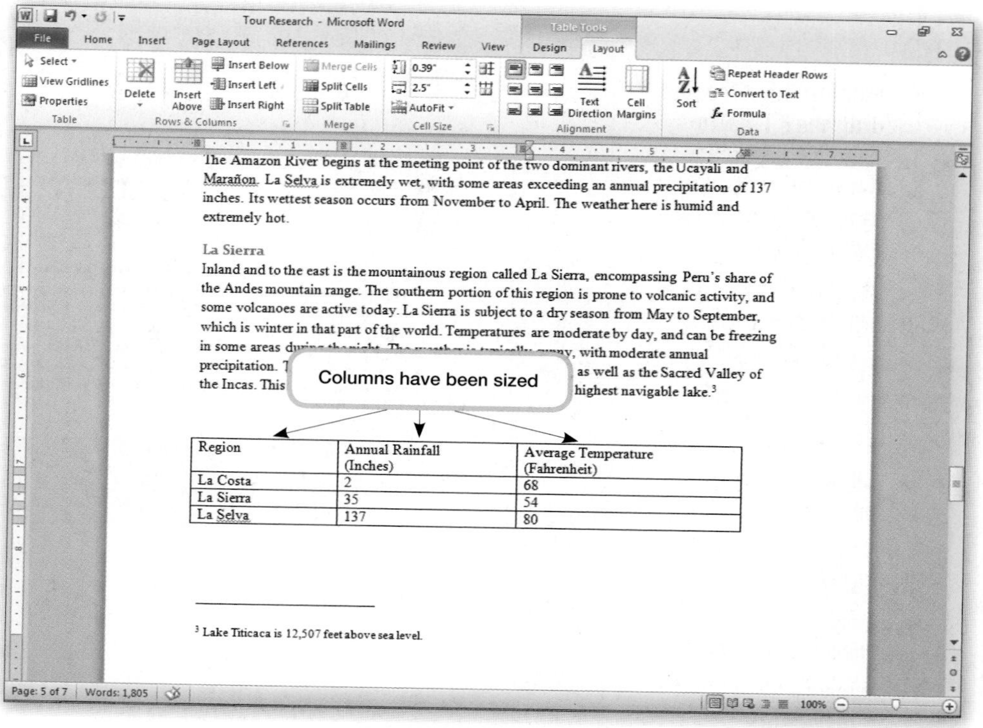

Your screen should be similar to Figure 3.53

The Amazon River begins at the meeting point of the two dominant rivers, the Ucayali and Marañon. La Selva is extremely wet, with some areas exceeding an annual precipitation of 137 inches. Its wettest season occurs from November to April. The weather here is humid and extremely hot.

La Sierra

Inland and to the east is the mountainous region called La Sierra, encompassing Peru's share of the Andes mountain range. The southern portion of this region is prone to volcanic activity, and some volcanoes are active today. La Sierra is subject to a dry season from May to September, which is winter in that part of the world. Temperatures are moderate by day, and can be freezing in some areas during the night. The weather is typically sunny, with moderate annual precipitation. [...] as well as the Sacred Valley of the Incas. This [...] highest navigable lake.[3]

Columns have been sized

Region	Annual Rainfall (Inches)	Average Temperature (Fahrenheit)
La Costa	2	68
La Sierra	35	54
La Selva	137	80

[3] Lake Titicaca is 12,507 feet above sea level.

Figure 3.53

SIZING A TABLE

The table is still wider than it needs to be. To quickly reduce the overall table size, you can drag the resize handle □. This handle appears in the lower-right corner whenever the mouse pointer rests over the table. Once the table is smaller, you will select the entire table by clicking the ⊞ move handle and center it between the margins.

- Point to the table and drag the ☐ resize handle to decrease the width of the table to 5 inches (see Figure 3.54).

Additional Information

The mouse pointer appears as ⬈ when you point to the ☐ resize handle.

- Click ⊞ to select the entire table.

Additional Information

The mouse pointer appears as 🕂 when you point to the ⊞ move handle.

- Click ≣ Center on the Mini toolbar.

Your screen should be similar to Figure 3.54

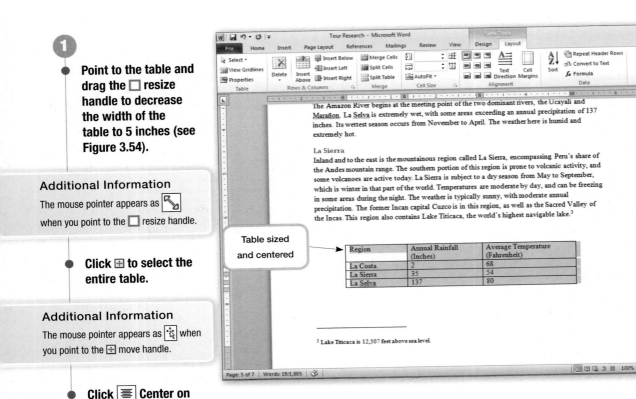

Figure 3.54

Another Method

You also can drag the ⊞ move handle to move the table to any location or click ⊞ Center in the Table Properties dialog box.

Having Trouble?

See Concept 8: Sort in Lab 2 to review this feature.

SORTING A TABLE

Next you decide you want the three regions to appear in alphabetical order as they are presented in the report. To make this change quickly, you can **sort** the table. The process is similar to sorting a list.

You will use the default Sort settings that will sort by text and paragraphs in ascending order. Additionally, when sorting a table, the program assumes the first row of the table is a header row and uses the information in that row for you to select the column to sort on. The default is to sort on the first column. In this case, this is acceptable because you want to sort the table by Region.

Click [Sort] in the Data group of the Table Tools Layout tab.

Click [OK] to accept all the default settings.

Click in the table to clear the highlight.

Your screen should be similar to Figure 3.55

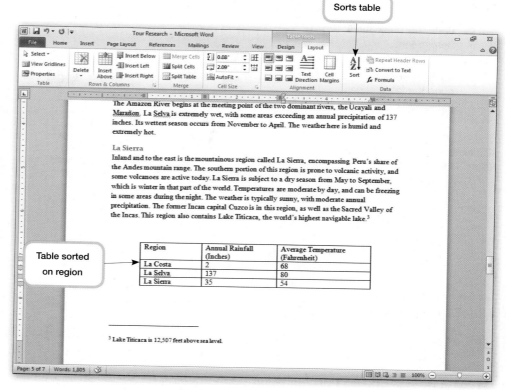

Table sorted on region

Figure 3.55

The three regions now appear in ascending sort order in the table.

FORMATTING A TABLE

To enhance the appearance of the table, you can apply many different formats to the cells. This process is similar to adding formatting to a document, except that the formatting affects the selected cells only or the entire table.

The quickest way to apply formats to a table is to use a table quick style. This feature includes built-in combinations of formats that consist of different fill or background colors, patterns, borders, fonts, and alignment settings.

Having Trouble?

Refer to Concept 9 Quick Styles in Lab 2 to review this feature.

1

- **Open the Table Tools Design tab.**

- **Click** **More to open the table styles gallery.**

Your screen should be similar to Figure 3.56

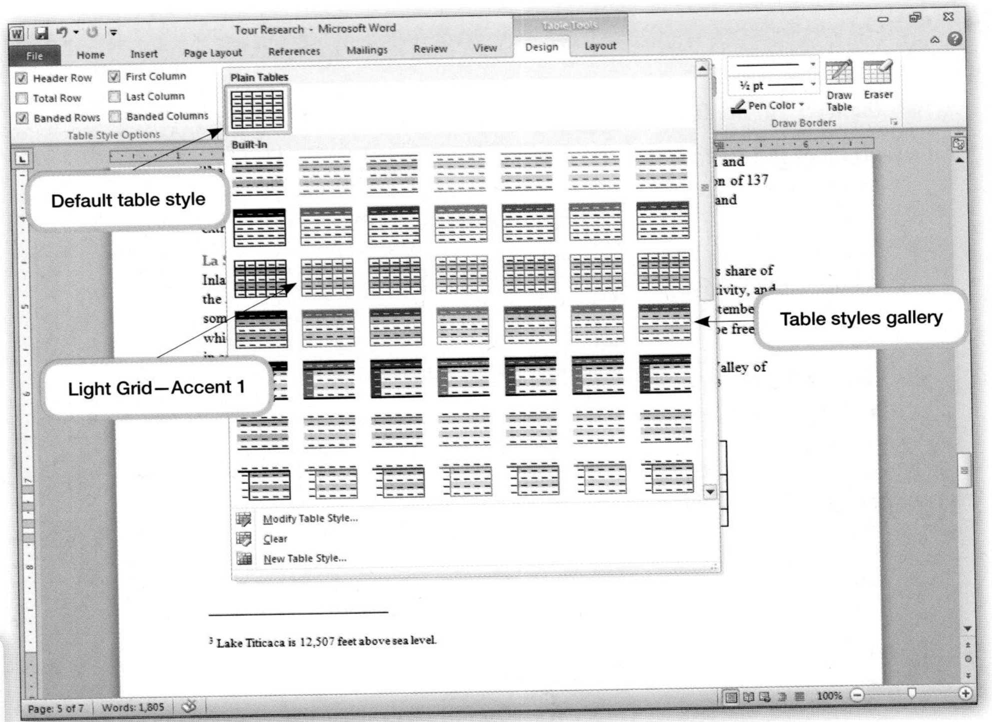

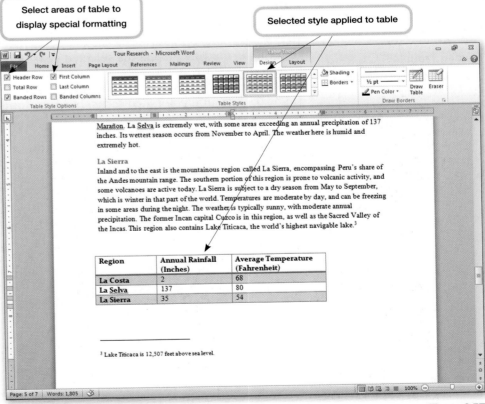

Figure 3.56

From the table styles gallery, you select the table design you want to use. There are 146 Built-in styles. As you point to the style, the style name appears in a ScreenTip and Live Preview shows how the table will look.

2

- **Choose Light Grid— Accent 1 (3rd row, 2nd column).**

Your screen should be similar to Figure 3.57

Marañon. La Selva is extremely wet, with some areas exceeding an annual precipitation of 137 inches. Its wettest season occurs from November to April. The weather here is humid and extremely hot.

La Sierra

Inland and to the east is the mountainous region called La Sierra, encompassing Peru's share of the Andes mountain range. The southern portion of this region is prone to volcanic activity, and some volcanoes are active today. La Sierra is subject to a dry season from May to September, which is winter in that part of the world. Temperatures are moderate by day, and can be freezing in some areas during the night. The weather is typically sunny, with moderate annual precipitation. The former Incan capital Cuzco is in this region, as well as the Sacred Valley of the Incas. This region also contains Lake Titicaca, the world's highest navigable lake.[3]

Region	Annual Rainfall (Inches)	Average Temperature (Fahrenheit)
La Costa	2	68
La Selva	137	80
La Sierra	35	54

[3] Lake Titicaca is 12,507 feet above sea level.

Figure 3.57

The entire table is reformatted to the new design. It includes banded shades of color for the table data. In addition, the first column and row heading text is bold. Notice that the table is no longer centered; however, the table size was not changed. The table alignment was changed because the new design includes left alignment. Using a table style was much faster than applying these features individually.

Even after applying a table style, you may want to make additional changes. For example, the selected table style applies bold formatting to the header row and first column. It also uses a banded row effect for the table data. If you do not want one or all of these features, you can turn them off using the quick styles options. You would like to see how the table would look without some of these features.

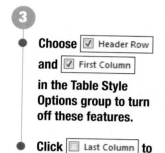

Choose ☑ Header Row **and** ☑ First Column **in the Table Style Options group to turn off these features.**

Click ☐ Last Column **to turn on this feature.**

Your screen should be similar to Figure 3.58

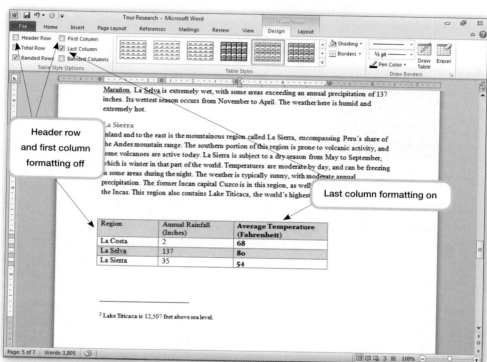

Figure 3.58

Additional Information

The gallery of table styles also reflects the changes in the style options.

The background of the first row is now shaded because of the Banded Rows setting and the bold effect was removed from the column and row headings. Bold was added to the last column to emphasize the data. As you can see you can quickly emphasize different areas of the table by selecting areas of the table to display special formatting. You prefer how the table looked before these changes and will restore these features.

4

● **Choose** ☑ Header Row **and** ☑ First Column **to restore these settings.**

● **Click** ☐ Last Column **to turn off this feature.**

However, there are a few changes you would like to make. As you continue to modify the table, many cells can be selected and changed at the same time. The table below describes the procedures to select information in a table.

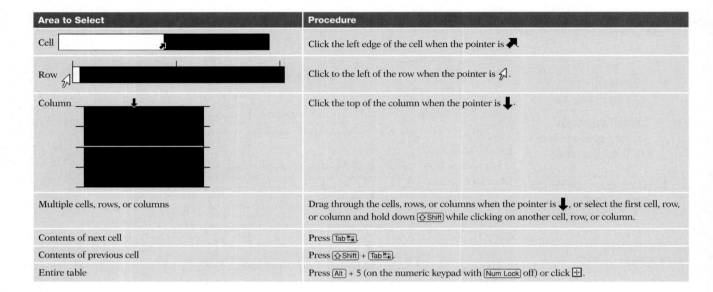

Area to Select	Procedure
Cell	Click the left edge of the cell when the pointer is ◢.
Row	Click to the left of the row when the pointer is ◿.
Column	Click the top of the column when the pointer is ⬇.
Multiple cells, rows, or columns	Drag through the cells, rows, or columns when the pointer is ⬇, or select the first cell, row, or column and hold down ⇧Shift while clicking on another cell, row, or column.
Contents of next cell	Press Tab⇥.
Contents of previous cell	Press ⇧Shift + Tab⇥.
Entire table	Press Alt + 5 (on the numeric keypad with Num Lock off) or click ⊞.

You want the entries in the header row (cells A1 through C1), and the table data in cells B2 through C4, to be centered in their cell spaces. You also want to increase the font size of the header text. Finally, you will add a caption below the table.

5

- Select cells A1 through C1 containing the table headings.

- Open the Table Tools Layout tab.

- Click ▤ Align Top Center from the Alignment group.

- In the same manner, center cells B2 through C4.

- Select the header row again.

- Click A̅ Grow in the Mini toolbar.

- Select the table and center it again.

- Add the caption **Table 1: Climate** below the table.

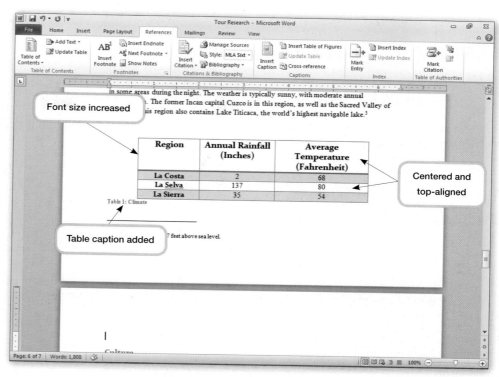

Figure 3.59

Having Trouble?

Follow the same steps for adding a figure caption, except choose Table as the caption label.

- Insert a blank line below the caption.

- Save the document.

Your screen should be similar to Figure 3.59

Including a Table of Figures

The report is near completion and you want to add a table of figures to the report.

Concept 8 Table of Figures

A **table of figures** is a list of the figures, tables, or equations used in a document and their associated page numbers, similar to how a table of contents lists topic headings. The table of figures is generated from captions that are included in the document and is a field that can be easily updated to reflect changes you may make to the document after the list is generated.

Table of Figures

Additionally, each entry in the table is a separate field that is a hyperlink to the caption in the document. It can then be used to quickly locate specific figures or other items in the document.

The table of figures is typically placed at the end of a long document.

CREATING A TABLE OF FIGURES

Because you have already added captions to several items in the report, creating a table of figures will be a simple process.

1

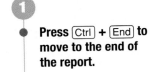

- **Press** Ctrl + End **to move to the end of the report.**

Having Trouble?

Do not be concerned if the layout of your document does not look exactly as you would like it to right now, you will make final adjustments to the layout after all the information has been added.

- **Enter the title** Table of Figures **and format it with a Heading 1 style.**

- **Press** Enter **to move to a blank line below the title.**

- **Open the References tab and click** Insert Table of Figures **in the Captions group.**

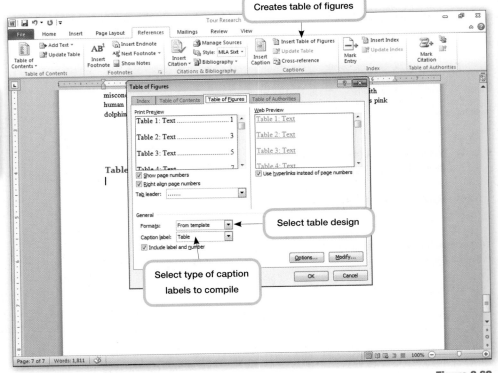

Figure 3.60

Your screen should be similar to Figure 3.60

The Table of Figures dialog box options are very similar to those in the Table of Contents dialog box. The default options to show and right-align page numbers are appropriate as well as the use of the tab leaders. The Formats box is used to select a design for the table of figures. The default design is the design included in the Normal template and is displayed in the Preview boxes. In the Caption label box, you select the type of caption label you want to compile in the table of figures. The default is to display Table caption labels. You will change the Format to another style and the caption label to compile figures.

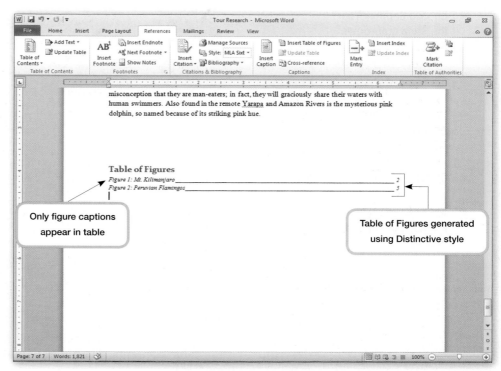

2

● **Choose Distinctive from the Formats drop-down list.**

● **Choose Figure from the Caption label drop-down list.**

● **Click** [OK].

Your screen should be similar to Figure 3.61

Only figure captions appear in table

Table of Figures generated using Distinctive style

Figure 3.61

The program searched for all figure captions in the document and displays them in the table of figures in sorted order by number. The table appears formatted in the selected style.

MODIFY A TABLE OF FIGURES

You also want to include the table references in the table of figures. To do this, you could create a second table of figures to display the table references only. Alternatively, you can modify the table of figures to display all types of captions in a single table. You decide, since there are only three captions, to use one table. You also decide that you do not like how the Distinctive format looks and will use the default template formatting instead.

1

- **Click** [Insert Table of Figures] **from the Captions group.**

- **Click** [Options...].

- **Choose Caption from the Style drop-down list.**

- **Click** [OK].

- **Change the Formats setting to From Template.**

- **Click** [OK].

- **Click** [Yes] **to replace the table of figures.**

Your screen should be similar to Figure 3.62

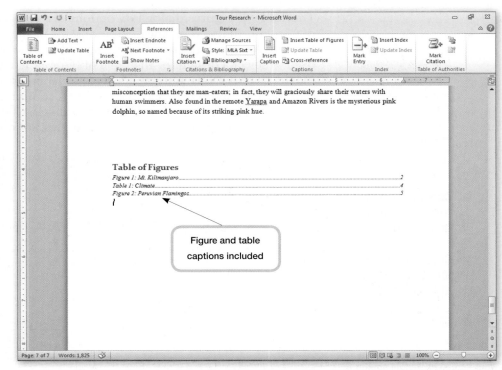

Figure 3.62

The table of figures now includes both table and figure captions using the default template style.

UPDATING A TABLE OF FIGURES

You have decided to change the table caption to Peru Climate to make it more descriptive of the table contents. Then you will update the table of figures to reflect this change.

1

- Use the Table 1: Climate hyperlink in the table of figures to jump to that location in the document.

- Click in the caption before the word Climate, type **Peru**, and press ⎵Spacebar⎵.

- Click on the table of figures to select it and click 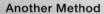 Update Table in the Captions group.

- Choose Update entire table and click OK .

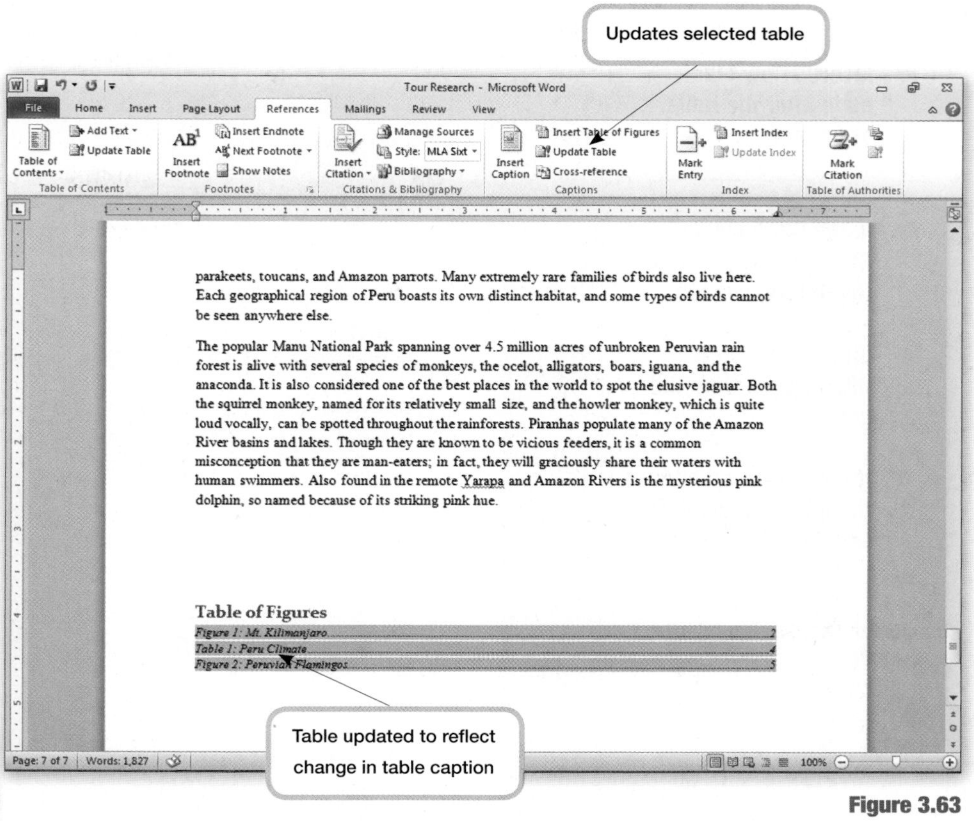

Another Method

You also could press F9 to update the table of figures or choose Update table from the table's context menu.

Updates selected table

Table updated to reflect change in table caption

Figure 3.63

The entry for the table is updated in the table of figures to reflect the change you made to the table caption.

Your screen should be similar to Figure 3.63

Creating a Bibliography

Finally, you are ready to create the bibliography for the report (see Concept 3). Word makes the process of creating a bibliography effortless by automatically generating the bibliography using the selected report style from the source information you entered when creating citations.

GENERATING THE BIBLIOGRAPHY

Additional Information

Word can automatically generate a complete bibliography that lists all sources associated with the document or an abbreviated bibliography that lists only those sources that have been cited.

The requirements for formatting a bibliography vary depending on the report style used. You are using the MLA style for this report. This style requires that each work directly referenced in the paper be listed in alphabetical order by author's last name on a separate page with the title "Works Cited."

Because you have already specified the MLA reference style, when the Works Cited bibliography is generated, the entries will automatically appear using the selected reference style.

1

- Insert a new blank page after the table of figures.

- Click 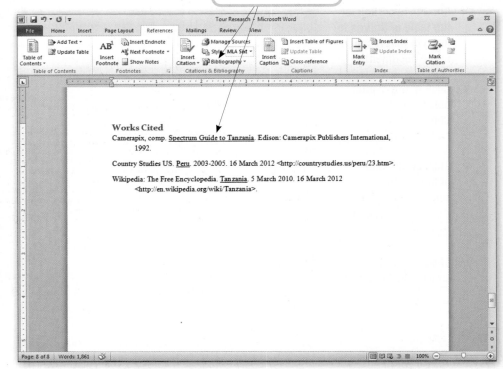 Bibliography ▾ in the Citations and Bibliography group of the References tab.

- Choose the Works Cited option from the gallery.

- If necessary, scroll to the top of the page to see the bibliography.

Your screen should be similar to Figure 3.64

> Generates bibliography from citation sources

Works Cited

Camerapix, comp. Spectrum Guide to Tanzania. Edison: Camerapix Publishers International, 1992.

Country Studies US. Peru. 2003-2005. 16 March 2012 <http://countrystudies.us/peru/23.htm>.

Wikipedia: The Free Encyclopedia. Tanzania. 5 March 2010. 16 March 2012 <http://en.wikipedia.org/wiki/Tanzania>.

Figure 3.64

The Works Cited bibliography is formatted using the selected MLA documentation style. The page is labeled with a Works Cited heading and each citation source is listed in ascending alphabetical order.

UPDATING A BIBLIOGRAPHY

Now, as you look at the Works Cited list, you believe you entered the wrong publisher information for the Camerapix source. Even though the bibliography has been generated, it can easily be updated to reflect additions and modifications to the sources. This is because the bibliography is a field that is linked to the sources in the Current List. You will fix the source information and update the bibliography. Rather than return to the citation in the document for this source to edit it, you will use the Source Manager.

1

Click

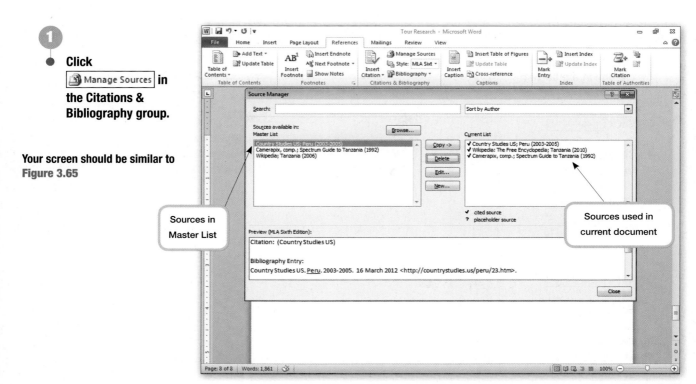

Manage Sources **in the Citations & Bibliography group.**

Your screen should be similar to Figure 3.65

Sources in Master List

Sources used in current document

Figure 3.65

Additional Information

The master list may display additional sources if they have been entered previously using this computer.

The Source Manager dialog box displays the three sources you entered in both the Master and Current List boxes. It is used to add, copy, delete, and edit sources. Notice that the items in the Current List are preceded with checkmarks. This indicates they have all been cited in the document. All items in the Current List will appear in the bibliography when it is generated. If a source appears in the Master List that you want to appear in the bibliography, you can select it and copy it to the Current List. You need to edit the Camerapix bibliography information.

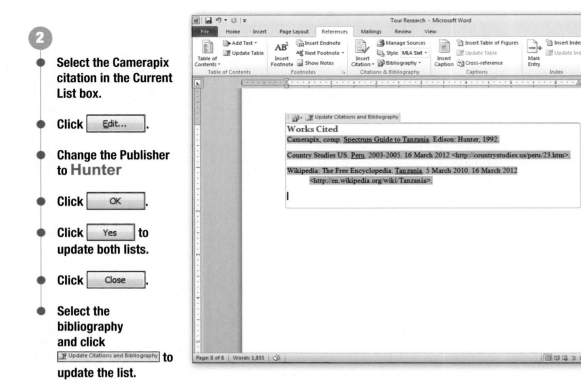

Figure 3.66

②

- Select the Camerapix citation in the Current List box.

- Click [Edit...].

- Change the Publisher to Hunter

- Click [OK].

- Click [Yes] to update both lists.

- Click [Close].

- Select the bibliography and click [Update Citations and Bibliography] to update the list.

Your screen should be similar to Figure 3.66

The bibliography information for the Camerapix source is now correct and the Works Cited list has been appropriately updated.

MODIFYING A BIBLIOGRAPHY

Finally, you will modify the format of the Works Cited page to more closely meet the MLA requirements. The page title should be centered at the top of the page. The bibliography entries must be formatted as hanging indents—the first line is even with the left margin and subsequent lines of the same work are indented 0.5 inch. Fortunately, your bibliography is already formatted this way. MLA formatting for the Works Cited page also requires that it should be double-spaced, as is the entire report.

First you will format the page title. In addition to centering the title at the top of the page, you decide to change the style of the title to the same as the table of contents title.

WD3.70   Lab 3: Creating Reports and Tables

WWW.MHHE.COM/OLEARY

Word 2010

- **Move to anywhere in the Works Cited title.**

- **Choose TOC Title from the Styles group of the Home tab.**

- **Click ▤ Center.**

Your screen should be similar to Figure 3.67

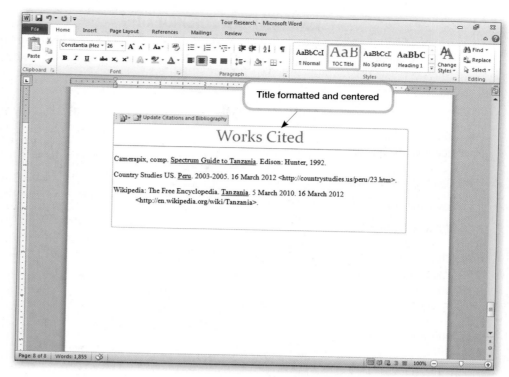

Title formatted and centered

Figure 3.67

Creating an Index

In a long document, a reader may remember seeing a particular item or term but not remember on which page to find it. To help your readers locate information quickly, you will create an index for your document.

Concept 9 Index

An **index** appears at the end of a long document as a list of major headings, topics, and terms with their page numbers. Word generates an index by compiling all of the entries and references to entries that you have previously marked in the content of your document, alphabetizing the list, and then assigning page numbers to the entries. An index subentry item is used to further define or explain the first index item. Once you've marked index entries in your document, you compile the entries into an index. The diagram below shows the relationship between index entries and subentries.

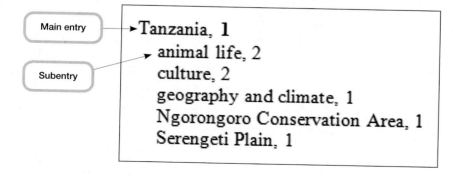

MARK ENTRIES FOR INDEXING

You decide to create index entries for the headings in the Tour Research document. You will mark your first entry by first selecting text.

- **Select the Tanzania heading on page 3.**

- **Open the References tab and click [Mark Entry] in the Index group.**

- **Choose Bold in the Page number format area.**

Your screen should be similar to Figure 3.68

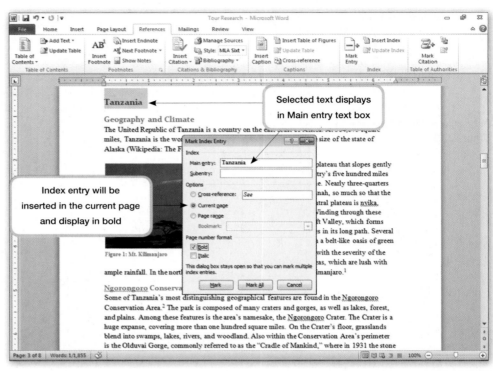

Figure 3.68

The selected text, Tanzania, is automatically displayed in the Main entry text box. The page number for this entry will be bold.

- **Click [Mark].**

Your screen should be similar to Figure 3.69

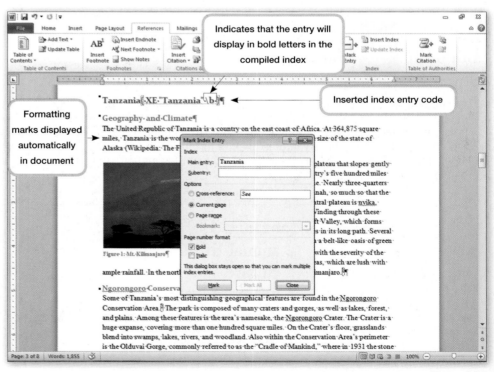

Figure 3.69

Notice that Word automatically turned on the display of formatting marks in your document and has inserted the field code "XE" with curly braces {} after the Tanzania heading. The XE field code will not print but will be used by Word later when generating the index. The Mark Index Entry dialog box is still open so that you can mark additional entries. Next you will create an index entry for the Geography and Climate heading by typing it in directly.

3

- If necessary, move the Mark Index Entry dialog box to the right side of your screen so that you can see more of your document.

- Click to the right of the Geography and Climate heading on page 3.

- Click in the Main entry text box and type **Tanzania**

- Type **geography and climate** in the Subentry text box.

- Click the Bold check box to remove the checkmark.

- Click **Mark**.

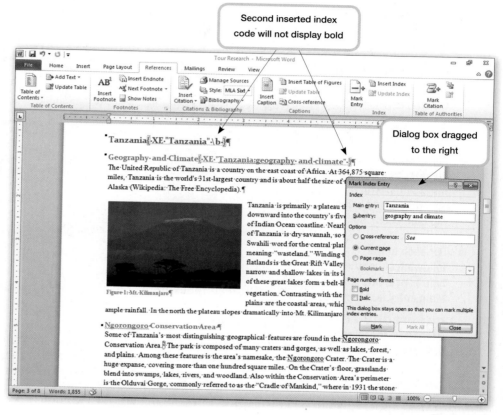

Second inserted index code will not display bold

Dialog box dragged to the right

Figure 3.70

Your screen should be similar to Figure 3.70

Another XE field code was inserted in the document. There was no need to capitalize the words "geography and climate" because they are not proper nouns. These words will be indented without bold letters below the Tanzania topic in the compiled index.

You will now mark thirteen additional index entries, all headings, in the Tour Research document. As you work, you may have to move the Mark Index Entry dialog box to another location on your screen to see the document text. Also, when marking subentries, it is usually easier to click to the right of the heading you want to include in your index before marking it. If you select the text instead, the selected text will appear in the Main entry text box and you will need to delete it.

4

- **For each of the following subentries, type** Tanzania **into the Main entry text box:**

  Ngorongoro Conservation Area

  Serengeti Plain

  culture

  animal life

- **Mark the Peru heading as a main index entry, with no subentries, and select the bold check box.**

- **For each of the following subentries, type** Peru **into the Main entry text box:**

  geography and climate (deselect the bold check box)

  La Costa

  La Selva

  La Sierra

  historical culture

  Machu Picchu

  current culture

  animal life

- **Close the Mark Index Entry dialog box.**

Your screen should be similar to Figure 3.71

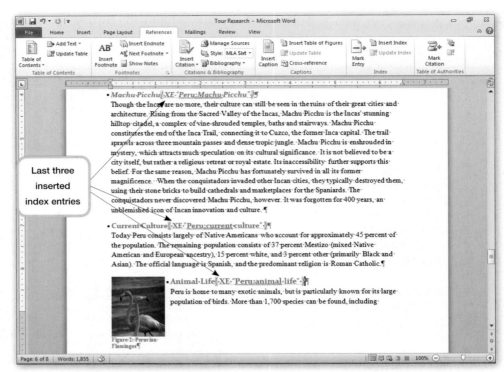

Last three inserted index entries

Figure 3.71

A total of fifteen index items have now been marked in your document.

CREATE THE INDEX

Now that all the entries are marked for your index, it is time to generate the index. Word collects the index entries, sorts them alphabetically, references their page numbers, finds and removes duplicate entries from the same page, and displays the index in the document.

1

● Turn off the display of formatting marks and then move to the end of the report.

● Insert a new blank page.

● Enter the title Index and format it with a Heading 1 style.

● Press Enter to move to a blank line below the title.

● Click 📄 Insert Index in the Index group of the References tab.

● Click OK .

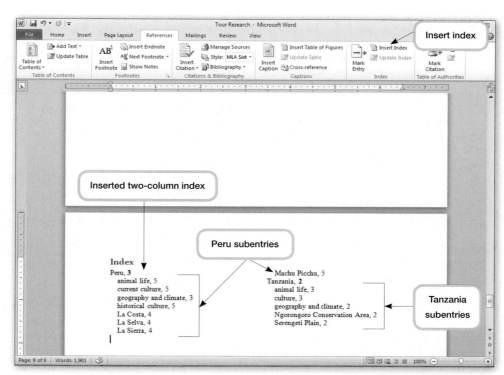

Figure 3.72

Your screen should be similar to Figure 3.72

Word has generated a two-column index with the entries you marked in the document. Notice that the page numbers for the main entries Tanzania and Peru are bold. Each subentry appears indented below its corresponding main entry.

UPDATE AND MODIFY THE INDEX

You decide that you should include items in your index from the body text of the Tour Research document. For example, you would like the index to include a reference to Mt. Kilimanjaro, the Olduvai Gorge, and several other sites. An index, like a table of contents, is a field that can easily be updated if you add, edit, format, or delete index entries after the index is generated. You will now mark several additional items in the Tour Research document as main entries.

Select and then mark each of the following words and phrases as main index entries with bold page numbers:

Location	Main Entry	
Tanzania topic		
Geography and Climate topic, second paragraph	**Great Rift Valley (select bold)**	
	Mt. Kilimanjaro	
Ngorongoro Conservation Area topic	**Ngorongoro Crater**	
	Olduvai Gorge	
Culture topic, first paragraph	**Swahili**	
Culture topic, second paragraph, first sentence	**Masai**	
Peru topic		
Geography and Climate topic, La Selva topic	**Amazon Basin**	
Historical Culture topic, first paragraph	**Incas**	
Historical Culture topic, second paragraph	**Francisco Pizarro**	
Animal Life topic, second paragraph	**Manu National Park**	

Additional Information

You may find the need to edit, format, or delete an index entry. To edit or format an existing index entry, click in the XE field in your document, and then change the text inside the quotation marks. Any formatting you apply to the text in the XE field will also be reflected in the compiled index. To delete an index entry, select the entire XE field, including the braces ({}), then press Delete.

- **Close the Mark Entry dialog box.**

- **Click on the index at the end of the document and press F9 to update the table.**

- **Turn off the display of formatting marks, and then click outside the index.**

Your screen should be similar to Figure 3.73

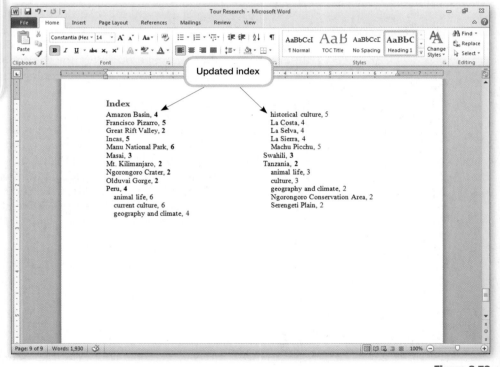

Figure 3.73

The index now includes displays all the newly added index entries. Finally, you decide to modify the design of the index so that the entries appear in a single column.

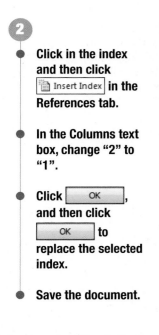

2

● **Click in the index and then click** [Insert Index] **in the References tab.**

● **In the Columns text box, change "2" to "1".**

● **Click** [OK]**, and then click** [OK] **to replace the selected index.**

● **Save the document.**

Your screen should be similar to Figure 3.74

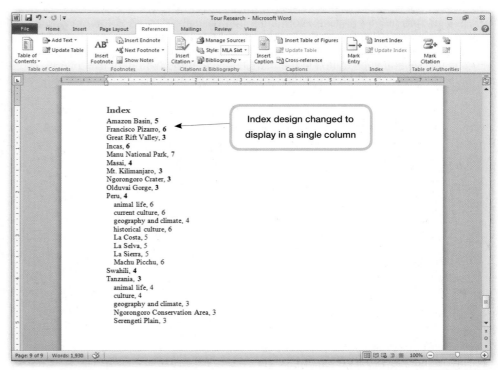

Figure 3.74

The index now displays as a single column.

Creating Headers and Footers

Next you want to add information in a header and footer to the report.

Concept Header and Footer

Headers and footers provide information that typically appears at the top and bottom of each page in a document and helps the reader locate information in a document. A **header** is a line or several lines of text in the top margin of each page. The header usually contains the title and the section of the document. A **footer** is a line or several lines of text in the margin space at the bottom of every page. The footer usually contains the page number and perhaps the date. Headers and footers also can contain graphics such as a company logo.

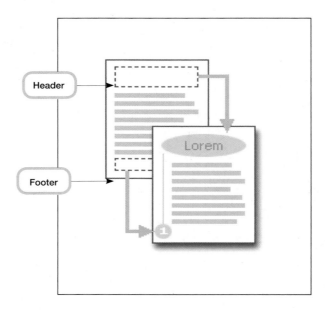

The same header and footer can be used throughout a document, or a different header and footer can be used in different sections of a document. For example, a unique header or footer can be used in one section and a different one in another section. You also can have a unique header or footer on the first page, or omitted entirely from the first page, or use a different header and footer on odd and even pages.

You want to add a header and footer to the entire document except for the first two pages.

USING A PREDESIGNED HEADER

Word includes many features that help you quickly create attractive headers and footers. Among these features are predesigned built-in header and footer designs that include placeholders to help you enter information. You will create a header for the report using this feature.

Because you do not want headers and footers on the first two pages of the document, you will first divide the document into two sections. You replace the hard page break that you inserted when creating the table of contents page with a Next Page section break.

①

- Move to the table of contents page.

- Turn on the display of formatting marks.

- Select the hard page break line below the table of contents and press Delete to remove it.

- At this location, insert a Next Page section break.

Having Trouble?

If you're having trouble inserting a Next Page section break, refer to the "Inserting a Section Break" topic in Lab 2.

- Turn off the display of formatting marks.

- Open the Insert tab and click ▤ Header ▾ in the Header & Footer group.

- From the gallery of header designs, choose Sideline.

Your screen should be similar to Figure 3.75

Additional Information

You can hide the display of the document text while working with headers and footers by deselecting ☑ Show Document Text in the Options group of the Design tab.

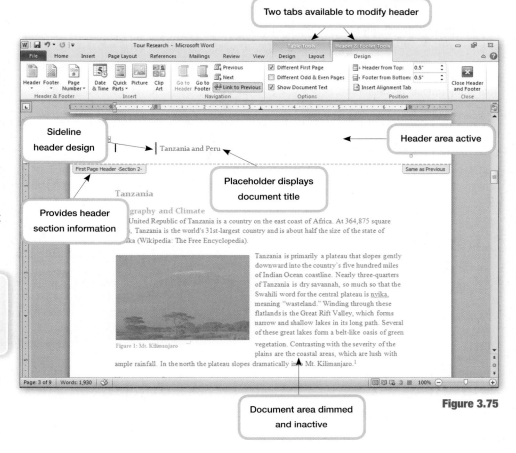

Two tabs available to modify header

Sideline header design

Tanzania and Peru

Header area active

First Page Header -Section 2-

Placeholder displays document title

Provides header section information

Tanzania

...graphy and Climate

United Republic of Tanzania is a country on the east coast of Africa. At 364,875 square ..., Tanzania is the world's 31st-largest country and is about half the size of the state of ...ka (Wikipedia: The Free Encyclopedia).

Tanzania is primarily a plateau that slopes gently downward into the country's five hundred miles of Indian Ocean coastline. Nearly three-quarters of Tanzania is dry savannah, so much so that the Swahili word for the central plateau is nyika, meaning "wasteland." Winding through these flatlands is the Great Rift Valley, which forms narrow and shallow lakes in its long path. Several of these great lakes form a belt-like oasis of green vegetation. Contrasting with the severity of the plains are the coastal areas, which are lush with ample rainfall. In the north the plateau slopes dramatically in...o Mt. Kilimanjaro.[1]

Figure 1: Mt. Kilimanjaro

Page: 3 of 9   Words: 1,930

Document area dimmed and inactive

Figure 3.75

The document area dims and the header area, above the dashed line, is active. The Header and Footer Tools Design tab is automatically displayed. Its buttons are used to add items to the header and footer and to navigate between headers and footers.

The Sideline design includes a graphic bar like that used in the cover page and the report title placeholder that displays the title from the document properties in orange. Notice that in addition to the Header and Footer Tools tab, the Table Tools tab is displayed. This is because the design is contained in a table consisting of a single cell that is used to control the placement of items.

MODIFYING HEADER SETTINGS

Notice the tab on the left below the dashed line of the header. This tab identifies the section information for each page of the document. Both sections of the Tour Research document have their own header areas that can be formatted differently.

1

● **Change the zoom to 39%.**

Your screen should be similar to Figure 3.76

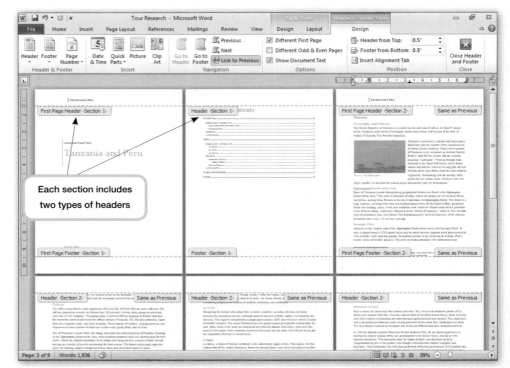

Each section includes two types of headers

Figure 3.76

Now you can see that the document contains two types of headers: "First Page Headers" and running "Headers." Word automatically added first page headers because it detected that the document includes a cover page. This allows you to create a unique header for the first page. Notice the Sidelines design has been inserted only in the "First Page Header" headers and that the headers on the following pages of the same section are blank.

Since it is not necessary to have a separate First Page Header in section 2, you will remove it and then insert the Sideline design again for the running header of that section.

2

- Click the "First Page Header—Section 2" tab below the dotted header line on page 3.

- Click ☑ Different First Page in the Options tab to turn off this feature for Section 2.

- Open the Insert tab, click 📄 Header ▾ in the Header & Footer group, and choose Sideline.

Your screen should be similar to Figure 3.77

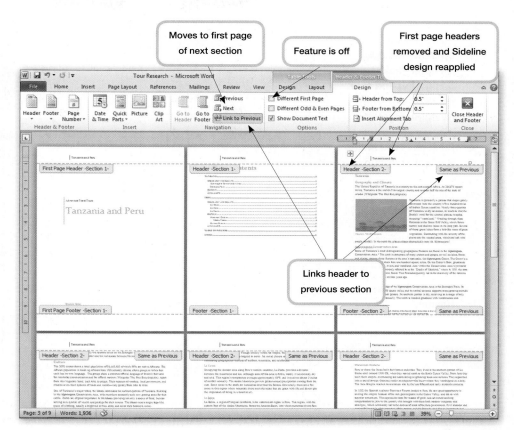

Moves to first page of next section

Feature is off

First page headers removed and Sideline design reapplied

Links header to previous section

Figure 3.77

Now all the headers in both sections of the document are formatted using this design. The same design was applied to both sections because the headers are initially linked even though the document is divided into sections. Notice the tab on the right displays "Same as Previous." When this setting is on, the header in the previous sections will have the same settings as the header in the section you are defining. Because you do not want the title or contents pages in section 1 to display information in the header, you will break the connection between sections 1 and 2 by turning off this option. Then you will remove the header from section 1.

● **Open the Header & Footer Tools Design tab and click** ⬚ Link to Previous **in the Navigation group.**

● **Click** ⬚ Previous **in the Navigation group.**

● **Click** ☑ Different First Page **in the Options group.**

● **Open the Insert tab and click** ⬚ Header ▾.

● **Choose Remove Header.**

Your screen should be similar to Figure 3.78

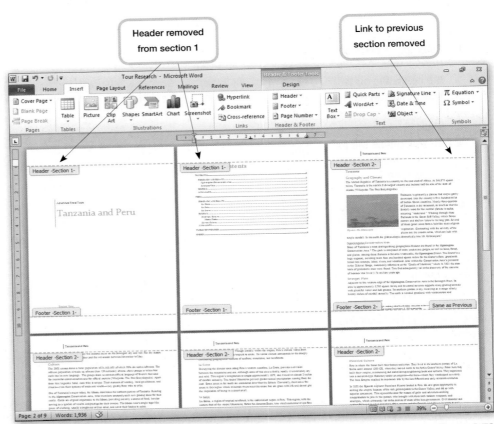

Header removed from section 1

Link to previous section removed

Figure 3.78

The header information is removed from section 1.

CHANGING HEADER CONTENT

The header text for your document is currently displaying in a single table cell. Before inserting your name in the header, you will add two columns to the right of the existing title. You will then insert your name into the cell on the right. To quickly add this information, you will use a Quick Parts entry.

1

- Open the Design tab and click Next in the Navigation group to move to the Section 2 header area.

- Increase the zoom to 100%.

- Click [📊 View Gridlines] on the Table Tools Layout tab to view the table's gridlines.

- Right-click the header text, select Insert and then choose Insert Columns to the Right from the context menu.

- Insert another column to the right of the newly inserted column.

Your screen should be similar to Figure 3.79

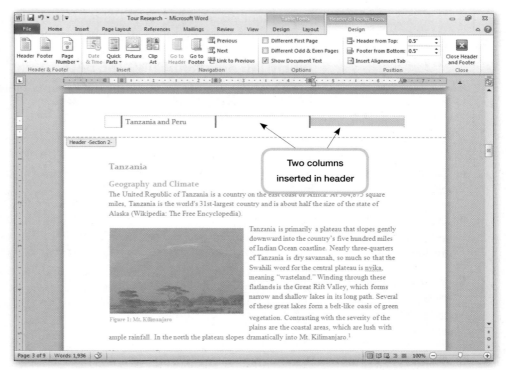

Figure 3.79

The table is now three cells wide. Now you will insert your name into the cell on the right.

2

- Click [📋 Quick Parts ▾] on the Insert tab.

- Select Document Property and choose Author.

- Right-align the contents of the cell on the right.

Your screen should be similar to Figure 3.80

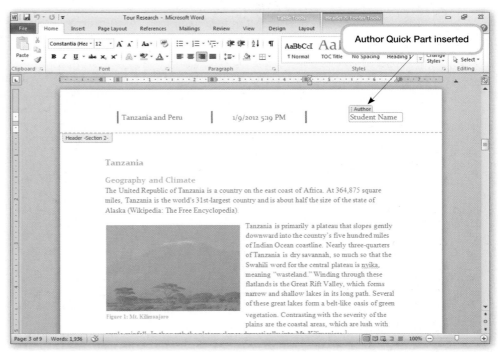

Figure 3.80

The Author placeholder is right-aligned in the header and displays your name because this information is stored in the document properties.

INSERTING AND MODIFYING THE DATE

Finally, you will add an automatic date stamp to display the current date in the middle cell of the header.

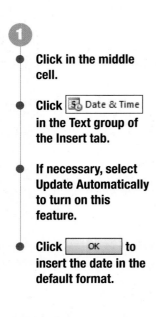

- Click in the middle cell.

- Click **⑤ Date & Time** in the Text group of the Insert tab.

- If necessary, select **Update Automatically** to turn on this feature.

- Click **OK** to insert the date in the default format.

Your screen should be similar to Figure 3.81

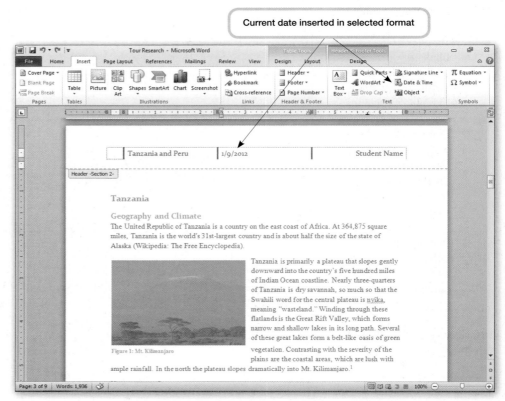

Current date inserted in selected format

Figure 3.81

The current date is inserted as a field and will update when the system date changes. Instead you decide to change the date to display the date and time the document was last saved using a Quick Parts entry.

2

- Select and delete the date placeholder.

- Click [≣ Quick Parts ▾] and choose Field.

- Choose Date and Time from the Categories list.

- Choose SaveDate from the Field Names list.

- Choose the M/d/yyyy h:mm am/pm date and time format (1/9/2012 4:05 PM).

- Click [OK] and then center the date.

- Click [≣ View Gridlines] on the Table Tools Layout tab to hide the table's gridlines.

- Reduce the zoom to 39%.

Your screen should be similar to Figure 3.82

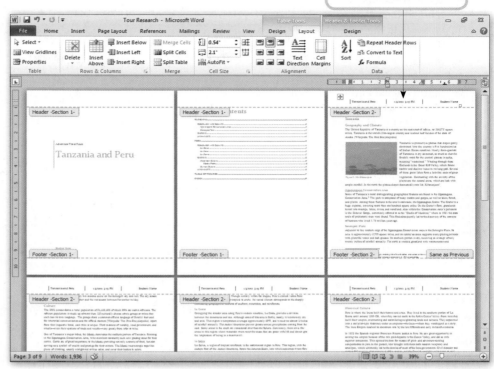

File save date and time inserted using Quick Parts

Figure 3.82

The date and time reflect the date and time the file was last saved. It can be updated when you save the file again.

INSERTING AND MODIFYING PAGE NUMBERS

Next, you will add information to the footer. You want the footer to display the page number. Page numbers can be added to the top, bottom, or side margins of the page. Word includes many built-in page number designs that include formatting and graphic elements to help you quickly create attractive page numbers. You will add the number to the bottom of the page, which inserts it in the footer.

1

Open the Insert tab and then click 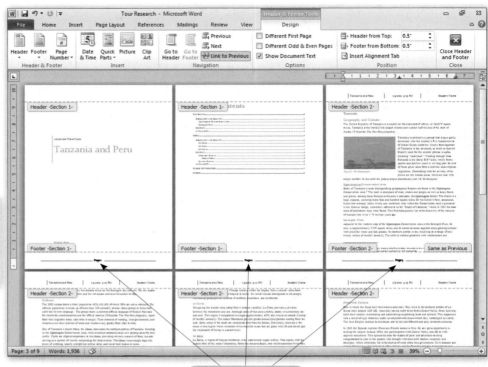 **Footer ▾** **in the Header & Footer group.**

Scroll the list and choose Conservative from the list of styles.

Additional Information

You also can easily change the built-in designs or create your own custom designs and save them to the gallery using the Save Selection as Page Number option.

Your screen should be similar to Figure 3.83

Additional Information

You also can display different information on odd and even pages for both headers and footers using Different Odd & Even Pages.

Additional Information

You also can change the format of page numbers from Arabic to Roman Numerals or letters and include chapter numbers.

Page number inserted for all sections

Figure 3.83

The footer area is active and the page number appears centered in the selected design in the footer of both sections. The number is a field that updates to reflect the document page. By default, when you insert sections, page numbering continues from the previous section. Because you do not want the title or contents pages in section 1 to display the footer information, you will break the connection between sections 1 and 2 by turning off this option. Then you will remove the footer from section 1 and begin page numbering with section 2.

- Move to the section 2 footer.

- Click 🔗 Link to Previous.

- Move to the footer of section 1.

- Click 📄 Footer ▾ on the Insert tab and choose Remove Footer.

- Move to the footer of section 2.

- Click 📄 Page Number ▾ in the Header & Footer group.

- Choose Format Page Numbers.

- Choose Start At.

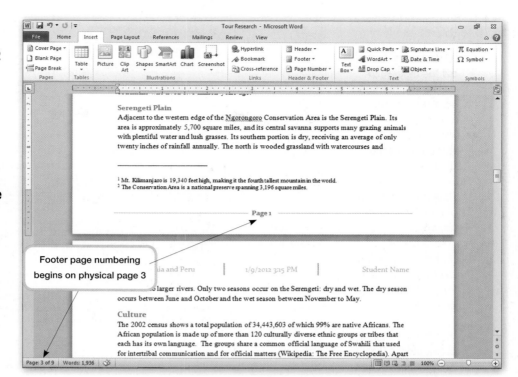

Figure 3.84

The section 2 footer now displays "1" as the current page number.

- Click ⬜ OK.

- Increase the zoom to 100%.

- Double-click outside the footer area to close the header and footer areas.

- Scroll the document so that your screen appears similar to Figure 3.84.

Your screen should be similar to Figure 3.84

Updating a Table of Contents

You have made many modifications to the report since generating the table of contents, so you want to update the listing. Because the table of contents is a field, if you add or remove headings, rearrange topics, or make other changes that affect the table of contents listing, you can quickly update the table of contents. In this case, you have added pictures, a table, a bibliography, a table of figures, and an index that have affected the paging and content of the document.

You will first review the overall layout of your document, and then update the table of contents to ensure that the page references are accurate and that any new content is included. You will also update the table of figures and the index to ensure that the correct page numbers are displaying.

- If necessary, turn off the display of paragraph marks in your document.

- Move to the third page of the document.

- Delete the blank line above the Tanzania heading.

- If necessary, delete the blank line above Peru's Culture heading.

- Insert a hard page break before Peru's Animal Life section so that the flamingo picture is not split between pages.

- Move to the table of contents page and click anywhere on the table of contents.

- Click **Update Table...** in the field tab.

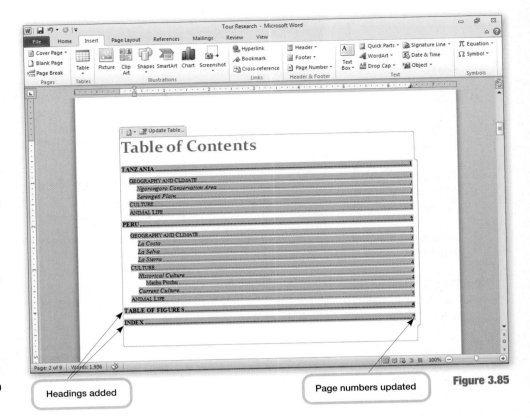

Headings added

Page numbers updated

Figure 3.85

Another Method

You also can use **Update Table** on the References tab, or choose Update Field from the table of contents context menu, or press F9 to quickly update a table of contents field.

- Choose Update entire table.

- Click **OK** and then scroll the document slightly to see the entire table of contents.

Your screen should be similar to Figure 3.85

The page numbers referenced by each table-of-contents hyperlink have been updated as needed and the Table of Figures and Index headings have been added to the list. However, the Works Cited page is not included. This is because the Works Cited page title is formatted using the TOC Title style, not a heading style. You will add the Works Cited page to the table of contents listing by marking the individual entry.

2

- Move to the Works Cited page title.

- Click 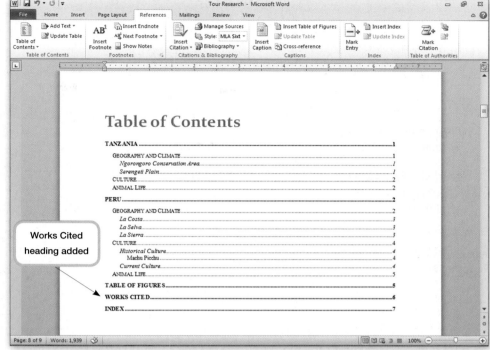 **Add Text** in the Table of Contents group of the References tab.

- Select Level 1 as the level for the heading.

- Click **Update Table** in the Table of Contents group.

- Choose Update entire table.

- Click **OK**.

- Move back to the table of contents page.

Your screen should be similar to Figure 3.86

Table of Contents

Works Cited heading added

Figure 3.86

The listing now includes a hyperlink to the Works Cited page. Finally, you will update the table of figures and the index.

3

- Use the Table of Figures link in the table of contents to quickly navigate to the table of figures.

- Right-click the table of figures and then choose Update Field.

- Choose Update entire table and then click **OK**.

- In a similar manner, update the index at the end of the document.

- Save the document.

The document has now been updated with the correct page numbers.

Printing Selected Pages

You are now ready to print the report.

1

- **Open the File tab and then choose Print.**

- **Reduce the zoom to 20% to display all nine pages.**

Your screen should be similar to **Figure 3.87**

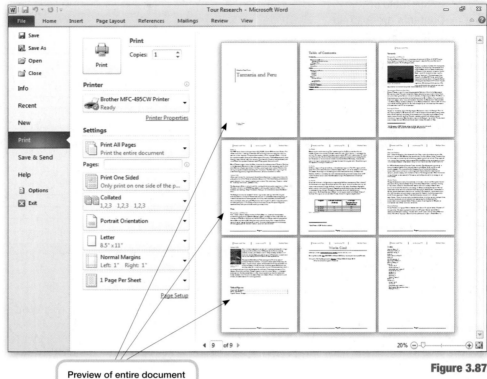

Preview of entire document

Figure 3.87

You would like to print only the first and second pages in section one, and the sixth, seventh, and eighth pages in section two of the document. To do this, you use the Pages text box to select the pages you want to print. When printing pages in different sections, the page number and section number (p#s#) must be identified in the page range.

2

● If necessary, select the appropriate printer for your computer system.

● Type **p1s1, p2s1, p6s2-p8s2** in the Pages text box.

● Click [Print].

● Exit Word.

Your printed output should be similar to that shown in the Case Study at the beginning of the lab.

CUS ON CAREERS

EXPLORE YOUR CAREER OPTIONS

Market Research Analyst

Have you ever wondered who investigates the market for new products? Ever thought about the people who put together phone surveys? Market research analysts are responsible for determining the potential sales for a new product or service. They conduct surveys and compile statistics for clients or their employer. These reports usually include report features like a table of contents, cross-references, headers and footers, and footnotes for references. Market research analysts may hold positions as faculty at a university, work for large organizations, or hold governmental positions. The average salary range for an entry-level market research analyst is $48,500, with demand higher in a strong economy.

Theme (WD3.17)

A theme is a predefined set of formatting choices that can be applied to an entire document in one simple step.

Table of Contents (WD3.23)

A table of contents is a listing of the topic headings that appear in a document and their associated page references

Citations and Bibliography (WD3.30)

Parenthetical source references, called citations, give credit for specific information included in the document. Complete source information for citations is included in a bibliography at the end of the report.

Footnotes and Endnotes (WD3.37)

Footnotes and endnotes are used in documented research papers to explain or comment on information in the text, or provide source references for text in the document.

Text Wrapping (WD3.42)

You can control the appearance of text around a graphic object by specifying the text wrapping style.

Captions and Cross-References (WD3.46)

A caption is a numbered label for a figure, table, picture, or graph. A cross-reference is a reference from one part of a document to related information in another part.

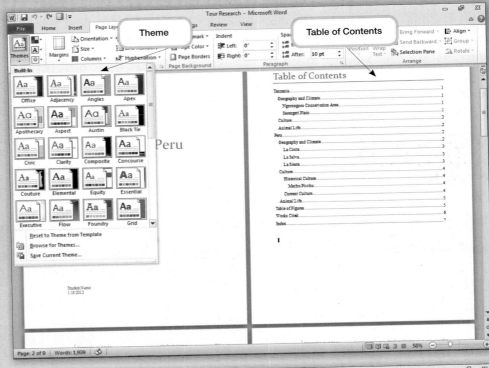

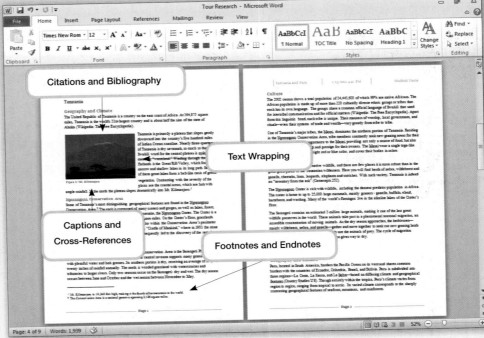

Table (WD3.53)

A table is used to organize information into an easy-to-read format of horizontal rows and vertical columns.

Table of Figures (WD3.64)

A table of figures is a list of the figures, tables, or equations used in a document and their associated page numbers.

Index (WD3.71)

An index appears at the end of a long document as a list of major headings, topics, and terms with their page numbers.

Header and Footer (WD3.77)

A header is a line or several lines of text in the top margin of each page. A footer is a line or several lines of text in the margin space at the bottom of every page.

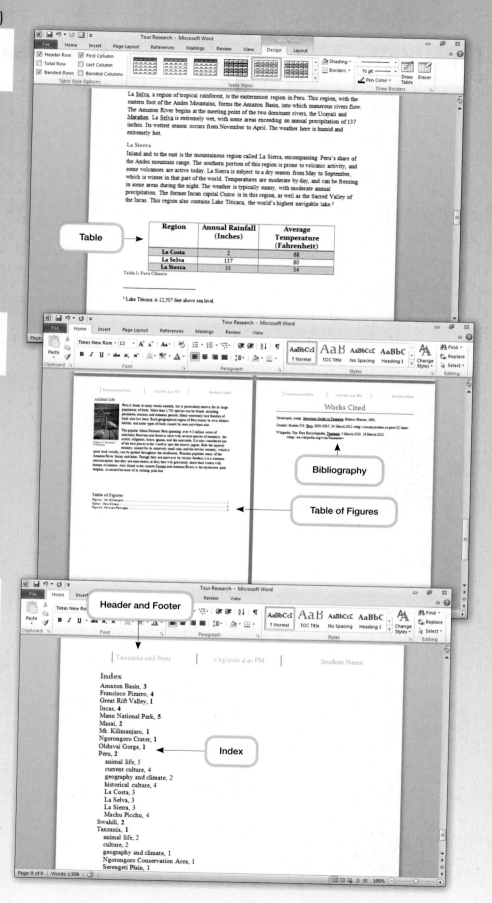

KEY TERMS

bibliography WD3.30
caption WD3.46
cell WD3.53
citations WD3.30
cross-reference WD3.46
drawing layer WD3.42
endnote WD3.37
floating object WD3.42
footer WD3.78
footnote WD3.37
header WD3.78
heading style WD3.5
index WD3.71

inline object WD3.42
note reference mark WD3.37
note separator WD3.37
sort WD3.58
split window WD3.48
table WD3.53
table of contents WD3.23
table of figures WD3.64
table reference WD3.53
text box WD3.47
text wrapping style WD3.42
theme WD3.17

COMMAND SUMMARY

Button/Command	Shortcut	Action
File tab		
Print		
🗐 Options /Proofing		Changes settings associated with Spelling and Grammar checking
Home tab		
Paragraph group		
↓A↓ Sort		Rearranges items in a selection into ascending alphabetical/ numerical order
Insert tab		
Pages group		
🗎 Cover Page ▾		Inserts a preformatted cover page
🗋 Blank Page		Inserts a blank page
Tables group		
Table		Inserts table at insertion point
Header and Footer group		
🗐 Header ▾		Inserts predesigned header style
🗐 Footer ▾		Inserts predesigned footer style
Page Layout tab		
Themes group		
Aa Themes		Applies selected theme to document
◼▾ Theme Colors		Changes colors for current theme
A▾ Theme Fonts		Changes fonts for current theme
Arrange group		
Wrap Text ▾		Controls how text wraps around a selected object
References tab		
Table of Contents group		
Table of Contents ▾		Generates a table of contents

COMMAND SUMMARY (CONTINUED)

Button/Command	Shortcut	Action
🖹 Add Text ▾		Adds selected text as an entry in table of contents
🖹 Update Table...	F9	Updates the table of contents field
Footnotes group		
AB¹ Insert Footnote	Alt + Ctrl + F	Inserts footnote reference at insertion point
Citations & Bibliography group		
Insert Citation ▾		Creates a citation for a reference source
🖹 Manage Sources		Displays list of all sources cited
Style: APA Fiftl ▾		Sets the style of citations
🖹 Bibliography ▾		Creates a bibliography list of sources cited
Captions group		
Insert Caption		Adds a figure caption
🖹 Cross-reference		Creates figure cross-references
Index Group		
Mark Entry		Mark an index entry
🖹 Insert Index		Inserts an index at the insertion point
View tab		
Window group		
Split		Divides a document into two horizontal sections
Picture Tools Format tab		
Arrange group		
Wrap Text ▾		Specifies how text will wrap around picture

COMMAND SUMMARY (CONTINUED)

Button/Command	Shortcut	Action
Table Tools Design tab		
Table Style Options group		
☑ Header Row		Turns on/off formats for header row
☑ First Column		Turns on/off formats for first column
☐ Last Column		Turns on/off formats for last column
Table Styles group		
⌄ More		Opens Table Styles gallery
Table Tools Layout tab		
Rows & Columns group		
Insert Above		Inserts a new row in table above selected row
Alignment group		
▤ Align Top Center		Aligns text at top center of cell space
Header & Footer Tools Design tab		
Header & Footer Group		
Page Number ▾		Inserts page number in header or footer
Insert group		
Date & Time		Inserts current date or time in header or footer
Quick Parts ▾ /Document Property		Inserts selected document property into header or footer
Quick Parts ▾ /Field		Inserts selected field Quick Part
Navigation group		
Link to Previous		Turns on/off link to header or footer in previous section
Option group		
☑ Different First Page		Specifies a unique header and footer for the first page
Position group		
Insert Alignment Tab		Inserts a tab stop to align content in header/footer

LAB EXERCISES

MATCHING

Match the item on the left with the correct description on the right.

1. index   _____ a. letter and number used to identify table cells
2. heading style _____ b. inserts built-in pieces of information automatically
3. table reference _____ c. parenthetical source reference
4. cross-reference _____ d. graphic positioned directly in the text
5. caption   _____ e. lists major headings, topics, and terms with their page numbers
6. inline image   _____ f. text closely follows contours around a graphic
7. citation   _____ g. combination of fonts, type sizes, bold, and italics used
                          to identify different topic levels in a document
8. bibliography   _____ h. reference from one part of the document to another part
9. document theme _____ i. numbered label for a figure, table, picture, or graph
10. tight wrap   _____ j. complete source information for citations

TRUE/FALSE

Circle the correct answer to the following questions.

1. You must be viewing your document in Draft view before using
   the Sort command.   **True   False**
2. Footnotes must be manually renumbered as you move text around
   in a document.   **True   False**
3. A table of contents and a cross-reference are fields.   **True   False**
4. Citations give credit for specific information included in the document. **True   False**
5. Indexes are used for compiling complete source information for citations. **True   False**
6. A document theme is applied to selected characters and paragraphs.   **True   False**
7. A table of contents hyperlink is used to jump directly to a specific location
   in a document.   **True   False**
8. Information that appears at the top of every page is referred to as an endnote. **True   False**
9. Floating objects are inserted into the drawing layer.   **True   False**
10. Once heading styles are applied to a document's titles, it becomes easier
    to navigate the document.   **True   False**

FILL-IN

Complete the following statements by filling in the blanks with the correct terms.

1. A(n) _____ is a set of formats that is assigned a name and can be quickly applied to a document.

2. The _____ for a footnote appears at the bottom of the page on which the reference mark appears.

3. The intersection of a row and a column creates a(n) _____.

4. A(n) _____ is a container for text and other graphic objects that can be moved like any other object.

5. A(n) _____ is used to identify topics and their associated page numbers in a document.

6. A(n) _____ identifies the content to be entered in a cover page.

7. A(n) _____ is used to organize information into horizontal rows and vertical columns.

8. By changing a graphic to a(n) _____, it is inserted into the drawing layer.

9. Specifying _____ controls how text appears around a graphic object.

10. A(n) _____ is a line or several lines of text at the top of each page in a document.

LAB EXERCISES

MULTIPLE CHOICE

Circle the correct response to the questions below.

1. A _____ is a reference from one part of a document to related information in another part of the same document.
   a. citation
   b. caption
   c. heading
   d. cross-reference

2. A(n) _____ displays information in horizontal rows and vertical columns.
   a. Document Map
   b. cell reference
   c. object
   d. table

3. _____ are lines of text at the top and bottom of a page outside the margin lines.
   a. Characters and paragraphs
   b. Headers and footers
   c. Tables and text wrappers
   d. Styles and sections

4. A _____ allows you to see two parts of the same document at the same time.
   a. divided window
   b. split window
   c. sectioned window
   d. note pane

5. A(n) _____ is inserted at the end of a document listing headings and topics with their associated page numbers.
   a. bibliography
   b. table of figures
   c. index
   d. caption list

6. You can control how text appears around a graphic with _____ styles.
   a. sorting
   b. text wrapping
   c. section
   d. caption

7. Floating objects are inserted into the _____.
   a. Navigation Pane
   b. drawing layer
   c. header and footer area
   d. table of figures

8. Which of the following would you insert at the end of a report to identify the sources you used when conducting research for a report?
   a. caption
   b. table of figures
   c. citation
   d. bibliography

9. A _____ is a line of text that describes the object that appears above it.
   a. citation
   b. cross-reference
   c. caption
   d. footnote

10. A(n) _____ is a predesigned set of formats that can be applied to an entire document.
    a. AutoFormat
    b. theme
    c. style
    d. Quick Part

STEP-BY-STEP

IMPROVING A REPORT ★

1. You have become the local composting expert in your community. Many of your friends and neighbors have asked you for more information about composting, so you've put together some information in a Word document. The document is in need of formatting to help your readers to more easily identify topics and lists. You would also like to add a picture to the document and a footer. Your completed document is similar to the one shown here:

   a. Open the file
      wd03_Composting.

   b. Apply the Heading 1 style to the title "Basic Information." Change the spacing before this heading to 0.

   c. Insert a line after the title that includes the following text: **Compiled by Student Name**. Center the first two lines of the document.

   d. Apply the Heading 2 style to the following text: "Did You Know That Compost Can . . ." on page 1, "Organic Materials" on page 1, "What to Compost—The IN List" at the bottom of page 1, and "What Not to Compost—The OUT List" on page 2.

   e. Apply bullets using the style of your choice to the list of items in the "Did You Know That Compost Can . . ." section. Apply this same bullet style to the list of items in the "What to Compost—The IN List" and "What Not to Compost—The OUT List" sections, not including the "Note" at the bottom of the page.

   f. Save the document as Composting Information.

Basic Information
Compiled¹ by Student Name

Compost is organic material that can be used as a soil amendment or as a medium to grow plants. Mature compost is a stable material with a content called humus that is dark brown or black and has a soil-like, earthy smell. It is created by: combining organic wastes (e.g., yard trimmings, food wastes, manures) in proper ratios into piles, rows, or vessels; adding bulking agents (e.g., wood chips) as necessary to accelerate the breakdown of organic materials; and allowing the finished material to fully stabilize and mature through a curing process.

Natural composting, or biological decomposition, began with the first plants on earth and has been going on ever since. As vegetation falls to the ground, it slowly decays, providing minerals and nutrients needed for plants, animals, and microorganisms. Mature compost, however, includes the production of high temperatures to destroy pathogens and weed seeds that natural decomposition does not destroy.

Did You Know That Compost Can...
- Suppress plant diseases and pests.
- Reduce or eliminate the need for chemical fertilizers.
- Promote higher yields of agricultural crops.
- Facilitate reforestation, wetlands restoration, and habitat revitalization efforts by amending contaminated, compacted, and marginal soils.
- Cost-effectively remediate soils contaminated by hazardous waste.
- Remove solids, oil, grease, and heavy metals from storm water runoff.
- Capture and destroy 99.6 percent of industrial volatile organic chemicals (VOCs) in contaminated air.
- Provide cost savings of at least 50 percent over conventional soil, water, and air pollution remediation technologies, where applicable.

Organic Materials
Yard trimmings and food residuals together constitute 23 percent of the U.S. waste stream, as documented by EPA. An estimated 56.9 percent of yard trimmings were recovered for composting or grass cycled in 2000, a dramatic increase from the 12 percent recovery rate in 1990. Accompanying this surge in yard waste recovery is a composting industry that has grown from less than 1,000 facilities in 1988 to nearly 3,800 in 2000. Once dominated by public sector operations, the composting industry is increasingly entrepreneurial and private-sector driven, led by firms that add value to compost products through processing and marketing. Compost prices have been as high as $26 per ton for landscape mulch to more than $100 per ton for high-grade compost, which is bagged and sold at the retail level.

¹ All the information in this document comes from the United States Environmental Protection Agency website at http://www.epa.gov/osw/conserve/rrr/composting/basic.htm.

g. Display the headings in the document using the Navigation Pane. Using the Navigation Pane, move the "What to Compost—The IN List" heading and associated text to after the "What Not to Compost—The OUT List" section.

h. Move the "Note" paragraph located at the end of the "What Not to Compost—The OUT List" section and the following blank line to the end of the document.

i. Insert the current page number in a footer using the Grid style.

j. Using the References tab, insert a footnote to the right of the word Compiled on the second line of the document that includes the following text: **All the information in this document comes from the United States Environmental Protection Agency website at http://www.epa.gov/osw/conserve/rrr/composting/basic.htm.**

While yard trimmings recovery typically involves leaf compost and mulch, yard trimmings can also be combined with other organic waste, such as food residuals, animal manure, and bio solids to produce a variety of products with slightly different chemical and physical characteristics. In contrast to yard trimmings recovery, only 2.6 percent of food waste was composted in 2000. The cost-prohibitive nature of residential food waste separation and collection is the primary deterrent to expanding food waste recovery efforts. Yet in many communities, edible food residuals are donated to the needy, while inedible food residuals are blended into compost or reprocessed into animal feed. In some areas, composting operations are working with high-volume commercial and institutional food producers to recover their food byproducts, saving these firms significant disposal costs.

What Not to Compost - The OUT List

- Black walnut tree leaves or twigs -- Releases substances that might be harmful to plants
- Coal or charcoal ash -- Might contain substances harmful to plants
- Dairy products (e.g., butter, milk, sour cream, yogurt) and eggs -- Create odor problems and attract pests such as rodents and flies
- Diseased or insect-ridden plants -- Diseases or insects might survive and be transferred back to other plants
- Fats, grease, lard, or oils -- Create odor problems and attract pests such as rodents and flies
- Meat or fish bones and scraps -- Create odor problems and attract pests such as rodents and flies
- Pet wastes (e.g., dog or cat feces, soiled cat litter) -- Might contain parasites, bacteria, germs, pathogens, and viruses harmful to humans
- Yard trimmings treated with chemical pesticides -- Might kill beneficial composting organisms

What to Compost - The IN List

- Animal manure
- Cardboard rolls
- Clean paper
- Coffee grounds and filters
- Cotton rags
- Dryer and vacuum cleaner lint
- Eggshells
- Fireplace ashes
- Fruits and vegetables
- Grass clippings
- Hair and fur
- Hay and straw
- Houseplants
- Leaves
- Nut shells
- Sawdust
- Shredded newspaper
- Tea bags
- Wood chips
- Wool rags
- Yard trimmings

NOTE: Finished compost can be applied to lawns and gardens to help condition the soil and replenish nutrients. Compost, however, should not be used as potting soil for houseplants because of the presence of weed and grass seeds.

k. Remove the formatting from the hyperlink.

l. Use the Clip Art pane to insert a picture related to composting at the beginning of the "Did You Know That Compost Can . . ." section. Size the picture appropriately.

m. Apply the Top and Bottom wrapping style to the picture. Move the picture so that it appears centered between the margins.

n. Apply the Austin theme to the document.

o. Save, print, and then close the file.

LAB EXERCISES

CREATING A TABLE ★

2. You work for the Animal Rescue Foundation and are putting together a list of contact information. You would like to display the information in a table. Your completed document will be similar to the one shown here.

a. Open a new document and enter the title **Animal Rescue Foundation** left-aligned at the top of the document on the first line and **Telephone Contacts** on the second line. Apply the Title style to the first line and the Subtitle style to the second line.

b. Enter the following introductory paragraph left-aligned below the subtitle.

> This listing of direct-dial telephone numbers will make it easy for you to contact the ARS department you need. If you are unsure of your party's extension, please dial the main number, (803) 555-0100. You will be greeted by an automated attendant, which will provide you with several options for locating the party with whom you wish to speak.

c. Several lines below the paragraph, insert a simple table with 3 columns and 7 rows. Enter the following information into the table:

Pet Adoption	Jack Rogers	803-555-0158
Behavior Helpline	Rachel Howard	803-555-0132
Education Department	Jon Willey	803-555-0122
Therapeutic Programs	Samantha Wilson	803-555-0132
Volunteer Services	James Thomas	803-555-0173
Job Hotline	Gavin Smith	803-555-0133
Membership & Giving	Mike Miller	803-555-0132

d. Insert a new row above the first entry and enter the following headings:

Department	Contact	Telephone Number

e. Change the sort order of the table so that it is sorted by department in ascending order.

f. Select a document theme and then apply a table style of your choice to the table.

g. If necessary, size the table to display the data in each row on a single line. Center the table.

h. Insert the footnote **If you need operator assistance, simply press "0" at any time.** using the * symbol instead of a number. Place the reference mark at the end of the introductory paragraph.

i. Add a footer to the document using the Alphabet design. Delete the "Type text" placeholder and then use the Author Quick Part to display your name left-aligned in the footer.

j. Save the document as ARS Department Contacts.

k. Print the document.

CREATING AN INFORMATIONAL SHEET ★★

3. You are the manager of Justice Bike Shop, a small bike repair and retail shop. Lately, you've had to repair many bikes due to accidents on the local college campus. As a result, you've decided to prepare an informational sheet about bike safety, and to then post it around town and on campus. Your completed document will be similar to the one shown here.

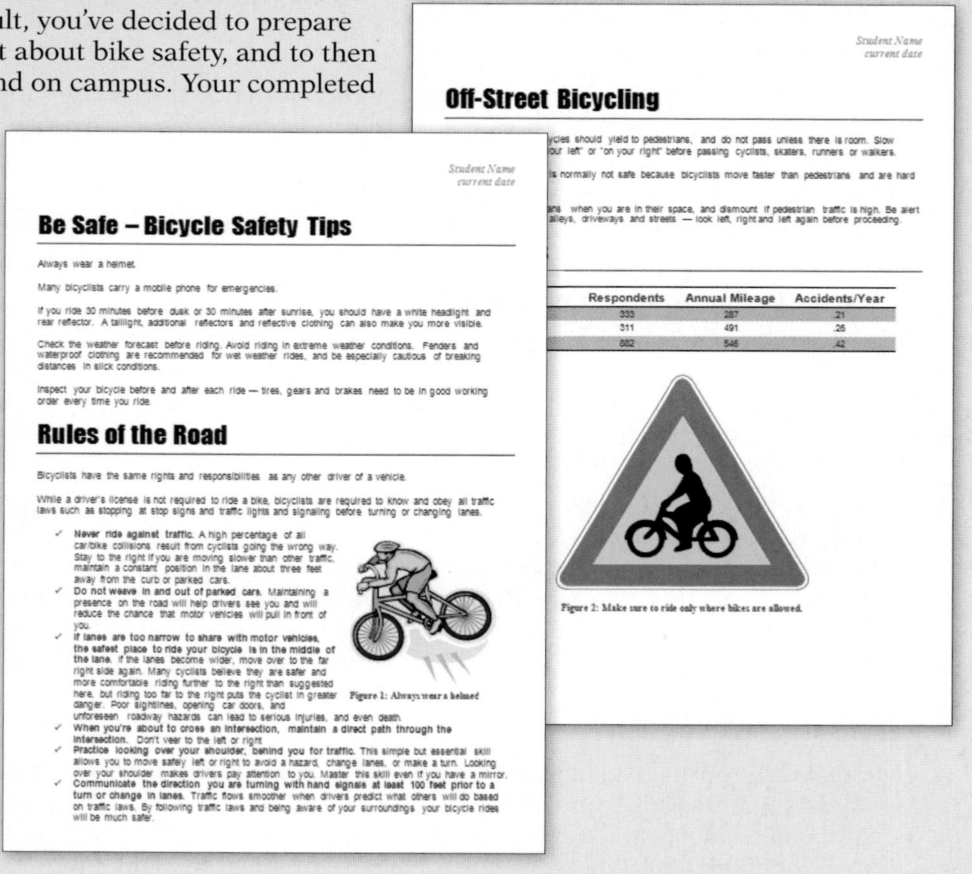

Student Name
current date

Off-Street Bicycling

...ycles should yield to pedestrians, and do not pass unless there is room. Slow ...our left" or "on your right" before passing cyclists, skaters, runners or walkers.

...is normally not safe because bicyclists move faster than pedestrians and are hard ...

...ans when you are in their space, and dismount if pedestrian traffic is high. Be alert ...alleys, driveways and streets — look left, right and left again before proceeding.

	Respondents	Annual Mileage	Accidents/Year
	333	287	.21
	311	491	.26
	882	546	.42

Figure 2: Make sure to ride only where bikes are allowed.

Student Name
current date

Be Safe – Bicycle Safety Tips

Always wear a helmet.

Many bicyclists carry a mobile phone for emergencies.

If you ride 30 minutes before dusk or 30 minutes after sunrise, you should have a white headlight and rear reflector. A taillight, additional reflectors and reflective clothing can also make you more visible.

Check the weather forecast before riding. Avoid riding in extreme weather conditions. Fenders and waterproof clothing are recommended for wet weather rides, and be especially cautious of breaking distances in slick conditions.

Inspect your bicycle before and after each ride — tires, gears and brakes need to be in good working order every time you ride.

Rules of the Road

Bicyclists have the same rights and responsibilities as any other driver of a vehicle.

While a driver's license is not required to ride a bike, bicyclists are required to know and obey all traffic laws such as stopping at stop signs and traffic lights and signaling before turning or changing lanes.

- ✓ **Never ride against traffic.** A high percentage of all car/bike collisions result from cyclists going the wrong way. Stay to the right if you are moving slower than other traffic, maintain a constant position in the lane about three feet away from the curb or parked cars.
- ✓ **Do not weave in and out of parked cars.** Maintaining a presence on the road will help drivers see you and will reduce the chance that motor vehicles will pull in front of you.
- ✓ **If lanes are too narrow to share with motor vehicles, the safest place to ride your bicycle is in the middle of the lane.** If the lanes become wider, move over to the far right side again. Many cyclists believe they are safer and more comfortable riding further to the right than suggested here, but riding too far to the right puts the cyclist in greater danger. Poor sightlines, opening car doors, and unforeseen roadway hazards can lead to serious injuries, and even death.
- ✓ **When you're about to cross an intersection, maintain a direct path through the intersection.** Don't veer to the left or right
- ✓ **Practice looking over your shoulder, behind you for traffic.** This simple but essential skill allows you to move safely left or right to avoid a hazard, change lanes, or make a turn. Looking over your shoulder makes drivers pay attention to you. Master this skill even if you have a mirror.
- ✓ **Communicate the direction you are turning with hand signals at least 100 feet prior to a turn or change in lanes.** Traffic flows smoother when drivers predict what others will do based on traffic laws. By following traffic laws and being aware of your surroundings your bicycle rides will be much safer.

Figure 1: Always wear a helmet

a. Open the file wd03_Bike Safety.

b. Apply the Title style to the document's three titles.

c. Create a bulleted list in the Rules of the Road section beginning with the third paragraph, selecting a bullet design of your choice.

d. Select a document theme of your choice.

e. Add the heading **Statistics** to the end of your document and then format it using the Title style. Enter the following information in a table below the Statistics heading:

1-Gear	333	287	.21
3-Gear	311	491	.26
5-15 Gear	882	546	.42

f. Insert a new row above the first entry and enter the following headings:

Gears	Respondents	Annual Mileage	Accidents/Year

g. Remove the space after paragraphs in the table. Apply a table style of your choice. Turn off the first column style effect. Center-align all the text in the table. Increase the font size of the column headings to 12 points. Size the table to the contents, keeping each row to a single line, and center the table.

h. Locate a clip art image showing a biker wearing a helmet and insert it in the Rules of the Road section of the document. Size and position the image by referring to the completed document. Add the following caption below the graphic: **Figure 1: Always wear a helmet!**

i. Locate the clip art image shown at the end of the completed document and then size and position it accordingly. Add the following caption to the image: **Figure 2: Make sure to ride only where bikes are allowed.**

j. Change your chosen theme, if desired, to better match the inserted images.

k. Insert the Grid style header. Insert your name in the header, replacing the existing text, if necessary. On the second line of the header, enter the current date as a field that updates automatically. Select both lines of the header and then apply the Intense Emphasis style. Right-align both lines of the header.

l. Make adjustments, if necessary, to make the information sheet look similar to the one pictured at the beginning of this exercise.

m. Save the document as Bike Safety. Print the document.

CREATING A BROCHURE ★ ★ ★

4. Your next project as marketing coordinator at Adventure Travel Tours is to create a brochure promoting three new adventures. You have already started working on the brochure and have added most of the text content. Because this brochure is for clients, you want it to be both factual and attractive. To do this, you plan to enhance the appearance of the document by adding some finishing formatting touches. Additionally, you want to include a table of contents on the second page of the document, several pictures, a table of tour dates, and an index. Your completed brochure will be similar to that shown here.

a. Open the file wd03_ATT Brochure.

b. Create a cover page using the Stacks design. Enter the title **Three New Adventures** and subtitle **Alaska Scenic Rail Tour, Hiking the Great Eastern Trail, Kayaking the Blue Waters of Mexico**. Add your name as the Author. Double-click to the right of your name and then press Enter to insert a blank line. Type **Adventure Travel Tours** on the blank line.

c. Create a custom document theme that includes custom colors and fonts for the brochure. Add a coordinating color to the title and subtitle on the cover page.

d. Apply the Title style to the first topic heading line. Apply the Heading 1 style to the following five topic headings.

e. Insert a new page as page 2 and insert a Contents listing.

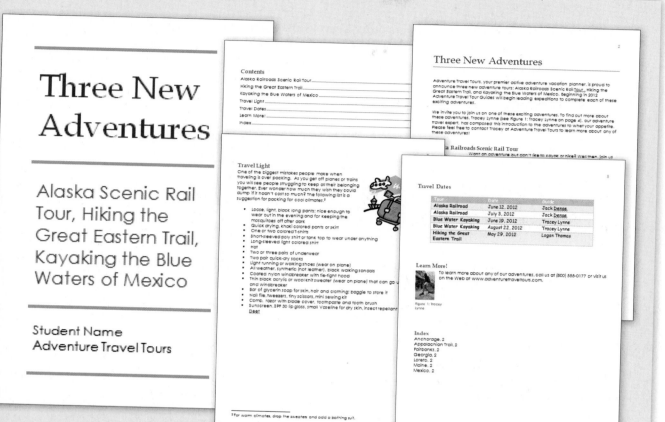

f. In this step, you will be inserting several graphics. For each of these, size the graphic appropriately. Wrap the text around the picture using a text wrapping style of your choice.

- Insert the graphic wd03_Train to the left of the paragraph in the "Alaska Railroads Scenic Rail Tours" section.
- Insert the graphic wd03_Hiking to the left of the first paragraph of the "Hiking the Great Eastern Trail" section.
- Insert the graphic wd03_Kayaking to the left of the first paragraph of the "Kayaking the Blue Waters of Mexico" section.
- Insert a picture from the clip art gallery in the Travel Light section.
- Insert wd03_Tracey to the left of the last paragraph in the last section of the report.

g. Add the caption **Tracey Lynne** below her photograph.

h. In the second paragraph of the "Three New Adventures" section, after the word "Lynne," add a cross-reference, with the figure number and caption, for the photo of Tracey. Use the split window feature to add the cross-reference.

i. Add a bullet style of your choice to the packing list items.

j. At the end of the first sentence in the section "Hiking the Great Eastern Trail," add the following text as a footnote: **The Appalachian Trail is 2,155 miles long.**

LAB EXERCISES

k. At the end of the first paragraph in the "Travel Light" section, add the following text as a footnote: **For warm climates, drop the sweaters and add a bathing suit.**

l. Add a new section titled **Travel Dates** before the "Learn More!" section. Apply a Heading 1 style to the section heading. Insert a hard page break above this section.

m. Enter the following information in a table:

Tour	Date	Guide
Hiking the Great Eastern Trail	May 29, 2012	Logan Thomas
Alaska Railroad	June 12, 2012	Jack Denae
Blue Water Kayaking	June 19, 2012	Tracey Lynne
Alaska Railroad	July 3, 2012	Jack Denae
Blue Water Kayaking	August 22, 2012	Tracey Lynne

n. Size the table appropriately. Apply formatting of your choice to the new table. Sort the table in ascending sort order by tour. Center the table.

o. Mark the following items as main entry index items:

Mexico, Loreto (Kayaking section)

Appalachian Trail, Georgia, Maine (Hiking section)

Anchorage, Fairbanks (Alaska Railroads section)

p. Insert a few extra lines at the end of the document. Type **Index** on the first line and then apply the Heading 1 style. Generate the index in a single column below the heading.

q. Add a header that includes a right-aligned page number.

r. Update the table of contents and adjust the document's formatting as needed.

s. Save the document as ATT Brochure. Print the report.

WRITING A REPORT ★ ★ ★

5. As a senior trainer at Lifestyle Fitness Club, you are responsible for researching new fitness trends and sharing your findings with other trainers and clients. You have written a Beginner's Guide to Yoga for this purpose. Pages two and three contain the body of your report. You still need to add several pictures, footnotes, and citations to the report. Your completed report will be similar to that shown here.

a. Open the file wd03_Yoga Guide.

b. Create a cover page using a design of your choice. Include the report title **Beginner's Guide to Yoga**, and your name as the author and the current date. Remove any other placeholders.

c. Apply a Heading 1 style to the five topic headings.

d. Create a table of contents on a separate page after the cover page.

e. Insert the graphic wd03_Yoga Pose to the right of the second paragraph in the "What is Yoga" section as shown in the example. Size the graphic appropriately and use the square text wrapping style. Include the figure caption **Yoga emphasizes breathing and meditation** below the graphic.

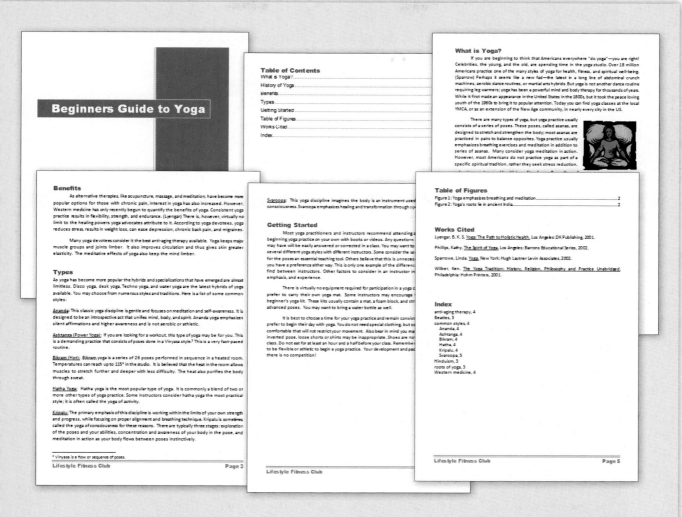

f. Insert the graphic wd03_History to the left of the first two paragraphs in the "History of Yoga" section as shown in the example. Size the graphic appropriately and use the square text wrapping style. Include the figure caption **Yoga's roots lie in ancient India** below the graphic.

g. Apply a document theme of your choice for the report.

h. In the "History of Yoga" section, move to the end of the second sentence in the first paragraph after the word "poses" and add the following text as a footnote:

Ancient ceramics found in the caves of Mojendro-Daro and Harappa depict recognizable yoga positions.

i. In the "Ashtanga (Power Yoga)" description, move to the end of the second sentence after the word "style" and add the following text as a footnote:

Vinyasa is a flow or sequence of poses.

j. Display the six types of yoga in alphabetical order.

k. Using MLA style, enter citations in the text at the locations specified below using the information in the following four reference sources:

Location	Source
First paragraph, end of third sentence	Sparrowe
End of third paragraph	Wilber
Fifth paragraph, end of third sentence	Iyengar
End of second paragraph	Phillips

Type	Author	Title	Year	City	Publisher
Book	Linda Sparrowe	Yoga	2002	New York	Hugh Lautner Levin Associates
Book	B. K. S. Iyengar	Yoga: The Path to Holistic Health	2001	Los Angeles	DK Publishing
Book	Kathy Phillips	The Spirit of Yoga	2002	Los Angeles	Barrons Educational Series
Book	Ken Wilber	The Yoga Tradition: History, Religion, Philosophy and Practice Unabridged	2001	Philadelphia	Hohm Printers

l. At the end of the document, on a new blank page, create a table of figures and a Works Cited bibliography. Add a title above the table of figures formatted using the Heading 1 style.

m. Add a title below the Works Cited section named Index. Apply the Heading 1 style. Mark the following index entries:

Main Entries	Subentries	Location
roots of yoga		History of Yoga section
Hinduism		
Beatles		
roots of yoga		
Western medicine		Benefits section
anti-aging therapy		
common styles		Types section, first paragraph
	Ananda	
	Ashtanga	
	Bikram	
	Hatha	
	Kripalu	
	Svaroopa	

n. Generate a single-column index below the Index title.

o. Update the table of contents and adjust any formatting in the document as necessary.

p. Use the Alphabet footer design and use the document Quick Part to add the company name, **Lifestyle Fitness Club**. Do not display the footer on the cover page.

q. Start the page numbering with "1" on the table of contents page.

r. Review the layout of the document and make adjustments as needed. Then, update tables and your index so that the correct page numbers display.

s. Save the document as Yoga Guide. Print the report.

ON YOUR OWN

DESIGNING A FLYER ★

1. The Sports Company is introducing a new line of kayaking equipment. It is holding a weekend promotional event to familiarize the community with paddling equipment. You have already started designing a flyer to advertise the event, but it still needs additional work.

- Open the file wd03_Kayaking Flyer.
- Create the following table of data below the " . . . boat giveaway!" paragraph. Use an appropriate table style.

TIME	EVENT
12:00 p.m.	Freestyle Whitewater Panel Discussion
1:15 p.m.	Kids Canoe Relay Race
1:30 p.m.	Becky Andersen & Brad Ludden Autographed Boats Charity Auction
2:30 p.m.	Drawing for Extrasport Joust Personal Flotation Device
3:00 p.m.	Team Dagger Autograph Session
5:00 p.m.	Free BBQ dinner

- Insert the picture wd03_Kayacking from your data files to the right of the text "Meet Team Dagger." Size and position the graphic appropriately.
- Add a caption below the image.
- Add formatting and styles of your choice to the document.
- Make any editing changes you feel are appropriate.
- Enter your name and the date centered in the footer.
- Save the document as Kayaking Flyer.
- Print the document.

LAB EXERCISES

CREATING A REPORT FROM AN OUTLINE ★ ★

2. You are working on the Downtown Internet Café Web site and want to include information about coffee characteristics, roasting, grinding, and brewing. You have created an outline that includes information on these topics. Open the file wd03_Coffee Outline and, using the Web as your resource, complete the report by providing the body text for the topics in the outline. Include the following features in your report:

- Create a cover page and table of contents.
- Select a Document theme.
- The body of the report should include at least three footnotes and two cross-referenced images.
- Include three citations. Generate a bibliography of your sources.
- Create an index that includes at least five main entries and three subentries.
- Add page numbers to the report, excluding the title page.
- Include your name, file name, and the date in the footer.

  Save the report as Coffee Report. Preview and print the title page, the first page, the works cited page, and the index page.

PREPARING FOR A JOB SEARCH ★ ★

3. You are graduating next June and plan to begin your job search early. To prepare for getting a job, locate three sources of information on how to conduct a job search. Use your school's career services department, the library, newspapers, magazine articles, and the Web as possible sources. Begin by creating an outline of the topics you will include in the report. Using the outline, write a brief report about your findings. Include the following features in your report:

- A cover page that displays the report title, your name, and the current date.
- An updated table of contents page.
- At least two levels of headings in the body of the paper.
- A minimum of three citations and three footnotes.
- A header that includes your name and page numbers on the top-right corner of every page (excluding the title page).
- At least one picture with a caption and cross-reference.
- A table that compares the jobs you are interested in and a table caption.
- A table of figures that has a formatted title that will appear in the table of contents.
- A bibliography of your reference sources. Format the bibliography appropriately.
- An index that includes at least five main entries and three subentries.

  Save the report as Job Search. Print the document.

WRITING A RESEARCH PAPER ★ ★ ★

4. Create a brief research report (or use a paper you have written in the past) on a topic of interest to you. The paper must include the following features:

- A cover page that displays the report title, your name, and the current date.
- A table of contents.
- At least two levels of headings and a minimum of three footnotes and three citations.
- At least one picture with a caption and cross-reference.
- A table of information with a caption.
- A table of figures.
- A bibliography page of your reference sources.
- A single-column index with at least 10 entries.
- A header and/or footer that displays the page numbers, file name, and date. Do not include this information on the cover page or table of contents page.

  Save the document as Research. Print the cover page, the table of contents page, and the last page of the report.

RESEARCHING VIRUS HOAXES ★ ★ ★

5. There are a lot of real computer viruses that can wreak havoc with your computer. This makes virus hoaxes even more annoying, as they may lead some users to ignore all virus warning messages, leaving them vulnerable to a genuine, destructive virus.

   Use the Web as a resource to learn more about virus hoaxes. Write a brief report defining virus hoaxes. Describe three hoaxes, how they are perpetuated, and the effect they could have if the receiver believes the hoax. The report must include the following features:

- A cover page that displays the report title, your name, and the current date.
- A table of contents.
- At least two levels of headings and a minimum of two footnotes and three citations in the body of the paper.
- At least one picture with a caption and cross-reference.
- A table of information with a caption.
- A table of figures.
- A bibliography page of your reference sources.
- The page numbers, file name, and date in a header and/or footer. Do not include this information on the cover page or table of contents page.

  Save the document as Computer Viruses. Print the document.

Working Together 1: Word 2010 and Your Web Browser

CASE STUDY

Adventure Travel Tours

The Adventure Travel Tours Web site is used to promote its products and broaden its audience of customers. In addition to the obvious marketing and sales potential, it provides an avenue for interaction between the company and the customer to improve customer service. The company also uses the Web site to provide articles of interest to customers. The articles, which include topics such as travel background information and descriptions, changes on a monthly basis as an added incentive for readers to return to the site.

You want to use the flyer you developed to promote the new tours and presentations on the Web site. To do this, you will use Word 2010's Web-editing features that help you create a Web page quickly and easily. While using the Web-editing features, you will be working with Word and with a Web browser application. This capability of all Microsoft Office 2010 applications to work together and with other applications makes it easy to share and exchange information between applications. Your completed Web pages are shown here.

NOTE The Working Together tutorial is designed to show how two applications work together and to present a basic introduction to creating Web pages.

Creating a Web Page

You want to create a Web page to be used on the company's Web site. A **Web page** is a document that can be used on the World Wide Web (WWW). The Web page you will create will provide information about the tour presentations. Word offers two ways to create or **author** Web pages. One way is to start with a blank Web page and enter text and graphics much as you would a normal document. Another is to quickly convert an existing Word document to a Web page.

SAVING A WORD DOCUMENT AS A WEB PAGE

Because the tour flyer has already been created as a Word document and contains much of the information you want to use on the Web page, you will convert it to a Web page document. You made a couple of changes to the flyer, giving it a title that is more appropriate for the Web page and removing the border and banner. You will use the modified version of the flyer as the basis for the Web page.

1

● **Start Word 2010.**

● **Open the file** wdwt_Presentations **from the appropriate location.**

Your screen should be similar to Figure 1

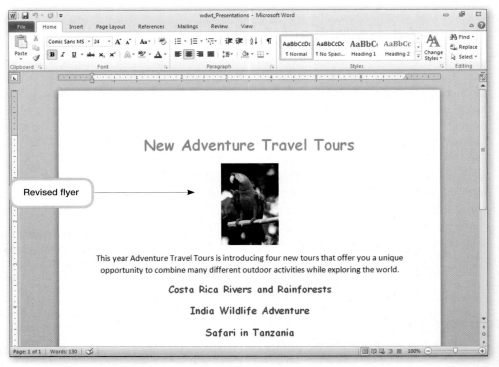

Figure 1

When you save a document as a Web page, Word translates the text, layout, images, and formatting of your document into HTML code. **HTML (HyperText Markup Language)** is a programming language used to create Web pages. HTML commands control the display of information on a page, such as font colors and size, and the way an item will be processed. HTML also allows users to click on hyperlinks and jump to other locations on the same page, other pages in the same site, or other sites and locations on the WWW. HTML commands are interpreted by the browser software you are using. A **browser** is a program that connects you to remote computers and displays the Web pages you request.

When saving a document as a Web page, Word provides three Web-related choices on the Save as Type drop-down list, as described in the following table:

Save as Type	File Type	Description
Single File Web Page	MTHML (.mht)	Creates a single file with the extension of .mht that includes all the elements of the Web site page in a single file, including text and graphics. Commonly used when e-mailing a Web page to someone or when posting the Web page to a shared network folder.
Web Page	HTML (.htm)	Creates a single file with the extension of .htm. Also creates a separate .xml file that contains instructions for locating and displaying images and text within a Web page. Converts images to a Web-compatible .gif or .jpg format, and then stores the. xml file and image files in a folder that uses the same name as your Web page file.
Web Page, Filtered	HTML (.htm)	Same as the Web Page option, except the size of the .htm file is smaller because certain HTML instructions, called **tags**, are filtered out. This option filters out tags used by Microsoft Office without changing the look of the displayed Web page. The main disadvantage to using this option is that when you open a filtered Web page in Microsoft Word, you might not have access to all the editing commands you had when creating the document.

For best results, Web page filenames should contain lowercase letters without spaces or symbols, except for underscores and hyphens. Names should also be as short as possible while describing as much as possible. You will save your document as New_Tour_Presentations using the Web Page (.htm) file type. Additionally, you will save all the Web page files in a new folder named ATT Web Page.

2

- **Open the File tab and click** 🖺 Save As .

- **If necessary, change the location to save to the appropriate save location.**

- **Click** New folder **and enter the folder name** **ATT Web Page**

- **Change the file name to** New_Tour_ Presentations

- **From the Save as type drop-down list, choose Web Page.**

Your screen should be similar to Figure 2

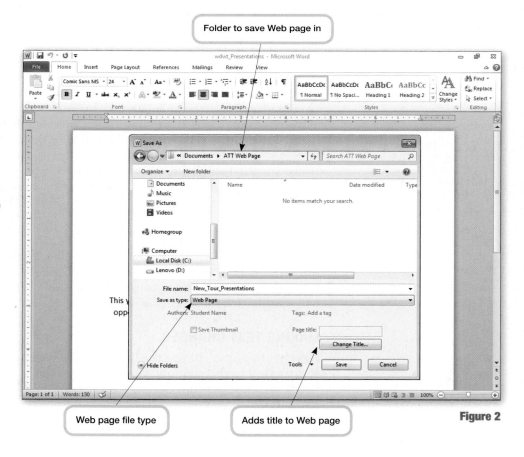

Folder to save Web page in

Web page file type

Adds title to Web page

Figure 2

You also need to provide a title for the page. This is the text that will appear in the title bar of the Web browser when the page is displayed. You want the title to be the same as the file name.

3

● **Click** [Change Title...].

● **The title to New Tour Presentations**

● **Click** [OK].

● **Click** [Save].

Your screen should be similar to Figure 3

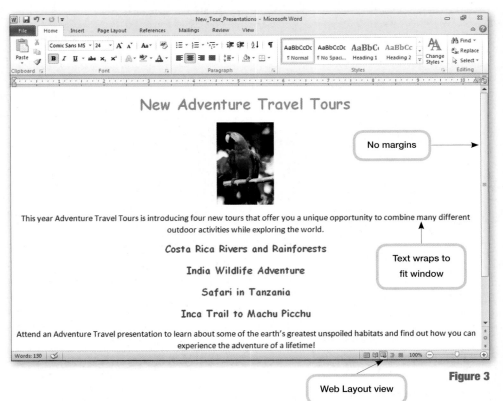

Figure 3

The flyer has been converted to an HTML document and is displayed in Web Layout view. This view displays the document as it will appear if viewed using a Web browser. This document looks very much like a normal Word document. In fact, the only visible difference is the margin settings. A Web page does not include margins. Instead, the text wraps to fit the window space. However, the formatting and features that are supported by HTML, in this case the paragraph and character formatting such as the font style, type size, and color attributes, have been converted to HTML format.

Additional Information

Some formatting features, such as emboss and shadow effects, are not supported by HTML or other Web browsers and are not available when authoring Web pages.

MODIFYING A WEB PAGE

Because you saved your Web page using the "Web Page" file type rather than the "Web Page, Filtered" file type, you now have full access to Word's editing features for making changes to your document. In the next few sections, you will modify several aspects of your document for optimal display on the Web.

MAKING TEXT CHANGES

Next, you want to change the layout of the Web page so that more information is displayed in the window when the page is viewed in the browser. To do this, you will delete any unnecessary text and change the paragraph alignment to left-aligned.

1

- Delete the last two paragraphs (beginning with "Presentation dates" and ending with "trip dates").

- Left-align all the text below the picture.

- Add bullets preceding the list of four tours.

- Select the title and increase the font size to 36 points.

- Click on the title to clear the selection.

Your screen should be similar to Figure 4

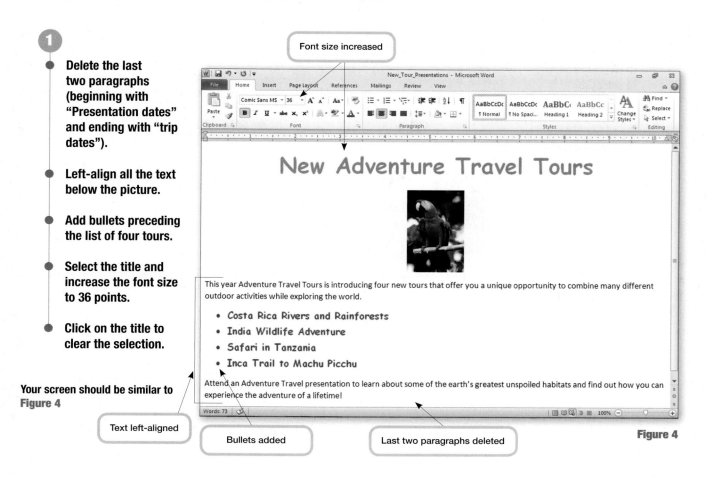

Figure 4

Now, all the information is visible within the window.

CHANGING THE PICTURE LAYOUT

Next, you want to move the picture to the left edge of the window and wrap the text to the right around it. Unlike a normal Word document, a Web page document does not have pictures and other graphic elements embedded in it. As mentioned earlier, when you save a document as an HTML Web page, each graphic object is stored as a separate file that is accessed and loaded by the browser when the page is loaded. Word creates a link to the object's file in the HTML file. The link is a tag that includes the location and file name of the graphic file.

Additionally, graphics are inserted into a Web page document as inline objects. You can change the wrapping style and move, size, and format graphic objects in a Web page just like embedded objects in a Word document.

- **Click on the picture to select it.**

- **Drag the picture to the "T" in "This" at the beginning of the first paragraph.**

- **From the Picture Tools Format tab, click 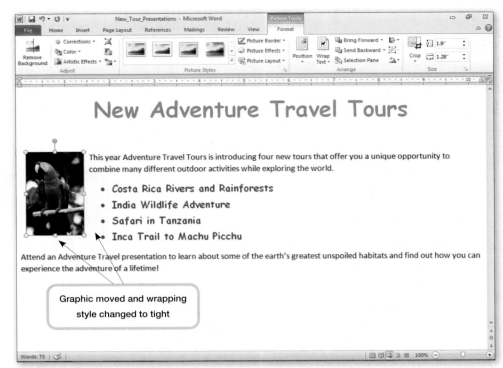 and choose Tight.**

Your screen should be similar to Figure 5

Figure 5

Next, you will make a few other adjustments to improve the appearance.

APPLYING PAGE COLOR

Because color and design are important elements of Web pages, you can add a background color to the Web page. You think a light blue may look good.

- **Deselect the graphic.**

- **Open the Page Layout tab.**

- **Click Page Color in the Page Background group.**

Additional Information

The gallery of colors associated with the default Office theme is displayed.

- **Point to several different shades of blue to see how they look in Live Preview.**

Your screen should be similar to Figure 6

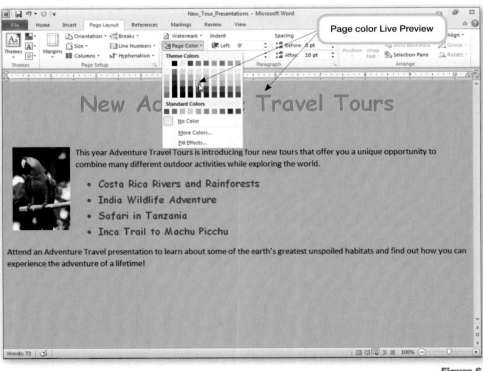

Figure 6

You do not really like how any of these colors look and decide to try a fill effect instead. Fill effects include gradient color, texture, patterns, or pictures. These effects should be used in moderation—you want them to enhance, not detract from, the content. You will try a blue gradient effect first.

2

● **Choose Fill Effects.**

● **Choose One color.**

● **Open the Color 1 gallery and choose, Blue, Accent 1, Lighter 40%.**

● **Drag the shade slider closer to the Light side (see Figure 7).**

● **If necessary, select Horizontal in the Shading styles options.**

● **Select the top to bottom variant (upper-right square).**

Your screen should be similar to Figure 7

Figure 7

The Sample area shows how your color selections will appear. Now you are ready to apply these settings to the page.

3

● **Click** OK **.**

Your screen should be similar to Figure 8

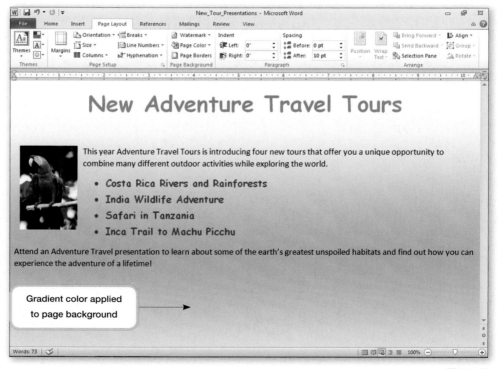

Figure 8

Although adding gradient color shading looks nice, you still are not satisfied. You will try a texture instead.

4

● Click Page Color.

● Choose Fill Effects.

● Open the Texture tab.

● Select the Stationery texture (fourth row, fourth column).

Having Trouble?

When you click on a texture, the texture name appears below the gallery.

● Click OK.

Your screen should be similar to Figure 9

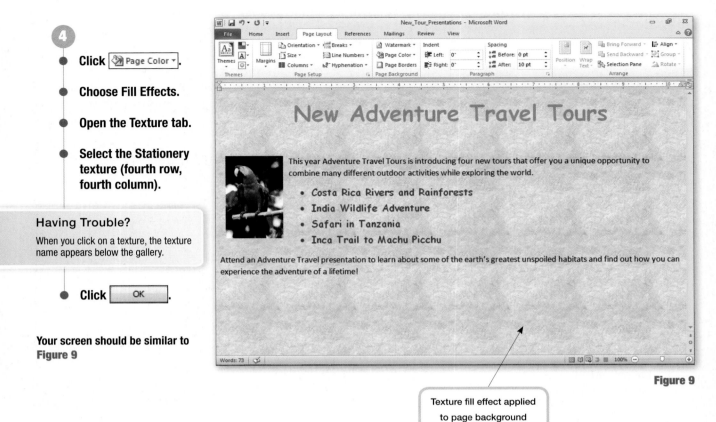

Texture fill effect applied to page background

Figure 9

You like the more natural effect of this background.

CHANGING BULLET STYLES

The last enhancement you want to make is to change the bullet style.

1

- Select the four bulleted items.

- Open the Home tab and then open the ☰▾ Bullets drop-down gallery.

- Choose ➤ from the Bullet Library.

- Click anywhere on the bulleted list to clear the selection.

- Save the changes you have made to the Web page.

Your screen should be similar to Figure 10

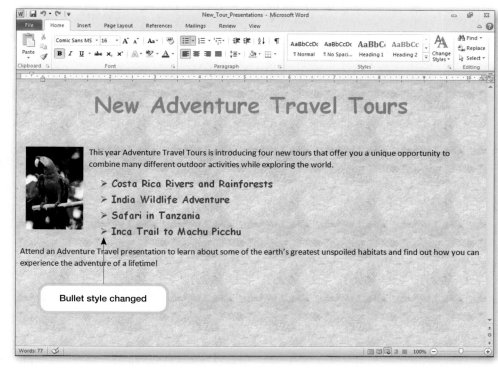

Figure 10

Additional Information

You can access many more graphic bullets by opening the ☰▾ Bullets drop-down gallery, choosing Define New Bullet, clicking Symbol... Picture... or Font... , and then selecting a bullet from the displayed list.

The new bullet style adds more emphasis to the items in the list.

Linking Pages

As you have learned, a hyperlink provides a quick way to jump to other documents, objects, or Web pages. Hyperlinks are the real power of the WWW. You can jump to sites on your own system and network as well as to sites on the Internet and WWW.

CREATING A HYPERLINK

Next, you want to create another Web page that will contain a list of presentation locations. You will then add a hyperlink to this information from the New Tour Presentations page. The list of tour locations has already been entered as a Word document and saved as a file.

1

- **Open the file** wdwt_Locations

- **Save the document as a Web page to the ATT Web Page folder with the file name** Tour_Locations **and a page title of** Tour Presentation Locations

- **Apply the same bullet style to this page.**

- **Apply the Stationery texture background page color.**

- **Save the page again.**

Your screen should be similar to Figure 11

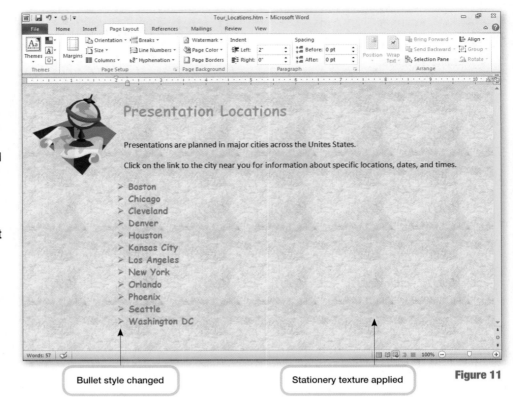

Bullet style changed

Stationery texture applied

Figure 11

Now you are ready to create the hyperlink from the New_Tour_Presentations page to the Tour_Locations page.

2

- **Switch to the New_Tour_Presentations window.**

- **Add the following text to the end of the last paragraph:** Find out about presentation locations, dates, and times.

- **Select the text "locations, dates, and times"**

- **Open the Insert tab.**

- **Click** Hyperlink **from the Links group.**

Your screen should be similar to Figure 12

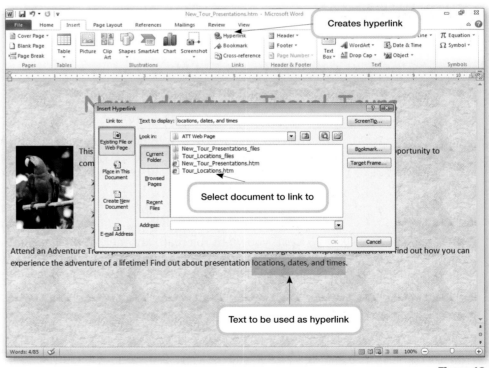

Creates hyperlink

Select document to link to

Text to be used as hyperlink

Figure 12

From the Insert Hyperlink dialog box, you need to specify the name of the document you want the link to connect to.

3

● **Select** Tour_ Locations **from the file list.**

● **Click** OK .

● **Save the document.**

Your screen should be similar to Figure 13

Figure 13

The selected text appears as a hyperlink in the design colors specified by the theme.

TESTING A HYPERLINK

You will now make sure that the hyperlink you inserted correctly links to and displays the Presentation Locations document.

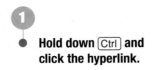

1 **Hold down Ctrl and click the hyperlink.**

Your screen should be similar to Figure 14

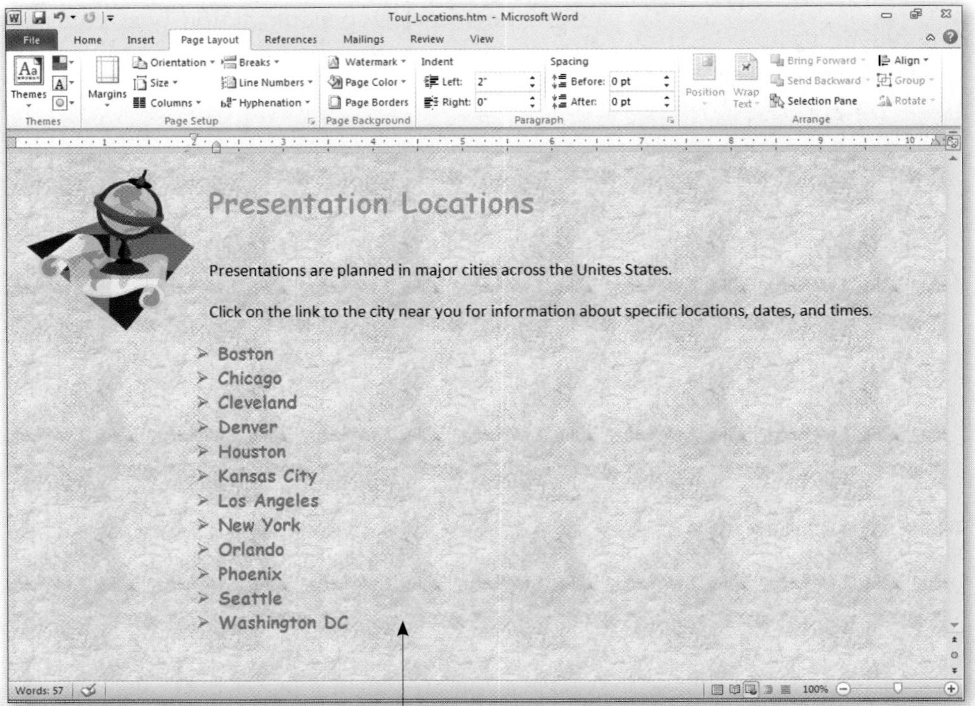

Tour_Locations.htm - Microsoft Word
File
Home
Insert
Page Layout
References
Mailings
Review
View
Presentation Locations
Presentations are planned in major cities across the Unites States.
Click on the link to the city near you for information about specific locations, dates, and times.
Boston
Chicago
Cleveland
Denver
Houston
Kansas City
Los Angeles
New York
Orlando
Phoenix
Seattle
Washington DC
Words: 57
100%
Linked page displayed

Figure 14

Additional Information

The following instructions and figures are based on using Internet Explorer 8. If you are using a different browser or a different version of Internet Explorer, your screens will look different. Additionally, you will need to substitute the equivalent procedures for your browser in the following steps.

Because the Locations document is already open in a window, clicking the hyperlink simply switches to the open Word window and displays the page. You plan to add hyperlinks from each location to information about specific location dates and times at a later time.

Previewing the Page

To see how your Web page will actually look when displayed by your browser, you can preview it.

1

- Open your Web browser.

- If necessary, maximize the browser window.

- Choose Open from the File menu.

- Click `Browse...` and then change to the location containing the ATT Web Page folder.

- Double-click New_Tour_Presentations to open it.

Your screen should be similar to Figure 15

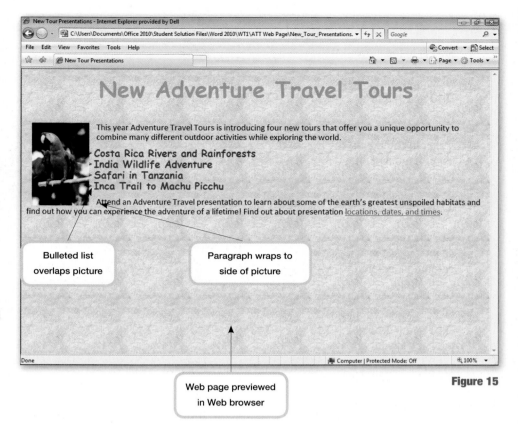

Bulleted list overlaps picture

Paragraph wraps to side of picture

Web page previewed in Web browser

Figure 15

The Web page you created is displayed in the browser window. Sometimes the browser may display a page slightly differently from the way it appears in Web Page view. In this case, the picture overlaps the bullets and the last paragraph wraps to the side of the picture. You will add space between the picture and bullets by indenting the bulleted list more. Then, to fix the paragraph wrapping, you will insert a special text wrapping break that is used in Web pages to separate text around objects.

2

- Switch to the New_ Tour_Presentations document in the Word 2010 application window.

- Select the bulleted list of tours and drag the left indent marker to the 2-inch position on the ruler.

- Move to the beginning of the last paragraph, before the word Attend.

- Click 📇 Breaks ▾ in the Page Setup group of the Page Layout tab.

- Choose Text Wrapping.

- Save the document.

- Turn on the display of formatting marks.

Your screen should be similar to Figure 16

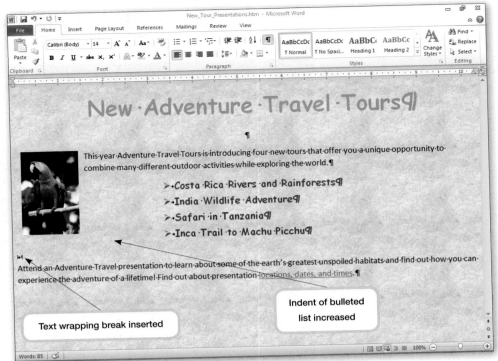

Figure 16

By increasing the indent, the list of bulleted items should now indent appropriately when viewed in the browser. Additionally, the text wrapping break that was inserted before the paragraph will stop the text following the break from wrapping around the object. The text wrapping break character 🔁 is not visible unless you display formatting marks.

3

- Switch to the browser window.

- Open the View menu and choose Refresh to see the revised version of the Web page.

Another Method

You can also click ↻ or press F5 to refresh the window.

Your screen should be similar to Figure 17

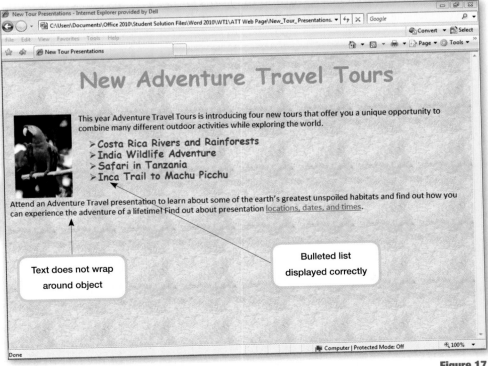

Figure 17

Increasing the indent for the bulleted list has added enough space to separate it from the graphic. Inserting the text wrapping break stopped the text in the last paragraph from wrapping around the object. Next, you will use the hyperlink to open the Presentation Locations Web page in the browser.

4

● **Click on the hyperlink.**

Your screen should be similar to Figure 18

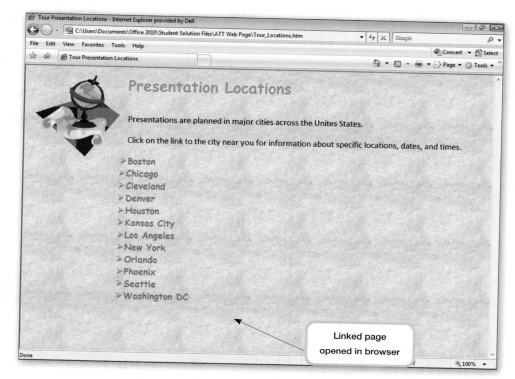

Figure 18

This page looks fine and does not need any additional formatting.

5

● Click [X] in the title bar to exit the browser program.

● Close both documents and exit Word 2010.

Making a Web Page Public

Now that you have created Web pages, you need to make them available on the Internet for others to see them. The steps that you take to make your pages public depend on how you want to share them. There are two main avenues: on your local network or intranet for limited access by people within an organization or on the Internet for access by anyone using the WWW. To make pages available to other people on your network, you'll need to move both the .htm file and its associated folder containing the .xml and image files to a shared folder on the network. To make your Web pages available on the WWW, you need to first either install Web server software on your computer or locate an Internet service provider that allocates space for Web pages. In both cases, the .htm file and associated folder will need to be moved to your Web server location for your new Web page to display and function properly.

KEY TERMS

author WDWT1.2
browser WDWT1.2
HTML (HyperText Markup
Language) WDWT1.2

tag WDWT1.3
Web page WDWT1.2

COMMAND SUMMARY

Command	Shortcut	Action
File tab		
Save As /Save as Type/ Web Page		Saves file as a Web page document
Insert tab		
Links group		
Hyperlink	Ctrl + K	Inserts hyperlink
Page Layout tab		
Page Setup group		
Breaks ▾		Stops text from wrapping around objects in a Web page
Page Background group		
Page Color ▾		Adds selected color to page background
Page Color ▾ /Fill Effects		Adds selected color effect to page background

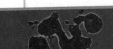

B EXERCISES

STEP-BY-STEP

ADDING A NEW WEB PAGE ★

1. You want to continue working on the Web pages about the new tour presentations for the Adventure Travel Web site. Your next step is to create links from each location on the Presentation Locations Web page to information about each location's presentation date and times. Your completed Web page for the Los Angeles area should be similar to the one shown here.

   a. In Word, open the Web page file Tour_Locations you created in this lab.

   b. Open the document wdwt_Los Angeles. Save the document as a Web page to the ATT Web Page folder with the file name Los_Angeles and a page title of **Los Angeles Presentation Information**.

   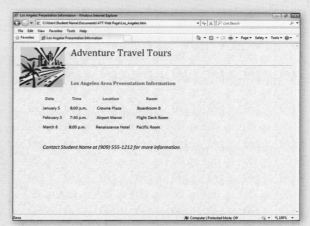

   c. Change the page color to a textured fill effect of your choice. Change the first title line to the Title style and the second title line to a Heading 1 style. Change the title lines to a color of your choice.

   d. Increase the size of the graphic appropriately.

   e. Increase the font size of the table to 12 points. Add color to the table headings. Enhance the Web page with any features you feel are appropriate.

   f. Two lines below the table, add the text **Contact [your name] at (909) 555-1212 for more information**. Apply the Emphasis style to this line and increase the font size to 14 points.

   g. On the Tour_Locations page, create a link from the Los Angeles text to the Los Angeles page. Test the link.

   h. Resave both Web pages and preview them in your browser. Print the Los Angeles Web page.

   i. Exit the browser and Word.

CONVERTING A FLYER TO A WEB PAGE ★ ★

2. The Westbrook Parks and Recreation Department has asked you to modify the Celebrate Bikes article you created and convert it into a Web page to add to the Web site. Your completed Web page should be similar to the one shown here.

   a. Open the file Bike Event you created in Step-by-Step Exercise 2 in Lab 1. If you don't have access to the Bike Event file, open wdwt_Biking Flyer from your data files location.

   b. Convert the article to a Web page and save it as Celebrate_Bicycling in a new folder. Include an appropriate page title.

LAB EXERCISES

c. Apply a page background color effect of your choice.

d. Increase the size of the title to 36 points.

e. Delete your name and the date from the end of the document. Add **[Your name] at** before the phone number in the last line.

f. Save the Web page. Preview the page in your browser. Adjust the layout as needed. Close your browser. Resave the Web page.

g. Print the Web page.

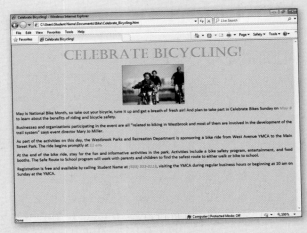

ADVERTISING ON THE WEB ★ ★ ★

3. You would like to advertise the grand re-opening of the Internet Café on the Web. You plan to use the information in the advertisement flyer you created as the basis for the Web pages. Your completed Web pages should be similar to those shown here.

a. Open the file Music Performances you created in Step-by-Step Exercise 3 in Lab 1. If you don't have access to the Music Performances file, open wdwt_ Café Performances from your data files location. Convert the document to a Web page, add a title of **Monthly Music Performances**, and save it as Café_Flyer in a new folder.

b. Delete the graphic. Insert a clip art image of your choice that is in keeping with the theme of the flyer. Change the picture text wrapping style to Behind Text. Move the picture to the left of the three title lines and size it appropriately. Insert a hard return after the word Performances in the title.

c. Save the changes.

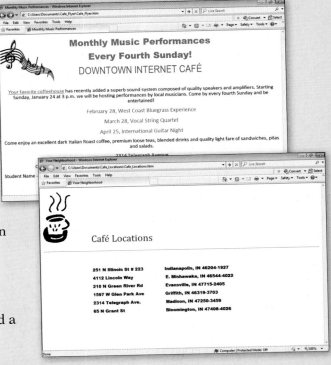

d. Open the file wdwt_Café Locations. Save the document as a Web page to your Web Page folder with the file name Café_Locations and a page title of **Your Neighborhood**.

e. Create a link from the text **Your favorite coffeehouse** in the Café Flyer page to the Café Locations page. Test the link.

f. Enhance the pages with any features you feel are appropriate.

g. Resave the Web pages and preview them in your browser.

h. Print the pages.

Creating and Editing a Worksheet

Objectives

After completing this lab, you will know how to:

1. Create new worksheets.
2. Enter and edit data.
3. Modify column widths and row heights.
4. Use proofing tools.
5. Copy and paste cell contents.
6. Create formulas.
7. Insert and delete rows and columns.
8. Format cells and cell content.
9. Hide and unhide rows and columns.
10. Create a basic chart.
11. Format values as a date.
12. Preview and print a worksheet.
13. Display and print formulas.
14. Change worksheet orientation and scale content.

Downtown Internet Café

You are excited about your new position as manager and financial planner for a local coffeehouse. Evan, the owner, has hired you as part of a larger effort to increase business at the former Downtown Café. Evan began this effort by completely renovating his coffeehouse and installing a wireless network. He plans to offer free Wi-Fi service for customers to use with their own laptop computers. In addition, he has set up several computer kiosks for customers to use who do not have laptops and has provided a printer and copier for all customers to use. He also has decided to rent an MP3 download kiosk for customers who may want to update the music on their iPods or PDAs. Finally, to reflect the new emphasis of the café, he has changed its name to the Downtown Internet Café.

You and Evan expect to increase sales by attracting techno-savvy café-goers, who you hope will use the Downtown Internet Café as a

place to meet, study, work, or download music for their iPods and PDAs. You also believe the rental computers will be a draw for vacationers who want to check e-mail during their travels.

Evan wants to create a forecast estimating sales and expenses for the first quarter. As part of a good business plan, you and Evan need a realistic set of financial estimates and goals.

In this lab, you will help with the first-quarter forecast by using Microsoft Office Excel 2010, a spreadsheet application that can store, manipulate, and display numeric data. You will learn to enter numbers, perform calculations, copy data, and label rows and columns as you create the basic structure of a worksheet for the Downtown Internet Café. You will then learn how to enhance the worksheet using formatting features and by adding color as shown here.

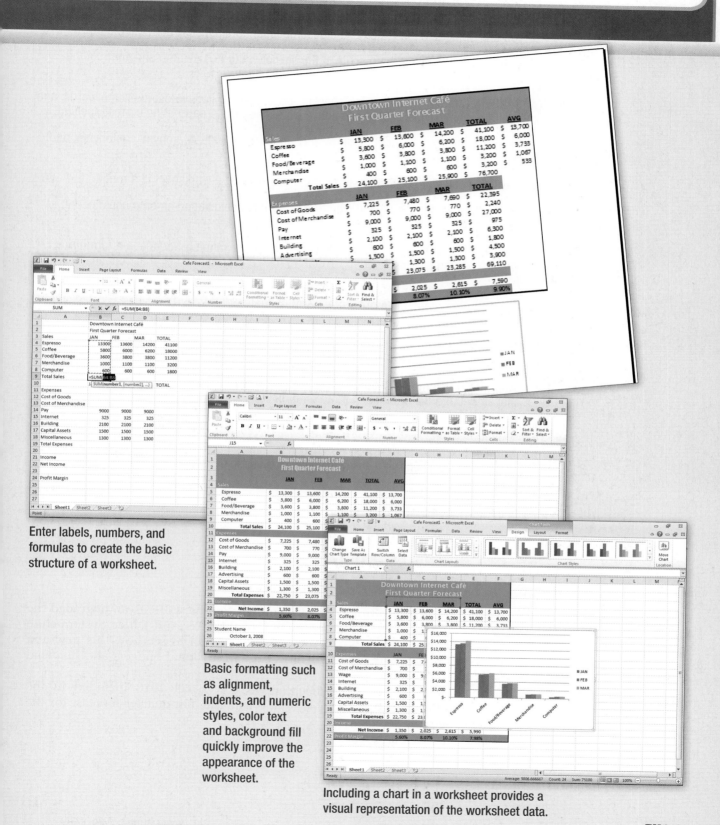

Enter labels, numbers, and formulas to create the basic structure of a worksheet.

Basic formatting such as alignment, indents, and numeric styles, color text and background fill quickly improve the appearance of the worksheet.

Including a chart in a worksheet provides a visual representation of the worksheet data.

The following concepts will be introduced in this lab:

1 Data The basic information or data you enter in a cell can be text or numbers.

2 AutoCorrect The AutoCorrect feature makes some basic assumptions about the text you are typing and, based on these assumptions, automatically corrects the entry.

3 Column Width The column width is the size or width of a column and controls the amount of information that can be displayed in a cell.

4 Spelling Checker The spelling checker locates misspelled words, duplicate words, and capitalization irregularities in the active worksheet and proposes the correct spelling.

5 Thesaurus The thesaurus is a reference tool that provides synonyms, antonyms, and related words for a selected word or phrase.

6 Range A selection consisting of two or more cells on a worksheet is a range.

7 Formula A formula is an equation that performs a calculation on data contained in a worksheet.

8 Relative Reference A relative reference is a cell or range reference in a formula whose location is interpreted in relation to the position of the cell that contains the formula.

9 Function A function is a prewritten formula that performs certain types of calculations automatically.

10 Recalculation When a number in a referenced cell in a formula changes, Excel automatically recalculates all formulas that are dependent upon the changed value.

11 Alignment Alignment settings allow you to change the horizontal and vertical placement and the orientation of an entry in a cell.

12 Row Height The row height is the size or height of a row measured in points.

13 Number Formats Number formats change the appearance of numbers onscreen and when printed, without changing the way the number is stored or used in calculations.

Creating a Workbook

As part of the renovation of the Downtown Internet Café, Evan upgraded the office computer with the latest version of the Microsoft Office System suite of applications, Office 2010. You are very excited to see how this new and powerful application can help you create professional budgets and financial forecasts for the Café.

You will use the spreadsheet application Excel 2010 included in the Microsoft Office 2010 System suite to create the first-quarter forecast for the Café.

1

- Start Microsoft Excel 2010.

- If necessary, maximize the Excel application window.

Having Trouble?

See "Common Office 2010 Features" page IO.13, for information on how to start the application and for a discussion of features common to all Microsoft Office 2010 applications.

Your screen should be similar to Figure 1.1

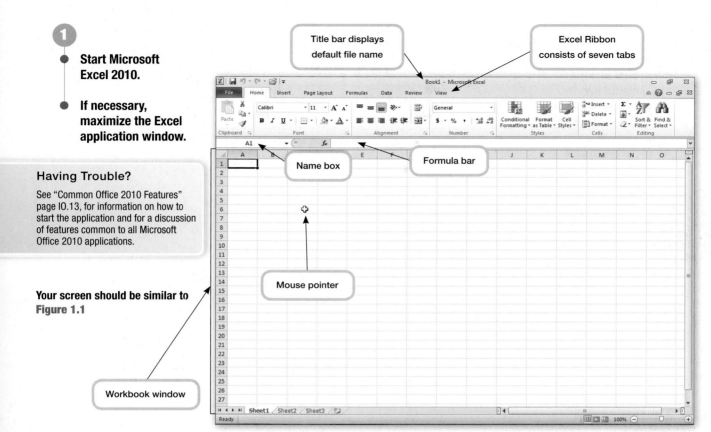

Figure 1.1

Additional Information

Because the Ribbon can adapt to the screen resolution and orientation, your Ribbon may look slightly different. It also may display additional tabs if other application add-ins associated with Office 2010 are on.

Additional Information

You will learn all about using these features throughout these labs.

Having Trouble?

If the workbook is floating in the workbook window, the title bar displays the file name and the [ ] Minimize, [ ] Maximize, and [ ] Close buttons. Click [ ] to maximize the workbook window.

After a few moments, the Excel application window is displayed. Because Excel remembers many settings that were in use when the program was last closed, your screen might look slightly different.

The Excel application window title bar displays the default file name, Book1, and program name. The Ribbon below the title bar consists of seven tabs that provide access to the commands and features you will use to create and modify a worksheet.

Below the Ribbon is the formula bar. The **formula bar** displays entries as they are made and edited in the workbook window. The **Name box**, located at the left end of the formula bar, provides information about the selected item.

The large center area of the program window is the **workbook window**. A **workbook** is an Excel file that stores the information you enter using the program. You will learn more about the different parts of the workbook window shortly.

The mouse pointer can appear as many different shapes. The mouse pointer changes shape depending upon the task you are performing or where the pointer is located on the window. Most commonly it appears as a ▷ or ✛. When it appears as a ✛, it is used to move to different locations in the workbook window; when it appears as a ▷, it is used to choose items, such as commands from the Ribbon.

2

- Move the mouse pointer into the center of the workbook window to see it appear as ⊕.

- Move the mouse pointer to the Ribbon to see it appear as ⬚.

Your screen should be similar to Figure 1.2

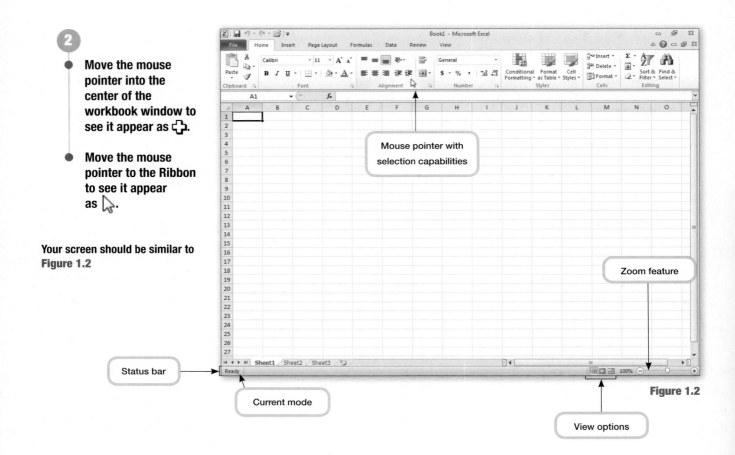

Mouse pointer with selection capabilities

Zoom feature

Status bar

Current mode

View options

Figure 1.2

The status bar at the bottom of the Excel window displays information about various Excel settings. The left side of the status bar displays the current mode or state of operation of the program, in this case, Ready. When Ready is displayed, you can move around the workbook, enter data, use the function keys, or choose a command. As you use the program, the status bar displays the current mode. The right side of the status bar contains buttons to change the view and a zoom feature.

Exploring the Workbook Window

Additional Information

See "Using Backstage View" in the Introduction to Microsoft Office 2010 to review these features.

When you first start Excel 2010, the workbook window displays a new blank workbook that includes many default settings. These default settings, are stored in the default workbook template file named Book.xltx.

The default workbook file includes three blank sheets. A **sheet** is used to display different types of information, such as financial data or charts. Whenever you open a new workbook, it displays a worksheet. A **worksheet**, also commonly referred to as a **spreadsheet**, is a rectangular grid of **rows** and **columns** used to enter data. It is always part of a workbook and is the primary type of sheet you will use in Excel. The worksheet is much larger than the part you are viewing in the window. The worksheet actually extends 16,384 columns to the right and 1,048,576 rows down.

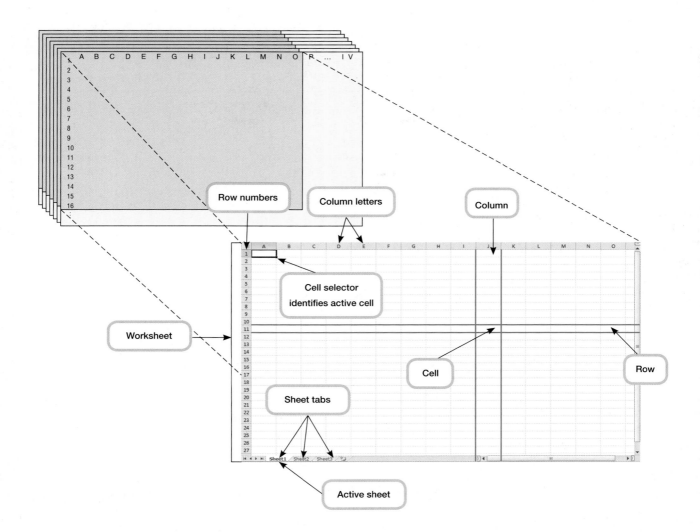

The **row numbers** along the left side and the **column letters** across the top of the workbook window identify each worksheet row and column. The intersection of a row and column creates a **cell**. Notice the black border, called the **cell selector**, surrounding the cell located at the intersection of column A and row 1. This identifies the **active cell**, which is the cell your next entry or procedure affects. Additionally, the Name box in the formula bar displays the **cell reference**, consisting of the column letter and row number of the active cell. The reference of the active cell is A1.

Each sheet in a workbook is named. Initially, the sheets are named Sheet1, Sheet2, and so on, displayed on **sheet tabs** at the bottom of the workbook window. The name of the **active sheet**, which is the sheet you can work in, appears bold. The currently displayed worksheet in the workbook window, Sheet1, is the active sheet.

1 ● **Click the Sheet2 tab.**

Another Method

You also can press [Ctrl] + [Page Down] to move to the next sheet and [Ctrl] + [Page Up] to move to the previous sheet.

Your screen should be similar to Figure 1.3

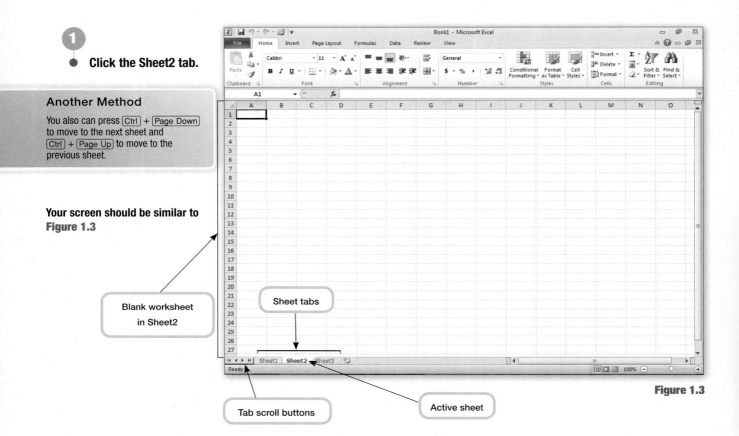

Blank worksheet in Sheet2

Sheet tabs

Active sheet

Tab scroll buttons

Figure 1.3

Additional Information

Do not be concerned if your workbook window displays more or fewer column letters and row numbers than shown here. This is a function of your computer monitor settings.

An identical blank worksheet is displayed in the window. The Sheet2 tab letters are bold, the background is highlighted, and it appears in front of the other sheet tabs to show it is the active sheet.

The sheet tab area also contains **tab scroll buttons**, which are used to scroll tabs right or left when there are more sheet tabs than can be seen. You will learn about these features throughout the labs.

MOVING AROUND THE WORKSHEET

Additional Information

You can use the directional keys in the numeric keypad (with [Num Lock] off) or, if you have an extended keyboard, you can use the separate directional keypad area.

The mouse or keyboard commands can be used to move the cell selector from one cell to another in the worksheet. To move using a mouse, simply point to the cell you want to move to and click the mouse button. Depending upon what you are doing, using the mouse to move may not be as convenient as using the keyboard, in which case the directional keys can be used. You will make Sheet1 active again and use the mouse, then the keyboard, to move in the worksheet.

1

- Click the **Sheet1** tab to make it the active sheet again.

- Click cell **B3**.

- Press ⇥ (3 times).

- Press ⬇ (4 times).

Your screen should be similar to Figure 1.4

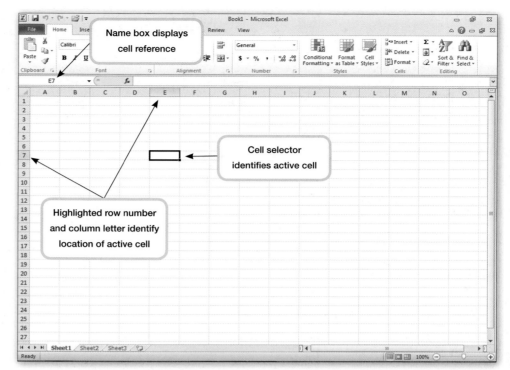

Name box displays cell reference

Cell selector identifies active cell

Highlighted row number and column letter identify location of active cell

Figure 1.4

Having Trouble?

Refer to the "Scrolling the Document Window" section of the Introduction to Office 2010 for more keyboard and mouse procedures.

Cell E7 is outlined in black, indicating this cell is the active cell. The Name box displays the cell reference. In addition, the row number and column letter are gold to further identify the location of the active cell.

As you have learned, the worksheet is much larger than the part you are viewing in the window. To see an area of the worksheet that is not currently in view, you need to scroll the window. The keyboard procedures shown in the table that follows can be used to move around the worksheet.

Keyboard	Action
Alt + Page Down	Moves right one full window.
Alt + Page Up	Moves left one full window.
Home	Moves to beginning of row.
Ctrl + Home	Moves to upper-left corner cell of worksheet.
Ctrl + End	Moves to last-used cell of worksheet.
End →	Moves to last-used cell in row.
End ⬇	Moves to last-used cell in column.

In addition, if you hold down the arrow keys, the Alt + Page Up or Alt + Page Down keys, or the Page Up or Page Down keys, you can quickly scroll through the worksheet. When you use the scroll bar, however, the active cell does not change until you click on a cell that is visible in the window.

You will scroll the worksheet to see the rows below row 27 and the columns to the right of column O.

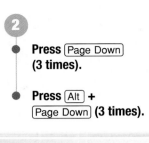

2

- Press ⌈Page Down⌉ (3 times).

- Press ⌈Alt⌉ + ⌈Page Down⌉ (3 times).

Having Trouble?

Do not use the numeric keypad ⌈Page Up⌉ and ⌈Page Down⌉ keys, as this may enter a character in the cell.

Your screen should be similar to Figure 1.5

Having Trouble?

Your screen may display more or fewer rows and columns and the active cell may be a different cell. This is a function of your screen and system settings.

Additional Information

If you have a mouse with a scroll wheel, rotating the wheel forward or back scrolls up or down a few rows at a time.

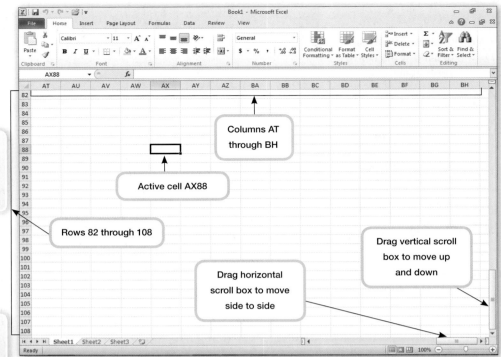

Columns AT through BH

Active cell AX88

Rows 82 through 108

Drag horizontal scroll box to move side to side

Drag vertical scroll box to move up and down

Figure 1.5

The worksheet scrolled downward and left three full windows, and the window displays rows 82 through 108 and columns AT through BH of the worksheet. The active cell is cell AX88. As you scroll the worksheet using the keyboard, the active cell also changes.

It is even more efficient to use the scroll bar to move long distances.

3

- Slowly drag the vertical scroll box up the scroll bar until row 1 is displayed.

- Slowly drag the horizontal scroll box left along the scroll bar until column A is displayed.

Additional Information

As you scroll, the scroll bar identifies the current row position at the top of the window or column position at the left side of the window in a ScreenTip.

Your screen should be similar to Figure 1.6

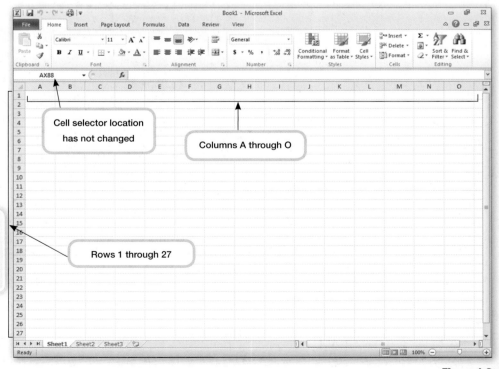

Cell selector location has not changed

Columns A through O

Rows 1 through 27

Figure 1.6

Another Method

You also can type a cell address in the Name box and press ⌐Enter⌐ to move to that location.

Rows 1 to 27 and columns A to O are displayed again. Notice that the Name box displays the active cell location as AX88. When you use the scroll bar to scroll the worksheet, the active cell does not change.

● Practice moving around the worksheet using the keys presented in the table on page EX1.9.

Additional Information

The ⌐Ctrl⌐ + ⌐End⌐ key presented in the table will not change the worksheet location until the worksheet contains data.

● Press ⌐Ctrl⌐ + ⌐Home⌐ to move to cell A1.

You can use the mouse or the keyboard with most of the exercises in these labs. As you use both the mouse and the keyboard, you will find that it is more efficient to use one or the other in specific situations.

DEVELOPING A WORKSHEET

Now that you are familiar with the parts of the workbook and with moving around the worksheet, you are ready to create a worksheet showing the forecast for the first three months of operation for the Downtown Internet Café.

Worksheet development consists of four steps: planning, entering and editing, testing, and formatting. The objective is to create well-designed worksheets that produce accurate results and are clearly understood, adaptable, and efficient.

Step	Description
1. Plan	Specify the purpose of the worksheet and how it should be organized. This means clearly identifying the data that will be input, the calculations that are needed to achieve the results, and the output that is desired. As part of the planning step, it is helpful to sketch out a design of the worksheet to organize the worksheet's structure. The design should include the worksheet title and row and column headings that identify the input and output. Additionally, sample data can be used to help determine the formulas needed to produce the output.
2. Enter and edit	Create the structure of the worksheet using Excel by entering the worksheet labels, data, and formulas. As you enter information, you are likely to make errors that need to be corrected or edited, or you will need to revise the content of what you have entered to clarify it or to add or delete information.
3. Test	Test the worksheet for errors. Use several sets of real or sample data as the input, and verify the resulting output. The input data should include a full range of possible values for each data item to ensure the worksheet can function successfully under all possible conditions.
4. Format	Enhance the appearance of the worksheet to make it more readable or attractive. This step is usually performed when the worksheet is near completion. It includes many features such as boldface text, italic, and color.

As the complexity of the worksheet increases, the importance of following the design process increases. Even for simple worksheets like the one you will create in this lab, the design process is important. You will find that you will generally follow these steps in the order listed above for your first draft of a worksheet. However, you will probably retrace steps such as editing and formatting as the final worksheet is developed.

During the planning phase, you have spoken with the Café manager, Evan, regarding the purpose of the worksheet and the content in general. The primary purpose is to develop a forecast for sales and expenses for the next year. First, Evan wants you to develop a worksheet for the first-quarter forecast and then extend it by quarters for the year. After reviewing past budgets and consulting with Evan, you have designed the basic layout for the first-quarter forecast for the Café, as shown below.

Entering and Editing Data

Now that you understand the purpose of the worksheet and have a general idea of the content, you are ready to begin entering the data. Each worksheet is like a blank piece of paper that already has many predefined settings. You will use the blank Sheet1 worksheet with the default settings to create the worksheet for the Café.

As you can see, the budget you designed above contains both descriptive text entries and numeric data. These are two types of data you can enter in a worksheet.

Concept 1 Data

The basic information or **data** you enter in a cell can be text, numbers, dates, or times. **Text** entries can contain any combination of letters, numbers, spaces, and any other special characters. **Number** entries can include only the digits 0 to 9 and any of the special characters + − ( ) , . / $ % ? =. Number entries can be used in calculations.

Text and number entries generally appear in the cell exactly as they are entered. However, some entries such as formulas direct Excel to perform a calculation on values in the worksheet. In these cases, the result of the formula appears in the cell, not the formula itself. You will learn about formulas later in the lab.

Adding Text Entries

You enter data into a worksheet by moving to the cell where you want the data displayed and typing the entry using the keyboard. First, you will enter the worksheet headings. Row and column **headings** are entries that are used to create the structure of the worksheet and describe other worksheet entries. Generally, headings are text entries. The column headings in this worksheet consist of the three months (January through March) and a total (sum of entries over three months) located in columns B through E. You will begin by entering the column heading for January in cell B2.

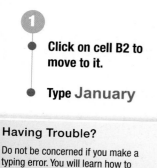

- **Click on cell B2 to move to it.**

- **Type January**

Having Trouble?

Do not be concerned if you make a typing error. You will learn how to correct it shortly.

Your screen should be similar to Figure 1.7

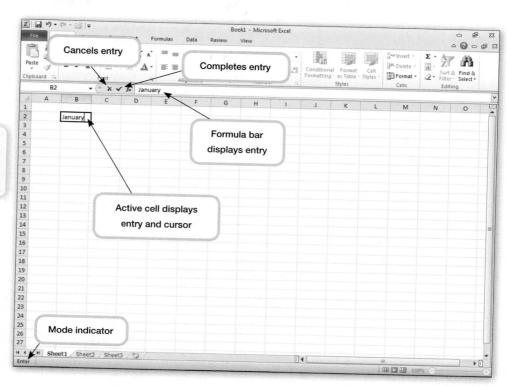

Figure 1.7

Several changes have occurred in the window. As you type, the entry is displayed both in the active cell and in the formula bar. The cursor appears in the active cell and marks your location in the entry. Two new buttons, ✖ and ✔, appear in the formula bar. They can be used with a mouse to cancel your entry or complete it.

Notice also that the mode displayed in the status bar has changed from Ready to Enter. This notifies you that the current mode of operation in the worksheet is entering data.

Although the entry is displayed in both the active cell and the formula bar, you need to press the ⌐Enter or Tab key, click ✔, or click on any other cell to complete your entry. If you press Esc or click ✖, the entry is cleared and nothing appears in the cell. Since your hands are already on the keyboard, it is quicker to press ⌐Enter or Tab than it is to use the mouse.

2

● Press ⏎Enter.

Your screen should be similar to Figure 1.8

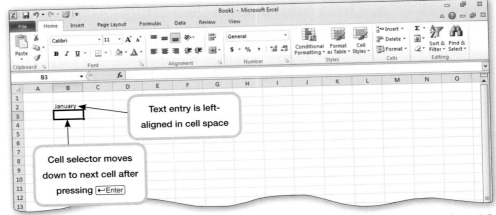

Text entry is left-aligned in cell space

Cell selector moves down to next cell after pressing ⏎Enter

Figure 1.8

The entry January is displayed in cell B2, and the mode has returned to Ready. In addition, the active cell is cell B3. Whenever you use the ⏎Enter key to complete an entry, the cell selector moves down one cell.

Notice that the entry is positioned to the left side of the cell space. This is one of the worksheet default settings.

Additional Information

Pressing ⇧Shift + ⏎Enter to complete an entry moves up a cell, and Ctrl + ⏎Enter completes the entry without moving to another cell.

CLEARING AN ENTRY

After looking at the entry, you decide you want the column headings to be in row 3 rather than in row 2. This will leave more space above the column headings for a worksheet title. The Delete key can be used to clear the contents from a cell. You will remove the entry from cell B2 and enter it in cell B3.

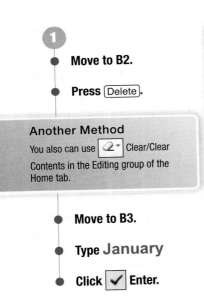

1

● **Move to B2.**

● **Press Delete.**

Another Method

You also can use ✐▾ Clear/Clear Contents in the Editing group of the Home tab.

● **Move to B3.**

● **Type January**

● **Click ✔ Enter.**

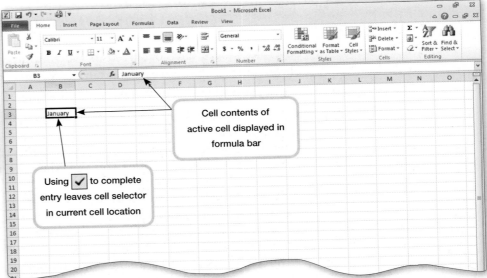

Cell contents of active cell displayed in formula bar

Using ✔ to complete entry leaves cell selector in current cell location

Figure 1.9

Your screen should be similar to Figure 1.9

The active cell does not change when you click ✔ to complete an entry. Because the active cell contains an entry, the cell content is displayed in the formula bar.

EDITING AN ENTRY

Next, you decide to change the heading from January to JAN. An entry in a cell can be entirely changed in the Ready mode or partially changed or edited in the Edit mode. To use the Ready mode, you move to the cell you want to change and retype the entry the way you want it to appear. As soon as a new character is entered, the existing entry is cleared.

Generally, however, if you need to change only part of an entry, using the Edit mode is quicker. To change to Edit mode, double-click on the cell whose contents you want to edit.

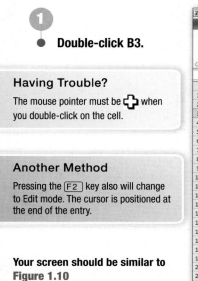

Double-click B3.

Having Trouble?

The mouse pointer must be ⊹ when you double-click on the cell.

Another Method

Pressing the F2 key also will change to Edit mode. The cursor is positioned at the end of the entry.

Your screen should be similar to Figure 1.10

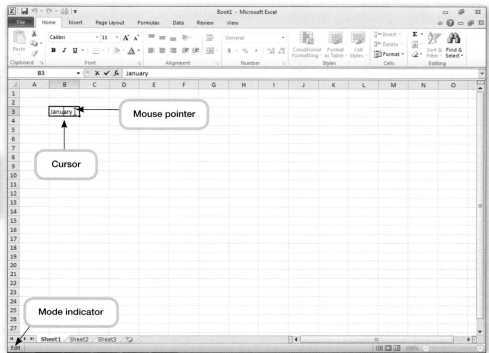

Figure 1.10

The status bar shows that the new mode of operation is Edit. The cursor appears at the location you clicked in the entry, and the mouse pointer changes to an I-beam when positioned on the cell. Now you can click again or use the directional keys to move the cursor within the cell entry to the location of the text you want to change.

After the cursor is appropriately positioned, you can edit the entry by removing the incorrect characters and typing the correct characters. To do this, you can use the Backspace and Delete keys to delete text character by character and enter the new text, or you can select the text to be changed and then type the correction. You will change this entry to JAN.

Having Trouble?

Refer to the "Entering and Editing Text" and "Selecting Text" sections of the Introduction to Office 2010 to review these features.

Additional Information

You also can use Ctrl + Delete to delete everything to the right of the cursor.

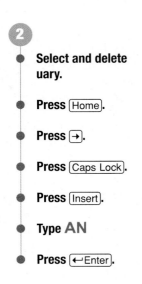

2

● **Select and delete**
uary.

● **Press** [Home].

● **Press** [→].

● **Press** [Caps Lock].

● **Press** [Insert].

● **Type** AN

● **Press** [←Enter].

Your screen should be similar to
Figure 1.11

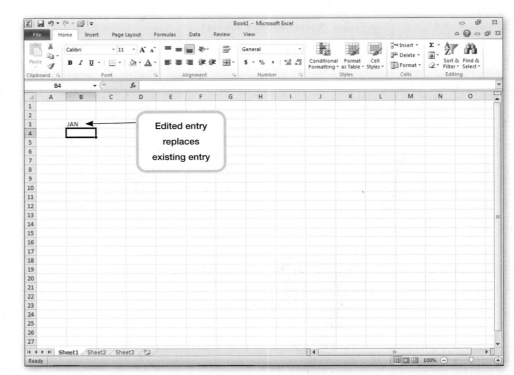

Figure 1.11

Additional Information

The Caps Lock indicator light on your keyboard is lit when this feature is on.

Additional Information

Overwrite is automatically turned off when you leave Edit mode or you press [Insert] again.

The four characters at the end of the entry were deleted. Turning on the Caps Lock feature produced the uppercase letters AN without having to hold down [⇧Shift]. Finally, by pressing Insert, the program switched from inserting text to overwriting text as you typed. When overwriting text is on, the cursor changes to a highlight to show that the character will be replaced with the new text you type.

The new heading JAN is entered into cell B3, replacing January. As you can see, editing will be particularly useful with long or complicated entries.

Next, you will enter the remaining three headings in row 3. Because you want to move to the right one cell to enter the next month label, you will complete the entries using [→] or [Tab↹].

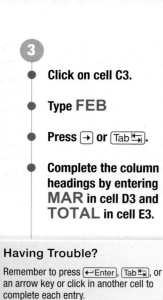

3

- Click on cell C3.

- Type **FEB**

- Press → or Tab⇥.

- Complete the column headings by entering **MAR** in cell D3 and **TOTAL** in cell E3.

Having Trouble?

Remember to press ←Enter, Tab⇥, or an arrow key or click in another cell to complete each entry.

- Press Caps Lock to turn off this feature.

Your screen should be similar to Figure 1.12

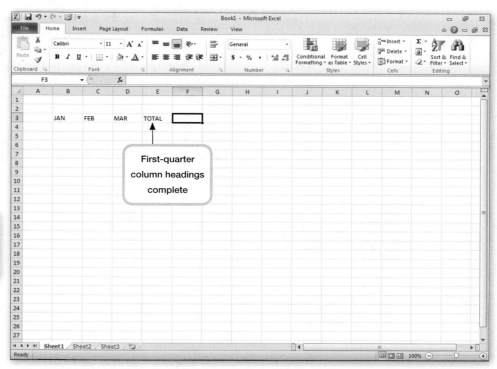

First-quarter column headings complete

Figure 1.12

The column headings are now complete for the first quarter. Above the column headings, you want to enter a title for the worksheet. The first title line will be the café name, Downtown Internet Café.

4

- Move to B1.

- Type **Downtown Café** and click ✓ Enter.

- Double-click on cell B1 to change to Edit mode.

- Move the cursor to the beginning of the word Café.

- Type **Internet** followed by a space.

- Press Ctrl + ←Enter.

Your screen should be similar to Figure 1.13

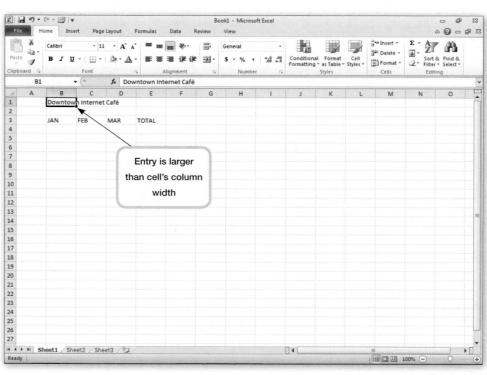

Entry is larger than cell's column width

Figure 1.13

This time, because you did not change to overwriting text as you edited the entry, the new text was inserted between the existing text. Inserting text while editing is the default setting. Also notice that the entry is longer than the cell's column width and overlaps into the cell to the right. As long as the cell to the right is empty, the whole entry will be displayed. If the cell to the right contains an entry, the overlapping part of the entry is not displayed.

USING AUTOCORRECT

Next, you will enter the second title line, First Quarter Report. As you enter text in a cell, Excel checks the entry for accuracy. This is part of the automatic correcting feature of Excel.

Concept AutoCorrect

The **AutoCorrect** feature makes some basic assumptions about the text you are typing and, based on these assumptions, automatically corrects the entry. The AutoCorrect feature automatically inserts proper capitalization at the beginning of sentences and in the names of days of the week. It also will change to lowercase letters any words that were incorrectly capitalized because of the accidental use of the Caps Lock key. In addition, it also corrects many common typing and spelling errors automatically.

One way the program automatically makes corrections is by looking for certain types of errors. For example, if two capital letters appear at the beginning of a word, the second capital letter is changed to a lowercase letter. If a lowercase letter appears at the beginning of a sentence, the first letter of the first word is capitalized. If the name of a day begins with a lowercase letter, the first letter is capitalized.

Another way the program makes corrections is by checking all entries against a built-in list of words that are commonly spelled incorrectly or typed incorrectly. If it finds the entry on the list, the program automatically replaces the error with the correction. For example, the typing error "aboutthe" is automatically changed to "about the" because the error is on the AutoCorrect list. You also can add words that you want to be automatically corrected to the AutoCorrect list. Words you add are added to the list on the computer you are using and will be available to anyone who uses the machine later.

You will enter the second title line and will intentionally misspell two words to demonstrate how the AutoCorrect feature works.

Move to B2.

Type Firts Quater Forecast

Press ⏎Enter.

Your screen should be similar to Figure 1.14

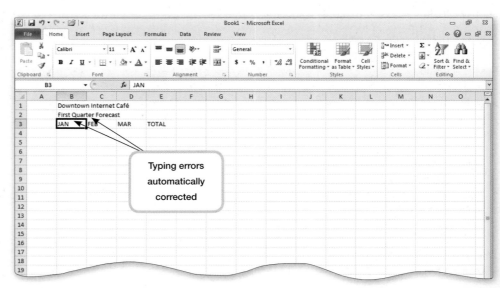

Figure 1.14

The two typing errors were automatically corrected as soon as you completed a word by pressing the spacebar. If the entry was a single word, it would be checked as soon as you completed the entry.

Next, the row headings need to be entered into column A of the worksheet. The row headings and what they represent are shown in the following table.

Heading	Description
Sales	
Espresso	Income from sales of espresso-based drinks
Coffee	Income from drip coffee sales
Food/Beverage	Income from sales of baked goods, sandwiches, salads, and other beverages
Merchandise	Income from sales of mugs, books, magazines, candy, etc.
Computer	Income from computer rental usage, printing, copier use, and MP3 downloads
Total Sales	Sum of all sales
Expenses	
Cost of Goods	Cost of espresso, coffee, and food items sold
Cost of Merchandise	Cost of merchandise other than food and beverage
Wages	Manager and labor costs
Internet	Wi-Fi access, MP3 kiosk rental, etc.
Building	Lease, insurance, electricity, water, etc.
Capital Assets	Equipment leases, interest, depreciation
Miscellaneous	Maintenance, phone, office supplies, outside services, taxes, etc.
Income	
Net Income	Total sales minus total expenses
Profit Margin	Net income divided by total sales

2

Complete the row headings for the Sales portion of the worksheet by entering the following headings in the indicated cells.

Cell	Heading
A3	Sales
A4	Espresso
A5	Coffee
A6	Food/ Beverage
A7	Merchandise
A8	Computer
A9	Total Sales

Figure 1.15

Your screen should be similar to Figure 1.15

Adding Text Entries   **EX1.19**

ADDING NUMBER ENTRIES

Next, you will enter the expected sales numbers for January into cells B4 through B8. As you learned earlier, number entries can include the digits 0 to 9 and any of these special characters: + − ( ) , . / $ % ? =. When entering numbers, it is not necessary to type the comma to separate thousands or the currency ($) symbol. You will learn about adding these symbols shortly.

1

● **Move to B4.**

● **Type 13300 and press ⏎Enter.**

● **In the same manner, enter the January sales numbers for the remaining items using the values shown below.**

Cell	Number
B5	5800
B6	3600
B7	1000
B8	600

Your screen should be similar to Figure 1.16

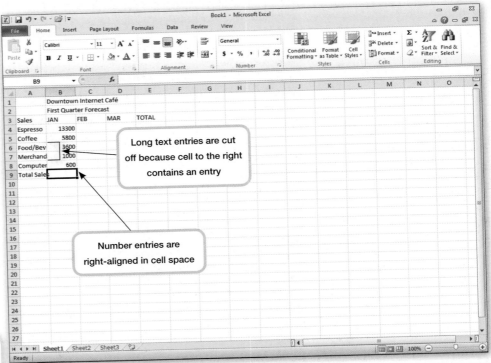

Figure 1.16

Unlike text entries, Excel displays number entries right-aligned in the cell space by default. Also notice that the entries in cells A6 and A7 are no longer completely displayed. They contain long text entries and because the cells to the right now contain an entry, the overlapping part of the entry is shortened. However, the entire entry is fully displayed in the formula bar. Only the display of the entry in the cell has been shortened.

Modifying Column Widths

To allow the long text entries in column A to be fully displayed, you can increase the column's width.

Concept 3 Column Width

The **column width** is the size or width of a column and controls the amount of information that can be displayed in a cell. A text entry that is larger than the column width will be fully displayed only if the cells to the right are blank. If the cells to the right contain data, the text is interrupted. On the other hand, when numbers are entered in a cell, the column width is automatically increased to fully display the entry.

The default column width setting is 8.43. The number represents the average number of digits that can be displayed in a cell using the standard type style. The column width can be any number from 0 to 255. If it is set to 0, the column is hidden.

When the worksheet is printed, it appears as it does currently on the screen. Therefore, you want to increase the column width to display the largest entry. Likewise, you can decrease the column width when the entries in a column are short.

There are several ways to change the column width. Using the mouse, you can change the width by dragging the boundary of the column heading. You also can set the column width to an exact value or to automatically fit the contents of the column.

DRAGGING THE COLUMN BOUNDARY

The column width can be quickly adjusted by dragging the boundary line located to the right of the column letter. Dragging it to the left decreases the column width, while dragging it to the right increases the width. As you drag, a temporary column reference line shows where the new column will appear and a ScreenTip displays the width of the column.

- **Point to the boundary line to the right of the column letter A, and when the mouse pointer changes to ✛, click and drag the mouse pointer to the right.**

- **When the ScreenTip displays 24.00, release the mouse button.**

Your screen should be similar to Figure 1.17

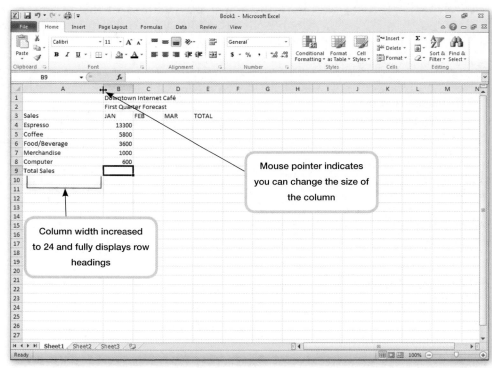

Figure 1.17

Now column A is more than wide enough to fully display all the row headings.

USING A SPECIFIED VALUE

Next, you will reduce the width of column A to 20.

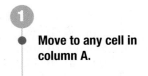

- Move to any cell in column A.

- Click **Format** in the Cells group and choose Column Width.

- Type **20** in the Column Width text box and click **OK**.

Your screen should be similar to Figure 1.18

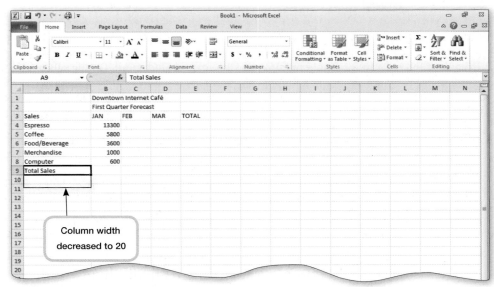

Column width decreased to 20

Figure 1.18

Additional Information

You can quickly return the column width to the default width setting using 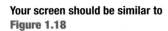/Default Width.

Although this is close, you would like to refine it a little more.

USING AUTOFIT

Another way to change the column width is to use the **AutoFit** feature to automatically adjust the width to fit the column contents. When using AutoFit, double-click the boundary to the right of the column heading of the column you want to fit to contents.

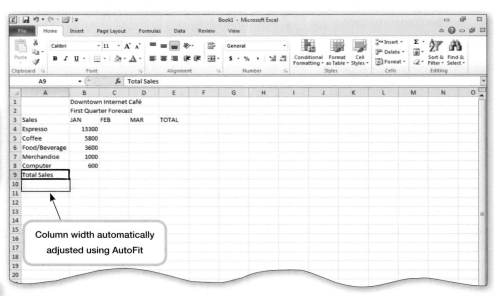

- Double-click the right boundary line of column A.

Having Trouble?

Make sure the mouse pointer changes to before you double-click on the column boundary line.

Your screen should be similar to Figure 1.19

Column width automatically adjusted using AutoFit

Figure 1.19

Another Method

You also can use **Format**/AutoFit Column Width.

The column width is sized to just slightly larger than the longest cell contents.

Saving, Closing, and Opening a Workbook File

Having Trouble?

Refer to the section "Saving a File" in the Introduction to Office 2010 to review this feature.

You have a meeting you need to attend shortly, so you want to save the work you have completed so far on the workbook to a file and then close the file. You will name the file Cafe Forecast and use the default file type settings of Excel Workbook (*.xlsx). The file extension .xlsx identifies the file as an Excel 2007 or 2010 workbook. The default file type saves the workbook file in XML (Extensible Markup Language) format.

Excel 2003 and earlier versions used the .xls file extension. If you plan to share a file with someone using Excel 2003 or earlier, you can save the file using the .xls file type; however, some features may be lost. Otherwise, if you save it as an .xlsx file type, the recipient may not be able to view all the features.

1

- Click 💾 **Save in the Quick Access Toolbar.**

- **Select the location where you want to save your file.**

- **Click in the File Name text box to highlight the proposed file name, or if necessary triple-click on the file name to select it.**

- **Type Cafe Forecast**

- **Click** [Save] **or press** [←Enter].

Your screen should be similar to Figure 1.20

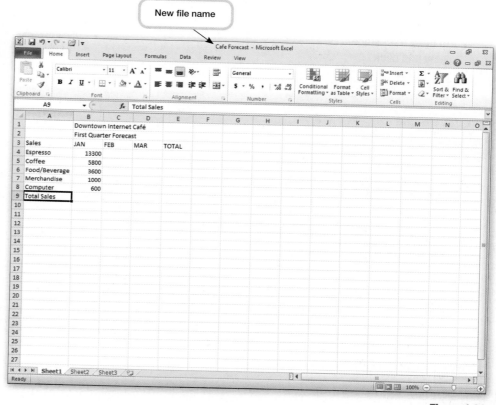

New file name

Figure 1.20

Additional Information

The file name in the title bar may display the workbook file extension, .xlsx, depending on your Windows Folder settings.

The new file name is displayed in the application window title bar. The worksheet data that was on your screen and in the computer's memory is now saved at the location you specified in a new file called Cafe Forecast.

You are now ready to close the workbook file.

Click the File tab to open Backstage view and click .

Because you did not make any changes to the workbook after saving it, the workbook file is closed immediately and the Excel window displays an empty workbook window. If you had made changes to the file before closing it, you would have been prompted to save the file to prevent the accidental loss of data.

After attending your meeting, you continued working on the Café forecast. To see what has been done so far, you will open the workbook file named ex01_CafeForecast1.

3

● **Click the File tab to open Backstage view and click** 📂 **Open** .

● **Select the location containing your data files.**

● **Select** ex01_Cafe Forecast1.

● **Click** Open ▼.

● **If necessary, maximize the workbook window.**

Your screen should be similar to Figure 1.21

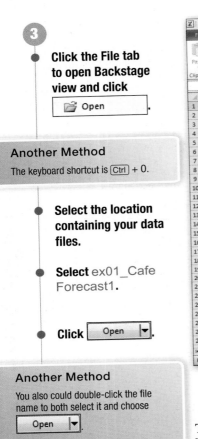

Figure 1.21

The workbook is opened and displayed in the workbook window. The workbook contains the additional sales values for February and March, the expense row headings, and several of the expense values for the month of January.

Using Proofing Tools

When entering information into a worksheet, you are likely to make spelling and typing errors. To help locate and correct these errors, the spelling checker feature can be used. Additionally, you may find that the descriptive headings you have entered may not be exactly the word you want. The thesaurus can suggest better words to clarify the meaning of the worksheet.

CHECKING SPELLING

In your rush to get the row headings entered you realize you misspelled a few words. For example, the Expenses label is spelled "Espenses." Just to make sure there are no other spelling errors, you will check the spelling of all text entries in this worksheet.

Concept 4 Spelling Checker

The **spelling checker** locates misspelled words, duplicate words, and capitalization irregularities in the active worksheet and proposes the correct spelling. This feature works by comparing each word to a dictionary of words, called the **main dictionary**, that is supplied with the program. You also can create a **custom dictionary** to hold words you commonly use but that are not included in the main dictionary. If the word does not appear in the main dictionary or in a custom dictionary, it is identified as misspelled.

When you check spelling, the contents of all cell entries in the entire active sheet are checked. If you are in Edit mode when you check spelling, only the contents of the text in the cell are checked. The spelling checker does not check spelling in formulas or in text that results from formulas.

Excel begins checking all worksheet entries from the active cell forward.

1

● **If necessary, move to A1.**

● **Open the Review tab.**

● **Click** 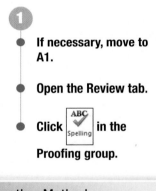 **in the Proofing group.**

Another Method

The keyboard shortcut is ⎡F7⎤.

Your screen should be similar to Figure 1.22

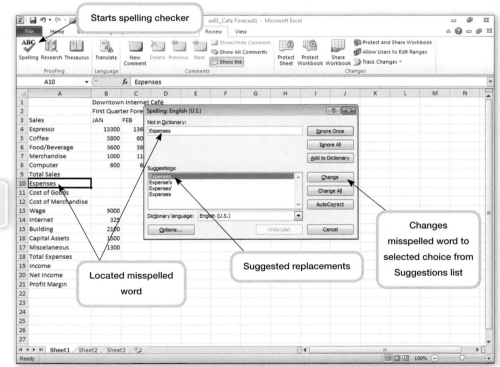

Figure 1.22

Additional Information

Spell-checking operates the same way in all Office 2010 programs. The dictionaries are shared between Office applications.

The spelling checker immediately begins checking the worksheet for words that it cannot locate in its main dictionary. The first cell containing a misspelled word, in this case Espenses, is now the active cell and the Spelling dialog box is displayed. The word it cannot locate in the dictionary is displayed in the Not in Dictionary text box. The Suggestions text box displays a list of possible replacements. If the selected replacement is not correct, you can select

Using Proofing Tools **EX1.25**

another choice from the suggestions list or type the correct word in the Not in Dictionary text box.

The option buttons shown in the table below have the following effects:

Option	Effect
Ignore Once	Leaves selected word unchanged.
Ignore All	Leaves this word and all identical words in worksheet unchanged.
Add to Dictionary	Adds selected word to a custom dictionary so Excel will not question this word during subsequent spell-checks.
Change	Changes selected word to word highlighted in Suggestions box.
Change All	Changes this word and all identical words in worksheet to word highlighted in Suggestions box.
AutoCorrect	Adds a word to the AutoCorrect list so the word will be corrected as you type.

You want to accept the suggested replacement, Expenses.

2

● Click [Change].

Your screen should be similar to Figure 1.23

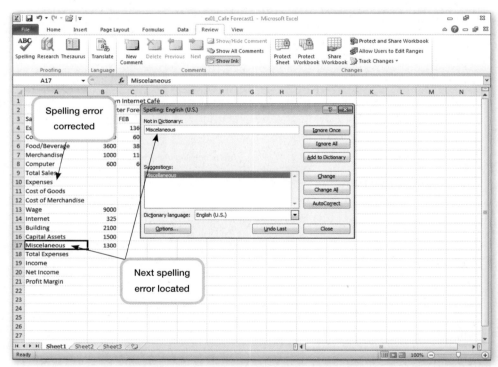

Figure 1.23

The correction is made in the worksheet, and the program continues checking the worksheet and locates another error, Miscelaneous. You will make this correction. When no other errors are located, a dialog box is displayed, informing you that the entire worksheet has been checked.

3

● **Change this word to Miscellaneous.**

● **Click [OK] to end spell-checking.**

The worksheet is now free of spelling errors.

USING THE THESAURUS

The next text change you want to make is to find a better word for "Wage" in cell A13. To help find a similar word, you will use the thesaurus tool.

Concept 5 Thesaurus

The **thesaurus** is a reference tool that provides synonyms, antonyms, and related words for a selected word or phrase. **Synonyms** are words with a similar meaning, such as "cheerful" and "happy." **Antonyms** are words with an opposite meaning, such as "cheerful" and "sad." Related words are words that are variations of the same word, such as "cheerful" and "cheer." The thesaurus can help to liven up your documents by adding interest and variety to your text.

To use the thesaurus, first move to the cell containing the word you want to change. If a cell contains multiple words, you need to select the individual word in the cell.

Move to A13.

Click [Thesaurus] **in the**
Proofing group.

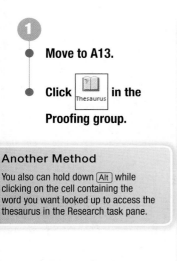

Another Method

You also can hold down [Alt] while clicking on the cell containing the word you want looked up to access the thesaurus in the Research task pane.

Your screen should be similar to Figure 1.24

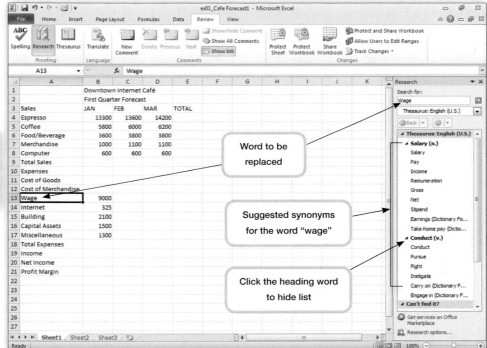

Figure 1.24

The Research task pane opens. The word in the active cell, Wage, is entered in the Search for text box and the list box displays words in the thesaurus that have similar meanings for this word. The list contains synonyms for "wage" used as a noun or as a verb. The first word at the top of each group is the group heading and is closest in meaning. It is preceded by a ▲ symbol, and the word is bold. The ▲ indicates the list of synonyms is displayed. Clicking the heading word will hide the list of synonyms.

When you point to a word in the list, a drop-down list of three menu options, Insert, Copy, and Lookup, becomes available. The Insert option inserts the word into the active cell. The Copy option is used to copy and then paste the word into any worksheet cell. The Lookup option displays additional related words for the current word. You decide to use the word "Pay" and will insert the word into cell A13 in place of "Wage."

2

- Point to "Pay" and click ⌄ to display the menu.

- Choose Insert.

- Click ✕ in the title bar of the Research task pane to close it.

Your screen should be similar to Figure 1.25

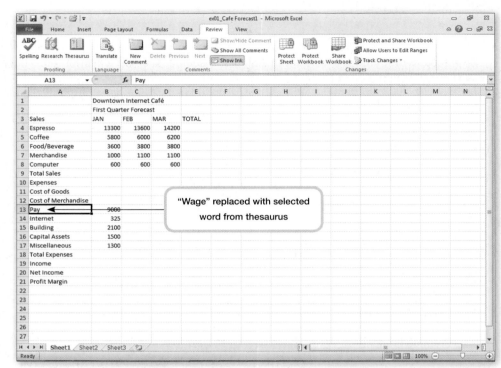

Figure 1.25

The word "Wage" is replaced with the selected word from the thesaurus. Notice the replacement word is capitalized correctly. This is because the replacement text follows the same capitalization as the word it replaces.

Copying and Pasting Cell Contents

Next, you want to enter the estimated expenses for salary, computers, lease, and miscellaneous for February and March. They are the same as the January expense numbers. Because these values are the same, instead of entering the same number repeatedly into each cell you can quickly copy the contents of one cell to another. You also want to move information from one location in the worksheet to another.

COPYING AND PASTING DATA

To use the Copy command, you first must select the cell or cells in the source containing the data to be copied. This is called the **copy area**. You will copy the Pay value in cell B13 into cells C13 and D13.

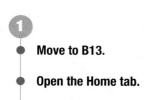

1

● Move to B13.

● Open the Home tab.

● Click 📋 Copy in the Clipboard group.

Your screen should be similar to Figure 1.26

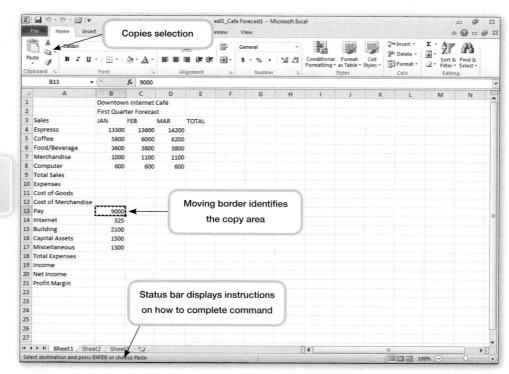

Figure 1.26

A moving border identifies the copy area and indicates that the contents have been copied to the system Clipboard. The instructions displayed in the status bar tell you to select the destination, called the **paste area**, where you want the contents copied. You will copy them to cell C13.

2

● Move to C13.

● Click the top part of the 📋 Paste button.

Additional Information

The 📋 Paste button is a split button. Clicking the top part of the button pastes using the default settings. Clicking the lower part displays a menu of options.

Your screen should be similar to Figure 1.27

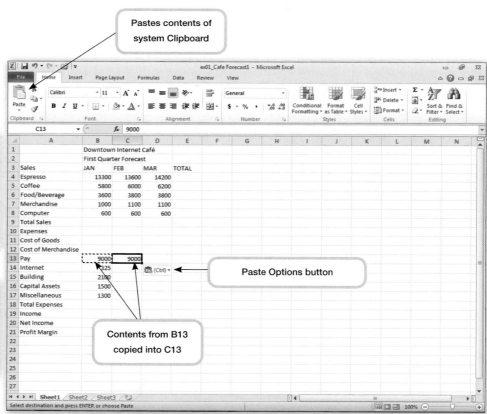

Figure 1.27

Copying and Pasting Cell Contents **EX1.29**

The contents of the system Clipboard are inserted at the specified destination location. Each time the Paste command is used, the  Paste Options button is available. Clicking on the button opens the Paste Options menu that allows you to control how the information you are pasting is inserted. Be careful when pasting to the new location because any existing entries are replaced.

The moving border is still displayed, indicating the system Clipboard still contains the copied entry. Now you can complete the data for the Pay row by pasting the value again from the system Clipboard into cell D13. While the moving border is still displayed, you also can simply press ←Enter to paste. However, as this method clears the contents of the system Clipboard immediately, it can only be used once.

3

● **Move to D13.**

● **Press** ←Enter.

Your screen should be similar to Figure 1.28

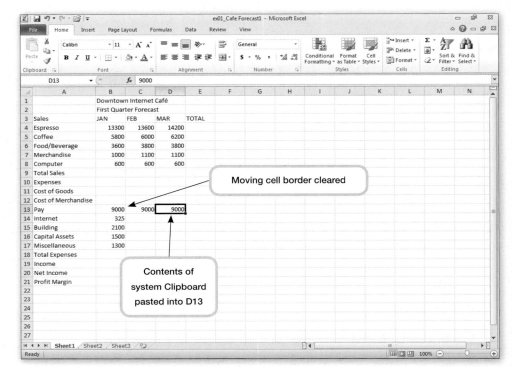

Figure 1.28

The contents of the system Clipboard are inserted at the specified destination location and the moving border is cleared, indicating the system Clipboard is empty.

SELECTING A RANGE

Now you need to copy the Internet value in cell B14 to February and March. You could copy and paste the contents individually into each cell as you did with the Pay values. A quicker method, however, is to select a range and paste the contents to all cells in the range at once.

Concept **6** Range

A selection consisting of two or more cells on a worksheet is a **range**. The cells in a range can be adjacent or nonadjacent. An **adjacent range** is a rectangular block of adjoining cells. A **nonadjacent range** consists of two or more selected cells or ranges that are not adjoining. In the example shown below, the shaded areas show valid adjacent and nonadjacent ranges. A **range reference** identifies the cells in a range. A colon is used to separate the first and last cells of an adjacent range reference. For example, A2:C4 indicates the range consists of cells A2 through C4. Commas separate the cell references of a nonadjacent range. For example, A10,B12,C14 indicates the range consists of cells A10, B12, and C14 of a nonadjacent range.

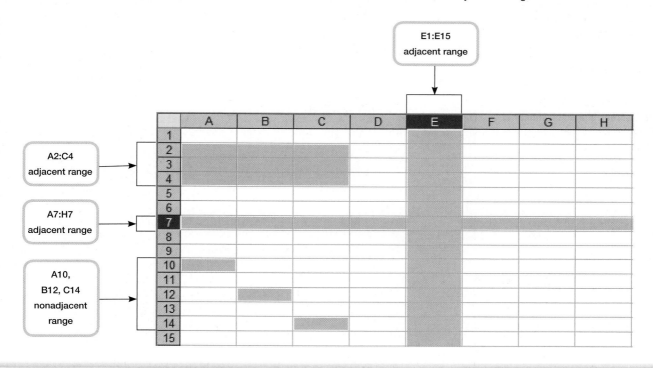

E1:E15
adjacent range

A2:C4
adjacent range

A7:H7
adjacent range

A10,
B12, C14
nonadjacent
range

You can select a range using the mouse procedures shown in the following table. You also can select using the keyboard by moving to the first cell of the range, holding down ⇧Shift or pressing F8 and using the navigational keys to expand the highlight. Using the F8 key turns on and off Extend mode. When this mode is on, Extend Selection appears in the status bar.

To Select	Mouse
A range	Click first cell of range and drag to the last cell.
A large range	Click first cell of range, hold down ⇧Shift, and click last cell of range.
All cells on worksheet	Click the [ ] All button located at the intersection of the row and column headings.
Nonadjacent cells or ranges	Select first cell or range, hold down Ctrl while selecting the other cell or range.
Entire row or column	Click the row number or column letter heading.
Adjacent rows or columns	Drag across the row number or column letter headings.
Nonadjacent rows or columns	Select first row or column, hold down Ctrl, and select the other rows or columns.

To complete the data for the Internet row, you want to copy the value in cell B14 to the system Clipboard and then copy the system Clipboard contents to the adjacent range of cells C14 through D14.

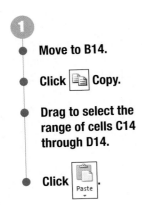

● Move to B14.

● Click 🗐 Copy.

● Drag to select the range of cells C14 through D14.

● Click [Paste].

Your screen should be similar to Figure 1.29

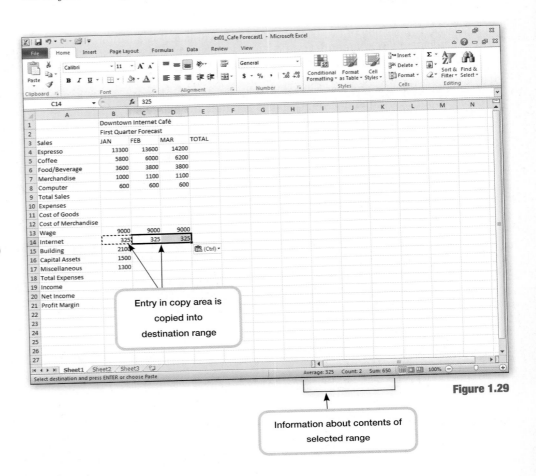

Entry in copy area is copied into destination range

Information about contents of selected range

Figure 1.29

Additional Information

The paste area does not have to be adjacent to the copy area.

The destination range is highlighted and identified by a dark border surrounding the selected cells. The source entry was copied from cell B14 and pasted into the selected destination range. Also notice the status bar now displays the average, count, and sum of values in the selected range.

USING THE FILL HANDLE

Next, you will copy the January Building expenses to cells C15 through D15, the Capital Assets expenses to cells C16 through D16, and the Miscellaneous expenses to cells C17 through D17. You can copy all values at the same time across the row by first specifying a range as the source. Another way to copy is to select the cells that contain the data you want to copy and drag the **fill handle**, the black box in the lower-right corner of a selection across or down the cells you want to fill.

1

- Press [Esc] to clear the moving border.

- Drag to select cells B15 through B17.

- Point to the fill handle and when the mouse pointer is a **+**, drag the mouse to extend the selection to cells D15 through D17.

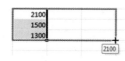

- Release the mouse button.

Another Method

You also can select the range B15:D17, click [icon] ▾ Fill in the Editing group, and choose Right. The shortcut key is [Ctrl] + R.

Your screen should be similar to Figure 1.30

Additional Information

You will learn more about the AutoFill feature in later labs.

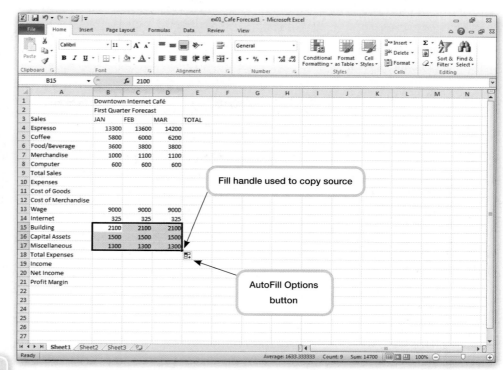

Figure 1.30

The range of cells to the right of the source is filled with the same values as in the source range. Using this method does not copy the source to the system Clipboard and therefore you cannot paste the source multiple times. When you copy by dragging the fill handle, the AutoFill Options button [icon] appears. Its menu commands are used to modify how the fill operation was performed. It will disappear as soon as you make an entry in the worksheet.

INSERTING COPIED CELL CONTENT

You also decide to include another row of month headings above the expenses to make the worksheet data easier to read. To do this quickly, you can insert copied data between existing data. To indicate where to place the copied content, you move the cell selector to the upper-left cell of the area where you want the selection inserted.

The column headings you want to copy are in cells B3 through E3. You will also copy cell A3, and clear the text in column A of the new row when you paste the contents.

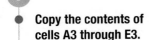

- Copy the contents of cells A3 through E3.

- Move to A10.

- Click ⊟ Insert ▾ in the Cells group.

- Select cell A10 and delete the word "Sales".

Your screen should be similar to Figure 1.31

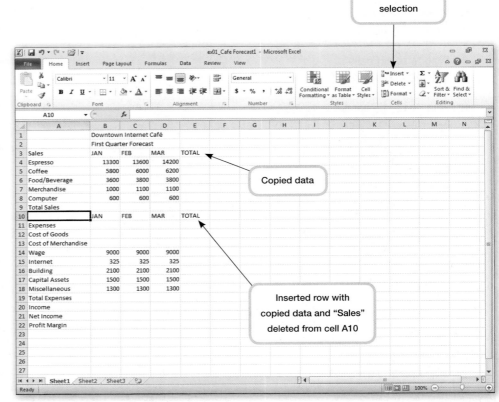

Figure 1.31

The copied data is inserted into the existing row (10) and all entries below are moved down one row.

CUTTING AND PASTING DATA

Next, you decide the Income, Net Income, and Profit Margin rows of data would stand out more if a blank row separated them from the expenses. Also, the Profit Margin row of data would be better separated from the Net Income row by a blank row. You will first remove the cell contents of the three cells using ✂ Cut and then paste the contents from the system Clipboard into the new location. The pasted content will copy over any existing content. You will use the keyboard shortcuts for these commands to complete this process.

1

- Select cells A20 through A22.

- Press Ctrl + X.

- Move to cell A21.

- Press Ctrl + V.

Your screen should be similar to Figure 1.32

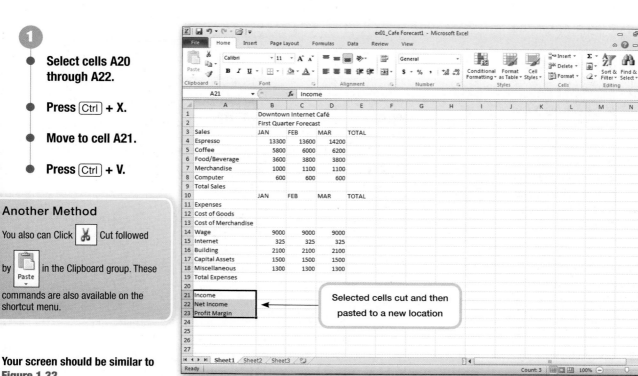

Figure 1.32

The contents of the three selected cells are copied to the system Clipboard. Then, when you paste, the cell contents are removed and inserted at the new location, copying over any existing content.

Another way you can cut and paste is to use drag and drop to move the cell contents. This method is quickest and most useful when the distance between cells is short and they are visible within the window, whereas cut and paste is best for long-distance moves. You will use this method to move the Profit Margin entry down one cell.

2

- Move to cell A23.

- Point to the border of the selection and when the mouse pointer shape is ⬆, drag the selection down one row to cell A24 and release the mouse button.

- Open the File tab and click 🖫 Save As .

- Save the changes you have made to the workbook as Cafe Forecast1 to your solution file location.

Your screen should be similar to Figure 1.33

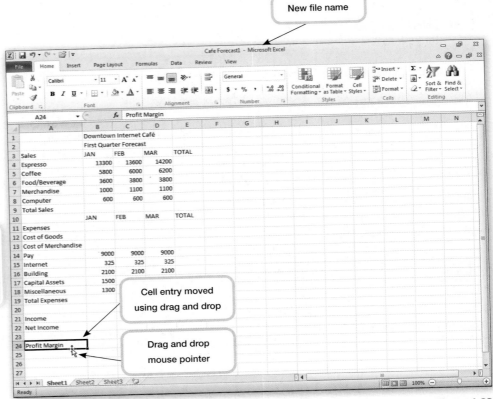

New file name

Cafe Forecast1 - Microsoft Excel

	A	B	C	D	E
1		Downtown Internet Café			
2		First Quarter Forecast			
3	Sales	JAN	FEB	MAR	TOTAL
4	Espresso	13300	13600	14200	
5	Coffee	5800	6000	6200	
6	Food/Beverage	3600	3800	3800	
7	Merchandise	1000	1100	1100	
8	Computer	600	600	600	
9	Total Sales				
10		JAN	FEB	MAR	TOTAL
11	Expenses				
12	Cost of Goods				
13	Cost of Merchandise				
14	Pay	9000	9000	9000	
15	Internet	325	325	325	
16	Building	2100	2100	2100	
17	Capital Assets	1500			
18	Miscellaneous	1300			
19	Total Expenses				
20					
21	Income				
22	Net Income				
23					
24	Profit Margin				
25					
26					
27					

Cell entry moved using drag and drop

Drag and drop mouse pointer

Figure 1.33

The cell contents were moved into cell A24 and cleared from the original cell.

When you use the Copy and Cut commands, the contents are copied to the system Clipboard and can be copied to any location in the worksheet, another workbook, or a document in another application multiple times. When you use 🔽 Fill or drag the fill handle, the destination must be in the same row or column as the source, and the source is not copied to the system Clipboard. Dragging the cell border to move or copy also does not copy the source to the system Clipboard.

NOTE If you are running short on lab time, this is an appropriate place to end your session. When you begin again, open the file Cafe Forecast1.

Working with Formulas

The remaining entries that need to be made in the worksheet are formula entries.

Concept 7 Formula

A **formula** is an equation that performs a calculation on data contained in a worksheet. A formula always begins with an equal sign (=) and uses arithmetic operators. An **operator** is a symbol that specifies the type of numeric operation to perform. Excel includes the following operators: + (addition), − (subtraction), / (division), * (multiplication), % (percent), and ^ (exponentiation). The calculated result from formulas is a **variable** value because it can change if the data it depends on changes. In contrast, a number entry is a **constant** value. It does not begin with an equal sign and does not change unless you change it directly by typing in another entry.

In a formula that contains more than one operator, Excel calculates the formula from left to right and performs the calculation in the following order: percent, exponentiation, multiplication and division, and addition and subtraction (see Example A). This is called the **order of precedence**. If a formula contains operators with the same precedence (for example, addition and subtraction), they are again evaluated from left to right. The order of precedence can be overridden by enclosing the operation you want performed first in parentheses (see Example B). When there are multiple sets of parentheses, Excel evaluates them working from the innermost set of parentheses out.

Example A: =5*4−3   Result is 17 (5 times 4 to get 20, and then subtract 3 for a total of 17)
Example B: =5*(4−3)   Result is 5 (4 minus 3 to get 1, and then 1 times 5 for a total of 5)

The values on which a numeric formula performs a calculation are called **operands**. Numbers or cell references can be operands in a formula. Usually cell references are used, and when the numeric entries in the referenced cell(s) change, the result of the formula is automatically recalculated.

ENTERING FORMULAS

The first formula you will enter will calculate the total Espresso sales for January through March (cell E4) by summing the numbers in cells B4 through D4. You will use cell references in the formula as the operands and the + arithmetic operator to specify addition. A formula is entered in the cell where you want the calculated value to be displayed. As you enter the formula, Excel helps you keep track of the cell references by identifying the referenced cell with a colored border and using the same color for the cell reference in the formula.

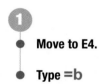

Move to E4.

Type =b

Your screen should be similar to
Figure 1.34

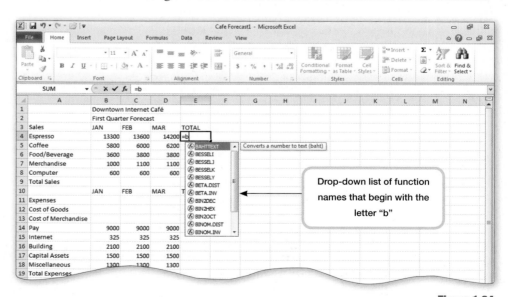

Figure 1.34

A drop-down list of function names that begin with the letter "b" is displayed. Functions are a type of formula entry that you will learn about shortly.

2
● Type **4+c4+d4**

Additional Information

Cell references can be typed in either uppercase or lowercase letters. Spaces between parts of the formula are optional.

Your screen should be similar to Figure 1.35

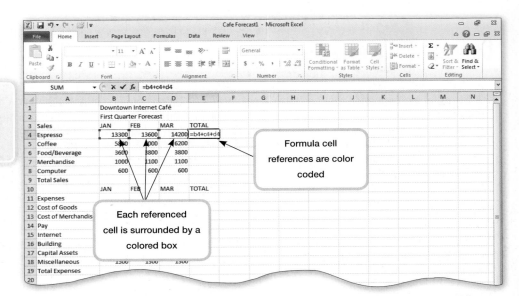

Figure 1.35

As you enter the formula, each cell that is referenced in the formula is surrounded by a colored box that matches the color of the cell reference in the formula.

3
● Press Ctrl + ←Enter or click ✔ Enter in the formula bar.

Your screen should be similar to Figure 1.36

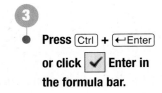

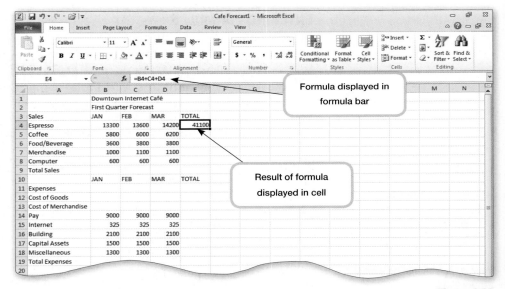

Figure 1.36

The number 41100 is displayed in cell E4, and the formula that calculates this value is displayed in the formula bar.

COPYING FORMULAS WITH RELATIVE REFERENCES

The formulas to calculate the total sales for rows 5 through 8 can be entered next. Just as you can with text and numeric entries, you can copy formulas from one cell to another.

- **Copy the formula in cell E4 to cells E5 through E8 using any of the copying methods.**

- **Move to E5.**

- **If necessary, press Esc to clear the moving border.**

Your screen should be similar to Figure 1.37

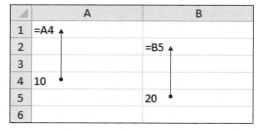

Cell references in the copied formula were adjusted relative to new location of formula in worksheet

Figure 1.37

The calculated result, 18000, is displayed in the cell. The formula displayed in the formula bar is =B5+C5+D5. The formula to calculate the Coffee total sales is not an exact duplicate of the formula used to calculate the Espresso total sales (=B4+C4+D4). Instead, the cells referenced in the formula have been changed to reflect the new location of the formula in row 5. This is because the references in the formula are relative references.

Concept 8 Relative Reference

A **relative reference** is a cell or range reference in a formula whose location is interpreted by Excel in relation to the position of the cell that contains the formula. When a formula is copied, the referenced cells in the formula automatically adjust to reflect the new worksheet location. The relative relationship between the referenced cell and the new location is maintained. Because relative references automatically adjust for the new location, the relative references in a copied formula refer to different cells than the references in the original formula. The relationship between cells in both the copied and the pasted formulas is the same although the cell references are different.

For example, in the figure here, cell A1 references the value in cell A4 (in this case, 10). If the formula in A1 is copied to B2, the reference for B2 is adjusted to the value in cell B5 (in this case, 20).

	A	B
1	=A4	
2		=B5
3		
4	10	
5		20
6		

Move to cell E6, E7, and then to cell E8.

Your screen should be similar to Figure 1.38

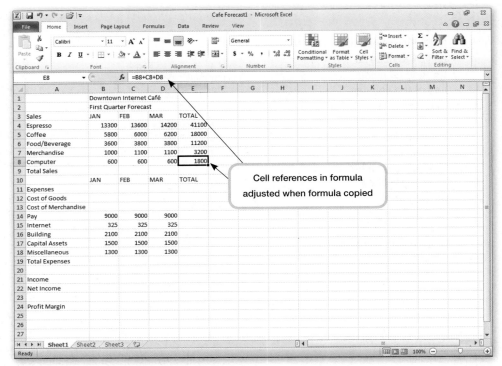

The formula bar shows **=B8+C8+D8** for cell E8.

	A	B	C	D	E	F	G	H	I	J	K	L	M	N
1		Downtown Internet Café												
2		First Quarter Forecast												
3	Sales	JAN	FEB	MAR	TOTAL									
4	Espresso	13300	13600	14200	41100									
5	Coffee	5800	6000	6200	18000									
6	Food/Beverage	3600	3800	3800	11200									
7	Merchandise	1000	1100	1100	3200									
8	Computer	600	600	600	1800									
9	Total Sales													
10		JAN	FEB	MAR	TOTAL									
11	Expenses													
12	Cost of Goods													
13	Cost of Merchandise													
14	Pay	9000	9000	9000										
15	Internet	325	325	325										
16	Building	2100	2100	2100										
17	Capital Assets	1500	1500	1500										
18	Miscellaneous	1300	1300	1300										
19	Total Expenses													
20														
21	Income													
22	Net Income													
23														
24	Profit Margin													
25														
26														
27														

Cell references in formula adjusted when formula copied

Figure 1.38

The formulas in these cells also have changed to reflect the new row location and to appropriately calculate the total based on the sales.

SUMMARIZING DATA

Next, you will calculate the monthly total sales. The formula to calculate the total sales for January needs to be entered in cell B9 and copied across the row. You could use a formula similar to the formula used to calculate the category sales in column E. The formula would be =B4+B5+B6+B7+B8. However, it is faster and more accurate to use a function.

Concept 9 Function

A **function** is a prewritten formula that performs certain types of calculations automatically. The **syntax** or rules of structure for entering all functions is as follows:

=Function name (argument1, argument2, . . .)

The function name identifies the type of calculation to be performed. Most functions require that you enter one or more arguments following the function name. An **argument** is the data the function uses to perform the calculation. The type of data the function requires depends upon the type of calculation being performed. Most commonly, the argument consists of numbers or references to cells that contain numbers. The argument is enclosed in parentheses, and commas separate multiple arguments. The beginning and ending cells of a range are separated with a colon.

Some functions, such as several of the date and time functions, do not require an argument. However, you still need to enter the opening and closing parentheses; for example, =NOW(). If a function starts the formula, enter an equal sign before the function name; for example, =SUM(D5:F5)/25.

Excel includes several hundred functions divided into 11 categories. Some common functions from each category and the results they calculate are shown in the following table.

Category	Function	Calculates
Financial	PMT	Calculates the payment for a loan based on constant payments and a constant interest rate.
	PV	Returns the present value of an investment—the total amount that a series of future payments is worth now.
	FV	Returns the future value of an investment—the total amount that a series of payments will be worth.
Date & Time	TODAY	Returns the serial number that represents today's date.
	DATE	Returns the serial number of a particular date.
	NOW	Returns the serial number of the current date and time.
Math & Trig	SUM	Adds all the numbers in a range of cells.
	ABS	Returns the absolute value of a number (a number without its sign).
Statistical	AVERAGE	Returns the average (arithmetic mean) of its arguments.
	MAX	Returns the largest value in a set of values; ignores logical values and text.
	MIN	Returns the smallest value in a set of values; ignores logical values and text.
	COUNT	Counts the number of cells in a range that contain numbers.
	COUNTA	Counts the number of cells in a range that are not empty.
	COLUMNS	Returns the number of columns in an array or reference.
Lookup & Reference	HLOOKUP	Looks for a value in the top row of a table and returns the value in the same column from a row you specify.
	VLOOKUP	Looks for a value in the leftmost column of a table and returns the value in the same row from a column you specify.
Database	DSUM	Adds the numbers in the field (column) or records in the database that match the conditions you specify.
	DAVERAGE	Averages the values in a column in a list or database that match conditions you specify.
Text	PROPER	Converts text to proper case in which the first letter of each word is capitalized.
	UPPER	Converts text to uppercase.
	LOWER	Converts text to lowercase.
	SUBSTITUTE	Replaces existing text with new text in a text string.
Logical	IF	Returns one value if a condition you specify evaluates to TRUE and another value if it evaluates to FALSE.
	AND	Returns TRUE if all its arguments are TRUE; returns FALSE if any arguments are FALSE.
	OR	Returns TRUE if any arguments are TRUE; returns FALSE if all arguments are FALSE.
	NOT	Changes FALSE to TRUE or TRUE to FALSE.
	IFERROR	Returns value-if-error if expression is an error and the value of the expression itself otherwise.
Information	ISLOGICAL	Returns TRUE if value is a logical value, either TRUE or FALSE.
	ISREF	Returns TRUE if value is a reference.
Engineering	BIN2DEC	Converts a binary number to decimal.
	CONVERT	Converts a number from one measurement system to another.
Cube	CUBESETCOUNT	Returns the number of items in a set.

You will use the SUM function to calculate the total sales for January. Because the SUM function is the most commonly used function, it has its own command button.

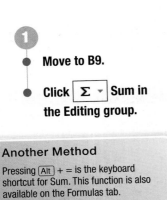

1

- Move to B9.

- Click Σ ▾ Sum in the Editing group.

Another Method

Pressing [Alt] + = is the keyboard shortcut for Sum. This function is also available on the Formulas tab.

Your screen should be similar to Figure 1.39

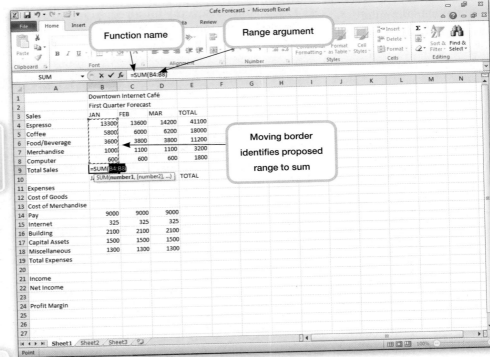

Figure 1.39

Additional Information

The Σ ▾ Sum button also can calculate a grand total if the worksheet contains subtotals. Select a cell below or to the right of a cell that contains a subtotal and then click Σ ▾ Sum.

Excel automatically proposes a range based upon the data above or to the left of the active cell. The formula bar displays the name of the function followed by the range argument enclosed in parentheses. You will accept the proposed range and enter the function.

2

- Click ✔ Enter.

Your screen should be similar to Figure 1.40

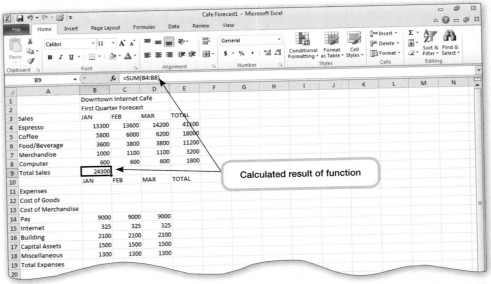

Figure 1.40

The result, 24300, calculated by the SUM function is displayed in cell B9. Next, you need to calculate the total sales for February and March and the Total column.

3

- Copy the function from cell B9 to cells C9 through E9.

- Move to C9.

Your screen should be similar to Figure 1.41

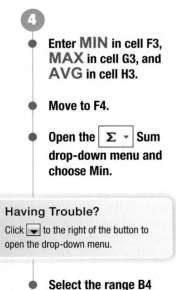

Figure 1.41

The result calculated by the function, 25100, is displayed in cell C9 and the copied function is displayed in the formula bar. The range reference in the function is adjusted relative to its new cell location because it is a relative reference.

You also decide to calculate the minimum, maximum, and average sales for each sales category. You will add appropriate column headings and enter the functions in columns F, G, and H. The Σ ▾ Sum button also includes a drop-down menu from which you can select several other common functions. As you enter these functions, the proposed range will include the Total cell. Simply select another range to replace the proposed range.

4

- Enter **MIN** in cell F3, **MAX** in cell G3, and **AVG** in cell H3.

- Move to F4.

- Open the Σ ▾ Sum drop-down menu and choose Min.

Having Trouble?

Click ▾ to the right of the button to open the drop-down menu.

- Select the range B4 through D4 to specify the January through March sales values and click ✔ Enter.

Your screen should be similar to Figure 1.42

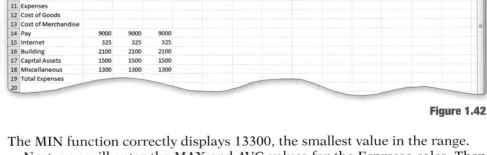

Figure 1.42

The MIN function correctly displays 13300, the smallest value in the range.

Next, you will enter the MAX and AVG values for the Espresso sales. Then you will copy the functions down the column through row 8.

5

- Enter the MAX function in cell G4 and the AVG function in cell H4 to calculate the Espresso sales values for January through March.

- Copy the functions in cells F4 through H4 to F5 through H8.

- Move to H8.

Your screen should be similar to Figure 1.43

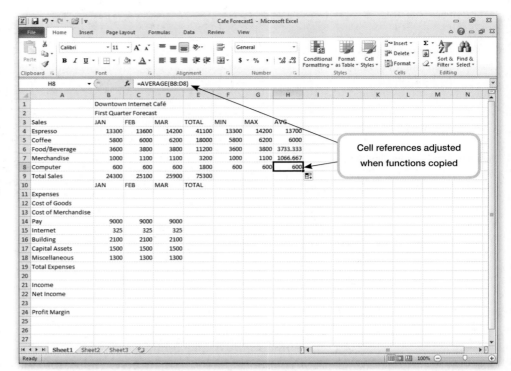

Figure 1.43

The minimum, maximum, and average values for the five sales categories have been calculated. The Average column displays as many decimal places as cell space allows.

USING POINTING TO ENTER A FORMULA

Next, you will enter the formula to calculate the cost of goods for espresso, coffee, and food and beverages sold. These numbers are estimated by using a formula to calculate the number as a percent of sales. Evan suggested using estimated percents for this worksheet so he could get an idea of what to expect from the first three months after the remodel. He wants you to calculate espresso expenses at 25 percent of espresso sales, coffee expenses at 30 percent of coffee sales, and food and beverage expenses at 60 percent of food sales.

Rather than typing in the cell references for the formula, you will enter them by selecting the worksheet cells. In addition, to simplify the process of entering and copying entries, you can enter data into the first cell of a range and have it copied to all other cells in the range at the same time by using [Ctrl] + [←Enter] to complete the entry. You will use this feature to enter the formulas to calculate the beverage expenses for January through March. This formula needs to calculate the beverage cost of goods at 25 percent first and add it to the food cost of goods calculated at 50 percent.

1

- Select B12 through D12.

- Type =

- Click cell B4.

Additional Information

Even when a range is selected, you can still point to specify cells in the formula. You also can use the direction keys to move to the cell.

Your screen should be similar to Figure 1.44

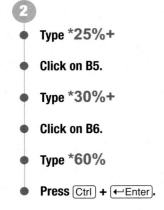

Figure 1.44

Additional Information

While entering the formula in Point mode, if you make an error, edit the entry like any other error and then continue entering the remainder of the formula.

Notice that the status bar displays the current mode as Point. This tells you that the program is allowing you to select cells by highlighting them. The cell reference, B4, is entered following the equal sign. You will complete the formula by entering the percentage value to multiply by and adding the Food percentage to the formula.

2

- Type *25%+

- Click on B5.

- Type *30%+

- Click on B6.

- Type *60%

- Press [Ctrl] + [←Enter].

Your screen should be similar to Figure 1.45

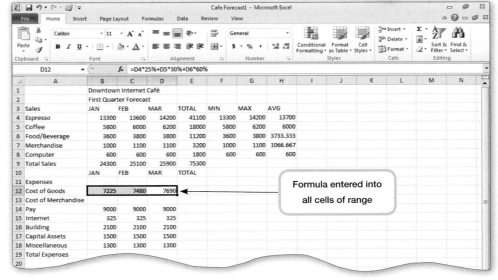

Figure 1.45

Having Trouble?

If you made an error in the formula, edit the entry in the formula bar and then press [Ctrl] + [←Enter] again to copy it to the selected range.

The formula to calculate the January Cost of Goods expenses was entered in cell B12 and copied to all cells of the selected range.

Now you will enter the Cost of Merchandise expenses by multiplying the value in B8 by 70%. Then you will calculate the total expenses in row 19 and column E. To do this quickly, you will preselect the range and use the Σ ▾ Sum button. Then you will enter the formula to calculate the net income. Net income is calculated by subtracting total expenses from total sales.

3

- Select cells B13 through D13.

- Type =

- Click on B7.

- Type *70%

- Press Ctrl + ←Enter.

- Select B12 through E19.

- Click Σ ▾ Sum.

- Select B22 through E22.

- Enter the formula =B9-B19 and press Ctrl + ←Enter.

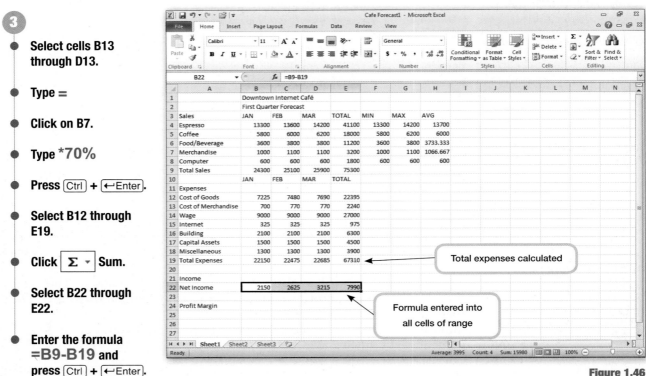

Figure 1.46

Your screen should be similar to Figure 1.46

The formulas were quickly entered into all cells of the specified ranges.

Finally, you will enter the formula to calculate the profit margin. Profit margin is calculated by dividing net income by total sales.

4

- Select B24 through E24.

- Enter the formula **=B22/B9** and press [Ctrl] + [←Enter].

Your screen should be similar to Figure 1.47

	A	B	C	D	E	F	G	H
1		Downtown Internet Café						
2		First Quarter Forecast						
3	Sales	JAN	FEB	MAR	TOTAL	MIN	MAX	AVG
4	Espresso	13300	13600	14200	41100	13300	14200	13700
5	Coffee	5800	6000	6200	18000	5800	6200	6000
6	Food/Beverage	3600	3800	3800	11200	3600	3800	3733.333
7	Merchandise	1000	1100	1100	3200	1000	1100	1066.667
8	Computer	600	600	600	1800	600	600	600
9	Total Sales	24300	25100	25900	75300			
10		JAN	FEB	MAR	TOTAL			
11	Expenses							
12	Cost of Goods	7225	7480	7690	22395			
13	Cost of Merchandise	700	770	770	2240			
14	Wage	9000	9000	9000	27000			
15	Internet	325	325	325	975			
16	Building	2100	2100	2100	6300			
17	Capital Assets	1500	1500	1500	4500			
18	Miscellaneous	1300	1300	1300	3900			
19	Total Expenses	22150	22475	22685	67310			
20								
21	Income							
22	Net Income	2150	2625	3215	7990			
23								
24	Profit Margin	0.088477	0.104582	0.124131	0.106109			
25								
26								
27								

Formula entered into all cells of range

Figure 1.47

The net income and profit margins are calculated and displayed in the worksheet.

RECALCULATING THE WORKSHEET

Now that you have created the worksheet structure and entered some sample data for the forecasted sales for the first quarter, you want to test the formulas to verify that they are operating correctly. A simple way to do this is to use a calculator to verify that the correct result is displayed. You can then further test the worksheet by changing values and verifying that all cells containing formulas that reference the value are appropriately recalculated.

Concept 10 Recalculation

When a number in a referenced cell in a formula changes, Excel automatically **recalculates** all formulas that are dependent upon the changed value. Because only those formulas directly affected by a change in the data are recalculated, the time it takes to recalculate the workbook is reduced. Without this feature, in large worksheets it could take several minutes to recalculate all formulas each time a number is changed in the worksheet. Recalculation is one of the most powerful features of electronic worksheets.

After considering the sales estimates for the three months, you decide that the estimated sales generated from Computer usage for January are too high and you want to decrease this number from 600 to 400.

Change the entry in cell B8 to 400

Your screen should be similar to Figure 1.48

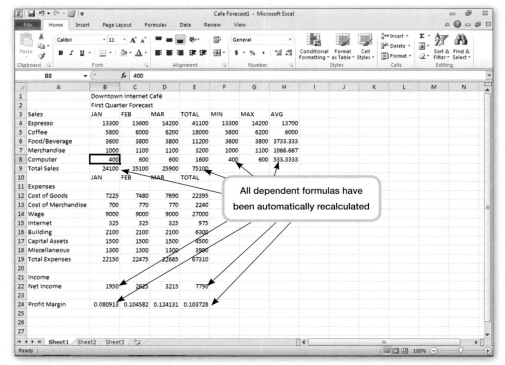

Figure 1.48

The Computer total in cell E8 has been automatically recalculated. The number displayed is now 1600. The MIN and AVG values in cells F8 and H8 have been recalculated to 400 and 533.3333 respectively. Likewise, the January total in cell B9 of 24100 and the grand total in cell E9 of 75100 each decreased by 200 from the previous totals to reflect the change in cell B8. Finally, the Net Income and Profit Margin values also have adjusted appropriately.

The formulas in the worksheet are correctly calculating the desired result. The Sales portion of the worksheet is now complete.

Inserting and Deleting Rows and Columns

As you are developing a worksheet, you may realize you forgot to include information or decide that other information is not needed. To quickly add and remove entire rows and columns of information, you can insert and delete rows and columns. A new blank row is inserted above the active cell location and all rows below it shift down a row. Similarly, you can insert blank cells and columns in a worksheet. Blank cells are inserted above or to the left of the active cell, and blank columns are inserted to the left of the active cell. Likewise, you can quickly delete selected cells, rows, and columns, and all information in surrounding cells, rows, or columns automatically shifts appropriately to fill in the space.

Additionally, whenever you insert or delete cells, rows, or columns, all formula references to any affected cells adjust accordingly.

INSERTING ROWS

You realize that you forgot to include a row for the Advertising expenses. To add this data, you will insert a blank row above the Capital Assets row.

1

- Move to A17.

- Open the 🔳 Insert ▾ drop-down menu in the Cells group and choose Insert Sheet Rows.

Another Method

You also can choose Insert from the active cell's context menu.

- Enter the heading **Advertising** in cell A17 and the value **600** in cells B17 through D17.

- Copy the function from cell E16 to E17 to calculate the total advertising expense.

- Move to cell B20.

- Click 🔳 Save to save the workbook using the same file name.

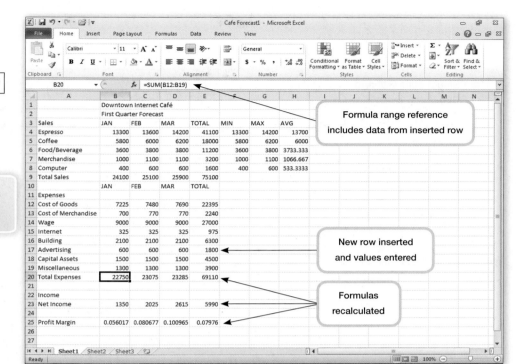

Figure 1.49

Your screen should be similar to Figure 1.49

Additional Information

Click 🔳 Insert ▾ to insert blank cells, shifting existing cells down, and 🔳 Insert ▾ /Sheet Columns to insert blank columns, shifting existing columns right.

A blank row was inserted in the worksheet and the cell references in all formulas and functions below the inserted row adjusted appropriately. The range in the formula to calculate monthly total expenses in row 20 has been adjusted to include the data in the inserted row, and the total expense for the first quarter is 69110. Additionally, the net income in row 23 and the profit margin in row 25 have been recalculated to reflect the change in data.

DELETING COLUMNS

As you look at the worksheet data, you decide the minimum and maximum values are not very useful since this data is so easy to see in this small worksheet. You will delete these two columns from the worksheet to remove this information. To specify which column to delete, select any cell in the column.

1

- Select cells F20 and G20.

- Open the
  Delete drop-down menu in the Cells group and choose Delete Sheet Columns.

Your screen should be similar to Figure 1.50

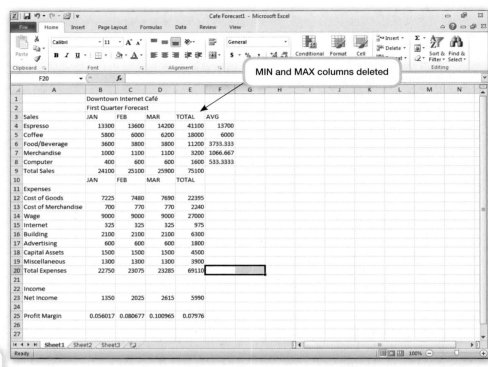

Figure 1.50

The two columns have been removed and the columns to the right of the deleted columns automatically shifted to the left.

Formatting Cells and Cell Content

Now that the worksheet data is complete, you want to improve the appearance of the worksheet. Applying different formatting to text and numbers can greatly enhance the appearance of the document. In Excel, formats control how entries are displayed in a cell and include such features as the position of data in a cell, character font and color, and number formats such as commas and dollar signs.

You want to change the appearance of the row and column headings and apply formatting to the numbers. Applying different formats greatly improves both the appearance and the readability of the data in a worksheet.

CHANGING CELL ALIGNMENT

You decide the column headings would look better if they were right-aligned in their cell spaces, so that they would appear over the numbers in the column. Alignment is a basic format setting that is used in most worksheets.

Concept Alignment

Alignment settings allow you to change the horizontal and vertical placement and the orientation of an entry in a cell.

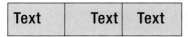

Horizontal placement allows you to left-, right-, or center-align text and number entries in the cell space. Entries also can be indented within the cell space, centered across a selection, or justified. You also can fill a cell horizontally with a repeated entry.

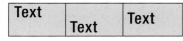

Vertical placement allows you to specify whether the cell contents are displayed at the top, the bottom, or the center of the vertical cell space or justified vertically.

You also can change the orientation or angle of text in a cell by varying the degrees of rotation.

The default workbook horizontal alignment settings left-align text entries and right-align number entries. The vertical alignment is set to Bottom for both types of entries, and the orientation is set to zero degrees rotation from the horizontal position. You want to change the horizontal alignment of the month headings in rows 3 and 10 to right-aligned.

The Alignment group contains commands to control the horizontal and vertical placement of entries in a cell. You can quickly apply formatting to a range of cells by selecting the range first. A quick way to select a range of filled cells is to hold down ⇧Shift and double-click on the edge of the active cell in the direction in which you want the range expanded. For example, to select the range to the right of the active cell, you would double-click the right border. You will use this method to select and right-align these entries.

Additional Information

If you do not hold down ⇧Shift while double-clicking on a cell border, the active cell moves to the last-used cell in the direction indicated.

1

● Move to B3.

● Hold down ⇧Shift and double-click the right cell border of cell B3.

Having Trouble?

The mouse pointer must be ‡ when you click the cell border.

● Click ▤ Align Text Right from the Alignment group.

● Select B10 through E10.

● Click ▤ Align Text Right.

Your screen should be similar to Figure 1.51

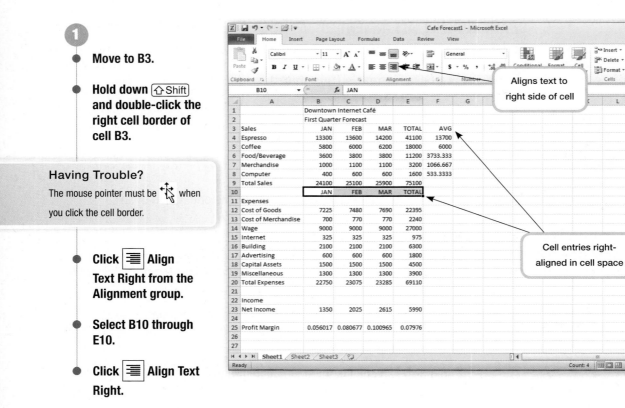

Figure 1.51

The entries in the selected ranges are right-aligned in their cell spaces. You notice the month labels do not stand out well and decide to try rotating them.

2

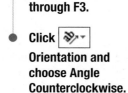

● Select cells B3 through F3.

● Click ▤ Orientation and choose Angle Counterclockwise.

Your screen should be similar to Figure 1.52

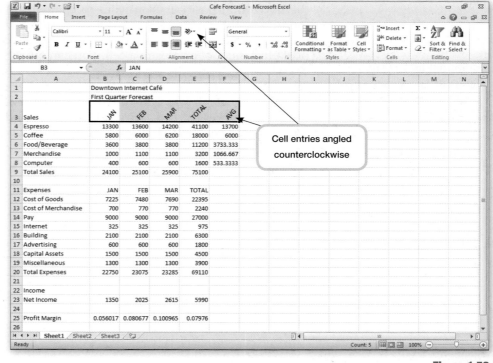

Figure 1.52

Notice how the row height increased automatically to accommodate the change in size.

CHANGING ROW HEIGHT

You don't like the way it looks rotated and decide to undo the change, add height to the row manually to help identify the month label row better, and center-align the labels. You also decide to move the month labels in row 10 down a row to match the first row of month labels.

Concept 12 Row Height

The **row height** is the size or height of a row measured in points. The default row height is 12.75 points which is slightly larger than the default font point size of 11. The row height can be any number from 0 to 409. If it is set to 0, the row is hidden. The row height automatically adjusts to changes in the character size, style and orientation.

The row height can also be changed manually using methods that are similar to those used to change the column width. The difference is that you drag or click the boundary below the row heading to adjust the row height.

- Click Undo.

- Move the entries in cells B10 through E10 into the same columns in row 11.

- Drag the bottom boundary of rows 3 and 11 to increase the row height to 22.5.

- Select the text in cells B3 through F3 and click Center.

- Do the same for cells B11 through E11.

Your screen should be similar to Figure 1.53

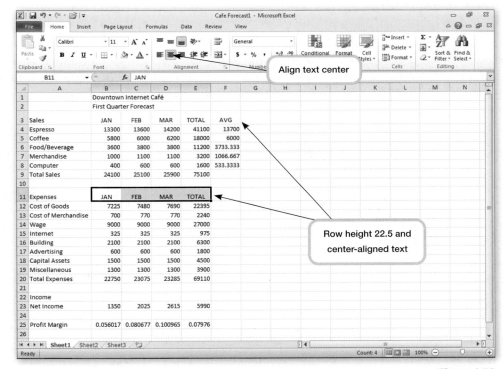

Figure 1.53

Increasing the row height of the month labels visually separates the labels from other worksheet entries.

INDENTING CELL CONTENT

Next, you would like to indent the row headings in cells A4 through A8 and A12 through A19 to show that the entries are subtopics below the Sales and Expense headings. You want to indent the headings in both ranges at the same time. To select nonadjacent cells or cell ranges, after selecting the first cell or range, hold down Ctrl while selecting each additional cell or range. You will select the cells and indent their contents.

Additional Information

You also can select entire nonadjacent rows or columns by holding down Ctrl while selecting the rows or columns.

Formatting Cells and Cell Content **EX1.53**

1

- Select A4 through A8.

- Hold down Ctrl.

- Select A12 through A19.

- Release Ctrl.

- Click 🔲 Increase Indent in the Alignment group.

- AutoFit the width of column A.

Your screen should be similar to Figure 1.54

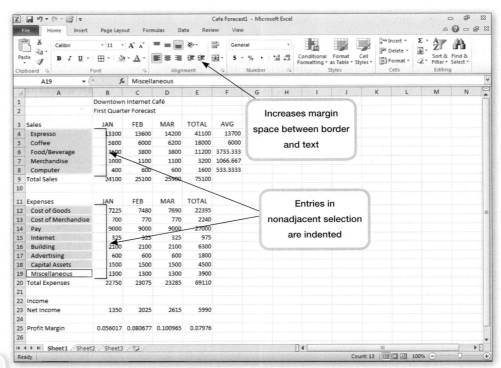

Figure 1.54

Additional Information

Clicking 🔲 Increase Indent multiple times indents the selection in two-space increments. Clicking 🔲 Decrease Indent reduces the margin between the border and the text in the cell.

Each entry in the selected range is indented two spaces from the left edge of the cell. Finally, you want to right-align the Total Sales, Total Expenses, and Net Income headings.

2

- Select A9, A20, and A23.

- Click ≡ Align Text Right.

Your screen should be similar to Figure 1.55

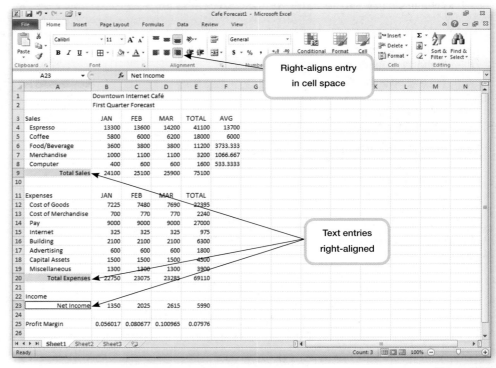

Figure 1.55

MERGING CELLS

Next, you want to center the worksheet titles across columns A through F so they are centered over the worksheet data. To do this, you will merge or combine the cells in the range over the worksheet data (A1 through F1) into a single large **merged cell** and then center the contents of the range in the merged cell. This process is easily completed in one simple step using the Merge & Center command.

1

- Select A1 through F1.

- Click Merge & Center in the Alignment group.

Your screen should be similar to Figure 1.56

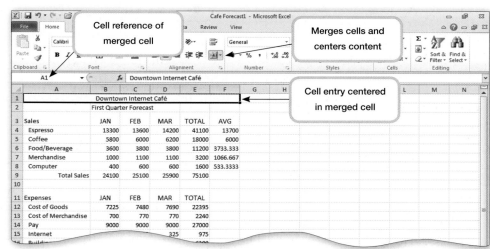

Figure 1.56

The six cells in the selection have been combined into a single large cell, and the entry that was in cell B1 is centered within the merged cell space. Only the contents of the first cell containing an entry in the upper-leftmost section of the selected range are centered in the merged cell. If other cells to the right of that cell contain data, it will be deleted. The cell reference for a merged cell is the upper-left cell in the original selected range, in this case A1.

2

- Merge and center the second title line across columns A through F.

Your screen should be similar to Figure 1.57

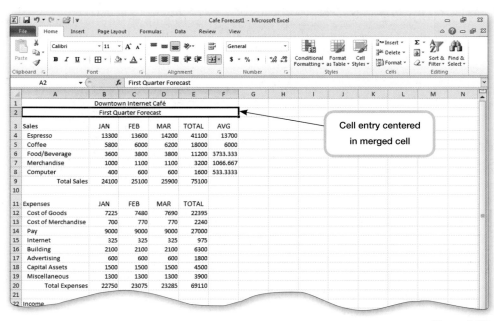

Figure 1.57

Formatting Cells and Cell Content   **EX1.55**

You also can use the commands in the [⊞ ▾] Merge & Center drop-down menu shown in the following table to control a merge. You can merge cells horizontally and vertically.

Merge Menu	Action
⊞ Merge & Center	Merges cells and centers entry
⊟ Merge Across	Merges cells horizontally
⊞ Merge Cells	Merges cells horizontally and vertically
⊞ Unmerge Cells	Splits cells that have been merged back into individual cells

CHANGING FONTS AND FONT SIZES

Having Trouble?

Refer to the section "Formatting Text" in the Introduction to Microsoft Office 2010 to review fonts.

Finally, you want to improve the worksheet appearance by enhancing the appearance of the title. One way to do this is to change the font and font size used in the title. There are two basic types of fonts: serif and sans serif. **Serif** fonts have a flare at the base of each letter that visually leads the reader to the next letter. Two common serif fonts are Roman and Times New Roman. Serif fonts generally are used in paragraphs. **Sans serif** fonts do not have a flare at the base of each letter. Arial and Helvetica are two common sans serif fonts. Because sans serif fonts have a clean look, they are often used for headings in documents. It is good practice to use only two types of fonts in a worksheet, one for text and one for headings. Too many styles can make your document look cluttered and unprofessional.

Here are several examples of the same text in various fonts and sizes.

Typeface	Font Size (12 pt/18 pt)
Calibri (Sans Serif)	This is 12 pt. This is 18 pt.
Times New Roman (Serif)	This is 12 pt. This is 18 pt.
Book Antiqua (Serif)	This is 12 pt. This is 18 pt.

Using fonts as a design element can add interest to your document and give readers visual cues to help them find information quickly. First you will try a different font for the title and a larger font size.

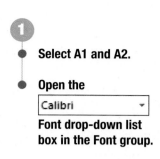

● **Select A1 and A2.**

● **Open the**

Calibri

Font drop-down list box in the Font group.

Your screen should be similar to Figure 1.58

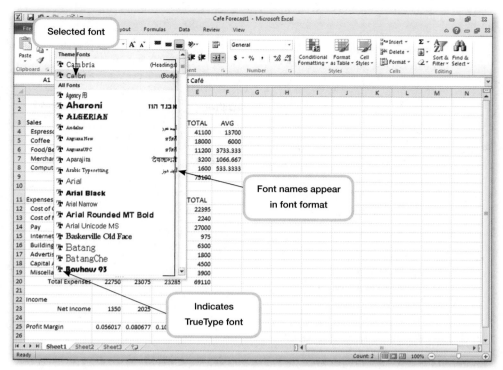

Figure 1.58

The Font drop-down list displays examples of the available fonts on your system in alphabetical order. The default worksheet font, Calibri, is highlighted. Notice the preceding the font name. This indicates the font is a TrueType font. TrueType fonts appear onscreen as they will appear when printed. They are installed when Windows is installed. Fonts that are preceded by a blank space are printer fonts. These fonts are supported by your printer and are displayed as closely as possible to how they will appear onscreen but may not match exactly when printed. You will change the font and increase the font size to 14. As you point to the font options, the Live Preview will show how it will appear if chosen.

Scroll the list and choose Lucida Sans.

Having Trouble?

You will not be able to see the Fonts Live Preview because the drop-down menu covers the selection to be formatted.

● **Open the** `11 ▾` **Font Size drop-down list box.**

● **Point to several different font sizes in the list to see the Live Preview.**

● **Choose 14.**

Your screen should be similar to Figure 1.59

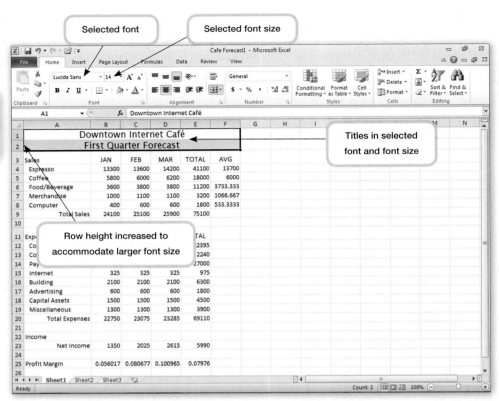

Figure 1.59

The title appears in the selected typeface and size, and the Font and Font Size buttons display the name of the font and the size used in the active cell. Notice that the height of the row has increased to accommodate the larger font size of the heading.

APPLYING TEXT EFFECTS

Another Method

The Font and Font Size commands are also available on the Mini toolbar.

In addition to changing font and font size, you can apply different text effects to enhance the appearance of text. The table below describes some of the text effects and their uses.

Having Trouble?

Refer to the section "Formatting Text" in the Introduction to Microsoft Office 2010 to review text effects.

Format	Example	Use
Bold	**Bold**	Adds emphasis.
Italic	*Italic*	Adds emphasis.
Underline	<u>Underline</u>	Adds emphasis.
Strikethrough	~~Strikethrough~~	Indicates words to be deleted.
Superscript	"To be or not to be."[1]	Used in footnotes and formulas.
Subscript	H_2O	Used in formulas.
Color	Color Color Color	Adds interest.

First you want to enhance the appearance of the column headings by increasing the font size and adding bold, italic, and underlines.

1

- Select B3 through F3.

- Increase the font size to 12.

- Click **B** Bold.

- Click **U** ▾ Underline.

Your screen should be similar to Figure 1.60

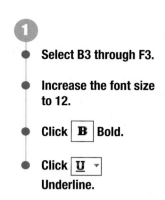

Adds underline effect

Adds bold effect

Entries bold and underlined

Figure 1.60

Having Trouble?

Refer to the section "Formatting Text" in the Introduction to Microsoft Office 2010 to review using the Mini toolbar.

Many of the formatting commands are also available on the Mini toolbar. In Excel, you must right-click on a cell to display the Mini toolbar and the shortcut menu. The selected formatting is applied to the entire cell contents. If you select text in a cell, the Mini toolbar appears automatically and the formatting is applied to the selected text only.

2

- Select A4 through A8.

- Right-click on the selection to display the Mini toolbar.

- Click **B** Bold.

- Click **I** Italic.

Another Method

The keyboard shortcut for bold is Ctrl + B; for italic, it is Ctrl + I; and for underline, it is Ctrl + U.

Your screen should be similar to Figure 1.61

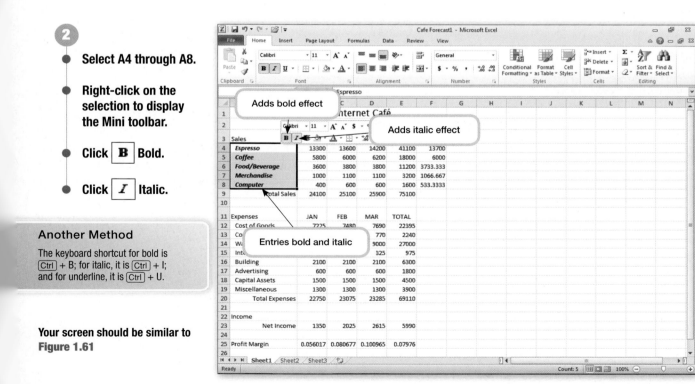

Adds bold effect

Adds italic effect

Entries bold and italic

Figure 1.61

Formatting Cells and Cell Content   **EX1.59**

CLEARING FORMATS

Sometimes formatting changes you make do not have the expected result. In this case, you feel that the sales category names would look better without the formatting. One way to remove the format from cells is to use ✐ Clear in the Editing group and choose Clear Formats. Because this will remove all formatting in the selected cells, you will need to redo the indenting in those cells.

1

- **With cells A4 through A8 still selected, open the ✐ Clear drop-down list in the Editing group.**

- **Choose Clear Formats.**

- **Click 📊 Increase Indent.**

Another Method

You could also use ↩ Undo to remove the formats by reversing your last actions.

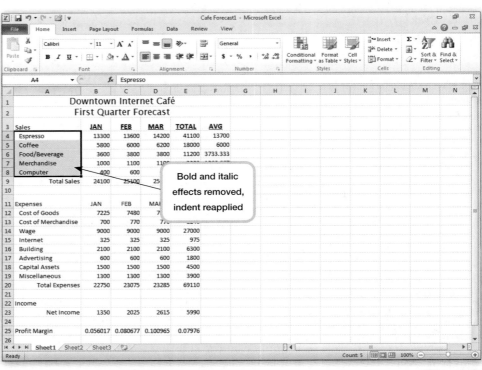

Bold and italic effects removed, indent reapplied

Figure 1.62

Your screen should be similar to Figure 1.62

Additional Information

You can remove both formatting and content using ✐ Clear/Clear All.

Having Trouble?

Refer to the section "Copying Formats" in the Introduction to Microsoft Office 2010 to review the Format Painter.

USING FORMAT PAINTER

You do think, however, that the Total Sales, Total Expenses, and Net Income headings would look good in bold. You will bold the entry in cell A9 and then copy the format from A9 to the other cells using Format Painter. You also will format the headings in row 11.

1

- Apply bold to cell A9.

- With cell A9 selected, double-click Format Painter in the Clipboard group.

- Click A20.

- Click A23.

- Click 🖌 Format Painter to turn it off.

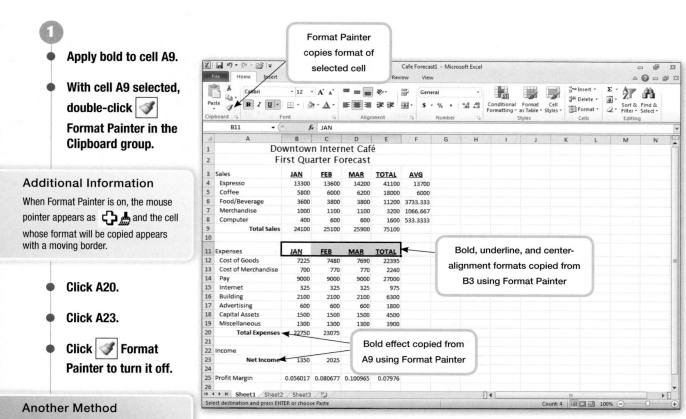

Figure 1.63

- Use Format Painter to copy the format from cell B3 to cells B11 through E11.

Your screen should be similar to Figure 1.63

The formatting was quickly added to each cell or range as it was selected.

FORMATTING NUMBERS

You also want to improve the appearance of the numbers in the worksheet by changing their format.

Concept ⑬ Number Formats

Number formats change the appearance of numbers onscreen and when printed, without changing the way the number is stored or used in calculations. When a number is formatted, the formatting appears in the cell, while the value without the formatting is displayed in the formula bar.

The default number format setting in a worksheet is General. General format, in most cases, displays numbers just as you enter them, unformatted. Unformatted numbers are displayed without a thousands separator such as a comma, with negative values preceded by a − (minus sign), and with as many decimal place settings as cell space allows. If a number is too long to be fully displayed in the cell, the General format will round numbers with decimals and use scientific notation for large numbers.

First, you will change the number format of cells B4 through F9 to display as currency with dollar signs, commas, and decimal places.

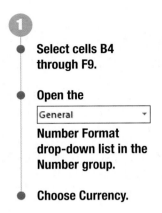

- Select cells B4 through F9.

- Open the

  | General ▼ |

  Number Format drop-down list in the Number group.

- Choose Currency.

Your screen should be similar to Figure 1.64

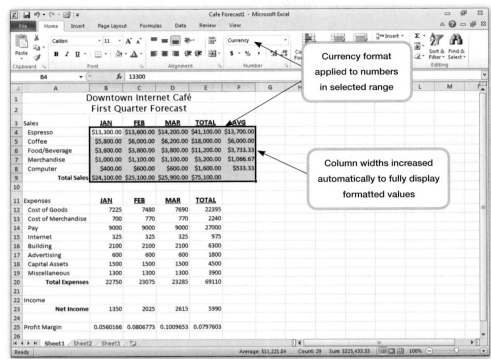

Figure 1.64

Another Method

Excel will also automatically apply a format to a cell based on the symbols you use when entering the number. For example, entering 10,000 in a cell formats the cell to Comma format, and entering $102.20 formats the cell to Currency with two decimal places.

The number entries in the selected range appear with a currency symbol, comma, and two decimal places. The column widths increased automatically to fully display the formatted values.

A second format category that displays numbers as currency is Accounting. You will try this format next on the same range. Additionally, you will specify zero as the number of decimal places because most of the values are whole values. To specify settings that are different than the default setting for a format, you can use the Format Cells dialog box.

2

- Make sure you still have cells B4 through F9 selected.

- Click 🔲 in the Number group to open the Format Cells: Number dialog box.

Another Method

The keyboard shortcut to open the Format Cells dialog box is Ctrl + 1.

- From the Category list box, choose Accounting.

- Reduce the decimal places to 0.

- Click ☐ OK ☐.

Your screen should be similar to Figure 1.65

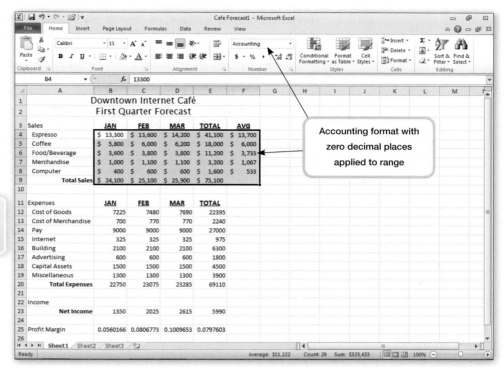

Figure 1.65

The numbers now appear in Accounting format. The primary difference between the Accounting and the Currency formats is that the Accounting format aligns numbers at the decimal place and places the dollar sign in a column at the left edge of the cell space. In addition, it does not allow you to select different ways of displaying negative numbers but displays them in black in parentheses.

You decide the Accounting format will make it easier to read the numbers in a column and you will use this format for the rest of the worksheet. An easier way to apply the Accounting format with 0 decimals is to use the commands in the Number group.

3

- Select the range B12 through E20.

- Click $ ▾ Accounting Number Format in the Number group.

- Click ☐ Decrease Decimal twice.

Your screen should be similar to Figure 1.66

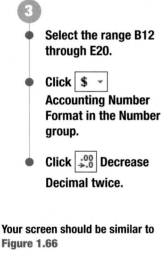

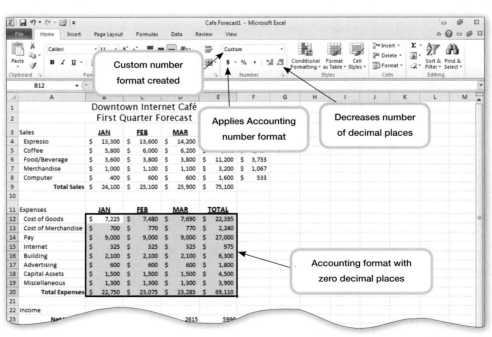

Figure 1.66

Notice the Number Format box displays Custom because you modified a copy of the existing Accounting number format code. The custom number format is added to the list of number format codes. Between 200 and 250 custom formats can be added depending on the language version of Excel you are using. You can then reapply the custom format by selecting it from the Custom category of the Format Cells: Number dialog box. This is useful for complicated formats, but not for formats that are easy to re-create.

Finally, you will format the Net Income values as Accounting with zero decimal places and the Profit Margin values as percentages with two decimal places. You will do this using the Mini toolbar. This feature is particularly helpful when working at the bottom of the worksheet window.

4

- Select B23 through E23.

- Click **$** Accounting Number Format on the Mini toolbar.

Having Trouble

Right-click on the selection to display the Mini toolbar.

- Click Decrease Decimal twice on the Mini toolbar.

- Select B25 through E25.

- Click **%** Percent Style on the Mini toolbar.

- Click Increase Decimal twice on the Mini toolbar.

Your screen should be similar to Figure 1.67

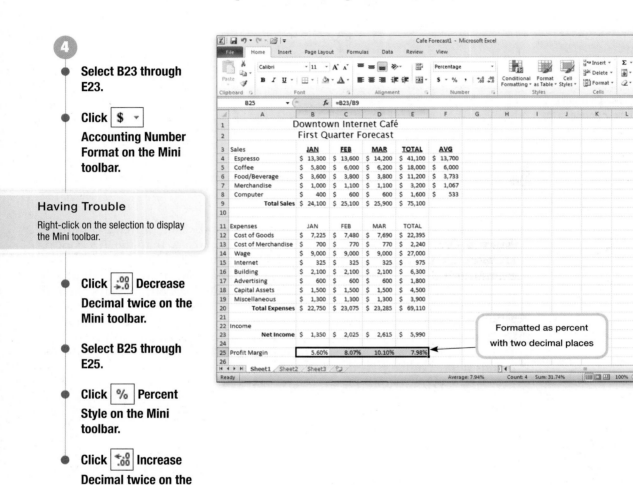

Figure 1.67

ADDING FONT COLOR

The last formatting change you would like to make to the worksheet is to add color to the text of selected cells. Font color can be applied to all the text in a selected cell or range or to selected words or characters in a cell.

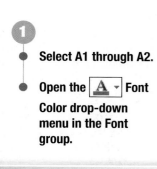

1

● Select A1 through A2.

● Open the Font Color drop-down menu in the Font group.

Another Method

Font Color is also available on the Mini toolbar.

Your screen should be similar to Figure 1.68

Figure 1.68

Additional Information

You will learn about using themes in Lab 2.

A palette of colors is displayed. Automatic is the default text color setting. This setting automatically determines when to use black or white text. Black text is used on a light background and white text on a dark background. The center area of the palette displays the theme colors. Theme colors are a set of colors that are associated with a **theme**, a predefined set of fonts, colors, and effects that can be applied to an entire worksheet. If you change the theme, the theme colors change. The Standard Colors bar displays 10 colors that are always the same.

As you point to a color, the entry in the selected cell changes color so you can preview how the selection would look. A ScreenTip displays the name of the standard color or the description of the theme color as you point to it.

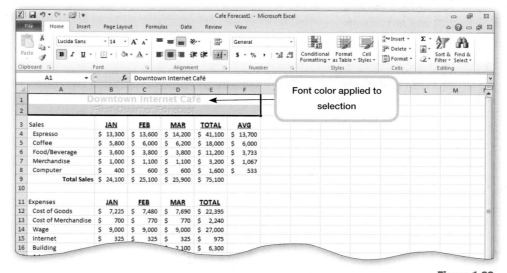

2

● Choose Yellow from the Standard Colors bar.

● Click **B** Bold.

Your screen should be similar to Figure 1.69

Figure 1.69

The font color of all the text in cells A1 and A2 has changed to the selected color and bold. The selected color appears in the button and can be applied again simply by clicking the button.

ADDING FILL COLOR

Next, you will change the cell background color, also called the fill color, behind the titles and in several other areas of the worksheet. Generally, when adding color to a worksheet, use a dark font color with a light fill color or a light font color with a dark fill color.

1

- Select cells A1 through F3.

- Open the 🪣 ▾ Fill Color drop-down color palette.

- Point to several colors to see a Live Preview.

- Select the Light Blue color from the Standard Colors bar.

- Select cells A11 through F11 and click 🪣 ▾ Fill Color to apply the last selected fill color.

- Apply the same fill color to A22 through F22 and A25 through F25.

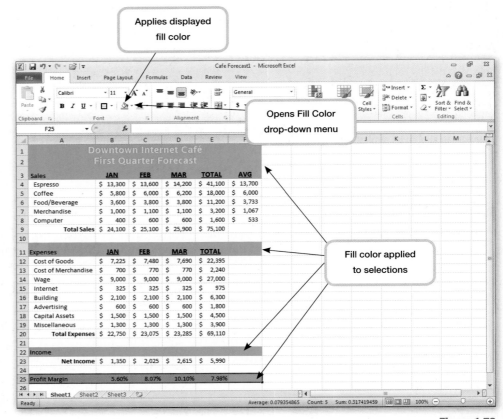

Figure 1.70

Your screen should be similar to Figure 1.70

The color highlight helps distinguish the different areas of the worksheet.

ADDING AND REMOVING CELL BORDERS

Finally, you decide to add a border around the entire worksheet area. Excel includes many predefined border styles that can be added to a single cell or to a range of cells. Then you will make several additional formatting changes to improve the appearance and readability of the worksheet.

1

- Select the range A1 through F25.

- Open the
  Borders drop-down menu in the Font group and choose the Thick Box Border style.

- Click outside the range to see the border.

Your screen should be similar to Figure 1.71

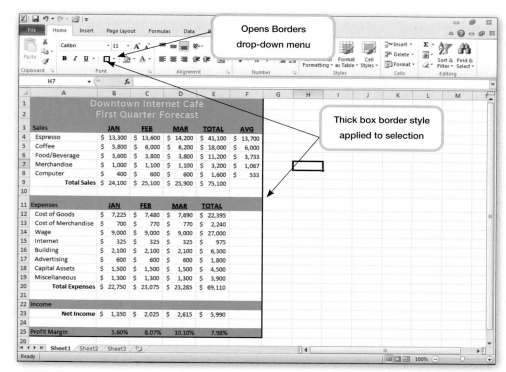

Figure 1.71

The range is considered a single block of cells, and the box border surrounds the entire worksheet selection.

When adding borders, the border also is applied to adjacent cells that share a bordered cell boundary. In this case, cells G1 through G25 acquired a left border and cells A26 through F26 acquired a top border. When pasting a cell that includes a cell border, the border is included unless you specify that the paste does not include the border. To see how this works, you will first copy a cell and its border, and then you will copy it again without the border.

2

- Copy cell A1 and paste it in cell G2.

- Move to G4, open the Paste drop-down menu, and choose No Borders.

- Move to G6 to see the changes.

Your screen should be similar to Figure 1.72

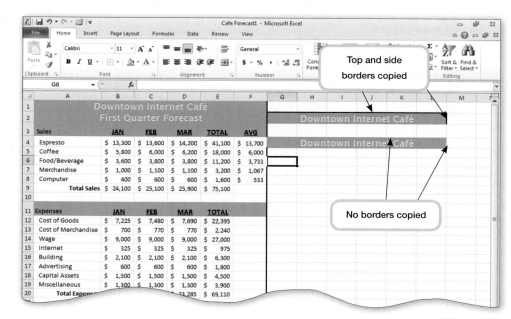

Figure 1.72

If you want to add additional borders or replace an existing border with another, select the range and then add the border. However, if you want to remove a border style from one area of a selection and add a border to another

Formatting Cells and Cell Content **EX1.67**

area, you need to remove all borders first and then apply the new border styles. You will try these features next on the entry in cell G2.

3
- Move to G2 and choose No Border from the Borders drop-down menu.
- Apply a Bottom Double Border to the selection.
- Move to G6 to see the changes.

Your screen should be similar to Figure 1.73

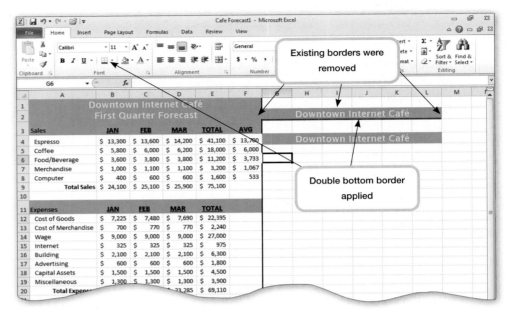

Figure 1.73

All existing borders were removed, including those that share a cell boundary, and the new double bottom border is applied to the selection. You will restore the worksheet to how it was prior to copying the title using Undo and then make some final adjustments to the worksheet.

4
- Undo your last four actions.
- Move to any cell in row 10 and choose Delete Sheet Rows from the Delete drop-down menu in the Cells group.
- In the same manner, delete the blank rows 20 and 23.
- Add bold and yellow font color to cells A3, A10, A20, and A22.
- Click Save to save the worksheet changes.

Your screen should be similar to Figure 1.74

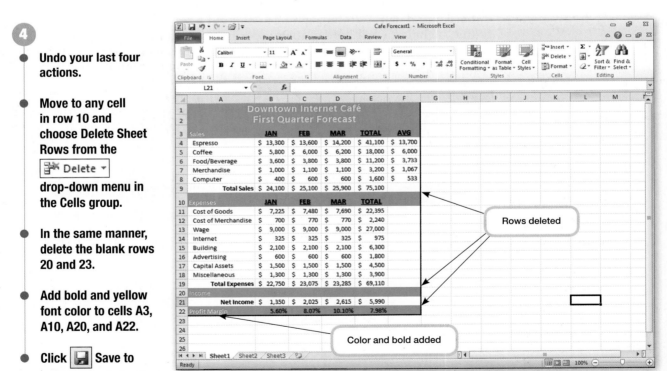

Figure 1.74

Hide and Unhide Rows and Columns

Now that the worksheet is nicely formatted, you want to focus on the data. One way to do this is to hide areas of data that you do not want to see in order to emphasize others. You will use this method to emphasize the total data.

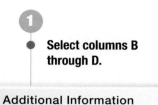

Select columns B through D.

Additional Information

Any range of cells within the area you want to hide can be selected.

Open the

Format ▾

drop-down menu in the Cells group and select Hide & Unhide.

Choose Hide Columns.

Your screen should be similar to Figure 1.75

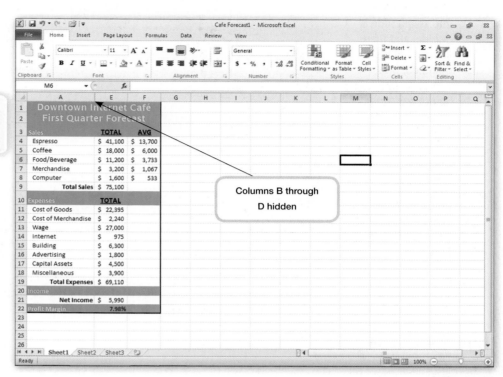

Figure 1.75

Another Method

You could also right-click on the selected columns and choose Hide from the context menu.

Now the worksheet focus is on the monthly total values, not the monthly values. The columns were hidden by reducing their column width to zero. Instead, you want to hide the rows.

Click on column A and drag to select columns A and E.

In the Cells group, click 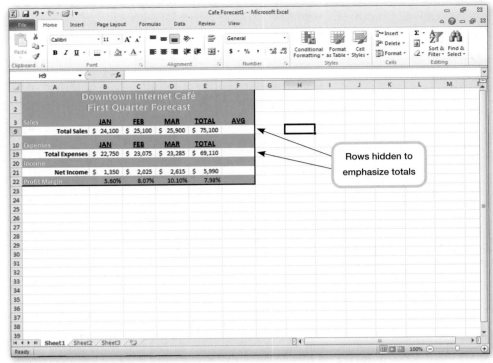 **Format ▼ and select Hide & Unhide, and then choose Unhide Columns.**

Select any range of cells within rows 4 through 8.

Open the ▦ Format ▼ **drop-down menu, select Hide & Unhide, and then choose Hide Rows.**

Repeat to hide rows 11 through 18.

Figure 1.76

Notice how hiding the rows emphasizes the monthly totals by category.

Your screen should be similar to Figure 1.76

Click ↩ **Undo twice to unhide the rows.**

Creating a Simple Chart

Another way to better understand the data in a worksheet is to create a chart. A **chart** is a visual representation of data that is used to convey information in an easy-to-understand and attractive manner. You decide to create a chart of the sales data for the three months.

SPECIFYING THE DATA TO CHART

To tell Excel what data to chart, you need to select the range containing the data you want to appear in the chart plus any row or column headings you want used in the chart.

1

• Select cells A3 through D8.

• Hold down the [Alt] key and press [F1].

Your screen should be similar to Figure 1.77

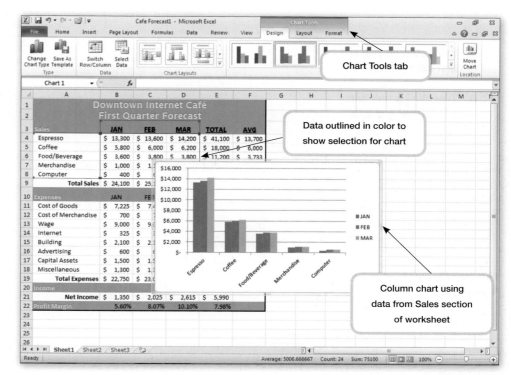

Figure 1.77

The information in the selected range was translated into a chart based on the shape and contents of the selection. A column chart showing the sales for the five items over three months was quickly created.

2

• Point to the edge of the chart object and drag to move it below the worksheet to cover rows 24 to 38.

• Click outside the chart object to deselect it.

Formatting Values as a Date

Now that the worksheet is complete, you want to include your name and the date in the worksheet as documentation. There are many ways to enter the date. For example, you could type the date using the format mm/dd/yy or as month dd, yyyy. When a date is entered as text, Excel converts the entry to a numeric entry that allows dates to be used in calculations. Excel stores all dates as **serial values** with each day numbered from the beginning of the 20th century. The date serial values are consecutively assigned beginning with 1, which corresponds to the date January 1, 1900, and ending with 2958465, which is December 31, 9999.

1

● Enter your first and last name in cell A40.

● Type the current date as mm/dd/yy in cell A41.

Your screen should be similar to Figure 1.78

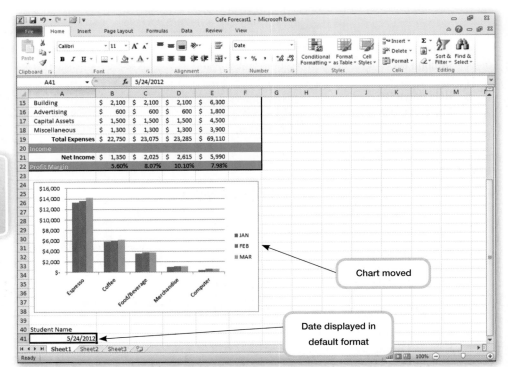

Figure 1.78

The date is displayed using the default date format, which is based on the settings in Windows. It is right-aligned in the cell because it is a numeric entry. You can change the date format in the worksheet without changing the Windows settings using the Format Cells: Number dialog box.

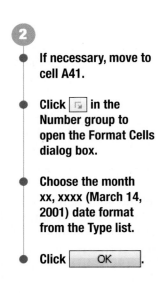

2

● If necessary, move to cell A41.

● Click ☐ in the Number group to open the Format Cells dialog box.

● Choose the month xx, xxxx (March 14, 2001) date format from the Type list.

● Click [OK].

Your screen should be similar to Figure 1.79

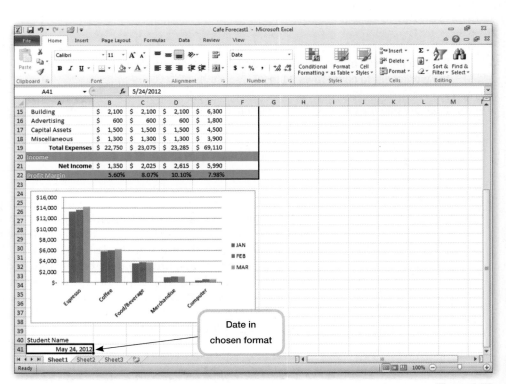

Figure 1.79

The date appears in the specified format.

Documenting a Workbook

Having Trouble?

Refer to the section "Specifying Document Properties" in the Introduction to Microsoft Office 2010 to review this feature.

You are finished working on the worksheet for now and want to save the changes you have made to the file. In addition, you want to update the file properties to include your name as the author, a title, and keywords.

- **Open the File tab.**

- **In the Backstage view Info window, enter the following information in the appropriate boxes.**

Title	Downtown Internet Café
Tags	Sales Projections
Author	Your Name

Additional Information

The Author text box may be blank or may show your school or some other name. Clear the existing contents first if necessary.

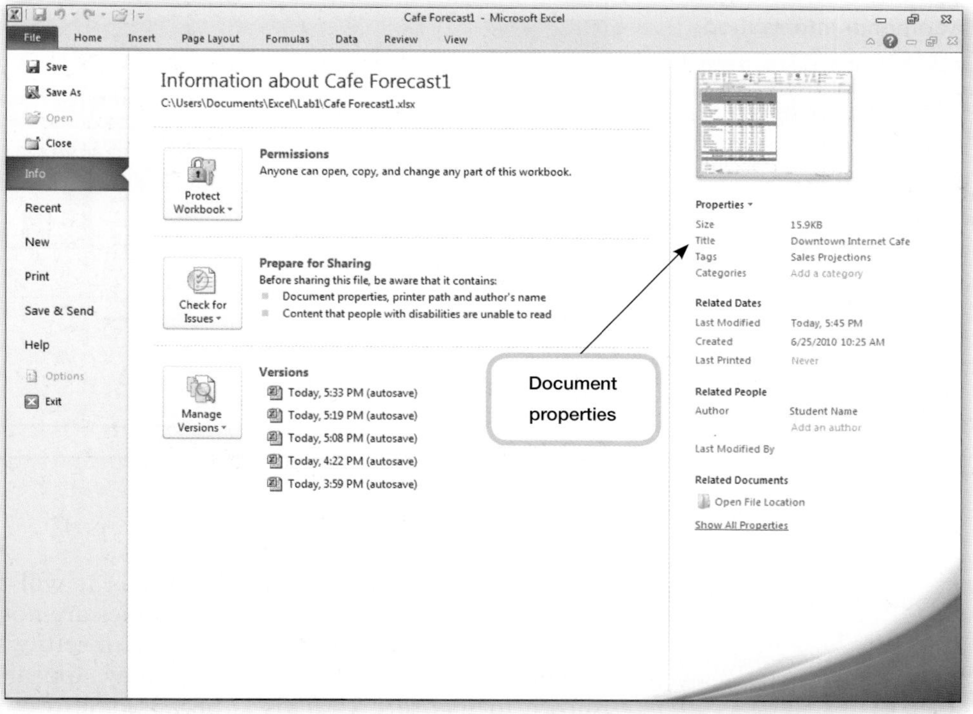

Cafe Forecast1 - Microsoft Excel

File   Home   Insert   Page Layout   Formulas   Data   Review   View

Save
Save As
Open
Close
Info
Recent
New
Print
Save & Send
Help
Options
Exit

Information about Cafe Forecast1
C:\Users\Documents\Excel\Lab1\Cafe Forecast1.xlsx

Permissions
Anyone can open, copy, and change any part of this workbook.

Protect Workbook ▾

Prepare for Sharing
Before sharing this file, be aware that it contains:
- Document properties, printer path and author's name
- Content that people with disabilities are unable to read

Check for Issues ▾

Versions
Today, 5:33 PM (autosave)
Today, 5:19 PM (autosave)
Today, 5:08 PM (autosave)
Today, 4:22 PM (autosave)
Today, 3:59 PM (autosave)

Manage Versions ▾

Document properties

Properties ▾
Size   15.9KB
Title   Downtown Internet Cafe
Tags   Sales Projections
Categories   Add a category

Related Dates
Last Modified   Today, 5:45 PM
Created   6/25/2010 10:25 AM
Last Printed   Never

Related People
Author   Student Name
                Add an author
Last Modified By

Related Documents
Open File Location

Show All Properties

Figure 1.80

Your screen should be similar to Figure 1.80

Previewing and Printing a Worksheet

Although you still plan to make more changes to the worksheet, you want to print a copy of the estimated first-quarter forecast for the owner to get feedback regarding the content and layout.

1 Choose Print and view the preview in the right pane.

Your screen should be similar to Figure 1.81

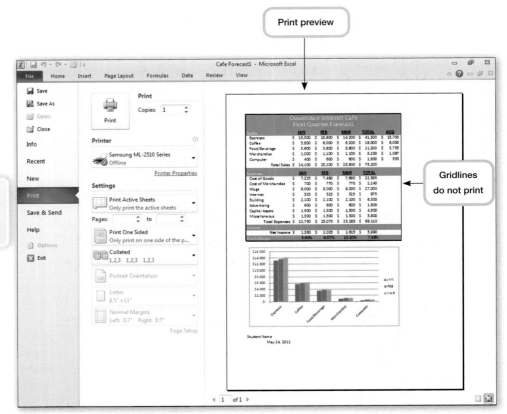

Figure 1.81

The preview displays the worksheet as it will appear on the printed page. Notice that the row and column gridlines are not displayed and will not print. This is one of the default worksheet print settings.

The preview of your worksheet may appear slightly different from that shown in Figure 1.81. This is because the way pages appear in the preview depends on the available fonts, the resolution of the printer, and the available colors. If your printer is configured to print in black and white, the preview will not display in color.

The Excel print settings let you specify how much of the worksheet you want printed. The options are described in the following table.

Option	Action
Print Active Sheets	Prints the active worksheet (default).
Print Entire Workbook	Prints all worksheets in the workbook.
Print Selection	Prints selected range only.
Pages	Prints pages you specify by typing page numbers in the text box.

The worksheet looks good and does not appear to need any further modifications immediately. Now you are ready to print the worksheet using the default print settings.

NOTE **Please consult your instructor for printing procedures that may differ from the following directions.**

②

● If necessary, make sure your printer is on and ready to print.

● If you need to change the selected printer to another printer, open the Printer drop-down list box and select the appropriate printer.

● Click 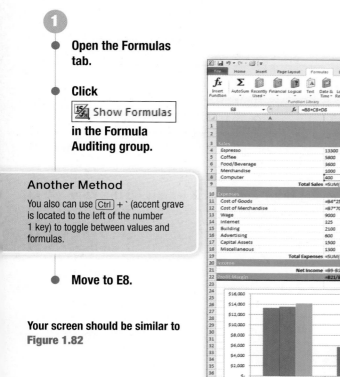.

The printed copy should be similar to the document shown in the preview area.

When printing is complete, Backstage view is automatically closed. A dotted line may appear between columns G and H. This is the automatic page break line that shows where one printed page ends and the next begins.

DISPLAYING AND PRINTING FORMULAS

Often, when verifying the accuracy of the data in a worksheet, it is helpful to display all the formulas in a worksheet rather than the resulting values. This way you can quickly verify that the formulas are referencing the correct cells and ranges.

①

● Open the Formulas tab.

● Click 15⅜ **Show Formulas** in the Formula Auditing group.

Another Method

You also can use Ctrl + ` (accent grave is located to the left of the number 1 key) to toggle between values and formulas.

● Move to E8.

Your screen should be similar to Figure 1.82

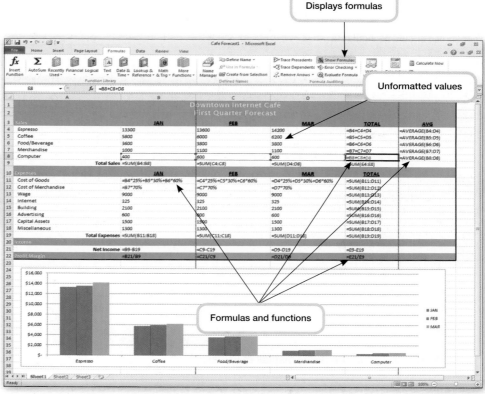

Figure 1.82

The display of the worksheet has changed to display unformatted values and the formulas and functions. It has automatically increased the column widths so the formulas and text do not overflow into the adjacent cells.

CHANGING WORKSHEET ORIENTATION AND SCALING CONTENT

Next, you will print the worksheet with formulas. Because the worksheet is so much wider, you will need to change the orientation to landscape, which prints across the length of the paper. Then you will reduce the scale of the worksheet so it fits on one page. The **scaling** feature will reduce or enlarge the worksheet contents by a percentage or to fit them to a specific number of pages by height and width. You want to scale the worksheet to fit on one page.

1

● **Open the File tab and choose Print.**

● **Change the orientation setting to Landscape Orientation.**

● **Open the**

drop-down menu and choose Fit Sheet on One Page.

Your screen should be similar to Figure 1.83

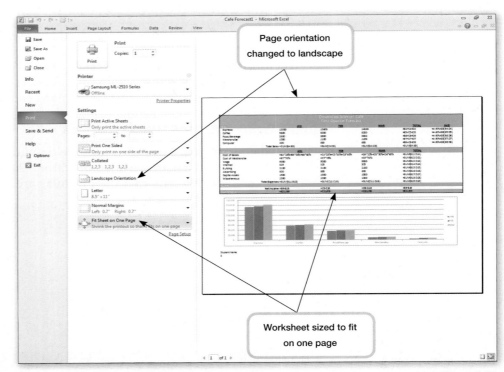

Figure 1.83

The entire worksheet will easily print across the length of the page when printed using landscape orientation and scaled to fit a single page.

Another Method

You also can scale the worksheet using Scale: in the Scale to Fit group of the Page Layout tab and setting the scale percentage.

2

● **Print the worksheet.**

● **Press** Ctrl **+ ` to return the display to values.**

Exiting Excel 2010

Having Trouble?

Refer to the "Closing a File" and "Exiting an Office 2010 Application" sections in the Introduction to Microsoft Office 2010 to review these features.

You are now ready to exit the Excel application. If you attempt to close the application without first saving the workbook, Excel displays a warning asking whether you want to save your work. If you do not save your work and you exit the application, all changes you made from the last time you saved will be lost.

1

● **Move to cell A1.**

● **Click** ☒ **Close (in the application window title bar).**

● **Click** [Save] **to resave the worksheet.**

Additional Information

Excel saves the file with the cell selector in the same cell location it is in at the time it is saved.

Because you added the date since last saving the worksheet, you were prompted to save it again before closing it.

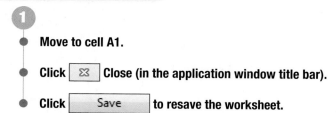

OCUS ON CAREERS

EXPLORE YOUR CAREER OPTIONS

Fan Coordinator

Did you know that 40 percent of the advertised positions in sports are for marketing and promotion? A marketing graduate hired as a basketball fan coordinator would use Excel to keep track of the income and expenses for coordinated halftime activities at professional sporting events. These worksheets would provide valuable information for promoting sponsors' products and services at games. A fan coordinator might start out as an unpaid intern, but after graduation could expect to earn from $25,000 to $45,000.

Data (EX1.12)

The basic information or data you enter in a cell can be text or numbers.

AutoCorrect (EX1.18)

The AutoCorrect feature makes some basic assumptions about the text you are typing and, based on these assumptions, automatically corrects the entry.

Column Width (EX1.21)

The column width is the size or width of a column and controls the amount of information that can be displayed in a cell.

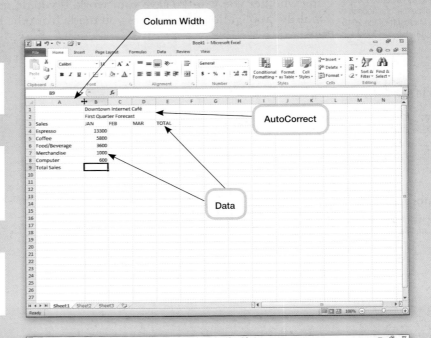

Spelling Checker (EX1.25)

The spelling checker locates misspelled words, duplicate words, and capitalization irregularities in the active worksheet and proposes the correct spelling.

Thesaurus (EX1.27)

The thesaurus is a reference tool that provides synonyms, antonyms, and related words for a selected word or phrase.

Range (EX1.31)

A selection consisting of two or more cells on a worksheet is a range.

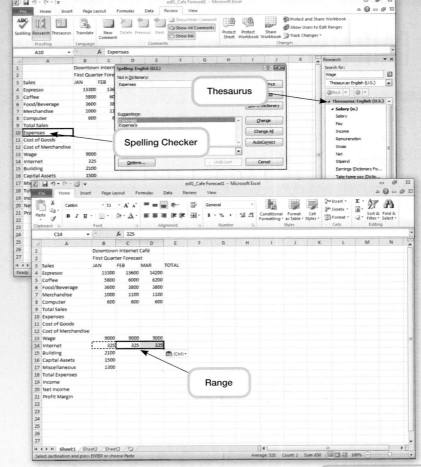

Formula (EX1.37)

A formula is an equation that performs a calculation on data contained in a worksheet.

Relative Reference (EX1.39)

A relative reference is a cell or range reference in a formula whose location is interpreted in relation to the position of the cell that contains the formula.

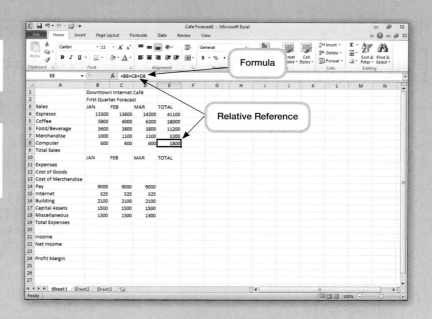

Function (EX1.40)

A function is a prewritten formula that performs certain types of calculations automatically.

Recalculation (EX1.47)

When a number in a referenced cell in a formula changes, Excel automatically recalculates all formulas that are dependent upon the changed value.

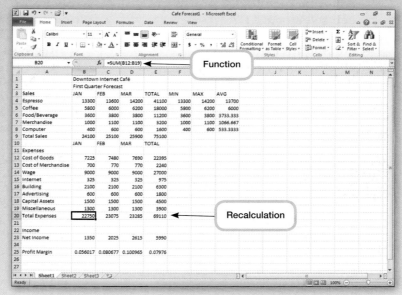

Alignment (EX1.51)

Alignment settings allow you to change the horizontal and vertical placement and the orientation of an entry in a cell.

Row Height (EX1.53)

The row height is the size or height of a row measured in points.

Number Formats (EX1.61)

Number formats change the appearance of numbers onscreen and when printed, without changing the way the number is stored or used in calculations.

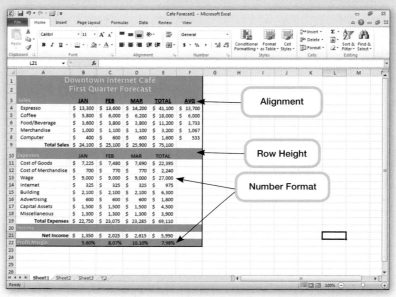

KEY TERMS

active cell EX1.7
active sheet EX1.7
adjacent range EX1.31
alignment EX1.51
antonym EX1.27
argument EX1.40
AutoCorrect EX1.18
AutoFit EX1.22
cell EX1.7
cell reference EX1.7
cell selector EX1.7
chart EX1.70
column EX1.6
column letter EX1.7
column width EX1.21
constant EX1.37
copy area EX1.28
custom dictionary EX1.25
data EX1.12
fill handle EX1.32
formula EX1.37
formula bar EX1.5
function EX1.40
heading EX1.12
main dictionary EX1.25
merged cell EX1.55
Name box EX1.5
nonadjacent range EX1.31
number EX1.12

number formats EX1.61
operand EX1.37
operator EX1.37
order of precedence EX1.37
paste area EX1.29
range EX1.31
range reference EX1.31
recalculation EX1.47
relative reference EX1.39
row EX1.6
row number EX1.7
sans serif EX1.56
scaling EX1.76
serial value EX1.71
serif EX1.56
sheet EX1.6
sheet tab EX1.7
spelling checker EX1.25
spreadsheet EX1.6
synonym EX1.27
syntax EX1.40
tab scroll buttons EX1.8
text EX1.12
theme EX1.65
thesaurus EX1.27
variable EX1.37
workbook EX1.5
workbook window EX1.5
worksheet EX1.6

COMMAND SUMMARY

Command	Shortcut	Action
File		
Open	Ctrl + O	Opens an existing workbook file
Save	Ctrl + S	Saves file using same file name
Save As	F12	Saves file using a new file name
Close	Ctrl + F4	Closes open workbook file
New	Ctrl + N	Opens a new blank workbook
Print/ Print	Ctrl + P	Prints a worksheet
Print/ No Scaling Print sheets at their actual size /Fit sheet on one page		Scales worksheet to fit on a single page
Exit	X or Alt + F4	Exits Excel program
Quick Access Toolbar		
Save	Ctrl + S	Saves document using same file name
Undo	Ctrl + Z	Reverses last editing or formatting change
Redo	Ctrl + Y	Restores changes after using Undo
Home tab		
Clipboard group		
Paste	Ctrl + V	Pastes selections stored in system Clipboard
Cut	Ctrl + X	Cuts selected data from the worksheet
Copy	Ctrl + C	Copies selected data to system Clipboard
Format Painter		Copies formatting from one place and applies it to another
Font group		
Calibri Font		Changes text font
11 Font Size		Changes text size
B Bold	Ctrl + B	Bolds selected text
I Italic	Ctrl + I	Italicizes selected text

LAB REVIEW

COMMAND SUMMARY (CONTINUED)

Command	Shortcut	Action
Underline	Ctrl +U	Underlines selected text
Borders		Adds border to specified area of cell or range
Fill Color		Adds color to cell background
Font Color		Adds color to text
Alignment group		
Align Text Left		Left-aligns entry in cell space
Center		Center-aligns entry in cell space
Align Text Right		Right-aligns entry in cell space
Increase Indent		Indents cell entry
Decrease Indent		Reduces the margin between the left cell border and cell entry
Merge & Center		Combines selected cells into one cell and centers cell contents in new cell
Number group		
General Number Format		Applies selected number formatting to selection
$ Accounting Number Format		Applies Accounting number format to selection
% Percent Style		Applies Percent Style format to selection
Increase Decimal		Increases number of decimal places
Decrease Decimal		Decreases number of decimal places
Cells group		
Insert /Insert Cells		Inserts blank cells, shifting existing cells down
Insert /Insert Cut Cells		Inserts cut row of data into new worksheet row, shifting existing rows down
Insert /Insert Copied Cells		Inserts copied row into new worksheet row, shifting existing rows down
Insert /Insert Sheet Rows		Inserts blank rows, shifting existing rows down
Insert /Insert Sheet Columns		Inserts blank columns, shifting existing columns right
Delete /Delete Sheet Rows		Deletes selected rows, shifting existing rows up

COMMAND SUMMARY (CONTINUED)

Command	Shortcut	Action
Delete ▾ /Delete Sheet Columns		Deletes selected columns, shifting existing columns left
Format ▾ /Row Height		Changes height of selected row
Format ▾ /AutoFit Row Height		Changes row height to match the tallest cell entry
Format ▾ /Column Width		Changes width of selected column
Format ▾ /AutoFit Column Width		Changes column width to match widest cell entry
Format ▾ /Default Width		Returns column width to default width
Editing group		
Σ ▾ Sum		Calculates the sum of the values in the selected cells
Σ ▾ Sum/Average		Calculates the average of the values in the selected range
Σ ▾ Sum/Min		Returns the smallest of the values in the selected range
Σ ▾ Sum/Max		Returns the largest of the values in the selected range
▾ Fill/Right	Ctrl + R	Continues a pattern to adjacent cells to the right
✐▾ Clear		Removes both formats and contents from selected cells
✐▾ Clear/Clear Formats		Clears formats only from selected cells
✐▾ Clear/Clear Contents	Delete	Clears contents only from selected cells
Formulas tab		
Formula Auditing group		
Show Formulas	Ctrl + `	Displays and hides worksheet formulas
Review tab		
Proofing group		
ABC✔ Spelling	F7	Spell-checks worksheet
Thesaurus		Opens the thesaurus for the selected word in the Research task pane

LAB EXERCISES

SCREEN IDENTIFICATION

1. In the following Excel 2010 screen, letters identify important elements. Enter the correct term for each screen element in the space provided.

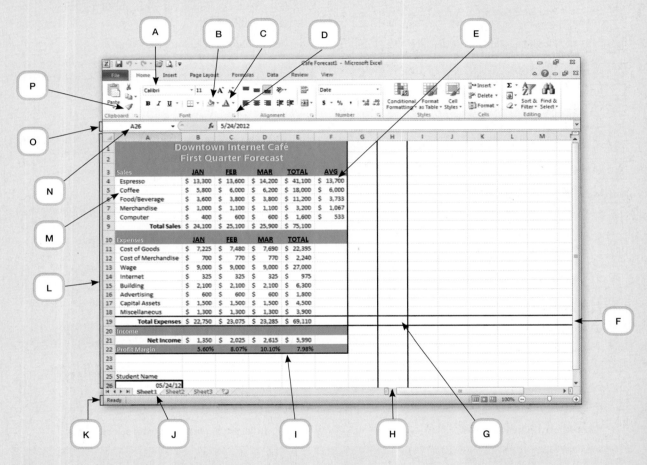

Possible answers for the screen identification are:

Column	Workbook window	**A.** _____	**I.** _____
Status bar	Cell	**B.** _____	**J.** _____
Font color	Formula bar	**C.** _____	**K.** _____
Numeric entry	Active sheet	**D.** _____	**L.** _____
Fill color	Text label	**E.** _____	**M.** _____
Font	Cell reference	**F.** _____	**N.** _____
Range	Format Painter	**G.** _____	**O.** _____
Formula	View buttons	**H.** _____	**P.** _____
Row	Border		
Column labels	Sheet tabs		

MATCHING

Match the lettered item on the right with the numbered item on the left.

1.   _____ a. an arithmetic operator
2. .xlsx   _____ b. changes the width of a column
3.   _____ c. a graphic representation of data
4. chart   _____ d. Excel workbook file name extension
5. /   _____ e. two or more worksheet cells
6.   _____ f. enters a SUM function
7. =C19*A21   _____ g. adds a cell border
8. D11   _____ h. merges cells and centers entry
9. range   _____ i. a formula multiplying the values in two cells
10.   _____ j. a cell reference
11.   _____ K. Format Painter

TRUE/FALSE

Circle the correct answer to the following questions.

1. Number formats affect the way that numbers are used in calculations. **True** **False**
2. Charts are visual representations of the data in a worksheet. **True** **False**
3. A colon is used to separate cell references in nonadjacent ranges. **True** **False**
4. A function is a prewritten formula that performs a calculation. **True** **False**
5. The default column width setting is 10.12. **True** **False**
6. When a formula containing relative references is copied, the cell references in the copied formula refer to the same cells that are referenced in the original formula. **True** **False**
7. An adjacent range is two or more selected cells or ranges that are adjoining. **True** **False**
8. The spellingchecker can only find misspelled words if they are entered in the main dictionary. **True** **False**
9. Recalculation is one of the most powerful features of electronic worksheets. **True** **False**
10. Cell alignment allows you to change the horizontal and vertical placement and the orientation of an entry in a cell. **True** **False**

LAB EXERCISES

FILL-IN

Complete the following statements by filling in the blanks with the correct key terms.

1. Cells or ranges that are included in the same selection but are not located next to each other are part of a(n) _____.

2. _____ are integers assigned to the days from January 1, 1900, through December 31, 2099, that allow dates to be used in calculations.

3. The _____ displays the cell selector and will be affected by the next entry or procedure.

4. A(n) _____ window is used to display an open workbook file.

5. By default, text entries are _____-aligned and number entries are _____-aligned.

6. A(n) _____ entry is used to perform a calculation.

7. The _____ function automatically adds all the numbers in a range of cells.

8. A(n) _____ is a rectangular grid of rows and columns.

9. The _____ dictionary holds words the user enters that are not included in the main dictionary.

10. A(n) _____ cell is a cell made up of several selected cells combined into one.

MULTIPLE CHOICE

Circle the correct response to the questions below.

1. _____ entries can contain any combination of letters, numbers, spaces, and any other special characters.
   a. Number
   b. Variable
   c. Constant
   d. Text

2. The _____ is a small black square, located in the lower-right corner of the selection, used to create a series or copy to adjacent cells.
   a. sheet tab
   b. fill handle
   c. scroll box
   d. sizing handle

3. Rotating entries, using color, and using character effects are three ways to _____.
   a. emphasize information
   b. create reports
   c. perform calculations
   d. update spreadsheets

4. The amount of information that is displayed in a cell is determined by the _____.
   a. column size
   b. row size
   c. column width
   d. row height

5. Which of the following is a valid Excel formula?
   a. =(5 + 8)(2 + 1)
   b. 5 + 8*2 + 1
   c. =5 + 8(2 + 1)
   d. =(5 + 8)*(2 + 1)

6. Whenever a formula containing _____ references is copied, the referenced cells are automatically adjusted.
   a. relative
   b. automatic
   c. fixed
   d. variable

7. The _____ feature in Excel automatically inserts proper capitalization at the beginning of sentences and in the names of days of the week.
   a. AutoName
   b. AutoCorrect
   c. CorrectWords
   d. Word Wrap

8. The Currency number format can display _____.
   a. dollar signs
   b. commas
   c. decimal places
   d. all of the above

9. When a number in a referenced cell is changed, all the formulas that use the cell reference are _____.
   a. recalculated
   b. reformatted
   c. redefined
   d. left unchanged

10. The _____ is a reference tool that provides synonyms and related words for a selected word.
    a. synonym locator
    b. thesaurus
    c. spelling checker
    d. research book

TEENAGE CELL PHONE USAGE DATA ANALYSIS ★

1. Mary Collins works for a cell phone company. She's been asked to analyze data gathered in a survey of teenage cell phone users to find possible service packages for the company to offer. After following the directions below to complete the worksheet, your solution will be similar to that shown here.

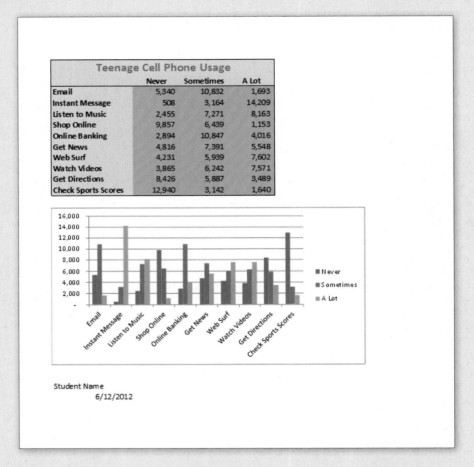

Teenage Cell Phone Usage

	Never	Sometimes	A Lot
Email	5,340	10,832	1,693
Instant Message	508	3,164	14,209
Listen to Music	2,455	7,271	8,163
Shop Online	9,857	6,439	1,153
Online Banking	2,894	10,847	4,016
Get News	4,816	7,391	5,548
Web Surf	4,231	5,939	7,602
Watch Videos	3,865	6,242	7,571
Get Directions	8,426	5,887	3,489
Check Sports Scores	12,940	3,142	1,640

Student Name
6/12/2012

a. Open an Excel 2010 workbook.

b. Enter the data here into the spreadsheet.

Row	Col A	Col B	Col C	Col D
1		Never	Sometimes	A Lot
2	Email	5340	10832	1693
3	Instant Message	508	3164	14209
4	Listen to Music	2455	7271	8163
5	Shop Online	9857	6439	1153
6	Online Banking	2894	10847	4016
7	Get News	4816	7391	5548
8	Web Surf	4231	5939	7602
9	Watch Videos	3865	6242	7571
10	Get Directions	8426	5887	3489
11	Check Sports Scores	12940	3142	1640

c. AutoFit the width of column A. Insert a new row above row 1.

d. In cell A1, enter the worksheet title **Teenage Cell Phone Usage**

e. Merge and center the worksheet title over columns A through D.

f. Change the font in cell A1 to 16 points.

g. Bold the column labels in row 2 and the row labels in column A.

h. Add an outside border around A1 through D2, and another around A3 through D12.

i. Center the column headings and data in cells B2 through D12. AutoFit column C.

j. Apply the Comma number format with zero decimal places to the data in B3 through D12.

k. Add fill colors of your choice, using one color for rows 1 and 2 and the row labels in column A and a different color for cells B3 through D12. Change the text color for readability if needed. Add a font color of your choice and bold to the worksheet title.

l. Create a chart using the data in the worksheet, and move the chart to row 14.

m. Type your name in cell A30 and the date in cell A31.

n. Save the workbook as Teenage Cell Phone Usage to your solution file location. Print the worksheet.

LAB EXERCISES

ANIMAL RESCUE FOUNDATION ADOPTION ANALYSIS ⋆

2. Edward Corwin works for the Animal Rescue Foundation. One of his responsibilities is to collect and analyze data on the animals that enter the shelters. He has compiled a list of the cost of housing animals by the local shelters for the past four years. After following the directions below to complete the worksheet, your solution will be similar to that shown here.

a. Open the workbook ex01_Animal Housing. Auto fit the column width of column A. Spell-check the worksheet and correct any misspelled words.

b. Modify the title in cell B2 so the first letter of each word is capitalized. Increase the font size to 14 point and change the row height to 22.5. Merge and center both title lines across columns A through E.

c. Bold and center the headings in row 5. Insert a blank row above row 6.

d. In row 17, enter a function to total the data under the 2009 column and a function to total the data under the 2010 column.

e. Format the numbers in rows 7 and 17 using the Accounting style with zero decimal places. Format the numbers in rows 8 through 16 using the Comma style with zero decimal places.

f. Adjust the column widths so all the data is fully displayed. Insert a blank row above row 17.

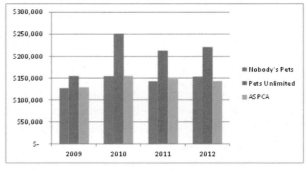

Animal Angels Housing Analysis
Years 2009 through 2012

	2009	2010	2011	2012
Nobody's Pets	$ 127,000	$ 154,200	$ 142,600	$ 152,800
Pets Unlimited	154,500	251,000	213,500	220,300
ASPCA	129,100	154,300	148,500	142,400
FOCAS	14,500	19,200	12,500	14,700
Wood Green Animal Shelter	2,300	2,500	2,200	4,200
Pet Where Shelter	1,200	1,500	1,400	1,600
New River Animal Shelter	11,200	1,530	11,700	10,500
New Pet Shelter	19,300	19,900	18,900	25,300
City of Dogs Shelter	10,200	11,500	14,200	13,500
Humane World	29,100	12,500	26,700	29,900
Total	$ 498,400	$ 628,130	$ 592,200	$ 615,200

Student Name
August 3, 2012

g. Edward has just received the information for the last two years. Enter the following data in the cells indicated.

Row	Col D	Col E
5	2011	2012
7	142600	152800
8	213500	220300
9	12500	14700
10	2200	4200
11	1400	1600
12	148500	142400
13	11700	10500
14	18900	25300
15	14200	13500
16	26700	29900

h. Format the column heads to match the style of the corresponding information in columns B and C.

i. Copy the Total function in cell B18 to calculate the total for each of the new years. Increase the indent in cell A18

j. Add font and fill colors to the worksheet as you like.

k. Add a thick box border around A1 through E18.

l. Move the row of ASPCA data to above the row of FOCAS data.

m. Delete the word "Shelter" in cell A5.

n. Next, you want to create a chart showing the annual data for the three largest shelter groups. Select the range A5 through E9 and create a chart displaying the data. Move the chart to cell A20.

o. Enter your name in cell A35 and the current date in cell A36. Format cell A36 to display the month, day, and year (March 14, 2001) date format.

p. Move to cell A1. Save the workbook as Animal Housing Analysis to your solution file location. Preview and print the worksheet.

q. Print the worksheet with formulas using landscape orientation so that it fits on one page.

LAB EXERCISES

HURRICANE ANALYSIS WORKSHEET ★

3. Mary Ellen is a manager for an insurance agency. One of her responsibilities is to collect and analyze data on weather conditions in geographical areas. She has compiled a list of hurricanes from the National Weather Service. After following the directions below to complete the worksheet, your solution will be similar to that shown here.

a. Open the workbook ex01_US Hurricanes. Spell-check the worksheet and correct any misspelled words.

b. Modify the title in cell A1 so the first letter of each word is capitalized, except "by." Merge and center the two worksheet titles across columns A through I. Increase the font size to 12 point. Bold the titles.

c. Enter the heading % Major to All in cell I3 and increase the widths of columns H and I to fully display their headings.

d. Merge and center cells A3 and A4. Merge and center cells I3 and I4.

e. Adjust the width of column A so all the data is fully displayed.

f. Insert new rows above row 1 and below row 3.

g. Bold the labels in rows 5 and 6. Merge and center cells B5 through H5. Underline and center the labels in cells B6 through H6.

h. Enter the formula =H7/G7 in cell I7. Copy the formula down column I for the rest of the states. Format the numbers in column I as a percent with one decimal place.

i. Center the data in cells B7 through I33.

j. Add font and fill colors to the worksheet as you like.

k. In the ALL column, locate the four states with the highest total number of major hurricanes and fill the cells with a different fill color.

l. In cells K7 through K10, enter the names of the four states with the highest total number of major hurricanes. In cells L7 through L10, enter the corresponding numbers. Enter "Total Hurricanes" in cell L6. Add color to the cells to match the data.

m. Create a chart using the data in the table you just created and move it to cell J12.

n. Enter your name and the current date on separate rows just below the chart. Format the date to display the month, day, and year (March 14, 2001) date format.

o. Move to cell A1. Save the workbook as US Hurricanes Analysis to your solution file location. Print the worksheet in landscape orientation on one page.

COMPARATIVE MEDIAN INCOME FOR FOUR-PERSON FAMILIES ★★★

4. Terrence Lewis works for an employment agency and needs to provide information about salaries in different states for his clients. He has started a worksheet with data from the years 2006–2008. After following the directions below to complete the worksheet, the first page of your solution will be similar to that shown here.

   a. Open the workbook ex01_Family Income. Spell-check the worksheet and correct any misspelled words.

   b. Edit the title in cell A1 by capitalizing the first letter of each word except the word "by" and by deleting the comma following "income." Merge and center the title across columns A through F. Increase the font size to 12, and bold and apply a font color of your choice to the title.

   c. Center-align and underline the column headings in row 2. Adjust the width of column A to fully display the labels. Insert blank rows above and below the title.

   d. Right-align cells B5 through D56 and format the cells as Accounting with zero decimal places.

   e. Enter the heading **Average** in cell E4. Center and underline the heading. Calculate the average income in cell E5 using the function =Average(B5:D5). Copy the formula to cells E6 through E56.

   f. Next, you would like to calculate the percent of change from 2006 to 2008. Enter the heading **% Change** in cell F4. Center and underline the title. Enter the formula =(D5−B5)/D5 in cell F5. Format the cell as a percentage with two decimal places. Copy the formula to cells F6 through F56.

   g. AutoFit columns B through F.

   h. Add font and fill colors to the worksheet as you like. Locate the state with the highest positive % change and the state with the highest negative % change. Surround their entire rows with a box border and a different fill color.

   i. Enter your name and the current date on separate rows just below the last lines. Format the date to day, month, year (14-Mar-01) date format.

LAB EXERCISES

j. Move to cell A1. Save the workbook as Family Income to your solution file location. Change page size to legal to fit on one page, and print the worksheet.

k. Print the worksheet again with formulas on one page using landscape orientation.

PECAN GROVES HOMEOWNERS ASSOCIATION ★ ★ ★

5. The Pecan Groves Homeowners Association is planning a large building project and wants to project how much there is likely to be in the cash budget after expenses. Using last year's final budget numbers, you will create a projected budget for 2012. After following the directions below to complete the worksheet, your solution will be similar to that shown here.

a. Open the workbook file ex01_ Pecan Groves Budget. Spell-check the worksheet and correct any misspelled words.

b. Change the font type, size, and color and fill color of the three worksheet title lines to a format of your choice. Merge and center the titles across columns A through E.

c. Set the width of column A to 25. Insert a column between columns B and C. Merge and center cell B5 across columns B and C. Merge and center cell D5 across columns D and E. Set the fill color of cells B5 and D5 to match the fill color in the titles.

d. Center the text in cell A6 and change the font color and fill color to a color of your choice. Apply the same formats to cell A13.

e. Right-justify the text in cells A12 and A25. Indent the text in cells A19:A23. Indent the text in cell A23 again. Move the data in cells B14:B17 to C14:C17. Move the data in cell B24 to C24.

Pecan Groves Homeowners Association Projected Budget for 2012				
		2011		2012
Income				
Cash on hand	$	16,701	$	17,703
Funds		2,200		2,332
Member Dues		219,500		232,670
Transfer Fees		1,700		1,802
Interest - savings		1,200		1,272
Total Income		$ 241,301		$ 255,779
Expenditures				
Administration		$ 120,000		$ 134,400
Insurance		16,000		17,920
Audit & Tax Preparation		21,200		23,744
Lawyer		27,000		30,240
Maintenance				
Street Repair	$	2,700	$	3,105
Street Cleaning		1,582		1,819
Snow Removal		550		633
Street Signs		4,985		5,733
Total Maintenance		9,817		11,290
Miscellaneous		3,000		3,360
Total Expenditures		$ 197,017		$ 220,954
Ending Cash Balance		$ 44,284		$ 34,826

Student Name
7/6/2012

f. In cell C12, sum the income data. In cell C23, sum the maintenance expenditure data. In cell C25, sum all the Expenditures items. In cell C27, enter a formula to calculate the ending cash balance (Hint: =C12-C25).

g. Each of the 2012 Income items is projected to increase by 6 percent over the previous year. Enter a formula in cell D7 to calculate the increase in cash on hand (Hint: =B7*1.06). Copy this formula down column D to the other Income items. Enter the appropriate function into cell E12 to calculate the 2012 total income value.

h. Each of the 2012 expenditure items except for the maintenance expenditures is projected to increase by 12 percent over the previous year. Enter the appropriate formulas in column E to reflect this change. Each maintenance expense is projected to increase 15 percent. Enter the appropriate formulas in column D. Enter the appropriate function in cell E23 to calculate the total maintenance expenses. Use formulas to calculate the value for total expenditures and ending cash balance for 2012.

i. Format cells B7, B19, C12, C14, C25, C27, D7, D19, E12, E14, E25, and E27 as Accounting with zero decimal places. Format all other cells containing numbers except for B5 and D5 to Comma with zero decimal places. Set the column widths of columns B through E to 12. Fill the cells A27:E27 with the same fill color used for the titles. Delete column F. Surround the entire worksheet with a thick box border.

j. Enter your name and the current date on separate rows just below the worksheet.

k. Save the workbook file as Pecan Groves Budget to your solution file location. Print the worksheet.

l. Print the worksheet again with formulas using landscape orientation.

ON YOUR OWN

TRACKING YOUR CALORIES ★

1. A worksheet can be used to track your calories for the day. Design and create a worksheet to record the food you consume and the exercise you do on a daily basis. The worksheet should include your food consumption for all meals and snacks and the activities you performed for a week. Use the Web as a resource to find out the calorie values for the items you consumed (or refer to the calorie information on the product packaging) and to find out the caloric expenditure for the exercises you do. Include an appropriate title, row and column headings, and formulas to calculate your total calorie intake and expenditure on a daily basis. Include a formula to calculate the percent deviation from your recommended daily calorie intake. Format the worksheet appropriately using features presented in this lab. Enter real or sample data. Include your name and date above the worksheet. Spell-check the worksheet. Save the workbook as Calorie Tracking and print the worksheet.

LAB EXERCISES

CREATING A PERSONAL BUDGET ★

2. In a blank Excel 2010 workbook, create a personal three-month budget. Enter an appropriate title and use descriptive labels for your monthly expenses (food, rent, car payments, insurance, credit card payments, etc.). Spell-check your worksheet. Enter your monthly expenses (or, if you prefer, any reasonable sample data). Use formulas to calculate total expenses for each month and the average monthly expenditures for each expense item. Add a column for projection for the next year showing a 2.5 percent increase in the cost of living. Enhance the worksheet using features you learned in this lab. Enter your name and the current date on separate rows just below the worksheet. Save the workbook as Personal Budget. Preview and print the worksheet.

TRACKING PROJECT HOURS ★ ★

3. Samantha Johnson is the project manager for a small publishing company. She has four part-time employees (Melanie, Bob, Vanessa, and Rudy). Using the steps in the planning process, plan and create a worksheet for Samantha that can be used to record and analyze the hours each employee works per day during the month on two projects: magazine and brochure. Hours-worked data for each employee will be entered into the worksheet. Using that data, the worksheet will calculate the total number of hours for each person per project. Additionally, it will calculate the total weekly hours for each project. Write a short paragraph describing how you used each of the planning steps. Enter sample data in a worksheet. Include your name and the current date on separate rows just below the worksheet. Spell-check the worksheet. Save the workbook as Project Hours. Preview and print the worksheet.

MUSIC ANALYSIS ★ ★ ★

4. Use the library and/or the Web to locate information on trends in CD sales versus music downloads on the Internet. Create a worksheet to display information relating to the increasing usage by country, age group, or any other trend you locate. Calculate totals or averages based on your data. Enhance the worksheet using features you learned in this lab. Enter your name and the current date on separate rows just below the worksheet. Spell-check the worksheet. Save the workbook as Music Analysis. Preview and print the worksheet.

HOME ELECTRONICS ANALYSIS ★ ★ ★

5. A national electronics retailer wants to analyze the trend in home electronics sales and usage for the past three years. Design and create a worksheet to record the number of households (one-person, two-person, and four-person) that have computers, Internet access, televisions, and cable TV access. Include an appropriate title, row and column headings, and formulas to calculate average by category and by year. Include a formula to calculate the percent growth over the three years. Format the worksheet appropriately using features presented in this tutorial. Enter sample data for the three years. Include your name and date above the worksheet. Spell-check the worksheet. Save the workbook as Home Electronics Analysis and print the worksheet.

Enhancing the Worksheet with Graphics and Charts

Lab 2

Objectives

After completing this lab, you will know how to:

1. Apply and customize themes.

2. Use cell styles.

3. Insert and size a graphic.

4. Create a chart.

5. Move, size, and format a chart.

6. Change the type of chart.

7. Create, explode, and rotate a pie chart.

8. Apply patterns and color to a chart.

9. Document a workbook.

10. Size and align a sheet on a page.

11. Add predefined headers and footers.

Downtown Internet Café

Evan is impressed with how quickly you were able to create the first-quarter sales forecast for the Downtown Internet Café. He made several suggestions to improve the appearance of the worksheet, including applying different formats and adding a graphic. Evan also expressed concern that the sales values seem a little low and has asked you to contact several other Internet cafés to inquire about their start-up experiences.

While speaking with other Internet café managers, you heard many exciting success stories. Internet connections attract more customers, and the typical customer stays longer at an Internet café than at a regular café. As a result, they spend more money.

You would like to launch an aggressive advertising campaign to promote the new Internet aspect of the Café. The new Café features include free Wi-Fi connection, computer rentals, and printing and copying services. You believe that the campaign will lead to an increase in customers and subsequently to an increase in sales. To convince Evan, you need an effective way to illustrate the sales growth you are forecasting. You will use Excel 2010's chart-creating and formatting features to produce several different charts of your sales estimates, as shown on the following page.

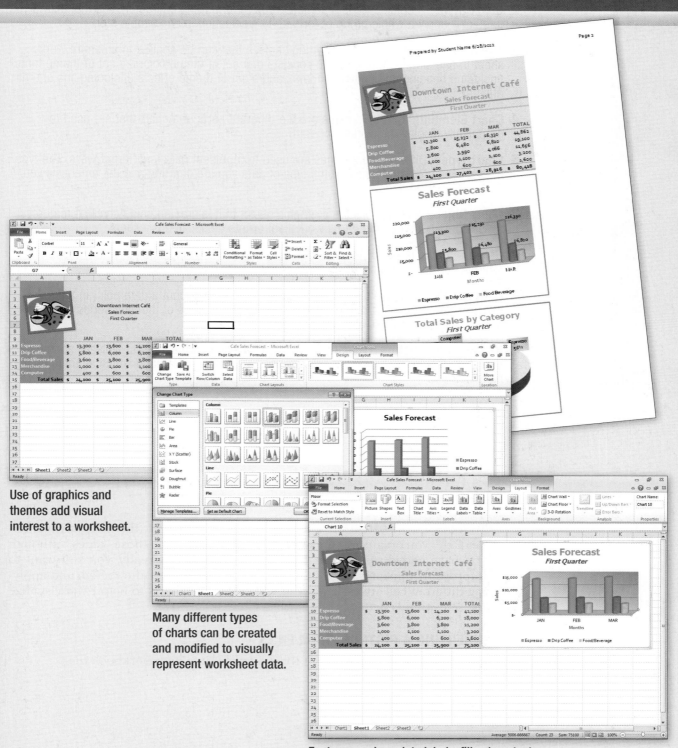

Use of graphics and themes add visual interest to a worksheet.

Many different types of charts can be created and modified to visually represent worksheet data.

Features such as data labels, fill colors, textures, and shadows add a professional appearance to your charts.

The following concepts will be introduced in this lab:

1 **Graphics** A graphic is a nontext element or object such as a drawing or picture that can be added to a document.

2 **Quick Style** A quick style is a named group of formatting characteristics that allows you to quickly apply a whole group of formats to a selection in one simple step.

3 **Theme** A theme is a set of formatting choices that can be applied to an entire worksheet in one simple step. A theme consists of a set of theme colors, a set of theme fonts (including heading and body text fonts), and a set of theme effects (including line and fill effects).

4 **Chart Elements** Chart elements are the different parts of a chart that are used to graphically display the worksheet data.

5 **Chart Types** Different chart types are used to represent data in different ways. The type of chart you create depends on the type of data you are charting and the emphasis you want the chart to impart.

6 **Chart Object** A chart object is a graphic object that is created using charting features. An object can be inserted into a worksheet or into a special chart sheet.

7 **Group** A group is two or more objects that behave as a single object when moved or sized. A chart is a group that consists of many separate objects.

8 **Data Labels** Data labels provide additional information about a data point in the data series. They can consist of the value of the point, the name of the data series or category, a percent value, or a bubble size.

9 **Headers and Footers** Headers and footers provide information that typically appears at the top and bottom of each page and commonly include information such as the date and page number.

Inserting and Formatting Illustrations

To focus Evan's attention solely on the sales values for the Downtown Internet Café, you created a new worksheet containing only those values. Although you have added some formatting to the worksheet already, you still want to improve its appearance by adding a graphic, changing the theme, and applying different cell styles. Then you will create the charts to help Evan visualize the sales trends better.

INSERTING A PICTURE FROM FILES

You saved the sales portion of the worksheet in a new workbook file.

Start Excel 2010.

If necessary, maximize the Excel application window.

Open the file ex02_ Cafe Sales.

Your screen should be similar to Figure 2.1

Figure 2.1

First you want to add a graphic next to the worksheet title to add interest.

Concept 1 Graphics

A **graphic** is a nontext element or **object** such as a drawing or picture that can be added to a document. An object is an item that can be sized, moved, and manipulated.

A graphic can be a simple **drawing object** consisting of shapes, such as lines and boxes, that can be created using features on the Drawing toolbar. A drawing object is part of the Excel workbook. A **picture** is an illustration such as a graphic illustration or a scanned photograph. Pictures are graphics that were created from another program and are inserted in the worksheet as embedded objects. An **embedded object** becomes part of the Excel workbook and can be opened and edited using the **source program**, the program in which it was created. Any changes made to the embedded object are not made to the original picture file because they are independent. Several examples of drawing objects and pictures are shown below.

Drawing object

Graphic illustration

Photograph

Add graphics to your worksheets to help the reader understand concepts, to add interest, and to make your worksheet stand out from others.

Graphic files can be obtained from a variety of sources. Many simple drawings called **clip art** are available in the Clip Organizer, a Microsoft Office tool that arranges and catalogs clip art and other media files stored on the computer's hard disk. Additionally, you can access Microsoft's Clip Art and Media Web site for even more graphics.

Digital images created using a digital camera are one of the most common types of graphic files. You also can create graphic files using a scanner to convert any printed document, including photographs, to an electronic format. Most images that are scanned are stored as Windows bitmap files (.bmp). All types of graphics, including clip art, photographs, and other types of images, can be found on the Internet. These files are commonly stored as .jpg or .pcx files. Keep in mind that any images you locate on the Internet may be protected by copyright and should be used only with permission. You also can purchase CDs containing graphics for your use.

You want to insert a picture to the left of the title in the worksheet. You located a graphic of a coffee cup and coffee beans and saved a copy of the graphic as a file on your computer.

1

● **Open the Insert tab.**

● **Click** 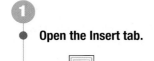 **in the Illustrations group.**

● **Change to the location of your data files.**

● **Select** ex02_ Internet Cafe.bmp.

● **If a preview of the selected graphic is not displayed, click** ⊞▾ **and choose Large Icons.**

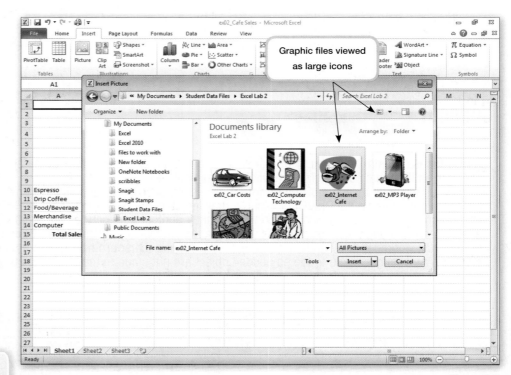

Figure 2.2

Having Trouble?

Depending on the version of Windows on your computer, you may need to click ▣ Views ▾ and choose Large Icons.

Only files that have a graphic file type are displayed in the file list. You think the selected picture illustrates the concept of a café and that it will look good in the worksheet.

Your screen should be similar to Figure 2.2

Click Insert ▼.

Your screen should be similar to
Figure 2.3

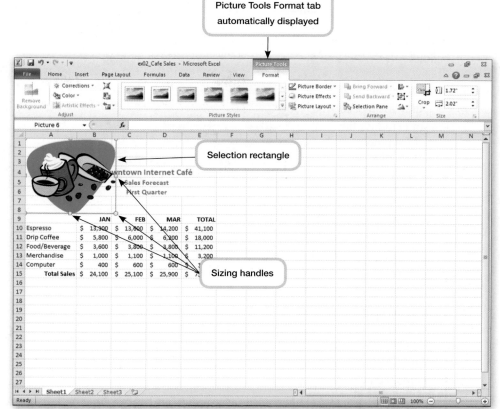

Picture Tools Format tab
automatically displayed

Selection rectangle

Sizing handles

Figure 2.3

The picture is inserted in the worksheet at the location of the cell selector. The picture is surrounded by a **selection rectangle** and eight squares and circles, called **sizing handles**, indicating it is a selected object and can now be deleted, sized, moved, or modified. The Picture Tools Format tab is automatically displayed and can be used to modify the selected picture object.

SIZING A GRAPHIC

Usually, when a graphic is inserted, its size will need to be adjusted. To size a graphic, you select it and drag the sizing handles to increase or decrease the size of the object. The mouse pointer changes to ⬉ when pointing to a corner handle and ⬌ or ⬍ when pointing to a side handle. The direction of the arrow indicates the direction in which you can drag to size the graphic. Dragging a corner handle maintains the scale of the picture by increasing both the width and length of the graphic equally. You also can move a graphic object by pointing to the graphic and dragging it to the new location. The mouse pointer changes to ⬌ when you can move the graphic.

Another Method

You also can size a picture to an exact measurement using commands in the Size group of the Picture Tools Format tab.

1

- Point to the lower-right corner sizing handle.

- With the pointer as a ⬉, drag the mouse inward to reduce the size of the graphic until the bottom of the graphic is even with row 6.

Additional Information

When you drag to size the graphic, the mouse pointer shape changes to a ✛.

- Point to the center of the graphic and, when the mouse pointer is ⬍, drag the graphic to position it as in Figure 2.4.

Your screen should be similar to Figure 2.4

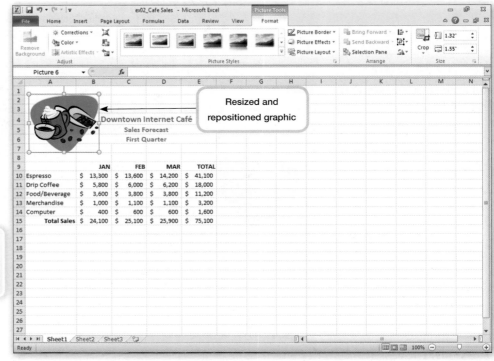

Figure 2.4

The graphic is smaller and moved to the left of the title as you want it.

INSERTING A PICTURE FROM THE CLIP ART GALLERY

Although you like the graphic, you decide to check the Clip Art gallery for pictures that show the use of a computer in a café environment.

1

● Move to cell F1 to deselect the graphic and choose the location where you want a new picture inserted.

● Open the Insert tab.

● Click 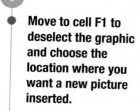 in the Illustrations group.

Your screen should be similar to Figure 2.5

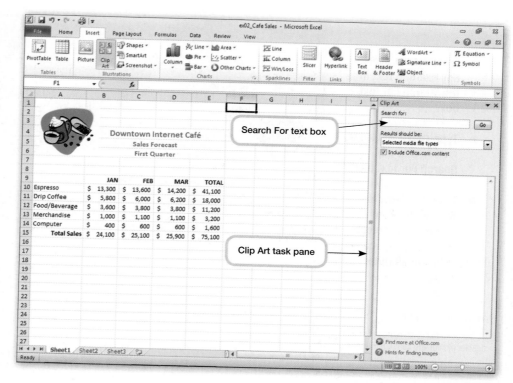

Figure 2.5

The Clip Art task pane appears in which you can enter a word or phrase that is representative of the type of picture you want to locate. You also can specify the locations to search and the type of media files, such as clip art, movies, photographs, or sound, to display in the results. You want to find photographs of computers and coffee.

- If necessary, select any existing text in the Search For text box.

- Type **computers, coffee** in the Search For text box.

- Open the Results Should Be drop-down menu, select Photographs, and deselect all other options.

Having Trouble?

Click the box next to an option to select or deselect (clear the checkmark).

- If necessary, select the Include Office.com content check box.

- Click [Go].

Your screen should be similar to **Figure 2.6**

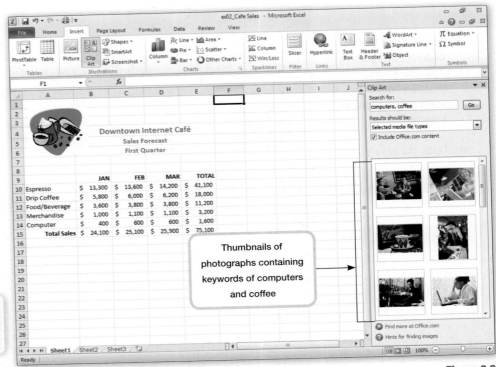

Figure 2.6

Having Trouble?

Your Clip Art task pane may display different pictures than those shown in Figure 2.6.

The program searches the Microsoft Clip Organizer on your computer and, if you have an Internet connection established, Microsoft's Office Online site for clip art and graphics that match your search terms. The Results area displays **thumbnails**, miniature representations of pictures, of all located graphics. The pictures stored on your computer in the Microsoft Clip Organizer appear first in the results list, followed by the Office Online clip art.

Pointing to a thumbnail displays a ScreenTip containing the **keywords** associated with the picture and information about the picture properties. It also displays a drop-down list bar that accesses the item's context menu.

3

● Scroll the list to view additional pictures.

● Point to the thumbnail shown in Figure 2.7 to see a ScreenTip.

Having Trouble?

If this graphic is not available, point to another of your choice.

Your screen should be similar to Figure 2.7

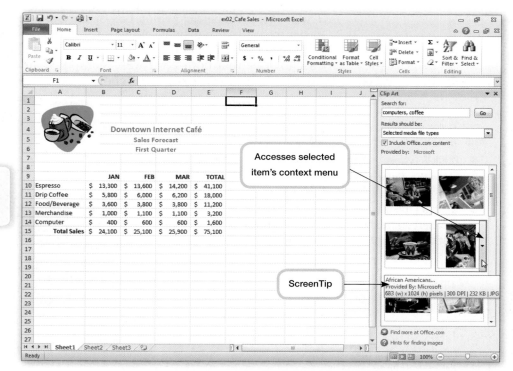

Figure 2.7

The ScreenTip displays the first keywords associated with the graphic as well as some basic information about the size and type of file. Additionally, because it is sometimes difficult to see the details in the graphic in the thumbnail, you can preview it in a larger size.

4

● Click ▾ next to the graphic to open the context menu.

● Choose Preview/ Properties.

Your screen should be similar to Figure 2.8

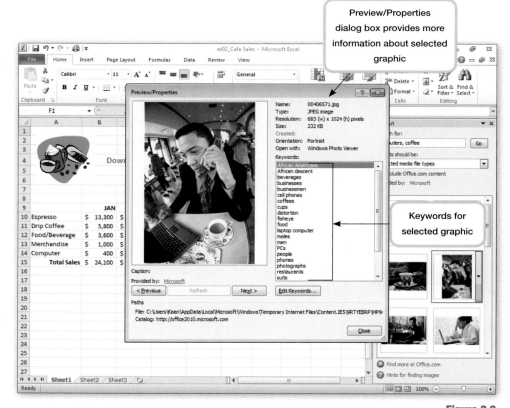

Figure 2.8

The Preview/Properties dialog box displays the selected graphic larger so it is easier to see. It also displays more information about the properties associated with the graphic, including all the keywords used to identify the graphic. You can now see that both keywords, "computer" and "coffee" appear in the list. You think this looks like a good choice and will insert it into the worksheet.

5

● Click [Close] to close the dialog box.

● Click on the graphic to insert it into the worksheet.

Another Method

You also could choose Insert from the thumbnail's context menu.

● Click [✕] in the Clip Art task pane to close it.

Your screen should be similar to Figure 2.9

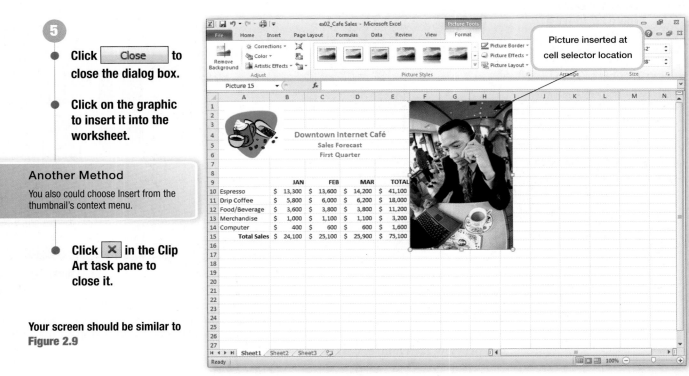

Figure 2.9

The picture is inserted in the worksheet at the location of the cell selector. You now have two graphic objects in the worksheet, a drawing and a photograph.

DELETING A GRAPHIC

You decide to use the drawing graphic and need to remove the photograph. To do this, you select the graphic and delete it.

If necessary, click on the photograph to select it.

Press Delete.

Your screen should be similar to Figure 2.10

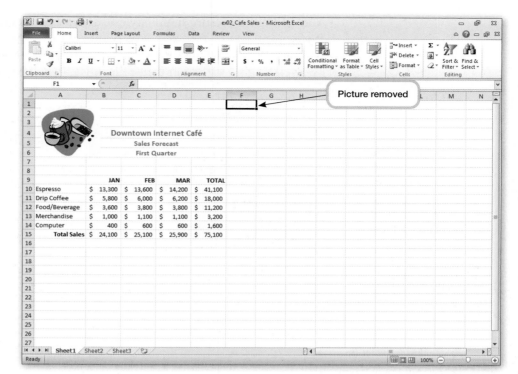

Figure 2.10

The photograph is deleted from the worksheet.

APPLYING AND MODIFYING A PICTURE QUICK STYLE

Next, you want to enhance the graphic by applying a quick style to it.

Concept 2 Quick Style

A **quick style** is a named group of formatting characteristics that allows you to quickly apply a whole group of formats to a selection in one simple step. The formatting options associated with the different quick styles vary depending upon the type of object. For example, a line quick style may consist of a combination of color, shadows, gradients, and three-dimensional (3-D) perspectives options, whereas a shape quick style may consist of a combination of fill color, line color, and line weight options.

Many quick styles are automatically applied when certain features, such as charts, are used. Others must be applied manually to the selected object. You also can create your own custom styles.

Quick styles are available for cell selections as well as many different types of objects. Some of the most common are described in the following table.

Type of Quick Style	Description
Cell style	Affects selected cells by applying effects such as fill color, text and number formatting, and bold and underline formats.
Shape style	Affects all aspects of a shape object's appearance, including fill color, outline color, and other effects.
Chart style	Provides a consistent look to charts by applying color, shading, line, and font effects.
Picture style	Adds a border around a graphic object that consists of combinations of line, shadow, color, and shape effects.

You will use a picture quick style to add a border around the picture to make it stand out more. You also can create your own picture style effects by selecting specific style elements such as borders and shadow individually using the  Picture Layout ▾, ✎ Picture Border ▾, and ◯ Picture Effects ▾ commands.

1

- Select the graphic.

- Click ▾ More in the Picture Styles group of the Format tab to open the Picture Styles gallery.

- Point to several styles to see the Live Preview.

Your screen should be similar to Figure 2.11

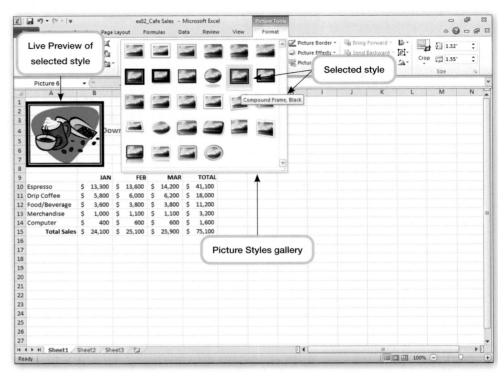

Figure 2.11

When you point to a style, the style name appears in a ScreenTip and the Live Preview shows how the selected picture style will look with your graphic. As you can see, many are not appropriate. However, you decide that the rotated style with a white border will enhance the graphic and the worksheet.

2

- Choose 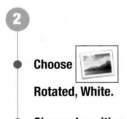 Rotated, White.

- Size and position the graphic as in Figure 2.12.

- Click outside the graphic to deselect the object.

Your screen should be similar to Figure 2.12

Figure 2.12

After seeing how the graphic looks with the selected picture style, you decide to modify the quick style by adding color to and changing the weight of the border.

3

- Click on the graphic to select it again.

- Click

  Picture Border ▾

  in the Picture Styles group of the Format tab.

- Choose the Red, Accent2 color from the Theme Colors category.

- Click

  Picture Border ▾,

  select Weight, and choose 6 pt.

- Click outside the graphic to deselect the object.

- Document the workbook by adding your name as author and the workbook title of Sales Forecast

- Save the revised workbook as Cafe Sales Forecast to your solution file location.

Your screen should be similar to Figure 2.13

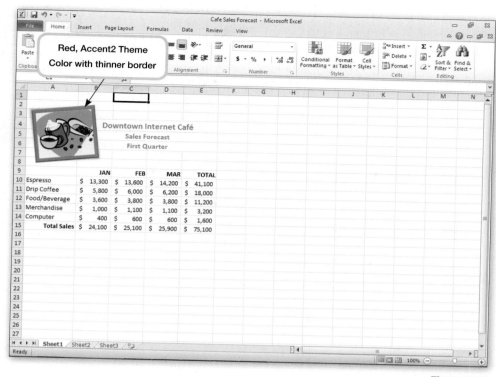

Figure 2.13

Using Themes

The addition of a graphic adds a nice touch to the worksheet title. Now, you want to continue to improve the worksheet appearance by selecting a different theme.

Concept 3 Theme

A **theme** is a set of formatting choices that can be applied to an entire workbook in one simple step. A theme consists of a set of theme colors, a set of theme fonts (including heading and body text fonts), and a set of theme effects (including line and fill effects). Excel includes 40 named built-in themes. Each theme includes three subsets of themes: colors, fonts, and effects. Each color theme consists of 12 colors that are applied to specific elements in a document. Each fonts theme includes different body and heading fonts. Each effects theme includes different line and fill effects. You also can create your own custom themes by modifying an existing document theme and saving it as a custom theme. The default workbook uses the Office theme. The font and fill colors and quick style effects that are available are determined by the current theme.

Using themes gives your documents a professional and modern look. Because themes are shared across Office 2010 applications, all your office documents can have the same uniform appearance.

APPLYING A THEME

You decide to see how the worksheet would look using a different theme.

1
- **Open the Page Layout tab.**

- **Click**  **from the Themes group.**

Your screen should be similar to Figure 2.14

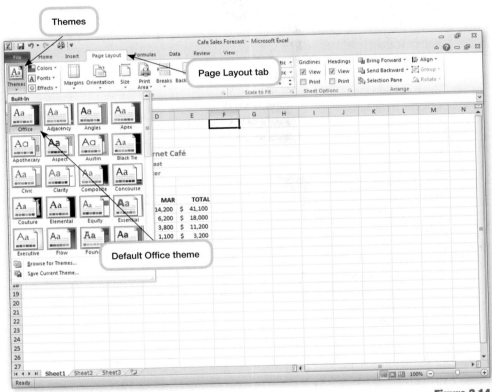

Figure 2.14

A gallery of 40 built-in named themes is displayed. A sample shows the color and font effects included in each theme. The Office theme is highlighted because it is the default theme. Pointing to each theme will display a Live Preview of how it will appear in the worksheet.

2

● Point to several themes to preview them.

● Scroll through the selections and choose the Horizon theme.

Your screen should be similar to Figure 2.15

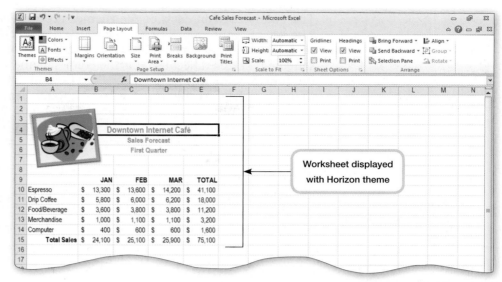

> Worksheet displayed with Horizon theme

Figure 2.15

Additional Information

If the border and font colors were colors on the Standard Colors bar, the color would not have updated to the new theme design.

The formatting settings associated with the selected theme have been applied to the worksheet. Most noticeable is the color change of the picture border and titles. This is because the colors in the theme category have been updated to the Horizon theme colors. Consequently the available picture quick style colors and font colors have been updated to the new theme colors. Additionally, the font style used in the worksheet has changed from Calibri to Arial Narrow.

Additional Information

Only one theme can be used in a workbook.

As you add other features to the worksheet, they will be formatted using the Horizon theme colors and effects. The same theme also has been applied to the other sheets in the workbook file.

CUSTOMIZING A THEME

Additional Information

The colors you see in the
[■■ Colors ▼] Theme Colors button
represent the current text and background colors.

Sometimes, you cannot find just the right combination of design elements in a built-in theme. To solve this problem, you can customize a theme by changing the color scheme, fonts, and effects. Although you like much of the Horizon theme design, you decide to try customizing the theme by changing the color scheme. Each theme has an associated set of colors that you can change by applying the colors from another theme to the selected theme.

1

● Click [■■ Colors ▼] Theme Colors in the Themes group.

Your screen should be similar to Figure 2.16

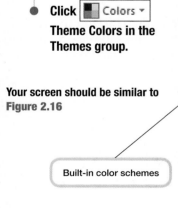

> Built-in color schemes

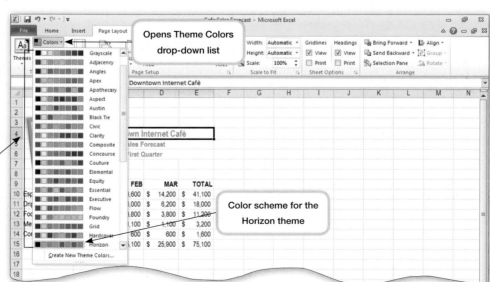

> Opens Theme Colors drop-down list

> Color scheme for the Horizon theme

Figure 2.16

The colors used in each of the themes are displayed in the drop-down list. The set of eight colors that appears next to each theme color name represents the text, background, accent, and hyperlink colors. The Horizon color scheme is selected because it is the color scheme currently in use. Notice that the fourth color from the left in the Horizon color bar is the Accent2 color that is used in the picture border. Although you like that color, you think some of the other colors are drab. Instead, you want to see how the Metro color scheme would look.

2

● Point to several color schemes to preview them.

● Choose the Metro theme color scheme.

Your screen should be similar to Figure 2.17

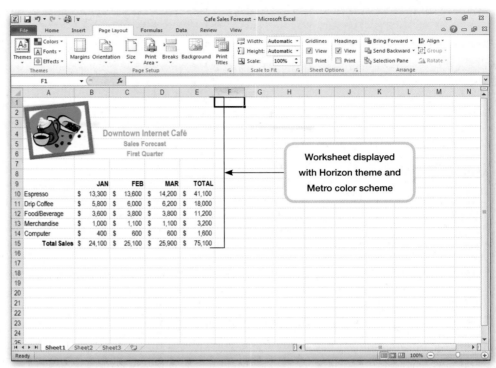

Worksheet displayed with Horizon theme and Metro color scheme

Figure 2.17

Additional Information

You can change the theme fonts and effects in a similar manner.

The new color scheme has been applied to the picture border and font color used in the worksheet titles. All other aspects of the Horizon theme are unchanged.

SAVING A CUSTOM THEME

Additional Information

Custom themes have the .thmx file extension, which identifies the file as an Office theme template file.

You decide to save the color change you have made to the Horizon theme as a custom theme. This will make it easy to reapply the same settings to another workbook in the future. Custom themes are saved in the Document Themes folder by default and are available in all Office applications that use themes.

1

Click 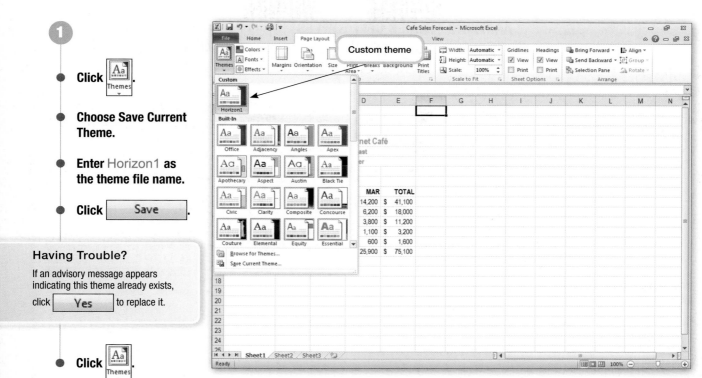.

Choose **Save Current Theme.**

Enter Horizon1 as the theme file name.

Click **Save**.

Having Trouble?

If an advisory message appears indicating this theme already exists, click **Yes** to replace it.

Click **Themes**.

Your screen should be similar to Figure 2.18

Additional Information

To remove a custom theme, choose Delete from the theme's shortcut menu.

Figure 2.18

The custom theme you created and saved appears at the top of the Themes gallery. Now you can quickly reapply this entire theme in one step to another workbook, just like the built-in themes, or to any other Office document.

Using Cell Styles

Next, you want to enhance the worksheet more by adding background cell shading to define areas of the worksheet, selecting heading styles for the title, and changing the format of the Food, Internet, and Merchandise values to display commas only, without dollar signs.

Although you could make these changes using individual formatting commands, a quicker way is to select a cell quick style. Excel includes 44 predefined cell styles, or you can create your own custom styles. Using cell styles allows you to apply several formats in one step and helps ensure that cells have consistent formatting. Cell styles are based on the theme that is applied to the entire workbook. When you switch to another theme, the cell styles are updated to match the new theme.

APPLYING THEMED CELL STYLES

First, you want to add background shading behind the entire worksheet.

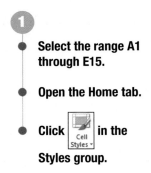

1 ● Select the range A1 through E15.

● Open the Home tab.

● Click 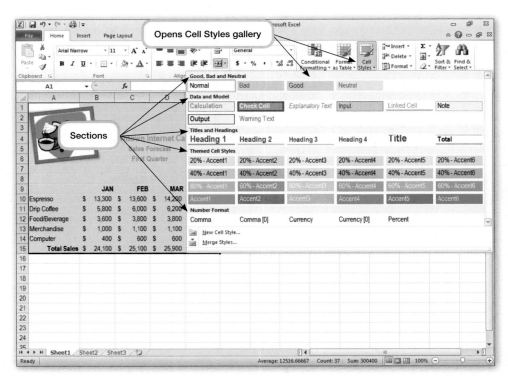 in the Styles group.

Your screen should be similar to Figure 2.19

Figure 2.19

The Cell Styles gallery is divided into five sections. The styles in each section are designed to identify different areas of a worksheet and types of cell entries, as explained in the following table:

Section	Identifies
Good, Bad and Neutral	Data trends or outcomes; for example, selecting Bad would be used to identify a bad outcome
Data and Model	Worksheet areas; for example, calculations and warning notes
Titles and Headings	Worksheet titles and headings
Themed Cell Styles	Basic worksheet data
Number Format	Number formats

You will use a cell style in the Themed Cell Styles section. These cell styles consist of background fill colors and either white or black text color. The colors are associated with the theme colors. Pointing to a cell style displays a Live Preview of the cell style.

2

- Point to several cell styles to see the Live Preview.

- Choose 40%—Accent3 in the Themed Cell Styles section.

- Click on the worksheet to clear the selection.

Your screen should be similar to Figure 2.20

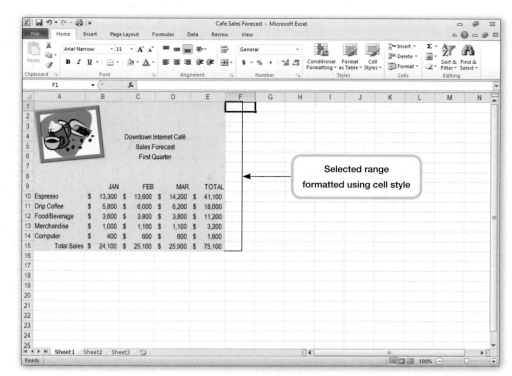

Selected range formatted using cell style

Figure 2.20

The selected range has been formatted using the selected cell style. It consists of a gold fill color for the cell background and black text in the theme font of Arial Narrow, 11 point. The green font color used in the titles was replaced with the font color associated with the cell style.

APPLYING HEADING AND TOTAL CELL STYLES

Next you will define the row headings area of the worksheet by selecting a different style from the Themed Cell Styles section. Then you will use two cell styles from the Titles and Headings section that will format the month column headings and the Total Sales row of data.

1

- Select A1 through A15.

- Click 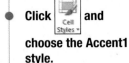 and choose the Accent1 style.

- Select cells A10 through A15 and make them bold.

- Select B9 through E9 and apply the Heading 3 cell style.

- Select A15 through E15 and apply the Total cell style.

- Click outside the selection to see the formatting changes.

Your screen should be similar to Figure 2.21

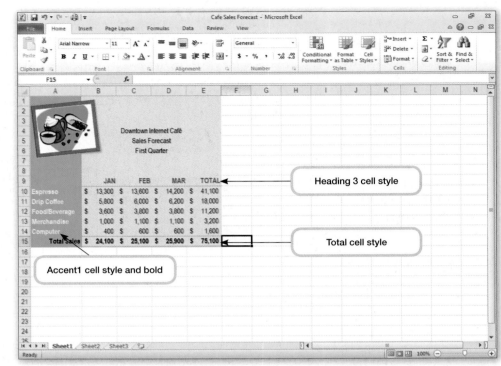

Figure 2.21

The Accent1 style uses a white font color with a green fill color. The Heading 3 style includes a gray font color and a bottom border. The Total cell style applies a black font color, bold text effect and a top and bottom border.

Next, you will add formatting to the worksheet titles by applying a Title style to the first title line, a Heading 1 style to the second line, and a Heading 2 style to the third line.

2

- Apply the Title cell style to cell B4.

- Apply the Heading 1 cell style to cell B5.

- Apply the Heading 2 cell style to cell B6.

- Click outside the selection to see the formatting changes.

- Resize and reposition the graphic as needed to show the full title text.

Your screen should be similar to Figure 2.22

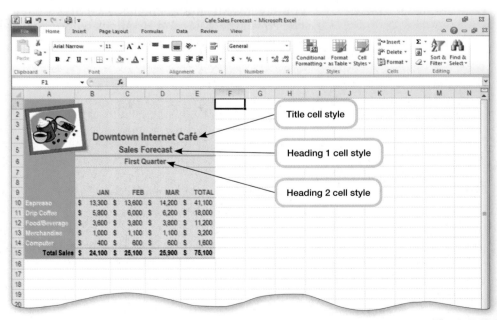

Figure 2.22

MODIFYING CELL STYLES

Although you like the font size change and the colored bottom border line, you feel the titles could be improved by changing the font color to the same color as the fill color used in column A. Instead of changing the font color for each cell containing the titles, you will modify the cell styles so that the color changes to these styles will be easily available again.

1

- Click [Cell Styles] and right-click on the Title cell style.

- Choose Modify from the shortcut menu.

- Click [Format...] and open the Font tab.

- Open the Color gallery and choose Green, Accent1 from the Theme Colors category.

- Click [OK] twice.

- Modify the Heading 1 and Heading 2 cell styles in the same manner.

Your screen should be similar to Figure 2.23

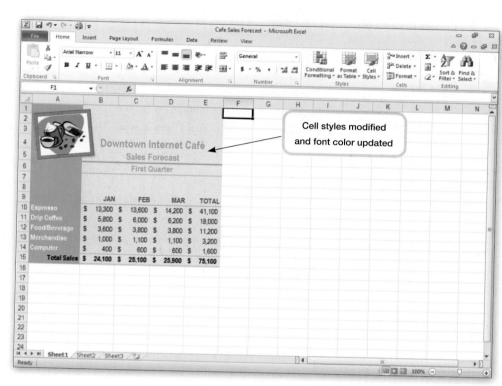

Figure 2.23

The three title lines have been updated to the new color associated with the three cell styles you modified. The changes to cell styles are saved with the current workbook file only.

APPLYING A NUMBER CELL STYLE

The final change you want to make is to change the format of some of the worksheet values. Currently all the values are formatted using the Accounting style with zero decimal places. The Cell Styles gallery also includes five predefined number format styles. Examples of the five predefined number styles are shown below.

Style	Example
Comma	89,522.00
Comma [0]	89,522
Currency	$ 89,522.00
Currency [0]	$ 89,522
Percent	89.52200%

You will use the Comma [0] style for the four middle rows of values.

- Select B11 through E14.

- Open the Cell Styles gallery.

- Choose Comma [0].

- Clear the selection.

- Save the file.

Additional Information

Using 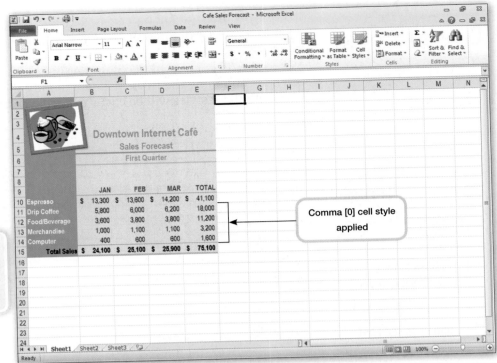 Comma Style in the Number group applies the Comma number format with two decimal places.

Your screen should be similar to Figure 2.24

Figure 2.24

The Comma [0] style applies the Comma number format with zero decimal places and does not display a currency symbol. Using a style applies many formats in one easy step, making it quicker to apply formats to cells.

Creating Charts

Although the worksheet shows the sales data for each category, it is difficult to see how the different categories change over time. To make it easier to see the sales trends, you decide to create a chart of this data.

SELECTING THE CHART DATA

As you learned in Lab 1, a **chart** is a visual representation of data in a worksheet. Because all charts are drawn from data contained in a worksheet, the first step in creating a new chart is to select the worksheet range containing the data you want displayed as a chart plus any row or column headings you want used in the chart. Excel then translates the selected data into a chart based upon the shape and contents of the worksheet selection.

A chart consists of a number of parts or elements that are important to understand so that you can identify the appropriate data to select in the worksheet.

Concept 4 — Chart Elements

Chart elements are the different parts of a chart that are used to graphically display the worksheet data. The entire chart and all its elements is called the **chart area**.

The basic elements of a two-dimensional chart are described in the following table.

Element	Description
Plot area	Area within the X- and Y-axis boundaries where the chart data series appears.
Axis	The lines bordering the chart plot area used as a frame of reference for measurement. The **Y axis**, also called the **value axis**, is usually the vertical axis and contains data. The **X axis**, also called the **category axis**, is usually the horizontal axis and contains categories.
Data series	Related data points that are distinguished by different colors or patterns, called **data markers**, and displayed in the plot area.
Data labels	Labels that correspond to the data points that are plotted along the X axis.
Chart gridlines	Lines extending from the axis line across the plot area that make it easier to read the chart data.
Legend	A box that identifies the chart data series and data markers.
Chart title	A descriptive label displayed above the charted data that explains the contents of the chart.
Category-axis title	A descriptive label displayed along the X axis.
Value-axis title	A descriptive label displayed along the Y axis.

The basic parts of a two-dimensional chart are shown in the figure below.

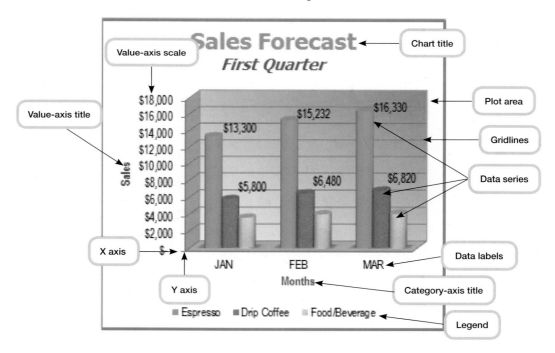

3-D column, 3-D cone, or 3-D pyramid charts have a third axis, the **depth axis** (also known as the **series axis** or **Z axis**), so that data can be plotted along the depth of a chart. Radar charts do not have horizontal (category) axes, and pie and doughnut charts do not have any axes.

The first chart you want to create will show the total sales pattern over the three months. This chart will use the month headings in cells B9 through D9 to label the X axis. The numbers to be charted are in cells B15 through D15. In addition, the heading Total Sales in cell A15 will be used as the chart legend, making the entire range A15 through D15.

Notice that the two ranges, B9 through D9 and A14 through D14, are not adjacent and are not the same size. When plotting nonadjacent ranges in a chart, the selections must form a rectangular shape. To do this, you will include the blank cell A9 in the selection. You will specify the range and create the chart.

Additional Information

If you select only one cell, Excel automatically plots all cells that contain data that is adjacent to that cell into a chart.

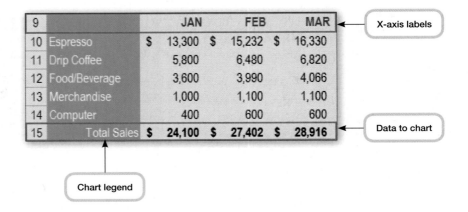

X-axis labels

Data to chart

Chart legend

1
Select cells A9 through D9.

Hold down [Ctrl].

Select cells A15 through D15.

Your screen should be similar to Figure 2.25

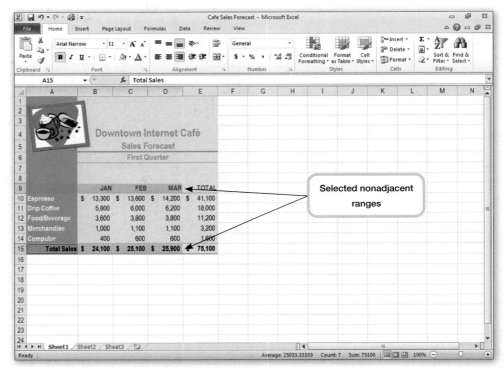

Selected nonadjacent ranges

Figure 2.25

SELECTING THE CHART TYPE

The next step is to select the chart type. There are many different types of charts that can be used to convey the information in a worksheet in an attractive and easy-to-understand manner.

Concept 5 Chart Types

Different chart types are used to represent data in different ways. The type of chart you create depends on the type of data you are charting and the emphasis you want the chart to impart.

Excel 2010 can produce 14 standard types of graphs or charts, with many different subtypes for each standard type. In addition, Excel includes professionally designed, built-in custom charts that include additional formatting and chart refinements. The basic chart types and how they represent data are described in the following table.

Type	Description	Type	Description
	Area charts show the magnitude of change over time by emphasizing the area under the curve created by each data series.		**Radar charts** display a line or area chart wrapped around a central point. Each axis represents a set of data points.
	Bar charts display data as evenly spaced bars. The categories are displayed along the Y axis and the values are displayed horizontally, placing more emphasis on comparisons and less on time.		**XY (scatter) charts** are used to show the relationship between two ranges of numeric data.
	Column charts display data as evenly spaced bars. They are similar to bar charts, except that categories are organized horizontally and values vertically to emphasize variation over time.		**Surface charts** display values in a form similar to a rubber sheet stretched over a 3-D column chart. These are useful for finding the best combination between sets of data.
	Line charts display data along a line. They are used to show changes in data over time, emphasizing time and rate of change rather than the amount of change.		**Bubble charts** compare sets of three values. They are similar to a scatter chart with the third value displayed as the size of bubble markers.
	Pie charts display data as slices of a circle or pie. They show the relationship of each value in a data series to the series as a whole. Each slice of the pie represents a single value in the series.		**Stock charts** illustrate fluctuations in stock prices or scientific data. They require three to five data series that must be arranged in a specific order.
	Doughnut charts are similar to pie charts except that they can show more than one data series.		

Each type of chart includes many variations. The Charts group in the Insert tab contains commands to create the most commonly used types of charts. In addition, it includes the [Other Charts] button, which accesses the less commonly used charts. You also can open the Charts group dialog box to have access to all the available chart types. You think a column chart may best represent this data.

1

Open the Insert tab.

Click 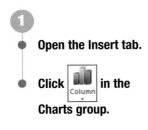 **in the Charts group.**

Your screen should be similar to Figure 2.26

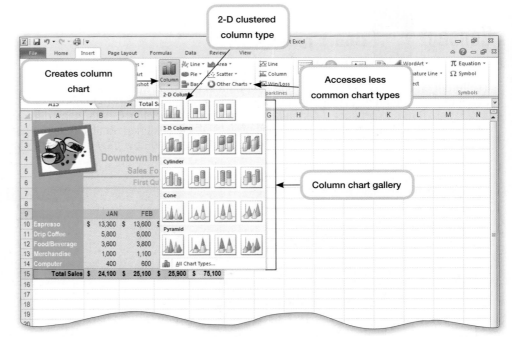

Figure 2.26

Additional Information

3-D displays the data in a 3-D perspective. This is different from a 3-D chart that has a third axis.

The column chart gallery contains five categories of column charts. From within the categories you can choose clustered, stacked, 100% stacked, and 3-D. You decide to use the two-dimensional clustered column. An enhanced ScreenTip containing a description of the selected column chart type displays as you point to each chart type.

2

Click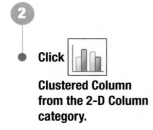

Clustered Column from the 2-D Column category.

Your screen should be similar to Figure 2.27

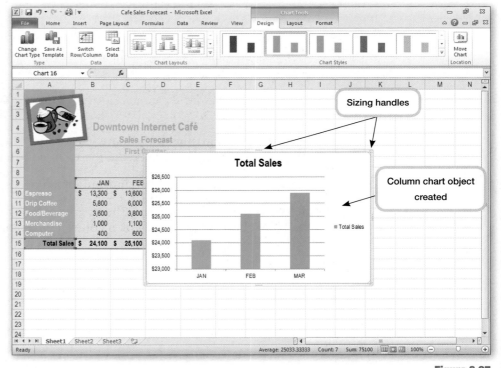

Figure 2.27

The column chart is created using the data from the worksheet and displayed as a chart object in the worksheet.

Concept 6 Chart Object

A **chart object** is a graphic object that is created using charting features. A chart object can be inserted into a worksheet or into a special chart sheet. By default, Excel inserts the chart object into the worksheet. Charts that are inserted into a worksheet are embedded objects. An **embedded chart** becomes part of the sheet in which it is inserted and is saved as part of the worksheet when you save the workbook file. Like all graphic objects, an embedded chart object can be sized and moved in a worksheet. A worksheet can contain multiple charts.

A chart that is inserted into a separate chart sheet also is saved with the workbook file. Only one chart can be added to a chart sheet, and it cannot be sized or moved.

Excel decides which data series to plot along the X and Y axes based on the type of chart selected and the number of rows and columns defined in the series. The worksheet data range that has the greater number of rows or columns appears along the X axis, and the smaller number is charted as the Y data series. When the data series is an equal number of rows and columns, as it is in this case, the default is to plot the rows. The first row defines the X-axis category labels and the second row the plotted data. The content of the first cell in the second row is used as the chart title and legend text.

MOVING AND SIZING A CHART

Notice that the new chart is on top of the worksheet data. As objects are added to the worksheet, they automatically **stack** in individual layers. The stacking order is apparent when objects overlap. Stacking allows you to create different effects by overlapping objects. Because you can rearrange the stacking order, you do not have to add or create the objects in the order in which you want them to appear.

First you want to move the chart so that it is displayed to the right of the worksheet data. In addition, you want to increase the size of the chart. A chart is moved by dragging the chart border and sized just like a graphic object. The sizing handles of a chart object are the dots that appear in the center and corners of the selected chart's border. If you hold down [Alt] while dragging to move and size a chart object, the chart automatically snaps into position or aligns with the closest worksheet cell when you release the mouse button. Release the mouse button before you release [Alt].

1

- Point to the chart border and drag the chart object so the upper-left corner is in cell F1.

- Point to the bottom-center sizing handle, hold down [Alt], and drag the chart border line down until it is even with the bottom of row 15.

Your screen should be similar to Figure 2.28

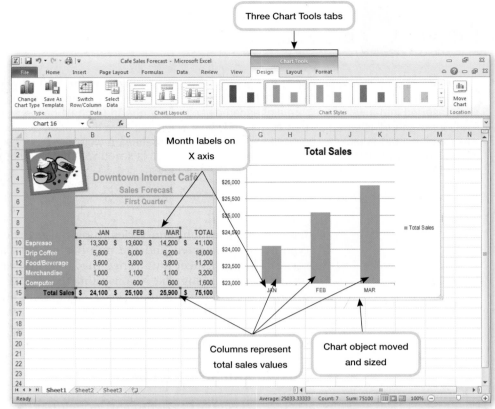

Figure 2.28

Additional Information

Dragging a side handle does not maintain the scale.

It is now easy to see how the worksheet data you selected is represented in the chart. Each column represents a value or data point in the data series (row 15) and provides a visual representation of the total sales for each month. The month labels in row 9 have been used to label the X-axis category labels. The range or scale of values along the Y axis is determined from the data in the worksheet. The upper limit is the maximum value in the worksheet rounded upward to the next highest interval. The row label in cell A15 is the chart title.

Three new Chart Tools tabs appear on the Ribbon to help you modify the chart. The Design tab contains options to change the chart orientation, redefine the source data, and change the chart location or type. The Layout tab commands are used to change the display of chart elements by modifying or adding features such as chart titles, text boxes, callout lines, and pictures. The Format tab is used to add embellishments such as fill colors and special effects to the chart.

APPLYING CHART LAYOUTS

Next, you want to improve the appearance of the chart. To help you do this quickly, Excel includes many predefined chart layouts (also called quick layouts) and quick styles from which you can select. First, you want to change the chart layout. A **chart layout** is a predefined set of chart elements that can be quickly applied to a chart. The elements include chart titles, a legend, a data table, or data labels. These elements are displayed in a specific arrangement in the chart. Each chart type includes a variety of layouts. You can then modify or customize these layouts further to meet your needs. However, the custom layouts cannot be saved.

To see the different chart layouts for a column chart, you will open the chart layout gallery.

1

● **Click ▾ More in the Chart Layouts group of the Chart Tools Design tab.**

Additional Information

The three chart layouts shown in the Ribbon are the most recently selected chart layouts.

Your screen should be similar to Figure 2.29

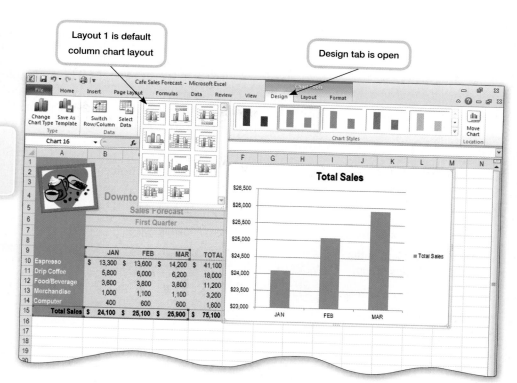

Figure 2.29

The chart layout gallery displays the 11 chart layouts for a column chart. The default chart layout is Layout 1. Since this chart contains only three columns, you decide to try Layout 10 because it shows a chart with wider columns and data labels.

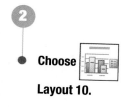

2

● **Choose Layout 10.**

Your screen should be similar to Figure 2.30

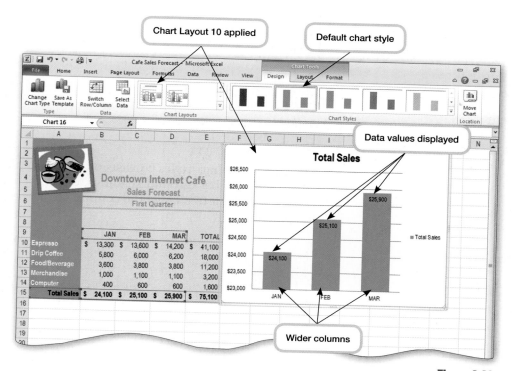

Figure 2.30

The columns are now wider and include the data values.

APPLYING CHART STYLES

Next, you want to change the color of the columns to further enhance the chart. Although you could manually format the chart elements individually, it is quicker to use a chart quick style. The available chart styles are based on the document theme that has been applied. This ensures that the formats you apply to the chart will coordinate with the worksheet formatting. The chart styles use the same colors, fonts, line, and fill effects that are defined in the theme.

The default chart style is selected in the Chart Styles group in the Ribbon. You want to see all available choices.

1

● **Click** ▾ **More in the Chart Styles group.**

Your screen should be similar to Figure 2.31

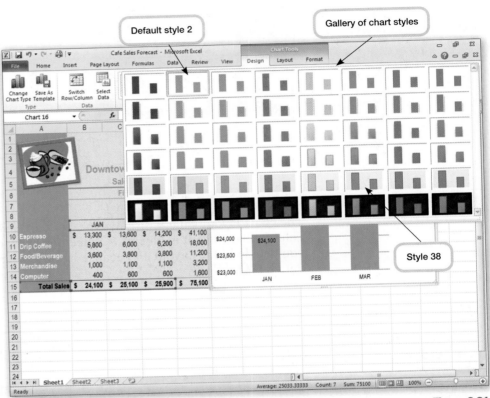

Figure 2.31

The gallery of chart styles consists of 48 sample designs that include different color columns, background shadings, column shapes, and three-dimensional effects. You want to change the column color and add background shading to the plot area.

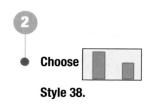

Choose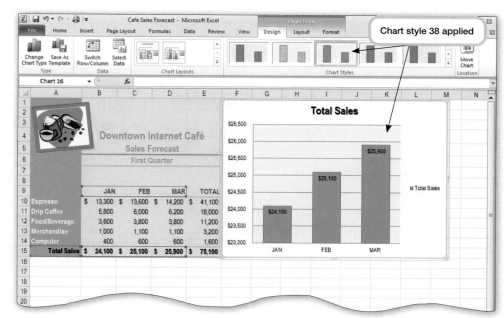
Style 38.

Your screen should be similar to
Figure 2.32

Figure 2.32

The columns are blue with a shaded background in the plot area.

ADDING AND REMOVING CHART LABELS

Finally, you want to clarify the data in the chart by adding labels along both chart axes, removing the legend, and adding a more descriptive chart title. The Labels group on the Layout tab contains options to add and remove chart labels.

You will start by adding titles along the X and Y axes. By default, the X- and Y-axis titles do not display.

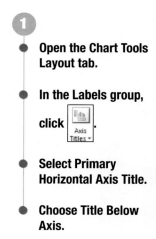

● **Open the Chart Tools Layout tab.**

● **In the Labels group, click** 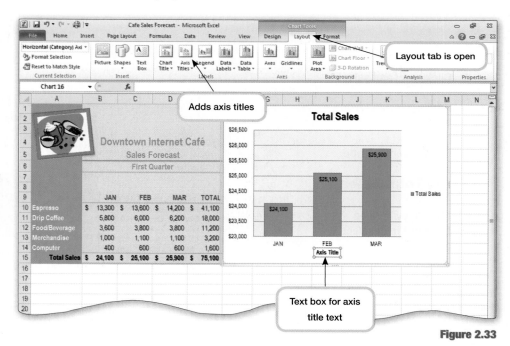 **.**

● **Select Primary Horizontal Axis Title.**

● **Choose Title Below Axis.**

Your screen should be similar to
Figure 2.33

Figure 2.33

A title text box is inserted below the X-axis. It is a selected object and displays the sample text, Axis Title. A **text box** is a graphic element that is a container for specific types of information. In this case, it is designed to contain text for the axis title. You will replace the sample text with the axis title.

To replace all the text in a text box, simply select the text box and type the new text. You also can edit text in a text box using the same features that are used to edit a cell entry.

2

● Type **Months**

● Click anywhere on the chart to deselect the text box.

Your screen should be similar to Figure 2.34

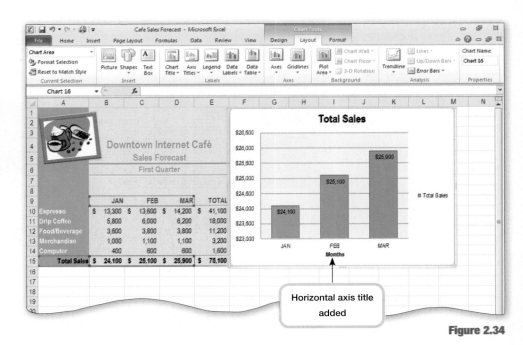

Figure 2.34

All the sample text in the text box was replaced by the text you typed. Next, you will add a title to the Y axis.

3

● Click  and select **Primary Vertical Axis Title.**

● Choose **Vertical Title.**

● Type **Total Sales**

● Click anywhere on the chart to deselect the text box.

Your screen should be similar to Figure 2.35

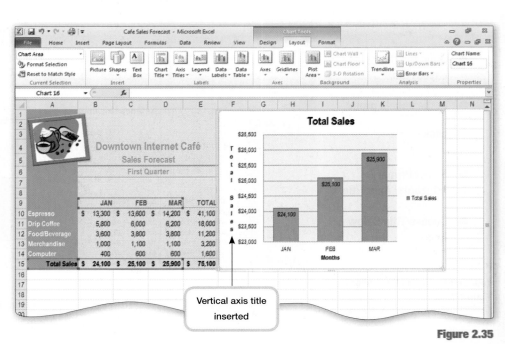

Figure 2.35

You decide the Y-axis title text would look better if it were rotated.

4

- **Click** .

- **Select Primary Vertical Axis Title.**

- **Choose Rotated Title.**

Your screen should be similar to Figure 2.36

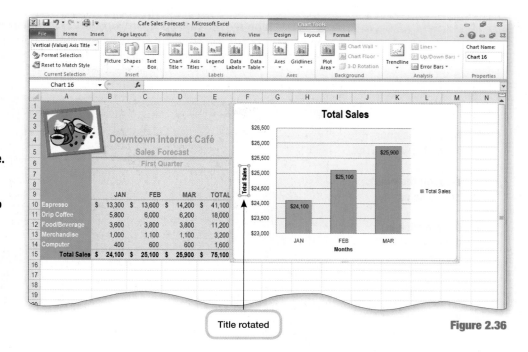

Title rotated

Figure 2.36

The titles clearly describe the information displayed in the chart. Now, because there is only one data range and the category title fully explains this data, you decide to remove the display of the legend.

Changes placement of legend

5

- **Click** **and choose None.**

Your screen should be similar to Figure 2.37

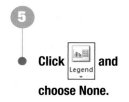

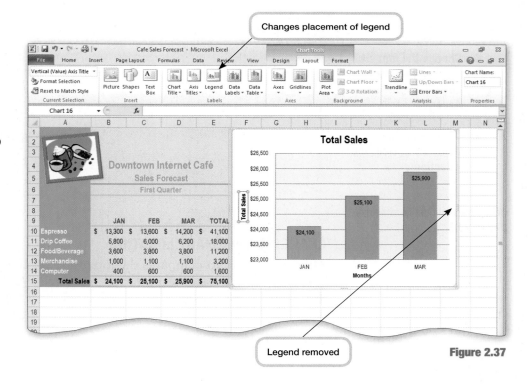

Legend removed

Figure 2.37

The legend is removed and the chart area resized to occupy the extra space. All chart labels can be removed in the same manner.

Finally, you want to add a more descriptive title to the chart and improve its appearance. The [Chart Title] button changes the location of the title on the chart, but the default selection of Above Chart works well. You just need to change the text, which you can do by editing and formatting the text in the text box. When you point to different areas in the chart, a chart ScreenTip appears that identifies the chart element that will be affected by your action.

6

- Point to the chart title to see the ScreenTip.

- Click on the chart title to select it.

- Double click on the word "Total" to select it and type **Downtown Internet Cafe**

- Select all the text in the text box and point to the Mini toolbar.

Additional Information

The Mini toolbar appears automatically when you select text and is dim until you point to it.

- Change the font size to 16 and the font color to Turquoise, Accent 4.

- Click anywhere in the chart to clear the selection.

Your screen should be similar to Figure 2.38

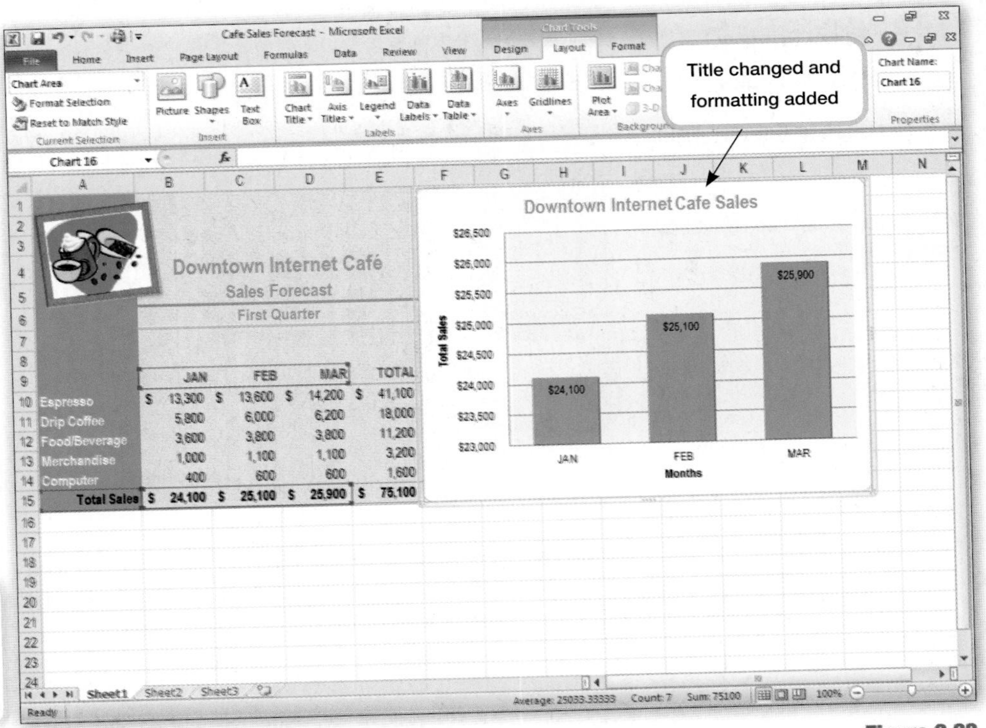

Figure 2.38

CHANGING THE CHART LOCATION

Although this chart compares the total sales for the three months, you decide you are more interested in seeing a comparison for the sales categories. You could delete this chart simply by pressing Delete while the chart area is selected. Instead, however, you will move it to a separate worksheet in case you want to refer to it again.

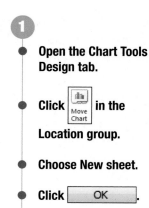

● Open the Chart Tools Design tab.

● Click 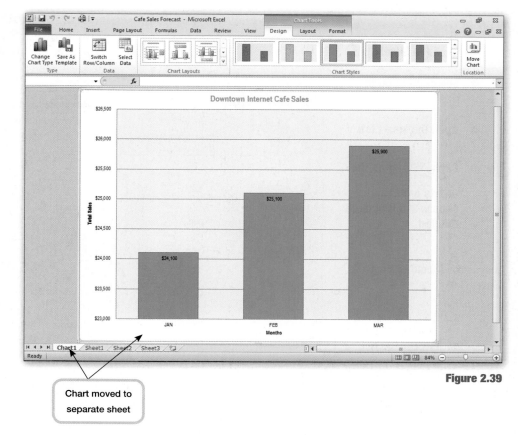 in the Location group.

● Choose New sheet.

● Click OK .

● Save the workbook.

Your screen should be similar to Figure 2.39

Chart moved to separate sheet

Figure 2.39

The column chart is now an object displayed in a separate chart sheet. Generally, you display a chart in a chart sheet when you want the chart displayed separately from the associated worksheet data. The chart is still automatically linked to the worksheet data from which it was created. The new chart sheet, named Chart1, was inserted to the left of the worksheet, Sheet1. The chart sheet is the active sheet, or the sheet in which you are currently working.

Creating a Multiple Data Series Chart

Now you are ready to continue your analysis of sales trends. You want to create a second chart to display the sales data for each category for the three months. You could create a separate chart for each category and then compare the charts; however, to make the comparisons between the categories easier, you will display all the categories on a single chart.

The data for the three months for the four categories is in cells B10 through D14. The month headings (X-axis data series) are in cells B9 through D9, and the legend text is in the range A10 through A14.

1

- Click the **Sheet1** tab.

- Select **A9** through **D14**.

- Open the **Insert** tab.

- Click 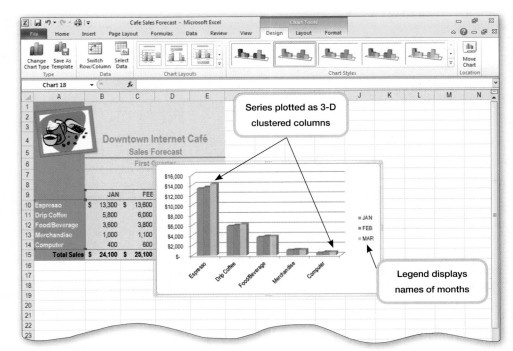 from the **Charts** group and choose **3-D Clustered Column**.

Your screen should be similar to Figure 2.40

Series plotted as 3-D clustered columns

Legend displays names of months

Figure 2.40

A three-dimensional column chart is drawn showing the monthly sales for each category. A different column color identifies each data series, and the legend identifies the categories. When plotting the data for this chart, Excel plotted the three months as the data series because the data range has fewer columns than rows. This time, however, you want to change the data series so that the months are along the X axis.

2

- Click 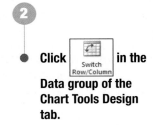 in the **Data** group of the **Chart Tools Design** tab.

Your screen should be similar to Figure 2.41

Changes chart orientation by switching rows and columns

Chart redrawn to show sales by month

Figure 2.41

The chart is redrawn with the new orientation. The column chart now compares the sales by month rather than by category. The legend displays the names of the sales categories.

Next, you will specify the chart titles and finish the chart.

3

- Change the chart style to Style 18.

- Change the chart layout to Layout 9.

- Replace the axis and title text box sample text with the titles shown below:

Title	Entry
Chart title	Sales Forecast
Horizontal Axis	Months
Vertical Axis	Sales

- Move and size the chart until it covers cells F2 through L15.

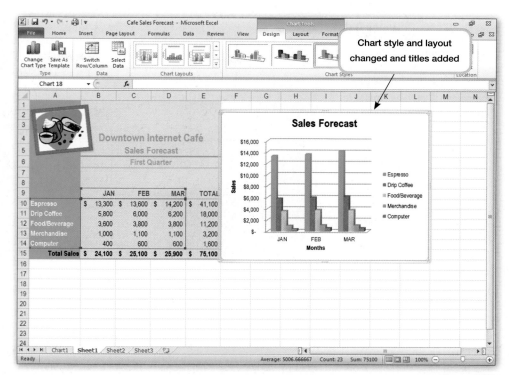

Figure 2.42

Your screen should be similar to Figure 2.42

The column chart shows that sales in all categories are increasing, with the greatest increase occurring in espresso sales.

CHANGING THE DATA SOURCE

As you look at the chart, you see that the Merchandise and Computer sales values are inconsequential to the forecast because they are so small and do not change much. You will remove these data series from the chart.

1

Click  in the Data group.

Your screen should be similar to Figure 2.43

Opens Select Data Source dialog box

Removes selected data series

Current chart data series

Figure 2.43

In the Select Data Source dialog box, you can change the chart data range, switch the row and column orientation, and add, edit, and remove specific data series. You will remove the Merchandise and Computer data series.

2

● Select the Merchandise series name and click ✗ Remove.

● Select the Computer series name and click ✗ Remove.

● Click OK.

Your screen should be similar to Figure 2.44

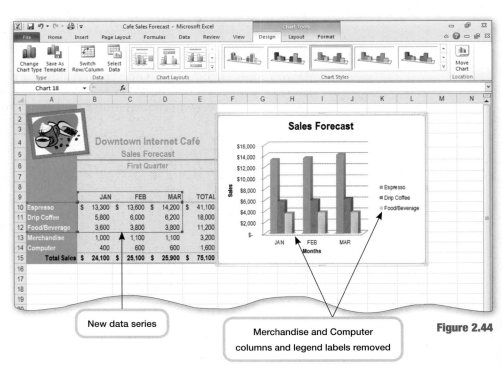

New data series

Merchandise and Computer columns and legend labels removed

Figure 2.44

The columns representing the Merchandise and Computer series were removed from the chart along with the legend labels. The new chart data series is identified in the worksheet.

CHANGING THE CHART TYPE: LINE, BAR, AREA, STACKED

Next, you would like to see how the same data displayed in the column chart would look as a line chart. A line chart displays data as a line and is commonly used to show trends over time. You can change the chart type easily using the 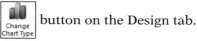 button on the Design tab.

1

Click 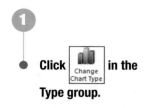 in the Type group.

Your screen should be similar to Figure 2.45

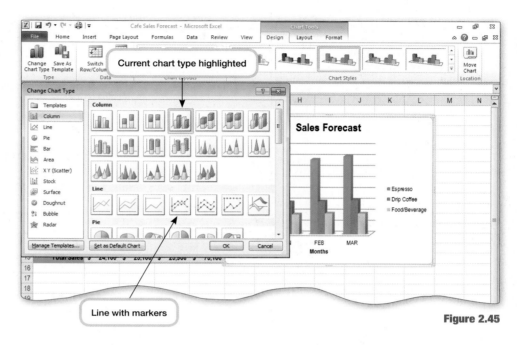

Current chart type highlighted

Line with markers

Figure 2.45

The Change Chart Type box displays all the available chart types. The current selection, Clustered Column, is highlighted. You want to change it to a line chart.

2

Choose 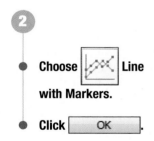 Line with Markers.

Click OK .

Your screen should be similar to Figure 2.46

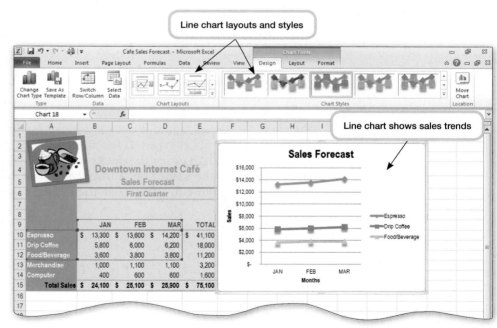

Line chart layouts and styles

Line chart shows sales trends

Figure 2.46

The line chart shows the sales trends from month to month. Notice the chart layouts and chart styles in the Ribbon reflect layouts and styles that are available for line charts.

You do not find this chart very interesting, so you will change it to a 3-D bar chart next.

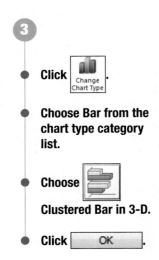

3

• **Click** [Change Chart Type].

• **Choose Bar from the chart type category list.**

• **Choose** [icon] **Clustered Bar in 3-D.**

• **Click** [OK].

Your screen should be similar to Figure 2.47

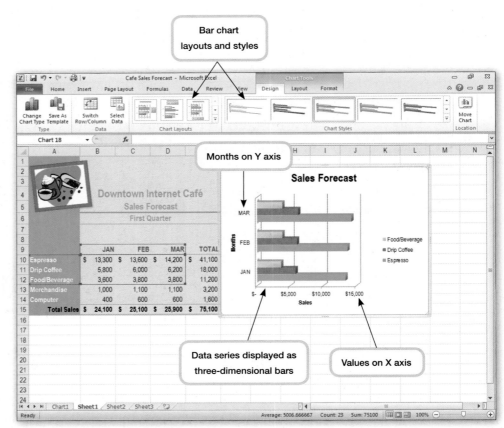

Figure 2.47

The 3-D bar chart reverses the X and Y axes and displays the data series as three-dimensional bars. As you can see, it is very easy to change the chart type and format after the data series are specified. The same data can be displayed in many different ways. Depending upon the emphasis you want the chart to make, a different chart style can be selected.

Although the 3-D bar chart shows the sales trends for the three months for the sales categories, again it does not look very interesting. You decide to look at several other chart types to see whether you can improve the appearance. First you would like to see the data represented as an area chart. An area chart represents data the same way a line chart does, but, in addition, it shades the area below each line to emphasize the degree of change.

4

Click 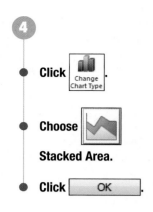 .

Choose

Stacked Area.

Click [OK] .

Your screen should be similar to
Figure 2.48

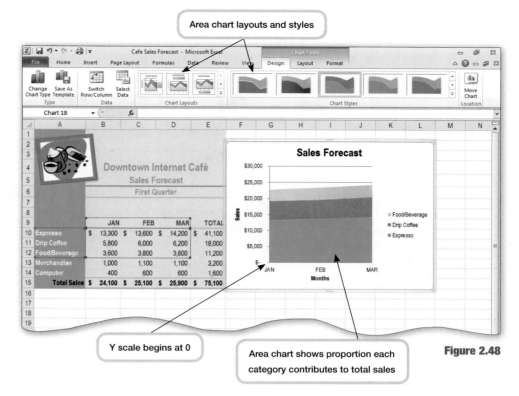

Area chart layouts and styles

Y scale begins at 0

Area chart shows proportion each
category contributes to total sales

Figure 2.48

The Y-axis scale has changed to reflect the new range of data. The new Y-axis
range is the sum of the four categories or the same as the total number in the
worksheet. Using this chart type, you can see the magnitude of change that
each category contributes to the total sales each month.

Again, you decide that this is not the emphasis you want to show and will continue looking at other types of charts. You want to see how this data will look as
a stacked-column chart. You also can double-click a chart type to select it.

5

Click 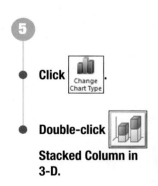 .

Double-click

Stacked Column in
3-D.

Your screen should be similar to
Figure 2.49

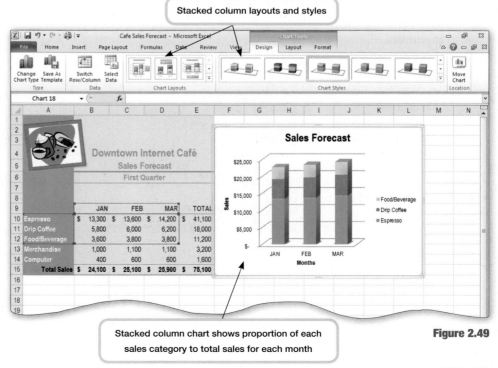

Stacked column layouts and styles

Stacked column chart shows proportion of each
sales category to total sales for each month

Figure 2.49

The chart is redrawn showing the data as a **stacked-column chart**. This type of chart also shows the proportion of each sales category to the total sales.

Although this chart is interesting, you feel that the data is difficult to read and want to see how the data will be represented in several other chart types.

6

● Choose several other chart types to see how the data appears in the chart.

● Change the chart to Clustered Cylinder in the Column category.

Your screen should be similar to Figure 2.50

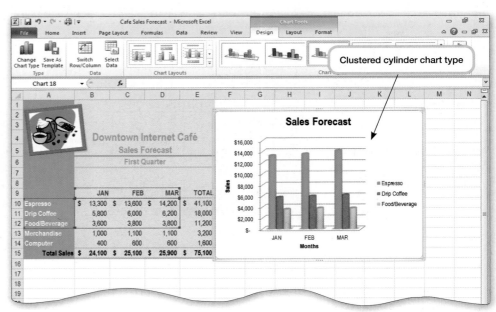

Figure 2.50

You like both the appearance of the clustered cylinders and how the data is represented.

MOVING THE LEGEND

While looking at the chart, you decide to move the legend below the X axis.

1

● Open the Chart Tools Layout tab.

● Click 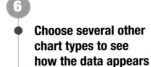 in the Labels group.

● Choose Show Legend at Bottom.

Your screen should be similar to Figure 2.51

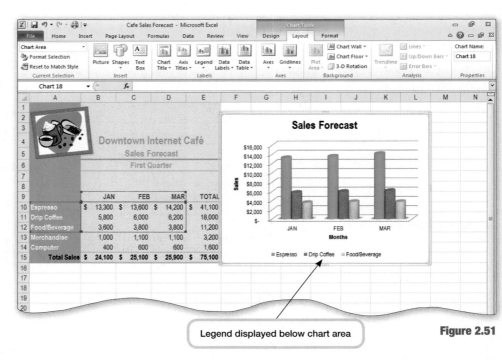

Legend displayed below chart area

Figure 2.51

The legend appears below the plot area of the chart.

FORMATTING CHART ELEMENTS

Next, you want to further improve the appearance of the chart by applying additional formatting to the chart titles. The chart is an object made up of many different objects or chart elements. Each element of a chart can be enhanced individually to create your own custom style chart. Because a chart consists of many separate objects, it is a group.

Concept **7** Group

A **group** is two or more objects that behave as a single object when moved or sized. A chart is a group that consists of many separate objects. For example, the chart title is a single object within the chart object. Some of the objects in a chart are also groups that consist of other objects. For example, the legend is a group object consisting of separate items, each identifying a different data series.

Other objects in a chart are the axis lines, a data series, a data marker, the entire plot area, or the entire chart.

There are several methods you can use to select chart elements. One as you have learned, is to click on the element. To help you select the correct chart element, the element name displays when you point to a chart element. Another method is to select the element from the Chart Area ▾ drop-down list in the Format tab. Finally, you also can use the arrow keys located on the numeric keypad or the directional keypad to cycle from one element to another. The keyboard directional keys used to select chart elements are described in the following table.

Press	To
↓	Select the previous group of elements in a chart.
↑	Select the next group of elements in a chart.
→	Select the next element within a group.
←	Select the previous element within a group.
Esc	Cancel a selection.
Tab ↹	Select the next object or shape in the chart.
Shift + Tab ↹	Select the previous object or shape in the chart.

There are also several different methods you can use to format chart elements. These methods will be demonstrated as you add formatting to the chart.

The first formatting change you want to make is to increase the font size and add color to the chart title.

1

- **Right-click on the chart title to select it and open the shortcut menu.**

- **From the Mini toolbar, choose Tahoma as the font type.**

- **Change the font size to 20.**

- **Select the Gold, Accent 3, Darker 25% theme font color.**

Your screen should be similar to Figure 2.52

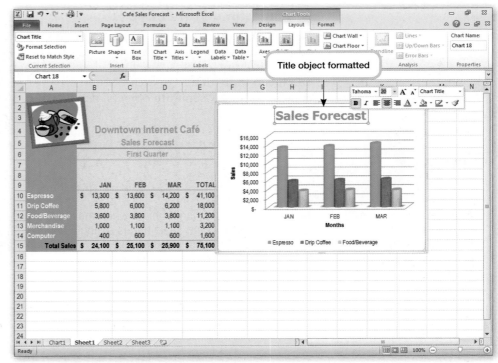

Figure 2.52

Your formatting selections were applied to all the text in the selected object.

Next, you want to add a subtitle below the main title. It will be in a smaller font size and italicized. You also can select individual sections of text in an object and apply formatting to them just as you would format any other text entry.

2

- Click at the end of the title to place the cursor.

- Press ⎆Enter.

- Type **First Quarter**

- Triple-click on the second title line to select it.

- Use the Mini toolbar to italicize the selection.

- Change the font size to 14.

- Apply the Gold, Accent 3, Darker 50% theme color to the subtitle.

- In a similar manner, apply the Gold, Accent 3, Darker 50% theme color to the axis titles.

- Click anywhere in the chart to clear the selection.

Your screen should be similar to Figure 2.53

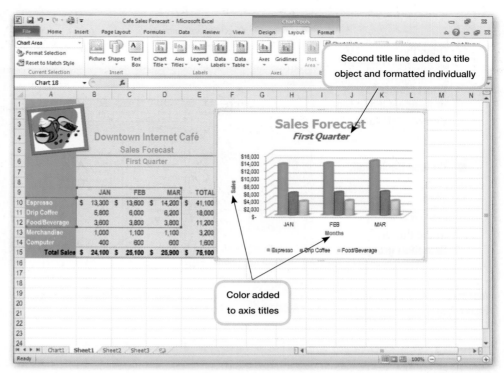

Second title line added to title object and formatted individually

Color added to axis titles

Figure 2.53

Next, you decide to add some formatting enhancements to the chart walls and floor.

3

● **Open the**

　Chart Area ▾

　Chart Elements drop-down list in the Current Selection group.

● **Choose Back Wall.**

● **Click**

　🖌 **Format Selection**

　in the Current Selection group.

Your screen should be similar to Figure 2.54

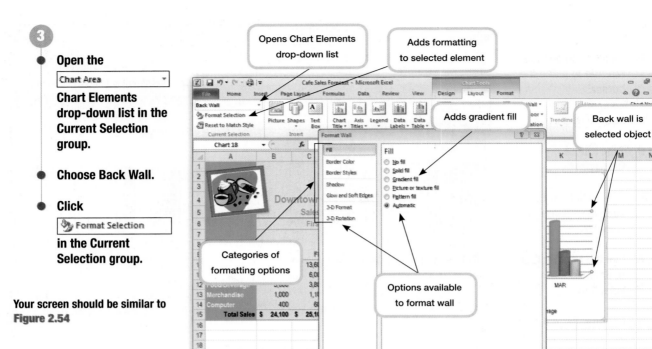

Figure 2.54

From the Format Wall dialog box, you can change the wall fill colors, outside border, and style, and add shadow, 3-D format, and rotation effects. Fill is the currently selected category and shows that the fill colors use the default fill settings that were automatically set by Excel. You decide to add a gradient fill to the background and a solid line around the chart wall. A **gradient** is a gradual progression of colors and shades that can be from one color to another or from one shade to another of the same color. Excel includes several preset colors that include combinations of gradient fills.

- Choose **Gradient Fill**.

- Open the **Preset Colors** gallery and choose **Daybreak**.

- Open the **Direction** gallery and choose **Linear Diagonal—Top Right to Bottom Left** (top row, option 3).

- Choose **Border Color** from the category list and choose **Solid line**.

- Click [Close].

Your screen should be similar to Figure 2.55

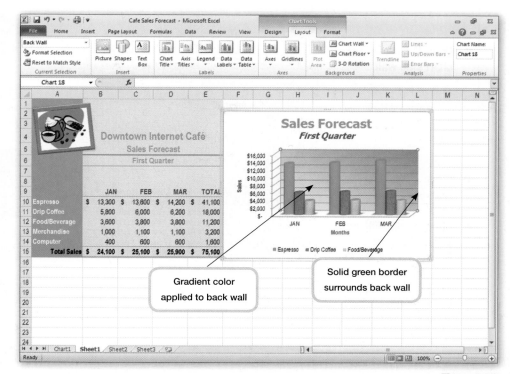

Gradient color applied to back wall

Solid green border surrounds back wall

Figure 2.55

Another Method

You also could use in the Background group of the Layout tab and choose More Walls Options. This option formats both the back and side walls at the same time.

Next, you will format the side wall and floor using a solid fill color with a slight transparency.

Press ← to select the chart side wall.

Additional Information

The Chart Element box displays the name of the selected element.

Click **Format Selection** .

Choose Solid Fill, and select the Light Blue, Background 2, Darker 25% fill color.

Increase the Transparency to 40%.

Having Trouble?

Drag the transparency slider, use the scroll arrows, use the ↑ and ↓ keys, or type the percentage value to change the transparency percentage.

Click on the chart floor to select it.

Change the chart floor to the same color and transparency as the side wall.

Click Close .

Your screen should be similar to **Figure 2.56**

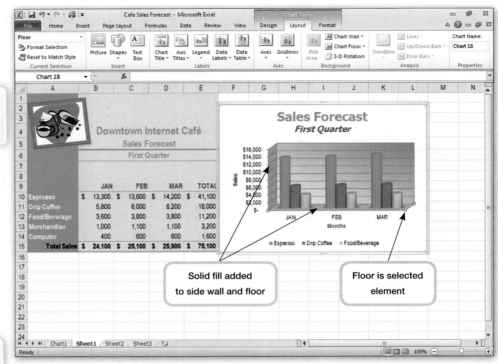

Figure 2.56

The last formatting change you will make is to modify the border line around the entire chart object.

- **Click on the chart area (the white background) to select the entire chart.**

- **Open the Format tab.**

- **Click** **Shape Outline ▾** **in the Shape Styles group.**

- **Select Weight and choose 2¼ points.**

- **Click Shape Outline ▾ and choose the Green, Accent 1, Darker 25% theme color.**

- **Click outside the chart to deselect it.**

Your screen should be similar to Figure 2.57

Figure 2.57

You have modified and enhanced many of the chart elements individually, creating a unique, professional-looking chart.

ADDING DATA LABELS

Finally, to make sure that Evan sees your projected increase in espresso and coffee sales, you will include data labels containing the actual numbers plotted on the column chart.

Concept 8 Data Labels

Data labels provide additional information about a data point in the data series. They can consist of the value of the point, the name of the data series or category, a percent value, or a bubble size. The different types of data labels that are available depend on the type of chart and the data that is plotted.

Value data labels are helpful when the values are large and you want to know the exact value for one data series. Data labels that display a name are helpful when the size of the chart is large and when the data point does not clearly identify the value. The percent data label is used when you want to display the percent of each series on charts that show parts of the whole. Bubble size is used on bubble charts to help the reader quickly see how the different bubbles vary in size.

You want to display the Espresso and Drip Coffee values as data labels for the three months.

- **Click on any Espresso data column to select the series.**

- **Right-click the selection and choose Add Data Labels.**

- **Add data labels for the Drip Coffee sales.**

Your screen should be similar to Figure 2.58

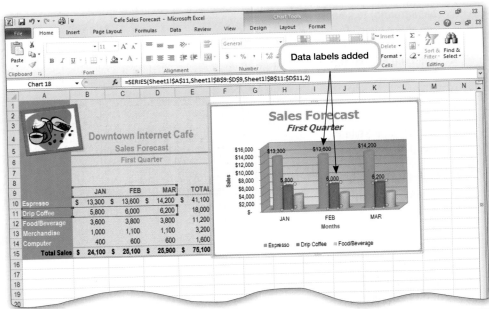

Figure 2.58

Another Method

You also could use the Data Labels in the Chart Tools Layout tab to add data labels.

Data labels containing the actual values for Espresso and Drip Coffee sales are displayed above the appropriate sales columns on the chart. They use the same formatting as the values in the worksheet.

Data labels, like other chart elements, can be further enhanced by adding fill colors, shadows, 3-D effects, lines, and text orientation to the data label. You will use this feature to add the currency symbol to the Drip Coffee data label so the format matches the Espresso labels.

- **Right-click on the Drip Coffee data labels and choose Format Data Labels from the shortcut menu.**

- **Select the Number category and choose Accounting.**

- **Reduce the decimal places to 0.**

- **Click Close.**

Your screen should be similar to Figure 2.59

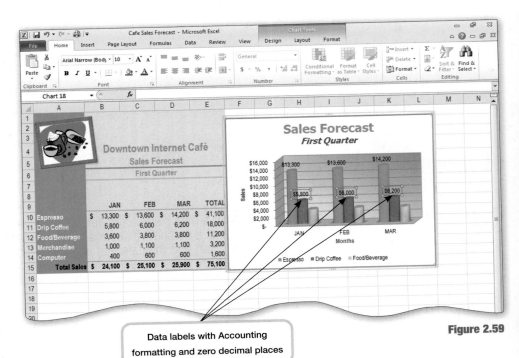

Data labels with Accounting formatting and zero decimal places

Figure 2.59

Next, you will reposition all the data labels so that they appear to the right of each column. Each data label needs to be selected and moved individually.

3

● **Click on the January Drip Coffee data label to select it and drag to position it as in Figure 2.60.**

Having Trouble?

To select an individual data label, first click on a data label to select the entire series, and then click on the individual label.

● **In the same manner, select the February and March Drip Coffee data labels and drag to position them as in Figure 2.60.**

● **Select each Espresso data label and drag to position it as in Figure 2.60.**

Your screen should be similar to Figure 2.60

Additional Information

You can delete individual data labels or the entire series by selecting the data label or series and pressing ⌈Delete⌉ or choosing Delete from the shortcut menu.

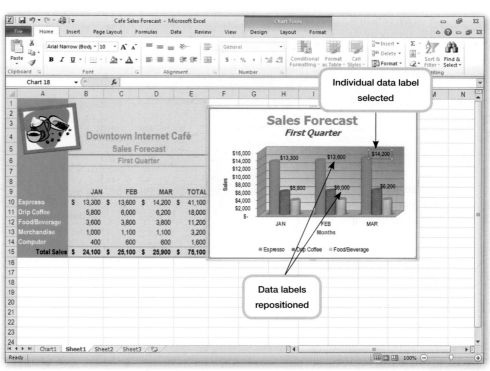

Figure 2.60

The data labels are positioned to the top right of each column.

CHANGING WORKSHEET DATA

So far, the charts you have created reflect your original sales estimates for the quarter. You are planning to heavily promote the new Internet aspect of the Café and anticipate that Espresso, Drip Coffee, and Food/Beverage sales in February and March will increase dramatically and then level off in the following months. You want to change the worksheet to reflect these increases.

1

Increase the February and March Espresso sales by 12% and 15%, respectively.

Having Trouble?

Change the entry to a formula by inserting an = sign at the beginning of the entry and then multiply by 1 + increase; for example, a 12 percent increase in the February Espresso sales is =13600*1.12.

Increase the February and March Drip Coffee sales by 8% and 10%.

Increase the February and March Food/Beverage sales by 5% and 7%.

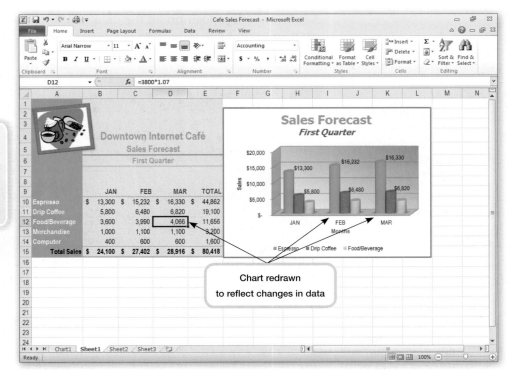

Figure 2.61

Your screen should be similar to Figure 2.61

The worksheet has been recalculated, and the chart columns that reference those worksheet cells have been redrawn to reflect the change in the sales data. Because the chart is linked to the source data, changes to the source data are automatically reflected in the chart. Likewise, the values in the data labels reflect the revised data.

2

Move the chart to its own chart sheet.

Make Sheet1 active again.

Save the workbook.

Creating and Formatting a Pie Chart

The last chart you will create will use the Total worksheet data in column E. You want to see what proportion each type of sales is of total sales for the quarter. The best chart for this purpose is a pie chart.

A pie chart compares parts to the whole in a similar manner to a stacked-column chart. However, pie charts have no axes. Instead, the worksheet data that is charted is displayed as slices in a circle or pie. Each slice is displayed as a percentage of the total.

SELECTING THE PIE CHART DATA

The use of X (category) and data series settings in a pie chart is different from their use in a column or line chart. The X series labels the slices of the pie rather than the X axis. The data series is used to create the slices in the pie. Only one data series can be specified in a pie chart.

The row labels in column A will label the slices, and the total values in column E will be used as the data series.

1

● **Select A10 through A14 and E10 through E14.**

Having Trouble?

Hold down [Ctrl] while selecting nonadjacent ranges.

● **Open the Insert tab.**

● **Click** 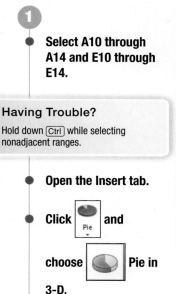 **and**

choose Pie in

3-D.

● **Move and size the pie chart to be displayed over cells F1 through L15.**

Additional Information

Hold down [Alt] while sizing to snap the chart to the cells.

Your screen should be similar to Figure 2.62

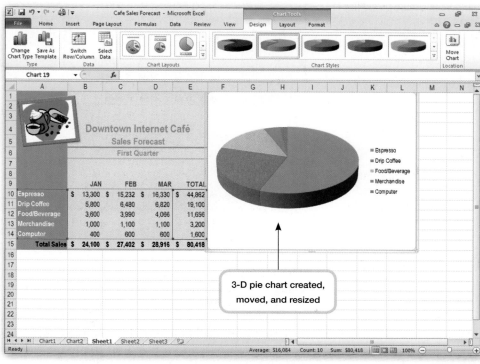

3-D pie chart created, moved, and resized

Figure 2.62

A three-dimensional pie chart is drawn in the worksheet. Each value in the data series is displayed as a slice of the pie chart. The size of the slice represents the proportion of total sales that each sales category represents.

ADDING TITLES AND DATA LABELS

To clarify the meaning of the chart, you need to add a chart title. In addition, you want to remove the legend and display data labels to label the slices of the pie instead. You will take a look at the predefined chart layouts to see if there is a layout that will accomplish all these things in one step.

①

● Click ⏷ More in the Charts Layout group of the Design tab.

● Choose Layout 1.

Your screen should be similar to Figure 2.63

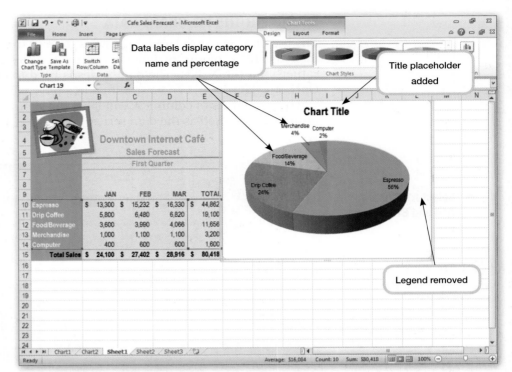

Figure 2.63

The legend has been removed and replaced with data labels that display the category name and the percentage each category is of total sales. The data labels display the category name on a separate line from the value and, if needed, include a leader line to identify the associated wedge. Also, a chart title text box has been added to the pie chart.

Next, you will add a title and then you will improve the appearance of the data labels by adding a gradient fill to them.

2

- Enter the chart title **Total Sales by Category**

- Add the subtitle **First Quarter**

- Change the first title line to Tahoma with the Gold, Accent 3, Darker 25% color.

- Change the subtitle line to Tahoma, 14 pt, with the Gold, Accent 3, Darker 50% color, and italic.

- Click on one of the data labels to select the data label series.

- Choose Format Data Labels from the context menu.

- Uncheck the Show Leader Lines box in the Label Contains area.

- Choose the Fill category and choose Gradient Fill.

- Move the dialog box to see the chart.

Your screen should be similar to **Figure 2.64**

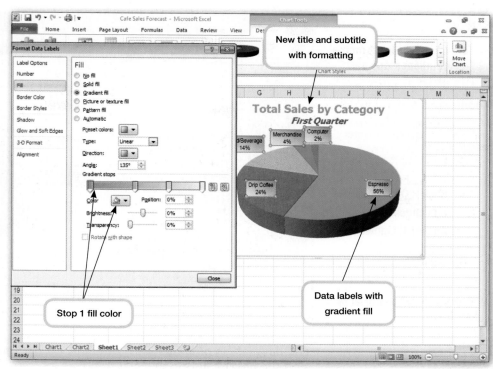

Figure 2.64

Additional Information

The maximum number of stops is 12 and the minimum is 2.

The default gradient fill has been added to each data label. You want to change the fill to a gradient fill composed of two colors. Currently the gradient fill consists of a range of light blue fading to white. The Gradient stops bar shows this gradient fill is made of four "**stops**," or specific points where the blending of two adjacent colors in the gradient ends. The Stop 1 fill color of blue is already correctly specified. You will change the Stop 2 color to green.

3

● **Click on Stop 2 on the Gradient stops bar.**

● **Click** 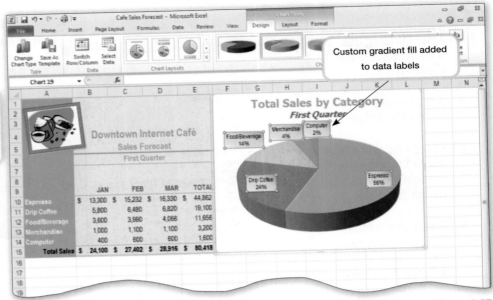 **Color and choose Green, Accent 1, Lighter 60%.**

● **Click** Close .

Your screen should be similar to Figure 2.65

Figure 2.65

The data labels now include a gradient fill background that coordinates well with the chart colors.

The pie chart clearly shows the percent each category is of the total sales. The industry standard for a successful espresso café generates 60 percent of sales from espresso-based drinks. With your suggested advertising campaign, your sales forecast is very close to this standard.

EXPLODING AND ROTATING THE PIE

Next, you want to separate slightly or **explode** the slices of the pie to emphasize the data in the categories.

1

● **Right-click the pie chart and choose Change Series Chart Type.**

● **Choose** 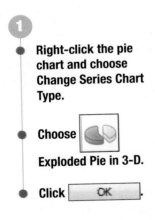 **Exploded Pie in 3-D.**

● **Click** OK .

Your screen should be similar to Figure 2.66

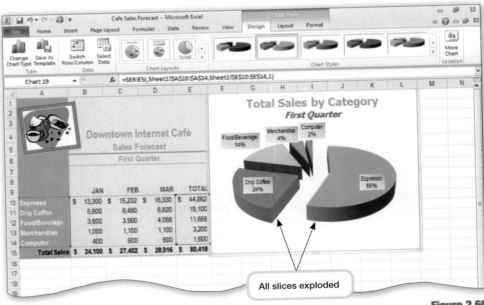

Figure 2.66

All slices are exploded from the center of the pie chart. However, you do not like how this looks. Instead, you decide you only want to explode the Espresso slice to give emphasis to the increase in sales in that category.

- Click 🔄 Undo to cancel your last action.

- Select the Espresso slice.

- Choose Format Data Point from the context menu.

Having Trouble?

If Format Data Point is not displayed, the slice is not selected. Double-click on the slice to select it and open the Format Data Point dialog box.

Your screen should be similar to Figure 2.67

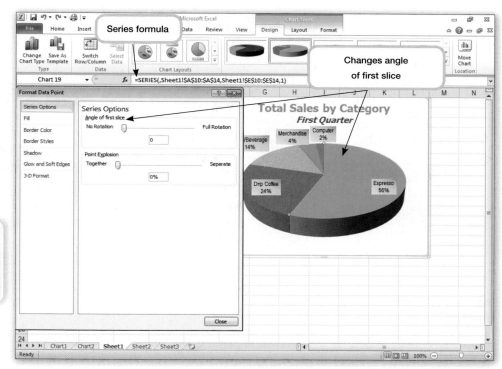

Figure 2.67

Notice that the formula bar displays a **series formula**. A series formula links the chart object to the source worksheet, in this case, Sheet1. The formula contains four arguments: a reference to the cell that includes the data series name (used in the legend), references to the cells that contain the categories (X-axis numbers), references to the numbers plotted, and an integer that specifies the number of data series plotted.

The Format Data Point dialog box has options to rotate the pie and control the amount of explosion of the slices. You want to rotate the pie approximately 330 degrees so that the Espresso slice is more to the right side of the pie. When a pie chart is created, the first data point is placed to the right of the middle at the top of the chart. The rest of the data points are placed in order to the right until the circle is complete. To change the angle of the first slice, you rotate the pie chart. Then you will explode the Espresso slice.

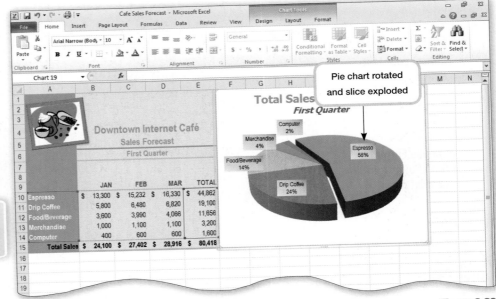

3

● Drag the slider to increase the Angle of first slice to 330 degrees.

● Increase the Point Explosion to 10%.

● Click [Close].

Another Method

You also can drag a slice away from the pie to explode it.

Your screen should be similar to Figure 2.68

Figure 2.68

Even though the program tries to determine the best position for the data labels, many of the labels are close together and look crowded. You will fix this by changing the position of the data labels.

4

● Select the data label series and choose **Format Data Labels** from the context menu.

● Choose **Outside End** from the Label Position area.

● Click [Close].

● Drag the Computer, Espresso, and Drip Coffee labels to the positions shown in Figure 2.69.

Your screen should be similar to Figure 2.69

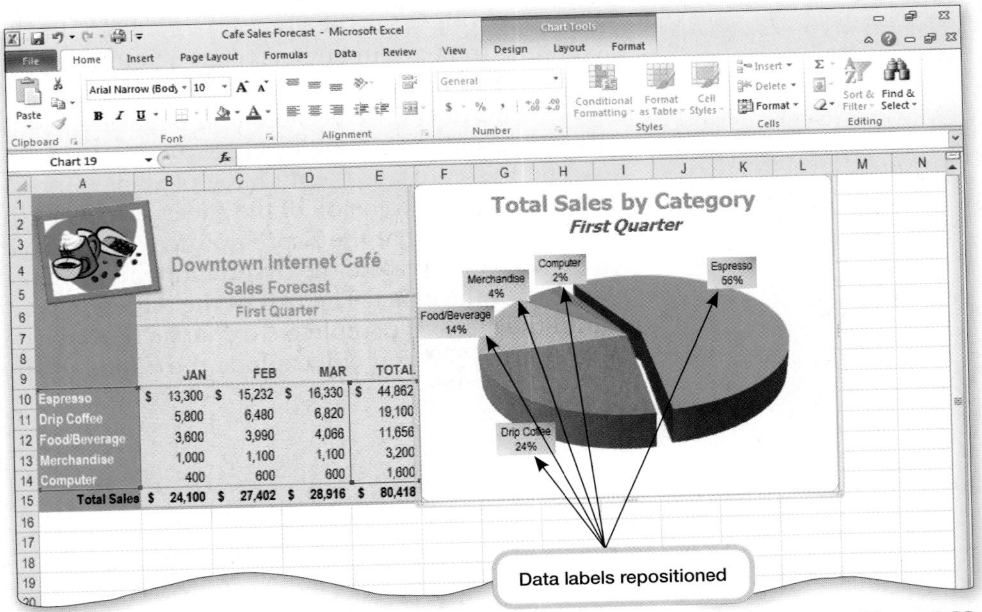

Figure 2.69

Now the labels are more evenly positioned on the pie chart.

APPLYING COLOR AND TEXTURE

The last change you would like to make is to change the color of the Drip Coffee slice and add a fill to the Espresso slice to make it stand out even further. First, you will enhance the Espresso slice by adding a texture.

1

- **Select the Espresso slice.**

- **Choose Format Data Point from the context menu.**

- **Choose Picture or texture fill from the Fill category.**

- **Open the Texture gallery.**

Your screen should be similar to Figure 2.70

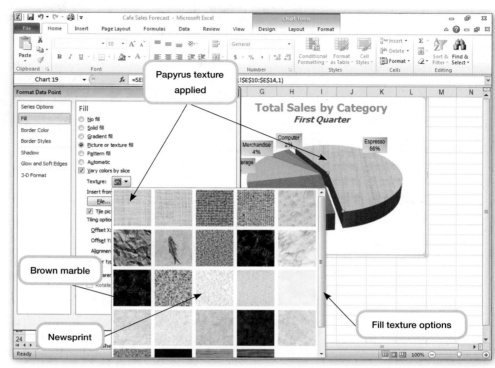

Figure 2.70

A variety of pictures and textures is displayed in the gallery. The Papyrus texture is applied by default. If none of the provided choices is suitable, you could use a picture from a file or clip art as the fill. Although you like how the Papyrus texture looks, you want to see how the brown marble texture would look instead.

- Choose several texture designs to see how they will look.

Having Trouble?

You will need to reopen the Texture gallery again after each selection.

- Choose the **Brown Marble** texture.

- Choose the **Papyrus** texture.

- Select the Drip Coffee slice.

- Choose **Gradient fill** from the Fill category.

- Click [Close].

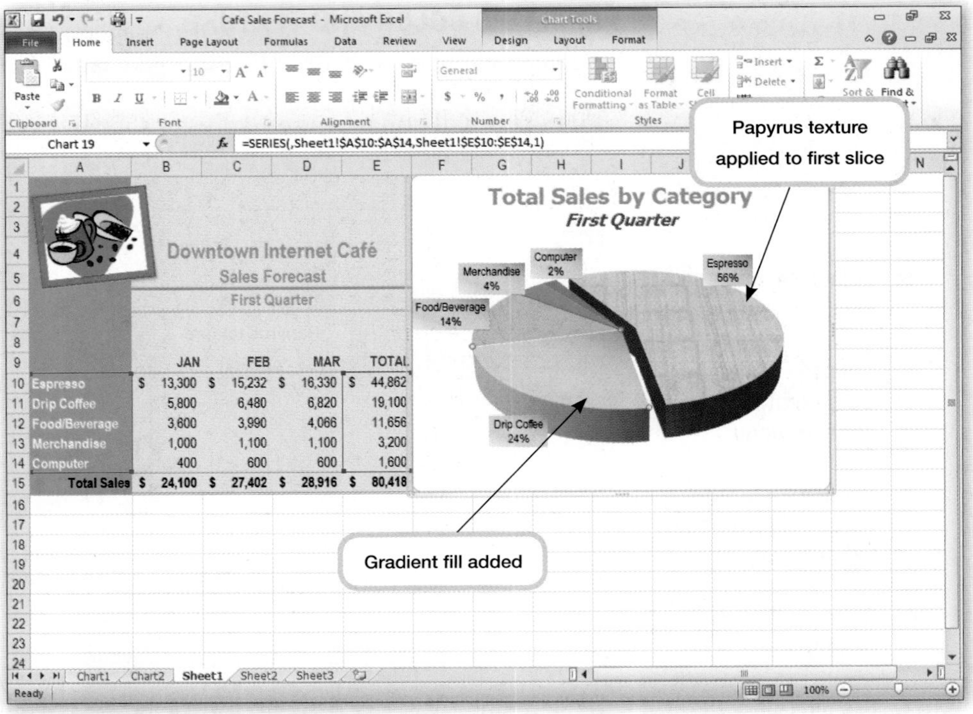

Your screen should be similar to Figure 2.71

The last-used gradient fill colors are automatically applied. You decide, however, that the gradient fill does not look good and instead will try using a shape style. Shape styles consist of predefined combinations of fills, outlines, and effects much like chart styles. Shape styles affect only the selected element.

Figure 2.71

3

- If necessary, select the Drip Coffee slice.

- Open the Format tab.

- Open the Shape Styles gallery in the Shape Styles group and point to several styles to see their effect on the slice.

- Choose the Subtle Effect—Green, Accent 1 Shape Style (4th row, 2nd column).

Additional Information

If the style you want to use is displayed in the Ribbon, you can select it without opening the gallery. You also can simply scroll the gallery line by line using the Shape Style scroll buttons.

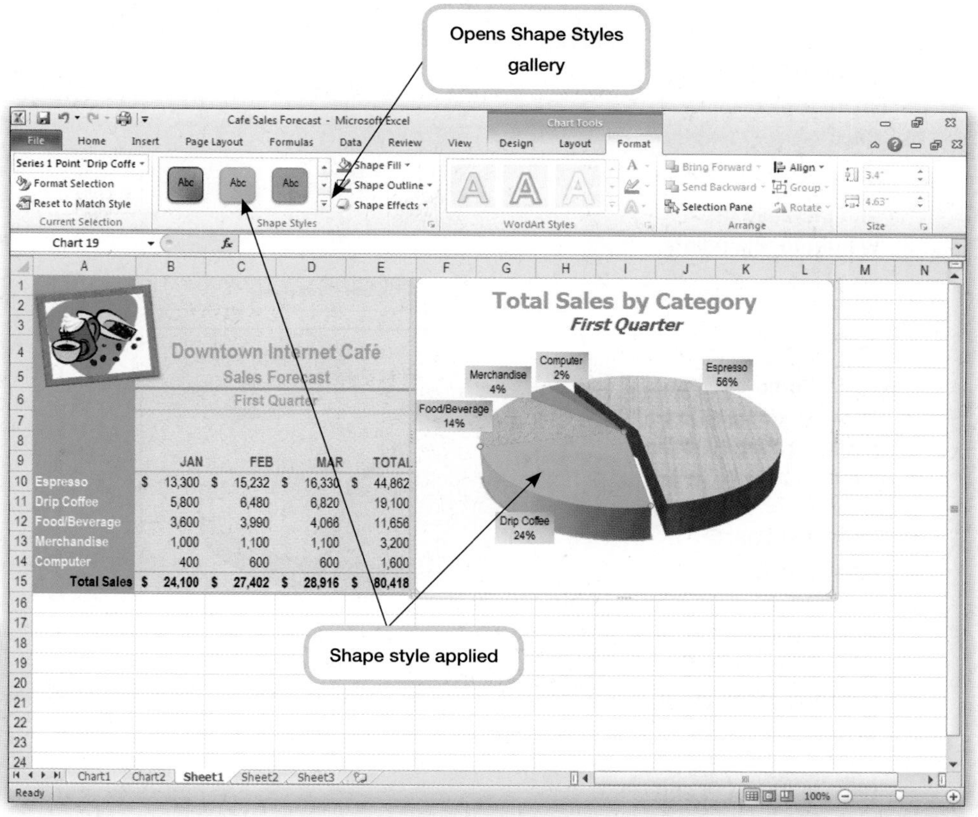

Your screen should be similar to Figure 2.72

Figure 2.72

Finally, you will add a colored outline border around the entire chart, like the one you used in the column chart. Then you will move the column chart from the chart sheet back into the worksheet.

4

- Select the chart area.

- Click
  [✎ Shape Outline ▾]
  and increase the
  Weight to 2¼ points.

- Click
  [✎ Shape Outline ▾]
  and change the line
  color to the Green,
  Accent 1, Darker 25%
  color.

- Make the Chart2
  sheet active.

- Click [Move Chart] in the
  Location group of the
  Design tab.

- Choose Object in and
  select Sheet1 from
  the drop-down menu.

- Click [OK].

- Move and size the
  column chart to fit
  A17 through F33.

- Move and size the
  pie chart to fit A35
  through F50.

- Deselect the chart.

- Save the workbook.

Your screen should be similar to
Figure 2.73

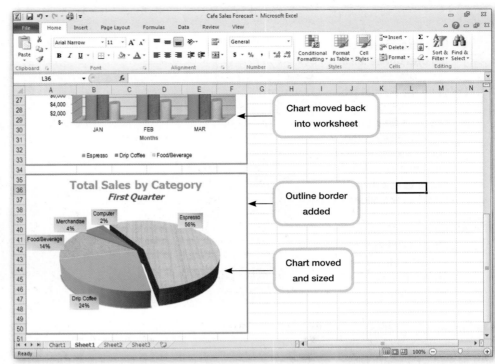

Figure 2.73

The column chart was moved back into the sheet as an embedded object, and the chart sheet it occupied was deleted.

Preparing the Worksheet and Charts for Printing

Before printing a large worksheet or a worksheet that contains charts, you can quickly fine-tune it in Page Layout view. Using this view, you can change the layout and format of data just as in Normal view, but, in addition, you can adjust the layout of the data on the page by changing the page orientation, page margins, scaling, and alignment. Additionally, you can easily add headers and footers.

SCALING THE WORKSHEET

To get the worksheet ready for printing, you will first make several adjustments to the layout in Page Layout view. While in this view, you also will zoom out on the worksheet to see more information in the workbook window by adjusting the zoom percentage.

Having Trouble?

Refer to the section "Using the Zoom Feature" in the Introduction to Microsoft Office 2010 for information on using this feature.

1

● Click ▦ **Page Layout view (in the status bar).**

Another Method

You also can use 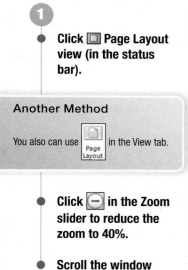 in the View tab.

● Click ⊖ **in the Zoom slider to reduce the zoom to 40%.**

● **Scroll the window up slightly to see the bottom of the pie chart.**

Your screen should be similar to Figure 2.74

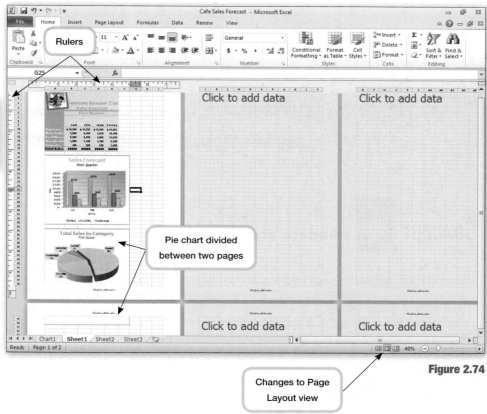

Pie chart divided between two pages

Changes to Page Layout view

Figure 2.74

This view shows how the data and charts lay out on each page of the worksheet. Because you reduced the zoom, you can quickly see that the pie chart is divided between two pages. You also notice that the worksheet and charts are not centered on the page. In Page Layout view, horizontal and vertical rulers are displayed so you can make exact measurements of cells, ranges, and objects in the worksheet. You will make several changes to the layout of the page to correct these problems.

First you will reduce the scale of the worksheet until all the data fits on one page. Because the width is fine, you will only scale the height.

2

● **Open the Page Layout tab.**

● **Open the**

 Height: Automatic ▾

drop-down menu and choose 1 page.

Your screen should be similar to Figure 2.75

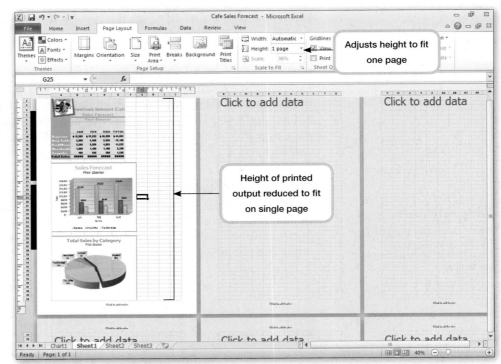

Figure 2.75

The height of the printed worksheet has been reduced to fit on a single page.

ADDING PREDEFINED HEADERS AND FOOTERS

Next, you want to include your name and the date in a header.

Concept ⑨ Headers and Footers

Headers and footers provide information that typically appears at the top and bottom of each page and commonly include information such as the date and page number. A **header** is a line or several lines of text that appear at the top of a page just above the top margin line. The header usually contains the file name or worksheet title. A **footer** is a line or several lines of text that appear at the bottom of a page just below the bottom margin line. The footer usually contains the page number and perhaps the date. Headers and footers also can contain graphics such as a company logo. Each worksheet in a workbook can have a different header and footer.

You can select from predefined header and footer text or enter your own custom text. The information contained in the predefined header and footer text is obtained from the file properties associated with the workbook and from the program and system settings.

Header and footer text can be formatted like any other text. In addition, you can control the placement of the header and footer text by specifying where it should appear: left-aligned, centered, or right-aligned in the header or footer space.

Additional Information

If the computer you are using has your name as the user name, you will not need to add your name as the author in the document properties.

You will add a predefined header to the worksheet that displays your name, the date, and page number. To have your name appear in a predefined header, you will need to first add your name as the author to the file properties.

1

- Open the File tab and in the Info window, enter your name in the Author box.

- Open the Home tab, increase the zoom to 90%, and scroll to the top of the worksheet.

- Click in the center section of the Header area to activate the header.

- Click 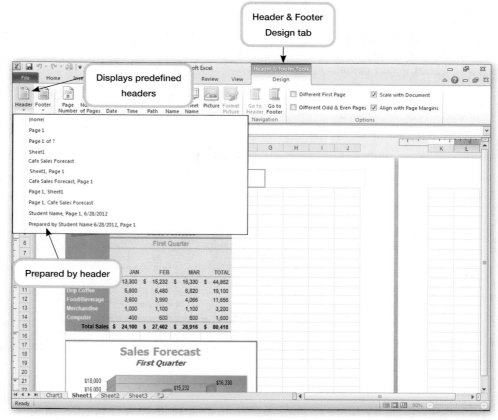 in the Header and Footer group of the Header & Footer Tools Design tab.

Your screen should be similar to Figure 2.76

Figure 2.76

Activating the worksheet header displays the Header & Footer Tools Design tab. It contains commands to add elements to, format, or navigate between a header or footer. The [Header] drop-down list includes many predefined headers that can be quickly inserted into the header. Notice that several of the predefined headers include information that was entered in the document properties.

Choose the Prepared by [your name] [date], Page 1 option.

Your screen should be similar to Figure 2.77

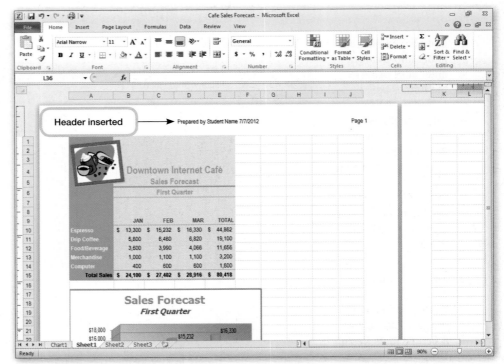

Figure 2.77

The selected header is displayed in the header area of the worksheet. It could then be edited or formatted to meet your needs.

PRINTING THE ENTIRE WORKBOOK

Finally, you are ready to print the workbook. Because it includes a chart sheet and a worksheet, you first need to change the print setting to print the entire workbook.

1 ●

- **Open the File tab.**

- **Choose Print and under Settings, click**

  Print Active Sheets
  Only print the active sheets

  and choose Print Entire Workbook.

- **If necessary, select the printer you will use from the Printer list box.**

Your screen should be similar to Figure 2.78

Preview of chart in Chart1 sheet

Workbook will print on two pages

Figure 2.78

Because the Chart1 sheet containing the column chart is the first sheet in the workbook, it is displayed in the preview area. It will be printed on a separate page by itself in landscape orientation. The page indicator shows that the workbook will print on two pages. The worksheet will print on the second page. In addition, if you are not using a color printer, the preview displays the chart colors in shades of gray as they will appear when printed on a black-and-white printer.

You decide to add a footer to the chart sheet. Each sheet can have its own header and footer definitions.

2

● Click <u>Page Setup</u>.

● Open the Header/
Footer tab.

**Your screen should be similar to
Figure 2.79**

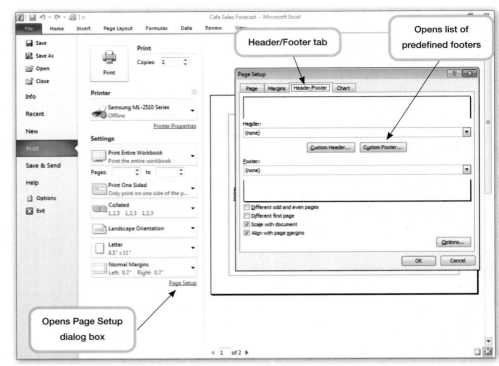

Figure 2.79

Many of the same elements that were available when adding a header in Page Layout view are available in the Page Setup dialog box. You will add a predefined footer to the chart sheet.

3

● Click ▾ More in
the Footer section
to open the list of
predefined footers.

● Scroll the list and
choose the footer
that displays your
name, Page 1, and
date.

● Click ▭ OK ▭.

**Your screen should be similar to
Figure 2.80**

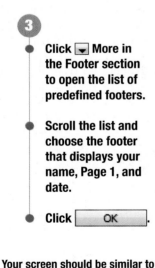

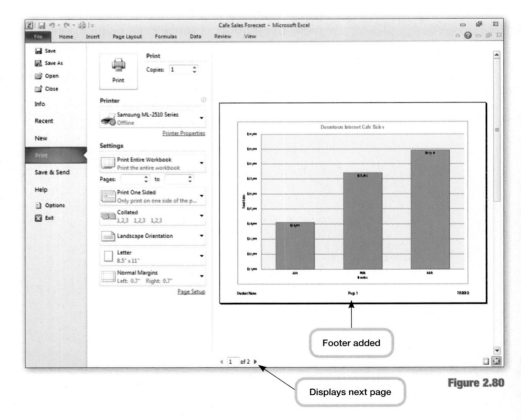

Figure 2.80

The preview shows the selected footer.

Next, you will preview the worksheet.

4

● **Click** ▶ **at the bottom of the Preview pane to see the worksheet and charts in Sheet1.**

Your screen should be similar to Figure 2.81

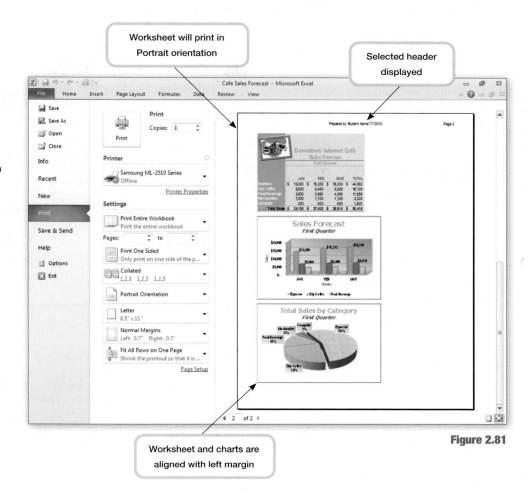

Worksheet will print in Portrait orientation

Selected header displayed

Worksheet and charts are aligned with left margin

Figure 2.81

The preview shows the header you added to the worksheet and because the worksheet was scaled vertically, all the data fits on a single page in portrait orientation.

ALIGNING A SHEET ON A PAGE

However, in the print preview, you can see that the worksheet and charts are all aligned with the left margin. You would like to center the worksheet horizontally on the page. The default worksheet margin settings include 1-inch top and bottom margins and 0.75-inch right and left margins. The **margins** are the blank space outside the printing area around the edges of the paper. The worksheet contents appear in the printable area inside the margins. You want to center the worksheet data horizontally within the existing margins.

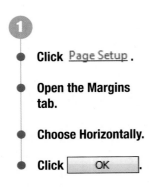

1

● Click Page Setup .

● Open the Margins tab.

● Choose Horizontally.

● Click OK .

Your screen should be similar to Figure 2.82

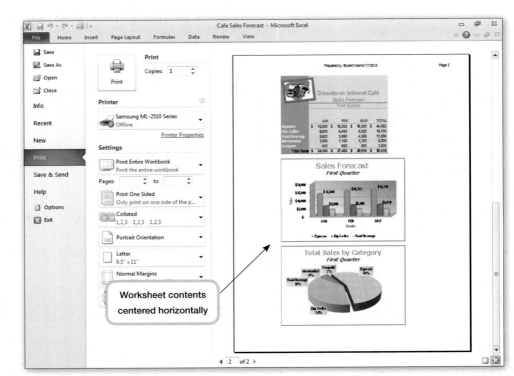

Worksheet contents centered horizontally

Figure 2.82

The preview window displays the worksheet centered horizontally between the right and left margins. It now appears the way you want it to look when printed.

Next, you will print a copy of the worksheet and chart. Then you will exit the application and save the file at the same time.

2

● **Click** 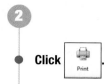 .

● **Change to Normal view and move to cell A9 of Sheet1.**

Additional Information

The dotted line between columns J and K shows the page margin.

● **Exit Excel, saving the workbook again.**

The page layout settings you specified have been saved with the workbook file.

OCUS ON CAREERS

EXPLORE YOUR CAREER OPTIONS

Financial Advisor

With the stock market fluctuations in the last few years, investors are demanding more from their financial advisors than ever before. An advisor needs to promote the company's potential and growth in order to get investors to buy stock. One way to do this is to create a worksheet of vital information and to chart that information so the investor can see why the stock is a good investment. The position of Financial Advisor usually requires a college degree and commands salaries from $35,000 to $60,000, depending on experience.

Graphic (EX2.5)

A graphic is a nontext element or object, such as a drawing or picture, that can be added to a document.

Quick Style (EX2.13)

A quick style is a named group of formatting characteristics that allows you to quickly apply a whole group of formats to a selection in one simple step.

Theme (EX2.16)

A theme is a set of formatting choices that can be applied to an entire workbook in one simple step. A theme consists of a set of theme colors, a set of theme fonts (including heading and body text fonts), and a set of theme effects (including line and fill effects).

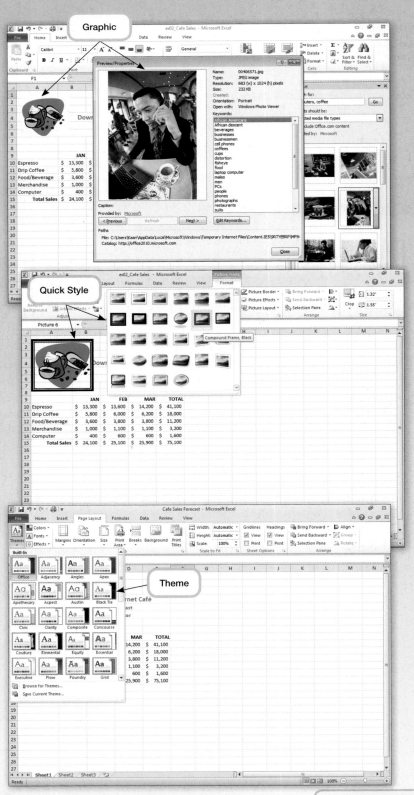

Chart Elements (EX2.25)

Chart elements are the different parts of a chart that are used to graphically display the worksheet data.

Chart Types (EX2.27)

Different chart types are used to represent data in different ways. The type of chart you create depends on the type of data you are charting and the emphasis you want the chart to impart.

Chart Object (EX2.29)

A chart object is a graphic object that is created using charting features. A chart object can be inserted into a worksheet or into a special chart sheet.

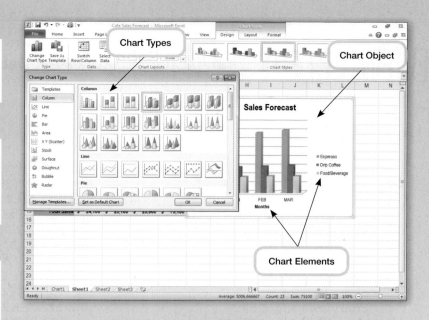

Group (EX2.45)

A group is two or more objects that behave as a single object when moved or sized. A chart is a group that consists of many separate objects.

Data Labels (EX2.51)

Data labels provide additional information about a data point in the data series. They can consist of the value of the point, the name of the data series or category, a percent value, or a bubble size.

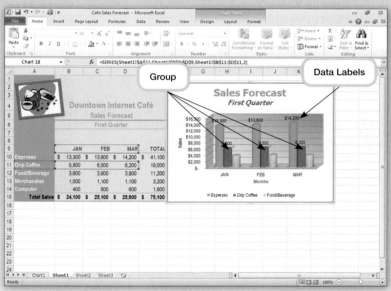

Headers and Footers (EX2.66)

Headers and footers provide information that typically appears at the top and bottom of each page and commonly includes the date and page number.

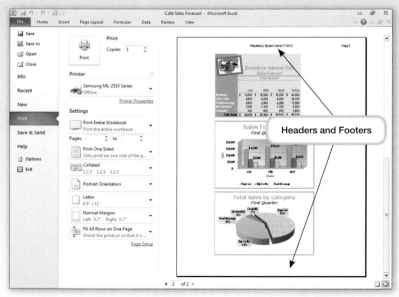

KEY TERMS

area chart EX2.27
axis EX2.25
bar chart EX2.27
bubble chart EX2.27
category axis EX2.25
category-axis title EX2.25
cell style EX2.13
chart EX2.24
chart area EX2.25
chart elements EX2.25
chart gridlines EX2.25
chart layout EX2.30
chart object EX2.29
chart style EX2.13
chart title EX2.25
clip art EX2.6
column chart EX2.27
data label EX2.25, EX2.51
data marker EX2.25
data series EX2.25
depth axis EX2.25
doughnut chart EX2.27
drawing object EX2.5
embedded chart EX2.29
embedded object EX2.5
explode EX2.58
footer EX2.66
gradient EX2.48
graphic EX2.5
group EX2.45
header EX2.66

keyword EX2.10
legend EX2.25
line chart EX2.27
margin EX2.71
object EX2.5
picture EX2.5
picture style EX2.13
pie chart EX2.27
plot area EX2.25
quick style EX2.13
radar chart EX2.27
selection rectangle EX2.7
series axis EX2.25
series formula EX2.59
shape style EX2.13
sizing handle EX2.7
source program EX2.5
stack EX2.29
stacked-column chart EX2.44
stock chart EX2.27
stops (gradient stops) EX2.57
surface chart EX2.27
text box EX2.34
theme EX2.16
thumbnail EX2.10
value axis EX2.25
value-axis title EX2.25
X axis EX2.25
XY (scatter) chart EX2.27
Y axis EX2.25
Z axis EX2.25

COMMAND SUMMARY

Command	Action
File tab	
Print/Settings/ [Print Active Sheets — Only print the active sheets] / Print Entire Workbook	Prints all sheets in workbook file
Page Setup	Opens Page Setup dialog box
Home tab	
Styles group Cell Styles	Applies predefined combinations of colors, effects, and formats to selected cells
Cell Styles /Modify	Modifies existing cell style
Insert tab	
Illustrations group Picture	Inserts a picture from a file
Clip Art	Inserts a graphic from the Clip Organizer or from Office.com
Charts group Column	Inserts a column chart
Pie	Inserts a pie chart
Text group Header & Footer	Adds header or footer to worksheet
Page Layout tab	
Themes group Themes	Applies selected theme to worksheet

LAB REVIEW

COMMAND SUMMARY (CONTINUED)

Command	Action
Aa Themes /Save Current Theme	Saves modified theme settings as a custom theme
Colors ▾	Changes colors for the current theme
Scale to Fit group	
Width:	Scales worksheet width to specified number of pages
Height:	Scales worksheet height to specified number of pages
Scale:	Scales worksheet by entering a percentage
Picture Tools Format tab	
Picture Styles group	
Picture Layout ▾	Converts selected picture to a SmartArt graphic
Picture Border ▾	Specifies color, width, and line style for outline of shape
Picture Effects ▾	Adds glow, shadow, and other effects to pictures
Chart Tools Design tab	
Type group	
Change Chart Type	Changes to a different type of chart
Data group	
Switch Row/Column	Swap the data over the axes
Select Data	Change the data range included in chart
Location group	
Move Chart	Moves chart to another sheet in the workbook

COMMAND SUMMARY (CONTINUED)

Command	Action
Chart Tools Layout tab	
Labels group	
Chart Title ▾	Adds, removes, or positions the chart title
Axis Titles ▾	Adds, removes, or positions the axis titles
Legend ▾	Adds, removes, or positions the chart legend
Data Labels ▾	Adds, removes, or positions the data labels
Background group	
Chart Wall ▾	Formats chart walls
Chart Tools Format tab	
Current Selection group	
Chart Area ▾	Selects an element on the chart
Format Selection	Opens Format dialog box for selected element
Shape Styles group	
▾ More	Opens Shape Styles gallery
Shape Fill ▾	Adds selected fill to shape
Shape Outline ▾	Specifies color, weight, and type of outline
Shape Effects ▾	Adds selected effect to shape
View tab	
Zoom group	
Zoom	Changes the magnification of the worksheet

LAB EXERCISES

MATCHING

Match the lettered item on the right with the numbered item on the left.

1. plot area   _____ a. bottom boundary line of the chart
2. value axis   _____ b. identifies each number represented in a data series
3. explode   _____ c. numbered scale along the left boundary line of the chart
4. theme   _____ d. area of chart bounded by X and Y axes
5. legend   _____ e. applies a set of colors, fonts, and effects
6. scaling   _____ f. separate location that holds only one chart
7. gradient   _____ g. a chart that displays data as vertical columns
8. X axis   _____ h. identifies the chart data series and data markers
9. category ranges   _____ i. to separate a slice slightly from other slices of the pie
10. column chart   _____ j. identifies the data along the X axis
11. chart sheet   _____ k. a gradual progression of colors and shades
12. data marker   _____ l. adjusting print size to fit on the selected number of
                             pages

TRUE/FALSE

Circle the correct answer to the following questions.

1.	The chart title is visually displayed within the X- and Y-axis boundaries.	**True**	**False**
2.	An object is an item that can be sized, moved, and manipulated.	**True**	**False**
3.	A group is two or more objects that behave as a single object when moved or sized.	**True**	**False**
4.	A line chart displays data commonly used to show trends over time.	**True**	**False**
5.	The X-axis title line is called the category-axis title.	**True**	**False**
6.	A chart style is a predefined set of chart formats that can be quickly applied to a chart.	**True**	**False**
7.	A header is a line or several lines of text that appear at the bottom of each page just above the bottom margin.	**True**	**False**
8.	A pie chart is best suited for data that compares parts to the whole.	**True**	**False**
9.	A data series links the chart object to the source worksheet.	**True**	**False**
10.	Exploding a slice of a pie chart emphasizes the data.	**True**	**False**

FILL-IN

Complete the following statements by filling in the blanks with the correct key terms.

1. A(n) _____ is a named combination of formats.

2. The small circles and squares that surround a selected object are called _____.

3. _____ is a collection of graphics that is usually bundled with a software application.

4. A(n) _____ is an object that contains other objects.

5. The axis of the chart that usually contains numerical values is called the _____ or _____.

6. A(n) _____ formula is a formula that links a chart object to the source worksheet.

7. _____ provide more information about a data marker.

8. The _____ is the part of the chart that gives a description of the symbols used in a chart.

9. _____ are combinations of formatting styles such as font, border, shadow, and shape effects that can be applied to a graphic.

10. The X axis of a chart is also called the _____ axis.

LAB EXERCISES

MULTIPLE CHOICE

Circle the correct response to the questions below.

1. A group is one or more _____ that behave as one when moved or sized.
   a. objects
   b. lines
   c. data markers
   d. symbols

2. A chart consists of a number of _____ that are used to graphically display the worksheet data.
   a. elements
   b. groups
   c. gridlines
   d. titles

3. 3-D charts have an additional axis called the _____.
   a. W axis
   b. X axis
   c. Y axis
   d. Z axis

4. A(n) _____ describes the symbols used within the chart to identify different data series.
   a. X axis
   b. legend
   c. Y axis
   d. chart title

5. Charts that are inserted into a worksheet are called _____.
   a. attached objects
   b. enabled objects
   c. embedded objects
   d. inserted objects

6. To change the appearance of the bars in a bar chart, select _____.
   a. format bars
   b. format data series
   c. format chart
   d. format data point

7. A visual representation of data in an easy-to-understand and attractive manner is called a(n) _____.
   a. object
   b. picture
   c. chart
   d. drawing

8. The _____ of a chart usually displays a number scale determined by the data in the worksheet.
   a. Z axis
   b. value axis
   c. X axis
   d. category axis

9. A _____ chart shows the relationship of each value in a data series to the series as a whole.
   a. line
   b. bar
   c. pie
   d. bubble

10. _____ provide additional information about information displayed in the chart.
    a. Data masks
    b. Data labels
    c. Headers
    d. Chart titles

STEP-BY-STEP

PATENTS BY REGION ★

1. Max's international studies paper is on patents. He has some data saved in a worksheet on how many computer technology patents are granted each year by region. He has asked you to help him chart the data and make the worksheet look more attractive. The completed worksheet with charts is shown here. (Your solution may look different depending upon the formatting selections you have made.)

   a. Open the workbook ex02_ Patent Data. Insert a graphic of your choice to the left of the worksheet data (or use ex02_ Computer Technology.bmp) and size it appropriately. Apply a picture style of your choice.

   b. Apply a theme of your choice. Use cell styles, cell fill color, and other formatting effects as needed.

   c. Document the workbook to include your name as the author. Save the workbook as Patents by Region to your solution file location.

   d. Create a Clustered Bar in 3-D chart and move it below the worksheet data.

   e. Apply the Layout 1 chart layout. Enter the chart title **Patents Granted**.

   f. Change the chart type to a Clustered Column. Switch the row and column orientation. Remove all except the top four data series.

   g. Select a chart style of your choice. Display the legend below the chart. Display data labels above the largest data series only.

   h. Add a second title line of **Top Four Regions**. Format the title appropriately.

   i. Size the chart to the same width as the worksheet. Increase the height of the chart to better show the data.

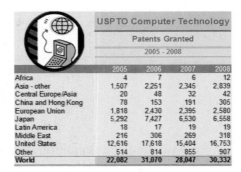

USPTO Computer Technology			
Patents Granted			
2005 - 2008			
2005	2006	2007	2008
Africa	4	7	6	12
Asia - other	1,507	2,251	2,345	2,839
Central Europe/Asia	20	48	32	42
China and Hong Kong	78	153	191	305
European Union	1,818	2,430	2,395	2,580
Japan	5,292	7,427	6,530	6,558
Latin America	18	17	19	19
Middle East	216	306	269	318
United States	12,616	17,618	15,404	16,753
Other	514	814	855	907
World	**22,082**	**31,070**	**28,047**	**30,332**

USPTO is U.S. Patent and Trademark Office

SOURCE: The Patent Board, Proprietary Patent Database, special tabulations (2009).
Science and Engineering Indicators 2010

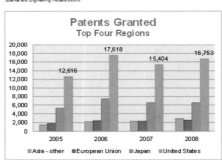

Student Name   Page 1   11/25/2012

j. Preview the worksheet. Add a predefined footer to the worksheet that displays your name, page number, and date. Center the worksheet horizontally on the page. Print the worksheet.

k. Save the workbook again.

CAR COSTS ★ ★

2. Larissa works for the Department of Transportation. She is preparing a report on the costs of owning and operating a car as part of a program to analyze transportation costs. She has compiled some recent data for her report and wants to create several charts to highlight the data. (Your completed solution may be slightly different depending upon the formatting choices you make.)

a. Open the file ex02_Vehicle Costs.

b. Apply a theme of your choice. Change the colors associated with the theme and save the theme as a custom theme. Use cell styles, font, and fill colors to enhance the worksheet as you like to improve its appearance.

c. Add a clip art image of your choice to the left of the title. If you do not have an Internet connection, you can use ex02_ Car Costs.bmp.

d. Save the workbook as Vehicle Costs to your solution file location.

e. Create a column chart of the worksheet data in rows 8 and 9. Enter a chart title. Enhance the chart using features presented in the lab. Move the chart to a separate chart sheet.

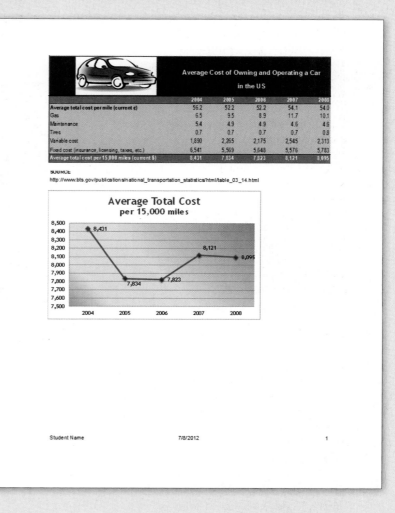

LAB EXERCISES

f. Create a line chart with markers of the data in row 10. Include and format an appropriate title. Select a chart layout and style of your choice. Include data labels. Position the data labels appropriately. Do not display the legend. Format the chart plot area with a gradient color of your choice. Move the chart to below the worksheet data and size appropriately.

g. Document the workbook by adding your name as author. Preview the workbook. Add a predefined footer to the worksheet and chart sheet that displays your name, page number, and date. Scale the worksheet to fit all columns on the page. Print the workbook.

h. Save the workbook again.

MUSIC DOWNLOAD ANALYSIS ★★

3. The Downtown Internet Café is considering providing MP3 download kiosks in the café. To help with the decision, you have collected some data on the number of people who download music. You want to graph the data to get a better idea of the popularity of this activity. The completed worksheet with charts is shown here. (Your completed solution may be slightly different depending upon the formatting choices you make.)

a. Open the workbook file ex02_Music Download Analysis.

b. Insert a clip art image of your choice to the left of the data. Size the image as necessary. If you do not have an image, you can use ex02_MP3 Player.bmp.

c. Change the theme to one of your choice. Apply cell styles and adjust column widths as needed.

d. Create a line chart using the data in cells A5 through C9. Title the chart appropriately.

e. Change the chart type to a bar chart of your choice. Apply a chart style of your choice. Adjust and format the chart title as needed and add a text color of your choice. Display the legend at the bottom of the chart.

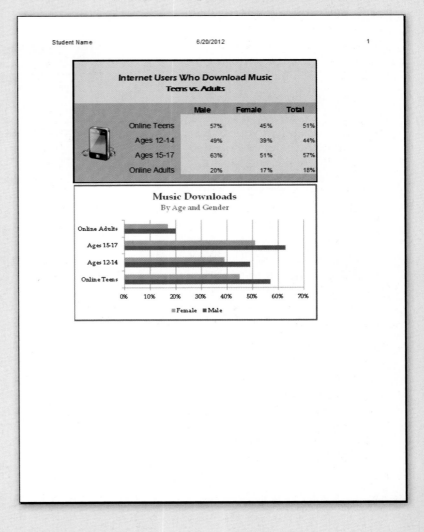

f. Position the chart below the worksheet data and size it appropriately. Add borders around the worksheet and chart.

g. Save the workbook as Music Download Analysis to your solution file location.

h. Create a 3-D column chart showing the total percentage. Select the Style 27 chart style. Title the chart appropriately using font sizes and colors of your choice.

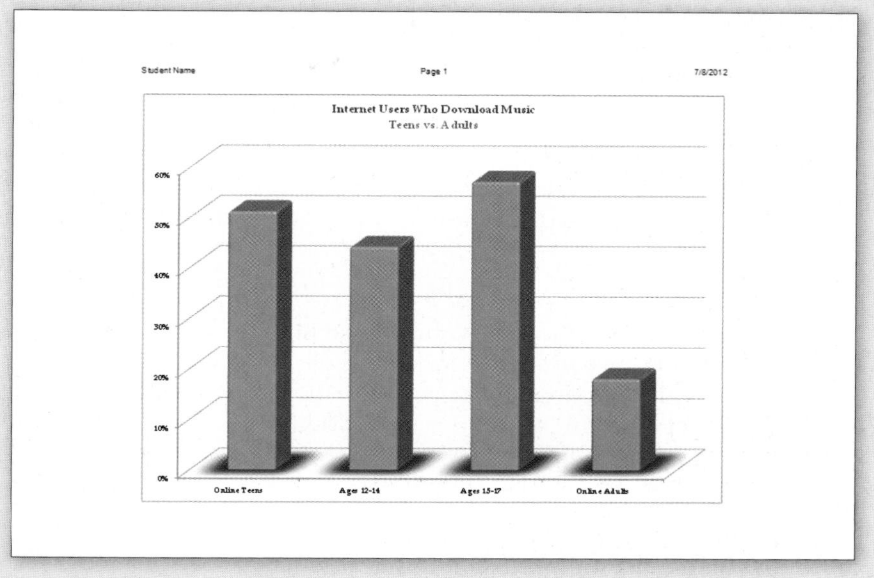

Internet Users Who Download Music
Teens vs. Adults

i. While reviewing the charts, you realize that the Male and Female columns of data were transposed. Correct the data using the table below.

	Male	Female
Online Teens	57	45
Ages 12–14	49	39
Ages 15–17	63	51
Online Adults	20	17

j. Move the chart to a separate chart sheet. Remove the legend.

k. Document the workbook file by adding your name as author.

l. Preview the workbook. Add a predefined header to the worksheet and chart sheet that displays your name, page number, and date. Center the worksheet horizontally on the page. Print the worksheet. Print the chart sheet.

m. Save the workbook again.

LAB EXERCISES

TRACKING ANIMAL ADOPTIONS ★ ★ ★

4. Richard Phillipe volunteers for Animal Angels, a volunteer group that supports the Animal Rescue Agency. He has compiled a worksheet of the number of adoptions in the downtown shelter for the last year. He would like to create a chart that shows how the adoptions differ by month and a chart that shows the total number of adoptions this year. The completed worksheet with charts is shown here. (Your completed solution may be slightly different depending upon the formatting choices you make.)

   a. Open the file ex02_Adoptions.

   b. Insert a clip art image of your choice in the top-left corner of the worksheet. Size and position the image as necessary. If you don't have an image, use ex02_Pets

   .bmp. (Hint: Use [Color] in the Adjust group and choose Set transparent color to change the picture background to transparent.)

   c. Save the workbook as Adoption Tracking to your solution file location.

   d. Chart the monthly data for the three animal categories as a column chart.

   e. Enter the chart title **Adoptions by Month** and the value (Y) axis title **Number of Animals**. Display the legend below the chart.

   f. Position the chart over cells A16 through N35.

   g. Change the chart type to a line chart with markers.

   h. Create a 3-D pie chart of the data in columns A11 through A13 and N11 through N13. Title the chart **Total Adoptions**. Turn off the legend and use the category names and percentages to label the data series.

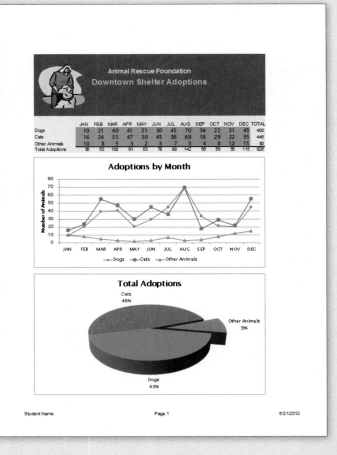

   i. Position the chart over cells A38 through N55. Add color and font refinements to the chart title as you like. Rotate the chart so the Dogs slice is at the front of the chart. Explode the Other Animals slice. Apply a chart style of your choice to the pie chart.

   j. Richard found an error in the data. Change the value of Other Animals in June to **3** and Dogs to **22** in October.

   k. Document the workbook file by adding your name as author.

   l. Save the workbook.

m. Preview the worksheet. Scale the worksheet and charts to fit on one page. Add a predefined footer to the worksheet that displays your name, page number, and date. Center the worksheet horizontally on the page. Print the worksheet.

n. Save the workbook file again.

INTERNET EXPERIENCE ★ ★ ★

5. Wendy Murray teaches a class on Internet technology at a local community college. She has discovered some intriguing research that shows how people use the Internet. She would like to share this information with her students by creating several charts of the data.

The completed worksheet with charts is shown here. (Your completed solution may be slightly different depending upon the formatting choices you make.)

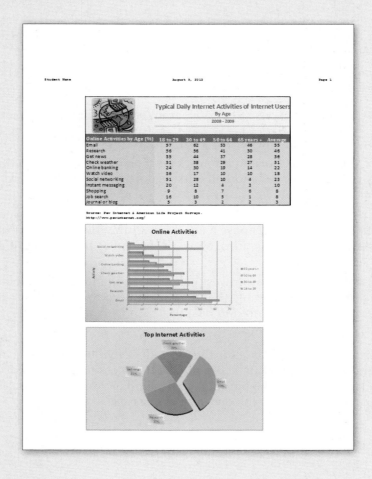

LAB EXERCISES

a. Create a worksheet of the data in the table below.

Online Activities by Age (%)	18 to 29	30 to 49	50 to 64	65 years +
Email	57	62	53	46
Research	56	56	41	30
Get news	35	44	37	28
Check weather	31	38	29	27
Online banking	24	30	19	14
Watch video	36	17	10	10
Social networking	51	28	10	4
Instant messaging	20	12	4	3
Shopping	9	8	7	6
Job search	16	10	5	1
Journal or blog	5	3	2	2

b. Add a column at the right that averages the percentages. Show zero decimal places. Include an appropriate heading for the column.

c. Include a title above the worksheet data. Insert a clip art graphic of your choice to the left of the title. If you do not have an Internet connection, you can use ex02_Online Usage.bmp. (Hint: Use [Color icon] in the Adjust group and choose Set transparent color to change the picture background to transparent.) Apply a picture style of your choice to the graphic.

d. Apply a theme of your choice. Format the worksheet using the cell styles, fill color, and other formatting features you have learned. Add an outside border around the worksheet data. Save the workbook as **Online Activities**.

e. Create a bar chart for the activities by age group (excluding the average data). Increase the size of the chart to show all the data. Choose a chart layout that displays chart titles and axis titles. Include appropriate chart and axis titles. Move the legend to the bottom of the chart. Add a gradient fill to the chart area.

f. Remove the four categories with the lowest percentages from the chart: Instant messaging, Journal or blog, Job search, and Shopping. (Hint: You will need to switch orientation before removing data, and then switch the orientation back.)

g. Display the chart below the worksheet. Size the chart appropriately.

h. Create a pie chart of the average data for the top four activities. Include an appropriate title. Remove the legend and display data labels outside the slices for the category names and values. Format the data labels. Format the pie chart to be similar to the bar chart. Explode a slice of the pie. Rotate the pie to display the exploded slice at the right.

i. Move the chart below the bar chart. Size it appropriately.

j. Add colored borders around both charts.

k. Document the workbook file by adding your name as author.

l. Preview the worksheet. Add a predefined header to the worksheet that displays your name, page number, and date. Center the worksheet horizontally on the page. Scale the worksheet to fit on one page. Print the worksheet.

m. Save the workbook file again.

ON YOUR OWN

JOB MARKET SEMINAR ★

1. Nancy Fernandez is preparing for an upcoming job market seminar she is presenting. She has collected data comparing the mean hourly pay rate for several computer and mathematical jobs in the Midwest and Northeast to the U.S. average rates. Open the workbook ex02_Job Market. Calculate the percent difference between the Midwest states and U.S. average in column E. Calculate the percent difference between the Northeast states and U.S. average in column F. Add appropriate fill and font colors to the worksheet. Add a graphic to the top-left corner of the worksheet. Nancy thinks the information would be much more meaningful and have greater impact if it were presented in a chart. Create an appropriate chart of the average hourly wage for Computer Programmers, Computer Support Specialists, Computer Systems Analysts, and Database Administrators on a separate chart sheet. Include appropriate chart titles. Add a pattern to the data series and change the plot area fill color. Enhance the chart in other ways using different font sizes and font colors. Position the legend at the bottom of the chart. Add a predefined header to the chart sheet that displays your name, page number, and date. Save the workbook as Seminar and print the chart.

GRADE TRACKING ★

2. Create a worksheet that tracks your GPA for at least four semesters or quarters. (If necessary, use fictitious data to attain four grading periods.) Create a chart that best represents your GPA trends. Use the formatting techniques you have learned to change the appearance of the worksheet and the chart. Save the workbook as Grades. Include a header or footer that displays your name and the current date in the worksheet. Print the worksheet with the chart.

LAB EXERCISES

STOCK MARKET WORKBOOK ★ ★

3. You are interested in the stock market. Use Help to learn more about the Stock chart type. Pick five related mutual funds and enter data about their performance over a period of time. Create a stock chart of the data. Save the worksheet with the chart as Mutual Funds. Include a header or footer that displays your name and the current date in the worksheet. Print the worksheet and the chart.

GRADUATE SCHOOL DATA ★ ★ ★

4. Andrew Romine is considering graduate school at Ohio State and has gathered some data to present to his parents to make a case for paying part of his tuition and fees. Open the file ex02_Graduate School, which has two worksheets, one that shows Earnings and the other Payback data if Andrew chooses Ohio State. Using what you learned in the lab, create two charts from the data on the Earnings worksheet. One chart should represent the lifetime earning potential of people based on their level of education and the other should represent median earning by level. Create a pie chart on the Payback worksheet to represent the number of years after graduation that it will take Andrew to earn back what he paid for the higher education. Use the difference in salary as the data labels. Use the features you have learned to enhance the appearance of the worksheets and charts. Include a header on both worksheets that displays your name and the current date. Save the worksheet as Graduate School2. Print the worksheet with the charts.

INSURANCE COMPARISONS ★ ★ ★

5. Roberto Sanchez is thinking about purchasing a new car. However, he is concerned about the insurance rates. Before purchasing, he wants to find out the insurance rates on the cars he is evaluating. Select three different car manufacturers and models. Use the Web and select three different comparable insurance companies to get the insurance premium cost information for different amounts of coverage (minimum required). Use your own personal information as the basis for the insurance quotes. Create a worksheet that contains the cost of minimum coverage, cost of optional coverage, deductibles available, and insurance premium quotes for each vehicle. Create a chart of the data that shows the coverage and premiums. Enhance the chart appropriately. Add pictures of the cars. Include a header or footer that displays your name and the current date in the worksheet. Save the workbook as Insurance. Print the worksheet and chart.

Managing and Analyzing a Workbook Lab 3

Objectives

After completing this lab, you will know how to:

1. Use absolute references.

2. Copy, move, name, and delete sheets.

3. Use AutoFill.

4. Reference multiple sheets.

5. Use Find and Replace.

6. Zoom the worksheet.

7. Split windows and freeze panes.

8. Use what-if analysis and Goal Seek.

9. Create Sparklines

10. Control page breaks.

11. Add custom headers and footers.

12. Print selected sheets and areas.

CASE STUDY

Downtown Internet Café

You presented your new, more-optimistic, first-quarter sales forecast for the Downtown Internet Café to Evan. He was impressed with the charts and the projected increase in sales if an aggressive advertising promotion is launched. However, because the Café's funds are low due to the cost of the recent renovations, he has decided to wait on launching the advertising campaign.

Evan wants you to continue working on the Café forecast using the original, more-conservative projected sales values for the first quarter. In addition, he asks you to include an average calculation and to extend the forecast for the next three quarters.

After discussing the future sales, you agree that the Café will likely make a small profit during the first quarter of operations. Then the Café should show increasing profitability. Evan stresses that the monthly profit margin should reach 20 percent in the second quarter.

As you develop the Café's financial forecast, the worksheet grows in size and complexity. You will learn about features of Office Excel 2010 that help you manage a large workbook efficiently. You also will learn how you can manipulate the data in a worksheet to reach a goal using the what-if analysis capabilities of Excel. The completed annual forecast is shown here.

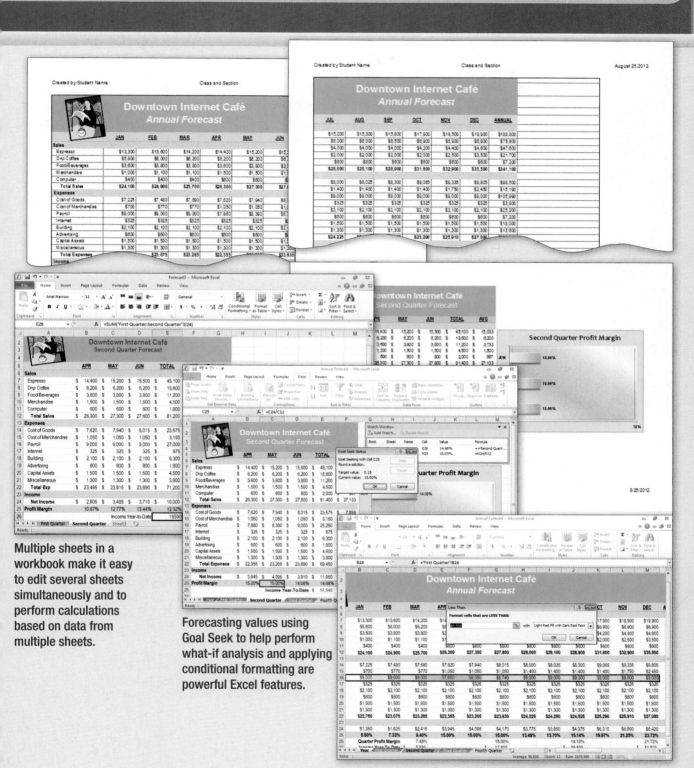

Multiple sheets in a workbook make it easy to edit several sheets simultaneously and to perform calculations based on data from multiple sheets.

Forecasting values using Goal Seek to help perform what-if analysis and applying conditional formatting are powerful Excel features.

Conditional formatting allows you to quickly emphasize worksheet data based on specified conditions.

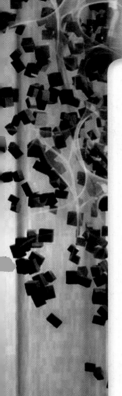

The following concepts will be introduced in this lab:

1 **Absolute Reference** An absolute reference is a cell or range reference in a formula whose location does not change when the formula is copied.

2 **Sheet Name** Each sheet in a workbook can be assigned a descriptive sheet name to help identify the contents of the sheet.

3 **AutoFill** The AutoFill feature makes entering a series of headings easier by logically repeating and extending the series. AutoFill recognizes trends and automatically extends data and alphanumeric headings as far as you specify.

4 **Sheet and 3-D References** Sheet and 3-D references in formulas are used to refer to data from multiple sheets and to calculate new values based on this data.

5 **Find and Replace** The Find and Replace feature helps you quickly find specific information and automatically replace it with new information.

6 **Split Window** The split window feature allows you to divide a worksheet window into sections, making it easier to view different parts of the worksheet at the same time.

7 **Freeze Panes** Freezing panes prevents the data in the pane from scrolling as you move to different areas in a worksheet.

8 **What-If Analysis** What-if analysis is a technique used to evaluate the effects of changing selected factors in a worksheet.

9 **Goal Seek** The Goal Seek tool is used to find the value needed in one cell to attain a result you want in another cell.

10 **Conditional Formatting** Conditional formatting changes the appearance of a range of cells based on a condition that you specify.

Correcting Formulas

After talking with Evan, the owner of the Café, about the first-quarter forecast, you are ready to begin making the changes he suggested. Evan returned the workbook file to you containing several changes he made to the format of the worksheet.

1

- **Start Excel 2010.**

- **Open the workbook** ex03_First Quarter Forecast.

- **If necessary, maximize the application and workbook windows.**

Your screen should be similar to Figure 3.1

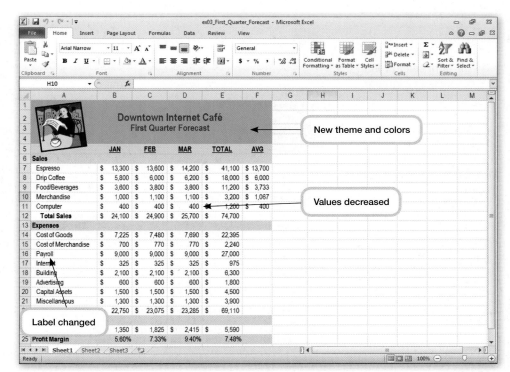

Figure 3.1

As you can see, Evan made several formatting changes to the worksheet. He added a graphic; changed the theme, fill, and text colors; and made several changes to the row headings. For example, the Pay heading has been changed to Payroll. Evan also decided to decrease the computer sales values to $400 for February and March.

IDENTIFYING FORMULA ERRORS

Now you are ready to enter the average formula for the expense values. To do this, you will copy the function down column F.

1

● Copy the function from cell F11 into cells F12 through F24.

● Move to cell F13.

Your screen should be similar to Figure 3.2

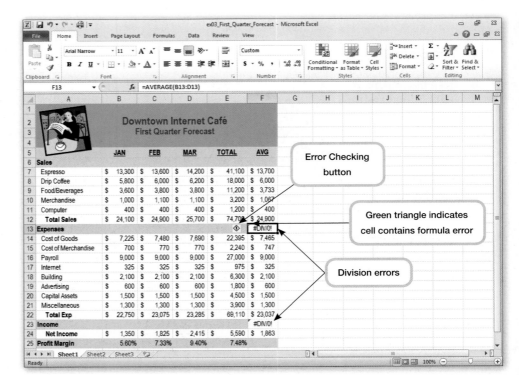

Figure 3.2

The average value has been correctly calculated for each row. Notice, however, that two cells display the error value #DIV/0!, indicating the cells contain a formula error. When a formula cannot properly calculate a result, an error value is displayed and a green triangle appears in the upper-left corner of the cell. In addition, the ⟨!⟩ Error Checking button appears when you select a cell containing an error.

Each type of error value has a different cause, as described in the following table.

Error Value	Cause
#####	Column not wide enough to display result, or negative date or time is used
#VALUE!	Wrong type of argument or operand is used
#DIV/0!	Number is divided by zero
#NAME?	Text in formula not recognized
#N/A	Value not available
#REF!	Cell reference is not valid
#NUM!	Invalid number values
#NULL!	Intersection operator is not valid

Having Trouble?

If you don't see the green triangle or the ⟨!⟩ Error Checking button when you click on a cell with a formula error, you may need to turn on background error checking. To do this, open the File tab, click [⬚ Options], choose Formulas, and choose Enable background error checking.

Excel 2010 includes several tools to help you find and correct errors in formula entries. These tools provide the capability to display the relationships between formulas and cells and to identify and suggest corrections to potential problems in formulas.

To correct this problem, you need to find out the cause of the error. Pointing to the ⟨!⟩ Error Checking button displays a ScreenTip identifying the cause of the error. Clicking the ⟨!⟩ Error Checking button displays a list of options for error checking the worksheet. In this case, the formula is attempting to divide by zero or empty cells.

2

- Point to Error Checking to see the ScreenTip.

- Click Error Checking.

- Choose Edit in Formula Bar.

Your screen should be similar to Figure 3.3

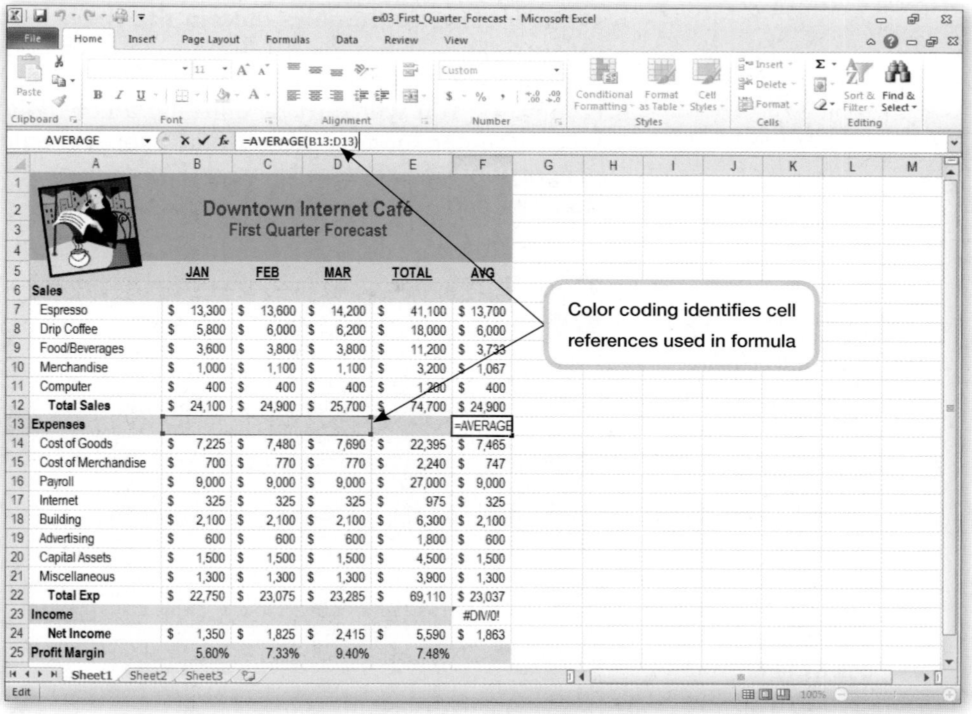

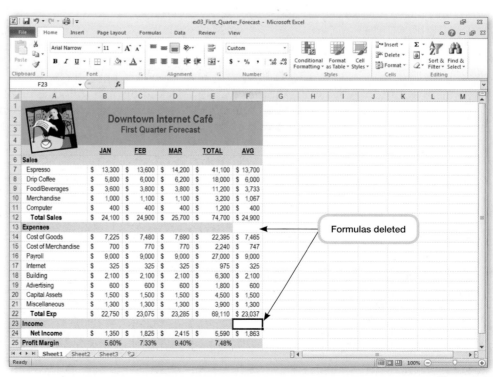

Figure 3.3

In Edit mode, the formula references are color coded to the referenced worksheet cells and you can now easily see the error is caused by references to blank cells when the function was copied.

Since you do not need this formula, you will delete it. Likewise, you need to delete the function that was copied into cell F23. You will clear the entry in this cell using the fill handle.

3

- Press Esc to exit Edit mode.

- Press Delete.

- Move to cell F23.

- Point to the fill handle and when the mouse pointer changes to +, drag upward until the cell is gray.

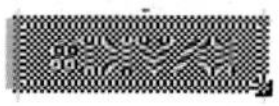

Your screen should be similar to Figure 3.4

Figure 3.4

While looking at the sales data in the worksheet, you decide it may be interesting to know what contribution each sales item makes to total sales. To find out, you will enter a formula to calculate the proportion of sales by each in column G. You will start by entering a new column heading in cell G5. Then you will enter the formula = Total Espresso Sales/Total Sales to calculate the proportion for Espresso sales in G7 and copy it to G8 to calculate the proportion for Drip Coffee sales.

4

- **Enter the heading Proportion in cell G5.**

- **Enter the formula =E7/E12 in cell G7.**

- **Drag the fill handle to copy the formula in cell G7 to G8.**

Your screen should be similar to Figure 3.5

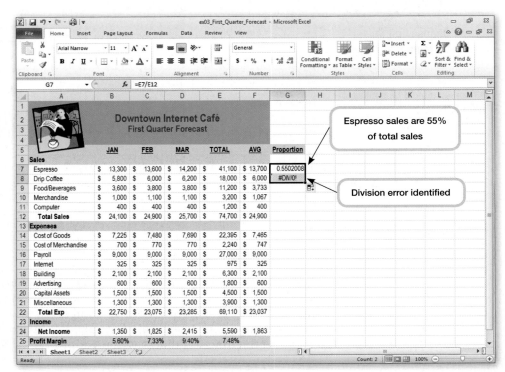

Figure 3.5

The value 0.5502008 is correctly displayed in cell G7. This shows that the Espresso sales are approximately 55 percent of Total Sales. However, a division by zero error has occurred in cell G8.

Another way to check a formula to locate errors or to confirm that the correct cell references are being used is to use the features in the Formula Auditing group of the Formulas tab.

5

● Move to G8.

● Open the Formulas
  tab.

● Open the

  menu in the Formula
  Auditing group and
  choose Trace Error.

Your screen should be similar to
Figure 3.6

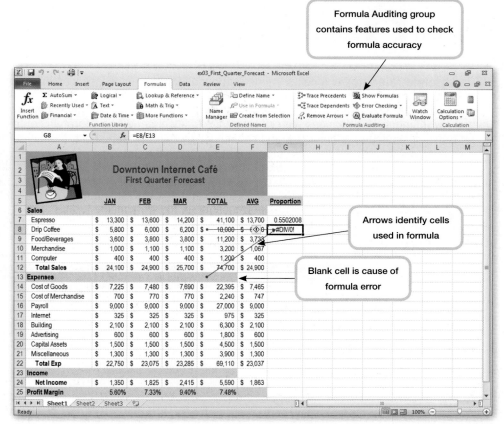

Figure 3.6

Additional Information

You also can use

⊞⊐ Trace Precedents | or

⊏⊐ Trace Dependents | to show

relationships between formulas and
cells.

Excel displays arrows from each cell that affects the value in the current cell.
You can now see the error occurred because the relative reference to cell E12
adjusted correctly to the new location when the formula was copied and now
references cell E13, a blank cell.

USING ABSOLUTE REFERENCES

The formula in G7 needs to be entered so that the reference to the Total Sales
value in cell E12 does not change when the formula is copied. To do this, you
need to make the cell reference absolute.

Concept Absolute Reference

An **absolute reference** is a cell or range reference in a formula whose location does not change when the formula is copied.

To stop the relative adjustment of cell references, enter a $ (dollar sign) character before the column letter and row number. This changes the cell reference to absolute. When a formula containing an absolute cell reference is copied to another row and column location in the worksheet, the cell reference does not change. It is an exact duplicate of the cell reference in the original formula.

A cell reference also can be a **mixed reference**. In this type of reference, either the column letter or the row number is preceded with the $. This makes only the row or column absolute. When a formula containing a mixed cell reference is copied to another location in the worksheet, only the part of the cell reference that is not absolute changes relative to its new location in the worksheet.

The table below shows examples of relative and absolute references and the results when a reference in cell G8 to cell E8 is copied to cell H9.

Cell Contents of G8	Copied to Cell H9	Type of Reference
E8	E8	Absolute reference
E$8	F$8	Mixed reference
$E8	$E9	Mixed reference
E8	F9	Relative reference

You will change the formula in cell G7 to include an absolute reference for cell E12. Then you will copy the formula to cells G8 through G10.

You can change a cell reference to absolute or mixed by typing in the dollar sign directly or by using the ABS (Absolute) key, F4. To use the ABS key, the program must be in Edit mode and the cell reference that you want to change must be selected. If you continue to press F4, the cell reference will cycle through all possible combinations of cell reference types.

1

● Click  **Remove Arrows** in the Formula Auditing group to remove the trace arrows.

● Move to G7.

● Click on the reference to E12 in the formula bar to enter Edit mode and select the reference.

● Press F4 four times to cycle through all reference types.

● Press F4 again to display an absolute reference.

Your screen should be similar to Figure 3.7

Figure 3.7

The cell reference now displays $ characters before the column letter and row number, making this cell reference absolute. Leaving the cell reference absolute, as it is now, will stop the relative adjustment of the cell reference when you copy it again.

2

● Click ✔ Enter or press ←Enter.

● Copy the revised formula to cells G8 through G11.

● Move to G8 and click  **Trace Precedents** in the Formula Auditing group.

Your screen should be similar to Figure 3.8

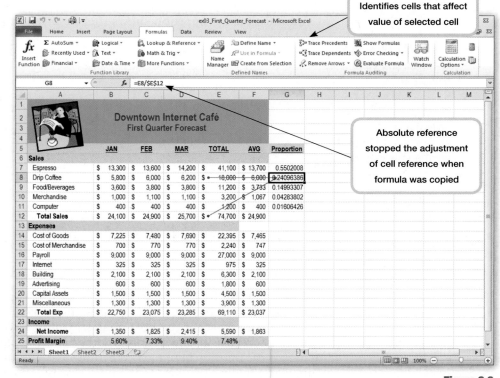

Figure 3.8

The trace arrows show that when the formula was copied it correctly adjusted the relative cell reference to Drip Coffee sales in cell E8 and did not adjust the reference to E12 because it is an absolute reference.

The last change you need to make to the proportion data is to format it to the Percent style.

③

- Click **Remove Arrows** in the Formula Auditing group.

- Select G7 through G11.

- Open the Home tab.

- Click **%** Percent Style in the Number group.

- Click **Increase Decimal** (twice).

- Extend the fill in the title area to column G.

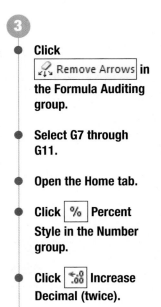

Figure 3.9

Having Trouble?
Use Format Painter to copy the fill colors.

- Extend the fill in rows 6, 13, 23, and 25 to column G.

- Move to cell A6 and save the workbook as Forecast3 to your solution file location.

Your screen should be similar to Figure 3.9

The calculated proportion shows the same values that a pie chart of this data would show.

Creating a Second-Quarter Worksheet

Next, you want to add the second-quarter forecast to the workbook. You want this data in a separate sheet in the same workbook file. To make it easier to enter the forecast for the next quarter, you will copy the contents of the first-quarter forecast in Sheet1 into another sheet in the workbook. Then you will change the month headings, the title, and the number data for the second quarter. Finally, you want to include a formula to calculate a year-to-date total for the six months.

COPYING BETWEEN WORKSHEETS

You want to copy the worksheet data from Sheet1 to Sheet2. Copying between sheets is the same as copying within a sheet, except that you switch to the new sheet to specify the destination.

1

- Select the worksheet range A1 through G25.

Having Trouble?

A quick way to select this range is to move to cell A1, hold down (Shift), and click on cell G25.

- Click 📋 Copy.

- Click on the Sheet2 tab.

- Click 📋 Paste.

Your screen should be similar to Figure 3.10

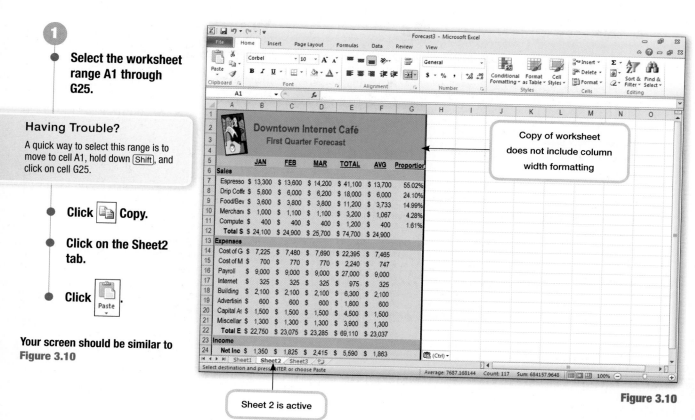

Copy of worksheet does not include column width formatting

Sheet 2 is active

Figure 3.10

All the worksheet data, graphic objects, and formatting, except for the column width, were copied into the existing Sheet2. You can change the column width settings by specifying that this feature be copied from the source. Notice that although the graphic was copied, it needs to be resized.

2

- Open the  menu and choose Paste Special.

- Choose Column Widths.

- Click [OK].

- Appropriately size and position the graphic.

- Click outside the graphic to clear the selection.

Your screen should be similar to Figure 3.11

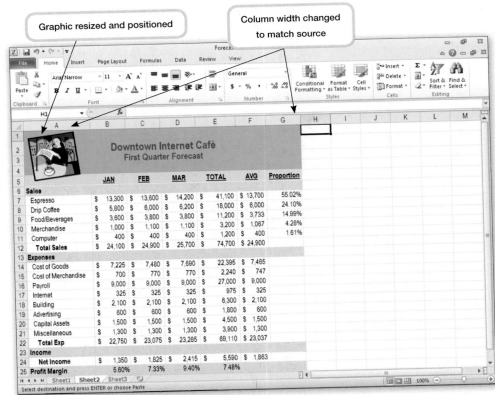

Graphic resized and positioned

Column width changed to match source

Figure 3.11

Another Method

You also can use [Format ▾]
Move or Copy Sheet in the Cells group or hold down Ctrl while dragging the active sheet tab to copy an entire sheet. All formatting, including column widths, is copied into the destination sheet.

The column widths from the copied selection are pasted into the new sheet. Sheet2 now contains a duplicate of the first-quarter forecast in Sheet1.

RENAMING SHEETS AND COLORING SHEET TABS

As more sheets are added to a workbook, remembering what information is in each sheet becomes more difficult. To help clarify the contents of the sheets, you can rename the sheets.

Concept Sheet Name

Each sheet in a workbook can be assigned a descriptive **sheet name** to help identify the contents of the sheet. The following guidelines should be followed when naming a sheet. A sheet name

- Can be up to 31 characters.
- Can be entered in uppercase or lowercase letters or a combination (it will appear as entered).
- Can contain any combination of letters, numbers, and spaces.
- Cannot contain the characters : ? * / \.
- Cannot be enclosed in square brackets [ ].

Double-clicking the sheet tab makes the sheet active and highlights the existing sheet name in the tab. The existing name is cleared as soon as you begin to type the new name. You will change the name of Sheet1 to First Quarter and Sheet2 to Second Quarter.

1

- Double-click the Sheet1 tab.

- Type **First Quarter**

- Press [←Enter].

- Change the name of the Sheet2 tab to **Second Quarter**

Another Method

You also can use 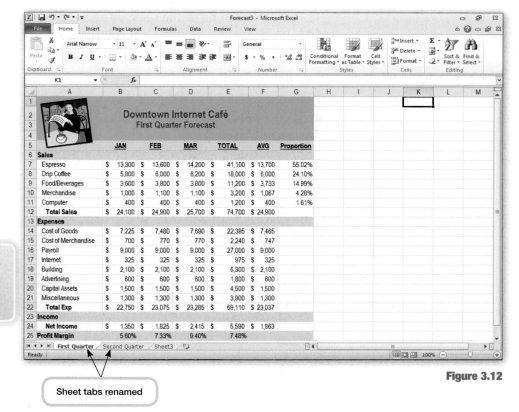 Format ▾ Rename Sheet in the Cells group of the Home tab.

Your screen should be similar to Figure 3.12

Sheet tabs renamed

Figure 3.12

To further differentiate the sheets, you can add color to the sheet tabs.

2

- Right-click on the First Quarter tab.

- Select Tab Color from the shortcut menu.

- Choose the Turquoise, Accent 4 theme color from the color palette.

- In the same manner, change the color of the Second Quarter sheet tab to the Pink, Accent 2 theme color.

Your screen should be similar to Figure 3.13

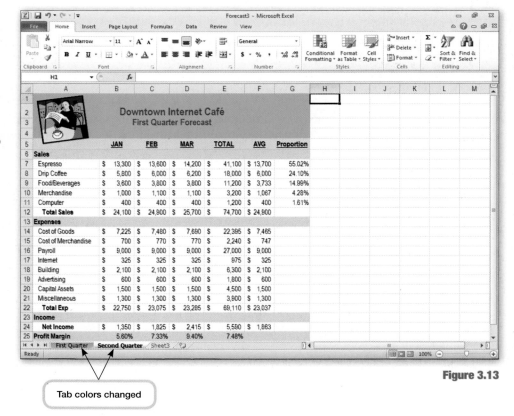

Tab colors changed

Figure 3.13

The sheet tab name of the selected sheet is underlined in the tab color of pink and the First Quarter sheet tab is turquoise. When a sheet is not selected, the sheet tab is displayed with the background color.

FILLING A SERIES

Now you can change the worksheet title and data in the Second Quarter sheet. First you will change the worksheet title to identify the worksheet contents as the second-quarter forecast. Then you will change the month headings to the three months that make up the second quarter: April, May, and June.

1

● Change the title in cell B3 to **Second Quarter Forecast**

● Change the month heading in cell B5 to **APR.**

Your screen should be similar to Figure 3.14

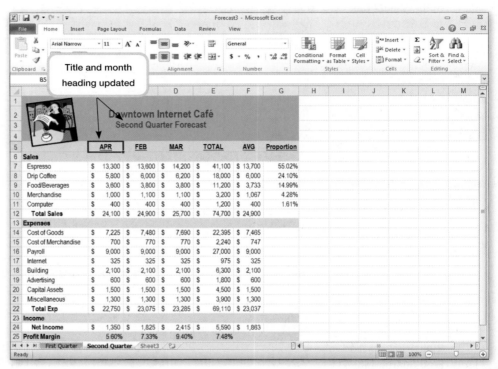

Figure 3.14

Now you need to change the remaining month headings to MAY and JUN. You will use the AutoFill feature to enter the month headings.

Concept 3 AutoFill

The **AutoFill** feature makes entering a series of numbers, numbers and text combinations, dates, or time periods easier by logically repeating and extending the series. AutoFill recognizes trends and automatically extends data and alphanumeric headings as far as you specify.

Dragging the fill handle activates the AutoFill feature if Excel recognizes the entry in the cell as an entry that can be incremented. When AutoFill extends the entries, it uses the same style as the original entry. For example, if you enter the heading for July as JUL (abbreviated with all letters uppercase), all the extended entries in the series will be abbreviated and uppercase. Dragging down or right increments in increasing order, and up or left increments in decreasing order. A linear series increases or decreases values by a constant value, and a growth series multiplies values by a constant factor. Examples of how AutoFill extends a series are shown in the table below.

Initial Selection	Extended Series
Qtr1	Qtr2, Qtr3, Qtr4
Mon	Tue, Wed, Thu
Jan, Apr	Jul, Oct, Jan

A starting value of a series may contain more than one item that can be incremented, such as JAN-02, in which both the month and year can increment. You can specify which value to increment by selecting the appropriate option from the AutoFill Options menu.

The entry in cell B5, APR, is the starting value of a series of months. You will drag the fill handle to the right to increment the months. The mouse pointer displays the entry that will appear in each cell as you drag.

2

- Drag the fill handle of cell B5 to extend the range from cell B5 through cell D5.

- Save the workbook.

Your screen should be similar to Figure 3.15

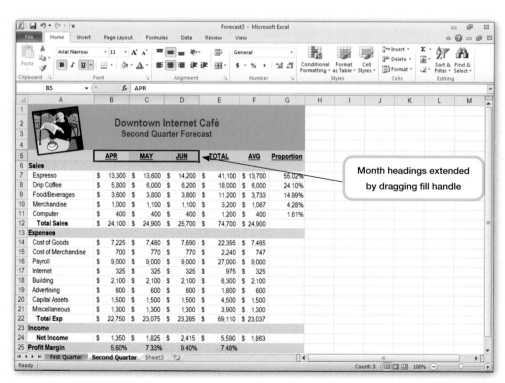

Figure 3.15

Additional Information

If you do not want a series created when you drag the fill handle, hold down Ctrl as you drag and the entries will be copied, not incremented. Alternatively, you can choose Copy Cells from the AutoFill Options menu.

The month headings now correctly reflect the three months for the second quarter. This is because the entry in cell B5 was a month that was recognized as an entry that can be incremented. Additionally, the months appear in uppercase characters, the same as the starting month. This is because AutoFill copies formatting when extending the series.

USING A 3-D REFERENCE

Finally, you need to update the forecast to reflect the April through June sales. You anticipate that sales will increase in all areas, except food and beverage sales, which will remain the same. Then you will enter a formula to calculate the year-to-date income total using data from both sheets.

1. **Enter the following values in the specified cells.**

Sales	Cell	Number
Espresso	B7	14400
	C7	15200
	D7	15500
Drip Coffee	B8	6200
	C8	6200
	D8	6200
Merchandise	B10	1500
	C10	1500
	D10	1500
Computer	B11	600
	C11	600
	D11	600

Your screen should be similar to Figure 3.16

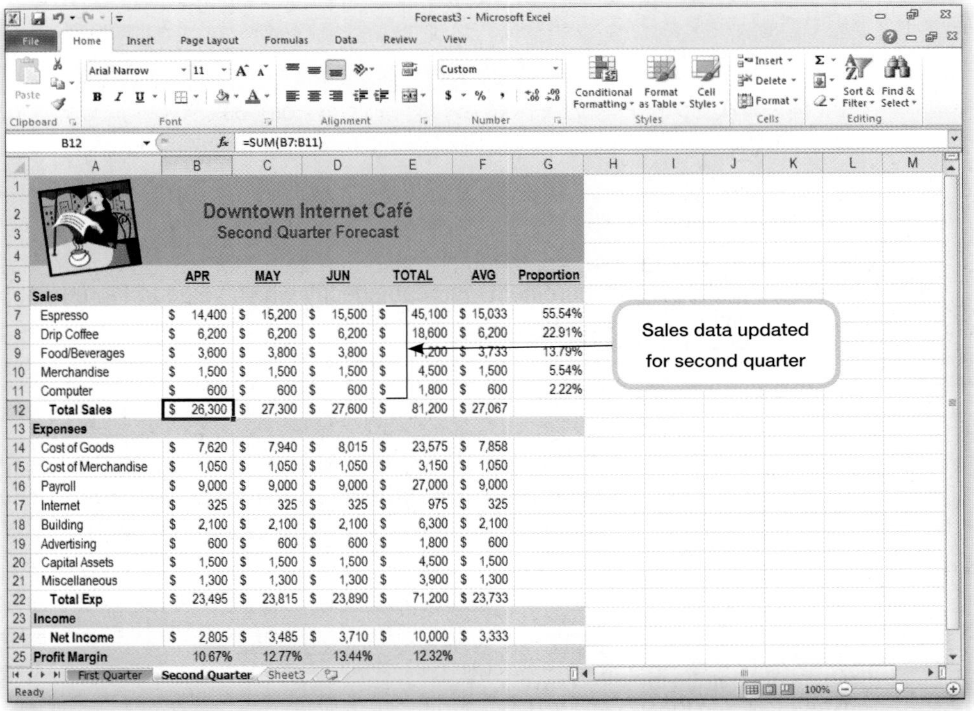

Figure 3.16

The worksheet now contains the data for the second quarter and all dependent formulas have been recalculated.

Now you can enter the formula to calculate a year-to-date income total. The formula to make this calculation will sum the total income numbers from cell E24 in the First Quarter sheet and cell E24 in the Second Quarter sheet. To reference data in another sheet in the same workbook, you enter a formula that references cells in other worksheets.

Concept 4 Sheet and 3-D References

Sheet and 3-D references in formulas are used to refer to data from multiple sheets and to calculate new values based on this data. A **sheet reference** in a formula consists of the name of the sheet, followed by an exclamation point and the cell or range reference. If the sheet name contains nonalphabetic characters, such as a space, the sheet name (or path) must be enclosed in single quotation marks.

If you want to use the same cell or range of cells on multiple sheets, you can use a **3-D reference**. A 3-D reference consists of the names of the beginning and ending sheets enclosed in quotes and separated by a colon. This is followed by an exclamation point and the cell or range reference. The cell or range reference is the same on each sheet in the specified sheet range. If a sheet is inserted or deleted, the range is automatically updated. 3-D references make it easy to analyze data in the same cell or range of cells on multiple worksheets.

Reference	Description
=Sheet2!B17	Displays the entry in cell B17 of Sheet2 in the active cell of the current sheet
=Sheet1!A1 + Sheet2!B2.	Sums the values in cell A1 of Sheet1 and B2 of Sheet2
=SUM(Sheet1:Sheet4!H6:K6)	Sums the values in cells H6 through K6 in Sheets 1, 2, 3, and 4
=SUM(Sheet1!H6:K6)	Sums the values in cells H6 through K6 in Sheet1
=SUM(Sheet1:Sheet4!H6)	Sums the values in cell H6 of Sheets 1, 2, 3, and 4

Just like a formula that references cells within a sheet, a formula that references cells in multiple sheets is automatically recalculated when data in a referenced cell changes.

You will enter a descriptive text entry in cell D26 and then use a 3-D reference in a SUM function to calculate the year-to-date total in cell E26.

The SUM function argument will consist of a 3-D reference to cell E24 in the First and Second Quarter sheets. Although a 3-D reference can be entered by typing it using the proper syntax, it is much easier to enter it by pointing to the cells on the sheets. To enter a 3-D reference, select the cell or range in the beginning sheet and then hold down ⇧Shift and click on the sheet tab of the last sheet in the range. This will include the indicated cell range on all sheets between and including the first and last sheets specified.

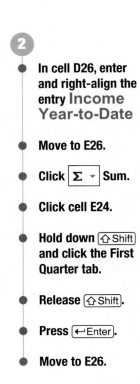

2

- In cell D26, enter and right-align the entry Income Year-to-Date

- Move to E26.

- Click Σ ▾ Sum.

- Click cell E24.

- Hold down ⇧Shift and click the First Quarter tab.

- Release ⇧Shift.

- Press ←Enter.

- Move to E26.

Your screen should be similar to Figure 3.17

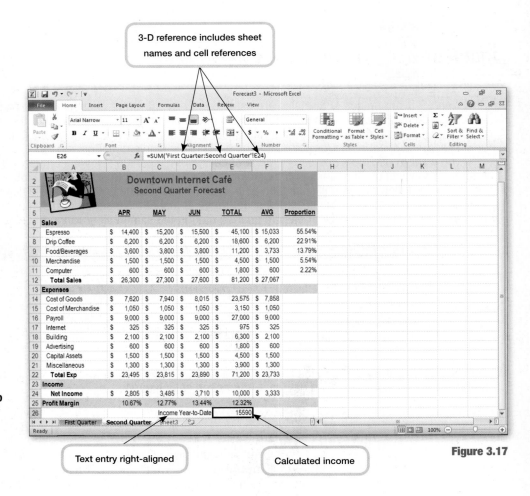

3-D reference includes sheet names and cell references

Text entry right-aligned

Calculated income

Figure 3.17

The calculated number 15,590 appears in cell E26, and the function containing a 3-D reference appears in the formula bar.

HIDING GRIDLINES AND HEADINGS

Just as you completed the forecast for the first half of the year, Evan, the Café owner, stopped in and you decide to show him the forecast. To simplify the screen display while showing Evan the worksheet, you will hide the gridlines and column and row headings.

1

- Move to cell A1 and open the View tab.

- Choose ☑ Gridlines from the Show group to clear the selection.

- Choose ☑ Headings from the Show group to clear the selection.

Your screen should be similar to Figure 3.18

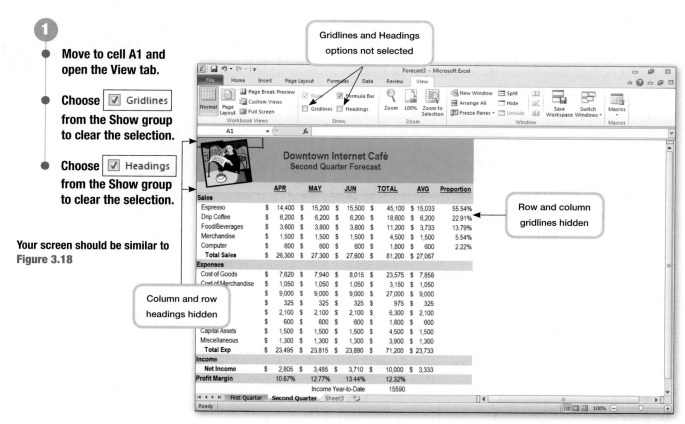

Gridlines and Headings options not selected

Row and column gridlines hidden

Column and row headings hidden

Figure 3.18

While these features are off, you will format the year-to-date income value to Accounting with zero decimal places. Rather than opening the Home tab to access these features, you will copy the format from another cell. The Paste Special menu option, Formatting, will do this quickly for you.

2

- Select any cell that is formatted in the Accounting format and choose Copy from the context menu.

- Right-click on cell E26 and choose %_ Formatting from the Paste Options section of the context menu.

Your screen should be similar to Figure 3.19

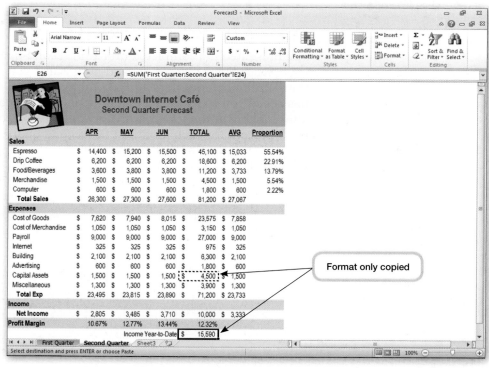

Format only copied

Figure 3.19

Creating a Second-Quarter Worksheet   **EX3.21**

Hiding gridlines and headers is convenient for presenting the worksheet to others; however, it is not as easy to work in the sheet with these features off. You will turn them back on, add file documentation, and then print a copy of the workbook for Evan.

3

- Choose [Gridlines] from the Show group to select it.

- Choose [Headings] from the Show group to select it.

- Enter the following information in the workbook file properties:

  Author   your name

  Title   Downtown Internet Cafe

  Subject   First and second quarter forecasts

Having Trouble?
Click Show All Properties to display the Subject box.

- Change the Print setting to print the entire workbook.

- Preview both worksheets.

- Add a predefined header containing your name, page number, and the date to both worksheets.

- Print the workbook.

- Move to cell A6 in both worksheets and save the workbook.

- Close the workbook.

DELETING AND MOVING WORKSHEETS

You presented the completed first- and second-quarter forecasts to Evan. He is very pleased with the results and now wants you to create worksheets for the third and fourth quarters and a combined annual forecast. Additionally, Evan has asked you to include a column chart of the data for each quarter. Finally, after looking at the forecast, Evan wants the forecast to show a profit margin of 15 percent for each month in the second quarter.

You have already made several of the changes requested and saved them as a workbook file. You will open this file to see the revised and expanded forecast.

1

● Open the workbook
file ex03_Annual
Forecast.

Your screen should be similar to
Figure 3.20

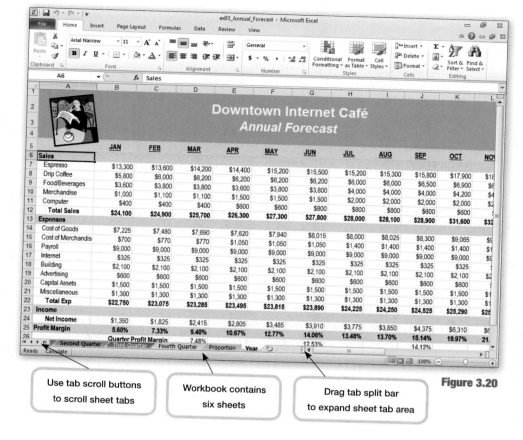

Use tab scroll buttons
to scroll sheet tabs

Workbook contains
six sheets

Drag tab split bar
to expand sheet tab area

Figure 3.20

The workbook file now contains six sheets: First Quarter, Second Quarter,
Third Quarter, Fourth Quarter, Proportion, and Year. The Proportion sheet
contains the proportion of sales values from the first and second quarters. The
Year sheet contains the forecast data for the entire 12 months. Each quarter
sheet also includes a chart of the profit margin for that quarter.

Notice also that the First Quarter sheet tab is not entirely visible. This is
because there is not enough space in the sheet tab area to display all the tabs.
To see the tabs, you can drag the tab split bar located at the right edge of the
sheet tab area to expand the area or use the sheet tab scroll buttons to scroll
the tabs into view.

- Click on each of the Quarter sheet tabs to view the quarterly data and profit margin chart.

- Display the Proportion sheet.

Your screen should be similar to Figure 3.21

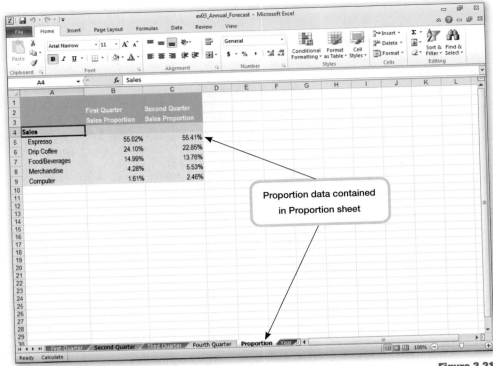

Figure 3.21

You decide this data, although interesting, is not needed in the forecast workbook and want to delete the entire sheet.

- In the Cells group of the Home tab, open the Delete ▾ menu and choose Delete Sheet.

- Click Delete to confirm that you want to permanently remove the sheet.

Another Method

You also can choose Delete from the sheet tab's shortcut menu to delete a sheet.

Your screen should be similar to Figure 3.22

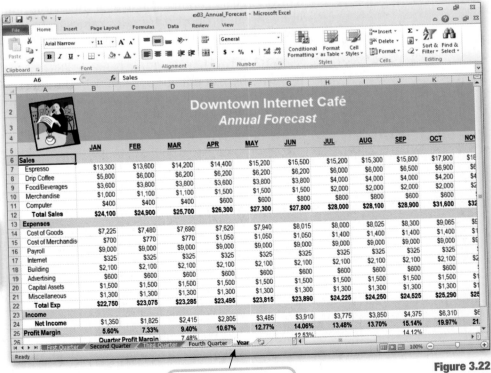

Figure 3.22

Proportion sheet deleted

The entire sheet is deleted, and the Year sheet is now the active sheet. Next you want to move the Year sheet from the last position in the workbook to the first. You can quickly rearrange the order of sheets in a workbook by dragging the selected sheet tab along the row of sheet tabs to the new location.

4

Drag the Year tab to the left of the First Quarter tab.

Additional Information

The mouse pointer appears as and the symbol ▾ indicates the location where the sheet will be moved.

Another Method

You also can use Move or Copy from the sheet tab's shortcut menu to move a sheet to another location in the workbook.

Your screen should be similar to Figure 3.23

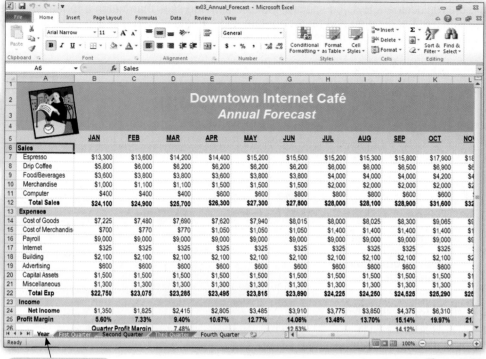

Sheet moved by dragging sheet tab

Figure 3.23

The Year sheet is now the first sheet in the workbook.

Finding and Replacing Information

As you look over the worksheets, you notice that the only abbreviation used in the entire workbook is for expenses in the Total Exp row heading. You want to change it to "Expenses" in all worksheets in the workbook.

You could change the word in each sheet by changing the text directly on the worksheet cells. However, the larger your workbook becomes, the more difficult it will be to find the data you want to modify. Therefore, you will use the Find and Replace feature to quickly locate the word and make the change.

Concept Find and Replace

The **Find and Replace** feature helps you quickly find specific information and automatically replace it with new information. The Find command locates all occurrences of the text or numbers you specify. The Replace command is used with the Find command to locate the specified entries and replace the located occurrences with the replacement text you specify. You also can find cells that match a format you specify and replace the format with another. Finding and replacing data and formats is both fast and accurate, but you need to be careful when replacing that you do not replace unintended matches.

FINDING INFORMATION

First, you will locate and correct the abbreviation using the Find command. This command can be used to locate data in any type of worksheet.

1

- **Click**  **in the Editing group and choose Find.**

- **If necessary, click** Options >> **to display the additional search options.**

> **Another Method**
>
> The keyboard shortcut is Ctrl + F.

Your screen should be similar to Figure 3.24

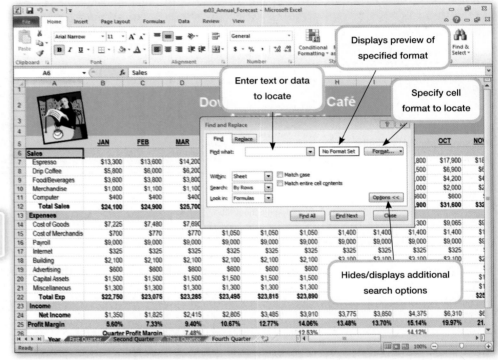

Figure 3.24

In the Find and Replace dialog box, you enter the information you want to locate in the Find what text box. It must be entered exactly as it appears in the worksheet. The additional options in the dialog box can be combined in many ways to help locate information. They are described in the table below.

Option	Effect
Within	Searches the active worksheet or workbook.
Search	Specifies the direction to search in the worksheet: By Columns searches down through columns and By Rows searches to the right across rows.
Look in	Looks for a match in the specified worksheet element: formulas, values, comments.
Match case	Finds words that have the same pattern of uppercase letters as entered in the Find what text box. Using this option makes the search case sensitive.
Match entire cell contents	Looks for an exact and complete match of the characters specified in the Find what text box.
Format	Used to specify a cell format to locate and replace. A sample of the selected format is displayed in the preview box.

You will enter the text to find, exp, and will search using the default options.

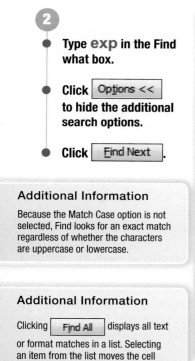

Type exp in the Find what box.

Click Options << **to hide the additional search options.**

Click Find Next **.**

Additional Information

Because the Match Case option is not selected, Find looks for an exact match regardless of whether the characters are uppercase or lowercase.

Additional Information

Clicking Find All displays all text or format matches in a list. Selecting an item from the list moves the cell selector to the cell containing the entry.

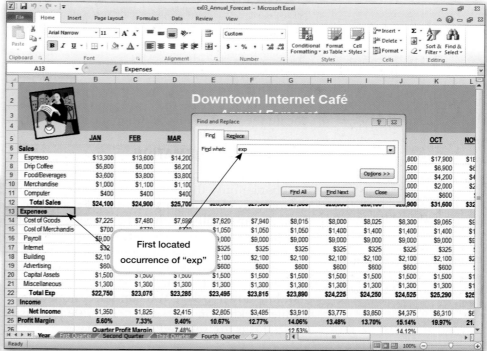

Figure 3.25

Your screen should be similar to Figure 3.25

The cell selector jumps to the first occurrence of "exp," in cell A13, which contains the word "Expenses." It located this word because the first three letters match. However, this is not the entry you are trying to locate. You will continue the search to locate the next occurrence. Then you will edit the cell to display the word "Expenses."

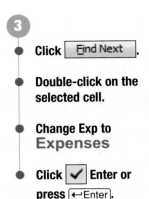

3

- Click **Find Next**.

- Double-click on the selected cell.

- Change Exp to **Expenses**

- Click ✔ **Enter** or press ←Enter.

Your screen should be similar to Figure 3.26

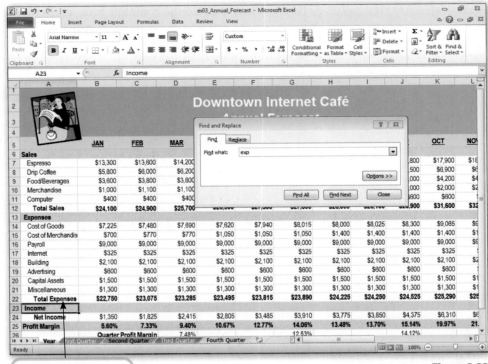

Located text changed

Figure 3.26

You manually made the correction to the label in cell A22. Next, you want to locate the word in all the other sheets and correct the entries.

REPLACING INFORMATION

You realize that "exp" will be located twice in every worksheet. Since you want to change only the Total Exp headings, you will refine your search term to locate only this heading and use the Replace command to make the correction automatically on the other sheets. The replacement text must be entered exactly as you want it to appear.

First, you will select all four quarter sheets as a group so that any changes you make are made to all selected sheets. To select two or more adjacent sheets, click on the tab for the first sheet and click on the last sheet tab while holding down ⇧Shift. You can select nonadjacent sheets by holding down Ctrl while clicking on each sheet. The title bar displays "[Group]" whenever multiple sheets are selected.

Additional Information

You can select all sheets using Select All Sheets from the sheet tab shortcut menu.

Additional Information

The tabs of all sheets appear with a white top, indicating they are selected; the active sheet tab name is bold.

Click on the First Quarter sheet tab, hold down ⇧Shift**, and click on the Fourth Quarter tab.**

Change the entry in the Find What box to total exp

Open the Replace tab.

Type Total Expenses **in the Replace with box.**

Click Find Next .

Click Replace All .

Your screen should be similar to Figure 3.27

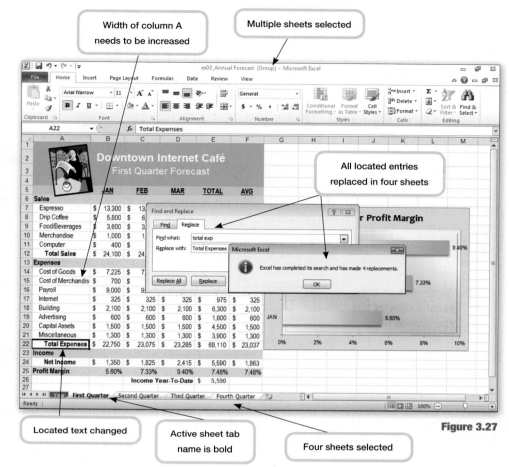

Width of column A needs to be increased

Multiple sheets selected

All located entries replaced in four sheets

Located text changed

Active sheet tab name is bold

Four sheets selected

Figure 3.27

Another Method

You also can use Find & Select ▾/Replace; the keyboard shortcut is Ctrl + H.

Four replacements were made, indicating that the heading was corrected on all four sheets. It is much faster to use Replace All than to confirm each match separately. However, exercise care when using Replace All because the search text you specify might be part of another word and you may accidentally replace text you want to keep.

Now, you also notice that the labels in column A are not fully displayed, so you need to increase the column width. You will expand the group selection to include the Year sheet and adjust the width of column A on all worksheets at the same time.

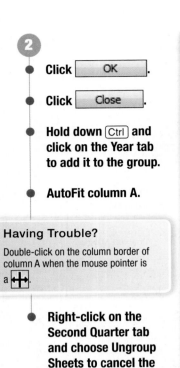

2

- Click **OK**.

- Click **Close**.

- Hold down Ctrl and click on the Year tab to add it to the group.

- AutoFit column A.

Having Trouble?

Double-click on the column border of column A when the mouse pointer is a ↔.

- Right-click on the Second Quarter tab and choose Ungroup Sheets to cancel the group selection and make it the active sheet.

Another Method

You also can click on any unselected sheet tab to cancel a group selection.

Your screen should be similar to Figure 3.28

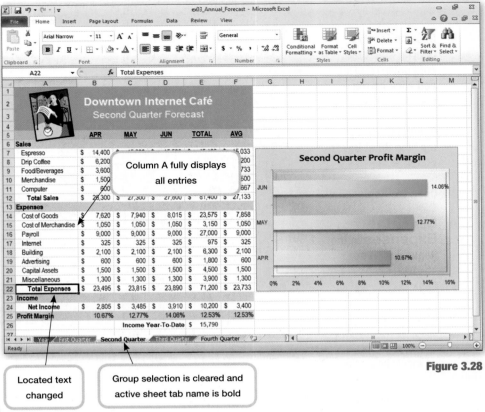

Figure 3.28

Located text changed

Group selection is cleared and active sheet tab name is bold

You can now see that the width of column A has been adjusted and that the Total Exp label has been replaced with Total Expenses, as it has in all other sheets. When multiple sheets are selected, be careful when making changes, as all selected sheets are affected.

Saving to a New Folder

You have made several changes to the workbook, and before continuing, you want to save it. Since the workbook is for projected forecasts, you decide to save it in a separate folder from the rest of the Café's financial workbooks. You will save the file to a new folder named Forecasts.

1

● Display the Year sheet.

● Open the File tab and choose Save As.

● If necessary, change the location to where you save your files.

● Enter **Annual Forecast** as the file name.

● Click | New folder | in the Save As dialog box.

Your screen should be similar to Figure 3.29

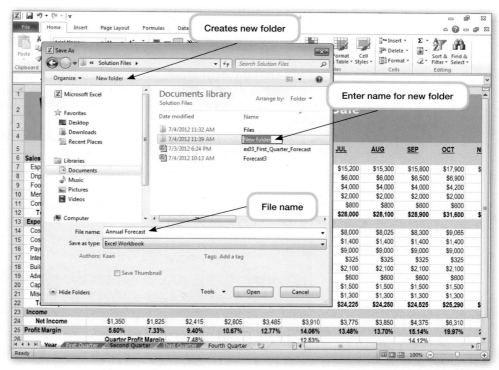

Figure 3.29

Having Trouble?

Your Save As dialog box may look slightly different depending upon the version of Windows you are using.

The file list displays a new folder with the default folder name, New Folder. You need to replace the default folder name with a descriptive folder name. Then you will open the new folder and save the file in it.

Additional Information

You also can rename an existing folder from the Save As dialog box by choosing Rename from the folder's shortcut menu and entering the new name.

2

● Type **Café Forecasts** in place of New Folder.

● Press ← Enter to complete the folder name.

● Double-click on the Café Forecasts folder to open it.

● Click | Save |.

Additional Information

If you are running short on lab time, this is an appropriate place to end this session and begin again at a later time.

The Annual Forecast workbook is saved in the new Café Forecasts folder.

Now that the Year worksheet is much larger, you are finding that it takes a lot of time to scroll to different areas within the worksheet. To make managing large worksheets easier, you can zoom a worksheet, split the workbook window, and freeze panes.

The Year worksheet includes all of the quarterly data. The entire worksheet, however, is not visible in the window.

1

● **Reduce the zoom percentage to 80%.**

● **Move to B7.**

Another Method

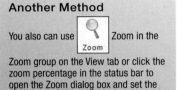

You also can use [Zoom] Zoom in the Zoom group on the View tab or click the zoom percentage in the status bar to open the Zoom dialog box and set the magnification.

Your screen should be similar to Figure 3.30

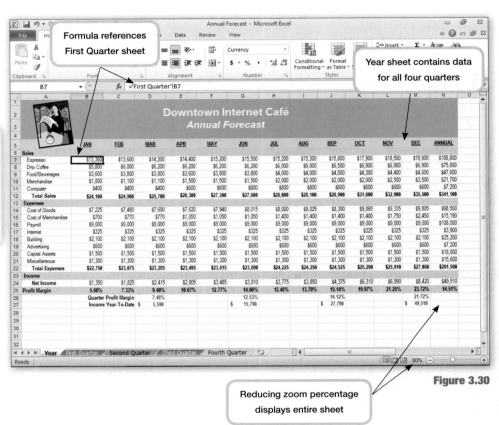

Figure 3.30

Reducing zoom percentage displays entire sheet

You can now see the entire worksheet. Most of the monthly values in the Year sheet, such as cell B7, contain linking formulas that reference the appropriate cells in the appropriate quarter sheets.

GOING TO A SPECIFIC CELL

The only formulas that do not reference cells outside the Year worksheet are those in the Annual column, N. Because you reduced the zoom, it is easy to see the values in column N and to move to a cell by clicking on the cell. However, when the worksheet is at 100 percent zoom, you would need to scroll the worksheet first. You will return the zoom to 100 percent and then use the Go To feature to quickly move to a cell that is not currently visible in the window.

1 **Return the zoom to 100%.**

Click in the Name box and type N16

Press ⏎Enter.

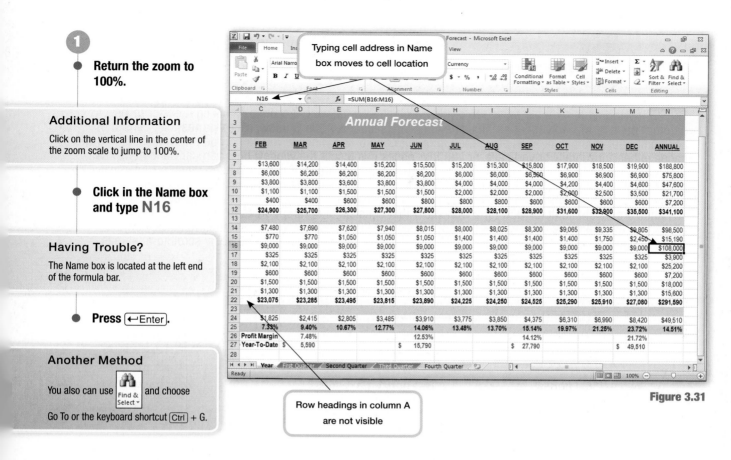

Typing cell address in Name box moves to cell location

N16   fx =SUM(B16:M16)

Annual Forecast

Row headings in column A are not visible

Figure 3.31

Your screen should be similar to Figure 3.31

The cell selector jumps directly to cell N16 in the Annual column. The formula in this cell calculates the total of the values in row 16 and does not reference another sheet. However, it is difficult to know what the numbers represent in this row because the row headings are not visible. For example, is this number the total for the lease expenses, advertising expenses, or miscellaneous expenses? Without scrolling back to see the row headings, it is difficult to know.

SPLITTING WINDOWS

Whenever you scroll a large worksheet, you will find that information you may need to view in one area scrolls out of view as you move to another area. Although you could reduce the zoom percent to view more of a worksheet in the window, you still may not be able to see the entire worksheet if it is very large. And as you saw, continuing to reduce the zoom makes the worksheet difficult to read. To view different areas of the same worksheet at the same time, you can split the window.

Concept 6 Split Window

The **split window** feature allows you to divide a worksheet window into sections, making it easier to view different parts of the worksheet at the same time. The sections of the window, called **panes**, can consist of any number of columns or rows along the top or left edge of the window. You can divide the worksheet into two panes either horizontally or vertically, or into four panes if you split the window both vertically and horizontally.

Each pane can be scrolled independently to display different areas of the worksheet. When split vertically, the panes scroll together when you scroll vertically, but scroll independently when you scroll horizontally. Horizontal panes scroll together when you scroll horizontally, but independently when you scroll vertically.

Panes are most useful for viewing a worksheet that consists of different areas or sections. Creating panes allows you to display the different sections of the worksheet in separate panes and then to quickly switch between panes to access the data in the different sections without having to repeatedly scroll to the areas.

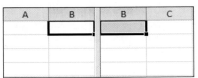

Two vertical panes   **Two horizontal panes**   **Four panes**

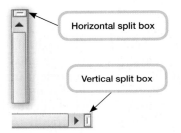

Horizontal split box

Vertical split box

Dragging the split box at the top of the vertical scroll bar downward creates a horizontal split, and dragging the split box at the right end of the horizontal scroll bar leftward creates a vertical split.

You will split the window into two vertical panes. This will allow you to view the headings in column A at the same time as you are viewing data in column N.

1

- **Point to the vertical split box in the horizontal scroll bar.**
- **Drag the split box to the left and position the bar between columns D and E.**

Additional Information

The mouse pointer changes to a ⟺ to show you can drag to create a split.

Your screen should be similar to Figure 3.32

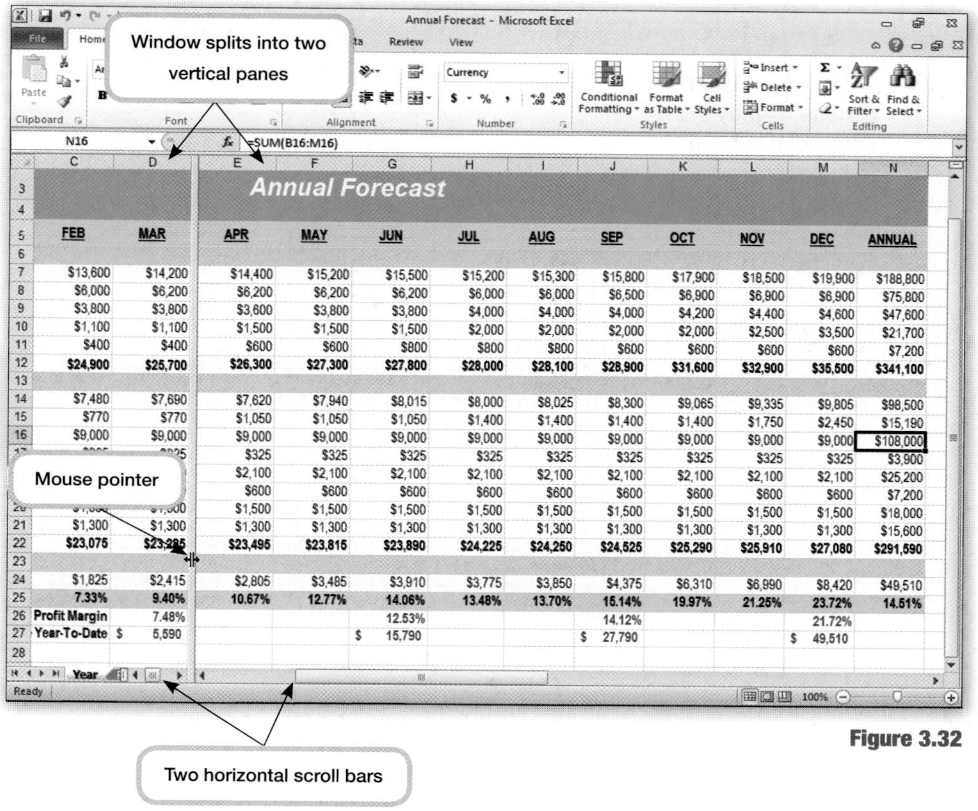

Figure 3.32

Additional Information

The Split command in the Window group on the View tab can be used to quickly create a four-way split at the active cell.

There are now two vertical panes with two separate horizontal scroll bars. The highlighted cell selector is visible in the right pane. The left pane also has a cell selector in cell N16, but it is not visible because that area of the worksheet is not displayed in the pane. When the same area of a worksheet is visible in multiple panes, the cell selector in the panes that are not active is highlighted whereas the cell selector in the active pane is clear. The active pane will be affected by your movement horizontally. The cell selector moves in both panes, but only the active pane scrolls.

You will scroll the left pane horizontally to display the month headings in column A.

2

● Click C16 in the left pane to display the active cell selector in the pane.

● Press ← twice.

Your screen should be similar to Figure 3.33

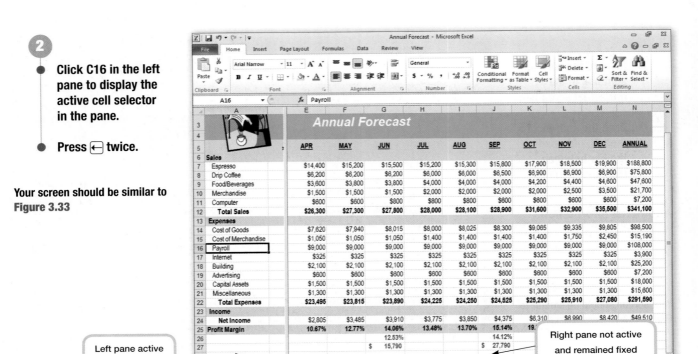

Left pane active and scrolled

Right pane not active and remained fixed

Figure 3.33

The right pane did not scroll when you moved horizontally through the left pane to display the row headings. The cell selector in the right pane is in the same cell location as in the left pane (A16), although it is not visible. You want to change the location of the split so that you can view an entire quarter in the left pane in order to more easily compare quarters.

3

● Drag the split bar to the right three columns.

● Click cell E16 in the right pane.

● Press End →.

● Press → (four times).

Your screen should be similar to Figure 3.34

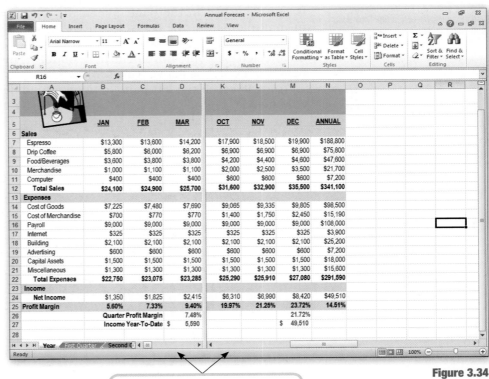

Split windows make comparing distant areas of a large worksheet easier

Figure 3.34

Now you can easily compare the first-quarter data to the last-quarter data. As you can see, creating panes is helpful when you want to display and access distant areas of a worksheet quickly. After scrolling the data in the panes to display the appropriate worksheet area, you can then quickly switch between panes to make changes to the data that is visible in the pane. This saves you the time of scrolling to the area each time you want to view it or make changes to it. You will clear the vertical split from the window.

Another Method

You also can use Split in the Window group on the View tab to clear the split.

4

- Double-click anywhere on the split bar.

- Scroll to the top of the window.

Your screen should be similar to Figure 3.35

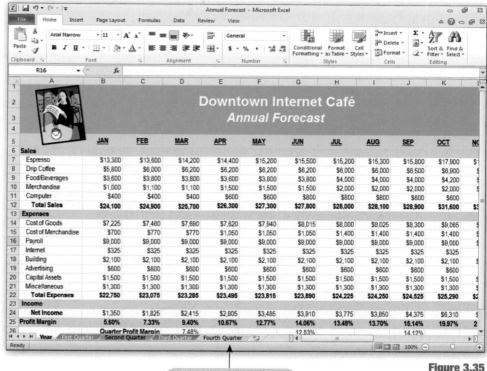

Double-clicking on split bar removes vertical split

Figure 3.35

FREEZING PANES

Another way to manage a large worksheet is to freeze panes.

 Concept **7** **Freeze Panes**

Freezing panes prevents the data in the pane from scrolling as you move to different areas in a worksheet. You can freeze the information in the top and left panes of a window only. This feature is most useful when your worksheet is organized using row and column headings. It allows you to keep the titles on the top and left edge of your worksheet in view as you scroll horizontally and vertically through the worksheet data.

You want to keep the month headings in row 5 and the row headings in column A visible in the window at all times while looking at the Income and Profit Margin data beginning in row 22. To do this, you will create four panes with the upper and left panes frozen.

When creating frozen panes, first position the worksheet in the window to display the information you want to appear in the top and left panes. This is because data in the frozen panes cannot be scrolled like data in regular panes. Then move to the location specified in the following table before using the ▦ Freeze Panes ▾ command in the Window group on the View tab to create and freeze panes.

To Create	Cell Selector Location	Example
Two horizontal panes with the top pane frozen	Move to the leftmost column in the window and to the row below where you want the split to appear.	<table><tr><td></td><td>A</td><td>B</td><td>C</td></tr><tr><td>13</td><td>Expenses</td><td></td><td></td></tr><tr><td>20</td><td>Capital Assets</td><td>$ 1,500</td><td>$ 1,500</td></tr><tr><td>21</td><td>Miscellaneous</td><td>$ 1,300</td><td>$ 1,300</td></tr><tr><td>22</td><td>Total Expenses</td><td>$ 22,750</td><td>$ 23,075</td></tr><tr><td>23</td><td>Income</td><td></td><td></td></tr><tr><td>24</td><td>Net Income</td><td>$ 1,350</td><td>$ 1,825</td></tr><tr><td>25</td><td>Profit Margin</td><td>5.60%</td><td>7.33%</td></tr></table> Top pane frozen
Two vertical panes with the left pane frozen	Move to the top row of the window and to the column to the right of where you want the split to appear.	<table><tr><td></td><td>A</td><td>D</td><td>E</td></tr><tr><td>13</td><td>Expenses</td><td></td><td></td></tr><tr><td>14</td><td>Cost of Goods</td><td>$ 9,805</td><td>$ 28,205</td></tr><tr><td>15</td><td>Cost of Merchandise</td><td>$ 2,450</td><td>$ 5,600</td></tr><tr><td>16</td><td>Payroll</td><td>$ 9,000</td><td>$ 27,000</td></tr><tr><td>17</td><td>Internet</td><td>$ 325</td><td>$ 975</td></tr></table> Left pane frozen
Four panes with the top and left panes frozen	Move to the cell below and to the right of where you want the split to appear.	<table><tr><td></td><td>A</td><td>B</td><td>E</td></tr><tr><td>13</td><td>Expenses</td><td></td><td></td></tr><tr><td>14</td><td>Cost of Goods</td><td>$ 9,065</td><td>$ 28,205</td></tr><tr><td>19</td><td>Advertising</td><td>$ 600</td><td>$ 1,800</td></tr><tr><td>20</td><td>Capital Assets</td><td>$ 1,500</td><td>$ 4,500</td></tr><tr><td>21</td><td>Miscellaneous</td><td>$ 1,300</td><td>$ 3,900</td></tr><tr><td>22</td><td>Total Expenses</td><td>$ 25,290</td><td>$ 78,280</td></tr></table> Top and left panes frozen

You want to split the window into four panes with the month column headings at the top of the window and the row headings in column A at the left side of the window.

1

- Move to B6.

- Open the View tab.

- Click 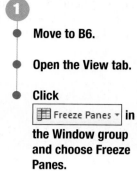 Freeze Panes ▾ in the Window group and choose Freeze Panes.

Your screen should be similar to Figure 3.36

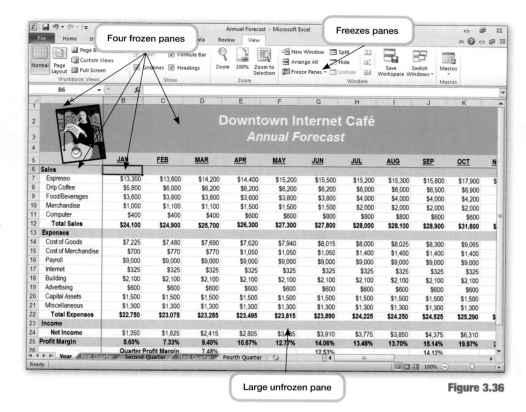

Figure 3.36

The window is divided into four panes at the cell selector location. Only one set of scroll bars is displayed because the only pane that can be scrolled is the larger lower-right pane. You can move the cell selector into a frozen pane, but the data in the frozen panes will not scroll. As you move the cell selector within the worksheet it moves from one pane to another over the pane divider, making it unnecessary to click on a pane to make it active before moving the cell selector into that pane.

Because Evan has asked you to adjust the Profit Margin values, you want to view this area of the worksheet only.

2

- Use the vertical scroll bar to scroll the window until row 25 is below row 5.

- Move to cell G25.

Your screen should be similar to Figure 3.37

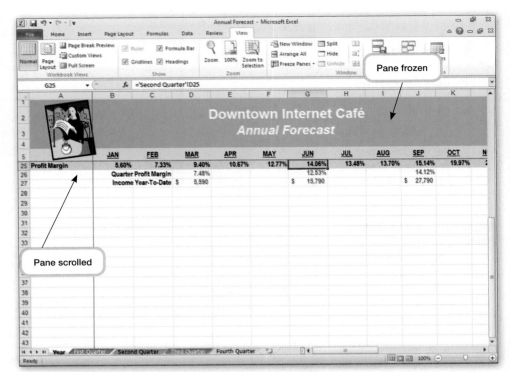

Figure 3.37

Now the Income and Profit Margin data are displayed immediately below the month headings in row 5. The data in rows 6 through 24 is no longer visible, allowing you to concentrate on this area of the worksheet.

WATCHING CELLS

While using a workbook with large worksheets and/or multiple sheets, you may want to keep an eye on how changes you make to values in one area affect cells in another. For example, if you change a value in one sheet that is referenced in a formula in another, you can view the effect on the calculated value using the Watch Window toolbar.

You will be changing values in the Second Quarter sheet next and want to be able to see the effect on the second-quarter profit margin (G26) and annual profit margin (N25) in the Year sheet at the same time.

1
- Select cells G26 and N25.

- Open the Formulas tab.

- Click in the Formula Auditing group.

- If the Watch Window toolbar is docked along an edge of the window, drag it into the workbook window area.

- Click  from the Watch Window toolbar.

Your screen should be similar to Figure 3.38

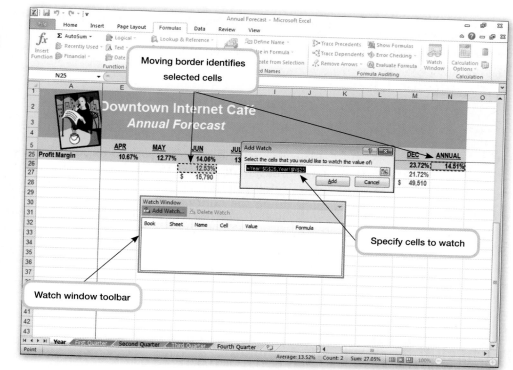

Figure 3.38

The Add Watch dialog box is used to specify the cells you want to see in the Watch Window toolbar. The currently selected cells are identified with a moving border. You will add these cells to the Watch Window.

2
- Click [Add].

- If necessary, move the Watch Window toolbar to the upper-right corner of the worksheet window below the column headings.

Your screen should be similar to Figure 3.39

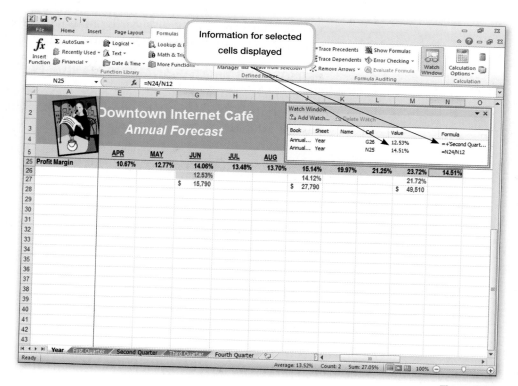

Figure 3.39

The values in the selected cells as well as the formula and location information are displayed in the Watch Window toolbar. The Watch Window toolbar will remain open on top of the worksheet as you move from one sheet to another.

Forecasting Values

Evan has asked you to adjust the forecast for the second quarter to show a profit margin of at least 15 percent for each month. After some consideration, you decide you can most easily reduce monthly payroll expenses by carefully scheduling the hours employees work during these three months. Reducing the monthly expense will increase the profit margin for the quarter. You want to find out what the maximum payroll value you can spend during that period is for each month to accomplish this goal. The process of evaluating what effect changing the payroll expenses will have on the profit margin is called what-if analysis.

Concept 8 What-If Analysis

What-if analysis is a technique used to evaluate the effects of changing selected factors in a worksheet. This technique is a common accounting function that has been made much easier with the introduction of spreadsheet programs. By substituting different values in cells that are referenced by formulas, you can quickly see the effect of the changes when the formulas are recalculated.

You can perform what-if analysis by manually substituting values or by using one of the what-if analysis tools included with Excel.

PERFORMING WHAT-IF ANALYSIS MANUALLY

To do this, you will enter different payroll expense values for each month and see what the effect is on that month's profit margin. You will adjust the April payroll value first.

1

● Display the Second
  Quarter sheet.

● Type **7000** in cell
  B16.

● Press ⎵Enter.

Your screen should be similar to Figure 3.40

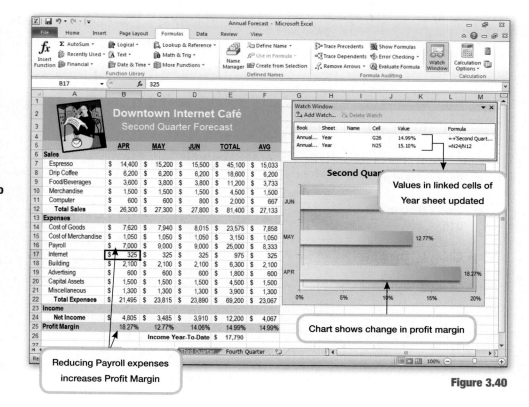

Reducing Payroll expenses
increases Profit Margin

Values in linked cells of
Year sheet updated

Chart shows change in profit margin

Figure 3.40

Now by looking in cell B25, you can see that decreasing the payroll expenses has increased the profit margin for the month to 18.27 percent. This is more than you need. Also notice the chart has changed to reflect the change in April's profit margin. The Watch Window shows that the values in the two linked cells in the Year sheet were updated accordingly.

You will continue to enter payroll values until the profit margin reaches the goal.

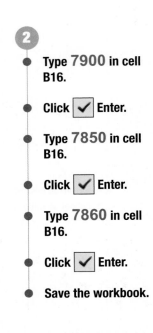

2

- Type **7900** in cell B16.
- Click ✔ Enter.
- Type **7850** in cell B16.
- Click ✔ Enter.
- Type **7860** in cell B16.
- Click ✔ Enter.
- Save the workbook.

Your screen should be similar to Figure 3.41

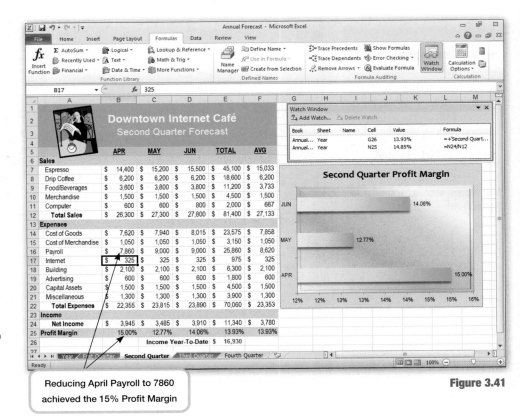

Reducing April Payroll to 7860 achieved the 15% Profit Margin

Figure 3.41

That's it! Reducing the payroll value from 9000 to 7860 will achieve the 15 percent profit margin goal for the month. Also notice that the column chart reflects the change in the April profit margin.

USING GOAL SEEK

It usually takes several tries to find the appropriate value when manually performing what-if analysis. A quicker way is to use the what-if analysis Goal Seek tool provided with Excel.

Concept 9 Goal Seek

The **Goal Seek** tool is used to find the value needed in one cell to attain a result you want in another cell. Goal Seek varies the value in the cell you specify until a formula that is dependent on that cell returns the desired result. The value of only one cell can be changed.

You will use this method to find the payroll value for May that will produce a 15 percent profit margin for that month. The current profit margin value is 12.77 percent in cell C25.

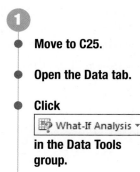

1

- Move to C25.

- Open the Data tab.

- Click

   What-If Analysis ▾

  in the Data Tools group.

- Choose Goal Seek.

Your screen should be similar to Figure 3.42

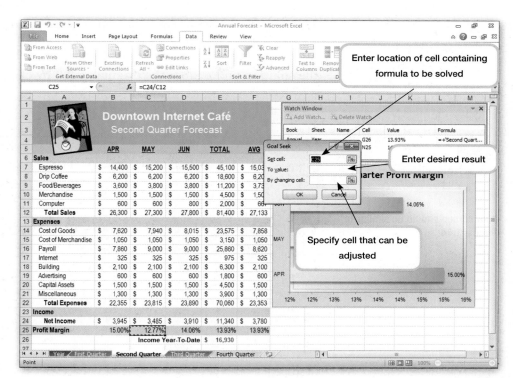

Figure 3.42

In the Goal Seek dialog box, you need to specify the location of the cell containing the formula to be solved, the desired calculated value, and the cell containing the number that can be adjusted to achieve the result. You want the formula in cell C25 to calculate a result of 15 percent by changing the payroll number in cell C16. The Set cell text box correctly displays the current cell as the location of the formula to be solved. You will enter the information needed in the Goal Seek dialog box.

2

- Click in the To value text box and enter **15.00%**

- Click in the By changing cell text box and then click on cell C16 in the worksheet to enter the cell reference.

- Click ⌷OK⌷.

Your screen should be similar to Figure 3.43

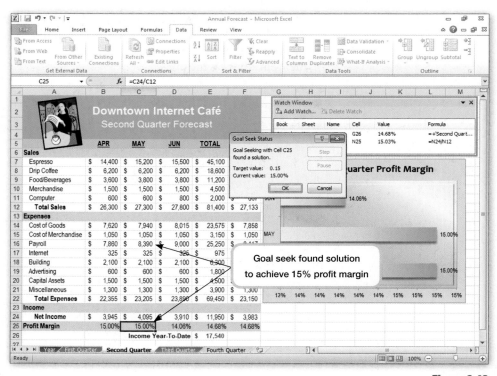

Figure 3.43

The Goal Seek dialog box tells you it found a solution that will achieve the 15 percent profit margin. The payroll value of 8390 that will achieve the desired result has been temporarily entered in the worksheet. You can reject the solution and restore the original value by choosing [Cancel]. In this case, however, you want to accept the solution.

3 ● Click [OK].

Your screen should be similar to Figure 3.44

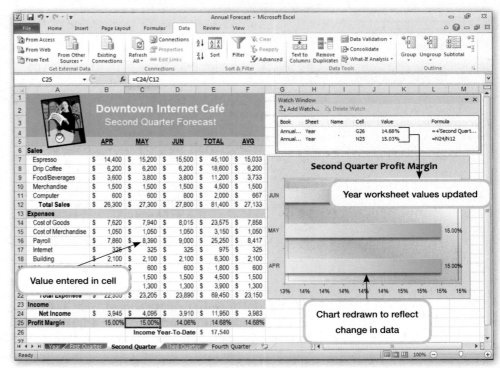

Figure 3.44

The payroll value is permanently updated and the chart redrawn to reflect the change in the May profit margin. Finally, you will adjust the June payroll value. When you are finished, you will close the Watch Window and unfreeze the Year sheet window.

4

- In a similar manner, use Goal Seek to adjust the June payroll value to achieve a 15% profit margin.

- Select both watch cell entries in the Watch Window and click <u>🐾 Delete Watch</u> .

- Click ✕ Close to close the Watch Window toolbar.

- Make the Year sheet active to further verify that the profit margin values for the second quarter were updated.

- Open the View tab.

- Click 🔲 Freeze Panes ▾ in the Window group and choose Unfreeze Panes.

- Save the workbook file again.

Your screen should be similar to Figure 3.45

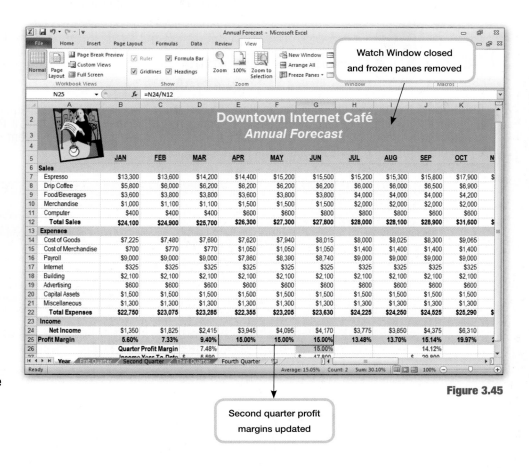

Watch Window closed and frozen panes removed

Second quarter profit margins updated

Figure 3.45

The second-quarter values are now at the 15 percent profit margin objective.

Using Conditional Formatting

Next, you want to highlight or emphasize certain values in the worksheet to help visualize the data and quickly analyze information in a worksheet. To do this, you can use conditional formatting.

Conditional formatting changes the appearance of a range of cells based on a condition that you specify. If the cells in the range meet the conditions (the condition is true), they are formatted. If they do not meet the conditions (the condition is false), they remain unformatted. There are several different ways you can apply conditional formatting as described in the following table.

Conditional Formatting	Description
Highlight Cells Rules	Highlights cells based on rules you specify, such as greater than or less than, between, or equal to. It also can highlight cells that contain certain text, dates, and duplicate values.
Top/Bottom Rules	Highlights the highest and lowest values in a range by number, percent, or average based on a cutoff value that you specify.
Data Bars	Displays a color bar in a cell to help you see the value of a cell relative to other cells. The length of the bar represents the value in the cell. A longer bar is a higher value and a shorter bar, a lower value.
Color Scales	Applies a two- or three-color graduated scale to compare values in a range. A two-color scale uses two different colors to represent high or low values and a three-color scale uses three colors to represent high, mid, and low values.
Icon Sets	Displays different color icons in the cell to classify data into three to five categories. Each icon represents a range of values.

CREATING CELL RULES

You will use the cell rules conditional formatting to highlight the payroll values that are less than $9,000 a month.

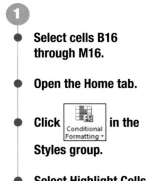

1

- Select cells B16 through M16.

- Open the Home tab.

- Click [Conditional Formatting] in the Styles group.

- Select Highlight Cells Rules.

- Choose Less Than.

Your screen should be similar to Figure 3.46

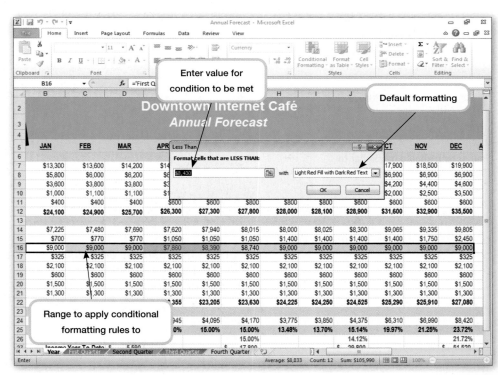

Figure 3.46

In the Less Than dialog box, you enter the value that will be used to determine which cells to highlight. In this case, you will enter the value 9000 so that all values below this amount in the selected range will be highlighted. It also lets you select the formatting to apply to those cells meeting the condition. The default formatting, a light red fill with dark red text, is acceptable.

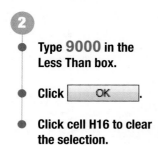

- Type **9000** in the Less Than box.

- Click [OK].

- Click cell H16 to clear the selection.

Your screen should be similar to Figure 3.47

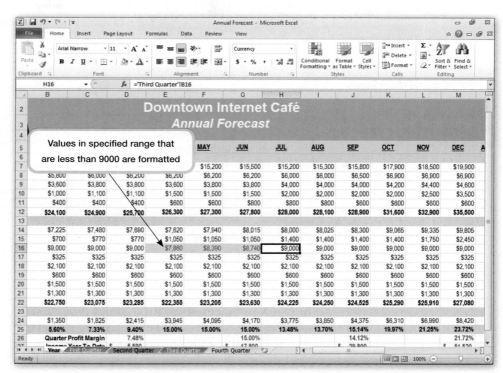

Figure 3.47

Only those cells in the Payroll row whose value is less than 9,000 are formatted using the light-red highlight and dark-red font color.

APPLYING TOP/BOTTOM RULES, DATA BARS, COLOR SCALES, AND ICON SETS CONDITIONAL FORMATTING

Next, you want to emphasize the Net Income values using the Top/Bottom Rules conditional formatting. This formatting identifies the highest and lowest values in a range of cells that are above or below a cutoff value you specify. You want to identify the net income values that are in the top 50% of the values in the range.

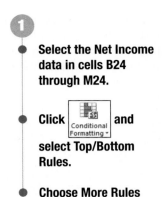

1

- Select the Net Income data in cells B24 through M24.

- Click and select Top/Bottom Rules.

- Choose More Rules

Your screen should be similar to Figure 3.48

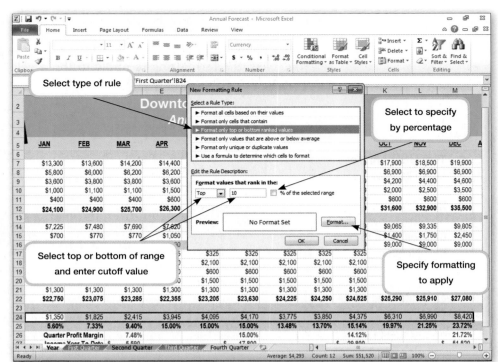

Select type of rule

Select to specify by percentage

Select top or bottom of range and enter cutoff value

Specify formatting to apply

Figure 3.48

In the New Formatting Rule dialog box, you select the type of rule to apply and the rule conditions. The current type of rule is already correctly specified. In the Edit the Rule Description you will specify to format values that are in the top 50% of values in the range using red font color.

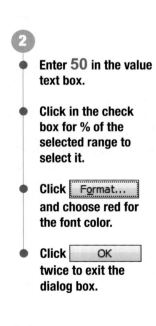

2

- Enter **50** in the value text box.

- Click in the check box for % of the selected range to select it.

- Click **Format...** and choose red for the font color.

- Click **OK** twice to exit the dialog box.

Your screen should be similar to Figure 3.49

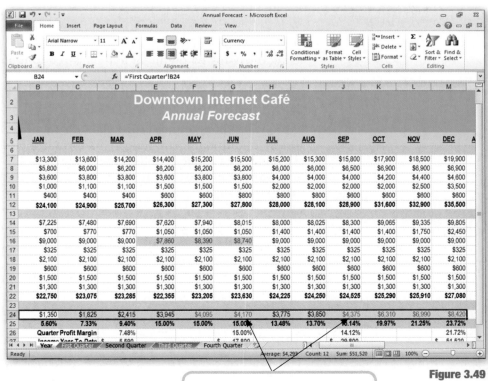

Values in specified range that are in the top 50% are shown in red

Figure 3.49

The net income values that are in the top 50% of values in the selection are now shown in red. Although this is interesting, it does not really provide much additional information. Instead, you decide to undo this formatting and see if applying data bars conditional formatting to the profit margin values is more informative. This option displays colored bars similar to a bar chart within each cell to show the relative values of the cell.

3

- Click 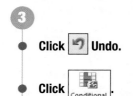 Undo.

- Click **Conditional Formatting** .

- Select **Data Bars** and point to the different data bar colors to see the live preview.

- Choose **Light Blue Data Bar** from the **Solid Fill** section.

Your screen should be similar to Figure 3.50

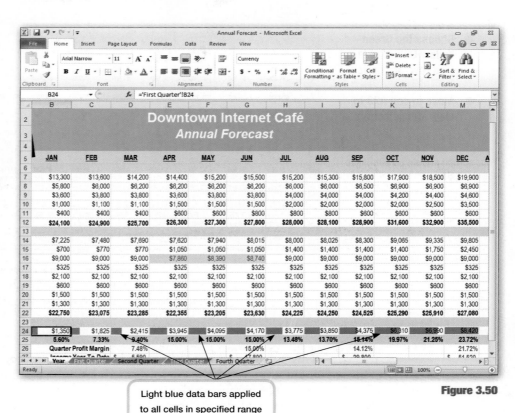

Light blue data bars applied to all cells in specified range

Figure 3.50

Color bars appear in each cell containing a number. The size of the number determines the length of the bar; the larger the value, the longer the bar. Again, you do not feel this adds much to the worksheet and will undo this formatting. Instead, you decide to try the Color Scales conditional formatting, which applies a scale consisting of a gradation of two colors to cells in a range. The shade of the color represents higher or lower values.

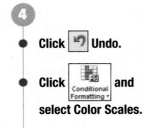

4

- Click **Undo.**

- Click **[Conditional Formatting]** and select **Color Scales.**

- Choose the **Green–Yellow Color Scale (3rd row, 3rd option).**

- Move to cell **A23** to clear the selection.

Your screen should be similar to Figure 3.51

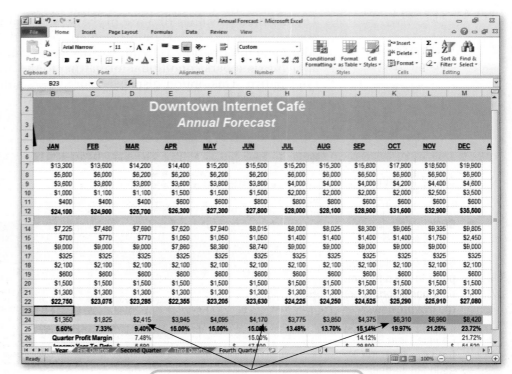

	B	C	D	E	F	G	H	I	J	K	L	M
2					**Downtown Internet Café**							
3					*Annual Forecast*							
5	**JAN**	**FEB**	**MAR**	**APR**	**MAY**	**JUN**	**JUL**	**AUG**	**SEP**	**OCT**	**NOV**	**DEC**
7	$13,300	$13,600	$14,200	$14,400	$15,200	$15,500	$15,200	$15,300	$15,800	$17,900	$18,500	$19,900
8	$5,800	$6,000	$6,200	$6,200	$6,200	$6,200	$6,000	$6,000	$6,500	$6,900	$6,900	$6,900
9	$3,600	$3,800	$3,800	$3,600	$3,800	$3,800	$4,000	$4,000	$4,000	$4,200	$4,400	$4,600
10	$1,000	$1,100	$1,100	$1,500	$1,500	$1,500	$2,000	$2,000	$2,000	$2,000	$2,500	$3,500
11	$400	$400	$400	$600	$600	$800	$800	$800	$600	$600	$600	$600
12	$24,100	$24,900	$25,700	$26,300	$27,300	$27,800	$28,000	$28,100	$28,900	$31,600	$32,900	$35,500
14	$7,225	$7,480	$7,690	$7,620	$7,940	$8,015	$8,000	$8,025	$8,300	$9,065	$9,335	$9,805
15	$700	$770	$770	$1,050	$1,050	$1,050	$1,400	$1,400	$1,400	$1,400	$1,750	$2,450
16	$9,000	$9,000	$9,000	$7,860	$8,390	$8,740	$9,000	$9,000	$9,000	$9,000	$9,000	$9,000
17	$325	$325	$325	$325	$325	$325	$325	$325	$325	$325	$325	$325
18	$2,100	$2,100	$2,100	$2,100	$2,100	$2,100	$2,100	$2,100	$2,100	$2,100	$2,100	$2,100
19	$600	$600	$600	$600	$600	$600	$600	$600	$600	$600	$600	$600
20	$1,500	$1,500	$1,500	$1,500	$1,500	$1,500	$1,500	$1,500	$1,500	$1,500	$1,500	$1,500
21	$1,300	$1,300	$1,300	$1,300	$1,300	$1,300	$1,300	$1,300	$1,300	$1,300	$1,300	$1,300
22	$22,750	$23,075	$23,285	$22,355	$23,205	$23,630	$24,225	$24,250	$24,525	$25,290	$25,910	$27,080
24	$1,350	$1,825	$2,415	$3,945	$4,095	$4,170	$3,775	$3,850	$4,375	$6,310	$6,990	$8,420
25	5.60%	7.33%	15.00%	15.00%	15.00%	13.48%	13.70%	15.14%	19.97%	21.25%	23.72%	
26	**Quarter Profit Margin**		7.48%			15.00%			14.12%			21.72%

Figure 3.51

Green–Yellow Color Scale rule identifies low values in yellow, midrange values in light green, and high values in dark green.

This formatting applies a color scale to the data in those cells, with yellow highlight identifying the lowest values, light green the middle values, and dark green the highest values.

Next, you decide to add icons as a visual indicator to the profit margin values.

5

- Select cells B25 through M25.

- Click 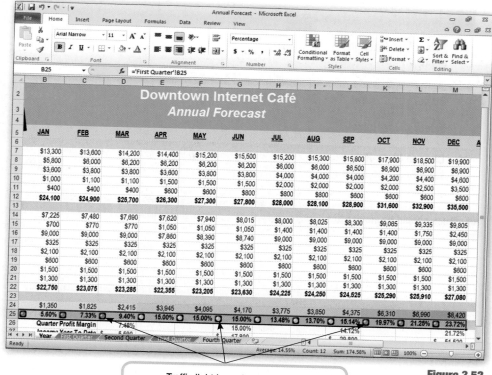 Conditional Formatting ▾

- Select Icon Sets and point to the different icon sets to see the live preview.

- Choose 3 Traffic Lights (Rimmed) in the Shapes group.

Your screen should be similar to Figure 3.52

Traffic light icons identify values in the lower third in red, middle third in yellow, and upper third in green.

Figure 3.52

The icons give a better indication of which months had a higher or lower profit margin. Red shows where the profit margin value was in the lower third, yellow indicates a profit margin in the middle third, and green shows values in the upper third. These icons reflect the same trends as the color scale used in the net income row of data.

CLEARING CONDITIONAL FORMATTING

Because the icon set formatting really duplicates the information provided by the conditional formatting in the Net Income row, you decide to just keep the Profit Margin formatting. This time you cannot use Undo to remove the conditional formatting from the Net Income row because it also would remove the formatting from the Profit Margin row. To remove conditional formatting, you will need to clear the rules from the range.

- **Select B24 through M24.**

- **Click**  **and select Clear Rules.**

- **Choose Clear Rules from Selected Cells.**

Your screen should be similar to Figure 3.53

Figure 3.53

The conditional formatting rules for the specified range were cleared and the formatting removed.

Using Sparklines

Although the icon set conditional formatting in the profit margin row identifies variances in a range, the trend is not entirely obvious. To show the data trends more clearly, you decide to create a sparkline. A **sparkline** is a tiny chart of worksheet data contained in the background of a single cell. Generally, a sparkline is positioned close to the data it represents, to have the greatest impact.

CREATING A SPARKLINE

You want to display the sparkline in cell O25, to the right of the profit margin row.

- Move to cell O25.

- Open the Insert tab.

- Click ⟋ Line in the Sparklines group.

- Select cells B25 through M25.

- Click [OK].

- Increase the width of column O to 30, and the height of row 25 to 50.

Your screen should be similar to Figure 3.54

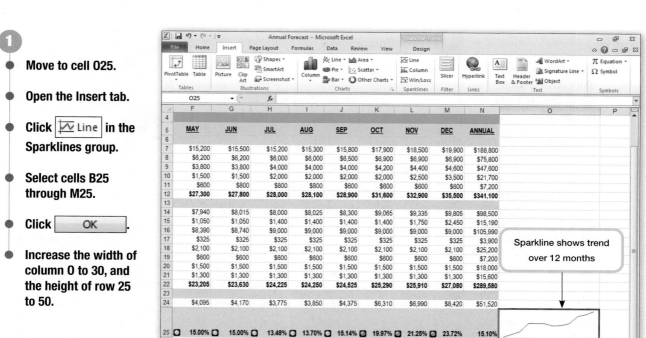

Figure 3.54

A simple line chart of the profit margin values clearly shows the increase in profit margin over the year.

ENHANCING A SPARKLINE

Next you want to improve the appearance of the sparkline by adding data markers and color. Then you will enter a descriptive label in the cell to clarify the meaning of the sparkline.

1

- If necessary, select cell O25 and open the Sparkline Tools Design tab.

- Choose **Markers** in the Show group.

- Open the Style gallery and choose Sparkline Style Colorful #1 (6th row, 1st column).

- Open the Home tab, click [icon] ▾ Fill Color, and choose Green, Accent 1, Lighter 80%.

- Type **Monthly Profit Margin** and press ⏎Enter.

- Click [icon] Top Align in the Alignment group.

- Save the workbook.

Your screen should be similar to Figure 3.55

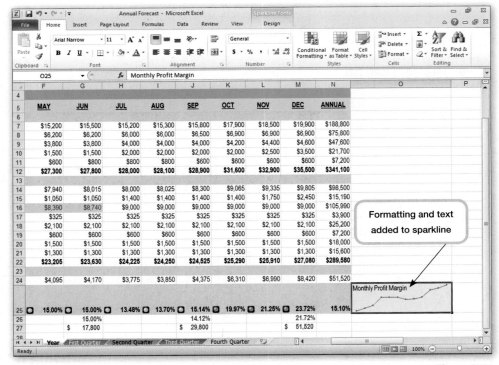

Figure 3.55

Additional Information

To delete a sparkline, select the cell containing the sparkline and choose

[🧽 Clear ▾] in the Group group of the Sparkline Tools Design tab.

The addition of the sparkline helps clarify the profit margin trend for the year. Just like a chart, if the data in a referenced cell changes, the sparkline will automatically update to reflect the change.

Customizing Print Settings

Now you are ready to print the workbook. Just because your worksheet looks great on the screen, this does not mean it will look good when printed. Many times you will want to change the default print and layout settings to improve the appearance of the output. Customizing the print settings by controlling page breaks, changing the orientation of the page, centering the worksheet on the page, hiding gridlines, and adding custom header and footer information are just a few of the ways you can make your printed output look more professional.

CONTROLLING PAGE BREAKS

First you want to preview the Year sheet.

1

● **Open the File tab and choose Print.**

● **Display page 2 of the worksheet.**

Your screen should be similar to Figure 3.56

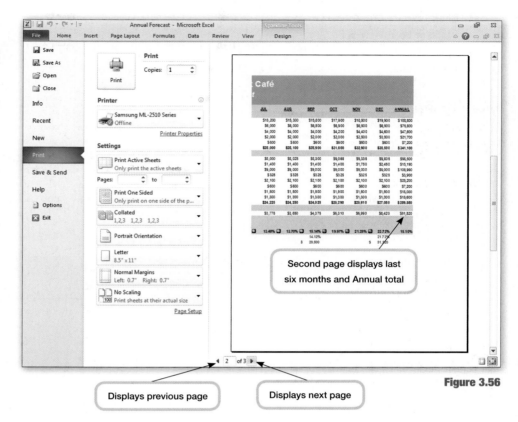

Second page displays last six months and Annual total

Displays previous page

Displays next page

Figure 3.56

The first page of the Year worksheet displays the first six months, and the second page, the remaining months and the annual total. The sparkline is by itself on a third page. Although you could change the orientation to landscape and use the Fit To feature to compress the worksheet to a single page, this would make the data small and difficult to read. Instead, you decide to fit the printout on two pages, with the sparkline on the second page.

To do this, you will change the location of the **page break**, the place where one printed page ends and another starts. Excel inserts automatic page breaks based on the paper size, margin settings, and orientation when the worksheet exceeds the width of a page. You can change the location of the automatic page break by inserting a manual page break location. To help you do this, Page Break Preview is used to adjust the location of page breaks.

2

● **Open the View tab.**

● **Click** [▣ Page Break Preview] **in the Workbook Views group.**

Another Method

You also could click 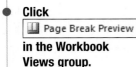 in the status bar to change to Page Break Preview.

● **If a Welcome to Page Break Preview box appears, click** [OK] **.**

● **Change the zoom to 80% and scroll the window horizontally to see the entire sheet.**

Your screen should be similar to Figure 3.57

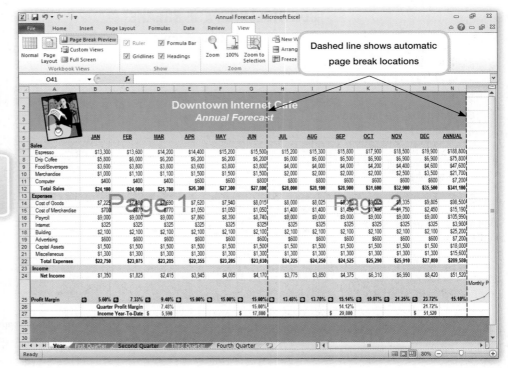

Figure 3.57

Additional Information

You can work in Page Break Preview just like in Normal view.

Now you can easily see the page break locations. The dashed line indicates the location of the automatic page breaks. You can change the location by dragging the page break line. When you move an automatic page break location to another location, the page break line changes to a solid line, indicating it is a manual page break. To include the sparkline on page two, you will move the second page break to the right of column O.

Additionally, you realize that the worksheet title will be split between the two pages You will fix the title by unmerging the cells, moving the title to the left on page 1 and copying the title to page 2.

3

- Point to the page break line after column N, and drag it to the right of column O.

Another Method

You also can insert page breaks by moving to the column location in the worksheet where you want the break inserted and using [Breaks] /Insert Page Break in the Page Layout tab.

- Select the two merged cells containing the titles.

- Open the Home tab.

- Open the [Merge & Center icon] Merge & Center drop-down menu and choose Unmerge Cells.

- Copy the contents of D2 through D3 to K2 through K3.

- Press [Esc] to clear the selection and move to cell K4.

Your screen should be similar to Figure 3.58

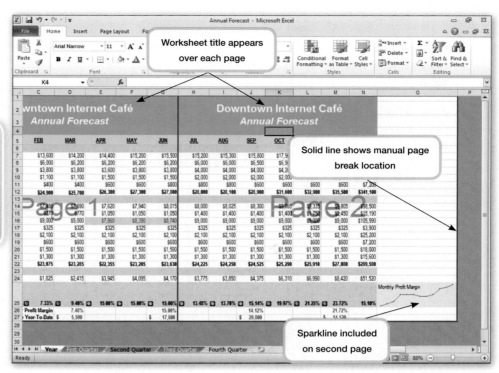

Figure 3.58

The entire worksheet will now print on two pages. Unmerging the cells split the merged cell into its original cells and moved the contents into the upper-left cell of the range of split cells. The center formatting was not removed. Now both pages of the worksheet printout will display a worksheet title.

ADDING A CUSTOM HEADER AND FOOTER

You also would like to add a custom header to this worksheet. You will do this in Page Layout view because you can add the header simply by clicking on the header area of the page and typing the header text.

Additional Information

You also can add a custom footer by clicking in the footer area of the page.

1

- **Switch to Page Layout view at 70% zoom.**

- **Click on the left end of the header area of page 1.**

Your screen should be similar to Figure 3.59

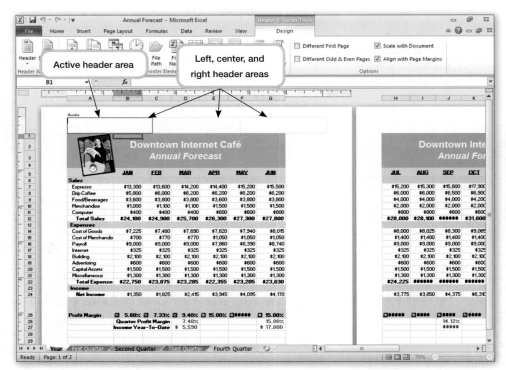

Figure 3.59

The header area is divided into three sections. The left section text box will display the text you enter aligned with the left margin; the center section will center the text; and the right section will right-align the text. You want to enter your name in the left section, class in the center, and the date in the right section. You will enter your name and class information by typing it directly in the box. You will enter the current date using the Current Date feature on the Header & Footer Tools Design tab.

2

● Type **Created by Your Name**

● Press Tab.

Another Method

You also could click on the section to move to it.

● Enter the name of your class and the section or time.

● Press Tab.

● Click [Current Date] in the

Header & Footer Elements group.

Your screen should be similar to Figure 3.60

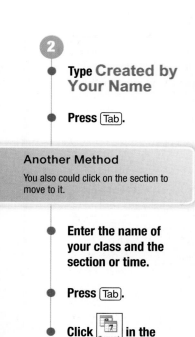

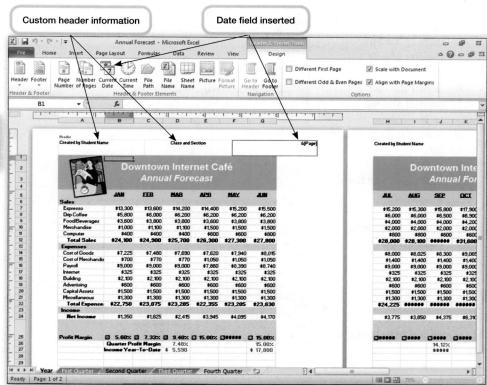

Figure 3.60

Additional Information

Be careful when making changes to multiple sheets as these changes may replace data on other sheets.

The Date field is entered in the header. It will enter the current date whenever the worksheet is opened. The actual date will display when you leave the header area.

Next, you want to add footers to the quarter sheets. It is faster to add the footer to all sheets at the same time. If you make changes to the active sheet when multiple sheets are selected, the changes are made to all other selected sheets.

3

- Display the First Quarter sheet.

- Select the four quarter sheets.

- Open the Page Layout tab.

- Open the Page Setup dialog box.

- Open the Header/Footer tab.

- Click

  Custom Footer... .

Your screen should be similar to Figure 3.61

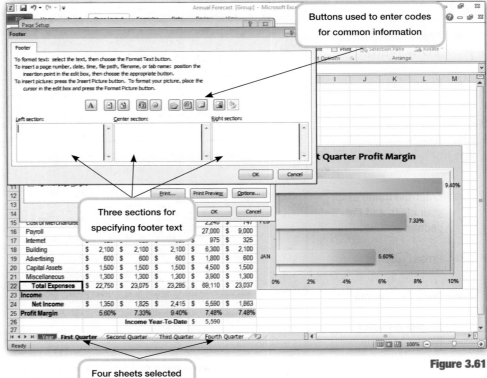

Figure 3.61

Just like in Page Layout view, the footer area consists of three sections. The buttons above the section boxes are used to enter the codes for common header and footer information. The cursor is currently positioned in the Left section text box.

You will enter your name in the left section, the file name in the middle section, and the date in the right section.

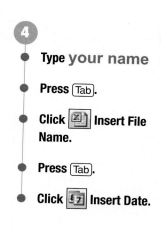

④

● Type **your name**

● Press Tab.

● Click 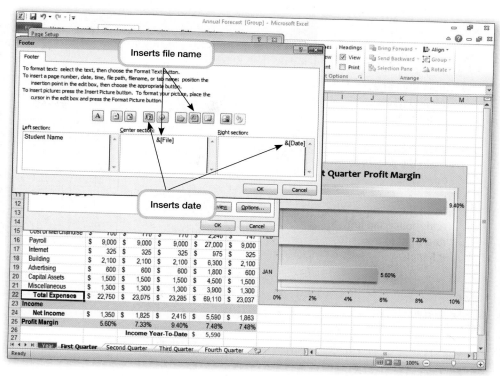 Insert File Name.

● Press Tab.

● Click Insert Date.

Your screen should be similar to Figure 3.62

Figure 3.62

Next you will change the orientation of the four sheets to landscape, change the margins to 0.5 inch, and scale the sheets to fit the page. Then you want to make one final check to see how the worksheets will look before printing the workbook.

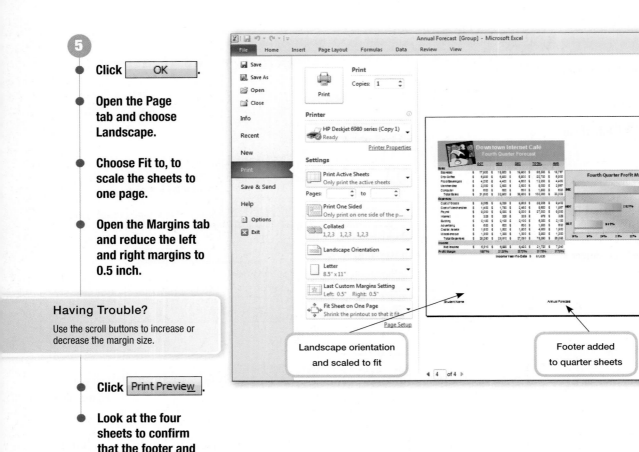

5

- Click [OK].

- Open the Page tab and choose Landscape.

- Choose Fit to, to scale the sheets to one page.

- Open the Margins tab and reduce the left and right margins to 0.5 inch.

Having Trouble?

Use the scroll buttons to increase or decrease the margin size.

- Click [Print Preview].

- Look at the four sheets to confirm that the footer and orientation changes were added to all the quarter sheets.

Your screen should be similar to Figure 3.63

Figure 3.63

Additional Information

You also could drag the right or left border of the margin area in the ruler while in Page Layout view to adjust the size of the margins.

The footer as you entered it appears on all selected worksheets and the page layout changes were made as well.

PRINTING SELECTED SHEETS

You want to print the Year and Second Quarter worksheets only. Because the annual worksheet is large, you also feel the worksheet may be easier to read if the row and column gridlines were printed. Although gridlines are displayed in Page Layout View and Normal view, they do not print unless you turn on this feature.

1

- Open the Home tab.

- Right-click on a sheet tab and choose Ungroup Sheets.

- Make the Year sheet active.

- Open the Page Layout tab and choose Print in the Gridlines section of the Sheet Options group.

- Save the workbook again.

- Hold down [Ctrl] and click the Second Quarter sheet tab to add it to the selection of sheets to print.

- Open the File tab and choose Print.

- Preview the three pages and then print the worksheets.

Another Method

You also can print gridlines by choosing Gridlines from the Page Setup dialog box.

Your printed output should look like that shown in the Case Study at the beginning of the lab.

PRINTING SELECTED AREAS

You are finished printing the Year and Second Quarter sheets and you have the information Evan requested. However, you think Evan also would like a printout of the First Quarter worksheet without the chart displayed. To print a selected area, you first select the cell range that you want to print.

1

- Make the First Quarter sheet active.

- Select cells A1 through F26.

- Open the Page Layout tab.

- Click in the Page Setup group and choose Set Print Area.

Your screen should be similar to Figure 3.64

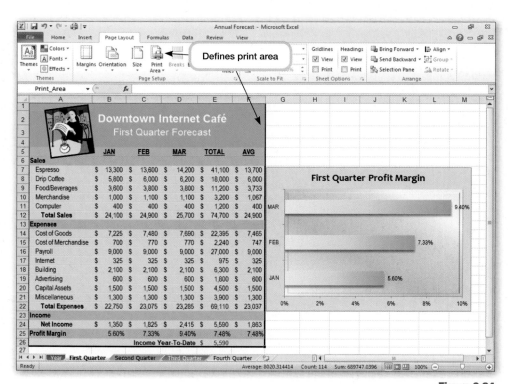

Figure 3.64

Customizing Print Settings **EX3.65**

The area you selected, called the **print area**, is surrounded with a heavy line that identifies the area.

2

● **Open the File tab and choose Print.**

● **Change the orientation to Portrait Orientation.**

Your screen should be similar to Figure 3.65

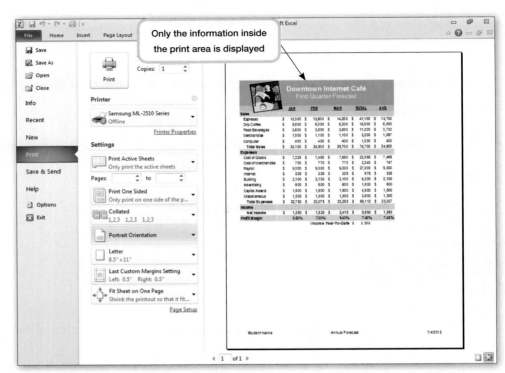

Figure 3.65

The Preview displays only the information contained in the defined print area. The print area is saved with the worksheet and will be used automatically whenever you print the worksheet. It can be cleared using Clear Print Area in the 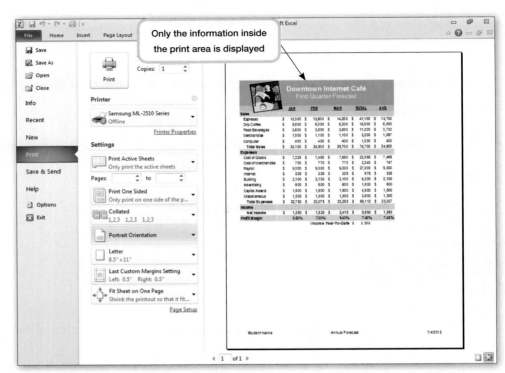 menu.

3

- If necessary, specify any printer settings.

- Print the worksheet.

- Change to Normal view and move to cell A6 in the First Quarter sheet.

- Close and save the workbook and exit Excel.

OCUS ON CAREERS

EXPLORE YOUR CAREER OPTIONS

Medical Sales Accountant

Medical sales accountants visit doctors and clinics to promote the pharmaceuticals and supplies made by the company they represent. The accountants usually specialize in a few pharmaceuticals or products so that they can help the doctor understand the benefits and risks associated with their products. Medical sales accountants must keep careful and complete records of the samples they have in inventory and what they have delivered to doctors. An Excel workbook is a useful tool to keep track of the many doctors and the deliveries made. A career as a medical sales accountant can start with a salary of $35,000 and go up to over $90,000 plus car and travel benefits.

Absolute Reference (EX3.10)

An absolute reference is a cell or range reference in a formula whose location does not change when the formula is copied.

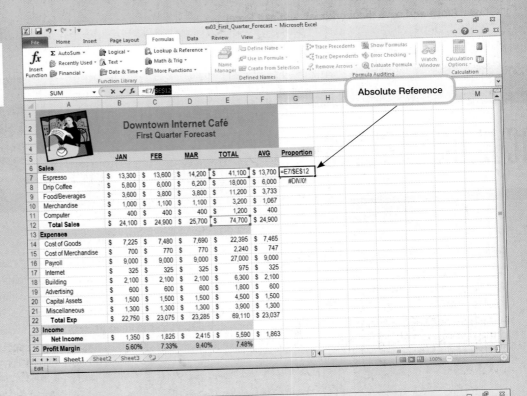

Sheet Name (EX3.14)

Each sheet in a workbook can be assigned a descriptive sheet name to help identify the contents of the sheet.

AutoFill (EX3.17)

The AutoFill feature makes entering a series of headings easier by logically repeating and extending the series. AutoFill recognizes trends and automatically extends data and alphanumeric headings as far as you specify.

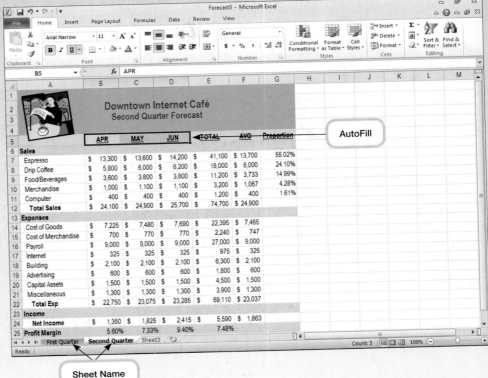

Sheet and 3-D References (EX3.19)

Sheet and 3-D references in formulas are used to refer to data from multiple sheets and to calculate new values based on this data.

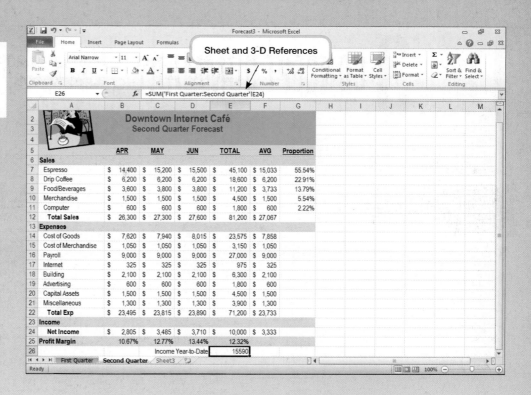

Find and Replace (EX3.26)

The Find and Replace feature helps you quickly find specific information and automatically replace it with new information.

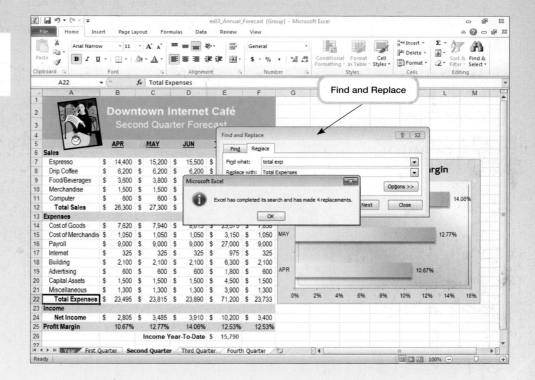

Lab 3 CONCEPT SUMMARY Managing and Analyzing a Workbook

Split Window (EX3.34)

The split window feature allows you to divide a worksheet window into sections, making it easier to view different parts of the worksheet at the same time.

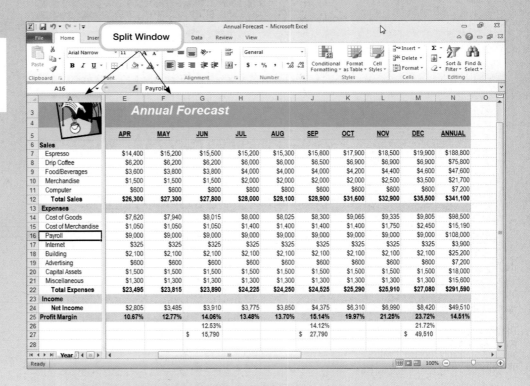

Freeze Panes (EX3.37)

Freezing panes prevents the data in the pane from scrolling as you move to different areas in a worksheet.

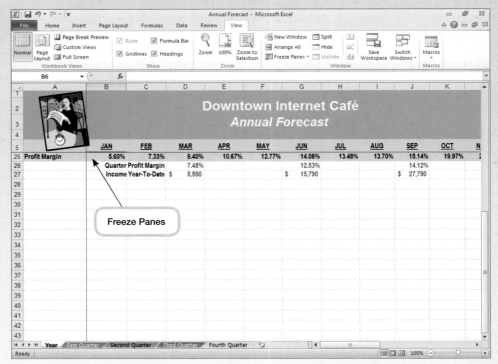

What-If Analysis (EX3.42)

What-if analysis is a technique used to evaluate the effects of changing selected factors in a worksheet.

Goal Seek (EX3.44)

The Goal Seek tool is used to find the value needed in one cell to attain a result you want in another cell.

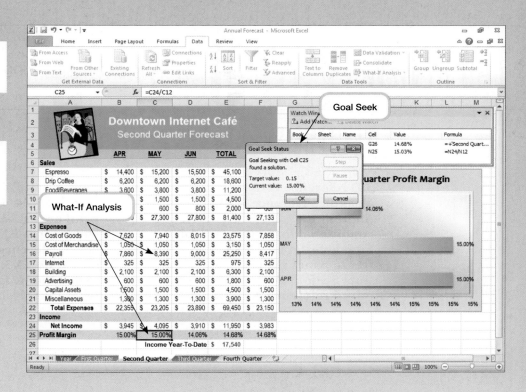

Conditional Formatting (EX3.48)

Conditional formatting changes the appearance of a range of cells based on a condition that you specify.

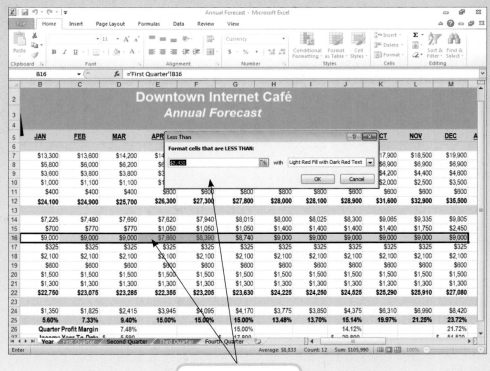

Conditional Formatting

KEY TERMS

3-D reference EX3.19
absolute reference EX3.10
AutoFill EX3.17
conditional formatting EX3.48
Find and Replace EX3.26
freeze panes EX3.37
Goal Seek EX3.44
mixed reference EX3.10

page break EX3.57
pane EX3.34
print area EX3.66
sheet name EX3.14
sheet reference EX3.19
sparkline EX3.54
split window EX3.34
what-if analysis EX3.42

COMMAND SUMMARY

Command	Shortcut	Action
Home tab		
Styles group		
Conditional Formatting ▾		Applies Highlight Cells Rules, Top/Bottom Rules, Data Bars, Color Scales, and Icons Sets to selected cells based on criteria
Cells group		
Delete ▾ /Delete Sheet		Deletes entire sheet
Format ▾ /Rename Sheet		Renames sheet
Format ▾ /Move or Copy Sheet		Moves or copies selected sheet
Format ▾ /Tab Color		Changes color of sheet tabs
Editing group		
Find & Select ▾ /Find	Ctrl + F	Locates specified text, numbers, and/or formats
Find & Select ▾ /Replace	Ctrl + H	Locates specified characters or formats and replaces them with specified replacement characters or format
Find & Select ▾ /Go To	Ctrl + G	Goes to a specified cell location in worksheet
Insert tab		
Sparklines group		
Line		Inserts sparkline in the selected cell
Design Sparklines Tool tab		
Style group		
		Applies pictured style to sparkline
Clear ▾		Removes sparkline

LAB REVIEW

COMMAND SUMMARY (CONTINUED)

Command	Shortcut	Action
Page Layout tab		
Page Setup group		
Margins /Narrow		Changes margin settings
Margins /Custom Margins/Horizontally		Centers worksheet horizontally on page
Margins /Custom Margins/Vertically		Centers worksheet vertically on page
Print Area /Set Print Area		Sets print area to selected cells
Breaks /Insert Page Break		Inserts page break at cell pointer location
Breaks /Remove Page Break		Removes page break at cell pointer location
Breaks /Reset all Page Breaks		Restores automatic page breaks
Scale to Fit group		
Height: /1 page		Scales worksheet vertically to fit one page
Sheet Options group		
Print Gridlines		Displays/hides gridlines for printing
Formulas tab		
Function Library group		
Σ AutoSum ▾		Enters Sum, Average, Minimum, Maximum, or Count function
Formula Auditing group		
Error Checking ▾		Checks worksheet for formula errors
Watch Window		Opens Watch Window toolbar

COMMAND SUMMARY (CONTINUED)

Command	Shortcut	Action
Data tab		
Data Tools group		
What-If Analysis ▾/Goal Seek		Adjusts value in specified cell until a formula dependent on that cell reaches specified result
View tab		
Workbook Views group		
Normal		Changes worksheet view to Normal
Page Layout		Displays worksheet as it will appear when printed
Page Break Preview		Displays where pages will break when a worksheet is printed
Show group		
☑ Gridlines		Turns on/off display of gridlines
☑ Headings		Turns on/off display of row and column headings
Zoom group		
Zoom		Changes magnification of window
Window group		
Freeze Panes ▾/Freeze Panes		Freezes top and/or leftmost panes
Freeze Panes ▾/Unfreeze Panes		Unfreezes window panes
Split		Divides window into four panes at active cell or removes split

LAB EXERCISES

MATCHING

Match the lettered item on the right with the numbered item on the left.

1. panes   ____ a. technique used to evaluate the effects of changing selected factors in a worksheet
2. Goal Seek   ____ b. 3-D reference
3. Sheet1:Sheet3!H3:K5   ____ c. a what-if analysis tool
4. freezing panes   ____ d. mixed cell reference
5. M34   ____ e. applies formatting based on cell rules
6. 'Third Quarter'!A23   ____ f. pane that contains the cell selector
7. what-if analysis   ____ g. the sections of a divided window
8. conditional formatting   ____ h. sheet reference
9. sparkline   ____ i. absolute cell reference
10. #DIV/0!   ____ j. indicates division by zero error
11. $B12   ____ k. prevents data in pane from scrolling
12. active pane   ____ l. a tiny chart of worksheet data contained in a single cell

TRUE/FALSE

Circle the correct answer to the following questions.

1. The sheet reference consists of the name of the sheet separated from the cell reference by a question mark.   **True**   **False**
2. A sparkline is a miniature chart contained in a single cell.   **True**   **False**
3. To create two horizontal panes with the left pane frozen, move the cell selector in the top row of the window and select the column to the right of where you want the split to appear.   **True**   **False**
4. Dragging the sizing handle activates the AutoFill feature and recognizes the cell entry as one that can be incremented.   **True**   **False**
5. Icon Sets conditional formatting applies a two- or three-color graduated scale to compare values in a range.   **True**   **False**
6. You can freeze the information in the top and right panes of a window only.   **True**   **False**
7. The Trace Errors formula auditing command outlines the cell causing the error with a colored border   **True**   **False**
8. A relative reference is a cell or range reference in a formula whose location does not change when the formula is copied   **True**   **False**
9. B$7 is an absolute reference.   **True**   **False**
10. What-if analysis varies the value in the cell you specify until a formula that is dependent on that cell returns the desired result.   **True**   **False**

FILL-IN

Complete the following statements by filling in the blanks with the correct key terms.

1. A worksheet window can be divided into _____, either horizontal or vertical, through which different areas of the worksheet can be viewed at the same time.

2. A technique used to evaluate what effect changing one or more values in formulas has on other values in the worksheet is called _____.

3. A $ character in front of either the column or the row reference in a formula creates a(n) _____ reference.

4. A(n) _____ reference is created when the reference is to the same cell or range on multiple sheets in the same workbook.

5. The _____ feature logically repeats and extends a series.

6. _____ formatting changes the appearance of a range of cells based on a set of conditions you specify.

7. Use a(n) _____ to show the incremental change in data over time in one cell.

8. _____ consist of the name of the sheet enclosed in quotes, and are separated from the cell reference by an exclamation point.

9. When specified rows and columns are _____, they are fixed when you scroll.

10. The _____ tool is used to find the value needed in one cell to attain a result you want in another cell.

LAB EXERCISES

MULTIPLE CHOICE

Circle the correct response to the questions below.

1. A formula that contains references to cells in other sheets of a workbook is a(n) _____.
   a. Sheet formula
   b. Sparkline formula
   c. 3-D formula
   d. Average formula

2. The number 32534 displayed with the Currency style would appear as _____ in a cell.
   a. $32534
   b. 32,534
   c. $32,534
   d. $32,534.00

3. The _____ error value indicates that the wrong type of argument or operand was used.
   a. #####
   b. #DIV/0
   c. #N/A
   d. #VALUE!

4. The _____ function key will change a selected cell reference to absolute.
   a. F4
   b. F7
   c. F3
   d. F10

5. Which of the following is NOT a valid sheet name?
   a. Week 8–10
   b. Qtr 1
   c. 3/12/12
   d. Second Quarter

6. The _____ feature enters a series of headings by logically repeating and extending the series.
   a. ExtendSelect
   b. AutoFill
   c. AutoRepeat
   d. ExtendFill

7. The cell reference that will adjust row 8 without adjusting column E when it is copied is
_____.
   a. E8
   b. E8
   c. $E8
   d. E$8

8. A cell or range reference in a formula whose location does not change when the formula is copied is
a(n) _____.
   a. absolute reference
   b. frozen cell
   c. mixed reference
   d. relative reference

9. The information in the worksheet can be _____ in the top and left panes of a window only.
   a. fixed
   b. aligned
   c. frozen
   d. adjusted

10. _____ is used to evaluate the effects of changing selected factors in a worksheet.
   a. Value analysis
   b. AutoCalculate
   c. AutoFill
   d. What-if analysis

11. A division of the worksheet window that allows different areas of the worksheet to be viewed at the same time is called a _____.
   a. pane
   b. part
   c. window
   d. section

STEP-BY-STEP

GELATO SALES FORECAST ★

1. Leah Miller owns seven Gelato Fresco franchises. She has created a worksheet to record each store's first-quarter sales. Now she would like to create a second worksheet in the workbook to record the projected second-quarter sales for each store. The completed worksheets should be similar to the one shown here.

   a. Open the workbook ex03_Gelato Fresco.

   b. Calculate the total sales for each location and for each month. Adjust column widths as needed.

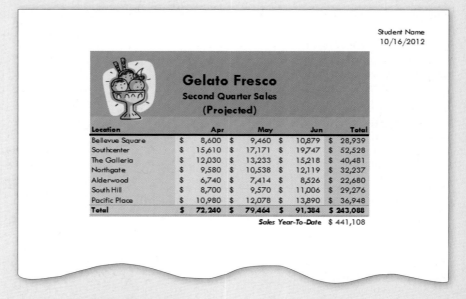

   c. Copy the worksheet data from Sheet1 to Sheet2 and maintain the column width settings. Check the height of the rows and adjust as needed to show text fully. Reposition the graphic as needed.

   d. Rename the Sheet1 tab **1st Quarter Sales** and the Sheet2 tab **2nd Quarter Sales**. Add color to the tabs. Delete Sheet3.

   e. In the 2nd Quarter Sales sheet, change the monthly labels to Apr, May, and Jun using AutoFill. Change the subtitle line to **Second Qtr Sales**. Enter and bold the heading **(Projected)** in cell A4. Merge and center the heading between columns A and E.

   f. Enter the following projected April sales figures:

Location	Number
Bellevue Square	8600
Southcenter	15610
The Galleria	12030
Northgate	9580
Alderwood	6740
South Hill	8700
Pacific Place	10980

   g. A new advertising campaign for May and June is expected to increase monthly sales. May sales for each location are expected to be 10 percent more than April sales, and June sales are expected to be 15 percent more than May sales. Enter formulas to calculate May and June sales for the "Bellevue Square" location and then copy these formulas into the other appropriate cells.

h. Select both sheets and make the following changes:
- Add a thick bottom border below the headings in row 5.
- Apply the Total cell style to the Total row heading and Total row values.
- Use the Find and Replace command to change "Qtr" to "Quarter."
- Reduce the font size of the subtitle line to 14 points.

i. In the Second Quarter sheet, enter, bold, italicize, and right-align the heading **Sales Year-To-Date:** in cell D14. In cell E14, enter a formula to calculate the total sales for the first six months by summing cells E13 on both sheets.

j. Document the workbook to include your name as the author.

k. In Page Layout view, add a custom header to both worksheets that displays your name and the date right-aligned on separate lines. Center the worksheet horizontally on the page.

l. Preview the workbook. Print the 2nd Quarter Sales worksheet.

m. Save the workbook as Gelato Fresco.

FORECASTING SALES ★ ★

2. The La Delice Cookies bakery has decided to add brownies to their offerings and wants to know the impact on sales. You are in the process of creating a worksheet of the cookie sales for the last six months. In addition, you want to add brownies to the items for sale and project how much of this item you would need to sell to increase the net income to $2,000 a month. Then, you want to set up a second sheet that you will use to enter the sales information for the second six months when it is available. When you are done, your completed worksheets should be similar to those shown here.

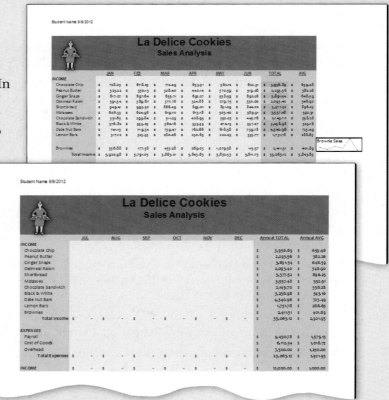

a. Open the workbook ex03_La Delice. Use AutoFill to complete the month headings. Save the workbook as La Delice.

b. Add a blank row below row 15 for brownies. Add the row heading **Brownies** in A16.

c. Edit the formula in B17 to include B16 and copy it across the row through column G.

d. Increase the cost of goods for each month by 12 percent to account for the added goods needed to make the brownies.

e. Enter the formulas to calculate the Total Expenses in row 23.

f. Correct all the formula errors in row 25.

g. Enter the functions to calculate the Total and Average values in row 6. Copy the functions down the columns through row 25. Clear the formulas from all cells that reference blank cells, except for row 16.

h. Freeze the window with the titles in column A and above row 5 frozen so you can scroll to see the Income values in row 25 while working on the brownie sales next.

i. Assuming other cookie sales remain the same, you want to know how much brownie sales would be necessary to generate a monthly net income of $2,000. Use Goal Seek to answer these questions and calculate the brownie sales figures. (Hint: Net income is displayed in row 25.)

j. Unfreeze the window.

k. Using conditional formatting, create a cell rule that will highlight those cookies that have total sales greater than $3,000. Use a highlight color of your choice.

l. You will soon be working on the sales figures for the second six months and want to set up a second sheet to hold this information when it is available. Copy the entire worksheet from Sheet1 to Sheet2, retaining the original column widths. Increase the row height of row 3 to 35.25 points and, if necessary, resize and move the graphic. Change the month headings using AutoFill for the second six months (JUL to DEC).

m. Rename Sheet1 to **January-June Sales**. Rename Sheet2 to **July-December Sales**. Add tab colors of your choice. Delete the extra sheet in the workbook.

n. In the July-December Sales sheet, delete the contents only in cells B6:G16 and B20:G22. In cell H6, enter a formula that adds the total from January through June with the monthly figures from July through December. Copy the formula down the column. Change the average formula to average the 12 months. Clear the formula from all cells that reference blank cells. Clear the conditional formatting from all cells in the July-December Sales sheet. Check the formulas by entering (and then removing) some sample data. Change the label in H4 to **Annual TOTAL** and I4 to **Annual AVG**. Best fit both columns.

o. In the January-June Sales sheet, add a line sparkline in cell J16 using the monthly sales numbers for brownies in row 16. Type **Brownie Sales** in the cell and top-align the text. Increase the row height and column width to show the sparkline. Display markers and choose a style of your choice. Add a thick box border to J16.

p. Use the Find and Replace command to change "bars" to "Bars" in both sheets. In Document Properties, type your name in the Author text box. Add a custom header with your name and the date left-aligned to both sheets.

q. Preview the workbook. Change the print orientation to landscape. Make the necessary adjustments to print each worksheet on a single page. Print both worksheets.

r. Add workbook documentation and save the workbook.

3. Colleen, a travel analyst for Adventure Travel Tours, is evaluating the profitability of a planned Italy Tour package. She has researched competing tours and has determined that a price of $5,000 is appropriate. Colleen has determined the following costs for the package.

Item	Cost
Air transport	$1,400 per person
Ground transportation	$460 per person
Lodging	$1,475 per person
Food	$900 per person
Tour guides	$3,000
Administrative	$1,200
Miscellaneous	$1,500

She has started a worksheet to evaluate the revenues and costs for the Italy Tour. She wants to know how many travelers are needed to break even (revenues equal costs), how many are needed to make $5,000, and how many are needed to make $10,000. When completed your Break Even and $10,000 Profit worksheets should be similar to those shown here.

a. Open the workbook ex03_Italy Tour. Notice that Colleen has already entered the tour price and an estimated number of travelers.

b. Revenue from reservations is calculated by multiplying the tour price times the number of travelers. Enter this formula into C9. Save the workbook as Italy Tour in a folder named Tour Analysis.

c. Based on Colleen's cost information, air transportation is $1,400 times the number of travelers. Enter this formula into C12. Enter formulas into C13, C14, and C15 for the other expenses (see table above) related to the number of travelers.

d. Enter the remaining expenses into cells C16, C17, and C18.

e. Calculate total costs in cell C19. Net revenue is the difference between revenue from reservations and total costs. Enter this formula into cell C21.

f. Format the currency values in the worksheet to Accounting with no decimal places.

g. Use Goal Seek to determine the number of travelers needed to just break even (net revenue equals zero).

LAB EXERCISES

h. Rename the Sheet1 tab to **Break Even**. Copy the data in the Break Even sheet to Sheet2, preserving column width settings. Rename the Sheet2 tab **$5,000**. Add color to both sheet tabs.

i. In the $5,000 sheet, change the title in B3 to **$5,000 Profit**. Use Goal Seek to determine the number of travelers needed to attain net revenues of $5,000.

j. Copy the $5,000 sheet data to Sheet3 and rename the tab of the copy **$10,000**. Change the tab color. Change the title in B3 to **$10,000 Profit**. Use Goal Seek to determine the number of travelers needed to attain net revenues of $10,000.

k. Use the Find and Replace command to change Trip Guides to Tour Guides in all sheets.

l. Select all three sheets and change the page layout to landscape. Change the left and right margins to 0.5 inch and scale the worksheet to fit on one printed page. Add a custom footer to the three sheets with your name and the date center-aligned.

m. Preview the worksheets. Adjust the picture size if needed.

n. Save the workbook. Print the Break Even sheet and the $10,000 sheet.

CALCULATING TOTAL POINTS AND GPA ★ ★ ★

4. George Lewis is a college student who has just completed the first two years of his undergraduate program as an architecture major. He has decided to create a worksheet that will calculate semester and cumulative totals and GPA for each semester. The completed Spring 2012 worksheet should be similar to the one shown here.

a. Open the workbook ex03_Grade Report. Look at the four sheets. Rename the sheet tabs **Fall 2010**, **Spring 2011**, **Fall 2011**, and **Spring 2012**. Add color to the tabs. Save the workbook as Grade Report in a folder named Grade Analysis.

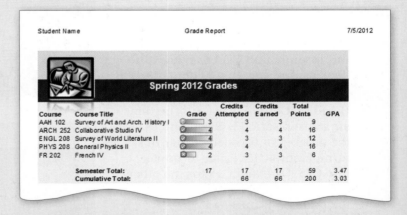

b. You need to enter the formulas to calculate the Total Points and GPA for the four semesters. You will do this for all four sheets at the same time. Select the four sheets. In the Fall 2010 sheet, multiply the Grade by the Credits Earned to calculate Total Points for Collaborative Studio I. Copy that formula down the column. Sum the Credits Attempted, Credits Earned, and Total Points columns and display the results in the Semester Total row.

c. In cell G13, divide the Semester Total's Total Points by the Semester Total's Credits Earned to calculate the GPA for the semester. Format the GPA to two decimal places. Ungroup the sheets.

d. Use what-if analysis to see the grade George would have had to earn in Western Civilization to get an overall 3.0 GPA for the Fall 2010 semester. Change the grade back to a 2.

e. Look at each sheet to see that the formulas were entered and the calculations performed.

f. Go to cell D14 in the Fall 2010 sheet. Enter the reference formula =D13 to copy the Semester Total Credits Attempted number to the Cumulative Total row. Copy the formula to cells E14 and F14 to calculate Credits Earned and Total Points.

g. Go to the Spring 2011 sheet and calculate a Cumulative Total for Credits Attempted by summing the Spring 2011 and Fall 2010 Semester Totals. (Hint: You can use pointing to enter the Cumulative Totals formula.)

h. Copy that formula to the adjacent cells to calculate Cumulative Totals for Credits Earned and Total Points. Repeat this procedure on the Fall 2011 and Spring 2012 sheets.

i. Go to the Fall 2010 sheet. Select all four sheets. In cell G14, calculate the GPA for the Cumulative Total. Format the Cumulative Total GPA to display two decimals. Look at each sheet to see the cumulative GPA for each semester. (Hint: George's cumulative GPA at the end of the Spring 2012 semester is 3.03.)

j. In each sheet, you want to highlight the information in the grade earned column. In the Fall 2010 sheet, apply a Color Scale conditional formatting to the grade column. In the Spring 2011 sheet, apply Data Bars conditional formatting to the grade column. In the Fall 2011 sheet, apply the 5 Arrows (Colored) Icon Set to the grade column. In the Spring 2012 sheet, apply the 3 Symbols (Circled) Icon Set and a Data Bars conditional formatting to the grade column.

k. Add a custom header with your name left-aligned, the sheet name centered, and the date right-aligned to all sheets.

l. Save the workbook. Print the Spring 2012 sheet.

YEAR-TO-DATE SALES ANALYSIS ★ ★ ★

5. Mei Liao is the owner of the Doggie Day Care Center, which offers full- and half-day care for dogs as well as grooming and training services. She has been asked to prepare a report on the year-to-date accounting totals. She has already entered the figures for January through June. Next, she will create a worksheet for the July through December data and compile the year's totals. Your completed worksheet should be similar to that shown here.

a. Open the file ex03_Doggie Day Care. Adjust the zoom to display all the data. Correct the formula errors. Save the workbook as Doggie Day Care.

b. Enter formulas in cells H9 and H10 to calculate the services totals.

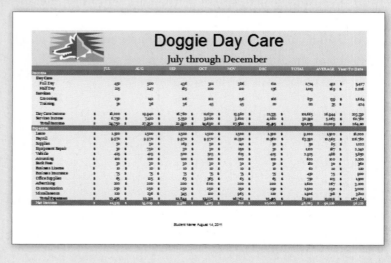

c. Enter the following formula in cell B12 to calculate the income from day care for January: =(B6*B32) + (B7*B33). Copy the formula across the row to calculate the Day Care income. Enter the appropriate formulas in the Total column to calculate the total income figures.

LAB EXERCISES

d. Enter formulas in cells H16 through H28 to calculate the total expenses. In cell H29, total the expenses.

e. In cell B30 enter a formula that subtracts the Total Expenses from the Total Income. Copy the formula across the row.

f. Enter the heading **AVERAGE** in cell I3. Adjust the formatting of the new column to match the other columns in the sheet. Enter a formula to calculate the average number of full-day dogs in cell I6. Copy the formula down the column. Delete the division by zero errors. Adjust the formatting of the sheet as needed.

g. Select the range A1:I30 and copy it to Sheet2, maintaining the original column widths. Adjust the graphic size and the row height to accommodate the graphic. Rename the new sheet **Jul-Dec**. Add tab colors to both sheets.

h. Change the title in the Jul-Dec sheet to **July through December**. Change the month heading in cell B3 to **JUL**. Use AutoFill to change the remaining month headings.

i. Adjust the references in the formulas of rows 12 and 13 by adding the sheet reference.

j. Select cells I14 and I30 and use Watch Window to view the changes made when you enter the following values in the specified cells:

	Jul	Aug	Sep	Oct	Nov	Dec
Full Day	450	500	436	321	386	402
Half Day	225	247	185	100	120	136
Grooming	130	142	116	122	156	166
Training	30	36	36	45	45	20

k. Delete the watch cells and close the Watch Window. Move to cell J3 and enter the heading **Year-to-Date**. In cell J6, enter a formula to compute the total full-day care in the first and second six-month periods. Copy the formula down the column to find the year-to-date totals for all of the rows. Adjust the formatting in column J to match the others in the sheet.

l. Delete Sheet3. Use Find and Replace to change the Marketing labels to **Advertising** in both sheets.

m. Use Goal Seek to calculate the number of full-day dogs needed to increase the Net Income for December to $10,000.

n. Add a custom footer with your name and the date to both sheets. Save the workbook.

o. Print the Jul-Dec sheet on one page.

ON YOUR OWN

EXPANDING BUDGET PROJECTIONS ★

1. In On Your Own exercise 2 of Lab 1, you created a Personal Budget workbook for a three-month budget. Extend the worksheet to add three more months for a total of six months. Add two additional sheets. One sheet will contain a budget for the next six months. The final sheet will present a full year's summary using 3-D references to the values in the appropriate sheets. You need to budget for a vacation. On a separate line below the total balance in the summary sheet, enter the amount you would need. Subtract this value from the total balance. If this value is negative, reevaluate your expenses and adjust them appropriately. Format the sheets using the features you have learned in the first three labs. Add your name in a custom header on all sheets. Preview, print, and save the workbook as Personal Budget2.

COMPANY EXPENSE COMPARISONS ★

2. Using the Internet or the library, obtain yearly income and expense data for three companies in a related business. In a workbook, record each company's data in a separate sheet. In a fourth sheet, calculate the total income, total expenses, and net income for each company. Also in this sheet, calculate the overall totals for income, expense, and net income. Format the sheets using the features you have learned in the first three labs. Add your name in a custom header on all sheets. Preview, print, and save the workbook as Company Expenses in a folder named Business.

HOUSE ANALYSIS ★ ★

3. Select three cities in which you would consider living after you graduate. Using the Internet or the library, select one price point of housing and determine each house's asking price, square footage, acreage, number of bedrooms, and number of bathrooms. In a workbook containing four sheets, record each city's housing prices and statistics in separate worksheets. In the fourth sheet, calculate the average, maximum and minimum for each city. Include a chart showing the average data for the three cities. Format the sheets using the features you have learned in the first three labs. Add your name in a custom header on all sheets. Preview, print, and save the workbook as House Analysis in a folder named Housing.

LAB EXERCISES

INVENTORY TRACKING ★ ★ ★

4. It's a good idea to have an inventory of your personal items for safe keeping. Design a worksheet that will keep track of your personal items divided by category; for example: living room, dining room, bedroom, and so forth. Each category may have as many detail lines as needed to represent the items. For example: sofa, vases, art, and so on. The worksheet should keep track of the number of items; the price paid for each item; the extended price (items * price), if applicable; and the replacement value. Determine the percentage increase in replacement value. Sum the price paid and replacement value in each category and the total value. Format the sheet using the features you have learned in the first three labs. Add your name in a custom header on all sheets. Change the worksheet orientation if necessary; preview, print, and save the workbook as Inventory Tracking.

START YOUR OWN BUSINESS ★ ★ ★

5. Owning and managing a small business is a dream of many college students. Do some research on the Web or in the library and choose a business that interests you. Create a projected worksheet for four quarters in separate worksheets. In a fifth sheet, show the total for the year. Include a year-to-date value in each quarterly sheet. In the last-quarter sheet, depending on the business you select, determine how many customers or sales you need in the last quarter to break even and to end the year with a 10 percent profit. Format the sheets using the features you have learned in the first three labs. Add your name in a custom header on all sheets. Preview, print, and save the workbook as My Business.

CASE STUDY

Downtown Internet Café

Your analysis of the sales data for the first quarter of operations for the Downtown Internet Café projects a small, steady increase in sales each month. If an advertising campaign promoting the new Internet aspect of the Café is mounted, you forecast that coffee and food sales in that quarter will increase sharply.

Evan, the Cafe owner, is still trying to decide if he should advertise and has asked you to send him a memo containing the worksheet data showing the expected sales without an advertising campaign and the chart showing the projected sales with an advertising campaign. Additionally, Evan wants a copy of the second-quarter forecast showing the 15-percent profit margins for each month. He also wants a copy of the workbook file so that he can play with the sales values to see their effects on the profit margin.

You will learn how to share information between applications while you create these memos. Your completed documents will look like those shown below.

NOTE This lab assumes that you know how to use Word 2010 and that you have completed Labs 2 and 3 of Excel 2010.

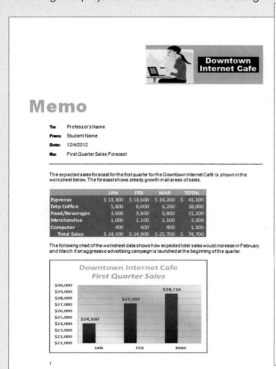

Sharing Information between Applications

All Microsoft Office 2010 applications have a common user interface such as similar Ribbon commands and galleries. In addition to these obvious features, they have been designed to work together, making it easy to share and exchange information between applications. For example, the same commands and procedures to copy information within an Excel 2010 worksheet are used to copy information to other Office 2010 applications such as Word. The information can be pasted in many different formats such as a worksheet object, a bitmap, a picture, a linked object, or an embedded object. How you decide to paste the object depends on what you want to be able to do with the data once it is inserted in the Word document.

COPYING BETWEEN EXCEL AND WORD

The memo to Evan about the analysis of the sales data has already been created using Word 2010 and saved as a document file.

1

Start Word 2010 and open the document exwt1_Sales Forecast Memo. docx.

In the memo header, replace Professor's Name with your instructor's name and Student Name with your name.

Save the file as Sales Forecast Memo **to your solution file location.**

Your screen should be similar to Figure 1

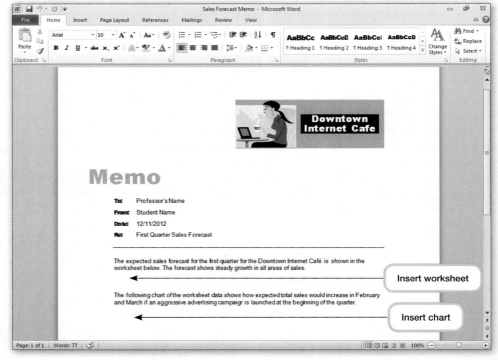

Figure 1

As you can see, you still need to add the Excel worksheet data and chart to the memo. To insert the information from the Excel workbook file into the Word memo, you need to open the workbook. You will then tile the two open application windows to make it easier to see and work with both files.

2

● **Start Excel and open the workbook** exwt1_Sales Charts.

Your screen should be similar to Figure 2

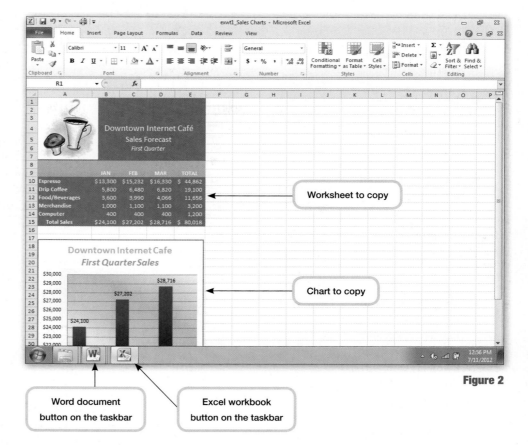

Worksheet to copy

Chart to copy

Word document button on the taskbar

Excel workbook button on the taskbar

Figure 2

There are now two open applications, Word and Excel. You will insert the worksheet data of the first-quarter sales forecast below the first paragraph. Below the second paragraph, you will display the chart.

You will begin by copying the chart from Excel into the Word document. While using Excel, you have learned how to use cut, copy, and paste to move or copy information within and between worksheets. You also can perform these operations between files in the same application and between files in different Office applications. You want to insert the chart as a picture object that can be edited using the Picture Tools commands in Word.

3

- Select the column chart.

- Click 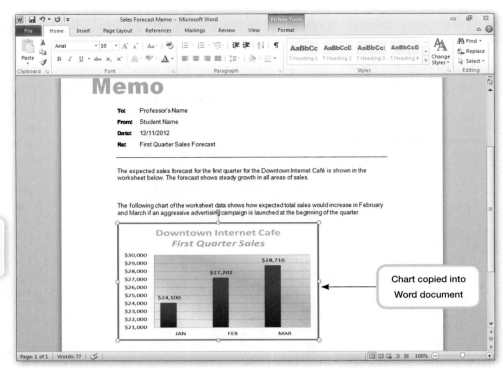 Copy to copy the selected chart object to the Clipboard.

- Switch to the Word document.

Having Trouble?

Click the Word document button in the taskbar.

- Move the cursor to the second blank line below the last paragraph of the memo.

- Click to open the Paste menu and choose Picture.

- Click on the chart object to select it.

- Open the Picture Tools Format tab.

- Click Wrap Text and choose Top and Bottom.

- Adjust the size of the chart and position it as in Figure 3.

Your screen should be similar to Figure 3

Figure 3

A copy of the chart has been inserted as a picture object into the Word document. By changing the text wrapping to top and bottom, the picture object can be moved anywhere in the document and the text will always appear above and below the object. It can be formatted, sized, and moved like any other picture object.

Linking between Applications

Next, you want to copy the worksheet showing the sales trends to below the first paragraph in the memo. You will insert the worksheet into the memo as **a linked object**. Information created in one application also can be inserted as a linked object into a document created by another application. When an object is linked, the data is stored in the **source file** (the document in which it was created). A graphic representation or picture of the data is displayed in the **destination file** (the document in which the object is inserted). A connection between the information in the destination file to the source file is established by the creation of an **external reference**, also called a **link**. The link contains references to the location of the source file and the selection within the document that is linked to the destination file.

When changes are made in the source file that affect the linked object, the changes are reflected automatically in the destination file when it is opened. This is called a **live link**. When you create linked objects, the date and time on your computer should be accurate. This is because the program refers to the date of the source file to determine whether updates are needed when you open the destination file.

You will copy the worksheet as a linked object so that it will be updated automatically if the source file is edited. To make it easier to work with the two applications, you will display the two open application windows side-by-side.

1

• **Right-click on a blank area of the taskbar and choose Show Windows Side by Side from the shortcut menu.**

• **Click in the Excel window and select cells A9 through E15.**

• **Click ⬛ Copy.**

• **Click in the Word document and move to the center blank line between the paragraphs of the memo.**

• **Open the ⬛ Paste menu and choose Paste Special.**

• **Choose Paste link from the Paste Special dialog box.**

Your screen should be similar to Figure 4

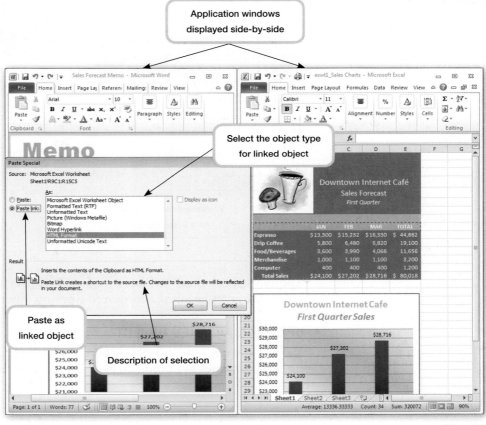

Figure 4

The Paste Special dialog box displays the type of object contained in the Clipboard and its location in the Source area. From the As list box, you select the type of format for the object you want inserted into the destination file. There are many different object types from which you can select. It is important to select the appropriate object format so that the link works correctly when inserted in the destination. In this case, you want to use the Microsoft Office Excel Worksheet Object format.

The Result area describes the effect of your selections. In this case, the object will be inserted as a picture, and a link will be created to the worksheet in the source file. Selecting the Display as Icon option changes the display of the object in the destination file from a picture to an icon. When inserted in this manner, double-clicking the icon displays the object picture.

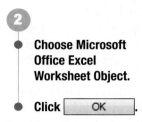

● **Choose Microsoft Office Excel Worksheet Object.**

● **Click** OK .

Your screen should be similar to Figure 5

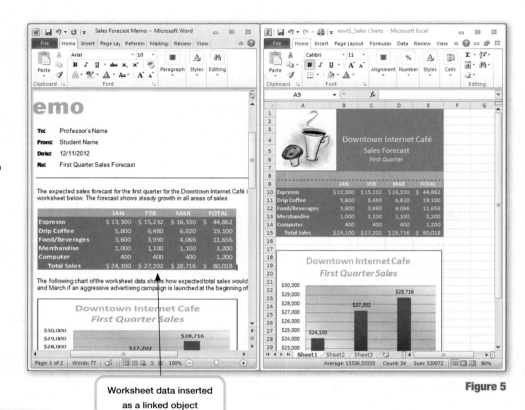

Worksheet data inserted as a linked object

Figure 5

The worksheet data has been copied into the Word document as a linked object that can be sized and moved like any other object.

UPDATING A LINKED OBJECT

Next, you want to return the sales data in the Excel worksheet to the original forecasted values assuming an aggressive marketing campaign is not mounted.

1

- Switch to the Excel window.

- Press Esc to clear the moving border.

- Change the entry in C10 to **13600** (you are removing the formula).

- In the same manner, replace the formulas in the following cells with the values shown.

Cell	Value
D10	**14,200**
C11	**6,000**
D11	**6,200**
C12	**3,800**
D12	**3,800**

Your screen should be similar to Figure 6

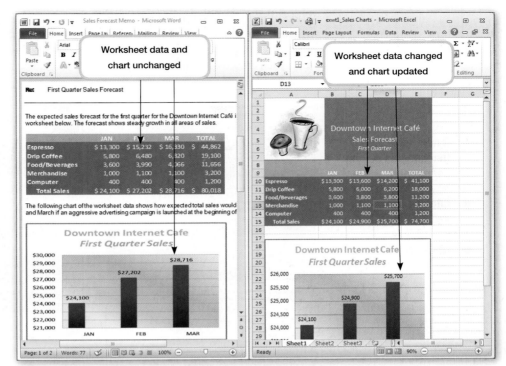

Figure 6

The Excel worksheet and chart have been updated; however, the worksheet data and chart in the Word document still reflect the original values. You will update the worksheet in the Word document next.

2

- Switch to the Word window.

- Select the worksheet object.

- Press F9 to update the linked object.

Another Method

You also can choose Update Link from the linked object's shortcut menu.

Your screen should be similar to Figure 7

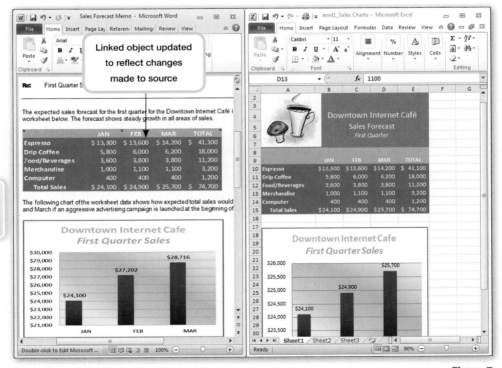

Figure 7

The linked worksheet object in the memo now reflects the changes you made in Excel for the sales data. This is because any changes you make in Excel will be reflected in the linked object in the Word document. Next, you will see if the chart has been updated also.

- **If necessary, scroll the memo to see the entire chart.**

- **Click on the chart and press** F9 .

- **Deselect the chart.**

Additional Information

The chart may have moved to the next page when the worksheet data was inserted. If this happened, reduce the size of the chart object.

Your screen should be similar to Figure 8

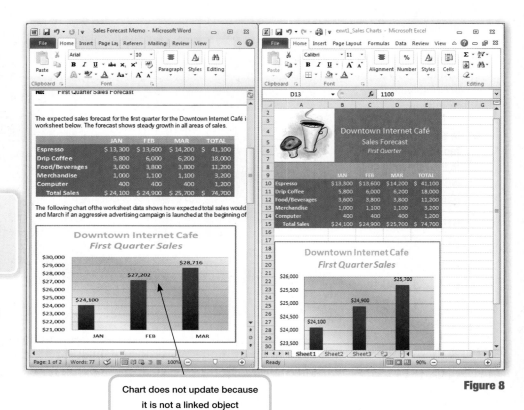

Chart does not update because it is not a linked object

Figure 8

Because the chart in the Word document is not a linked object, it does not update to reflect the changes in data that you made in Excel.

EDITING LINKS

When a document is opened that contains links, the application looks for the source file and automatically updates the linked objects. If the document contains many links, updating can take a lot of time. Additionally, if you move the source file to another location or perform other operations that may interfere with the link, your link will not work. To help with situations like these, you can edit the settings associated with links. You will look at the links to the worksheet data created in the Word document.

1

- Open the taskbar shortcut menu and choose Undo Show Side by Side.

- If necessary, maximize the Word window.

- If necessary, adjust the size of the chart to the same width as the worksheet object.

- Right-click the worksheet object and select Linked Worksheet Object.

- Choose Links from the submenu.

Your screen should be similar to Figure 9

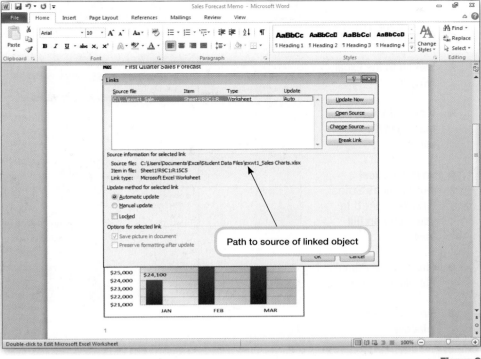

Figure 9

The Links dialog box displays the object path for all links in the document in the list box. The field code specifies the path and name of the source file, the range of linked cells or object name, the type of file, and the update status. Below the list box, the details for the selected link are displayed.

The other options in this dialog box are described in the table below.

Option	Effect
Automatic update	Updates the linked object whenever the destination document is opened or the source file changes. This is the default.
Manual update	The destination document is not automatically updated and you must use the Update Now command button to update the link.
Locked	Prevents a linked object from being updated.
Open Source	Opens the source document for the selected link.
Change Source	Used to modify the path to the source document.
Break Link	Breaks the connection between the source document and the active document.

The links in the Word document are to the exwt1_Sales Charts workbook file. Next, you will save the Excel workbook file using a new file name. Then you will recheck the link settings.

2

- Click [OK].

- Switch to the Excel window.

- If necessary, maximize the window.

- Save the Excel workbook as Sales Charts Linked to your solution file location.

- Close the workbook file (do not exit Excel).

- Switch to the Word window.

Having Trouble?

Click the application taskbar button to switch between windows.

- From the worksheet object's shortcut menu, select Linked Worksheet Object and choose Links.

Your screen should be similar to Figure 10

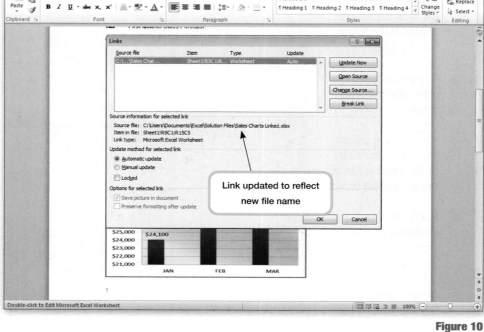

Figure 10

You can now see that the link has been updated to reflect the new workbook file name.

3

- Click [OK].

- Open the File tab and choose the Print group.

- Check the layout of the document in the preview and if necessary return to the document and make any needed adjustments.

- Print and then close the document, saving any changes if needed.

EMBEDDING AN OBJECT

Additional Information

The source data is stored in an Excel worksheet that is incorporated in the Word file.

The last thing you need to send Evan is a memo that describes and shows the second-quarter forecast. To do this, you will open the memo already created for you in Word and embed the worksheet containing the second-quarter data that Evan wants in the appropriate location. An **embedded object** is stored in the destination file and becomes part of that document. The entire file, not just the selection that is displayed in the destination file, becomes part of the document. This means that you can modify it without affecting the source document where the original object resides.

1

- Open the Word document exwt1_ Second Quarter Memo.docx.

- In the memo header, replace Student Name with your name.

- Save the document as Second Quarter Memo to your solution file location.

- Switch to Excel and open the workbook file exwt1_Second Quarter.

Your screen should be similar to Figure 11

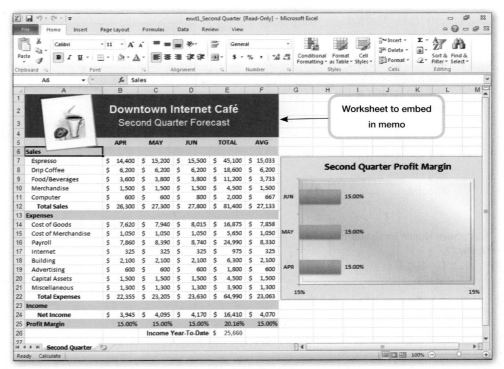

Figure 11

This workbook file contains a copy of the second-quarter worksheet from the Annual Forecast workbook. You will embed the second-quarter forecast worksheet in the Word document.

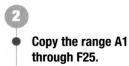

2

● Copy the range A1 through F25.

● Switch to the Word window.

● Move to the middle blank line below the first paragraph of the memo.

● Open the  menu and choose Paste Special.

Your screen should be similar to Figure 12

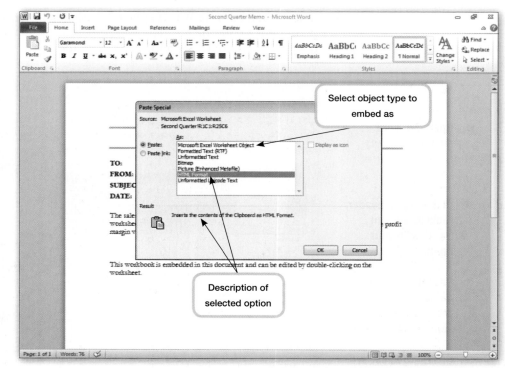

Figure 12

The Paste option inserts or embeds the Clipboard contents in the format you specify from the As list box. The default is to insert the Clipboard contents in HTML format. You want to embed the contents of the Clipboard into the document so it can be edited using the source program. To do this, you select the option that displays the source name, in this case Excel.

3

● Select Microsoft Excel Worksheet Object.

● Click ___OK___ .

Your screen should be similar to Figure 13

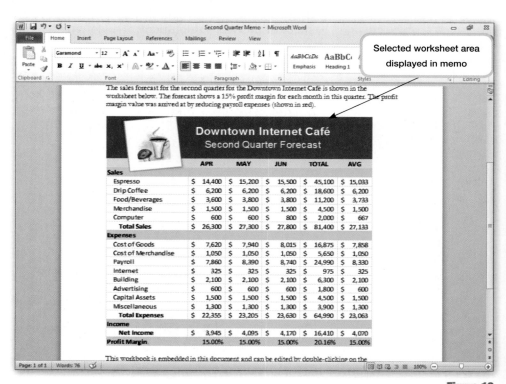

Figure 13

The selected portion of the worksheet is displayed in the memo at the location of the insertion point.

UPDATING AN EMBEDDED OBJECT

You want to add color to the payroll range of cells you adjusted to arrive at the 15 percent profit margin. Because the worksheet is embedded, you can do this from within the Word document. The source program is used to edit data in an embedded object. To open the source program and edit the worksheet, you double-click the embedded object.

Double-click the worksheet object in Word.

Having Trouble?

If the worksheet does not fully display the numbers, click outside the worksheet to return to the document, make the worksheet object larger, and then open the source program again.

Your screen should be similar to Figure 14

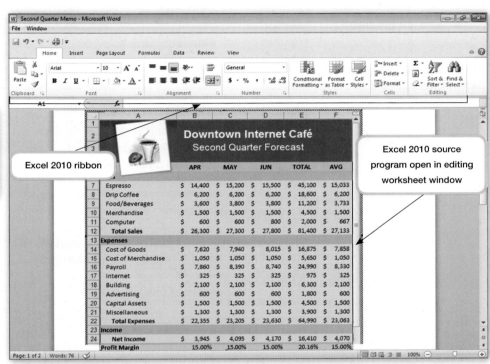

Figure 14

Additional Information

The source program must be installed on the computer system to be able to open and edit the embedded object.

The source program, in this case Excel 2010, is opened. The Excel Ribbon replaces the Word Ribbon and the embedded object is displayed in an editing worksheet window. Now you can use the source program commands to edit the object.

2

● **Change the font color of cells B16 through D16 to the Red, Accent 2 theme color.**

● **Close the source program by clicking anywhere outside the object.**

● **Save the document.**

Your screen should be similar to Figure 15

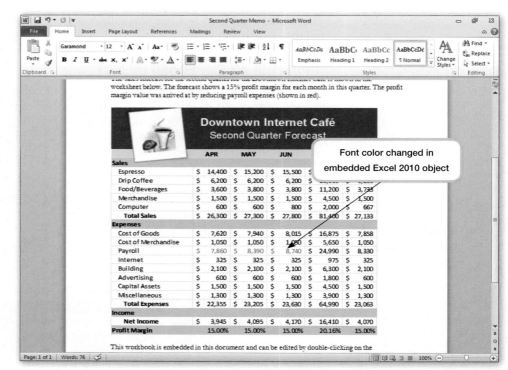

Figure 15

The embedded object in the memo is updated to reflect the changes you made. However, the Excel worksheet is unchanged.

3

● **Preview and print the memo.**

● **Exit Word.**

● **Look at the Excel worksheet to confirm that the worksheet has not changed.**

● **Exit Excel.**

Deciding When to Link or Embed Objects

Linking documents is a very handy feature, particularly in documents whose information is updated frequently. If you include a linked object in a document that you are giving to another person, make sure the user has access to the source file and application. Otherwise the links will not operate correctly.

Keep the following in mind when deciding whether to link or embed objects.

Use linking when:	Use embedding when:
File size is important.	File size is not important.
Users have access to the source file and application.	Users have access to the application but not to the source file.
The information is updated frequently.	The data changes infrequently.
	You do not want the source data to change.

LAB REVIEW | Working Together 1

KEY TERMS

destination file EXWT1.5
embedded object EXWT1.10
external reference EXWT1.5
link EXWT1.5

linked object EXWT1.4
live link EXWT1.5
source file EXWT1.4

COMMAND SUMMARY

Command	Shortcut	Action
Home tab		
Clipboard group		
/Paste Special/Paste		Inserts object as an embedded object
/Paste Special/Paste Link		Inserts object as a linked object
Linked Object shortcut menu (Word)		
Update Link	F9	Updates linked object
Linked Worksheet Object/Links		Modifies selected link

STEP-BY-STEP

RESCUE FOUNDATION INCOME MEMO ★ ★

1. The Animal Rescue Foundation's agency director has asked you to provide her with information about income for 2011. She is particularly interested in the two pet show fund-raising and membership drive events that are held in April and October. You will create a memo to her that will include a copy of the worksheet analysis of this data. Your completed memo will be similar to that shown here.

   a. Start Word and open the document exwt1_ Rescue Memo.docx.

   b. In the memo header, replace the From placeholder with your name.

   c. Start Excel and open the workbook exwt1_ Contributions.

   d. Insert both worksheets as Microsoft Excel Worksheet Object links below the first paragraph in the Word memo. Reduce the size of the worksheets until the memo fits on one page.

   e. You notice the April raffle ticket sales value looks low and after checking your records, you see it was entered incorrectly. In Excel, change the April raffle ticket sales income to $3,120.

   f. In the memo, update the linked worksheet.

   g. Save the Excel workbook as Contributions. Exit Excel.

   h. Save the Word document as Rescue Memo Linked. Preview and print the document.

Memo

To:	Barbara Wood, Director
From:	Student Name
CC:	Mark Wilson
Date:	6/27/2012
Re:	Income

Below is the completed income analysis for 2011. As you can see, the income for Fall/Winter is much higher due to corporate donations.

Animal Rescue Foundation

	March	April	May	June	July	August	Total
Annual Memberships	$9,200	$18,783	$8,595	$9,934	$5,684	$5,781	$57,977
Private Donations	$625	$1,400		$1,225			$3,250
Corporate Donations		$17,000	$15,000		$4,000	$9,000	$45,000
Raffle Tickets		$3,120					$3,120
Pet Show		$8,000					$8,000
Other	$3,000	$3,000	$3,000	$3,000	$3,000	$3,000	$18,000
Total	$12,825	$51,303	$26,595	$14,159	$12,684	$17,781	$135,347

Animal Rescue Foundation

	September	October	November	December	January	February	Total	Annual Total
Annual Memberships	$6,740	$23,723	$10,595	$22,134	$11,584	$10,781	$85,557	$143,534
Private Donations	$800	$2,200	$5,600	$79,900	$1,900	$3,000	$93,400	$96,650
Corporate Donations		$15,000		$312,000		$10,000	$337,000	$382,000
Raffle Tickets		$3,294					$3,294	$3,414
Pet Show		$11,000					$11,000	$19,000
Other	$3,000	$3,000	$3,000	$3,000	$3,000	$3,000	$18,000	$36,000
Total	$10,540	$58,217	$19,195	$417,034	$16,484	$26,781	$548,251	$680,598

Also, the pet show fundraising events have been very successful in boosting income during the slow periods of each year.

1

LAB EXERCISES

STUDENT RETENTION MEMO ★★

2. As part of your job at the State College, you keep track of the number of students who return each year and how many of those students graduate in four or five years. You record this data in a worksheet and are preparing to include the results for the class of 2012 in a department memo. Your completed memo will be similar to that shown here.

a. Start Word and open the exwt1_Student Retention.docx document. Replace Student Name with your name on the From line in the heading.

b. Start Excel and open the exwt1_College Student Retention workbook.

c. Copy the worksheet as a linked object to below the paragraph of the memo.

d. In Excel, enter the fourth-year graduation data for 2012 of **1495** in cell E11 and the fifth-year graduation rate for 2012 of **67** in E13.

e. Save the workbook as Student Retention to your solution file location. Exit Excel.

f. In Word, update the linked worksheet object.

g. Save the Word document as Student Retention Rates to your solution file location. Print the memo.

INTEROFFICE MEMORANDUM

TO: STATE COLLEGE ADMISSIONS STAFF
FROM: STUDENT NAME
SUBJECT: STUDENT RETENTION RATES
DATE: 7/11/2012

The rate of student retention for the past four years is displayed in the worksheet below. The number of students who return to State College every year and finish their degrees in four years is laudable, but there is growing concern at the increasing number of students who either do not return for the fourth year, or don't graduate after four years. There is a meeting scheduled for next week to discuss this issue and possible ways to decrease the rate of change. Please review this information prior to the meeting.

State College
Student Retention Rates

	2009	2010	2011	2012	Average
Enrolled First Year Students	1537	1579	1670	1700	1622
Returning Second Year Students	1397	1433	1571	1598	1500
Returning Third Year Students	1285	1398	1520	1562	1441
Returning Fourth Year Students	1221	1324	1484	1555	1396
Graduating Fourth Year Students	1211	1312	1461	1495	1370
Percent Graduate In Four Years	**79%**	**83%**	**87%**	**88%**	**84%**
Graduating Fifth Year Students	44	55	62	67	57
Percent Graduate In Five Years	**82%**	**87%**	**91%**	**92%**	**88%**

HOME SALE PRICE MEMO ★ ★

3. Jennifer works in the marketing department for a local real estate company. She has recently researched the median home prices and number of days on the market over the last three years for existing homes in the local market area. She has created a worksheet and column charts of the data. Now Jennifer wants to send a memo containing the information to her supervisor. The completed memo will be similar to that shown here.

a. Start Word and open the document exwt1_Home Price Memo.docx.

b. In the header, replace the CC: placeholder information in brackets with your name.

c. Start Excel and open the workbook exwt1_Real Estate Prices. Embed the worksheet data including the charts below the paragraph in the Word memo. Exit Excel.

d. Open the embedded worksheet object in Word and scroll to see the column chart of the Average Price. Change the title to Median Price and the chart type to a clustered cylinder.

e. Change the Days on Market chart to a clustered bar in 3-D. Select a more colorful chart style.

f. Reduce the size of the embedded worksheet object until it is just large enough to display the Median Price chart only. (Hint: Drag the sizing handles of the editing worksheet window until only the chart is displayed.) Close the embedded object, leaving the chart displayed in the memo.

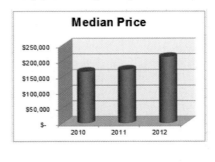

g. Save the Word document as Home Price Memo to your solution file location. Preview and print the document.

Creating a Database

Objectives

After completing this lab, you will know how to:

1. Plan, create, and modify a database.

2. Create and save a table structure.

3. Define field names, data types, field properties, and primary key fields.

4. Enter and edit data.

5. Add attachments.

6. Change views.

7. Adjust column widths.

8. Use the Best Fit feature.

9. Create a second table.

10. Navigate among records.

11. Add, copy, and move fields.

12. Add and delete records.

13. Document a database.

14. Preview and print a table.

15. Change page orientation.

16. Close and open a table and database.

Lifestyle Fitness Club

You have recently accepted a job as a human resources administrator with Lifestyle Fitness Club. Like many fitness centers, Lifestyle Fitness Club includes exercise equipment, free weights, aerobics classes, tanning and massage facilities, a swimming pool, a steam room and sauna, and child-care facilities. In addition, it promotes a healthy lifestyle by including educational seminars on good nutrition and proper exercise. It also has a small snack bar that serves healthy drinks, sandwiches, and snacks.

The Lifestyle Fitness Clubs are a franchised chain of clubs that are individually owned. You work at a club owned by Felicity and Ryan Albright, who also own two others in California. Accounting and employment functions for all three clubs are handled centrally at the Landis location.

You are responsible for maintaining the employment records for all employees, as

well as records for traditional employment activities such as hiring and benefits. Currently the club employment records are maintained on paper forms and are stored in file cabinets organized alphabetically by last name. Although the information is well organized, it still takes time to manually look through the folders to locate the information you need and to compile reports from this data.

The club has recently purchased new computers, and the owners want to update the employee record-keeping system to an electronic database management system. The software tool you will use to create the database is the database application Microsoft Access 2010. In this lab, you will learn about entering, editing, previewing, and printing information in the database you create for the club.

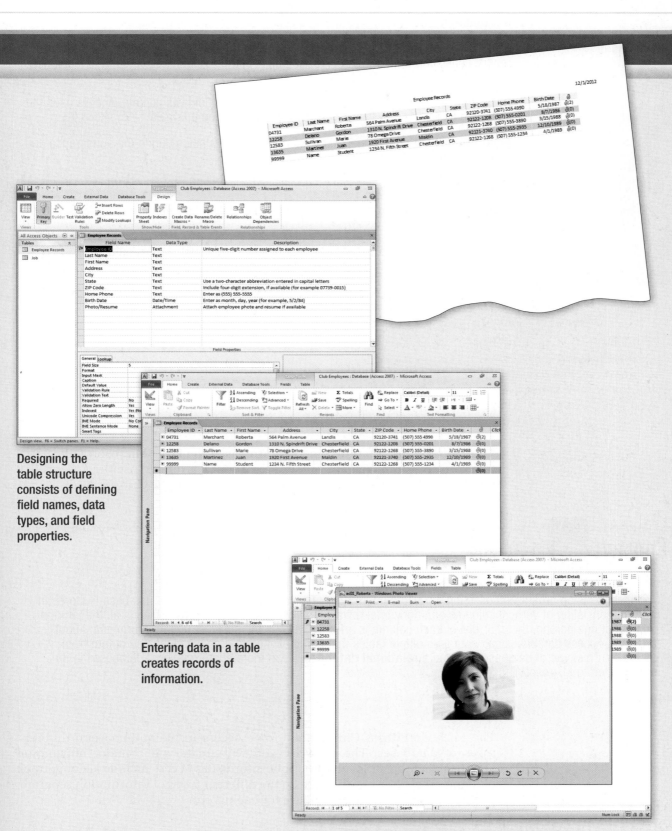

Designing the table structure consists of defining field names, data types, and field properties.

Entering data in a table creates records of information.

Fields can contain attachments such as pictures or files.

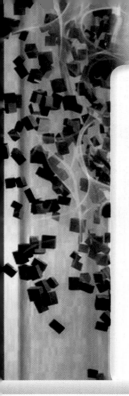

The following concepts will be introduced in this lab:

1 Database A database is an organized collection of related information.

2 Object An Access database is made up of several types of objects, such as a table or report, consisting of many elements. An object can be created, selected, and manipulated as a unit.

3 Data Type The data type defines the type of data the field will contain. Access uses the data type to ensure that the right kind of data is entered in a field.

4 Field Property A field property is a characteristic that helps define the appearance and behavior of a field.

5 Primary Key A primary key is a field that uniquely identifies each record.

6 Relationship A relationship establishes the association between common fields in two tables.

7 Subdatasheet A subdatasheet is a data table nested within a main data table; it contains information that is related or joined to the main table.

Designing a New Database

The Lifestyle Fitness Club recently purchased the 2010 Microsoft Office System software suite. You are very excited about learning to use the Access 2010 database management system to store and maintain the club's records.

Concept Database

A **database** is an organized collection of related information. Typically, the information in a database is stored in a **table** consisting of vertical columns and horizontal rows. Each row contains a **record**, which is all the information about one person, thing, or place. Each column is a **field**, which is the smallest unit of information about a record. Access databases can contain multiple tables that can be linked to produce combined output from all tables. This type of database is called a **relational database**. Read more about relational databases in the Introduction to Microsoft Office 2010.

The Lifestyle Fitness Club plans to use Access to maintain several different types of databases. The database you will create will contain information about each club employee. Other plans for using Access include keeping track of members and inventory. To keep the different types of information separate, the club plans to create a database for each group.

Good database design follows two basic principles: Do not include duplicate information (also called redundant data) in tables and enter accurate and complete information. Redundant data wastes space, wastes the time that is required to enter the same information multiple times, and consequently increases the possibility of errors and inconsistencies between tables. The information that is stored in a database may be used to make business decisions and if the information is inaccurate, any decisions that are based on the information will be misinformed.

To attain these principles, the database design process is very important and consists of the following steps: plan, design, develop, implement, and refine and review. You will find that you will generally follow these steps in order as you create your database. However, you will probably retrace steps as the final database is developed.

Step	Description
Plan	The first step in the development of a database is to define the purpose of the database in writing. This includes establishing the scope of the database, determining its feasibility, and deciding how you expect to use it and who will use it.
Design	Using the information gathered during the planning step, you can create an implementation plan and document the functional requirements. This includes finding and organizing the information required for the database and deciding how this information should be divided into subject groups. You also need to think about the types of questions you might want the database to answer and determine the types of output you need such as reports and mailings.
Develop	Using the design you created, you are ready to create tables to hold the necessary data. Create separate tables for each of the major subjects to make it easier to locate and modify information. Define fields for each item that you want to store in each table. Determine how tables are related to one another, and include fields to clarify the relationships as needed. Try not to duplicate information in the different tables.
Implement	After setting up the tables, populate the tables by entering sample data to complete each record. Then work with the data to make sure it is providing the information you need.
Refine and Review	Refine the design by adding or removing fields and tables and continue to test the data and design. Apply the data normalization rules to see if the tables are structured correctly. Periodically review the database to ensure that the initial objectives have been met and to identify required enhancements.

As you develop the employee database for the Lifestyle Fitness Club, you will learn more about the details of the design steps and how to use Access 2010 to create a well-designed and accurate database.

PLANNING THE CLUB DATABASE

Your first step is to plan the design of your database tables: the number of tables, the data they will contain, and the relationship between the tables. You need to decide what information each table in the employee database should contain and how it should be structured or laid out.

You can obtain this information by analyzing the current record-keeping procedures used in the company. You need to understand the existing procedures so that your database tables will reflect the information that is maintained by different departments. You should be aware of the forms that serve as the basis for the data entered into the department records and of the information that is taken from the records to produce periodic reports. You also need to determine whether there is information that the department heads would like to be able to obtain from the database that may be too difficult to generate with current procedures.

After looking over the existing record-keeping procedures and the reports that are created from the information, you decide to create several separate tables of data in the database file. Each table should only contain information about the subject of the table. Additionally, try not to duplicate information in different tables. If this occurs, create a separate table for this information. Creating several smaller tables of related data rather than one large table makes it easier to use the tables and faster to process data. This is because you can join several tables together as needed.

The main table will include the employee's basic information, such as employee number, name, birth date, and address. Another will contain the employee's job title and work location only. A third will contain data on pay rate and hours worked each week. To clarify the organization of the database, you sketched the structure for the employee database as shown below.

Club Records Database

Employee Records Table

Emp #	Last Name	First Name	Street	City	State	Zipcode	Phone	Birth Date
7721	Brown	Linda	—	—	—	—	—	—
7823	Duggan	Michael	—	—	—	—	—	—
• • •	• • •	• • •	• • •	• • •	• • •	• • •	• • •	• • •

link on common field

link on common field

Clubs Table

Emp #	Location	Position
7721	Iona	Greeter
7823	Fort Myers	Server
• • •	• • •	• • •

Pay Table

Emp #	Pay	Hours
7721	8.25	30
7823	7.50	20
• • •	• • •	• • •

Creating and Naming the Database File

Now that you have decided what information you want to include in the tables, you are ready to create a new database for the employee information using the Microsoft Access 2010 database management program.

1

- **Start the Access 2010 application.**

Having Trouble?

See the Introduction to Microsoft Office 2010 for information about starting an Office application and for a discussion of features that are common to all Office 2010 applications.

Your screen should be similar to Figure 1.1

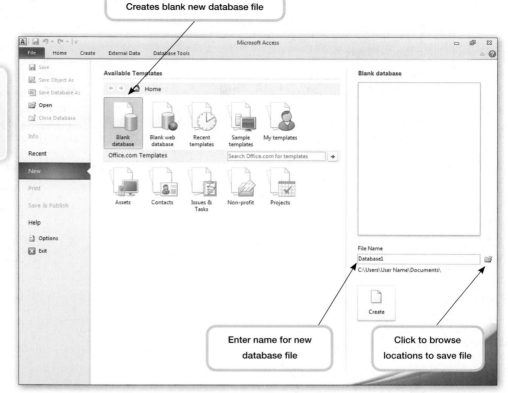

Creates blank new database file

Enter name for new database file

Click to browse locations to save file

Figure 1.1

Additional Information

Backstage view can be accessed anytime by opening the File tab.

When Microsoft Access first opens, the New tab of Backstage view is open and ready for you to create a new database. Several methods can be used to create a new database. One method is to use one of the many templates that are provided by Microsoft as the basis for your new database. A database template generally includes the data structure, tables, queries, forms, and reports for the selected type of database. Another method is to start with a blank database that contains the basic database objects and then add your own content. Although using a template is sometimes the fastest way to create a database, it often requires a lot of work to adapt the template to suit the needs of the existing data. A third option is to copy or import data from another source into an Access database file. Finally, you can use a custom template that you created and saved as the basis for your new database.

You decide to create the club database from a blank database file. The Blank Database template includes the basic structure for a database file, but it does not include a data structure that is specific to a type of database.

Additionally, when creating a new database, you need to enter a file name and specify the location on your computer where you want it saved. The File Name box displays Database1, the default database file name. After you specify the file name you want to use and the location to which it should be saved, Access will display the file extension .accdb after the file name. This identifies the file as an Access 2010 database.

Additional Information

Depending on your Windows settings, your screens may not display file extensions.

Having Trouble?

For information on how to save a file, refer to the Saving a File section in the Introduction to Microsoft Office 2010 lab.

2

- If necessary, click [Blank Database] in the Available Templates section of the New window.

- Replace the text in the File Name text box with Club Employees

Having Trouble?

If the default file name is not highlighted, triple-click on it to select the entire file name.

Additional Information

You do not need to type the file extension, as Access will add it automatically for you.

- Click 📂 to browse locations.

- Specify the appropriate drive and folder where you will save your database files (check with your instructor if you are not sure).

- Click ☐ OK ☐.

- Click [Create].

Your screen should be similar to Figure 1.2

Having Trouble?

If your screen looks slightly different, this is because Access remembers settings that were on when the program was last used.

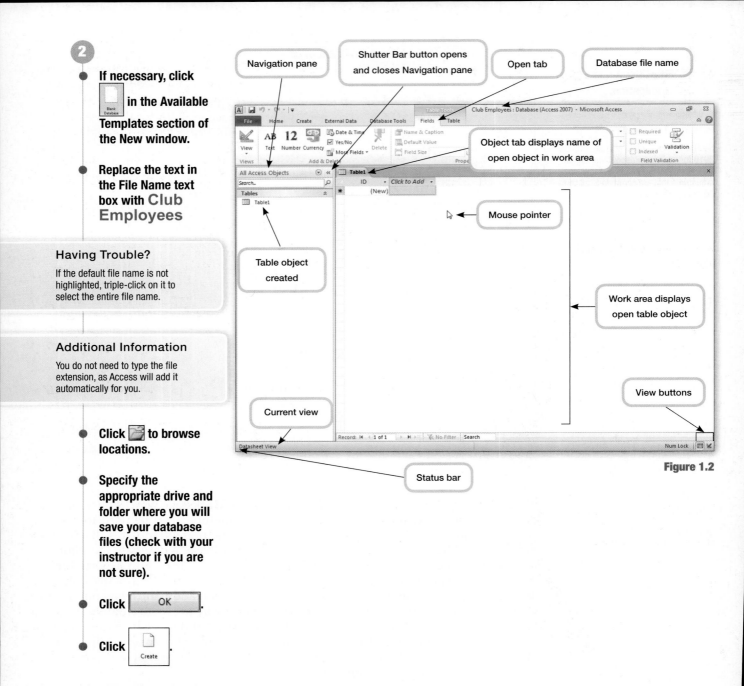

Figure 1.2

The blank database file is opened in the Access application window. The name of the database, Club Employees, followed by the application name appears in the window title bar.

EXPLORING THE ACCESS WINDOW

Located below the title bar is the Access 2010 Ribbon, which contain the commands and features you will use to create and modify database objects. The Access Ribbon always has four main tabs available: Home, Create, External Data, and Database Tools. Additional contextual tabs will appear as you perform different tasks and open various windows. In this case, the Table Tools Fields and Table contextual tabs are available to help you create a new table. The Table Tools Fields tab is currently open and contains command buttons that are used to perform basic database functions specifically relating to the fields within the table.

The mouse pointer appears as on your screen. The mouse pointer changes shape depending upon the task you are performing or where the pointer is located in the window.

The large area below the Ribbon is the work area where different Access components are displayed as you are using the program. When a new database file is created, it includes one empty table named Table1. A table is the main structure in a database that holds the data. It is one of several different database components or objects that can be included within the database file.

Concept 2 Object

An Access database is made up of several types of objects, such as a table or report, consisting of many elements. An **object** is a database component that can be created, selected, and manipulated as a unit. The basic database objects are described below.

Object	Use
Table	Store data.
Query	Find and display selected data.
Form	View, add, and update data in tables.
Report	Analyze and print data in a specific layout.

The table object is the basic unit of a database and must be created first, before any other types of objects are created. Access displays each different type of object in its own window. You can open multiple objects from the same database file in the work area; however, you cannot open more than one database file at a time in a single instance of Access. To open a second database file, you need to start another instance of Access and open the database file in it.

The work area displays a tab containing the table name for the open table. It is used to switch between open objects in the work area. There is currently just one tab because only one object is open.

Just below the work area, the status bar provides information about the task you are working on and about the current Access operation. Currently, the left end of the status bar displays Datasheet view and the right end displays two buttons that are used to change the view. In addition, the status bar displays messages such as instructions to help you use the program more efficiently.

USING THE NAVIGATION PANE

The **Navigation pane** along the left edge of the work area displays all the objects in the database and is used to open and manage the objects. Because your database only contains one object, Table1, that is the only object listed in the pane. When there are many different objects, the pane organizes the objects into categories and groups within each category. It is used to quickly access the different objects.

The Navigation pane is always displayed, but it can be collapsed to a bar to provide more space in the work area. The Shutter Bar close button « , located in the upper-right corner of the pane, is used to show or hide the pane.

Additional Information

The items in the Navigation pane can be organized differently by using the menu at the top of the pane.

● Click « to close the Navigation pane.

Your screen should be similar to Figure 1.3

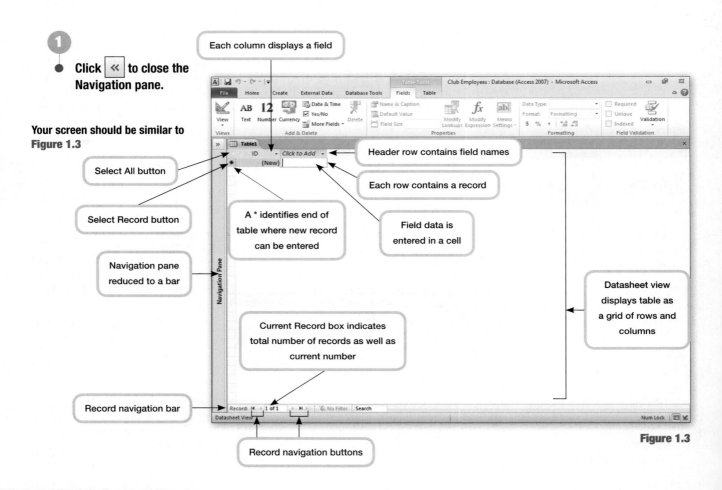

Each column displays a field

Header row contains field names

Each row contains a record

Select All button

Select Record button

A * identifies end of table where new record can be entered

Field data is entered in a cell

Navigation pane reduced to a bar

Datasheet view displays table as a grid of rows and columns

Current Record box indicates total number of records as well as current number

Record navigation bar

Record navigation buttons

Figure 1.3

Another Method

You also can press F11 to open/close the Navigation pane.

The Navigation pane is reduced to a bar along the left side of the window, and the work area expands to fill the space. The pane can be easily displayed again by clicking » . You will learn more about using the Navigation pane throughout the labs.

Creating a Table

In anticipation of your entering information in the table, Access displays the blank table in Datasheet view, one of several different window formats, called **views**, that are used to display and work with the objects in a database. Each view includes its own Ribbon tab that contains commands that are designed to work with the object in that view. The available views change according to the type of object you are using. For example, when working with reports the available views are report view, print preview, layout view, and design view; yet when working with datasheets the viewing options are design view and datasheet view. The basic views are described in the following table.

View	Purpose
Datasheet view	Provides a row-and-column view of the data in tables or query results.
Form view	Displays the records in a form.
Report view	Displays the table data in a report layout.
Design view	Used to create a table, form, query, or report. Displays the underlying design structure, not the data.
Layout view	Displays the object's data while in the process of designing the object.
Print Preview	Displays a form, report, table, or query as it will appear when printed.

Additional Information

Entering information in Datasheet view is very similar to working in a Microsoft Excel worksheet.

Datasheet view is a visual representation of the data that is contained in a database table. It consists of a grid of rows and columns that is used to display each field of a table in a column and each record in a row. The field names are displayed in the **header row** at the top of the datasheet.

Below the header row is a blank row. The intersection of the row and column creates a **cell** where you will enter the data for the record. The square to the left of each row is the **Select Record** button and is used to select an entire record. The record containing the insertion point is the **current record** and is identified by the color in the Select Record button. The * in the Select Record button signifies the end of the table or where a new record can be entered.

The bottom of the work area displays a Current Record box and record navigation buttons. The **Current Record box** shows the number of the current record as well as the total number of records in the table. Because the table does not yet contain records, the indicator displays "Record: 1 of 1" in anticipation of your first entry. On both sides of the record number are the **record navigation buttons**, which are used to move through records with a mouse. In addition, two buttons that are used to filter and search for data in a table are displayed. You will learn about using all these features throughout the text.

DEFINING TABLE FIELDS

Now you are ready to begin defining the fields for the table. You have already decided that the main table in this database will include the employee's basic information such as employee number, name, birth date, and address. Next, you need to determine what information you want to appear in each column (field) about the subject recorded in the table. For example, you know you want to include the employee's name. However, should the entire name be in a single column or should it appear as two separate columns: first name and last name? Because you may want to sort or search for information based on the employee's name, it is better to store the information in separate columns. Similarly, because the address actually consists of four separate parts—address, city, state, and zip code—it makes sense to store them in separate columns as well.

Generally, when deciding how to store information about a subject in a table, break down the information into its smallest logical parts. If you combine more than one kind of information in a field, it is difficult to retrieve individual facts later.

After looking at the information currently maintained in the personnel folder for each employee, you have decided to include the following fields in the table: Employee #, Hire Date, Last Name, First Name, Address, City, State, Zip Code, Home Phone, Birth Date, and Photo. The data for the first employee record you will enter is shown below.

Field Name	Data
Employee #	04731
Hire Date	August 19, 2005
Last Name	Marchant
First Name	Roberta
Address	564 Palm Avenue
City	Landis
State	CA
Zip Code	92120–3741
Home Phone	(507) 555–4990
Birth Date	May 18, 1987
Photo/Resume	Roberta.jpg

ENTERING FIELD DATA

Having Trouble?

For more information on moving through, entering, and editing text, refer to the section Entering and Editing Text in the Introduction to Microsoft Office 2010.

Notice that the first field in the table, ID, is already defined. The ID field is always included in a table when it is first created. It automatically assigns a number to each record as it is added to a table and is useful for maintaining record order. The second column header displays *Click to Add* and is used to add a new field in the table.

In Datasheet view, you can enter data for a record and create a new field at the same time. The first field of data you will enter is the employee number, which is assigned to each employee when hired. Each new employee is given the next consecutive number, so that no two employees can have the same number. Each number is a maximum of five digits.

When you enter data in a record, it should be entered accurately and consistently. The data you enter in a field should be typed exactly as you want it to appear. This is important because any printouts of the data will display the information exactly as entered. It is also important to enter data in a consistent form. For example, if you decide to abbreviate the word "Avenue" as "Ave." in the Address field, then it should be abbreviated the same way in every record where it appears. Also be careful not to enter a blank space before or after a field entry. This can cause problems when using the table to locate information.

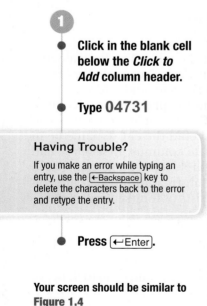

1

- **Click in the blank cell below the *Click to Add* column header.**

- **Type 04731**

Having Trouble?

If you make an error while typing an entry, use the ⟵Backspace key to delete the characters back to the error and retype the entry.

- **Press ⟵Enter.**

Your screen should be similar to Figure 1.4

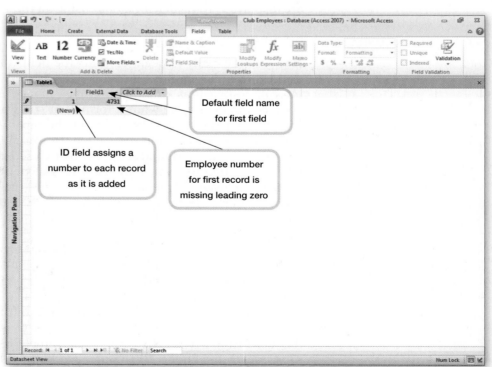

Figure 1.4

The employee number for the first record is entered in the table and Access is ready for you to enter the data for the next field. However, notice the leading zero is no longer displayed in the employee number you just typed. You will learn the reason for this and how to correct it shortly.

The new field has been assigned the default field name of Field1. Also notice that the ID field displays the number 1 for the first record entered in the table.

CHANGING FIELD NAMES

Before entering more data, you want to replace the default field name with a more descriptive field name. A **field name** is used to identify the data stored in the field. A field name should describe the contents of the data to be entered in the field. It can be up to 64 characters long and can consist of letters, numbers, spaces, and special characters, except a period, an exclamation point, an accent grave (`` ` ``), or brackets ([]). You also cannot start a field name with a space. It is best to use short field names to make the tables easier to manage.

1

● **Double-click on the Field1 column header.**

● **Type Employee # (be sure to include a space before the #).**

Another Method

You also can choose Rename Column from the column header's shortcut menu.

Additional Information

The field name can be typed in uppercase or lowercase letters. It will be displayed in your database table exactly as you enter it.

Your screen should be similar to Figure 1.5

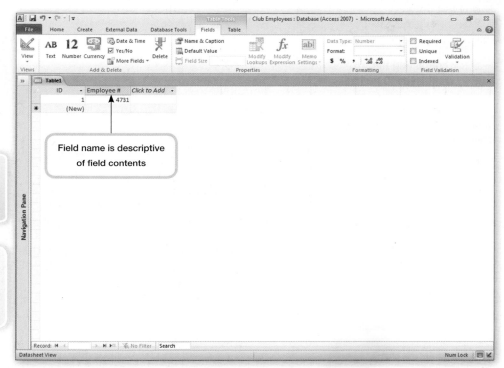

Field name is descriptive of field contents

Figure 1.5

The highlighted text is deleted and replaced by the new field name you typed. You realize that "Employee ID" is the more common term used on company forms, so you decide to use this as the field name instead. As you enter text, you are bound to make typing errors that need to be corrected. You also may want to edit or update information. In this case, you want to edit the field name you are currently working on. The insertion point is already in the correct position and you just need to delete the character to the left of it.

2

- Press ←Backspace to delete the # symbol.

- Type ID

- Press ←Enter.

- Press Esc to close the Data Type shortcut menu that appears for the next field.

Additional Information

You will learn about the Data Type shortcut menu shortly.

- Click in the cell containing the Employee ID number.

Your screen should be similar to Figure 1.6

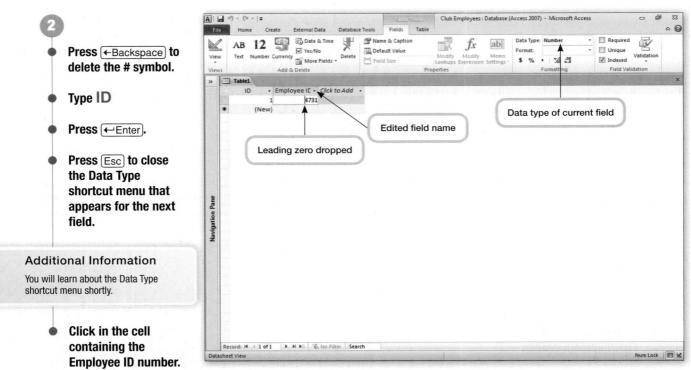

Figure 1.6

The field name has been completed, and it is now easy to know what the data in that column represents.

DEFINING FIELD DATA TYPE

As you noticed, the leading zero of the Employee ID number has been dropped. This is because Access automatically detects and assigns a data type to each field based upon the data that is entered. In this case, the field entry consisted of numbers only, and Access assigned the field a Number data type. This data type drops any leading zeros.

Concept ❸ Data Type

The **data type** defines the type of data the field will contain. Access uses the data type to ensure that the right kind of data is entered in a field. It is important to choose the right data type for a field before you start entering data in the table. You can change a data type after the field contains data, but if the data types are not compatible, such as a text entry in a field whose data type accepts numbers only, you may lose data. The data types are described in the following table.

Data Type	Purpose
Text	Use in fields that contain alphanumeric data (words, combinations of words and numbers, and numbers that are not used in calculations). Text field entries can be up to 255 characters in length. Names and phone numbers are examples of Text field entries. Text is the default data type.
Memo	Use in fields where you want to store more than 255 characters of alphanumeric data. A Memo field holds up to 1 GB of characters or 2 GB of storage, of which 65,535 characters can be displayed. Text in this field can be formatted.
Number	Use in fields that contain numeric data only and that will be used to perform calculations on the values in the field. Number of units ordered is an example of a Number field entry. Leading zeros are dropped. Do not use in fields involving money or that require a high degree of accuracy because Number fields round to the next highest value. Fields that contain numbers only but will not be used in calculations are usually assigned a Text data type.
Date/Time	Use in fields that will contain dates and times. Access allows dates from AD January 1, 100, to December 31, 9999. Access correctly handles leap years and checks all dates for validity. Even though dates and times are formatted to appear as a date or time, they are stored as **serial values** so that they can be used in calculations. The date serial values are consecutively assigned beginning with 1, which corresponds to the date January 1, 1900, and ending with 2958465, which is December 31, 9999.
Currency	Use in number fields that are monetary values or that you do not want rounded. Numbers are formatted to display decimal places and a currency symbol.
AutoNumber	Use when you need a unique, sequential number that is automatically incremented by one whenever a new record is added to a table. After a number is assigned to a record, it can never be used again, even if the record is deleted.
Yes/No	Use when the field contents can only be a Yes/No, True/False, or On/Off value. Yes values are stored as a 1 and No values as 0 so that they can be used in expressions.
OLE Object	Use in fields to store an object from another Microsoft Windows program, such as a document or graph. Stores up to 1 GB. The object is converted to a bitmap image and displayed in the table field, form, or report. An OLE server program must be on the computer that runs the database in order to render the object. Generally, use the Attachment field type rather than OLE Object field type because the objects are stored more efficiently and doing so does not require the OLE server.
Hyperlink	Use when you want the field to store a link to an object, document, Web page, or other destination.
Attachment	Use to add multiple files of different types to a field. For example, you could add a photograph and set of resumes for each employee. Unlike OLE Object fields, the files are not converted to bitmap images and additional software is not needed to view the object, thereby saving space. Attachments also can be opened and edited from within Access in their parent programs. Size limit is 256 MB per individual file, with a total size limit of 2 GB.
Calculated	Use this data type to create a calculated field in a table. For example, you could calculate the units on hand by the cost to determine the inventory value. You can then easily display or use the results of the calculation throughout your database. Whenever a record is edited, Access automatically updates the Calculated fields, thereby constantly maintaining the correct value in the field. Note that a Calculated field cannot refer to fields in other tables or queries.

Additional Information

If Access does not have enough information to determine the data type, it sets the data type to Text.

Notice in Figure 1.6 that the Data Type box in the Formatting group shows the current data type for the field is Number. Access accurately specified this data type because the Employee ID field contains numbers. However, unless the numbers are used in calculations, the field should be assigned the Text data type. This designation allows other characters, such as the parentheses or hyphens in a telephone number, to be included in the entry. Also, by specifying the type as Text, leading zeros will be preserved.

You need to override the data type decision and change the data type for this field to Text.

Open the

Data Type: Number ▾

drop-down menu in the Formatting group of the Table Tools Fields tab.

● **Choose Text.**

● **Click at the beginning of the Employee ID entry to place the insertion point and type 0**

● **Press End to move to the end of the entry.**

● **Press → to move to the next column.**

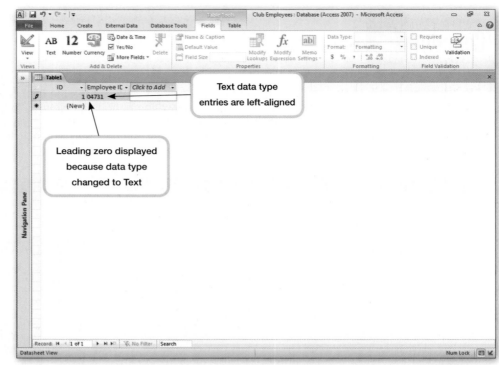

Text data type entries are left-aligned

Leading zero displayed because data type changed to Text

Figure 1.7

Your screen should be similar to Figure 1.7

The leading zero is now correctly displayed. Also notice that the entry is now left-aligned in the cell space whereas it was right-aligned when the data type was set to Number. Many data types also include formatting settings that control the appearance of the data in the field. In this case, the Text field format is to align the text with the left edge of the cell space. You will learn more about formatting later in the lab.

Now you are ready to enter the data for the next field, Hire Date.

● **Type Aug 19, 2001**

● **Press ←Enter.**

● **Right-click the Field1 column name and choose Rename Field from the shortcut menu.**

● **Type Hire Date**

● **Press ←Enter.**

● **Press Esc to close the Data Type shortcut menu that appears for the next field.**

● **Click on the hire date.**

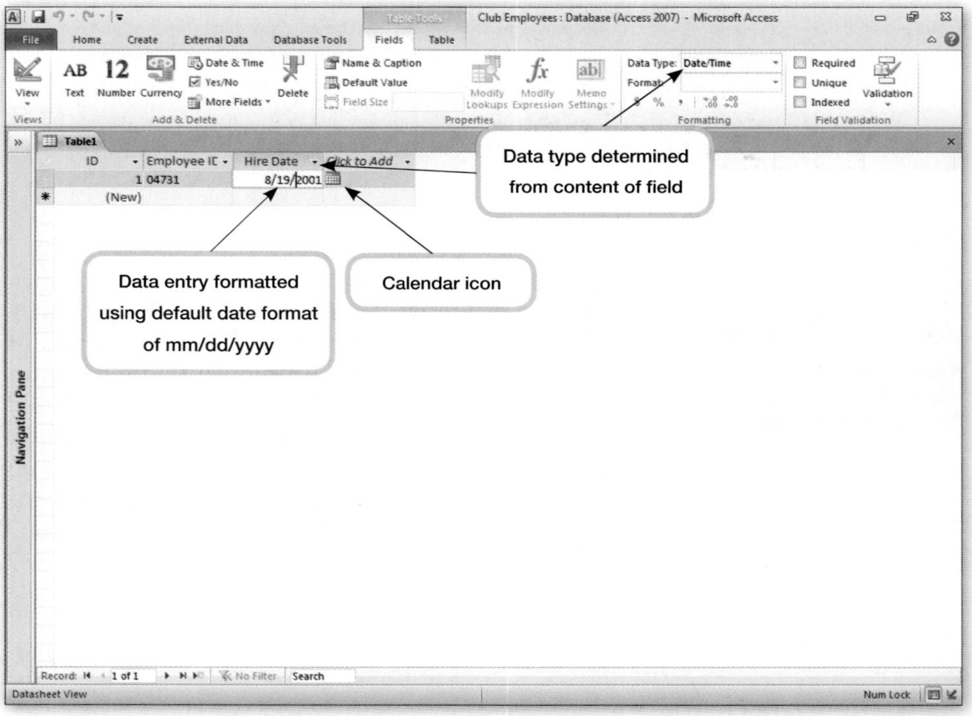

Data type determined from content of field

Data entry formatted using default date format of mm/dd/yyyy

Calendar icon

Your screen should be similar to Figure 1.8

Figure 1.8

Access correctly determined that the entry is a Date type and displays the date using the default date format of mm/dd/yyyy.

USING THE QUICK ADD FEATURE

The next few fields you need to enter include employee name and address information.

First you will add a field for the employee's last name.

1

● **Click on *Click to Add.***

Your screen should be similar to Figure 1.9

Clicking on *Click to Add* activates the Data Type Quick Add feature

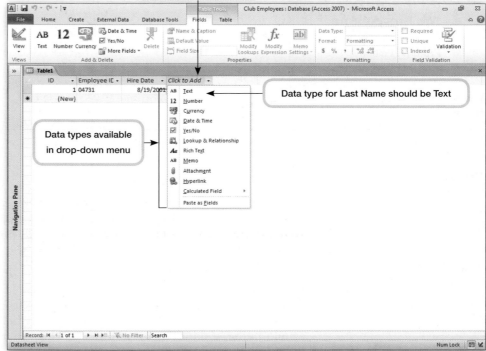

Figure 1.9

The Data Type Quick Add menu displays. It lists available data types as well as formatting that can be used. For example, the Rich Text option is really the Memo data type with the format property set to Rich Text.

You will choose the Text data type for this field and then define the same data type for the next field, First Name.

2

- **Choose Text from the Data Type drop-down menu.**

- **Type** Last Name

- **Press** ⏎Enter.

- **Press** T key to select Text as the data type from the Quick Add menu.

- **Type** First Name

- **Press** ⏎Enter.

Your screen should be similar to Figure 1.10

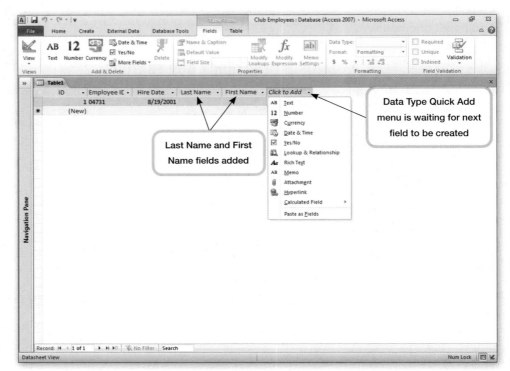

Last Name and First Name fields added

Data Type Quick Add menu is waiting for next field to be created

Figure 1.10

Using the Data Type Quick Add menu made it easy to quickly define the data type and specify the field name. It is again waiting for you to choose your next field type. You will add the remaining address fields using a different technique.

USING FIELD MODELS

Another way you can specify field names is to select them from a menu of predefined fields called **field models**. Each field model definition includes a field name, a data type, and other settings that control the appearance and behavior of the field.

Some field models consist of a set of several fields that are commonly used together. For example, the Address field model comes with a field for the street address, city, state, and zip code. You will use the Address field model to add the address fields next.

Click

More Fields ▾

in the Add & Delete group of the Table Tools Fields tab.

● **Scroll the menu until you see the Quick Start section.**

● **Choose Address.**

Your screen should be similar to Figure 1.11

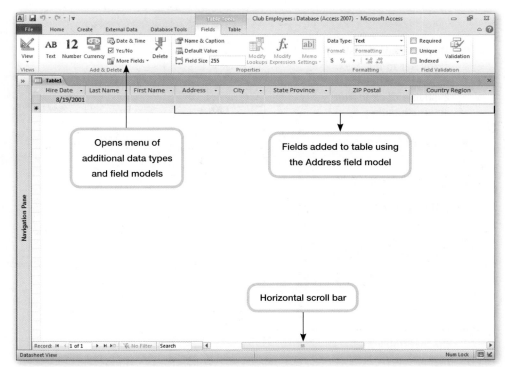

Figure 1.11

The Address, City, State Province, ZIP Postal and Country Region field names quickly appear in the table headings. Using field models saves time and provides the basis from which you can start. Once inserted, the field name and data type can be modified like any other fields.

A horizontal scroll bar may display at the bottom of the work area. This means there are more fields in the datasheet than can be viewed in the currently visible work space.

The last remaining field to add is Home Phone. You might have noticed the Phone option in the More Fields menu of Quick Start Field Models. Because the Phone field model contains three fields (Home Phone, Fax, and Mobile), it would not be the best option to use for this table. You will add the Home Phone field using the Add & Delete group.

2

- Move the horizontal scroll bar to the right to see the next available *Click to Add* column heading.

- Click on *Click to Add.*

- Click [12 Number] in the Add & Delete group.

- Type **Home Phone** for the field name.

- Press (←Enter).

- Press (Esc) to close the last Quick Add menu.

Your screen should be similar to Figure 1.12

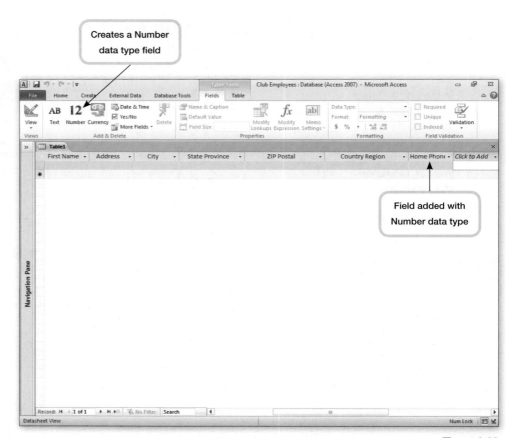

Creates a Number data type field

Field added with Number data type

Figure 1.12

DELETING A FIELD IN DATASHEET VIEW

The Country Region field that was added as part of the Address field model is not needed, so you will delete it. Deleting a field permanently removes the field column and all the data in the field from the table.

- Click in the Country Region field.

- Click Delete in the Add & Delete group.

- Click Yes in response to the message to confirm that you want to permanently delete the field.

Your screen should be similar to Figure 1.13

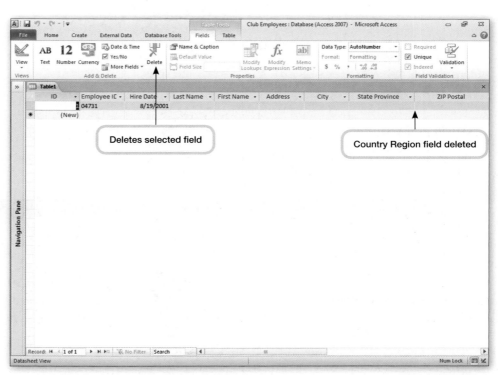

Figure 1.13

The field is permanently removed from the table.

Another Method
You also can delete a field in Datasheet view by choosing Delete Column from the shortcut menu for the field column you want to delete.

Modifying Field Properties

In addition to data type, there are many other field properties associated with a field.

Concept 4 Field Property

A **field property** is a characteristic that helps define the appearance and behavior of a field. Each field has a set of field properties associated with it, and each data type has a different set of field properties. Setting field properties enhances the way your table works. Some of the more commonly used properties and their functions are described in the following table.

Field Property	Description
Field Size	Sets the maximum number of characters that can be entered in the field.
Format	Specifies the way data displays in a table and prints.
Input Mask	Simplifies data entry by controlling the data that is required in a field and the way the data is to be displayed.
Caption	Specifies a field label other than the field name that is used in queries, forms, and reports.
Default Value	Automatically fills in a certain value for this field in new records as you add to the table. You can override a default value by typing a new value into the field.
Validation Rule	Limits data entered in a field to values that meet certain requirements.
Validation Text	Specifies the message to be displayed when the associated Validation Rule is not satisfied.
Required	Specifies whether a value must be entered in a field.
Allow Zero Length	Specifies whether an entry containing no characters is valid. This property is used to indicate that you know no value exists for a field. A zero-length string is entered as "" with no space between the quotation marks.
Indexed	Sets a field as an index field (a field that controls the order of records). This speeds up searches on fields that are searched frequently.

To view and change the field properties, you use Design view.

SWITCHING VIEWS

You can easily switch between views using the button in the Table Tools

Fields tab. The graphic in the button changes to indicate the view that will be displayed when selected. Currently the button displays the graphic for Design view. If the view you want to change to is displayed in the button, you can simply click on the upper part of the button to change to that view. Otherwise, you can click on the lower part of the button to open the button's drop-down menu and select the view you want to use. Before you can change views, you will be asked to save the table.

1

- Click ⟫ to open the Navigation pane.

- Click ✎ Design View in the Views group.

Another Method

You also can click View to open the View drop-down menu and choose Design View or click ✎ Design View in the status bar. Alternatively, you can right-click the object tab and choose Design View.

Your screen should be similar to **Figure 1.14**

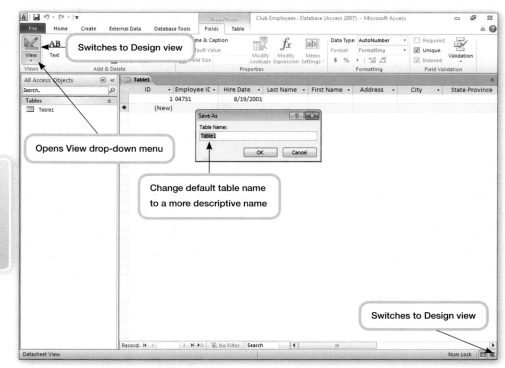

Figure 1.14

Additional Information

You also could click 🖫 Save in the Records group of the Home tab, or use the keyboard shortcut ⇧Shift + ⏎Enter, or click 🖫 Save in the Quick Access Toolbar to save changes to the table at any time.

When you first create a new table and switch views, you are asked to save the table by replacing the default table name, Table1, with a more descriptive name. A table name follows the same set of standard naming conventions or rules that you use when naming fields. It is acceptable to use the same name for both a table and the database, although each table in a database must have a unique name. You will save the table using the table name Employee Records.

2

- Type **Employee Records**

- Click OK.

Your screen should be similar to **Figure 1.15**

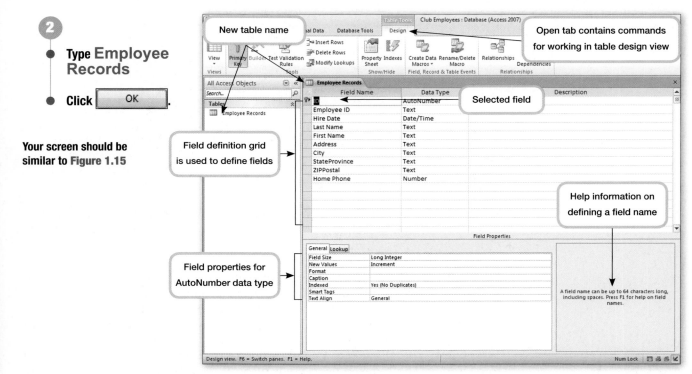

Figure 1.15

The work area now displays the table in design view. This view displays the structure of the table, not the table data. Therefore, it is only used to make changes to the layout and field properties of the table.

Additionally, the new table name appears in the Navigation pane and in the Table tab. You have created a table named Employee Records in the Club Employees database file. The table structure and data are saved within the database file.

SETTING FIELD SIZE

The Table Tools Design tab is displayed and open. The upper section of the design view window consists of a field definition grid that displays the field names, the data type associated with each field, and an area in which to enter a description of the field. The lower section displays the properties associated with each field and a Help box that provides information about the current task. The first field in the field definition grid, ID, is the selected field or **current field** and will be affected by any changes you make. It has a data type of AutoNumber. The properties associated with the current field are displayed in the Field Properties section.

You will look at the properties associated with the first field you added to the table, Employee ID. Positioning the insertion point in any column of the field definition grid will select that field and display the associated field properties.

1

● **Click on the Employee ID field name.**

Your screen should be similar to Figure 1.16

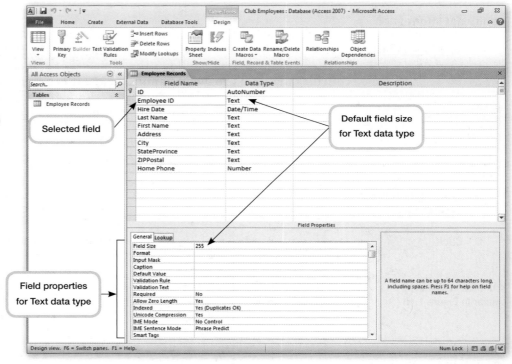

Figure 1.16

The data type of this field is Text, and the default properties associated with a Text data type are displayed in the Field Properties area. Although some of the properties are the same as those for the AutoNumber data type, most are different. Access sets the field size for a Text field to default maximum of 255 characters. It also sets the Required property to No, which allows the field to be blank. The Allow Zero Length property is set to Yes, which allows a field to be empty. The Indexed property is also set to Yes, meaning indexing is on, and duplicate entries are allowed in the field, as, for example, the same name could be entered in the Name field of multiple records. All these settings seem appropriate, except for the field size, which is much too large.

Although Access uses only the amount of storage space necessary for the text you actually store in a Text field, setting the field size to the smallest possible size can decrease the processing time required by the program. Additionally, if the field data to be entered is a specific size, setting the field size to that number restricts the entry to the maximum number.

Because the employee number will never be more than five digits long, you will change the field size from the default of 255 to 5.

2

● **Click the Field Size property text box.**

Another Method

You also can press F6 to switch between the upper and lower areas of the Design window.

● **Click the words Field Size in the row header to automatically select its contents of 255.**

Another Method

You can select text (highlight by dragging or double-clicking) and then press the Delete key to erase the selection.

● **Type 5 to replace the default entry.**

Additional Information

You can cancel changes you are making in the current field at any time before you move on to the next field. Just press Esc and the original entry is restored.

Your screen should be similar to Figure 1.17

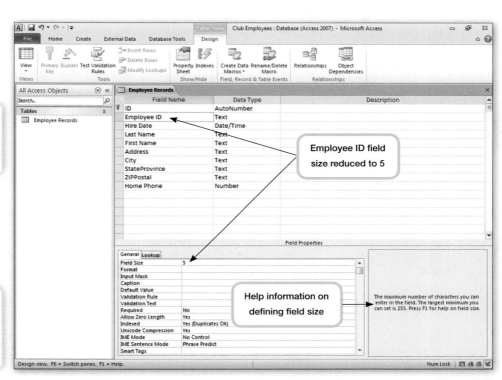

Figure 1.17

The maximum number of characters that can be entered in this field is now restricted to 5. Notice the Help box displays a brief description of the selected property.

Likewise, you will adjust the field sizes of several other fields.

3 ● Change the field sizes to those shown for the fields in the following table.

Field	Size
Last Name	25
First Name	25
Address	50
City	25
StateProvince	2
ZIPPostal	10

Your screen should be similar to Figure 1.18

Figure 1.18

CHANGING DATA TYPE

As you look at the field definitions, it is important to make sure the correct data type has been assigned to the field. You can see that the ZIPPostal field has been correctly assigned a data type of Text because it will not be used in calculations and you may use a dash to separate the digits. For the same reasons, you realize the Home Phone field should have a Text data type instead of Number. You will correct the data type for the Home Phone field.

1 ● Click in the Data Type column for the Home Phone field.

● Click ▼ to open the drop-down menu and choose Text.

● Change the field size for Home Phone to 15

Your screen should be similar to Figure 1.19

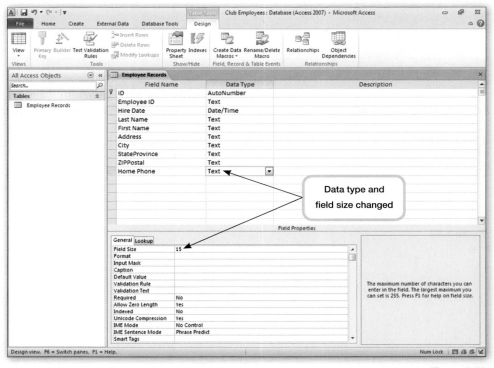

Figure 1.19

EDITING FIELD NAMES

As you continue to look over the fields, you decide to change the field names for the StateProvince and ZIPPostal fields that were assigned when you selected the Address field model.

1

● **Click on the StateProvince field.**

Your screen should be similar to Figure 1.20

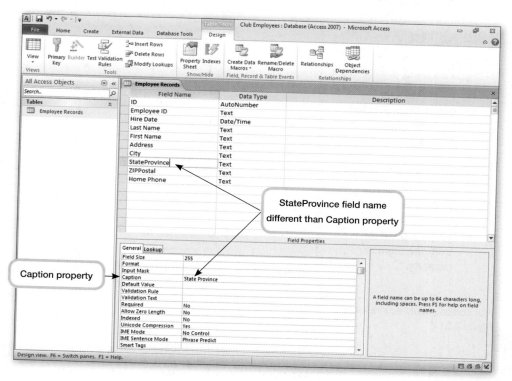

Figure 1.20

Notice that the StateProvince field name appears spelled with no space between the words, while the Caption property displays the State Province with a space. A **caption** is the text that displays in the column heading while in Datasheet view. It is used when you want the label to be different from the actual field name. If there is no text in the Caption field property, the field name will appear as the column heading in Datasheet view. You will change the field name to State and remove the caption for this field. Likewise, you will change the ZIPPostal field name to ZIP Code and clear the caption.

2

- **Change the StateProvince field name to State**

Having Trouble?

Double-click on the field name to select it.

- **Delete State Province from the Caption property.**

- **Change the ZIPPostal field name to ZIP Code**

- **Delete Zip Postal from the Caption property.**

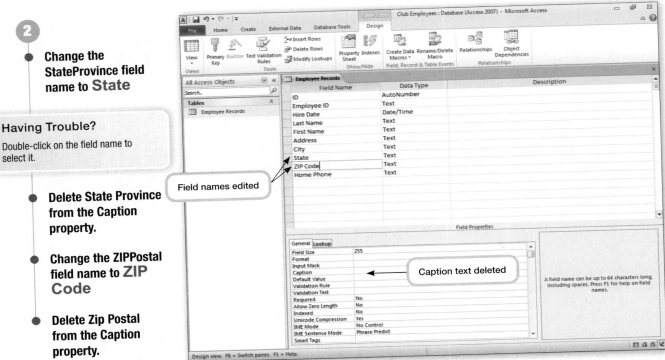

Field names edited

Caption text deleted

Figure 1.21

Your screen should be similar to
Figure 1.21

The field names have been corrected and captions removed. The field names
will automatically be used as the default text for the column headings.

DEFINING A FIELD AS A PRIMARY KEY

The next change you want to make is to define the Employee ID field as a primary key field.

Concept 5 Primary Key

A **primary key** is a field that uniquely identifies each record and is used to associate data from multiple tables. To qualify as a primary key field, the data in the field must be unique for each record. For example, a Social Security Number field could be selected as the primary key because the data in that field is unique for each employee. Other examples of primary key fields are part numbers or catalog numbers. (One example of a field that should not be used as the primary key is a name field because more than one person can have the same last or first name.) A second requirement is that the field can never be empty or null. A third is that the data in the field never, or rarely, changes.

A primary key prevents duplicate records from being entered in the table and is used to control the order in which records display in the table. This makes it faster for databases to locate records in the table and to process other operations.

Most tables have at least one field that is selected as the primary key. Some tables may use two or more fields that, together, provide the primary key of a table. When a primary key uses more than one field, it is called a **composite key**.

Notice the  icon that is displayed to the left of the ID field. This indicates that this field is a primary key field. You want to define the Employee ID field so that duplicate employee ID numbers will not be allowed.

1

- Click on the **Employee ID** field name.

- Click [Primary Key] in the **Tools** group.

Your screen should be similar to Figure 1.22

Figure 1.22

Notice the Indexed property setting for this field has changed to Yes (No Duplicates) because the field is defined as the primary key field. This setting prohibits duplicate values in a field. Also, the primary key status has been removed from the default ID field.

ENTERING FIELD DESCRIPTIONS

To continue defining the Employee ID field, you will enter a brief description of the field. Although it is optional, a field description makes the table easier to understand and update because the description is displayed in the status bar when you enter data into the table.

1

● **Click the Description text box for the Employee ID field.**

● **Type Unique five-digit number assigned to each employee**

Additional Information

The Description box scrolls horizontally as necessary to accommodate the length of the text entry. The maximum length is 255 characters.

Your screen should be similar to Figure 1.23

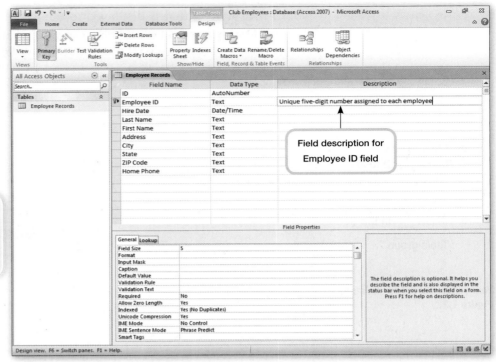

Figure 1.23

You also want to add field descriptions to several other fields. As you do, the Property Update Options button will appear when you complete the entry by moving outside the Description text box. Clicking on this button opens a menu whose option will update the description in the status bar everywhere the field is used. Because this database only contains one table, there is no need to update the description anyplace else. The button will disappear automatically when you continue working.

2

● **Add descriptions to the fields as shown in Figure 1.24.**

Your screen should be similar to Figure 1.24

Figure 1.24

DELETING A FIELD IN DESIGN VIEW

Because the ID field essentially duplicates the purpose of the Employee ID field, you will delete the ID field. Just like deleting a field in Datasheet view, deleting a field in Design view permanently removes the field column and all the data in the field from the table.

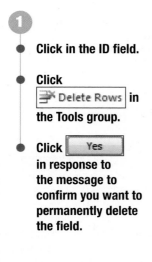

● **Click in the ID field.**

● **Click** ⟶ Delete Rows **in the Tools group.**

● **Click** Yes **in response to the message to confirm you want to permanently delete the field.**

Your screen should be similar to Figure 1.25

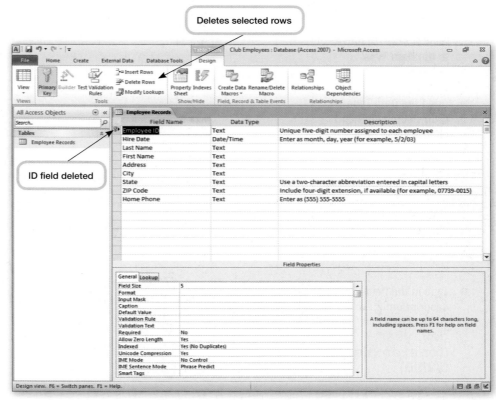

Figure 1.25

The field is permanently removed from the table.

CREATING A FIELD IN DESIGN VIEW

You still need to add two fields to the table: one for the employee's date of birth and the other to display the employee's photo. You will add the new fields and define their properties in Design view.

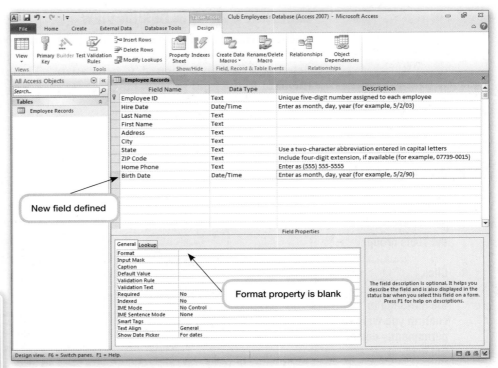

1

- Click in the blank Field Name row below the Home Phone field name.

- Type **Birth Date**

- Press ⏎Enter, Tab⇥, or → to move to the Data Type column.

- Open the Data Type drop-down menu and choose Date/Time.

Another Method

You also can enter the data type by typing the first character of the type you want to use. For example, if you type D, the Date/Time data type will be automatically selected and displayed in the field.

- Type in the field description: **Enter as month, day, year (for example, 5/2/90)**

Your screen should be similar to Figure 1.26

Figure 1.26

The default field properties for the selected data type are displayed. Because the format line is blank, you decide to check the format to make sure that the date will display as you want.

● **Click in the Format property box.**

● **Click to open the drop-down menu of format options.**

Your screen should be similar to Figure 1.27

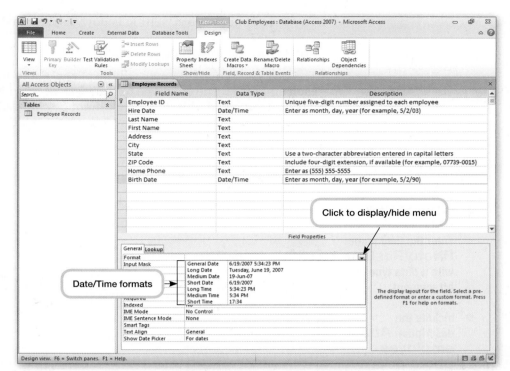

Figure 1.27

The names of the seven predefined layouts for the Date/Time field type are displayed in the list. An example of each layout appears to the right of the name. Although not displayed in the Format property box, the General Date format is the default format. It displays dates using the Short Date format. If a time value is entered, it also will display the time in the Long Time format. You will choose this format so that the setting will be displayed in the Format property box.

3

● **Choose General Date.**

Your screen should be similar to Figure 1.28

Additional Information

Access automatically assumes the first two digits of a year entry. If you enter a year that is between /30 and /99, Access reads this as a 20th century date (1930 to 1999). A year entry between /00 and /29 is assumed to be a 21st century date (2000 to 2029).

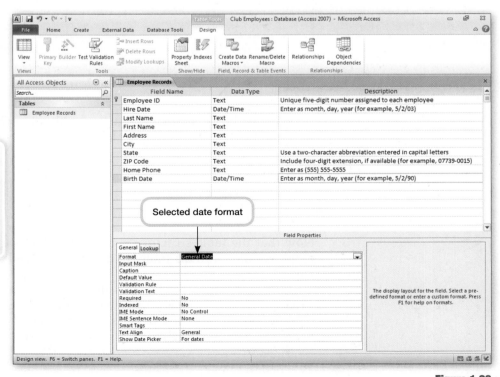

Figure 1.28

Modifying Field Properties **AC1.33**

The Date/Time property setting is now displayed in the Format text box.

CREATING AN ATTACHMENT FIELD

The last field you will enter will display a photo and resume if available for each employee. The data type for this type of input is Attachment. Once a field has been assigned, this data type cannot be changed. You can, however, delete the field and then redefine it if you think you made an error.

1

- In the next blank field name row, enter the field name **Photo/Resume** with a data type of Attachment.

- Include the description **Attach employee photo and resume if available**

Your screen should be similar to Figure 1.29

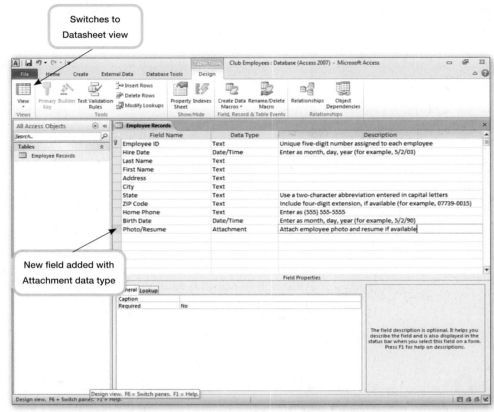

Figure 1.29

Specifying the Attachment data type allows you to store multiple files of different file types in a single field.

Entering and Editing Records

Now that the table structure is complete, you want to continue entering the employee data into the table. To do this, you need to switch back to Datasheet view.

Because you have made many changes to the table design, you will be asked to save the changes before you switch views. You also will be advised that data may be lost because you decreased field sizes in several fields. Since there is very little data in the table, this is not a concern.

1

- Click 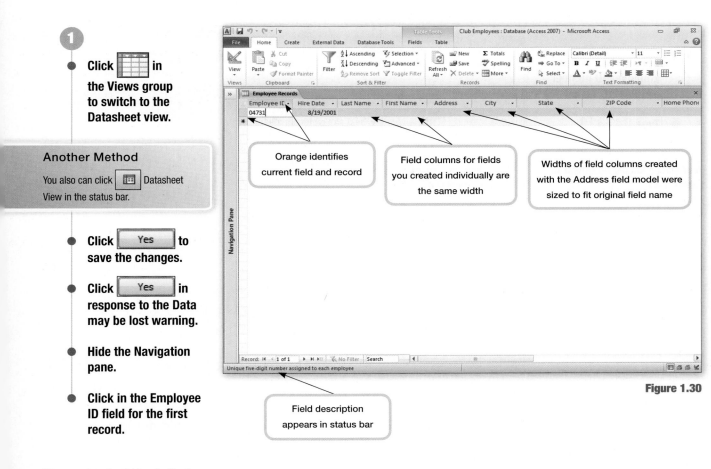 in the Views group to switch to the Datasheet view.

- Click **Yes** to save the changes.

- Click **Yes** in response to the Data may be lost warning.

- Hide the Navigation pane.

- Click in the Employee ID field for the first record.

Your screen should be similar to Figure 1.30

Figure 1.30

Orange identifies current field and record

Field columns for fields you created individually are the same width

Widths of field columns created with the Address field model were sized to fit original field name

Field description appears in status bar

Because you deleted the ID field, it is no longer displayed and the new fields you defined are ready for you to enter the remaining data for the first record. The first field, Employee ID, of the first record is outlined in orange, indicating that the program is ready to accept data in this field. The field name and Select Record button also are highlighted in orange to identify the current field and current record. The status bar displays the description you entered for the field.

Notice also in this view that the column widths for the fields you created individually are all the same, even though you set different field sizes in the Table Design window. This is because the Table Datasheet view has its own default column width setting. The column widths of the fields that were created using the Address field model were sized to fit the original field name for each column.

VERIFYING DATA ACCURACY AND VALIDITY

To see how field properties help ensure data accuracy, you will reenter the employee number for the first record and try to enter a number that is larger than the field size of five that you defined in Table Design view.

1

- Double-click on the Employee ID number to select it.

- Type **047310**

Your screen should be similar to Figure 1.31

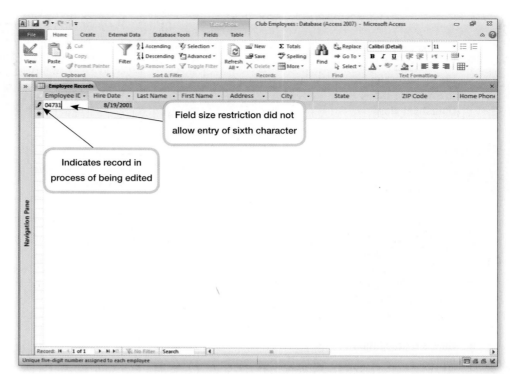

Field size restriction did not allow entry of sixth character

Indicates record in process of being edited

Figure 1.31

The program accepted only the first five digits and would not let you type a sixth. The field size restriction helps control the accuracy of data by not allowing an entry larger than has been specified. Notice also that the current record symbol has changed to 🖉. The pencil symbol means the record is in the process of being entered or edited and has not yet been saved.

Next, you will intentionally enter an invalid date to see what happens.

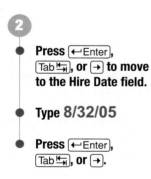

2

- Press ←Enter, Tab ⇥, or → to move to the Hire Date field.

- Type **8/32/05**

- Press ←Enter, Tab ⇥, or →.

Your screen should be similar to Figure 1.32

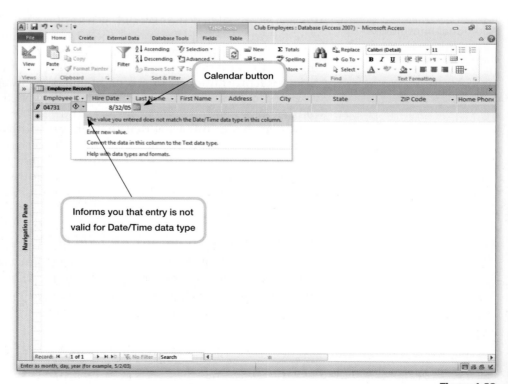

Calendar button

Informs you that entry is not valid for Date/Time data type

Figure 1.32

Additional Information

The calendar button appears automatically whenever a Date data type field is active. Clicking it displays a calendar for the current month from which you can quickly find and choose a date.

An informational message box is displayed advising you that the entry is not valid. In this case, the date entered (8/32/05) could not be correct because a month cannot have 32 days. Access automatically performs some basic checks on the data as it is entered based upon the field type specified in the table design. This is another way that Access helps you control data entry to ensure the accuracy of the data.

You will need to edit the date entry to correct it.

3

- Select **Enter new value** from the message box.

- Double-click on **32** to select it.

- Type **19**

- Press (Tab ⇥).

Your screen should be similar to **Figure 1.33**

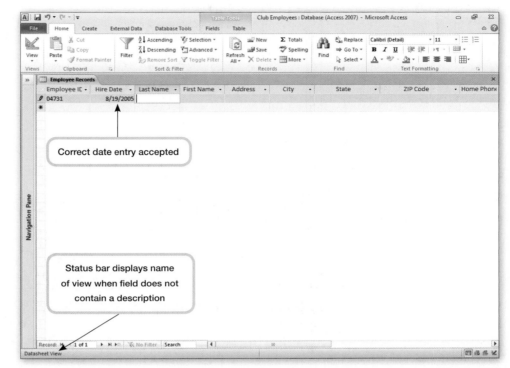

Figure 1.33

The corrected date is accepted, and the insertion point moves to the Last Name field. The year in the date changed to four digits, which reflects the date format you specified in the field's property.

Because you did not enter a description for the Last Name field, the status bar displays "Datasheet View," the name of the current view, instead of a field description.

USING AUTOCORRECT

Now you are ready to continue entering the data for the first record. As you are typing, you may make errors and they may be corrected automatically for you. This is because the AutoCorrect feature automatically corrects obvious errors such as capitalizing names of days, the first letter of sentences, and other common typing errors and misspellings such as words starting with two initial capital letters. The AutoCorrect Options button 🔣 will appear next to any text that was corrected. You have the option of undoing the correction or leaving it as is. Most of the time, the typing error is not corrected, and you will need to fix it manually.

To see how this works, you will enter the last name incorrectly by typing the first two letters using capital letters.

● Type **MArchant**

● Press $\boxed{\text{Tab} \rightleftharpoons}$.

Your screen should be similar to Figure 1.34

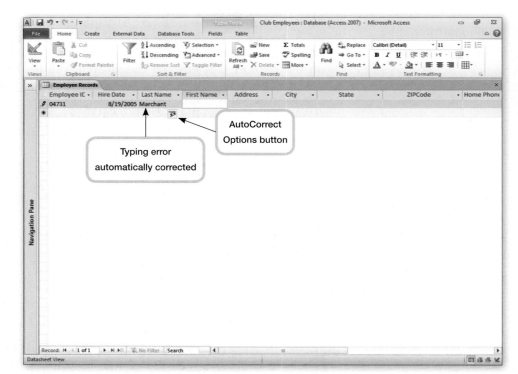

AutoCorrect
Options button

Typing error
automatically corrected

Figure 1.34

The name was automatically corrected, and the AutoCorrect Options button appears. You will leave the correction as is and continue to enter data for this record.

2

● **Enter the data shown in the table on the next page for the remaining fields, typing the information exactly as it appears.**

Additional Information

The fields will scroll in the window as you move to the right in the record.

Your screen should be similar to Figure 1.35

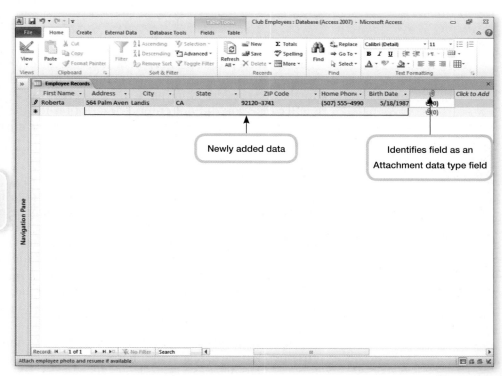

Newly added data

Identifies field as an Attachment data type field

Figure 1.35

Field Name	Data
First Name	Roberta
Address	564 Palm Avenue
City	Landis
State	CA
ZIP Code	92120–3741
Home Phone	(507) 555–4990
Birth Date	May 18, 1987 (press Tab⇆ to complete the entry)

All the information for the first record is now complete, except for the last field for the employee photo and resume.

ATTACHING FILES TO RECORDS

Notice that the field name in the header for this field is not Photo/Resume, as you defined in Design view. This is because Access does not use the field name for Attachment data types. Instead it displays a paper clip icon in the field header to show that the field has an Attachment data type. However, you can specify a caption for this field that will display as the field name. Before making this change, you want to add the data for this field.

You plan to attach the employee photo and a copy of the employee's resume if it is available. A photo is one of several different types of graphic objects that can be added to a database table. A **graphic** is a nontext element or object. A graphic can be a simple **drawing object** consisting of shapes such as lines and boxes that can be created using a drawing program such as Paint, or it can be a picture. A **picture** is an illustration such as a scanned photograph. A resume is a text document that is typically created using a word processor application.

Because you have not organized all the employees' badge photographs yet, you will only insert the photo for Roberta Marchant to demonstrate this feature to the club owners. You also will attach a sample resume that was created using Word 2010.

1
- **Double-click on the Attachment field cell for this record.**

Another Method

You also can choose Manage Attachments from the field's shortcut menu.

Your screen should be similar to Figure 1.36

Figure 1.36

The Attachments dialog box is used to manage the items that are in an attachment field. Because there are currently no attachments associated with this field, it is empty. You will select the photo and resume files you want to add to the field.

2

● Click [Add...].

● If necessary, specify the location of your data files in the Choose File dialog box.

● Select ac01_ Roberta **and** ac01_ Resume **from the file list box.**

Having Trouble?

Hold down Ctrl while clicking on the file names to select multiple files.

● Click [Open] in the Choose File dialog box.

Your screen should be similar to Figure 1.37

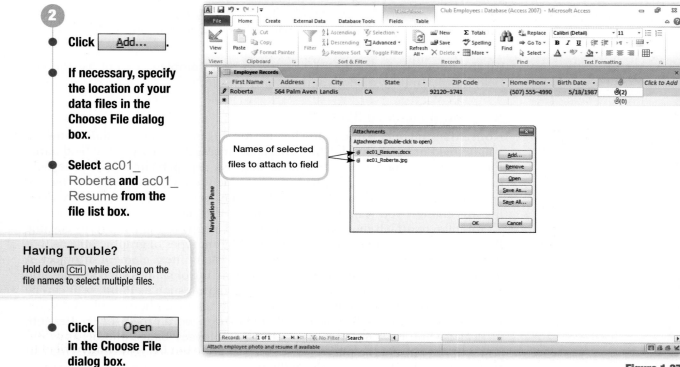

Names of selected files to attach to field

Figure 1.37

Additional Information

To remove a file from the Attachment field, select the file name from the list and click [Remove].

The Attachments dialog box is displayed again and now displays the names of the selected files.

3

● Click ⬚ OK ⬚ in the Attachments dialog box.

Your screen should be similar to Figure 1.38

> Two attachments in field

Figure 1.38

The selected files are inserted as attachments and identified with the number 2 in the cell. The number indicates how many attachments have been added to the field. You will now display the photograph from the Attachment field to check that it has been inserted properly.

4

● Double-click the cell containing the attachments for Roberta.

● Select the ac01_ Roberta file from the Attachments dialog box.

● Click ⬚ Open ⬚.

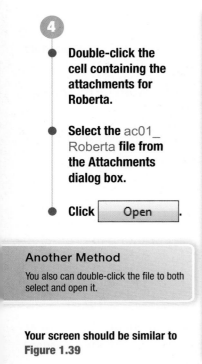

Another Method

You also can double-click the file to both select and open it.

Your screen should be similar to Figure 1.39

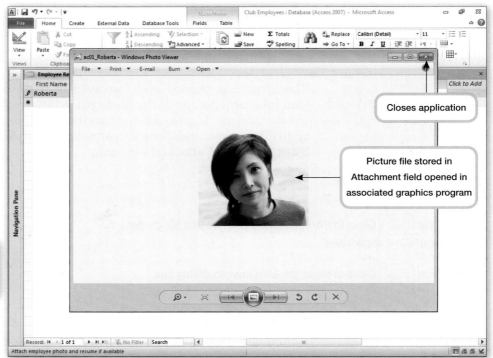

> Closes application

> Picture file stored in Attachment field opened in associated graphics program

Figure 1.39

Additional Information

Image files that open in Microsoft Picture and Fax Viewer can only be viewed, not edited. If you want to edit the image, right-click on the image and choose Edit. The program used to create the file, if available on your computer, will open.

The picture object is opened and displayed in the graphics program that is associated with this type of file—in this case, Windows Photo Viewer. Yours may open and display in a different graphics program such as Paint. The application that opens is not necessarily the application in which the file was created. If the application in which it opens includes features that can be used to edit the file, you will be prompted to save any changes before closing the Attachments dialog box. If you do not save them, the changes will be lost.

5

- Click ☒ Close in the graphics application window title bar to close the application.

- Select and open the ac01_Resume attachment.

- If necessary, maximize the Word application window.

Your screen should be similar to Figure 1.40

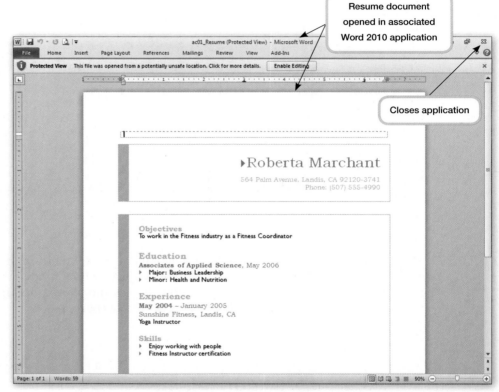

Figure 1.40

The resume is opened and displayed in the associated Word 2010 application program. A copy of the file is placed in a temporary folder. If you change the document, the changes are saved to the temporary copy. Then, when you return to Access and close the Attachments dialog box, you are asked if you want to save the attached file again.

6

- Click ☒ Close in the application window title bar to close the Word 2010 application.

- Click ☒ Close to close the Attachments dialog box.

Finally, you want to add the caption for the Attachment field. Rather than switching to Design view to make this change, you can use the 📝 Name & Caption button in the Properties group of the Table Tools Fields tab.

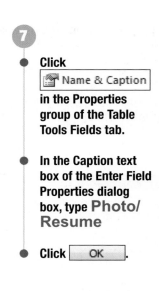

7

- Click  **Name & Caption** in the Properties group of the Table Tools Fields tab.

- In the Caption text box of the Enter Field Properties dialog box, type **Photo/ Resume**

- Click **OK**.

Your screen should be similar to Figure 1.41

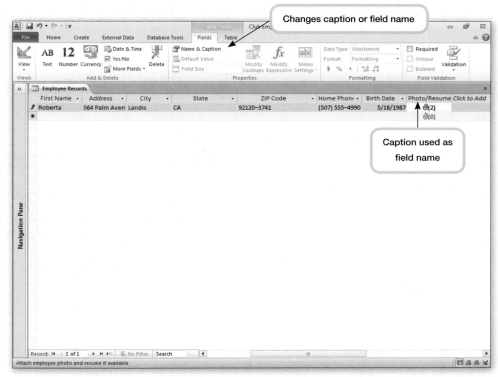

Figure 1.41

The field column now displays the caption associated with the field. This clarifies the field contents and makes it much easier for others to understand.

8

- Press **←Enter** to move to the beginning of the next record.

Your screen should be similar to Figure 1.42

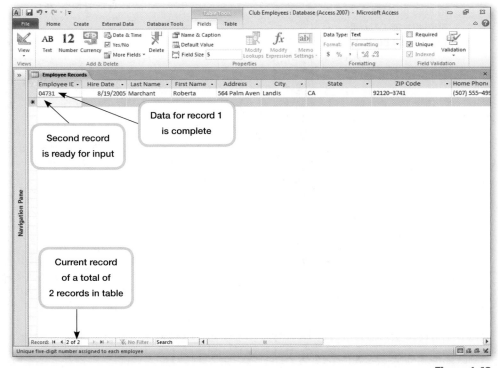

Figure 1.42

The information for the first record is now complete. The cursor moves to the first field in the next row and waits for input of the employee number for the next record. As soon as the cursor moves to another record, the data is saved to the table file and the number of the new record appears in the status bar. The second record was automatically assigned the record number 2.

MOVING BETWEEN FIELDS

Next, you will check the first record for accuracy. To quickly move from one field to another in a record, you can first select (highlight) the entire field contents and then you can use the keyboard keys shown in the following table to move quickly between field columns.

Key	Movement
→ or Tab ⇆	Next field
← or ⇧ Shift + Tab ⇆	Previous field
↑	Current field in previous record
↓	Current field in next record
Home	First field in record
End	Last field in record

You will select the Employee ID field for the first record and then move to the Address field to check its contents.

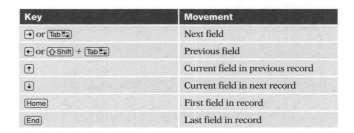

1

- Point to the left end of the Employee ID field for the first record. When the mouse pointer appears as ⇩, click the mouse button.

- Press → four times.

Your screen should be similar to Figure 1.43

Figure 1.43

Additional Information

If you press Delete or ←Backspace while the entire field is selected, the entire field contents will be deleted.

Because the entire field contents are selected, you need to be careful that you do not type a character, as that will delete the selection and replace it with the new text. To switch back to editing, you need to display the cursor in the field and then edit the entry.

2

● Click the Address field with the mouse pointer shaped as an I-beam.

Your screen should be similar to Figure 1.44

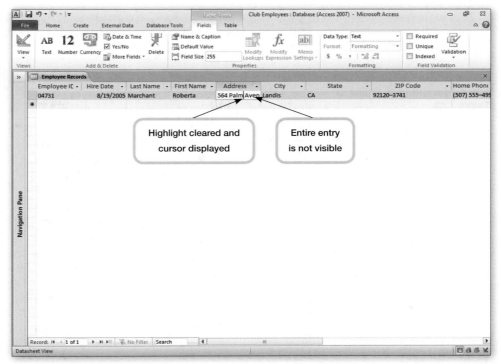

Highlight cleared and cursor displayed

Entire entry is not visible

Figure 1.44

Additional Information

You can press [F2] to switch between editing an entry (the cursor is displayed) and navigating (the field is selected) through the datasheet.

The highlight is cleared and the cursor is visible in the field. Now, using the directional keys moves the cursor within the field and you can edit the field contents if necessary.

ZOOMING A FIELD

The beginning of the field looks fine, but because the column width is too narrow, you cannot see the entire entry. You will move the cursor to the end of the address so you can check the rest of the entry.

1

● Press End.

Your screen should be similar to
Figure 1.45

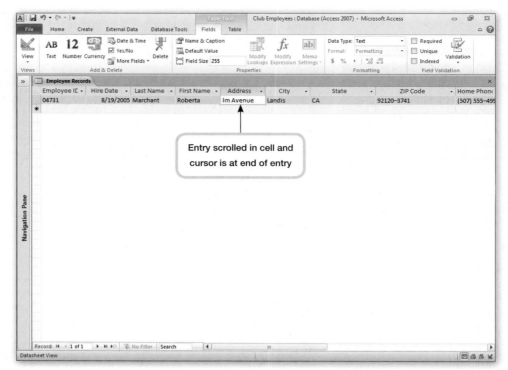

Entry scrolled in cell and
cursor is at end of entry

Figure 1.45

The text scrolled in the field, and the cursor is positioned at the end of the entry. However, now you cannot see the beginning of the entry, which makes it difficult to edit. Another way to view the field's contents is to expand the field.

2

● Press ⇧Shift + F2.

Your screen should be similar to
Figure 1.46

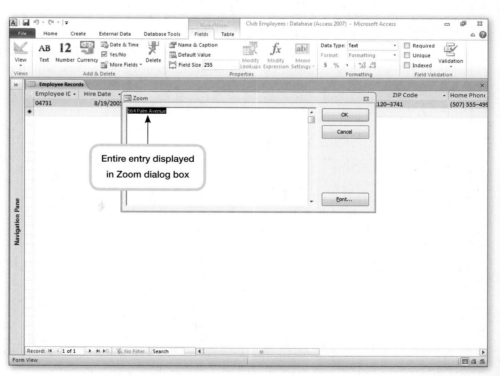

Entire entry displayed
in Zoom dialog box

Figure 1.46

The entry is fully displayed in the Zoom dialog box. You can edit in the dialog box just as you can in the field.

- If the entry contains an error, correct it.

- Click [OK] to close the Zoom dialog box.

- Press Tab⇥ to move to the next field.

- Continue to check the first record for accuracy and edit as needed.

- Enter the data for the second record as shown in the table to the right (you will leave the Attachment field empty).

- Check the second record for accuracy and edit it if necessary.

- Move to the first field of the blank record row.

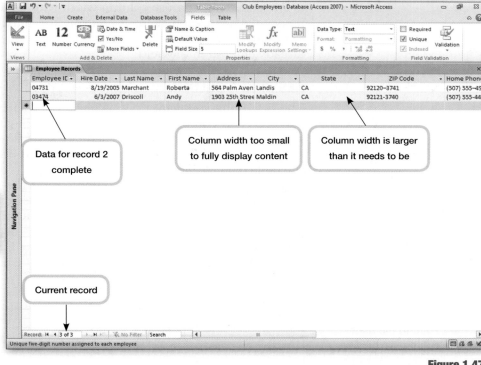

Figure 1.47

Field Name	Data
Employee ID	03474
Hire Date	June 3, 2007
Last Name	Driscoll
First Name	Andy
Address	1903 25th Street
City	Maldin
State	CA
ZIP Code	92121-3740
Home Phone	(507) 555-4494
Birth Date	October 10, 1986

Your screen should be similar to Figure 1.47

The record indicator in the status bar tells you that record 3 is the current record of a total of three records.

Changing Column Width

As you have noticed, some of the fields (such as the Address field) do not display the entire entry, while other fields (such as the State field) are much larger than the field's column heading or contents. This is because the default width of a column in the datasheet is not the same size as the field sizes you specified in Design view. **Column width** refers to the size of a field column in a datasheet. The column width does not affect the amount of data you can enter into a field, but it does affect the data that you can see.

You can adjust the column width to change the appearance of the datasheet. Usually you should adjust the column width so that the column is slightly larger than the column heading or longest field contents, whichever is longer. Do not confuse column width with field size. Field size is a property associated with each field; it controls the maximum number of characters that you can enter in the field. If you shorten the field size, you can lose data already entered in the field.

RESIZING A COLUMN

The first thing you want to do is make the Address column wider so that you can see each complete field entry without having to move to the field and scroll or expand the field box. There are several ways that you can manipulate the rows and columns of a datasheet so that it is easier to view and work with the table data.

To quickly resize a column, simply drag the right column border line in the field selector in either direction to increase or decrease the column width. The mouse pointer shape is ✛ when you can drag to size the column. As you drag, a column line appears to show you the new column border. When you release the mouse button, the column width will be set. First you will increase the width of the Address field so that the entire address will be visible.

1

- Point to the right column border line for the Address field.

- When the mouse pointer shape is ✛, click and drag to the right until you think the column width will be wide enough to display the field contents.

- Adjust the column width again if it is too wide or not wide enough.

Another Method

You also can adjust the column width to a specific number of characters using ⊞ More ▾ in the Records group of the Home tab and choosing Field Width. This command is also on the shortcut menu when an entire column is selected.

Your screen should be similar to Figure 1.48

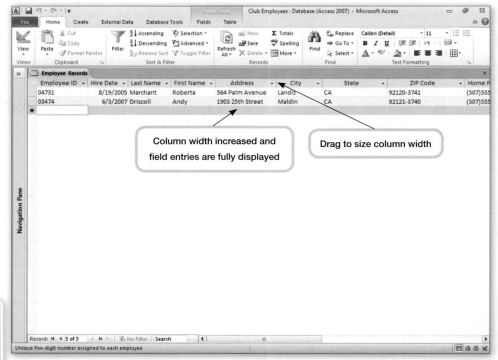

Figure 1.48

USING BEST FIT

Rather than change the widths of all the other columns individually, you can select all columns and change their widths at the same time using the **Best Fit** feature. To select multiple columns, point to the column heading in the header row of the first or last column you want to select. Then, when the mouse pointer changes to ⬇, click, and without releasing the mouse button, drag in either direction across the column headings. You also can quickly select the entire table by clicking the ◢ Select All button to the left of the first field name.

● Drag across the first four field columns ⬇ to select them.

● Click the ◢ Select All button to select the entire table.

Your screen should be similar to Figure 1.49

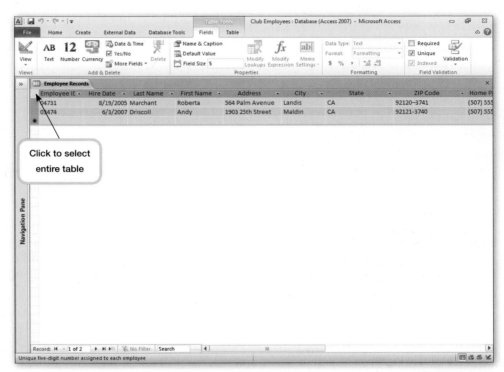

Figure 1.49

All the table columns are highlighted. Now, if you were to drag the column border of any selected column, all the selected columns would change to the same size. However, you want the column widths to be adjusted appropriately to fit the data in each column. To do this, you can double-click the column border to activate the Best Fit feature. The Best Fit feature automatically adjusts the column widths of all selected columns to accommodate the longest entry or column heading in each of the selected columns.

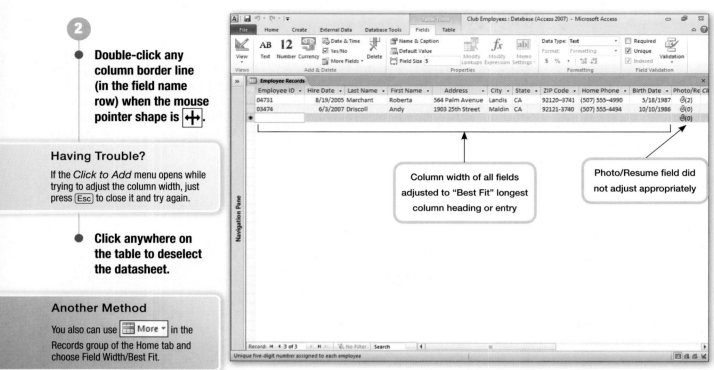

2

- Double-click any column border line (in the field name row) when the mouse pointer shape is [↔].

Having Trouble?

If the *Click to Add* menu opens while trying to adjust the column width, just press [Esc] to close it and try again.

- Click anywhere on the table to deselect the datasheet.

Another Method

You also can use [⊞ More ▾] in the Records group of the Home tab and choose Field Width/Best Fit.

Column width of all fields adjusted to "Best Fit" longest column heading or entry

Photo/Resume field did not adjust appropriately

Figure 1.50

Your screen should be similar to Figure 1.50

The column widths for each field have been sized to accommodate the longest entry or column heading. Also, as you add more records to the table that contain longer field entries, you will need to use Best Fit again to readjust the column widths.

3

● Check each of the records again and edit any entries that are incorrect.

● Add the data shown in the following table as record 3.

● Press ⏎Enter twice to skip the Photo/Resume field and complete the record.

Your screen should be similar to Figure 1.51

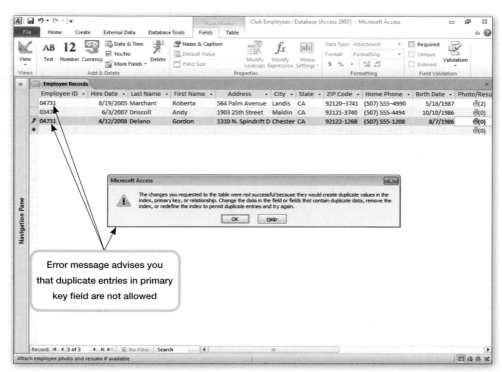

Error message advises you that duplicate entries in primary key field are not allowed

Figure 1.51

Field Name	Data
Employee ID	04731
Hire Date	April 12, 2008
Last Name	Delano
First Name	Gordon
Address	1310 N. Spindrift Drive
City	Chesterfield
State	CA
ZIP Code	92122-1268
Phone	(507) 555-1208
Birth Date	August 7, 1986

As soon as you complete the record, an error message dialog box appears indicating that Access has located a duplicate value in a primary key field. The key field is Employee ID. You realize you were looking at the employee number from Roberta Marchant's record when you entered the employee number for this record. You need to clear the message and enter the correct number.

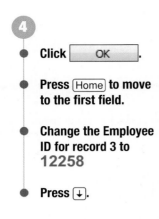

4

● Click [OK].

● Press (Home) to move to the first field.

● Change the Employee ID for record 3 to **12258**

● Press ↓.

Your screen should be similar to Figure 1.52

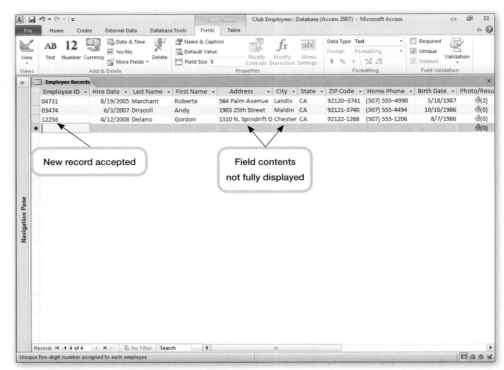

New record accepted

Field contents not fully displayed

Figure 1.52

The record is accepted with the new employee number. However, you notice that the address and city for this record are not fully displayed in the fields.

5

● Best Fit the Address and City fields.

Your screen should be similar to Figure 1.53

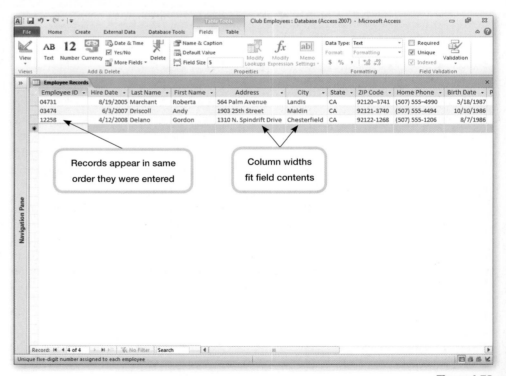

Records appear in same order they were entered

Column widths fit field contents

Figure 1.53

When you add new records in a datasheet, the records are displayed in the order in which you enter them. However, they are stored inside the database file in order by the primary key field.

You will add three more records to the table. If data for some fields, such as the City, State, or ZIP Code, is the same from record to record, you can save yourself some typing by copying the data from one of the other records. Just select the field contents and click 📋 Copy in the Clipboard group on the Home ribbon. Then move to the field where you want the copy to appear and click 📋 Paste in the Clipboard group.

6

● Enter the data for the two records shown in the following table.

● Enter a final record using your first and last name. Enter **99999** as your employee ID and the current date as your date hired. Use **Chesterfield, CA 92122-1268** for the city, state, and zip code. The information you enter in all other fields can be fictitious.

Field	Record 4	Record 5
Employee ID	13635	12583
Hire Date	January 2, 2011	April 20, 2011
Last Name	Martinez	Sullivan
First Name	Juan	Marie
Address	1920 First Avenue	78 Omega Drive
City	Maldin	Chesterfield
State	CA	CA
ZIP Code	92121-3740	92122-1268
Phone	(507) 555-2935	(507) 555-3890
Birth Date	December 10, 1989	March 15, 1988

● Check each of the records and correct any entry errors.

Your screen should be similar to Figure 1.54

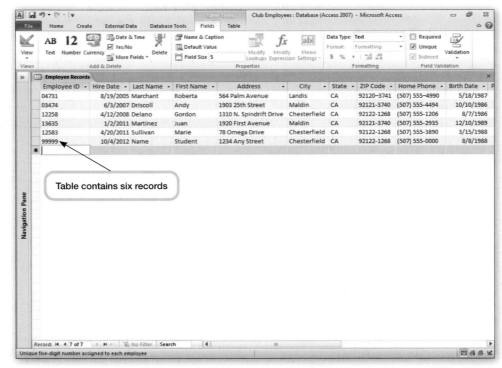

Figure 1.54

There are now a total of six records in the table.

You have found that with the addition of records, it takes longer to move around in the datasheet. Typical database tables are very large and consequently can be cumbersome to navigate. Learning how to move around in a large table will save time and help you get the job done faster.

MOVING USING THE KEYBOARD

In a large table, there are many methods you can use to quickly navigate through records in Datasheet view. You can always use the mouse to move from one field or record to another. However, if the information is not visible in the window, you must scroll the window using the scroll bar first. The following table presents several keyboard methods that will help you move around in the datasheet.

Keys	Effect
Page Down	Down one window
Page Up	Up one window
Ctrl + Page Up	Left one window
Ctrl + Page Down	Right one window
Ctrl + End	Last field of last record
Ctrl + Home	First field of first record
Ctrl + ↑	Current field of first record
Ctrl + ↓	Current field of last record

Currently, records 1 through 6 of the Employee Records table are displayed in the work area. You will use many of these methods to move around the datasheet.

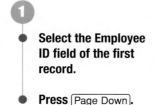

- **Select the Employee ID field of the first record.**

- **Press** Page Down.

Your screen should be similar to Figure 1.55

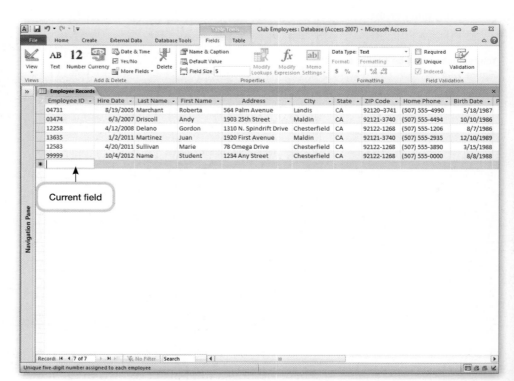

Figure 1.55

If you were working on a very large table, the next page of records would display, with the first record in the window being the current record. Because this table is small, pressing [Page Down] moved the cursor to the last position in the window, the row to add a new record. To see an example of moving in a wide table, you will expand the Navigation pane. Because there are numerous fields of various widths, not all of the fields are able to display in the window at the same time. Rather than scrolling the window horizontally to see the additional fields, you can quickly move to the right one window at a time.

2

● **Expand the Navigation pane.**

● **Click on First Name field for the second record.**

● **Press** [Ctrl] + [Page Down].

Your screen should be similar to Figure 1.56

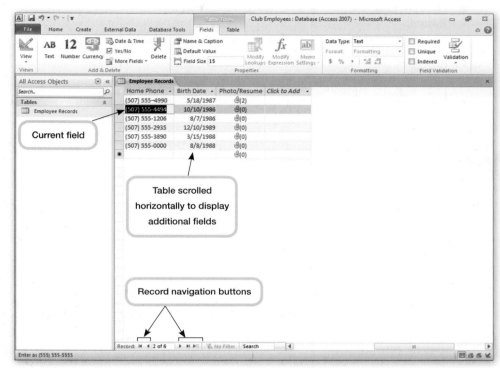

Figure 1.56

The table scrolled horizontally one window to the right, and the last three field columns in the table are now visible. The current field is the first field of this screen, but on the second record's row.

MOVING USING THE RECORD NAVIGATION BUTTONS

The record navigation buttons in the status bar also provide navigation shortcuts. These buttons are described in the following table.

Another Method

You also can use ⇒ Go To ▾ in the Find group of the Home tab to access the record navigation buttons.

Button	Effect
I◀	First record, same field
◀	Previous record, same field
▶	Next record, same field
▶I	Last record, same field
▶✳	New (blank) record

You will use the record navigation buttons to move to the same field that is currently selected in the last record, and then back to the same field of the first record. Then you will move to the first field of the first record.

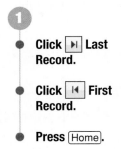

● Click ▶| Last Record.

● Click |◀ First Record.

● Press Home.

Your screen should be similar to Figure 1.57

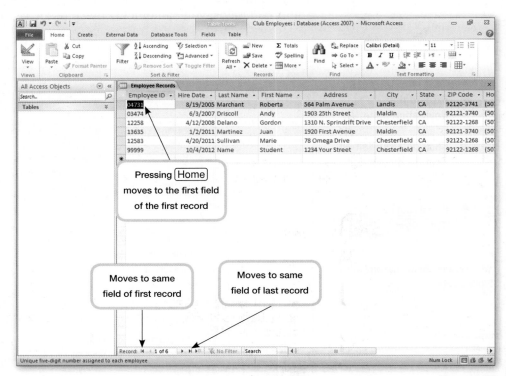

Figure 1.57

The first field of the first record is selected.

MOVING TO A SPECIFIC RECORD

You have moved the location of the cursor to the first record by using the record navigation buttons. You can also quickly move to a specific record by simply typing the record number into the Current Record box in the record navigation bar. This method is especially helpful when navigating around a large table when you know the record number you are looking for. Now you will practice moving to a specific record number.

1

- **Click in the Current Record box.**

- **Press** ←Backspace **or** Delete **to delete the number 1.**

- **Type in** 5 **and press** ←Enter**.**

Your screen should be similar to Figure 1.58

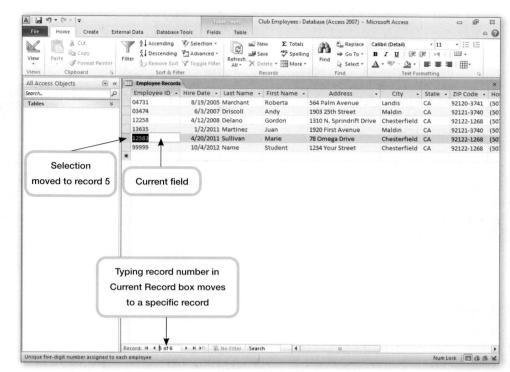

Selection moved to record 5

Current field

Typing record number in Current Record box moves to a specific record

Figure 1.58

The specified record is now selected.

Deleting Records

Additional Information

You can select multiple noncontiguous records by holding down Ctrl while clicking the Select Record button of each record. To select contiguous records, click and drag along the Select Record buttons.

While you are entering the employee records, you find a memo from one of your managers stating that Andy Driscoll is no longer working at the club and asking you to remove his record from the employee files.

You can remove records from a table by selecting the entire record and pressing the Delete key. After pressing Delete, you will be asked to confirm that you really want to delete the selected record. This is because this action cannot be reversed.

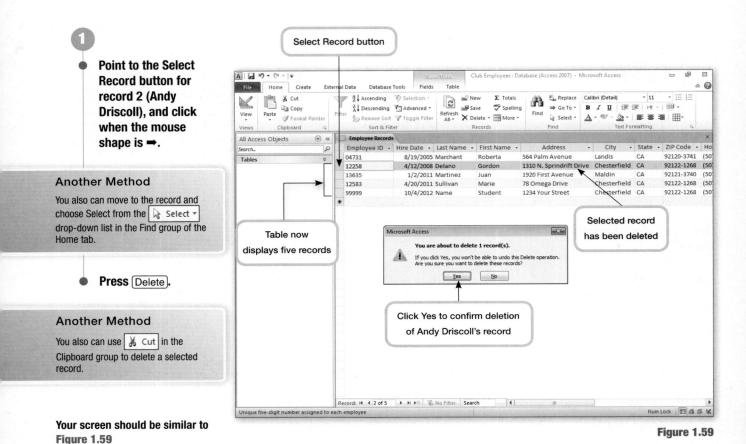

1

● **Point to the Select Record button for record 2 (Andy Driscoll), and click when the mouse shape is ➡.**

Another Method

You also can move to the record and choose Select from the [⬚ Select ▾] drop-down list in the Find group of the Home tab.

● **Press** ⏷Delete⏷.

Another Method

You also can use [✂ Cut] in the Clipboard group to delete a selected record.

Your screen should be similar to Figure 1.59

Select Record button

Table now displays five records

Selected record has been deleted

Click Yes to confirm deletion of Andy Driscoll's record

Figure 1.59

Although Andy Driscoll's record has been removed from the table, it will not be permanently deleted from the database until you confirm the deletion. If you change your mind, you can click [No] to restore the record.

2

● **Click** [Yes] **to confirm that you want to delete the record.**

Another Method

You also can choose Delete Record from the [✕ Delete] drop-down list in the Records group of the Home tab. The current record is both selected and deleted at the same time.

The record has been permanently deleted and the table now consists of five employee records.

Creating a Table in Design View

Following your plan for the employee database, you will add another table to the existing database file. This table will hold information about the employee's work location and job title.

There are several ways to create a new table in an existing database. You can insert a blank table and define the fields in Datasheet view as you already have done, or you can create a table based on a table model. You also can import from or link to data from another source, such as another database, an Excel worksheet, or a SharePoint list. Finally, you can create a new table starting in Design view. You will use this last method to define the two fields in the table, Location and Job Title.

Additional Information

A SharePoint list is a list of data that is stored on a SharePoint server and is available to others in an organization.

1

- **Open the Create tab and click** [Table Design] **in the Tables group.**

- **Define the fields using the settings shown in the following table.**

Your screen should be similar to Figure 1.60

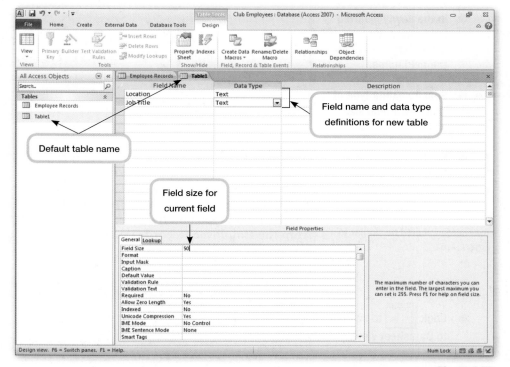

Figure 1.60

Field Name	Data Type	Field Size
Location	Text	20
Job Title	Text	50

The new table has a default table name of Table1.

INSERTING A FIELD

As you look at the table you realize you need a field to identify which employee the information belongs to. You want this field to be the first field in the table. To do this, you will insert the new field above the Location field.

1

- Make Location the current field.

- Click  in the Tools group of the Table Tools Design tab.

Another Method

You also can use Insert Rows on the shortcut menu.

- In the newly inserted field row, enter **Employee ID** as the field name.

- Specify a data type of Text and a field size of **5**

- Set the Employee ID field as the primary key for this table.

Your screen should be similar to Figure 1.61

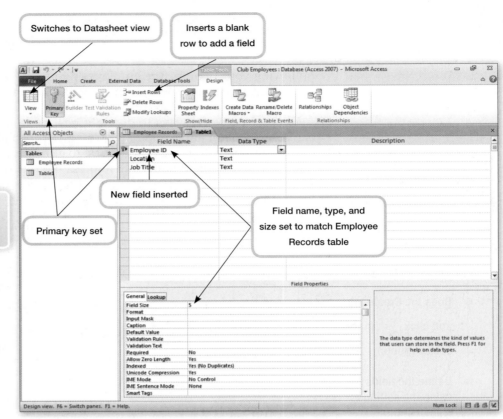

Figure 1.61

The Employee ID field is now inserted above the Location field in Design view. The Text data type and field size of 5 will match the existing property settings from the Employee Records table. Now you will switch to Datasheet view and save the table.

2

- Click 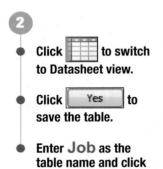 to switch to Datasheet view.

- Click **Yes** to save the table.

- Enter **Job** as the table name and click **OK**.

Your screen should be similar to Figure 1.62

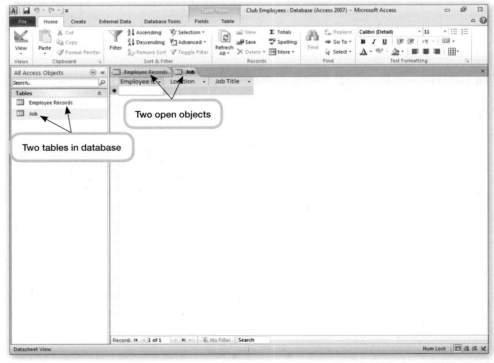

Figure 1.62

As you consider the contents of the two tables, you realize that the Hire Date information should be in the Job table because the subject matter is related to the employee's job, not to his or her personal information.

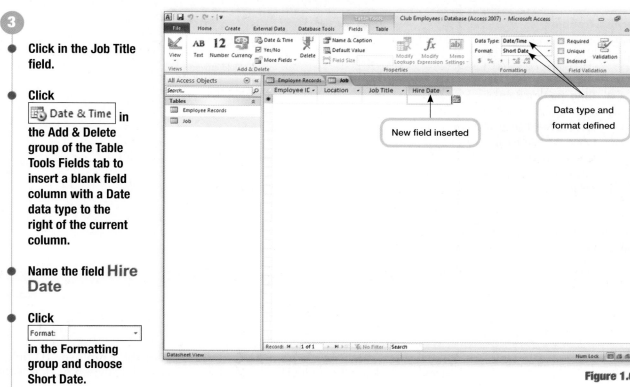

Figure 1.63

3

- Click in the Job Title field.

- Click [icon] **Date & Time** in the Add & Delete group of the Table Tools Fields tab to insert a blank field column with a Date data type to the right of the current column.

- Name the field **Hire Date**

- Click Format: in the Formatting group and choose Short Date.

- Click in the Hire Date field to confirm your settings.

Your screen should be similar to Figure 1.63

The new field has been inserted and defined.

MOVING A FIELD

The Hire Date field was inserted as the last field in the Job table. While in Datasheet view, you decide to move the Hire Date field next to the Employee ID field. To move a field column, select the column and then drag the selected column to the new location. As you drag, a heavy black bar shows where the column will be placed when you stop dragging.

1

● Select the Hire Date column.

Having Trouble?

Point to the field column name and click when the mouse pointer appears as ↓.

● Drag the Hire Date field to the left and release the mouse when the black bar is to the right of the Employee ID field column.

Your screen should be similar to Figure 1.64

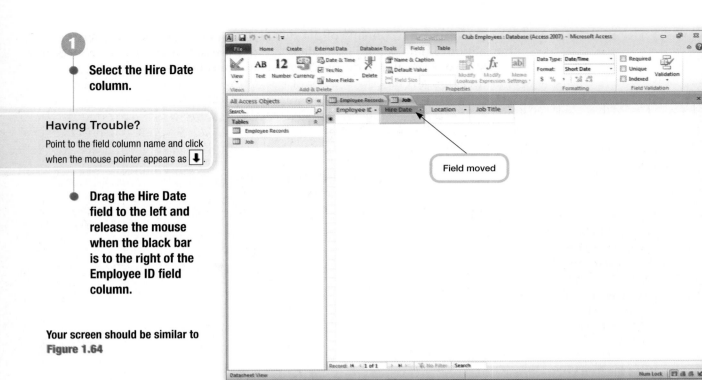

Field moved

Figure 1.64

The Hire Date field has been moved to the right of the Employee ID field. To compare the Datasheet view to the Design view, you will switch back to Design view.

2

● Click  to switch back to Design view.

Your screen should be similar to Figure 1.65

Hire Date field still in last position, even though moved in Datasheet view

Figure 1.65

Notice the Hire Date field is still last in the list of field names in Design view, even though you moved it to the second position in Datasheet view. The order in which the fields display can differ between the two views. This enables you to aesthetically display the order of the fields in the table and yet be able to arrange them in a specific structural order in Design view. Usually it is best for the field order to be the same in both views. You want to move the Hire Date below the Employee ID to match the placement in the datasheet. Moving a field in Design view is similar to doing so in Datasheet view, except that a row rather than a column is selected.

3

- Position the mouse in the gray row selector button next to Hire Date.

- Click when the mouse symbol changes to ➡ to select the Hire Date field row.

- While pointing to the row selector for the Hire Date row, drag up until the black move indicator line is below the Employee ID field.

- Release the mouse to place the Hire Date field row in its new position in Design view.

Your screen should be similar to Figure 1.66

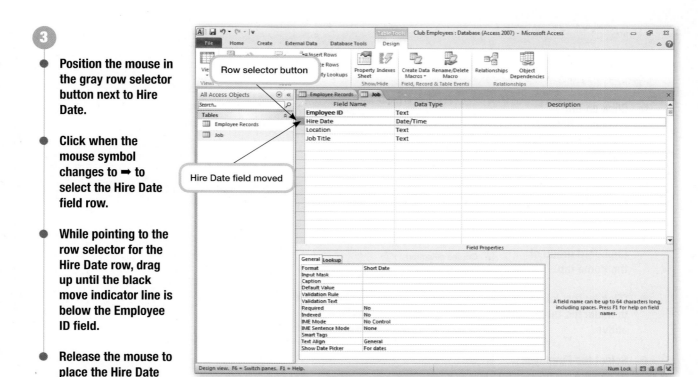

Figure 1.66

The field order in Design view now matches the order in which the fields are displayed in the datasheet.

4

- Click 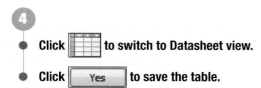 to switch to Datasheet view.

- Click | Yes | to save the table.

The Job table is now ready for you to input the data.

COPYING FIELD CONTENT

To save yourself time and prevent possible errors in typing, you will copy the data from the Employee ID and Hire Date fields in the Employee Records table into the new fields in the Job table. To switch between open tables, simply click on the table's tab. It then becomes the active table, or the table you can work in.

Having Trouble?

To review how to copy and paste, refer to the Copying and Moving Selections section in the Introduction to Microsoft Office 2010 lab.

Another Method

You can also press [Ctrl] + [F6] to cycle between open table windows.

1

● Click on the Employee Records tab to make the table active.

● Select the Employee ID column.

● Click 🗐 Copy in the Clipboard group of the Home tab.

● Click on the Job tab to make the table active.

● Select the Employee ID column.

● Click [Paste] in the Clipboard group of the Home tab.

● Click [Yes] to confirm the paste operation.

● Repeat these steps to copy the hire date information from the Employee Records table into the Job table.

Your screen should be similar to Figure 1.67

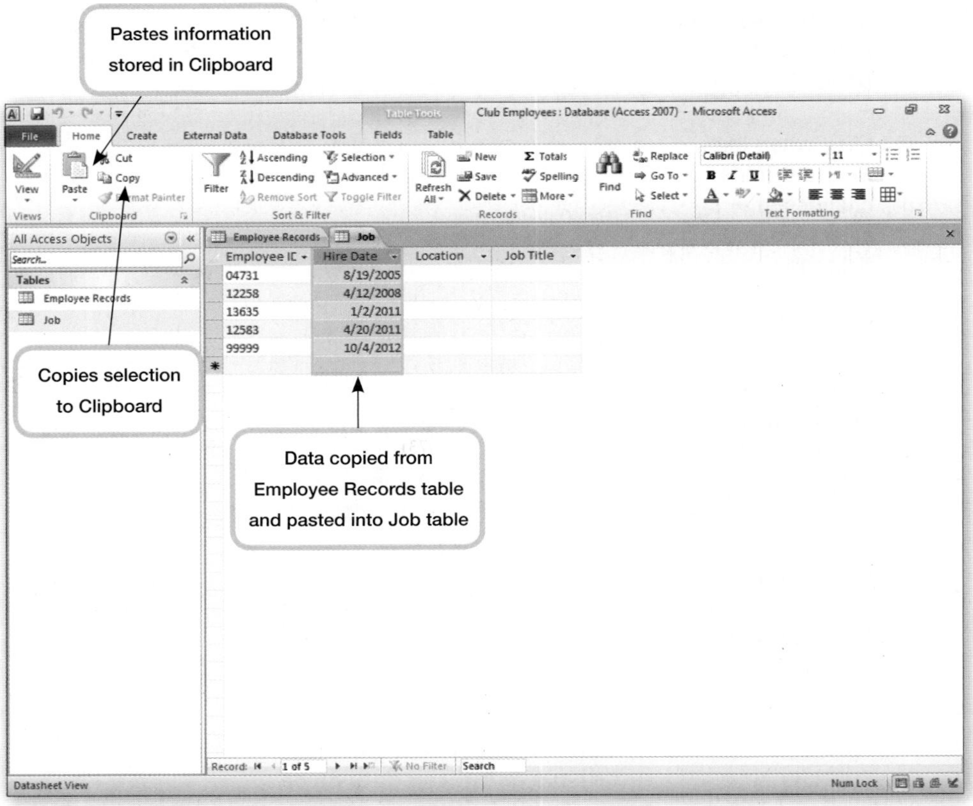

Figure 1.67

The table now includes information on the employee ID and hire date for the same records as in the Employee Records table. Now, all you need to do is delete the Hire Date field in the Employee Records table and then enter the rest of the data for the employees' job locations and titles.

2

- Make the Employee Records table active.

- Press Delete and click [Yes] to remove the still-selected Hire Date field from the Employee Records table.

- Add the information shown below to the appropriate records in the Job table.

- Best Fit the columns.

Your screen should be similar to Figure 1.68

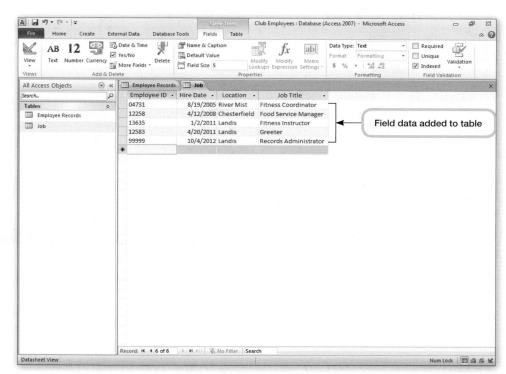

Field data added to table

Figure 1.68

Employee ID	Location	Job Title
04731	River Mist	Fitness Coordinator
12258	Chesterfield	Food Service Manager
12583	Landis	Greeter
13635	Landis	Fitness Instructor
99999	Landis	Records Administrator

Now the Employee Records table only contains the employee's personal information, and the Job table contains information about the employee's job.

Creating Relationships

Now that the database contains two tables, a relationship needs to be created between the tables to link the data together.

Concept 6 Relationship

A **relationship** establishes the association between common fields in two tables. The related fields must be of the same data type and contain the same kind of information but can have different field names. The exception to this rule occurs when the primary key field in one of the tables is the AutoNumber type, which can be related to another AutoNumber field or to a Number field, as long as the field size property is the same for both. This is also the case when both fields are AutoNumber or Number—they always have to be the same field size in order to be related.

There are three types of relationships that can be established between tables: one-to-one, one-to-many, and many-to-many.

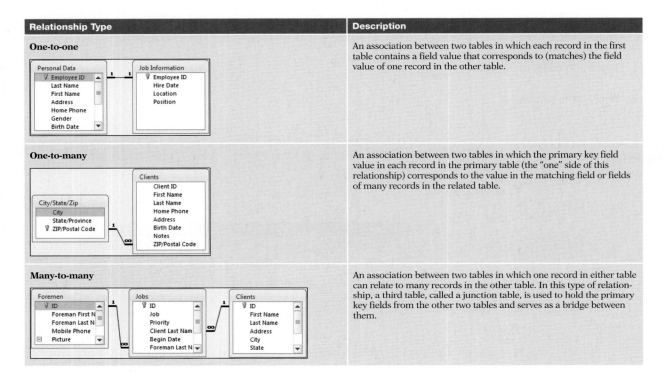

Relationship Type	Description
One-to-one	An association between two tables in which each record in the first table contains a field value that corresponds to (matches) the field value of one record in the other table.
One-to-many	An association between two tables in which the primary key field value in each record in the primary table (the "one" side of this relationship) corresponds to the value in the matching field or fields of many records in the related table.
Many-to-many	An association between two tables in which one record in either table can relate to many records in the other table. In this type of relationship, a third table, called a junction table, is used to hold the primary key fields from the other two tables and serves as a bridge between them.

Once relationships are established, rules can be enforced, called the rules of **referential integrity**, to ensure that relationships between tables are valid and that related data is not accidentally changed or deleted. The rules ensure that a record in a primary table cannot be deleted if matching records exist in a related table, and a primary key value cannot be changed in the primary table if that record has related records.

The Employee ID field is the field that the two tables have in common in this database and on which you will establish a relationship to link the tables together. To be able to create or edit relationships, you must close all open objects.

CLOSING TABLES

You close a table by closing its window and saving any layout changes you have made. Because you changed the column widths of the table, you will be prompted to save the layout changes before the table is closed. If you do not save the table, your column width settings will be lost.

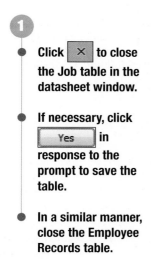

1

• Click [X] to close the Job table in the datasheet window.

• If necessary, click [Yes] in response to the prompt to save the table.

• In a similar manner, close the Employee Records table.

Your screen should be similar to Figure 1.69

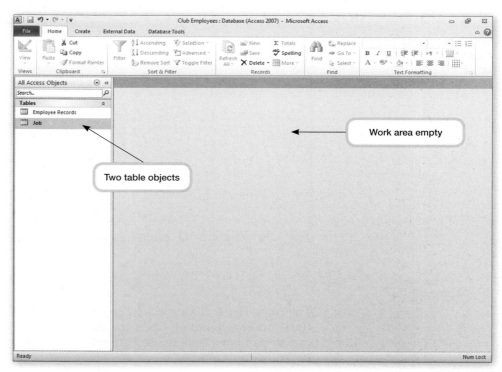

Figure 1.69

Both tables are closed and the work area is empty. The Navigation pane continues to display the names of the two table objects.

VIEWING RELATIONSHIPS

The Relationships window is used to create and edit relationships. It displays a field list for each table in the database and identifies how the tables are associated with relationship lines. However, the first time you open the Relationships window for a database, you need to select the tables to display in the window and then establish the relationship between the tables.

1

● Click 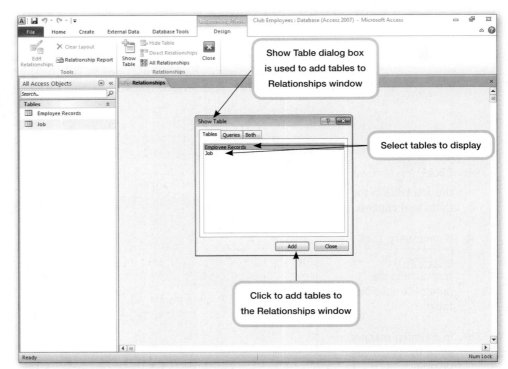 in the
**Relationships group
of the Database Tools
tab.**

Your screen should be similar to
Figure 1.70

Show Table dialog box
is used to add tables to
Relationships window

Select tables to display

Click to add tables to
the Relationships window

Figure 1.70

The Show Table dialog box appears automatically the first time you open the
Relationships window for a database. It displays the names of both tables
in the database and is used to select the tables you want displayed in the
Relationships window.

2

● Click [Add]
**to add the selected
table, Employee
Records, to the
Relationships
window.**

● **Click Job in the
Tables list to select
the table and then
click** [Add].

● **Click** [Close].

Your screen should be similar to
Figure 1.71

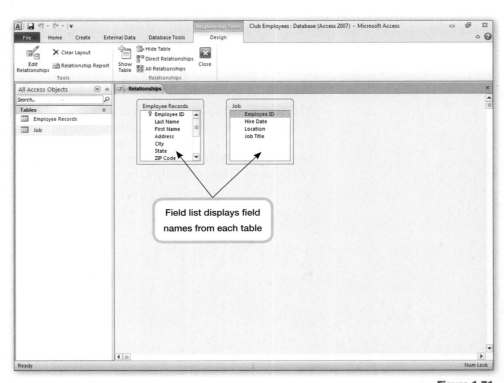

Field list displays field
names from each table

Figure 1.71

As you selected each table, a field list box displaying the field names from the table was added to the Relationships window. Next, you need to establish the relationship between the tables.

DEFINING RELATIONSHIPS

When creating relationships between the tables, study them first to determine what field the two tables have in common, and then determine which table is the main table. The common field in the lesser table, called a **foreign key** field, will be used to refer back to the primary key field of the main table. The field names of these two fields do not have to match, although their data types must be the same. As we have established, the Employee ID field is the common field between the two tables in this database. The Employee Records table is the main table, as it contains the main information about the employee. The Employee ID field in the Job table is the foreign key field.

Now you must connect the Employee Records' Employee ID field to its related field in the Job table. To create the relationship, you drag the field from the field list of one table to the common field in the field list of the other table.

As you point to the foreign key field, the mouse pointer will appear as 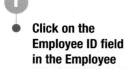, indicating a relationship is being established.

1

Click on the Employee ID field in the Employee Records table and drag to the same field in the Job table.

Your screen should be similar to Figure 1.72

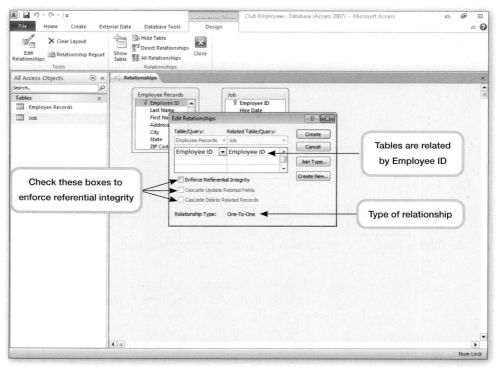

Figure 1.72

The Edit Relationships dialog box appears and shows how the tables will be related. You also want to enforce referential integrity between the tables. Selecting this option will make the Cascade Update and Cascade Delete options available. Again, you will select these options to ensure that if you change a primary key or delete a record, all fields that reference the primary key of that record are likewise updated or deleted in both tables. This prevents inconsistent and **orphaned records** (records that do not have a matching primary key record in the associated table). In addition, you can see that Access has correctly defined the type of relationship as one-to-one.

2

● **Choose Enforce Referential Integrity.**

● **Choose both Cascade options.**

● **Click** Create .

● **Click on the Job field list title bar to clear the selection from the relationship line.**

Your screen should be similar to Figure 1.73

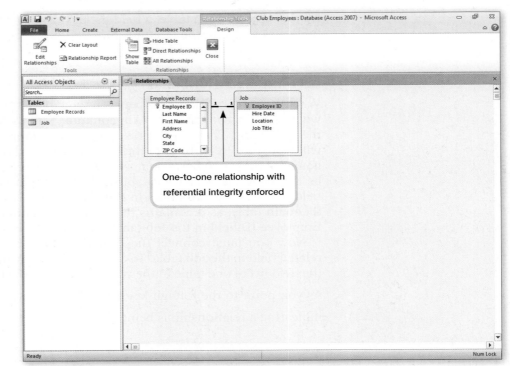

One-to-one relationship with referential integrity enforced

Figure 1.73

The two tables now display a relationship line that shows the tables are related on the Employee ID field. You can tell from the number 1 above each end of the relationship line that the relationship type is one-to-one. You can also tell that referential integrity is enforced because the relationship line is thicker near each end. If referential integrity were not enforced, the line would not be thicker at the ends.

3

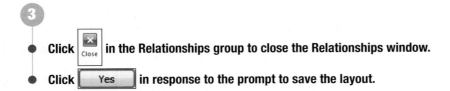

● **Click** [Close] **in the Relationships group to close the Relationships window.**

● **Click** Yes **in response to the prompt to save the layout.**

The relationships and layout are saved. Now that a relationship has been established and referential integrity enforced, a warning message will automatically appear if one of the rules is broken, and you will not be allowed to complete the action you are trying to do.

OPENING TABLES

Now that you have established relationships between the tables, you will open the Employee Records table to see how the change has affected it. To open a table object, double-click on the name in the Navigation pane.

Double-click Employee Records in the Navigation pane.

Another Method

You also can drag the object from the Navigation pane to the work area to open it, or right-click the object name in the Navigation pane and choose Open.

Your screen should be similar to Figure 1.74

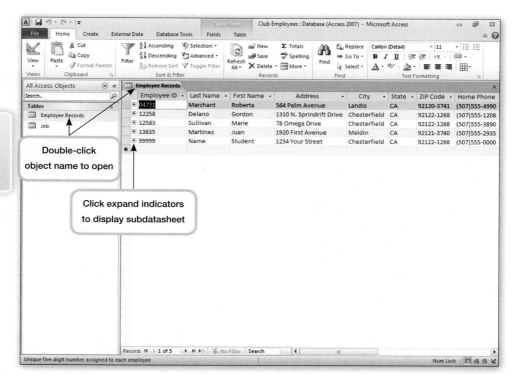

Figure 1.74

The Employee Records table is open in the work area. Notice the records are no longer in the same order they were entered, but are now in ascending order by the primary key, Employee ID. There are also expand indicators ⊞ at the beginning of each row. This indicates there is a subdatasheet linked to the records in this table.

Concept Subdatasheet

A **subdatasheet** is a data table nested within a main data table that contains information that is related or joined to the main table. A subdatasheet allows you to easily view and edit related data. Subdatasheets are created automatically whenever relationships are established between tables.

In this case, the subdatasheet is the Job table. Clicking ⊞ will expand the table to show the information in the subdatasheet table, Job.

2

●   Click ⊞ next to the
     first record.

**Your screen should be similar to
Figure 1.75**

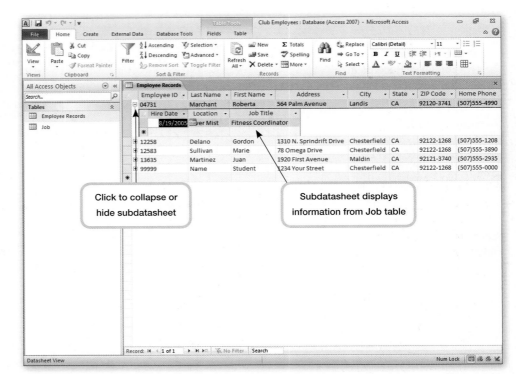

Figure 1.75

Additional Information

You will learn more about relationships
and subdatasheets in later labs.

A subdatasheet appears and displays the location and job title information
contained in the Job table for Roberta Marchant. Similarly, the Job table will
display a subdatasheet to the Employee Records table.

Then, to hide or collapse the subdatasheet again, you click the collapse
indicator ⊟.

3

●   Click ⊟ next to the first record.

●   Close the table.

You have created a database file that contains two tables and follows the two
basic principles of database design: Do not include redundant information in
tables, and enter accurate and complete information. Although you may think
the employee number is redundant data, it is the only way the information in
the two tables can be associated. The database attains the goals of **normalization**, a design technique that identifies and eliminates redundancy by applying a set of rules to your tables to confirm that they are structured properly.

Closing and Opening a Database

You are ready to show the manager your database to get approval on the setup
of the data. But first you want to make sure you know how to close and open
the file.

It is always a good idea to close all open objects in the work area before
closing the database. Since you have already closed the tables, the work area
is empty and there are no open objects. Next, you will close the database, but
not the Access program.

CLOSING A DATABASE

When closing a database file, unlike other types of files, you do not need to save first, as each time changes are made to the data they are automatically saved as part of the process. Changes to an object's design, however, need to be saved for the changes to be permanent.

1 • **Open the File tab and click** Close Database .

Your screen should be similar to Figure 1.76

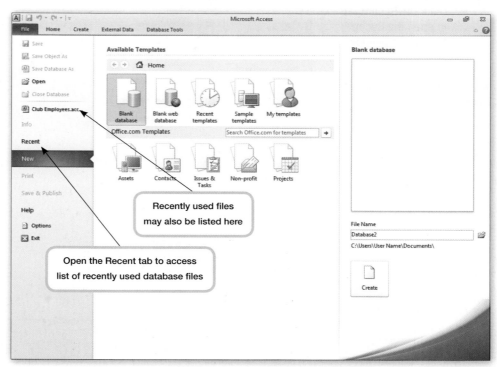

Figure 1.76

Additional Information

To review file types, refer to the Saving a File section in the Introduction to Microsoft Office 2010 lab.

The New tab in Backstage view is displayed again so you can create another new database or open an existing one. If you plan to share an Access 2007 or 2010 .accdb file with someone using Access 2003 or earlier, before closing the database open the Save & Publish tab in Backstage view, choose the Save Database As option and save it as the .mdb file type. Be aware some features may be lost when saving to an older version of Access.

OPENING A DATABASE

Additional Information

See the section Opening a File in the Introduction to Microsoft Office 2010 to review the basics on how to open a file.

Just as there are several methods to create a new database, there are several methods you can use to open an existing database. The first is to click

Open , which displays the Open dialog box through which you browse to specify the location and name of the file you want to open. Another is to open the Recent tab and select from a list of recently used database files. A third is to select from the list of recently used database files above the Info tab if the feature to display recent databases in this location is selected.

You also can open database files that were created in previous versions of Access that used the .mdb file extension. These older file types must be converted to the Access 2010 file format if you want to take advantage of the new features in Access 2010.

You will open the Recent Databases window list to see the list of recently opened database files and use this method to open the database.

1

● **Click the Recent tab to open the Recent Databases window.**

Your screen should be similar to Figure 1.77

Recent tab opens list of recently used files

Figure 1.77

Additional Information

Items can be removed from the Recent list by right-clicking the file name and choosing Remove from list.

The Recent Databases window by default displays up to 17 names of recently used database files on the computer you are using. The file names listed, however, are not always accurate as files may have been moved or deleted since they were last accessed.

2

● **Choose** Club Employees **from the Recent Databases list.**

● **If necessary, click**

> **Enable Content**

in the Security Warning message bar below the Ribbon to fully utilize the database.

Having Trouble?

Depending upon the security settings on your system, a Security Warning may be displayed below the Ribbon.

● **Double-click on the Employee Records table.**

Another Method

You also can drag the object from the Navigation pane to the work area to open it.

Your screen should be similar to Figure 1.78

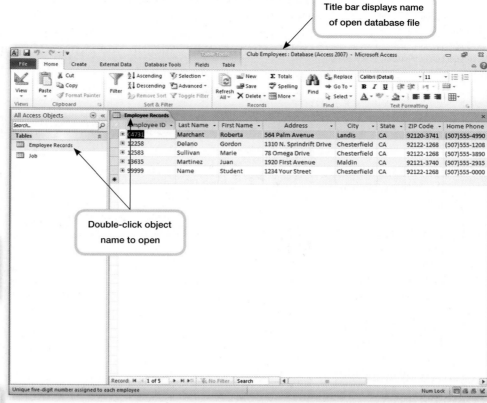

Title bar displays name of open database file

Double-click object name to open

Figure 1.78

The database file and table are open again and appear just as they were when you closed them.

Setting Database and Object Properties

Now, you want to look at the file properties or settings that are associated with the database file. Some of these properties are automatically generated. These include statistics such as the date the file was created and last modified. Others such as a description of the file are properties you can add.

DOCUMENTING A DATABASE

The information you can associate with the file includes a title, subject, author, keywords, and comments about the file. You will look at the file properties and add documentation to identify you as the author and a title for the database.

Having Trouble?

See Specifying Document Properties in the Introduction to Microsoft Office 2010 for more information about this feature.

- Open the File tab and, if necessary, choose Info.

- Click on the View and edit database properties link, located below the database preview.

- Open each tab in the Properties dialog box and look at the recorded information.

- Open the Summary tab.

- Enter the following information in the Summary tab.

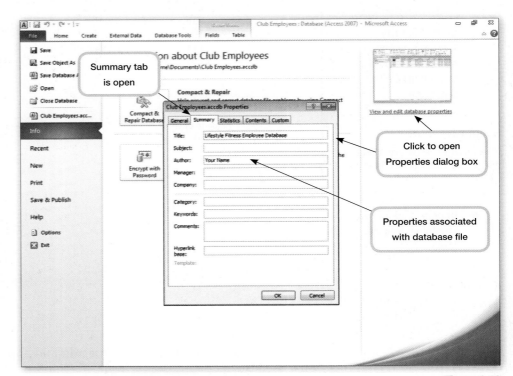

Figure 1.79

Title	**Lifestyle Fitness Employee Database**
Author	**Your Name**

Having Trouble?

The Title and Author text boxes may be blank or may already show information. Clear the existing contents first if necessary.

You also want to create a custom property to identify the completion date.

Your screen should be similar to Figure 1.79

2

- Open the Custom tab.
- Choose Date completed from the Name list.
- Choose Date as the Type.
- Enter the current date in the Value text box.
- Click [Add].

Your screen should be similar to Figure 1.80

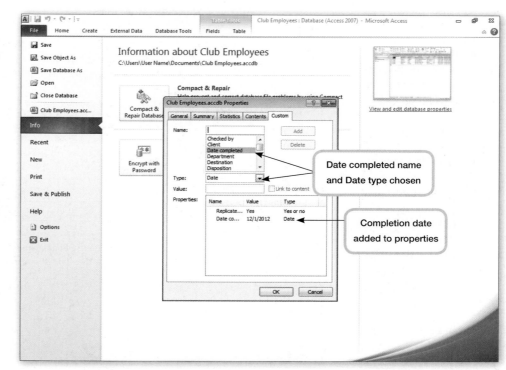

Date completed name and Date type chosen

Completion date added to properties

Figure 1.80

You are now finished entering information in the Database properties.

3

- Click [OK].

- Click the Home tab to close Backstage view.

DOCUMENTING A TABLE OBJECT

You have completed adding the properties to the file. You also can add limited documentation to each object in a database. You will add documentation to the Employee Records table object.

1

- **Right-click the Employee Records table object in the Navigation pane.**

- **Choose Table Properties from the drop-down menu.**

- **In the Description text box, type** This table is under construction and currently contains 5 records.

Your screen should be similar to Figure 1.81

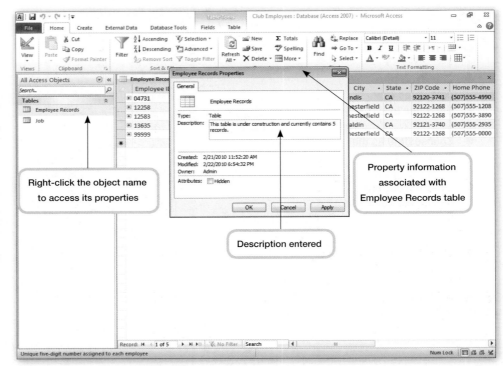

Right-click the object name to access its properties

Property information associated with Employee Records table

Description entered

Figure 1.81

You have added property information to both the database file and the Employee Records table.

2

- **Click** OK **to close the Properties dialog box.**

Previewing and Printing a Table

Now that you have completed designing and entering some sample data in the two tables, you want to print a copy of the tables to get your manager's approval before you begin entering more employee records. Before printing the tables, you will preview them onscreen to see how they will look when printed.

PREVIEWING THE TABLE

Previewing a table displays each page in a reduced size so you can see the layout. Then, if necessary, you can make changes to the layout before printing to save time and avoid wasting paper.

1

- **Open the Job table.**
- **Open the File tab.**
- **Open the Print tab and choose Print Preview.**
- **Hide the Navigation pane.**

Your screen should be similar to Figure 1.82

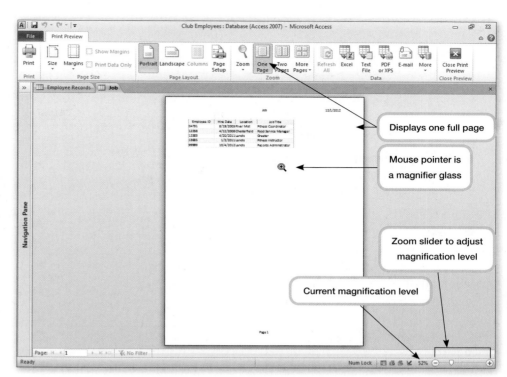

Displays one full page

Mouse pointer is a magnifier glass

Zoom slider to adjust magnification level

Current magnification level

Figure 1.82

Additional Information

The current magnification level is displayed in the status bar.

The Print Preview window displays how the table will appear when printed. The Print Preview contextual tab is open and includes commands that are used to modify the print settings.

2

- **Click on the table.**

Additional Information

The location where you click will determine the area that is displayed initially.

Your screen should be similar to Figure 1.83

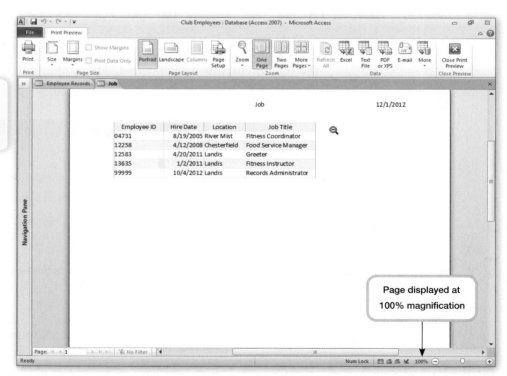

Page displayed at 100% magnification

Figure 1.83

The table appears in 100 percent magnification. This is the size it will appear when printed.

PRINTING A TABLE

The [Print] button in the Print group of the Print Preview tab is used to define the printer settings and print the document.

1

● If necessary, make sure your printer is on and ready to print.

● Click [Print].

Another Method

The keyboard shortcut is Ctrl + P.

Having Trouble?

Please consult your instructor for printing procedures that may differ from the directions given here.

Your screen should be similar to Figure 1.84

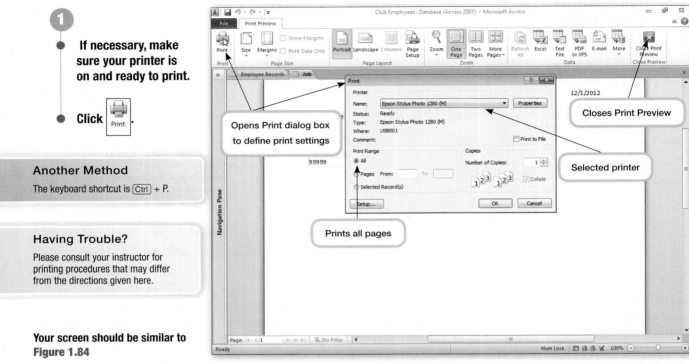

Figure 1.84

The Print Range area of the Print dialog box is used to specify the amount of the document you want printed. The range options are described in the following table.

Option	Action
All	Prints the entire document.
Pages	Prints pages you specify by typing page numbers in the text box.
Selected Records	Prints selected records only.

You will print the entire document.

2

● If you need to change the selected printer to another printer, open the Name drop-down list box and select the appropriate printer (your instructor will tell you which printer to select).

● Click [OK].

A status message box is displayed briefly, informing you that the table is being printed.

CHANGING THE PAGE ORIENTATION AND MARGINS

Next, you will preview and print the Employee Records table.

1

Click  in the
Close Preview group.

● Make the Employee
Records table active.

● Open the File tab.

● Open the Print tab
and then choose
Print Preview.

● Click on the table to
zoom the preview.

Your screen should look similar
to **Figure 1.85**

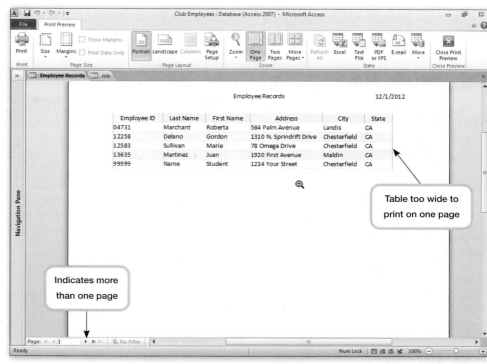

Figure 1.85

Notice that because the table is too wide to fit across the width of a page, only
the first six fields are displayed on the page. Tables with multiple columns are
typically too wide to fit on an 8½- by 11-inch piece of paper. You would like to
see both pages displayed onscreen.

2

Click 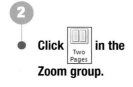 in the
Zoom group.

Your screen should be similar to
Figure 1.86

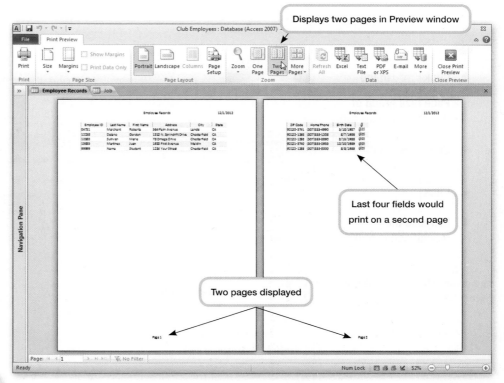

Figure 1.86

Having Trouble?

Refer to the section Printing a Document
in the Introduction to Microsoft Office
2010 lab to review page orientation.

Rather than print the table on two pages, you decide to see whether changing the page orientation from portrait to landscape will allow you to print the
table on one page.

3

Click 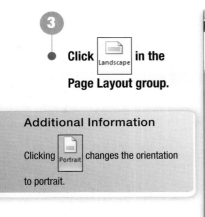 in the **Page Layout group.**

Additional Information

Clicking **Portrait** changes the orientation to portrait.

Your screen should be similar to Figure 1.87

Changes orientation to landscape

Still two fields that don't fit on first page

Figure 1.87

Although this helps, there are still two fields that do not fit on the page. To fix this, you will try reducing the size of the page margins. The **margin** is the blank space around the edge of a page. You will decrease the right and left margin settings to 0.25 inch to see if this allows all fields to fit on one page.

4

Click 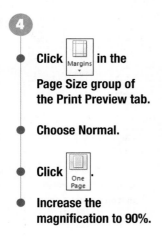 in the **Page Size group of the Print Preview tab.**

Choose **Normal.**

Click **One Page.**

Increase the magnification to 90%.

Your screen should be similar to Figure 1.88

Adjust page margins

Normal margins have .25" left and right and .75" top and bottom

All fields fit on one page

Grayed-out arrow indicates there are no more pages after page 1

Magnification at 90%

Figure 1.88

You can now see that all the fields will print on one page.

5

● **Print the table.**

● **Close the Print Preview window.**

Exiting Access

You will continue to build and use the database of employee records in the next lab. Until then, you can exit Access.

1

● **Click** **Close in the Access window title bar.**

Another Method

You also can open the File tab and choose ✕ Exit .

Notice that this time you were not prompted to save the tables because you did not made any layout changes to them since opening them. If you had made layout changes, you would be prompted to save the tables before exiting Access.

OCUS ON CAREERS

EXPLORE YOUR CAREER OPTIONS

Admitting Nurse

Can you imagine trying to organize the information of hundreds of patients in a busy emergency room? This is the job of an admitting nurse, who must be able to enter, edit, and format data; add and delete records; and so on. This information is used by all departments of the hospital, from the doctors, to the pharmacy, and to the billing department. Without a proper understanding of database software, a hospital cannot run efficiently. The average salary of an admitting nurse is in the $40,000 to $50,000 range. The demand for nurses is expected to remain high.

Database (AC1.4)

A database is an organized collection of related information.

Object (AC1.9)

An Access database is made up of several types of objects, such as a table or report, consisting of many elements. An object can be created, selected, and manipulated as a unit.

Data Type (AC1.15)

The data type defines the type of data the field will contain. Access uses the data type to ensure that the right kind of data is entered in a field.

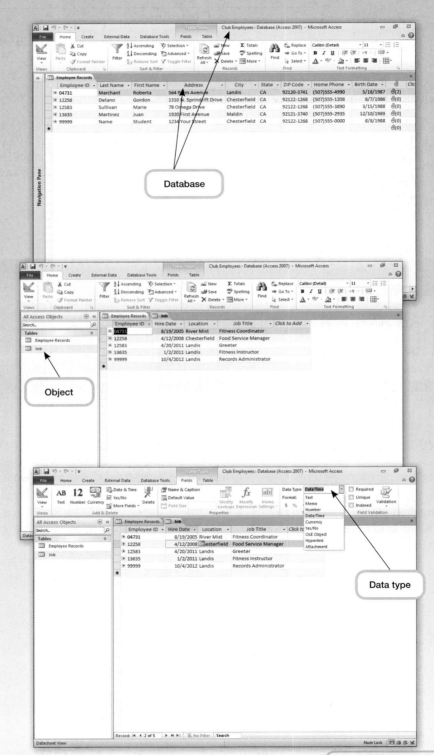

Field Property (AC1.22)

A field property is a characteristic that helps define a field. A set of field properties is associated with each field.

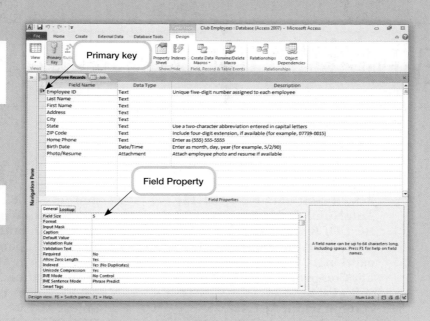

Primary Key (AC1.28)

A primary key is a field that uniquely identifies each record.

Relationship (AC1.66)

A relationship establishes the association between common fields in two tables.

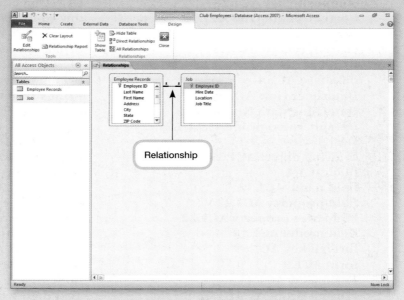

Subdatasheet (AC1.71)

A subdatasheet is a data table nested within a main data table; it contains information that is related or joined to the main table.

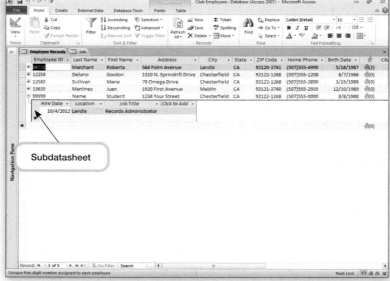

LAB REVIEW | Lab 1 Creating a Database

KEY TERMS

Allow Zero Length property AC1.22
Attachment data type AC1.15
AutoNumber data type AC1.15
Best Fit feature AC1.49
Calculated data type AC1.15
caption AC1.27
Caption property AC1.22
cell AC1.11
column width AC1.47
composite key AC1.28
Currency data type AC1.15
current field AC1.24
current record AC1.11
data type AC1.15
database AC1.4
Datasheet view AC1.11
Date/Time data type AC1.15
Default Value property AC1.22
Design view AC1.11
drawing object AC1.39
field AC1.4
field name AC1.13
field property AC1.22
Field Size property AC1.22
field model AC1.18
foreign key AC1.69
form AC1.9
Form view AC1.11
Format property AC1.22
graphic AC1.39
header row AC1.11
Hyperlink data type AC1.15
Indexed property AC1.22
Input Mask property AC1.22

Layout view AC1.11
margin AC1.82
Memo data type AC1.15
navigation buttons AC1.11
Navigation pane AC1.10
normal form AC1.72
normalization AC1.72
Number data type AC1.15
object AC1.9
OLE Object data type AC1.15
one-to-many AC1.66
one-to-one AC1.66
orphaned records AC1.69
picture AC1.39
primary key AC1.28
Print Preview AC1.11
query AC1.9
record AC1.4
referential integrity AC1.66
relational database AC1.4
relationship AC1.66
report AC1.9
Report view AC1.11
Required property AC1.22
Select Record button AC1.11
serial value AC1.15
subdatasheet AC1.71
table AC1.4, 9
Text data type AC1.15
Validation Rule property AC1.22
Validation Text property AC1.22
view AC1.10
Yes/No data type AC1.15

COMMAND SUMMARY

Command	Shortcut	Action
File Tab		
New		Opens a new blank database
Open	Ctrl + O	Opens an existing database
Save	Ctrl + S	Saves database object
Recent		Displays a list of recently used database files
Print/Print	Ctrl + P	Specifies print settings and prints current database object
Print/Print Preview		Displays file as it will appear when printed
Close Database		Closes open window
✕ Exit		Closes Access
Home Tab		
Views group		
☑ Design View	☑	Displays object in Design view
▦ Datasheet View	▦	Displays object in Datasheet view
Clipboard group		
✂ Cut	Ctrl + X	Removes selected item and copies it to the Clipboard
📋 Copy	Ctrl + C	Duplicates selected item and copies to the Clipboard
📋 Paste	Ctrl + V	Inserts copy of item from Clipboard
Records group		
✕ Delete	Delete	Deletes current record
▦ More ▾ /Field Width		Adjusts width of selected column
Find group		
▷ Select ▾ /Select		Selects current record

LAB REVIEW

COMMAND SUMMARY (CONTINUED)

Command	Shortcut	Action
Table Tools Field Tab		
Views group		
Design View	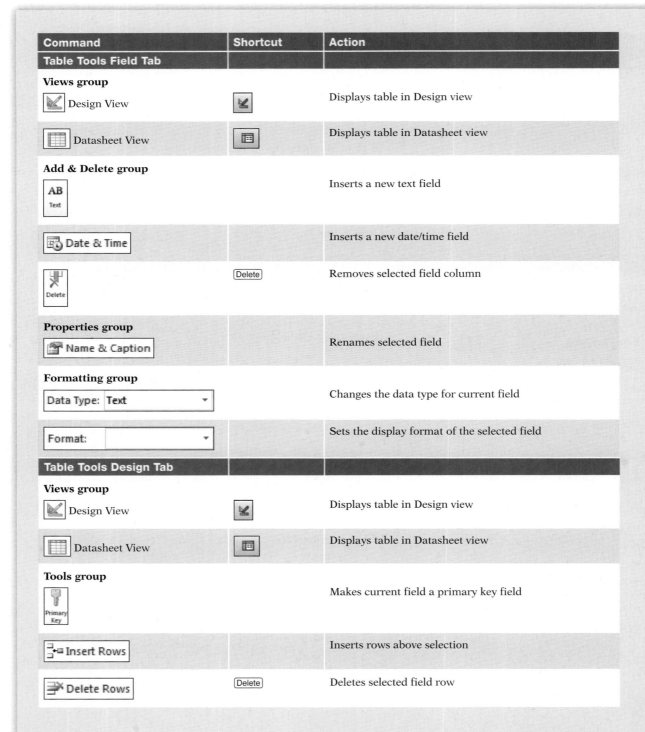	Displays table in Design view
Datasheet View		Displays table in Datasheet view
Add & Delete group		
AB Text		Inserts a new text field
Date & Time		Inserts a new date/time field
Delete	Delete	Removes selected field column
Properties group		
Name & Caption		Renames selected field
Formatting group		
Data Type: Text		Changes the data type for current field
Format:		Sets the display format of the selected field
Table Tools Design Tab		
Views group		
Design View		Displays table in Design view
Datasheet View		Displays table in Datasheet view
Tools group		
Primary Key		Makes current field a primary key field
Insert Rows		Inserts rows above selection
Delete Rows	Delete	Deletes selected field row

COMMAND SUMMARY (CONTINUED)

Command	Shortcut	Action
Database Tools Tab		
Relationships		Opens relationships window
Print Preview Tab		
Print group		
Print	Ctrl + P	Prints displayed object
Page Layout group		
Portrait		Changes print orientation to portrait
Landscape		Changes print orientation to landscape
Zoom group		
One Page		Displays one entire page in Print Preview
Two Pages		Displays two entire pages in Print Preview
Close Preview group		
Close Print Preview		Closes Print Preview window

LAB EXERCISES

SCREEN IDENTIFICATION

1. On the following Access screen, several items are identified by letters. Enter the correct term for each item in the spaces provided.

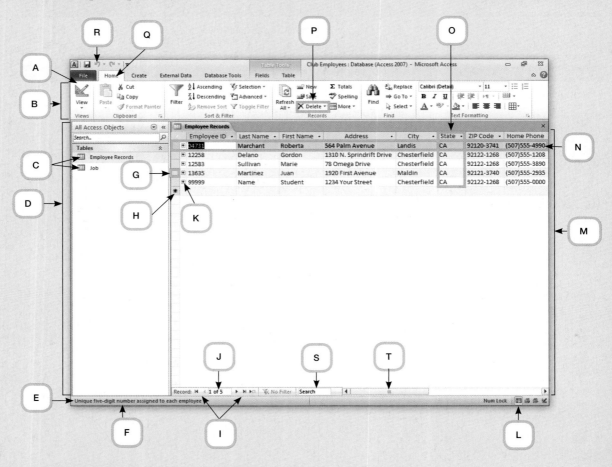

Possible answers for the screen identification are:

Cell
Current Record box
Datasheet View button
Delete record
Design view
Field
Field description
Navigation pane
New Record/End of table marker
Object
Open object tab
Primary key indicator

Quick Access Toolbar
Record
Record navigation buttons
Ribbon
Scroll bar
Search
Select Record button
Status bar
Subdatasheet indicator
Tab
Work area

A. _____   K. _____
B. _____   L. _____
C. _____   M. _____
D. _____   N. _____
E. _____   O. _____
F. _____   P. _____
G. _____   Q. _____
H. _____   R. _____
I. _____   S. _____
J. _____   T. _____

MATCHING

Match the numbered item with the correct lettered description.

1. Datasheet view   ____ a. contains multiple tables linked by a common field
2. Attachment   ____ b. used to define the table structure
3. Design view   ____ c. used to open and manage database objects
4. field size   ____ d. a data type that stores multiple files of different file types in a single field
5. data type   ____ e. field that uniquely identifies each record
6. object   ____ f. displays table in row and column format
7. record   ____ g. defines the type of data the field will contain
8. relational database   ____ h. controls the maximum number of characters that can be entered in a field
9. primary key   ____ i. collection of related fields
10. Navigation pane   ____ j. a unit of a database

TRUE/FALSE

Circle the correct answer to the following statements.

1. A foreign key is a field in one table that refers to the primary key field in another table and indicates how the tables are related.	True	False
2. Tables and queries are two types of database objects.	True	False
3. Caption text can be different from the field's name.	True	False
4. A table is a required object in a database.	True	False
5. Changing the column width in the datasheet changes the field size.	True	False
6. A field description is a required part of the field definition.	True	False
7. Interactive databases define relationships between tables by having common data in the tables.	True	False
8. A field contains information about one person, thing, or place.	True	False
9. The data type defines the information that can be entered in a field.	True	False
10. You can format the text in a Memo field.	True	False

LAB EXERCISES

FILL-IN

Complete the following statements by filling in the blanks with the correct terms.

1. The _____ data type can be used to store a graphic file in a field.
2. A(n) _____ is used to create a preformatted field or a set of several fields commonly used together.
3. An Access database is made up of several types of _____.
4. A(n) _____ is a data table nested in another data table that contains data that is related or joined to the table where it resides.
5. The field property that limits a Text data type to a certain size is called a(n) _____.
6. Using _____ orientation prints across the length of the paper.
7. The _____ data type restricts data to digits only.
8. A field name is used to identify the _____ stored in a field.
9. The _____ field property specifies how data displays in a table.
10. You use the _____ located at the left of the work area to select the type of object you want to work with.

MULTIPLE CHOICE

Circle the letter of the correct response.

1. _____ view is only used to modify the table structure.
   a. Design
   b. Report
   c. Datasheet
   d. Query

2. The basic database objects are _____.
   a. panes, tables, queries, and reports
   b. tables, queries, forms, and reports
   c. forms, reports, data, and files
   d. portraits, keys, tables, and views

3. Graphics can be inserted into a field that has a(n) _____ data type.
   a. Graphic
   b. Text
   c. Attachment
   d. Memo

4. Another way to create fields is to select from a list of predefined fields called _____.
   a. value fields
   b. data types
   c. field models
   d. attachment fields

5. A _____ is a field in one table that refers to the primary key field in another table and indicates how the tables are related.
   a. foreign key
   b. common key
   c. related key
   d. data key

6. _____ affects the amount of data that you can enter into a field.
   a. Column width
   b. Field size
   c. Format
   d. Description size

7. You may lose data if your data and _____ are incompatible.
   a. field name
   b. data type
   c. default value
   d. field size

8. A _____ is often used as the primary key.
   a. phone number
   b. catalog number
   c. last name
   d. first name

9. _____ is a design technique that identifies and eliminates redundancy by applying a set of rules to your tables.
   a. Database development
   b. Normalization
   c. Validation
   d. Orientation

10. The last step of database development is to _____.
    a. design
    b. develop
    c. review
    d. plan

LAB EXERCISES   Hands-On Exercises

STEP-BY-STEP

OAK RIDGE SCHOOL PARENT CONTACT DATABASE ★

1. Oak Ridge Elementary School has decided to set up a database with the contact information for all students. As a parent, you have volunteered to do the initial database creation and teach the secretary at the school to maintain it. The database table you create will have the following information: student's last name, student's first name, guardian's name, home address, and home phone number. When you have finished, a printout of your completed database table should look similar to the one shown here.

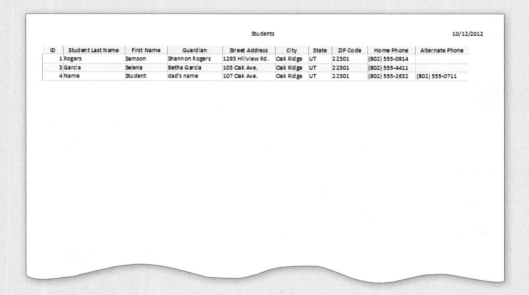

   a. Create a blank database named Oak Ridge School. Create a table in Datasheet view using the following field information. When creating the address fields, use the Address field model to create the Address, City, State, and ZIP Code fields. Switch to Design view and save the table as **Students**. Make the ID field the primary key field. Delete the Country Region field generated from the Address field model and then modify the field names and properties to match those shown below.

Field Name	Data Type	Description	Field Size/Format
ID	AutoNumber		Long Integer
Student Last Name	Text	Student's legal last name	25
First Name	Text	Include student's nickname in parentheses	25
Guardian	Text	First and last names of primary guardian	55
Street Address	Text		75
City	Text		20
State	Text	Two-letter abbreviation	2
ZIP Code	Text		5
Home Phone	Text		15

b. In Datasheet view, enter the following records into the table, using Copy and Paste for fields that have the same data (such as the city):

	Record 1	Record 2	Record 3
Student Last Name	Rogers	Wilson	Garcia
First Name	Samson	Avette	Selena
Guardian	Shannon Rogers	Rita Wilson-Montoya	Betha Garcia
Street Address	1293 Hillview Rd.	102 4th Street	103 Oak Ave.
City	Oak Ridge	Oak Ridge	Oak Ridge
State	UT	UT	UT
ZIP Code	22301	22301	22301
Home Phone	(802) 555-0914	(802) 555-3375	(802) 555-4411

c. Adjust the column widths appropriately.

d. Delete record 2. Add another record with the following data:

[Your last name]

[Your first name]

[Your parent's name]

107 Oak Ave.

Oak Ridge

UT

22301

(802) 555-2632

e. Add a new field after the Home Phone field with the following definitions:

Field Name: Alternate Phone

Data Type: Text

Field Size: 15

f. Change the ZIP Code field size to **10**

g. Enter the Alternate Phone number of **(802) 555-0711** and the ZIP Code of **22301-4459** for the record with ID number **4**

h. Best Fit all columns.

i. In the database properties, add **your name** as the author and **Oak Ridge School** as the title. Add the description **Exercise 1 in Access Lab 1** to the table properties.

i. View the table in Print Preview; change the page orientation to landscape and margins to Normal.

j. Print, save, and close the table.

LAB EXERCISES

PEPPER RIDGE RENTALS DATABASE ★ ★

2. You manage a real estate rental business and decide to implement a database to track the rental properties. A database will be useful to look up any information about the rental, including its location, how many bedrooms and bathrooms, square footage, and date available. This will help you find rentals within the desired home size and price range of your clients. When you are finished, your printed database table should be similar to the one shown here.

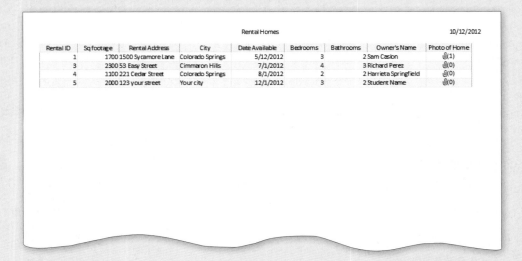

Rental ID	Sq footage	Rental Address	City	Date Available	Bedrooms	Bathrooms	Owner's Name	Photo of Home
1	1700	1500 Sycamore Lane	Colorado Springs	5/12/2012	3	2	Sam Casion	📎(1)
3	2300	53 Easy Street	Cimmaron Hills	7/1/2012	4	3	Richard Perez	📎(0)
4	1100	221 Cedar Street	Colorado Springs	8/1/2012	2	2	Harrieta Springfield	📎(0)
5	2000	123 your street	Your city	12/1/2012	3	2	Student Name	📎(0)

Rental Homes — 10/12/2012

a. Create a blank database named PepperRidgeRentals

b. Add the following fields to the new table:

Rental Address

City

Date Available

Bedrooms

Bathrooms

Sq Footage

Owner's Name

c. Switch to Design view. Save the table as **Rental Homes**

d. Change the ID field name to **Rental ID**

e. Add an Attachment field and name it **Photo of Home**. Use this name for the Caption property as well.

f. Change the field size of the Address and Owner's Name fields to **40**

g. Change the field size of the City field to **20**

h. Set the Date Available data type to Date, Short format.

i. The data type for Bedrooms, Bathrooms, and Sq Footage should be Number.

j. Return to Datasheet view. Add the following records to the table:

Address	1500 Sycamore Lane	8900 Sparrows Nest	53 Easy Street	221 Cedar Street
City	Colorado Springs	Cascade	Cimarron Hills	Colorado Springs
Date Available	5/12/2012	6/1/2012	7/1/2012	8/1/2012
Bedrooms	3	2	4	2
Bathrooms	2	1	3	2
Sq Footage	1700	840	2300	1100
Owner's Name	Sam Caslon	Betty Rose	Richard Perez	Harrieta Springfield

k. Insert the image file ac01_1500SycamoreHouse in the Attachment field of the first record.

l. Adjust the column widths using the Best Fit feature.

m. Delete the record for the address 8900 Sparrows Nest. Add a new record with fictional information, your name in the Owner's Name field, and the current date in the Date Available field.

n. In the database properties, add **your name** as the author and **Pepper Ridge Rentals** as the title. Add the description **Exercise 2 in Access Lab 1** to the table properties.

o. Preview and print the table in landscape orientation with normal margins.

p. Save and close the table. Exit Access.

LAB EXERCISES

CAR CLUB MEMBERS DATABASE ★★

3. You are a member of the local car club. Even though the club was founded only last year, the membership has grown considerably. Because of your computer skills, you have been asked to create a database with the membership number, membership date, first name, last name, address, city, state, zip, phone number, car year, and car model. This will help the club president contact members about events, the treasurer to mail out dues notices, and the events coordinator to mail out newsletters. Your printed database tables and relationships should be similar to those shown here.

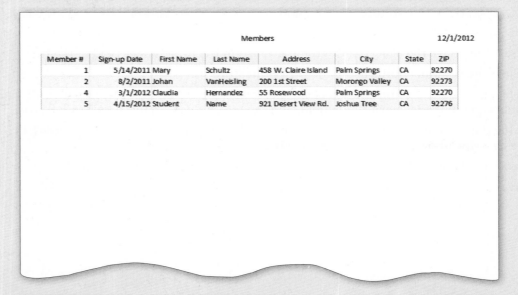

Member #	Sign-up Date	First Name	Last Name	Address	City	State	ZIP
1	5/14/2011	Mary	Schultz	458 W. Claire Island	Palm Springs	CA	92270
2	8/2/2011	Johan	VanHeisling	200 1st Street	Morongo Valley	CA	92273
4	3/1/2012	Claudia	Hernandez	55 Rosewood	Palm Springs	CA	92270
5	4/15/2012	Student	Name	921 Desert View Rd.	Joshua Tree	CA	92276

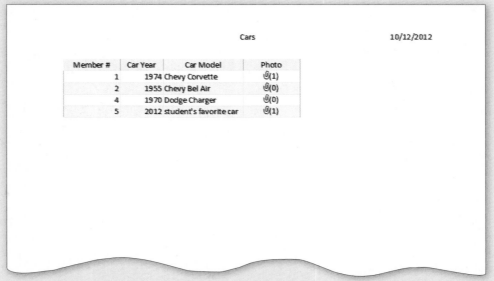

Member #	Car Year	Car Model	Photo
1	1974	Chevy Corvette	(1)
2	1955	Chevy Bel Air	(0)
4	1970	Dodge Charger	(0)
5	2012	student's favorite car	(1)

a. Create a blank database named Classics Car Club

b. Add the following fields to the new table:

Sign-up Date

Member Name

Address (use the Address field model)

c. Switch to Design view. Save the table as **Members**

d. Edit the field properties using the following information:

Field Name	Data Type	Description	Field Size/Format
Change ID to **Member #**	AutoNumber		
Sign-up Date	Date/Time	Date member joined club	Short Date
Change Member Name to **First Name**	Text	Member's first name	25
Address		Mailing address	50
Change State Province to **State**		Two-letter state abbreviation	2
Change ZIP Postal to **ZIP**		ZIP code, ex: 99999 or 99999-1234	10

e. Insert a row above the Address field and add the following field there:

Field Name	Data Type	Description	Field Size
Last Name	Text	Member's last name	25

f. Delete the Country Region field that was created as part of the Address field model.

g. Switch to Datasheet view and enter the following records into the table:

	Record 1	Record 2	Record 3	Record 4
Membership date	5/14/2011	8/2/2011	12/20/2011	3/1/2012
First Name	Mary	Johan	Frank	Claudia
Last Name	Schultz	Van Heisling	Bonaire	Hernandez
Address	458 W. Claire Island	200 1st Street	890 Lakeside Dr.	55 Rosewood Circle
City	Palm Springs	Morongo Valley	Indio	Palm Springs
State	CA	CA	CA	CA
ZIP	92270	92273	92275	92270

h. Best Fit all column widths.

i. Create a second table named **Cars** with the following fields:

Field Name	Data Type	Description	Field Size
Car Year	Number	Car's year of manufacture	
Car Model	Text	Car's make and model (e.g., Ford Mustang)	50
Vehicle Photo	Attachment	Photo of car in Classics Car show	

j. Change the Caption property for the Vehicle Photo to read **Photo**

Since you need a way to link the two tables together, you will obtain the member information from the Members table and paste it into the Cars table.

k. Switch to Datasheet view. Make the Members table active. Copy the Member # column.

l. Make the Cars table active. Right-click the Car Year field name and choose Insert field from the shortcut menu. Click Paste to complete the copy process, bringing the Member # field and information into the Cars table.

m. Enter the following records into the Cars table:

Member #	1	2	3	4
Car Year	1974	1955	1930	1970
Car Model	Chevy Corvette	Chevy Bel Air	Studebaker	Dodge Charger
Photo	ac01_1974Corvette			

n. Best Fit all column widths.

o. Close the tables. Establish the relationship between the Members table and the Cars table (hint: one member can have many cars). Enforce referential integrity and check the Cascade delete and update options. Close and save the relationship.

p. Open the Members table. Delete record 3. Add a new record with the following data:

Membership Date: **4/15/2012**

First Name: **Your first name**

Last Name: **Your last name**

Address: **921 Desert View Rd**

City: **Joshua Tree**

State: **CA**

Zip: **92276**

q. Open the Cars table and add your car information as a new record. (Your Member # should be 5.)

Car Year: **your favorite car year** or use **1961**

Car Model: **your favorite car model** or use **Ferrari**

Photo: attach photo of your car or use ac01_1961Ferrari

r. Check the tables in Print Preview. Print in portrait orientation with normal margins. Save and close both tables. Exit Access.

DOWNTOWN INTERNET CAFÉ INVENTORY DATABASE ★ ★ ★

4. The Downtown Internet Café, which you helped get off the ground, is an overwhelming success. The clientele is growing every day, as is the demand for the beverages the café serves. Up until now, the information about the vendors has been kept in an alphabetical card file. This has become quite unwieldy, however, and Evan, the owner, would like a more sophisticated tracking system. He would like you to create a database containing each supply item and the contact information for the vendor that sells that item. When you are finished, your database tables should be similar to those shown here.

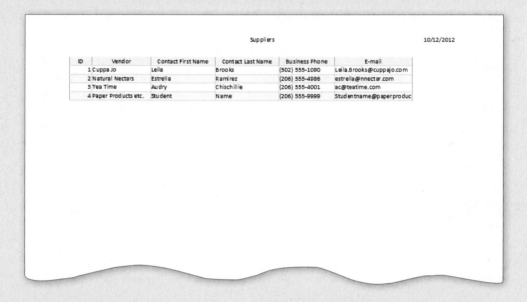

Suppliers   10/12/2012

ID	Vendor	Contact First Name	Contact Last Name	Business Phone	E-mail
1	Cuppa Jo	Leila	Brooks	(502) 555-1090	Leila.Brooks@cuppajo.com
2	Natural Nectars	Estrella	Ramirez	(206) 555-4986	estrella@nnectar.com
3	Tea Time	Audry	Chischillie	(206) 555-4001	ac@teatime.com
4	Paper Products etc.	Student	Name	(206) 555-9999	Studentname@paperproduc

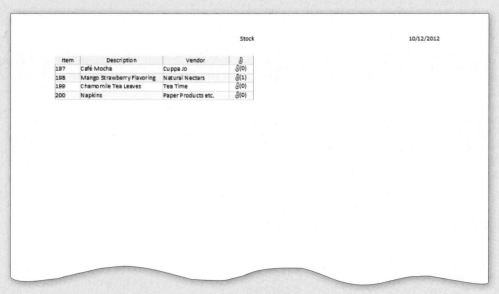

Stock   10/12/2012

Item	Description	Vendor	🔗
197	Café Mocha	Cuppa Jo	🔗(0)
198	Mango Strawberry Flavoring	Natural Nectars	🔗(1)
199	Chamomile Tea Leaves	Tea Time	🔗(0)
200	Napkins	Paper Products etc.	🔗(0)

LAB EXERCISES

a. Create a blank database named Cafe Inventory

b. Design a table with the field names **Item** and **Description**

c. Switch to Design view. Save the table as **Stock**

d. Delete the ID field. Make Item the primary key field.

e. Add the following information to the field properties:

Field Name	Data Type	Description	Field Size
Item	Text	Unique three-digit product number	3
Description	Text	Name of product	50

f. Create a second table using the following field names:

Company

First Name

Last Name

Business Phone

E-mail Address

g. Switch to Design view. Save the table as **Suppliers**

h. Edit the field properties as shown here:

Field Name	Data Type	Description	Field Size
Change Company to **Vendor**	Text	Company name of supplier	50
Change First Name to **Contact First Name**	Text		50
Change Last Name to **Contact Last Name**	Text		50
Business Phone	Text	Include the area code in parentheses: (800) 555-5555	15
Change E-mail Address to **E-mail**	Text	E-mail address of contact person	50

i. Enter the following records into the Stock and Suppliers tables:

Stock table		
Record 1	**Record 2**	**Record 3**
197	198	199
Café Mocha	Mango Strawberry Flavoring	Chamomile Tea Leaves

Suppliers table			
Record 1	**Record 2**	**Record 3**	**Record 4**
Cuppa Jo	Natural Nectars	Tea Time	Paper Products etc.
Leila	Estrella	Audry	Enter your first name
Brooks	Ramirez	Chischillie	Enter your last name
(502) 555-1090	(206) 555-4986	(206) 555-4001	(206) 555-9999
lbrooks@cuppajo.com	estrella@nnectar.com	ac@teatime.com	Yourname@paperproducts.com

j. Add the existing field, Vendor, from the Suppliers table as the last field in the Stock table.

k. In the Stock table, select Cuppa Jo as the vendor for the first record, Natural Nectars for the second record, and Tea Time for the third record.

l. In the Suppliers table, edit the record for ID 1 by changing the e-mail address to **Leila.Brooks@ cuppajo.com**

m. Add a new attachment data type field to the Stock table. Assign the new field the name and caption of **Picture**. For item number 198 insert the file ac01_Flavoring

n. Add the following new item to the Stock file.

Item:	**200**
Description:	**Napkins**
Vendor:	**Paper Products etc**

o. Adjust the column widths in both tables using Best Fit.

p. Make sure there is a relationship line connecting the Suppliers table ID field to the Stock table Vendor field. Edit the relationship line to enforce referential integrity, and the cascade update and delete options.

q. Preview the Suppliers table. Change to landscape orientation. Change the margins to wide and print the table.

r. Preview the Stock table. Change to landscape orientation. Change the margins to wide and print the table.

s. Close the database. Exit Access.

KODIAK CONSTRUCTION DATABASE ★ ★ ★

5. You have just been hired by Kodiak Paint and Construction to create and maintain a database containing information about their clients and jobs. The company has grown rapidly, and they need ready access to information about jobs spread across the city. When you are finished, your tables should be similar to those shown here.

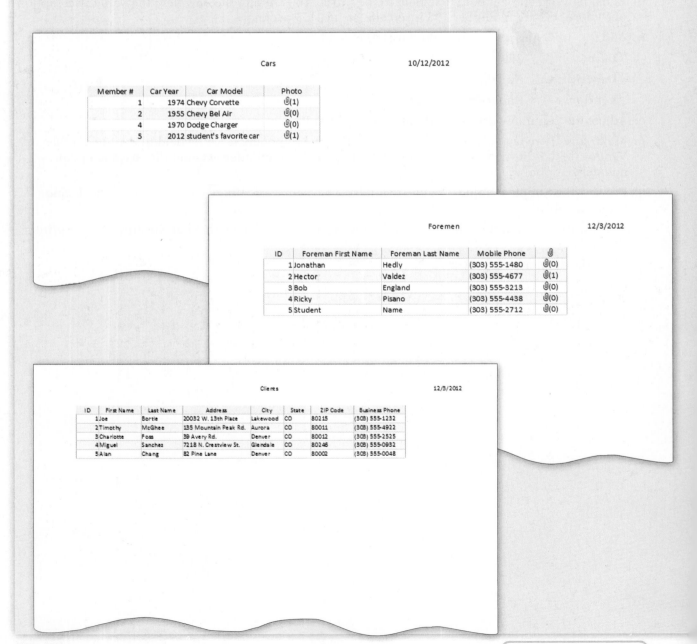

Cars   10/12/2012

Member #	Car Year	Car Model	Photo
1	1974	Chevy Corvette	(1)
2	1955	Chevy Bel Air	(0)
4	1970	Dodge Charger	(0)
5	2012	student's favorite car	(1)

Foremen   12/3/2012

ID	Foreman First Name	Foreman Last Name	Mobile Phone	
1	Jonathan	Hedly	(303) 555-1480	(0)
2	Hector	Valdez	(303) 555-4677	(1)
3	Bob	England	(303) 555-3213	(0)
4	Ricky	Pisano	(303) 555-4438	(0)
5	Student	Name	(303) 555-2712	(0)

Clients   12/3/2012

ID	First Name	Last Name	Address	City	State	ZIP Code	Business Phone
1	Joe	Bortle	20032 W. 13th Place	Lakewood	CO	80215	(303) 555-1232
2	Timothy	McGhee	135 Mountain Peak Rd.	Aurora	CO	80011	(303) 555-4922
3	Charlotte	Foss	39 Avery Rd.	Denver	CO	80012	(303) 555-2525
4	Miguel	Sanchez	721B N. Crestview St.	Glendale	CO	80246	(303) 555-0932
5	Alan	Chang	82 Pine Lane	Denver	CO	80002	(303) 555-0048

a. Create a blank database named Kodiak Construction. Design a table using the following field names:

Project Name

Begin Date

End Date

b. Add the following additional fields to the table.

Field Name	Type
Job Description	Memo
Job Location	Text
Job Estimate	Currency

c. Save the table as **Jobs**. Switch to Design view.

d. Change the Project Name field name to **Job**. Delete the End Date field. Add field descriptions and make the changes to the field properties shown in the following table:

Field Name	Data Type	Description	Field Size	Format
ID	Text	Unique three-digit job ID	3	
Job		Project Name	75	
Begin Date				Short date
Job Description		Brief description of project		
Job Location	Text	Enter city only	25	

e. Enter the following records into the table:

Record 1	Record 2	Record 3	Record 4	Record 5
034	062	010	053	112
Summit Lakes	Sandalwood Villa	Ridgeline Condos	R Bar C Ranch	Williams Retreat
4/13/2008	9/15/2008	2/18/2008	7/18/2008	12/13/2008
Remodel golf club	Remodel restaurant	New construction of 75 condo units	Private home guest addition	New construction
Denver	Aurora	Aurora	Glendale	Golden
1,200,000	750,000	2,500,000	125,000	925,000

f. Adjust the column widths using Best Fit.

g. Delete the record for the Summit Lakes job.

h. Create a second table for the client information using the following field names: (Use the Address field model to create the address fields.)

First Name

Last Name

Address

City

State Province

ZIP Postal Code

Business Phone

i. Save the table as **Clients**

j. Add field descriptions and make the changes to the field properties shown in the following table:

Field Name	Data Type	Description	Field Size
First Name	Text	First name of client	25
Last Name	Text	Last name of client	25
Address		Mailing address	50
City	Text		50
Change State Province to State		Use two-character abbreviation	2
Change ZIP Postal Code to ZIP Code		Enter 10 digit code, if available	10
Business Phone	Text	Enter phone as (###) ###-####	14

k. Add the following client information:

	Record 1	Record 2	Record 3	Record 4	Record 5
First Name	Joe	Timothy	Charlotte	Miguel	Alan
Last Name	Bortle	McGhee	Foss	Sanchez	Chang
Address	20032 W. 13th Place	135 Mountain Peak Rd.	39 Avery Rd.	7218 N. Crestview St.	82 Pine Lane
City	Lakewood	Aurora	Denver	Glendale	Denver
State	CO	CO	CO	CO	CO
ZIP Code	80215	80011	80012	80246	80002
Business Phone	(303) 555-1232	(303) 555-4922	(303) 555-2525	(303) 555-0932	(303) 555-0048

l. Create a third table for the foreman information with the following fields:

Field Name	Data Type	Description	Field Size
Foreman First Name	Text		25
Foreman Last Name	Text		25
Mobile Phone	Text	Enter phone as (###) ###-####	14
Picture	Attachment	Photo of foreman	

m. Save the table as **Foremen**

n. Enter the following information for the five foremen.

Jonathan Hedly	Hector Valdez	Bob England	Ricky Pisano	Your Name
(303) 555-1480	(303) 555-4677	(303) 555-3213	(303) 555-4438	(303) 555-2712

o. Add the file ac01_Valdez to the Attachment field for Hector Valdez.

p. Create a new field in the Jobs table that matches the Foreman Last Name from the Foreman table. Place the field after the Begin Date field. Use the field name **Foreman Last Name**

q. Enter the following foremen for each job:

Job	Foreman
010	Pisano
053	England
062	Your Name
112	Valdez

r. Create a field that matches the Last Name from the Client table after the Job field in the Jobs table. Rename the field **Client Last Name**

s. Enter the following clients for each job:

Job	Client
010	Foss
053	Sanchez
062	McGhee
112	Bortle

t. Establish relationships between tables: create a relationship between the Client Last Name field of the Client table and the Client Last Name field of the Jobs table; create another relationship between the Foreman Last Name field of the Foremen table and the Foreman Last Name field of the Jobs table.

u. Best Fit all fields in all tables.

v. Preview and print the Jobs table in landscape orientation with normal margins. Print the Foremen table in portrait orientation with wide margins. Print the Client table in landscape orientation with wide margins.

w. Save and close all tables and exit Access.

LAB EXERCISES

ON YOUR OWN

MUSIC COLLECTION DATABASE ★

1. You have just purchased a 200-disc CD carousel, and now you would like to organize and catalog your CDs. You realize that without an updatable list, it will be difficult to maintain an accurate list of what is in the changer. To get the most out of your new purchase, you decide a database is in order. Create a new database called Music Collection and a table called **CD Catalogue**. The table you create should include Artist's Name, Album Title, Genre, and Position Number fields. Make the Position Number field the primary key (because you may have multiple CDs by a given artist). Enter at least 15 records. Include an entry that has your name as the artist. Preview and print the table when you are finished.

VALLEY VIEW NEWSLETTER ADVERTISING DATABASE ★

2. Your homeowner's association distributes a monthly newsletter, *Valley View News*, to keep residents up to date with neighborhood news. In the past year, there has been rapid growth in building, including more houses and small office complexes. There are also plans to build an elementary school, fire station, and shopping center in the community. Consequently, the newsletter is now the size of a small newspaper, and the homeowners' dues are not covering the expense of publishing it.

   The editorial staff has already begun selling ad space in the newsletter to local businesses, and, based on your background in database management, they have asked you to set up a database to keep track of the advertiser contact information. You agree to design such a database, called Valley View News, and tell them you will have something to show them at the next meeting. Your finished database should include each advertiser's billing number, business name and address, and contact name and phone number in a table named **Advertisers**. Enter 10 records and include a record that has your name as the contact name. Preview and print the table when you are finished.

PATIENT DATABASE ★

3. You are the manager of a newly opened dental office. As one of your first projects, you need to create a patient database. Create a database called Dental Patients and a table named **Patient Information**. The database table you set up should contain patient identification numbers, last and first names, addresses, and phone numbers. Also include a field named "Referred by" and another field named "Patient since." Use appropriate field sizes and make the ID number field the primary key. Enter at least 10 records, adjusting the column widths as necessary. Include a record that contains your name as the patient. Preview and print the table.

OLD WATCH DATABASE USING THE WEB ★ ★

4. You have a small online business, Timeless Treasures, that locates and sells vintage wrist and pocket watches. Your business and inventory have grown large enough now that you have decided to use a database to track your inventory. Create a simple database named Timeless Treasures with a table named **Watches** that contains identification numbers, manufacturer (Waltham, Hamilton, Melrose), category (pocket watch, wrist watch), description, price, and quantity on hand. Size the fields appropriately and assign a primary key to one of them. Enter at least 10 records in the table. To obtain data about watches to include in your table, do a Web search on "old watches." Use the information you locate to complete the data for the records in your table. Adjust column widths as necessary. Include your name as the manufacturer in one of the records. Preview and print the table.

EXPENSE TRACKING DATABASE ★ ★ ★

5. You work in the accounting department at a start-up company called AMP Enterprises. One of your duties is to reimburse employees for small, company-related expenses, which up until now has been a simple task of having the employees fill out a form that they submit to you for payment. You then cut checks for them that are charged to the general expense fund of the company. However, the company has grown tremendously in the last year, adding employees and departments at a rapid rate, and the executive team has decided that it is time to start managing the income and expenses on a much more detailed level. To this end, you need to create a database that includes the employee ID, employee name, submission date, expense type, and expense amount for each expense report that is turned in. Name the database AMP Enterprises. Create two tables, one for the employee information named **Employee Info** and the other for employee expenses named **Employee Expenses**. Include the Employee ID, First Name, and Last Name fields in the Employee Info table. Include the Employee ID, Submission Date, Expense Type, and Expense Amount fields in the Employee Expenses table. Use the Currency data type for the Expense Amount field, and appropriate data types for all other fields. Size the fields appropriately. Delete the ID field from the Employee Info table and make the Employee ID field the primary key. Enter at least 15 records. Adjust the column widths as necessary. Delete one of the records you just entered, and then edit one of the remaining records so it contains your name as the employee. Enter 10 records in the Employee Expenses table (one should be an expense record for the record containing your name). Preview and print both tables.

Modifying and Filtering a Table and Creating a Form Lab 2

Objectives

After completing this lab, you will know how to:

1. Change field format properties.

2. Set default field values.

3. Define validation rules.

4. Hide and redisplay fields.

5. Create a lookup field.

6. Search, find, and replace data.

7. Sort records.

8. Format a datasheet.

9. Filter a table.

10. Create and use a form.

11. Modify the layout of a form.

12. Add a record using a form.

13. Organize the Navigation Pane

14. Preview, print, close, and save a form.

15. Identify object dependencies.

Lifestyle Fitness Club

Lifestyle Fitness Club owners, Ryan and Felicity, are very pleased with your plans for the organization of the database and with your progress in creating the first table of basic employee data. As you have seen, creating a database takes planning and a great deal of time to set up the structure and enter the data. As you have continued to add more employee records to the table, you have noticed several errors. You also realize that you forgot to include a field for the employee's gender. Even with the best of planning and care, errors occur and the information may change. You will see how easy it is to modify the database structure

and to customize field properties to provide more control over the data that is entered in a field.

Even more impressive, as you will see in this lab, is the program's ability to locate information in the database. This is where all the hard work of entering data pays off. With a click of a button, you can find data that might otherwise take hours to locate. The result saves time and improves the accuracy of the output.

You also will see how you can make the data you are looking at onscreen more pleasing and easier to read by creating and using a form.

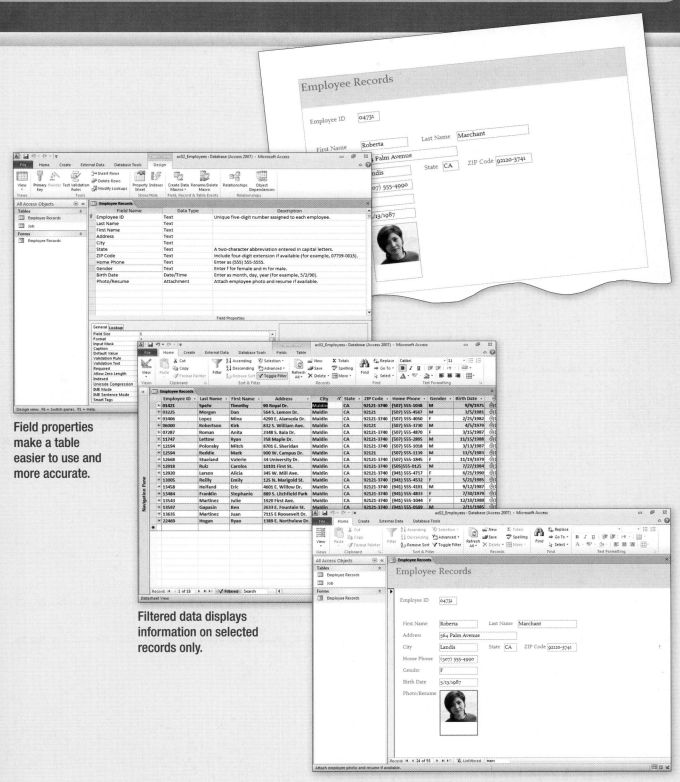

Field properties make a table easier to use and more accurate.

Filtered data displays information on selected records only.

Forms can be used to display information in an easy-to-read manner and make data entry easier.

The following concepts will be introduced in this lab:

1 Format Property The Format property is used to specify the way that numbers, dates, times, and text in a field are displayed and printed.

2 Default Value Property The Default Value property is used to specify a value that is automatically entered in a field when a new record is created.

3 Validation Rule Validation rules are used to control the data that can be entered in a field by defining the input values that are valid or allowed.

4 Expression An expression is a formula consisting of a combination of symbols that will produce a single value.

5 Lookup Field A lookup field provides a list of values from which the user can choose to make entering data into that field simpler and more accurate.

6 Find and Replace The Find and Replace feature helps you quickly find specific information and automatically replace it with new information.

7 Sorting Sorting rearranges the order of the records in a table based on the value in each field.

8 Filter A filter is a restriction placed on records in the open datasheet or form to quickly isolate and display a subset of records.

9 Form A form is a database object used primarily to display records onscreen to make it easier to enter new records and to make changes to existing records.

10 Controls Controls are objects that display information, perform actions, or enhance the design of a form or report.

11 Theme A theme is a predefined set of formatting choices that can be applied to an entire document in one simple step.

Customizing Fields

You have continued to add more records to the Lifestyle Fitness Club employee database. You want to open the expanded database to continue working on and refining the Employee Records table.

NOTE Before you begin, you may want to create a backup copy of the ac02_Employees **file by copying and renaming it.**

1

● **Start Microsoft Access 2010.**

● **Open the database file ac02_Employees.**

● **If necessary, click**

[**Enable Content**]

in the Security Warning bar below the Ribbon.

● **Open the Employee Records table.**

Your screen should be similar to Figure 2.1

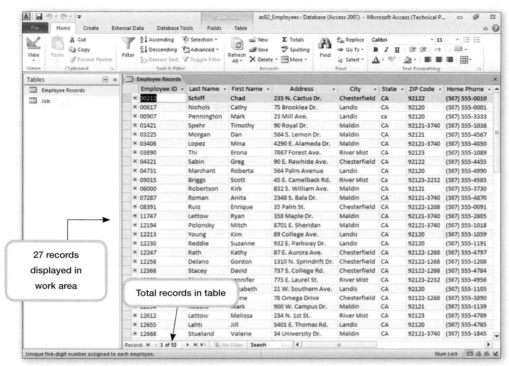

Figure 2.1

Having Trouble?

Your screen may display more or fewer records, depending upon your monitor settings.

As you can see from the record number indicator, the updated table now contains 53 records, but only the first 27 records are displayed. To see the rest of the records, you will move about the table using the keyboard and the record navigation buttons.

2

● **Press** [Page Down] **to look at the next page of records.**

● **Press** [Ctrl] + [End] **to move to the last field of the last record.**

Your screen should be similar to Figure 2.2

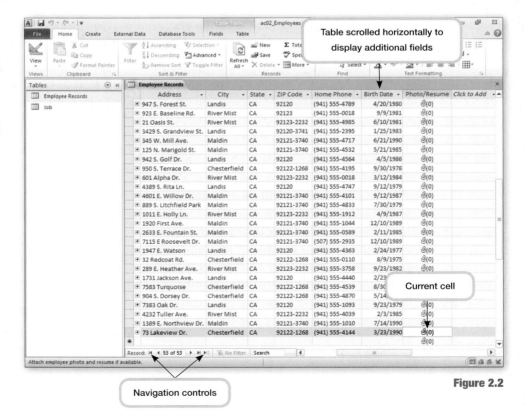

Figure 2.2

First the table moved down one full window to display records 27 through 53. Then the table scrolled horizontally one window to the right, and now the last fields in the table are visible. The last field in the last record is currently active.

3

Click the ◄ First record navigation button to move to the first record.

Press Home to move to the first field of the first record.

Your screen should be similar to Figure 2.3

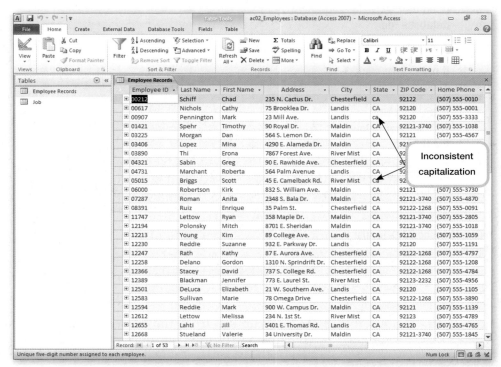

Figure 2.3

As you look through the records, you notice that record 3 has a lowercase entry in the State field and that record 10 has a mixed-case entry. You want all the State field entries to be consistently entered in all uppercase letters. Also, because all the club locations are in California, it is unlikely that any club employees live in another state. Rather than repeatedly entering the same state for each record, you want the State field to automatically display CA. You will make these changes to the State field by modifying its properties.

Additionally, you realize that you forgot to include a field for each employee's gender. While developing a table, you can modify and refine how the table operates. You can easily add and delete fields and add restrictions on the data that can be entered in a field as well as define the way that the data entered in a field will be displayed.

SETTING DISPLAY FORMATS

You will begin by fixing the display of the entries in the State field. Instead of manually editing each field, you will fix the entries by defining a display format for the field to customize the way the entry is displayed.

Concept ① **Format Property**

The **Format property** is used to specify the way that numbers, dates, times, and text in a field are displayed and printed. Format properties do not change the way Access stores data, only the way the data is displayed. To change the format of a field, you can select from predefined formats or create a custom format by entering different symbols in the Format text box. For example, four common format symbols used in Text and Memo data types are shown in the following table.

Symbol	Meaning	Example
@	Requires a text character or space	@@@-@@-@@@@ would display 123456789 as 123-45-6789. Nine characters or spaces are required.
>	Forces all characters to uppercase	> would display SMITH whether you entered SMITH, smith, or Smith.
<	Forces all characters to lowercase	< would display smith whether you entered SMITH, smith, or Smith.
&	Allows an optional text character	@@-@@@& would display 12345 as 12-345 and 1234 as 1-234. Four out of five characters are required, and a fifth is optional.

You want to change the format of the State field to display the entries in all uppercase characters.

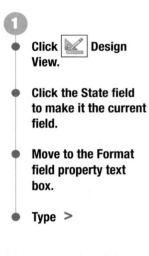

1

- Click 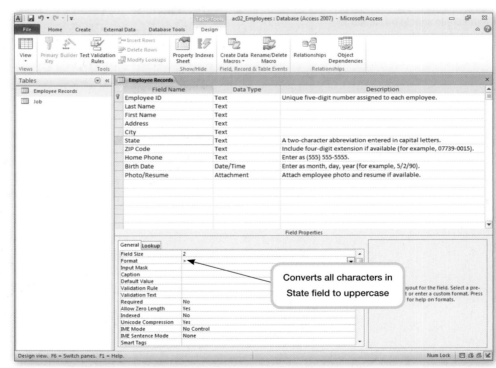 Design View.

- Click the State field to make it the current field.

- Move to the Format field property text box.

- Type >

Your screen should be similar to Figure 2.4

Converts all characters in State field to uppercase

Figure 2.4

SETTING DEFAULT VALUES

Next, you want to change the State field for new records to automatically display CA. To do this, you specify a Default Value property.

Concept 2 Default Value Property

The **Default Value property** is used to specify a value that is automatically entered in a field when a new record is created. This property is commonly used when most of the entries in a field will be the same for the entire table. That default value is then displayed automatically in the field. When users add a record to the table, they can either accept this value or enter another value. This saves time while entering data.

You will set the State field's default value to display CA.

- Click in the Default Value property text box.

- Type **CA**

- Press ⏎Enter.

Your screen should be similar to Figure 2.5

Enters default value of CA in State field

Figure 2.5

The default value is automatically enclosed in quotation marks to identify the entry as a group of characters called a **character string**. To see the effect on the table of setting a default value, you will return to Datasheet view and look at a new blank record.

First, you want to see the effect of the modifications to the State field's properties on the table.

2

● Click 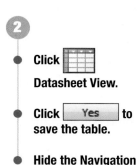 **Datasheet View.**

● Click **Yes** to save the table.

● **Hide the Navigation pane.**

Your screen should be similar to Figure 2.6

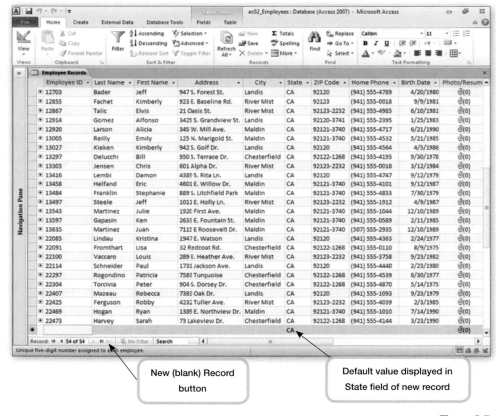

Converted to uppercase

Figure 2.6

You can see that records 3 (Mark Pennington) and 10 (Scott Briggs) now correctly display the state in capital letters. Setting the format for the field will prevent this type of error from occurring again.

3

● Click  **New (blank) Record on the navigation bar to move to a new record.**

Your screen should be similar to Figure 2.7

New (blank) Record button

Default value displayed in State field of new record

Figure 2.7

The new blank record at the end of the table displays CA as the default value for the State field. If you did need to enter a different state, it would display in all capital letters because of the Format property setting associated with the field.

DEFINING VALIDATION RULES

After looking at the fields, you decide to add a Gender field between the Home Phone and Birth Date fields. The field will need to have restrictions set so that it only accepts a single character, either "f" or "m", and formats it for uppercase. To create this customized field, you will switch to Design view to insert and define the new field.

- **Switch to Design view.**

- **Make the Birth Date field current.**

- **Click ⌐⊐ Insert Rows in the Tools group of the Design tab to insert a blank field definition row.**

- **Enter the new field definitions from the table shown here:**

Field Name	Gender
Data Type	Text
Description	Enter f for female and m for male.
Field Size	1
Format	>

Your screen should be similar to Figure 2.8

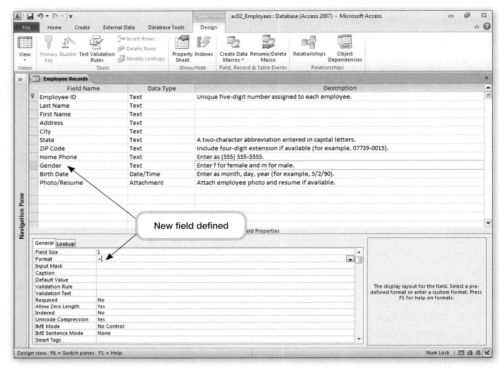

Figure 2.8

The only two characters you want the Gender field to accept are F for female and M for male. To specify that these two characters are the only entries acceptable in the Gender field, you will add a validation rule to the field's properties.

Concept ③ Validation Rule

A **validation rule** is used to control the data that can be entered in a field by defining the input values that are valid or allowed. Certain checks on the validity of the data that is entered in a field are performed automatically based on the field's data type and size. For example, in a field whose data type is Number and size is five, the type of data that can be entered in the field is restricted to a maximum of five numeric entries. You can further refine these basic restrictions by adding a validation rule to the field's properties that defines specific restrictions for the type of data that can be entered in the field.

You also can include a validation text message. **Validation text** is an explanatory message that appears if a user attempts to enter invalid information in a text field for which there is a validity check. If you do not specify a message, Access will display a default error message, which may not clearly describe the reason for the error.

You will create a validation rule for the Gender field to restrict the data entry to the two valid characters. A validation rule is specified by entering an expression in the **Validation Rule property** that limits the values that can be entered in the field.

Concept 4 Expression

An **expression** is a formula consisting of a combination of symbols that will produce a single value. You create an expression by combining identifiers, operators, constants, and functions to produce the desired results.

An **identifier** is an element that refers to the value of a field, a graphical object, or a property. In the expression [Sales Amount] + [Sales Tax], [Sales Amount] and [Sales Tax] are identifiers that refer to the values in the Sales Amount and Sales Tax fields. Identifiers are separated by dots or exclamation points. Each part of an identifier is surrounded by square brackets.

An **operator** is a symbol or word that indicates that an operation is to be performed. Common mathematical operators are + for addition, - for subtraction, * for multiplication, and / for division. A **comparison operator** is a symbol that allows you to make comparisons between two items. The following table describes the comparison operators:

Operator	Meaning
=	Equal to
< >	Not equal to
<	Less than
>	Greater than
<=	Less than or equal to
>=	Greater than or equal to

In addition, the OR and AND operators allow you to enter additional criteria in the same field or different fields.

Constants are numbers, dates, or character strings. Character strings such as "F", "M", or "Workout Gear" are enclosed in quotation marks. Dates are enclosed in pound signs (#), as in #1/1/99#. **Functions** are built-in formulas that perform certain types of calculations automatically. Functions begin with the function name, such as SUM, and are followed by the function **argument**, which specifies the data the function should use. Arguments are enclosed in parentheses.

The following table shows some examples of possible expressions.

Expression	Result
[Sales Amount] + [Sales Tax]	Sums values in two fields.
"F" OR "M"	Restricts entry to the letters F or M only.
>= #1/1/99# AND <= #12/31/99#	Restricts entries to dates greater than or equal to 1/1/99 and less than or equal to 12/31/99.
"Workout Gear"	Allows the entry Workout Gear only.
SUM([Pay])	Totals the values in the Pay field.

You will learn much more about entering expressions in later labs.

You will enter the expression to restrict the data entry in the Gender field to the letters "f" or "m." As you do, a drop-down list of available functions that begin with the character you are typing, in this case f or m, will be displayed. The context-sensitive menu appears anytime you can enter an expression and suggests identifiers and functions that could be used. This is the **IntelliSense** feature, which is designed to help you quickly type expressions and ensure their accuracy. You can continue typing to narrow the list of functions or identifiers, or you can select an item from the list and press ⏎Enter or Tab⇥, to have the highlighted suggestion entered for you. By continuing to type or by pressing an arrow key to move on, you can continue entering the expression and ignore the IntelliSense suggestions. You will also enter text in the **Validation Text property** to display a message to the user if data is entered incorrectly.

1

- **Move to the Validation Rule field property text box.**

- **Type f or m**

Additional Information

The AND and OR operators can be entered using uppercase or lowercase characters.

- **Press Esc to clear the drop-down list of functions, and then press Enter to complete the entry.**

- **For the validation text, type The only valid entry is f or m.**

Your screen should be similar to Figure 2.9

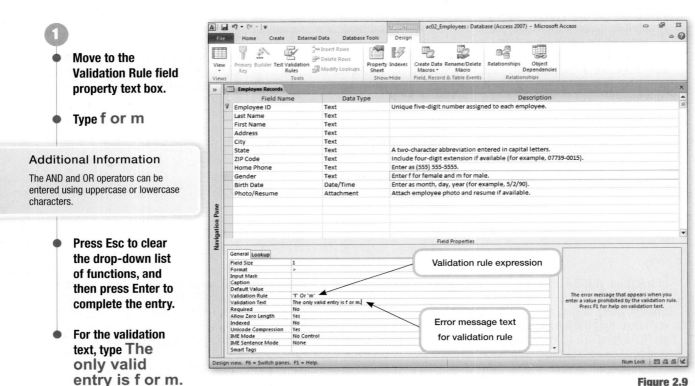

Figure 2.9

The expression you entered for the validation rule states that the only acceptable data values for this field must be equal to an F or an M. Notice that when you finished typing the validation rule, Access automatically added quotation marks around the two character strings and changed the "o" in "or" to uppercase. Because the Format property has been set to convert all entries to uppercase, a lowercase entry of f or m is as acceptable as the capitalized letters F or M.

Next, you will switch back to Datasheet view to test the validation rule by entering data for the Gender field. In addition to a message box asking whether you want to save the design changes, another message box will appear to advise you that the data integrity rules have been changed. When you restructure a table, you often make changes that could result in a loss of data. Changes such as shortening field sizes, creating validation rules, or changing field types can cause existing data to become invalid. Because the field is new, it has no data values to verify, and a validation check is unnecessary at this time.

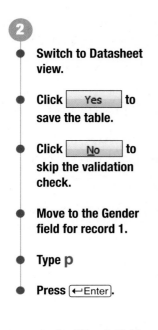

2

● **Switch to Datasheet view.**

● Click [Yes] to save the table.

● Click [No] to skip the validation check.

● **Move to the Gender field for record 1.**

● **Type p**

● Press [←Enter].

Your screen should be similar to Figure 2.10

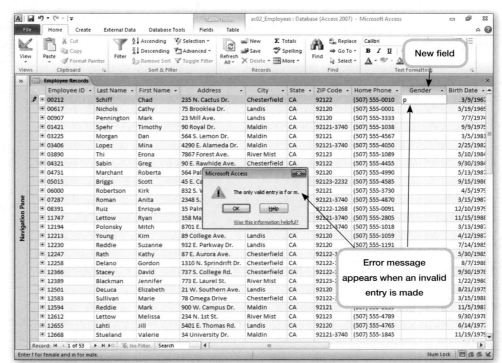

Figure 2.10

The new field was added to the table between the Home Phone and Birth Date fields. Because the letter p is not a valid entry, Access displays the error message you entered as the validation text for the field. You will clear the error message and correct the entry.

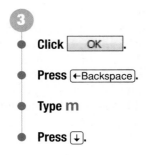

● **Click** OK .

● **Press** ←Backspace .

● **Type** m

● **Press** ↓ .

Your screen should be similar to Figure 2.11

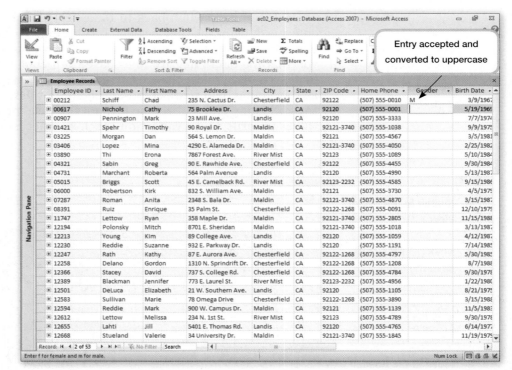

Figure 2.11

The entry for the first record is accepted and displayed as an uppercase M.

Hiding and Redisplaying Fields

To enter the gender data for the rest of the fields, you will use the First Name field as a guide. Unfortunately, the First Name and Gender fields are currently on opposite sides of the screen and will require you to look back and forth across each record. You can eliminate this problem by hiding the fields you do not need to see, and then redisplaying them when you have finished entering the gender data.

HIDING FIELDS

A quick way to view two fields side by side (in this case, the First Name and Gender fields) is to hide the fields that are in between (the Address through Home Phone fields).

1

Select the Address field through the Home Phone field.

Additional Information

Drag along the column headings when the mouse pointer is ↓ to select the fields.

Right-click on the selection.

Choose Hide Fields from the shortcut menu.

Another Method

You also can click ⊞ More ▾ in the Records group of the Home tab and choose Hide Fields.

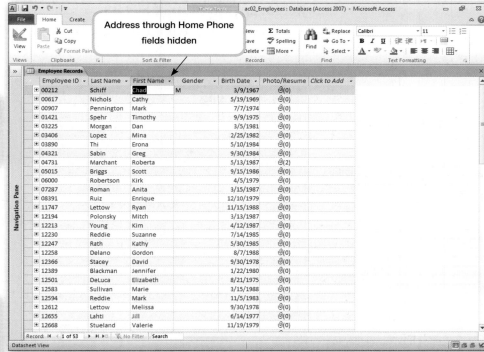

Figure 2.12

Your screen should be similar to Figure 2.12

Now that the First Name and Gender columns are next to each other, you can refer to the first name in each record to enter the correct gender data.

2

Enter the Gender field values for the remaining records by looking at the First Name field to determine whether the employee is male or female.

Reduce the size of the Gender column using the Best Fit command.

Having Trouble?

Remember, to Best Fit data in a column, you double-click its right border.

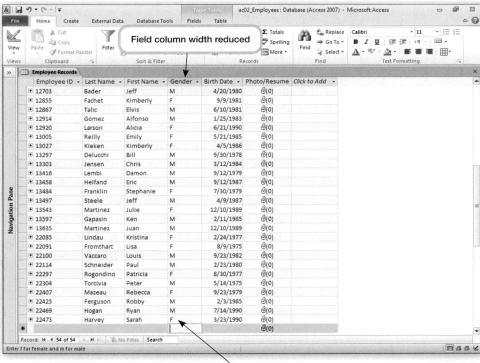

Your screen should be similar to Figure 2.13

Figure 2.13

Gender data entered for all records

REDISPLAYING HIDDEN FIELDS

After you have entered the gender data for all of the records, you can redisplay the hidden fields.

- **Right-click on any column header.**

- **Choose Unhide Fields from the shortcut menu.**

Another Method

You also can click [More ▾] in the Records group of the Home tab and choose Unhide Columns.

Your screen should be similar to Figure 2.14

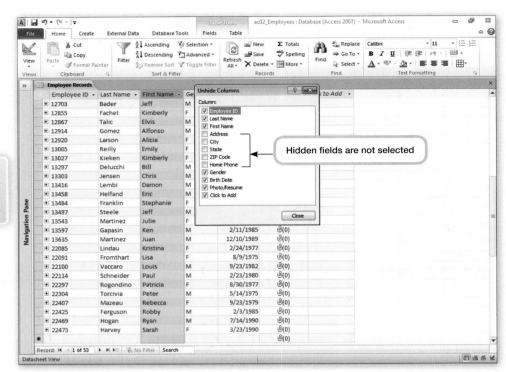

Figure 2.14

You use the Unhide Columns dialog box to select the currently hidden columns you want to redisplay. A checkmark in the box next to a column name indicates that the column is currently displayed; column names with no checkmarks indicate that they are currently hidden. You want to unhide all hidden columns in your table.

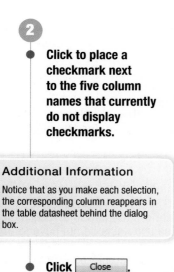

2 Click to place a checkmark next to the five column names that currently do not display checkmarks.

Additional Information

Notice that as you make each selection, the corresponding column reappears in the table datasheet behind the dialog box.

● Click **Close**.

Your screen should be similar to Figure 2.15

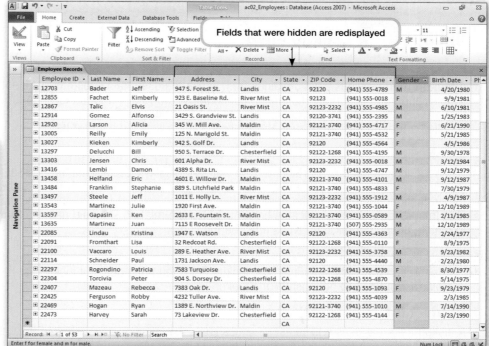

Fields that were hidden are redisplayed

Figure 2.15

All of the fields are displayed again.

Creating a Lookup Field

Next you decide to change the Location field in the Job table to a lookup field that will make entering the location information easier, faster, and less prone to errors.

Concept ⑤ Lookup Field

A **lookup field** provides a list of values from which the user can choose to make entering data into that field simpler and more accurate. The lookup field can get the values from an existing table or a fixed set of values that are defined when the lookup field is created. A lookup field that uses another table as the source for values is called a **lookup list**, and one that uses fixed values is called a **value list**.

Lookup List

When the lookup field uses a table for the values it displays, an association is created between the two tables. Picking a value from the lookup list sets the foreign key value in the current record to the primary key value of the corresponding record in the related table. A foreign key is a field in one table that refers to the primary key field in another table and indicates how the tables are related. The field names of these two fields do not have to match, although their data types must be the same.

The related table displays but does not store the data in the record. The foreign key is stored but does not display. For this reason, any updates made to the data in the related table will be reflected in both the list and records in the table containing the lookup field. You must define a lookup list field from the table that will contain the foreign key and display the lookup list.

Value List

A lookup field that uses a fixed list of values looks the same as a lookup field that uses a table, except the fixed set of values is entered when the lookup field is created. A value list should be used only for values that will not change very often and do not need to be stored in a table. For example, a list for a Salutation field containing the abbreviations Mr., Mrs., or Ms. would be a good candidate for a value list. Choosing a value from a value list will store that value in the record—it does not create an association to a related table. For this reason, if you change any of the original values in the value list later, they will not be reflected in records added before this change was made.

There are three club locations: Landis, Chesterfield, and River Mist. You want the club locations to be displayed in a drop-down list so that anyone entering a new employee record can simply choose from this list to enter the club location.

USING THE LOOKUP WIZARD

The **Lookup Wizard** is used to create a lookup field that will allow you to select from a list of values. A **wizard** is a feature that guides you step by step through the process to perform a task. You will use the Lookup Wizard to change the existing Location field to a lookup field that uses fixed values.

1

- **Close the Employee Records table, saving any changes.**

- **Display the Navigation pane and open the Job table.**

- **Hide the Navigation pane and switch to Design view.**

- **Make the Location field active.**

- **Open the Data Type drop-down menu and choose Lookup Wizard.**

Your screen should be similar to Figure 2.16

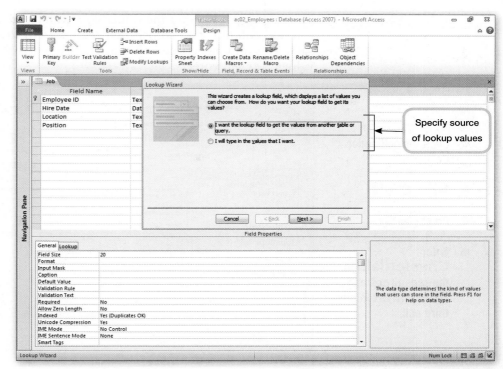

Figure 2.16

Additional Information

In Datasheet view, you can use in the Add & Delete group of the Table Tools Fields tab and choose More Fields ▾ to create a new field column and start the Lookup Wizard.

In the first Lookup Wizard dialog box, you specify the source for the values for the lookup field. You will enter your own values, the club locations, for this field.

2

- **Choose "I will type in the values that I want."**

- **Click** Next > .

Your screen should be similar to Figure 2.17

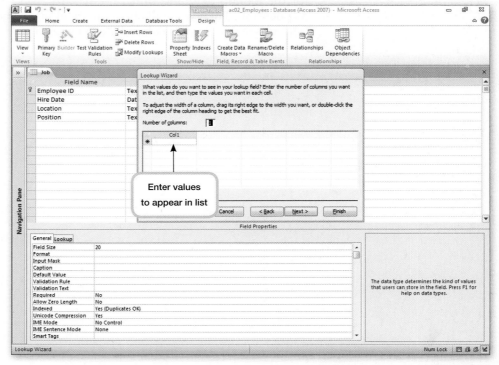

Figure 2.17

Creating a Lookup Field **AC2.19**

The next step is to enter the values you want listed in the lookup field. You also can add columns and adjust their widths to fit the values you enter, if necessary. You only need one column, and the current width is sufficient for the values you will enter.

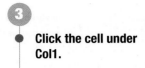

- Click the cell under Col1.

- Type **Landis**

- Press Tab.

- Enter **Chesterfield** in the second cell and **River Mist** in the third cell.

Having Trouble?

You can correct these entries the same way you do when entering data into any other field.

Your screen should be similar to Figure 2.18

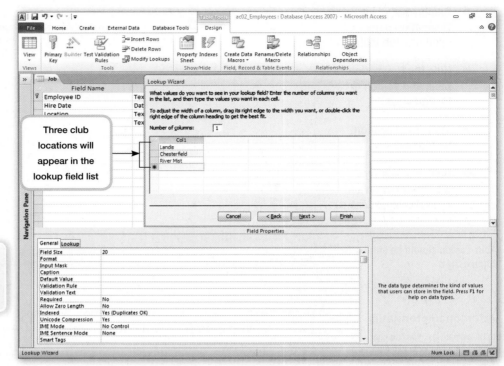

Figure 2.18

After entering the field values, you will move to the next step to enter a label for the lookup field and finish the wizard. You will leave the field name label as Location. Then you will check the field property settings established for this field to see whether any changes are necessary.

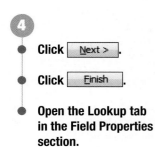

- Click [Next >].

- Click [Finish].

- **Open the Lookup tab in the Field Properties section.**

Your screen should be similar to Figure 2.19

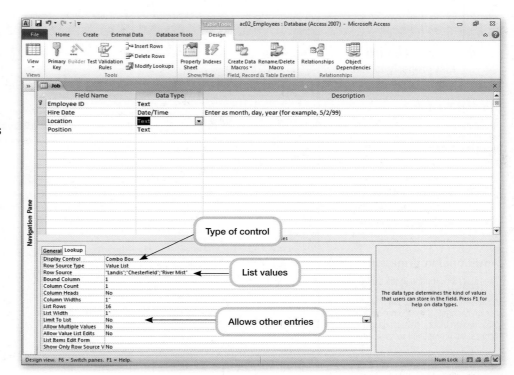

Figure 2.19

Before you clicked on the Lookup tab, you may have noticed that the property settings for the Location field looked like nothing had changed; the data type is still Text. By clicking the Lookup tab, you can see the values you typed in the Lookup Wizard listed in the Row Source property box. The Row Source Type is a Value List and will display in a Combo Box (drop-down list) control when in Datasheet view, as well as on any forms where this field is used. The other properties are set to the defaults for lookup fields. The only change you want to make is to restrict the data entry in that field to values in the lookup list. Then you will test that the Location field is performing correctly by entering a location that is not in the list.

5

Change the Limit To List property to Yes.

Having Trouble?

Select the property and click ▼ at the end of the box to open the drop-down menu of options.

Save the table design and switch to Datasheet view.

Additional Information

The 💾 Save button in the Quick

Access Toolbar will save the table design changes. If you do not save the table design before switching views, Access will prompt you to save it.

Click in the Location field of the first record.

Select and replace the current entry by typing Maldin and pressing ⏎Enter.

Your screen should be similar to Figure 2.20

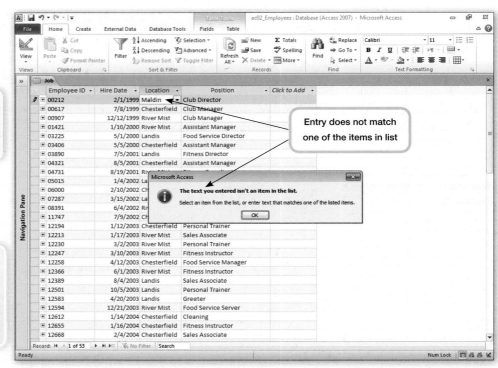

Figure 2.20

A warning box advises you that the entry is not one of the listed items because you restricted the field entries in the Location field to the lookup values you specified.

6

Click [OK].

Choose Landis from the list of locations.

Press [←Enter].

Your screen should be similar to Figure 2.21

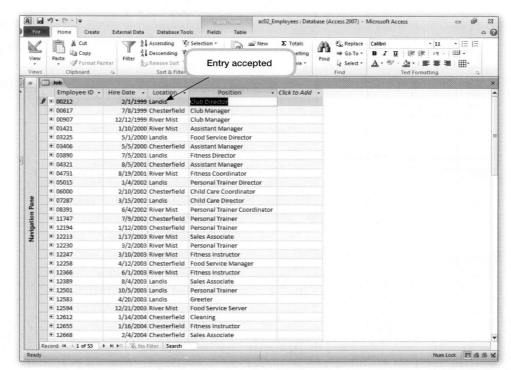

Figure 2.21

The Location lookup field is working correctly. Using a lookup field makes entering repetitive information faster and more accurate.

Searching for, Finding, and Replacing Data

Over the past few days, you have received several change request forms to update the employee records and a request to know how many fitness instructors there are in the company. Rather than having to scroll through all the records to locate the ones that need to be modified, you can use various methods to search for, find, and/or replace the data.

SEARCHING FOR DATA

While working in the Job table, you decide to find out how many fitness instructors are employed in the company first. One way to do this is to use the Search box to locate this information. The Search box is a useful tool to find any character(s) anywhere in the database. For example, it could be used to quickly locate a particular Employee ID number in order to update an address change. When you type in the Search box, Access will simultaneously highlight any possible fields that match. The more characters you type in the Search box, the more accurate the search response will be. Additionally, this feature is not case sensitive.

You want to search for "Fitness Instructor".

1

● Click in the Search
box in the record
navigation bar.

● Type in **fi**

Your screen should be similar to
Figure 2.22

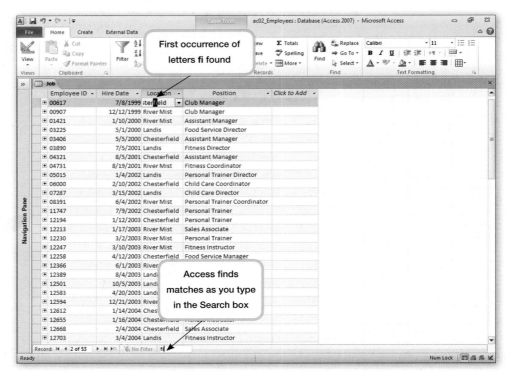

Figure 2.22

Notice that Access highlighted the "fi" in Chester**fi**eld. You will continue to
type the word "Fitness" in the Search box, and notice that as you enter more
text, the search is refined to more closely locate what you are looking for.

2

● Continue to type the
word **fitness** in the
Search box (Fitness
Director is located)

● Press Spacebar and
type **in** to locate
the first record
containing the text
Fitness Instructor.

● Press ←Enter to
move to the next
record containing
the search text.

Your screen should be similar to
Figure 2.23

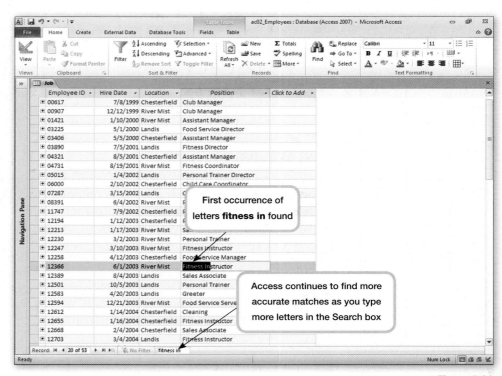

Figure 2.23

The next record in the search that matches the characters "fitness in" is selected. Because it is now locating the information you want to find, you do not need to complete the word "instructor". Notice that each time the enter key is pressed, the selection moves to the next record until it reaches the last matching set of characters.

Continue pressing ⎡←Enter⎤ **to locate all fitness instructor records.**

When the last field matching the search text is selected, it will remain highlighted and Access will go no further; no message will appear telling you there are no more matches. If you were counting, there were seven fitness instructors. Although this method worked to find out the number of fitness instructors, you will learn later in this lab about another, more effective way to gather this information.

FINDING DATA

Now you will work on making the changes to update the employee records from the change requests forms you have received. Rather than use the Search box to locate the records to change, you will use the Find and Replace feature.

Concept ·6· Find and Replace

The **Find and Replace** feature helps you quickly find specific information and automatically replace it with new information. The Find command will locate all specified values in a field, and the Replace command will both find a value and automatically replace it with another. For example, in a table containing supplier and item prices, you may need to increase the price of all items supplied by one manufacturer. To quickly locate these items, you would use the Find command to locate all records with the name of the manufacturer and then update the price appropriately. Alternatively, you could use the Replace command if you knew that all items priced at $11.95 were increasing to $15.99. This command would locate all values matching the original price and replace them with the new price.

Finding and replacing data is fast and accurate, but you need to be careful when replacing not to replace unintended matches.

The first change request is for Melissa Lettow, who recently married and has both a name and address change. To quickly locate the correct record, you will use the Find command. This information is in the Last Name field of the Employee Records table.

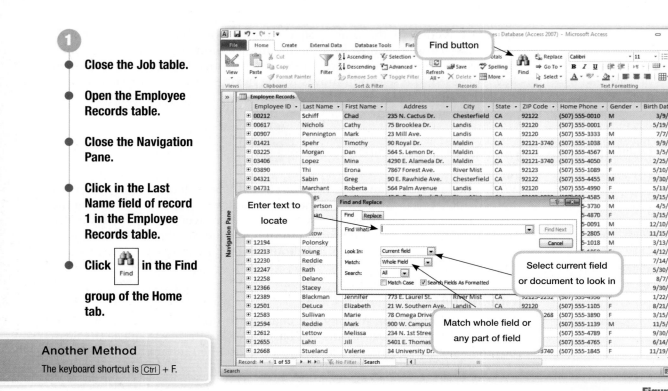

1

- Close the Job table.

- Open the Employee Records table.

- Close the Navigation Pane.

- Click in the Last Name field of record 1 in the Employee Records table.

- Click [Find] in the Find group of the Home tab.

Another Method

The keyboard shortcut is Ctrl + F.

Your screen should be similar to Figure 2.24

Figure 2.24

You use the Find and Replace dialog box to specify the information you are looking for and the way that you want Access to search the table. In the Find What text box, you specify the **criteria**, or a set of limiting conditions, records must meet by entering the text you want to locate. You can enter a specific character string or use wildcards to specify the criteria. **Wildcards** are symbols that are used to represent characters. The * symbol represents any collection of characters and the ? symbol represents any individual character. For example, ?ar will locate any three-letter text such as bar, far, and car. In contrast, *ar will locate the same text, but in addition will expand the criteria to locate any text ending with ar, such as star, popular, and modular.

Access defaults to search the entire current document, and matches any part of the field. You can change these settings and further refine your search by using the options described in the following table.

Option	Effect
Look In	Searches the current field or the entire table for the specified text.
Match	Locates matches to the whole field, any part of the field, or the start of the field.
Search	Specifies the direction in which the table will be searched: All (search all records); Down (search down from the current insertion point location in the field); or Up (search up from the current insertion point location in the field).
Match Case	Finds words that have the same pattern of uppercase letters as entered in the Find What text box. Using this option makes the search case sensitive.
Search Fields as Formatted	Finds data based on its display format.

With the cursor in the field you want to search, you will change the Look In location to search only that field. If you wanted to search on a different field, you could click on the field you want in the datasheet without closing the dialog box. You also will change it to match the whole field. The other default option to search all records is appropriately set.

Once your settings are as you want them, you will use the * wildcard to find all employees whose last names begin with "L".

2

- Change the Look In setting to Current field.

- Change the Match setting to Whole Field.

- Type **l*** in the Find What text box.

- Click [Find Next] eight times to move from one located record to the next.

Your screen should be similar to Figure 2.25

Figure 2.25

Using the wildcard located seven employees whose last names start with the letter "L". The more specific you can make your criteria, the more quickly you can locate the information you want to find. In this case, you want to find a specific last name, so you will enter the complete name in the Find What text box.

3

- Click [OK] to close the finished searching informational box.

- Select the entry in the Find What text box and type **lettow**

Additional Information

Because the Match Case option is not selected in the Find and Replace dialog box, you can enter the text to be located in uppercase, lowercase, or mixed-case letters—Access will ignore the case and look for the specified text.

- Click [Find Next].

Your screen should be similar to Figure 2.26

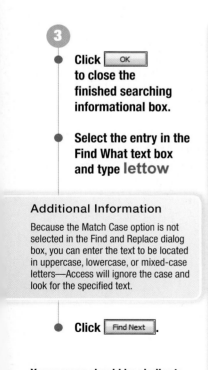
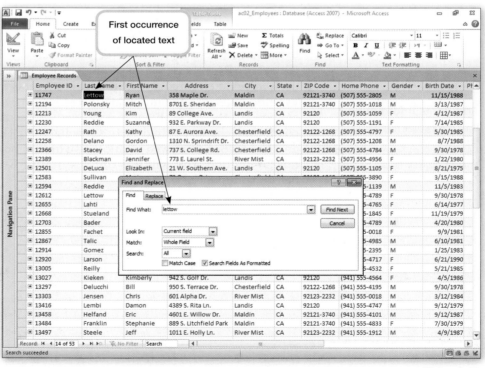

Figure 2.26

Access searches the table and moves to the first located occurrence of the entry you specified. The Last Name field is highlighted in record 14. You need to change the last name from Lettow to Richards.

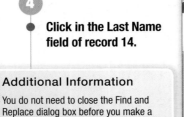

4

- **Click in the Last Name field of record 14.**

Additional Information

You do not need to close the Find and Replace dialog box before you make a change to the table. You will be using this dialog box again to perform more searches, so leave it open for now.

- **Double-click Lettow to select the entry.**

- **Type Richards**

- **Press ← Enter.**

Your screen should be similar to Figure 2.27

Figure 2.27

Now that the highlight is on the First Name field, you notice that this is the record for Ryan Lettow, not Melissa. You changed the wrong record. You will use the Undo command next to quickly fix this error.

Additional Information

Refer to the section Undoing and Redoing Editing Changes in the Introduction to Microsoft Office 2010 to review the Undo feature.

Undo will cancel your last action as long as you have not made any further changes to the table. Even if you save the record or the table, you can undo changes to the last edited record by clicking 🔄 Undo. After you have changed another record or moved to another window, however, the earlier change cannot be undone. You will use Undo to return Ryan's record to the way it was before you made the change.

5 ● Click  Undo.

Your screen should be similar to
Figure 2.28

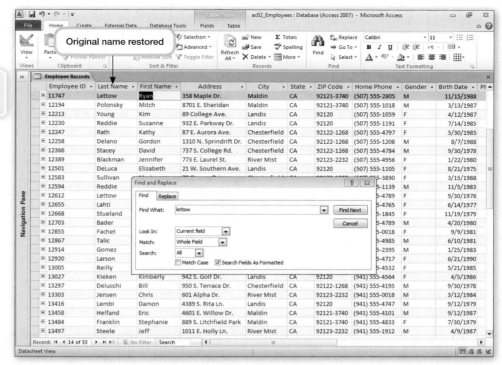

Figure 2.28

The original field value of Lettow is restored. Now you want to continue the search to locate the next record with the last name of Lettow.

6

● **Move back to the Last Name field of record 14.**

● **Click** [Find Next] **in the Find and Replace dialog box.**

● **When Access locates the record for Melissa Lettow (record 25), change her last name to Richards and the address to 5522 W. Marin Lane**

Having Trouble?
If necessary, move the Find and Replace dialog box.

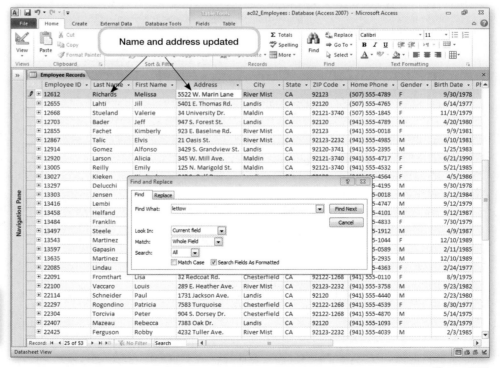

Figure 2.29

Your screen should be similar to
Figure 2.29

The Find method works well when you need to locate an individual field in order to view the data and/or modify it. However, when you need to make the same change to more than one record, the Replace command is the quicker method because it both finds and replaces the data.

REPLACING DATA

You have checked with the U.S. Postal Service and learned that all ZIP Codes of 92120 have a four-digit extension of 3741. To locate all the records with this ZIP Code, you could look at the ZIP Code field for each record to find the match and then edit the field to add the extension. If the table is small, this method would be acceptable. For large tables, however, this method could be quite time-consuming and more prone to errors. A more efficient way is to search the table to find specific values in records and then replace the entry with another.

● **Move to the ZIP Code field of record 1.**

● **Open the Replace tab.**

Another Method

You can use ⌐ₐᵦ Replace in the Find group, or the keyboard shortcut of Ctrl + H, to open the Find and Replace dialog box and display the Replace tab.

Your screen should be similar to Figure 2.30

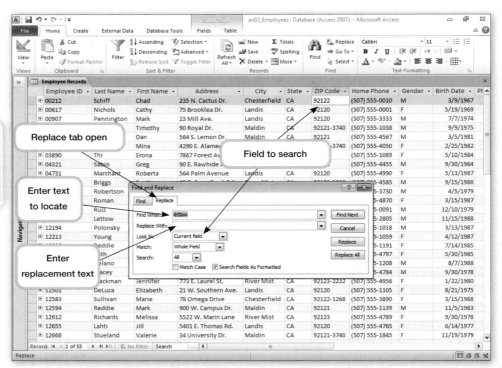

Figure 2.30

The options in the Replace tab are the same as those in the Find tab, with the addition of a Replace With text box, where you enter the replacement text exactly as you want it to appear in your table.

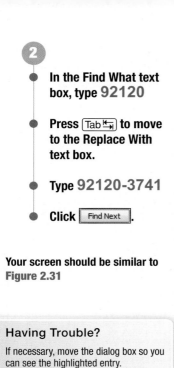

2

- In the Find What text box, type **92120**

- Press [Tab ⇆] to move to the Replace With text box.

- Type **92120-3741**

- Click [Find Next].

Your screen should be similar to Figure 2.31

Having Trouble?

If necessary, move the dialog box so you can see the highlighted entry.

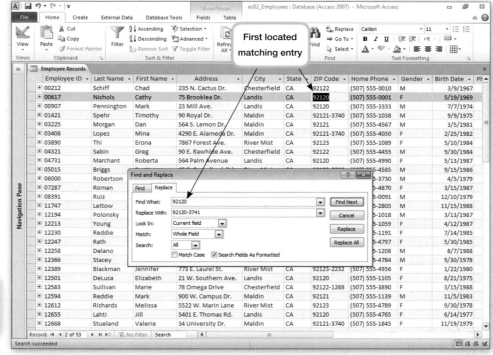

First located matching entry

Figure 2.31

Immediately, the highlight moves to the first occurrence of text in the document that matches the Find What text and highlights it. You can now replace this text with the click of a button.

3

- Click  [Replace].

Your screen should be similar to Figure 2.32

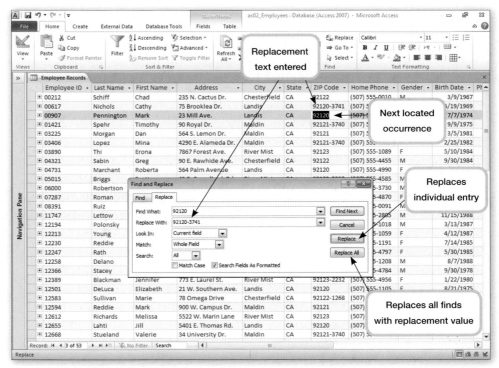

Replacement text entered

Next located occurrence

Replaces individual entry

Replaces all finds with replacement value

Figure 2.32

The original ZIP Code entry is replaced with the new ZIP Code. The program immediately continues searching and locates a second occurrence of the entry. You decide that the program is locating the values accurately and that it will be safe to replace all finds with the replacement value.

4

● Click [Replace All].

● Click [Yes] in response to the advisory message.

● Close the Find and Replace dialog box.

Your screen should be similar to Figure 2.33

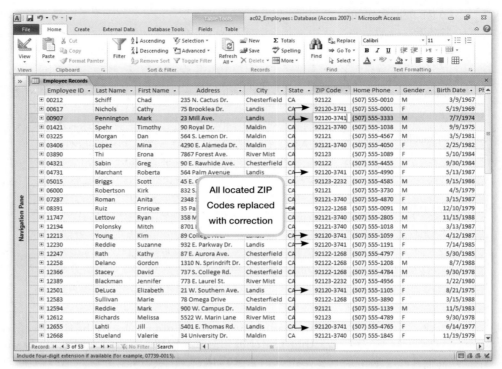

All located ZIP Codes replaced with correction

Figure 2.33

All matches are replaced with the replacement text. It is much faster to use Replace All than to confirm each match separately. However, exercise care when using Replace All because the search text you specify might be part of another field and you may accidentally replace text you want to keep.

Sorting Records

As you may recall from Lab 1, the records are ordered according to the primary key field, Employee ID. The accounting manager, however, has asked you for an alphabetical list of all employees. To do this, you will sort the records in the table.

Concept 7 Sorting

Sorting rearranges the order of the records in a table based on the value in each field. Sorting data helps you find specific information more quickly without having to browse the data. You can sort data in **ascending sort order** (A to Z or 0 to 9) or **descending sort order** (Z to A or 9 to 0).

You can sort all records in a table by a single field, such as State, or you can select adjacent columns and sort by more than one field, such as State and then City. When sorting on multiple fields, you begin by selecting the columns to sort. Access sorts records starting with the column farthest left (the outermost field) and then moves to the right across the selected columns to sort the innermost fields. For example, if you want to sort by state, and then by city, the State field must be to the left of the City field. The State field is the outermost field and the city field is the innermost field.

Access saves the new sort order with your table data and reapplies it automatically each time you open the table. To return to the primary key sort order, you must remove the temporary sort.

SORTING ON A SINGLE FIELD

You will sort the records on a single field, Last Name. To perform a sort on a single field, you move to the field on which you will base the sort and click the button that corresponds to the type of sort you want to do. In this case, you will sort the Last Name field in ascending alphabetical order.

1

- **Move to the Last Name field of any record.**

- **Click** [A↓ Ascending] **in the Sort & Filter group of the Home tab.**

Additional Information

Clicking [Z↓ Descending] arranges the data in descending sort order.

Your screen should be similar to Figure 2.34

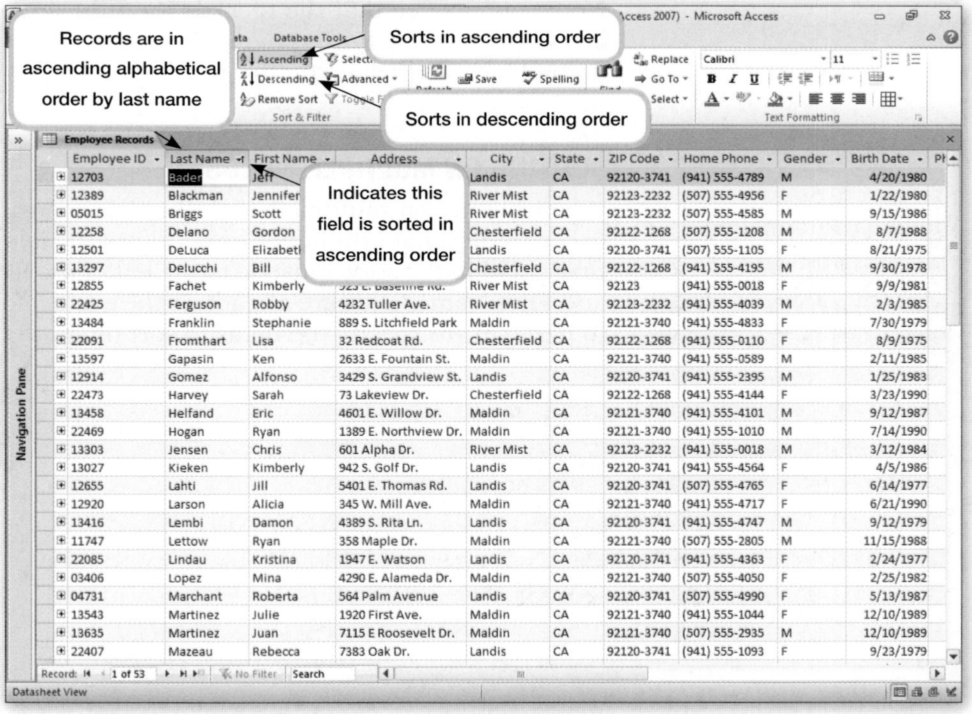

Figure 2.34

The employee records are displayed in alphabetical order by last name. The Last Name field header displays a ⌐↑ to show that the field is in ascending sorted order. Next, you want to check the rest of the table to see if there is anything else you need to do.

2

● **Use the scroll box to scroll down to record 25.**

Additional Information

As you drag the scroll box, the record location is displayed in a Screen Tip (for example, "Record 25 of 53").

Your screen should be similar to Figure 2.35

Employee ID	Last Name	First Name	Address	City	State	ZIP Code	Home Phone	Gender	Birth Date
13543	Martinez	Julie	1920 First Ave.	Maldin	CA	92121-3740	(941) 555-1044	F	12/10/1989
13635	Martinez	Juan	7115 E Roosevelt Dr.	Maldin	CA	92121-3740	(507) 555-2935	M	12/10/1989
22407	Mazeau	Rebecca	7383 Oak Dr.	Landis	CA	92120-3741	(941) 555-1093	F	9/23/1979
03225	Morgan	Dan	564 S. Lemon Dr.	Maldin	CA	92121	(507) 555-4567	M	3/5/1981
00617	Nichols	Cathy	75 Brooklea Dr.	Landis	CA	92120-3741	(507) 555-0001	F	5/19/1969
00907	Pennington	Mark	23 Mill Ave.	Landis	CA	92120-3741	(507) 555-3333	M	7/7/1974
12194	Polonsky	Mitch	8701 E. Sheridan	Maldin	CA	92121-3740	(507) 555-1018	M	3/13/1987
12247	Rath	Kathy	87 E. Aurora Ave.	Chesterfield	CA	92122-1268	(507) 555-4797	F	5/30/1985
12230	Reddie	Suzanne	932 E. Parkway Dr.	Landis	CA	92120-3741	(507) 555-1191	F	7/14/1985
12594	Reddie	Mark	900 W. Campus Dr.	Maldin	CA	92121	(507) 555-1139	M	11/5/1983
13005	Reilly	Emily	125 N. Marigold St.	Maldin	CA	92121-3740	(941) 555-4532	F	5/21/1985
12612	Richards	Melissa	5522 W. Marin Lane	River Mist	CA	92123	(507) 555-4789	F	9/30/1978
06000	Robertson	Kirk	832 S. William Ave.	Maldin	CA	92121	(507) 555-3730	M	4/5/1979
22297	Rogondino	Patricia	7583 Turquoise	Chesterfield	CA	92122-1268	(941) 555-4539	F	8/30/1977
07287	Roman	Anita	2348 S. Bala Dr.	Maldin	CA	92121-3740	(507) 555-4870	F	3/15/1987
08391	Ruiz	Enrique	35 Palm St.	Chesterfield	CA	92122-1268	(507) 555-0091	M	12/10/1979
04321	Sabin	Greg	90 E. Rawhide Ave.	Chesterfield	CA	92122	(507) 555-4455	M	9/30/1984
00212	Schiff	Chad	235 N. Cactus Dr.	Chesterfield	CA	92122	(507) 555-0010	M	3/9/1967
22114	Schneider	Paul	1731 Jackson Ave.	Landis	CA	92120-3741	(941) 555-4440	M	2/23/1980
01421	Spehr	Timothy	90 Royal Dr.	Maldin	CA	92121-3740	(507) 555-1038	M	9/9/1975
12366	Stacey	David	737 S. College Rd.	Chesterfield	CA	92122-1268	(507) 555-4784	M	9/30/1978
13497	Steele	Jeff	1011 E. Holly Ln.	River Mist	CA	92123-2232	(941) 555-1912	M	4/9/1987
12668	Stueland	Valerie	34 University Dr.	Maldin	CA	92121-3740	(507) 555-1845	F	11/19/1979
12583	Sullivan	Marie	78 Omega Drive	Chesterfield	CA	92122-1268	(507) 555-3890	F	3/15/1988
12867	Talic	Elvis	21 Oasis St.	River Mist	CA	92123-2232	(941) 555-4985	M	6/10/1981
03890	Thi	Erona	7867 Forest Ave.	River Mist	CA	92123	(507) 555-1089	F	5/10/1984
22304	Torcivia	Peter	904 S. Dorsey Dr.	Chesterfield	CA	92122-1268	(941) 555-4870	M	5/14/1975

Record: 1 of 53 No Filter Search

Datasheet View

Records with same last name not sorted by first name

Figure 2.35

Now you can see that the records for Julie and Juan Martinez are sorted by last name but not by first name. You want all records that have the same last name to be further sorted by first name. To do this, you need to sort using multiple sort fields.

SORTING ON MULTIPLE FIELDS

Additional Information

If the columns to sort were not already adjacent, you would hide the columns that are in between. If the columns were not in the correct order, you would move the columns.

When sorting on multiple fields, the fields must be adjacent to each other in order to designate the inner and outer sort fields. The **outer sort field** (primary field in the sort) must be to the left of the inner sort field. The Last Name and First Name fields are already in the correct locations for the sort you want to perform. To specify the fields to sort on, both columns must be selected.

- Select the Last Name and First Name field columns.

- Click .

- Scroll down to record 25 again.

Your screen should be similar to Figure 2.36

Records with same last name also sorted by first name

Employee ID	Last Name	First Name	Address	City	State	ZIP Code	Home Phone	Gender	Birth Date	Ph
13635	Martinez	Juan	7115 E Roosevelt Dr.	Maldin	CA	92121-3740	(507) 555-2935	M	12/10/1989	
13543	Martinez	Julie	1920 First Ave.	Maldin	CA	92121-3740	(941) 555-1044	F	12/10/1989	
22407	Mazeau	Rebecca	7383 Oak Dr.	Landis	CA	92120-3741	(941) 555-1093	F	9/23/1979	
03225	Morgan	Dan	564 S. Lemon Dr.	Maldin	CA	92121	(507) 555-4567	M	3/5/1981	
00617	Nichols	Cathy	75 Brooklea Dr.	Landis	CA	92120-3741	(507) 555-0001	F	5/19/1969	
00907	Pennington	Mark	23 Mill Ave.	Landis	CA	92120-3741	(507) 555-3333	M	7/7/1974	
12194	Polonsky	Mitch	8701 E. Sheridan	Maldin	CA	92121-3740	(507) 555-1018	M	3/13/1987	
12247	Rath	Kathy	87 E. Aurora Ave.	Chesterfield	CA	92122-1268	(507) 555-4797	F	5/30/1985	
12594	Reddie	Mark	900 W. Campus Dr.	Maldin	CA	92121	(507) 555-1139	M	11/5/1983	
12230	Reddie	Suzanne	932 E. Parkway Dr.	Landis	CA	92120-3741	(507) 555-1191	F	7/14/1985	
13005	Reilly	Emily	125 N. Marigold St.	Maldin	CA	92121-3740	(941) 555-4532	F	5/21/1985	
12612	Richards	Melissa	5522 W. Marin Lane	River Mist	CA	92123	(507) 555-4789	F	9/30/1978	
06000	Robertson	Kirk	832 S. William Ave.	Maldin	CA	92121	(507) 555-3730	M	4/5/1979	
22297	Rogondino	Patricia	7583 Turquoise	Chesterfield	CA	92122-1268	(941) 555-4539	F	8/30/1977	
07287	Roman	Anita	2348 S. Bala Dr.	Maldin	CA	92121-3740	(507) 555-4870	F	3/15/1987	
08391	Ruiz	Enrique	35 Palm St.	Chesterfield	CA	92122-1268	(507) 555-0091	M	12/10/1979	
04321	Sabin	Greg	90 E. Rawhide Ave.	Chesterfield	CA	92122	(507) 555-4455	M	9/30/1984	
00212	Schiff	Chad	235 N. Cactus Dr.	Chesterfield	CA	92122	(507) 555-0010	M	3/9/1967	
22114	Schneider	Paul	1731 Jackson Ave.	Landis	CA	92120-3741	(941) 555-4440	M	2/23/1980	
01421	Spehr	Timothy	90 Royal Dr.	Maldin	CA	92121-3740	(507) 555-1038	M	9/9/1975	
12366	Stacey	David	737 S. College Rd.	Chesterfield	CA	92122-1268	(507) 555-4784	M	9/30/1978	
13497	Steele	Jeff	1011 E. Holly Ln.	River Mist	CA	92123-2232	(941) 555-1912	M	4/9/1987	
12668	Stueland	Valerie	34 University Dr.	Maldin	CA	92121-3740	(507) 555-1845	F	11/19/1979	
12583	Sullivan	Marie	78 Omega Drive	Chesterfield	CA	92122-1268	(507) 555-3890	F	3/15/1988	
12867	Talic	Elvis	21 Oasis St.	River Mist	CA	92123-2232	(941) 555-4985	M	6/10/1981	
03890	Thi	Erona	7867 Forest Ave.	River Mist	CA	92123	(507) 555-1089	F	5/10/1984	
22304	Torcivia	Peter	904 S. Dorsey Dr.	Chesterfield	CA	92122-1268	(941) 555-4870	M	5/14/1975	

Record: 1 of 53   No Filter   Search

Datasheet View

Figure 2.36

The record for Juan Martinez now appears before the record for Julie. As you can see, sorting is a fast, useful tool. The sort order remains in effect until you remove the sort or replace it with a new sort order. Although Access remembers your sort order even when you exit the program, it does not actually change the table records.

You can remove the sort at any time to restore the records to the primary key sort order. You decide to return to primary key sort order and re-sort the table alphabetically for the Accounting department later, after you have finished making changes to it.

Click [🔽 Remove Sort].

● **Click anywhere in the datasheet to clear the selection.**

Your screen should be similar to Figure 2.37

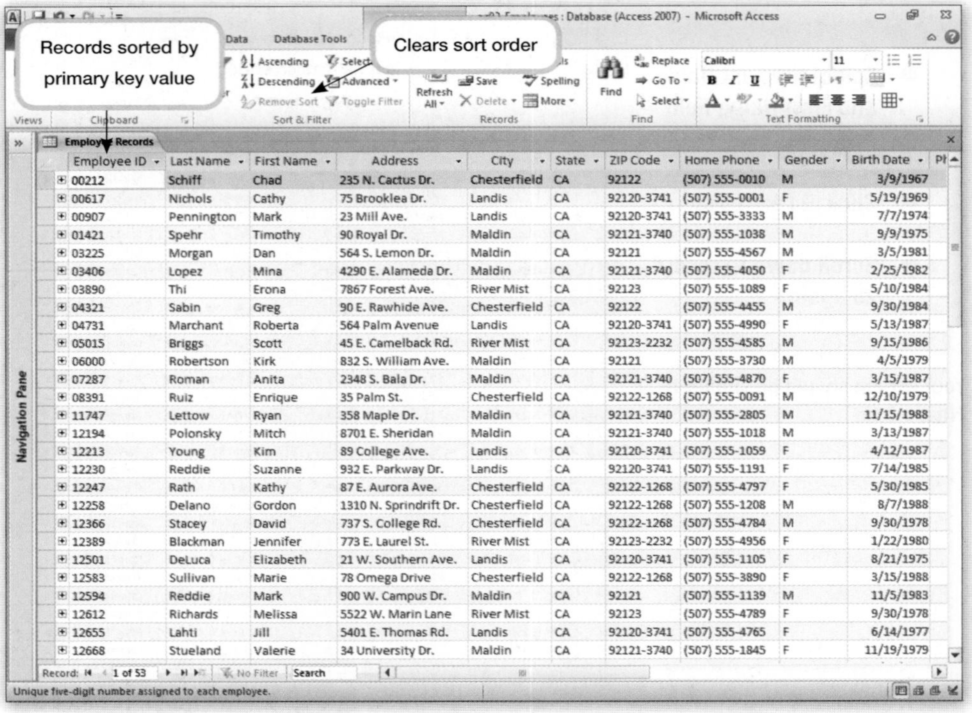

Records sorted by primary key value

Clears sort order

Figure 2.37

All the sorts are cleared, and the data in the table is now in order by the primary key field, Employee ID.

FORMATTING THE DATASHEET

Finally, you want to format or enhance the appearance of the datasheet on the screen to make it more readable or attractive by applying different effects. Datasheet formats include settings that change the appearance of the cell, gridlines, background and gridline colors, and border and line styles. In addition, you can change the text color and add text effects such as bold and italics to the datasheet. Datasheet formats affect the entire datasheet appearance and cannot be applied to separate areas of the datasheet.

Additional Information

Refer to the section Formatting Text in the Introduction to Microsoft Office 2010 to review formatting features.

CHANGING BACKGROUND AND GRIDLINE COLORS

The default datasheet format displays alternate rows in white and light gray backgrounds with a gridline color of blue. The text color is set to black. You want to see the effect of changing the color of the alternate rows and gridlines in the datasheet.

1

Click 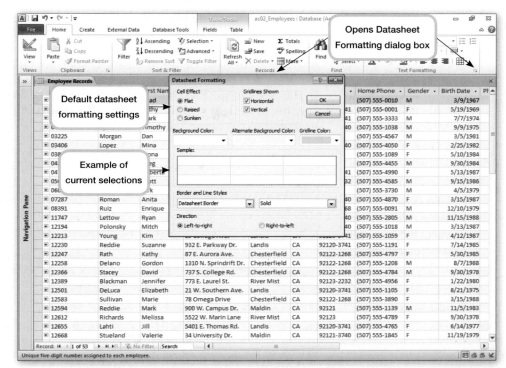 in the Text
Formatting group
of the Home tab to
open the Datasheet
Formatting dialog
box.

Your screen should be similar to
Figure 2.38

Figure 2.38

The default datasheet formatting settings are displayed in the dialog box, and
the Sample area shows how the settings will appear in the datasheet. You will
leave the background color white and change the color of the alternate rows.

2

Open the Alternate
Background Color
drop-down menu.

Your screen should be similar to
Figure 2.39

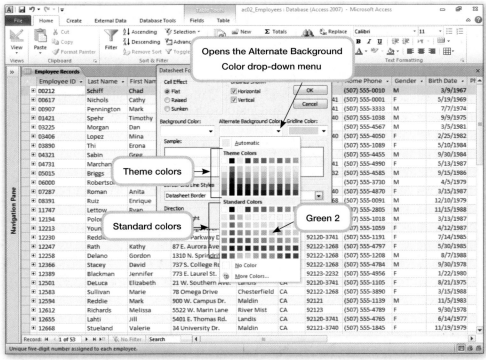

Figure 2.39

The color gallery displays the Access theme colors in the upper section and standard colors in the lower section. **Theme colors** are a combination of coordinating colors that are used in the default datasheet. Each color is assigned to a different area of the datasheet, such as label text or table background. Pointing to a theme color identifies the name of the color and where it is used in the ScreenTip. The colors in the Standard Colors gallery are not assigned to specific areas on the datasheet. Pointing to a standard color displays the name assigned to the color.

3

- **Point to several theme colors to see where they are used in the datasheet.**

- **Click on the Green 2 color in the Standard Colors area.**

Another Method

You also can use [icon] Alternate Row Color in the Text Formatting group to change the color.

Your screen should be similar to Figure 2.40

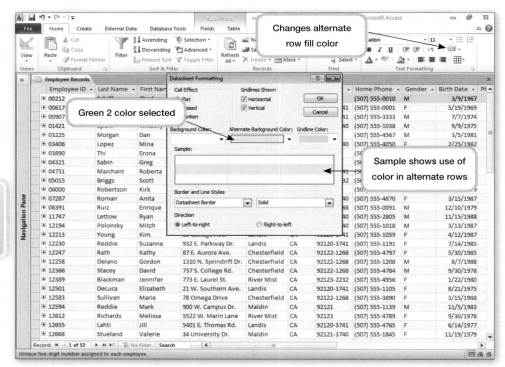

Figure 2.40

The sample area displays how the alternate background color selection will appear in the datasheet. You like the green shading and want to change the gridline color to a darker shade of the same green.

4

● Open the Gridline
Color drop-down
menu.

● Choose Green 5 from
the Standard Colors
area.

● Click [OK].

Your screen should be similar to
Figure 2.41

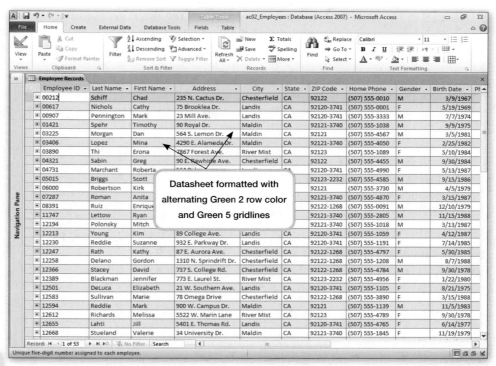

Figure 2.41

The selected alternating row and gridline color formatting has been applied to the datasheet.

Additional Information
You can use ⊞ ▾ Gridlines in the Text Formatting group to change the display of the gridlines.

CHANGING THE TEXT COLOR

The datasheet background colors brighten the screen appearance, but you think the text is a little light, making it difficult to read. You will change the text color to a dark blue and bold.

1

● Open the Font
Color drop-down
menu in the Text
Formatting group.

● Select Dark Blue from
the Standard Colors
section of the color
gallery.

● Click **B** Bold in
the Text Formatting
group.

Your screen should be similar to
Figure 2.42

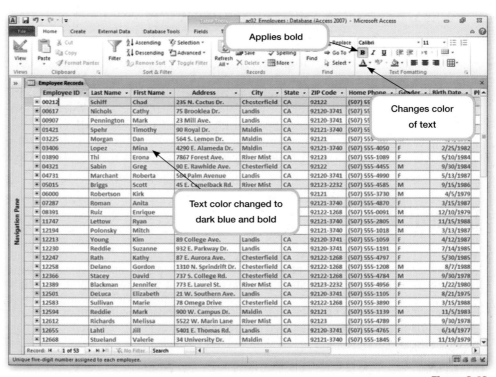

Figure 2.42

You do not like how the blue text color looks and want to change it back to the default color. You cannot use Undo to remove formatting, so you will need to select the text color again.

- Open the 🅰️ Font Color drop-down menu.
- Choose Automatic to restore the default font color.

Your screen should be similar to Figure 2.43

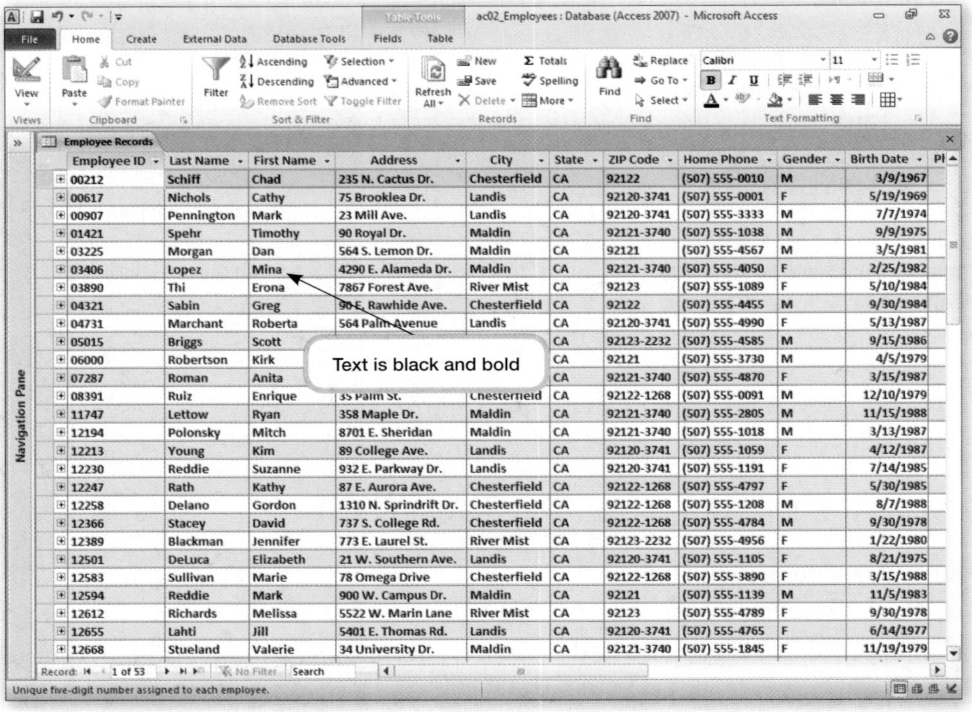

Figure 2.43

The black text color is restored. The text is still bolded and is easier to read.

Filtering a Table

Juan Martinez, an employee at the Landis location, is interested in forming a car pool. He recently approached you about finding other employees who also may want to carpool. You decide this would be a great opportunity to use the table of employee data to find this information. To find the employees, you could sort the table and then write down the needed information. This could be time-consuming, however, if you had hundreds of employees in the table. A faster way is to apply a filter to the table records to locate this information.

Concept 8 Filter

A **filter** is a restriction placed on records in the open table or form to quickly isolate and display a subset of records. A filter is created by specifying the criteria that you want records to meet in order to be displayed. A filter is ideal when you want to display the subset for only a brief time and then return immediately to the full set of records. You can print the filtered records as you would any form or table. A filter is only temporary, and all records are redisplayed when you remove the filter or close and reopen the table or form. The filter results cannot be saved. However, the last filter criteria you specify can be saved with the table, and the results can be quickly redisplayed.

USING FILTER BY SELECTION

Juan lives in Maldin and works at the Lifestyle Fitness Club located in Landis. You can locate other employees who live in Maldin quite easily by using the Filter by Selection feature. Filter by Selection displays only records containing a specific value. This method is effective when the table contains only one value that you want to use as the criterion for selecting and displaying records.

The process used to select the value determines the results that will be displayed. Placing the cursor in a field selects the entire field's contents. The filtered subset will include all records containing an exact match. Selecting part of a value in a field (by highlighting it) displays all records containing the selection. For example, in a table for a book collection, you could position the cursor anywhere in a field containing the name of the author Stephen King, choose the Filter by Selection command, and only records for books whose author matches the selected name, "Stephen King," would be displayed. Selecting just "King" would include all records for authors Stephen King, Martin Luther King, and Barbara Kingsolver.

You want to filter the table to display only those records with a City field entry of Maldin. To specify the city to locate, you select an example of the data in the table.

Additional Information

If the selected part of a value starts with the first character in the field, the subset displays all records with values that begin with the same selected characters.

1

● **Move to the City field of record 4.**

● **Click** [Selection ▾] **in the Sort & Filter group of the Home tab.**

Your screen should be similar to Figure 2.44

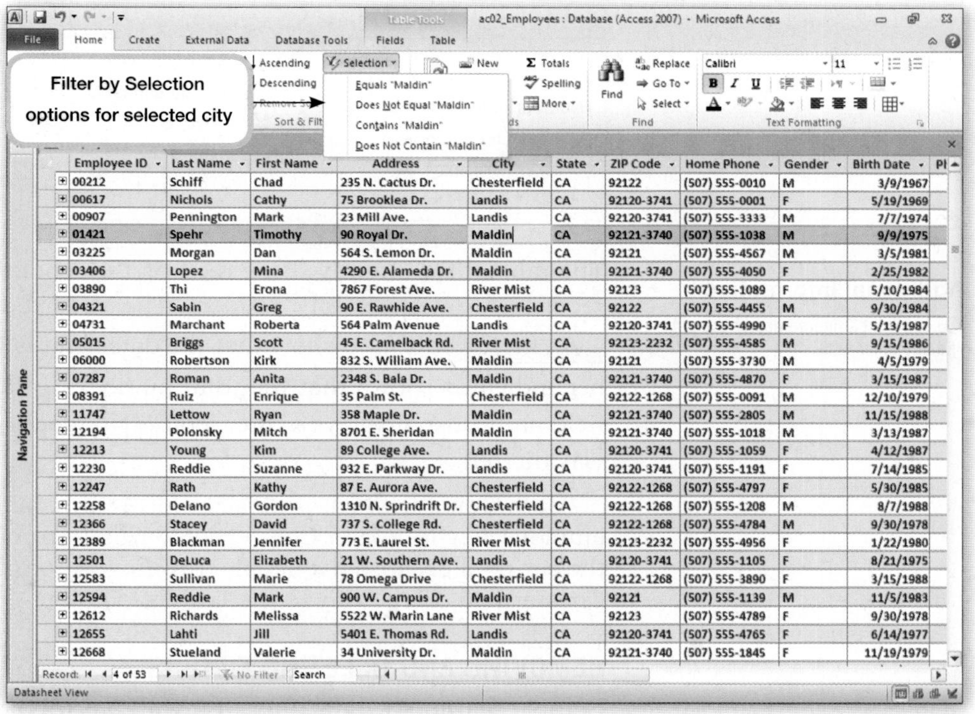

Figure 2.44

The drop-down menu of commands contains the current selected value in the field. The commands that appear will vary depending on the data type of the selected value. Also, the commands will vary depending on how much of the value is selected. If the selection is a partial selection, the commands allow you to specify a filter using the beginning, middle, or end of a field value. In this case, the entire value is selected and the four commands allow you to specify whether you want the selection to equal, not equal, contain, or not contain the value.

Choose Equals "Maldin".

Another Method

You also can display the Filter by Selection commands using the selection's shortcut menu.

Your screen should be similar to Figure 2.45

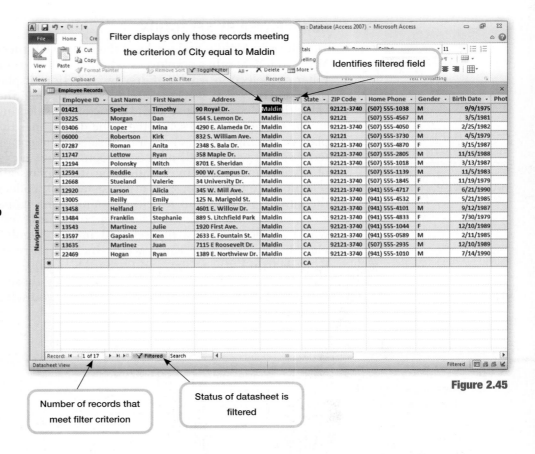

Filter displays only those records meeting the criterion of City equal to Maldin

Identifies filtered field

Number of records that meet filter criterion

Status of datasheet is filtered

Figure 2.45

Additional Information

You can print a filtered datasheet just like any other table.

The table displays only those records that contain the selected city. All other records are temporarily hidden. The record navigation bar displays the **Filtered** button to show that the datasheet is filtered, and the record number indicator shows that the total number of filtered records is 17. The City field name also displays a filter icon to identify the field on which the table was filtered.

After seeing how easy it was to locate this information, you want to locate employees who live in Chesterfield. This information may help in setting up the car pool because the people traveling from the city of Maldin pass through Chesterfield on the way to the Landis location.

REMOVING AND DELETING FILTERS

Before creating the new filter, you will remove the current filter and return the table to its full display.

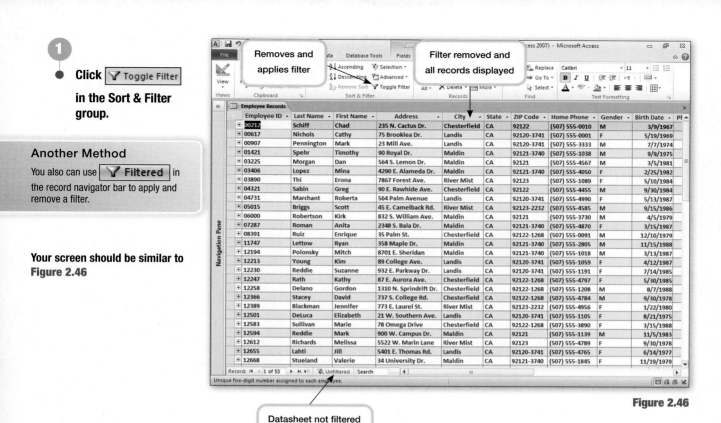

Your screen should be similar to Figure 2.46

Figure 2.46

The filter is temporarily removed from the field and all the records are displayed again. The status bar displays ⚑ Unfiltered. The filter is still available and can be reapplied quickly by clicking ▼ Toggle Filter or ⚑ Unfiltered.

You will reapply the filter, and then you will permanently remove these filter settings.

2

● Click ▼ Toggle Filter to redisplay the filtered datasheet.

● Click ⚏ Advanced ▾ in the Sort & Filter group.

● Choose Clear All Filters.

The filter is removed and all the records are redisplayed. The ▼ Toggle Filter button is dimmed because the table does not include any filter settings.

FILTERING USING COMMON FILTERS

To filter the employee data by two cities, Chesterfield and Maldin, you can select from a list of several popular filters. Using this list allows you to perform filters on multiple criteria within a single field.

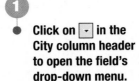

1

● Click on ⏷ in the City column header to open the field's drop-down menu.

Another Method

You also can move to the field to filter on and click 🔽 in the Sort & Filter group to display the Filter list.

Your screen should be similar to Figure 2.47

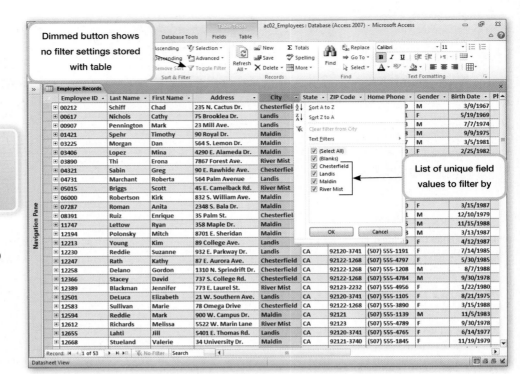

Figure 2.47

A list of all the unique values that are stored in the current field is displayed. Selecting a value from the list filters the table based on the selected value. Depending on the data type of the selected value, you may be able to filter for a range of values by clicking on a value and specifying the appropriate range. In this case, because the field is not filtered, all the values are selected. You will first clear the selection from all values, and then select the names of the two cities you want displayed in the filtered list.

2

● Click the Select All check box to clear the selection from all values.

● Click the Chesterfield and Maldin check boxes to select them.

● Click OK.

Your screen should be similar to Figure 2.48

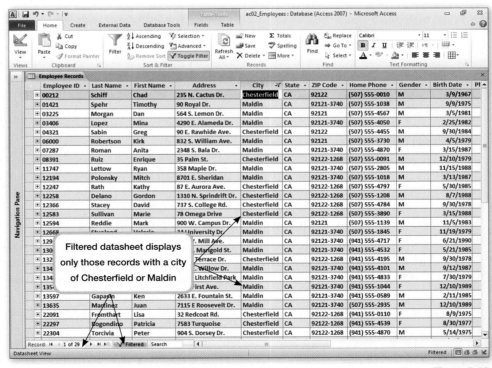

Figure 2.48

The filtered datasheet displays the records for all 29 employees who live in the cities of Chesterfield or Maldin.

FILTERING ON MULTIPLE FIELDS

As you look at the filtered results, you decide to further refine the list by restricting the results to those records that have the same ZIP Code as Juan's ZIP Code of 92121. Although you can only specify one filter per field, you can specify a different filter for each field that is present in the view.

1

● **Open the ZIP Code field's drop-down menu to display the field list.**

● **Clear the checkmark from the 92121-3740 value.**

● **Click** [OK].

Your screen should be similar to Figure 2.49

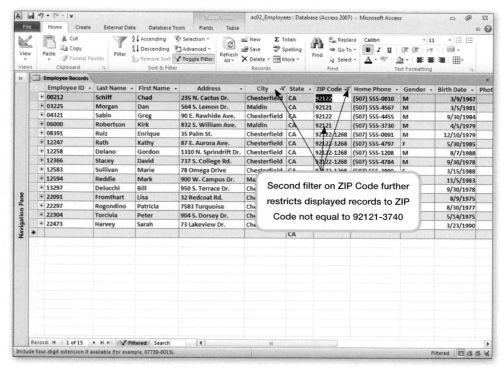

Figure 2.49

Now there are only 15 records displayed in the filtered table. Applying the second filter refined the results by removing all records from the filtered list that had a ZIP Code of 92121-3740.

Although you would like to provide a copy of this information to Juan, you realize that it contains more information about each employee than someone would need (or should even have access to) in order to form a car pool. Also, because you are not finished adding records to the employee database, these findings may not be complete.

You will redisplay all the records in the table, but you will not clear the filter settings. If you do not clear the filters, the filter criteria you last specified are stored with the table, and the results can be redisplayed simply by applying the filter again.

2

● **Click** [🔽 Toggle Filter] **to display the unfiltered datasheet.**

● **Close the table, saving your design changes.**

● **Redisplay the Navigation pane.**

The table is closed and the work area is empty. Next you will learn how to create and use a form in Access.

NOTE **If you are ending your session now, close the database file and exit Access. When you begin again, start Access and open the** ac02_Employees **database file.**

Creating a Simple Form

One of your objectives is to make the database easy to use. You know from experience that long hours of viewing large tables can be tiring. Therefore, you want to create an onscreen form to make this table easier to view and use.

Concept 9 Form

A **form** is a database object used primarily to display records onscreen and to make it easier to enter new records and make changes to existing records. Forms can control access to data so that any unnecessary fields or data is not displayed, which makes it easier for people using the database. They enable people to use the data in the tables without having to sift through many lines of data to find the exact record.

Forms are based on an underlying table and can include design elements such as descriptive text, titles, labels, lines, boxes, and pictures. Forms also can use calculations to summarize data that is not listed on the actual table, such as a sales total. The layout and arrangement of information can be customized in a form. Using these features creates a visually attractive form that makes working with the database more enjoyable, more efficient, and less prone to data-entry errors.

You want the onscreen form to be similar to the paper form that is completed by each new employee when hired (shown below). The information from that form is used as the source of input for the new record that will be added to the table for the new employee.

EMPLOYEE DATA
Employee ID _____
First Name _____   Last Name _____
Street _____
City _____   State _____   Zip _____
Phone Number _____
Gender _____
Birth Date _____

There are several different methods you can use to create forms, as described in the following table. The method you use depends on the type of form you want to create.

Method	Use to
Form tool	Create a form containing all the fields in the table.
Split Form tool	Create a form that displays the form and datasheet in a single window
Blank Form tool	Build a form from scratch by adding the fields you select from the table
Datasheet tool	Create a form using all the fields in the table and display it in Datasheet view
Multiple Items tool	Create a form that displays multiple records but is more customizable than a datasheet
Form Wizard	Create a form using a wizard that guides you through the steps to create a complex form that displays selected fields, data groups, sorted records, and data from multiple tables

USING THE FORM TOOL

Using the Form tool is the quickest method to create a simple form. You decide to see if the Form tool will create the form you need.

- **If necessary, select the Employee Records table in the Navigation pane.**

- **Open the Create tab.**

- **Click [Form] in the Forms group.**

Your screen should be similar to Figure 2.50

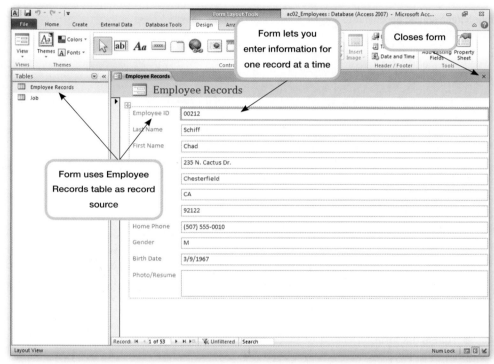

Figure 2.50

A form that allows you to enter data for one record at a time was quickly created. The fields from the Employee Records table were used to create the form because it was the selected object in the Navigation pane. The underlying table that is used to create a form is called the **record source**. The fields are in the same order as in the datasheet.

This form does not quite meet your needs, and you decide to try another method to create the form.

- **Close the form.**

- **Click [No] to the prompt to save the form.**

USING THE MULTIPLE ITEMS TOOL

Next, you will use the Multiple Items tool to create a form.

- If necessary, open the Create tab.

- Click  More Forms ▾ in the Forms group.

- Choose Multiple Items.

Your screen should be similar to Figure 2.51

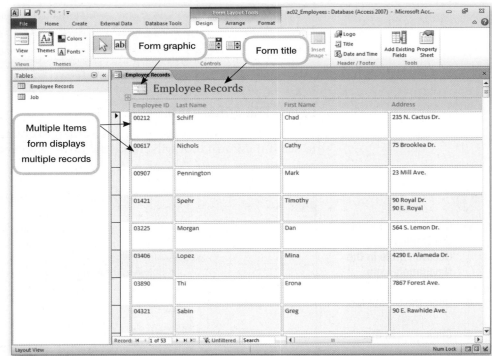

Figure 2.51

A form that displays multiple records at a time was quickly created. Although it looks similar to Datasheet view, it is easier to read and includes a title and graphic. However, this form still does not work and you decide to use the Form Wizard to create a form that is closer to your needs.

- Close the form.

- Click [No] to the prompt to save the form.

USING THE FORM WIZARD

The **Form Wizard** will help you create a form that is closer to your needs by guiding you through a series of steps that allow you to specify different form features.

Open the Create tab and click [⬛ Form Wizard] **in the Forms group.**

Your screen should be similar to Figure 2.52

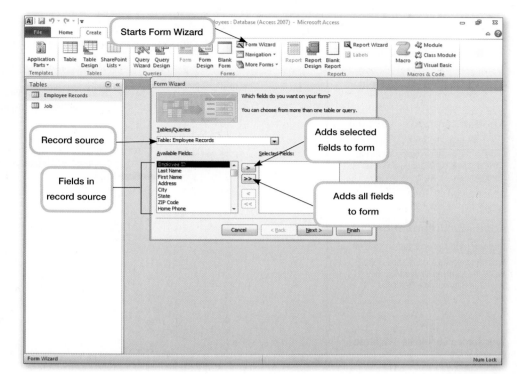

Starts Form Wizard

Record source

Fields in record source

Adds selected fields to form

Adds all fields to form

Figure 2.52

The Form Wizard dialog box displays the name of the current table, Employee Records, in the Tables/Queries list box. This is the table that will be used as the record source. If you wanted to use a different table as the record source, you could open the Tables/Queries drop-down list to select the appropriate table.

The fields from the selected table are displayed in the Available Fields list box. You use this box to select the fields you want included on the form, in the order in which you want them to appear. This order is called the **tab order** because it is the order in which the highlight will move through the fields on the form when you press the [Tab ⬐] key during data entry. You decide that you want the fields to be in the same order as they are on the paper form shown in the illustration on page AC2.46.

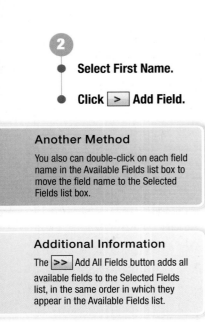

2

- Select First Name.

- Click > Add Field.

Another Method

You also can double-click on each field name in the Available Fields list box to move the field name to the Selected Fields list box.

Additional Information

The >> Add All Fields button adds all available fields to the Selected Fields list, in the same order in which they appear in the Available Fields list.

Your screen should be similar to Figure 2.53

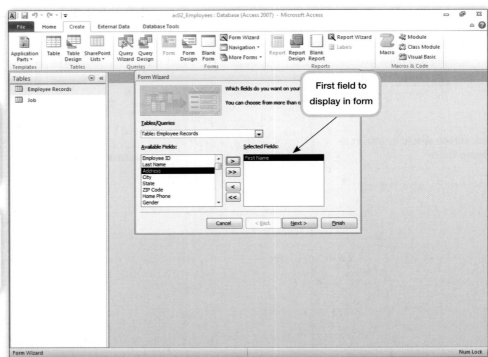

First field to display in form

Figure 2.53

The First Name field is removed from the Available Fields list and added to the top of the Selected Fields list box. It will be the first field in the form.

3

- In the same manner, add the following fields to the Selected Fields list in the order shown here:

  Last Name

  Address

  City

  State

  ZIP Code

  Home Phone

  Gender

  Birth Date

  Employee ID

Your screen should be similar to Figure 2.54

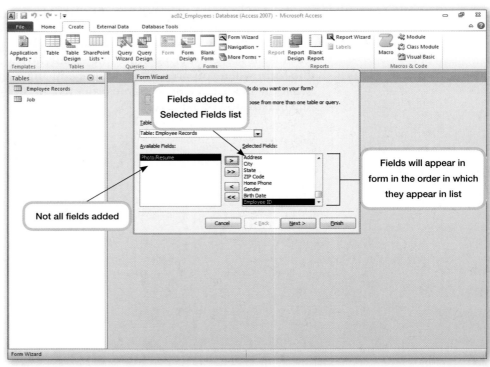

Fields added to Selected Fields list

Not all fields added

Fields will appear in form in the order in which they appear in list

Figure 2.54

When finished, the only remaining field in the Available Fields list box is the Photo/Resume field. The Selected Fields list box contains the fields in the order in which you added them.

You are now ready to move on to the next Form Wizard screen.

4

Click  .

Your screen should be similar to Figure 2.55

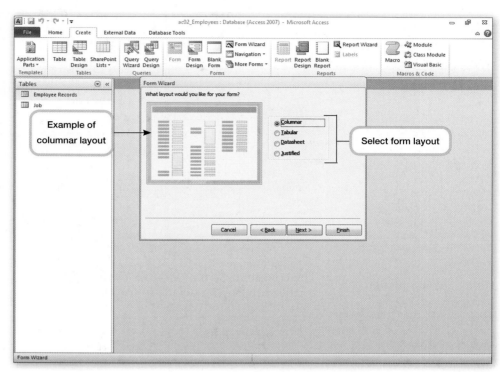

Figure 2.55

In this Form Wizard screen, you are asked to select the control layout for the form. **Layouts** determine how the data is displayed in the form by aligning the items horizontally or vertically to give the form a uniform appearance. Layouts act as a guide for the placement of items on the form.

Layouts are usually configured in a tabular or stacked format. **Tabular formats** arrange the data in rows and columns, with labels across the top. **Stacked formats** arrange data vertically with a field label to the left of the field data. A form can have both types of layouts in different sections.

The four form layouts offered by the Form Wizard are variations of the two basic layouts as described in the following table.

Format		Description
Columnar	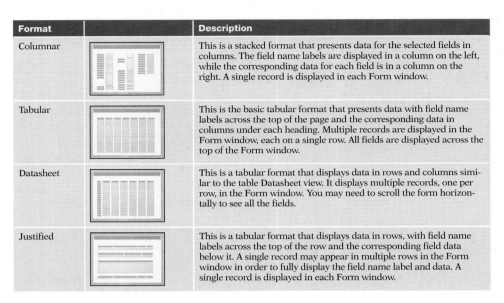	This is a stacked format that presents data for the selected fields in columns. The field name labels are displayed in a column on the left, while the corresponding data for each field is in a column on the right. A single record is displayed in each Form window.
Tabular		This is the basic tabular format that presents data with field name labels across the top of the page and the corresponding data in columns under each heading. Multiple records are displayed in the Form window, each on a single row. All fields are displayed across the top of the Form window.
Datasheet		This is a tabular format that displays data in rows and columns similar to the table Datasheet view. It displays multiple records, one per row, in the Form window. You may need to scroll the form horizontally to see all the fields.
Justified		This is a tabular format that displays data in rows, with field name labels across the top of the row and the corresponding field data below it. A single record may appear in multiple rows in the Form window in order to fully display the field name label and data. A single record is displayed in each Form window.

The columnar format appears most similar to the paper form currently in use by the club, so you decide to use that configuration for your form.

Additional Information

Using 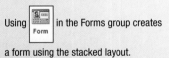 in the Forms group creates a form using the stacked layout.

5

● If necessary, choose **Columnar**.

● Click 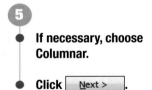 Next > .

Your screen should be similar to Figure 2.56

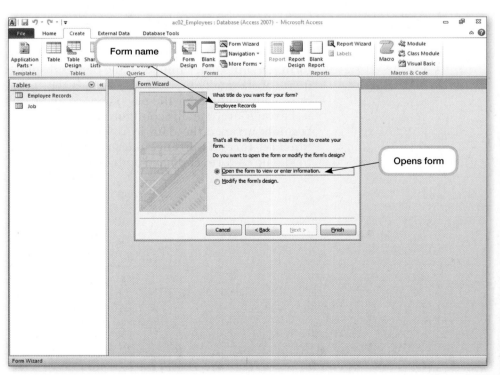

Figure 2.56

In the final Form Wizard dialog box, you can enter a form title to be used as the name of the form, and you can specify whether to open the form or to modify it. The Form Wizard uses the name of the table as the default form title. You will keep the proposed form title and the default of opening the form.

6 Click **Finish**.

Your screen should be similar to Figure 2.57

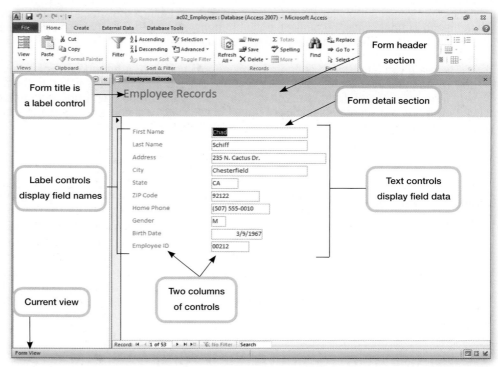

Figure 2.57

The completed form is displayed in the work area in Form view. The form title appears at the top of the form in the form header section. The employee information for Chad Schiff, the first record in the table, is displayed in the form detail section.

The form displays the chosen fields in columnar format with the default form design. The field name labels display in a column on the left, while the data for each corresponding field is displayed in a column on the right.

Each item in the form is a separate object contained in boxes, called controls.

Additional Information

You will learn about changing the form design shortly.

Concept ⑩ Controls

Controls are objects that display information, perform actions, or enhance the design of a form or report. Access provides controls for many types of objects, including labels, text boxes, check boxes, list boxes, command buttons, lines, rectangles, option buttons, and more. The most common controls are text controls and label controls. **Text controls** display the information in the field from the record source. **Label controls** display descriptive labels.

There are two basic types of controls: bound and unbound. A **bound control** is linked to a field in an underlying table. An example of a bound control is a text control that is linked to the record source (usually a field from a table) and displays the field data in the form or report. An **unbound control** is not connected to an underlying record source. Examples of unbound controls are labels such as the title of a form or elements that enhance the appearance of the form such as lines, boxes, and pictures.

Additional Information

You will learn about reports in Lab 3.

This form contains two types of controls: label controls that display the form title and field names and text controls that display the field data. The text controls are bound controls. Changing information in the text controls will change the data for the record in the underlying table. Even though the label controls display the field names that are used in the underlying table, they are unbound controls. If you were to change the text in the form's label control, the field name in the table would not change. The columnar format determines the layout and position of these controls.

Modifying a Form

Although you are generally satisfied with the look of the form, there are a few changes that you want to make. You see that you accidentally placed the Employee ID field at the bottom of the form. The first change you will make is to move the Employee ID field to the top of the form and size it to more closely fit the data.

You can use Form Layout view or Form Design view to modify the design and layout of a form. As in Datasheet Design view, Form Design view displays the structure of the form, not the data in the form. It is used to make extensive changes to the form. Form Layout view displays the underlying data and allows you to make many basic modifications.

USING FORM LAYOUT VIEW

You will use Form Layout view to make the change to the Employee ID field controls because you want to be able to see the data in the Employee ID field as you adjust the size of the control.

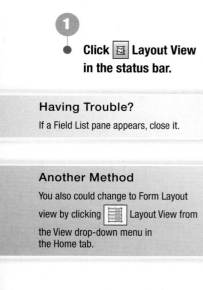

1 Click ⊞ **Layout View in the status bar.**

Having Trouble?

If a Field List pane appears, close it.

Another Method

You also could change to Form Layout view by clicking ⊞ Layout View from the View drop-down menu in the Home tab.

Your screen should be similar to Figure 2.58

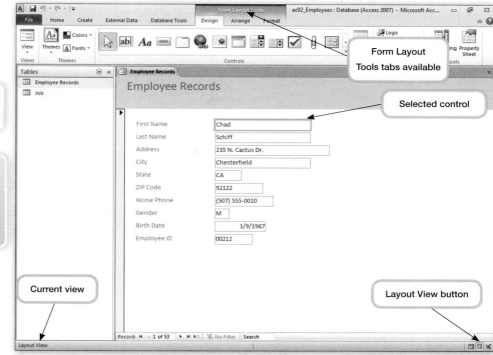

Figure 2.58

The Form Layout Tools Design, Arrange, and Format tabs are now available to help you modify the form design. Currently, the First Name text box control is surrounded with a solid orange box, indicating the control is selected and is the control that will be affected by your actions.

MOVING CONTROLS

First you will select the Employee ID control to move it.

1 Click on the Employee ID text control to select it.

Your screen should be similar to Figure 2.59

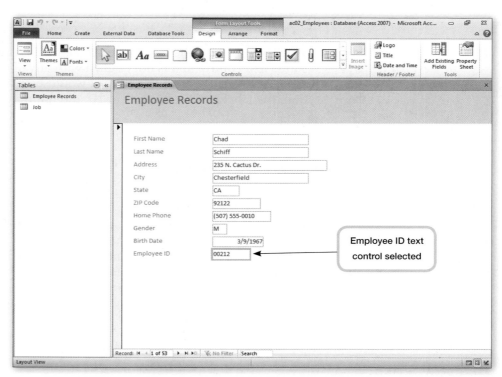

Figure 2.59

Modifying a Form **AC2.55**

The Employee ID text control is selected and surrounded in an orange box. Once controls are selected, they can be moved, sized, deleted, or modified. You will move the control to above the First Name control. When you point to the selected control and the mouse pointer appears as ⁺⃗k, you can move the control by dragging it.

2

- Point to the selected control, and when the mouse pointer appears as ⁺⃗k, drag the control up above the First Name text control.

- When you think the mouse is where you want the control to appear, stop dragging and release the mouse.

Your screen should be similar to Figure 2.60

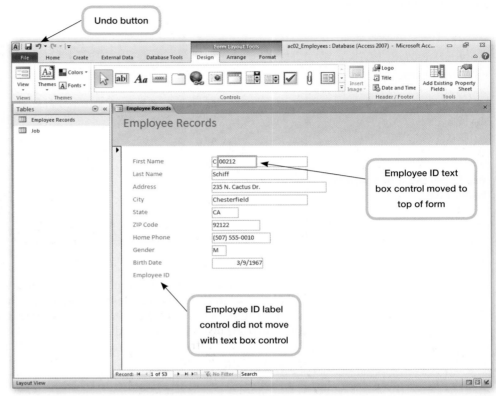

Figure 2.60

When you release the Employee ID control, it probably is on top of the First Name text control and is not aligned with any of the other controls. It also was difficult to know where the control would be placed as you dragged. In addition, the label control, Employee ID, did not move with the text control.

3

- Click 🔄 Undo to cancel moving the Employee ID control.

APPLYING A LAYOUT

To make it easier to move and arrange controls, you will group the controls by applying the stacked layout. This will position the controls in a layout consisting of cells arranged in rows and columns, which behave much like a table in Word. When the Wizard created this form, it arranged the controls in a tabular format but did not group the controls in a layout. You want to include all the form controls except the form title in the stacked layout. You first need to select all the controls you want to include in the new layout.

- Press Ctrl + A to select all the controls on the form.

- Press Ctrl + click on the Employee Records label in the Form header to deselect it.

- Open the Arrange tab and click in the Table group.

Your screen should be similar to Figure 2.61

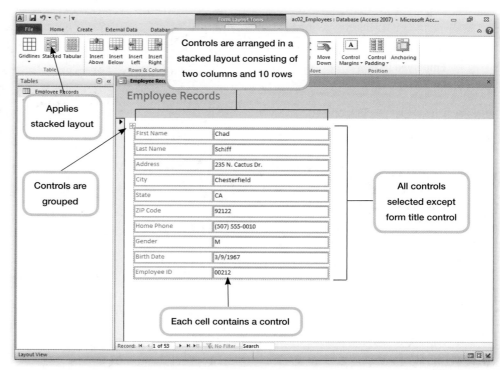

Figure 2.61

All controls in the record's detail section of the form are selected and surrounded with a solid orange border. They are grouped and arranged in the basic stacked layout with the label controls in one column to the left of the text controls. The controls in each column are now all the same size. Notice also that the group is surrounded with a dotted border with a ⊞ in the upper left corner. This indicates the controls are grouped in the layout.

The layout is a guide that helps you align your controls horizontally and vertically. It is similar in appearance to a table, which consists of rows and columns, but the layout differs in that it only allows controls to be placed in the cells. This layout has two columns and 10 rows. Each cell contains a single control.

You will again move the Employee ID control. This time, you also will select the Employee ID label so that both controls will move together. As you move the controls in the layout, a solid orange line will appear showing you where the controls will be placed when you stop dragging.

2

- Click on the Employee ID text control.

- Press ⸢Shift⸥ + click on the Employee ID label control.

- Point to the selected controls and drag upward to move them.

Additional Information

Using [Move Up] in the Move group of the Arrange tab moves the control up one row at a time.

- When the light orange line appears above the First Name control, release the mouse button to drop the controls in the new location.

Your screen should be similar to Figure 2.62

Figure 2.62

The Employee ID label and text controls have moved to the top row of the table and all other controls have moved down one row.

SIZING AND MOVING CONTROLS IN A LAYOUT

Next, you want to reduce the size of the Employee ID text control to match the size of the entry. When you position the mouse pointer on the orange box surrounding the selected control, the pointer changes to ↔ and can be used to size the control. The direction of the arrow indicates in which direction dragging the mouse will alter the shape of the object. This action is similar to sizing a window.

Click on the Employee ID text control to select it.

Point to the right edge of the control box and, when the mouse pointer is ←→, drag to the left to decrease the size of the control as in Figure 2.63.

Your screen should be similar to Figure 2.63

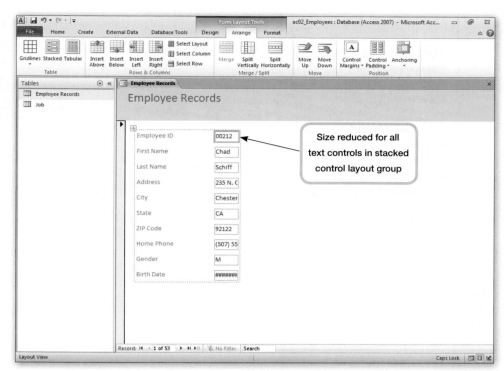

> Size reduced for all text controls in stacked control layout group

Figure 2.63

Unfortunately, the size of all the text box controls in the column has been reduced. This is because, in order for the stacked control layout to maintain a uniform appearance, it groups the controls so that they size as a unit. To size a control individually, it must be in its own separate column or in a separate layout group. You decide you will move the Employee ID control to a separate layout group so that it stands alone at the top of the form. Then you will size it to fit the contents.

First you resize all the controls in the layout to fully display the information. Then you will make space at the top of the form for the Employee ID controls by moving all the controls in this layout group down.

②

• Increase the size of the text controls to fully display the data as shown in Figure 2.64.

• Click the ⊞ layout selector box at the top-left corner of the layout to select all the controls in the layout.

• Drag the selection down 2 rows.

Having Trouble?

The control layout changes to dark blue as you move it to show the new position of the object.

Your screen should be similar to Figure 2.64

Figure 2.64

Additional Information

You also can remove controls from a layout without placing them in another layout using Layout/Remove Layout on the control's shortcut menu.

SPLITTING A LAYOUT

Now that you have space at the top of the form for the Employee ID information, you will remove the Employee ID control from the layout into a separate stacked layout and then move and size it to fit the contents.

①

• Select the Employee ID text and label controls.

• Click in the Stacked Table group of the Arrange tab.

Your screen should be similar to Figure 2.65

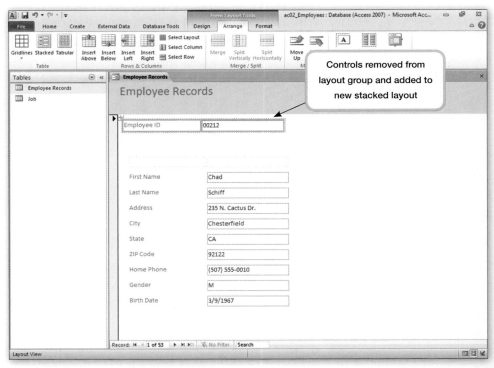

Figure 2.65

The Employee ID controls have been removed from the original stacked layout and added to a separate stacked layout. There are now two stacked layouts in the form that can be sized individually. You will reposition and size the controls in both layouts next.

2

● Using the ⊞ layout selector, drag the Employee ID object to the position shown in Figure 2.66.

● Reduce the size of the Employee ID text and label controls as in Figure 2.66.

● Click on the First Name label control to select it, and size it to match the size of the Employee ID label control.

Your screen should be similar to Figure 2.66

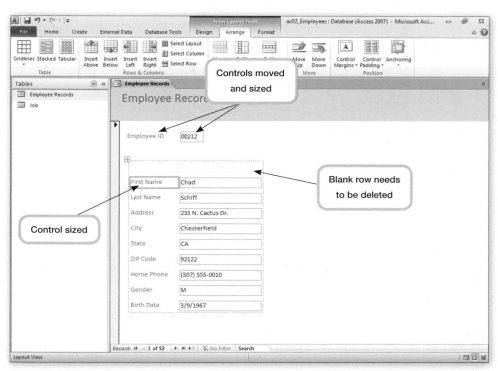

Figure 2.66

The Employee ID is clearly separate from the personal data on the form, and the text control has been sized to fit the data more closely.

REMOVING ROWS FROM A LAYOUT

Notice, however, there is a blank row in the layout where the Employee ID was previously. You will delete the blank row and then move the Last Name controls to the right of the First Name text control, as they appear in the company's paper form.

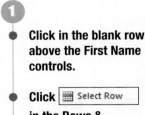

Click in the blank row above the First Name controls.

Click Select Row **in the Rows & Columns group of the Arrange tab.**

Press Delete.

Select the Last Name controls and drag them to the right of the First Name text control.

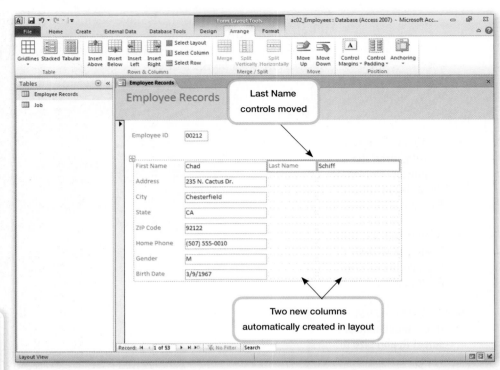

Figure 2.67

Having Trouble?

The orange indicator line should be at the right of the First Name text control when you release the mouse.

Your screen should be similar to Figure 2.67

Additional Information

You can delete a column by selecting a cell in the column, clicking

Select Column, and pressing

Delete.

The blank row was deleted and two new columns were added to the layout to accommodate the moved controls. You will continue to arrange the elements on the form so the form appears similar to the paper form the company uses. This will make the process of entering data from the paper form into the database easier for the user.

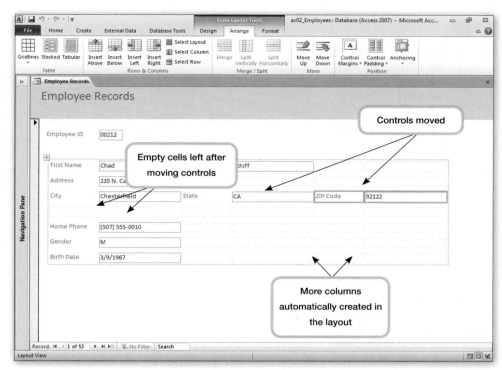

2

- Select the State controls and move them to the blank cell to the right of City text control.

- Select the ZIP Code controls and move them to the right of the State text control.

- Close the Navigation Pane so you have more room to work.

Your screen should be similar to Figure 2.68

Figure 2.68

The controls are now placed where you want them, but they need to be resized to better fit their contents. Also, you notice the Last Name and State labels are a little close to the boxes on their left and would look better with some space added between them.

INSERTING, MERGING, AND SPLITTING CELLS

Working with layouts also allows you to easily insert columns and rows, and merge and split cells to achieve the design you want for the form. The next change you want to make is to insert a narrow blank column to the left of the Last Name controls to separate the controls.

1

● Reduce the width of the Last Name label control to better fit the label.

● Click 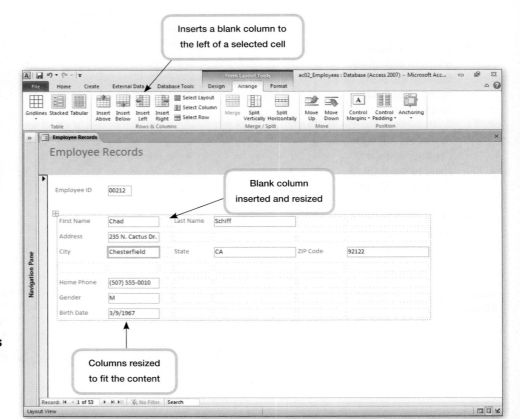 to insert a blank column to the left of the Last Name label control and add separation.

● Reduce the width of the blank column as in Figure 2.69.

● Resize the columns of the text controls on the left so they better fit the contents of the Phone Number control.

Your screen should be similar to Figure 2.69

Figure 2.69

The form now has a nice visual separation between the controls on the left and those added on the right.

Now, however, you feel the Address text control could be larger. To fix this, you will merge it with the cells on the right to allow for longer address entries. When you **merge cells** any selected adjacent cells are combined into one big cell spanning the length of the previously selected cells.

You cannot merge cells containing more than one control, because each cell can contain only one control. You can merge any number of empty adjacent cells.

First you must select the cells to be merged.

- Select the Address text control.

- Hold down ⇧Shift and click the two empty cells to the right of the Address control.

- Click 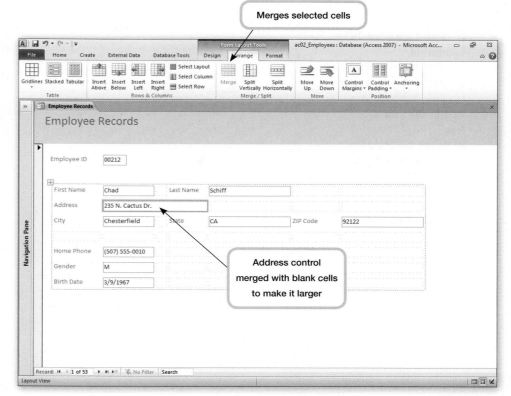 in the Merge/Split group.

Your screen should be similar to Figure 2.70

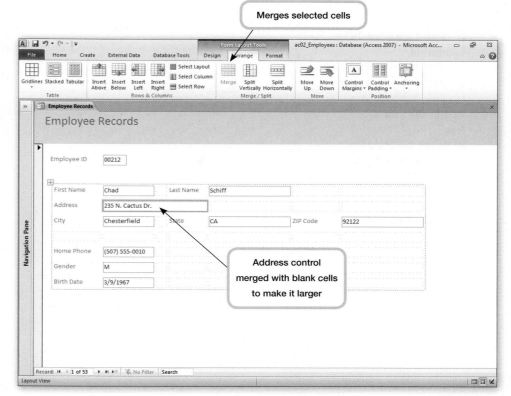

Figure 2.70

The three cells have been combined into one cell that should be large enough to display most addresses. When merging cells, it is better to adjust column sizes as much as possible before merging, as the underlying row and column structure can become complicated and make it difficult to resize just the cells you want.

To further enhance the form, the State and ZIP Code controls could be resized to better fit the text they contain. However, if you resize the State field, it will make the Last Name controls too narrow. Since the State text control only needs to be wide enough for two characters, you think it would fit next to the State label if you could utilize the extra space in the cell. To make one cell into two, you can split the cell.

You can **split cells** horizontally or vertically. Splitting a cell vertically creates a new row and splitting a cell horizontally creates a new column. Splitting can be performed on only one cell at a time. The affected cell can be an empty cell or contain a control. When splitting a cell containing a control, the control is kept in the far left box and an empty cell is created on the right side. You want to split the cell containing the State label.

3

- Select the State label control.

- Click [Split Horizontally] to split the cell into two.

- Move the State text control into the new empty cell.

Your screen should be similar to Figure 2.71

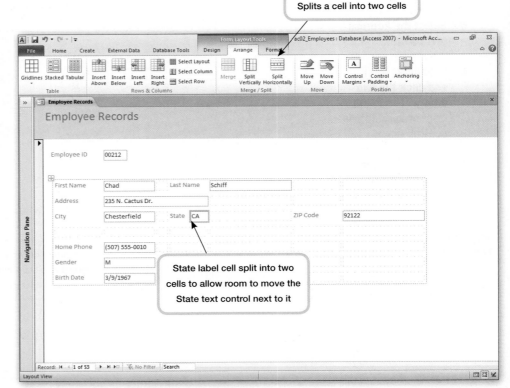

Figure 2.71

Both State controls now reside within the same column containing the last name label. You notice the Address text control also ends in this column. If you were to try and resize the State or Address text controls, it would affect the entire column, including the cell containing the Last Name label.

Your form has room for the ZIP Code label and text controls to be moved to the right of the State control. You will split the empty cell and move both ZIP Code controls into the new position.

4

- Click the empty cell to the right of the State text control.

- Click .

- Select both ZIP Code controls and move them to the empty cells to the right of the State text control.

- Select the ZIP Code label control, and click ≣ Align Text Right in the Font group of the Format tab.

Your screen should be similar to Figure 2.72

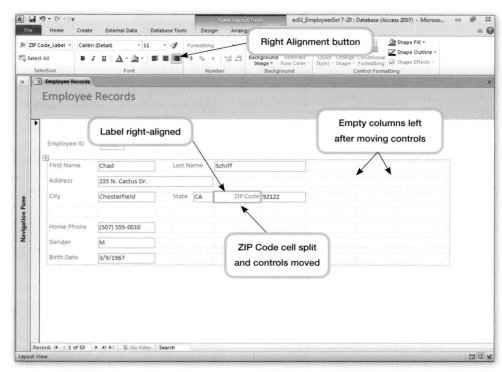

Figure 2.72

Aligning the label to the right gives the appearance of space between the label and the State text control. Now you need to delete the extra columns in the layout and move the last three fields up below the City field. To specify the column to be removed, select any cell in the column and the entire column will be deleted.

5

- Click an empty cell in the column to the right of the Last Name text control.

- Press Delete.

- In the same manner, delete the second empty column.

- Select the label and text controls for the last three fields.

- Drag the selected controls up to the blank cell under the City label.

Your screen should be similar to Figure 2.73

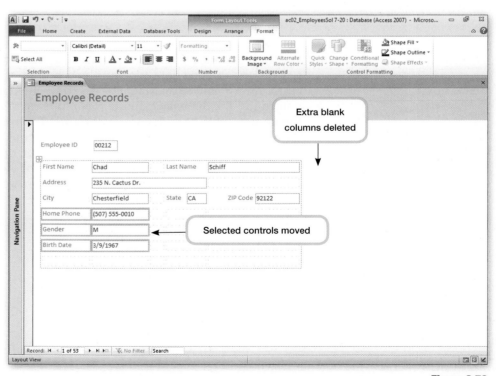

Figure 2.73

The form you have created is getting closer to matching the layout of the company's paper form.

ADDING EXISTING FIELDS

The only element missing on your new form is the Photo/Resume field. You will add the field to the form layout and then merge cells to make room for the photo.

1

- Open the Format Layout Tools Design tab.

- Click [Add Existing Fields] in the Tools group to open the field list.

- Drag the Photo/Resume field from the Field List pane to the empty cell below the Birth Date label.

Your screen should be similar to Figure 2.74

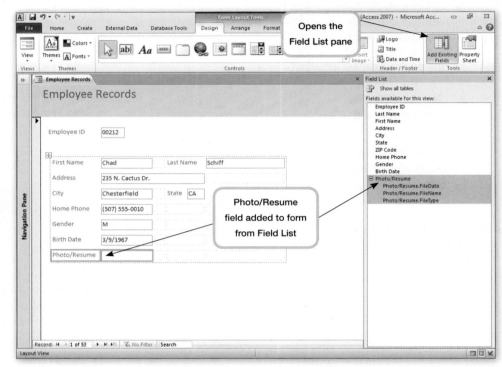

Figure 2.74

The Photo/Resume field is now placed in the layout. The Photo/Resume field has an attachment data type and is a bound control that allows you to add, edit, remove, and save attached files to the field directly from the form, just as you can in the datasheet. In the form, it uses an attachment control to display the contents of the field. The **attachment control** displays image files automatically. Other types of attachments, such as Word documents, appear as icons that represent the file type and must be opened to be viewed. Currently the attachment control that will display the photo is too small to be functional. To enlarge the control, you will insert four rows below it and then merge the new cells for the attachment control.

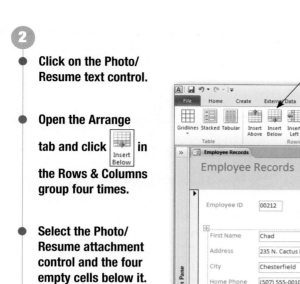

2

- Click on the Photo/ Resume text control.

- Open the Arrange tab and click in the Rows & Columns group four times.

- Select the Photo/ Resume attachment control and the four empty cells below it.

- Click [Merge].

- Close the Field List.

Your screen should be similar to Figure 2.75

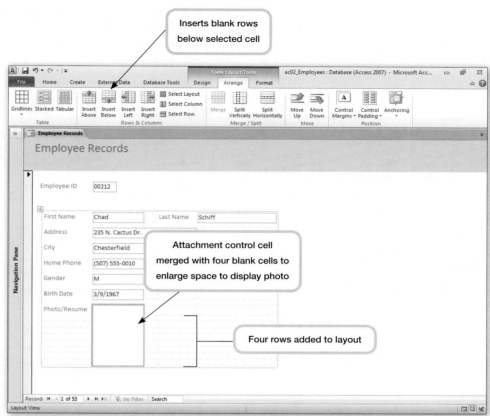

Figure 2.75

Now the Photo/Resume attachment control is large enough to display a photo. The Photo/Resume field's control is currently empty because there are no attachments for this record.

CHANGING THE DESIGN STYLE

Next you want to enhance the form's appearance by making changes to the form colors and fonts. To make it easy to quickly change the appearance of the form you will change the form's design theme.

Concept 11 Theme

A **theme** is a predefined set of formatting choices that can be applied to an entire document in one simple step. Access includes 40 named, built-in themes that can be applied to forms and reports. Each theme includes two subset of themes: colors and fonts. Each color theme consists of 12 colors that are applied to specific elements in the form or report. Each fonts theme includes a set of different body and heading fonts. You also can create your own custom themes by modifying an existing theme and saving it as a custom theme. The blank database file uses the default Office theme for any forms or reports you create.

The same themes also are available in Word 2010, Excel 2010 and PowerPoint 2010. Using themes gives your documents a professional and modern look. Because document themes are shared across 2010 Office applications, all your Office documents can have the same uniform look.

Currently this form uses the built-in Office theme, which consists of a certain set of colors and the fonts Cambria and Calibri. You decide to look at the other themes to see if there is one that may coordinate well with the colors used in the Employee Records table.

1

● **Open the Design tab.**

● **Click** 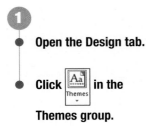 **in the Themes group.**

Your screen should be similar to Figure 2.76

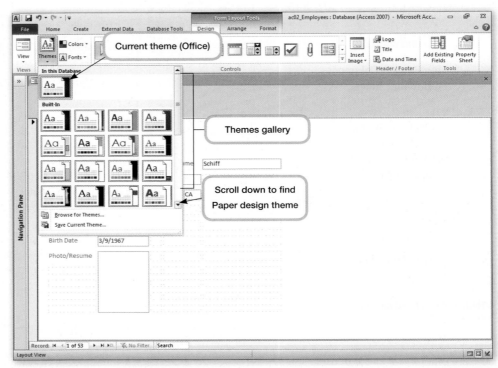

Figure 2.76

A gallery of 40 built-in named themes is displayed. A sample shows the color and font used in each theme. The Office theme is the default theme and is the theme that is used in the form. When you point to each theme, the theme name appears in a ScreenTip and a live preview of how the theme's settings will look is displayed in the form. You think the Paper theme will match the colors you chose for the Employee Records table.

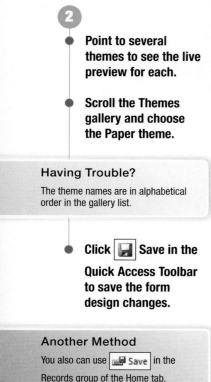

2

- **Point to several themes to see the live preview for each.**

- **Scroll the Themes gallery and choose the Paper theme.**

Having Trouble?

The theme names are in alphabetical order in the gallery list.

- **Click 🖫 Save in the Quick Access Toolbar to save the form design changes.**

Another Method

You also can use 🖫 Save in the Records group of the Home tab.

Additional Information

If you do not save the design changes at this time, you will be prompted to save them before closing the form.

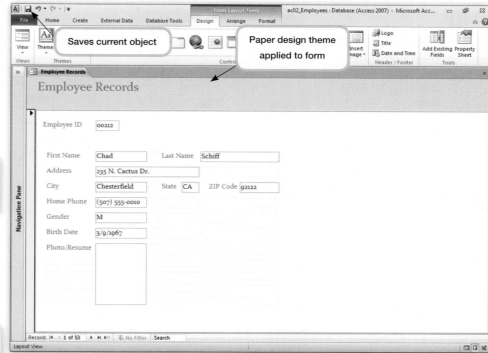

Figure 2.77

The formatting settings associated with the selected theme have been applied to the form. Because themes are available in the other Office applications, you can coordinate the design styles used in documents created in the other applications by choosing the same theme.

Your screen should be similar to Figure 2.77

Using a Form

Now that you have created the form and enhanced its appearance, you are ready to utilize the form by switching to Form view. Using a form, you can do many of the same things you can do in Datasheet view. For example, you can update and delete records, search for records, and sort and filter the data.

NAVIGATING IN FORM VIEW

You use the same navigation keys in Form view that you used in Datasheet view. You can move between fields in the form by using the Tab⇄, ⏎Enter, or Shift + Tab⇄ keys. The → and ← keys are used to move character by character through the entry. You can use Page Up and Page Down, as well as the navigation buttons at the bottom of the form, to move between records.

You will try out several of these navigation keys as you try to locate the record for Roberta Marchant. First, you must switch to Form view.

1

- Change the view to Form View.

- Press Tab ⇥ three times.

- Press Page Down two times.

Your screen should be similar to Figure 2.78

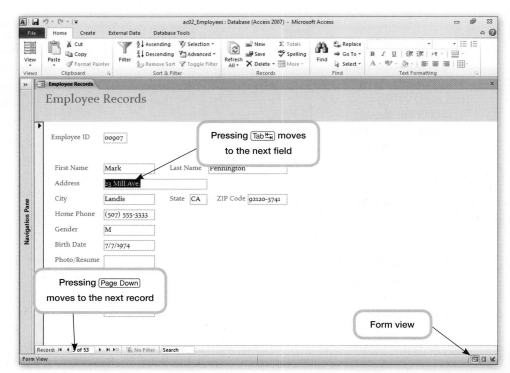

Figure 2.78

First you moved three fields to the Address field in the current record. Then you moved down two records to record three. The field that was selected in the previous record remains the selected field when you move between records.

Searching in Form View

A quicker way to locate a record is to use the Find command or the Search feature. Both features work just as they do in Datasheet view. You will use the Search feature to locate the record for Roberta Marchant by entering the first few characters of her last name in the Search box. As you type the characters, watch how the search advances through the table and highlights matching text.

1

● Click in the Search text box.

● Type **marc**

Your screen should be similar to Figure 2.79

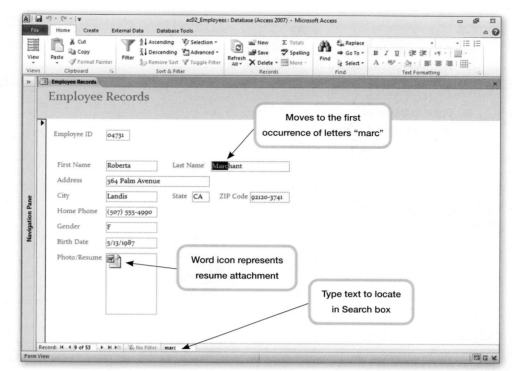

Moves to the first occurrence of letters "marc"

Word icon represents resume attachment

Type text to locate in Search box

Figure 2.79

The Search feature located Roberta Marchant's record and displays it in the form. The Photo/Resume field displays a Word icon for the resume file. To open the resume file, simply double-click on the Word icon and choose [Open] from the Attachments dialog box. To display the next attachment, click on the Attachment control to make it active. This will display the Mini toolbar, which contains three buttons that are used to work with attachment controls. When the Mini toolbar first displays above the Attachment control, it will appear transparent and may be hard to discern. By pointing to the Mini Toolbar, it will become solid and easier to see. Using the Mini toolbar, you can scroll through attached files using the 🔘 and 🔘 buttons, or you may add or view attachments using 📎 to open the Attachments dialog box. You will use the Mini toolbar to display the photo attachment.

Additional Information

Refer to the Formatting Text section in the Introduction to Microsoft Office 2010 to review the Mini toolbar feature.

2

- Click on the Photo/ Resume field to make it active.

- Point to the Mini toolbar and click 🔄 to move to the next attachment.

Your screen should be similar to Figure 2.80

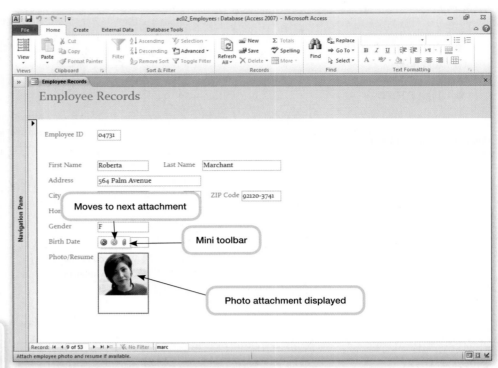

Figure 2.80

Now the photo is displayed in the Photo/Resume field control.

SORTING AND FILTERING DATA IN A FORM

Just as in the table datasheet, you can sort and filter the data that is displayed in a form. You will use these features to sort the records in alphabetical order by last name and display only records for employees who live in River Mist.

1

- Right-click on the Last Name field.

- Choose Sort A to Z.

- Move to any record that displays River Mist and right-click on the City field.

- Choose Equals "River Mist".

- Display the last record.

Your screen should be similar to Figure 2.81

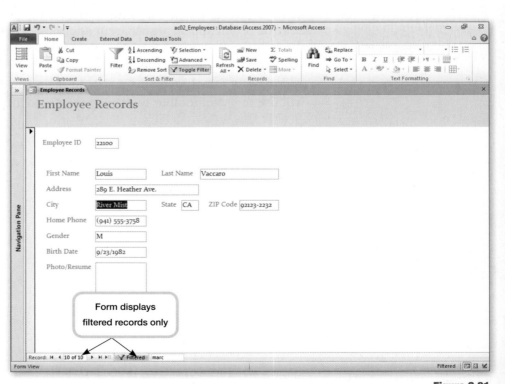

Figure 2.81

The record number indicator tells you that there are only 10 records and the table is filtered. The records are also in sorted order by last name. The sort and filter settings apply only to the object in which they were specified, in this case the form.

ADDING RECORDS USING A FORM

Now you need to add a new employee record to the database whose paper employee record form is shown here. You will add the record while in Form view, using the information on the paper form to input the data into the form's fields. You also will attach a picture to the Photo/Resume field.

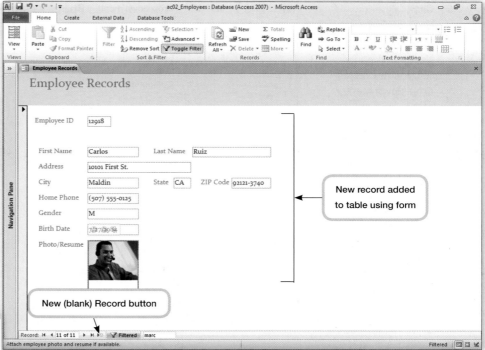

EMPLOYEE DATA

Employee ID   12918

First Name   Carlos   Last Name   Ruiz
Street   10101 First St.
City   Maldin   State CA   Zip Code 92121-3740
Phone Number (507) 555-0125
Gender   M
Birth Date   July 27, 1984

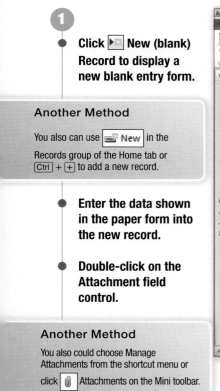

1

Click New (blank) **Record to display a new blank entry form.**

Another Method

You also can use New in the Records group of the Home tab or Ctrl + + to add a new record.

Enter the data shown in the paper form into the new record.

Double-click on the Attachment field control.

Another Method

You also could choose Manage Attachments from the shortcut menu or click Attachments on the Mini toolbar.

Add the file ac02_ Carlos **from your data file location.**

Your screen should be similar to Figure 2.82

New (blank) Record button

New record added to table using form

Figure 2.82

Using the form makes entering the new employee data much faster because the fields are in the same order as the information on the paper Employee Data form used by the Personnel department.

Before you end this lab, you will add a record for yourself.

2

- Enter another record using your special Employee ID **99999** and your first and last names. The data in all other fields can be fictitious.

- Remove the filter.

- Open the Navigation Pane.

The table now contains 55 records. Next, you need to add these two records to the Job table.

Organizing the Navigation Pane

Notice the name of the form does not appear in the Navigation pane. This is because initially the pane is set to display table objects only. To display other objects in the pane, you can change what objects are displayed in the pane and how they are grouped.

- **Click**

  Tables

  at the top of the Navigation pane to open the Tables drop-down menu.

Your screen should be similar to Figure 2.83

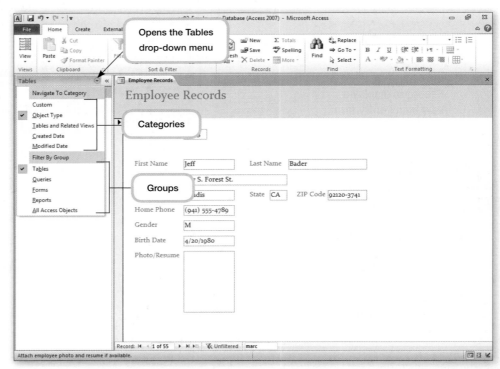

Figure 2.83

The upper section of the menu contains categories, and the lower section contains groups. The groups change as you select different categories. Currently, Object Type is the selected category and Tables is the selected group. You want to keep the category selection as Object Type but want to change the group selection to display all object types in the pane at the same time.

2

- From the Filter By Group section, choose **All Access Objects**.

- Double-click the **Job** table in the Navigation Pane.

Another Method

You also can drag an object from the Navigation pane to the work area to open it.

- Add the information for the two records shown below to the table.

Your screen should be similar to Figure 2.84

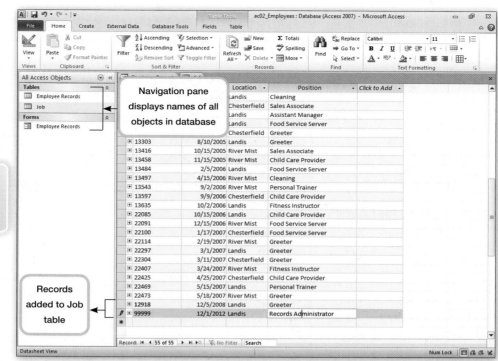

Navigation pane displays names of all objects in database

Records added to Job table

Figure 2.84

Field	Record 54	Record 55
Employee ID	12918	99999
Hire Date	12/5/2008	Today's date
Location	Landis	Landis
Position	Greeter	Records Administrator

Now both tables contain 55 records.

You want to preview and print only the form that displays your record.

1

- **Click the Employee Records tab to display the form.**

- **Open the File tab and choose Print.**

- **Choose Print Preview.**

Having Trouble?

Your form may display fewer records than in Figure 2.85.

Your screen should be similar to Figure 2.85

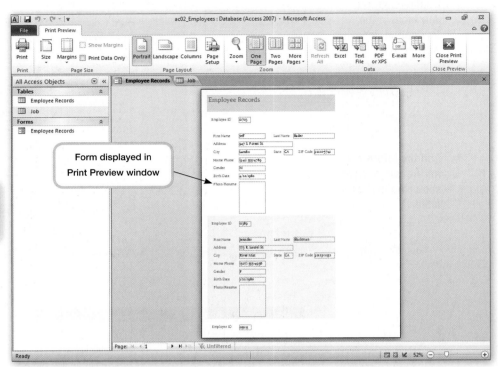

Form displayed in Print Preview window

Figure 2.85

The form object is displayed in the Print Preview window.

PRINTING A SELECTED RECORD

Access prints as many records as can be printed on a page using the Form layout. You want to print only the form displaying your record. To do this, you need to select your record first in Form view.

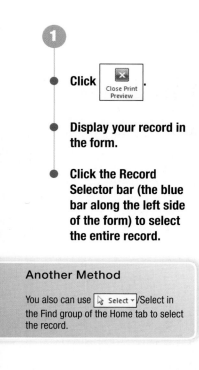

1

● Click [Close Print Preview].

● **Display your record in the form.**

● **Click the Record Selector bar (the blue bar along the left side of the form) to select the entire record.**

Another Method

You also can use [Select ▾]/Select in the Find group of the Home tab to select the record.

Your screen should be similar to Figure 2.86

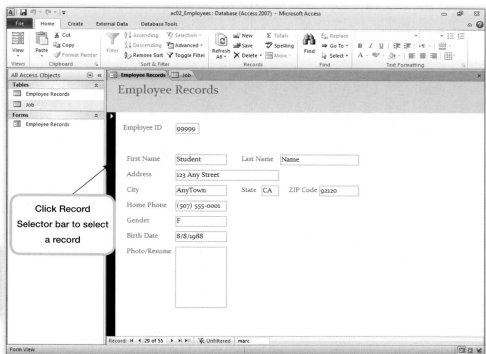

Click Record Selector bar to select a record

Figure 2.86

Now that the record is selected, you can print it.

2

● **Open the File tab and choose Print.**

● **Choose Print.**

● **Choose the Selected Record(s) option from the Print dialog box.**

● **If necessary, make sure your printer is on and select the appropriate printer.**

● **Click [OK].**

Identifying Object Dependencies

The form is the third database object that has been added to the file. Many objects that you create in a database have **object dependencies**, meaning they are dependent upon other objects for their content. In this case, the form is dependent upon the Employee Records database table for its content. Sometimes it is helpful to be able to find out what objects an object is dependent on or what depend on it. To help in these situations, you can display the object dependencies.

1

- **Select the Employee Records table object in the Navigation pane.**

- **Open the Database Tools tab.**

- **Click** 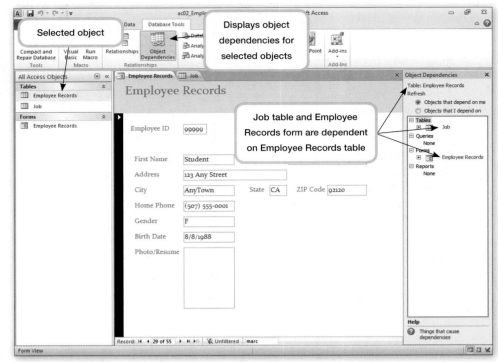 **in the Relationships group.**

- **If necessary, select "Objects that depend on me" from the Object Dependencies task pane.**

Your screen should be similar to Figure 2.87

Figure 2.87

The Object Dependencies task pane identifies the two objects that are dependent on the table: the Job table and the Employee Records form. Next, you will see which objects depend on the Employee Records form.

2

- **Select Employee Records in the Forms category of the Navigation pane.**

- **Click Refresh in the Object Dependencies task pane.**

Your screen should be similar to Figure 2.88

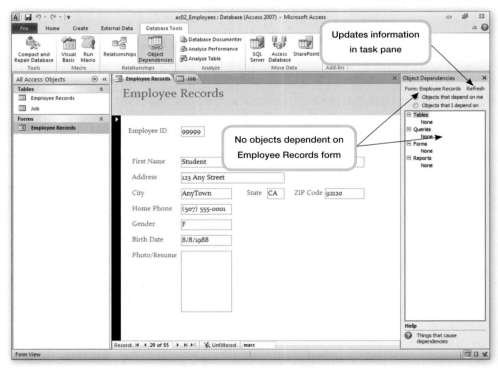

Figure 2.88

You can now see that the Employee Records form object does not have any objects dependent on it.

3

● Choose "Objects that I depend on" from the Object Dependencies task pane.

Your screen should be similar to Figure 2.89

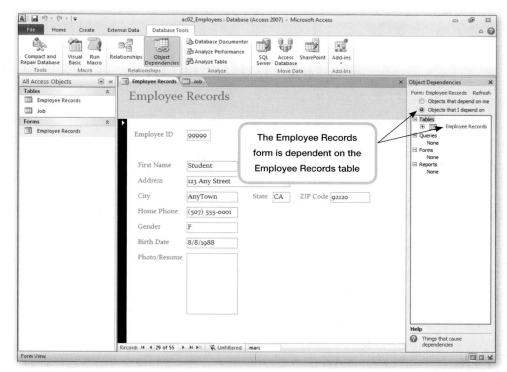

Figure 2.89

The Object Dependencies task pane identifies that the only object that the form depends on is the Employee Records table.

4

● Close the Object Dependencies task pane.

● Close the form and table objects, saving any changes.

● In the database properties, add your name as the author, and in the Comments box, add **This database contains 55 records and is still under construction**.

● Exit Access.

)CUS ON CAREERS

EXPLORE YOUR CAREER OPTIONS

Administrative Assistant

Administrative assistants are typically responsible for the efficient management of office operations. This position may involve conducting research, training new staff, scheduling meetings, and maintaining databases. As an administrative assistant, you could be responsible for updating an inventory or staffing database. The typical salary range of an administrative assistant is $27,000 to $64,000. Demand for experienced administrative assistants, especially in technology and health fields, is expected to increase through 2018.

Format Property (AC2.7)

The Format property is used to specify the way that numbers, dates, times, and text in a field are displayed and printed.

Default Value Property (AC2.8)

The Default Value property is used to specify a value that is automatically entered in a field when a new record is created.

Validation Rule (AC2.11)

Validation rules are used to control the data that can be entered in a field by defining the input values that are valid or allowed.

Expression (AC2.11)

An expression is a formula consisting of a combination of symbols that will produce a single value.

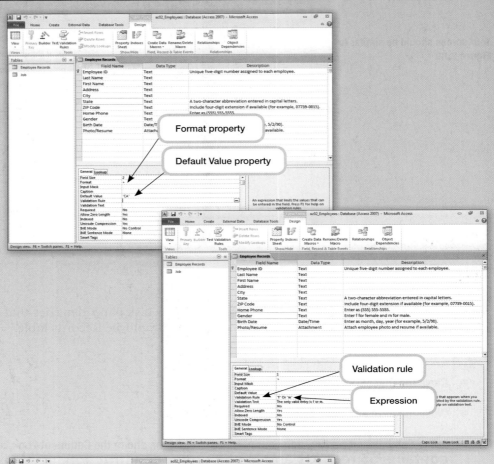

Lookup Field (AC2.18)

A **lookup field** provides a list of values from which the user can choose to make entering data into that field simpler and more accurate.

Find and Replace (AC2.25)

The Find and Replace feature helps you quickly find specific information and automatically replace it with new information.

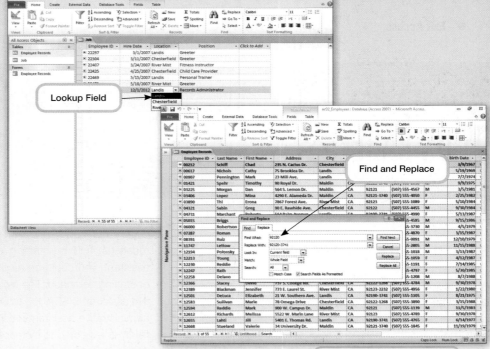

Sorting (AC2.33)

Sorting rearranges the order of the records in a table based on the value in each field.

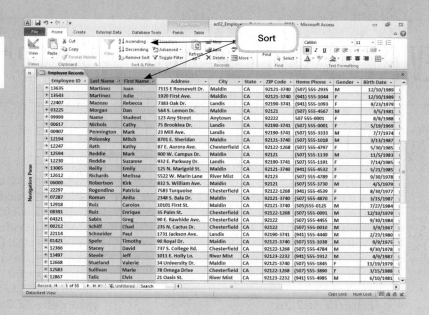

Filter (AC2.40)

A filter is a restriction placed on records in the open table or form to quickly isolate and display a subset of records.

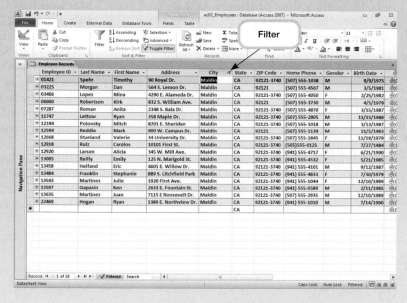

Form (AC2.46)

A form is a database object used primarily to display records onscreen to make it easier to enter new records and to make changes to existing records.

Controls (AC2.54)

Controls are objects that display information, perform actions, or enhance the design of a form or report.

Theme (AC2.69)

A **theme** is a predefined set of formatting choices that can be applied to an entire document in one simple step.

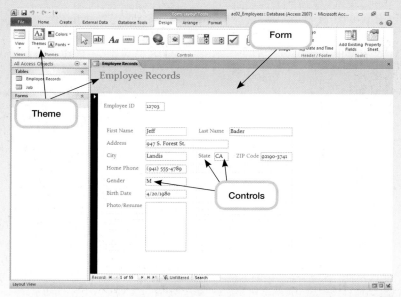

KEY TERMS

argument AC2.11
ascending sort order AC2.33
attachment control AC2.68
bound control AC2.54
character string AC2.8
comparison operator AC2.11
constant AC2.11
control AC2.54
criteria AC2.26
Default Value property AC2.8
descending sort order AC2.33
expression AC2.11
filter AC2.40
Find and Replace AC2.25
form AC2.46
format AC2.7
Format property AC2.7
Form Wizard AC2.48
function AC2.11
identifier AC2.11
IntelliSense AC2.12
label control AC2.54
layout AC2.51
lookup field AC2.18

lookup list AC2.18
Lookup Wizard AC2.18
merge cells AC2.64
object dependencies AC2.79
operator AC2.11
outer sort field AC2.34
record source AC2.47
sorting AC2.33
split cells AC2.65
stacked format AC2.51
tab order AC2.49
tabular format AC2.51
text control AC2.54
theme AC2.68
theme colors AC2.38
unbound control AC2.54
validation rule AC2.11
Validation Rule property AC2.11
validation text AC2.11
Validation Text property AC2.11
value list AC2.18
wildcards AC2.26
wizard AC2.18

COMMAND SUMMARY

Command	Shortcut	Action
Quick Access Toolbar		
↩ Undo	Ctrl + Z	Cancels last action
💾 Save	Ctrl + S	Saves the current object
Home tab		
Views group		
Form View		Changes to Form view
Form Layout View		Changes to Form Layout view
Text Formatting group		
B Bold	Ctrl + B	Applies bold effect to all text in datasheet
A ▾ Font Color		Applies selected color to all text in datasheet
▦▾ Gridlines		Changes the display of gridlines in the datasheet
▦ ▾ Alternate Row Color		Changes background color of alternate rows in datasheet
Sort & Filter group		
A↓ Ascending		Changes sort order to ascending
Z↓ Descending		Changes sort order to descending
ᴬ↓ Remove Sort		Clears all sorts and returns sort order to primary key order
▼ Filter		Used to specify filter settings for selected field
Selection ▾ /Equals		Sets filter to display only those records containing selected value
Advanced ▾ /Clear All Filters		Deletes all filters from table
▼ Toggle Filter		Applies and removes filter from table
Records group		
💾 Save	⇧ Shift + ↵ Enter	Saves changes to object design
New	Ctrl + +	Adds new record
More ▾ /Hide Fields		Hides selected columns in Datasheet view

COMMAND SUMMARY (CONTINUED)

Command	Shortcut	Action
More ▾ /Unhide Fields		Redisplays hidden columns
Find group		
Find	Ctrl + F	Locates specified data
Replace	Ctrl + H	Locates specified data and replaces it with specified replacement text
Go To ▾		Moves to First, Previous, Next, Last, or New record location
Select ▾ /Select		Selects current record
Select ▾ /Select All		Selects all records in database
Create tab		
Tables group		
Table		Creates a new table in Datasheet view
Table Design		Creates a new table in Design view
Forms group		
Form		Creates a new form using all the fields from the underlying table
Blank Form		Displays a blank form to which you add the fields from the table that you want to appear on the form
Form Wizard		Creates a new form by following the steps in the Form Wizard
Database Tools tab		
Relationships group		
Object Dependencies		Shows the objects in the database that use the selected object
Table Tools Design tab		
Tools group		
Insert Rows		Inserts a new field in Table Design view

COMMAND SUMMARY (CONTINUED)

Command	Shortcut	Action
Table Tools Fields tab		
Add & Delete group		
More Fields ▾ / Lookup & Relationship		Creates a lookup field
Form Design Tools Design tab		
Themes group		
Aa Themes ▾		Opens gallery of theme styles
Tools group		
Add Existing Fields		Adds selected existing field to form
Form Design Tools Arrange tab		
Table group		
Stacked		Applies Stacked layout to the controls
Rows & Columns group		
Select Layout		Selects entire layout
Select Column		Selects column in a layout
Select Row		Selects row in a layout
Insert Left		Inserts a blank column to the left of the selected cell in a layout
Insert Below		Inserts a blank row below the selected cell in a layout
Merge/Split group		
Split Horizontally		Divides a layout cell horizontally into two cells
Merge		Combines two or more layout cells into a single cell
Form Design Tools Format tab		
Font group		
≡ Align Text Right		Right aligns contents of cell

LAB EXERCISES

MATCHING

Match the numbered item with the correct lettered description.

1. record source   ____ a. wildcard character
2. form   ____ b. underlying table for a form
3. *   ____ c. locates specified values in a field
4. filter   ____ d. an expression
5. tab order   ____ e. database object used primarily for onscreen display
6. character string   ____ f. order that the selection point moves in a form when Tab⇆ is used
7. find   ____ g. temporarily displays subset of records
8. >=   ____ h. operator
9. ascending sort   ____ i. a group of characters
10. ="Y" Or "N"   ____ j. rearranges records in A to Z or 0 to 9 order

TRUE/FALSE

Circle the correct answer to the following statements.

1. Values are numbers, dates, or pictures.   **True**   **False**
2. An expression is a sequence of characters (letters, numbers, or symbols) that must be handled as text, not as numeric data.   **True**   **False**
3. Label controls are bound controls.   **True**   **False**
4. A contrast operator is a symbol that allows you to make comparisons between two items.   **True**   **False**
5. A validation rule is an expression that defines acceptable data entry values.   **True**   **False**
6. Filter results can be saved with the database and quickly redisplayed.   **True**   **False**
7. Database objects are not dependent on one another.   **True**   **False**
8. The Default Value property determines the value automatically entered into a field of a new record.   **True**   **False**
9. Forms are database objects used primarily for viewing data.   **True**   **False**
10. Text controls display descriptive labels.   **True**   **False**

FILL-IN

Complete the following statements by filling in the blanks with the correct terms.

1. The two basic form layouts are _____ and _____.

2. The _____ property is used to specify a value that is automatically entered in a field when a new record is created.

3. A(n) _____ is a guide that helps you align controls in a form horizontally and vertically.

4. The most common controls are _____ controls and _____ controls.

5. The _____ property changes the way data appears in a field.

6. Format _____ is used to create custom formats that change the way numbers, dates, times, and text display and print.

7. _____ is displayed when an invalid entry is entered.

8. _____ restrict the type of data that can be entered in a field.

9. A(n) _____ is a symbol or word that indicates that an operation is to be performed.

10. The upper section of the Navigation pane contains _____, and the lower section contains _____.

LAB EXERCISES

MULTIPLE CHOICE

Circle the letter of the correct response.

1. A _____ is a feature that guides you step by step through a process.
   a. dialog box
   b. wizard
   c. task pane
   d. gallery

2. _____ properties change the way that data is displayed.
   a. Format
   b. Field
   c. Data
   d. Record

3. The _____ property is commonly used when most of the entries in a field will be the same for the entire table.
   a. AutoNumber
   b. Default Value
   c. Field Data
   d. Best Fit

4. A(n) _____ control is linked to its underlying data source.
   a. bound
   b. label
   c. field
   d. unbound

5. _____ is/are an explanatory message that appears if a user attempts to enter invalid information in a text field.
   a. Validation text
   b. Validation rule
   c. Expressions
   d. Validity checks

6. The _____ is used to specify a value that is automatically entered in a field when a new record is created.
   a. Default Value property
   b. Sort property
   c. field value
   d. Format property

7. _____ layouts arrange data vertically with a field label to the left of the field data.
   a. Datasheet
   b. Justified
   c. Tabular
   d. Stacked

8. A _____ is a temporary restriction placed on a table to display a subset of records.
   a. wildcard
   b. control
   c. filter
   d. sort

9. A form is _____ an underlying table for its content.
   a. independent of
   b. reliant on
   c. contingent on
   d. dependent on

10. _____ control(s) how data is displayed in a form.
    a. Design styles
    b. Controls
    c. Layouts
    d. Tab order

STEP-BY-STEP

RATING SYSTEM

★	Easy
★ ★	Moderate
★ ★ ★	Difficult

NOTE Before you begin, you may want to create a backup copy of each data file by copying and renaming it.

SECOND TIME AROUND INVENTORY DATABASE ★

1. You have already set up an inventory database for the Second Time Around consignment shop. It currently contains fields for the item number, description, price, and consignor last name, and it has records for the inventory currently in stock. The owner of the shop is quite pleased with the database as it stands but has asked you to change the name of the existing Price field to show that it is the original price and to add a new field for the current selling price of the item. Also, she would like you to modify some existing records, create a form to ease data entry, and print a copy of the form. Your completed table and form will be similar to those shown here.

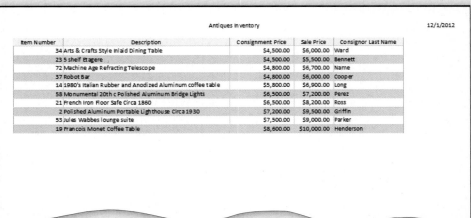

    a. Open the database named ac02_Second Time Around and the table named Antiques Inventory.

    b. Change the Price field name to **Consignment Price**. Change the data type for this field to Currency.

    c. Insert the following field before the Consignor Last Name field:

    Field Name: Sale Price

    Data Type: Currency

    d. Make all fields except Sale Price required. (Hint: Set the Required property to Yes.) Reduce the field size of the Consignor Last Name field to **25**.

    e. Switch to Datasheet view and respond "yes" to all prompts and warnings when saving the design changes. (When the Consignment Price field is converted to the currency data type, the "contact dealer" text will be deleted from the field.)

f. Update the table by entering **0.00** in the Consignment Price field for all records that have a blank entry in this field. (Hint: Use copy and paste.)

g. Enter appropriate values in the Sale Price field for each record. (Generally the sale price is 33 percent more than the consignment price.) Leave the Sale Price field blank for those items with $0.00 in the Consignment Price field.

h. Appropriately size all columns to fully display the data.

i. Find all occurrences of dates that include an apostrophe (1930's) and are preceded with the word circa. Manually delete the 's from each located item.

j. Filter the table to display all records with a consignment price greater than or equal to $4,500. Sort the filtered records in ascending sort order by consignment price.

k. Format the datasheet using alternate row fill colors. Print the filtered table in landscape orientation with normal margins. Close the table object.

l. Use the Form tool to create a simple form for the Antiques Inventory table.

m. Display the form in Layout view. Change the form Theme style to another of your choice. Reduce the size of all the text controls to best fit the contents.

n. Use the new form to enter the following new records:

	Record 1	Record 2
Description	Machine Age Refracting Telescope	Mid Century School House Globe
Consignment Price	$4,800	$1,100
Consignor Last Name	[Your Last Name]	Lewis

o. Print the form for the record containing your name. Close the form, saving it as **Inventory**.

p. Open the table and rerun the filter to display your record in the results. Print the filtered datasheet in landscape orientation using the normal margin setting. Close the table.

q. Display all object types in the Navigation pane.

r. Add your name to the database properties and exit Access.

ENTERPRIZE EMPLOYMENT CLIENT DATABASE ★★

2. You work for a private employment agency as an administrative assistant. As part of your responsibilities, you maintain a client database that contains the job candidates' basic contact information: name, address, and phone number. The office manager has asked you to add to the database the date each candidate applied at your office, the date they were placed with an employer, and the employer's name. Also, because the database is getting rather large, you decide to create a form to make it easier to enter and update records. Your completed table and form will be similar to those shown here.

a. Open the database named ac02_ Enterprize Employment Agency and the table named Candidates.

b. Reduce the State field size to **2**. Change the State field Format property to display all entries in uppercase. Make the default value for the State field **FL**.

c. Change the ZIP Code data type to Text with a field size of **10**.

d. Insert the following field after the Application # field.

Field Name:	**Application Date**
Data Type:	Date/Time
Format:	Short Date

e. Add the following two fields to the end of the table:

Field Name:	**Hire Date**
Data Type:	Date/Time
Format:	Short Date
Field Name:	**Employed By**
Data Type:	Text
Description:	**Enter the name of the employer**
Field Size:	**45**

f. Switch to Datasheet view and save the table design changes.

g. All ZIP Codes of 72725 need to be changed to **72725-1016**. Use Find and Replace to make this change in the database. Best Fit the columns.

h. Use the Form Wizard to create a form for the Candidates table. Include all the table fields in their current order. Use the columnar layout and a theme of your choice. Title the form **Candidate Information**.

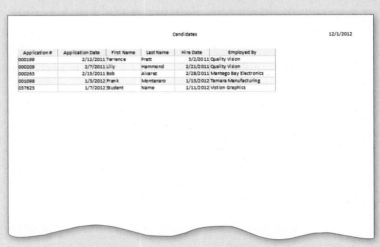

i. In Form Layout view, select the label and text box controls for all the fields except the Application # and Application Date. Apply the stacked layout, then adjust the column widths so they best fit the contents in the form.

j. Insert a column on the right side of the layout. Make the following changes to the placement of the controls:

- Move the Last Name label and control to the right of the First Name field.
- Move the State label and control to the right of the City field.
- Horizontally split the cell containing the State label and then move the State control next to the label.
- Move the ZIP Code field to the right of the State field. Horizontally split the cell containing the ZIP Code; then move the ZIP Code control next to the label.
- Move the Phone label and control underneath the City field.
- Select the Last Name label. Insert a blank row above and a blank column to the left. Adjust the blank column width so that it is about .25" wide, just enough to give some space between the fields.
- Merge the Address control with the two blank cells on the right.
- Merge the Employed By control with the two blank cells on the right.
- Delete any empty row or column placeholders in the layout, but leave one empty row above the First Name and the Hire Date. Resize all columns to best fit the contents.

k. Use the new form to enter the following records in Form view:

Application #	001098	037623
Application Date	1/5/12	1/7/12
First Name	Frank	Your first name
Last Name	Montanaro	Your last name
Address	124 Beach Front Way	802 Valimara Way
City	Lexington	Palmdale
State	FL	FL
ZIP Code	72724	72725-1016
Phone	(726) 555-4623	(726) 555-0909
Hire Date	1/13/12	1/11/12
Employed By	Tamara Manufacturing	Vistion Graphics

l. Use the Search feature to locate the following records and update their data.

Locate	Application Date	Hire Date	Employed By
Lilly Hammond	2/7/11	2/21/11	Paper Products etc.
Terrence Pratt	2/12/11	3/2/11	Quality Vision
Bob Alvarez	2/15/11	2/28/11	Mantego Bay Electronics

m. Display all object types in the Navigation pane.

n. Print the form for the record containing your name.

o. Filter the Candidates table to display only those records displaying a hire date. Sort the records in ascending order by last name. Hide the Address through Phone columns.

LAB EXERCISES

p. Print the filtered datasheet using the wide margin setting in landscape orientation.

q. Remove the filter and unhide the columns.

r. Add your name to the database properties. Close all objects and exit Access.

ARF TRACKING DATABASE ★ ★

3. You have created a database for tracking the animals that come into and go out of the Animal Rescue Foundation. Now you need to modify the database structure and customize field properties to control the data entered by the foundation's volunteers who are assigned this task. You also want to create a form to make it easier for the volunteers to enter the necessary information. Your completed datasheet and form will be similar to those shown here.

a. Open the file ac02_ARF Database and the table Rescues in Datasheet view.

b. Use the Replace command to change the Age field from abbreviations to spelled out information. Make Y = Young, A = Adult, and B = Baby.

c. Use Find to locate ID # R-904. Add the adoption date 6/13/2012.

d. Use Search to locate the animal named **Spreckels**; change the age to **B** and enter **12/01/2012** as the Foster Date.

e. Create a values lookup field to select Boarded, Foster Care, or Adopted. Place the field before the Arrival Date field, with the following specifications:

Field Name:	**Status**
Description:	**Select Boarded, Foster Care, or Adopted**
Field Size:	**15**

f. Make the following additional changes to the database structure:

- Restrict the entries in the Status field to list items only. Make **Boarded** the default value for Status.

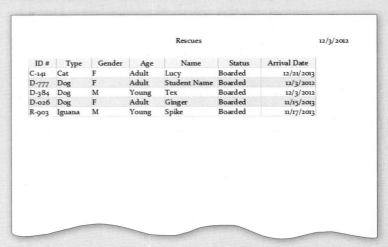

- Add a validation rule and validation text to the Gender field to accept only M or F (male or female). Format the field to display the information in uppercase.

- Change the Age field to a lookup field to accept only the values of Baby, Young, or Adult. Increase the field size to **5**. Restrict the entries to items on the list only.

g. In Datasheet view, complete the data for the Status by entering F (if there is a Foster Date only), A (if there is an adoption date), or B (if there is neither a foster nor an adoption date).

h. Add formatting of your choice to the Datasheet. Change the font of the datasheet to Constantia, 12 point.

i. Best Fit all columns.

j. Use the Form Wizard to create a columnar form. Include all the fields except for the Photo attachment field. Add the fields in their current order and title the form **Animals**.

k. Switch to Form Layout view and make the following changes to the form:

- Choose a theme design style of your choice.
- Apply the stacked layout to all the controls except the form title.
- Insert three columns to the right. Move the Name label and control to the right of the ID text control, in the second empty column.
- Add the Photo attachment field under the Name label, on the right side of the form. Select the attachment control box and the four empty cells beneath it. Merge these cells together.
- Adjust the widths of the empty column, labels, and controls to better fit their contents.

l. Search in Form view to locate the animal named Titus and add the picture ac02_WhiteDog to the Attachment field.

m. Add two records using the new form. Use the ID # **D-384** for the first record and attach the picture of ac02_Tex_dog, a young male dog. In the second record you add, use the ID # **D-777** and enter your name in the Name field. Attach the picture of ac02_Lilly_dog, who is an adult female dog, to your record. For both records, use the current date as the arrival date, and make the status Boarded.

n. Save the form and print the record with your name as the animal name.

o. Filter the Rescues datasheet to display only those animals with a status of Boarded. Sort the filtered datasheet by Type. Hide the Foster Date, Adoption Date, and Photo attachment columns. Print the Rescues datasheet in portrait orientation using the wide margin setting.

p. Unhide all columns. Clear all sorts and remove the filter.

q. Display all object types in the Navigation pane.

r. Identify object dependencies.

s. Add your name to the database properties. Close all objects and exit Access.

LAB EXERCISES

PEPPER RIDGE RENTALS DATABASE ★ ★ ★

4. Pepper Ridge Rentals is a property rental business, and you recently put the rental homes into a database to track the rental properties. The database initially began with basic facts about each home, but now you see the need for more detailed information. A database will be useful to look up any information about the rental, including its location, how many bedrooms and bathrooms, square footage, and date available. You decide to make some additional changes to help with inventory control and make data entry even easier. This will help you find rentals within the desired home size and price range of your clients. When you are finished, your printed database table and form should be similar to the ones shown here.

   a. Open the database file you created in Lab1, PepperRidgeRentals. Save the file as PepperRidgeRentals2.

   b. Open the table Rental Homes.

   c. Add a Currency field after the Sq Footage field. Name the new field **Monthly Rent**.

   d. Add a Memo field at the end of the table and name it **Comments**.

   e. You want to add a new field to show the condition of each home. This field can only contain four possible values: Pets not okay, Pets okay, Horses and pets allowed, or Assistant animals only. Insert a new field after Sq Footage named **Animal Permission**. Use a data type of Lookup and enter the following as list values: **Pets not okay, Pets okay, Horses and pets allowed**, or **Assistant animals only**. Set the field's default value to **Pets not okay**, and limit entries to the list items.

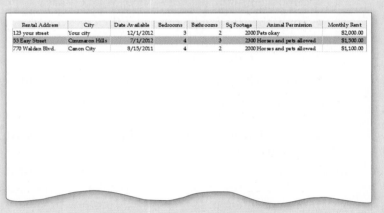

f. In Datasheet view, add two new records:

Rental Address:	770 Walden Blvd.	654 Sunset Lane
City:	Canon	Canon
Date Available:	8/15/2011	7/1/2011
Bedrooms:	4	3
Bathrooms:	2	2
Sq Footage:	2000	1500
Animal Permission:	Horses and pets allowed	Assistant animals only
Monthly Rent:	$1100	$850
Owner's Name:	George Mitchel	Gretchen Heinz
Comments:	Beautiful home with horse barn and corrals	Located in the city in a new subdivision with amenities

g. Widen the fields to best fit the data.

h. Hide the Rental ID, Bedrooms, Bathrooms, Sq Footage, Owner's Name, and Photo Attachment fields.

i. Update the other records with information for the new fields (Monthly Rent, Animal Permission, and Comments):

Record	Monthly Rent	Animal Permission	Comments
1500 Sycamore Lane	$1000	Pets not okay	Townhome with homeowners association rules
53 Easy Street	$1500	Horses and pets allowed	Big ranch house with acreage and horse facilities
221 Cedar Street	$650	Pets okay	Older home close to nice parks
Your street	name your price	Pets okay	your comments

j. Unhide all fields.

k. Find all instances of Canon in the City field and replace with **Canon City**.

l. Insert a new field after the Date Available field named **Rented** with a field size of **1**, data type of Text. Add "**Y**" or "**N**" as a validation rule. Add **Must be Y or N** as the Validation text. Format the field to display in uppercase.

m. Use Search to find the record for 221 Cedar Street. The home has been rented out, so delete the entry in Date Available and type in **Y** for the Rented field. Enter **N** for all other Rented fields.

n. Add formatting of your choice to the datasheet. Change the font of the datasheet to one of your choice. Adjust column widths as needed.

o. Use the Form Wizard to create a form for the Rentals table. Include all of the fields except Rental ID and Photo of Home from the Rentals table, in order. Use the columnar form layout and accept the form name **Rentals**.

p. Switch to Layout view. Select a Theme style. Select the Comments label and text control and apply the stacked layout. Resize the Comments controls so they are the same size as the controls above. Move the Comments stacked control group to the right side of the other fields. Add the Photo of Home form field below the Comments field. Resize the height of the row containing the Photo control so the bottom of the photo box aligns with the bottom of the Owner's Name control. Resize the fields to fit their labels and data.

LAB EXERCISES

q. Use the form to enter another new record with an address of your choice, **Colorado Springs** for the city, and your name as the owner. Include **Pets not okay** for the Animal Permission field, a monthly rent price of **$750**, today's date as the date available, and comments of your choice in the Comments field. Insert the picture ac02_pine_cottage for the Photo of Home field.

r. Preview and print the form for your new record in landscape orientation. Save and close the form.

s. Filter the Rental Homes table to display only those records with Rented N, and Pets okay (hint: select both pets okay and pets allowed options). Hide the Rental ID, Rented, Owner Name, Attachments, and Comments fields. Print the filtered datasheet in landscape orientation with narrow margins.

t. Display all object types in the Navigation pane.

u. Add your name to the database properties as the author. Save the database and exit Access.

KODIAK CONSTRUCTION DATABASE ★ ★ ★

5. Although the database you designed for the expanding Kodiak Construction Company was well received, you have been asked to make several additions and improvements to the original design. In addition, they have asked you to create a form to make the process of entering new records in the database easier. Your completed database table and form will be similar to those shown here.

   a. Open the file ac02_Kodiak Construction.

   b. Open the Clients table and switch to Design view. Insert a new field before the Business Phone field named **Home Phone**. Include a description. Set the field size to **14**.

   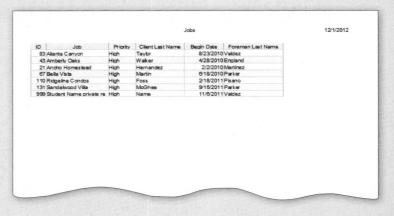

   c. Enter the following Home Phone numbers into the table. Hide the fields between the Last Name and Home Phone fields. Use Find to locate the records. Unhide the columns when you are done.

Last Name	Home Phone
Lopez	(303) 555-3772
Miller	(303) 555-0831
Walker	(303) 555-4613
Young	(303) 555-0912

   d. Change the City column to a Lookup Field data type. Include the following cities as the lookup list values: Aurora, Denver, Glendale, Lakewood, Littleton, and Parker.

   e. Open the City field drop-down list for each record and select a city.

   f. Make the default value for the State field **CO**. Change the format to uppercase.

   Next, you want to add a field for the job priority to the Jobs table. This field can only contain three possible values: High, Normal, or Low. Instead of typing this information in the field, you will make the field a lookup field.

g. Open the Jobs table in Design view and insert the new field named **Priority** after the Job field. Select the Lookup Wizard from the Data Type list. Select the "I will type in the values that I want." option. In column 1, enter **High** in the first cell, **Normal** in the second cell, and **Low** in the third cell. Accept the field name. Set the field's size to **15** and the default value to **Normal**. Limit entries to values from the list.

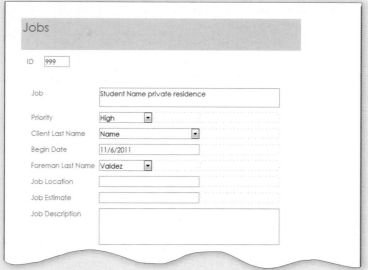

You decide to use the Lookup Wizard for the Client Last Name and Foreman Last Name fields as well because this will save input time and reduce the chance of any entry errors.

h. Create a lookup for the Client Last Name field to obtain its values from the Clients table. Display the Last Name and First Name fields in the lookup. Choose ascending sort order by Last Name. Adjust the column widths for the lookup fields as needed. Use the default name for the label of the lookup field (Client Last Name).

i. In a similar fashion, use the Lookup Wizard to establish the lookup for the Foreman Last Name, using the Foremen table.

j. Switch to Datasheet view, saving your design changes.

k. Open the Priority field drop-down list for each record and select a priority level. Using this same technique, assign clients and foremen to each job.

l. Best Fit the columns.

m. Add formatting of your choice to the Jobs datasheet. Change the font to Arial. Close the table.

n. Enforce referential integrity in the relationships between all tables. Close the Relationships window and save your changes.

o. Use the Form Wizard to create a form for the Jobs table. Include all of the fields from the Jobs table in order. Use the columnar form layout. Accept the default form name (**Jobs**).

p. In Form view, search for the record for R Bar C Ranch. Change the foreman to **Valdez**.

q. In Form Layout view, make the following changes:

- Group the controls in stacked layout, and then move them down about 1″.
- Move the ID field outside the layout.
- Add a column to the right side of the main set of stacked fields.
- Horizontally split the cells containing the text controls for Priority and Begin Date.
- Merge the Job Description text control with the cell to the right.
- Merge the Job text control with the cell on the right.
- Appropriately size the label and text controls for all fields.
- Remove the empty row at the top of the stacked layout.

LAB EXERCISES

r. Change the Theme to one of your choice and then change the Font Theme to Austin (Century Gothic).

s. Create similar forms for the Clients and Foremen tables. Keep the default form layout. Size the ID controls appropriately. The Theme design should match the Job table.

t. Using the Client form, add a new record to the Client table using your first and last names as the client name. Save the changes and close the form.

u. Using the Job form, add a new record to the Jobs table with **999** as the ID and **[your last name] private residence** as the job; select your name as the client last name, priority of high, the current date as the begin date, and a foreman of your choice.

v. Print your record in the form.

w. Open the Jobs table and complete the following:

- Filter the records to display only those with a high priority. Sort the filtered records by Job in ascending sort order.
- Hide the Job Location, Job Estimate, and Job Description columns. Print the filtered Jobs datasheet in landscape orientation.
- Unhide all columns. Clear all sorts and remove the filter.

x. Display all object types in the Navigation pane.

y. Add your name to the database properties. Save and close the database.

ON YOUR OWN

ADVENTURE TRAVEL PACKAGES FORM ★

1. You have heard from the employees of Adventure Travel Tours that the database table you created is a bit unwieldy for them to enter the necessary data because it now contains so many fields that it requires scrolling across the screen to locate them. You decide to create a form that will make entering data not only easier, but more attractive as well. Open the ac02_ATT database. Best fit the columns. Change the order of the Length and Description field columns in Design view. Apply formatting of your choice to the datasheet. Sort the table on Destination in ascending order. Use the Form Wizard to create a form called **Travel Packages** for the Packages table. Use the form to enter five new records with tour package information of your choice (use the newspaper travel section or the Web for ideas). Enter your name as the contact in one of the new records. Print the form containing your name. Print the datasheet in landscape orientation.

AMP ACCOUNT TRACKING ★★

2. While creating the database table for AMP Enterprises, you learned that some employees have been receiving advances for anticipated expenses (such as for travel). You also have been informed that the CEO wants to start tracking the expenses by department. Open the database file AMP Enterprise (Lab 1, On Your Own 5). Add a new field named **Advanced Amount** with a Currency data type to the Employee Expenses table. Also add a Yes/No field named **Payment Made** to record whether or not the expense has been paid, with a corresponding validation rule and message. In the Employee Info table, add a new field named **Department** for the department's charge code number. Update both tables to include appropriate values in the new fields in the existing records. Apply formatting of your choice to the Employee Expenses datasheet. Sort the Employee Expenses table on the Expense Amount field in descending sort order. Close the table, saving the changes. Use the Form Wizard to create a form named **Expenses** for the Employee Expenses table. Include the form title **Your Name Expenses**. Modify the form in Layout view to make it more attractive and user friendly. To test the form, enter a new expense record using the employee ID number for the record containing your name in the Employee Info table. Select your record in the form and print it.

DENTAL PATIENT DATABASE UPDATE ★★

3. The dentist office for which you created a patient database has expanded to include a second dentist and receptionist. The two dentists are Dr. Jones and Dr. Smith. You now need to modify the database to identify required fields and to add a new field that identifies which patient is assigned to which dentist. You also decide that creating a form for the database would make it easier for both you and the other receptionist to enter and locate patient information. Open the Dental Patients database (Lab 1, On Your Own 3) and the Patient Information table. Make the patient identification number, name, and phone number required fields. Add a **Dentist Name** Lookup list field, with the two dentists' names and an appropriate validation rule and message. Update the table to "assign" some of the patients to one of the dentists and some patients to the other dentist. Assign the record containing your name to Dr. Jones. Sort the table by dentist name to see the results of your new assignments. "Reassign" one of the displayed patients and then remove the sort. Filter the table to display only those patients for Dr. Jones. Apply formatting of your choice to the datasheet. Print the filtered datasheet and then remove the filter. Create a form called **Patient Data** for the table using the Form Wizard. Modify the form in Layout view to make it more attractive and user friendly. Enter two new records, one for each of the dentists. Use the Search feature to locate the record that has your name as the patient, and then select and print the displayed record in the form.

LEWIS & LEWIS EMPLOYEE DATABASE ★★

4. You work in the Human Resource Management department at Lewis & Lewis, Inc. You recently created a simple database containing information on each employee's department and work telephone extension. Several of your coworkers also want to use the database. You decide to add a field for the employee's job title and enhance the table. You also want to create a form that will make it easier for others to update the information in the database. Open the ac02_Lewis Personnel database and Phone List table and add the **Job Title** field after the Department field. Update the table to include information in the new field for the existing records (hint: use job titles such as Accounts Payable Clerk, Graphic Design Coordinator, Personnel Manager, etc.). Add a new record that

includes your name and Administrative Assistant for the job title. Apply formatting of your choice to the datasheet. Sort the table by Department and Last Name. Use the Search feature to locate and delete the record for Anna Tai, who has left the company. Print the datasheet in landscape orientation. Remove the sort and close the table, saving the changes. Create a form called **Phone List** for the Phone List table using the Form Wizard. Modify the form using Layout view and place the controls in a more user-friendly order (for example, place the Last Name control to the right of the First Name control.) Enter five new records. Use the Replace command to locate and change the last name for Alexa Hirsch to Alexa **Muirhead**, who has gotten married since you first created the database. Use the Search feature to locate the record form that has your name as the employee. Select and print the displayed record.

TIMELESS TREASURES INVENTORY DATABASE ★ ★ ★

5. You realize that you have left out some very important fields in the Inventory table you created in the Timeless Treasures database (Lab 1, On Your Own 4)—fields that identify the sources where you can obtain the vintage watches your customers are looking for. Repeat your Web search for old watches and note the resources (for example, online shopping services, specialty stores, or individual collectors who are offering these items at online auctions) for the watches in your table. Add a **Source Name** field, a **Source E-mail** field, and a **Source Phone** field to the table. Update the table to include this information in the existing records. Apply formatting of your choice to the datasheet. Sort the records according to the Source Name field and adjust the column widths to accommodate the new information. Print the datasheet. Remove the sort and close the table, saving the changes. Now, to make data entry easier, create a form named **Watches** using the Form Wizard. Modify the arrangement of controls to make the form more visually appealing. Use the form to locate the record with your name as the manufacturer, and then print it.

Objectives

After completing this lab, you will know how to:

1. Evaluate table design.

2. Modify relationships.

3. Enforce referential integrity.

4. Create and modify a simple query.

5. Query two tables.

6. Filter a query.

7. Find unmatched and duplicate records.

8. Create a parameter query.

9. Create reports from tables and queries.

10. Display a Totals row.

11. Modify a report design.

12. Select, move, and size controls.

13. Change page margins.

14. Preview and print a report.

15. Compact and back up a database.

Lifestyle Fitness Club

After modifying the structure of the table of personal data, you have continued to enter many more records. You also have created a second table in the database that contains employee information about location and job titles. Again, the owners are very impressed with the database. They are eager to see how the information in the database can be used.

As you have seen, compiling, storing, and updating information in a database is very useful. The real strength of a database program, however, is its ability to find

the information you need quickly, and to manipulate and analyze it to answer specific questions. You will use the information in the tables to provide the answers to several inquiries about the club's employees. As you learn about the database's analytical features, imagine trying to do the same tasks by hand. How long would it take? Would your results be as accurate or as well presented? In addition, you will create several reports that present the information from the database attractively.

A report created from a multitable query displaying selected fields.

A report showing the relationships between tables.

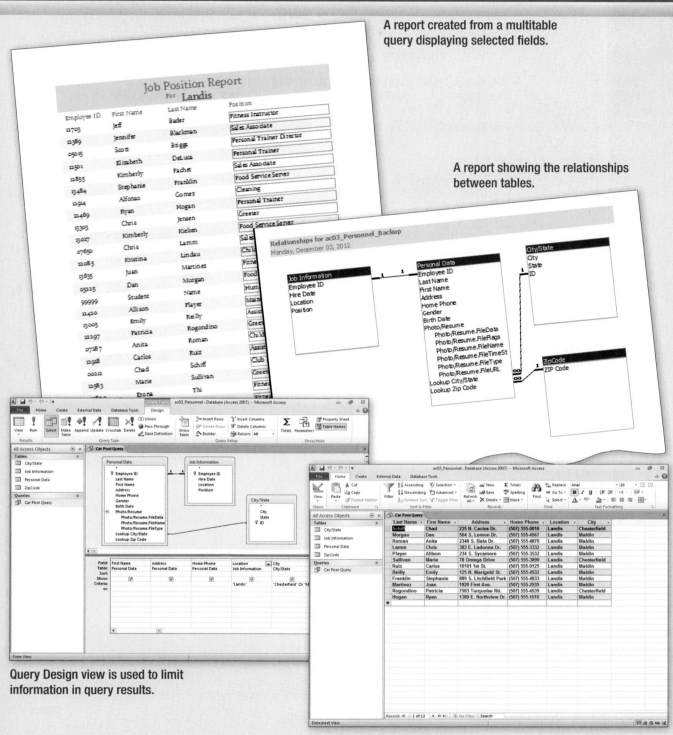

Query Design view is used to limit information in query results.

Creating queries of data limits the information that is displayed in the results.

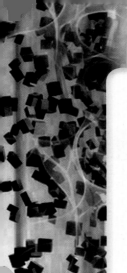

The following concepts will be introduced in this lab:

1 Query A query is a request for specific data contained in a database. Queries are used to view data in different ways, to analyze data, and even to change existing data.

2 Join A join is an association between a field in one table or query and a field of the same data type in another table or query.

3 Query Criteria Query criteria are expressions that are used to restrict the results of a query to display only records that meet certain limiting conditions.

4 Report A report is professional-appearing output generated from tables or queries that may include design elements, groups, and summary information.

Refining the Database Design

You have continued to enter data into the Employee Records table. The updated table has been saved for you as Personal Data in the ac03_Personnel database file.

NOTE Before you begin, you may want to create a backup copy of the ac03_Personnel file by copying and renaming it.

Start Microsoft Access 2010.

Open the ac03_Personnel **database file from your data file location.**

If necessary, click

Enable Content

in response to the Security Warning in the message bar.

Your screen should be similar to Figure 3.1

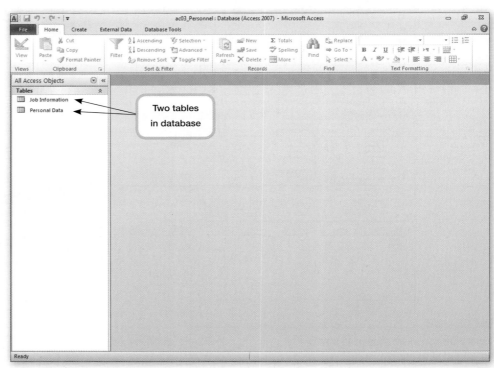

Figure 3.1

The Navigation pane displays the names of two tables in this database: Personal Data and Job Information.

2

- Open the Personal Data table.

- Add your information as record number 70 using your special ID number **99999** and your name. Enter **Maldin** as the city and **92121** as the zip code. Fill in the remaining fields as desired.

- Return to the first field of the first record.

- Hide the Navigation pane.

Your screen should be similar to Figure 3.2

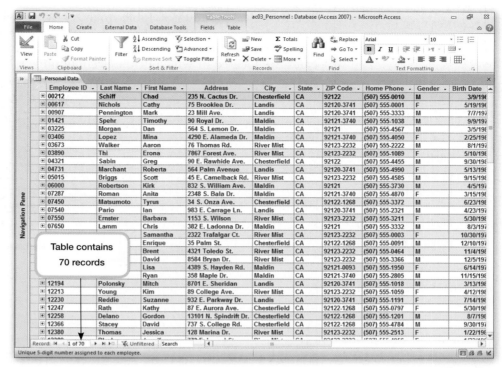

Figure 3.2

EVALUATING TABLE DESIGN

As you continue to use and refine the database, you have noticed that you repeatedly enter the same city, state, and zip code information in the Personal Data table. You decide there may be a better way to organize the table information and will use the Table Analyzer tool to help evaluate the design of the Personal Data table.

1

- Open the Database Tools tab.

- Click  in the Analyze group.

Your screen should be similar to Figure 3.3

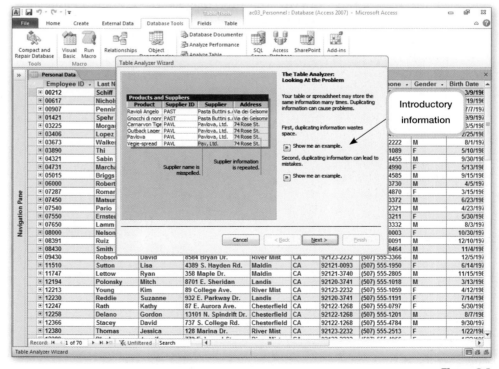

Figure 3.3

The first two windows of Table Analyzer Wizard are introductory pages that review the process that will be used. First, the wizard will analyze the information stored in the table by looking for duplicate information. Then, if duplicates are located, it will split the original table and create new tables to store the information a single time to solve the problem.

Click Next > to see the next introductory page.

Click Next > to move to the first step.

Your screen should be similar to Figure 3.4

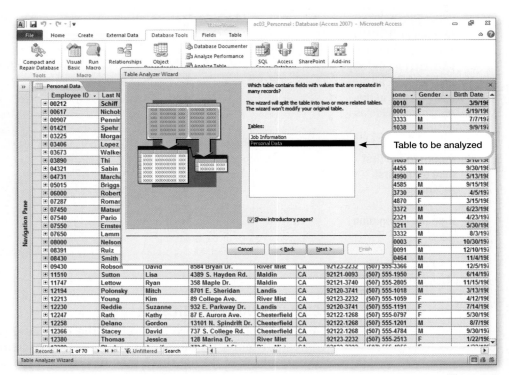

Figure 3.4

In the next two steps, you identify the table you want to evaluate and whether you want the wizard to decide what fields to place in the new table or whether you would rather make that determination yourself.

- Click [Next >] to accept analyzing the Personal Data table.

- Click [Next >] to accept letting the wizard decide.

- If the field names in the Table2 and Table3 list boxes are not visible, increase the length and/or width of the box.

Having Trouble?

Drag the top or bottom border to size the object vertically. Drag the right border to change the object's width.

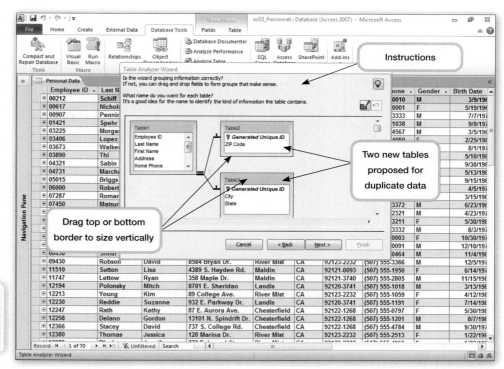

Figure 3.5

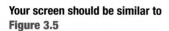

Your screen should be similar to Figure 3.5

The wizard has identified duplicate data in the ZIP Code, City, and State fields and proposes to move these fields into two additional tables—one for ZIP Codes and the other for city and state—where the information would be stored only once. The instructions at the top of the Table Analyzer Wizard box ask you to revise the grouping if needed and to create names for the tables. You agree that creating the two new tables will prevent duplicate data. You will then rename the new tables and move to the next step.

4

- Increase the length of the Table1 list to display all the field names.

- Double-click on the Table2 title bar and enter **ZipCode** as the table name.

- Click [OK].

- In the same manner, enter **City/State** as the table name for Table 3.

- Click [Next >] to move to the next step.

Your screen should be similar to Figure 3.6

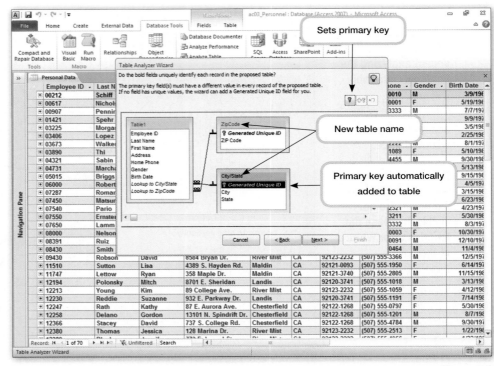

Figure 3.6

This step identifies the fields to use as primary keys in the new tables by bolding the field names. The wizard automatically added a Generated Unique ID field (AutoNumber) to the ZIPCode and City/State tables and defined it as the primary key field. In both tables, this field is unnecessary because the values in the City and ZIP Codes fields are unique and therefore can be used as the primary key fields. You will define the City and ZIP Code fields as the primary key field in each table, which will also remove the Unique ID field.

5

- Select the ZIP Code field and then click [🔑].

- In the same manner change the City field to the primary key field.

- Click [Next >] to move to the next step.

Your screen should be similar to Figure 3.7

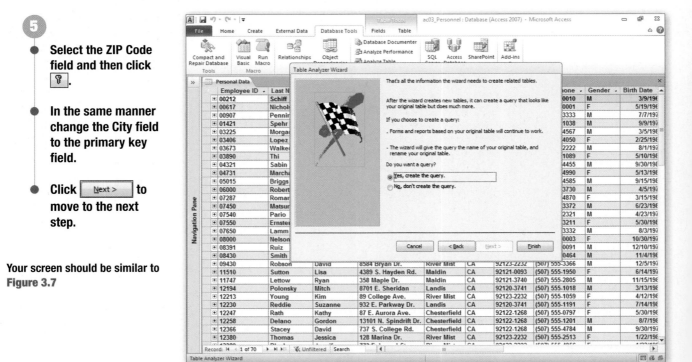

Figure 3.7

The final wizard step asks if you want to create a query. You will be learning about queries shortly, so you will not create a query at this time.

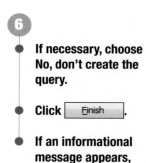

● If necessary, choose No, don't create the query.

● Click [Finish].

● If an informational message appears, click [OK] to continue.

Your screen should be similar to Figure 3.8

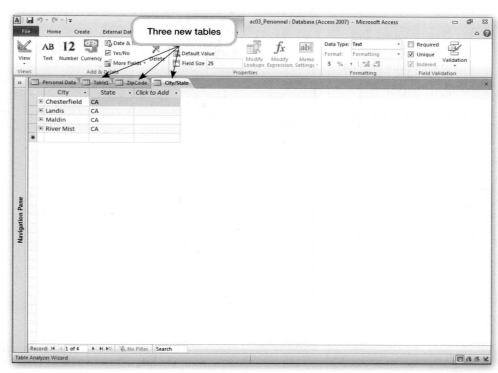

Figure 3.8

There are now three new tables open: City/State, ZipCode, and Table1. Table1 was automatically created by the Table Analyzer Wizard. It is a replica of the Personal Data table but with lookup fields for the City/State and ZipCode tables. The City/State table is currently displayed and consists of two fields, City and State with the City field as the primary key field. You will take a look at the ZipCode table, which only contains the ZIP Code field set as the primary key, and then examine Table1. The primary key fields in the City/State and Zip-Code tables have been associated with the data in the new Table1.

7

- Display the ZipCode table.

- Display Table1 and move to the Lookup to City/State field for the first record.

- Display the Lookup to City/State field lookup list.

Your screen should be similar to Figure 3.9

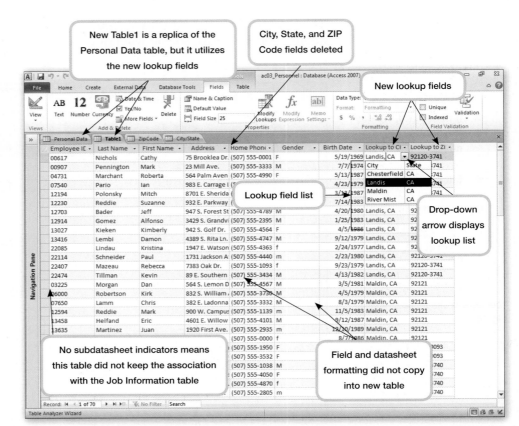

Figure 3.9

Table1 displays the ZIP code, city, and state information as lookup fields with data from their associated tables. Clicking the drop-down arrow in a lookup field displays the list of possible choices from the originating table. The individual fields that stored this information for each record have been deleted from Table1. You can now see how using separate tables to store this data saves space by not repeating the information and also makes data entry easier and more accurate.

CREATING A TABLE LIST LOOKUP FIELD

Now your database contains two tables that hold duplicate data, Table1 and Personal Data, and you need to decide which table to keep. You notice that Table1 did not maintain the association to the Job Information table and the field and datasheet formatting. Rather than make these same changes again to Table1, you decide to modify the Personal Data table by creating lookup fields to the City/State and ZipCode tables.

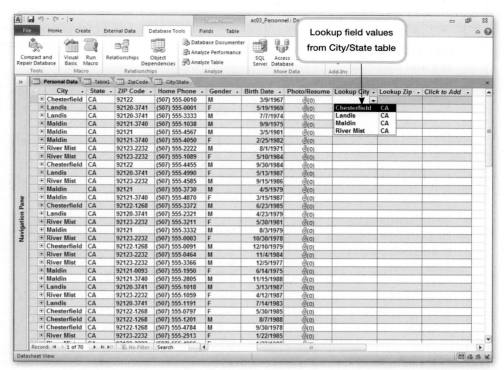

Figure 3.10

1

- Display the Personal Data table.

- Scroll to the right to display the last column.

- Open on the *Click to Add* menu and choose Lookup & Relationship.

- Run the Lookup Wizard and specify the following settings:

  - Look up the values in a table or query.

  - Use the City/State table.

  - Add the City and State fields to the Selected Fields list.

  - Specify ascending sort order by City.

  - Clear the checkmark in Hide key column and size the State column to best fit.

  - Choose the City field as the value to store in the database.

  - Enter the field name **Lookup City/State**

- Repeat the steps to add a lookup field for the ZIP Code using the ZipCode table to look up the values and the ZIP Code field in the Selected Fields list. Name the field **Lookup Zip Code**

- Click in the Lookup City/State field for the first record and display the drop-down list.

Your screen should be similar to Figure 3.10

You have added two new lookup fields to the table. Now you need to add the data for these fields. Instead of selecting the City and ZIP code for each record, you will copy the data from the existing City and ZIP Code field columns into the new lookup columns. Then, because you will no longer need them, you will delete the original City, State, and ZIP Code fields. Finally, you will move the Lookup field columns after the Address field column.

Copy the data in the City field column to the Lookup City/State column.

Having Trouble?

Remember: To select an entire column, click on its column heading when the mouse pointer is ⬇.

Copy the data in the ZIP Code field column to the Lookup Zip Code column.

Delete the City, State, and ZIP Code columns.

Select both lookup field columns and move them to the right of the Address field.

Having Trouble?

Refer to the Moving a Field topic in Lab 1 to review this feature.

Add a caption of City for the Lookup City/State field.

Having Trouble?

Instead of changing the caption in Design view, use the

🗐 Name & Caption button in the Fields tab.

Add the caption of Zip Code for the Lookup Zip Code field.

Best fit the City and Zip Code columns.

Your screen should be similar to Figure 3.11

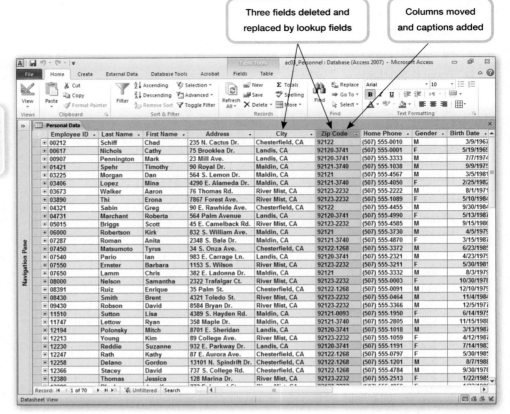

Three fields deleted and replaced by lookup fields

Columns moved and captions added

Figure 3.11

DELETING A TABLE

Now that the Personal Data table is modified, you will delete the duplicate Table1.

1

- Close all tables, saving layout changes when prompted.

- Display the Navigation pane.

- Select Table1 and click ✕ Delete in the Records group of the Home tab.

- Click Yes to confirm the deletion from all groups.

Another Method

You also could press Delete or choose Delete from the object's shortcut menu.

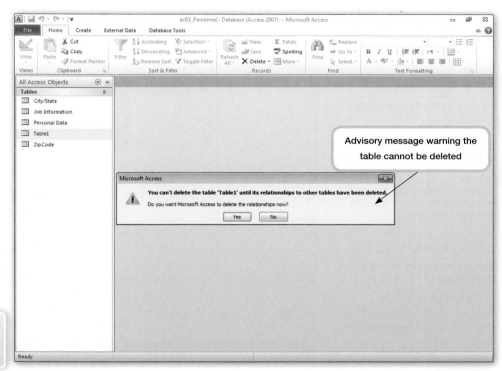

Figure 3.12

Your screen should be similar to Figure 3.12

The advisory message warns that the table cannot be deleted until its relationships to other tables have been deleted. Rather than have the program remove the relationships for you, you will look at the relationships that have been created between all tables first.

2

- Click No.

- Click OK.

Defining and Modifying Relationships

When you create lookup fields, Access automatically establishes relationships between the tables. You will open the Relationships window to edit these relationships.

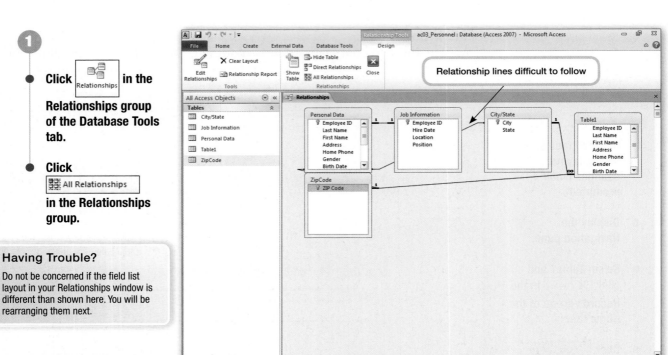

Step 1

● Click [Relationships] in the **Relationships group of the Database Tools tab.**

● Click [All Relationships] **in the Relationships group.**

Having Trouble?

Do not be concerned if the field list layout in your Relationships window is different than shown here. You will be rearranging them next.

Your screen should be similar to Figure 3.13

Figure 3.13

When the field lists for each table display, the relationship lines show how the tables are associated. However, the lines may appear tangled and untraceable when the tables first display. To see the relationships better, you will rearrange and size the field lists in the window. The field list can be moved by dragging the title bar and sized by dragging the border.

2

● Click on the Job Information field list title bar, and drag the field list to the left of the Personal Data field list.

● Continue to move the field lists until they are in the locations shown in Figure 3.14.

● Drag the bottom border of the Personal Data field list down so that all fields are displayed.

● Increase the length of the Table1 field list so that all fields are displayed.

Your screen should be similar to Figure 3.14

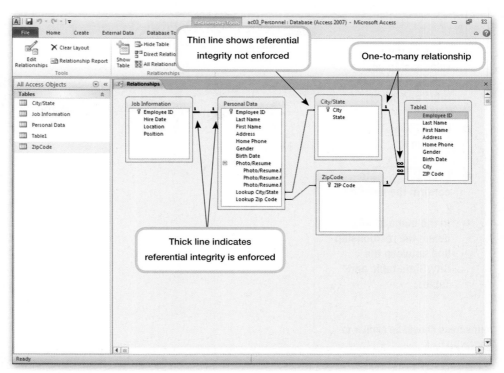

Figure 3.14

Having Trouble?

Refer to the Creating Relationships section of Lab 1 to review this feature.

Now it is easier to follow the relationship lines. The Personal Data and Job Information tables are related by the Employee ID key fields and are connected by a relationship line indicating they have a one-to-one relationship. This relationship was established when you created the Job Information table.

There is also a relationship line between the Lookup Zip Code field in the Personal Data table and the ZIP Code field in the ZipCode table. A thin line between common fields shows that the relationship does not support referential integrity. The third relationship that exists is between the Lookup City/State field and the City field in the City/State table.

Lastly, the ZIP Code field in the ZipCode table and the City field in the City/State table connect to their matching fields in Table1. These lines are thicker at both ends, which indicates referential integrity has been enforced. It also displays a 1 at one end of the line and an infinity symbol (∞) over the other end. This tells you the relationship is a one-to-many type relationship.

DELETING RELATIONSHIPS

The first relationship changes you want to make are to remove the relationships between Table1 and the City/State and ZipCode tables so that you can delete Table1. To edit or delete a relationship, click on the relationship line to select it. It will appear thicker to show it is selected. Then it can be modified.

- Click on the relationship line between the ZipCode table and Table1.

- Press Delete to remove it.

- Click Yes to confirm the deletion.

- In the same manner, delete the relationship line between the City/State table and Table1.

Your screen should be similar to Figure 3.15

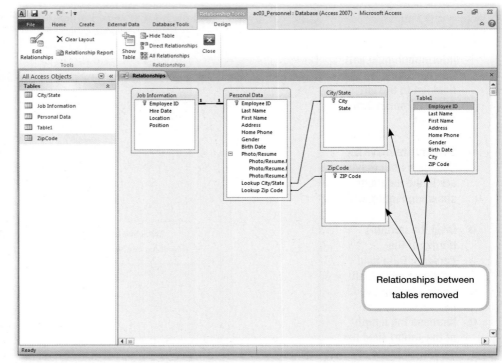

Relationships between tables removed

Figure 3.15

The relationship lines have been removed between the tables. Now you can delete the table.

- Click on the Table1 field list to select it and then press Delete.

Your screen should be similar to Figure 3.16

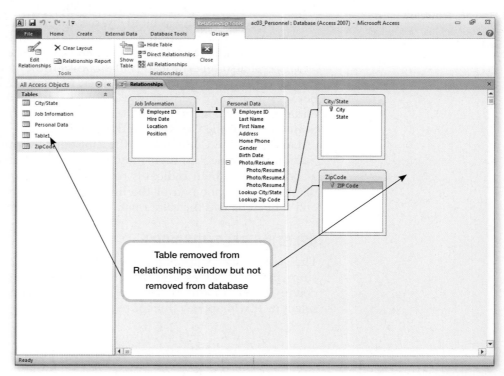

Table removed from Relationships window but not removed from database

Figure 3.16

The Table1 field list is removed from the Relationships window. However, the Table1 object has not been removed from the Navigation pane, indicating that the table has not been deleted from the database. Now that the relationships have been removed from Table1, you can delete the actual table.

3

- **Right-click Table1 in the Navigation Pane.**

- **Choose Delete from the shortcut menu.**

- **Click** Yes **to confirm deleting the table.**

Your screen should be similar to Figure 3.17

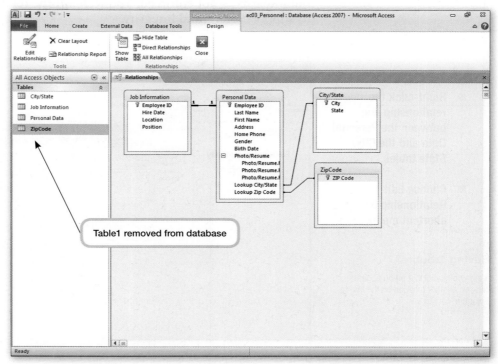

Figure 3.17

Table1 no longer appears in the Tables list in the Navigation Pane, showing that it has been deleted from the database.

EDITING RELATIONSHIPS TO ENFORCE REFERENTIAL INTEGRITY

The next change you want to make is to enforce referential integrity between the tables to ensure that the relationships are valid and that related data is not accidentally changed or deleted. The thin relationship lines connecting the City/State and ZIP Code fields to the Personal Data table indicate that referential integrity is not enforced. You will edit the relationships between the tables to support referential integrity.

Having Trouble?

Refer to the Defining Relationships section of Lab 1 to review referential integrity.

- **Right-click the relationship line between the Personal Data and the City/State tables.**

- **Choose Edit Relationship from the shortcut menu.**

Having Trouble?

If the wrong shortcut menu appears, click on another location on the line to try again.

Another Method

You also can double-click the relationship line or click  in the Tools group to open the Edit Relationships dialog box.

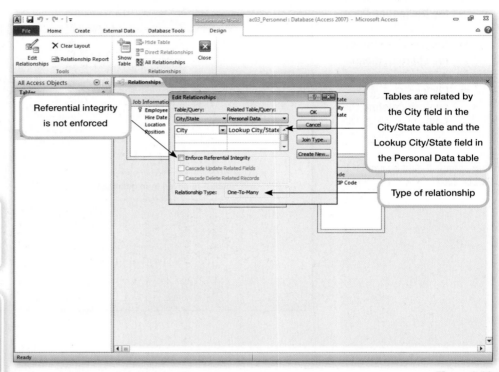

Figure 3.18

Your screen should be similar to Figure 3.18

The Edit Relationships dialog box shows the City field in the City/State table is related to the Lookup City/State field in the Personal Data table. In addition, you can see the relationship type is one-to-many.

You will enforce referential integrity to prevent users from entering a city or ZIP code in the Personal Data table that is not in the associated lookup table. To enter a new city or ZIP code would require that the new city or ZIP code values be entered in the lookup tables first. This prevents cities and ZIP codes that are not in the lookup tables from being used in the Personal Data table and would maintain an accurate lookup field list.

2

- Choose Enforce Referential Integrity.

- Click [OK].

- In a similar manner, edit the relationship line between the Personal Data table and the ZipCode table to enforce referential integrity.

- Click on the ZipCode field list to deselect the relationship line.

Your screen should be similar to Figure 3.19

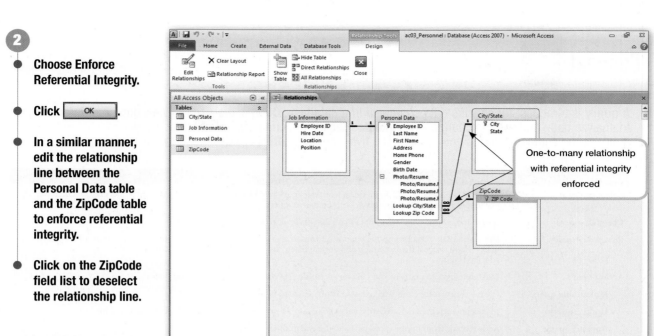

Figure 3.19

Once referential integrity is enforced, the relationship line changes and identifies the type of relationship.

3

- Click [Close] to close the Relationships window.

- Click [Yes] in response to the prompt to save the layout.

The relationship and layout changes are saved. Now that referential integrity is enforced between these tables, a warning message will automatically be displayed if one of the rules is broken while entering or editing data, and you will not be allowed to complete the action you are trying to do.

Creating a Query

You are ready to start gathering information from the database. Your fellow employee, Juan, would like to create a car pool and has enlisted your help as the database expert. In Lab 2, you were able to filter the table to obtain the information needed for the car pool list, but it contained more data about each employee than someone would need, or should have access to. To obtain the exact information you need to give Juan for his car pool, you will use a query.

Concept 1 Query

A **query** is a request for specific data contained in a database. Queries are used to view data in different ways, to analyze data, and even to change existing data. Because queries are based on tables, you also can use a query as the source for forms and reports. The five types of queries are described in the following table.

Query Type	Description
Select query	Retrieves the specific data you request from one or more tables, then displays the data in a query datasheet in the order you specify. This is the most common type of query.
Crosstab query	Summarizes large amounts of data in an easy-to-read, row-and-column format.
Parameter query	Displays a dialog box prompting you for information, such as the criteria for locating data. For example, a parameter query might request the beginning and ending dates, then display all records matching dates between the two specified values.
Action query	Makes changes to many records in one operation. There are four types of action queries:
Make-table query	Creates a new table from selected data in one or more tables.
Update query	Makes update changes to records, when, for example, you need to raise salaries of all sales staff by 7 percent.
Append query	Adds records from one or more tables to the end of other tables.
Delete query	Deletes records from a table or tables.
SQL query	Creates a query using SQL (Structured Query Language), an advanced programming language used in Access.

You will create a simple select query to obtain the results for the car pool. Creating a query adds a query object to the database file. It is a named object, just like a form, that can be opened, viewed, and modified at any time.

USING THE QUERY WIZARD

Query Design view or the Query Wizard can be used to create a query. The process is much like creating a table or form. You will first use the Query Wizard to guide you through the steps. Selecting the table object in the Navigation Pane will help start the process in the right direction but is not a required step.

1

- **Click the Personal Data table object in the Navigation Pane.**

- **Open the Create tab and click** Query Wizard **in the Queries group.**

Your screen should be similar to Figure 3.20

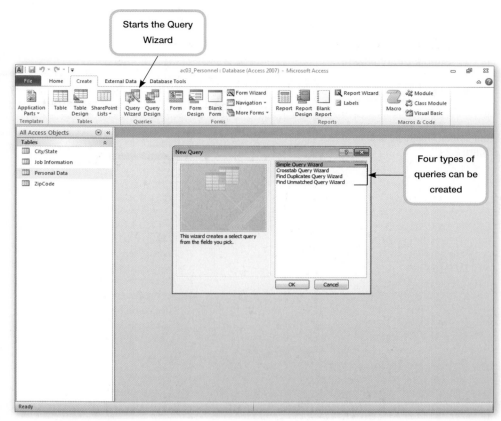

Starts the Query Wizard

Four types of queries can be created

Figure 3.20

From the New Query dialog box, you select the type of query you want to create using the wizard.

Query Wizard	Type of Query
Simple	Select query.
Crosstab	Crosstab query.
Find Duplicates	Locates all records that contain duplicate values in one or more fields in the specified tables.
Find Unmatched	Locates records in one table that do not have records in another. For example, you could locate all employees in one table who have no hours worked in another table.

You will use the Simple Query Wizard to create a select query to see if it gives you the results you want.

2

● If necessary, select Simple Query Wizard.

● Click [OK].

Your screen should be similar to Figure 3.21

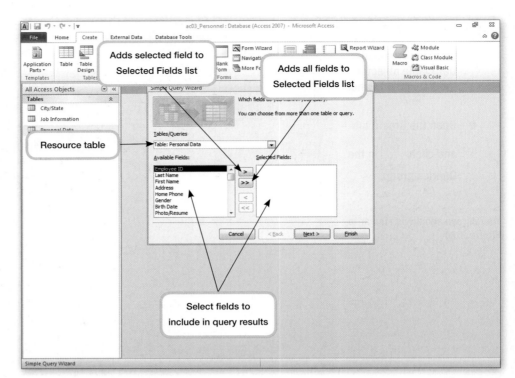

Figure 3.21

In the first Simple Query Wizard dialog box, you specify the resource table that will be used to supply the data and the fields that you want displayed in the query result, just as you did when creating a form. You will use the Personal Data table as the resource table and select the fields you want displayed in the query output.

3

● If necessary, select the Personal Data table from the Tables/Queries drop-down list.

● Add the Last Name, First Name, Address, Lookup City/State and Home Phone fields to the Selected Fields list in that order.

Additional Information

The quickest way to add a field to the Selected Fields list is to double-click its field name in the Available Fields list.

● Click [Next >].

Your screen should be similar to Figure 3.22

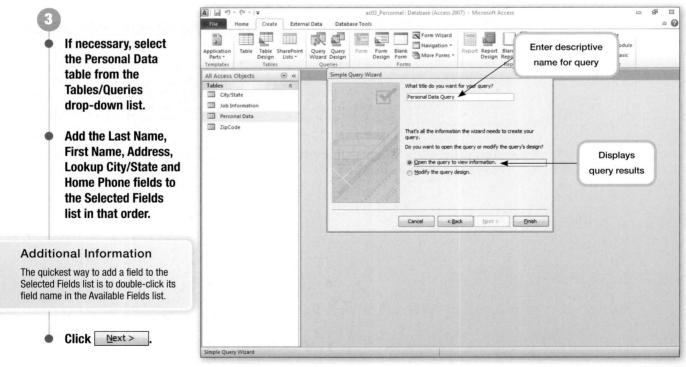

Figure 3.22

In the last Simple Query Wizard dialog box, you specify a name for your query and whether you want to open it to see the results or modify it in Design view. You also can have Access display Help messages while you are working on your query by clicking the corresponding box at the bottom of this wizard screen. You decide that you just want to display the query results, and you want to give the query a name that will identify it.

4

● Replace the suggested title in the text box with Car Pool Query

● Click [Finish].

Your screen should be similar to Figure 3.23

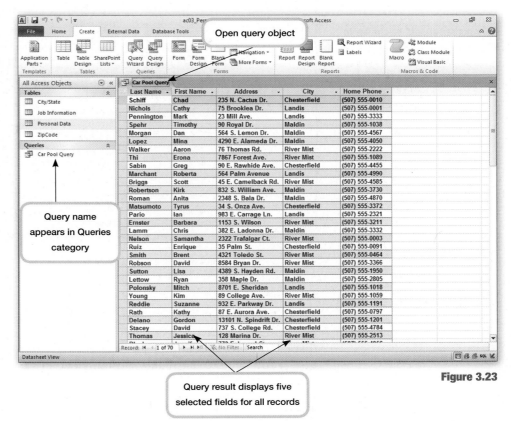

Figure 3.23

The query result displays the five specified fields for all records in the table in a new query datasheet object. The object's tab displays the query name. The Navigation pane also displays the name of the new query object in the Queries category.

FILTERING A QUERY

Although the query result displays only the fields you want to see, it includes all the records in the table. To display only those records with the cities needed for the car pool information for Juan, you will filter the query results.

Having Trouble?

Refer to the Filtering a Table section of Lab 2 to review this feature.

1

Filter the query to display only records with a city name of Chesterfield or Maldin.

Your screen should be similar to Figure 3.24

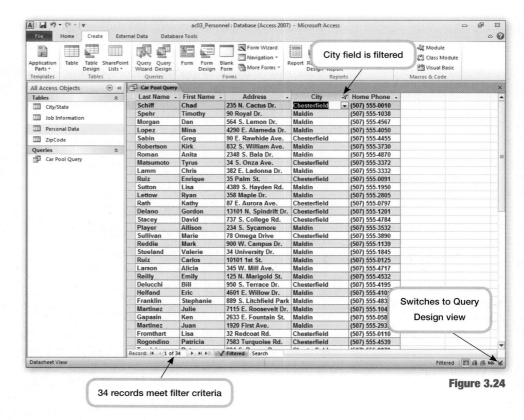

Figure 3.24

34 records meet filter criteria

Now the Car Pool Query results display 34 records. Although these results are close to what you need, you are still not satisfied. You want the results to display the work location as well as the city. To make these refinements to the query, you need to use Query Design view.

2

Click ⬚ Design View in the status bar to switch to Query Design view.

Your screen should be similar to Figure 3.25

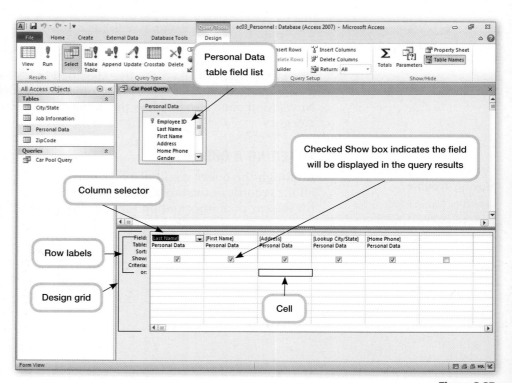

Figure 3.25

USING QUERY DESIGN VIEW

Query Design view can be used to create a new query as well as modify the structure of an existing query. This view automatically displays the Query Tools Design tab, which contains commands that are used to create, modify, and run queries.

Query Design view is divided into two areas. The upper area displays a list box of all the fields in the selected table. This is called the **field list**. The lower portion of the window displays the **design grid** where you enter the settings that define the query. Each column in the grid holds the information about each field to be included in the query datasheet. The design grid automatically displays the fields that are specified when a query is created using the Query Wizard.

Above the field names is a narrow bar called the **column selector bar**, which is used to select an entire column. Each **row label** identifies the type of information that can be entered. The intersection of a column and row creates a cell where you enter expressions to obtain the query results you need.

The boxes in the Show row are called Show boxes. The **Show box** for a field lets you specify whether you want that field displayed in the query result. A checked box indicates that the field will be displayed; an unchecked box means that it will not.

ADDING A SECOND TABLE TO THE QUERY

To display the work location information for each employee in the query results, you need to add the Job Information table to the query design. A query that uses information from two or more tables to get the results is called a **multitable query**.

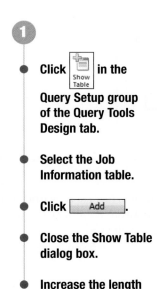

1

- Click 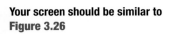 in the Query Setup group of the Query Tools Design tab.

- Select the Job Information table.

- Click **Add**.

- Close the Show Table dialog box.

- Increase the length of the Personal Data field list to display all the fields.

Your screen should be similar to Figure 3.26

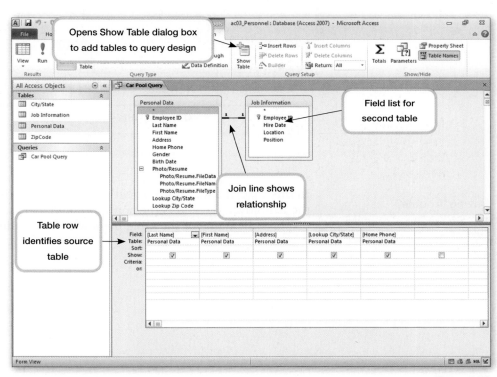

Figure 3.26

The field list for the Job Information table has been added to the Query Design window. When multiple tables are added to a query, Access automatically creates joins between the tables.

Concept 2 Join

A **join** is an association that is created in a query between a field in one table or query and a field of the same data type in another table or query. The join is based on the relationships that have already been defined between tables. A **join line** between the field lists identifies the fields on which the relationship is based.

If a table did not already have a relationship defined, a join would be created between common fields in the tables if one of the common fields is a primary key. If the common fields have different names, however, Access does not automatically create the join. In those cases, you would create the join between the tables using the same procedure that is used to create table relationships.

The difference between a relationship line and a join line in a query is that the join line creates a temporary relationship that establishes rules that the data must match to be included in the query results. Joins also specify that each pair of rows that satisfies the join conditions will be combined in the results to form a single row.

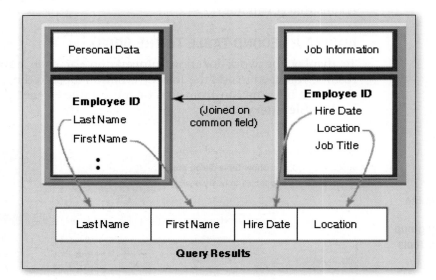

In this case, the join line correctly indicates that the tables are related and that the Employee ID field is the common field. Notice the Table row in the grid. It displays the name of the table from which each field is selected.

ADDING FIELDS

You want the query results to display the work location for each record. To do this, you need to add the Location field from the Job Information field list to the design grid. You can use the following methods to add fields to the design grid:

- Select the field name and drag it from the field list to the grid. To select several adjacent fields, press ⇧Shift while you click the field names. To select nonadjacent fields, press Ctrl while clicking the field names. To select all fields, double-click the field list title bar. You can then drag all the selected fields into the grid, and Access will place each field in a separate column.

- Double-click on the field name. The field is added to the next available column in the grid.

- Select the field cell drop-down arrow in the grid, and then choose the field name.

In addition, if you select the asterisk in the field list and add it to the grid, Access displays the table or query name in the field row followed by a period and asterisk. This indicates that all fields in the table will be included in the query results. Also, using this feature will automatically include any new fields that may later be added to the table and will exclude deleted fields. You cannot sort records or specify criteria for fields, however, unless you also add those fields individually to the design grid.

1

● **Double-click Location in the Job Information field list to add it to the grid.**

Your screen should be similar to Figure 3.27

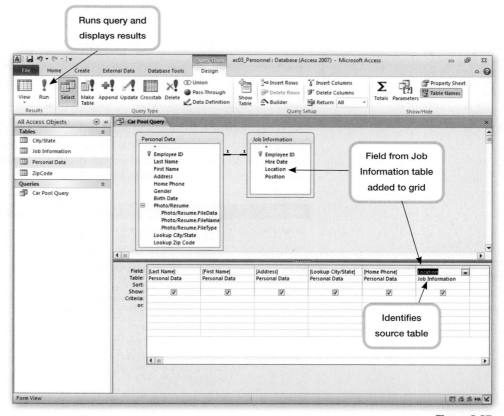

Figure 3.27

Notice the Table row displays the name of the table from which the Location field was drawn. Sometimes when multiple tables are specified in a query, they have fields with the same names. For example, two tables may have fields named Address; however, the address in one table may be a personal address and the one in the other table may be a business address. It is important to select the appropriate field from a table that contains the data you want to appear in the query. The Table row makes it clear from which table a field was drawn.

Now you want to see the query results. To do this, you run the query.

● Click [Run] in the **Results group of the Query Tools Design tab.**

Your screen should be similar to Figure 3.28

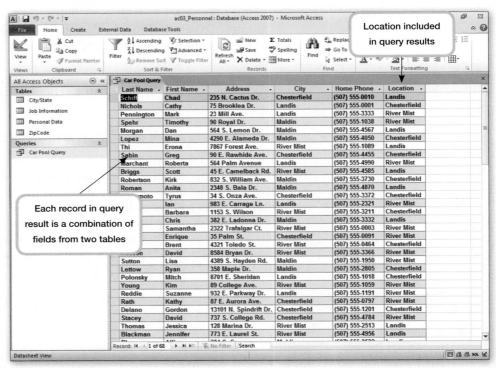

Figure 3.28

The work location for each record is displayed in the results. Now each record in the query results datasheet shows information from both tables. This is because of the type of join used in the query. There are three basic types of joins, as described in the following table.

Join Type	Description
Inner join	Tells a query that rows from one of the joined tables correspond to rows in the other table on the basis of the data in the joined fields. Checks for matching values in the joined fields; when it finds matches, it combines the records and displays them as one record in the query results.
Outer join	Tells a query that although some of the rows on both sides of the join correspond exactly, the query should include all rows from one table even if there is no match in the other table. Each matching record from two tables is combined into one record in the query results. One table contributes all of its records even if the values in its joined field do not match the field values in the other table. Outer joins can be left outer joins or right outer joins. In a query with a left outer join, all rows in the left table are included in the results, and only those rows from the other table where the joining field contains values common to both tables are included. The reverse is true with a right outer join.
Unequal joins	Records to be included in the query results are based on the value in one join field being greater than, less than, not equal to, greater than or equal to, or less than or equal to the value in the other join field.

In a query, the default join type is an inner join. In this case, it checked for matching values in the Employee ID fields, combined matching records, and displayed them as one record in the query result.

Having Trouble?

See Concept 4, Expression, in Lab 2 to review this feature.

SPECIFYING QUERY CRITERIA

You have created a query that displays the employees' names, cities, and work locations. However, you only want to display those with a work location in Landis. You can limit the results of a query by specifying query criteria in the query design grid.

Concept 3   Query Criteria

Query criteria are expressions that are used to restrict the results of a query to display only records that meet certain limiting conditions. In addition to comparison operators that are commonly used in expressions, other commonly used criteria are described in the following table.

Criterion	Description
Is Null	This can be used to find any records where field contents are empty, or "null."
Is Not Null	Returns records only where there is a value in the field.
Not	Return all results *except* those meeting the Not criteria.
DateDiff	Used with Date/Time fields to determine the difference in time between dates.
Like	Returns records where there is a match in content.
Not Like	Returns records that do not contain the text string.

The Criteria row in the query design grid is used to enter the query criteria. Entering the **criteria expression** is similar to using a formula and may contain constants, field names, and/or operators. To instruct the query to locate records meeting multiple criteria, also called **compound criteria**, you use the **AND** or **OR operators**. Using AND narrows the search because a record must meet both conditions to be included. This condition is established by typing the word "and" in a field's Criteria cell as part of its criteria expression. It is also established when you enter criteria in different fields in the design grid. Using OR broadens the search because any record meeting either condition is included in the output. This condition is established by typing the word "or" in a field's Criteria cell or by entering the first criteria expression in the first Criteria cell for the field and the second expression in the Or criteria row cell for the same field.

The following table shows some sample query criteria and their results.

Criteria	Result
DateDiff ("yyyy", [BirthDate], Date()) > 40	Determines the difference between today's year and the BirthDate field. If the difference is greater than 40, the corresponding records will display.
Not Like M*	Returns records for all states whose names start with a character other than "M".
Like "*9.99"	Returns records where the price ends with "9.99", such as $9.99, $19.99, $29.99, and so on.
>= "Canada"	Returns a list of countries starting with Canada and ascending through the rest of the alphabet.
Not "Smith"	Returns all records with names other than Smith.
1 OR 2	Returns all records with either a 1 or a 2 in the selected field.
"Doctor" AND "Denver"	Returns only those records that have the text string of Doctor and Denver within the same record.
"Mi*"	Finds all words starting with the letters "Mi". Example: Michigan, Missouri, Minnesota.
"*Main*"	Finds all records with that contain the text "Main" within it. Example: 590 Main Street, 11233 W. Mainland Dr.

You will enter the query criteria in the Criteria row of the Location column to restrict the query results to only those records where the location is Landis. It is not necessary to enter = (equal to) in the criteria because it is the assumed comparison operator.

1

- Display the query in Design view again.

- Move to the Location Criteria cell.

Another Method

As with other Access tables and forms, you can use ←Enter, Tab⇄, and the arrow keys to move from cell to cell in the query design grid.

- Type **Landis**

- Press ←Enter.

Additional Information

The criteria expression is not case-sensitive.

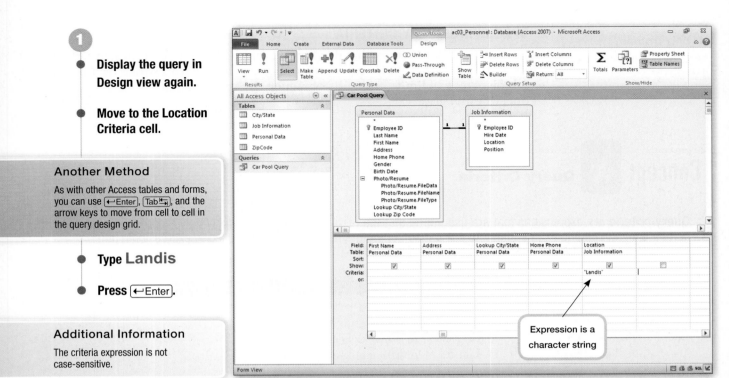

Figure 3.29

Your screen should be similar to Figure 3.29

The query criterion is enclosed in quotation marks because it is a character string. To display the query results, you will run the query. Another way to run a query is to change to Datasheet view.

2

- Click 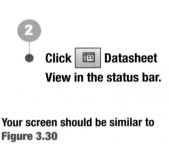 Datasheet View in the status bar.

Your screen should be similar to Figure 3.30

Figure 3.30

Now the query datasheet displays 23 records meeting the location criterion. However, the results do not show only those who reside in Chesterfield or Maldin and commute to the Landis location. You could apply a filter for these cities, but each time you run the query, you would need to reapply the filter. Rather than do this, you decide to specify the criteria in the query design so it will automatically return the results you want each time the query is run.

To include those who live in Chesterfield and Maldin, you will add a second criterion to the City field. Because you want to display the records for employees who live in either city, you will use the OR operator.

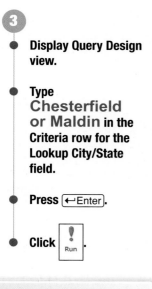

- **Display Query Design view.**

- **Type Chesterfield or Maldin in the Criteria row for the Lookup City/State field.**

- **Press** ⏎Enter.

- **Click** 🔴Run.

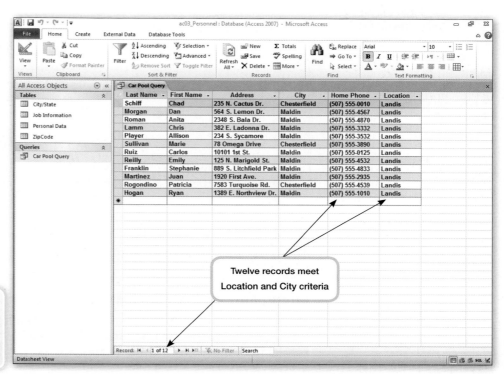

Twelve records meet Location and City criteria

Figure 3.31

Your screen should be similar to Figure 3.31

The results are closer to what you need to create the car pool list. The last step is to exclude those who do not need a car pool because they live close to the Landis work location, in the ZIP code 92121-3740. You will need to add the Lookup ZIP Code field to the query grid and then enter the criteria to exclude the ZIP code of 92121-3740. Then you will run the query.

● **Switch to Design view.**

● **Add the Lookup ZIP Code field from the Personal Data field list to the query grid.**

● **Enter <>92121-3740 in the ZIP Code Criteria cell.**

● **Run the query.**

Your screen should be similar to Figure 3.32

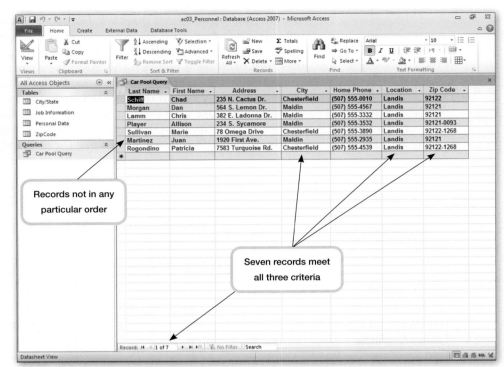

Records not in any particular order

Seven records meet all three criteria

Figure 3.32

The query located seven records that met the specified criteria, and you are pleased with the results so far.

HIDING AND SORTING COLUMNS

However, you still want to make a few additional changes to the query design. You do not want the Zip Code fields displayed in the results and would like the results to be sorted by last name and city.

1

- Switch to Design view.

- Click the Show box of the Lookup Zip Code field to clear the checkmark.

- Click in the Sort row of the Last Name

Having Trouble?

Scroll the grid to bring field columns into view.

field.
- Open the Sort drop-down menu and choose Ascending.

- Hide the Navigation Pane so you can see all the fields in the query grid.

Your screen should be similar to Figure 3.33

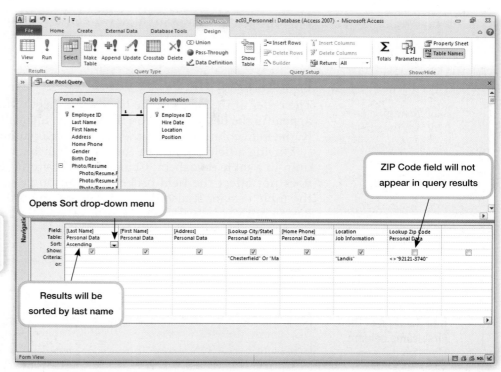

Figure 3.33

Now you can display the results.

2

- Run the query.

Your screen should be similar to Figure 3.34

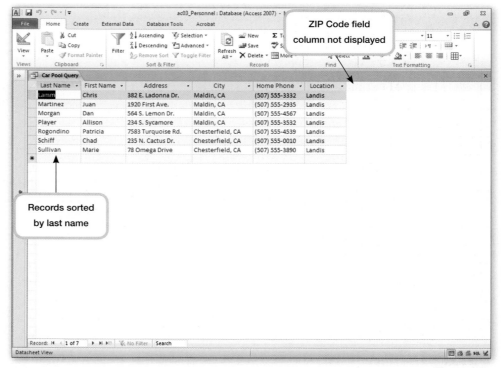

Figure 3.34

The query result shows that seven employees meet all the criteria. The ZIP Code field is not displayed, and last names are sorted in ascending alphabetical order.

REARRANGING THE QUERY DATASHEET

The order of the fields in the query datasheet reflects the order in which they appear in the design grid. You think the results will be easier to read if the Last Name field column follows the First Name column.

Moving a field column in the query datasheet is the same as moving a column in a table datasheet. Changing the column order in the query datasheet does not affect the field order in the resource table, which is controlled by the table design. It also does not change the order of the fields in the query design grid.

- Select the Last Name column and move it to the right of the First Name column.

Another Method

You also could move the field columns in the design grid and then run the query to obtain the same results.

Your screen should be similar to Figure 3.35

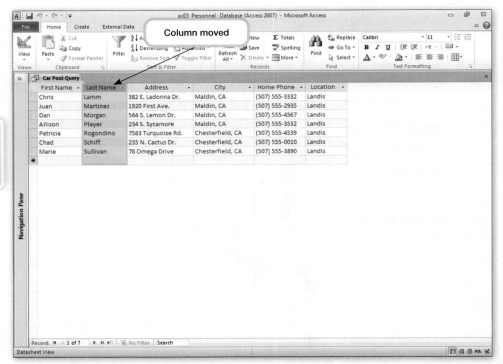

Figure 3.35

This is the information Juan needs to form his car pool. However, as you look at the results, you realize your record should have been included in the list because you live in Maldin and work at the Landis location. You need to determine why your record was not included.

FINDING UNMATCHED RECORDS

When working with a database containing several tables, occasionally a record may be created in one table without any correlating data entered into the corresponding table. This can happen accidentally (for example, when the data entry person forgets to update the related table) or on purpose (when a customer may not have an order pending). The Find Unmatched query is a helpful tool that will locate records in one table that do not have related records in another table. You will use the Find Unmatched query to locate any records that are missing corresponding information in the Job Information table. First, however, you decide to do a manual inspection of the record count in the tables, which will reveal if there are potentially missing records.

1

● Display the Navigation Pane.

● Display the Personal Data table.

● Scroll to the bottom of the table to see your record.

You can see that the Personal Data table has 70 records from the record indicator and that your record is the last record. Now, however, you realize that you did not add your information to the Job Information table.

You will check the Job Information table to see how many records it contains.

2

● Open the Job Information table.

Your screen should be similar to Figure 3.36

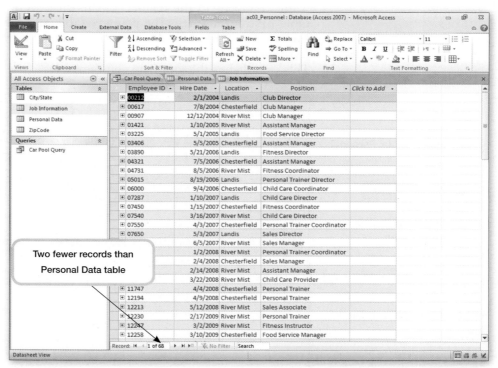

Two fewer records than Personal Data table

Figure 3.36

This table has 68 records, whereas the Personal Data table has 70. You know your record is one of the missing records, but you need to locate the other missing record. You can do this quickly using the Find Unmatched Query Wizard.

3

● Click 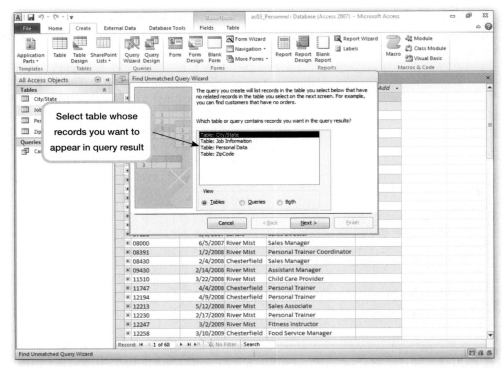 in the
Queries group of the
Create tab.

● Choose Find
Unmatched Query
Wizard.

● Click **OK** .

Your screen should be similar to
Figure 3.37

Figure 3.37

In the first wizard dialog box, you select the table that contains records you
want to appear in the results. In this case, you will select the Personal Data
table first because it is the primary table and has more records than the Job
Information table, and these are the records you want to appear in the results.
In the second dialog box, you will select the table to compare the first table to.
This establishes the join between the tables.

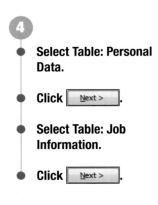

4

● Select Table: Personal
Data.

● Click **Next >** .

● Select Table: Job
Information.

● Click **Next >** .

Your screen should be similar to
Figure 3.38

Figure 3.38

The third step is to identify the matching (common) fields. The two highlighted fields, Employee ID, in both tables are already correctly highlighted.

5

● Click <=> to mark these fields as the matching fields.

Additional Information

The field names of the selected matching fields appear in the Matching Fields text box.

● Click Next >.

Your screen should be similar to Figure 3.39

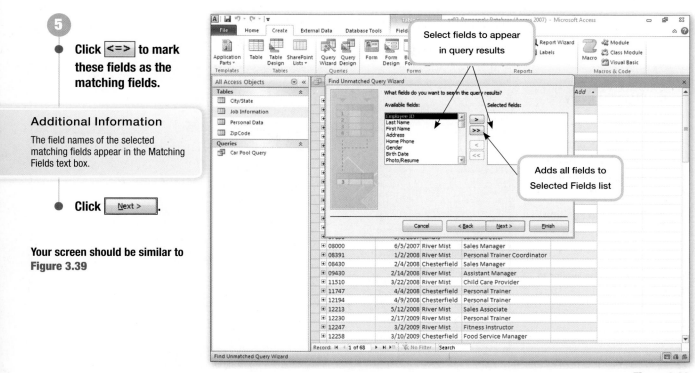

Figure 3.39

Next, you need to identify the fields you want to appear in the query results.

6

● Click >> to add all the fields to the Selected Fields list.

● Click Next >.

● Click Finish.

Your screen should be similar to Figure 3.40

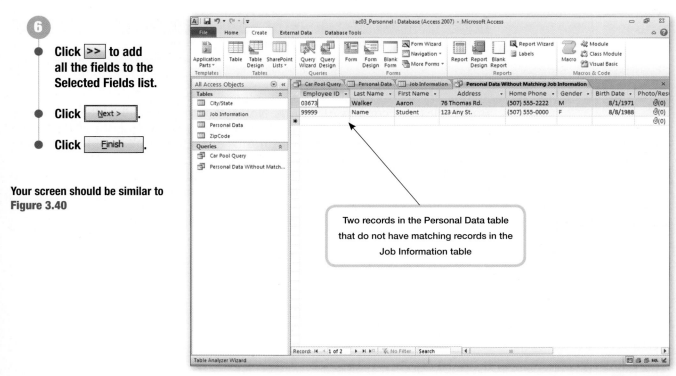

Figure 3.40

The two records in the Personal Data table that do not have matching records in the Job Information table are displayed in the query results. One record is the matching information for your own record that you added earlier to the Personal Data table. Now, you just need to add the information to the Job Information table for these two employees.

7

- Close the query datasheet.

- Add the records to the Job Information table shown in the table below.

- Best fit the Position field.

Your screen should be similar to Figure 3.41

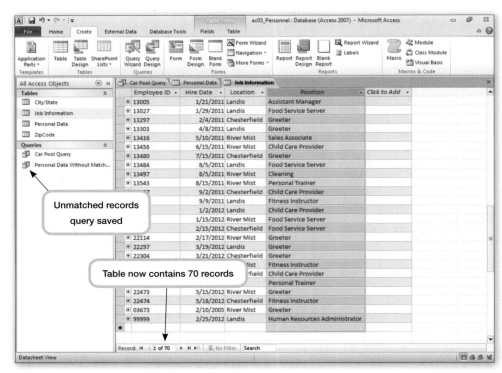

Figure 3.41

Employee ID	Hire Date	Location	Position
03673	2/10/2005	River Mist	Greeter
99999	2/25/2012	Landis	Human Resources Administrator

Both tables now contain 70 records. Notice that the Unmatched Records query was automatically saved and the object is listed in the Queries group of the Navigation pane. If you were to rerun this query, no results would be located because there are no longer any missing records.

Finally, you want to update all objects that use the Location field as the underlying record source to reflect the addition of the new records.

8

- Display the Car Pool Query datasheet.

- Click [Refresh All] in the Records group of the Home tab to refresh the screen image with the change in data.

Your screen should be similar to Figure 3.42

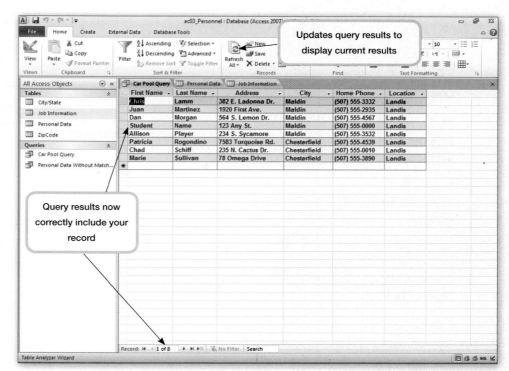

Figure 3.42

The query results list eight records that meet the criteria and now correctly include your record.

FINDING DUPLICATE RECORDS

Next, you want to check the Personal Data table for possible duplicate records. Even though this table uses the Employee ID field as the primary key, it is possible to enter the same record with two different IDs. To check for duplication, you will use the Find Duplicates Query Wizard.

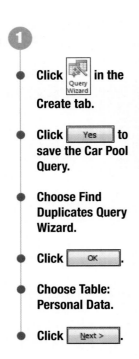

1

- Click  in the Create tab.

- Click **Yes** to save the Car Pool Query.

- Choose **Find Duplicates Query Wizard.**

- Click **OK**.

- Choose **Table: Personal Data.**

- Click **Next >**.

Your screen should be similar to Figure 3.43

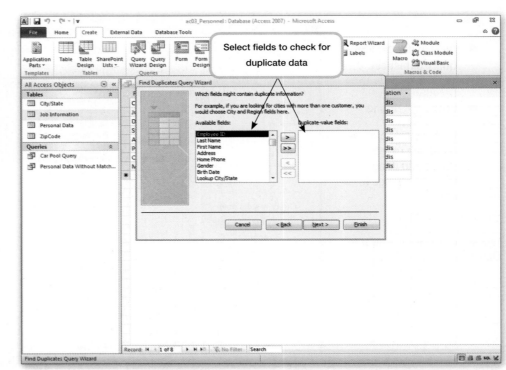

Figure 3.43

In this wizard dialog box, you identify the fields that may contain duplicate data. In this case, you will check the Last Name fields for duplicate values.

2

- Add the **Last Name** field to the Duplicate-Value Fields list.

- Click **Next >**.

Your screen should be similar to Figure 3.44

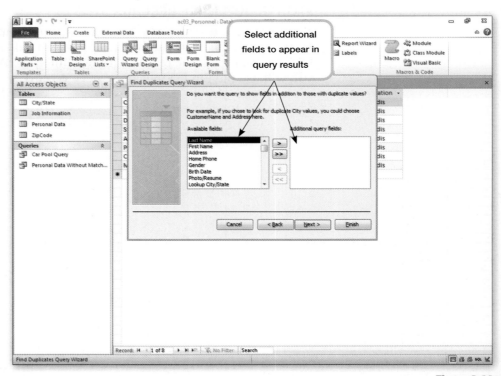

Figure 3.44

Next, you need to identify the additional fields you want to appear in the query results.

3
- Add the First Name, Birth Date, and Gender fields to the Additional Query Fields list.

- Click **Next >** .

- Click **Finish** .

Your screen should be similar to Figure 3.45

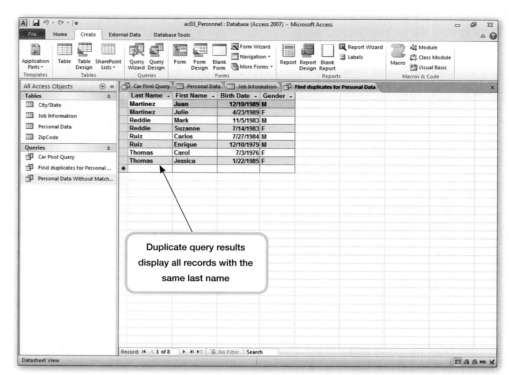

Duplicate query results display all records with the same last name

Figure 3.45

All records with the same last name are listed. These all look like valid records, so you will not make any changes.

CREATING A PARAMETER QUERY

Periodically, the club director wants to know the employee numbers and names of the employees at each club and their job positions. To find this information, you will create a simple query and sort the Location field to group the records.

To create this query, you will modify the existing Car Pool Query design, since it already includes the two tables—Personal Data and Job Information—that you need to use. You will clear the design grid and save the modified query using a new name.

1

- **Display the Car Pool Query in Design view.**

- **Drag across the top of the seven fields in the grid to select them and press** Delete.

- **Open the File tab and choose Save Object As.**

- **In the Save 'Car Pool Query' to: text box, enter Location Query and click** OK.

- **Click the Query Tools Design tab to close the Backstage view.**

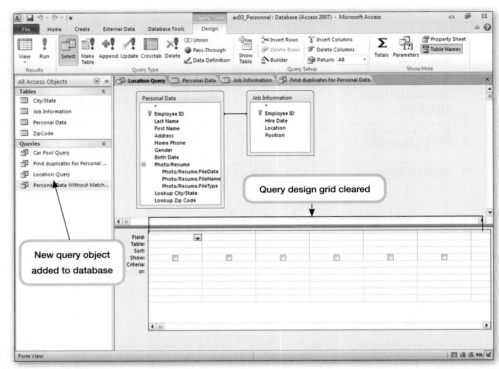

Figure 3.46

Your screen should be similar to Figure 3.46

The query object is added to the Navigation pane and you are ready to define the query. You will add all the fields from the Personal Data table to the grid, along with the Location field from the Job Information table.

2

- Double-click * in the Personal Data field list.

- Double-click Location in the Job Information table.

- Sort the Location field in ascending sort order.

- Run the query.

- Hide the Navigation pane.

- Scroll the window to the right to see the Location field.

Your screen should be similar to Figure 3.47

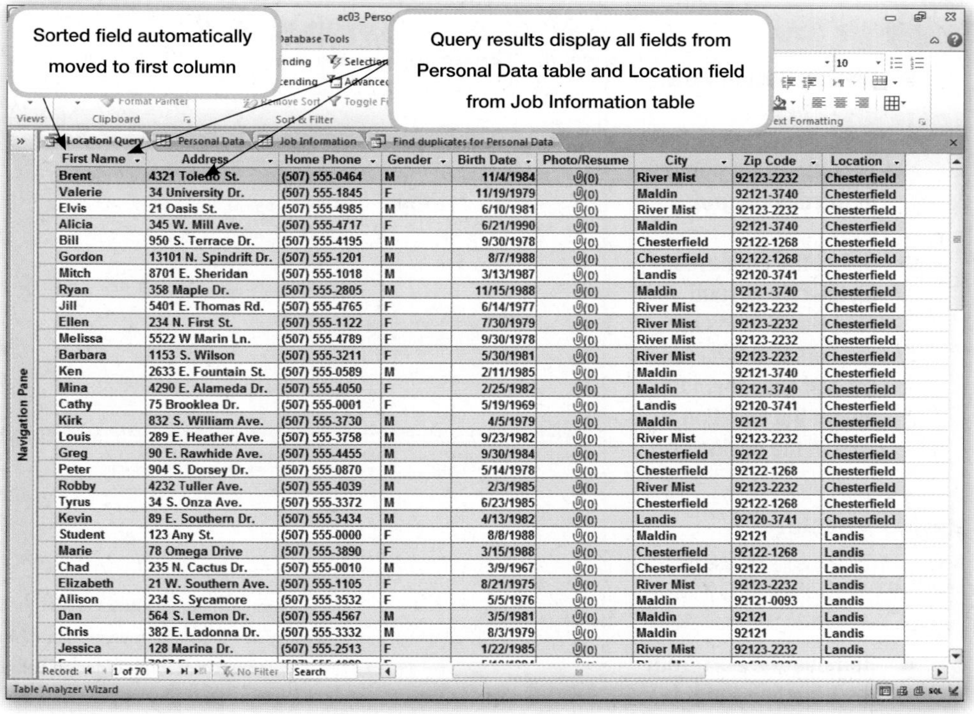

Sorted field automatically moved to first column

Query results display all fields from Personal Data table and Location field from Job Information table

First Name	Address	Home Phone	Gender	Birth Date	Photo/Resume	City	Zip Code	Location
Brent	4321 Toledo St.	(507) 555-0464	M	11/4/1984	(0)	River Mist	92123-2232	Chesterfield
Valerie	34 University Dr.	(507) 555-1845	F	11/19/1979	(0)	Maldin	92121-3740	Chesterfield
Elvis	21 Oasis St.	(507) 555-4985	M	6/10/1981	(0)	River Mist	92123-2232	Chesterfield
Alicia	345 W. Mill Ave.	(507) 555-4717	F	6/21/1990	(0)	Maldin	92121-3740	Chesterfield
Bill	950 S. Terrace Dr.	(507) 555-4195	M	9/30/1978	(0)	Chesterfield	92122-1268	Chesterfield
Gordon	13101 N. Spindrift Dr.	(507) 555-1201	M	8/7/1988	(0)	Chesterfield	92122-1268	Chesterfield
Mitch	8701 E. Sheridan	(507) 555-1018	M	3/13/1987	(0)	Landis	92120-3741	Chesterfield
Ryan	358 Maple Dr.	(507) 555-2805	M	11/15/1988	(0)	Maldin	92121-3740	Chesterfield
Jill	5401 E. Thomas Rd.	(507) 555-4765	F	6/14/1977	(0)	River Mist	92123-2232	Chesterfield
Ellen	234 N. First St.	(507) 555-1122	F	7/30/1979	(0)	River Mist	92123-2232	Chesterfield
Melissa	5522 W Marin Ln.	(507) 555-4789	F	9/30/1978	(0)	River Mist	92123-2232	Chesterfield
Barbara	1153 S. Wilson	(507) 555-3211	F	5/30/1981	(0)	River Mist	92123-2232	Chesterfield
Ken	2633 E. Fountain St.	(507) 555-0589	M	2/11/1985	(0)	Maldin	92121-3740	Chesterfield
Mina	4290 E. Alameda Dr.	(507) 555-4050	F	2/25/1982	(0)	Maldin	92121-3740	Chesterfield
Cathy	75 Brooklea Dr.	(507) 555-0001	F	5/19/1969	(0)	Landis	92120-3741	Chesterfield
Kirk	832 S. William Ave.	(507) 555-3730	M	4/5/1979	(0)	Maldin	92121	Chesterfield
Louis	289 E. Heather Ave.	(507) 555-3758	M	9/23/1982	(0)	River Mist	92123-2232	Chesterfield
Greg	90 E. Rawhide Ave.	(507) 555-4455	M	9/30/1984	(0)	Chesterfield	92122	Chesterfield
Peter	904 S. Dorsey Dr.	(507) 555-0870	M	5/14/1978	(0)	Chesterfield	92122-1268	Chesterfield
Robby	4232 Tuller Ave.	(507) 555-4039	M	2/3/1985	(0)	River Mist	92123-2232	Chesterfield
Tyrus	34 S. Onza Ave.	(507) 555-3372	M	6/23/1985	(0)	Chesterfield	92122-1268	Chesterfield
Kevin	89 E. Southern Dr.	(507) 555-3434	M	4/13/1982	(0)	Landis	92120-3741	Chesterfield
Student	123 Any St.	(507) 555-0000	F	8/8/1988	(0)	Maldin	92121	Landis
Marie	78 Omega Drive	(507) 555-3890	F	3/15/1988	(0)	Chesterfield	92122-1268	Landis
Chad	235 N. Cactus Dr.	(507) 555-0010	M	3/9/1967	(0)	Chesterfield	92122	Landis
Elizabeth	21 W. Southern Ave.	(507) 555-1105	F	8/21/1975	(0)	River Mist	92123-2232	Landis
Allison	234 S. Sycamore	(507) 555-3532	F	5/5/1976	(0)	Maldin	92121-0093	Landis
Dan	564 S. Lemon Dr.	(507) 555-4567	M	3/5/1981	(0)	Maldin	92121	Landis
Chris	382 E. Ladonna Dr.	(507) 555-3332	M	8/3/1979	(0)	Maldin	92121	Landis
Jessica	128 Marina Dr.	(507) 555-2513	F	1/22/1985	(0)	River Mist	92123-2232	Landis

Record: 1 of 70   No Filter   Search

Table Analyzer Wizard

Figure 3.47

All the fields from the Personal Data table and the Location field are displayed. The location is in sorted order. However, because the director wants the information for each location on a separate page when printed, sorting the Location field will not work. To display only the records for a single location at a time, you could filter the Location field, or change the criteria in the Location field to provide this information, and then print the results.

Another method, however, is to create a parameter query that will display a dialog box prompting you for location information when the query is run. This saves having to change to Design view and enter the specific criteria or applying a filter. Criteria that are entered in the Criteria cell are **hard-coded criteria**, meaning they are used each time the query is run. In a parameter query, you enter a **parameter value** in the Criteria cell rather than a specific value. The parameter value tells the query to prompt you for the specific criteria you want to use when you run the query.

Additionally, the director does not need all the information from the Personal Data table, so you will change the design to include only the necessary fields. First, you will change the fields in the design grid to display only the Employee ID and the First Name and Last Name fields from the Personal Data table.

3

● **Display Design view.**

● **Select and delete the Personal Data column in the design grid.**

● **Select the Employee ID, Last Name, and First Name fields in the Personal Data field list and drag them to before the Location field in the design grid.**

Having Trouble?

Hold down ⇧Shift while clicking on each field name to select all three.

● **Remove the Sort from the Location field.**

● **Type [Enter Location] in the Location Criteria cell.**

Your screen should be similar to Figure 3.48

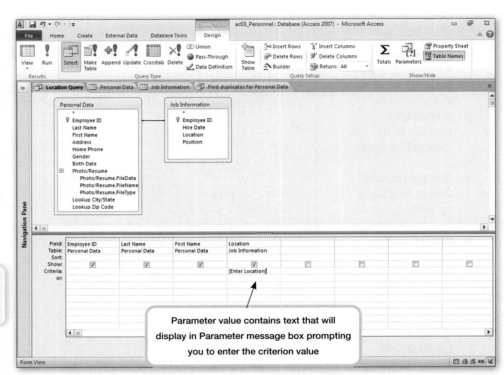

Figure 3.48

The Location criterion you entered is the parameter value. Parameter values are enclosed in square brackets and contain the text you want to appear when the parameter prompt is displayed. The parameter value cannot be a field name because Access will assume you want to use that particular field and will not prompt for input.

4

● **Run the query and type Landis in the Enter Parameter Value dialog box.**

● **Click   OK   .**

Your screen should be similar to Figure 3.49

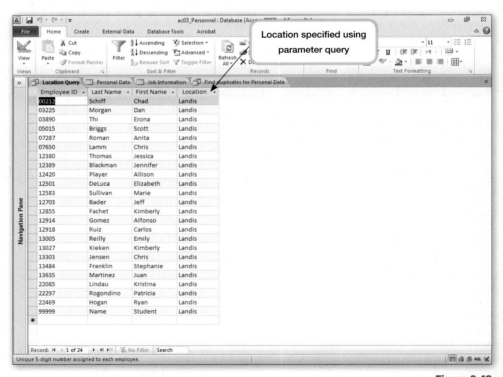

Figure 3.49

Only those records whose location is Landis are displayed. Additionally, only the fields you specified are included in the result. Now, each time you run the query, you simply need to specify the location in the Enter Parameter Value dialog box to obtain results for the different locations.

Displaying a Totals Row

As you look at the query results, you can see the record indicator tells you there are 24 records. The record indicator is a simple count of the total number of records in the table and only appears when you view the datasheet. You decide to display a Totals row in the datasheet that will display this information when you print the datasheet.

In addition to count totals, the Totals row can perform other types of calculations such as averages and sums on a column of data. Calculations that are performed on a range of data are called **aggregate functions**. Because aggregate functions perform calculations, the data type in a column must be a Number, Decimal, or Currency data type. The Personal Data table does not use any of these data types. However, the Count function can be used on all data types.

You will add a Totals row and then use the Count aggregate function to display the record count. The Totals row appears below the star (new record) row in the table and remains fixed on the window as you scroll the table. Clicking in a column of the Totals row selects the field to be calculated. Then you open the drop-down list to select the function you want to use. For Text data types, only the Count function is listed.

> **Additional Information**
>
> Some functions also can use a Date/Time data type.

1
- Click **Σ Totals** in the Records group of the Home tab.

- Click on the **Last Name** field in the Totals row.

- Open the drop-down list and choose **Count**.

Your screen should be similar to Figure 3.50

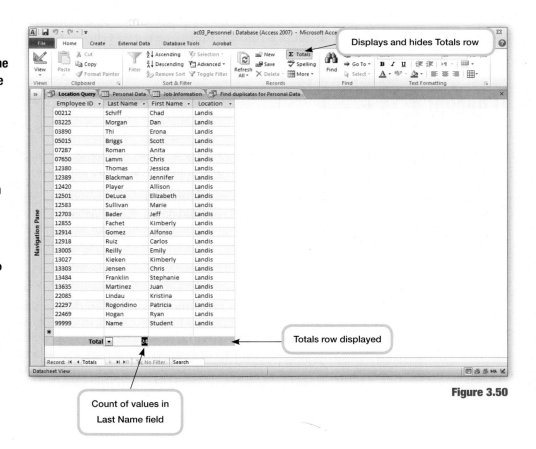

Displays and hides Totals row

Totals row displayed

Count of values in Last Name field

Figure 3.50

The Totals row displays 24 as the number of values in the column. The Totals label in the first column identifies the meaning of this value.

You can turn the display of the Totals row on and off any time by clicking [Σ Totals]. When you redisplay the row, any functions that were selected are displayed again. A Totals row also can be displayed in a table datasheet.

You will print this query datasheet and then close all open objects.

2

- Click [💾] Save in the Quick Access Toolbar to save the query.

- Preview and then print the query datasheet.

- Close the query, saving the layout changes if prompted.

- Close all remaining open objects, saving the layout when prompted.

- Display the Navigation pane.

NOTE If you are running short on time, this is an appropriate place to end your Access session. When you begin again, open the ac03_Personnel database.

Creating Reports

As you know, you can print the table and query datasheets to obtain a simple printout of the data. However, there are many times when you would like the output to look more professional. To do this, you can create custom reports using this information.

Concept 4 Report

A **report** is professional-appearing output generated from tables or queries that may include design elements, groups, and summary information. A report can be a simple listing of all the fields in a table, or it might be a list of selected fields based on a query. Reports generally include design elements such as formatted labels, report titles, and headings, as well as different theme design styles, layouts, and graphics that enhance the display of information. In addition, when creating a report, you can group data to achieve specific results. You can then display summary information such as totals by group to allow the reader to further analyze the data. Creating a report displays the information from your database in a more attractive and meaningful format.

The first step in creating a report is to decide what information you want to appear in the report. Then you need to determine the tables or queries (the report's record source) that can be used to provide this information. If all the fields you want to appear in the report are in a single table, then simply use that table. However, if the information you want to appear in the report is contained in more than one table, you first need to create a query that specifically fits the needs of the report.

There are several different methods you can use to create reports, as described in the following table. The method you use depends on the type of report you need to create.

Report tool	Creates a simple report containing all the fields in the table.
Blank Report tool	Builds a report from scratch in Report Layout view by adding the fields you select from the table.
Report design	Builds a report from scratch in Report Design view by adding the fields you select from the table.
Report Wizard	Guides you through the steps to create a report.

USING THE REPORT TOOL

Although you could give Juan a simple printout of the car pool query results, you decide to create a report of this information. Because the fastest way to create a report is to use the Report tool, you decide to try this method first. This tool uses the selected or displayed table or query object as the report source.

1

- Select the Car Pool Query in the Navigation pane.

- Click [Report] in the Reports group of the Create tab.

- Hide the Navigation pane.

Your screen should be similar to Figure 3.51

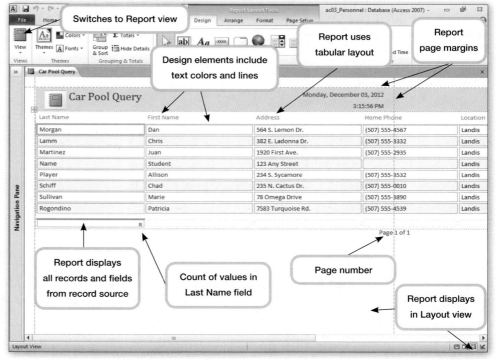

Figure 3.51

The Report tool creates a report that displays all fields and records from the record source in a predesigned report layout and style. It uses a tabular layout in which each field name appears at the top of the column and each record appears in a line, much like in Datasheet view. The fields are displayed in the order in which they appear in the query design. Notice the records are not sorted by last name as they are in the query results. This is because the query sort order is overridden by the report sort order, which is by default unsorted. It also displays the object name as the report title and the current date and time in the title area. The report design elements include blue font color for the report title and field names and blue fill color behind the title. The title is also in a larger text size. The last row displays a total value of the number of records in the report. The dotted lines identify the report page margins and show that the Home Phone field data will be split between two pages.

VIEWING THE REPORT

The report is displayed in Layout view. As in Form Layout view, you could modify the report design if needed in this view. Instead, you will switch to Report view to see how the report will look when printed.

1

● **Click** ⊞ **Report View in the Views group of the Report Layout Tools Design tab.**

● **Scroll to the right to see the last field column.**

Your screen should be similar to Figure 3.52

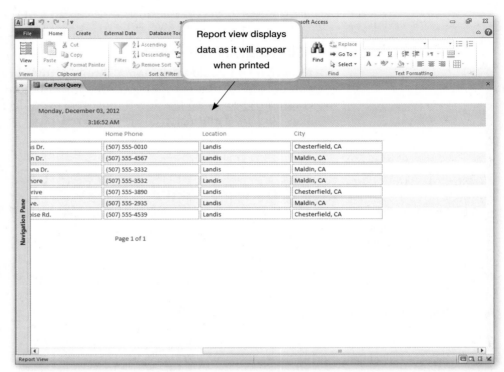

Figure 3.52

Additional Information

The report date and time will reflect the current date and time on your computer.

Report view displays the data in the report as it will appear when printed. It does not show how the data will fit on a page. This view is useful if you want to copy data from the report and paste it into another document such as a Word file. It also can be used to temporarily change what data is displayed in the report by applying a filter.

The last view you can use is Print Preview. This view will show you exactly how the report will look when printed and can be used to modify the page layout and print-related settings. Another way to display this view is from the object's shortcut menu.

- **Right-click on the report tab or an empty area of the report and choose Print Preview.**

Another Method

You also can right-click an object in the Navigation pane to display this shortcut menu.

- **Click** 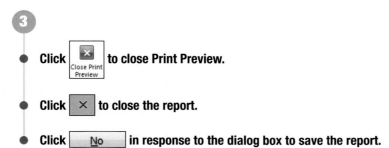 **in the Zoom group.**

Your screen should be similar to Figure 3.53

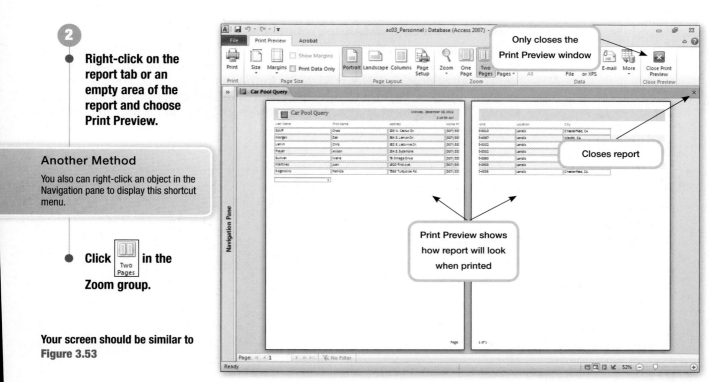

Figure 3.53

It is now easy to see exactly how the report will look when printed. After looking over the report, you decide that although the tabular layout is appropriate for your report, you do not want the report to include all the fields from the query. Rather than modify the report design by removing the unneeded fields, you will close this report without saving it and then use the Report Wizard to create a report that is more appropriate for your needs.

3

- **Click** [Close Print Preview] **to close Print Preview.**

- **Click** [×] **to close the report.**

- **Click** [No] **in response to the dialog box to save the report.**

USING THE REPORT WIZARD

Using the Report Wizard, you can easily specify the fields you want to include in the report. The Report Wizard consists of a series of dialog boxes, much like those in the Form and Query Wizards. In the first dialog box, you specify the table or query to be used in the report and add the fields to be included. The Car Pool Query object is already correctly specified as the object that will be used to create the report.

1

- Click 🔍 Report Wizard in the Reports group of the Create tab.

- Add the First Name field to the Selected Fields list.

- Add all the remaining fields to the list.

- Remove the Location field.

- Click Next >.

Your screen should be similar to Figure 3.54

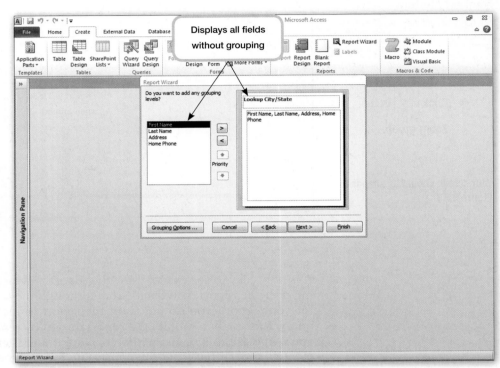

Figure 3.54

In this dialog box, you are asked if you want to add any grouping levels to the report. As suggested, you will group the report by city.

2

Click [Next >].

Your screen should be similar to Figure 3.55

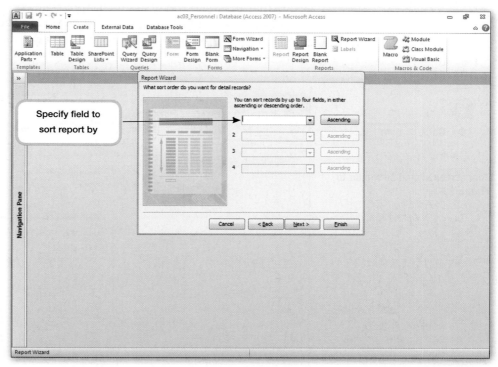

Figure 3.55

You can specify a sort order for the records in this dialog box. Because you want the last names sorted within each city group, you will specify to sort by last name.

3

- **Open the first list box drop-down menu and choose Last Name.**

- **Click** [Next >].

Your screen should be similar to Figure 3.56

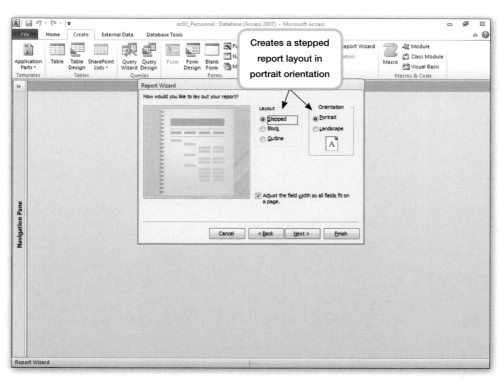

Figure 3.56

This dialog box is used to change the report layout and orientation. The default report settings for a grouped report uses a stepped report design layout with portrait orientation. The stepped design displays the report data using a tabular format in which the field labels appear in columns above the rows of data. The data in each group is indented or stepped to clearly identify the groups. In addition, the option to adjust the field width so that all fields fit on one page is selected. The default settings are acceptable.

5

● Click [Next >].

Your screen should be similar to Figure 3.57

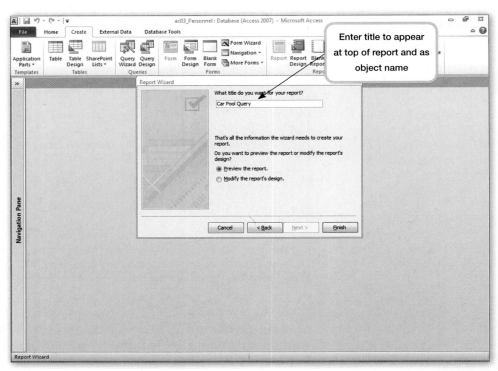

Enter title to appear at top of report and as object name

Figure 3.57

The last Report Wizard dialog box is used to add a title to the report and to specify how the report should be displayed after it is created. The only change you want to make is to replace the query name with a more descriptive report title.

6

- Enter **Car Pool Report: Maldin to Landis** as the title.

- Click [**Finish**].

Your screen should be similar to Figure 3.58

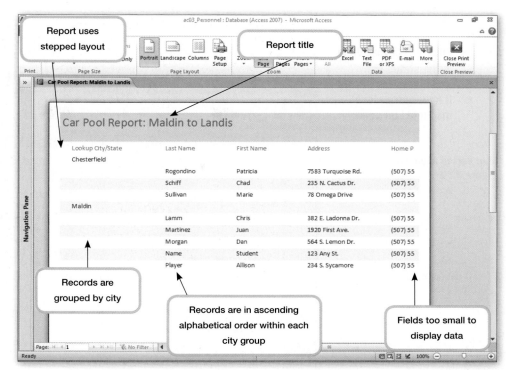

Report uses stepped layout

Report title

Car Pool Report: Maldin to Landis

Records are grouped by city

Records are in ascending alphabetical order within each city group

Fields too small to display data

Figure 3.58

In an instant, the completed report with the data from the resource query is displayed in Print Preview. The report appears in the stepped layout, grouped by city. The title reflects the title you specified. The records appear in alphabetical order within each group, as you specified in the Report Wizard.

However, there are a few problems with the report. The most noticeable is that the city field is much larger than it needs to be; consequently, the Home Phone field is truncated. Additionally, you want to change the Lookup City/State column heading to City and to display the first name field column before the last name.

MODIFYING THE REPORT IN LAYOUT VIEW

To make these changes, you need to modify the report design. You can modify a report in either Design view or Layout view. To make these simple changes, you will use Layout view.

1

Click ⊞ Layout View
in the status bar.

If necessary, close
the Field List pane.

Your screen should be similar to
Figure 3.59

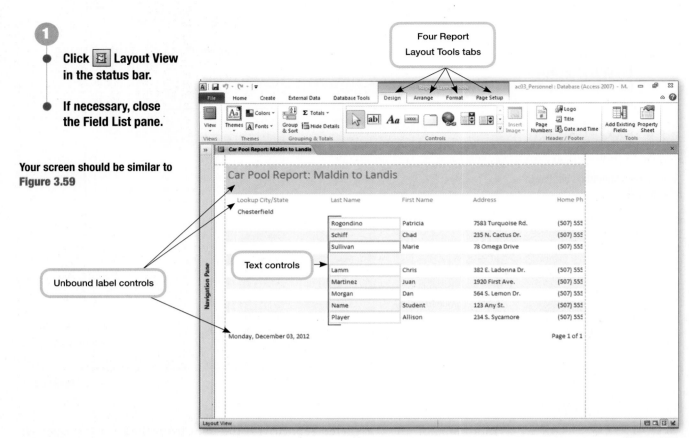

Four Report
Layout Tools tabs

Unbound label controls

Text controls

Figure 3.59

Having Trouble?

See Concept 10 in Lab 2 to review
controls.

In Layout view, four tabs are available to help you modify the report. The Design tab features are used to add fields, controls, totals, and other elements to the report. The Arrange tab is used to modify the overall layout of the report or of individual elements. The Format tab contains commands to format shapes as well as make text enhancements such as changing the font and font color. The Page Setup tab is used to control the page layout of the report for printing purposes.

Just as in forms, each item in the report is a separate control. The field names are label controls and the field information is a text control. The text controls are bound to the data in the underlying table. The field names and report title are unbound label controls. The stepped report design controls the layout and position of these controls.

The same features you learned when working in Form Layout view are available in Report Layout view. Additionally, just like forms, reports can use a stacked or tabular table layout to make it easier to work with controls. Generally, reports use a tabular layout in which controls are arranged in rows and columns like a spreadsheet, with labels across the top. Currently, although the stepped design you selected in the Report Wizard displays the controls using a tabular design, it did not group the controls in a table layout. You will apply a tabular layout to the report controls so that you can easily modify the report.

Additional Information

The commands in the Rows & Columns group of the Arrange tab are not available until a table layout has been applied.

2

- Press Ctrl + A to select all the controls on the report.

- Hold down Ctrl while clicking on the title, date, and page # label controls to deselect them.

- Click [Tabular] in the Table group of the Arrange tab to group the selected controls in a tabular layout.

- Double-click on the Lookup City/State label control and change the label to City.

- Click anywhere in the First Name field and click [Select Column] in the Rows & Columns group to select the column.

- Drag the First Name field column to the left of the Last Name field column.

Having Trouble?

When you move a field column, a yellow bar indicates where the column will be placed when you stop dragging.

- Adjust the size of the fields as in Figure 3.60.

Your screen should be similar to Figure 3.60

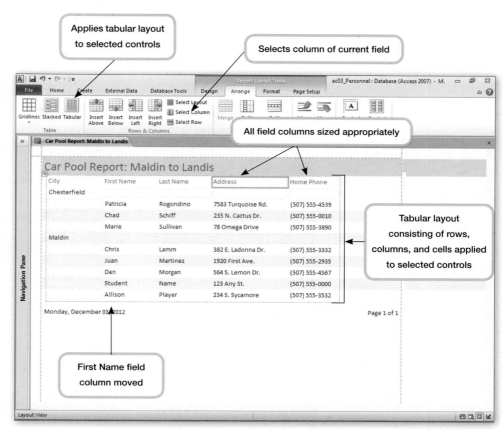

Applies tabular layout to selected controls

Selects column of current field

All field columns sized appropriately

Tabular layout consisting of rows, columns, and cells applied to selected controls

First Name field column moved

Figure 3.60

Applying the tabular layout made it easy to size and move the controls. Now the report easily fits on a single page and all the fields fully display their contents.

CHANGING THE REPORT THEME

The last changes you want to make are to the appearance of the report. You decide to change the report theme design style to another, more colorful style.

1

● Click [Themes] in the Themes group of the Design tab.

● Choose Flow.

Having Trouble?

The theme names are in alphabetical order and appear in a ScreenTip when you point to the different designs in the Themes gallery.

● Click on the title label control and size it to fully display the text.

Your screen should be similar to Figure 3.61

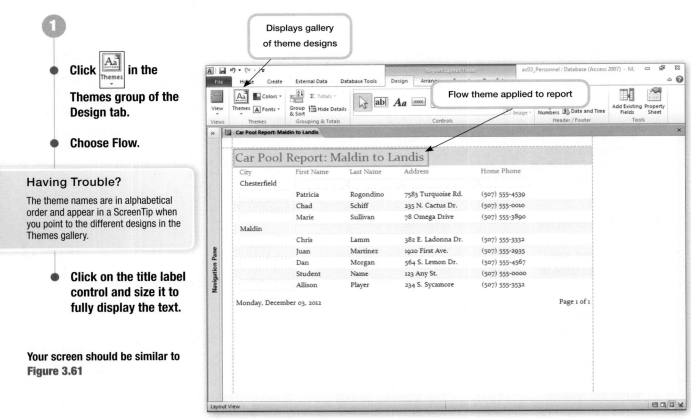

Figure 3.61

The selected theme is applied to the report. It includes brighter colors and different fonts. You are finished making changes to the report and will close and save the report.

2

● Close the report, saving the changes when prompted.

● Display the Navigation pane.

The name of the report you created appears in the Reports category of the Navigation pane.

MODIFYING A REPORT IN DESIGN VIEW

After seeing how easy it was to create a report for the car pool information, you decide to create a custom report for the job position and location information requested by the club director. You will create the report using the Report Wizard. Then you will modify the report in Design view.

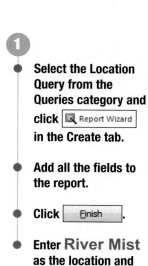

1

- Select the Location Query from the Queries category and click 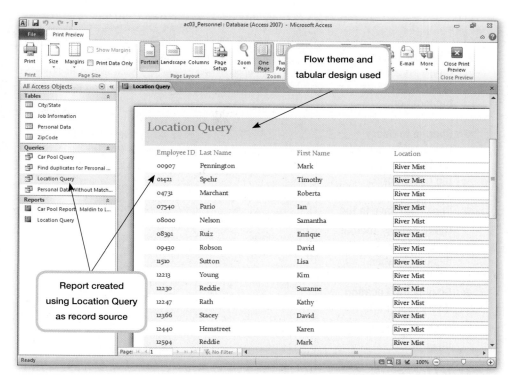 Report Wizard in the Create tab.

- Add all the fields to the report.

- Click Finish.

- Enter **River Mist** as the location and click OK.

Your screen should be similar to Figure 3.62

Figure 3.62

Because you knew that you would be using the default or last-used wizard settings, you were able to end the wizard without moving through all the steps. The report displays the specified fields and uses a tabular design and the Flow theme. The tabular design was used because it is the default setting for the Report wizard and the Flow theme was used because it was the last-used theme in the database.

As you look at the report, you realize you forgot to include the Position field. You will modify the query and then add this field in Design view to the report.

2

- Open the Location Query and enter **River Mist** as the location.

- Change to Query Design view and add the Position field to the design grid.

- Click 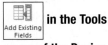 Save in the Quick Access Toolbar to save the query design changes.

- Display the Location Query report and click Design View.

- Hide the Navigation pane.

- If the Field List pane is not displayed, click 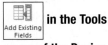 in the Tools group of the Design tab.

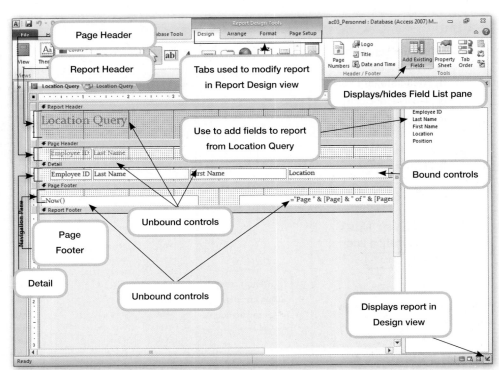

Figure 3.63

Another Method

You also can use the shortcut key Alt + F8 to hide and display the Field List pane.

Your screen should be similar to Figure 3.63

The report is displayed in Report Design view. This view displays the same four tabs—Design, Arrange, Format, and Page Setup—that were available in Report Layout view.

The Field List task pane displays the field names from the design grid of the Location Query. You will use the Field List task pane shortly to add the missing field to the report.

The Report Design window is divided into five sections: Report Header, Page Header, Detail, Page Footer, and Report Footer. The contents of each section appear below the horizontal bar that contains the name of that section. The sections are described in the following table.

Section	Description
Report Header	Contains information to be printed once at the beginning of the report. The report title is displayed in this section.
Page Header	Contains information to be printed at the top of each page. The column headings are displayed in this section.
Detail	Contains the records of the table. The field column widths are the same as the column widths set in the table design.
Page Footer	Contains information to be printed at the bottom of each page such as the date and page number.
Report Footer	Contains information to be printed at the end of the report. The Report Footer section currently contains no data.

The controls in the Page Header section are unbound label controls whereas those in the Detail section are bound text controls. The control in the Report Header that displays the report title and those in the Page Footers that display the date and page numbers are also unbound label controls.

First, you will group the controls in the Page Header and Detail sections together by applying a tabular layout to the selected fields. Then you will add the missing field to the report.

Click in the ruler area to the left of the fields in the Page Header section to select all the controls in that section.

Additional Information

When positioning the mouse in the ruler, the pointer will appear as a selection arrow ➡ indicating that you can select all fields in the section.

⇧Shift click on the ruler area next to the Detail section to select all the controls in that section as well.

Having Trouble?

You can also select the controls individually by using the ⇧Shift key.

Click ▦ Tabular in the Table group of the Arrange tab.

Scroll the window horizontally to view the Location controls and the right edge of the report.

Drag the Position field from the Field List to the right of the Location text control in the Detail section and when a vertical orange bar appears, release the mouse to drop it at that location.

Another Method

You also can double-click on a field in the Field List to move it into the Detail section of the report.

Close the Field List pane.

If necessary, scroll to the left to view all the controls in the report.

Your screen should be similar to Figure 3.64

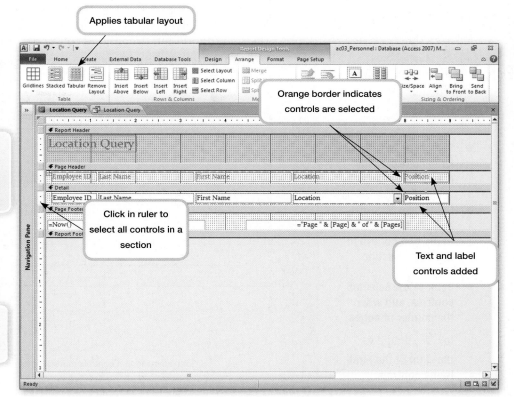

Figure 3.64

The Position field text and label controls have been added to the report. The Position label control was inserted in the Page Header section, and the Position text control was inserted in the Detail section. This is because the controls were inserted into the tabular control layout and comply with the horizontal and vertical alignment settings of the layout. The text control is a bound control that is tied to the Position field data. Both controls are surrounded by an orange border indicating that they are selected.

Now you want to move the Last Name controls to the right of the First Name controls. A control can be moved to any location within the control layout by selecting it and then dragging it to the new location. The mouse pointer changes to ⬚ to indicate that a selected control can be moved.

4

● **Select the Last Name label control in the Page Header section.**

● **Hold down ⇧Shift and click on the Last Name text control in the Detail section.**

● **Point to the selected controls, and when the pointer changes to ⬚, drag it to the right of the First Name controls.**

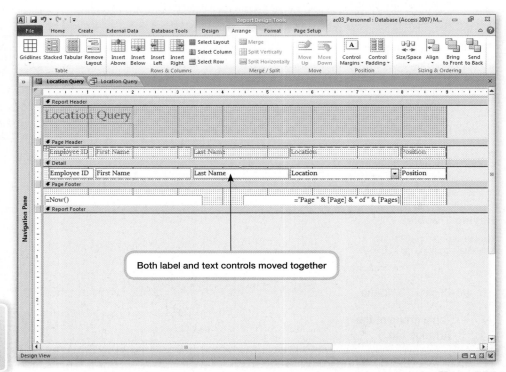

Figure 3.65

Your screen should be similar to Figure 3.65

Notice that the Last Name label and text controls moved together because they were both selected. The controls in both the **Page Header** and Detail sections are horizontally and vertically aligned and spaced an equal distance apart.

FORMATTING CONTROLS

Next, you decide to change the text of the report title and center it over the report. First you will enlarge the title control to extend the width of the report, and then center the text within the control.

1

- Select the report title control.

- Drag the right edge of the control toward the right margin; stop at approximately 8" on the ruler.

- Click ▤ Center in the Font group of the Report Design Tools Format tab.

- Click in the report title control to place the cursor in the text and select the text.

- Type **Job Position Report** and then press ⏎Enter.

Your screen should be similar to Figure 3.66

Centers text in selected control

Report title edited and centered

Right edge of control lined up with 8" on ruler

Use right-middle handle to resize control width

Job Position Report

Figure 3.66

The revised title is centered over the report columns. Changing the title text does not change the name of the report object. You also want the work location to be included in the title because the report results could vary depending on what location you entered into the parameter dialog box when the report was opened. To make the title reflect the contents of the report, you will add the Location field to the Report Header area and then use the formatting tools to change its appearance.

2

- Click [Add Existing Fields] in the Design tab to open the Field List task pane.

- Drag the Location field into the Report Header section, below the title.

- Select and replace the text in the Location label control with **For**

Your screen should be similar to Figure 3.67

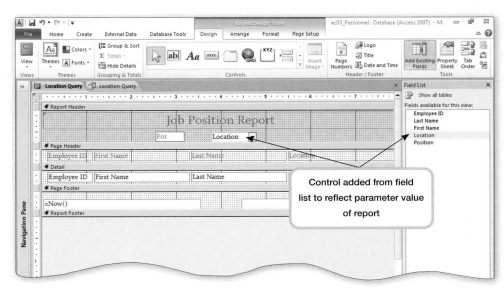

Control added from field list to reflect parameter value of report

Figure 3.67

Next you will format the Location controls by making them transparent, removing the outline border and changing the font size and color.

3

- Click on the Location text control.

- Click 🖌 Shape Fill ▾ in the Control Formatting group of the Format tab and choose Transparent.

- Click 📝 Shape Outline ▾ in the Control Formatting group and choose Transparent.

- Click 11 ▾ Font Size in the Font group and choose 18.

- Enlarge the Location text control to fully display the text.

Having Trouble?

In order to grab the corner sizing handles to increase the size of the control, you may need to expand the report header section. Do this by positioning the mouse on the top edge of the Page Header section bar and, when the mouse becomes ✛, drag the bar down slightly.

- Click 🅰 Font Color and choose Dark Red from the Standard Colors section of the color gallery (last row, first column).

- Position and resize both control boxes as shown in Figure 3.68.

Having Trouble?

Use the large gray handle in the upper-left corner of a control to move each control individually.

- Close the Field List pane.

Your screen should be similar to **Figure 3.68**

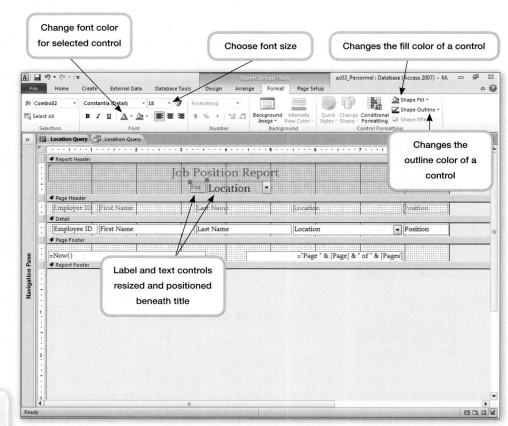

Change font color for selected control

Choose font size

Changes the fill color of a control

Changes the outline color of a control

Label and text controls resized and positioned beneath title

Figure 3.68

When you were attempting to position the Location text and label controls, you may have noticed how they moved together. When the controls are associated and act as one when moved, they are called **compound controls**.

Now you want to see the effects of your changes. You will be prompted to enter the location. This time, you will enter Landis as the location, and the report title now will update to include the location information.

● Switch to Layout view.

● Enter the location of **Landis**

Your screen should be similar to Figure 3.69

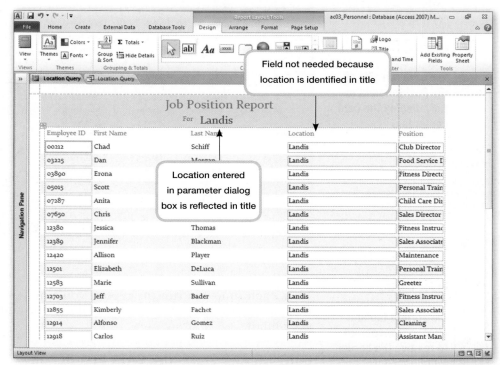

Figure 3.69

The report is really shaping up. However, there are still a few changes you need to make. You want to remove the Location field because the report title now identifies the location. Then you will adjust the sizes of the fields to make the report fill more of the width of the page.

DELETING A FIELD

You will delete the Location field and make adjustments to the other fields in Layout view so you can see the field content and layout while working with them.

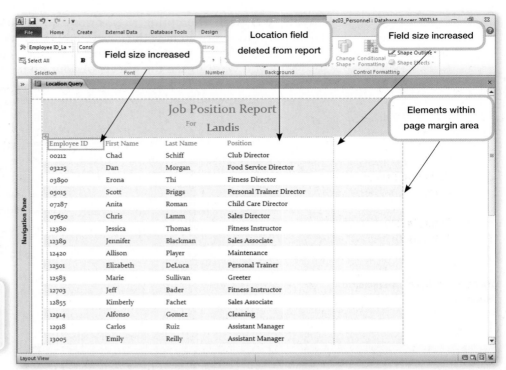

1

- **Click in the Location field.**

- **Click** [Select Column] **in the Rows & Columns group of the Arrange tab.**

- **Press** Delete.

- **Increase the size of the Position field to fully display the field contents.**

Having Trouble?

Scroll to the end of the report to make sure that the largest text entry in the Position field is fully displayed.

- **Click** [Shape Outline ▼] **in the Control Formatting group of the Format tab and choose Transparent to remove the border around the Position field.**

- **Decrease the width of the First Name and Last Name columns to better fit the text.**

- **Increase the size of the Employee ID field slightly.**

Your screen should be similar to Figure 3.70

Figure 3.70

Now, each time you run the report, you simply need to enter the location in the query parameter message box and the title and report contents will reflect your input.

SORTING AND FILTERING DATA IN A REPORT

You also notice that the records in the report are in order by employee ID. This is because a sort order was not specified in the query or the report when they were created. Just as in a table datasheet, query, or form, you can sort and filter the data that is displayed in a report. You will use these features to sort the records in alphabetical order by last name and display only the records for employees whose job is fitness instructor.

Right-click on the Last Name field of any record.

Choose Sort A to Z.

Right-click on the Position field of any record that displays Fitness Instructor.

Choose Equals "Fitness Instructor".

Your screen should be similar to Figure 3.71

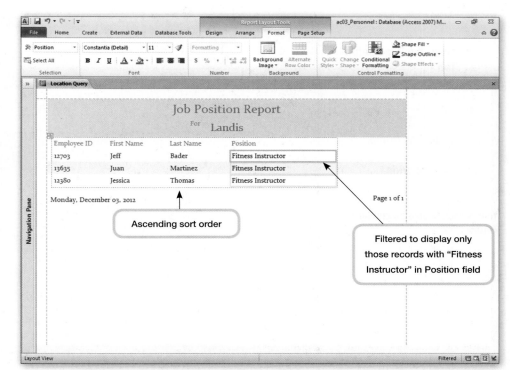

Figure 3.71

Only the three records meeting the filter requirements are displayed in the report. They are in alphabetical order by last name. You will remove the filter but maintain the sorted record order.

2

Right-click on the Position field of any record.

Choose Clear filter from Position.

Additional Information

You also can click [Toggle Filter] in the Home tab to remove the filter.

All the records are redisplayed again.

Preparing Reports for Printing

You can print the report from any view or even when the report is closed. However, unless you are sure the page settings are correct, it is a good idea to check how its elements are arranged in Layout view or Print Preview before printing. The advantage to Layout view is that you can instantly see how any changes made to the page layout will affect the printed report and you can make any needed adjustments.

MODIFYING THE PAGE SETUP

Additional Information

The default margin setting is Narrow, which sets all margins to 0.25 inch.

As you look at the layout of the report on the page, you see the report is not centered horizontally on the page and there is a lot of empty space to the right of the Position column. To fix this, you will increase the size of the margins, which will push the columns to the right and better center the elements on the page. Then you will readjust the column widths.

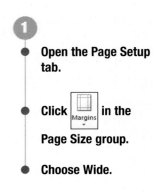

1

- Open the Page Setup tab.

- Click 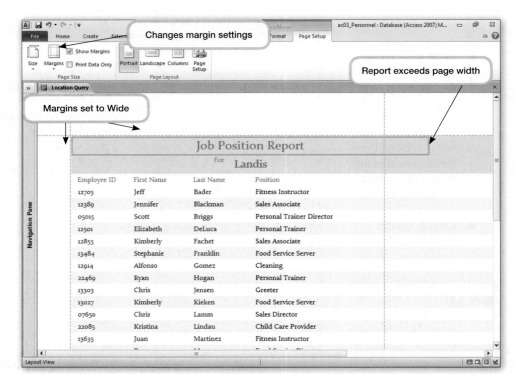 in the Page Size group.

- Choose Wide.

Your screen should be similar to Figure 3.72

Figure 3.72

The Wide margin option increases the left and right margins to 0.75 inch. The columns now begin at 0.75 inch, and the report appears more balanced on the page; however, now the report width exceeds a single page. This is because some of the controls in the report exceed the new page margins. Additionally, the title is no longer centered because the control is wider than the new page width. These problems can be quickly fixed by reducing the size of the controls that are causing the problem. You decide to increase the margins to 1 inch and then make the adjustments to the controls to fit the new page width. To do this, you will set custom left and right margins.

2

- Click  in the Page Layout group.

- Enter **1** in the Left and Right Margin text boxes.

- Click [OK].

- Size the title control to fit the new page width.

- Click on the Landis Location control in the title area, then ⇧Shift click on the For label control.

- Move the controls so they are once again centered under the Job Position Report title.

- Scroll to the bottom of the report and click on the Page Number control in the footer.

- Reduce the Page Number control size (from the right edge) until it is inside the right margin line.

- If the report still exceeds the margins, further adjust the sizes of the field columns until the report fits within the margins.

- Scroll to the top of the report.

Your screen should be similar to Figure 3.73

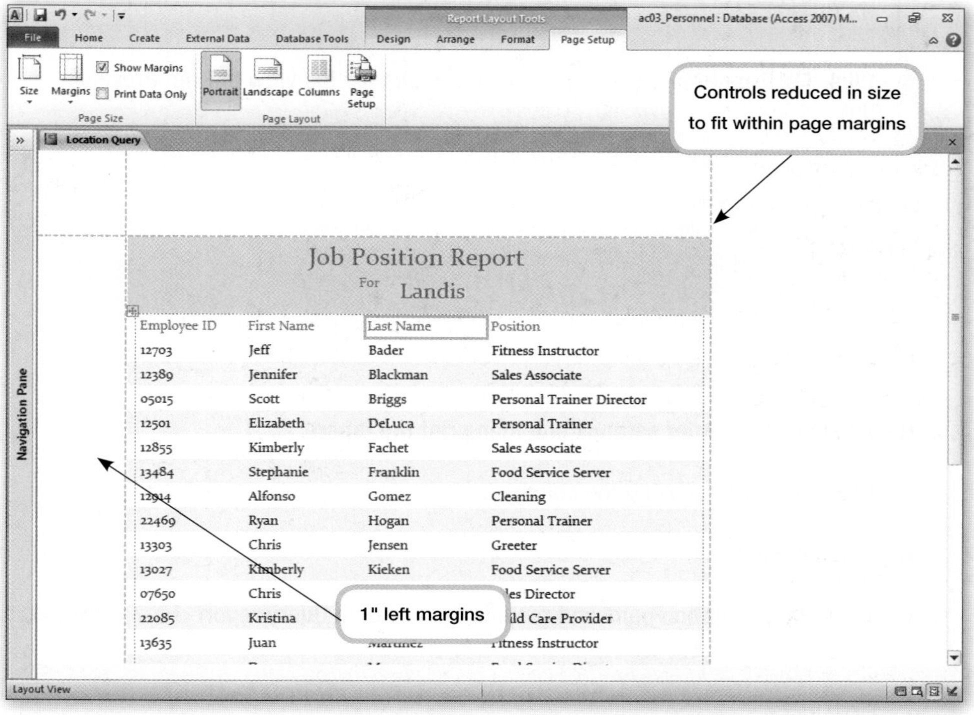

Controls reduced in size to fit within page margins

Job Position Report
For **Landis**

Employee ID	First Name	Last Name	Position
12703	Jeff	Bader	Fitness Instructor
12389	Jennifer	Blackman	Sales Associate
05015	Scott	Briggs	Personal Trainer Director
12501	Elizabeth	DeLuca	Personal Trainer
12855	Kimberly	Fachet	Sales Associate
13484	Stephanie	Franklin	Food Service Server
12914	Alfonso	Gomez	Cleaning
22469	Ryan	Hogan	Personal Trainer
13303	Chris	Jensen	Greeter
13027	Kimberly	Kieken	Food Service Server
07650	Chris		les Director
22085	Kristina		ild Care Provider
13635	Juan	Martinez	Fitness Instructor

1" left margins

Figure 3.73

Now the columns are spaced attractively across the page. The page layout settings you specify are saved with the report, so unless you make changes to the report design, you only need to set them once.

PREVIEWING AND PRINTING REPORTS

Although you believe the report is ready to print, you will preview it first and then print it.

● Click **Print Preview** in the status bar to change the view to Print Preview.

Additional Information

You also can specify margins and page setup using the same features in the Print Preview ribbon.

● Click [Print].

● Specify your printer settings and then print the report.

● Close the report, saving the changes.

● Close the query.

● Open the Navigation pane and rename the Location Query report **Job Position Report**

Your printed report should look like the one shown in the case study at the beginning of the lab.

PRINTING A RELATIONSHIPS REPORT

Before exiting Access, you want to print a report that shows the relationships between the tables in your database.

● **Open the Database Tools tab.**

● **Click** [Relationships].

● **If necessary, click** [All Relationships] **to show all table relationships.**

● **Click** [Relationship Report] **in the Tools group.**

● **Print the report.**

Your screen should be similar to Figure 3.74

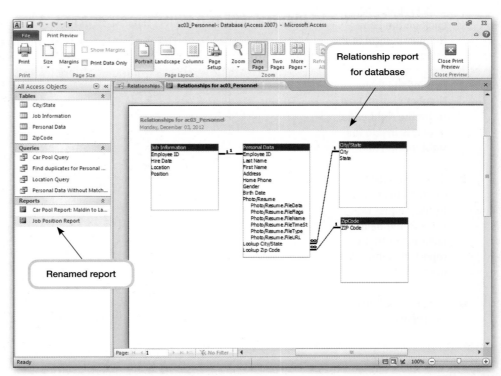

Figure 3.74

A preview of how the report will look when printed is displayed on the screen. The database name and creation date are automatically used as the report header. You can print this report as well as save it for future reference.

● **Close the relationship report without saving it.**

● **Close the Relationships window.**

Compacting and Backing Up the Database

Additional Information

A file is fragmented when it becomes too large for your computer to store in a single location on your hard disk. When this happens, the file is split up and stored in pieces in different locations on the disk, making access to the data slower.

As you modify a database, the changes are saved to your disk. When you delete data or objects, the database file can become fragmented and use disk space inefficiently. To make the database perform optimally, you should **compact** the database on a regular basis. Compacting makes a copy of the file and rearranges the way that the file is stored on your disk.

● **Open the File tab and if necessary, choose Info.**

● **Click** **to compact and repair the database.**

Although it appears that nothing has happened, the database file has been compacted and repaired as needed. It is also a good idea to back up your databases periodically. This will ensure that you have a copy of each database in case of a power outage or other system failure while you are working on a file, or in case you need to access a previous version of a database that you have changed.

2

● Open the File tab and choose Save & Publish.

● Double-click Back Up Database.

Your screen should be similar to Figure 3.75

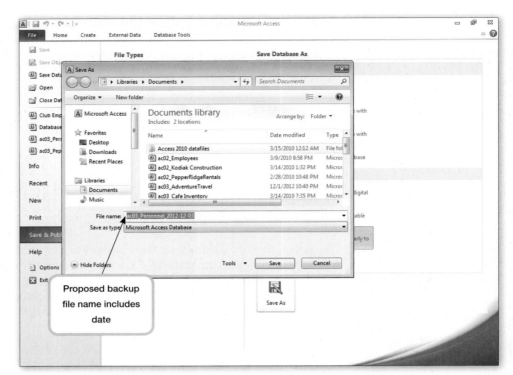

Proposed backup file name includes date

Figure 3.75

The Save As dialog box displays your database name (which in this case is ac03_Personnel) with the current date appended to it. This is a good way to keep track of when you performed the backup on the database, so you will not change this file name.

3

● If necessary, change to the location where you save your solution files.

● Click [Save].

● Close the database and exit Access.

The backup database file has been saved to your solution file location. If you need to restore a backed-up database, you just change the name of the backup file (so it does not conflict with another file of the same name that you may have created since the backup) and then open it in Access.

XPLORE YOUR CAREER OPTIONS

atabase Administrator

atabase administrators are responsible for organizing and aintaining an organization's information resources by work-j with database management software to implement, ana-e, and organize the presentation and use of the data. The ministrator usually controls user access, tests new objects, cks up the data, and trains new users to use the database.

As a database administrator, your position also would include safeguarding the system from threats, whether internal or via the Internet. The typical salary range of a database adminis-trator is $40,000 to $65,000, but with years of experience an administrator can earn as much as $100,000. A bachelor's degree in computer science is typically preferred in addition to practical experience. Demand for skilled database admin-istrators is expected to make this one of the fastest-growing occupations.

Query (AC3.20)

A query is a request for specific data contained in a database. Queries are used to view data in different ways, to analyze data, and even to change existing data.

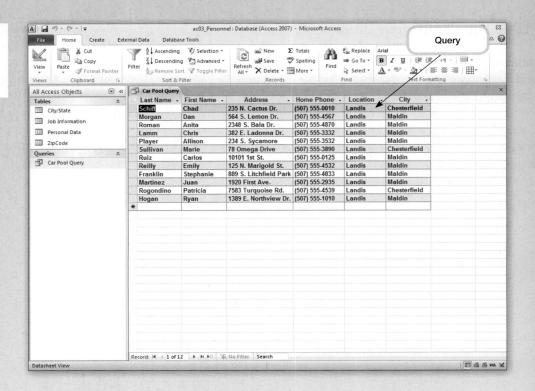

Join (AC3.26)

A join is an association that is created in a query between a field in one table or query and a field of the same data type in another table or query.

Query Criteria (AC3.29)

Query criteria are expressions that are used to restrict the results of a query to display only records that meet certain limiting conditions.

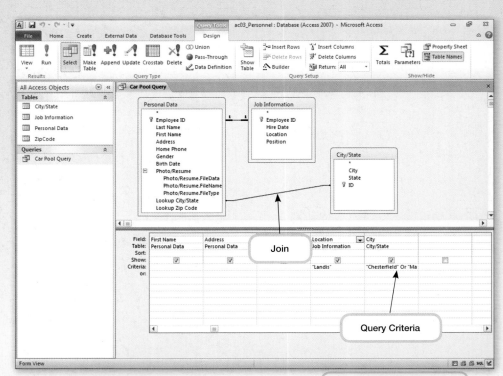

Report (AC3.46)

A report is professional-appearing output generated from tables or queries that may include design elements, groups, and summary information.

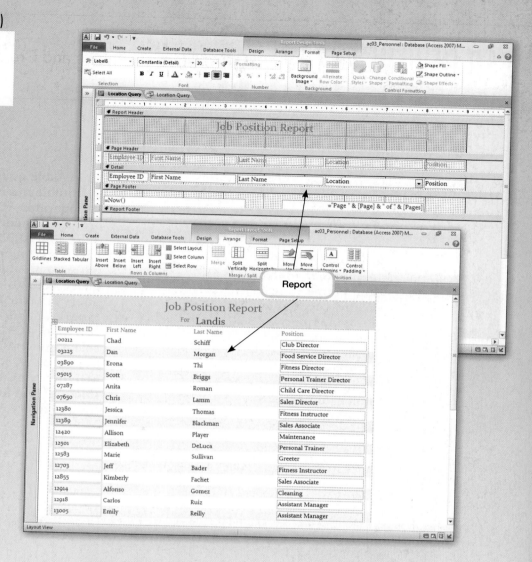

KEY TERMS

action query AC3.20
aggregate functions AC3.45
AND operator AC3.29
append query AC3.20
column selector bar AC3.25
compact AC3.69
compound control AC3.63
compound criteria AC3.29
criteria expression AC3.29
crosstab query AC3.20
delete query AC3.20
design grid AC3.25
field list AC3.25
hard-coded criteria AC3.43
inner join AC3.28
join AC3.26
join line AC3.26

make-table query AC3.20
multitable query AC3.25
OR operator AC3.29
orphaned records AC3.18
outer join AC3.28
parameter query AC3.20
parameter value AC3.43
query AC3.20
query criteria AC3.29
report AC3.18
row label AC3.25
select query AC3.20
Show box AC3.25
SQL query AC3.20
unequal join AC3.28
update query AC3.20

COMMAND SUMMARY

Command	Shortcut	Action
File Tab		
Save Database As		Saves database object with a new file name
Save & Publish>Back Up Database		Backs up database
Info> Compact & Repair Database		Compacts and repairs database file
Home tab		
Views group		
Report View		Displays report in Report view
Report Layout View		Displays report in Layout view
Records group		
Refresh All		Updates selected object
Σ Totals		Displays/hides Totals row
Create tab		
Queries group		
Query Wizard		Creates a query using the Query Wizard
Query Design		Creates a query using Query Design view
Reports group		
Report		Creates a report using all fields in current table
Report Design		Creates a report using Report Design view
Report Wizard		Creates a report using the Report Wizard

LAB REVIEW

COMMAND SUMMARY (CONTINUED)

Command	Shortcut	Action
Database Tools tab		
Relationships group		
Relationships		Defines how the data in tables is related
Analyze group		
Analyze Table		Evaluates table design
Query Tools Design tab		
Results group		
Run		Displays query results in Query Datasheet view
Query Setup group		
Show Table		Displays/hides Show Table dialog box
Show/Hide group		
Table Names		Displays/hides the Table row
Report Layout Tools Arrange tab		
Tabular		Arranges controls in a stacked tabular arrangement
Select Column		Selects column
Report Layout Tools Format tab		
Font group		
Align Text Left		Aligns text at left edge of control
Center		Centers text in selected control
11		Used to change the font size of text
A Font color		Changes color of text

COMMAND SUMMARY (CONTINUED)

Command	Shortcut	Action
Controls Formatting group		
Shape Fill ▾		Changes the color fill inside a control
Shape Outline ▾		Opens menu to change the border color and line thickness
Report Layout Tools Design tab		
Tools group		
Add Existing Fields		Displays/hides Add Existing Fields task pane
Themes		Applies predesigned theme styles to report
Report Layout Tools Page Setup tab		
Page Size group		
Margins		Sets margins of printed report
Page Layout group		
Page Setup		Sets features related to the page layout of printed report
Relationship Tools Design tab		
Tools group		
Relationship Report		Creates a report of the displayed relationships
Print Preview tab		
Page Size group		
Margins		Adjusts margins in printed output

LAB EXERCISES

MATCHING

Match the numbered item with the correct lettered description.

1. select query   _____ a. query that uses data from more than one table

2. [Run]   _____ b. used to ask questions about database tables

3. cell   _____ c. the most common type of query

4. query   _____ d. makes a copy of the file and rearranges the way that the file is stored on your disk

5. aggregate functions _____ e. records that do not have a matching primary key record in the associated table

6. multitable query   _____ f. runs a query and displays a query datasheet

7. compact   _____ g. calculations that are performed on a range of data

8. orphaned   _____ h. intersection of a column and row

9. parameter value   _____ i. prompts you for the specific criteria you want to use when you run the query

10. query criteria   _____ j. set of limiting conditions

TRUE/FALSE

Circle the correct answer to the following statements.

1.	A compound control consists of two controls that are associated.	True	False
2.	A query can be created with information from more than one table.	True	False
3.	Reports can be generated from tables only.	True	False
4.	Queries are used to view data in different ways, to analyze data, and to change existing data.	True	False
5.	Values that tell Access how to filter the criteria in a query are called filter expressions.	True	False
6.	Hard-coded criteria are used each time the query is run.	True	False
7.	A delete query is the most common type of query.	True	False
8.	A compound criterion is created using the AND operator.	True	False
9.	A field cannot be added to a report without using the Report Wizard.	True	False
10.	A join line shows how different tables are related.	True	False

FILL-IN

Complete the following statements by filling in the blanks with the correct terms.

1. Aggregate functions perform _____.
2. A(n) _____ is used to display the results of a query.
3. A(n) _____ is a request for specific data contained in a database.
4. A(n) _____ control is used to enter multiple criteria.
5. The _____ operator narrows the search for records that meet both conditions.
6. The Page Setup tab is used to control the page layout of the report for _____ purposes.
7. To be joined, tables must have at least one _____ field.
8. _____ are the set of limiting conditions used in filters and queries.
9. In a report, a(n) _____ is not connected to a field.
10. The _____ is where you enter the settings that define the query.

LAB EXERCISES

MULTIPLE CHOICE

Circle the letter of the correct response.

1. Bound and unbound are types of _____.
   a. buttons
   b. forms
   c. properties
   d. controls

2. The operator that broadens the filter, because any record meeting either condition is included in the output, is _____.
   a. AND
   b. OR
   c. MOST
   d. ALL

3. _____ view can be used to view the data in a report and modify the report design and layout.
   a. Layout
   b. Design
   c. Print Preview
   d. Datasheet

4. When a file is _____, it uses disk space inefficiently.
   a. broken
   b. fragmented
   c. compacted
   d. repaired

5. _____ view is used to create and modify the structure of a query.
   a. Design
   b. Update
   c. Layout
   d. Datasheet

6. A(n) _____ query prompts you for the specific criteria you want to use when you run the query.
   a. parameter
   b. SQL
   c. update
   d. append

7. A report title is a(n) _____ control because it is not connected to a field.
   a. bound
   b. associated
   c. unbound
   d. text

8. The _____ operator is assumed when you enter criteria in multiple fields.
   a. OR
   b. AND
   c. BETWEEN
   d. EQUAL TO

9. The query _____ is where you enter the settings that define the query.
   a. field list
   b. Show box
   c. design grid
   d. object

10. A join line creates a _____ relationship that establishes rules that the data must match to be included in the query results.
    a. permanent
    b. partial
    c. temporary
    d. complete

STEP-BY-STEP

PEPPER RIDGE RENTALS ★

1. As your property rental business has grown, you've noticed that potential renters usually want to search by price and date availability. You decide to create a query to determine inventory according to these parameters. Your completed query will be similar to that shown here.

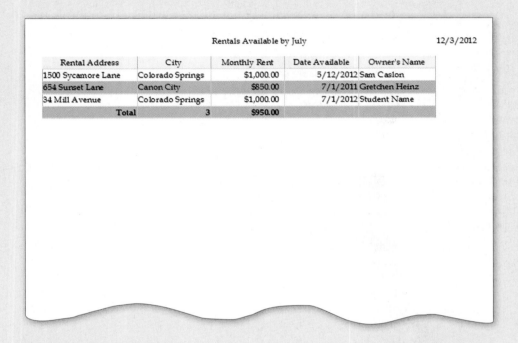

Rentals Available by July   12/3/2012

Rental Address	City	Monthly Rent	Date Available	Owner's Name
1500 Sycamore Lane	Colorado Springs	$1,000.00	5/12/2012	Sam Caslon
654 Sunset Lane	Canon City	$850.00	7/1/2011	Gretchen Heinz
34 Mill Avenue	Colorado Springs	$1,000.00	7/1/2012	Student Name
Total		3	$950.00	

a. Open the PepperRidgeRentals2 database you modified in Lab 2, Step-by-Step Exercise 4, and save as PepperRidgeRentals3.

b. Open the Rental form and add the following two new records:

Rental Address:	901 W. Sunnyslope	34 Mill Avenue
City:	Cimmaron Hills	Colorado Springs
Rented:	Y	N
Date Available:	6/15/2012	7/1/2012
Bedrooms/Baths:	3/2	2/2
Sq Footage:	1400	1300
Monthly Rent:	$750	$1000
Owner's Name:	Kim Ming	Your name

c. Create a query based on the Rentals table. Include, in this order, the Rental Address, City, Monthly Rent, Date Available, Rented, and Owner's Name fields. Save the query as **Rentals Available by July**. Use the criteria of **<=July 1, 2012** for the available date and **<=1000** for the price.

d. Filter the query to show only the records for the homes that are not currently rented. Best fit the query datasheet columns. Display a Totals row with a count in the City column and an Average in the Monthly Rent column. Print the query results.

e. Close all objects. Compact and repair the database. Exit Access.

SCENSATIONS SPA DATABASE ★ ★

2. The Scensations Salon and Day Spa offers hair and spa treatments exclusively for women. The owner of the spa is offering a new spa package that would include various anti-aging skin treatments and massages. She wants to send an announcement about this package to her clients who are over the age of 45. You will get this information for her from the client information that is stored in an Access 2010 database file. Your printed report will be similar to that shown here.

a. Open the database file named ac03_Scensations Spa and the table named Clients.

b. Find and delete any duplicate records using the Last Name field as the field to check for duplicate data. Delete the record with the higher Client ID#.

c. Use the Table Analyzer Wizard to create a second table containing the city, state, and zip code information. Name the new table **City/State/Zip**. Make the Zip Code field the primary key in this table.

Clients 45+ Report

Last Name	First Name	Address	City	State/Province	ZIP/Postal Code
Anderson	Lisa	7428 S. Hill	Yerington	NV	89447
Arnold	Beatrice	369 N. Main	Yerington	NV	89447
Austin	Alma	560 E. Hickory	Smith Valley	NV	89430
Chavez	Kristen	861 S. Tenth	Smith Valley	NV	89430
Cook	Gloria	224 E. Laurel	Dayton	NV	89403
Foster	Phyllis	27984 W. Dogwood	Fernley	NV	89408
Hayes	Robin	861 N. Fourth	Fernley	NV	89408
Henderson	Andrea	8666 N. 9th	Dayton	NV	89403
Jones	Barbara	738 N. Eighth	Smith Valley	NV	89430
Kelley	Elsie	1008 W. 11th	Silver City	NV	89428
Matthews	Erica	738 E. Sixth	Yerington	NV	89447
Myers	Peggy	492 S. Lincoln	Fernley	NV	89408
Name	Student	123 Any Street	Smith Valley	NV	89430
Peters	Sue	1238 E. Fourth	Silver City	NV	89428
Reed	Doris	10494 N. Forest	Dayton	NV	89403
Sims	Vanessa	784 N. Cherry	Smith Valley	NV	89430
Sullivan	Dawn	369 E. 8th	Fernley	NV	89408
Taylor	Dorothy	1238 E. Fifth	Smith Valley	NV	89430
Williams	Linda	495 W. Cherry	Smith Valley	NV	89430

Saturday, December 01, 2012   Page 1 of 1

d. Delete the Clients table. Rename Table1 **Clients**. Move the Lookup field after the Address field. Best fit all the fields in the table.

e. Query the Clients table to display the First Name, Last Name, and Address fields for those records with a birth date before **1/1/65**. Add all the fields from the City/State/Zip table. Move the Birth Date field to the first position in the datasheet. Run the query. If you get an error message, click OK as necessary.

LAB EXERCISES

f. Display a Totals row showing a count of the Last Name field. Save the query as **Clients 45+**. Print the query results.

g. Use the Report Wizard to create a report with the client names and addresses, based on the Clients 45+ query. Choose landscape orientation and tabular layout. Save the report as **Clients 45+ Report**.

h. Change the report margins to Normal. Apply tabular layout to the controls and then adjust the controls to fit the report on a single page widthwise.

i. Add a new record to the Clients table that includes your name in the First Name and Last Name fields and a birth date of **2/11/62**.

j. Refresh the query and report to update them.

k. Print the report.

l. Compact and repair the database. Back up the database.

m. Close the database, saving as needed, and exit Access.

DOWNTOWN INTERNET CAFÉ INVENTORY ★ ★

3. The Inventory database you created for the Downtown Internet Café (Lab 1, Step-by-Step Exercise 4) has been in use several weeks now and is working well. During this time, you have modified the table design and added more information to the table. Evan, the owner, has asked you to submit a daily report on all low-quantity items so he can place the necessary orders. You will use the database to monitor inventory levels and respond to Evan's request. First, you decide to run a query to find the low-stock items, and then you can generate the requested report from the query. Your completed report should look similar to the report below.

a. Open the database file named ac03_Cafe Inventory. Open the Stock table to view its contents. In the Suppliers table, replace the contact for Cuppa Jo (Joseph Tan) with your name.

b. Use the Query Wizard to create a query based on the Stock table. Include all fields, except Item, in their current order. Name the query **Low Stock**.

c. In Query Design view, enter the criteria to display only those records with an In Stock value less than **30**, and run the query.

Low Stock Report

Supplier	Description	In Stock	Special Order?	Contact	Phone Number	E-mail
ABC Restaurant Supply	Sugar	26	N	Richard Price	(206) 555-0037	brs@email.net
ABC Restaurant Supply	Cups-large	27	N	Richard Price	(206) 555-0037	brs@email.net
ABC Restaurant Supply	Cups-medium	28	N	Richard Price	(206) 555-0037	brs@email.net
ABC Restaurant Supply	Cups-small	29	N	Richard Price	(206) 555-0037	brs@email.net
Aquatics	Bottled water	14	N	Lee Branson	(207) 555-1122	thirst@net.com
By Design	T-Shirts	12	Y	Anna Parker	(502) 555-6973	design@email.com
Cuppa Jo	Italian Roast	12	N	Student Name	(206) 555-9090	jo@dial.com
Cuppa Jo	Espresso	11	Y	Student Name	(206) 555-9090	jo@dial.com
Cuppa Jo	Kona coffee	10	N	Student Name	(206) 555-9090	jo@dial.com
Tea and Toast, Inc.	Darjeeling Tea	13	Y	Mavis Dunhill	(206) 555-6001	tea@net.com

d. Upon reviewing the query results, you realize that the query needs to include the contact names, phone numbers, and e-mail addresses for Evan to use when he places orders. Add these fields from the Suppliers table to the query design, then run and save the query.

e. Use the Report Wizard to create a report based on the Low Stock query. Include all the fields in the order listed. Select Supplier as the only sort field. Select the tabular layout and landscape orientation. Name the report **Low Stock Report**.

f. In Design view, select the label and text box controls in both the Page Header and Detail sections. Apply the tabular layout arrangement. In Report Layout view, change the theme design for the report to Essential. Resize the control box for the title, and then change the title font color to a color of your choice. Make the shape outline for the Supplier control transparent. Adjust the field column widths as needed to appropriately display the data. Center the data in the Special Order column. Change the margin setting to Normal, and resize or move any controls that cause the report to overlap to a second page.

g. Preview and print the report. Close the Report window, saving the changes.

h. Compact and repair the database.

i. Back up the database. Exit Access.

ADVENTURE TRAVEL TOURS ★ ★

4. You have continued working on the database you created for Adventure Travel in Lab 2, On Your Own Exercise 1. Although you are pleased with it, it still needs some revisions to make booking trips easier, as well as a price sheet for selected packages to give to potential customers. Your finished report will appear similar to that shown below.

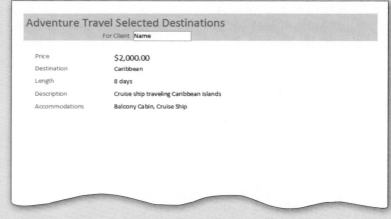

a. Open ac03_AdventureTravel and then open the Clients table. Add a new record with your name as Client **99999**, and fill out the remaining information for your client record.

b. Create a new table named **Trip Sales**. In Design view, enter **Sale #** as an AutoNumber ID field and set it as the primary key. Create a lookup field called **Client**, based on the Client table, and use the last name and first name fields sorted in ascending order. Create a lookup field called **Package**, using the Package table. Include the Destination and Length fields, and sort in ascending order by destination. Lastly, create a lookup field called **Agent**, based on the Agent table, and use the agent's last and first name, sorted in ascending order. For the Package field, look up the Destination and Length fields, and sort by destination. Adjust all column widths in the lookup as needed.

c. Switch to Datasheet view and assign trips to these customers:

Client	Package	Agent
Your Name	Caribbean	Mary Cook
Frank Cider	Hawaii	Mark Milligan
Torri Dun	Atlantic City	Lynn Sims
Scott Berco	Lake Tahoe	Mary Cook

d. Create relationships for the four tables. Enforce referential integrity for all relationships. Print the relationships report.

LAB EXERCISES

e. Create a parameter query named **Destination Query** that displays all fields from the Packages table and the Client field from the Trip Sales table. Enter **[Enter Destination]** for the criteria. Run and test the query using the destination of **Caribbean**.

f. Using the Report Wizard, create a report using the Destination Query. Include the Destination, Length, Description, Accommodations, and Price fields. Sort by price in ascending order. Use columnar layout. Save the report as **Adventure Travel Selected Destinations**.

g. Change the font size for the Price text box control to 14 point, and align the text to the left. Add the Client field to the report header, under the Adventure Travel Selected Destinations title. In the Client label, type in the word **For** to the left of Client. In Layout view, apply tabular layout to the labels and text controls before adjusting the width of any controls as needed. Print the report.

h. Add your name as the author to the database properties.

i. Compact and repair the database. Save any changes and exit Access.

ARF REPORTS ★ ★ ★

5. The Animal Rescue Foundation volunteers are successfully using the database you created in Lab 2, Step-by-Step Exercise 3, to enter information for all the rescued animals. Meanwhile, you created another table containing information about the foster homes (including names, addresses, and phone numbers). The Animal Rescue Foundation management has now asked you for a report, shown below, of all animals placed in foster homes in the past year (2011), and the names and addresses of those providing foster care, so the appropriate thank-you notes can be sent. Your completed report will be similar to the report shown here.

a. Open the database file named ac03_ARF3. Open both tables to review their content.

b. In the Rescues table, search for the dog named Tasha, update the information for Foster Date to **4/15/2011**, and attach the photo ac03_Tasha. Update her Current Status to reflect that she is now being fostered.

c. Find and delete any duplicate records in the Fosters table using the Last Name field as the field to check for duplicate data. Delete the duplicate records that have the highest Foster ID number.

d. Add your name as a new foster parent with the ID number **999** with the city of **Tempe**. Close the Fosters table.

2011 Foster Parents Report

Foster First Name	Foster Last Name	Foster Street	Foster City	Foster State	Foster Zip	Type
Gloria	Atherton	808 McDonald Rd.	Mesa	AZ	85205-0346	Cat
Katherine	Burke	834 Forest Ln.	Mesa	AZ	85205-0346	Cat
Katherine	Burke	834 Forest Ln.	Mesa	AZ	85205-0346	Cat
Theresa	Fox	969 Price Rd.	Tempe	AZ	85201-1268	Cat
Tricia	Franko	1289 S. Hayden Rd.	Mesa	AZ	85205-0346	Dog
Judith	Gold	663 Alameda Dr.	Scottsdale	AZ	85201-6760	Dog
Lucy	Granger	61 Lincoln Blvd.	Mesa	AZ	85205-0346	Cat
Bradley	Hawkins	789 University Ave.	Tempe	AZ	85201-1268	Dog
Mark	Lemon	900 Thomas Rd.	Phoenix	AZ	82891-9999	Dog
Cathy	Lind	1271 Rawhide Circle	Chandler	AZ	83174-2311	Dog
Susan	Malik	22 Sunrise Dr.	Mesa	AZ	85205-0346	Dog
Allyn	McMurphey	111 S. Central Rd.	Phoenix	AZ	82891-9999	Dog
Student	Name	123 Any Street	Tempe	AZ	85201-1268	Pig
Jennifer	Shane	22 Mill Ave.	Mesa	AZ	85205-0346	Cat
Kurt	Valdez	44 Franklin Dr.	Phoenix	AZ	82891-9999	Goat
Mike	Zito	3030 Tenth St.	Phoenix	AZ	82891-9999	Monkey

Saturday, December 01, 2012   Page 1 of 1

e. To generate the requested information, you need to add a new field to the Rescues table that identifies the foster person that was assigned to the animal. Instead of checking the Fosters table to find the number and then entering the number in the Rescues table, you will make the new field a lookup field that will display values from the Fosters table.

In Design view, add the **Foster ID#** field after the Foster Date field of the Rescues table. Select Lookup Wizard from the Data Type list. Select the following options from the Lookup Wizard:

- Look up values in a table.
- Use the Fosters table.
- Display the Foster ID#, Foster Last Name, and Foster First Name fields.
- Sort by the last and first names.
- Clear the Hide key column option, and then adjust the widths as needed.
- Select Foster ID# as the value to store.
- Use the Foster ID# field name.

f. Switch to Datasheet view. Now you need to enter the Foster ID# for all animals that have been in a foster home. Create a query to display only the pets that have had a foster in 2011. Display the animal's Name, Current Status, Foster Date, and Foster ID# columns only. Type in **>=#1/1/2011#** for the Foster Date criteria. Name the query **Fosters for 2011**. When you run the query, only the pets with a foster in 2011 should display. From the Foster ID# drop-down list, select a foster name for each record (the foster list is quite long, and you can scroll to choose more names). Select your name as the foster parent for the last animal.

g. Next you will modify the query to display the information you need in the report. Add the Fosters table to the query design and resize both table field lists to fully display their information. Delete the Foster ID# field from the grid. Add the following fields from the tables specified in the order listed below.

Rescues table

- Type

Fosters table

- Foster First Name
- Foster Last Name
- Foster Street
- Foster City
- Foster State
- Foster Zip

h. Sort the Foster Last Name column in ascending order. Run the query and review the resulting datasheet. Hide the Current Status field. Save the query again as **2011 Foster Parents**.

LAB EXERCISES

i. Use the Report Wizard to create a report based on the 2011 Foster Parents query you just saved. Include the following fields in the order listed below:

- Foster First Name
- Foster Last Name
- Foster Street
- Foster City
- Foster State
- Foster Zip
- Type

j. Group the data by Rescues; use the tabular layout and landscape orientation. Name the report **2011 Foster Parents Report**.

k. Change the page margin setting to Wide. Center the Report Header control at the top of the page. Change the theme to one of your choice. Apply the tabular table layout to all the controls in the Page Header and Detail sections. Size the controls as needed to enhance the report appearance and fit the entire report on a single page.

l. Preview and then print the report. Close the report window, saving the changes you made.

m. Compact and repair the database.

n. Back up the database and exit Access.

ON YOUR OWN

TIMELESS TREASURES REPORT ★

1. The owners of Timeless Treasures have decided to expand their offerings to include vintage clocks as well as watches. Open the database file Timeless Treasures that you worked on in Lab 2, On Your Own Exercise 5. Revisit the Web to obtain information on vintage clocks. Create a second table in the database with the same fields as the Watches table to use for maintaining the clock inventory. Name this table **Clocks**. Enter 10 records in the new table. Create an inventory report called **Timeless Treasures Watches Inventory** that displays the Identification Number, Description, Price, and Quantity on Hand fields of information. Use a layout and theme design style of your choice. Modify the report design as needed to improve its appearance. Create the same report for the Clocks table and name it **Timeless Treasures Clocks Inventory**. Preview and print both reports. Compact and back up the database.

DENTAL OFFICE CAR POOL LIST ★

2. As the office manager at Jones & Smith Dentistry, you see a need to arrange carpooling for the employees. Open the Dental Patients database you worked with in Lab 2, On Your Own Exercise 3. Create a table named **Employees** that includes fields for the employee ID number, first and last names, and home contact information (street, city, state, zip code, and phone). Enter eight records in the table. For the employee's city, choose from these three cities: **Williams**, **Flagstaff**, and **Munds Park**. Include your name as the employee name in one of the records. Then use this table to create a query that includes only the employee first and last names and home address fields of information. Sort the query by city. Enter the criteria of Williams OR Munds Park for the city. Save the query as **Employees Outside of Flagstaff**. Create a report named **Employee Car Pool List** using the query as the record source. Use tabular layout and a theme design style of your choice. Modify the report design as needed to improve its appearance. Compact and back up the database.

LEARNSOFT DEVELOPERS ★★

3. Learnsoft Inc. develops computer-based curricula for grades K–8. The company uses a database to track which software titles have been worked on by the project managers. The program manager for Learnsoft wants a report of this information so he can use it for employee reviews the following week. Open the database file ac03_Learnsoft and the table named Software. Add a new field named **Project Manager** before the Release Date field to include the name of the project manager for each title. Make this field a lookup list field that will look up the names of the five project managers. (Use names of your choice, but include your name as one of the project managers.) Complete the data for this field by selecting a project manager for each record. Assign your name as project manager to one of the records with a release date in 2012. Create a report named **Project Manager Report** that shows the titles, subject, and project manager names for the years 2010 through 2012. Use a theme design style and layout of your choice. Modify the report design as needed to improve its appearance. Compact and back up the database.

AMP EXPENSE ACCOUNT REPORT ★★

4. One of the department managers at AMP Enterprises has requested a report showing who in her department has submitted an expense reimbursement request but has not yet been paid. You decide this would be a good report to generate for all departments. In the AMP Enterprises database, open the Employee Expenses table you updated in Lab 2, On Your Own Exercise 2. Create a one-to-many relationship between the Employee Info table and the Employee Expenses table based on the Employee ID fields. Enforce referential integrity and select the Cascade Update option. Create a query that displays all fields from both tables, sorted by department. View the query results. Modify the query to not show the Employee ID field and to display only those employees who have not been paid. Apply an ascending sort to the Submission Date field. Save the query as **Pending Payment**. Use the Report Wizard to create a report named **Open Expense Requests** based on the Pending Payment query. Use a theme design style and layout of your choice. Modify the report design as needed to improve its appearance. Preview and print the report. Compact and back up the database.

LAB EXERCISES

KODIAK CONSTRUCTION REPORTS ★ ★ ★

5. The database you created for Kodiak Construction has been very well received. A few requests for changes to the database have been made, so you will create a query and a report to fulfill these requests. Open the database file named ac02_Kodiak Construction that you modified in Lab 2, Step-by-Step Exercise 5. Create a parameter query named **Priority** that displays the ID, Job, Priority, Client Last Name, and Begin Date from the Jobs table and the Foreman Last Name from the Foremen table. For the Priority field criteria, type in the parameter question **[Enter priority level]**. Create a report using the Priority query for jobs with a high priority. Include the ID, Job, Priority, Begin Date, and Foreman Last Name fields. Sort the report by begin date. Use the tabular layout in portrait orientation. Name the report **Job Priority Report**. Change the page margins to Wide. Adjust the size of the report controls in Layout view to appropriately display the data on one page. Use the Flow theme style. Preview and print the report. Create and print a relationships report. Compact and repair the database.

CASE STUDY

Lifestyle Fitness Club

Periodically, the club director wants to know the names of the employees at each club and their job positions. You created a parameter query to obtain this information and a custom report to display it professionally. Now you want to provide this information to the director.

You will learn about exporting Access data to Excel and Word using the Export Wizard. Then you will learn how to copy and paste objects and selections between Access and Word to create a memo to the director.

Your memo containing a copy of the query results and the report generated by Access will look like the one shown here.

NOTE This tutorial assumes that you already know how to use Word 2010 and that you have completed Lab 3 of Access 2010.

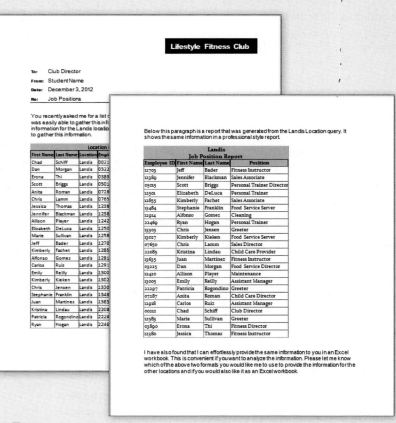

Exporting Data

There are often circumstances when you will want to provide data from an Access database for use in another program or method of presentation. The process of copying this information to a file outside the database is called

exporting. There are a variety of methods you can use, depending upon the type of output needed. The most common export types are described below:

Export to	Description
Excel	Creates a copy of the selected data, table, query, or form object and stores the copy in an Excel worksheet.
Word	Creates a copy of the selected data, table, query, form, or report, including formatting, in a new rich text file (*.rtf) that can be utilized in Word.
Access database	Creates a copy of the table definition and data or just the table definition in another Access database.
Text file	Creates a copy of the selected data, table, query, form, or report, approximating formatting if possible, in a new text file (*.txt) document.
SharePoint site	Creates a copy of a table or query and stores it on a SharePoint site as a list.

The Export Wizard is used for all types of exports. In addition, in some cases, you can copy and paste an object in another application. The file that you export from is the **source file** and the file that is created is the **destination file**.

EXPORTING TO EXCEL 2010

The director does not have Access 2010 installed on his computer, so you need to export the data to either Word 2010 or Excel 2010 format. You will try both methods to see what the output in each application looks like.

When exporting to Excel, the database file you want to copy from must be open in Access. Then you select the object you want to export. The Export Wizard can copy selected data, a table, a query, or a form object, but it cannot export a report to Excel. Because you cannot export a report, you will export the Job Positions query instead.

Additional Information

If you want to export a selection, you need to open the object and select the records you want to export.

Additional Information

Only one object can be exported at a time.

1

● Start Access 2010 and open the database file acwt1_ Personnel **from your data file location.**

● **If necessary, respond appropriately to the Security Warning.**

● **Select Location Query in the Navigation pane.**

● Click **in the Export group of the External Data tab.**

Your screen should be similar to Figure 1

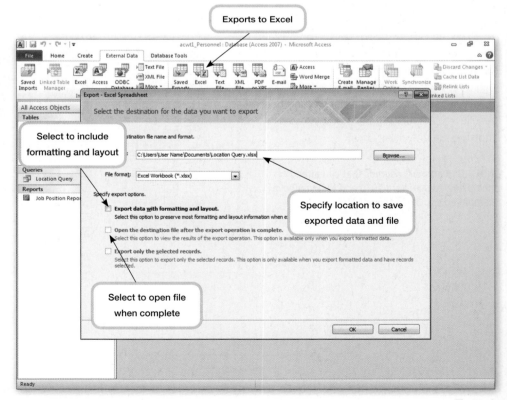

Figure 1

In the first Export-Excel Spreadsheet wizard dialog box, you specify the name of the destination file and the file format. The default file format of an Excel 2010 workbook file (.xlsx) is acceptable; however, you need to change the file location and name. In addition, you want to include the formatting from the query object and see the new Excel workbook file after it is created. Because the query is a parameter query, you also will be asked to enter which fitness club location you want the exported query results to display.

2

● Click **Browse...** and specify the location to save the file.

● In the File Save dialog box, enter the file name **Landis Job Positions** and click **Save**.

● Choose Export data with formatting and layout.

● Choose Open the destination file after the export operation is complete.

● Click **OK**.

● Type **Landis** in the Enter Parameter Value dialog box.

● Click **OK**.

● If necessary, maximize the Excel application window.

Your screen should be similar to Figure 2

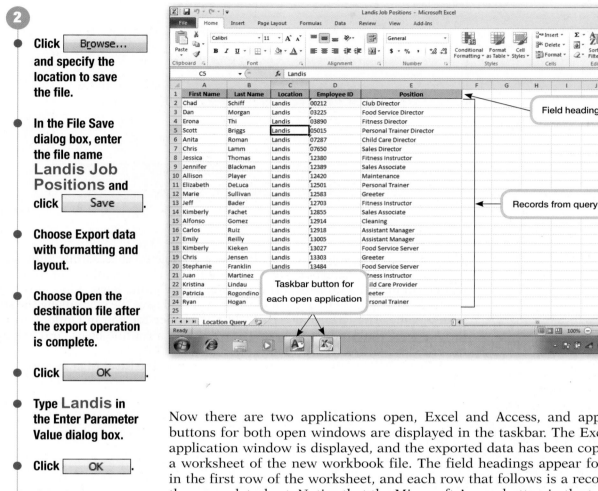

Figure 2

Now there are two applications open, Excel and Access, and application buttons for both open windows are displayed in the taskbar. The Excel 2010 application window is displayed, and the exported data has been copied into a worksheet of the new workbook file. The field headings appear formatted in the first row of the worksheet, and each row that follows is a record from the query datasheet. Notice that the Microsoft Access button in the taskbar is flashing. This is to tell you that the wizard is not yet done.

3

● **Click on the** **Microsoft Access button in the taskbar to switch to the Access application window.**

Having Trouble?

If your taskbar is hidden, point to the thin line at the bottom of the screen to redisplay it.

Your screen should be similar to Figure 3

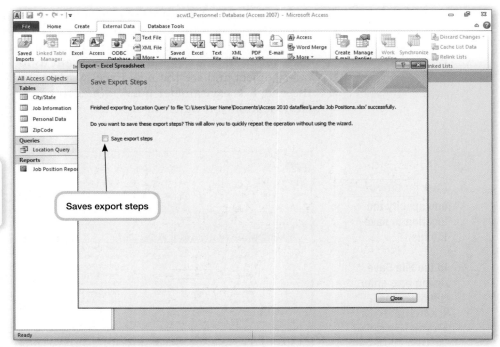

Figure 3

The final step tells you the export has been completed successfully and asks if you want to save the export steps. Saving the steps is useful if you think you will be running the same export operation on a routine basis. Since you need to repeat this operation for each location, you will save the steps using the suggested name. The wizard also can add a reminder for you in Outlook to run the export if you need to generate the results on a routine basis. You will not include this feature at this time.

Then you will use the saved export steps to export the River Mist location data.

4

- Choose Save Export Steps.

- Click **Save Export**.

- Click  in the Export group to start the next export process.

Your screen should be similar to Figure 4

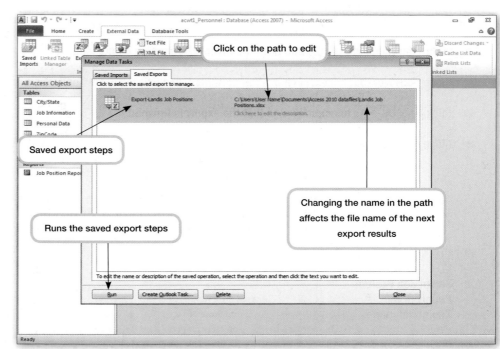

Figure 4

The Saved Exports dialog box contains options for running export steps that have been previously executed and saved. The only change you will make to the saved export is to edit the file name that is used to save the exported data in Excel to reflect the River Mist location.

5

- Click on the path, select Landis in the file name, and change it to **River Mist**

- Press ⏎Enter to complete the change.

- Click **Run**.

- In the Enter Parameter Value dialog box, type **River Mist** as the location.

- Click **OK**.

Your screen should be similar to Figure 5

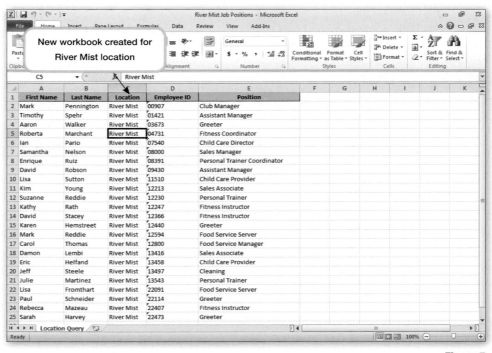

Figure 5

A separate workbook file was created and contains the data for the River Mist location. Now all the Excel features can be used to analyze the data in the worksheets. After exporting each location to a workbook, you could combine the workbooks by copying the worksheet data from each worksheet into one workbook file.

- Enter your name in cell A26 and print the River Mist location worksheet.

- Close both workbook files, saving when prompted, and exit the Excel application.

- Click [OK] to acknowledge that the export is finished.

- Close the Manage Data Tasks dialog box.

EXPORTING TO WORD 2010

Next, you will try exporting the Job Position Report to a Word document. When you use the Export Wizard to do this, a copy of the object's data is inserted into a Microsoft Word Rich Text Format file (.rtf).

1

- Select Job Position Report in the Navigation pane.

- Click [More ▾] in the Export group, and then choose [Word — Export the selected object to Rich Text]

- If necessary, change the file location to your solution file location.

Having Trouble?
The report will be saved using the default file name of Job Position Report.

- Choose Open the destination file after the export operation is complete.

- Click [OK].

- Type Landis in the Enter Parameter Value dialog box and click [OK].

Your screen should be similar to Figure 6

Having Trouble?
If WordPad is the open application, this is because your system has associated .rtf file types with this application. You could close WordPad and open the document in Word 2010.

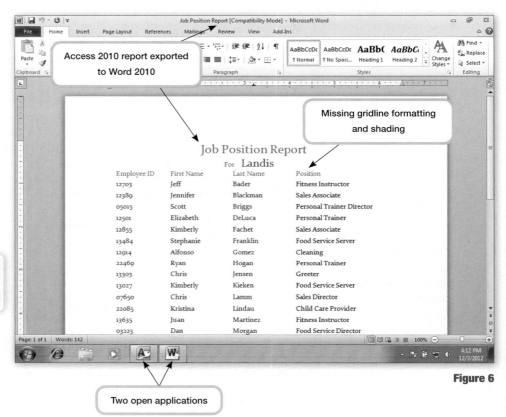

Figure 6

Now there are two applications open, Word 2010 and Access 2010, and application buttons for both open windows are displayed in the taskbar. The Word 2010 application window is displayed, and the exported data has been copied into a document file and saved as Job Position Report. The report resembles the Access report as closely as possible. The problem with the exported report is that the gridlines and shading did not copy.

Again, the Microsoft Access button in the taskbar is flashing. This time you will not save the steps.

2

● Switch to the Access application window.

● Click [Close] to close the Export Wizard.

COPYING A QUERY OBJECT TO WORD 2010

Finally, you decide to try copying an Access object to an existing Word document without using the Export Wizard. To do this, you can use the Copy and Paste commands or drag and drop to copy a database object between the Access and Word applications.

You have already started a memo to the club director about the Job Position query and report you created.

1

● Switch to the Word application window and close the Job Position Report document.

● Open the document acwt1_Job Positions from your data file location.

● In the memo header, replace Student Name with your name.

Your screen should be similar to Figure 7

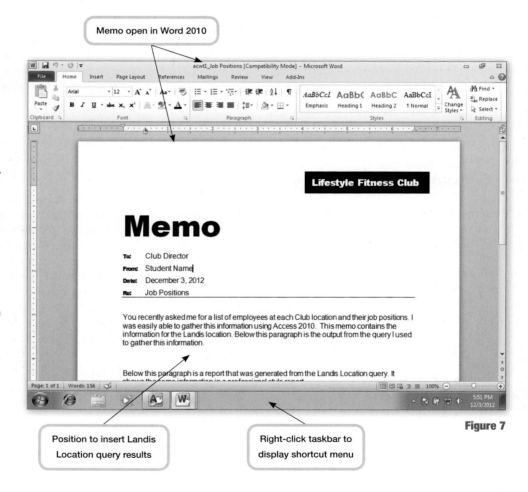

Memo open in Word 2010

Position to insert Landis Location query results

Right-click taskbar to display shortcut menu

Figure 7

This document contains the text of the memo to the director. Below the first paragraph, you want to copy the output from the Landis Location query results using drag and drop. To do this, both applications must be open and visible, which you will do by displaying the application windows side by side.

2

- **Right-click on a blank area of the taskbar to open the shortcut menu.**

- **Choose Show Windows Side by Side.**

- **Click in the Word application window to make it the active window.**

Your screen should be similar to Figure 8

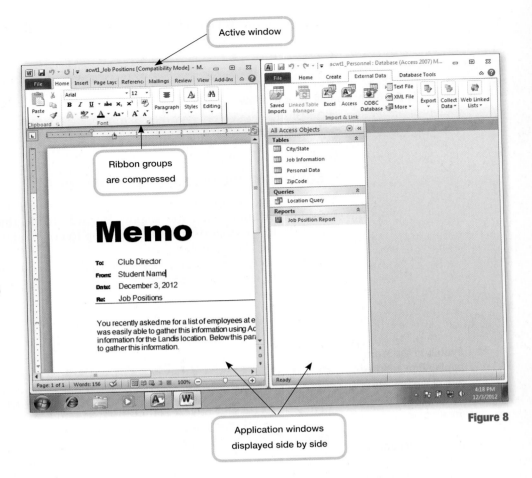

Active window

Ribbon groups are compressed

Application windows displayed side by side

Figure 8

You can now see the contents of both the Access and Word applications. The Word document contains the insertion point, and the window title bar text is not dimmed, which indicates that it is the **active window**, or the window in which you can work. Simply clicking on the other document makes it active. Because the windows are side by side and there is less horizontal space in each window, the Ribbon groups are compressed. To access commands in these groups, simply click on the group button and the commands appear in a drop-down list.

You will copy the query results using drag and drop to below the first paragraph of the memo. As you drag the object you want to copy from Access into the Word document, a temporary cursor shows the location in the document where the content will be inserted and the mouse pointer appears as .

- **Select Location Query in the Access Navigation pane.**

- **Drag the selected object to the blank line below the first paragraph of the memo.**

- **Enter Landis as the Location parameter and click [OK].**

- **Click in the Word document to deselect the table.**

- **Scroll the document to see the table.**

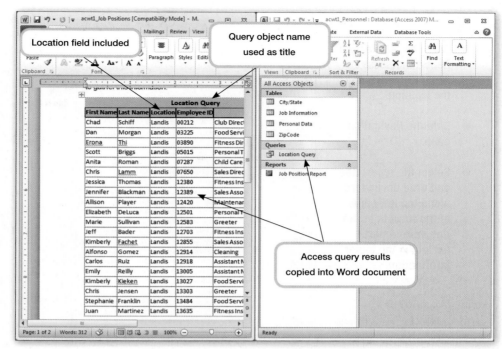

Figure 9

Your screen should be similar to Figure 9

The query results have been copied into the Word document as a table that can be edited and manipulated within Word. The formatting associated with the copied object also is included. However, the title is the same as the query name and the Location field is displayed. To change this, you could edit the title and then delete the table column using Word 2010.

COPYING A REPORT

Next, you will copy the report into the memo to show how it will look. To copy report data, you run the report in Access and then use the Copy and Paste commands to copy the contents to a Word document.

1

- Open the Job Position Report in Access using **Landis** as the location.

- Hide the Navigation pane.

- Select the report title and drag downward along the left edge of the rows to select the entire report, excluding the footer information.

Having Trouble?

If you accidentally select the footer, hold down ⇧Shift and click to the left of the last record to remove the selection from the footer.

- Open the Home tab and click Copy in the Clipboard group.

Your screen should be similar to Figure 10

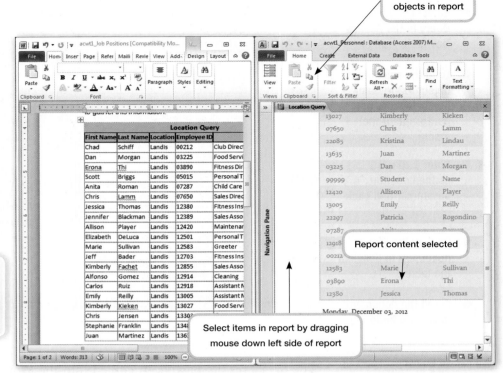

Figure 10

Next, you need to select the location in the memo where you want the copied data inserted.

2

- Scroll the Word document and click on the blank line between the second and third paragraphs.

- Click Paste in the Home tab.

- Scroll the document up to see the top of the report.

Your screen should be similar to Figure 11

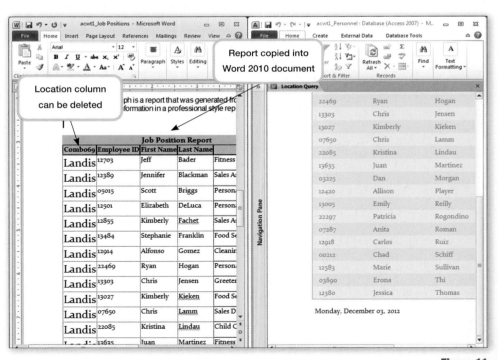

Figure 11

The copied report is similar to the copied query. The location is displayed in a column in the Word document, even though it was not displayed in the report. You will remove the column and add the location to the report title.

3

- **Select the cells in the column containing the heading Combo69 and the Landis text.**

Having Trouble?

You will have to scroll up to the previous page to select the column heading at the beginning of the table.

- **Right-click the selection and choose Delete Cells.**

- **Click [OK] to shift the cells left.**

- **Click in front of the Job Position Report title.**

- **Type Landis and press ←Enter.**

Your screen should be similar to Figure 12

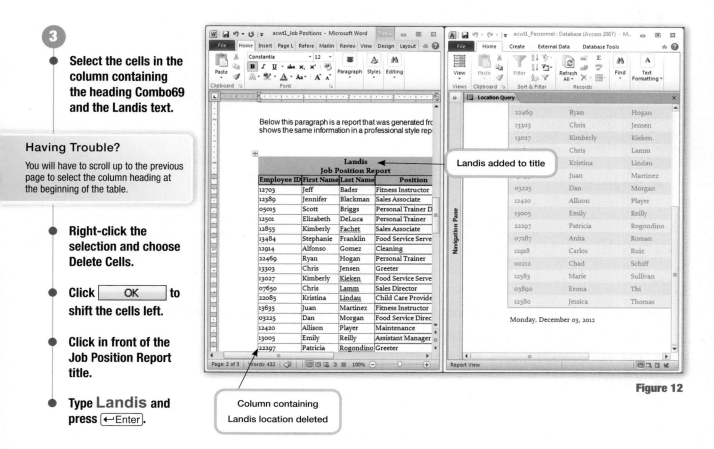

Landis added to title

Column containing Landis location deleted

Figure 12

The Location column has been removed and the table title is now descriptive of the table contents.

4

- Switch to Access and close the report.

- Click [No] to not save the copied data that was placed on the Clipboard.

- Display the Navigation pane.

- Undo the side-by-side windows.

Having Trouble?

Choose Undo Show Side by Side from the taskbar shortcut menu.

- Exit Access.

Currently the Word document is three pages long and the Location Query table is split between pages. To correct this, you will remove the MEMO heading at the top of the document.

5

- Move to the top of the document and select and delete the word "MEMO". Add a blank line at that location.

- Delete the blank line above both tables in the memo.

- Save the memo as Landis Job Positions to your solution file location.

- Print the memo.

- Exit Word.

Deleting the MEMO heading allowed enough room for each table to fit on its own page. Your printed memo should now be only two pages long and look similar to the one shown in the case study at the beginning of this lab.

KEY TERMS

active window ACWT1.8	export ACWT1.2
destination file ACWT1.2	source file ACWT1.2

COMMAND SUMMARY

Command	Shortcut	Action
Home tab		
Clipboard group		
Copy	Ctrl + C	Copies selection to Clipboard
Paste	Ctrl + V	Pastes selection into document at insertion point
External Data tab		
Export group		
Saved Exports		Views and runs saved exports
Excel		Exports selected object to an Excel workbook
More ▾ / Word Export the selected object to Rich Text		Exports selected object to a Rich Text Format (*.rtf) file

LAB EXERCISES | Hands-On Exercises

STEP-BY-STEP

SPA MARKETING MEMO ★

1. The Scensations Salon and Day Spa database has been used extensively. The owner asked you for a list of clients who are over the age of 45 to get an idea of how much interest there would be in an anti-aging spa package she is considering offering. You already filtered the Clients table to locate this information and now want to include the results in a memo to Latisha. The first page of the memo is shown here.

   a. Open the ac03_Scensations Spa database file and the Clients table that you modified in Lab 3, Step-by-Step Exercise 2. Display the results of the Clients 45+ query.

   b. Start Word 2010 and enter the following text in a new document.

   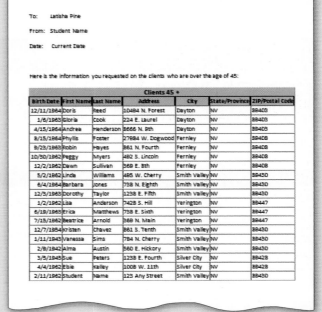

To:	Latisha Pine
From:	[Your Name]
Date:	[current date]

   Here is the information you requested on the clients who are over the age of 45:

   c. Select the Clients 45+ query results and copy them into the Word document.

   d. Save the memo as **45+ Spa Clients**. Print the memo.

   e. Close the document and exit Word.

   f. Close the table and database.

LOW STOCK ANALYSIS ★ ★

2. Evan, the owner of the Downtown Internet Café, continues to be impressed with the café's inventory database (Lab 3, Step-by-Step Exercise 3). He has asked you for a list of all special-order items and how many of these items are currently in stock. He wants this information as an Excel 2010 worksheet so that he can further analyze the data. You will provide this information by exporting the data from Access 2010 to Excel 2010. Your completed worksheet of this data should be similar to that shown here.

Item	Description	In Stock	Special Order?	Supplier
121	Powdered cream	31	Y	ABC Restaurant Supply
131	T-Shirts	10	Y	By Design
171	Decaf Viennese	33	Y	Pure Processing
172	Decaf Sumatra	35	Y	Pure Processing
200	Business cards	43	Y	Pro Printing
257	Coffee mints	30	Y	Sweet Stuff
273	French Roast	47	Y	Café Ole
753	Guatamala coffee	45	Y	Cuppa Jo
754	Java coffee	46	Y	Cuppa Jo
755	Arabian coffee	47	Y	Cuppa Jo
759	Espresso	11	Y	Cuppa Jo
859	Darjeeling Tea	13	Y	Tea and Toast, Inc.

a. Open the ac03_Cafe Inventory database that you modified in Lab 3, Step-by-Step Exercise 3.

b. Create a new query named **Special Orders** that will display items with Y in the Special Order? field, and include the Description, In Stock, Special Order?, and Supplier fields (in that order). Run the query, then save it.

c. Export the data to Excel using the file name **Special Orders**. Include formatting but do not choose Open to view the file. Close the workbook file.

d. Save the export steps.

e. In Access, with the query still open, change the InStock for t-shirts to **10** and coffee mints to **30**. Rerun the export using the saved steps, replacing the Special Orders file.

f. Print the worksheet and exit Excel.

g. Save the query. Close the table and database.

LAB EXERCISES

FOSTER PARENTS MEMO ★★

3. The Foster Parents Report you created for the Animal Rescue Foundation needs to be sent to management. (See Lab 3, Step-by-Step Exercise 5.) You want to include a brief note with the report and decide to export the report to a memo you create using Word. Your completed memo should be similar to that shown here.

a. Open the ac03_ARF3 database that you created in Lab 3, Step-by-Step Exercise 5. Save the database as acWT1_ARF. Modify the 2011 Foster Parents query to show only the Name, Foster Date, Foster First Name, and Foster Last Name fields. Leave the criteria for the foster date at >=#1/1/2011#. Save the query as **2011 Foster Names**.

b. Export the 2011 Foster Names query results to a Word document named **ARF Foster Parents**.

c. Enter the following text appropriately spaced above the table in the document.

To: **ARF Management**
From: **[Your Name]**
Date: **[current date]**
Re: **Foster Parents for 2011**

As you requested, here is a list of foster parents and pets for the year 2011.

To: ARF Management

From: [Your Name]

Date: [Current Date]

Re: Foster Parents for 2011

As you requested, here is a list of foster parents and pets for the year 2011.

Name	Foster Date	Foster First Name	Foster Last Name
Sylvester	7/30/2011	Gloria	Atherton
Grey	9/1/2011	Katherine	Burke
Tiny	11/12/2011	Katherine	Burke
Taz	12/23/2011	Theresa	Fox
Tasha	4/15/2011	Tricia	Franko
Samson	7/1/2011	Judith	Gold
Muffin	10/25/2011	Lucy	Granger
Lorelei	7/19/2011	Bradley	Hawkins
Fred	8/12/2011	Mark	Lemon
Ruff	11/15/2011	Cathy	Lind
Sandi	11/30/2011	Susan	Malik
Ralph	1/15/2011	Allyn	McMurphy
Babe	2/1/2011	Student	Name
Tabby	6/20/2011	Jennifer	Shane
Billy	11/3/2011	Kurt	Valdez
George	3/2/2011	Mike	Zito

d. Apply formatting of your choice to the table. Size and center the table appropriately.

e. Save the memo. Print the document.

f. Close the document and database.

Objectives

After completing this lab, you will know how to:

1 Use a template to create a presentation.

2 View and edit a presentation.

3 Copy and move selections.

4 Move, copy, and delete slides.

5 Move, demote, and promote items.

6 Use a numbered list.

7 Check spelling.

8 Size and move placeholders.

9 Change fonts and formatting.

10 Insert and modify clip art.

11 Run a slide show.

12 Document a file.

14 Preview and print a presentation.

Animal Rescue Foundation

You are the volunteer coordinator at the local Animal Rescue Foundation. This nonprofit organization rescues unwanted pets from local animal shelters and finds foster homes for them until a suitable adoptive family can be found. The agency has a large volunteer group called the Animal Angels that provides much-needed support for the foundation.

The agency director has decided to launch a campaign to increase community awareness about the foundation. As part of the promotion, you have been asked to create a powerful and persuasive presentation to entice more members of the community to join Animal Angels.

The agency director has asked you to preview the presentation at the weekly staff meeting tomorrow and has asked you to present a draft of the presentation by noon today.

To help you create the presentation, you will use Microsoft PowerPoint 2010, a graphics presentation application that is designed to create presentation materials such as slides, overheads, and handouts. Using PowerPoint 2010, you can create a high-quality and interesting onscreen presentation with pizzazz that will dazzle your audience.

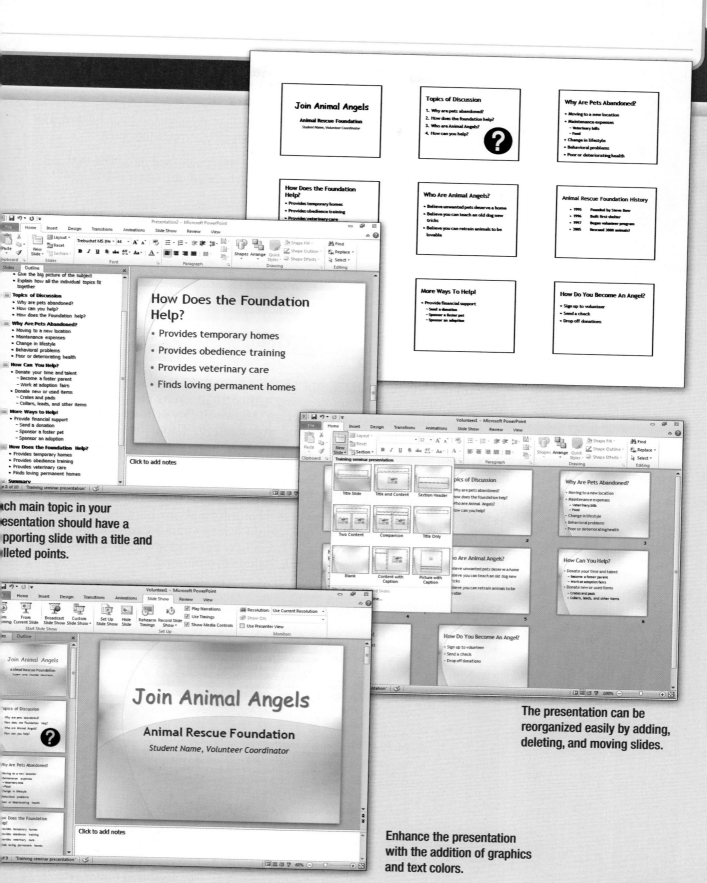

The presentation can be reorganized easily by adding, deleting, and moving slides.

Enhance the presentation with the addition of graphics and text colors.

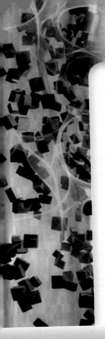

The following concepts will be introduced in this lab:

1 Slide A slide is an individual "page" of your presentation.

2 Spelling Checker The spelling checker locates all misspelled words, duplicate words, and capitalization irregularities as you create and edit a presentation, and proposes possible corrections.

3 AutoCorrect The AutoCorrect feature makes some basic assumptions about the text you are typing and, based on those assumptions, automatically corrects the entry.

4 Layout A layout defines the position and format for objects and text on a slide. A layout contains placeholders for the different items such as bulleted text, titles, charts, and so on.

5 Graphic A graphic is a nontext element or object such as a drawing or picture that can be added to a slide.

Starting a New Presentation

The Animal Rescue Foundation has just installed the latest version of the Microsoft Office suite of applications, Office 2010, on its computers. You will use the graphics presentation program, Microsoft PowerPoint 2010, included in the Office suite, to create your presentation. Using this program, you should have no problem creating the presentation in time for tomorrow's staff meeting.

DEVELOPING A PRESENTATION

During your presentation, you will present information about the Animal Rescue Foundation and why someone should want to join the Animal Angels volunteer group. As you prepare to create a new presentation, you should follow several basic steps: plan, create, edit, enhance, and rehearse.

Step	Description
Plan	The first step in planning a presentation is to understand its purpose. You also need to find out the length of time you have to speak, who the audience is, what type of room you will be in, and what kind of audiovisual equipment is available. These factors help to determine the type of presentation you will create.
Create	To begin creating your presentation, develop the content by typing your thoughts or notes into an outline. Each main idea in your presentation should have a supporting slide with a title and bulleted points.
Edit	While typing, you will probably make typing and spelling errors that need to be corrected. This is one type of editing. Another type is to revise the content of what you have entered to make it clearer, or to add or delete information. To do this, you might insert a slide, add or delete bulleted items, or move text to another location.
Enhance	You want to develop a presentation that grabs and holds the audience's attention. Choose a design that gives your presentation some dazzle. Wherever possible, add graphics to replace or enhance text. Add effects that control how a slide appears and disappears and that reveal text in a bulleted list one bullet at a time.
Rehearse	Finally, you should rehearse the delivery of your presentation. For a professional presentation, your delivery should be as polished as your materials. Use the same equipment that you will use when you give the presentation. Practice advancing from slide to slide and then back in case someone asks a question. If you have a mouse available, practice pointing or drawing on the slide to call attention to key points.

After rehearsing your presentation, you may find that you want to go back to the editing phase. You may change text, move bullets, or insert a new slide. Periodically, as you make changes, rehearse the presentation again to see how the changes affect your presentation. By the day of the presentation, you will be confident about your message and at ease with the materials.

EXPLORING THE POWERPOINT DOCUMENT WINDOW

During the planning phase, you have spoken with the foundation director regarding the purpose of the presentation and the content in general. The purpose of your presentation is to educate members of the community about the organization and to persuade many to volunteer. In addition, you want to impress the director by creating a professional presentation.

1

● **Start the PowerPoint 2010 application.**

● **If necessary, maximize the window.**

Your screen should be similar to Figure 1.1

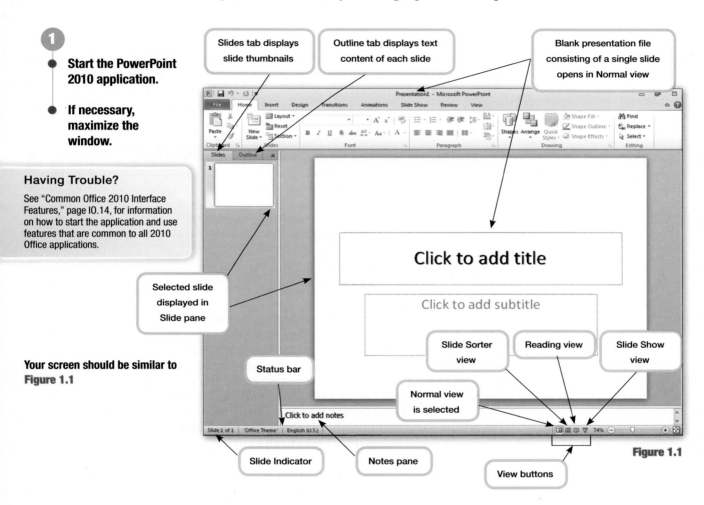

Figure 1.1

When you first start PowerPoint, a new blank presentation file, named Presentation1, is opened and displayed in the document window. It is like a blank piece of paper that already has many predefined settings. These default settings are generally the most commonly used settings and are stored in the Blank Presentation template file.

Many other templates that are designed to help you create professional-looking presentations are also available within PowerPoint and from the Microsoft Office Online Web site. They include design templates, which provide a design concept, fonts, and color scheme; and content templates, which suggest content for your presentation based on the type of presentation you are making. You also can design and save your own presentation templates.

The Blank Presentation template consists of a single slide that is displayed in the document window.

Concept 1 Slide

A **slide** is an individual "page" of your presentation. The first slide of a presentation is the title slide, which is used to introduce your presentation. Additional slides are used to support each main point in your presentation. The slides give the audience a visual summary of the words you speak, which helps them understand the content and keeps them engaged. The slides also help you, the speaker, organize your thoughts and prompt you during the presentation.

When you first start PowerPoint, it opens in a view called Normal view. A **view** is a way of looking at a presentation and provides the means to interact with the presentation. PowerPoint provides several views you can use to look at and modify your presentation. Depending on what you are doing, one view may be preferable to another.

View	Button	Description
Normal		Provides four working areas of the window that allow you to work on all aspects of your presentation in one place.
Slide Sorter		Displays a miniature of each slide to make it easy to reorder slides, add special effects such as transitions, and set timing between slides.
Reading View		Displays each slide in final form within the PowerPoint window so you can see how it will look during a presentation but still have access to the Windows desktop.
Slide Show		Displays each slide in final form using the full screen space so you can practice or present the presentation.

Normal view is displayed by default because it is the main view you use while creating a presentation. Normal view has four working areas: Outline tab, Slides tab, Slide pane, and Notes pane. These areas allow you to work on all components of your presentation in one convenient location. The **Outline tab** displays the text content of each slide in outline format, and the **Slides tab** displays a miniature version or **thumbnail** of each slide. You can switch between the Slides and Outline tabs by clicking on the tab. The **Slide pane** displays the selected slide. The **Notes pane** includes space for you to enter notes that apply to the current slide.

Below the document window is the status bar, which displays the slide indicator, messages and information about various PowerPoint settings, buttons to change the document view, and a window zoom feature. The **slide indicator** identifies the number of the slide that is displayed in the Slide pane, along with the total number of slides in the presentation. You will learn about the other features of the status bar shortly.

You decide to try to create your first presentation using the Blank Presentation template. It is the simplest and most generic of the templates. Because it has minimal design elements, it is good to use when you first start working with PowerPoint, as it allows you to easily add your own content and design changes.

Notice the slide contains two boxes with dotted borders. These boxes, called **placeholders**, are containers for all the content that appears on a slide. Slide content consists of text and **objects** such as, graphics, tables and charts. In this case, the placeholders are text placeholders that are designed to contain text and display standard **placeholder text** messages that prompt the user to enter a title and subtitle.

ENTERING AND EDITING TEXT

As suggested, you will enter the title for the presentation. As soon as you click on the placeholder, the placeholder text will disappear and will be replaced by the text you want to appear in the slide.

1

Click the "Click to add title" placeholder.

Your screen should be similar to Figure 1.2

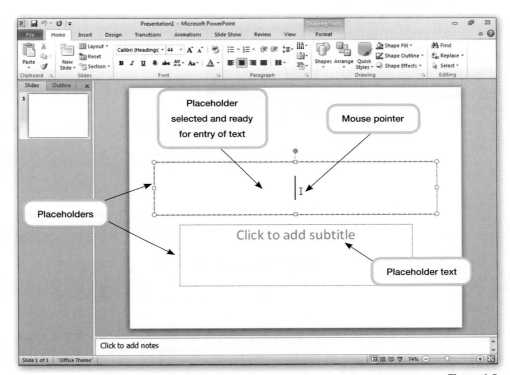

Figure 1.2

Additional Information

A solid border indicates that you can format the placeholder box itself. Clicking the dashed-line border changes it to a solid border.

Notice that the placeholder is surrounded with a dashed-line border. This indicates that you can enter, delete, select, and format the object inside the placeholder. Because this placeholder contains text, the cursor is displayed to show your location in the text and to allow you to select and edit the text. Additionally, the mouse pointer appears as a I to be used to position the cursor.

Next you will type the title text you want to appear on the slide. Then you will enter the subtitle.

Having Trouble?

See the section "Entering and Editing Text" in the Introduction to Microsoft Office 2010 to review this feature.

Type Join
Animal Angels

Having Trouble?

If you make a typing error, press
Backspace to delete the characters
back to the error and retype the entry.

**Click in the "Click
to add subtitle"
placeholder and type
Animal Rescue
Foundation**

Your screen should be similar to
Figure 1.3

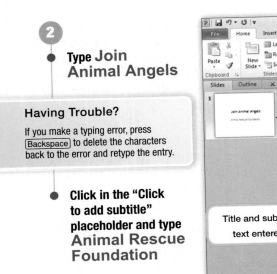

Figure 1.3

The content for the first slide is complete. Notice that the thumbnail of the
slide in the Slides tab now displays the text you just entered.

INSERTING A SLIDE

Next you want to add the content for a second slide. To continue creating the
presentation, you need to add another slide.

1

**If necessary, click the
Home tab to open it.**

Click New Slide **in the
Slides group.**

Another Method

You also can use the keyboard shortcut
Ctrl + M to insert a new slide.

Your screen should be similar to
Figure 1.4

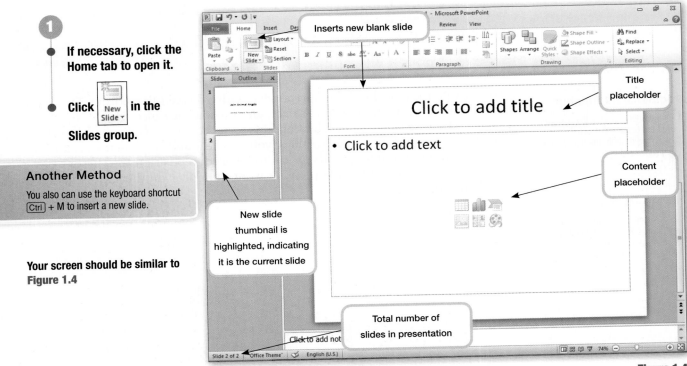

Figure 1.4

A new slide with a slide title placeholder and a content placeholder was added to the presentation. It is displayed in the Slide pane and is the **current slide**, or the slide that will be affected by any changes you make. The Slides tab displays a second slide thumbnail. It is highlighted, further indicating it is the current slide. The status bar displays the number of the current slide and the total number of slides in the presentation.

Now you could add text to the new slide and continue adding slides to create the presentation.

OPENING A PRESENTATION TEMPLATE

Although the Blank presentation template is opened automatically when you start PowerPoint, it is not the only method that can be used to create a presentation. Another is to use one of the many supplied design templates. A third is to save the design elements of an existing presentation as a custom template, which you would then use as the basis for your new presentation. Finally, you can open an existing presentation and modify the design and content as needed for the new presentation.

Because you have not decided exactly what content should be presented next in the presentation, you decide that it might be easier to use one of the templates that will suggest the content to include. You will close this file without saving it and then open a presentation template file.

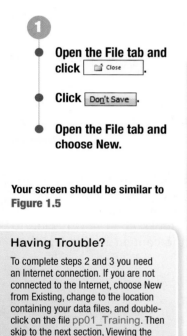

- Open the File tab and click ▭ Close.

- Click Don't Save.

- Open the File tab and choose New.

Your screen should be similar to Figure 1.5

Having Trouble?

To complete steps 2 and 3 you need an Internet connection. If you are not connected to the Internet, choose New from Existing, change to the location containing your data files, and double-click on the file pp01_Training. Then skip to the next section, Viewing the Presentation.

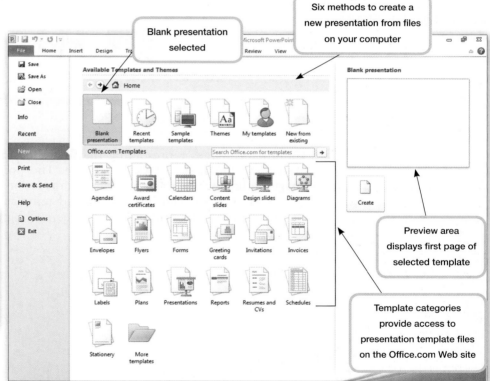

Figure 1.5

The Available Templates and Themes window of Backstage view is open. The upper section of this window displays six options from which you can choose to start a new presentation from files that are stored on your computer. The Blank presentation template is selected, as this is the default template that is opened when you first start PowerPoint. The five other choices provide the means of

Additional Information

The template categories and files may vary as the content from the Office.com Web site is updated frequently.

starting a presentation from recent templates you have opened, templates you have created, or other existing presentations.

The lower section of the window displays categories of templates that are available online from Microsoft. When you choose a category, folders of additional subcategories are displayed that contain the available presentation template files. For this presentation, you want to look at the online templates.

2

● **Choose Presentations from the Office.com Templates category.**

● **Choose the Training folder.**

● **Scroll the list of template files in the Training folder and select "Employee Training Presentation".**

Your screen should be similar to Figure 1.6

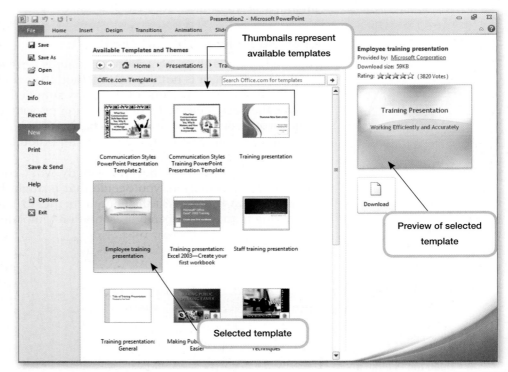

Figure 1.6

Thumbnail images representing the first slide in each template file are displayed in alphabetical order by name. The preview area displays a larger image of the selected thumbnail and information about the template.

You think the design of the selected template looks good and decide to begin your presentation for the volunteers using the content in this template as a guide.

Click ___ .

● **If necessary, close the Help window.**

Your screen should be similar to Figure 1.7

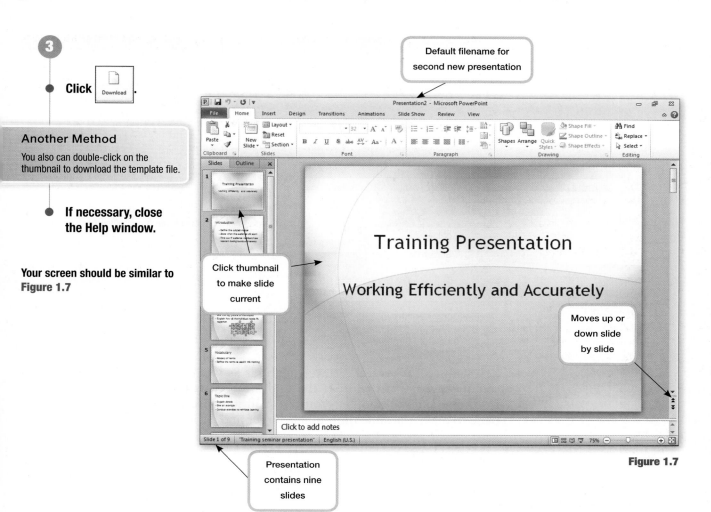

Default filename for second new presentation

Click thumbnail to make slide current

Moves up or down slide by slide

Figure 1.7

Presentation contains nine slides

The template file is downloaded and opened in PowerPoint. It contains a total of nine slides. Because this is the second new presentation you have worked on since starting PowerPoint 2010, the default file name is Presentation2.

MOVING AMONG SLIDES

You want to look at the slides in the presentation to get a quick idea of their content. There are many ways to move from slide to slide in PowerPoint. Most often, the quickest method is to click on the slide thumbnail in the Slides tab. Clicking on a slide in the Slides tab displays it in the Slide pane and makes it the current slide. However, if your hands are already on the keyboard, you may want to use the keyboard directional keys. The following table shows both keyboard and mouse methods to move among slides in Normal view.

To Display	Action
Previous slide	Click ▲
	Click above scroll box
	Press Page Up
	↑ One slide up
Next slide	Click ▼
	Click below scroll box
	Press Page Down
	↓ One slide down
Any slide	Drag the Slide pane's scroll box until the ScreenTip displays the slide you want to view.
Last slide in presentation	End
First slide in presentation	Home

You will try out several of these methods as you look at the slides in the presentation. First you will use the Slides tab. This tab makes it easy to move from one slide to another. You also will increase the width of the Slide tab pane to make the slide thumbnails larger and easier to see.

1

- Point to the splitter bar between the Slide pane and the Slides tab pane and when the mouse pointer is shaped as ↔ drag to the right to increase the width of the pane as in Figure 1.8.

- Press ↓ or Page Down to move to the next slide.

- Scroll the Slides tab to display slides 4 to 7.

- Click on slide 4.

Your screen should be similar to Figure 1.8

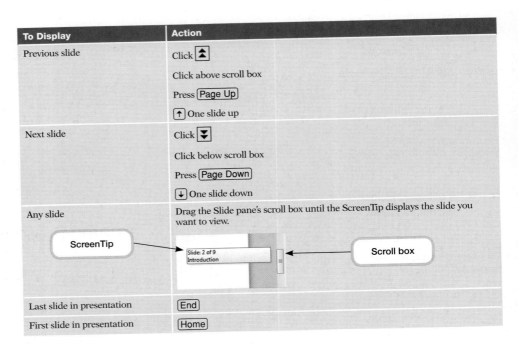

Figure 1.8

Slide 4 is the current slide and is displayed in the Slide pane. This slide contains two placeholders: title and content. The content placeholder consists of two bulleted items as well as a graphic. Next you will use the Slide pane scroll bar to display the next few slides.

Click ⏷ Next Slide to display slide 5.

Having Trouble?

The ⏶ Previous Slide and ⏷ Next Slide buttons are located at the bottom of the Slide pane's vertical scroll bar.

Drag the scroll box and stop when the ScreenTip displays Slide 6 of 9.

Click below the scroll box to display slide 7.

Press End to display the last slide.

Your screen should be similar to Figure 1.9

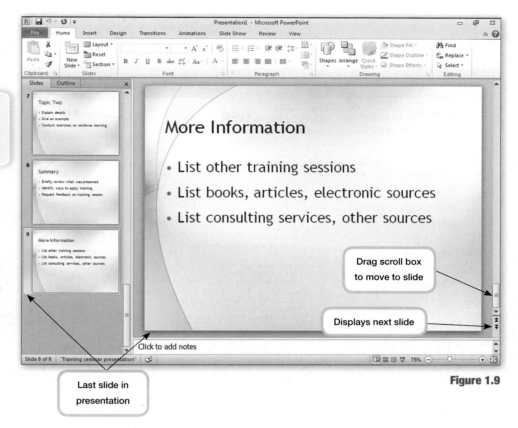

Last slide in presentation

Drag scroll box to move to slide

Displays next slide

Figure 1.9

You can see this template will help you to create your presentation because the content provides some basic guidance as to how to organize a presentation.

Editing a Presentation

Now you need to edit the presentation to replace the sample content with the appropriate information for your presentation. Editing involves making text changes and additions to the content of your presentation. It also includes making changes to the organization of content. This can be accomplished quickly by rearranging the order of bulleted items on slides as well as the order of slides.

USING THE OUTLINE TAB

You have already entered text in a slide in the Slide pane. Another way to make text-editing changes is to use the Outline tab in Normal view. The Outline tab displays the content of the presentation in outline form, making it easy to see the organization of your presentation as you enter and edit content. The first change you want to make is to enter a title for the presentation on slide 1. First, you will open the Outline tab and select the sample title text on the slide and delete it.

1

- Click the Outline tab to open it.

- Scroll the Outline tab to the top to display the text for slide 1.

- Click anywhere on the text for slide 1 in the Outline tab to make it the current slide.

- Select the text "Training Presentation".

Having Trouble?

Refer to the topic "Selecting Text" in the Introduction to Microsoft Office 2010 to review these features.

- Press Delete.

Your screen should be similar to Figure 1.10

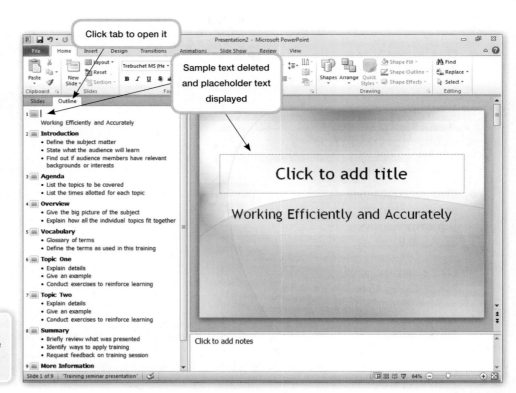

Figure 1.10

The sample text is deleted. As you change the text content in the Outline tab, it also appears in the slide displayed in the Slide pane. Notice that although you deleted the sample text, the slide still displays the title placeholder text.

You will enter the title and subtitle for the presentation next.

2

Type Join Animal Angels

Having Trouble?

If you make a typing error, use Backspace or Delete to correct the errors.

● **Select the text "Working Efficiently and Accurately" on the second line of slide 1 in the Outline tab and type Animal Rescue Foundation**

Your screen should be similar to Figure 1.11

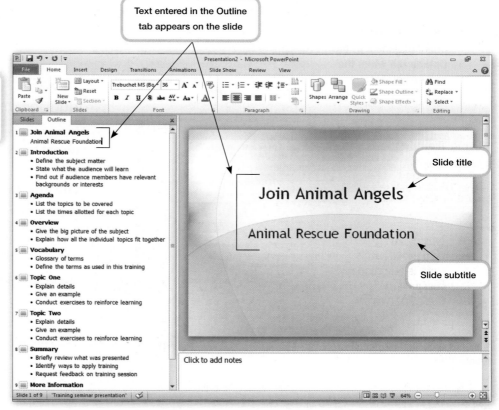

Figure 1.11

Additional Information

If you click the slide icon to the right of the slide number in the Outline tab, all text on the slide is selected.

As soon as you pressed a key, the selected text was deleted and replaced with the text you typed. When entering the title for a slide, it is a common practice to use title case, in which the first letter of most words is capitalized.

The next change you want to make is in the Introduction slide. The sample text recommends that you define the subject of the presentation and what the audience will learn. You will replace the sample text next to the first bullet with the text for your slide. In the Outline tab, you can select an entire paragraph and all subparagraphs by pointing to the left of the line and clicking when the mouse pointer is a ✛.

3

● **Click on the first bullet of slide 2 in the Outline tab when the mouse pointer is a** **.**

Having Trouble?

If you accidentally drag selected text, it will move. To return it to its original location, immediately click [↺] ▾ Undo on the Quick Access Toolbar.

● **Type Your Name, Volunter (this word is intentionally misspelled) Coordinator**

Your screen should be similar to Figure 1.12

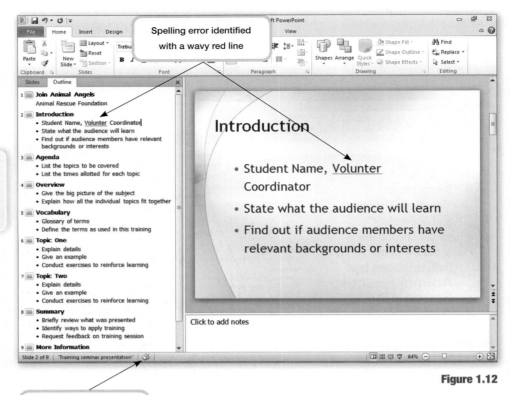

Figure 1.12

Having Trouble?

Do not be concerned if the spelling checker identifies your name as misspelled.

Having Trouble

If the Spelling indicator is not displayed, right click on the status bar and choose Spell Check from the context menu.

The sample text has been replaced with the text you typed. Depending on the length of your name, the text in this bullet may not have wrapped to a second line.

CORRECTING ERRORS

As you enter text, the program checks each word for accuracy. In this case, a spelling error was located. PowerPoint identified the word as misspelled by underlining it with a wavy red line. The Spelling indicator in the status bar also shows a spelling error has been detected in the document.

Concept **2** Spelling Checker

The **spelling checker** locates all misspelled words, duplicate words, and capitalization irregularities as you create and edit a presentation, and proposes possible corrections. This feature works by comparing each word to a dictionary of words. If the word does not appear in the main dictionary or in a custom dictionary, it is identified as misspelled. The **main dictionary** is supplied with the program; a **custom dictionary** is one you can create to hold words you commonly use, such as proper names and technical terms, that are not included in the main dictionary.

If the word does not appear in either dictionary, the program identifies it as misspelled by displaying a red wavy line below the word. You can then correct the misspelled word by editing it. Alternatively, you can display a list of suggested spelling corrections for that word and select the correct spelling from the list to replace the misspelled word in the presentation.

To quickly correct the misspelled word, you can select the correct spelling from a list of suggested spelling corrections displayed on the shortcut menu.

1

● **Right-click on the misspelled word in the Outline tab to display the shortcut menu.**

Your screen should be similar to Figure 1.13

Additional Information

Sometimes the spelling checker cannot suggest replacements because it cannot locate any words in its dictionary that are similar in spelling. Other times the suggestions offered are not correct. If either situation happens, you must edit the word manually.

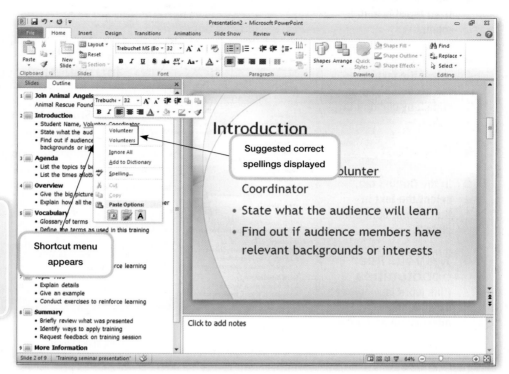

Figure 1.13

The shortcut menu displays two suggested correct spellings. The menu also includes several related menu options described below.

Additional Information

The spelling checker works just as it does in the other Microsoft Office 2010 applications.

Option	Effect
Ignore All	Instructs PowerPoint to ignore the misspelling of this word throughout the rest of this session.
Add to Dictionary	Adds the word to the custom dictionary list. When a word is added to the custom dictionary, PowerPoint will always accept that spelling as correct.
Spelling	Opens the Spelling dialog box to check the entire presentation.

You will replace the word with the correct spelling and then enter the information for the second bullet.

2

- Choose "Volunteer" from the shortcut menu.

- In the Outline tab, select the text in the second bullet on slide 2 by clicking the bullet.

- Press [Delete].

- In the Outline tab, select the text in the second bullet on slide 2.

- Type volunteer oppotunities (this word is intentionally misspelled) and press [Spacebar].

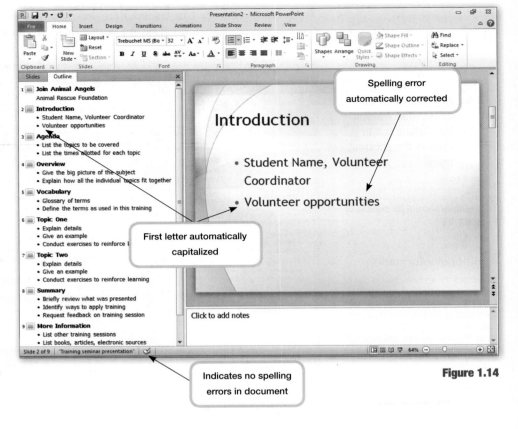

Figure 1.14

Your screen should be similar to Figure 1.14

Additional Information

Bulleted items in a presentation are capitalized in sentence case format. Ending periods, however, are not included.

Notice that the first letter of "volunteer" was automatically capitalized. Also notice that the incorrect spelling of the word "oppotunities" was corrected. These corrections are part of the AutoCorrect feature of PowerPoint.

Concept AutoCorrect

The **AutoCorrect** feature makes some basic assumptions about the text you are typing and, based on those assumptions, automatically corrects the entry. The AutoCorrect feature automatically inserts proper capitalization at the beginning of sentences and in the names of days of the week. It also will change to lowercase letters any words that were incorrectly capitalized due to the accidental use of the [Caps Lock] key. In addition, it also corrects many common typing and spelling errors automatically.

One way the program makes corrections automatically is by looking for certain types of errors. For example, if two capital letters appear at the beginning of a word, the second capital letter is changed to a lowercase letter. If a lowercase letter appears at the beginning of a sentence, the first letter of the first word is capitalized. If the name of a day begins with a lowercase letter, the first letter is capitalized.

Another way the program makes corrections is by automatically replacing a misspelled word with the correct spelling in situations where the spelling checker offers only one suggested spelling correction. AutoCorrect also checks all words against the AutoCorrect list, a built-in list of words that are commonly spelled or typed incorrectly. If it finds the entry on the list, the program automatically replaces the error with the correction. For example, the typing error "aboutthe" is automatically changed to "about the" because the error is on the AutoCorrect list. You also can add words to the AutoCorrect list that you want to be corrected automatically. Any such words are added to the list on the computer you are using and will be available to anyone who uses the machine after you.

COPYING AND MOVING SELECTIONS

You are now ready to enter the text for the next slide in your presentation by entering the three main topics of discussion. You want to enter a new slide title, Topics of Discussion, with three bulleted items describing the topics to be discussed. Two placeholder bullets with sample text are displayed. You will edit these and then add a third bulleted item.

1

- Move to slide 3.

- In the Outline tab, replace the sample title, Agenda, with **Topics of Discussion**

- Select and replace the text in the first bullet with **Why are pets abandoned?**

- Select and replace the text in the second bullet with **How can you help?**

- Press [Enter].

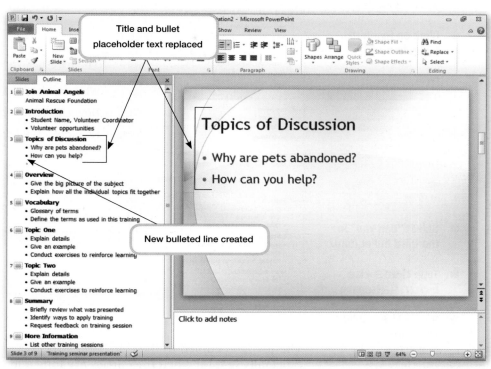

Figure 1.15

Having Trouble?

If you accidentally insert an extra bullet and blank line, press [Backspace] twice to remove them.

Your screen should be similar to Figure 1.15

Having Trouble?

Refer to "Copying and Moving Selections" in the Introduction to Microsoft Office 2010 to review this feature.

A new bulleted line is automatically created whenever you press [Enter] at the end of a bulleted item. Because the text you want to enter for this bullet is similar to the text in the second bullet, you decide to save time by copying and pasting the bullet text. Then you will modify the text in the third bullet.

- Select the second bulleted item.

- Click Copy in the Clipboard group of the Home tab.

- Click on the third bullet line and click Paste.

Another Method

You also can press Ctrl + C to copy a selection and Ctrl + V to paste a selection.

- Select "can you" in the third bullet item.

- Type **does the Foundation**

- If necessary, delete the fourth blank bullet line.

Your screen should be similar to Figure 1.16

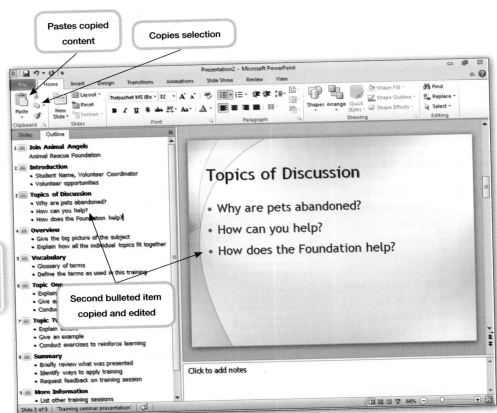

Figure 1.16

The text you copied to the third bullet has been quickly modified. Copying is especially helpful when the entries are long and complicated.

As you review what you have entered so far in your presentation, you decide that it would be better to introduce yourself on the first slide. Rather than retyping this information, you will move your introduction from slide 2 to slide 1. You will do this using drag and drop.

3

- In the Outline tab, press [Enter] at the end of the subtitle in slide 1 to create a blank line.

- Select the first bulleted item on aslide 2.

- Drag the selection to the blank line on slide 1.

Another Method

You can also use ✂ Cut or [Ctrl] + X to cut a selection and then paste it to the new location.

- Move to the blank line at the end of slide 1 and press [Backspace] to delete it.

Your screen should be similar to Figure 1.17

Additional Information

You can also delete and move slides in the Outline tab by clicking on the slide icon next to the slide number to select the entire slide and then use the appropriate command.

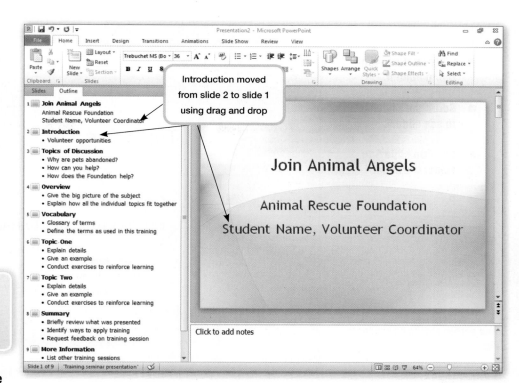

Figure 1.17

Because the Outline tab lets you see the content in multiple slides at once, it makes it easy to see the organization of the presentation and to quickly make text changes within and between slides.

MOVING, COPYING, AND DELETING SLIDES

As you continue to plan the presentation content and organization, you decide you will not use the Vocabulary slide and want to delete it. You also think a more appropriate location for the Overview slide may be above the agenda. Finally, you plan to have three slides to present the three main topics you plan to cover in the presentation. For this purpose, you want to add a third topic slide. Because you are not working with slide content, you will use the Slides tab to make these changes.

First you will delete slide 5, Vocabulary.

- **Click on the Slides tab to open it.**

- **Scroll the Slides tab to see slide 5.**

- **Click on slide 5 to select the slide.**

- **Press** Delete.

Another Method

You can also choose Delete Slide from the selected slide's context menu.

Your screen should be similar to Figure 1.18

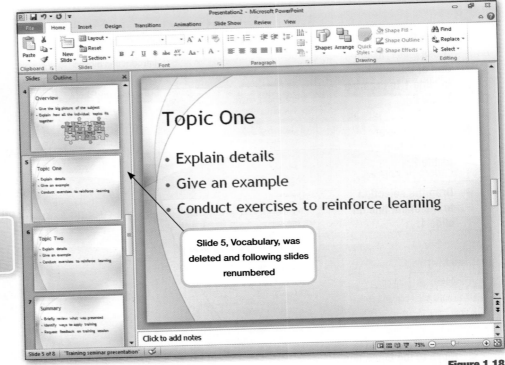

Figure 1.18

The slide has been deleted and all subsequent slides renumbered. Next, you will move the Overview slide (4) above slide 3 using drag and drop

②

- **Select slide 4 in the Slides tab.**

- **If necessary, scroll the Slides tab to show slide 3.**

- **Drag slide 4 above slide 3 in the Slides tab.**

Additional Information

A solid horizontal line identifies the location where the slide will be placed when you stop dragging.

Your screen should be similar to Figure 1.19

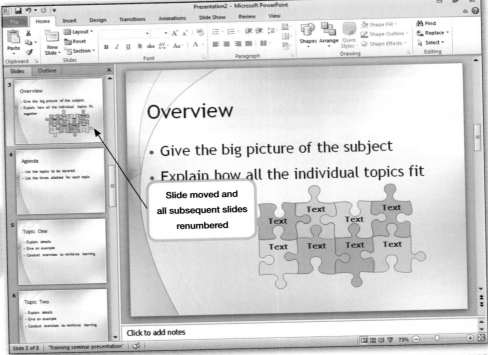

Figure 1.19

The Overview slide is now slide 3 and, again, all following slides are appropriately renumbered. Finally, you will make a copy of slide 6.

3

- Select slide 6 in the Slides tab.

- Open the 🔲 ▾ drop-down menu and choose Duplicate.

Another Method

You could also copy and paste the slide to duplicate it or use ⬛ New Slide ▾ in the Slides group and choose Duplicate Selected Slides from the drop-down menu.

- Scroll the Slides tab to see slides 5 to 7.

Your screen should be similar to Figure 1.20

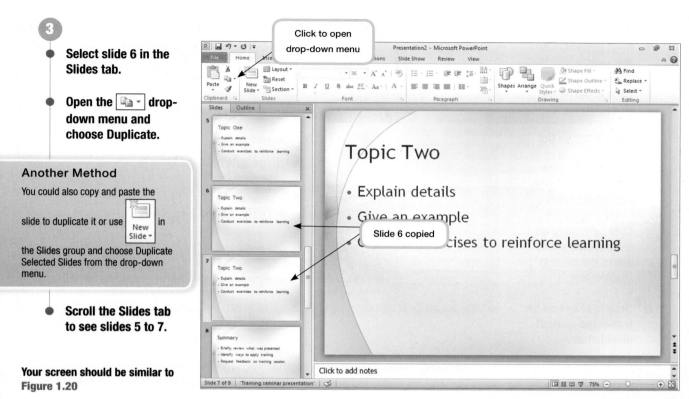

Figure 1.20

There are now three topic slides. The duplicate slide was inserted directly below the slide that was copied and is the selected slide.

MOVING, DEMOTING, AND PROMOTING BULLETED ITEMS

Now you are ready to enter the text for the three topic slides. You decide to enter the text for these slides using the Slide pane rather than the Outline tab. Simply clicking in an area of the slide in the Slide pane will make it the active area.

1

- Make slide 5 the current slide.

- Click anywhere in the sample title text of slide 5 in the Slide pane to select the title placeholder.

- Triple-click on the sample title to select it and type **Why Are Pets Abandoned?**

- Click anywhere on the bulleted list to select the content placeholder.

- Drag to select all the text in the content placeholder.

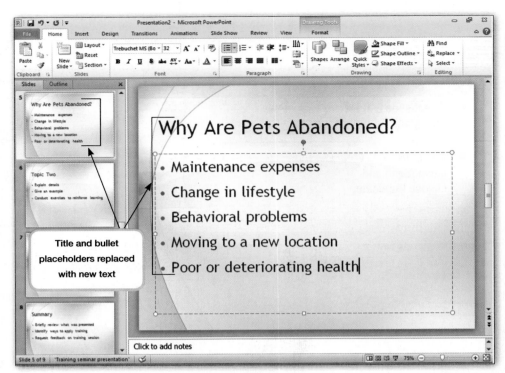

Figure 1.21

In reviewing slide 5, you realize that moving to a new location is one of the most common reasons for pets to be abandoned, so you decide to move that to the top of the list. You can rearrange bulleted items in the Slide pane by selecting the item and dragging it to a new location in the same way you moved selections in the Outline tab.

Another Method

You also can click ⟦ Select ▾ ⟧ in the Editing group of the Home tab and click ⟦ Select ▾ ⟧ or use the shortcut key Ctrl + A to select everything in a placeholder box.

- Enter the following bulleted items (Press Enter after each line, except the last, to create a new bullet):

Maintenance expenses

Change in lifestyle

Behavioral problems

Moving to a new location

Poor or deteriorating health

Your screen should be similar to Figure 1.21

2

● Select all the text in the fourth bulleted item in the Slide pane.

● Drag the selection to the beginning of the first bulleted item.

Your screen should be similar to Figure 1.22

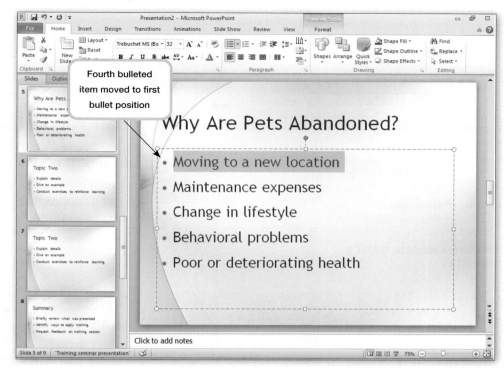

Figure 1.22

The fourth bullet is now the first bulleted item in the list.

In the next slide, you will enter information about how people can help the Animal Rescue Foundation.

3

● Make slide 6 the current slide.

● Replace the sample title text with **How Can You Help?**

● Select all the text in the bulleted text placeholder.

● Type **Donate your time and talent**

● Press Enter.

Your screen should be similar to Figure 1.23

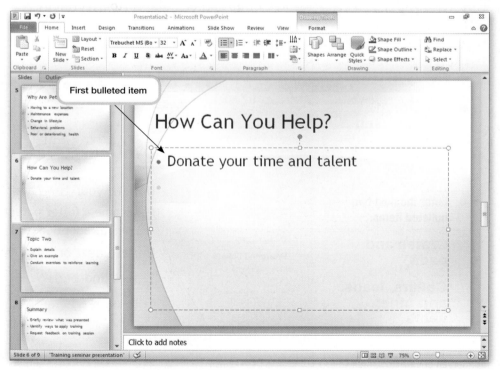

Figure 1.23

You want the next bulleted item to be indented below the first bulleted item. Indenting a bulleted point to the right **demotes** it, or makes it a lower or subordinate topic in the outline hierarchy.

4

- Press Tab.

- Type **Become a foster parent**

- Press Enter.

- Type **Work at adoption fairs**

- Press Enter.

Your screen should be similar to Figure 1.24

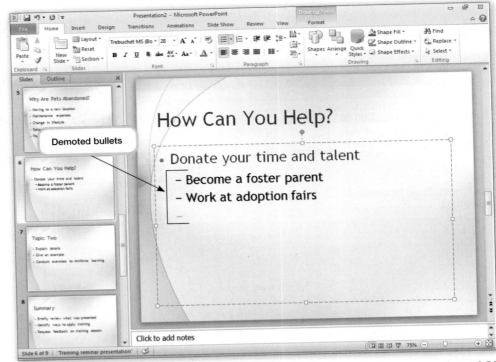

Figure 1.24

When you demote a bulleted point, PowerPoint continues to indent to the same level until you cancel the indent. Before entering the next item, you want to remove the indentation, or **promote** the line. Promoting a line moves it to the left, or up a level in the outline hierarchy.

5

- Press Shift + Tab.

- Type **Donate new or used items**

- Press Enter.

- Enter the next two bulleted items:

  Crates and pads

  Collars, leads, and other items

Your screen should be similar to Figure 1.25

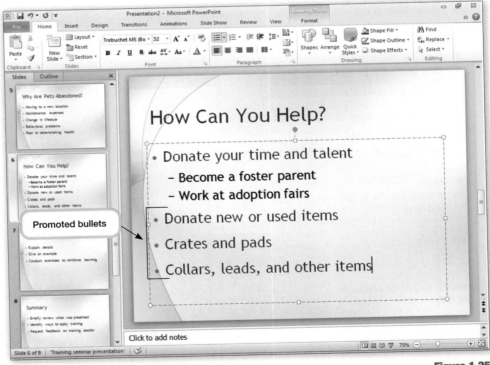

Figure 1.25

You also can promote or demote bulleted items after the text has been entered. The insertion point must be at the beginning of the line to be promoted or demoted, or all the text must be selected. You will demote the last two bulleted items.

6

● Select the two bulleted items "Crates and pads" and "Collars, leads, and other items".

● Press Tab.

● Move to the end of "Collars, leads, and other items".

● Press Enter.

Your screen should be similar to Figure 1.26

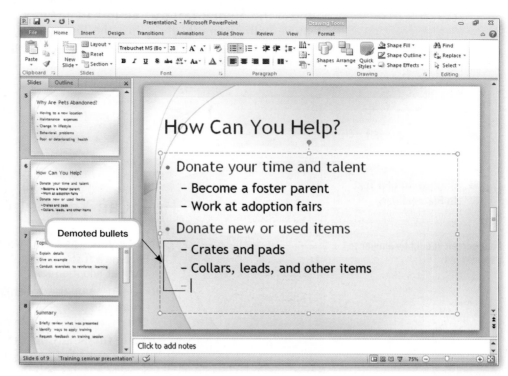

Figure 1.26

The last two items have been demoted. Next you will add more items to the bulleted list.

7

● Type **Provide financial support**

● Press Enter.

● Enter the following three bulleted items:

Send a donation

Sponsor a foster pet

Sponsor an adoption

● Promote the "Provide financial support" bullet.

Your screen should be similar to Figure 1.27

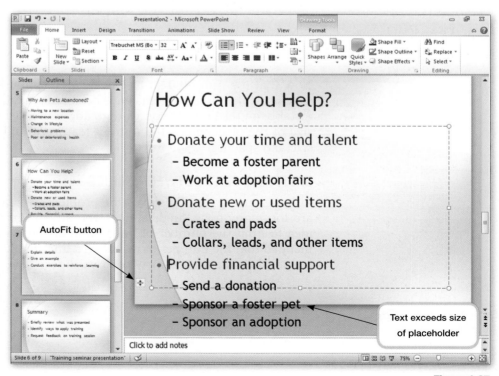

Figure 1.27

Editing a Presentation   **PP1.27**

As you entered more bulleted items, the slide's text exceeds the size of the placeholder. When this happens a  AutoFit Options button appears at the bottom left corner of the placeholder. It provides options that allow you to control the AutoFit feature and to handle any overspilling text. The AutoFit feature will automatically adjust the line spacing and text size as needed to display the content inside the placeholder appropriately. Currently, this feature is off in this template.

8

● Click  AutoFit Options.

● Choose AutoFit Text to Placeholder.

Your screen should be similar to Figure 1.28

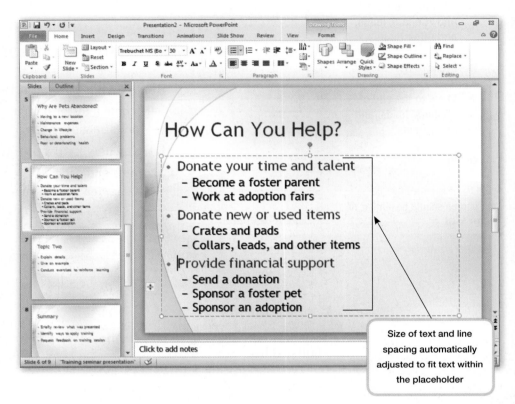

Figure 1.28

Now that the AutoFit Text to Placeholder option is on, the text size and line spacing of the bulleted items have been reduced to display the text more comfortably on the slide. If you were to add more text or increase or decrease the size of the placeholder, the AutoFit feature would continue to adjust the text size and spacing.

SPLITTING TEXT BETWEEN SLIDES

Although using AutoFit solved the problem, you decide that 10 bulleted items are too many for a single slide. Generally, when creating slides, it is a good idea to limit the number of bulleted items on a slide to six. It also is recommended that the number of words on a line should not exceed five. You decide to split the slide content between two slides.

With the bullet placeholder in slide 6 still selected, click ∸ AutoFit Options and choose Split Text Between Two Slides.

If necessary, scroll the Slides tab so that slides 6 and 7 are visible.

Your screen should be similar to **Figure 1.29**

Having Trouble?

You may have noticed that slide 6 in the Slides tab still displays all the bulleted items. Do not be concerned. The five bullets have been removed; however, the Slides tab has not updated to reflect the change.

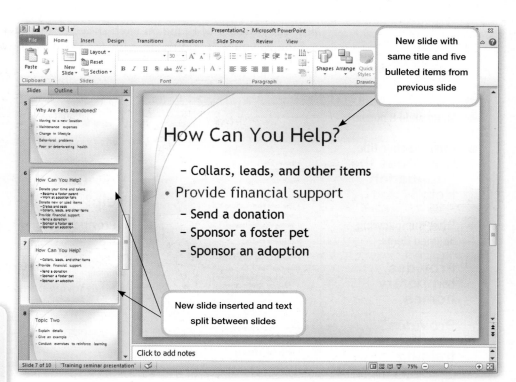

Figure 1.29

A new slide containing the same title as the previous slide and five of the bulleted items from the previous slide is inserted into the presentation. Often when splitting text between slides, the content may not split appropriately and you may still need to make adjustments to the slides. You will move the first bulleted item on slide 7 to the last item on slide 6 using the keyboard shortcuts for the Cut and Paste commands. You also will edit the slide title of slide 7.

On slide 7, replace the title text with More Ways to Help!

Select the first bulleted item on slide 7 and press Ctrl + X to cut the selection.

Move to the end of the last item on slide 6 and press Enter.

Press Ctrl + V to paste the item.

If necessary, delete the new blank bullet line.

Your screen should be similar to **Figure 1.30**

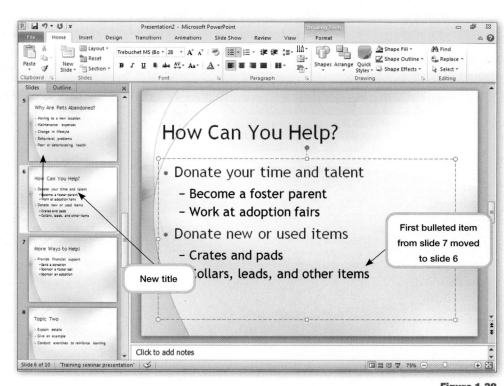

Figure 1.30

Editing a Presentation **PP1.29**

Now the number of items on each slide seems much more reasonable. Finally, you will add the text for the third topic slide.

3

- Make slide 8 current.

- Enter the slide title **How Does the Foundation Help?**

- Enter the following bulleted items:

  Provides temporary homes

  Provides obedience training

  Provides veterinary care

  Finds loving permanent homes

- Open the Outline tab and scroll the tab to see slides 4 through 8.

Your screen should be similar to Figure 1.31

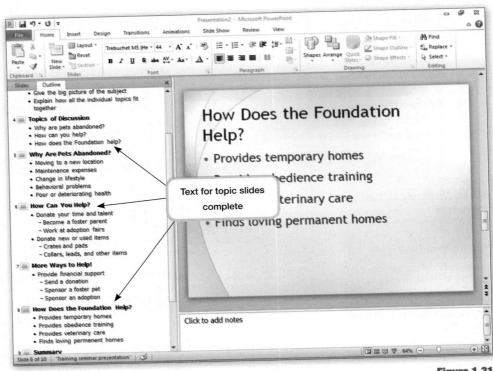

Figure 1.31

The text for the three topic slides reflects the order of the topics in the Topics of Discussion slide.

CREATING A NUMBERED LIST

After looking at slide 4, you decide that it would be better if the topics of discussion were a numbered list. You can easily change the format of the bulleted items to a numbered list using the [≣▾] Numbering command in the Paragraph group on the Home tab.

1

- Open the Slides tab and make slide 4 current.

- Click anywhere in the bulleted items placeholder on slide 4.

- Click on the dashed-line border of the placeholder box to change it to a solid line.

- Click 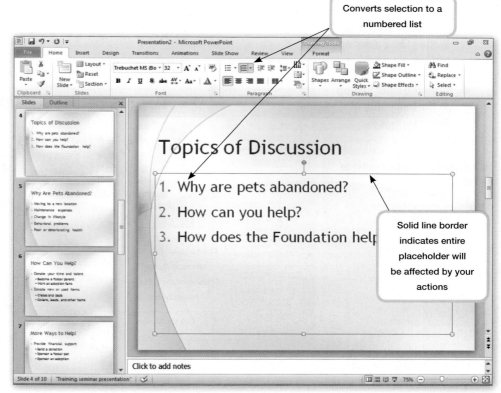 Numbering in the Paragraph group on the Home tab.

Your screen should be similar to Figure 1.32

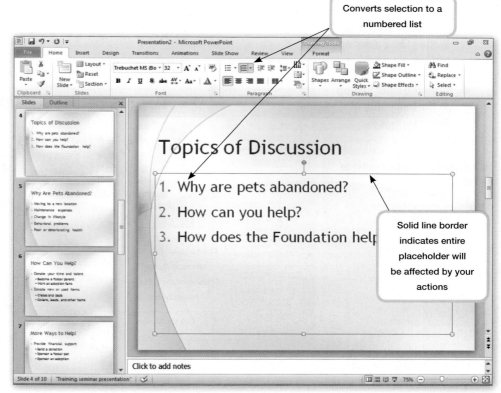

Figure 1.32

Notice the cursor does not appear in the placeholder box. This is because a solid line around the placeholder indicates your action will affect the entire placeholder rather than individual parts, such as the text, of the placeholder. The bullets have been replaced with an itemized numbered list.

MOVING, DEMOTING, AND PROMOTING NUMBERED ITEMS

Now it is obvious to you that you entered the topics in the wrong order. You want to present the information about the Foundation before information about how individuals can help. Just like a bulleted item, an item in a numbered list can be moved easily by selecting it and dragging it to a new location.

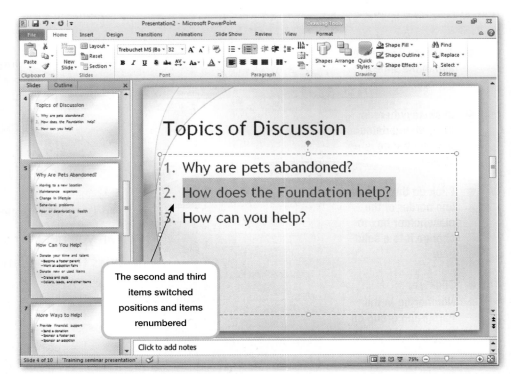

1

- Select the third item in the placeholder on slide 4.

- Drag the selection up to the beginning of the second line.

Your screen should be similar to Figure 1.33

Figure 1.33

As soon as you clicked inside the placeholder, the cursor appeared and the solid-line border changed to a dashed-line border, indicating you can edit the contents of the placeholder. The third item in the numbered list is now the second item, and PowerPoint automatically renumbered the list for you.

Because you don't want to miss anything, you decide to go back and review the information you've entered so far. As you go back through the slides, you realize that you forgot to include the Animal Angels volunteer group as a topic to be discussed. You will add it to the Topics of Discussion slide as a subtopic below the "How can you help?" topic.

Open the Outline tab to review the slide content.

Click at the end of the third numbered list item on slide 4 and press Enter.

Press Tab **and type** Who are Animal Angels?

Your screen should be similar to Figure 1.34

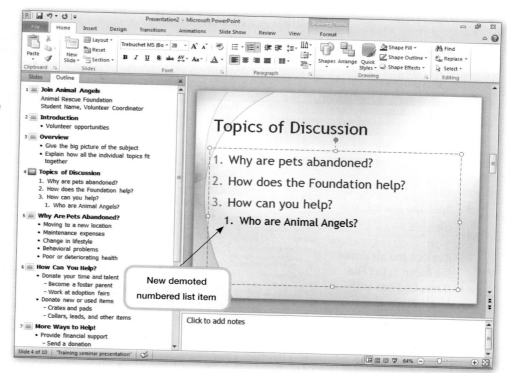

New demoted numbered list item

Figure 1.34

The numbering for the subtopic begins with one again. The new item is too important to be demoted on the list, so you decide to promote it and move it higher on the list.

Select the entire fourth line.

Press Shift + Tab **to promote the fourth line.**

Drag the selected item to the beginning of the third line.

Your screen should be similar to Figure 1.35

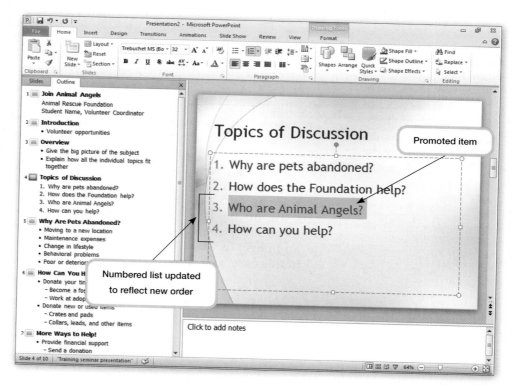

Promoted item

Numbered list updated to reflect new order

Figure 1.35

The numbered list has again been appropriately adjusted.

SAVING A PRESENTATION

Having Trouble?

See "Saving a File," in the Introduction to Microsoft Office 2010 to review this feature.

You have just been notified about an important meeting that is to begin in a few minutes. Before leaving for the meeting, you want to save the presentation so that you don't lose your work.

The Save or Save As commands on the File tab are used to save files. When a presentation is saved for the first time, either command can be used to display the Save As dialog box, in which you specify the location to save the file and the file name.

1

● **Open the File tab and click** ▣ Save As **.**

● **Replace the proposed file name in the File Name text box with Volunteer**

Having Trouble?

If you used the student data file pp01_Training for this lab, choose Save As from the File tab. The file name in the Save As dialog box will be the name of the file you opened.

● **Select the location where you will save your solution files.**

Your screen should be similar to Figure 1.36

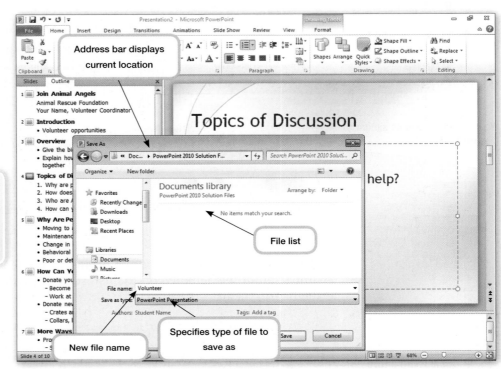

Figure 1.36

Additional Information

The file extensions may or may not be displayed, depending upon your Windows folder settings.

The file list displays folder names as well as the names of PowerPoint files (if any) stored in the current location. Only PowerPoint presentation files are listed, because the selected file type in the Save As Type list box is PowerPoint Presentation. Depending on what file type you choose, a different file extension will be added to the file name. Presentation files have a default file extension of .pptx.

You can also save PowerPoint presentations as an image file using the .gif, .tif, or .jpg file extension. When you save a presentation as an image file, you are given the choice to save the Current Slide Only or Every Slide as an image, in which case each slide will be saved as a separate image file.

In this case, you will use the default presentation file type (.pptx).

2 Click [Save].

Your screen should be similar to Figure 1.37

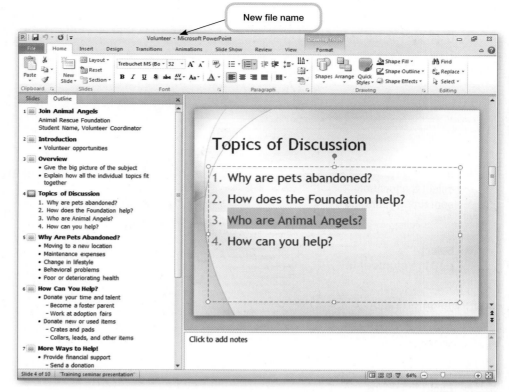

New file name

Figure 1.37

The presentation is now saved to the location you specified in a new file named Volunteer and the new file name is displayed in the application window title bar. The view in use at the time the file is saved also is saved with the file.

You are now ready to close the file.

3 Open the File tab and click

The presentation is closed, and an empty workspace is displayed. Always save your slide presentation before closing a file or leaving the PowerPoint program. As a safeguard against losing your work if you forget to save the presentation, PowerPoint will remind you to save any unsaved presentation before closing the file or exiting the program.

Opening an Existing Presentation

Additional Information

If you are ending your lab session now, open the File tab and click [×] Exit to exit the program.

After returning from your meeting, you continued to work on the presentation. You revised the content of several of the slides and added information for several new slides. Then you saved the presentation using a new file name. You will open this file to see the changes and will continue working on the presentation.

1

Open the File tab and click 📂 Open.

If necessary, select the location containing your data files.

Select pp01_Volunteer1.

Click Open ▼.

Open the Outline tab.

Replace "Your Name" in slide 1 with your name.

Scroll the Outline tab to see the additional content that has been added to the presentation.

Your screen should be similar to Figure 1.38

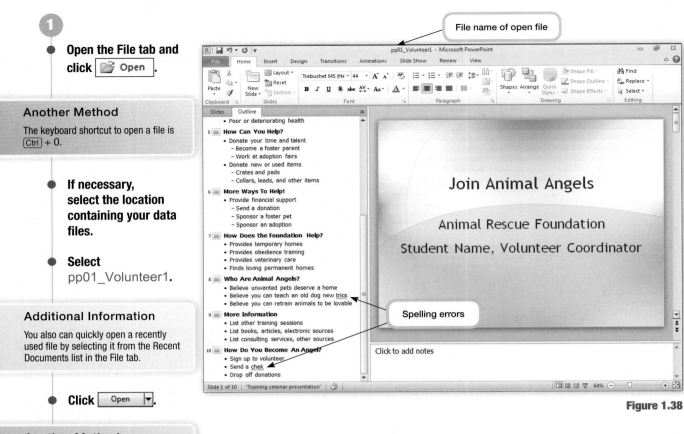

Figure 1.38

The presentation now contains 10 slides, and all the sample text has been replaced with text for the volunteer recruitment presentation, except for slide 9.

Using Spelling Checker

Additional Information

Unlike Word 2010, Powerpoint does not check for grammar errors.

As you entered the information on the additional slides, you left some typing errors uncorrected. To correct the misspelled words, you can use the shortcut menu to correct each individual word or error, as you learned earlier. However, in many cases, you may find it more efficient to wait until you are finished writing before you correct any spelling or grammatical errors. Rather than continually break your train of thought to correct errors as you type, you can check the spelling on all slides of the presentation at once by running the spelling checker.

1

- **Open the Review tab.**
- **Click** 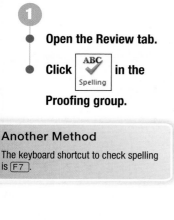 **in the Proofing group.**

Another Method

The keyboard shortcut to check spelling is [F7].

Your screen should be similar to Figure 1.39

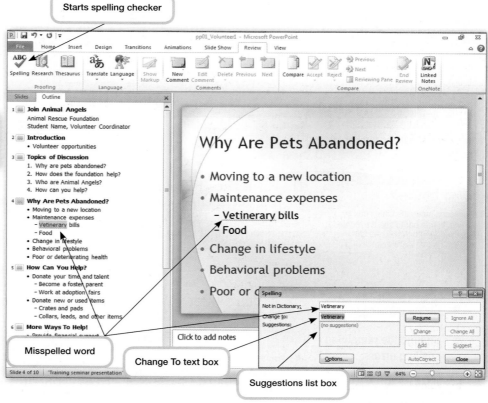

Figure 1.39

Additional Information

The spelling checker identifies many proper names and technical terms as misspelled. To stop this from occurring, use the Add Words To option to add those names to the custom dictionary.

The program jumps to slide 4; highlights the first located misspelled word, "Vetinerary," in the Outline pane; and opens the Spelling dialog box. The Spelling dialog box displays the misspelled word in the Not in Dictionary text box. The Suggestions list box typically displays the words the spelling checker has located in the dictionary that most closely match the misspelled word.

In this case, the spelling checker does not display any suggested replacements because it cannot locate any words in the dictionaries that are similar in spelling. If there are no suggestions, the Not in Dictionary text box simply displays the word that is highlighted in the text. When none of the suggestions is correct, you must edit the word yourself by typing the correction in the Change To text box.

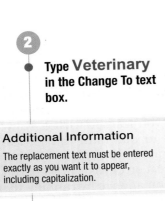

2

● Type **Veterinary** in the Change To text box.

Additional Information

The replacement text must be entered exactly as you want it to appear, including capitalization.

● Click [Change].

Additional Information

You also can edit words directly in the presentation and then click [Resume] to continue checking spelling.

Your screen should be similar to Figure 1.40

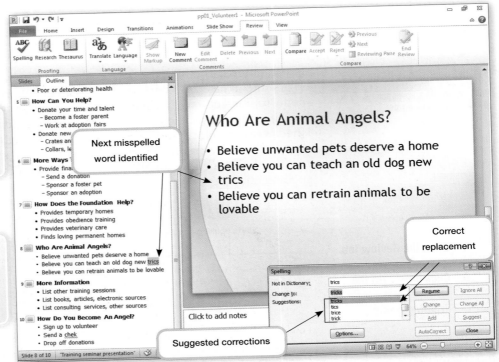

Figure 1.40

The corrected replacement is made in the slide. After the Spelling dialog box is open, the spelling checker continues to check the entire presentation for spelling errors. The next misspelled word, "trics," is identified. In this case, the suggested replacement is correct.

Having Trouble?

If necessary, move the dialog box by dragging its title bar to see the located misspelled word.

3

● Click [Change].

● Change the remaining spelling errors.

● Click [OK] in response to the message telling you that the spelling check is complete.

● Open the File tab, click [Save As] and save the revised presentation as **Volunteer1** to your solution file location.

Your screen should be similar to Figure 1.41

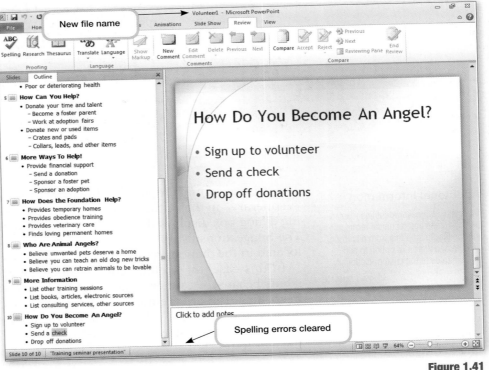

Figure 1.41

The Spelling indicator in the Status bar shows that all spelling errors have been resolved.

Using Slide Sorter View

To get a better overall picture of the presentation, you will switch to Slide Sorter view. This view displays thumbnail images of each slide in the work area and is particularly useful for rearranging slides to improve the flow and organization of the presentation. Clicking on a thumbnail selects the slide and makes it the current slide.

1

● **Click** 🔲 **Slide Sorter in the status bar.**

Having Trouble?

Pointing to a view button displays its name in a ScreenTip.

Another Method

You also could switch to Slide Sorter view by clicking 🔲 **Slide Sorter** in the Presentation Views group of the View tab.

● **Set the zoom to 90%.**

● **Click on slide 1.**

Your screen should be similar to Figure 1.42

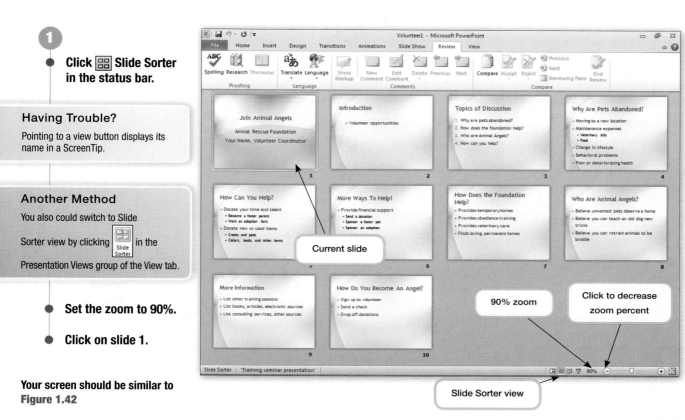

Figure 1.42

Having Trouble?

Do not be concerned if your screen displays a different number of slides per row. This is a function of the size of your monitor and your monitor settings.

The currently selected slide, slide 1, appears with a yellow border around it. Viewing all the slides side by side helps you see how your presentation flows. You realize that the second slide is no longer necessary because you added your name to the opening slide. You also decide to delete slide 9 because you plan to add any necessary information to other slides. As you continue to look at the slides, you can now see that slides 7 and 8 are out of order and do not follow the sequence of topics in the Topics of Discussion slide.

SELECTING AND DELETING SLIDES

You will delete slides 2 and 9. In this view, it is easy to select and work with multiple slides at the same time. To select multiple slides, hold down [Ctrl] while clicking on each slide to select it.

Select slide 2, hold down Ctrl**, and click on slide 9.**

Press Delete**.**

Increase the zoom to 100%.

Additional Information

You can use Delete to delete a slide in Slide Sorter view and in the Slides tab. However, in the Slide pane, using Delete deletes text or placeholder content.

Additional Information

The zoom setting for each view is set independently and remains in effect until changed to another zoom setting.

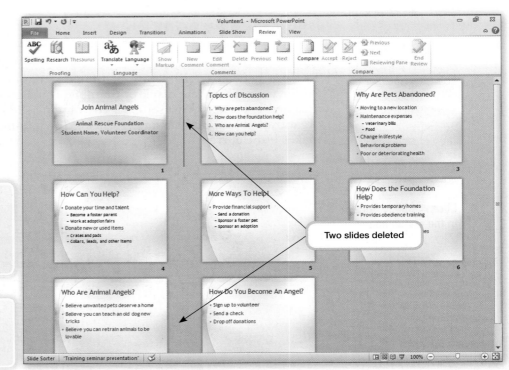

Figure 1.43

Your screen should be similar to Figure 1.43

The slides have been deleted, and all remaining slides have been appropriately renumbered.

MOVING SLIDES

Now you want to correct the organization of the slides by moving slides 6 and 7 before slide 4. To reorder a slide in Slide Sorter view, you drag it to its new location using drag and drop. As you drag the mouse, an indicator line appears to show you where the slide will appear in the presentation. When the indicator line is located where you want the slide to be placed, release the mouse button. You will select both slides and move them at the same time.

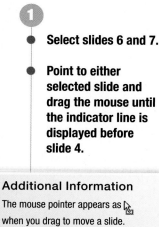

1

- Select slides 6 and 7.

- Point to either selected slide and drag the mouse until the indicator line is displayed before slide 4.

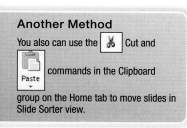

Additional Information

The mouse pointer appears as [cursor] when you drag to move a slide.

- Release the mouse button.

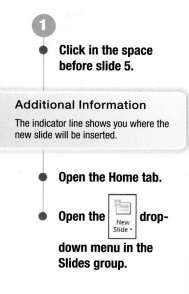

Another Method

You also can use the ✂ Cut and [Paste] commands in the Clipboard group on the Home tab to move slides in Slide Sorter view.

Your screen should be similar to Figure 1.44

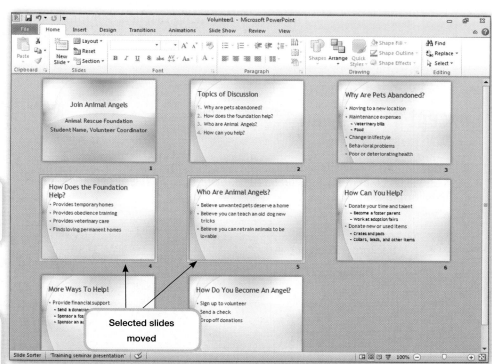

Figure 1.44

The slides now appear in the order in which you want them.

SELECTING A SLIDE LAYOUT

During your discussion with the foundation director, it was suggested that you add a slide showing the history of the organization. To include this information in the presentation, you will insert a new slide after slide 4.

1

- Click in the space before slide 5.

Additional Information

The indicator line shows you where the new slide will be inserted.

- Open the Home tab.

- Open the New Slide drop-down menu in the Slides group.

Your screen should be similar to Figure 1.45

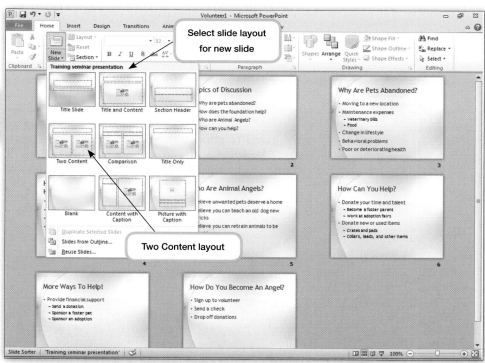

Figure 1.45

The drop-down menu displays 9 built-in slide layouts. The number of available layouts varies with the template you are using.

Concept ④ Layout

A layout defines the position and format for objects and text on a slide. Layouts provide placeholders for slide titles and slide content such as text, tables, diagrams, charts, or clip art. Many of these placeholders are shown in the following diagram.

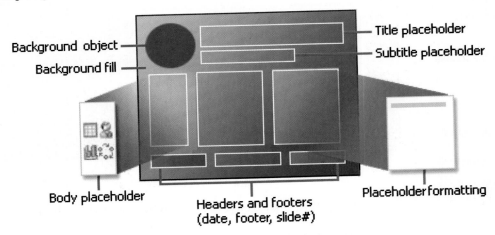

You can change the layout of an existing slide by selecting a new layout. If the new layout does not include placeholders for objects that are already on your slide (for example, if you created a chart and the new layout does not include a chart placeholder), you do not lose the information. All objects remain on the slide, and the selected layout is automatically adjusted by adding the appropriate type of placeholder for the object. Alternatively, as you add new objects to a slide, the layout automatically adjusts by adding the appropriate type of placeholder. You also can rearrange, size, and format placeholders on a slide any way you like to customize the slide's appearance.

To make creating slides easy, use the predefined layouts. The layouts help you keep your presentation format consistent and, therefore, more professional.

You need to choose the layout that best accommodates the changes you discussed with the director. Because this slide will contain two columns of text about the history of the organization, you will use the Two Content layout.

2

- Choose Two Content.

- Double-click on the slide to switch back to Normal view.

Additional Information
The current slide does not change when you switch views.

- Open the Slides tab.

Your screen should be similar to Figure 1.46

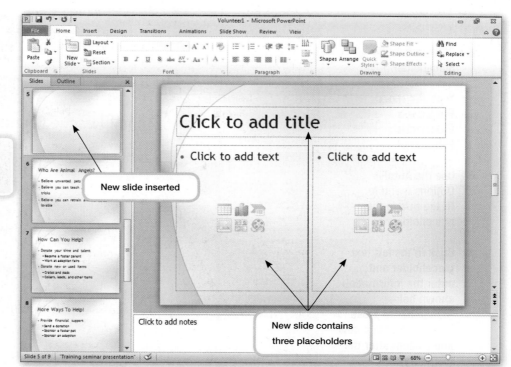

Figure 1.46

A new Two Content slide is inserted with the same design elements as the other slides in the presentation. The Two Content layout contains three placeholders, but unlike the template slides, the placeholders on the inserted slide do not contain sample text. When you select the placeholder, you can simply type in the text without having to select or delete any sample text.

CHANGING A PLACEHOLDER

You will add text to the slide presenting a brief history of the Animal Rescue Foundation. First, you will enter the slide title and then the list of dates and events.

1

- **Click in the title placeholder.**

- **Type Animal Rescue Foundation History**

- **Use the AutoFit Options menu to fit the title to the placeholder.**

- **Click in the left text placeholder and enter the information shown below. Remember to press [Enter] to create a new line (except after the last entry).**

  1995

  1996

  1997

  2005

- **In the same manner, enter the following text in the right text placeholder:**

  Founded by Steve Dow

  Built first shelter

  Began volunteer program

  Rescued 3000 animals!

Your screen should be similar to Figure 1.47

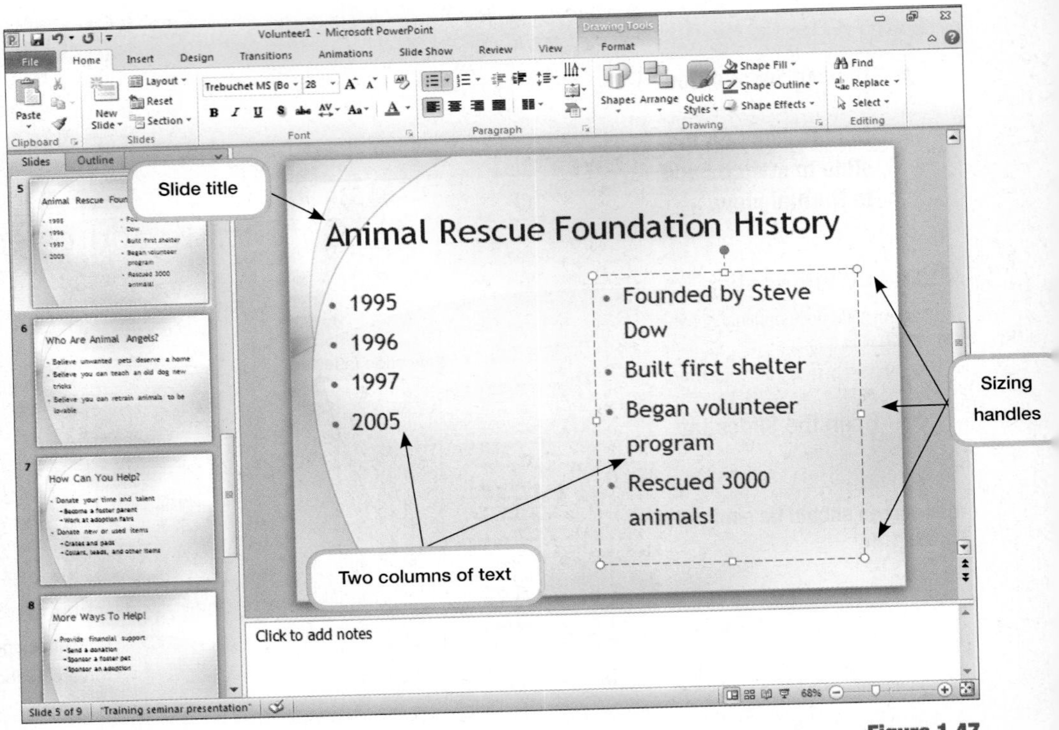

Figure 1.47

The left placeholder is too big for its contents and the right is too small, forcing some items to wrap to a second line. To correct the size, you can adjust the size of the placeholders.

SIZING A PLACEHOLDER

The four circles and squares that appear at the corners and sides of a selected placeholder's border are **sizing handles** that can be used to adjust the size of the placeholder. Dragging the corner sizing handles will adjust both the height and width at the same time, whereas the center handles adjust the associated side borders. When you point to the sizing handle, the mouse pointer appears as ⤢, indicating the direction in which you can drag the border to adjust the size.

1

- On the right placeholder, drag the left-center sizing handle to the left until each item appears on one line.

- Select the left text placeholder and drag the right-center sizing handle to the left (see Figure 1.48).

- With the left placeholder still selected, hold down [Shift] while clicking on the right placeholder border to select both.

- Use the bottom-middle sizing handle to decrease the height of the placeholders to fit the text.

Your screen should be similar to Figure 1.48

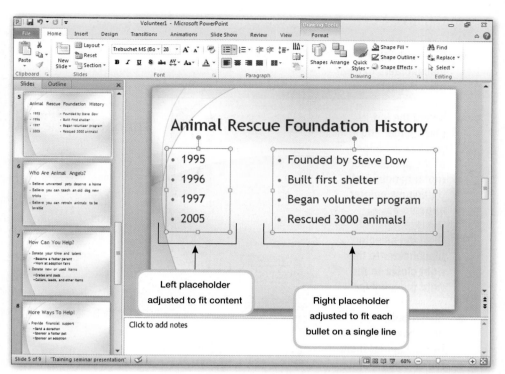

Figure 1.48

MOVING A PLACEHOLDER

Next, you want to decrease the blank space between the two columns. Then you want to move both placeholders so they appear more centered in the space. An object can be moved anywhere on a slide by dragging the place-holder's border. The mouse pointer appears as ❊ when you can move a place-holder. As you drag the placeholder, an opaque white copy of the placeholder is displayed to show your new location.

1

- Click outside the placeholders to clear the selection.

- Select the left placeholder and point to the edge of the placeholder (not a handle) until the mouse pointer appears as .

- Drag the selected placeholder to the right closer to the right placeholder.

- Select both placeholders and drag to center them horizontally in the slide as shown in Figure 1.49.

- Save your changes to the presentation.

Your screen should be similar to Figure 1.49

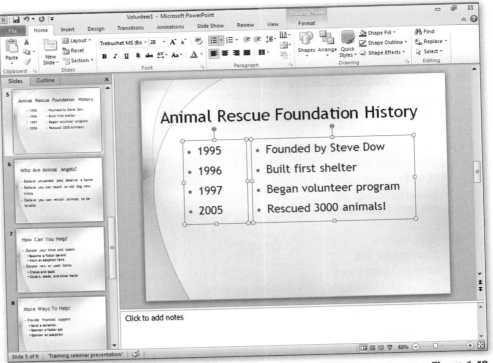

Figure 1.49

ADDING AND REMOVING BULLETS

Next, you want to remove the bullets from the items on the history slide. You can quickly apply and remove bullets using ⬛ Bullets in the Paragraph group on the Home tab. This button applies the bullet style associated with the design template you are using. Because the placeholder items already include bullets, using this button will remove them.

1

- With both text placeholders still selected, click ⬛ Bullets from the Paragraph group in the Home tab to remove all bullets.

Your screen should be similar to Figure 1.50

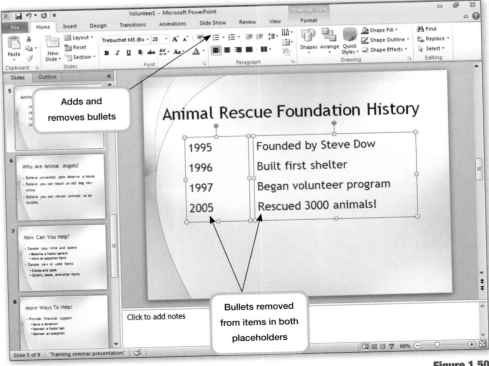

Figure 1.50

The bullets are removed from all the items in both placeholders. Now, however, you think it would look better to add bullets back to the years in the first column.

2

● Select the four years in the left column.

● Click ≣ ▾ Bullets from the Paragraph group in the Home tab.

● Click outside the selected placeholder to deselect it.

● Save the presentation again.

Your screen should be similar to Figure 1.51

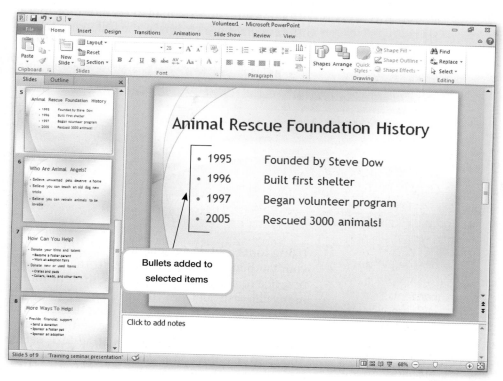

Figure 1.51

Bullets appear before the selected text items only.

Formatting Slide Text

The next change you want to make to the presentation is to improve the appearance of the title slide. Although the design template you are using already includes many formatting features, you want this slide to have more impact.

Applying different formatting to characters and paragraphs can greatly enhance the appearance of the slide. **Character formatting** features affect the selected characters only. They include changing the character style and size, applying effects such as bold and italics, changing the character spacing, and adding animated text effects. **Paragraph formatting** features affect an entire paragraph. A paragraph is text that has an (Enter) at the end of it. Each item in a bulleted list, title, and subtitle is a paragraph. Paragraph formatting features include the position of the paragraph or its alignment between the margins, paragraph indentation, spacing above and below a paragraph, and line spacing within a paragraph.

CHANGING FONTS

First, you will improve the appearance of the presentation title by changing the font of the title text. There are two basic types of fonts: serif and sans serif. **Serif fonts** have a flair at the base of each letter that visually leads the reader to the next letter. Two common serif fonts are Roman and Times New Roman.

Having Trouble?

Refer to the section "Formatting Text" in the Introduction to Microsoft Office 2010 to review this feature.

Serif fonts generally are used for text in paragraphs. **Sans serif fonts** do not have a flair at the base of each letter. Arial and Helvetica are two common sans serif fonts. Because sans serif fonts have a clean look, they are often used for headings in documents.

Each font can appear using a different font size. Several common fonts in different sizes are shown in the following table.

Font Name	Font Type	Font Size
Calibri	Sans serif	This is 10 pt. This is 16 pt.
Courier New	Serif	This is 10 pt. This is 16 pt.
Garamond	Serif	This is 10 pt. This is 16 pt.

Using fonts as a design element can add interest to your presentation and give your audience visual cues to help them find information quickly. It is good practice to use only two or three different fonts in a presentation, because too many can distract from your presentation content and can look unprofessional.

To change the font before typing the text, use the command and then type. All text will appear in the specified setting until another font setting is selected. To change a font setting for existing text, select the text you want to change and then use the command. If you want to apply font formatting to a word, simply move the insertion point to the word and the formatting is automatically applied to the entire word.

The [Trebuchet MS (He ▾)] Font button in the Font tab or on the Mini toolbar that appears when you select text is used to change the font style. As you select a font from the drop-down menu, a live preview of how the selected font will appear is displayed in the document.

Additional Information

The font used in the title is Trebuchet MS (Headings), as displayed in the [Trebuchet MS (He ▾)] Font button. It is automatically used in all headings in this template.

● Select the text "Join Animal Angels" in the Slide pane on slide 1.

● Open the Font drop-down list in the Mini toolbar.

● Point to several fonts to see the live preview.

Having Trouble?

Refer to the section "Using the Mini Toolbar" in the Introduction to Microsoft Office 2010 to review this feature.

Additional Information

The Live Preview feature is also available with many other formatting features.

Your screen should be similar to Figure 1.52

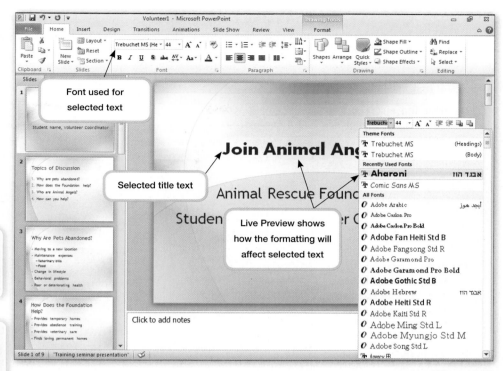

Figure 1.52

The selected text in the document appears in the font style you have selected in the menu. With Live Preview, you can see how the text will look with the selected font before you click the one that you want. You want to change the font to a design that has a less serious appearance.

● Scroll the menu and choose Comic Sans MS.

Another Method

You also could use Trebuchet MS (He ▾ Font in the Font group of the Home tab to change the font.

Your screen should be similar to Figure 1.53

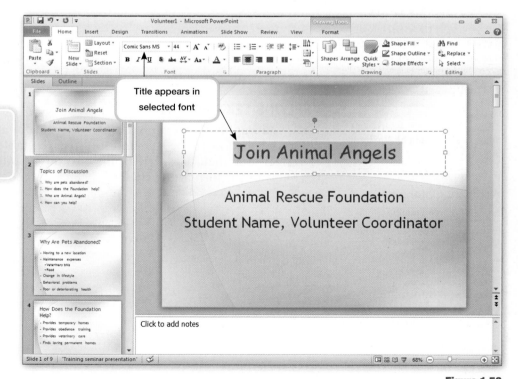

Figure 1.53

The text has changed to the new font style, and the Font button displays the font name used in the current selection.

CHANGING FONT SIZE

The title text is also a little smaller than you want it to be.

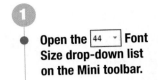

- **Open the** `44 ▾` **Font Size drop-down list on the Mini toolbar.**

Having Trouble?

If the Mini toolbar is no longer displayed, right click on the selection to display it again.

- **Point to several different sizes to see how the font size changes using Live Preview.**

- **Scroll the list and choose 60.**

Another Method

You also could use `44 ▾` Font Size in the Font group.

Another Method

Using `A˄` Increase Font Size in the Font group or the Mini toolbar will incrementally increase the font size. The keyboard shortcut is Ctrl + Shift + >.

Your screen should be similar to Figure 1.54

Additional Information

Use `A˅` Decrease Font Size or Ctrl + Shift + < to incrementally decrease the point size of selected text.

Additional Information

If a selection includes text in several different sizes, the smallest size appears in the Font Size button followed by a plus sign.

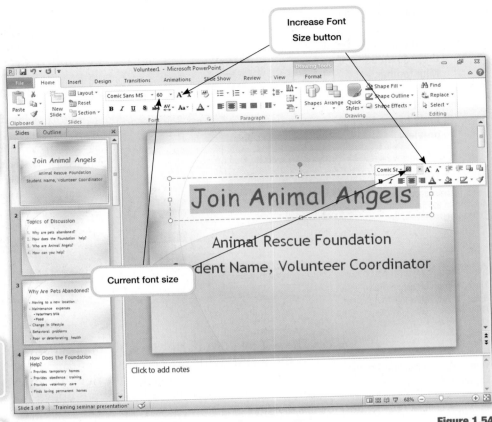

Figure 1.54

The font size increased from 44 points to 60 points. The Font Size button displays the point size of the current selection.

APPLYING TEXT EFFECTS

Next, you want to further enhance the title slide by adding **text effects** such as color and shadow to the title and subtitle. The table below describes some of the effects and their uses. The Home tab and the Mini toolbar contain buttons for many of the formatting effects.

Format	Example	Use
Bold, italic	***Bold Italic***	Adds emphasis
Underline	<u>Underline</u>	Adds emphasis
Superscript	"To be or not to be."[1]	Used in footnotes and formulas
Subscript	H_2O	Used in formulas
Shadow	**Shadow**	Adds distinction to titles and headings
Color	**Color Color Color**	Adds interest

You decide to add color and a shadow effect to the main title first.

1

- **If necessary, select the title text.**

- **Click** $\boxed{S}$ **Text Shadow in the Font group.**

- **Open the** $\boxed{A}$ **Font Color menu to display a gallery of colors.**

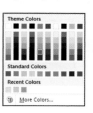

- **Choose Green, Accent 1, Darker 25% in the Theme Colors section.**

- **Click the subtitle placeholder to select it.**

Your screen should be similar to Figure 1.55

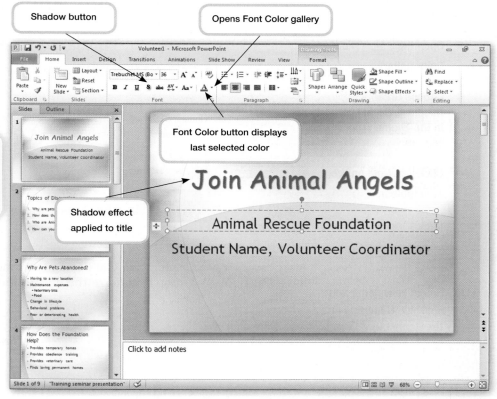

Figure 1.55

The selected color and slight shadow effect make the title much more interesting. Also notice the color in the Font Color button is the green color you just selected. This color can be quickly reapplied to other selections now simply by clicking the button.

Next you will enhance the two subtitle lines. Notice that the subtitle placeholder box does not include the second subtitle line. Although the second line was included in the placeholder when it was moved to this slide, the placeholder did not automatically increase in size to accommodate the new text. You will increase the size of the placeholder to visually include this text.

2

- Drag the bottom-middle sizing handle down to increase the size of the placeholder to include both subtitle lines.

- Select the text "Animal Rescue Foundation".

- Open the A ▾ Font Color gallery.

- Choose Green, Accent 1, Darker 50% in the Theme Colors section.

- Click B Bold on the Mini toolbar.

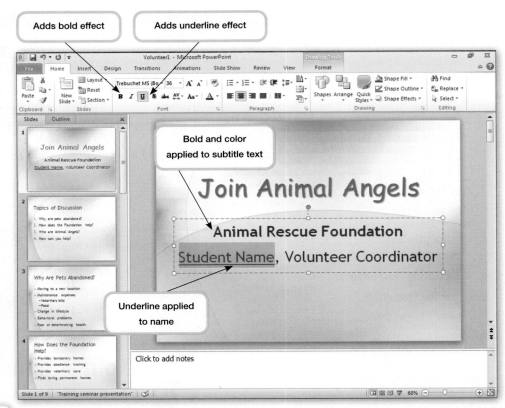

Figure 1.56

Another Method

The keyboard shortcut is Ctrl + B.

- Select your name and click U Underline on the Home tab.

Another Method

The keyboard shortcut is Ctrl + U.

Your screen should be similar to Figure 1.56

After reviewing your changes, you decide that underlining your name doesn't have the right look. You'll italicize the entire line instead and make the font smaller.

3

- Click **U** Underline.

- Select the entire second line of the subtitle.

- Click **I** Italic.

- Click **A˅** Decrease Font Size three times.

- Click somewhere outside the placeholder.

Your screen should be similar to Figure 1.57

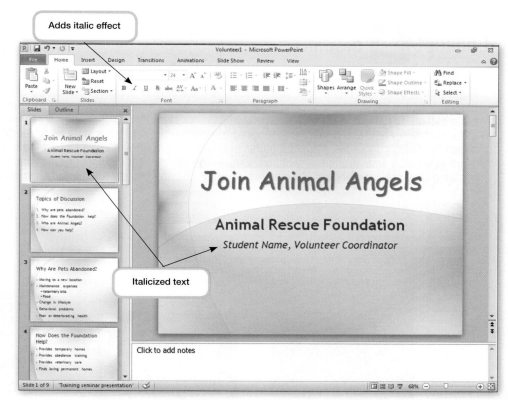

Figure 1.57

Now the title slide has much more impact.

Working with Graphics

Finally, you want to add a picture to the presentation. A picture is one of several different graphic objects that can be added to a slide.

Concept 5 Graphics

A **graphic** is a nontext element or object, such as a drawing or picture, that can be added to a slide. A graphic can be a simple drawing object consisting of shapes such as lines and boxes. A **drawing object** is part of your presentation document. A **picture** is an image such as a graphic illustration or a scanned photograph. Pictures are graphics that were created from another program and are inserted in a slide as **embedded objects**. An embedded object becomes part of the presentation file and can be opened and edited using the **source program**, the program in which it was created. Any changes made to the embedded object are not made to the original picture file because they are independent. Several examples of drawing objects and pictures are shown below.

Photograph

Graphic illustration

Drawing object

Add graphics to your presentation to help the audience understand concepts, to add interest, and to make your presentation stand out from others.

Graphic files can be obtained from a variety of sources. Many simple drawings called **clip art** are available in the Clip Organizer, a Microsoft Office tool that arranges and catalogs clip art and other media files stored on the computer's hard disk. The Clip Organizer's files, or clips, include art, sound, animation, and movies you can add to a presentation. Additionally, if you are connected to the Internet, Microsoft's Office.com Web site is automatically accessed for even more graphics.

Digital images created using a digital camera are one of the most common types of graphic files. You also can create graphic files using a scanner to convert any printed document, including photographs, to an electronic format. Most images that are scanned and inserted into documents are stored as Windows bitmap files (.bmp). All types of graphics, including clip art, photographs, and other types of images, can be found on the Internet. These files are commonly stored as .jpg or .pcx files. Keep in mind that any images you locate on the Internet may be protected by copyright and should only be used with permission. You also can purchase CDs containing graphics for your use.

Additional Information

When your computer is connected to a scanner, you also can scan a picture and insert it directly into a slide without saving it as a file first.

INSERTING A GRAPHIC FROM THE CLIP ORGANIZER

You want to add a graphic to the second slide. First you decide to check the Clip Art gallery to see if you can find an image that will work as an attention getter. The Insert tab includes commands that are designed to enhance a presentation by adding features such as shapes and illustrations to movies and sounds.

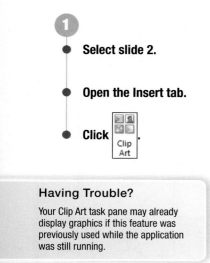

1

- **Select slide 2.**

- **Open the Insert tab.**

- **Click** Clip Art.

Having Trouble?

Your Clip Art task pane may already display graphics if this feature was previously used while the application was still running.

Your screen should be similar to Figure 1.58

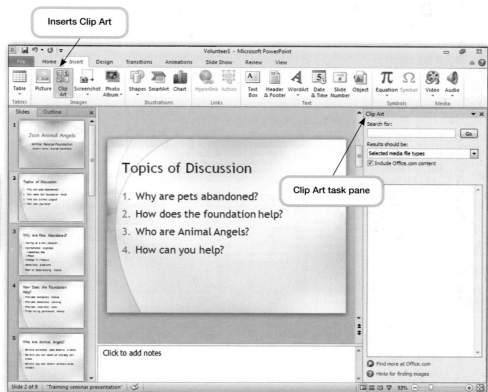

Figure 1.58

In the Clip Art task pane, you enter a word or phrase that is representative of the type of picture you want to locate. You also can specify the location to search and the type of media files, such as clip art, movies, photographs, or sound, to display in the search results. Since each of the items on this slide is a question, you decide to look for graphics of question marks.

2

● If necessary, select any existing text in the Search For text box.

● In the Search For text box, type **question**

● If necessary, select the Include Office.com content check box.

● Open the Results Should Be drop-down list, if necessary, choose Illustrations to select it, and deselect the all other options.

Having Trouble?

Click the box next to an option to select or deselect (clear the checkmark).

● Click outside the drop-down list to close it.

● Click [Go].

Having Trouble?

If your thumbnails appear in a single column, increase the width of your task pane by dragging the left edge of the pane until two columns are displayed.

Having Trouble?

Do not worry if the thumbnails displayed on your screen do not match those shown in Figure 1.59, because the online clip art is continuously changing.

Your screen should be similar to Figure 1.59

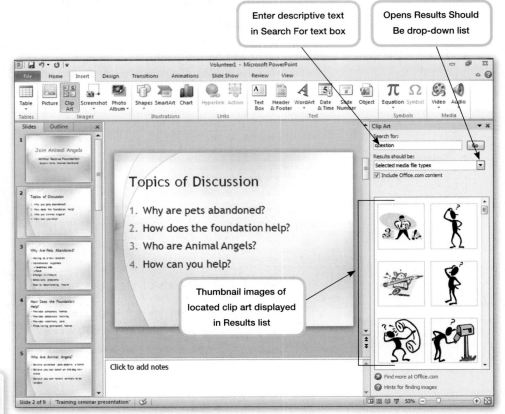

Figure 1.59

The program searches the Microsoft Clip Organizer on your computer and, if an Internet connection is established, searches Microsoft's Office.com Web site for clip art and graphics that match your search term. The Results list displays thumbnails of all located graphics. The pictures stored on your computer in the Microsoft Clip Art gallery appear first in the results list, followed by the Office Online clip art.

Pointing to a thumbnail displays a ScreenTip containing the **keywords**, descriptive words or phrases, associated with the graphic and other information about the picture properties. It also displays a drop-down list bar that accesses the item's shortcut menu. The shortcut menu commands are used to work with and manage the items in the Clip Organizer. Because it is sometimes difficult to see the graphic in the thumbnail, you can preview it in a larger size.

- **Scroll the Results list to view additional images.**

- **Point to any graphic and click ⌄ to open the thumbnail menu.**

- **Choose Preview/ Properties.**

Your screen should be similar to Figure 1.60

Having Trouble?

Do not worry if your preview image does not match Figure 1.60. It will only match if you selected the same graphic in the results area.

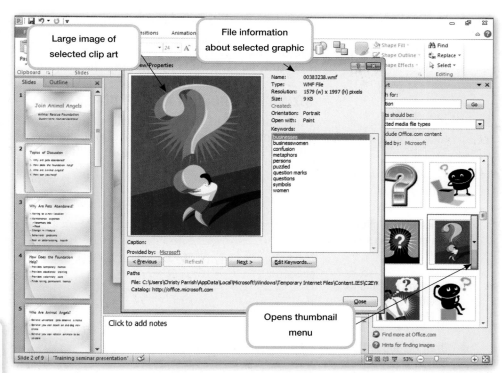

Figure 1.60

The Preview/Properties dialog box displays the selected graphic in a larger size so it is easier to see. It also displays more information about the properties associated with the graphic. Notice the search word you entered appears as one of the keywords. Now you will scroll the results list of graphics to find one you like.

- **Click Close to close the dialog box.**

- **Scroll the Results list to locate the graphic shown in Figure 1.61.**

- **Click on the graphic to insert it in the slide.**

Another Method

You also could choose Insert from the thumbnail's shortcut menu to insert the graphic.

Your screen should be similar to Figure 1.61

Having Trouble?

If this graphic is not available in the Clip Organizer, just choose a question mark graphic that you like from the results list.

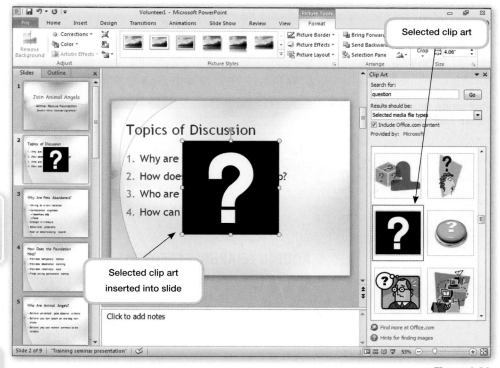

Figure 1.61

Working with Graphics   **PP1.57**

The clip art image is inserted in the center of the slide on top of the text. It is a selected object and can be sized and moved like any other selected object. The Picture Tools Format tab is automatically displayed in the Ribbon, in anticipation that you may want to modify the graphic.

SIZING AND MOVING A GRAPHIC

First you need to size and position the picture on the slide. A graphic object is sized and moved just like a placeholder. You want to decrease the graphic size slightly and move it to the bottom right of the slide.

1

- **If necessary, click on the graphic to select it.**

- **Drag the graphic to position it as shown in Figure 1.62.**

- **Drag the top left corner sizing handle inward to decrease its size to that shown in Figure 1.62.**

Additional Information

To maintain an object's proportions while resizing it, hold down **Shift** while dragging the sizing handle.

- **Close the Clip Art task pane.**

Your screen should be similar to Figure 1.62

Additional Information

Be careful when increasing the size of a picture (bitmap) image, as it can lose sharpness and appear blurry if enlarged too much.

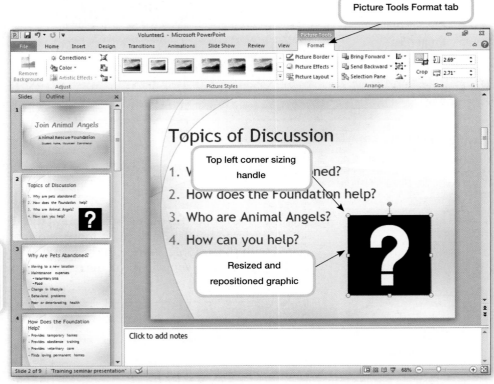

Figure 1.62

The clip art image is now smaller and placed in the correct position on the slide.

ADDING GRAPHIC EFFECTS

You can use the picture effects on the Picture Tools Format tab to customize the look of the graphic to suit your presentation. There are many effects that you can use to improve the appearance of graphics in your presentation. The first enhancement you would like to make is to change the color of the question mark so it coordinates with the slide design.

1

- With the clip art selected, click Color in the Adjust group of the Picture Tools Format tab.

- Point to the choices in the Recolor gallery to see live previews.

- Choose Light Green, Accent Color 5 Dark from the gallery (second row, fifth column).

Your screen should be similar to Figure 1.63

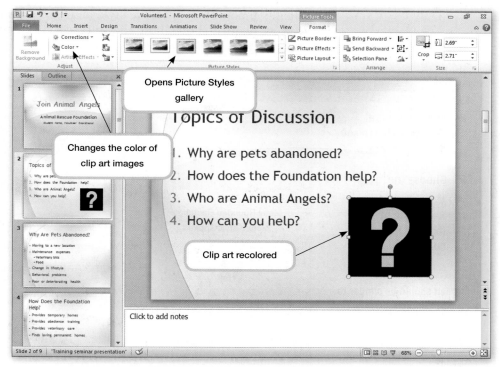

Figure 1.63

Next, you want to enhance the graphic by applying a picture style to it. A **style** is a combination of formatting options that can be applied in one easy step. In the case of **picture styles**, the combinations consist of border, shadow, and shape effects. You also can create your own picture style effects by selecting specific style elements, such as borders and shadows, individually using the Picture Border ▾, Picture Effects ▾, and Picture Layout ▾ commands.

2

- Click ▾ More in the Picture Styles group to open the Picture Styles gallery.

Your screen should be similar to Figure 1.64

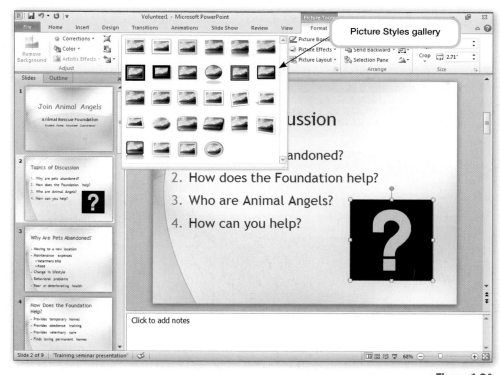

Figure 1.64

Working with Graphics **PP1.59**

When you point to a style, the style name appears in a ScreenTip, and the Live Preview feature shows how the selected graphic will look with the selected picture style.

3

● **Point to several picture styles to see the live previews.**

● **Choose the** 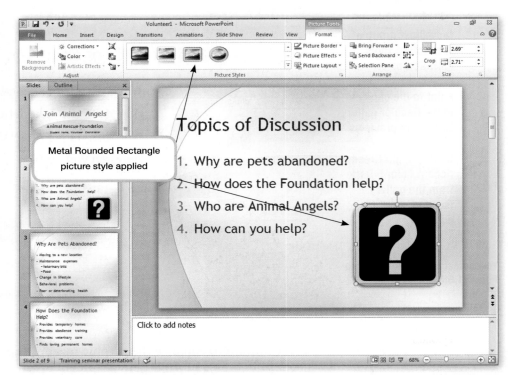 **Metal Rounded Rectangle style (bottom row, third column).**

Your screen should be similar to Figure 1.65

Figure 1.65

As you look at the picture, you decide to remove the rectangle and use the oval shape with the thin black border instead. You will then modify the picture style by changing the border color and removing the reflection.

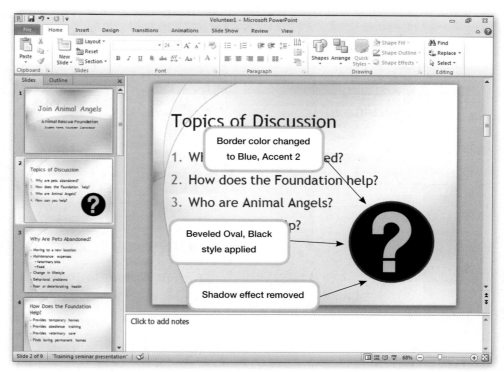

4

- Choose the Beveled Oval, Black style in the Picture Styles gallery.

- Click **Picture Border ▼** in the Picture Styles group.

- Choose Blue, Accent 2 from the Theme Colors group.

- Click **Picture Effects ▼** in the Picture Styles group.

- From the Shadow group, choose No Shadow.

- Click outside the graphic to deselect the object.

Your screen should be similar to Figure 1.66

Figure 1.66

The addition of a customized graphic image gives your presentation a more polished look. Now that the slides are in the order you want and formatted, you would like to see how the presentation will look when viewed by an audience.

Rehearsing a Presentation

Rather than projecting the presentation on a large screen as you would to present it for an audience, a simple way to rehearse a presentation is to view it on your computer screen as a **slide show**. A slide show displays each slide full screen and in order. While the slide show is running during this rehearsal, you can plan what you will say while each slide is displayed.

USING SLIDE SHOW VIEW

When you view a slide show, each slide fills the screen, hiding the PowerPoint application window, so you can view the slides as your audience would. You will begin the slide show starting with the first slide.

1

- **Select slide 1 in the Slides tab.**
- **Click Slide Show (in the status bar).**

Additional Information

Using Slide Show runs the slide show beginning with the currently selected slide.

Another Method

You also can use From Beginning or From Current Slide on the Slide Show tab or the shortcut keys F5 and Shift + F5, respectively, to start the slide show.

Your screen should be similar to Figure 1.67

First slide of the presentation displayed full screen

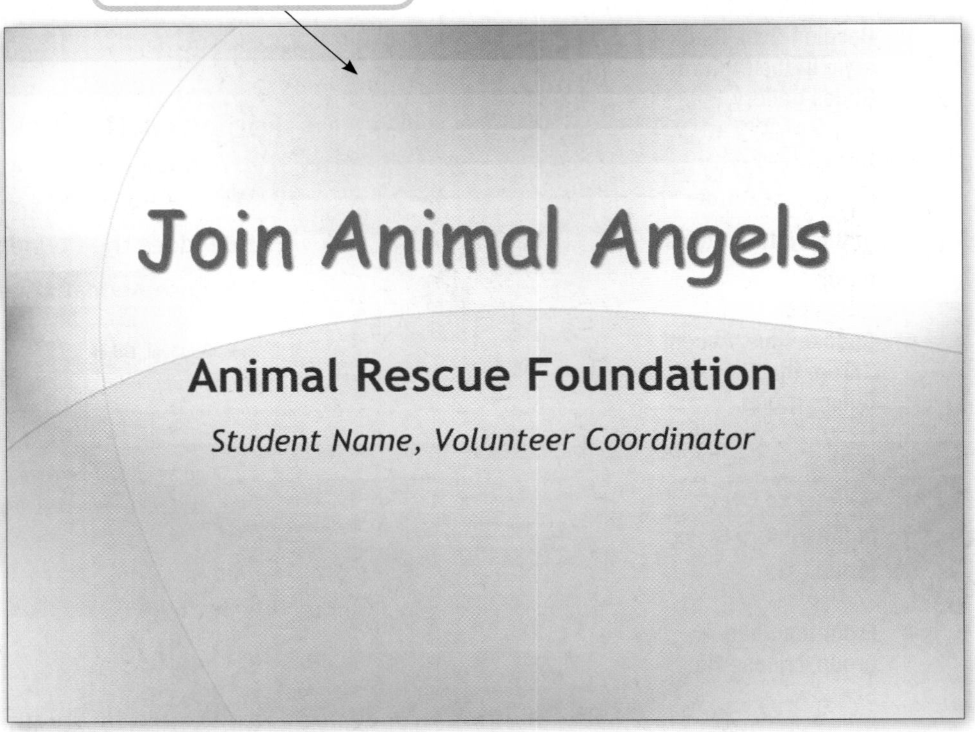

Join Animal Angels
Animal Rescue Foundation
Student Name, Volunteer Coordinator

Figure 1.67

The presentation title slide is displayed full screen, as it will appear when projected on a screen using computer projection equipment. The easiest way to see the next slide is to click the mouse button. You also can use the keys shown below to move to the next or previous slide.

Next Slide	Previous Slide
Spacebar	Backspace
Enter	
→	←
↓	↑
Page Down	Page Up
N (for Next)	P (for Previous)

You also can select Next, Previous, or Last Viewed from the shortcut menu. Additionally, moving the mouse pointer to the lower-left corner of the window in Slide Show displays the Slide Show toolbar. Clicking ⇦ or ⇨ moves to the previous or next slide, and ▤ opens the shortcut menu.

2

- Click to display the next slide.

- Using each of the methods described, slowly display the entire presentation.

- When the last slide displays a black window, click again to end the slide show.

Additional Information

You can press [Esc] or use End Show on the shortcut menu at any time to end the slide show.

Your screen should be similar to Figure 1.68

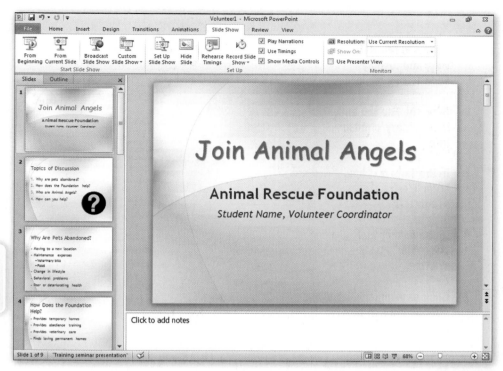

Figure 1.68

After the last slide is displayed, the program returns to the view you were last using, in this case, Normal view.

Documenting a File

Having Trouble?

Refer to the section "Specifying Document Properties" in the Introduction to Microsoft Office 2010 to review this feature.

Finally, you want to update the presentation file properties by adding your name as the author, and a tag. The default title does not need to be changed.

- **Return to Normal view and display slide 1, if necessary.**

- **Open the File tab and, if necessary, choose Info.**

- **In the Tags text box, enter Volunteer, Recruit**

- **In the Author text box, enter your name**

- **Click anywhere outside the text box.**

Your screen should be similar to Figure 1.69

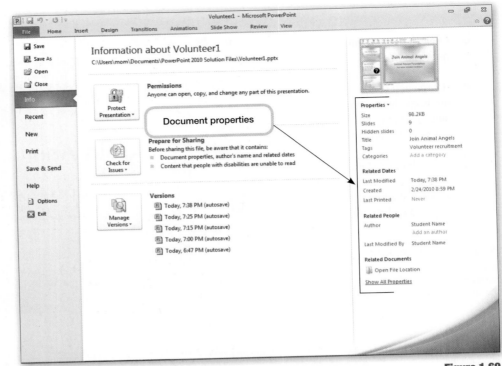

Figure 1.69

Previewing and Printing the Presentation

Although you still plan to make many changes to the presentation, you want to provide a printed copy of the presentation to the foundation director to get feedback regarding the content and layout.

PRINTING A SLIDE

Although your presentation looks good on your screen, it may not look good when printed. Shading, patterns, and backgrounds that look good on the screen can make your printed output unreadable. Fortunately, PowerPoint displays a preview of how your printed output will appear as you specify the print settings. This allows you to make changes to the print settings before printing and reduces unnecessary paper waste.

From the File tab choose Print.

Your screen should be similar to **Figure 1.70**

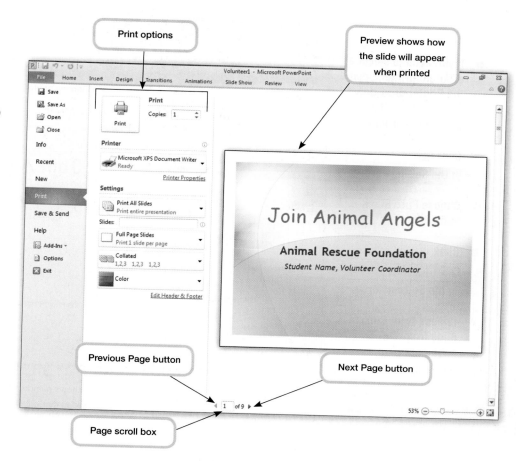

Print options

Preview shows how the slide will appear when printed

Previous Page button

Next Page button

Page scroll box

Figure 1.70

The Print window displays the print options in the left pane that are used to modify the default print settings. The preview area displays the first slide in the presentation as it will appear when printed using the current settings. It appears in color if your selected printer is a color printer; otherwise, it appears in grayscale (shades of gray). Even if you have a color printer, you can print the slides in grayscale or pure black and white. You want to print using the black and white option. The page scroll box shows the page number of the page you are currently viewing and the number of total pages. The scroll buttons on either side are used to scroll to the next and previous page.

The other change you want to make to the print settings is to only print the first slide in the presentation. To do this, you will change the settings to print the current slide only.

Additional Information

Use grayscale when your slides include patterns whose colors you want to appear in shades of gray.

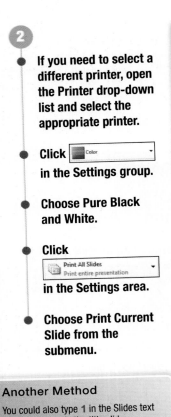

2

- If you need to select a different printer, open the Printer drop-down list and select the appropriate printer.

- Click [Color] in the Settings group.

- Choose **Pure Black and White**.

- Click [Print All Slides / Print entire presentation] in the Settings area.

- Choose **Print Current Slide** from the submenu.

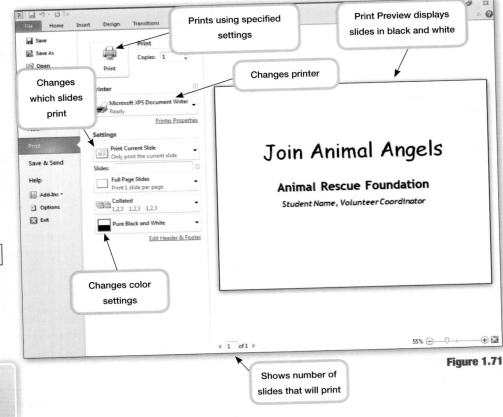

Figure 1.71

Another Method
You could also type **1** in the Slides text box to select only the title slide.

Your screen should be similar to Figure 1.71

The preview area displays how the slide will look when printed in black and white. Notice the page scroll box in the preview area now show 1 of 1, indicating that only the first slide will be printed.

Additional Information
Please consult your instructor for printing procedures that may differ from the following directions.

3

- If necessary, make sure your printer is on and ready to print.

A printing progress bar appears in the status bar, indicating that the program is sending data to the printer and the title slide should be printing.

- Click **Print**.

PRINTING HANDOUTS

You also can change the type of printed output from full page slides to any one of the output settings described in the table below. Only one type of output can be printed at a time.

Additional Information
You will learn about notes in Lab 2.

Output Type	Description
Full Page Slides	Prints one slide on a page.
Notes Pages	Prints the slide and the associated notes on a page.
Outline	Prints the slide content as it appears in Outline view.
Handouts	Prints multiple slides on a page.

To help the foundation's director get a better feel for the flow of the presentation, you decide to also print out the presentation as a handout. The handout format will allow him to see each slide as it appears onscreen.

1

- **Open the File menu and choose Print.**

- **Click**

  Print Current Slide
  Only print the current slide

  in the Settings area and choose Print All Slides.

- **Click**

  Full Page Slides
  Print 1 slide per page

  in the Settings area and choose 6 Slides Vertical **.**

Your screen should be similar to **Figure 1.72**

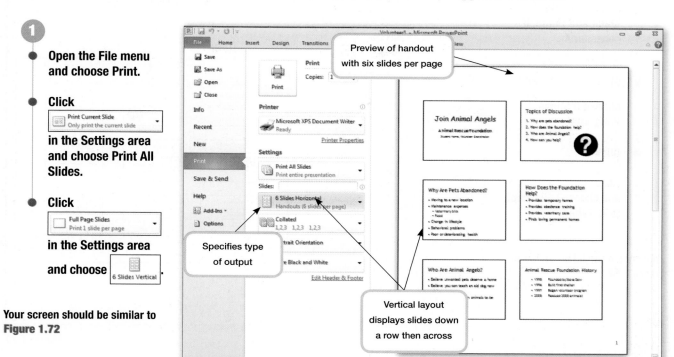

Figure 1.72

The preview area shows the handouts as they will print. The vertical arrangement of the slides displays the slides down a row and then across. You decide to change the orientation from the default of portrait to landscape so that the slides print across the length of the paper, to change the arrangement to horizontal, and also to increase the number of slides per page so that the entire presentation fits on one page.

Change the Color setting to Pure Black and White, if necessary.

Click 6 Slides Vertical **and choose 9 Slides Horizontal.**

Click Portrait Orientation ▼ **and choose Landscape Orientation.**

Your screen should be similar to Figure 1.73

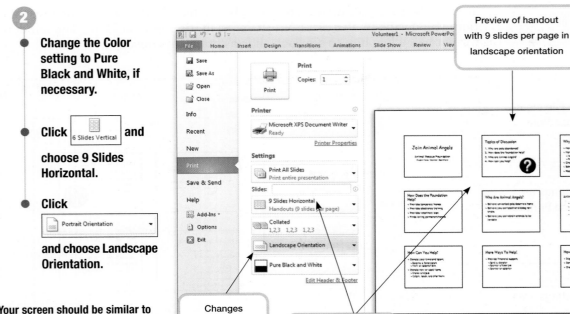

Figure 1.73

The preview area reflects your changes to the print settings. The horizontal layout displays the slides in order across a row and then down, making the presentation easier to follow.

③

Click  **Print.**

Your printed output should be similar to that shown in the Case Study at the beginning of the lab.

PRINTING AN OUTLINE

The final item you want to print is an outline of the presentation. An outline will make it easier for the director to provide feedback on the overall organization of the presentation.

1

● Open the File tab and choose Print.

● Change the Color setting to Pure Black and White again, if necessary.

● Change the orientation to Portrait Orientation.

● Click | 9 Slides Horizontal / Handouts (9 slides per page) ▾ | and choose .

● Ensure that the correct printer is selected and ready and click .

The printed outline will be a two-page document that looks similar to the preview.

Exiting PowerPoint

Another Method
You also can exit PowerPoint using ⊠ Exit in the File tab.

You have finished working on the presentation for now and will exit the PowerPoint program.

1

● Click ⊠ Close in the title bar.

● If asked to save the file again, click .

OCUS ON CAREERS

EXPLORE YOUR CAREER OPTIONS

Account Executive

Sales is an excellent entry point for a solid career in any company. Account executive is just one of many titles that a sales professional may have; field sales and sales representative are two other titles. Account executives take care of customers by educating them on the company's latest products, designing solutions using the company's product line, and closing the deal to make the sale and earn their commission. These tasks require the use of effective PowerPoint presentations that educate and motivate potential customers. The salary range of an account executive is limited only by his or her ambition; salaries range from $30,000 to more than $120,540. To learn more about this career, visit the Web site for the Bureau of Labor Statistics of the U.S. Department of Labor.

Slide (PP1.6)

A slide is an individual "page" of your presentation.

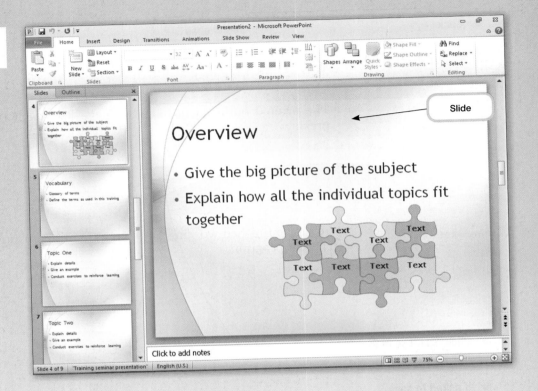

Spelling Checker (PP1.16)

The spelling checker locates most misspelled words, duplicate words, and capitalization irregularities as you create and edit a presentation, and proposes possible corrections.

AutoCorrect (PP1.18)

The AutoCorrect feature makes some basic assumptions about the text you are typing and, based on those assumptions, automatically corrects the entry.

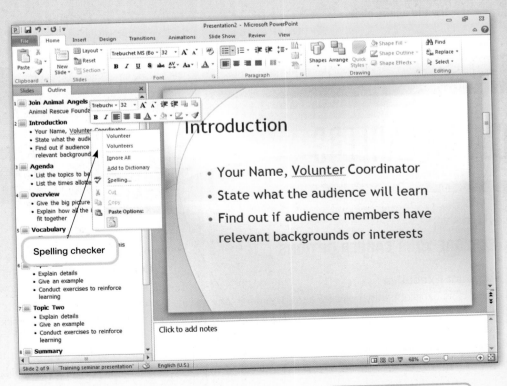

Layout (PP1.42)

A layout defines the position and format for objects and text on a slide. A layout contains placeholders for the different items such as bulleted text, titles, charts, and so on.

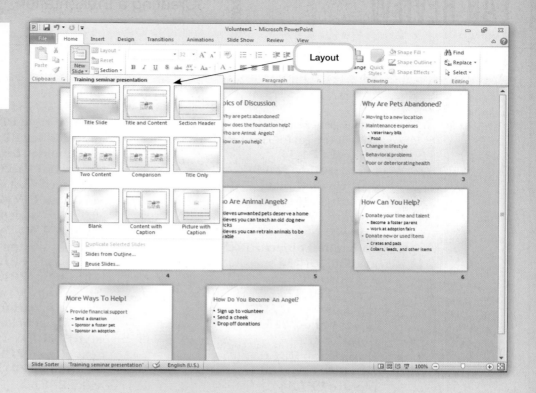

Graphic (PP1.54)

A graphic is a nontext element or object, such as a drawing or picture, that can be added to a slide.

KEY TERMS

AutoCorrect PP1.18
character formatting PP1.47
clip art PP1.54
current slide PP1.9
custom dictionary PP1.16
default settings PP1.5
demote PP1.25
drawing object PP1.54
embedded object PP1.54
graphic PP1.54
keyword PP1.56
layout PP1.42
main dictionary PP1.16
Notes pane PP1.6
object PP1.6
Outline tab PP1.6
paragraph formatting PP1.47
picture PP1.54

picture style PP1.59
placeholder PP1.6
placeholder text PP1.6
promote PP1.26
sans serif font PP1.48
serif font PP1.47
sizing handles PP1.44
slide PP1.6
Slide indicator PP1.6
Slide pane PP1.6
slide show PP1.61
Slides tab PP1.6
source program PP1.54
spelling checker PP1.16
style PP1.59
text effects PP1.50
thumbnail PP1.6
view PP1.6

COMMAND SUMMARY

Command	Shortcut	Action
File tab		
Save	Ctrl + S	Saves presentation
🖺 Save As	F12	Saves presentation using new file name and/or location
📂 Open	Ctrl + O	Opens existing presentation
📁 Close		Closes presentation
Info		Document properties
New	Ctrl + N	Opens New Presentation dialog box
Print	Ctrl + P	Opens print settings and a preview pane
☒ Exit		Closes PowerPoint
Quick Access Toolbar		
🖫 Save	Ctrl + S	Saves presentation
↺ ▾ Undo	Ctrl + Z	Reverses last action
Home tab		
Clipboard group		
Paste	Ctrl + V	Pastes item from Clipboard
✂ Cut	Ctrl + X	Cuts selection to Clipboard
📋 ▾ Copy	Ctrl + C	Copies selection to Clipboard
Slides group		
New Slide ▾	Ctrl + M	Inserts new slide with selected layout
📄 Layout ▾		Changes layout of a slide
Font group		
Trebuchet MS (He ▾) Font		Changes font type
44 ▾ Size		Changes font size

LAB REVIEW

COMMAND SUMMARY (CONTINUED)

Command	Shortcut	Action
A˄		Increases font size
A˅		Decreases font size
I		Italicizes text
U		Underlines text
S		Applies a shadow effect
A ▾		Changes font color
Paragraph group		
☰ ▾ Bullets/Bullets		Formats bulleted list
☰ ▾ Numbering/Bulleted		Formats numbered lists
Editing group		
▷ Select ▾ / ☰ Select All	Ctrl + A	Selects everything in the placeholder box
Insert tab		
Illustrations group		
Clip Art		Inserts clip art
Slide Show tab		
Start Slide Show group		
From Beginning	F5	Displays presentation starting with the first slide
From Current Slide	Shift + F5	Displays presentation starting with the current slide
Review tab		
Proofing group		
ABC Spelling	F7	Spell-checks presentation

COMMAND SUMMARY (CONTINUED)

Command	Shortcut	Action
View tab		
Presentation Views group		
Normal		Switches to Normal view
Slide Sorter		Switches to Slide Sorter view
Picture Tools Format tab		
Adjust group		
9 Slides Horizontal — Handouts (9 slides per page)		Modifies the color of the picture
Picture Styles group		
More		Opens Picture styles gallery to choose an overall visual style for a picture
Picture Layout ▾		Changes layout of a drawing
Picture Border ▾		Applies a border style to picture
Picture Effects ▾		Applies a visual effect to picture

LAB EXERCISES

SCREEN IDENTIFICATION

1. In the following PowerPoint screen, letters identify important elements. Enter the correct term for each screen element in the space provided.

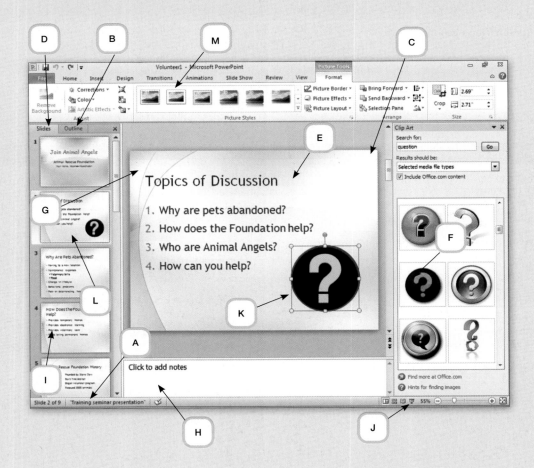

Possible answers for the screen identification are:

Clip art	Presentation template	**A.** _____	**H.** _____
Object	Outline tab	**B.** _____	**I.** _____
Picture Styles	Sizing handle	**C.** _____	**J.** _____
Slide Show view	Slides tab	**E.** _____	**K.** _____
Slide pane	Note pane	**F.** _____	**L.** _____
Slide title	Thumbnail	**G.** _____	**M.** _____
Current slide			

MATCHING

Match the item on the left with the correct description on the right.

1. AutoFit   _____ a. small image
2. demote   _____ b. sample text that suggests the content for the slide
3. embedded object   _____ c. moves the slide back to the previous slide in a presentation
4. Previous Slide button   _____ d. individual page of a presentation
5. layout   _____ e. displays each slide as a thumbnail
6. Notes pane   _____ f. indents a bulleted point to the right
7. placeholder text   _____ g. defines the position and format for objects and text that will be added to a slide
8. slide   _____ h. includes space to enter notes that apply to the current slide
9. Slides tab   _____ i. becomes part of the presentation file and can be opened and edited using the source program
10. thumbnail   _____ j. tool that automatically resizes text to fit within the placeholder

TRUE/FALSE

Circle the correct answer to the following questions.

1. A layout contains placeholders for different items such as bulleted text, titles, and charts.   **True**   **False**

2. PowerPoint will continue to indent to the same level when you demote a bulleted point until you cancel the indent.   **True**   **False**

3. A slide is a set of characters with a specific design.   **True**   **False**

4. PowerPoint identifies a word as misspelled by underlining it with a wavy blue line.   **True**   **False**

5. PowerPoint can print multiple types of output at a time.   **True**   **False**

6. The Previous Slide and Next Slide buttons are located at the bottom of the horizontal scroll bar.   **True**   **False**

7. Content templates focus on the design of a presentation.   **True**   **False**

8. Graphics are objects, such as charts, drawings, pictures, and scanned photographs, that provide visual interest or clarify data.   **True**   **False**

9. You can rely on AutoCorrect to ensure your document is error free.   **True**   **False**

10. After the final slide is displayed in Slide Sorter view, the program will return to the view you were last using.   **True**   **False**

LAB EXERCISES

FILL-IN

Complete the following statements by filling in the blanks with the correct terms.

1. _____ is a set of picture files or simple drawings that comes with Office 2010.
2. The size of a _____ can be changed by dragging its sizing handles.
3. A _____ is an individual "page" of your presentation.
4. _____ define the position and format for objects and text that will be added to a slide.
5. A _____ is text or graphics that appears at the bottom of each slide.
6. When selected, a placeholder is surrounded with eight _____.
7. A _____ is a miniature of a slide.
8. _____ is a PowerPoint feature that advises you of misspelled words as you add text to a slide and proposes possible corrections.
9. A _____ is a file containing predefined settings that can be used as a pattern to create many common types of presentations.
10. An embedded object is edited using the _____ program.

MULTIPLE CHOICE

Circle the correct response to the questions below.

1. The step in the development of a presentation that focuses on determining the length of your speech, the audience, the layout of the room, and the type of audiovisual equipment available is _____.
   a. editing
   b. creating
   c. planning
   d. enhancing

2. A _____ is a file containing predefined settings that can be used as a pattern to create many common types of presentations.
   a. presentation
   b. slide
   c. template
   d. graphic

3. The _____ feature makes some basic assumptions about the text you are typing and, based on those assumptions, automatically corrects the entry.
   a. grammar checker
   b. AutoCorrect
   c. spelling checker
   d. template

4. If you want to work on all aspects of your presentation, switch to _____ view, which displays the Slide pane, Outline pane, and Notes pane.
   a. Normal
   b. Outline
   c. Slide
   d. Slide Sorter

5. _____ displays a miniature of each slide to make it easy to reorder slides, add special effects such as transitions, and set timing between slides.
   a. Slide Show view
   b. Normal view
   c. Reading view
   d. Slide Sorter view

6. If you want to provide copies of your presentation to the audience showing multiple slides on a page, you would print _____.
   a. note pages
   b. slides
   c. handouts
   d. outline area

7. A(n) _____ is an onscreen display of your presentation.
   a. slide
   b. handout
   c. outline
   d. slide show

8. A _____ is a nontext element or object, such as a drawing or picture, that can be added to a slide.
   a. slide
   b. template
   c. text box
   d. graphic

9. When the spelling checker is used, you can create a(n) _____ dictionary to hold words that you commonly use but are not included in the main dictionary.
   a. official
   b. common
   c. personal
   d. custom

10. The keyboard shortcut to view a slide show is _____.
    a. [F5]
    b. [Alt] + V
    c. [F3]
    d. [Ctrl] + V

STEP-BY-STEP

TRIPLE CROWN PRESENTATION ★

1. Logan Thomas works at Adventure Travel Tours. He is working on a presentation about lightweight hiking to be presented to a group of interested clients. Logan recently found some new information to add to the presentation. He also wants to rearrange some slides and make a few other changes to improve the appearance of the presentation. The handouts of your completed presentation will be similar to those shown here.

   a. Open the file pp01_Triple Crown. Run the slide show.

   b. Enter your name in the subtitle on slide 1.

   c. Spell-check the presentation, making the appropriate corrections.

   d. Change the layout of slide 5 to Title Only.

   e. Move slide 6 before slide 5.

   f. Insert an appropriate photograph from the Clip Art gallery on slide 4. Size and position it appropriately.

   g. Insert a new slide using the Two Content layout after slide 4.

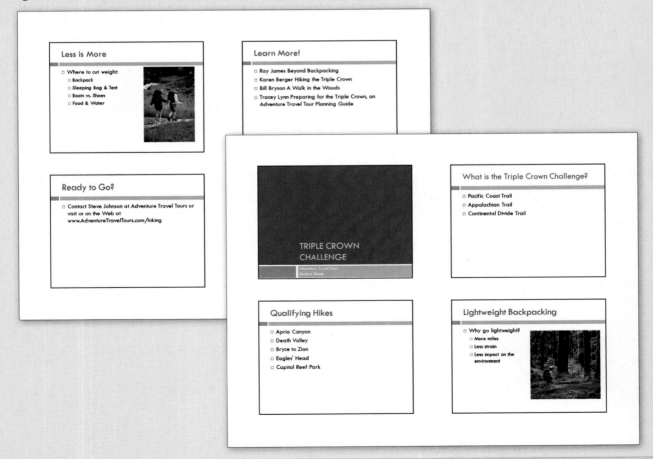

h. Enter the title **Less is More**. Insert an appropriate photograph on hiking from the Clip Art gallery in the right content placeholder. Move to slide 4 and select the second promoted bullet, "Where to cut weight:", and its subpoints. Cut this text and paste it in the left content placeholder of slide 5.

i. Change the layout of slide 7 to Title and Content layout. Add the following text in the text placeholder: **Contact Steve Johnson at Adventure Travel Tours or visit us on the Web at www. AdventureTravelTours.com/hiking**.

j. Run the slide show.

k. Save the presentation as Triple Crown Presentation. Print the slides in landscape orientation as handouts (four per page).

EMERGENCY DRIVING TECHNIQUES ★★

2. The Department of Public Safety holds monthly community outreach programs. Next month's topic is about how to handle special driving circumstances, such as driving in rain or snow. You are responsible for presenting the section on how to handle tire blowouts. You have organized the topics to be presented and located several clip art graphics that will complement the talk. Now you are ready to begin creating the presentation. Handouts of the completed presentation are shown here.

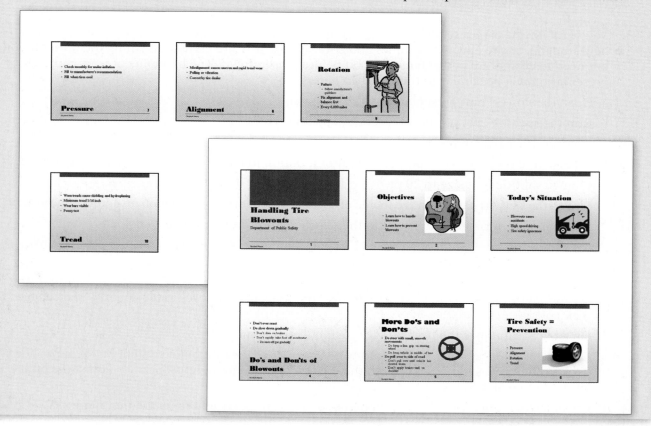

LAB EXERCISES

a. Open the PowerPoint presentation pp01_Handling Blowouts.

b. Run the spelling checker and correct any errors.

c. On slide 1, replace "Student Name" with your name.

Increase the title text to 54 pts.

Change title text color to Dark Red, Accent 1, Darker 50%.

d. On slide 5:

Promote bullet 4.

Demote the last bullet.

AutoFit the content text to the placeholder

e. On slide 6, insert a clip art image on the theme of tires and position it in the lower-right corner of the slide.

f. On slide 3, change the color of the clip art to Dark Red, Accent 6, Light. Apply the Bevel Rectangle picture style to the clip art image.

g. Save the presentation as Handling Blowouts.

h. Run the slide show.

i. Print the slides as handouts (six per page, horizontal) and close the presentation.

WRITING EFFECTIVE RESUMES ★ ★

3. You work for the career services center of a major university and are working on a presentation to help students create effective resumes and cover letters. You are close to finishing the presentation but need to clean it up and enhance it a bit before presenting it. The handouts of your completed presentation will be similar to those shown here.

a. Open the PowerPoint presentation pp01_Resume.

b. Run the spelling checker and correct any spelling errors.

c. On slide 1: Display in normal view.

Change title font size to 54 pt. Use the AutoFit option to fit the text into the placeholder.

Change subtitle font size to 20 pt.

Search the Clip Art gallery on the theme of success. Insert, size, and position an appropriate graphic.

Apply an appropriate picture style to the selected graphic and change its color.

d. On slide 2, replace "Student Name" with your name. Use picture styles and effects to improve the appearance of the picture.

e. On slides 3 and 4, search the Clip Art gallery on the theme of success. Insert, size, and position an appropriate graphic on each slide. Apply an appropriate picture styles to the graphics and change their colors.

f. On slide 5, capitalize the first word of each bulleted item.

g. On slide 6, split the slide content into two slides. Move the first bulleted item on the new slide (7) back to slide 6 so slide 7 begins with the "Other" bulleted item. Appropriately adjust the bullet level and font size of the moved item on slide 6.

h. On slide 10, reorganize the bulleted items so "Types of cover letters" is the first item.

i. To match the slide order with the way the topics are now introduced, move slide 13 before slide 11.

j. On slide 13: Break each bulleted item into two or three bullets each as appropriate.

Capitalize the first word of each bulleted item.

Remove any commas and periods at the end of the bullets.

k. Save the presentation as Resume1.

l. Run the slide show.

m. Print the slides as handouts (nine per page, horizontal, in landscape orientation) and close the presentation.

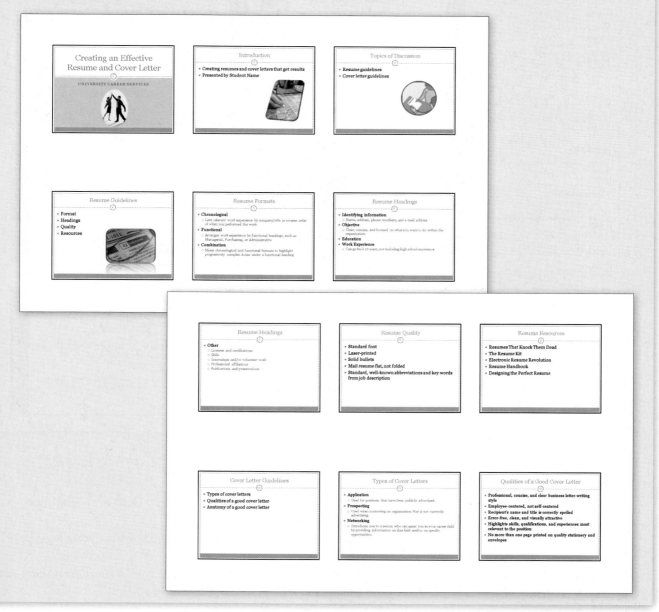

LAB EXERCISES

EMPLOYEE ORIENTATION ★ ★ ★

4. As the front desk manager of the Essex Inn, you want to make a presentation to your new employees about all of the amenities your hotel offers its guests as well as information on activities and dining in the area. The purpose of this presentation is to enable employees to answer the many questions that are asked by the guests about both the hotel and the town. The handouts of your completed presentation will be similar to those shown here.

a. Open pp01_Essex Inn, which uses the Opulent content template from Microsoft Online.

b. On slide 1:

Enter **Essex Inn** as the company name. Set the font to Constantia; apply Bold and Shadow. Change the font color to Ice Blue, Background 2, and size 66.

Insert, size, and position a clip art image suitable as a hotel logo in place of the "your logo here" graphic.

Insert a line after the title. Type your name on the line, and change the font size to Trebuchet MS and the font size to 20. Change the font color to White and apply italics.

c. On slide 2:

Enter **Amenities and Activities for Guests** as the title.

Change the font size of the title to 31.

Enter the sample bulleted text **What is there to do?** as the first bullet.

Enter **At the hotel or in the town?** as the second bullet.

Remove the remaining bulleted items.

d. Insert a new slide after slide 2. In this slide:

Set the layout to Title and Content.

Enter **Hotel Amenities and Activities** as the title.

Enter **Dining** as the first bullet.

Enter **Activities** as the second bullet.

Enter **Other amenities** as the third bullet.

Insert, size, and position a clip art image suitable for a hotel at the bottom center of the slide. Apply picture styles and effects.

e. Insert a new slide after slide 3. In this slide:

Set the layout to Title and Content.

Enter **Dining** as the title.

Enter **Breakfast** as the first bullet under Dining.

Enter **Eggs Benedict or custom omelet** and demote to appear as the first bullet under Breakfast.

Enter **Daily chef's special** as the second bullet under Breakfast.

Enter **Lunch** and promote to appear as the second bullet under Dining.

Enter **Custom-pack lunch for outings** and demote to appear as the first bullet under Lunch.

Enter **Build-your-own sandwich bar** as the second bullet under Lunch.

Enter **Dinner** and promote to appear as the third bullet under Dining.

Enter **Four course meal (salad, soup, entrée, dessert)** as the first bullet under Dinner.

Enter **Three nightly chef specials** as the second bullet under Dinner.

f. Insert a new slide after slide 4. In this slide:

Set the layout to Title and Content.

Enter **Activities** as the title.

Enter **Morning** as the first bullet under Activities.

Enter **Bird watching on the veranda** and demote to appear as the first bullet under Morning.

Enter **Lecture/Tour of gardens and hotel** as the second bullet under Morning.

Enter **Afternoon** and promote to appear as the second bullet under Activities.

Enter **Daily guest lecture or class** as the first bullet under Afternoon.

Enter **Historic walking tour of downtown** as the second bullet under Afternoon.

Enter **Evening** and promote to appear as the third bullet under Activities.

Enter **Champagne meet/greet** and demote to appear as the first bullet under Evening.

Enter **Live music/dancing with dinner** as the second bullet under Evening.

LAB EXERCISES

g. Insert a new slide after slide 5. In this slide:

Set the layout to Title and Content.

Enter **Other Amenities** as the title.

Enter **Special dining events** as the first bullet under Other Amenities.

Enter **Sunday champagne brunch** and demote to appear as the first bullet under Special Dining Events.

Enter **Saturday afternoon tea** as the second bullet under Special Dining Events.

Enter **Extras** and promote to appear as the second bullet for Other Amenities.

Enter **Third Tuesday cooking class** and demote to appear as the first bullet under Extras.

Enter **Tour of haunted houses on Saturdays at nine** as the second bullet under Extras.

Insert, size, and position a clip art image suitable for a hotel at the bottom center of the slide. Apply picture styles and effects.

h. Delete slides 7 through 13.

i. On the Summary slide 7.

Enter **Hotel amenities and activities** as the first bullet under Summary.

Enter **Dining** and demote to appear as the first bullet under Hotel amenities and activities.

Enter **Activities** as the second bullet under Hotel amenities and activities.

Enter **Other amenities** as the third bullet under Hotel amenities and activities.

Enter **Always remember** and promote to appear as the second bullet under Summary.

Enter **Our guests are our customers** and demote to appear as the first bullet under Always remember.

Enter **Treat our guests as friends** as the second bullet under Always remember.

Enter **Thanks for attending and put these ideas into practice** and promote to appear as the third bullet under Summary.

Delete any remaining bullet placeholders.

j. Save the presentation as Essex Inn Orientation.

k. Run the slide show.

l. Print the slides as handouts (four per page, horizontal, in landscape orientation).

WORKPLACE ISSUES ★ ★ ★

5. Tim is preparing for his lecture on "Workplace Issues" for his Introduction to Computers class. He uses PowerPoint to create presentations for each of his lectures. He has organized the topics to be presented, and located several clip art graphics that will complement the lecture. He is now ready to begin creating the presentation. Several slides of the completed presentation are shown here.

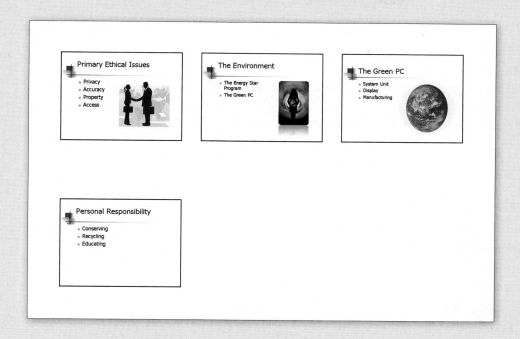

a. Open a new presentation using the Staff Training Presentation template. If you don't have access to the Internet, you can use the file pp01_Staff Training.

b. On slide 1:

Change the title to **Workplace Issues**. Change the font size to 48 and apply a bold effect.

Change the subtitle text to **Lecture 4**.

Add a line beneath the subtitle and type **Presented by Your Name**. Change the font size of this line to 24.

Insert, size, and position a clip art image suitable for the theme of an office meeting. Apply a picture style to the image.

c. On slide 2:

Enter **Topics of Discussion** as the title text.

Enter **Ergonomics** as bullet 1.

Enter **Ethics** as bullet 2.

Enter **Environment** as bullet 3.

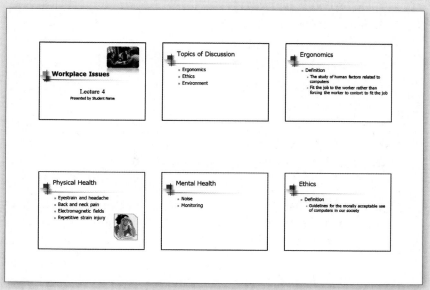

d. On slide 3:

Enter **Ergonomics** as the title.

Enter **Definition** as the first bullet.

Enter **Fit the job to the worker rather than forcing the worker to contort to fit the job** as the second bullet.

Enter **The study of human factors related to computers** as the third bullet.

e. Change the order of bullets 2 and 3 on slide 3.

Demote bullets 2 and 3.

f. On slide 4:

Change the title to **Mental Health**.

Include two bulleted items: **Noise** and **Monitoring**.

g. Change the title of slide 5 to **Physical Health** and include the following bulleted items:

Bullet 1: **Eyestrain and headache**

Bullet 2: **Back and neck pain**

Bullet 3: **Electromagnetic fields**

Bullet 4: **Repetitive strain injury**

Insert, size, and position a suitable clip art image. Use the picture formatting tools to customize the image to suit the presentation.

h. On slide 6:

Change the title to **Ethics**.

Include two bullets: **Definition** and **Guidelines for the morally acceptable use of computers in our society**.

Demote bullet 2.

i. Change the title of slide 7 to **Primary Ethical Issues**.

Enter **Privacy** as bullet 1.

Enter **Accuracy** as bullet 2.

Enter **Property** as bullet 3.

Enter **Access** as bullet 4.

Insert, size, and position a suitable clip art image. Use the picture formatting tools to customize the image to suit the presentation.

j. Insert a new Two Content layout slide between slides 7 and 8. On the new slide 8:

Enter **The Environment** as the title.

Enter **The Energy Star Program** as the first bullet.

Enter **The Green PC** as the second bullet.

In the right placeholder, insert, size, and position a suitable clip art image. Use the picture formatting tools to customize the image to suit the presentation.

k. Create a duplicate of slide 8. On the new slide 9:

Enter **The Green PC** as the title.

Enter **System Unit** as the first bullet.

Enter **Display** as the second bullet.

Enter **Manufacturing** as the third bullet.

In the right placeholder, insert, size, and position an appropriate clip art image.

l. On slide 10:

Enter **Personal Responsibility** as the title.

Enter **Conserving** as the first bullet.

Enter **Recycling** as the second bullet.

Enter **Educating** as the third bullet.

m. In Slide Sorter view, move slide 5 before slide 4.

n. Change the font of the words "Lecture 4" in the subtitle on the title slide to Times New Roman and the size to 44 pt.

o. Save the presentation as Workplace Issues.

p. Run the slide show. Revised PowerPoint_2010_Brief_Solutions

q. Print the slides as handouts (six per page in landscape orientation).

ON YOUR OWN

INTERNET POLICY PRESENTATION ★

1. You are working in the information technology department at International Sales Incorporated. Your manager has asked you to give a presentation on the corporation's Internet policy to the new-hire orientation class. Create your presentation with PowerPoint, using the information in the Word file pp01_Internet Policy as a resource. Use a template of your choice. When you are done, run the spelling checker, then save your presentation as Internet Policy and print it.

TELEPHONE TRAINING COURSE ★ ★

2. You are a trainer with Super Software, Inc. You received a memo from your manager alerting you that many of the support personnel are not using proper telephone protocol or obtaining the proper information from customers who call in. Your manager has asked you to conduct a training class that covers these topics. Using the Word document pp01_Memo data file as a resource, prepare the slides for your class. When you are done, save the presentation as Phone Etiquette and print the handouts.

LAB EXERCISES

VISUAL AIDS ★ ★

3. You are a trainer with Super Software, Inc. Your manager has asked you to prepare a presentation on various visual aids that may be used in presentations. Using the pp01_VisualAids data file as a resource, create an onscreen presentation using an appropriate template. Add clip art that illustrates the type of visual aid. Include your name on the title slide. When you are done, save the presentation as Presentation Aids and print the handouts.

WEB DESIGN PROPOSAL ★ ★ ★

4. Your company wants to create a Web site, but it is not sure whether to design its own or hire a Web design firm to do it. You have been asked to create a presentation to management relaying the pros and cons of each approach. To gather information, search the Web for the topic "Web design," and select some key points about designing a Web page from one of the "how-to" or "tips" categories. Use these points to create the first part of your presentation, and call it something like "Creating Our Own Web Page." Then search the Web for the topic "Web designers," and select two Web design firms. Pick some key points about each firm (for example, Web sites they have designed, design elements they typically use, and/or their design philosophy). Finally, include at least one slide that lists the pros and cons of each approach. Include your name on the title slide. When your presentation is complete, save it as Web Design and print the slides as handouts.

    You will expand on this presentation in On Your Own Exercise 4 of Lab 2.

CAREERS WITH ANIMALS ★ ★ ★

5. You have been volunteering at the Animal Rescue Foundation. The director has asked you to prepare a presentation on careers with animals to present to local schools in hopes that some students will be inspired to volunteer at the foundation. Using the Word document pp01_Animal Careers data file as a resource, create the presentation. Add photos or clip art where appropriate. When you are done, save the presentation as Careers with Animals and print the handouts.

Modifying and Refining a Presentation Lab 2

Objectives

After completing this lab, you will know how to:

1. Find and replace text.
2. Create and enhance a table.
3. Insert pictures.
4. Modify graphic objects.
5. Create and enhance shapes.
6. Create a text box.
7. Change the theme.
8. Modify slide masters.
9. Add animation, sound, and transitions.
10. Control a slide show.
11. Add speaker notes.
12. Add and hide slide footers.
13. Customize print settings.

CASE STUDY

Animal Rescue Foundation

The Animal Rescue Foundation director was very impressed with your first draft of the presentation to recruit volunteers and asked to see the presentation onscreen. While viewing it together, you explained that you plan to make many more changes to improve the appearance of the presentation. For example, you plan to use a different color theme and to include more art and other graphic features to enhance the appearance of the slides. You also explained that you will add more action to the slides using the special effects included with PowerPoint to keep the audience's attention.

The director suggested that you include more information on

ways that volunteers can help. Additionally, because the organization has such an excellent adoption rate, the director wants you to include a table to illustrate the success of the adoption program.

PowerPoint 2010 gives you the design and production capabilities to create a first-class onscreen presentation. These features include artist-designed layouts and color themes that give your presentation a professional appearance. In addition, you can add your own personal touches by modifying text attributes, incorporating art or graphics, and including animation to add impact, interest, and excitement to your presentation.

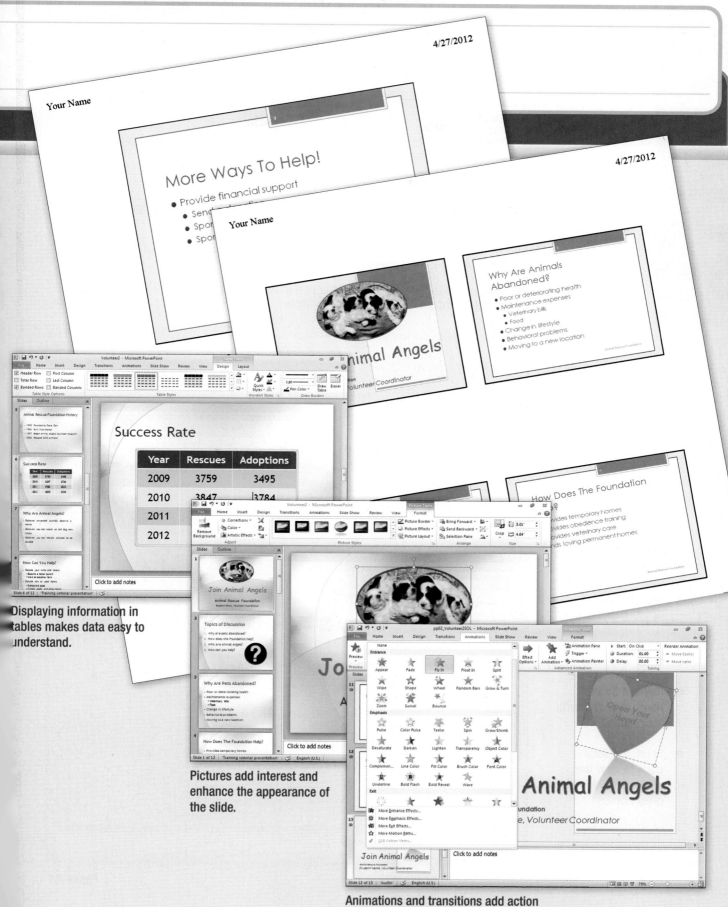

Displaying information in tables makes data easy to understand.

Pictures add interest and enhance the appearance of the slide.

Animations and transitions add action to a slide show.

The following concepts will be introduced in this lab:

1 Find and Replace To make editing easier, you can use the Find and Replace feature to find text in a presentation and replace it with other text.

2 Table A table is used to organize information into an easy-to-read format of horizontal rows and vertical columns.

3 Alignment Alignment controls the position of text entries within a space.

4 Theme A theme is a predefined set of formatting choices that can be applied to an entire document in one simple step.

5 Master A master is a special slide or page that stores information about the formatting for all slides or pages in a presentation.

6 Animations Animations are special effects that add action to text and graphics so they move around on the screen during a slide show.

Finding and Replacing Text

After meeting with the foundation director, you want to update the content to include the additional information on ways that volunteers can help the Animal Rescue Foundation.

- **Start PowerPoint 2010.**

- **Open the file** pp02_Volunteer2

- **If necessary, switch to Normal view.**

- **Replace Student Name in slide 1 with your name.**

- **Scroll the Slide pane to view the content of the revised presentation.**

Your screen should be similar to Figure 2.1

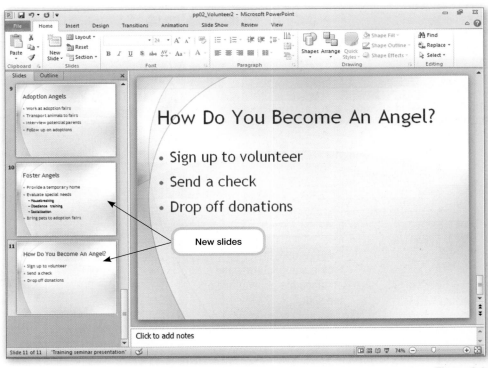

Figure 2.1

You added two new slides, 9 and 10, with more information about the Animal Angels volunteer organization, bringing the total number of slides in the presentation to 11. As you reread the content of the presentation, you decide to edit the text by finding the word "pet" and replacing it with the word "animal." To do this, you will use the Find and Replace feature.

Concept Find and Replace

To make editing easier, you can use the **Find and Replace** feature to find text in a presentation and replace it with other text. The Find feature will locate and identify any text string you specify in the presentation by highlighting it. When used along with the Replace feature, not only will the string be identified, but it will be replaced with the replacement text you specify if you choose. For example, suppose you created a lengthy document describing the type of clothing and equipment needed to set up a world-class home gym, and then you decided to change "sneakers" to "athletic shoes." Instead of deleting every occurrence of "sneakers" and typing "athletic shoes," you can use the Find and Replace feature to perform the task automatically.

The Replace feature also can be used to replace a specified font in a presentation with another. When using this feature, however, all text throughout the presentation that is in the specified font is automatically changed to the selected replacement font.

The Find and Replace feature is fast and accurate; however, use care when replacing so that you do not replace unintended matches.

FINDING TEXT

First, you will use the Find command to locate all occurrences of the word "pet" in the presentation. Because it is easier to read the text in the Slide pane, you will make that pane active before starting. If the Outline tab is active at the time you begin using Find and Replace, the located text will be highlighted in the Outline tab instead.

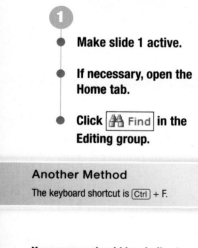

1

● Make slide 1 active.

● If necessary, open the Home tab.

● Click 🔍 Find in the Editing group.

Another Method
The keyboard shortcut is Ctrl + F.

Your screen should be similar to Figure 2.2

Figure 2.2

Finding and Replacing Text **PP2.5**

In the Find dialog box, you enter the text you want to locate in the Find what text box. The two options described in the following table allow you to refine the procedure that is used to conduct the search.

Option	Effect on Text
Match Case	Distinguishes between uppercase and lowercase characters. When selected, finds only those instances in which the capitalization matches the text you typed in the Find what box.
Find WholeWords Only	Distinguishes between whole and partial words. When selected, locates matches that are whole words and not part of a larger word. For example, finds "cat" only and not "catastrophe," too.

You want to find all occurrences of the complete word "pet." You will not use either option described above, because you want to locate all words regardless of case and because you want to find "pet" as well as "pets" in the presentation.

2

● **Type pet in the Find what text box.**

● **Click** Find Next .

● **If necessary, move the dialog box so you can see the located text.**

Your screen should be similar to Figure 2.3

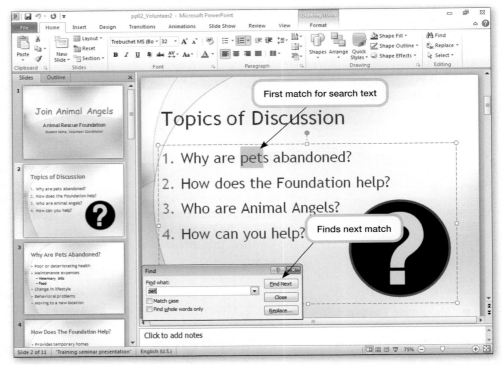

Figure 2.3

PowerPoint begins searching beginning at the cursor location for all occurrences of the text to find and locates the first occurrence of the word "pet."

3

● **Continue to click** Find Next **to locate all occurrences of the word.**

● **Click** OK **when PowerPoint indicates the entire document has been searched.**

The word "pet" is used five times in the document. Using the Find command is a convenient way to quickly navigate through a document to locate and move to specified information.

REPLACING TEXT

You want to replace selected occurrences of the word "pet" with "animal" throughout the presentation. You will use the Replace feature to specify the text to enter as the replacement text.

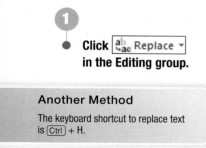

Click ab̲ac **Replace** ▾ **in the Editing group.**

> **Another Method**
>
> The keyboard shortcut to replace text is Ctrl + H.

Your screen should be similar to Figure 2.4

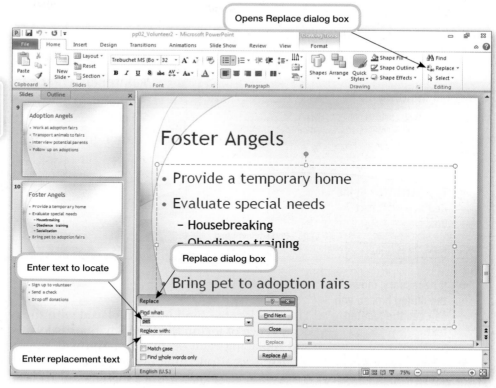

Figure 2.4

The Find dialog box changes to the Replace dialog box, and the Find text is still specified in the Find what text box. You can now enter the replacement text in the Replace with text box. The replacement text must be entered exactly as you want it to appear in your presentation.

2

● Press `Tab` or click in the Replace with text box.

Having Trouble?

If necessary, type **pet** in the Find what text box.

Additional Information

After entering the text to find, do not press `Enter` or this will choose `Find Next` and the search will begin.

● Type **animal** in the Replace with text box.

● Click `Find Next`.

● If necessary, move the dialog box so you can see the located text.

● Click `Replace`.

Having Trouble?

Click `Find Next` to move to the next occurrence if the search does not advance automatically.

Your screen should be similar to Figure 2.5

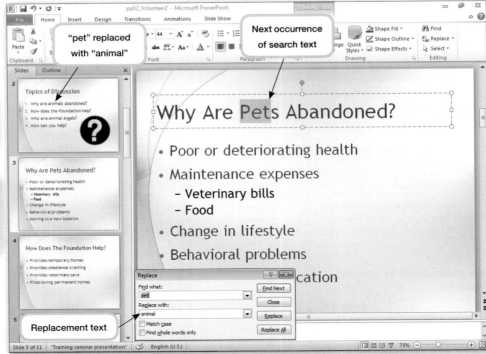

Figure 2.5

The first located Find text is replaced with the replacement text, and the next occurrence of text in the Find what box is located. You could continue finding and replacing each occurrence. You will, however, replace all the remaining occurrences at one time. As you do, the replacement is entered in lowercase even when it replaces a word that begins with an uppercase character. You will correct this when you finish replacing.

3

- Click **Replace All** to continue.

- Click **OK** in response to the finished searching dialog box.

- Click **Close** to close the Replace dialog box.

- Edit the word "animals" to "Animals" in slide 3.

- Click somewhere outside the placeholder.

- Save the presentation as Volunteer2 to you solution file location.

Your screen should be similar to Figure 2.6

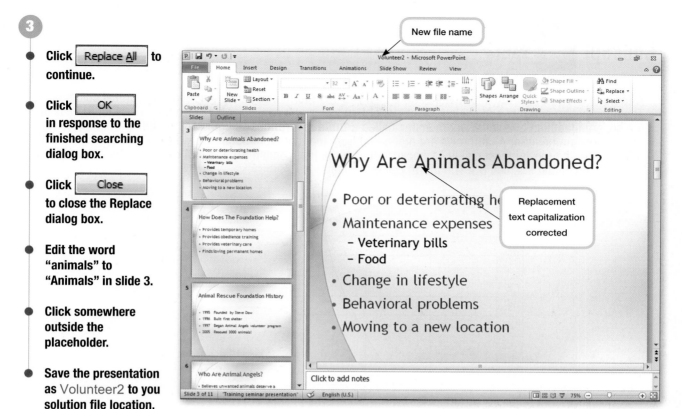

Figure 2.6

If you plan to change all occurrences, it is much faster to use **Replace All**. Exercise care when using Replace All, however, because the search text you specify might be part of another word and you may accidentally replace text you want to keep.

Creating a Simple Table

During your discussion with the director, he suggested that you add a slide containing data showing the success of the adoption program. The information in this slide will be presented using a table layout.

Concept 2 Table

A **table** is used to organize information into an easy-to-read format of horizontal rows and vertical columns. The intersection of a row and column creates a **cell** in which you can enter data or other information. Cells in a table are identified by a letter and number, called a **table reference**. Columns are identified from left to right beginning with the letter A, and rows are numbered from top to bottom beginning with the number 1. The table reference of the top-leftmost cell is A1 because it is in the first column (A) and first row (1) of the table. The third cell in column 2 is cell B3. The fourth cell in column 3 is C4.

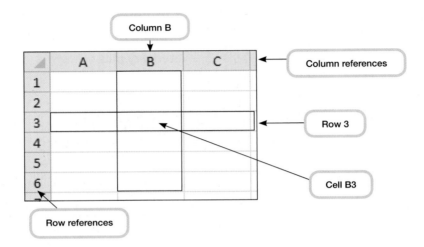

Tables are a very effective method for presenting information. The table layout organizes the information for readers and greatly reduces the number of words they have to read to interpret the data. Use tables whenever you can to make the information in your presentation easier to read.

The table you will create will display columns for the year and for the number of rescues and adoptions. The rows will display the data for the past four years. Your completed table will be similar to the one shown here.

Year	Rescues	Adoptions
2009	3759	3495
2010	3847	3784
2011	3982	3833
2012	4025	3943

CREATING A TABLE SLIDE

To include this information in the presentation, you will insert a new slide after slide 5. Because this slide will contain a table showing the adoption data, you want to use the Title and Content layout.

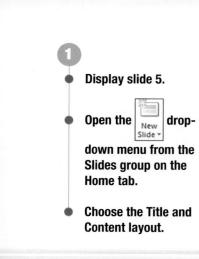

1

● Display slide 5.

● Open the  drop-down menu from the Slides group on the Home tab.

● Choose the Title and Content layout.

Additional Information

PowerPoint remembers the last slide layout used while working in this presentation or during the current session and inserts it when you click the top part of New Slide ▾.

Your screen should be similar to Figure 2.7

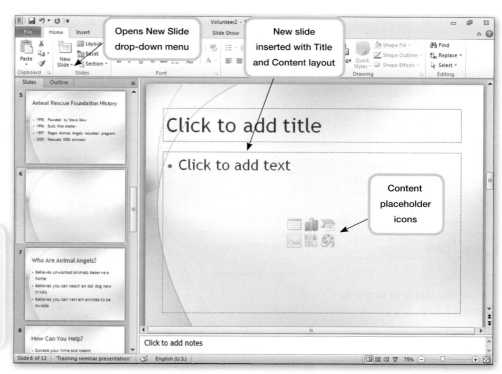

Figure 2.7

Six icons appear inside the content placeholder, each representing a different type of content that can be inserted. Clicking an icon opens the appropriate feature to add the specified type of content.

INSERTING THE TABLE

First, you will add a slide title, and then you will create the table to display the number of adoptions and rescues.

1

● Enter the title **Success Rate** in the title placeholder.

● Click the [ ] Insert Table icon in the center of the slide.

Your screen should be similar to Figure 2.8

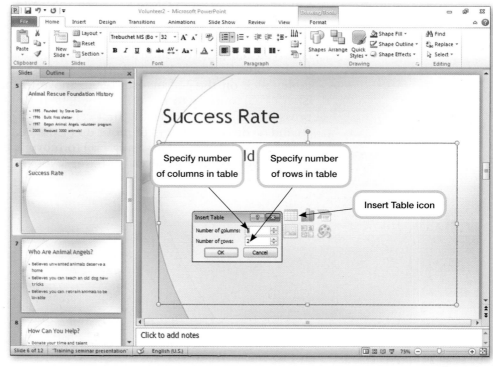

Figure 2.8

Creating a Simple Table **PP2.11**

In the Insert Table dialog box, you specify the number of rows and columns for the table.

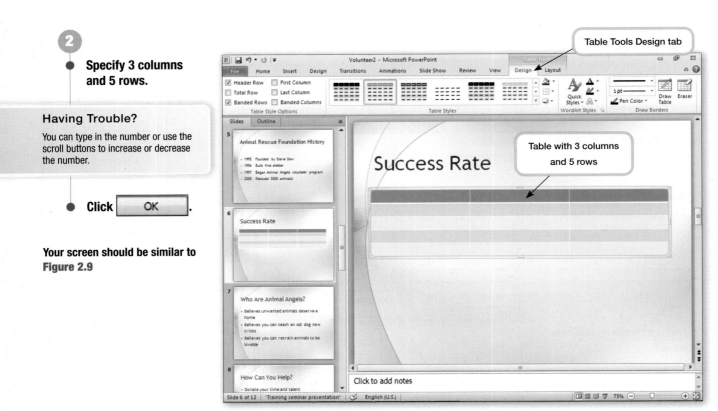

2

● **Specify 3 columns and 5 rows.**

Having Trouble?

You can type in the number or use the scroll buttons to increase or decrease the number.

● **Click** [OK].

Your screen should be similar to Figure 2.9

Figure 2.9

A basic table consisting of three columns and five rows is displayed as a selected object. In addition, the Table Tools Design tab opens in anticipation that you will want to modify the design of the table.

ENTERING DATA IN A TABLE

Now you can enter the information into the table. The insertion point appears in the top-left corner cell, cell A1, ready for you to enter text. To move in a table, click on the cell or use ⎯Tab⎯ to move to the next cell to the right and ⎯Shift⎯ + ⎯Tab⎯ to move to the cell to the left. If you are in the last cell of a row, pressing ⎯Tab⎯ takes you to the first cell of the next row. You also can use the ↑ and ↓ directional keys to move up or down a row. When you enter a large amount of text in a table, using ⎯Tab⎯ to move is easier than using the mouse because your hands are already on the keyboard.

Type Year

Press `Tab` **or click on the next cell to the right.**

Having Trouble?

Do not press `Enter` to move to the next cell, as this adds a new line to the current cell. If this happens, press `Backspace` to remove it.

Your screen should be similar to Figure 2.10

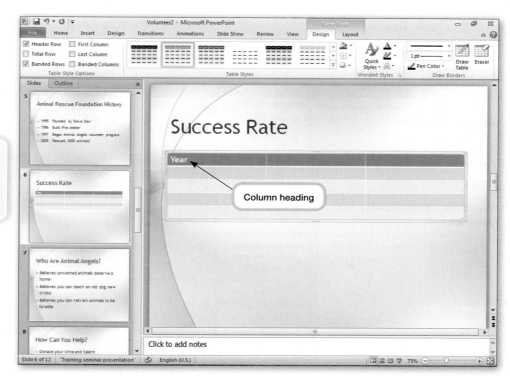

Figure 2.10

Next, you will complete the information for the table by entering the data shown below.

	Column A	Column B	Column C
Row 1	Year	Rescues	Adoptions
Row 2	2009	3759	3495
Row 3	2010	3847	3784
Row 4	2011	3982	3833
Row 5	2012	4025	3943

2 ● Add the remaining information shown above to the table.

Additional Information

You can also use the directional keys to move from cell to cell in the table.

Your screen should be similar to Figure 2.11

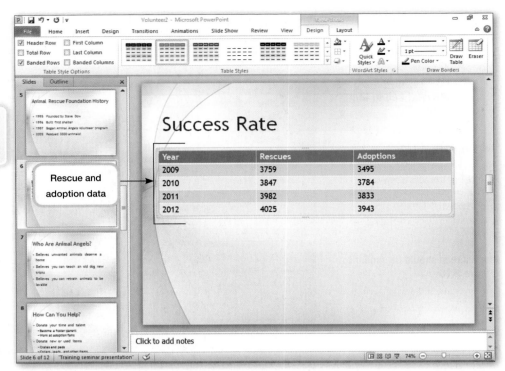

Figure 2.11

You are happy with the table but would like to increase the font size of the text to make it more readable onscreen. The size of the font in a table can be changed like any other text on a slide. However, selecting text in a table is slightly different. The following table describes how to select different areas of a table.

Area to Select	Procedure
Cell	Drag across the contents of the cell.
Row	Drag across the row or click in front of the row when the mouse pointer is a ➡.
Column	Drag down the column or click in front of the row when the mouse pointer is a ⬇.
Multiple cells, rows, or columns	Drag through the cells, rows, or columns when the mouse pointer is a ◢ or [.
	Or select the first cell, row, or column, and hold down ⇧Shift while clicking on another cell, row, or column.
Contents of next cell	Press Tab⇥.
Contents of previous cell	Press ⇧Shift + Tab⇥.
Entire table	Drag through all the cells or click anywhere inside the table and press Ctrl + A.

- **Select all the text in the table.**

- **Open the Home tab.**

- **Click** 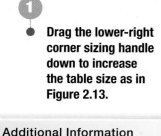 **Increase Font Size in the Font group four times.**

Additional Information

Clicking $\boxed{A^{\blacktriangledown}}$ increases the font size by units.

Your screen should be similar to Figure 2.12

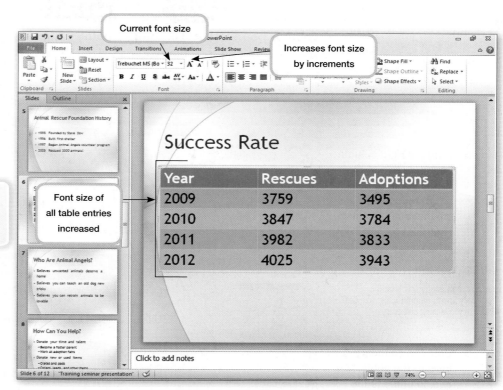

Figure 2.12

The font size has quickly been increased by four units, and at 32 points the text is much easier to read.

SIZING THE TABLE AND COLUMNS

You now want to increase the overall size of the table to better fill the space on the slide and then adjust the size of the columns to fit their contents.

1

- **Drag the lower-right corner sizing handle down to increase the table size as in Figure 2.13.**

Additional Information

The mouse pointer will appear as ⬉ when you can drag the corner sizing handle and as ＋ while dragging.

Your screen should be similar to Figure 2.13

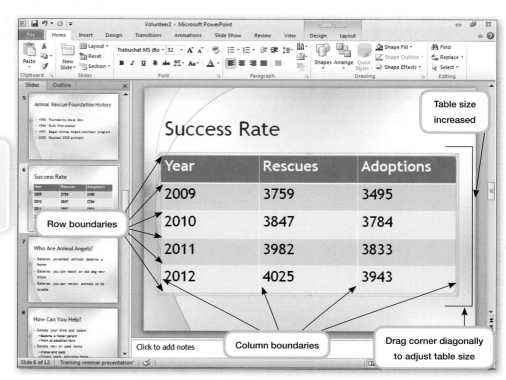

Figure 2.13

Creating a Simple Table   **PP2.15**

To adjust the individual column width or row height, you drag the row and column boundaries. The mouse pointer appears as a ✥ when you can size the column and ✥ when you can size the row. The mouse pointer appears as a ✥ when you can move the entire table.

2

● **Drag the right column boundary line of the year column to the left to reduce the column width as in Figure 2.14.**

Additional Information

You also can double-click on the boundary line to automatically size the width to the largest cell entry.

● **Drag the boundary lines of the other two columns to the left to reduce the column widths as in Figure 2.14.**

Your screen should be similar to Figure 2.14

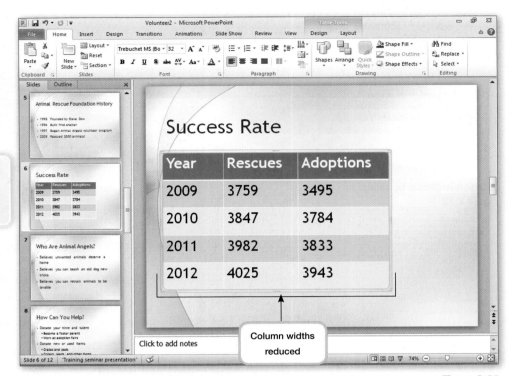

Figure 2.14

Now the columns are more appropriately sized to the data they display and the overall table size is good. You decide it would look best to align the table in the center of the slide as well. You could do this manually by moving the object to center it. A more precise method is to use the built-in alignment feature.

3

- Open the Table Tools Layout tab.

- Click 📄▾ Align in the Arrange group to display the drop-down menu.

- Choose Align Center.

Your screen should be similar to Figure 2.15

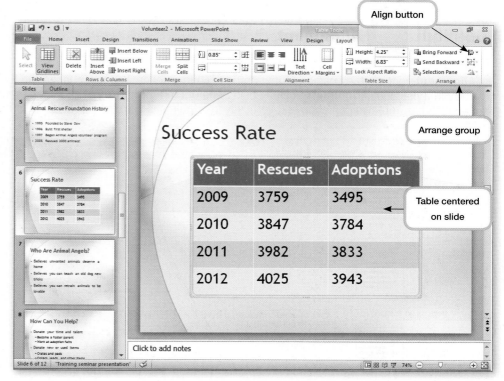

Figure 2.15

ALIGNING TEXT IN CELLS

The next change you want to make is to center the text and data in the cells. To do this, you can change the alignment of the text entries.

Concept ③ Alignment

Alignment controls the position of text entries within a space. You can change the horizontal placement of an entry in a placeholder or a table cell by using one of the four horizontal alignment settings: left, center, right, and justified. You also can align text vertically in a table cell with the top, middle, or bottom of the cell space.

Horizontal Alignment	Effect on Text	Vertical Alignment	Effect on Text
Left	Aligns text against the left edge of the placeholder or cell, leaving the right edge of text, which wraps to another line, ragged.	Top	Aligns text at the top of the cell space.
Center	Centers each line of text between the left and right edges of the placeholder or cell.	Middle	Aligns text in the middle of the cell space.
Right	Aligns text against the right edge of the placeholder or cell, leaving the left edge of multiple lines ragged.	Bottom	Aligns text at the bottom of the cell space.
Justified	Aligns text evenly with both the right and left edges of the placeholder or cell.		

The commands to change horizontal alignment are on the Home tab in the Paragraph group. However, using the shortcuts shown below or the Mini toolbar is often much quicker.

Alignment	Keyboard Shortcut
Left	Ctrl + L
Center	Ctrl + E
Right	Ctrl + R
Justified	Ctrl + J

The data in the table is not centered within the cells. You want to center the cell entries both horizontally and vertically in their cell spaces.

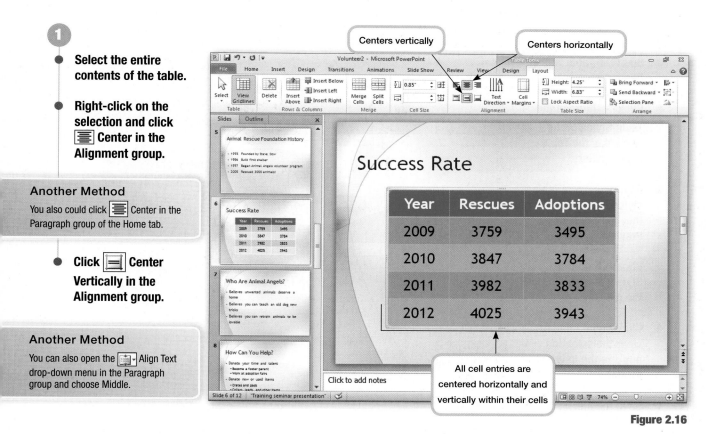

- Select the entire contents of the table.

- Right-click on the selection and click ≡ Center in the Alignment group.

Another Method

You also could click ≡ Center in the Paragraph group of the Home tab.

- Click ⊟ Center Vertically in the Alignment group.

Another Method

You can also open the ⊞▾ Align Text drop-down menu in the Paragraph group and choose Middle.

Your screen should be similar to Figure 2.16

Figure 2.16

CHANGING THE TABLE STYLE

Next, you will add a color and other formatting changes to the table. To quickly make these enhancements, you will apply a table style. Like picture styles, **table styles** are combinations of shading colors, borders, and visual effects such as shadows and reflections that can be applied in one simple step. You also can create your own table style effects by selecting specific style elements such as borders and shadows individually using the ⬧▾ Shading, ⊞▾ Borders, and ⬨▾ Effects commands from the Table Styles group on the Table Tools Design tab.

1

- Open the Table Tools Design tab.

- Click ☑ More in the Table Styles group to display the Table Styles gallery.

- Point to several table styles to see how they look in Live Preview.

- Choose Medium Style 2, Accent 2 from the gallery.

- Click in the table to clear the selection and see the new format.

- Save the file.

Your screen should be similar to Figure 2.17

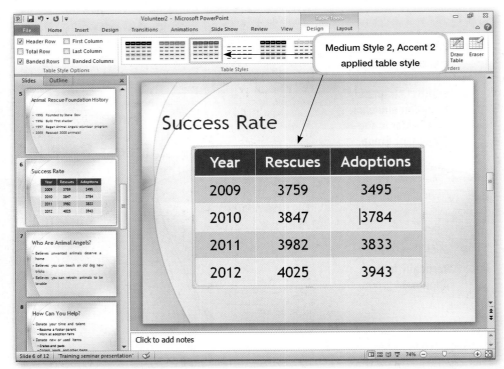

Figure 2.17

The selected table style has been applied to the table. The enhancements added to the table greatly improve its appearance, and the table now displays the information in an attractive and easy-to-read manner.

Inserting and Enhancing Pictures

Now you are ready to enhance the presentation by adding several more graphics. As you have seen, you can easily locate and add Clip Art graphics to slides. Next you want to add a picture to the presentation that you have saved as a file on your computer. You will insert the picture and then learn how to crop and enhance it using a picture style.

INSERTING A GRAPHIC FROM A FILE

You want to add the picture to the opening slide, but before you can begin, you need to reposition the placeholders to make more room for an image.

1

● Select slide 1.

● Select the title and subtitle placeholders and drag them down to position them as shown in Figure 2.18.

Having Trouble?

Click on the second placeholder while holding down Ctrl to select them both.

Your screen should be similar to Figure 2.18

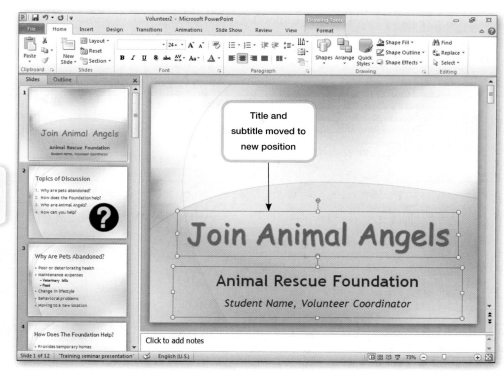

Figure 2.18

You want to see how a digital photograph of a litter of puppies you recently received from one of the foster parents would look.

2

● Open the Insert tab.

● Click 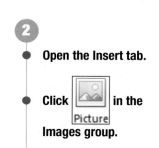 in the Images group.

● Change the location to your data file location.

● If necessary, click 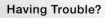 and choose Large Icons to display thumbnails.

Having Trouble?

In Windows Vista, click ▓ Views ▼ and choose Large Icon.

Your screen should be similar to Figure 2.19

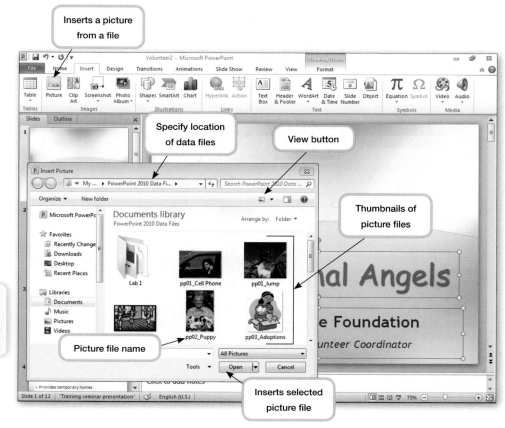

Figure 2.19

Having Trouble?

Your screen may display additional
picture files or it may only display the
file name.

The Insert Picture dialog box is similar to the Open and Save dialog boxes,
except that the only types of files listed are those with picture file extensions. A
thumbnail preview of each picture is displayed above the file name.

3

● **Select** pp02_Puppy

● **Click** [Insert ▼].

**Your screen should be similar to
Figure 2.20**

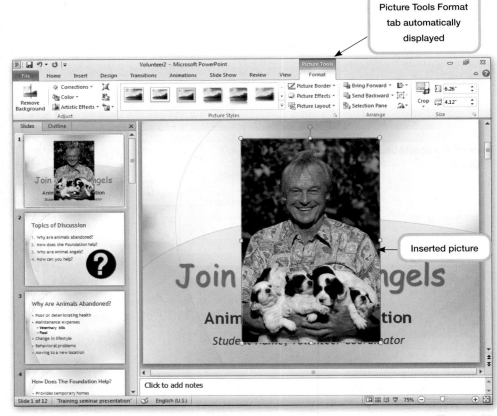

Picture Tools Format
tab automatically
displayed

Inserted picture

Figure 2.20

The picture is inserted in the center of the slide on top of the text. The Picture
Tools Format tab is automatically displayed in the Ribbon, in anticipation that
you may want to modify the graphic.

4 ● Drag the bottom-right corner sizing handle inward to decrease its size to that shown in Figure 2.21.

Additional Information

To maintain an object's proportions while resizing it, hold down Shift while dragging the sizing handle.

Your screen should be similar to Figure 2.21

Figure 2.21

Although this is better, you decide it is not the right shape for the space. You decide that you can draw more attention to the dogs by cropping the picture on the slide.

CROPPING A GRAPHIC

Trimming or removing part of a picture is called **cropping**. Cropping removes the vertical or horizontal edges of a picture to help focus attention on a particular area. You will remove the upper part of the picture by cropping it to show the puppies only. This will make the picture smaller and rectangular shaped.

- Click ![Crop] **from the**

  Size group.

Additional Information

The mouse pointer appears as ![crop icon] or

![corner icon] when it is used to crop a picture.

- **Point to the upper-left corner of the photo, and when the mouse pointer changes to a ![corner icon], drag down to just above the puppies.**

- Click ![Crop] **from the**

  Size group to turn off this feature.

Your screen should be similar to Figure 2.22

Additional Information

Be careful when increasing the size of a picture (bitmap) image, as it can lose sharpness and appear blurry if enlarged too much.

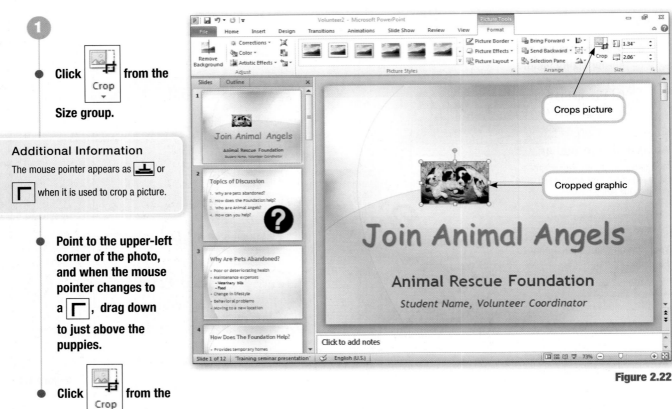

Figure 2.22

The upper part of the picture has been removed, leaving the puppies as the focus of attention. Next you want to increase the graphic's size and position it in the space above the title.

2

- Size the picture as in Figure 2.23 (approximately 3 by 4.5 inches).

Additional Information

The Shape Height and Shape Width buttons in the Size group display the current shape's size as you drag.

- Open the  Align drop-down menu in the Arrange group of the Picture Tools Format tab and choose Align Center.

- If necessary, position the graphic vertically on the slide as shown in Figure 2.23.

Your screen should be similar to Figure 2.23

Figure 2.23

ENHANCING A PICTURE

You decide to enhance the graphic on the title slide to match the picture effects that you applied to the question mark clip art image on slide 2. Repeating the same picture effects here will add consistency to the presentation. First you will select a picture style.

1

- Click ⊽ **More** in the Picture Styles group to display all the options in the Picture Styles gallery.

- Choose  **Beveled Oval, Black** from the Picture Styles group.

- Click 📝 **Picture Border** ▾ and choose **Blue, Accent 2** in the Theme Colors section of the gallery.

- Click 🔲 **Picture Effects** ▾ and choose **No Shadow** from the Shadow group.

Your screen should be similar to Figure 2.24

Figure 2.24

The addition of the picture of the puppies makes the title slide much more interesting and effective.

Inserting and Enhancing Shapes

At the end of the presentation, you want to add a concluding slide. This slide needs to be powerful, because it is your last chance to convince your audience to join Animal Angels.

ADDING A SHAPE

Additional Information

Most shapes also can be inserted from the Clip Organizer as well.

To create the concluding slide, you will duplicate slide 1 and then replace the picture with a graphic of a heart that you will create. To quickly add a shape, you will use one of the ready-made shapes supplied with PowerPoint. These shapes include rectangles and circles, lines, a variety of basic shapes, block arrows, flowchart symbols, stars and banners, action buttons, and callouts.

- Duplicate slide 1.

- Move slide 2 to the end of the presentation.

- Select the picture and press Delete.

- Click in the Drawing group of the Home tab.

Having Trouble?

If a small gallery of shapes is displayed in the Drawing group instead of Shapes, click ▼ to open the Shapes gallery.

Another Method

You also can access the Shapes gallery using Shapes on the Insert tab.

Your screen should be similar to Figure 2.25

Additional Information

The selected shape will be added to the Recently Used Shapes section of the Shapes gallery.

Figure 2.25

Next, you need to select the shape you want from the Shapes gallery and then indicate where you want the shape inserted on the slide. When inserting a shape, the mouse pointer appears as ✛ when pointing to the slide. Then, to insert the shape, click on the slide and drag to increase the size.

● Click Heart in the Basic Shapes section.

● Click above the title on the slide and drag to insert and enlarge the heart.

Another Method

To maintain the height and width proportions of the shape, hold down (Shift) while you drag.

● Size and position the heart as in Figure 2.26.

Additional Information

A shape can be sized and moved just like any other object.

Your screen should be similar to Figure 2.26

Figure 2.26

The heart shape is inserted and the Drawing Tools Format tab is available.

ENHANCING A SHAPE

Next, you will enhance the heart graphic's appearance by selecting a shape style and adding a reflection. Just like the other styles in PowerPoint 2010, **shape styles** consist of combinations of fill colors, outline colors, and effects.

1

- **Open the Drawing Tools Format tab.**

- **Click ☑ More in the Shape Styles group to open the Shape Styles gallery.**

- **Choose Intense Effect—Green, Accent 1 from the Shape Styles gallery.**

- **Click ⬚ Shape Effects ▾ and choose Half Reflection, 4 pt offset from the Reflection gallery.**

Additional Information

The offset controls the amount of space between the object and the reflection.

Your screen should be similar to Figure 2.27

Figure 2.27

The addition of style and reflection effects greatly improves the appearance of the heart.

ADDING TEXT TO A SHAPE

Next, you will add text to the heart object. Text can be added to all shapes and becomes part of the shape; when the shape is moved, the text moves with it.

1

- **Right-click on the heart to open the shortcut menu, and choose Edit Text.**

- **Type Open Your Heart**

Having Trouble?

If the inserted text does not fit into the heart shape, increase the size of the heart.

Your screen should be similar to Figure 2.28

Figure 2.28

Next, you want to improve the appearance of the text using character effects.

2

- Select the text in the heart.

- Click **B** Bold and **I** Italic on the Mini toolbar.

- Increase the font size to 24 points.

- Open the **A** ▾ Font Color gallery and choose Blue, Accent 2 in the Theme Colors section.

- Click outside the heart to deselect the shape.

Your screen should be similar to Figure 2.29

Figure 2.29

Additional Information

Holding down (Shift) while slowly dragging the rotate handle rotates the object in 15-degree increments.

Another Method

You also can use 🔄 ▾ in the Arrange group of the Drawing Tools Format tab to rotate an object.

ROTATING THE OBJECT

Finally, you want to change the angle of the heart. You can rotate an object 90 degrees left or right, flip it vertically or horizontally, or specify an exact degree of rotation. You will change the angle of the heart to the right using the 🔄

rotate handle for the selected object, which allows you to rotate the object to any degree in any direction.

1

- Select the heart graphic.

- Drag the rotate handle to the right slightly.

Additional Information

The mouse pointer appears as 🔁 when positioned on the rotate handle, and Live Preview shows how the object will look as you rotate it.

Your screen should be similar to Figure 2.30

Figure 2.30

The graphic is a nice addition to the final slide of the presentation.

Working with Text Boxes

On slide 12, you want to add the foundation's contact information. To make it stand out on the slide, you will put it into a text box. A **text box** is a container for text or graphics. The text box can be moved, resized, and enhanced in other ways to make it stand out from the other text on the slide.

CREATING A TEXT BOX

First you create the text box, and then you add the content. When inserting a text box, the mouse pointer appears as when pointing to the slide. Then, to create the text box, click on the slide and drag to increase the size.

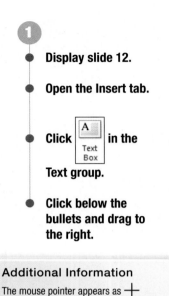

1
- Display slide 12.

- Open the Insert tab.

- Click 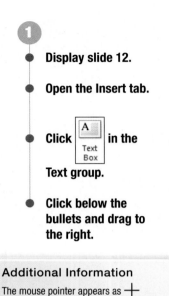 in the Text group.

- Click below the bullets and drag to the right.

Additional Information
The mouse pointer appears as 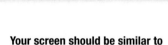 when dragging to create the text box.

Your screen should be similar to Figure 2.31

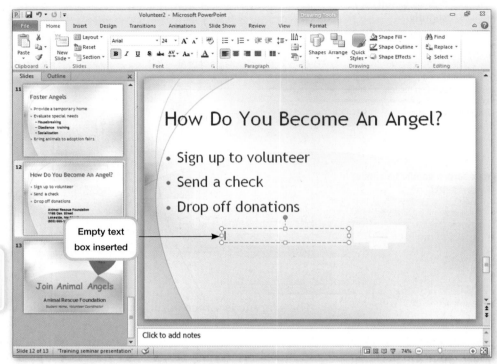

Figure 2.31

The text box is created and is a selected object. It is surrounded with a dashed border indicating you can enter, delete, select, and format the text inside the box.

ADDING TEXT TO A TEXT BOX

The text box displays a cursor, indicating that it is waiting for you to enter the text. As you type the text in the text box, it will increase in length automatically as needed to display the entire entry.

1

- Type the organization's name and address shown below in the text box. Press [Enter] to start a new line.

Having Trouble?

If your text box displays a solid border and no cursor, when you start to type, the cursor will appear and it will change to a dashed border.

Animal Rescue Foundation

1166 Oak Street

Lakeside, NH 03112

(603) 555-1313

- Select all the text and increase the font size to 24 points and bold.

- If necessary, increase the width of the text box to display the name of the foundation on a single line.

Additional Information

You also could copy text from another location and paste it into the text box.

Your screen should be similar to Figure 2.32

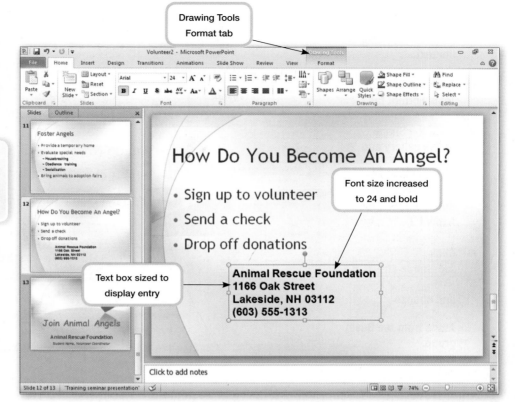

Figure 2.32

The text box is now more prominent and the content is easier to read.

ENHANCING THE TEXT BOX

Like any other object, the text box can be sized and moved anywhere on the slide. It also can be enhanced by adding styles and effects. You want to change the color and add a bevel effect around the box to define the space.

If necessary, deselect the text.

Open the Drawing Tools Format tab.

Open the Shape Styles gallery and choose **Subtle Effect, Blue Accent 2.**

Click 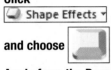 **and choose Angle from the Bevel group.**

Your screen should be similar to Figure 2.33

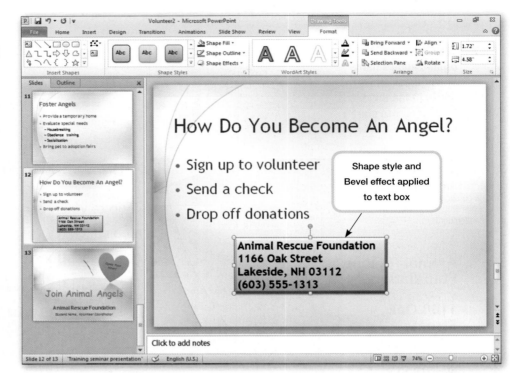

Figure 2.33

Next, you will position the text within the text box and the box on the slide. You want to expand the margin on either side of the text to focus the attention on the text and not the box. By default, PowerPoint uses the AutoFit feature on text boxes, which automatically sizes the text box to fit around the text. You'll want to turn off the AutoFit feature so that you control the position of the text.

- **Right-click within the text of the text box and choose Format Text Effects.**

- **Select Do Not AutoFit.**

- **Change the left and right internal margins to .3.**

- **Choose Middle Centered in the Vertical Alignment drop-down box.**

- **Close the Format Text Effects dialog box.**

- **Adjust the size of the text box to display the information as in Figure 2.34.**

- **Move the text box to the position shown in Figure 2.34.**

- **Deselect the text box.**

- **Save the presentation.**

Your screen should be similar to Figure 2.34

NOTE If you are ending your session now exit PowerPoint 2010. When you begin again, open this file.

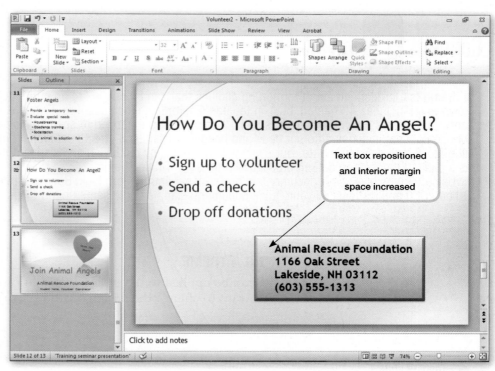

Figure 2.34

The information in the text box now stands out from the other information on the slide.

Changing the Presentation Design

When you first started this presentation, you used a PowerPoint template that included sample text as well as color and design elements. Now you are satisfied with the presentation's basic content and organization, but you would like to change its design style and appearance by applying a different document theme.

Concept 4 Theme

A **theme** is a predefined set of formatting choices that can be applied to an entire document in one simple step. PowerPoint includes 40 named, built-in themes. Each theme includes three subsets of components: colors, fonts, and effects. Each theme consists of 12 colors that are applied to specific elements in a document. Each font component includes different body and heading fonts. Each effects component includes different line and fill effects. You also can create your own custom themes by modifying an existing document theme and saving it as a custom theme. The default presentation uses the Office Theme.

Using themes gives your documents a professional and modern look. Because themes are shared across Office 2010 applications, all your Office documents can have the same uniform look.

APPLYING A THEME

A theme can be applied to the entire presentation or to selected slides. In this case, you want to change the design for the entire presentation.

1

- Display slide 1.

- Open the Design tab.

- Click 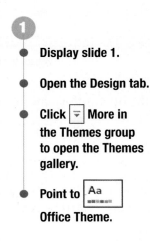 More in the Themes group to open the Themes gallery.

- Point to Aa Office Theme.

Your screen should be similar to Figure 2.35

Figure 2.35

The Themes gallery displays samples of the document themes. The This Presentation area displays a preview of the theme that is currently used in the presentation. This is the theme associated with the presentation template you used to start the presentation. The Built-In area displays examples of the themes that are available in PowerPoint. The Live Preview shows how the presentation would look if the Office Theme were used. As you can see, the slide colors, background designs, font styles, and overall layout of the slide are affected by the theme.

You will preview several other themes, and then use the Austin theme for the presentation.

2

● Preview several other themes.

● Choose the 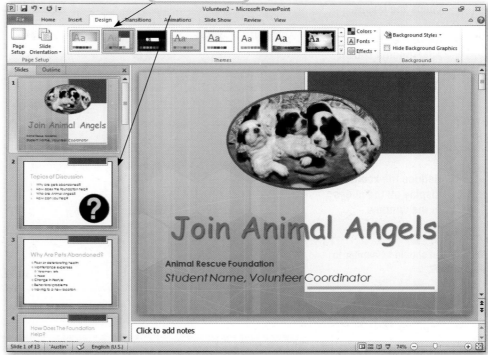 Austin theme.

Your screen should be similar to Figure 2.36

Austin theme applied to all slides in the presentation

Figure 2.36

Additional Information

To apply a theme to selected slides, preselect the slides to apply the themes to in the Slide pane, and use the Apply to Selected Slides option from the theme's shortcut menu.

The Austin theme has been applied to all slides in the presentation. When a new theme is applied, the text styles, graphics, and colors that are included in the design replace the previous design settings. Consequently, the layout may need to be adjusted. For example, the photo on slide 1 will need to be repositioned and sized.

However, if you had made individual changes to a slide, such as changing the font of the title, these changes are not updated to the new theme design. In this case, the title font is still the Comic Sans MS that you selected; however, it has a smaller point size.

3

- Use the Slides tab to select each slide and check the layout.

- Make the adjustments shown in the table below to the indicated slides.

- Switch to Slide Sorter view to see how all your changes look.

- Reduce the zoom to display all the slides in the window.

Your screen should be similar to Figure 2.37

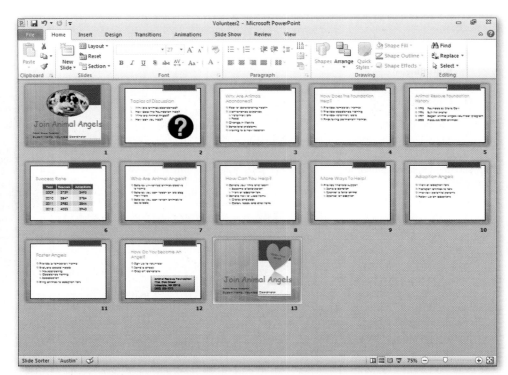

Figure 2.37

Slide	Adjustment
1	Increase the size of the graphic slightly. Realign the graphic to the center of the slide.
2	If needed, adjust the position of the text content placeholder so the bullets align with the title text. If needed, adjust the size of the graphic and reposition it slightly.
5	Select both content placeholders and move them slightly to the right to align the bullets with the title text.
6	Appropriately adjust the size and position of the table.
7	Reduce the width of the content placeholder so that more than one word wraps to a second line.
12	Adjust the position of the text box as needed.
13	If necessary, rotate, move, and resize the heart to fit the upper-right area of the slide.

CHANGING THE THEME COLORS

To make the presentation livelier, you decide to try changing the colors associated with the selected theme. Although each theme has an associated set of colors, you can change the colors by applying the colors from another theme to the selected theme.

Display slide 1 in Normal view.

Open the Design tab.

Click  Colors ▼ in the Themes group.

Your screen should be similar to Figure 2.38

Figure 2.38

Additional Information

The colors in the **▣ Colors ▼** button reflect the current theme colors.

The colors used in each of the themes are displayed in the Built-In drop-down list. Each theme's colors consist of eight coordinated colors that are applied to different slide elements. The Austin theme colors are selected because they are the set of colors associated with the Austin theme. You want to see how the colors used in the Oriel theme would look.

Preview several other color themes.

Select the Oriel theme colors.

Your screen should be similar to Figure 2.39

Figure 2.39

Changing the Presentation Design   **PP2.39**

The slides are all converted to the colors used in the Oriel theme. You like the slightly softer colors associated with the Oriel theme. Using predefined theme colors gives your presentation a professional and consistent look.

CHANGING THE BACKGROUND STYLE

Although you like the color theme of the presentation now, you think it is a bit too dark. The quickest way to brighten up the look of a presentation is to change the background style. **Background styles** are a set of theme colors and textures that you can apply to the back of your slides.

The PowerPoint Background Styles gallery contains four background colors that can be combined with the three theme backgrounds, giving you twelve different background style options. In addition to the preselected background colors, you can also apply a picture, clip art, or watermark as a background style. When you apply one of these elements or use one of the built-in styles, you can make your presentation truly unique.

Click

Background Styles ▾

in the Background group of the Design tab.

Choose Style 2.

Your screen should be similar to Figure 2.40

Figure 2.40

Background Style 2 has been applied to all slides in the presentation. Whenever you change the background style or theme colors of a presentation, you should go back through the presentation and adjust font and graphic colors as necessary. For example, the picture border on slide 1 needs to be changed to make it stand out more from the background. Also you want to change the title text color on the opening and closing slides from orange to a deep red.

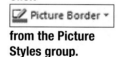

- Select the picture on slide 1 and change the border color to the Red, Accent 3 theme color (top row, seventh column).

- Click Picture Border ▾ from the Picture Styles group.

- Select Weight and then choose 2¼ pt.

- Change the color of the title font on slides 1 and 13 to the Red, Accent 3 Theme color.

- Make slide 1 active.

- Save the presentation.

Your screen should be similar to Figure 2.41

Figure 2.41

Working with Master Slides

While viewing the slides, you think the slide appearance could be further improved by changing the bullet design on all slides. Although you can change each slide individually, you can make the change much faster to all the slides by changing the slide master.

Concept 5 Master

A **master** is part of a template that stores information about the formatting for the three key components of a presentation—slides, speaker notes, and handouts. Each component has a master associated with it. The masters are described below.

Slide master	Defines the format and layout of text and objects on a slide, text and object placeholder sizes, text styles, backgrounds, color themes, effects, and animation.
Handout master	Defines the format and placement of the slide image, text, headers, footers, and other elements that will appear on every handout.
Notes master	Defines the format and placement of the slide image, note text, headers, footers, and other elements that will appear on all speaker notes.

Any changes you make to a master affect all slides, handouts, or notes associated with that master. Each theme comes with its own slide master. When you apply a new theme to a presentation, all slides and masters are updated to those of the new theme. Using the master to modify or add elements to a presentation ensures consistency and saves time.

You can create slides that differ from the slide master by changing the format and placement of elements in the individual slide rather than on the slide master. For example, when you changed the font settings of the title on the title slide, the slide master was not affected. Only the individual slide changed, making it unique. If you have created a unique slide, the elements you changed on that slide retain their uniqueness, even if you later make changes to the slide master. That is the reason that the title font did not change when you changed the theme.

MODIFYING THE SLIDE MASTER

You will change the title text font color and the bullet style in the slide master so that all slides in the presentation will be changed.

1

- Open the View tab.

- Click 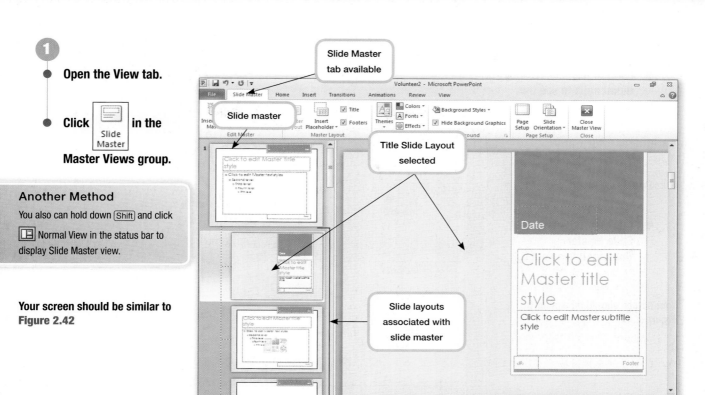 in the Master Views group.

Another Method

You also can hold down Shift and click 🔳 Normal View in the status bar to display Slide Master view.

Your screen should be similar to Figure 2.42

Figure 2.42

Additional Information

Every presentation contains at least one slide master. Each slide master contains one or more built-in or custom layouts.

The view has changed to Slide Master view, and a new tab, Slide Master, is displayed. Slide Master view consists of two panes: the slide thumbnail pane on the left containing slide thumbnails for the slide master and for each of the layouts associated with the slide master and the Slide pane on the right displaying the selected slide. In the slide thumbnail pane, the slide master is the larger slide image, and the associated layouts are positioned below the slide master. The slide master and all supporting layouts appear in the current theme, Austin, with the Oriel theme colors. Each slide layout displays a different layout arrangement. The thumbnail for the Title Slide Layout is selected, and the Slide pane displays the slide.

If you modify the slide master, all layouts beneath the slide master are also changed. If you modify a slide layout, although you are essentially also modifying the slide master, the changes effect only that layout under the slide master. You want to change the slide master so that your changes effect all the associated layouts.

2

Point to the thumbnails to see the ScreenTip.

Click on the Austin Slide Master thumbnail to select it.

Your screen should be similar to Figure 2.43

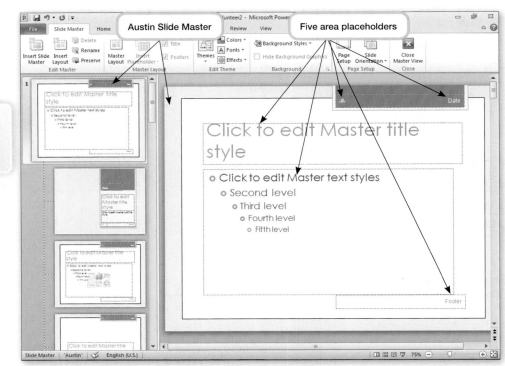

Figure 2.43

The Austin Slide Master consists of five area placeholders that control the appearance of all slides: title, content, date, slide number, and footer. The title and content areas display sample text to show you how changes you make in these areas will appear. You make changes to the slide master in the same way that you change any other slide. First you will change the font color for the title text throughout the presentation to match the dark red you applied to slides 1 and 13.

3

Click on the title area placeholder border to select it.

Open the Home tab.

Click 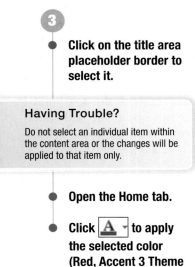 **to apply the selected color (Red, Accent 3 Theme color).**

Your screen should be similar to Figure 2.44

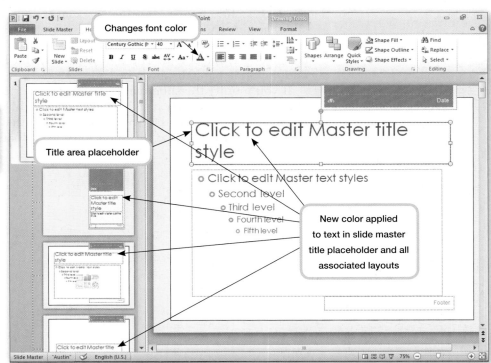

Figure 2.44

Next, you will modify the content area placeholder and change the current round bullet style to a picture bullet style.

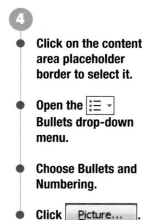

4

- Click on the content area placeholder border to select it.

- Open the ≔ ▾ Bullets drop-down menu.

- Choose Bullets and Numbering.

- Click Picture... .

Your screen should be similar to Figure 2.45

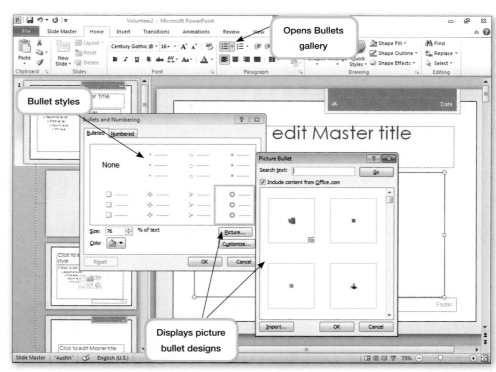

Figure 2.45

From the Picture Bullet dialog box, you select the bullet design you want to use from the bullet styles listed. You will use a round bullet design in a color that coordinates with the theme colors.

5

- Scroll the gallery and choose ● bullets, network blitz (first column of the seventh row).

Having Trouble?

If this bullet style is not available, select another of your choice.

- Click OK .

Your screen should be similar to Figure 2.46

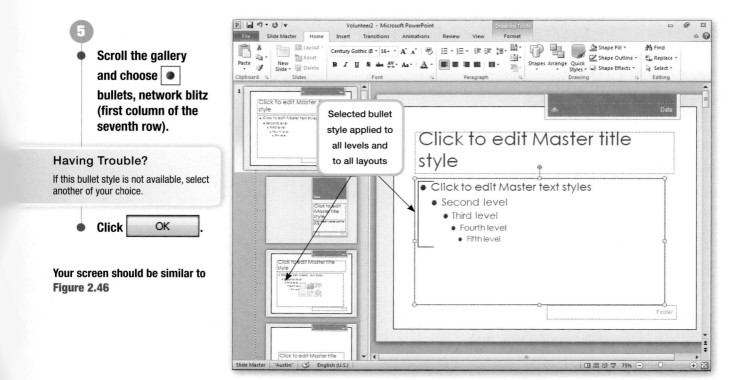

Figure 2.46

Working with Master Slides   **PP2.45**

The selected bullet style has been applied to all levels of items in the content area and to all layouts under the slide master that have bulleted items.

Now you want to see how the changes you have made to the slide master have affected the actual slides in the presentation.

- Click 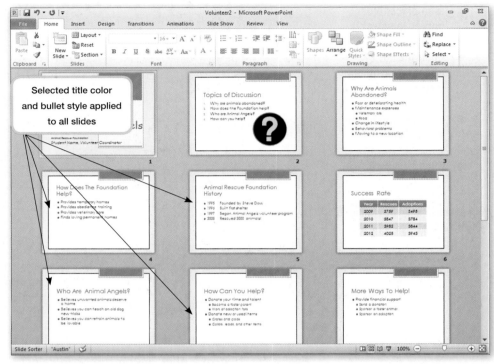 Slide Sorter view.

- Increase the magnification to 100%.

Your screen should be similar to Figure 2.47

Figure 2.47

You can now see that the change you made to the bullet style in the slide master is reflected in all slides in the presentation. Using the slide master allows you to quickly make global changes to your presentation.

You will run the slide show next to see how the changes you have made look full screen.

- Run the slide show beginning with slide 1.

- Click on each slide to advance through the presentation.

- Save the presentation.

Now that you are happy with the look of the presentation, you want to incorporate animation effects to change the way the text appears on the slides.

Animating the Presentation

You are pleased with the changes you have made to the presentation so far. However, you have several places in mind where using animation will make the presentation more interesting.

Concept 6 Animations

Animations are special effects that add action to text and graphics so they move around on the screen during a slide show. Animations provide additional emphasis for items or show the information on a slide in phases. There are two basic types of animations: object animations and transitions.

Object animations are used to display each bullet point, text, paragraph, or graphic independently of the other text or objects on the slide. You set up the way you want each element to appear (to fly in from the left, for instance) and whether you want the other elements already on the slide to dim or shimmer when a new element is added. For example, because your audience is used to reading from left to right, you could select animations that fly text in from the left. Then, when you want to emphasize a point, bring a bullet point in from the right. That change grabs the audience's attention.

Transitions control the way that the display changes as you move from one slide to the next during a presentation. You can select from many different transition choices. You may choose Dissolve for your title slide to give it an added flair. After that, you could use Wipe Right for all the slides until the next to the last, and then use Dissolve again to end the show. As with any special effect, use slide transitions carefully.

When you present a slide show, the content of your presentation should take center stage. You want the animation effects to help emphasize the main points in your presentation—not draw the audience's attention to the special effects.

ADDING TRANSITION EFFECTS

First, you want to add a transition effect to the slides. Although you can add transitions in Normal view, you will use Slide Sorter view so you can more easily preview the action on the slides.

1

- **Switch to Slide Sorter view, if necessary.**

- **Select slide 1.**

- **Open the Transitions tab.**

- **Click ▼ More in the Transition to This Slide group to open the Transitions gallery.**

Your screen should be similar to Figure 2.48

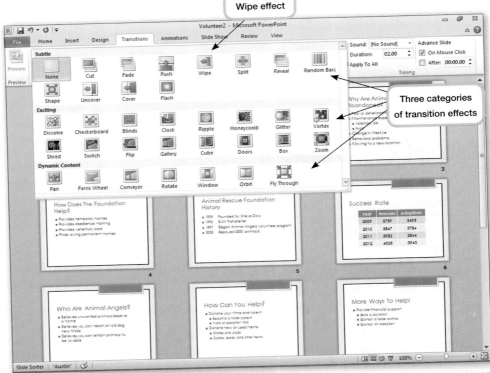

Figure 2.48

Additional Information

Use the None transition option to remove transition effects.

There are three transition categories, Subtle, Exciting and Dynamic Content, with each containing variations on the category effect. You want to use a simple transition effect that will display as each slide appears. As you choose a transition effect next, watch the live preview of the effect on the selected slide.

2

- Click 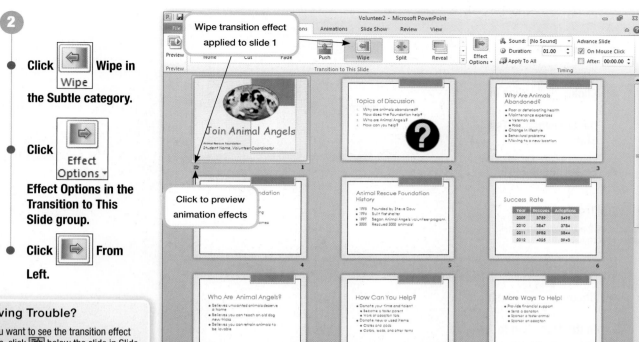 Wipe in the Subtle category.

- Click Effect Options ▾ Effect Options in the Transition to This Slide group.

- Click From Left.

Having Trouble?

If you want to see the transition effect again, click ⬚ below the slide in Slide Sorter view.

Another Method

You can also see the transition effect that is applied to a slide by selecting the slide and clicking Preview in the Preview group of the Transitions tab.

Your screen should be similar to Figure 2.49

Additional Information

You also can select transition effects from the Transitions gallery by scrolling the list in the Transition to This Slide group.

Figure 2.49

The selected slide displays the Wipe Left transition effect. This effect displays the next slide's content by wiping over the previous slide from the right with the new slide content. You want to use the same effect on slide 13. For the final slide, you want to use the default Wipe direction, which is from the right. You also want to try a similar effect on the other slides using the Push transition effect.

● **Select slide 13.**

● **Click** 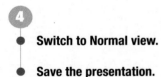 **Wipe in the Transition to This Slide group.**

● **Select slides 2–12.**

> **Having Trouble?**
>
> Select slide 2 and hold down ⇧Shift while selecting slide 12.

● **Choose** Push **in the Transition to This Slide group.**

Your screen should be similar to Figure 2.50

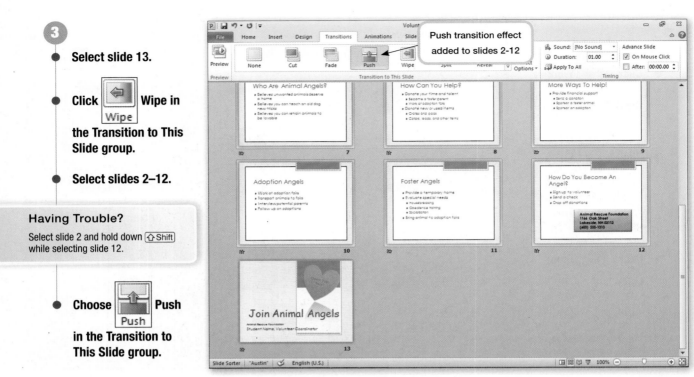

Figure 2.50

The transition animation effects associated with the selected slides were individually previewed beginning with slide 2, and each slide now displays a transition icon.

4

● **Switch to Normal view.**

● **Save the presentation.**

Notice an animation icon appears below each slide number in the Slides tab.

ANIMATING AN OBJECT

Next, you want to add an animation effect to the heart shape on the final slide. There are four different types of animation effects, described below. Animation effects can be used by themselves or in combination with other effects.

Type	Effect
Entrance	Makes an object appear on the slide using the selected effect.
Exit	Makes an object leave the slide using the selected effect.
Emphasis	Makes an object more noticeable by applying special effects to the object such as changing the text size and colors or adding bold or underlines.
Motion Path	Makes an object move in a selected pattern such as up, down, or in a circle.

1

● Display slide 13 in Normal view.

● Select the heart shape.

● Open the Animations tab.

● Point to several effects in the Animation group to see the Live Preview.

● Choose 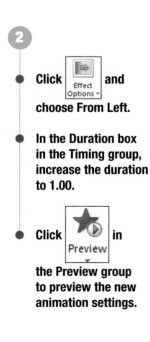 .

Your screen should be similar to Figure 2.51

Fly In animation effect applied to heart graphic

Numbered tag indicates this is first animation effect on slide

Figure 2.51

As you add animated items to a slide, each item is numbered. The number determines the order in which they display. A nonprinting numbered tag appears on the slide near each animated item that correlates to the effects in the list. This number does not appear during a slide show.

Next, you want to change the Fly In effect to come in from the left and to run slower.

2

● Click Effect Options ▾ and choose From Left.

● In the Duration box in the Timing group, increase the duration to 1.00.

● Click Preview in the Preview group to preview the new animation settings.

Your screen should be similar to Figure 2.52

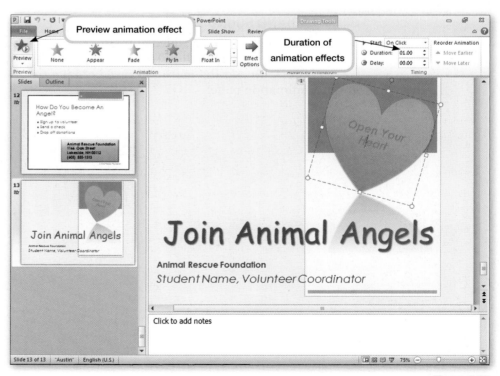

Preview animation effect

Duration of animation effects

Figure 2.52

You like the way the animation effect livens up the final slide of the presentation, so you decide to apply the same effect to the text box on slide 12. Since you plan to use the same animation settings for both slides, the easiest way to duplicate an effect is to use the Animation Painter.

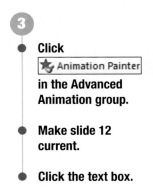

- **Click** 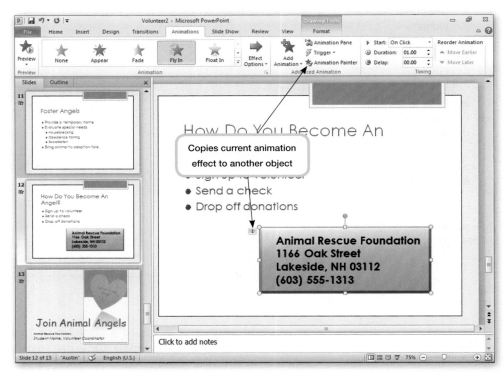 **Animation Painter in the Advanced Animation group.**

- **Make slide 12 current.**

- **Click the text box.**

Your screen should be similar to Figure 2.53

Figure 2.53

The Fly In animation effect is applied to the text box and previewed for you.

ADDING SOUND EFFECTS

Now that you have added animations to your presentation, you decide to give the animation on slide 13 extra emphasis by adding sound to the animation effect. To add the more advanced animation effects, you need to display the Animation pane.

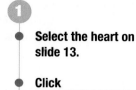

1

● Select the heart on slide 13.

● Click
[Animation Pane]
in the Advanced Animation group.

● Click [▶ Play] in the Animation pane.

Your screen should be similar to Figure 2.54

Figure 2.54

Additional Information

You will learn more about using the Animation pane in later labs.

This pane shows information about each animation effect on a slide. This includes the type of effect, the order of multiple effects in relation to one another, the name of the object affected, and the duration of the effect. It also is used to manage the animations and to add advanced effects to existing animations. You will use it to add a sound to the Fly In effect.

2

● Open the [1 ★ Heart 1: Open... ▼] drop-down menu and choose Effect Options.

● From the Sound drop-down list choose Chime.

● Click [OK].

Additional Information

You must have a speaker and a sound card to hear the sound.

● Run the slide show beginning with the current slide.

● Click on the slide to start the animation.

● Press [Esc] to end the slide show.

The slide transition effect is followed by the heart fly-in animation and the sound effect being played as it will when the slide show is run. You had to click the mouse button to start the heart animation, because this is the default setting to start an animation.

ANIMATING A SLIDE MASTER

The next effect you want to add to the slides is an animation effect that will display each bullet or numbered item progressively on a slide. When the animation is applied to a slide, the slide initially shows only the title. The bulleted text appears as the presentation proceeds. You want to add this effect to all the slides that have bulleted items (slides 2–5 and 7–12). However, you do not want slide 5, which contains the foundation's history, to display with an animation because you want the history to appear all at the same time.

To apply the animation to the bulleted items, you could add the effect to each slide individually. However, when there are many slides, it is faster to add the effect to the slide master so all slides based on the selected slide layout display the effect. You will move to slide 2, the first slide in the presentation to use bullets, and apply the animation effects to the associated slide layout under the slide master.

1

- Make slide 2 current.

- Change to Slide Master view.

- Point to the slide layout thumbnail to see the slide layout name and confirm that the correct slides will be affected (Title and Content Layout: used by slide(s) 2–4, 6–9, 12).

Having Trouble?

If this is not your selected slide master, change the selection to this master.

- Select the content placeholder.

- Open the Animations tab.

- Scroll the Animation gallery to see the second row of effects.

- Click  .

- Click  and choose From Right.

Your screen should be similar to Figure 2.55

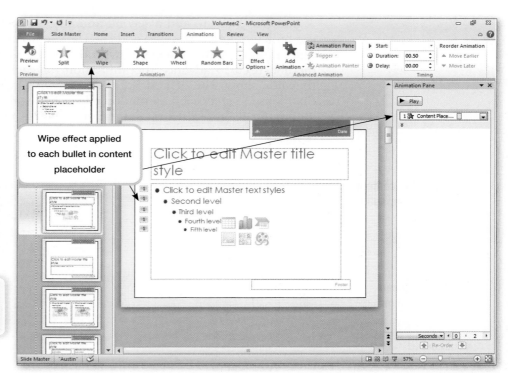

Figure 2.55

Animation icons appear next to each bulleted item in the content placeholder, and the Animation pane displays the information about the animation. The preview demonstrated how this effect will appear on the slide. Although the slide master preview does not show it, each bullet will appear individually on the slide. You can confirm this because a number tab appears next to each bullet in the content area indicating that the effect will be applied to each line.

You also want to add a second animation effect to give more emphasis to the bulleted items. You will add the Darken animation effect and change the Start timing setting associated with the effect. The Start settings control the method used to advance the animation for each bullet item while you run the slide show. The default Start setting, On Click, means you need to click the mouse to start each animation effect. You want the Darken effect to begin automatically after the first animation effect is finished.

2

- Select the content placeholder again.

- Click [Add Animation] in the Advanced Animation group.

- Choose [Darken] Darken from the Emphasis category.

- Click [Start:] in the Timing group and choose After Previous.

- Click [▶ Play] to view the effect.

Your screen should be similar to Figure 2.56

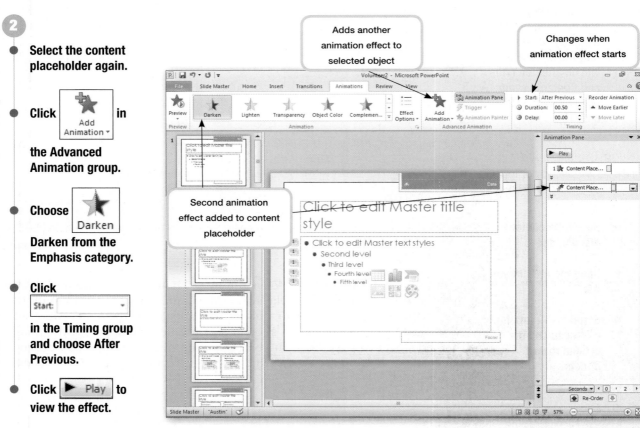

Figure 2.56

The preview showed that the Darken effect correctly started after the Wipe effect ended. You are concerned, however, that the timing for the Wipe effect is too fast and the Darken emphasis is too subtle. You will lengthen the duration for the Wipe effect and change the Darken emphasis to another.

3

- Click on `1 ⭐ Content Place... ▢` in the Animation pane to select it.

- Increase the Duration setting in the Timing group to 3.00.

- Click on `⭐ Content Place...` in the Animation pane to select it.

- Choose **Bold Reveal** from the Animation gallery.

- Click `▶ Play`.

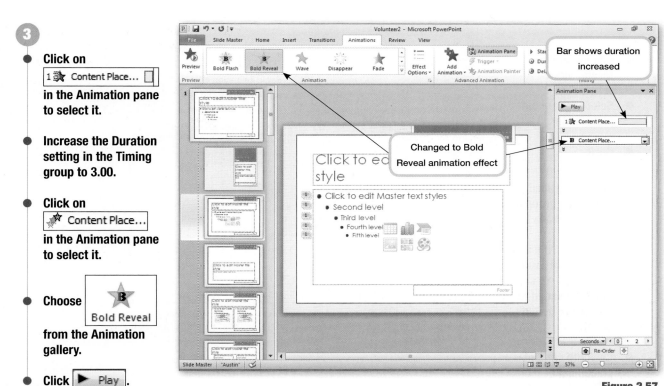

Figure 2.57

Your screen should be similar to Figure 2.57

The changes in the animation effects are shown in the Animation pane and have been applied to slides 2–4, 6–9, and 12. To check how the animation effects actually appear in a slide, you will return to Normal view and preview the animations.

4

- Change to Normal view and preview the animation on slide 2.

The preview demonstrates how the Wipe effect and then the Bold Reveal emphasis appears one-by-one on each bullet. Since you like the way the animation looks, you want to apply it to all the other bulleted slides except 5.

5

● Change to Slide Master view.

● Select the content placeholder.

● Click 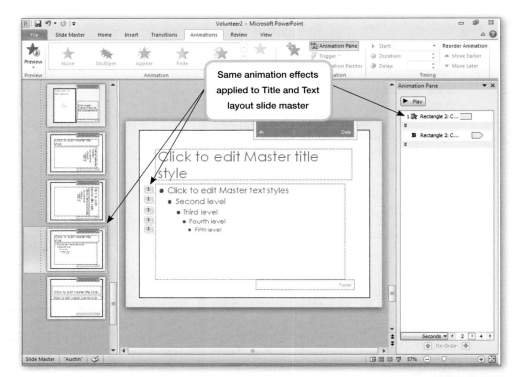 **Animation Painter** in the Advanced Animation group of the Animations tab.

● Select the Title and Text Layout: used by slide(s) 10–11 slide master (second to last layout in Slide pane).

● Click the content placeholder.

Your screen should be similar to Figure 2.58

Figure 2.58

The same animation effects that are on the Title and Content Layout (slides 2–4, 6–9, and 12) have been quickly copied to the Title and Text Layout (slides 10–11). If a new slide were inserted using one of these layouts, it would have the same animation effects. However, if the layout for a slide containing animations were changed to another layout, it would then have the animation effects (if any) associated with that layout.

Now slides 1 and 5 are the only slides that are not animated. You will change back to Normal view and check the animation effects in several slides.

6

● Return to Normal view.

● Preview the animation on slides 10 and 11.

● Move to slide 5 and verify that there are no animations associated with it.

● Play the animation on slide 6.

You noticed on slide 11 that the animation effects were applied individually to first-level bullets, and any sub-bullets were included with the first-level bullets. This seems appropriate. The animation effect on slide 6 was applied to the table as a whole. This is because the slide was created using the Title and Content layout and the table is considered a single bulleted item.

REMOVING ANIMATION EFFECTS

You want to remove the animation from slide 6. However, because the animation is associated with the slide master, removing it would remove it from all slides using that layout. Instead, you will change the slide layout to another layout that does not have an animation associated with it. Then you will add some other animation effects to this slide and apply these same effects to slide 5.

1

- Change the slide layout of slide 6 to the Title Only layout.

- Center the table in the slide space.

- Select the title placeholder and apply the Fly In from Left animation.

- Change the Start setting to With Previous.

- Select the table, click  and choose the Random Bars animation.

- Copy the title placeholder animation to the title placeholder of slide 5.

- Copy the table animation from slide 6 to both content placeholders on slide 5.

- Preview the animations on slide 5.

Your screen should be similar to Figure 2.59

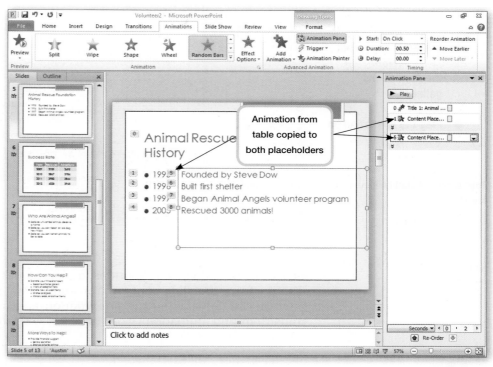

Figure 2.59

You like the title animation; however, you decide to remove the animations associated with the two content placeholders.

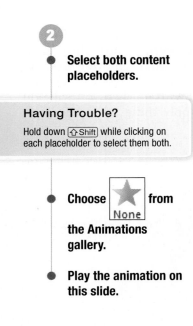

2

Select both content placeholders.

Having Trouble?

Hold down ⇧Shift while clicking on each placeholder to select them both.

Choose 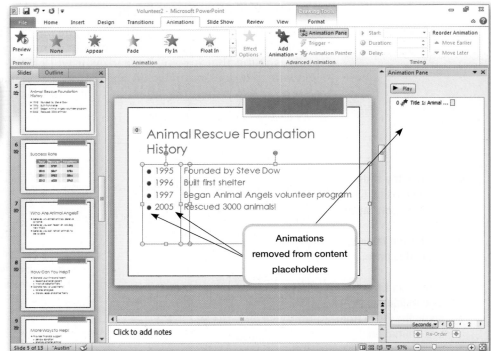 **from the Animations gallery.**

Play the animation on this slide.

Your screen should be similar to Figure 2.60

Figure 2.60

Be careful when using animations, as sometimes too many animation effects distract from the slide content. You think your animation changes will add interest without making the presentation appear too lively. To see how the transitions and animations work together, you will run the slide show next.

3

Close the Animation pane.

Save the presentation.

Preparing for the Slide Show

As you run the slide show to see the animation effects, you will also practice preparing for the presentation. As much as you would like to control a presentation completely, the presence of an audience usually causes the presentation to change course. PowerPoint has several ways to control a slide show during the presentation.

NAVIGATING IN A SLIDE SHOW

Running the slide show and practicing how to control the slide show help you to have a smooth presentation. For example, if someone has a question about a previous slide, you can go backward and redisplay it. You will try out some of the features you can use while running the slide show.

1

● **Start the slide show from the beginning.**

● **Click to advance to slide 2.**

● **Click 4 times to display the four bullets.**

Your screen should be similar to Figure 2.61

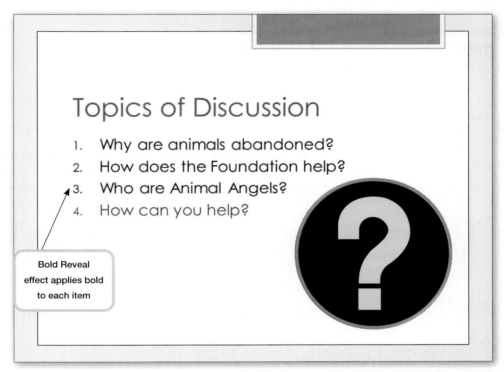

Figure 2.61

Another Method

You can also use the mouse wheel to move forward or backward through a presentation.

The first slide appeared using the Wipe From Left transition effect associated with the slide. The second slide appeared using the Push transition effect. Each bulleted item on slide 2 appeared when you clicked using the Wipe animation effect, and the Bold Reveal animation effect started automatically as soon as the last bullet appeared.

When an animation is applied to the content area of a slide, the content items are displayed only when you click or use any of the procedures to advance to the next slide. This is because the default setting to start an animation is On Click. This allows the presenter to focus the audience's attention and to control the pace of the presentation. The Bold Reveal associated with slide 2 started automatically because you changed the Start setting to After Previous.

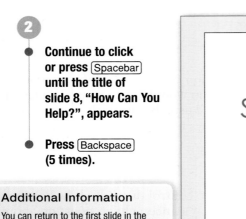

2

● Continue to click or press Spacebar until the title of slide 8, "How Can You Help?", appears.

● Press Backspace (5 times).

Additional Information

You can return to the first slide in the presentation by holding down both mouse buttons for two seconds.

Your screen should be similar to Figure 2.62

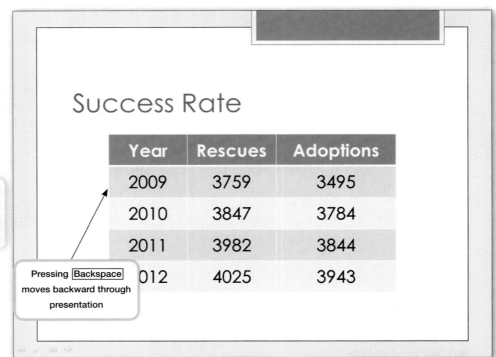

Figure 2.62

You returned the onscreen presentation to slide 6, but now, because the audience has already viewed slide 7, you want to advance to slide 8. To go to a specific slide number, you type the slide number and press Enter.

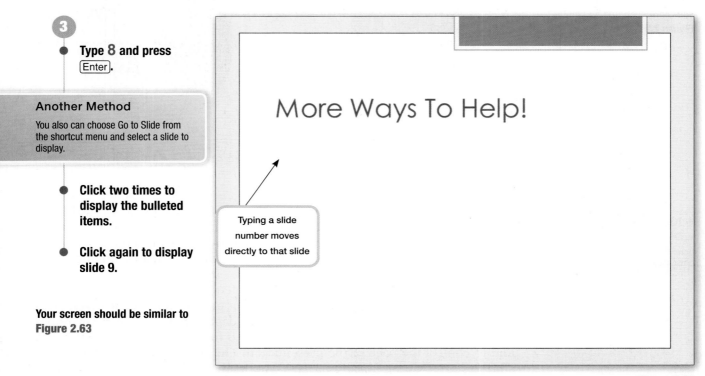

3

● Type **8** and press Enter.

Another Method

You also can choose Go to Slide from the shortcut menu and select a slide to display.

● Click two times to display the bulleted items.

● Click again to display slide 9.

Your screen should be similar to Figure 2.63

Figure 2.63

Slide 9, More Ways To Help!, is displayed.

Sometimes a question from an audience member can interrupt the flow of the presentation. If this happens to you, you can black out the screen to focus attention on your response.

● **Press b or B.**

The screen goes to black while you address the topic. When you are ready to resume the presentation, you can bring the slide back.

● **Click, or press b.**

● **Click to display the bulleted items on slide 9.**

ADDING FREEHAND ANNOTATIONS

During your presentation, you may want to point to an important word, underline an important point, or draw checkmarks next to items that you have covered. To do this, you can use the mouse pointer during the presentation. When you move the mouse, the mouse pointer appears and the Slide Show toolbar is displayed in the lower-left corner of the screen. The mouse pointer in its current shape can be used to point to items on the slide. You also can use it to draw on the screen by changing the mouse pointer to a ballpoint pen, felt-tip pen, or highlighter, which activates the associated freehand annotation feature.

● **Move the mouse on your desktop to display the mouse pointer and the Slide Show toolbar.**

● **Click in the Slide Show toolbar to display the Pointer Options menu.**

Another Method
You also can select Pointer Options from the shortcut menu.

Your screen should be similar to Figure 2.64

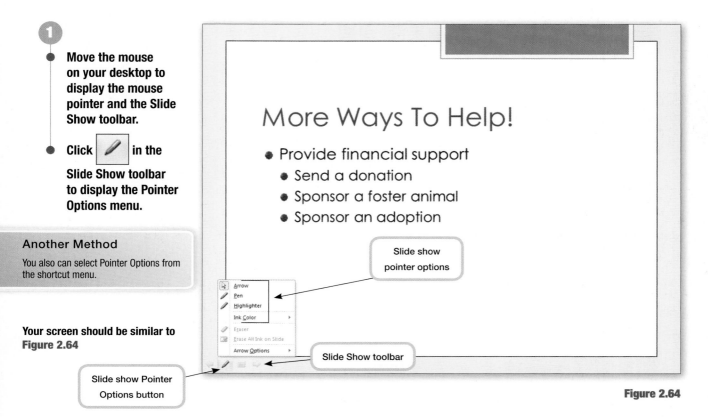

Figure 2.64

The mouse pointer and arrow options are described in the following table.

Pointer Options	Effect
Arrow	Displays the mouse pointer as an arrow.
Pen	Changes the mouse pointer to a diamond shape and turns on ballpoint pen annotation.
Highlighter	Changes the mouse pointer to a bar shape and turns on highlighter.
Ink Color	Displays a color palette to select a color for the annotation tool.
Eraser	Erases selected annotations.
Erase All Ink on Slide	Removes all annotations from the slide.
Arrow Options	(These options apply only if Arrow is selected.)
Automatic	Hides the mouse pointer if it is not moved for 15 seconds. It reappears when you move the mouse. This is the default setting.
Visible	Displays the mouse pointer as an arrow and does not hide it.
Hidden	Hides the mouse pointer until another pointer option is selected.

You will try out several of the freehand annotation features to see how they work. To draw, you select the pen style and then drag the pen pointer in the direction you want to draw.

● **Choose Pen.**

Another Method

You also can use Ctrl + P to display the Pen.

● **Move the dot pointer to near the word "Send" and then drag the dot pointer until a circle is drawn around the word "Send".**

● **Select Ink Color from the Pointer Options menu and choose Light Blue from the Standard Colors bar.**

Additional Information

The Automatic ink color setting determines the default color to use for annotations based upon the slide theme colors.

● **Draw three lines under the word "Help!".**

● **Choose Highlighter from the Pointer Options menu and highlight the word "donation".**

Additional Information

The mouse pointer changes shape depending upon the selected annotation tool.

Your screen should be similar to Figure 2.65

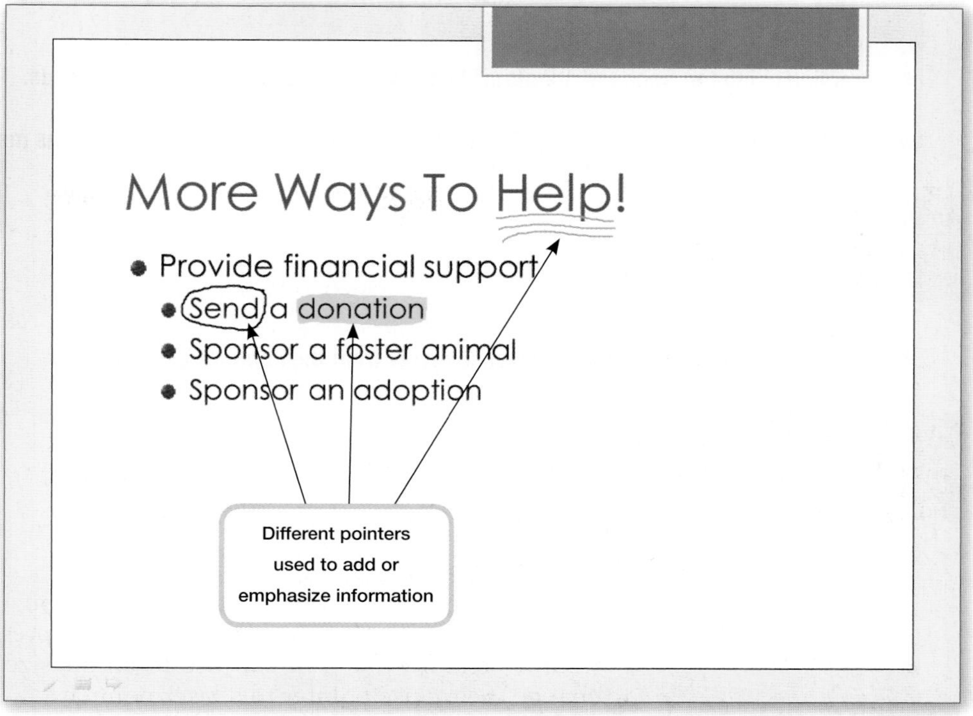

More Ways To Help!

- Provide financial support
- Send a donation
- Sponsor a foster animal
- Sponsor an adoption

Different pointers used to add or emphasize information

Figure 2.65

The freehand annotation feature allows you to point out and emphasize important information on a slide during the presentation.

3

● Practice using the freehand annotator to draw any shapes you want on the slide.

● To erase the annotations, choose Erase All Ink on Slide from the Pointer Options menu.

Another Method

The keyboard shortcut to erase annotations is E.

● To turn off freehand annotation, choose Arrow from the Pointer Options menu.

Another Method

You also can use Ctrl + A to display the arrow.

The freehand annotation feature allows you to point out and emphasize important information on a slide during the presentation.

Another feature that you can use to emphasize information on a slide is to change the mouse pointer to a laser pointer.

4

● Click to display the four bulleted items on slide 10.

● Press Ctrl and hold down the left mouse button to turn the mouse pointer into a laser light.

Additional Information

You can control the color of the laser light by clicking Set Up Slideshow on the Slide Show tab. You can then click the Laser pointer color drop-down list to choose a different color.

● Use the laser pointer to point to the first bulleted item on the slide.

Your screen should be similar to Figure 2.66

Figure 2.66

The laser pointer is much brighter than the regular mouse pointer; however, it is not as convenient because you have to hold Ctrl while using the feature.

If you do not erase annotations before ending the presentation, you are prompted to keep or discard the annotations when you end the slide show. If you keep the annotations, they are saved to the slides and will appear as part of the slide during a presentation.

Adding Speaker Notes

When making your presentation, there are some critical points you want to be sure to discuss. To help you remember the important points, you can add notes to a slide and then print the **notes pages**. These pages display the notes below a small version of the slide they accompany. You can create notes pages for some or all of the slides in a presentation. You decide to add speaker notes on slide 9 to remind you to suggest foster care donations.

1

- Press Esc to end the slide show.

- Display slide 9 in Normal view.

- Increase the size of the Notes pane to that shown in Figure 2.67.

Having Trouble?

Adjust the size of the notes pane by dragging the pane splitter bar.

- Click in the Notes pane and type the following:

Suggested foster animal donations per month

Cat: $10

Dog: $15/small $20/medium $25/large

Having Trouble?

Press Tab to separate the dollar amounts.

Your screen should be similar to Figure 2.67

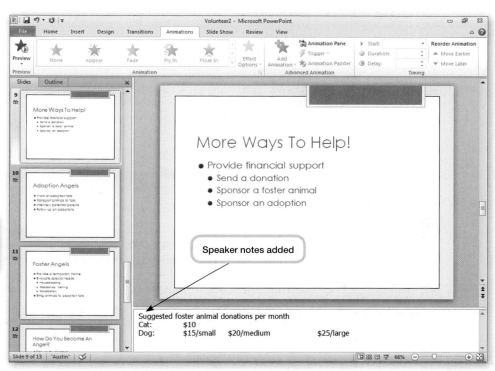

Figure 2.67

You will preview the notes page to check its appearance before it is printed.

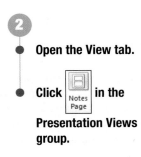

● Open the View tab.

● Click [Notes Page] in the **Presentation Views group.**

Your screen should be similar to Figure 2.68

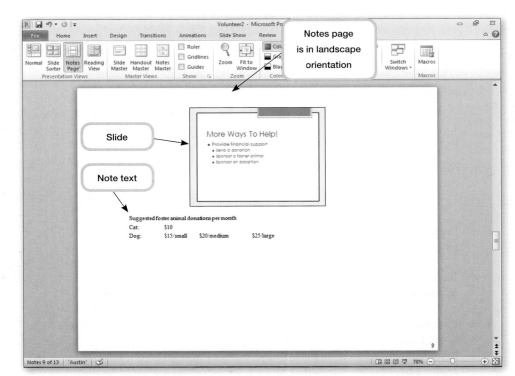

Figure 2.68

The notes pages display the note you added below the slide that the note accompanies. The notes page is in landscape orientation because the orientation for handouts was set to landscape (end of Lab 1). The page orientation setting affects both handouts and notes pages and is saved with the file.

To make the speaker notes easier to read in a dimly lit room while you are making the presentation, you will increase the font size of the note text.

● **Click on the note text to select the placeholder.**

● **Select the note text.**

● **Use the Mini toolbar to increase the font size to 20.**

● **Click outside the note text border.**

Your screen should be similar to Figure 2.69

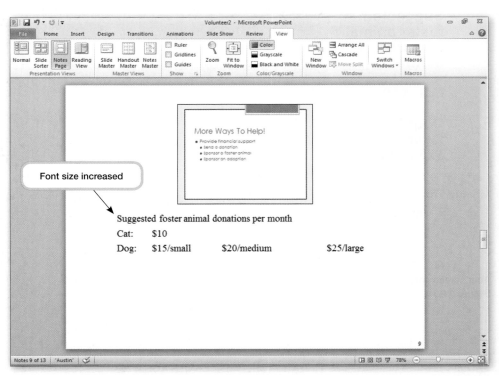

Figure 2.69

Adding Headers and Footers

Currently, the only information that appears in the footer of the notes page is the page number. You want to include additional information in the header and footer of the notes and handouts. The header and footer typically display information inside the margin space at the top and bottom of each printed page. Additionally, slides also may include header and footer information.

ADDING A HEADER TO A NOTES PAGE

You want to include the date and your name in the header of the notes pages.

1

● **Open the Insert tab.**

● **Click** 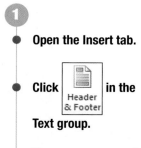 **in the Text group.**

● **If necessary, open the Notes and Handouts tab.**

Your screen should be similar to Figure 2.70

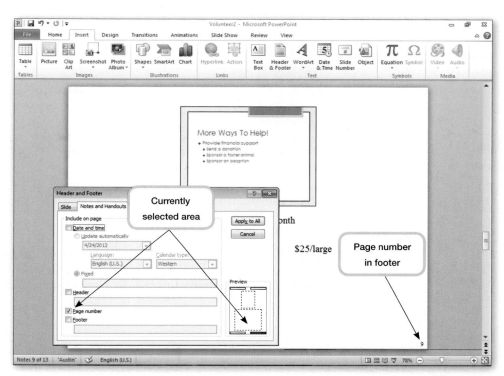

Figure 2.70

On notes and handouts, you can include header text and a page number. The Preview box identifies the four areas where this information will appear and identifies the currently selected areas, in this case page number, in bold.

- **Choose Date and Time to turn on this option and, if necessary, choose Update Automatically.**

- **Choose Header and enter your name in the Header text box.**

- **Click** Apply to All .

Your screen should be similar to Figure 2.71

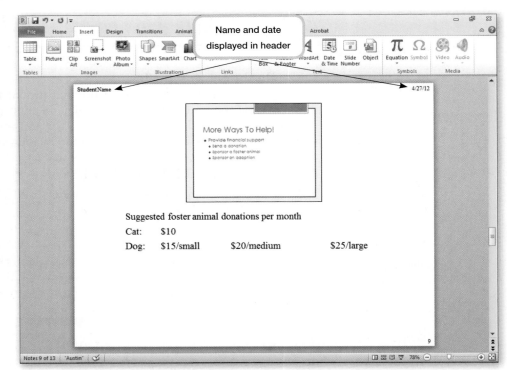

Name and date displayed in header

Figure 2.71

The information is displayed in the header as specified.

ADDING SLIDE FOOTER TEXT

You also would like to include the name of the foundation and slide number in a footer on the slides. The slide master controls the placement and display of the footer information but does not control the information that appears in those areas.

1

- **Switch to Slide Sorter view.**

- **Click** [Header & Footer] **in the Text group.**

- **If necessary, open the Slide tab.**

Your screen should be similar to Figure 2.72

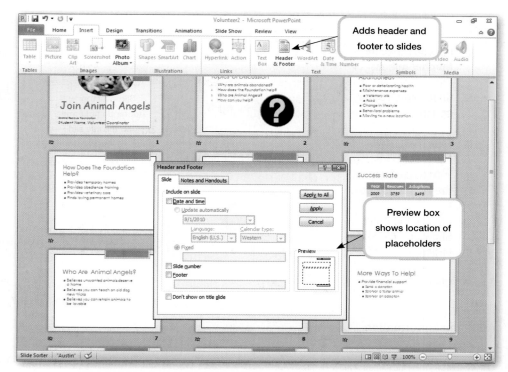

Figure 2.72

Slides can display the date and time, slide number, or footer text. The Preview box shows the location of the placeholders for each of these elements on the selected slide. When specified, this information can be displayed on all slides or selected slides only. You also can turn off the display of this information in title slides only. You would like to add the foundation name in the footer and the slide number to all slides, except the title slides.

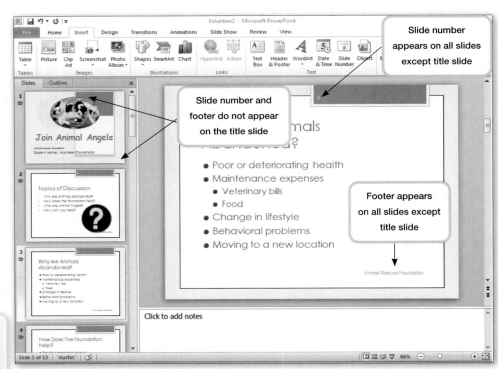

2

- Choose the Slide Number option.

- Choose the Footer option.

- Type **Animal Rescue Foundation** in the Footer text box.

- Choose the Don't Show on Title Slide option.

- Click [Apply to All].

Additional Information

The [Apply] command button applies the settings to the current slide or selected slides only.

- Double-click slide 3.

- Save the presentation.

Your screen should be similar to Figure 2.73

Additional Information

You can also delete the footer and slide number placeholders from individual slides to remove this information.

Figure 2.73

The text you entered is displayed in the Footer area placeholder, and the slide number appears in the blue bar. No footer information is displayed on the first or last slides in the presentation because they use the Title Slide layout.

Customizing Print Settings

You have created both slides and a notes page for the presentation. Now you want to print the notes page and some of the slides. Customizing the print settings by selecting specific slides to print and scaling the size of the slides to fill the page are a few of the ways to make your printed output look more professional.

PRINTING NOTES PAGES

First you will print the notes page for the slide on which you entered note text.

1

- Make slide 9 current.

- Open the File tab and choose Print.

- If necessary, select the printer.

- Choose Print Current Slide as the slide to print.

- Choose Notes Pages as the layout.

- Change the orientation to Portrait Orientation.

- If necessary, change the color setting to Grayscale.

Your screen should be similar to Figure 2.74

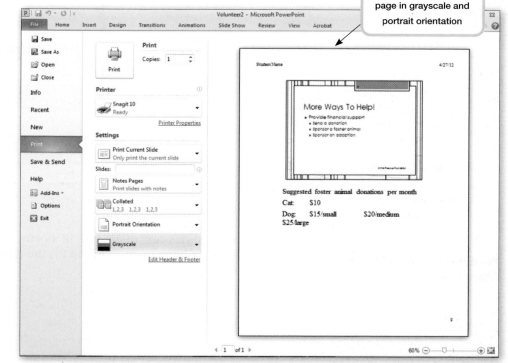

Figure 2.74

The notes page is displayed in grayscale and in portrait orientation, as it will appear when printed.

2

- Click .

Additional Information

To print multiple Notes pages, enter the slide number of each slide (separated by commas) you want to print in the Slides text box.

PRINTING SELECTED SLIDES

Next you will print a few selected slides to be used as handouts. You will change the orientation to portrait and scale the slides to fit the paper size.

1

- **Open the File tab and choose Print.**

- **In the Slides text box, type 1,6,12,13**

Additional Information

The print setting automatically changes to Custom Range.

- **Specify Handouts 4 Slides Horizontal as the layout.**

- **Choose Scale to Fit Paper from the Layout drop-down menu.**

- **If necessary, change the color setting to Grayscale.**

Your screen should be similar to Figure 2.75

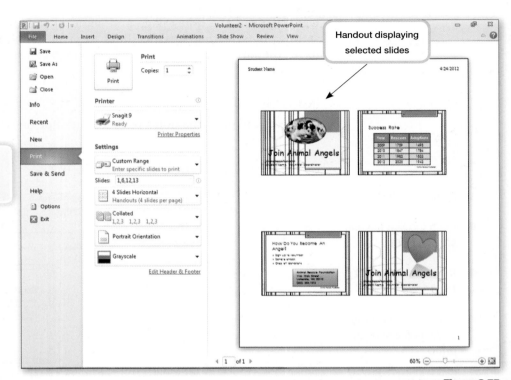

Figure 2.75

The four selected slides are displayed in portrait orientation, and the slide images were sized as large as possible to fill the page.

- **Print the handout.**

- **Open the File tab and if necessary, choose Info.**

- **In the Properties pane, enter your name in the Author text box.**

- **In the Tags text box, enter Volunteer, Recruit**

- **Save the completed presentation.**

- **Exit PowerPoint.**

The view you are in when you save the file is the view that will be displayed when the file is opened.

FOCUS ON CAREERS

EXPLORE YOUR CAREER OPTIONS

Communications Specialist

Are you interested in technology? Could you explain technology in words and pictures? Communications specialists, also known as public relations specialists, assist sales and marketing management with communications media and advertising materials that represent the company's products and services to customers. In high-tech industries, you will take information from scientists and engineers and use PowerPoint to transform the data into eye-catching presentations that communicate effectively. You also may create brochures, develop Web sites, create videos, and write speeches. If you thrive in a fast-paced and high-energy environment and work well under the pressure of deadlines, then this job may be for you. Typically a bachelor's degree in journalism, advertising, or communications is desirable. Typical salaries range from $38,400 to $98,000, depending on the industry. To learn more about this career, visit the Web site for the Bureau of Labor Statistics of the U.S. Department of Labor.

Find and Replace (PP2.5)

To make editing easier, you can use the Find and Replace feature to find text in a presentation and replace it with other text as directed.

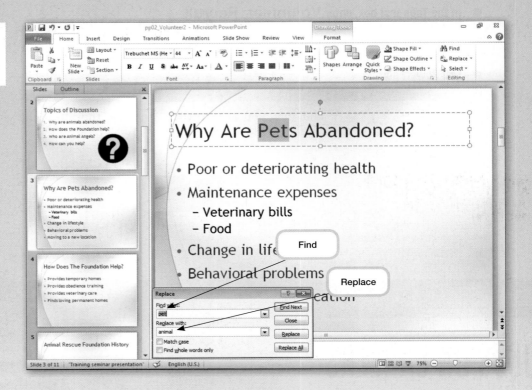

Table (PP2.10)

A table is used to organize information into an easy-to-read format of horizontal rows and vertical columns.

Alignment (PP2.18)

Alignment controls how text entries are positioned within a space.

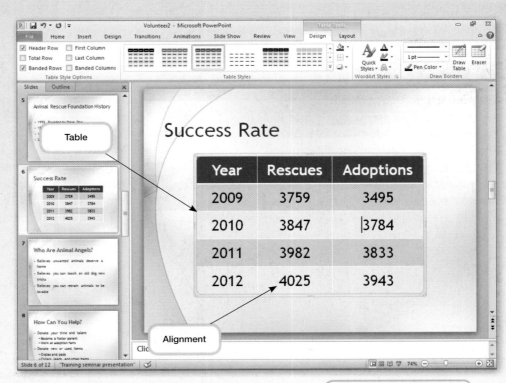

Theme (PP2.36)

A theme is a predefined set of formatting choices that can be applied to an entire document in one simple step.

Master (PP2.42)

...ter is a special slide or page ...ores information about ...tmatting for all slides in a ...tation.

Animations (PP2.47)

An...re special effects that ad...text and graphics so the...ound on the screen du...show.

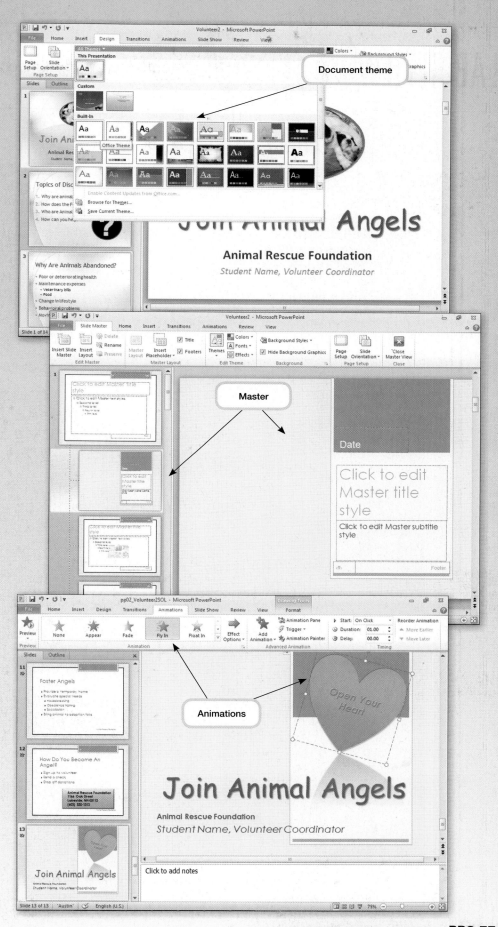

KEY TERMS

alignment PP2.18
animation PP2.47
background styles PP2.40
cell PP2.10
cropping PP2.23
Find and Replace PP2.5
master PP2.42
notes pages PP2.67
object animations PP2.47

rotate handle PP2.30
shape styles PP2.28
table PP2.10
table reference PP2.10
table styles PP2.19
text box PP2.31
theme PP2.36
transition PP2.47

COMMAND SUMMARY

Command	Shortcut	Action
Home tab		
Paragraph group		
Align Left	Ctrl + F	Aligns text to the left
Align Center	Ctrl + E	Centers text
Align Right	Ctrl + R	Aligns text to the right
Justify	Ctrl + F	Aligns text to both the left and right margins
Align Text		Sets vertical alignment of text
...wing group		
		Inserts a shape
...ng group		
...nd	Ctrl + F	Finds specified text
...place ▾	Ctrl + H	Replaces located text with replacement text
...t tab		
...s group		
		Inserts picture from a file
...tions group		
		Inserts a shape
...up		
		Inserts text box or adds text to selected shape
		Inserts a header and footer
...up		
		Opens gallery of document themes

COMMAND SUMMARY (CONTINUED)

Command	Shortcut	Action
◼ Colors ▾		Changes the color for the current theme
Transitions tab		
Preview group		
Preview		Displays the transition effect
Transition to This Slide group		
Effect Options ▾		Opens a gallery of effect options
▼		Opens gallery of transition effects
Animations tab		
Preview group		
Preview		Displays the transition effect
Animation group		
Effect Options ▾		Opens a gallery of effect options
▼		Opens a gallery of animation effects
Advanced Animation group		
Preview		Adds animation effect to selected object
Animation Pane		Opens the Animation pane
Animation Painter		Copies animation effect to another object
Timing group		
Start:		Sets the trigger for the animation
Duration: 00.50 ↕		Controls the amount of time for the animation to complete
View tab		
Presentation Views group		
Notes Page		Displays current slide in Notes view to edit the speaker no
Slide Master		Opens Slide Master view to change the design and layout the master slides

COMMAND SUMMARY (CONTINUED)

Command	Shortcut	Action
Drawing Tools Format tab		
Shapes Styles group		
☰ More		Opens the Shape Styles gallery to select a visual style to apply to a shape
🔵 Shape Effects ▾		Applies a visual effect to a shape
Arrange group		
🔄 ▾		Rotates or flips the selected object
Picture Tools Format tab		
Adjust group		
🖼 Color ▾		Recolors picture
Picture Styles		
☰ More		Opens Picture Styles gallery to select an overall visual style for picture
🔵 Picture Effects ▾		Applies a visual effect to picture
Arrange group		
▤ ▾ Align		Aligns edges of multiple selected objects
Size group		
🖼 Crop ▾		Crops off unwanted section of a picture
Table Tools Design tab		
Table Styles group		
☰ More		Opens the Table Styles gallery to choose a visual style for a table
🪣 ▾ Shading		Colors background behind selected text or paragraph
▦ ▾ Border		Applies a border style
🔵 ▾ Effects		Applies a visual effect to the table such as shadows and reflections
Table Tools Layout group		
Alignment group		
☰ Center		Centers the text within a cell
▤ Center Vertically		Centers the text vertically within a cell
Arrangement group		
▤ ▾ Align		Aligns edges of multiple selected objects

LAB EXERCISES

MATCHING

Match the item on the left with the correct description on the right.

1. rotate handle   _____ a. consists of 12 colors that are applied to specific elements in a document
2. color theme   _____ b. organizes information into an easy-to-read format of horizontal rows and vertical columns
3. table   _____ c. allows you to spin an object to any degree in any direction
4. object animation   _____ d. controls the way the display changes as you move from one slide to the next
5. animation   _____ e. predefined set of formatting choices that can be applied to an entire document
6. theme   _____ f. the intersection of a row and column
7. transition   _____ g. motion, such as clip art that flies in from the left
8. Animation Painter   _____ h. special effects that add action to text and graphics
9. master   _____ i. quickly copies an animation effect and applies it to a different object
10. cell   _____ j. slide that stores information about the formatting for all slides or pages in a presentation

TRUE/FALSE

Circle the correct answer to the following questions.

1.	A master is a special slide or page on which the formatting for all slides or pages in your presentation is defined.	True	False
2.	You can print 12 slides per page using notes pages.	True	False
3.	Columns in a table are identified by letters.	True	False
4.	When you create a footer, it is automatically applied to every slide in the presentation.	True	False
5.	Masters are professionally created slide designs that can be applied to your presentation.	True	False
6.	A theme can be applied to selected slides in a presentation.	True	False
7.	Find and Replace makes it difficult to locate specific words or phrases.	True	False
8.	Tables contain rows and columns.	True	False
9.	Alignment controls the position of text entries in a placeholder.	True	False
10.	When adding text to a text box in PowerPoint, the text box will lengthen automatically to display the entire entity.	True	False

FILL-IN

Complete the following statements by filling in the blanks with the correct terms.

1. _____ provides access to a combination of different formatting options such as edges, gradients, line styles, shadows, and three-dimensional effects.

2. Cells in a table are identified by a letter and number, called a _____.

3. Object _____ are used to display each bullet point, text, paragraph, or graphic independently of the other text or objects on the slide.

4. A _____ is a container for text or graphics.

5. The _____ slide is a special slide that stores information about the formatting for all slides or pages in a presentation.

6. _____ add action to text and graphics so they move on the screen.

7. _____ controls the position of text entries within a space.

8. The _____ tool allows you to change the shape of a graphic.

9. A _____ is part of a template that stores information about the formatting for the three key components of a presentation—slides, speaker notes, and handouts.

10. You can align text _____ in a table cell with the top, middle, or bottom of the cell space.

LAB EXERCISES

MULTIPLE CHOICE

Circle the letter of the correct response to the questions below.

1. A(n) _____ is a predefined set of formatting choices that can be applied to an entire document in one simple step.
   a. theme
   b. animation
   c. slide layout
   d. master

2. Each _____ theme consists of eight coordinated colors that are applied to different slide elements.
   a. color
   b. document
   c. master
   d. slide layout

3. _____ control the way that the display changes as you move from one slide to the next during a presentation.
   a. Graphics
   b. Transitions
   c. Animations
   d. Slide masters

4. If you want to display information in columns and rows, you would create a _____.
   a. slide layout
   b. shape
   c. table
   d. text box

5. You can change the horizontal placement of an entry in a placeholder or a table cell by using one of the four horizontal alignment settings: left, center, right, and _____.
   a. located
   b. marginalized
   c. highlighted
   d. justified

6. To substitute one word for another in a presentation, you would use the _____ feature.
   a. Find and Replace
   b. Duplicate
   c. Copy
   d. Locate and Move

7. If you wanted to add a company logo on each slide in your presentation, you would place it on the _____.
   a. master
   b. notes page
   c. handout
   d. outline slide

8. To help you remember the important points during a presentation, you can add comments to slides and print _____.
   a. notes pages
   b. handouts
   c. slide handouts
   d. preview handouts

9. The _____ defines the format and placement of the slide image, note text, headers, footers, and other elements that will appear on all speaker notes.
   a. handouts master
   b. title master
   c. slide master
   d. notes master

10. _____ add action to text and graphics so they move around on the screen.
   a. Animations
   b. Slides
   c. Transitions
   d. Masters

LAB EXERCISES | Hands-On Exercises

STEP-BY-STEP

ENHANCING A STAFF TRAINING PRESENTATION ★

1. You are working on the staff training presentation for the Sleepy Time Inn. You have already created the introductory portion of the presentation and need to reorganize the topics and make the presentation more visually appealing. Three slides from your modified presentation will be similar to those shown here.

a. Open the file pp02_Sleepy Time Staff Training.

b. Run the slide show to see the progress so far.

c. Spell-check the presentation, making the appropriate corrections.

d. Find and replace any occurrence of "city" with the word **town**.

e. In slide 1:

Insert a text box below the subtitle.

Type **Presented by Your Name**.

Set the font size to 24 and position the text box appropriately on the slide.

Add the following speaker note: **Be sure to introduce yourself and play the name game**.

f. In slide 4:

Add a shape of your choice to emphasize the text on the inserted shape.

Enter and format the text **Terms to Know**.

Position and size the shape appropriately. Add an animation effect of your choice to the shape.

g. In slide 5:

Set the Picture Style to Reflected Bevel, Black.

Set the Picture Effect to Half Reflection, 4 pt offset.

h. Move slide 4 after slide 12.

i. Change the design of the slides to one of your choice from the Themes gallery. Check all slides and make any needed adjustments.

j. Duplicate slide 1 and move it to the end of the presentation. Delete the speaker note from slide 15.

k. Add a transition effect of your choice to all slides. Add an animation effect and sound to the first slide.

l. Add your name to the File properties. Save the file as Sleepy Time Training.

m. Print slides 1, 4, 12, and 15 as handouts (four slides horizontal in portrait orientation).

EMERGENCY DRIVING TECHNIQUES ★

2. To complete this problem, you must have completed Step-by-Step Exercise 2 in Lab 1. You have completed the first draft of the presentation on tire blowouts, but you still have some information to add. Additionally, you want to make the presentation look better using many of the presentation features. Several slides of the modified presentation are shown here.

a. Open the presentation Handling Blowouts, which was saved at the end of Step-by-Step Exercise 2 in Lab 1. If necessary, switch to Normal view.

LAB EXERCISES

b. In Slide Master view, make the following adjustments to the Title Slide Layout:

Delete the page number placeholder.

Change the font of the title and subtitle to Tahoma or a similar font. Add a shadow.

Decrease the title text to 54 pts.

Change title text color to Dark Red, Accent 1, Darker 50%.

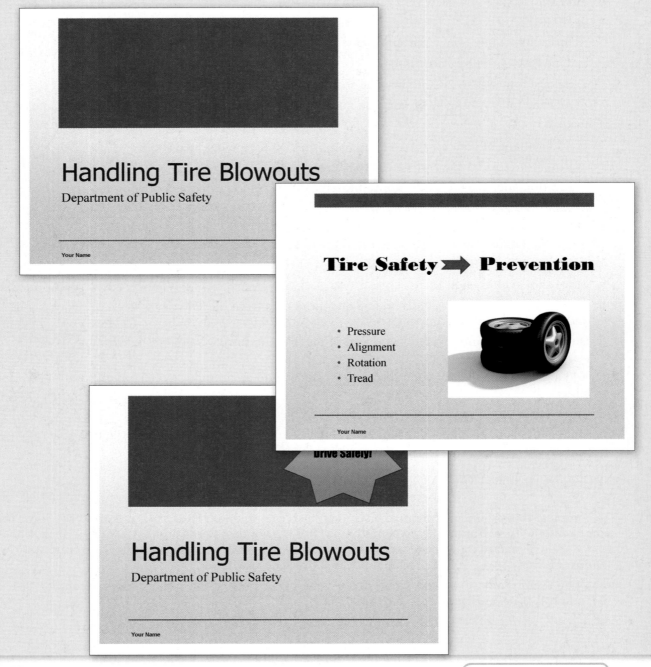

c. On slide 6, replace the = in the title with a right-facing block arrow AutoShape. Add a Fly In from the Left animation to the AutoShape. Modify slide title text as necessary to fit on one line.

d. Select slide 1. On the Home tab, click Reset in the slides group to see the changes you made to the Title Slide Layout in slide master view.

e. Duplicate the title slide and move it to the end of the presentation. Add a drawing object to this slide that includes the text **Drive Safely!**. Modify the shape style.

e. Select an animation scheme of your choice to add transition effects to all the slides. Run the slide show.

f. Add the following note to slide 7 in a point size of 18:

   Underinflation is the leading cause of tire failure.

   Maximum inflation pressure on tire is not recommended pressure.

g. Add the following note to slide 10 in a point size of 18:

   Penny test–tread should come to top of the head of Lincoln.

h. Add file documentation and save the completed presentation as Blowouts2.

i. Print the notes page for slide 7. Print slides 1, 6, and 11 as handouts with three slides per page.

ENHANCING THE ASU PRESENTATION ★★

3. Bonnie is the Assistant Director of New Admissions at Arizona State University. Part of her job is to make presentations at community colleges and local high schools about the university. She has already created the introductory portion of the presentation and needs to reorganize the topics and make the presentation more visually appealing. Several slides of the modified presentation are shown here.

a. Open the file pp02_ASU Presentation.

b. Run the slide show to see what Bonnie has done so far.

c. Spell-check the presentation, making the appropriate corrections.

d. Move slide 5 before slide 4.

e. Use the Find and Replace feature to locate all occurrences of "Arizona State University" and replace them with "ASU" on all slides except the first and second slides.

f. Enter your name as the subtitle in slide 1. Insert the picture pp02_PalmWalk on the title slide. Size the picture and position the placeholders on the slide appropriately.

g. Demote all the bulleted items on slides 8 and 9 except the first item.

h. Change the document theme to one of your choice. Change the color theme to a color of your choice. If necessary, reposition graphics and change font sizes.

i. Modify the text color of the all titles in the presentation using the slide master.

j. Duplicate slide 1 and move the duplicate to the end of the presentation. Replace your name with **Apply Now!**.

k. Bonnie would like to add some picture of the building at the end of presentation. Switch to Slide Sorter view and select slides 12, 13, and 14. Apply the Two Content layout. Insert the picture pp02_Student Services in slide 12, the picture pp02_Library in slide 13, and the picture pp02_Fine Arts in slide 14. (Hint: Use the Insert/Picture command to insert the picture and then drag the inserted picture into the clip art placeholder.)

l. Add a custom animation and sound to the picture on the title slide.

m. Apply random transitions to all slides in the presentation.

n. Apply the Fly In From Right build effect to all slides with bullet items.

o. Run the slide show.

p. Add file documentation and save the presentation as ASU Presentation1. Print slides 1, 2, and 12–15 as handouts (six per page).

4. To complete this problem, you must have completed Step-by-Step Exercise 1 in Lab 1. Logan's work on the Triple Crown Presentation was well received by his supervisor. She would like to see some additional information included in the presentation, including a table of upcoming qualifying hikes. Four slides from your updated presentation will be similar to those shown here.

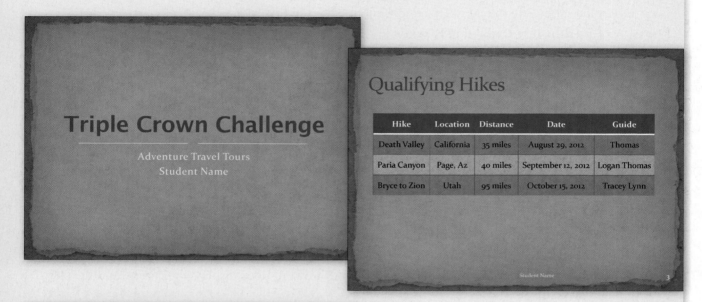

LAB EXERCISES

a. Open the file Triple Crown Presentation.

b. Change the document theme to one of your choice. Change the color theme to a color of your choice. If necessary, reposition graphics and change font sizes.

c. Using the slide master, change the text color of the titles and subtitles. Change the bullet styles.

d. Use the Find and Replace command to replace any occurrence of "Paria Canyon" with **Emerald Pools**.

e. Replace slide 3 with a new Title and Content slide. In this slide:

Enter the title **Qualifying Hikes**.

Create a table with five columns and four rows.

Enter the following information in the table:

Hike	Location	Distance	Date	Guide
Death Valley	California	35 miles	August 29, 2012	Logan Thomas
Paria Canyon	Page, AZ	40 miles	September 12, 2012	Logan Thomas
Bryce to Zion	Utah	95 miles	October 15, 2012	Tracey Lynn

Adjust the column and row size as needed.

Center the cell entries both horizontally and vertically in their cell spaces.

Change the table style to one of your choice.

Position the table appropriately.

f. Add a footer that does not display the date and time but does display your name and the slide number on all slides except the title slide.

g. Add the Float In animation to the graphics on slides 4 and 5. Add an animation effect of your choice to all slides that include bullets. Add a transition effect of your choice to all slides.

h. Duplicate slide 1 and place the copy at the end of the presentation. In this slide:

Change the title to **Adventure is Waiting!**.

Add the slide footer. (Hint: Use Copy and Paste to copy your name and the slide number to the final slide.)

Add a shape of your choice to the final slide with the text: **Call us Today!**.

i. Add the following information to the file properties:

Author: **Your Name**

Title: **Triple Crown Presentation**

j. Save the file as Triple Crown Presentation2.

k. Print slides 1, 3, 5, and 8 as a handout with four slides, horizontal, on one page.

5. To complete this problem, you must have completed Step-by-Step Exercise 5 in Lab 1. Tim has completed the first draft of the presentation for his class lecture on workplace issues, but he still has some information he wants to add to the presentation. Additionally, he wants to make the presentation look better using many of the PowerPoint design and slide show presentation features. Several slides of the modified presentation are shown here.

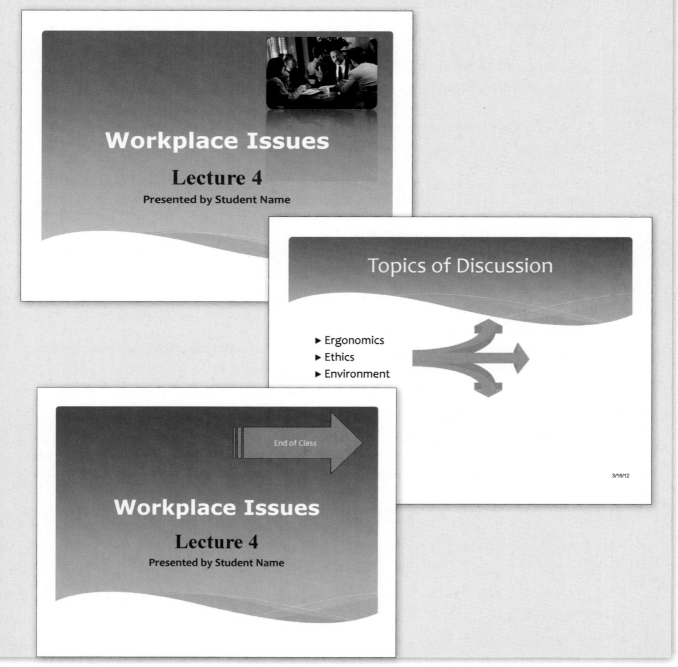

LAB EXERCISES

a. Open the presentation Workplace Issues, which was saved at the end of Step-by-Step Exercise 5 in Lab 1. If necessary, switch to Normal view.

b. Change the design template to Waveform. Change the color scheme to a color of your choice. Modify fonts as appropriate.

c. Change to Slide Sorter view and check the slide layouts. Make the following adjustments:

    Title Slide Layout (in Slide Master view):

      Delete the date area and number area placeholders.

      Change the text color of the subtitle to a color of your choice and bold it.

    Slide master:

      Change the bullet style to a picture style of your choice.

      Reduce the size of the object area placeholder and center it on the slide.

    Slide 1:

      Change the font of the title to Verdana or a similar font. Apply the shadow effect.

d. Check the slide layouts again in Slide Sorter view and fix the placement and size of the placeholders as needed.

e. Apply the Two Content layout to slide 2. Insert the clip art pp02_Arrows into the slide. Modify the AutoShape color to coordinate with the colors in your color scheme. Add a custom animation and sound to the clip art.

f. Change the angle of the clip art in slide 4.

g. Duplicate the title slide and move it to the end of the presentation. Delete the graphic and add a drawing object to this slide that includes the text **End of Class**. Format the object and text appropriately.

h. Add transition effects to all the slides. Run the slide show.

i. Add the following notes to slide 3 in a point size of 18:

    Computers used to be more expensive—focus was to make people adjust to fit computers

    Now, people are more expensive—focus is on ergonomics

    Objective—design computers and use them to increase productivity and avoid health risks

    Physical as well as mental risks

j. Add a bullet format to the notes on slide 3.

k. Add file documentation and save the completed presentation as Workplace Issues2.

l. Print the notes page for slide 3. Print slides 1, 2, 6, and 11 as handouts with four slides per page.

ON YOUR OWN

CLUTTER CONTROL ★

1. You work for a business that designs and builds custom closet solutions. You have been asked to prepare a presentation for new clients that will help them prepare for the construction phase. Clients need to organize and categorize their items before the crews arrive on-site; your presentation will serve as an organization guide. Research ideas on reducing clutter on the Web. Add transitions, animations, and a document theme that will catch the viewer's attention. Include your name and the current date in a slide footer. When you are done, save the presentation as Custom Closets, and print the presentation as handouts, nine per page.

PROMOTING A TRIP ★ ★

2. Your travel club is planning a trip next summer. You want to visit Rome and Venice, and you want to prepare a presentation on cost and key tourist attractions to help convince your club to add those cities to the itinerary. Research these two cities on the Web to determine flight costs, train costs between cities, hotel costs, and key tourist attractions. Start a new presentation and add appropriate text content. Include a table. Add transitions, graphics, animations, and a document theme that will catch the viewer's attention. Include your name and the current date in the slide footer. When you are done, save the presentation as Travel Italy and print the handouts.

ENHANCING THE CAREERS WITH ANIMALS PRESENTATION ★ ★ ★

3. To add interest to the Careers with Animals presentation that you created in Lab 1, On Your Own Exercise 5, select a document theme and color theme of your choice. Add clip art, animation, sound, and transitions that will hold your audience's interest. Add speaker notes with a header that displays your name. Include your name and the current date in a slide footer. When you are done, add appropriate documentation to the file, save the presentation as Careers with Animals2, print the presentation as handouts, and print the notes pages for only the slides containing notes.

ENHANCING THE INTERNET POLICY PRESENTATION ★ ★ ★

4. After completing the Internet Policy presentation you created in Lab 1, On Your Own Exercise 1, you decide it could use a bit more sprucing up. You want to add some information about personal computing security. Do some research on the Web to find some helpful tips on protecting personal privacy and safeguarding your computer. Enter this information in one or two slides. Add some animated clip art pictures and transitions to help liven up the presentation. Make these and any other changes that you think would enhance the presentation. Add a table and format it appropriately. Include speaker notes for at least one slide. Add appropriate documentation to the file. When you are done, save it as Internet Policy2; print the presentation as handouts, nine per page; and print the notes pages (with a header displaying your name and the current date) for only the slides containing notes.

LAB EXERCISES

ENHANCING THE WEB DESIGN PRESENTATION ★ ★ ★

5. After completing the Web Design presentation in Lab 1, On Your Own Exercise 4, you decide it needs a bit more sprucing up. First of all, it would be more impressive as an onscreen presentation with a custom design. Also, the pros and cons information would look better as a table, and a few animated clip art pictures, nonstandard bullets, builds, and transitions wouldn't hurt. Make these and any other changes that you think would enhance the presentation. Include speaker notes for at least one slide. Include your name and the current date in a slide footer. When you are done, add appropriate documentation to the file and save it as Web Design2. Print the presentation as hand-outs and print the notes pages for only the slides containing notes.

Working Together 1: Copying, Embedding, and Linking between Applications

CASE STUDY

Animal Rescue Foundation

The director of the Animal Rescue Foundation has reviewed the PowerPoint presentation you created and has asked you to include an adoption success rate chart that was created using Excel. Additionally, the director has provided a list of dates for the upcoming volunteer orientation meetings that he feels would be good content for another slide.

Frequently you will find that you want to include information that was created using a word processing, spreadsheet, or database application in your slide show. As you will see, you can easily share information between applications, saving you both time and effort by eliminating the need to re-create information that is available in another application. You will learn how to share information between applications while you create the new slides. The new slides containing information from Word and Excel are shown here.

NOTE The Working Together section assumes that you already know how to use Microsoft Word and Excel 2010 and that you have completed PowerPoint Lab 2.

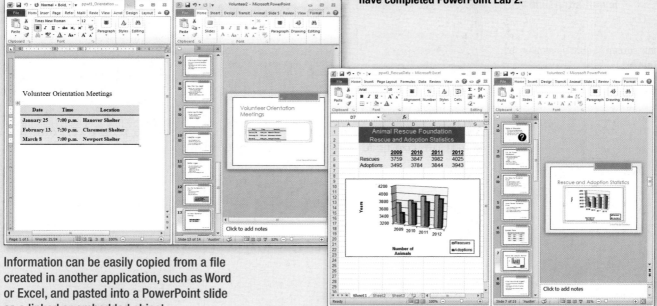

Information can be easily copied from a file created in another application, such as Word or Excel, and pasted into a PowerPoint slide as a linked or embedded object.

The orientation meeting information was already prepared in a document using Word 2010. As you have learned, all the Microsoft Office system applications have a common user interface, such as similar Ribbons and commands. In addition to these obvious features, the applications have been designed to work together, making it easy to share and exchange information between applications.

Rather than retype the list of orientation meeting dates provided by the director, you will copy the list from the Word document into the presentation. You also can use the same commands and procedures to copy information from PowerPoint or other Office applications into Word.

COPYING FROM WORD TO A POWERPOINT SLIDE

First, you need to modify the PowerPoint presentation to include a new slide for the orientation meeting dates.

1

- **Start PowerPoint 2010.**

- **Open the presentation** Volunteer2 **(saved at the end of Lab 2).**

Having Trouble?

If this file is not available, open ppwt1_Volunteer2. Be sure to change Student Name on the first slide to your name

- **Insert a new slide using the Title Only layout after slide 12.**

Your screen should be similar to Figure 1

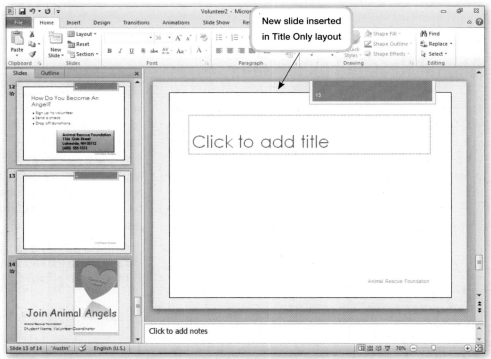

Figure 1

To copy information from the Word document file into the PowerPoint presentation, you need to open the Word document.

2

- **Start Word 2010.**

- **Open the document** ppwt1_Orientation Meetings

- **If necessary, maximize the window, hide the rulers, and set the magnification to 100%.**

Having Trouble?

Click 🖺 View Ruler at the top of the vertical scroll bar to view/hide the ruler.

Your screen should be similar to Figure 2

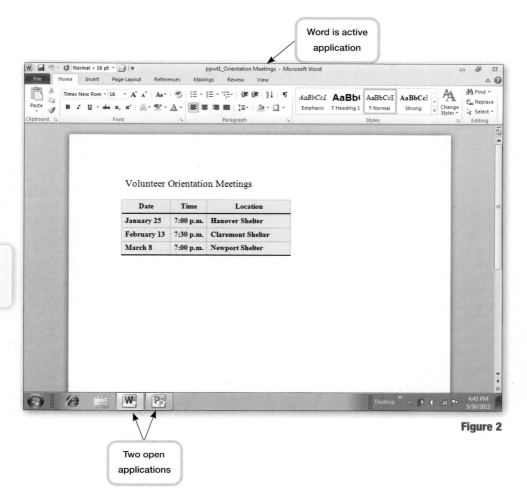

Word is active application

Two open applications

Figure 2

There are now two open applications, Word and PowerPoint. PowerPoint is open in a window behind the Word application window. Both application buttons are displayed in the taskbar. There are also two open files, ppwt1_Orientation Meetings in Word and Volunteer2 in PowerPoint. Word is the active application, and ppwt1_Orientation Meetings is the active file. To make it easier to work with two applications, you will display the windows next to each other to view both on the screen at the same time.

3

- Right-click on a blank area of the taskbar to open the shortcut menu.

- Choose Show Windows Side by Side.

- If necessary, click in the Word window to make it the active window.

Another Method

With Microsoft Windows 7, you also can use the Snap feature to quickly tile your windows. Simply drag the Word application window all the way to the left side of the screen and the PowerPoint window all the way to the right. The windows will automatically resize so that they each take up half the screen.

Your screen should be similar to Figure 3

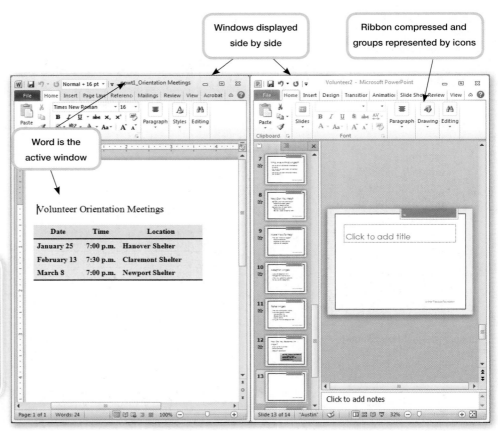

Figure 3

The active window is the window that displays the cursor and does not have a dimmed title bar. It is the window in which you can work. Because the windows are side by side and there is less horizontal space in each window, the Ribbon groups are compressed. To access commands in these groups, simply click on the group button and the commands appear in a drop-down list.

First, you will copy the title from the Word document into the title placeholder of the slide. While using the Word and PowerPoint applications, you have learned how to use cut, copy, and paste to move or copy information within the same document. You can also perform these same operations between documents in the same application and between documents in different applications. The information is pasted in a format that the application can edit, if possible.

4

- Select the title "Volunteer Orientation Meetings."

- Click [icon] · **Copy** on the Home tab in Word.

- Click on the PowerPoint window to make it the active window.

- Right-click in the title placeholder in the Slide pane in PowerPoint.

- Choose [A] **Keep Text Only** in the Paste Options area of the shortcut menu to apply the slide formatting to the title.

Another Method

You also could use drag and drop to copy the text to the slide.

- Click on the slide to deselect the placeholder.

Your screen should be similar to Figure 4

Additional Information

You could also click [icon] Reset Reset in the Slides group of the Home tab to quickly convert all the text on the slide to match the presentation's theme.

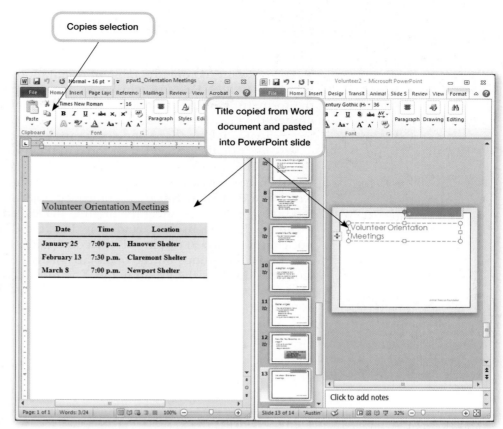

Copies selection

Title copied from Word document and pasted into PowerPoint slide

Figure 4

The title has been copied into the slide and can be edited and manipulated within PowerPoint. Because you used the Keep Text Only paste option, the formats associated with the slide master were applied to the copied text.

Next, you want to copy the table of orientation dates and place it below the title in the slide. Because you know that you are going to want to change the formatting of the table to match the look of your presentation, you will **embed** the table in the slide. Embedding the object will give you the freedom to modify the table's shape and appearance.

An object that is embedded is stored in the file in which it is inserted, called the **destination file**, and becomes part of that file. The embedded object can then be edited using features from the source program, the program in which it was created. Since the embedded object is part of the destination file, modifying it does not affect the original file, called the **source file**.

Notice that because the window is tiled, the Ribbon is smaller and there is not enough space to display all the commands. Depending on how small the Ribbon is, the groups on the open tab shrink horizontally and show a single icon that displays the group name. The most commonly used commands or features are left open. Clicking the icon opens the group and displays the commands.

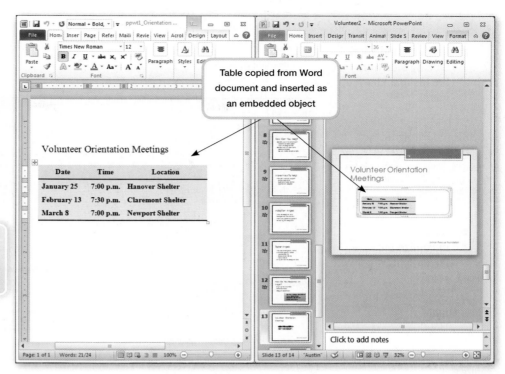

Figure 5

1

- Make the Word window active.

- Click within the table and open the Layout tab.

- Click ⌀ Select ▾ in the Table group and choose Select Table.

- Open the Home tab and click 📋 ▾ Copy.

- Click on the PowerPoint window.

- Open the Paste drop-down menu and choose 📋 Embed.

Your screen should be similar to Figure 5

The table, including the table formatting, is copied into the slide as an embedded object that can be manipulated. The object container is larger than the table it holds.

EDITING AN EMBEDDED OBJECT

As you look at the table, you decide to change the size and appearance of the table. To do this, you will edit the embedded object using the source program.

1

● **Choose Undo Show Side by Side from the taskbar shortcut menu.**

● **If necessary, maximize the PowerPoint window.**

● **Double-click the table.**

Your screen should be similar to Figure 6

Word Ribbon

Word's Table Tools Design and Layout tabs available for editing the table

Source program opened in editing window

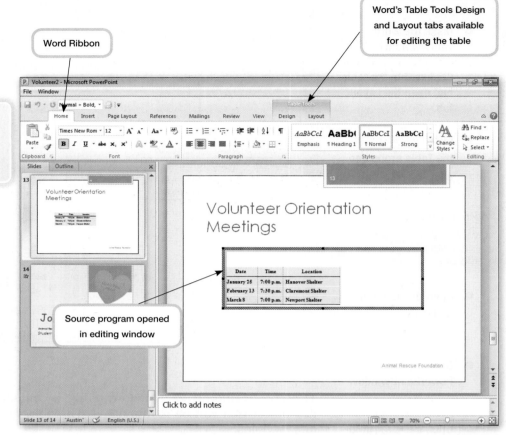

Figure 6

The source program, in this case Word 2010, is opened. The Word Ribbon replaces the PowerPoint Ribbon. The embedded object is displayed in an editing window. If your table does not display gridlines, this is because this feature is not on in your application. First, you will increase the size of the embedded object so that you can increase the size of the table within it.

2

● Drag the bottom-center sizing handle down to increase the object's size as in Figure 7.

Your screen should be similar to Figure 7

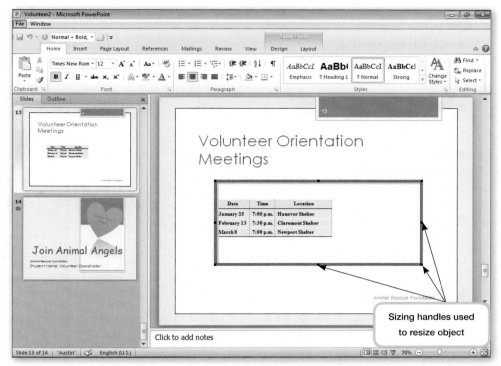

Figure 7

Now that the embedded object's container is larger, you can resize and reposition the table within the container.

- Click inside the table and open the Layout tab.

- Click  Properties in the Tables group.

- Click Positioning... in the Properties dialog box.

- In the Vertical area, open the Position drop-down menu and choose Top.

- Click OK and then click OK.

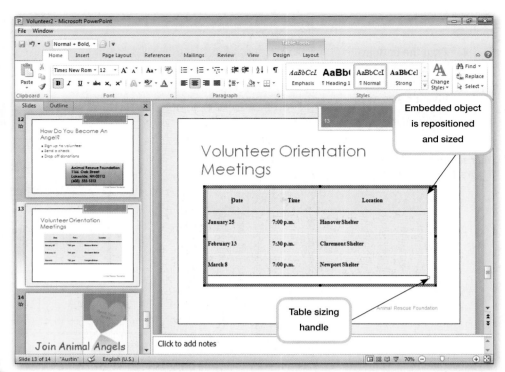

Figure 8

Next, you will use the Word commands to edit the object. You want to apply a different table design style, change the appearance of the text in the table.

Having Trouble?

If the entire table is not visible, click in the table and press Shift + Tab until the first column is visible. You can also use the scroll wheel to adjust it vertically.

- Drag the bottom-right corner sizing handle of the table to increase the size of the table in the object's container.

Having Trouble?

If you can't see the table's bottom-right corner sizing handle, try clicking in the table and scrolling up and down until it appears.

Having Trouble?

If the table gets too large to fit in the container, click Undo to reset it and try again.

Your screen should be similar to Figure 8

4

- Open the Design tab.

- Click ⏷ More in the Table Styles group.

- Choose 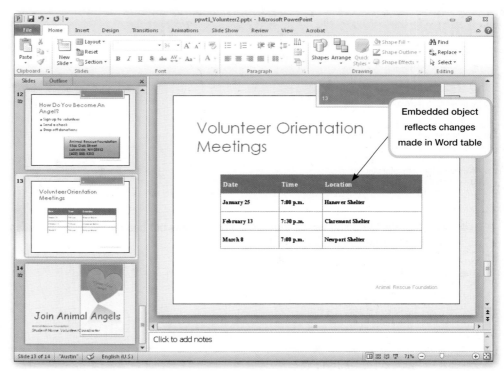 Light List, Accent 1 from the Table Styles gallery (third column, eighth row).

- Drag to select the table and open the Layout tab.

- In the Alignment group, choose ☰ Align Center Left.

- With the table still selected, open the Home tab and click A⌃ Grow Font once to increase the font size to 14.

- Drag to select the first row of table headings and click A⌃ Grow Font two more times to increase the font size of the three headings to 18.

- Click anywhere outside the object twice to close the source program and deselect the object.

Your screen should be similar to Figure 9

Figure 9

The embedded object in the PowerPoint slide is updated to reflect the changes you made in the Word table.

● Click in the taskbar to switch to the Word application.

Having Trouble?

Don't worry if your Word application taskbar image looks different than this one. Applications will look different depending on which version of Windows is installed on the computer you are using.

● **Deselect the table and notice that the source file has not been affected by the changes you made to the embedded object.**

● **Exit Word.**

Linking between Applications

Next, you want to copy the chart of the rescue and adoption data into the presentation. You will insert the chart object into the slide as a **linked object**, which is another way to insert information created in one application into a document created by another application. With a linked object, the actual data is stored in the source file (the document in which it was created). A graphic representation or picture of the data is displayed in the destination file (the document in which the object is inserted). A connection between the information in the destination file and the source file is established by creating a link. The link contains references to the location of the source file and the selection within the document that is linked to the destination file.

When changes are made in the source file that affect the linked object, the changes are automatically reflected in the destination file when it is opened. This connection is called a **live link**. When you create linked objects, the date and time on your machine should be accurate. This is because the program refers to the date of the source file to determine whether updates are needed when you open the destination file.

LINKING AN EXCEL CHART TO A POWERPOINT PRESENTATION

The chart of the rescue and adoption data will be inserted into another new slide following slide 6.

1

- Insert a new slide following slide 6 using the Title Only layout.

- Start Excel 2010 and open the workbook ppwt1_RescueData from your data files.

- Display the application windows side by side.

Your screen should be similar to Figure 10

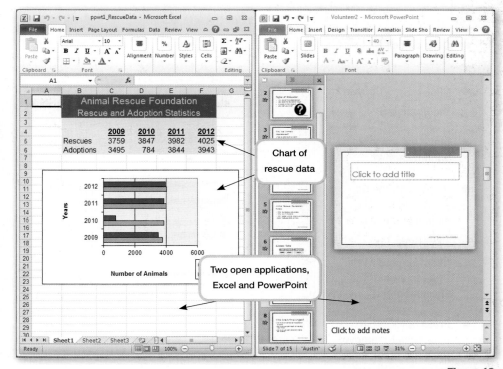

Figure 10

The worksheet contains the rescue and adoption data for the past four years as well as a bar chart of the data. Again, you have two open applications, PowerPoint and Excel. Next you will copy the second title line from the worksheet into the slide title placeholder.

- **Click on cell B2 to select it.**

- **Click** 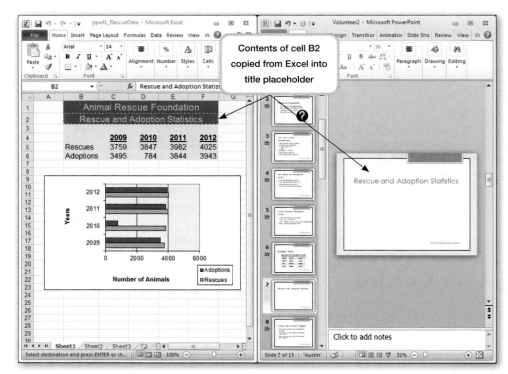 **Copy in the Home tab.**

- **Make the PowerPoint window active.**

- **Right-click the title placeholder in the slide and choose** **A Keep Text Only from the Paste Options area of the shortcut menu.**

- **Press** Backspace **five times to remove the extra blank lines below the title and the extra space at the end of the title.**

- **Click on the slide to deselect the placeholder.**

Your screen should be similar to Figure 11

Figure 11

Now you are ready to copy the chart. By making the chart a linked object, it will be updated automatically if the source file is edited.

3

Make the Excel window active.

Press Esc **to deselect B2 and the click on the chart object in the worksheet to select it.**

Having Trouble?

Click on the chart to select it when the ScreenTip displays "Chart Area."

Click **Copy.**

Click on the slide.

Open the  **drop-down menu and choose Paste Special.**

Your screen should be similar to Figure 12

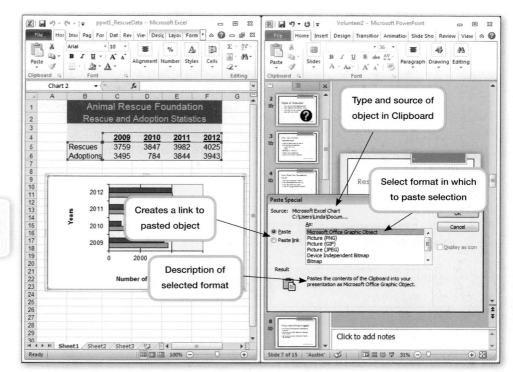

Figure 12

The Paste Special dialog box displays the type of object contained in the Clipboard and its location in the Source area. From the As list box, you select the type of format in which you want the object pasted into the destination file. The Result area describes the effect of your selections. In this case, you want to insert the chart as a linked object to Microsoft Excel.

4

Choose Paste link.

Click OK **.**

Appropriately size and center the linked object on the slide.

Your screen should be similar to Figure 13

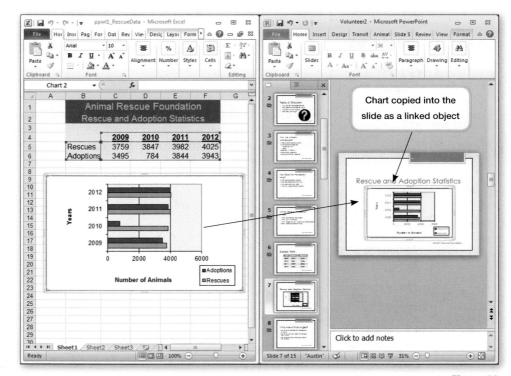

Figure 13

The chart object was inserted as a picture, and a link was created to the chart in the source file.

UPDATING A LINKED OBJECT

While looking at the chart in the slide, you decide to change the chart type from a bar chart to a column chart. You believe that a column chart will show the trends more clearly. You also notice the adoption data for 2010 looks very low. After checking the original information, you see that the wrong value was entered in the worksheet and that it should be 3784.

To make these changes, you need to switch back to the Excel application. Double-clicking on a linked object quickly switches to the open source file. If the source file is not open, it opens the file for you. If the application is not started, it both starts the application and opens the source file.

- **Double-click the chart object in the slide.**

Another Method

You can also right-click the edge of the object and select Linked Worksheet Object/Edit.

- **Make the Excel window active.**

- **Maximize the Rescue Data workbook within Excel.**

- **Click on the chart object to select it, if necessary.**

- **Open the Design tab and click** Change Chart Type.

Another Method

You could also right-click one of the columns and choose Change Series Chart Type.

- **Choose Column.**

- **Choose 3-D Clustered Column (first row, fourth item)**

- **Click** OK .

- **Change the value in cell D6 to 3784 and press Enter.**

Your screen should be similar to Figure 14

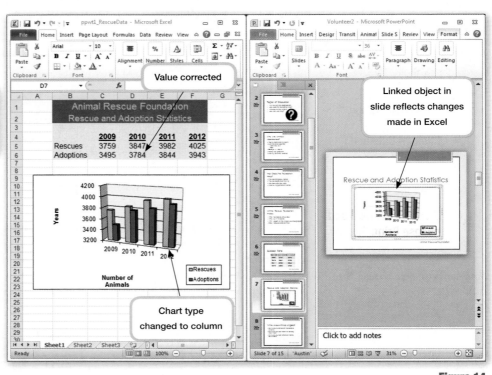

Figure 14

The chart in both applications has changed to a column chart, and the chart data series has been updated to reflect the change in data. This is because any changes you make in the chart in Excel will be automatically reflected in the linked chart in the slide.

2

- Undo the side-by-side window display.

- Save the revised Excel workbook.

- Exit Excel.

- If necessary, maximize the PowerPoint window.

Linking documents is a very handy feature, particularly in documents whose information is updated frequently. If you include a linked object in a document, make sure the source file name and location do not change. Otherwise the link will not operate correctly.

Printing Selected Slides

Next, you will print the two new slides.

1

- Open the File tab and choose Print.

- If necessary, select the printer.

- Enter 7,14 in the Slides text box to specify the slides to print.

- Specify Handouts (2 slides) as the type of output.

- Change the color setting to Grayscale.

- If necessary, click the Edit Header & Footer link and change the header to display your name.

- Print the page.

- Save the PowerPoint presentation as Volunteer3 Linked and exit PowerPoint.

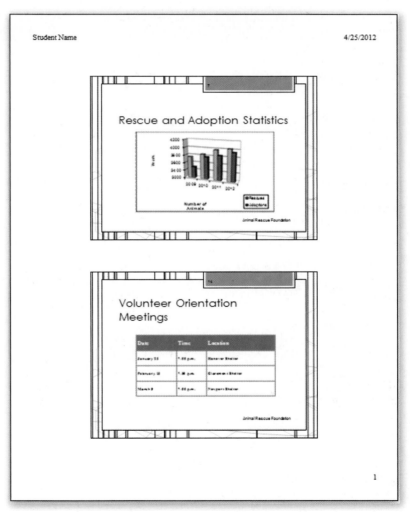

Figure 15

Your screen should be similar to Figure 15

Your printed output will be similar to that shown here.

LAB REVIEW Working Together 1

Copying, Embedding, and Linking between Applications

KEY TERMS

destination file PPWT1.6
embed PPWT1.6
linked object PPWT1.12
live link PPWT1.12
source file PPWT1.6

COMMAND SUMMARY

Command	Shortcut	Action
Home tab		
Clipboard group		
Paste / Embed		Embeds an object from another application
Paste /Paste Special/Paste Link		Inserts an object as a linked object
Paste	Paste	Inserts the copied text or object
A	Keep Text Only	Keeps the format associated with the destination format.
Slides group		
Reset	Reset	Converts all the slides content to match the presentation's theme.

STEP-BY-STEP

EMBEDDING A TABLE OF MASSAGE PRICES ★

1. At the Hollywood Spa and Fitness Center, you have been working on a presentation on massage therapy. Now that the presentation is almost complete, you just need to add some information to the presentation about prices. Your manager has already given you this information in a Word document. You will copy and embed this information into a new slide. The completed slide is shown below.

   a. Start Word and open the file ppwt1_MassagePrices.

   b. Start PowerPoint and open the Massage Therapy2 presentation.

   c. Add a new slide after slide 9 using the Title Only layout.

   d. Copy the title from the Word document into the slide title placeholder. Use the Keep Text Only option.

   e. Copy the table into the slide as an embedded object. Exit Word.

   f. Size and position the object on the slide appropriately.

   g. Edit the table to change the font color to an appropriate font color.

   h. Change the fill color of the table to match the slide design.

   i. If necessary, change the footer to display your name.

   j. Save the presentation as Massage Therapy.

   k. Print the new slide.

Swedish Massage	**$65 per hour**
Reflexology	**$65 per hour**
Shiatsu and Acupressure	**$75 per hour**
Sports Massage Therapy	**Make appointment for evaluation**

EMBEDDING A TABLE OF BLOWOUT INDICATORS ★ ★

2. To complete this problem, you must have completed Step-by-Step Exercise 2 in Lab 2. The Blowouts section for the Department of Safety presentation is almost complete. You just need to add some information to the presentation about the indicators of a flat tire. This information is already in a Word document as a table. You will copy and embed it into a new slide. The completed slide is shown below.

   a. Start Word and open the ppwt1_BlowoutSigns file.

   b. Start PowerPoint and open the Blowouts2 presentation. If this file is not available, you can use ppwt1_Blowouts2.

   c. Add a new slide after slide 3 using the Title Only layout.

   d. Copy the title from the Word document into the slide title placeholder.

   e. Copy the table into the slide as an embedded object. Exit Word.

   f. Size and position the object on the slide appropriately.

   g. Change the design of the table to suit your presentation.

   h. Change the fonts and font sizes of the table headings.

   i. If necessary, change the footer to display your name.

   j. Save the presentation as Blowouts3.

   k. Print the new slide.

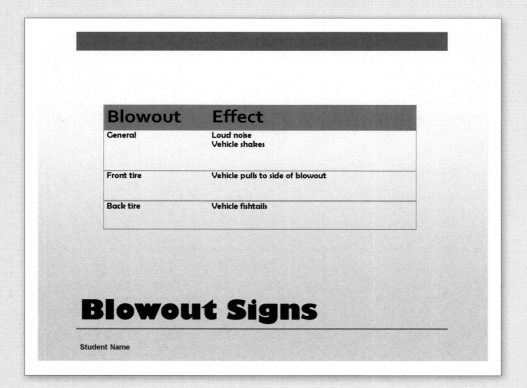

LINKING A WORKSHEET ON FOREST USE ★ ★ ★

3. To complete this problem, you must have completed Step-by-Step Exercise 4 in Lab 2. Logan has found some interesting data on the increase in Americans hiking and wants to include this information in his lecture presentation. The completed slide is shown below.

   a. Start PowerPoint and open the Triple Crown Presentation2 file. If this file is not available, you can use ppwt1_Triple Crown Presentation2. Save the presentation as Triple Crown Presentation3.

   b. Start Excel and open the ppwt1_Forest Use worksheet. Save the worksheet as Forest Use Linked.

   c. Add a new slide after slide 6 using the Title Only layout.

   d. Copy the worksheet cell A1 and paste it in the title placeholder using the Keep Text Only.

   e. Change the look of the presentation by apply the Hardcover theme and the Austin color theme.

   f. Copy the worksheet range A2 through B6 as a linked object into slide 7. Size and position it appropriately.

   g. Format the linked data so that it blends appropriately with the presentation.

   h. Add an appropriate Shape Outline to the linked object's container in the slide.

   i. You notice that the percentage for hiking seems low. After checking the original source, you see you entered the value incorrectly. In Excel, change the value in cell B5 to 42%.

   j. Copy the text in cell A8 and paste it into the Notes for slide 7.

   k. Exit Excel.

   l. If necessary, change the footer to display your name.

   m. Save the changes to the presentation as Triple Crown Presentation3.

   n. Print the new slide.

WORD 2010 COMMAND SUMMARY

COMMAND	SHORTCUT	ACTION
Quick Access Toolbar		
Save	Ctrl + **S**	Saves document using same file name
Undo	Ctrl + **Z**	Restores last editing change
Redo	Ctrl + **Y**	Restores last Undo or repeats last command or action
File Tab		
Save Save	Ctrl + **S**	Saves document using same file name
Save As Save As	F12	Saves document using a new file name, type, and/or location
Save/Save as Type/Web Page		Saves file as a Web page document
Open	Ctrl + **O**	Opens existing document file
/Inspect Document		Checks your document for hidden data or personal information
/Check Compatibility		Checks your document for features that aren't compatible with previous versions
Close	Ctrl + F4	Closes document
New	Ctrl + **N**	Opens new blank document or specialized template
Print/Print	Ctrl + **P**	Prints document
Print		Displays document as it will appear when printed
Share/ Send as Attachment		Sends a document as an e-mail attachment
Options		Change options for working with Word
Options /Proofing		Changes settings associated with Spelling and Grammar checking
Exit	Alt + F4	Exit Word application
Home Tab		
Clipboard Group		
Paste	Ctrl + **V**	Pastes items from Clipboard

WORD 2010 COMMAND SUMMARY

COMMAND	SHORTCUT	ACTION
✂ Cut	Ctrl + X	Cuts selection to Clipboard
📋 Copy	Ctrl + C	Copies selection to Clipboard
Font Group		
Calibri (Body) ▾ Font		Changes typeface
11 ▾ Font Size		Changes font size
B Bold	Ctrl + B	Adds/removes bold effect
I Italic	Ctrl + I	Adds/removes italic effect
U Underline	Ctrl + U	Underlines selected text with single line
Aa Clear Formatting		Removes all formatting from selection
A ▾ Font Color		Changes text to selected color
Aa ▾ Change Case	Shift + F3	Changes case of selected text
Paragraph Group		
☰ Bullets		Creates a bulleted list
☰ Numbering		Creates a numbered list
☰ Decrease Indent		Decreases indent of paragraph to previous tab stop
☰ Increase Indent		Increases indent of paragraph to next tab stop
☰ Align Text Left	Ctrl + L	Aligns text to left margin
☰ Center	Ctrl + E	Centers text between left and right margins
☰ Align Text Right	Ctrl + R	Aligns text to right margin
☰ Justify	Ctrl + J	Aligns text equally between left and right margins
☰ Line Spacing	Ctrl + 1 or 2	Changes spacing between lines of text
↕ Sort		Rearranges information in a list into ascending alphabetical/numerical order

WORD 2010 COMMAND SUMMARY

COMMAND	SHORTCUT	ACTION
¶ Show/Hide	Ctrl + *	Displays or hides formatting marks
/ Tabs...		Specifies types and positions of tab stops
/Indents and Spacing/Special/First Line	Tab	Indents first line of paragraph from left margin
/Indents and Spacing/Line Spacing	Ctrl + 1 or 2	Changes the spacing between lines of text
Editing Group		
Find	Ctrl + F	Locates specified text
Replace	Ctrl + H	Locates and replaces specified text
Insert Tab		
Pages Group		
Cover Page ▾		Inserts a preformatted cover page
Blank Page		Inserts a blank page
Page Break	Ctrl + Enter	Inserts hard page break
Tables Group		
Table		Inserts table at insertion point
Illustrations Group		
Picture		Inserts selected picture
Clip Art		Accesses Clip Organizer and inserts selected clip
Shapes		Inserts graphic shapes
Links Group		
Hyperlink	Ctrl + K	Inserts hyperlink
Header and Footer Group		
Header ▾		Inserts predesigned header style
Footer ▾		Inserts predesigned footer style

WORD 2010 COMMAND SUMMARY

COMMAND	SHORTCUT	ACTION
Text Group		
Quick Parts ▾		Inserts Building Blocks
Date & Time		Inserts current date or time, in selected format
Page Layout Tab		
Themes Group		
Themes		Applies selected theme to document
■▾		Changes colors for current theme
A▾		Changes fonts for current theme
Page Setup Group		
Margins		Sets margin sizes
Breaks ▾		Inserts page and section breaks
Breaks ▾ /**Text Wrapping**		Stops text from wrapping around objects in a Web page
Page Background Group		
Watermark ▾		Inserts ghosted text behind page content
Page Color ▾		Adds selected color to page background
Page Color ▾ /**Fill Effects**		Adds selected color effect to page background
Page Borders		Inserts and customizes page borders
Arrange Group		
Wrap Text ▾		Controls how text wraps around a selected object
References Tab		
Table of Contents Group		
Table of Contents ▾		Generates a table of contents
Add Text ▾		Adds selected text as an entry in table of contents
Update Table...	F9	Updates the table of contents field

COMMAND	SHORTCUT	ACTION
Footnotes Group		
Insert Footnote	Alt + Ctrl + **F**	Inserts footnote reference at insertion point
Citations & Bibliography Group		
Insert Citation		Creates a citation for a reference source
Manage Sources		Displays list of all sources cited
Style: APA Fifth		Sets the style of citations
Bibliography		Creates a bibliography list of sources cited
Captions Group		
Insert Caption		Adds a figure caption
Cross-reference		Creates figure cross-references
Index Group		
Mark Entry		Mark an index entry
Insert Index		Inserts an index at the insertion point
Mailings Tab		
Create Group		
Envelopes		Prepares and prints an envelope
Review Tab		
Proofing Group		
Spelling & Grammar		Opens Spelling and Grammar dialog box
Spelling & Grammar	F7	Starts Spelling and Grammar Checker
Thesaurus	Shift + F7	Opens Thesaurus tool

WORD 2010 COMMAND SUMMARY

COMMAND	SHORTCUT	ACTION
View Tab		
Document Views Group		
Print Layout		Shows how text and objects will appear on printed page
Full Screen Reading		Displays document only, without application features
Web Layout		Shows document as it will appear when viewed in a Web browser
Outline		Shows structure of document
Draft		Shows text formatting and simple layout of page
Show Group		
Ruler		Displays/hides ruler
Zoom Group		
Zoom		Opens Zoom dialog box
100%		Zooms document to 100% of normal size
One Page		Zooms document so an entire page fits in window
Page Width		Zooms document so width of page matches width of window
Window Group		
Arrange All		Arranges all open windows horizontally on the screen
Split		Divides a document into two horizontal sections
View Side by Side		Displays two document windows side by side to make it easy to compare content

WORD 2010 COMMAND SUMMARY

COMMAND	SHORTCUT	ACTION
Special Tabs		
Table Tools Design Tab		
Table Style Options Group		
☑ Header Row		Turns on/off formats for header row
☑ First Column		Turns on/off formats for first column
☐ Last Column		Turns on/off formats for last column
Table Styles Group		
⊟ More		Opens Table Styles gallery
Table Tools Layout Tab		
Rows & Columns Group		
Insert Above		Inserts a new row in table above selected row
Alignment Group		
Align Top Center		Aligns text at top center of cell space
Picture Tools Format Tab		
Picture Styles Group		
Picture Border ▾		Customize a picture's border
Picture Effects ▾		Add special effects to a picture
Arrange Group		
Wrap Text ▾		Specifies how text will wrap around picture
Header & Footer Tools Design Tab		
Header & Footer Group		
Page Number ▾		Inserts page number in header or footer
Insert Group		
Date & Time		Inserts current date or time in header or footer
Quick Parts ▾ /Document Property		Inserts selected document property into header or footer

WORD 2010 COMMAND SUMMARY

COMMAND	SHORTCUT	ACTION
Quick Parts ▾ /Field		Inserts selected field Quick Part
Navigation Group		
Link to Previous		Turns on/off link to header or footer in previous section
Options Group		
☑ Different First Page		Specifies a unique header and footer for the first page
Position Group		
Insert Alignment Tab		Inserts a tab stop to align content in header/footer

COMMAND	SHORTCUT	ACTION
[x] Excel Button		Starts Excel program
Quick Access Toolbar		
[Save] Save	Ctrl + S	Saves document using same file name
Undo	Ctrl + Z	Reverses last editing or formatting change
Redo	Ctrl + Y	Restores changes after using Undo
File Tab		
Save	Ctrl + S	Saves file using same file name
Save As	F12	Saves file using a new file name
Open	Ctrl + O	Opens an existing workbook file
Close	Ctrl + F4	Closes open workbook file
New	Ctrl + N	Opens a new blank workbook
Print	Ctrl + P	Opens Print dialog box
Print /Quick Print	Ctrl + P	Prints selection, worksheets, or workbook using the default printer settings
Print/Orientation/Landscape		Changes page orientation to landscape
Print/Scale:/Fit To		Scales the worksheet to fit a specified number of pages
Options		Displays and changes program settings
Exit or [X]	Alt + F4	Exits Excel program
Home Tab		
Clipboard Group		
Paste	Ctrl + V	Pastes selections stored in system Clipboard
Paste Special/Paste		Inserts object as an embedded object
Paste Special/Paste Link		Inserts object as a linked object
Cut	Ctrl + X	Cuts selected data from the worksheet

EXCEL 2010 COMMAND SUMMARY

COMMAND	SHORTCUT	ACTION
Copy	Ctrl + C	Copies selected data to system Clipboard
Format Painter		Copies formatting from one place and applies it to another
Font Group		
Calibri ▾ Font		Changes text font
11 ▾ Font Size		Changes text size
B Bold	Ctrl + B	Bolds selected text
I Italic	Ctrl + I	Italicizes selected text
U ▾ Underline	Ctrl + U	Underlines selected text
Borders		Adds border to specified area of cell or range
Fill Color		Adds color to cell background
A ▾ Font Color		Adds color to text
Alignment Group		
Align Text Left		Left-aligns entry in cell space
Center		Center-aligns entry in cell space
Align Text Right		Right-aligns entry in cell space
Decrease Indent		Reduces the margin between the left cell border and cell entry
Increase Indent		Indents cell entry
Merge & Center		Combines selected cells into one cell and centers cell contents in new cell
Number Group		
General ▾ Number Format		Applies selected number formatting to selection
$ ▾ Accounting Number Format		Applies Accounting number format to selection
% Percent Style		Applies Percent Style format to selection
Increase Decimal		Increases number of decimal places

EXCEL 2010 COMMAND SUMMARY

COMMAND	SHORTCUT	ACTION
Decrease Decimal		Decreases number of decimal places
Styles group		
Cell Styles		Applies predefined combinations of colors, effects, and formats to selected cells
Cell Styles /Modify		Modifies existing cell style
Conditional Formatting		Applies Highlight Cells Rules, Top/Bottom Rules, Data Bars, Color Scales, and Icon Sets to selected cells based on criteria
Cells Group		
Insert /Insert Cells		Inserts blank cells, shifting existing cells down
Insert /Insert Cut Cells		Inserts cut row of data into new worksheet row, shifting existing rows down
Insert /Insert Copied Cells		Inserts copied row into new worksheet row, shifting existing rows down
Insert /Insert Sheet Rows		Inserts blank rows, shifting existing rows down
Insert /Insert Sheet Columns		Inserts blank columns, shifting existing columns right
Delete /Delete Sheet Rows		Deletes selected rows, shifting existing rows up
Delete /Delete Sheet Columns		Deletes selected columns, shifting existing columns left
Delete /Delete Sheet		Deletes entire sheet
Format /Row Height		Changes height of selected row
Format /AutoFit Row Height		Changes row height to match the tallest cell entry
Format /Column Width		Changes width of selected column
Format /AutoFit Column Width		Changes column width to match widest cell entry
Format /Default Width		Returns column width to default width
Format /Rename Sheet		Renames sheet
Format /Move or Copy Sheet		Moves or copies selected sheet

EXCEL 2010 COMMAND SUMMARY

COMMAND	SHORTCUT	ACTION
Format ▾ /Tab Color		Changes color of sheet tabs
Editing Group		
Σ ▾ Sum		Calculates the sum of the values in the selected cells
Σ ▾ Sum/Average		Calculates the average of the values in the selected range
Σ ▾ Sum/Max		Returns the largest of the values in the selected range
Σ ▾ Sum/Min		Returns the smallest of the values in the selected range
▾ Fill/Right	Ctrl + R	Continues a pattern to adjacent cells to the right
▾ Clear		Removes both formats and contents from selected cells
▾ Clear/Clear Formats		Clears formats only from selected cells
▾ Clear/Clear Contents	Delete	Clears contents only from selected cells
Find & Select ▾ /Find	Ctrl + F	Locates specified text, numbers, and/or formats
Find & Select ▾ /Replace	Ctrl + H	Locates specified characters or formats and replaces them with specified replacement characters or format
Find & Select ▾ /Go To	Ctrl + G	Goes to a specified cell location in worksheet

Insert Tab

Illustrations Group

COMMAND	SHORTCUT	ACTION
Picture		Inserts a picture from a file

Charts Group

COMMAND	SHORTCUT	ACTION
Column ▾		Inserts a column chart
Pie ▾		Inserts a pie chart

Sparklines Group

COMMAND	SHORTCUT	ACTION
Line		Inserts sparkline in the selected cell

ce 2010

EXCEL 2010 COMMAND SUMMARY

COMMAND	SHORTCUT	ACTION
Text Group		
Header & Footer		Adds header or footer to worksheet
Page Layout Tab		
Themes Group		
Themes		Applies selected theme to worksheet
Themes	/Save Current Theme	Saves modified theme settings as a custom theme
Colors ▾		Changes colors for the current theme
Page Setup Group		
Margins	/Narrow	Changes margin settings
Margins	/Custom Margins/Horizontally	Centers worksheet horizontally on page
Margins	/Custom Margins/Vertically	Centers worksheet vertically on page
Orientation	/Landscape	Changes page orientation to landscape
Print Area ▾	/Set Print Area	Sets print area to selected cells
Breaks	/Insert Page Break	Inserts page break at cell pointer location
Breaks	/Remove Page Break	Removes page break at cell pointer location
Breaks	/Reset All Page Breaks	Restores automatic page breaks
Scale to Fit Group		
Width:		Scales worksheet width to specified number of pages
Height:		Scales worksheet height to specified number of pages

EXCEL 2010 COMMAND SUMMARY

COMMAND	SHORTCUT	ACTION
⬍️ Height: /1 page		Scales worksheet vertically to fit one page
📊 Scale:		Scales worksheet by entering a percentage
📊 Scale: /Fit To		Scales the worksheet to fit a specified number of pages
Sheet Options Group Print Gridlines		Displays/hides gridlines for printing
Formulas Tab		
Function Library Group		
Σ AutoSum ▾		Enters Sum, Average, Minimum, Maximum, or Count function
Formula Auditing Group		
🔢 Show Formulas	Ctrl + '	Displays and hides worksheet formulas
◆ Error Checking ▾		Checks worksheet for formula errors
👓 Watch Window		Opens Watch Window toolbar
Data Tab		
Data Tools Group		
🔀 What-If Analysis ▾ /Goal Seek		Adjusts value in specified cell until a formula dependent on that cell reaches specified result
Review Tab		
Proofing Group		
ABC✓ Spelling	F7	Spell-checks worksheet
📖 Thesaurus	Shift + F7	Opens the Thesaurus for the selected word in the Research task pane
View Tab		
Workbook Views Group		
▦ Normal		Changes worksheet view to Normal
🗐 Page Layout		Displays worksheet as it will appear when printed
🗏 Page Break Preview		Displays where pages will break when a worksheet is printed

EXCEL 2010 COMMAND SUMMARY

COMMAND	SHORTCUT	ACTION
Show Group		
☑ Gridlines		Turns on/off display of gridlines
☑ Headings		Turns on/off display of row and column headings
Zoom Group		
Zoom		Changes magnification of window
Window Group		
Freeze Panes ▾ /Freeze Panes		Freezes top and/or leftmost panes
Freeze Panes ▾ /Unfreeze Panes		Unfreezes window panes
Split		Divides window into four panes at active cell or removes split
Picture Tools Format Tab		
Picture Styles Group		
Picture Border ▾		Specifies color, width, and line style for outline of shape
Picture Effects ▾		Adds glow, shadow, and other effects to pictures
Picture Layout ▾		Converts selected picture to a SmartArt graphic
Chart Tools Design Tab		
Type Group		
Change Chart Type		Changes to a different type of chart
Data Group		
Switch Row/Column		Swaps the data over the axes
Select Data		Changes the data range included in chart
Location Group		
Move Chart		Moves chart to another sheet in the workbook

EXCEL 2010 COMMAND SUMMARY

COMMAND	SHORTCUT	ACTION
Chart Tools Layout Tab		
Labels Group		
Chart Title ▾		Adds, removes, or positions the chart title
Axis Titles ▾		Adds, removes, or positions the axis titles
Legend ▾		Adds, removes, or positions the chart legend
Data Labels ▾		Adds, removes, or positions the data labels
Background Group		
Chart Wall ▾		Formats chart walls
Chart Tools Format Tab		
Current Selection Group		
Chart Area ▾		Selects an element on the chart
Format Selection		Opens Format dialog box for selected element
Shape Styles Group		
▾/More		Opens Shape Styles gallery
Shape Fill ▾		Adds selected fill to shape
Shape Outline ▾		Specifies color, weight, and type of outline
Shape Effects ▾		Adds selected effect to shape
Design Sparklines Tool Tab		
Style Group		
⟋⟍		Applies pictured style to sparkline
Clear ▾		Removes sparkline

ACCESS 2010 COMMAND SUMMARY

COMMAND	SHORTCUT	ACTION
Quick Access Toolbar		
💾 Save	Ctrl + **S**	Saves the current object
↩ Undo	Ctrl + **Z**	Cancels last action
File Tab		
Save	Ctrl + **S**	Saves database object
Save Database As		Saves database object with a new file name
Open	Ctrl + **O**	Opens an existing database
Close Database		Closes open window
Info> Compact & Repair Database		Compacts and repairs database file
New		Opens a new blank database
Print/Print	Ctrl + **P**	Specifies print settings and prints current database object
Print/Print Preview		Displays file as it will appear when printed
Save & Publish > Back Up Database		Backs up database
✕ Exit		Closes Access
Home Tab		
Views Group		
Datasheet View	▦	Displays object in Datasheet view
Design View	◪	Displays object in Design view
Form View	▤	Changes to Form view
Form Layout View	▣	Changes to Form Layout view
Report View	▣	Displays report in Report view
Report Layout View	▣	Displays report in Layout view
Clipboard Group		
Paste	Ctrl + **V**	Inserts copy of item from the Clipboard
✂ Cut	Ctrl + **X**	Removes selected item and copies it to the Clipboard
📋 Copy	Ctrl + **C**	Duplicates selected item and copies to the Clipboard

ACCESS 2010 COMMAND SUMMARY

COMMAND	SHORTCUT	ACTION
Sort & Filter Group		
Filter		Specifies filter settings for selected field
A↓ Ascending		Changes sort order to ascending
Z↓ Descending		Changes sort order to descending
Remove Sort		Clears all sorts and returns sort order to primary key order
Selection ▾ /Equals		Sets filter to display only those records containing selected value
Advanced ▾ /Clear All Filters		Removes all filters from table
Toggle Filter		Applies and removes filter from table
Records Group		
Refresh All ▾		Updates selected object
New	Ctrl + +	Adds new record
Save	⇧ Shift + ←Enter	Saves changes to object design
Delete	Delete	Deletes current record
Σ Totals		Displays/hides Totals row
More ▾ /Hide Fields		Hides selected columns in Datasheet view
More ▾ /Unhide Fields		Redisplays hidden columns
More ▾ /Field Width		Adjusts width of selected column
Find Group		
Find	Ctrl + F	Locates specified data
Replace	Ctrl + H	Locates specified data and replaces it with specified replacement text
Go To ▾		Moves to First, Previous, Next, Last, or New record location
Select ▾ /Select		Selects current record

WWW.MHHE.COM/OLEARY

ACCESS 2010 COMMAND SUMMARY

COMMAND	SHORTCUT	ACTION
Select ▾ /Select All		Selects all records in database
Text Formatting Group		
B Bold	Ctrl + B	Applies bold effect to all text in datasheet
A ▾ Font Color		Applies selected color to all text in datasheet
Alternate Row Color		Changes background color of datasheet
Gridlines		Changes display of gridlines in the datasheet
Create Tab		
Tables Group		
Table		Creates a new table in Datasheet view
Table Design		Creates a new table in Design view
Queries Group		
Query Wizard		Creates a query using the Query Wizard
Query Design		Creates a query using Query Design view
Forms Group		
Form		Creates a new form using all the fields from the underlying table
Blank Form		Displays a blank form to which you add the fields from the table that you want to appear on the form
Form Wizard		Creates a new form by following the steps in the Form Wizard
Reports Group		
Report		Creates a report using all fields in current table
Report Design		Creates a report using Report Design view
Report Wizard		Creates a report using the Report Wizard

ACCESS 2010 COMMAND SUMMARY

COMMAND	SHORTCUT	ACTION
External Data Tab		
Export Group		
Saved Exports		Views and runs saved exports
Excel		Exports selected object to an Excel workbook
More ▾		Displays more export choices
More ▾ / Word Export the selected object to Rich Text		Exports selected object to a Rich Text Format (*.rtf) file
Database Tools Tab		
Relationships Group		
Relationships		Opens relationships window
Object Dependencies		Shows the objects in the database that use the selected object
Analyze Group		
Analyze Table		Evaluates table design
Table Tools Fields Tab		
Views Group		
Datasheet View		Displays table in Datasheet view
Design View		Displays table in Design view
Add & Delete Group		
AB Text		Inserts a new text field
Date & Time		Inserts a new Date/time field
More Fields ▾		Creates more fields
More Fields ▾ / Lookup & Relationship		Creates a lookup field

ACCESS 2010 COMMAND SUMMARY

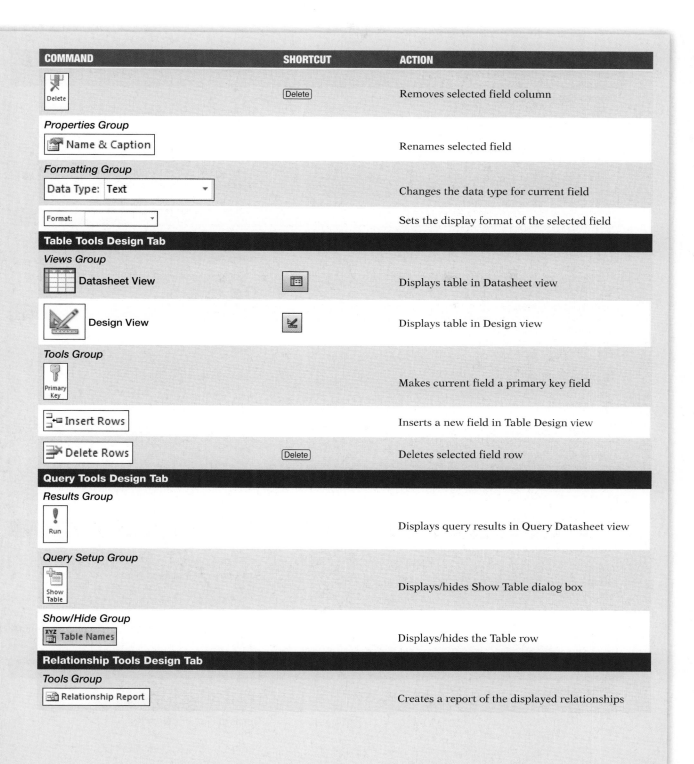

COMMAND	SHORTCUT	ACTION
Delete	Delete	Removes selected field column
Properties Group		
Name & Caption		Renames selected field
Formatting Group		
Data Type: Text		Changes the data type for current field
Format:		Sets the display format of the selected field
Table Tools Design Tab		
Views Group		
Datasheet View		Displays table in Datasheet view
Design View		Displays table in Design view
Tools Group		
Primary Key		Makes current field a primary key field
Insert Rows		Inserts a new field in Table Design view
Delete Rows	Delete	Deletes selected field row
Query Tools Design Tab		
Results Group		
Run		Displays query results in Query Datasheet view
Query Setup Group		
Show Table		Displays/hides Show Table dialog box
Show/Hide Group		
Table Names		Displays/hides the Table row
Relationship Tools Design Tab		
Tools Group		
Relationship Report		Creates a report of the displayed relationships

ACCESS 2010 COMMAND SUMMARY

COMMAND	SHORTCUT	ACTION
Report Layout Tools Design Tab		
Themes Group		
Themes		Applies predesigned theme styles to report
Tools Group		
Add Existing Fields		Displays/hides Add Existing Fields task pane
Report Layout Tools Arrange tab		
Tabular		Arranges controls in a stacked tabular arrangement
Select Column		Selects column
Report Layout Tools Format Tab		
Font Group		
A Font color		Changes color of text
Align Text Left		Aligns text at left edge of control
Center		Centers text in selected control
11		Used to change the font size of text
Control Formatting Group		
Shape Fill		Changes the color fill inside a control
Shape Outline		Opens menu to change the border color and line thickness of a selected control
Report Layout Tools Page Setup Tab		
Page Size Group		
Margins		Sets margins of printed report
Page Layout Group		
Page Setup		Sets features related to the page layout of printed report
Form Design Tools Tab		
Themes Group		
Themes		Opens gallery of theme styles

ACCESS 2010 COMMAND SUMMARY

COMMAND	SHORTCUT	ACTION
Tools Group		
Add Existing Fields		Adds selected existing field to form
Font Group		
		Right aligns contents of cell
Form Design Tools Arrange Tab		
Table Group		
Stacked		Applies Stacked layout to the controls
Rows and Columns Group		
Insert Below		Inserts a blank row below the selected cell
Insert Left		Inserts a blank column to the left of the selected cell
Select Layout		Selects entire layout
Select Column		Selects column in a layout
Select Row		Selects row in a layout
Merge/Split Group		
Merge		Merges two or more layout cells into a single cell
Split Horizontally		Splits a layout cell horizontally into two cells
Print Preview Tab		
Print Group		
Print	Ctrl + P	Prints displayed object
Page Size Group		
Margins		Adjusts margins in printed output

COMMAND	SHORTCUT	ACTION
Page Layout Group		
Portrait		Changes print orientation to portrait
Landscape		Changes print orientation to landscape
Zoom Group		
One Page		Displays one entire page in Print Preview
Two Pages		Displays two entire pages in Print Preview
Close Preview Group		
Close Print Preview		Closes Print Preview window

POWERPOINT 2010 COMMAND SUMMARY

COMMAND	SHORTCUT	ACTION
Quick Access Toolbar		
🖫 Save	Ctrl + **S**	Saves presentation
↺ Undo	Ctrl + **Z**	Reverses last action
File Tab		
Save	Ctrl + **S**	Saves presentation
Save As	F12	Saves presentation using new file name and/or location
Open	Ctrl + **O**	Opens existing presentation
Close		Closes presentation
Info		Document properties
New	Ctrl + **N**	Opens New Presentation dialog box
Print	Ctrl + **P**	Opens print settings and a preview pane
Exit		Closes PowerPoint
Home Tab		
Clipboard Group		
Paste	Ctrl + **V**	Pastes item from Clipboard
Paste /		Embeds an object from another application
/Paste Special/Paste Link		Inserts an object as a linked object
Cut	Ctrl + **X**	Cuts selection to Clipboard
Copy	Ctrl + **C**	Copies selection to Clipboard
Slides Group		
New Slide	Ctrl + **M**	Inserts new slide with selected layout
Layout		Changes layout of a slide
Paste /Paste		Inserts the copied text or object

POWERPOINT 2010 COMMAND SUMMARY

COMMAND	SHORTCUT	ACTION
A /Keep Text Only		Keeps the format associated with the destination format.
Reset /Reset		Converts all the slides content to match the presentation's theme.
Font Group		
Trebuchet MS (He ▾) Font		Changes font type
44 ▾ Size		Changes font size
A Increase Font Size	Ctrl + Shift + >	Increases font size of selected text
A Decreases font size		
I Italicizes text		
U Underlines text		
S Applies a shadow effect		
A ▾ Changes font color		
Paragraph Group		
Bullets/Bullets		Formats bulleted list
Numbering/Bulleted		Formats numbered lists
Align Text		Sets vertical alignment of text
Align Left	Ctrl + F	Aligns text to the left
Align Center	Ctrl + E	Centers text
Align Right	Ctrl + R	Aligns text to the right
Justify	Ctrl + F	Aligns text to both the left and right margins
Drawing Group		
Shapes		Inserts a shape
Editing Group		
Find	Ctrl + F	Finds specified text

POWERPOINT 2010 COMMAND SUMMARY

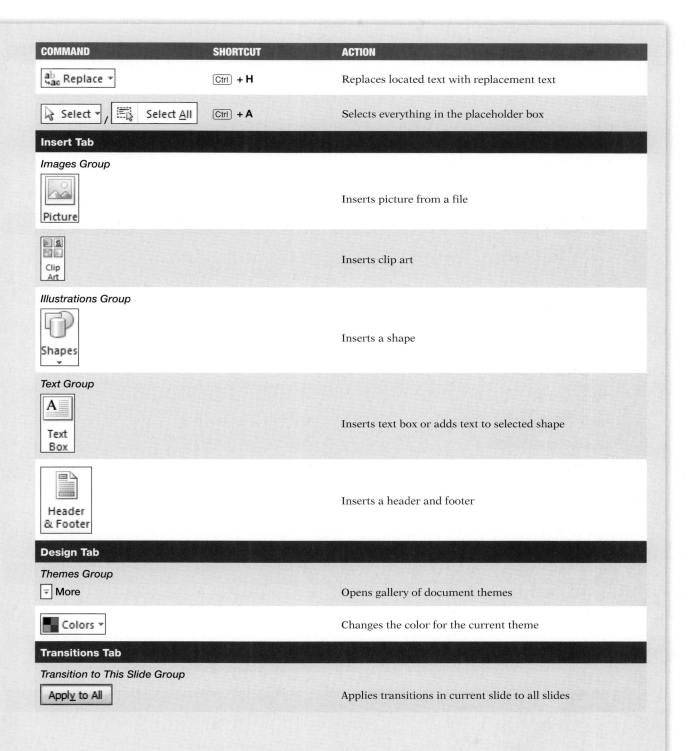

COMMAND	SHORTCUT	ACTION
ab/ac Replace ▾	Ctrl + H	Replaces located text with replacement text
⟋ Select ▾ / ⊟ Select All	Ctrl + A	Selects everything in the placeholder box
Insert Tab		
Images Group		
Picture		Inserts picture from a file
Clip Art		Inserts clip art
Illustrations Group		
Shapes		Inserts a shape
Text Group		
Text Box		Inserts text box or adds text to selected shape
Header & Footer		Inserts a header and footer
Design Tab		
Themes Group		
▾ More		Opens gallery of document themes
■ Colors ▾		Changes the color for the current theme
Transitions Tab		
Transition to This Slide Group		
Apply to All		Applies transitions in current slide to all slides

POWERPOINT 2010 COMMAND SUMMARY

COMMAND	SHORTCUT	ACTION
Effect Options ▾		Opens a gallery of effect options
▼		Opens a gallery of transition effects
Preview Group		
Preview		Displays the transition effect
Animations Tab		
Preview Group		
Preview		Displays the transition effect
Animation Group		
Effect Options ▾		Opens a gallery of effect options
▼		Opens a gallery of animation effects
Animation Pane		Opens the Animation pane
Advanced Animation Group		
Animation Painter		Copies animation effect to another object
Timing Group		
Start:		Sets the trigger for the animation
Duration: 00.50		Controls the amount of time for the animation to complete
Slide Show Tab		
Start Slide Show Group		
From Beginning	F5	Displays presentation starting with the first slide
From Current Slide	Shift + F5	Displays presentation starting with the current slide
Review Tab		
Proofing Group		
Spelling	F7	Spell-checks presentation

POWERPOINT 2010 COMMAND SUMMARY

COMMAND	SHORTCUT	ACTION
View Tab		
Presentation Views Group		
Normal		Switches to Normal view
Slide Sorter		Switches to Slide Sorter view
Notes Page		Displays current slide in Notes view to edit the speaker notes
Master Views Group		
Slide Master		Opens Slide Master view to change the design and layout of the master slides
Picture Tools Format Tab		
Adjust Group		
9 Slides Horizontal — Handouts (9 slides per page)		Modifies the color of the picture
Picture Styles Group		
More		Applies an overall visual style to picture
Picture Border		Applies a border style to picture
Picture Effects		Applies a visual effect to picture
Picture Layout		Changes layout of a drawing
Arrange Group		
		Opens a gallery of alignment options
Size Group		
Crop		Crops off unwanted section of a picture
Drawing Tools Format Tab		
Shapes Styles Group		
More		Opens the Shape Styles gallery to select a visual style to apply to a shape
Shape Effects		Applies a visual effect to a shape

POWERPOINT 2010 COMMAND SUMMARY

COMMAND	SHORTCUT	ACTION
Arrange Group		
		Rotates or flips the selected object
Table Tools Design Tab		
Table Styles Group		
More		Opens gallery of table designs
Shading		Colors background behind selected text or paragraph
Border		Applies a border style
Effects		Applies a visual effect to the table, such as shadows and reflections
Table Tools Layout Tab		
Table Group		
Properties		Edit table properties within the embedded object
Alignment Group		
		Centers the text within a cell
		Centers the text vertically within a cell
Arrangement Group		
		Opens a gallery of alignment options

b

Backstage view: Contains commands that allow you to work with your document, unlike the Ribbon that allows you to work in your document; contains commands that apply to the entire document.

Buttons: Graphical elements that perform the associated action when you click on them using the mouse.

c

Clipboard: Where a selection is stored when it is cut or copied.

Commands: Options that carry out a selected action.

Context menu: Also called a shortcut menu; opened by right-clicking on an item on the screen.

Contextual tabs: Also called on-demand tabs; tabs that are displayed only as needed. For example, when you are working with a picture, the Picture Tools tab appears.

Cursor: The blinking vertical bar that marks your location in the document and indicates where text you type will appear; also called the insertion point.

d

Database: A collection of related data.

Default: The standard options used by Office 2010.

Destination: The new location into which a selection that is moved from its original location is inserted.

Dialog box launcher: A button that is displayed in the lower-right corner of a tab group if more commands are available; clicking opens a dialog box or task pane of additional options.

Document window: The large center area of the program window where open application files are displayed.

e

Edit: To revise a document by changing the parts that need to be modified.

Enhanced ScreenTip: Displayed by pointing to a button in the Ribbon; shows the name of the button and the keyboard shortcut.

f

Field: The smallest unit of information about a record; a column in a table.

Font: Type style; also called typeface.

Font size: Size of typeface, given in points.

Format: The appearance of a document.

g

Groups: Part of a tab that contains related items.

h

Hyperlink: Connection to information located in a separate location, such as on a Web site.

i

Insertion point: Also called the cursor; the blinking vertical bar that marks your location in a document and indicates where text you type will appear.

k

Keyboard shortcut: A combination of keys that can be used to execute a command in place of clicking a button.

Keyword: A descriptive word that is associated with the file and can be used to locate a file using a search.

l

Live Preview: A feature that shows you how selected text in a document will appear if a formatting option is chosen.

m

Metadata: Details about the document that describe or identify it, such as title, author name, subject, and keywords; also called document properties.

Mini toolbar: Appears automatically when you select text; displays command buttons for often-used commands from the Font and Paragraph groups that are used to format a document.

O

Office Clipboard: Can store up to 24 items that have been cut or copied.

On-demand tabs: Also called contextual tabs; tabs that are displayed only as needed.

p

Paste Preview: Shows how a Paste Option will affect a selection.

Properties: Shown in a panel along the right side of the Info tab, divided into four groups; information such as author, keywords, document size, number of words, and number of pages.

q

Quick Access Toolbar: Located to the right of the Window button; provides quick access to frequently used commands such as Save, Undo, and Redo.

r

Records: The information about one person, thing, or place; contained in a row of a table.

Ribbon: Below the title bar; provides a centralized location of commands that are used to work in your document.

s

ScreenTip: Also called a tooltip; appears with the command name and the keyboard shortcut.

Scroll bar: Horizontal or vertical, it is used with a mouse to bring additional information into view in a window.

Selection cursor: Cursor that allows you to select an object.

Shortcut menu: A context-sensitive menu, meaning it displays only those commands relevant to the item or screen location; also called a context menu, it is opened by right-clicking on an item on the screen.

Slide: An individual page of a presentation.

Slide shows: Onscreen electronic presentations.

Source: The original location of a selection that is inserted in a new location.

Status bar:

At the bottom of the application window; displays information about the open file and features that help you view the file.

t

Tables: A database object consisting of columns and rows.

Tabs: Used to divide the Ribbon into major activity areas.

Tag: A descriptive word that is associated with the file and can be used to locate a file using a search; also called a keyword.

Task pane: A list of additional options opened by clicking the dialog box launcher; also called a dialog box.

Text effects: Enhancements such as bold, italic, and color that are applied to selected text.

Tooltip: Also called a ScreenTip; appears displaying a command name and the keyboard shortcut.

Typeface: A set of characters with a specific design; also commonly referred to as a font.

U

User interface: A set of graphical elements that are designed to help you interact with the program and provide instructions for the actions you want to perform.

V

View buttons: Used to change how the information in the document window is displayed.

W

Worksheet: An electronic spreadsheet, or worksheet, that is used to organize, manipulate, and graph numeric data.

Z

Zoom slider: Located at the far right end of the status bar; used to change the amount of information displayed in the document window by "zooming in" to get a close-up view or "zooming out" to see more of the document at a reduced view.

a

Active Window: The window in which you can work.

Alignment: The positioning of text on a line between the margins or indents. There are four types of paragraph alignment: left, centered, right, and justified.

Antonym: A word with an opposite meaning.

Attachment: A file that is sent with the e-mail message but is not part of the e-mail text.

Author: The creator of a Web page or document.

AutoCorrect: A feature that makes some basic assumptions about the text you are typing and, based on these assumptions, automatically corrects the entry.

b

Bibliography: Located at the end of the report, it includes the complete source information for citations.

Browser: A program that connects you to remote computers and displays the Web pages you request.

Building blocks: Reusable pieces of content or document parts included in the Quick Parts feature.

Bulleted list: A list to which bullets have been added before the items to organize information and make the writing clear and easy to read.

c

Caption: A numbered label for a figure, table, picture, or graph.

Case sensitive: In a search, this means that lowercase letters will not match uppercase letters in the text and vice versa.

Cell: The intersection of a row and column in a table.

Character formatting: Formatting features that affect selected characters only. This includes changing the character style and size, applying effects such as bold and italics to characters, changing the character spacing, and adding animated text effects.

Citations: Parenthetical source references that give credit for specific information included in the document.

Clip art: Simple drawings, available in the Clip Organizer, a Microsoft Office tool that arranges and catalogs clip art and other media files stored on the computer's hard disk. Additionally, you can access Microsoft's Clip Art and Media Web site for even more graphics.

Compatibility Checker: Lists any features that aren't compatible with the previous version of Word, and the number of occurrences in the document.

Control: A graphic element that is a container for information or objects. Controls, like fields, appear shaded when you point to them.

Cross-reference: A reference from one part of a document to related information in another part.

Cursor: The insertion point in the document; the blinking vertical bar that marks your location in the document.

Custom dictionary: A list of words such as proper names, technical terms, and so on, that are not in the main dictionary and that you want the spelling checker to accept as correct. Adding words to the custom dictionary prevents the flagging as incorrect of specialized words that you commonly use. Word shares custom dictionaries with other Microsoft Office applications such as PowerPoint.

d

Default: A document's predefined settings, generally the most commonly used. The default settings include a standard paper-size setting of 8.5 by 11 inches, 1-inch top and bottom margins, and 1-inch left and right margins.

Document theme: A predefined set of formatting choices that can be applied to an entire document in one simple step.

Document window: The large area below the Ribbon in a Word document. A vertical and horizontal ruler may be displayed along both edges of the document window.

Drawing layer: A separate layer from the text that allows graphic objects to be positioned precisely on the page.

Drawing object: A simple graphic consisting of shapes such as lines and boxes. A drawing object is part of your Word document.

e

Edit: Revising a document to correct typing, spelling, and grammar errors, as well as adding and deleting information and reorganizing it to make the meaning clearer.

Embedded object: Graphics that were created using another program and are inserted in a Word document. An embedded object becomes part of the Word document and can be opened and edited from within the Word document using the source program, the program in which it was created.

Endnote: Used in documented research papers to explain or comment on information in the text, or provide source references for text in the document. Appears at the end of a document.

End-of-file marker: The solid horizontal line that marks the last-used line in a document.

f

Field: A placeholder that instructs Word to insert information into a document.

Field code: Contains the directions as to the type of information to insert or action to perform in a placeholder. Field codes appear between curly brackets { }, also called braces.

Field result: The information that is displayed as a result of the field code.

Find and Replace: A feature that finds text in a document and replaces it with other text as directed.

Floating object: Can be placed anywhere in the document, including in front of or behind other objects including the text.

Font: Also commonly referred to as a typeface, a font is a set of characters with a specific design.

Font size: The height and width of the character, commonly measured in points, abbreviated "pt."

Footer: A line or several lines of text in the margin space at the bottom of every page.

Footnote: Used in documented research papers to explain or comment on information in the text, or provide source references for text in the document. Appears at the bottom of a page containing the material that is being referenced

Format: Any effects added to a document that alters its appearance. Formatting changes can include many features such as font, font size, boldfaced text, italics, and bulleted lists.

Format Painter: Applies the formats associated with the current selection to new selections.

g

Gradient: A gradual progression of colors and shades, usually from one color to another, or from one shade to another of the same color.

Grammar checker: Advises you of incorrect grammar as you create and edit a document, and proposes possible corrections.

Graphic: A nontext element or object such as a drawing or picture that can be added to a document.

h

Hard page break: A manually inserted page break at a specific location. A hard page break instructs Word to begin a new page regardless of the amount of text on the previous page. When used, its location is never moved regardless of the changes that are made to the amount of text on the preceding page.

Header: A header is a line or several lines of text in the top margin of each page.

Heading style: Combinations of fonts, type sizes, color, bold, italics, and spacing to be applied to topic headings.

HTML: Hypertext Markup Language, a programming language used to create Web pages.

Hyperlink: A connection to a location in the current document, another document, or a Web site. It allows the reader to jump to the referenced location by clicking on the hyperlink text when reading the document on the screen.

i

Indent: To help your reader find information quickly, you can indent paragraphs from the margins. Indenting paragraphs sets them off from the rest of the document.

Index: Appears at the end of a long document as a list of major headings, topics, and terms with their page numbers.

Inline object: An object that is positioned directly in the text at the position of the insertion point. It becomes part of the paragraph and any paragraph alignment settings that apply to the paragraph also apply to the object.

Insert mode: Allows new characters to be inserted into the existing text by moving the existing text to the right to make space for the new characters.

Insertion point: Also called the cursor, the blinking vertical bar that marks your location in the document.

l

Leader character: Solid, dotted, or dashed lines that fill the blank space between tab stops.

Line spacing: The vertical space between lines of text and paragraphs.

Live Preview: A feature of Word that displays how the selected text in the document will appear when formatting options are chosen.

m

Main dictionary: The dictionary supplied with the spelling checker; includes most common words.

n

Navigation Pane: When the Find feature is activated, the Navigation pane appears to the left of your document, and provides a convenient way to quickly locate and move to specified text. The Search text box at the top of the pane is used to specify the text you want to locate.

Normal document template: Automatically opens whenever you start Word 2010. Settings such as a Calibri 11-point font, left-alignment, and 1-inch margin are included.

Note reference mark: A superscript number appearing in the document at the end of the material being referenced.

Note separator: The horizontal line separating the footnote text from the document text.

Numbered list: A list to which numbers have been added before the items to organize information and make the writing clear and easy to read.

o

Object: An item such as a drawing or a picture that can be added to a document. An object can be sized, moved, and manipulated.

Outline numbered list: Displays multiple outline levels that show a hierarchical structure of the items in the list.

p

Page break: A page break marks the point at which one page ends and another begins. Two types of page breaks can be used in a document: soft page breaks and hard page breaks.

Page margin: The blank space around the edge of the page. Standard single-sided documents have four margins: top, bottom, left, and right.

Paragraph: Formatting that affects an entire paragraph, including how the paragraph is positioned or aligned between the margins, paragraph indentation, spacing above and below a paragraph, and line spacing within a paragraph.

Picture: A graphic such as an illustration or a scanned photograph.

Placeholder: Graphic elements, usually set apart with brackets, designed to contain specific types of information.

q

Quick Parts: A feature that includes reusable pieces of content or document parts for document building.

r

Ruler: Shows the line length in inches, and is used to set margins, tab stops, and indents and also shows your line location on the page.

s

Sans serif font: Fonts that don't have a flair at the base of each letter and are generally used for text in paragraphs. Arial and Calibri are two common sans serif fonts.

Section break: Identifies the end of a section and stores the document format settings associated with that section of the document.

Selection rectangle: A rectangle surrounding an object, indicating it is selected and can now be deleted, sized, moved, or modified.

Serif font: Fonts that have a flair at the base of each letter that visually leads the reader to the next letter. Two common serif fonts are Roman and Times New Roman.

Sizing handles: Four circles and four squares, located on the selection rectangle surrounding an object, used to resize the selected object.

Soft page break: Word inserts a soft page break automatically when the bottom margin is reached and starts a new page. As you add or remove text from a page, Word automatically readjusts the placement of the soft page break.

Soft space: Extra spaces that adjust automatically whenever additions or deletions are made to the text when using justified alignment, created so the columns of text are even.

Sort: Word can quickly arrange or sort text, numbers, or data in lists or tables in alphabetical, numeric, or date order based on the first character in each paragraph.

Source program: The program in which an object was created.

Spelling checker: Advises you of misspelled words as you create and edit a document, and proposes possible corrections.

Split window: Splits the document window into separate viewing areas.

Style: A named group of formatting characteristics.

Synchronized: When synchronized, the documents in two windows will scroll together so you can compare text easily.

Synonym: A word with a similar meaning

t

Tab stop: A marked location on the horizontal ruler that indicates how far to indent text each time the Tab key is pressed.

Table: Used to organize information into an easy-to-read format of horizontal rows and vertical columns.

Table of contents: A listing of the topic headings that appear in a document and their associated page references.

Table of figures: A list of the figures, tables, or equations used in a document and their associated page references.

Table reference: A letter and number used to identify cells in a table.

Tag: HTML instructions that can include information such as location and file name.

Template: A document file that stores predefined settings and other elements such as graphics for use as a pattern when creating documents.

Text box: A container for text and other graphic objects that can be moved like any other object.

Text wrapping style: Controls the appearance of text around a graphic object.

Thesaurus: A reference tool that provides synonyms, antonyms, and related words for a selected word or phrase.

Thumbnail: Miniature representation of a graphic object.

TrueType: Fonts that are automatically installed when you install Windows. They appear onscreen exactly as they will appear when printed.

Typeface: A font; a set of characters with a specific design.

U

URL: Uniform Resource Locator, a Web site's address.

W

Watermark: Text or pictures that appear behind document text.

Web page: A document that can be used on the World Wide Web (WWW).

Word wrap: A feature that automatically decides where to end a line and wraps text to the next line based on the margin settings.

3-D Reference: A formula that contains references to cells in other sheets of a workbook; allows you to use data from multiple sheets and to calculate new values based on this data.

a

Absolute Reference: A cell or range reference in a formula whose location does not change when the formula is copied.

Active Cell: The cell your next entry or procedure affects, indicated by a black outline.

Active Sheet: The sheet in which you can work, the name of which appears bold.

Adjacent Range: A rectangular block of adjoining cells.

Alignment: The settings that allow you to change the horizontal and vertical placement and the orientation of an entry in a cell.

Antonym: Words with an opposite meaning.

Area Chart: Shows the magnitude of change over time by emphasizing the area under the curve created by each data series.

Argument: The data a function uses to perform a calculation.

AutoCorrect: A feature that makes some basic assumptions about the text you are typing and, based on these assumptions, automatically corrects the entry.

AutoFill: A feature that makes entering a series of headings easier by logically repeating and extending the series. AutoFill recognizes trends and automatically extends data and alphanumeric headings as far as you specify.

AutoFit: Automatically adjusts the width of the columns to fit the column contents.

AutoRecover: A feature that, when enabled, will automatically save your work and can recover data if the program unexpectedly closes.

Axis: A line bordering the chart plot area used as a frame of reference for measurement.

b

Bar Chart: Displays data as evenly spaced bars. The categories are displayed along the Y axis and the values are displayed horizontally, placing more emphasis on comparisons and less on time.

Bubble Chart: Compares sets of three values. They are similar to a scatter chart with the third value determining the size of the bubble markers.

c

Category Axis: The X axis, usually the horizontal axis; contains categories.

Category-Axis Title: Clearly describes the information on and/or format of the X axis.

Cell: The intersection of a row and a column.

Cell Reference: The column letter and row number of the active cell (e.g., A1).

Cell Selector: The black border that surrounds the active cell.

Cell Style: A defined theme-based combination of formats that have been named and that can be quickly applied to a selection.

Character Effect: Font formatting, such as color, used to enhance the appearance of the document.

Chart: A visual representation of data in a worksheet.

Chart Area: The entire chart and all its elements.

Chart Gridlines: Lines extending from the axis line across the plot area that make it easier to read the chart data.

Chart Layout: A predefined set of chart elements that can be quickly applied to a chart. The elements include chart titles, a legend, a data table, or data labels.

Chart Object: A graphic object that is created using charting features. An object can be inserted into a worksheet or into a special chart sheet.

Chart Style: A predefined set of chart formats that can be quickly applied to a chart.

Chart Title: A descriptive label displayed above the charted data that explains the contents of the chart.

Clip Art: Simple drawings.

Column: The vertical stacks of cells in a workbook.

Column Chart: Displays data as evenly spaced bars. They are similar to bar charts, except that categories are organized horizontally and values vertically to emphasize variation over time.

Column Letter: Located across the top of the workbook window; identifies each worksheet column.

Conditional Formatting: Changes the appearance of a range of cells based on a condition that you specify.

Constant: A value that does not begin with an equal sign and does not change unless you change it directly by typing in another entry.

Copy Area: Range of data to be copied and pasted.

Custom Dictionary: In the spelling checker, holds words you commonly use but that are not included in the main dictionary.

d

Data Label: Labels that correspond to the headings for the worksheet data that is plotted along the X axis.

Data Marker: A bar, area, dot, slice, or other symbol in a chart, representing a single data point or value that originates from a worksheet cell.

Data Series: Related data markers in a chart.

Default: Predefined settings, used on new blank workbooks.

Depth Axis: The Z axis; a third axis, in a 3-D column, 3-D cone, or 3-D pyramid chart; allows data to be plotted along the depth of a chart.

Destination File: The document into which an object is inserted.

Doughnut Chart: Similar to pie charts except that they can show more than one data series.

Drawing Object: A graphic element.

e

Embedded Chart: Chart that is inserted into a worksheet; it becomes part of the sheet in which it is inserted and is saved as part of the worksheet when you save the workbook file.

Embedded Object: An object, such as a graphic, created from another program and inserted in the worksheet, becoming part of the sheet in which it is inserted; it is saved as part of the worksheet.

Explode: Separation between the slices of a pie chart to emphasize the data in the categories.

External Reference: References the location of a source file and the selection within a document that is linked to the destination file.

f

Fill Handle: The black box in the lower-right corner of a selection.

Find and Replace: A feature that helps you quickly find specific information and automatically replaces it with new information.

Footer: Provides information that appears at the bottom of each page; commonly includes information such as the date and page number.

Formula: An equation that performs a calculation on data contained in a worksheet. A formula always begins with an equal sign (=) and uses arithmetic operators.

Formula Bar: Below the Ribbon; displays entries as they are made and edited in the workbook window.

Freeze Panes: Prevents the data in the pane from scrolling as you move to different areas in a worksheet.

Function: A prewritten formula that performs certain types of calculations automatically.

g

Goal Seek: A tool used to find the value needed in one cell to attain a result you want in another cell.

Gradient: A fill option consisting of a gradual progression of colors and shades that can be from one color to another or from one shade to another of the same color.

Graphic: A nontext element or object such as a drawing or picture that can be added to a document.

Group: Two or more objects that behave as a single object when moved or sized. A chart is a group that consists of many separate objects.

h

Header: Information appearing at the top of each page.

Heading: Entries that are used to create the structure of the worksheet and describe other worksheet entries.

k

Keyword: Descriptive term associated with a graphic.

l

Legend: A box that identifies the chart data series and data markers.

Line Chart: Displays data along a line; used to show changes in data over time, emphasizing time and rate of change rather than the amount of change.

Link: Contains references to the location of a source file and the selection within a document that is linked to the destination file.

Linked Object: Information created in one application that is inserted into a document created by another application.

Live Link: A link that updates the linked object when changes are made to the source file.

m

Main Dictionary: The dictionary that is supplied with the spelling checker program.

Margin: The blank space outside the printing area around the edges of the paper.

Merged Cell: Two or more cells combined into one.

Mixed Reference: In a formula, either the column letter or the row number is preceded with the $. This makes only the row or column absolute. When a formula containing a mixed cell reference is copied to another location in the worksheet, only the part of the cell reference that is not absolute changes relative to its new location in the worksheet.

n

Name Box: Displays the cell reference.

Nonadjacent Range: Two or more selected cells or ranges that are not adjoining.

Number: The digits 0 to 9.

Number Format: Changes the appearance of numbers onscreen and when printed, without changing the way the number is stored or used in calculations.

o

Object: An element that is added to a document.

Operand: The values on which a numeric formula performs a calculation, consisting of numbers or cell references.

Operator: A symbol that specifies the type of numeric operation to perform, such as + (addition), − (subtraction), / (division), * (multiplication), % (percent), and ^ (exponentiation).

Order of Precedence: In a formula that contains more than one operator, Excel calculates the formula from left to right and performs the calculation in the following order: percent, exponentiation, multiplication and division, and addition and subtraction.

p

Page Break: The place where one printed page ends and another starts.

Pane: The sections of the window when using the split window feature.

Paste Area: Location you paste material you have copied.

Picture: A graphic element.

Picture Style: Adds a border around a graphic object that consists of combinations of line, shadow, color and shape effects.

Pie Chart: Displays data as slices of a circle or pie; shows the relationship of each value in a data series to the series as a whole. Each slice of the pie represents a single value in the series.

Plot Area: The area within the X- and Y-axis boundaries where the chart appears.

Print Area: The area you selected for printing; surrounded by a heavy line that identifies the area.

r

Radar Chart: Displays a line or area chart wrapped around a central point. Each axis represents a set of data points.

Range: A selection consisting of two or more cells on a worksheet.

Range Reference: Identifies the cells in a range.

Recalculation: When a number in a referenced cell in a formula changes, Excel automatically recalculates all formulas that are dependent upon the changed value.

Relative Reference: A cell or range reference in a formula whose location is interpreted in relation to the position of the cell that contains the formula.

Row: Horizontal strings of cells in a workbook.

Row Number: Along the left side of the workbook window; identifies each worksheet row.

s

Sans Serif: Fonts that do not have a flare at the base of each letter, such as Arial and Helvetica.

Scaling: Reducing or enlarging the worksheet contents by a percentage or to fit it to a specific number of pages by height and width.

Selection Rectangle: Box that surrounds a selected object, indicating that it is a selected object and can now be deleted, sized, moved, or modified.

Serial Value: Data stored as consecutively assigned numbers, such as dates where each day is numbered from the beginning of the 20th century. The date serial values begin with 1.

Series Axis: The Z axis; a third axis, in a 3-D column, 3-D cone, or 3-D pyramid chart; allows data to be plotted along the depth of a chart.

Series Formula: Links a chart object to the source worksheet.

Serif: Fonts that have a flare at the base of each letter that visually leads the reader to the next letter. Two common serif fonts are Roman and Times New Roman.

Sheet: Used to display different types of information, such as financial data or charts.

Sheet Name: Descriptive name that can be assigned to each sheet in a workbook. A sheet name helps identify the contents of the sheet.

Sheet Reference: The name of the sheet, followed by an exclamation point and the cell or range reference, in a formula.

Sheet Tab: Where the name of each sheet in a workbook is displayed, shown at the bottom of the workbook window.

Size: The width of a column.

Sizing Handle: Eight squares and circles located on the selection rectangle that allow the object to be resized.

Source File: The document that houses information that is referenced elsewhere.

Source Program: The program in which an object was created.

Sparkline: A tiny chart of worksheet data contained in the background of a single cell.

Spelling Checker: Locates misspelled words, duplicate words, and capitalization irregularities in the active worksheet and proposes the correct spelling.

Split Window: A feature that allows you to divide a worksheet window into sections, making it easier to view different parts of the worksheet at the same time.

Spreadsheet: A worksheet; a rectangular grid of rows and columns used to enter data.

Stacked-Column Chart: Displays data as evenly spaced bars, this type of chart also shows the proportion of each category to the total.

Stock Chart: Illustrates fluctuations in stock prices or scientific data; requires three to five data series that must be arranged in a specific order.

Stops (Gradient Stops): Specific points where the blending of two adjacent colors in the gradient ends.

Surface Chart: Displays values in a form similar to a rubber sheet stretched over a 3-D column chart. These are useful for finding the best combination between sets of data.

Synonym: Words with a similar meaning.

Syntax: Rules of structure for entering all functions.

t

Tab Scroll Buttons: Located in the sheet tab area; used to scroll tabs right or left when there are more sheet tabs than can be seen.

Template: A file that contains settings that are used as the basis for a new file you are creating.

Text: Any combination of letters, numbers, spaces, and any other special characters.

Text box: A graphic element that is designed to contain specific types of information.

Theme: A predefined set of formatting choices that can be applied to an entire worksheet in one simple step.

Thesaurus: A reference tool that provides synonyms, antonyms, and related words for a selected word or phrase.

Thumbnail: Miniature representations of graphic objects.

V

Value Axis: The Y axis, usually the vertical axis; contains data.

Value-Axis Title: Describes the information on and/or format of the Y axis.

Variable: A value that can change if the data it depends on changes.

W

What-If Analysis: A technique used to evaluate the effects of changing selected factors in a worksheet.

Workbook: An Excel file that stores the information you enter using the program.

Workbook Window: The large center area of the program window.

Worksheet: Also commonly referred to as a spreadsheet; a rectangular grid of rows and columns used to enter data.

X

X Axis: Also called the category axis; is usually the horizontal axis and contains categories

XY (Scatter) Chart: Used to show the relationship between two ranges of numeric data.

y

Y Axis: Also called the value axis; usually the vertical axis and contains data.

Z

Z Axis: Also called the depth axis or series axis; a third axis, in a 3-D column, 3-D cone, or 3-D pyramid chart; allows data to be plotted along the depth of a chart.

a

Action query: Used to make changes to many records in one operation. There are four types of action queries.

Active window: The window in which you can work.

Aggregate functions: Calculations that are performed on a range of data; to use, the data type in the column must be a number, decimal, or currency.

Allow Zero Length property: Specifies whether an entry containing no characters is valid. This property is used to indicate that you know no value exists for a field. A zero-length string is entered as "" with no space between the quotation marks.

AND operator: Instructs the query to locate records meeting multiple criteria, narrowing the search because any record must meet both conditions included in the output.

Append query: Adds records from one or more tables to the end of other tables.

Argument: Specifies the data the function should use; enclosed in parentheses.

Ascending sort order: Data arranged A to Z or 0 to 9.

Attachment control: A bound control that allows you to add, edit, remove, and save attached files to the field directly from the form, just as you can in the datasheet.

Attachment data type: Used to add multiple files of different types to a field.

AutoNumber data type: Automatically assigns a number to each record as it is added to a table; useful for maintaining record order.

b

Best Fit feature: Automatically adjusts the column widths of all selected columns to accommodate the longest entry or column heading in each of the selected columns.

Bound control: A control linked to a field in an underlying table, such as a text control that is linked to the record source and displays the field data in the form or report.

c

Calculated data type: Use to create a calculated field in a table.

Caption: The text that displays in the column heading while in Datasheet view. It is used when you want the label to be different from the actual field name.

Caption property: Specifies a field label other than the field name that is used in queries, forms, and reports.

Cell: The intersection of the row and column.

Character string: Constants such as "F" or "M"; enclosed in quotation marks.

Clipboard: A temporary storage area in memory.

Column selector bar: A narrow bar above the field names in Query Design view; used to select an entire column.

Column width: Adjusts to change the appearance of the datasheet.

Common field: A field shared between two tables.

Compact: Makes a copy of the database file and rearranges the way that the file is stored on your disk.

Comparison operator: A symbol that allows you to make comparisons between two items.

Composite key: A primary key that uses more than one field.

Compound controls: The controls are associated, and the two controls will act as one when moved, indicated by both controls being surrounded by an orange border.

Compound criteria: Using more than one type of criteria in a query.

Control: Objects that display information, perform actions, or enhance the design of a form or report.

Criteria: Expressions that are used to restrict the results of a query to display only records that meet certain limiting conditions.

Criteria expression: Defines the query criteria in the query design grid; similar to using a formula and may contain constants, field names, and/or operators.

Crosstab query: Summarizes large amounts of data in an easy-to-read, row-and-column format.

Currency data type: Use in number fields that are monetary values or that you do not want rounded. Numbers are formatted to display decimal places and a currency symbol.

Current field: The selected field.

Current record: The record containing the insertion point.

d

Data type: Defines the type of data the field will contain. Access uses the data type to ensure that the right kind of data is entered in a field.

Database: An organized collection of related information.

Datasheet view: Provides a row-and-column view of the data in tables or query results.

Date/Time data type: Used in fields that will contain dates and times; checks all dates for validity. Even though dates and times are formatted to appear as a date or time, they are stored as serial values so that they can be used in calculations.

Default Value property: Used to specify a value that is automatically entered in a field when a new record is created.

Delete query: Deletes records from a table or tables.

Descending sort order: Data arranged Z to A or 9 to 0.

Design grid: In Query Design view, the lower portion of the window where you enter the settings that define the query.

Design view: Used to create a table, form, query, or report. Displays the underlying design structure, not the data.

Destination: The location where you paste the copied data from the Clipboard.

Destination file: The file that is created by exporting information from a database.

Drawing object: A graphic consisting of shapes such as lines and boxes that can be created using a drawing program such as Paint.

e

Export: The process of copying information to a file outside of a database.

Expression: A formula consisting of a combination of symbols that will produce a single value.

f

Field: Information that appears in a column about the subject recorded in the table.

Field list: List of fields contained in a table.

Field model: A predefined field or set of fields that includes a field name, a data type, and other settings that control the appearance and behavior of the field.

Field name: Displayed in the header row at the top of the datasheet in Datasheet view.

Field property: A characteristic that helps define the appearance and behavior of a field.

Field Size property: The maximum number of characters that can be entered in the field.

Filter: A restriction placed on records in the open datasheet or form to quickly isolate and display a subset of records.

Find and Replace: A feature that helps you quickly find specific information and automatically replace it with new information

Foreign key: A field in one table that refers to the primary key field in another table and indicates how the tables are related.

Form: A database object used primarily to display records onscreen to make it easier to enter new records and to make changes to existing records.

Form view: Displays the records in a form.

Form Wizard: Guides you through the steps to create a complex form that displays selected fields, data groups, sorted records, and data from multiple tables.

Format: The way the data is displayed.

Format property: Used to specify the way that numbers, dates, times, and text in a field are displayed and printed.

Function: Built-in formulas that perform certain types of calculations automatically.

g

Graphic: A nontext element or object, such as a picture or shape.

h

Hard-coded criteria: Criteria that are entered in the criteria cell; they are used each time the query is run.

Header row: The row at the top of the datasheet where field names are displayed.

Hyperlink data type: Used when you want the field to store a link to an object, document, Web page, or other destinations.

i

Identifier: An element that refers to the value of a field, a graphical object, or a property.

Indexed property: Sets a field as an index field (a field that controls the order of records).

Inner join: Tells a query that rows from one of the joined tables corresponds to rows in the other table on the basis of the data in the joined fields. Checks for matching values in the joined fields; when it finds matches, it combines the records and displays them as one record in the query results.

Input Mask property: Controls the data that is required in a field and the way the data is to be displayed.

IntelliSense: The context-sensitive menu that appears anytime you can enter an expression; suggests identifiers and functions that could be used.

j

Join: An association that is created in a query between a field in one table or query and a field of the same data type in another table or query.

Join line: Identifies the fields on which the relationship is based.

l

Label control: Displays descriptive labels in a form or report.

Layout: Determines how the data is displayed in a form by aligning the items horizontally or vertically to a uniform appearance.

Layout view: Displays the object's data while in the process of designing the object.

Lookup field: Provides a list of values from which you can choose to make entering data into a field simpler and more accurate.

Lookup list: A lookup field that uses another table as the source for values.

Lookup Wizard: A feature that guides you step by step through creating a lookup field that will allow you to select from a list of values.

m

Make-table query: Creates a new table from selected data in one or more tables.

Margin: The blank space around the edge of a page.

Memo data type: Field entry consisting of a long block of text, such as a product description.

Merging cells: Combines any selected adjacent cells into one big cell spanning the length of the previously selected cells.

Mini toolbar: Appears when the attachment control is made active; contains three buttons that are used to work with attachment controls.

Multitable query: A query that uses information from two or more tables to get results.

n

Navigation buttons: Found on the bottom of the work area on both sides of the record number; used to move through records with a mouse.

Navigation pane: Located along the left edge of the work area; displays all the objects in the database and is used to open and manage the objects.

Normal form: A set of constraints that must be satisfied. There are five sequential normal form levels; the third level, commonly called 3NF, is the level that is required for most database designs. This level requires that every nonkey column be dependent on the primary key and that nonkey columns be independent of each other.

Normalization: A design technique that identifies and eliminates redundancy by applying a set of rules to your tables to confirm that they are structured properly.

Number data type: Field entry consisting of numbers only; this data type drops any leading zeros.

o

Object: Items that make up a database, such as a table or report, consisting of many elements. An object can be created, selected, and manipulated as a unit.

OLE Object data type: Used in fields to store an object from other Microsoft Windows programs, such as a document or graph; the object is converted to a bitmap image and displayed in the table field, form, or report.

One-to-many: An association between two tables in which the primary key field value in each record in the primary table corresponds to the value in the matching field or fields of many records in the related table.

One-to-one: An association between two tables in which each record in the first table contains a field value that corresponds to (matches) the field value of one record in the other table.

Operator: A symbol or word that indicates that an operation is to be performed.

OR operator: Instructs the query to locate records meeting multiple criteria, broadening the search because any record meeting either condition is included in the output.

Orientation: Refers to the direction that text prints on a page.

Orphaned records: Records that do not have a matching primary key record in the associated table.

Outer join: Tells a query that although some of the rows on both sides of the join correspond exactly, the query should include all rows from one table even if there is no match in the other table.

Outer sort field: The primary field in a sort; must be to the left of the inner sort field.

p

Parameter query: Displays a dialog box prompting you for information, such as the criteria for locating data.

Parameter value: Tells the query to prompt you for the specific criteria you want to use when you run the query.

Picture: A graphic such as a scanned photograph.

Primary key: A field that uniquely identifies each record and is used to associate data from multiple tables.

Print Preview: Displays a form, report, table, or query as it will appear when printed.

q

Query: Finds and displays specific data contained in a database.

Query criteria: Expressions that are used to restrict the results of a query in order to display only records that meet certain limiting conditions.

r

Record: All the information about one person, thing, or place.

Record number indicator: Shows the number of the current record as well as the total number of records in the table.

Record source: The underlying table that is used to create a form.

Referential integrity: Ensures that relationships between tables are valid and that related data is not accidentally changed or deleted.

Relational database: Databases containing multiple tables that can be linked to produce combined output from all tables.

Relationship: Establishes the association between common fields in two tables.

Report: A professional-appearing output generated from tables or queries that may include design elements, groups, and summary information; analyzes and displays data in a specific layout.

Report view: Displays the table data in a report layout.

Required property: The data that is required in a field.

Row label: Identifies the type of information that can be entered in the fields of a query design grid.

S

Search: Finds any character(s) anywhere in the database.

Select query: Retrieves the specific data you request from one or more tables, then displays the data in a query datasheet in the order you specify.

Select Record button: The square to the left of each row in Datasheet view; used to select an entire record.

Serial value: Data stored as sequential numbers, such as dates and times.

Show box: The box in the row label of a query design grid; lets you specify whether you want a field displayed in the query result.

Source: The original information.

Source file: The database file from which you export information.

Splitting cells: Divides a cell into two or more adjacent cells.

SQL query: A query created using SQL (Structured Query Language), an advanced programming language used in Access.

Stacked layout: Arranges data vertically with a field label to the left of the field data.

Subdatasheet: A data table nested in another data table that contains data related or joined to the table where it resides.

t

Tab order: The order in which the highlight will move through fields on a form when you press the [Tab ⇆] key during data entry.

Table: Organized collection of information, consisting of vertical columns and horizontal rows.

Tabular layout: Arranges the data in rows and columns, with labels across the top.

Template: Document model provided by Microsoft; generally includes the data structure, tables, queries, forms, and reports for the selected type of database.

Text control: Displays the information in a field from a record source.

Text data type: Field designation for text and special numbers. It allows other characters, such as the parentheses or hyphens in a telephone number, to be included in the entry. Also, by specifying the type as Text, leading zeros will be preserved.

Theme: A predefined set of font and color formats that can be applied to an entire document in one simple step.

Theme colors: A set of 12 colors that are applied to specific elements in a document.

U

Unbound control: A text control that is not connected to an underlying record source.

Unequal join: Records to be included in query results that are based on the value in one join field being greater than, less than, not equal to, greater than or equal to, or less than or equal to the value in the other join field.

Update query: Makes update changes to records.

V

Validation rule: Limits data entered in a field to values that meet certain requirements.

Validation Rule property: Specifies a validation rule, which limits the values that can be entered in the field to those that meet certain requirements.

Validation text: An explanatory message that appears if a user attempts to enter invalid information in a text field for which there is a validity check.

Validation Text property: The message to be displayed when the associated validation rule is not satisfied.

Value: Data entered in a field.

Value list: A list of options for a drop-down list.

View: Window formats that are used to display and work with the objects in a database.

W

Wildcards: Symbols that are used to represent characters. The * symbol represents any collection of characters; the ? symbol represents any individual character.

Wizard: A feature that guides you step by step through the process to perform a task.

Y

Yes/No data type: Use when the field contents can only be a Yes/No, True/False, or On/Off value. A Yes value is stored as a 1 and a No value is stored as a 0 so that they can be used in expressions.

a

Alignment: Controls the position of text entries within a space.

Animation: Special effects that add action to text and graphics so they move around on the screen during a slide show.

AutoCorrect: A feature that makes some basic assumptions about the text you are typing and, based on those assumptions, automatically corrects the entry.

b

Background styles: A set of theme colors and textures that you can apply to the background of your slides.

c

Cell: The intersection of a row and a column in a table.

Character formatting: Applies changes such as color and size to the selected characters only.

Clip art: Simple drawings; available in the Clip Organizer, a Microsoft Office tool that arranges and catalogs clip art and other media files stored on the computer's hard disk.

Cropping: Trimming or removing part of a graphic.

Current slide: The slide that will be affected by any changes you make.

Custom dictionary: The dictionary you can create to hold words you commonly use, such as proper names and technical terms, that are not included in the spelling checker's main dictionary.

d

Default settings: The most commonly used settings, automatically used in a new blank presentation file.

Demote: Indenting a bulleted point to the right, making it a lower or subordinate topic in the outline hierarchy.

Destination file: The file into which an object is embedded.

Document theme: A predefined set of formatting choices that can be applied to an entire document in one simple step.

Drawing object: A graphic consisting of shapes such as lines and boxes.

e

Embedded object: Graphics that were created from another program and are inserted in a slide. An embedded object becomes part of the presentation file and can be opened and edited using the program in which it was created.

f

Find and Replace: A feature used to find text in a presentation and replace it with other text.

g

Graphic: A nontext element or object, such as a drawing or picture, that can be added to a slide.

k

Keyword: Descriptive words or phrases associated with a graphic or figure that give information about the properties of the object.

l

Layout: Defines the position and format for objects and text that will be added to a slide. A layout contains placeholders for the different items such as bulleted text, titles, charts, and so on.

Linked object: A way to insert information created in one application into a document created by another application. With a linked object, the actual data is stored in the source file.

Live link: Connection that allows changes made in the source file that affect the linked object to be automatically reflected in the destination file when it is opened.

m

Main dictionary: The dictionary that is supplied with the spelling checker program.

Master: A special slide or page that stores information about the formatting for all slides or pages in a presentation.

Metadata: Additional data saved by PowerPoint as part of the presentation, may include author's name and other personal information.

n

Notes pages: Pages that display notes below a small version of the slide they accompany.

Notes pane: View that includes space for you to enter notes that apply to the current slide.

o

Object animations: Used to display each bullet point, text, paragraph, or graphic independently of the other text or objects on the slide.

Outline tab: Displays the text content of each slide in outline format.

p

Paragraph formatting: Formatting features that affect an entire paragraph.

Picture: An image such as a graphic illustration or a scanned photograph, created in another program.

Picture style: Effects added to a picture, such as borders and shadows.

Placeholder: Boxes with dotted borders that are used to contain content such as text, graphics and other objects.

Placeholder text: Messages inside placeholders that prompt you to enter text.

Promote: Removes the indentation before a line. Promoting a line moves it to the left, or up a level in the outline hierarchy.

r

Rotate handle: Allows you to rotate the selected object to any degree in any direction.

s

Sans serif font: A font without a flair at the base of each letter, such as Arial or Helvetica.

Serif font: A font that has a flair at the base of each letter, such as Roman or Times New Roman.

Shape styles: Combinations of fill colors, outline colors, and effects used to enhance the appearance of a shape.

Sizing handles: The four circles and squares that appear at the corners and sides of a selected placeholder's border.

Slide: An individual "page" of your presentation.

Slide indicator: Identifies the number of the slide that is displayed in the workspace, along with the total number of slides in the presentation.

Slide pane: View that displays the selected slide.

Slide show: Displays each slide full screen and in order.

Slides tab: View that displays a miniature version, or thumbnail, of each slide.

Source file: The original file used to create an embedded object.

Source program: The program in which an object was created.

Spelling checker: Locates all misspelled words, duplicate words, and capitalization irregularities as you create and edit a presentation, and proposes possible corrections.

Style: A combination of formatting options that can be applied in one easy step.

t

Table: Used to organize information into an easy-to-read format of horizontal rows and vertical columns.

Table reference: A letter and number used to identify cells in a table. Columns are identified from left to right beginning with the letter A, and rows are numbered from top to bottom beginning with the number 1.

Table styles: Combinations of shading colors, borders, and visual effects such as shadows and reflections that can be applied to a table.

Template: A file containing predefined settings that can be used as a pattern to create many common types of presentations.

Text box: A container for text or graphics.

Text effects: Enhancements to the text such as color and shadow.

Thumbnail: A miniature version of a slide, picture, or object.

Transition: Controls the way that the display changes as you move from one slide to the next during a presentation.

v

View: A way of looking at a presentation that provides the means to interact with the presentation.

Word

WD1.2	Brand X Pictures/PunchStock
WD2.2	Getty Images
WD3.2	Royalty-Free/CORBIS

Excel

EX1.2	TRBfoto/Getty Images
EX2.2	BlueMoon stock/agefotostock
EX3.2	Hill Street Studios/Getty Images

Access

AC1.2	Ryan Mcvay/Getty Images
AC2.2	Jupiterimages
AC3.2	Corbis Super R/Alamy

Powerpoint

| PP1.2 | Blend Images/PunchStock |
| PP2.2 | Thinkstock/PunchStock |

Notes